Clans and Clearance:
The Highland Clearances Volume One

"The past is never dead. It's not even past."
William Faulkner, *Requiem for a Nun.*

The Highland Clearances

ALWYN EDGAR

M.A. (Oxon.), LL.B. (Lond.),
Barrister-at-law (Inner Temple)

Volume One: Clans And Clearance

The Highland Clearances

Volume One: Clans and Clearance
Volume Two: Eighteenth-century Clearances
Volume Three: The Sutherland Clearances
Volume Four: Clearances 1800-40 (except in Sutherland)
Volume Five: Clearances 1840-1900

Copyright Alwyn Edgar 2019

Published by Theory and Practice 2019

www.theoryandpractice.org.uk

ISBN 978-0-9956609-3-9 (ebook)
ISBN 978-0-9956609-9-1 (hardback)

This work is dedicated to my mother
Harriet Maria Edgar, née Downs (1894-1967)
who enabled me to begin it,
and to my wife
Janet Edgar, née Stimpson,
who enabled me to finish it.

Contents

Preface	ix
Introduction	1
Chapter One: The Clearances in History	25
Chapter Two: The Highlands and Islands	155
Chapter Three: Power Within the Clan	210
Chapter Four: Chiefs and Charters	326
Chapter Five: The Life of the Highlanders	408
Chapter Six: Character of the Highlanders	485
Chapter Seven: Customs of the Highlanders	582
Bibliography	692
Appendix A	700
Appendix B	702
Index	705

PREFACE

1. Five volumes

I have to start with an apology. I have never been able to devote my whole time, or even my whole spare time, to history, and therefore writing this work has been a lengthy business. I began writing it in 1963, and only now is it at the point of publication. Many years ago I sent a section of it, with a letter explaining what I was doing, to Sorley MacLean, often called the greatest Gaelic poet of the twentieth century. He wrote back, on 29th August 1994: "Dear Mr Edgar, Your 'MacKinnon Clearances' fills me with hope that I will live to see your whole history of the Clearances published in parts or as a whole. It will supersede everything written on the Clearances at all times and places." Of course that did not happen: Sorley MacLean died in November 1996. I am sorry that my procrastination has prevented my being able to send the whole work to him.

There are five volumes altogether. This first volume contains something over 330,000 words, including notes; the other four average much the same length. If a project is that long, there is enough room for errors to creep in: no one could write a million and a half words without risking many blunders. I have tried to find and correct any mistakes; but if any reader finds a fault, I would be glad to hear about it. I can take consolation from the fact that since I have had the temerity to disagree with much of what many other people have written about the Highlands and about the clearances, it seems probable that any slips I have made will rapidly (and raucously) be revealed, if only in revenge.

Here, briefly, is what each volume is about.

Volume one, *Highland Clans and Clearance*. This volume looks at the clearances generally, and at some of the surprising orthodox beliefs about them; and then examines the Highland clans as they were in the centuries before the Jacobite rebellion of 1745-6, an account which sometimes differs from what is now often affirmed.

Volume two, *Eighteenth-century Clearances*. This deals with the clearances which took place before 1800, and with the position of the Highlanders at the end of the eighteenth century, as shown by contemporary observers including the writers of the Old Statistical Account of Scotland, which was published in twenty-one volumes between 1791 and 1799.

Volume three, *The Sutherland Clearances*. This tells the story of the sweeping changes carried out under the direction of the Countess of Sutherland on her estate in that county in the first quarter of the nineteenth century; and the similar clearances which took place on the other Sutherland estates, owned by lesser Sutherland landlords, at about the same time.

Volume four, *Highland Clearances 1800-40*. This covers the clearances in the first forty years of the nineteenth century (except those which took place in Sutherland, dealt with in volume three), and also the position of the Highlanders in about 1840, as indicated by contemporary observers including the writers of the New Statistical Account, the reports in which were compiled between 1833 and 1844.

Volume five, *Highland Clearances 1840-1900*. This considers the clearances from 1840 to the end of the century; the growing resistance of the Highlanders, both before and after the "Crofters' War"; and also the position of the Highlanders towards the end of the century, as revealed for example in the enquiries carried out by the Napier Commission (1883) and the Brand Commission (1893).

2. Style

Various questions as to style have arisen. Is the term "the Highlands" singular or plural? Does it need a singular or plural verb? I fear that on different occasions I have inconsistently treated them (or it) as both. When I have written of the Highlands as a distinct district, I have treated it as singular; when a particular usage seems to view the Highlands mainly as a collection of mountains, I have regarded them as plural. The same variation (to call it by no stronger word) will be seen when I mention the famous Highland regiments: for example the 92nd Regiment, the Gordon Highlanders. The regiment itself, the 92nd, must be singular; but when the topic is the men in it, the Gordon Highlanders themselves, I have used the plural. I am sorry if I have displeased any pedants among my readers by this duplicity, being partial to pedantry myself.

The names of glens, straths, and lochs, are normally given as two words – Glen Kingie, Strath Errick, Loch Rannoch. Four exceptions have been made to this rule. Where a name that began life as the appellation of a particular place is later taken to apply to the whole of a wider area, for example Glenelg, Glengarry, or Strathglass, the name – when it has this wider meaning – is written as one word. So Strath Naver, meaning the valley of the River Naver, is so written; while Strathnaver, meaning much of north Sutherland, is so written. The second exception is that where a locality forms part of the title of a chief or chieftain, again it is written as one word: hence Strath Garve, but MacKenzie of Strathgarve; Loch Nell, but Campbell of Lochnell; Glen Coe, but MacDonald of Glencoe; Loch Eil, but Cameron of Lochiel (common usage usually reverses the vowels in "Eil" when it is used as part of the chief's designation). A third exception is where the name of a glen or strath has been thriftily employed also as the name of a neighbouring feature – perhaps a village or a parish: thus Glen Finnan the glen, Glenfinnan the village; Strath Peffer the valley, Strathpeffer the village; Glen Isla the glen, Glenisla the parish; Strath Carron the valley, Strathcarron the railway station; Strath Carnach the valley, Strathcarnach the sheep farm. A fourth exception is that when the name of a loch is used as part of a term covering the area nearby, again it is incorporated into a single word – Loch Arkaig, but Locharkaigside, and Loch Tay, but Lochtayside.

I have standardized the spelling of surnames beginning M', Mc, and Mac, whether followed by a small letter or a capital, into Mac followed by a capital; especially since many of those with those surnames seem to have been happy themselves to spell their names in different ways, particularly in times past. If I have offended anyone who prefers a different spelling, I apologize. (The only exception is where some contemporary or recent figure seems invariably to prefer one of the other spellings: then I have tried to follow suit.)

Early in the twentieth century the authorities of the council centred on Dumbarton decided to call the county Dunbartonshire. This seems illogical, and in any case the writers of previous centuries, whose work I occasionally quote, used the earlier and more reasonable name (so does *Nelson's World Gazetteer* of 1941): so I have continued calling the shire of Dumbarton by the original and more tenable term.

One must distinguish the clan from the clan chief. In the case of those MacDonalds who lived in South Uist, in Eigg and Canna, and in Moidart and Morar, this has been done by calling the clan itself Clan Ranald, and the chief Clanranald.

I had thought that, since every British publisher of any size rejected this work (many of them twice), the only people who would ever read it would be members of my own family. So from time to time I have put in odd bits of information which might be of interest to near relatives, though perhaps to no one else. Readers may (and no doubt will) ignore such irrelevancies.

3. Parish names

Some parish names in Scotland are shared by two – or more – parishes, so where in the notes a reference has been made to a parish report in the Old Statistical Account of 1791-9, or the New Statistical Account of 1845, a shortened form of the relevant county has been added. These briefer styles have been used: Sutherland, Suth; Ross and Cromarty, Ross; Inverness-shire, Inv; Argyllshire, Arg; Buteshire, Bute; Stirlingshire, Stir; Dumbartonshire, Dumb; Perthshire, Perth; Angus, Ang; Aberdeenshire, Aberd; Banffshire, Banff; Morayshire, Moray; Nairnshire, Nairn; Caithness, Caith; Renfrewshire, Renfr.

The reader should also note that some Highland parishes have alternative names. In Ross-shire, Knockbain is also known as Kilmuir Wester and Suddie; Resolis as Kirkmichael; and Urquhart as Logie Wester. In Argyllshire, Glassary is also known as Kilmichael; and Strathlachlan was sometimes shortened to Stralachlan. In Buteshire, Kilmory could be spelled Kilmorie; in Inverness-shire Dunlichity could be Dunlichty, and Petty could be Pettie.

A number of Highland parishes were combined with a neighbour to make a joint-parish. In these cases, a reference to the main parish may be taken also to refer to the subsidiary parish, unless the context dictates otherwise. These are the Highland joint-parishes –

Ross-shire: Kilmuir Wester & Suddie.

Inverness-shire: Abernethy & Kincardine, Boleskine & Abertarff, Croy & Dalcross, Daviot & Dunlichity, Duthil & Rothiemurchus, Kingussie & Inch, Moy & Dalarossie, Urquhart & Glenmoriston.

Argyllshire: Ardchattan & Muckairn, Dunoon & Kilmun, Gigha & Cara, Glenorchy & Inishail, Jura & Colonsay, Kilarrow & Kilmeny, Kilbrandon & Kilchattan, Kilcalmonell & Kilberry, Kilchrenan & Dalavich, Kilfinichen & Kilvickeon, Killean & Kilchenzie, Kilmore & Kilbride, Kilninian & Kilmore, Kilninver & Kilmelfort, Lismore & Appin, Lochgoilhead & Kilmorich, Saddell & Skipness, Strachur & Strathlachlan, Tiree & Coll.

Perthshire: Dunkeld & Dowally, Monzievaird & Strowan.

Aberdeenshire: Crathie & Braemar, Glenmuick Tullich & Glengairn.

INTRODUCTION

1. Ruined Houses

Any visitor to the Highlands of Scotland must become curious about their history. Archaeology shows that people lived in the Highland straths and glens for thousands of years: why are they so empty now? What were these so-called "clearances" and "evictions" that are occasionally mentioned? And what happened to the people whose ruined habitations still dot the landscape in many remote areas?

When these questions first occurred to me in the middle of the last century, I naively assumed that most events in history, particularly when they concerned our own islands, and even more particularly when they occurred within the last two or three hundred years, must be adequately covered in a book somewhere, if I could only find it. But several years' searching at that time – in the 1950s – yielded very little to explain the emptiness of the Highlands. It was true that one Scottish journalist and author, Alexander MacKenzie (who was born on a croft in Wester Ross, and later became Dean of Guild in Inverness), had published in 1883 a somewhat over-titled *History of the Highland Clearances*, which was a collection of articles, pamphlets, speeches, and memoirs, some produced by himself and some by other opponents of the clearances; but the book had had very little effect on the basic currents of historical thought.[1] Many serious Scottish historians, who had after all spent their entire adult lives studying Scottish history at Scottish universities, discounted these "clearances" almost completely, and so did other responsible authors. They had occurred, it appeared, in only a few places, and any upset they had caused had been the result of the bunglings of a handful of incompetent or unusually harsh estate managers. By and large, the landlords were blameless.

There had certainly been many emigrations from the Highlands, which had led to many districts becoming almost deserted by the human race: but this was the result (we were persistently told) solely of a catastrophic population explosion, which had left the Highlands so desperately overcrowded that everyone, rich and poor, had seen the necessity for the Highlanders to leave their homeland at the first opportunity. (Though for some reason only the poor Highlanders acted on this – apparently joint – conviction, despite the fact that their poverty added greatly to the difficulties and dangers of emigration; the rich Highlanders, who could have emigrated almost in comfort, stayed at home, and – unless they were very foolish, which of course a few were – added to their fortunes.) The owners of the Highland estates, who had been attacked at the time by some irresponsible troublemakers, had in fact been completely innocent: they had acted merely from a desire to improve the welfare of their small tenants. They had not aimed to make a profit for themselves; the last thing on their minds had been any wish to make money or become prosperous. They had indeed – most of them – ruined themselves by their altruism, or been ruined by economic adversity. C. R. MacKinnon of Dunakin said of the years after 1746, when the Jacobite rising was defeated at Culloden: "The 'rebel' chiefs were either imprisoned or had fled, and their estates were forfeit. Those who managed to maintain their possessions [i.e., all the other chiefs] were gradually starved out."[2] So any pity we might feel on reading the Highland history of the last few centuries should be reserved entirely for the landlords.

This was the view taken by most leading historians, and by nearly all the great figures of Scotland's academia. Indeed, Professor Dr Gordon Donaldson, the Poet Laureate, as it were, of Scottish history, having been for fourteen years (1979-93) the Historiographer Royal in Scotland, declared a few years ago as he approached retirement age that until recently he "had hardly heard of these Highland clearances";[3] and in the books he wrote, summing up a lifetime's toil in the vanguard of Scottish historical writing, he felt that the historical reality of any such occurrences was so uncertain that whenever the unsavoury allegations had to be mentioned, the words "clearances" and "evictions" were admitted to his work only in quotation marks. Many modern commentators admit that clearances did occur, but say that there was such an enormous increase in the Highland population that they were unavoidable. A new school has now emerged, whose views are closer to Donaldson's. Those belonging to this school say that there were no clearances, or almost none, and anyone placing confidence in such stories is merely lazily accepting a myth. So now modern intellectual thought can boast two schools of denial: one pours cold water on the idea that millions of people were murdered in European concentration camps during the Second World War, while the other ridicules the view that there were ever any serious attempts to clear the Highlanders off all the good land.

2. *The footprint on the sand*

Since sixty-odd years ago, when I first went to the Highlands, there was so little material available on the clearances, I began – as a matter of personal curiosity – to collect what scraps of information I could discover. After a few years' gleaning, my appetite was whetted (as often occurs) by the scarcity of anything to satisfy it; so I went about the business more systematically, haunting the Reading Room of the British Museum, as it then was (I lived at the time in London), and paying visits to other libraries when time allowed, trying to find out what had happened. As I did this, I began more and more to think that I ought ultimately to find time to set down what I had unearthed. I had to earn my living, like most other people, and this naturally cut down my time for research. In 1963 I happened to be employed by a publishing firm, and I was looking through *The Bookseller* one day when I found that a book called "The Highland Clearances", by John Prebble, was coming out later that year. I felt like Robinson Crusoe when he saw the footprint on the sand: I was not alone. That evening I put a blank sheet of paper in my typewriter, and began the first of these volumes.

Fifty-five years later, this account has grown to over 1,600,000 words – rather long. (The Bible is said to have about 783,000 words; half as many.)[4] Of course I found that as I wrote I had more research to do; and every new book touching on Scottish history which came out, as well as any chance discovery in the second-hand bookshops, besides any volume encountered in the great libraries, had to be scoured for any help it might give, any unknown (to me) incident it might mention, or new avenue it might suggest. Hence the half-century of delay. I always hoped that I might find time one day to look at unpublished sources, as soon as I had completed my examination of the published material; but since I have not succeeded in exploring even all the writings in the public domain, I have not been able (with one or two insignificant exceptions) to turn my attention to unpublished documents. I had my hands more than full, merely considering what is already recorded in print (however obscure many of the printed sources may be). Sherlock Holmes once said, as he pondered the mysterious disappearance of a racehorse on Dartmoor: "It is one of those cases where the art of the reasoner should be used rather for the sifting of details than for the acquiring of fresh evidence."[5] That may serve as a description of what I have been trying to do since I first began to study the Highland clearances.

I have not been able to make my account proportionate with the events it describes. Ideally one should give as much space to a clearance in 1755 as to one in 1877: but much less can now be discovered about earlier events than about later ones. Sometimes information about entire counties for whole years in, say, the 1760s is scantier than what is known about single days in individual parishes in the 1880s. What one can now write about particular years or particular places depends not on their probable relative importance but on the amount of material that is available. In the words of an early history of the Britons, I can only say, "I have piled up everything I have discovered";[6] and I can only apologize if the size of the piles concerning different eras is disproportionate.

I ought to add a further apology here. It might be thought extraordinarily arrogant for someone who has yet to earn the slightest monetary return from all this historical research, to presume to offer criticism of those whose lives have

INTRODUCTION

been spent at the universities, earning reasonable salaries, winning higher offices, and pluming themselves on the prestige of professorial preferment. I can only say that I did not plan anything this way, and I have made repeated attempts to get this work published, but without success. I would have had no objection to any payment if it had ever arrived. But lack of financial reward should not mean that this account is never available.

3. What happened?

From the start, I was merely trying to find out what had actually happened. Schools of historiography come and go: my own belief is that history is simply a search for reality – the reality, so far as it can now be discovered, about a particular country or area during particular years. Of course one cannot put down every fact. The largest encyclopaedia in the world could not cover a single day in a single country if one did. One therefore has to choose as honestly as one can what seems to be significant. The problem is perhaps less acute when one is writing not a general history but the history of a particular phase or movement in the history of one particular region, as I am doing; by the definition in the title, I am writing about whether any mass evictions occurred, or did not occur, in a particular area, the Highlands, during a particular period, the eighteenth and nineteenth centuries, rather than about cattle prices or domestic architecture or any other strand of social life.

However, the key is still accuracy. Did clearances happen, or did they not? If they happened, where and how did they happen? What were their causes and what their results? What can reasonably be taken as proved, and what must be left blank, or at best offered as a possibility?

Firstly, accuracy is essential. Professor T. C. Smout, the present Historiographer Royal in Scotland, writing a foreword to another writer's survey of Scotland, said "in points that do not matter greatly, except to academics like myself, he is not always accurate".[7] Without embarking on the question of whether the criticism of this particular author was justified, it is necessary to defend the importance of accuracy; it is essential at all times, at all places, and to everyone – not merely "to academics". It could be claimed that it is not a matter of great moment whether the train from London to Edinburgh leaves at nine o'clock or ten past nine; but to anyone bound for Scotland who arrives at King's Cross at five past nine, it is very important indeed. Besides that, the implication that academics worship accuracy cannot survive an examination of what professional historians have written about the Highland clearances. Despite this author having claimed that he belonged to the only body of people – academics – to whom accuracy "mattered greatly", what he asserted when he wrote about the Highland clearances can only be described as (to use his own hesitant phrase) "not always accurate". For example, he said that in the history "of the Hebrides", during the years up to 1830, evictions were few and far between. "There is little hint (except on Rum and Jura in 1826 and on Arran in 1828) of men at this date being turned out to make room for sheep."[8] The sad reality of the matter is that in the 1820s alone, people were "turned out to make room for sheep" in practically every parish in the Hebrides; and there were also virtually ubiquitous clearances in those islands both before and after that decade. (These events are covered in volume four of this work.)

4. Time to be in earnest

All this time I have been actively engaged in finding out more about my chosen subject, since I wanted to make my account as comprehensive as possible. But now, after over half a century of labour, I am ninety – well past the biblical allotment, so a long future period of active life cannot be guaranteed, to say the least. A. E. Housman regretted that of his "threescore years and ten, twenty will not come again"; in my case, I have left not only the "twenty" but also the "threescore years and ten" well behind. So if publication is much longer delayed, it may well be deferred for ever: postponement will ripen into cancellation.

I have constantly tried to bring this account up-to-date, if only to avoid the criticism that the beliefs I am questioning were abandoned decades ago: and as (pursuing this objective) I was splicing into my work some remarks about another book on the Highlands, I suddenly realized that when I began writing my account of the clearances, the writer from whose work I was quoting had not only not commenced his career as a historian, but in fact *had not been born*.[9] From that point I had to admit that chronology was not on my side. "At seventy-seven", as Dr Johnson said, "it is time to be in earnest"; and I am well past that particular milestone. (Johnson, paradoxically, never reached it.)

Authors not infrequently apologize for the shortcomings of their work in their preliminary remarks. I have to do the same, and in my case the reader will see that there is certainly no false modesty involved. What is here published is really only work in progress. I know I could have made the work more complete and could have added to and improved what I have written; and if anyone could pledge me another decade of industrious existence, I would have done it. Such guarantees not being available, this is all I have time for.

5. Archive of the head

All historians of distant events rely completely on what they have been informed by other people, such information being almost always in writing. Of myself, I

INTRODUCTION

know nothing of the Highland clearances: I was not there when they occurred. I am in the same position as the schoolboy who complained that his history teacher kept asking him about things which had happened before he was born. All historians are would-be acrobats, attempting to balance on the shoulders of other commentators; all writers about past events have to derive much of their material from other writings. (Spoken words are important, but what people say only certainly endures in a completely reliable form if it is accurately recorded in one way or another.) All any author can do, and what every author must do, is to evaluate his information. Simon Schama talks of the "archive of the feet" – go and visit, he says, the places you are writing about. That is, of course, very valuable advice, which all historians should follow wherever possible. Equally important, in my view, is what might be termed the "archive of the head": in other words, every writer should use all he knows, should exercise all his wits, continually to ask and to answer numerous questions about his material, in order to decide the significance of each piece of apparent evidence. All one's knowledge and reasoning power (such as they are) must be brought into play to answer the many questions which continually arise, such as these – Is this likely, when measured against the other evidence? Is the witness a reliable one? Does he or she have "an axe to grind"? Is the testimony simply what he/she might have been expected to say, or is it so far as one can see disinterested? (Mandy Rice-Davies' pithy comment in the Stephen Ward trial – "He would say that, wouldn't he?" – should always be kept in mind.) Does it, even more significantly, go against the interest of the witness? (In the law courts, there are some cases where evidence is admitted only when it is against the interest of the person speaking.) Was he/she really the kind of person – always remembering the importance of a witness's economic and social background – who would understand what he/she is attempting to describe? Does this fit in with what we know of human behaviour? Is there an assumption that everyone always tells the truth? If I accept that the memories of poor and unimportant people may not always be accurate, do I nevertheless assume that the statements of important people, wealthy people, official people, must always be correct? If a document looks weighty and imposing, must it be believed? (If all documents must be accepted without question, then the man who writes the document makes the history.) In every case one's experience of the world, for example one's comprehension of the way people behave under certain pressures, cannot be ignored, but must be brought fully into play.

Not every piece of evidence points inescapably in one direction: a skilled polemicist could use a single fact to support two completely opposite conclusions. If (say in 1700) a meteorite had fallen by great ill-luck directly on to a Highlander and killed him, the event could be used by different writers in very different ways. One writer might say that this was the only such event during several centuries and was therefore very rare; another writer might give great prominence to it, alleging that Highlanders ran great risks from falling meteorites, and then, "for example", relate this particular incident, and allege that it was "typical". It is as if one was to write about twentieth-century Britain: "Doctors murdered large numbers of their patients; for example, one doctor was suspected to be guilty of killing 200 of the people he treated." This "example", of course, proves nothing. In the same way, there is apparently one man now alive who is eight foot five inches tall; but it would be unacceptable to claim that in the twenty-first century human beings generally were over eight feet high, then offering the example of this one individual as "proof". To know how useful such an assertion is, it would be essential to apply what I have called the "archive of the head". (In passing, one may say that the appearance of the phrase "for example" or the word "typically" should make the reader even more wary than – one trusts – he or she normally is. Of course it is perfectly allowable for a writer to give an example "for instance", if the point really does represent many similar cases; it is when the point is not at all typical that it becomes inadmissible.) In the field of Highland history, many historians "prove" that the Highland population rose dramatically, or tremendously, or amazingly, by quoting those parishes where the figures seem to show a great rise, while ignoring all those other Highland parishes where the figures showed a great fall. Other writers repeat the allegation of a vast Highland population rise without even that much evidence: reminding one of Kipling's monkeys, who cried, "We all say so, and so it must be true."[10]

This healthy suspicion should apply to all sources of information. It is not uncommon to see a writer examining with great scepticism any evidence that is hostile to his theory, only to accept without demur anything – however dubious – that supports his contentions. That is a double standard of the worst kind. Lytton Strachey said that we could not be sure what had happened at a certain interview between Pope Pius IX and the man who later became Cardinal Manning, since no one else was present. One commentator gave him the lie direct: yes, we did know, he said, because the Pope later left an account of their meeting. I trust it will not be considered too heretical to back Strachey on this issue: no one, whoever it may be, should be considered as being beyond or above the "archive of the head".

Nearly all this work is based on printed and published sources. I have tried to give, and I hope I have given, credit to those whose work I have used. Where I have taken information from other writers, I have accepted it only when the "archive of the head" would recognize it as probable. Other information that does not pass this test, even from the same writers, I have sometimes criticized and rejected. The criterion is not, and it cannot be, who provided the report; it is, and it must be, whether the report is convincing. In my opinion this is a reasonable procedure.

INTRODUCTION

6. Nothing personal

I have four points to make about notes.

1. Firstly, I confess I prefer an account to be as uninterrupted as possible and get annoyed to find my progress through the text (perhaps when I am trying to follow a complicated argument) to be continually ambushed by little numbers. (However, since much of what I have written goes against the received wisdom on these matters, and therefore may invite scepticism, I have been persuaded to put in a number of footnotes showing my authorities – as the reader can see.)

2. As I say above, I know nothing from my personal experience about these matters, and I have tried to underline this unhappy reality by putting a source – author and volume – in the text, wherever I have written about a fact that may be thought questionable.

3. Much of my work disagrees with orthodox history. Often I have quoted an orthodox belief merely to question it, and very often the theory I have outlined, or the wording I have cited, is merely one example out of dozens or even hundreds of similar assertions; in such cases there is no point in identifying a writer too closely, in case it seems that I am merely concerned with scoring points off a particular individual. Nothing in these volumes is personal; I am only concerned with trying to establish what actually happened. However, if the context seems to require that a particular writer with whom I am disagreeing has to be named, I have named him.

4. When I have written something that may be thought dubious, I have tried to support it by using the archive of the head. Some academic historians seem to feel that directing a reader to a particular written document is the same thing as proving what you have just asserted: and of course it is not. I am sometimes reluctant to put in a note of this kind in case I may be suspected of doing the same. Professor Eric Richards, who has written several books about the Highland clearances, assured his readers, when dealing with the Sutherland clearances in particular, that the population there was expanding fast. "The population of the Highlands had increased at an unprecedented rate, even in the most remote locations . . . Signs of accumulating population pressure were evident across the [Sutherland] estate . . . The local population was increasing rapidly . . . [Strath Naver had] a large population; [it was] densely populated."[11] Professor Richards referred to two documents in order to support his assertion of rapid population growth in Sutherland, one of which referred to a very small area of the county which was not at all typical, and could quickly be revealed to be not at all typical[12] and the other of which was a propagandist assertion by the Sutherland estate factor which was false, and could easily be shown to be false;[13] both of these

allegations, however, were supported by meticulous notes showing exactly where the documents concerned could be found. (In fact, the Sutherland population was extremely sparse to begin with, and experienced in 1750-1800 only a very mild increase – about seven per cent. Further particulars are given in the third volume of this work, which describes the Sutherland clearances.) This is merely one instance of the way in which a detailed note giving the exact provenance of assertions is used instead of employing the archive of the head, that is to say attempting to decide whether the information offered is true or not. I have been reluctant to let it be assumed that my work shares any of these techniques.

I was trying to find out about the Highland clearances for some years, merely satisfying my own curiosity, before I began to think about possible publication. So in those early years I merely used to jot down what others had said in order to remind myself of their information, and though I put down the name of the author and the title of the book, sometimes I failed to record the name of the publisher, or the date of publication, or the location of the firm, or the exact page. As a result, though I believe that nearly all references in this volume (over two thousand of them) are complete, it may be that in some few cases this detailed information is still absent. If any reader knows of any of these few missing details, and would tell me, I would be very grateful.

7. References

My original feeling about notes was this. After some years of searching for material about the clearances I decided that I ought to write about them in order to challenge what many historians had maintained about Highland history, for example what Professor Dr George Macaulay Trevelyan, Order of Merit, late Regius Professor of Modern History at the University of Cambridge, and late Master of Trinity College Cambridge, had asserted in his *English Social History*. Since I was writing what I hoped would be an answer to Trevelyan, I put down as many notes as Trevelyan had done: that is, almost none. If Trevelyan could describe what he alleged were the features of the Highland clan system while giving neither any instances from the actual history of the clans, nor any reasoned argument to back up his assertions, then I, giving both many historical instances and what I considered to be much reasoned argument (as will be seen later in these volumes), along with incorporating sources of any importance in the text itself, then I was already going much beyond what the Regius Professor of Modern History at Cambridge University thought was necessary. I put down the same number of notes – i.e. none – as Professor Gordon Donaldson had done when he said there were few clearances, or when Michael Fry said that there were practically none, or when Magnus Linklater said the clearances were "largely myth", or when Professor Rosalind Mitchison wrote that "typically" Caithness was not reported as Gaelic speaking, or when Professor T. C. Smout asserted that there was "little hint" of clearances (except in three places) in the Hebrides in the decade and a half after Waterloo, or when a number of experts repeatedly said there were Highland estates "which never cleared", or (on the other side of this controversy) when several commentators said the Highlanders after Culloden were forbidden to speak Gaelic, or when a number of writers alleged that 2000 families were evicted "in one day". (None of these avowals is, unfortunately, in accordance with the facts.) Another prominent work on these subjects, *The Highland Clans* by Sir Iain Moncreiffe of Moncreiffe, abstained from offering a single reference, even declining to name a source when using a direct extract in quotation marks; despite this apparent defect it was described by Professor Bruce Lenman, Professor Emeritus of Modern History at the University of St Andrews, as "the best introduction to the many strands in Celtic chieftainship . . . a book at once learned and attractive",[14] and by Magnus Linklater, historian and formerly chairman of the Scottish Arts Council, as "very well-informed".[15]

Now that I have come to the point of publication, however, I have begun to feel that the system adopted or approved of by Trevelyan, Moncreiffe, Lenman, Linklater and the rest, of professing one's opinions without providing any provenance (even my adaptation of that system) may be criticized, and I have put in some notes. Where what I have written is not supported by adequate annotation, I hope to remedy the deficiency in later volumes. In the meantime, if anyone doubting any statements I have made cares to write to me, I will gladly do my best to explain why I made them.

Readers will soon observe that I have been unable to agree with much of what is now accepted as the standard narrative of Highland history. I have therefore been under the necessity of criticizing, directly or indirectly, a number of other writers in this field. This volume, however, is only the first of five; and if anyone who feels that they have been unjustly maligned cares to make any answer to what I have said, I will print in a forthcoming volume any rebuttal or criticism (of reasonable length), and then try to justify what I have written.

8. Second-hand evidence

Much emphasis is placed in the history schools on the distinction between first- and second-hand evidence, between primary and secondary sources. This is very useful, as far as it goes. It is clearly better to hear from someone present at an event than from someone who arrived after it was all over, and can only report what everything looked like then, and what other people said. However, is first-hand evidence always accurate? It is often given credence which perhaps in some cases it does not merit. In the law reports, describing past cases in the English courts, there are some surprising accounts. In one case a family relationship had to be proved; and a vital link was the wording on a memorial tablet in a church – which had now, for some reason, disappeared. The opposing sides brought forward numbers of witnesses who claimed to have seen the tablet. The versions they gave of what was on the tablet, what names it mentioned, what relationships it indicated, even where in the church the tablet was – were often contradictory. Yet many of the witnesses had frequently attended services in the church, and must often have seen the tablet: so they were all giving first-hand evidence. Again, a television programme decided to investigate the same kind of phenomenon. In a crowded city street, without warning, a car drew up, some men jumped out and hustled a woman back into the car, and then drove off. This was all done by actors, and recorded on camera. Further actors, pretending to represent the law, then appeared in the street, and began questioning the bystanders. The eye-witnesses gave conflicting versions of what make the car was, what was its colour, what persons had emerged from the car, what they had done – and so on. If I remember correctly, there was an even more remarkable circumstance: none of the people near the incident, when the questioning began, had seen nothing. No one wished to admit having missed all the excitement, and having been simply staring into a shop window when it happened. Many of them, however, were volunteering to give first-hand evidence which was incorrect; that was certain because the entire incident had been preserved on film. And one remembers the judge who said, on his last day in court, that he felt he had spent much of his time having to adjudicate on collisions which had occurred between cars each of which had been stationary on its own side of the road.

This is not to say that all first-hand evidence is wrong; obviously no one could say that. But it is necessary to check what people assert by using the archive of the head. Every historian must remember Mr Jaggers' advice to Pip in *Great Expectations* – "Not a particle of evidence, Pip. Take nothing on its looks; take everything on evidence. There's no better rule."[16]

The over-riding distinction to be made, according to the operation of the archive of the head, is not between first- and second-hand; it is simply this – is the information (all things considered) probably true? There have often been cases (both in the past and at the present day) where strange things have been alleged, apparently at first hand; but the evidence has not necessarily been persuasive.

9. Fifteen rabbits

In November 1726 one Mary Toft, a married woman of Godalming in Surrey, reported that she had been frightened by a rabbit while working in a field during her pregnancy, and "as a result" had surprisingly given birth to a litter of fifteen rabbits.[17] They had appeared consecutively, day after day. The local man-midwife, Mr John Howard, affirmed that he had been present during some of these unusual arrivals. One Mr St André, "surgeon and anatomist to His Majesty" (in 1726 that was George I), said that he had been there while Mrs Toft gave birth to two more rabbits. (As Bergen Evans, detailing these events, remarked, such fertility would have been remarkable even in a rabbit.) So we have not one, but three first-hand witnesses of a woman giving birth to rabbits: one of them the woman herself, who (in the popularly sanctified phrase) "should know", and the others two professionals, one of them a particularly eminent practitioner.

Does this mean that one has to accept this story as true? Or should one believe subsidiary avowals from either contemporary or subsequent sceptics, who were not present at these deliveries, and whose words can therefore be ranked only as second-hand? For me, the second-hand evidence prevails over the first-hand, because my view of the universe does not have room for women who give birth to rabbits. Mrs Toft later confessed that her actions had been fraudulent, to gain notoriety, and that she had not in fact given birth to rabbits – thus confirming what the archive of the head would have urgently suggested from the beginning; but so strong is the desire to be amazed that many people, even after her confession, preferred to continue believing that she had. In fact years after she had abandoned her story, as late as 1752, William Whiston declared – according to the *Dictionary of National Biography* – that "she had clearly fulfilled the prophecy in *Esdras* [in the *Apocrypha*] that monstrous women should bring forth monsters", which is an extravagant description of baby rabbits.

Further problems are caused by the numerous cases reported in history of people who defied reality, and "lived without eating", for example during the eighteenth and nineteenth centuries. (If this ability was genuine, it would have solved many problems associated with poverty down the years.) Sarah Jacob, born in 1857, survived without taking food, according to her parents, and became renowned as "the Welsh Fasting Girl".[18] People came to see her, and left her money. Unfortunately it was decided to test her claim; and with her parents' approval, a strict watch was kept on her by four nurses from Guy's Hospital in London, supported by seven local doctors: and eight days later she died of starvation, at the age of twelve. No doubt the arrangements which must have been made to get food to her surreptitiously had not been effective: and Sarah must have ranked her desire to remain famous as more important than her desire to eat, thus becoming an early victim of the celebrity cult. And there were numbers of women during the eighteenth century, and later, who claimed to have given birth to various animals, just as there were numbers of people who claimed to be able to live without eating: indeed, in the twenty-first century a woman gained publicity for herself by making exactly that latter claim. But I cannot bring myself to believe her.

Earlier still, there was the case of Catharina Geisslerin, who in 1642 coughed up numbers of toads in front of crowds of witnesses.[19] She had, she said, inadvertently drunk some swamp water, with tadpoles in it; and now toads were living in her stomach. She could feel them hopping about, an assertion which was taken as a further proof of her story. The toads, by her account, continued to breed in this unpromising milieu for the next twenty years, until she died, in 1662. Doctors then dissected her corpse, but were apparently disappointed to find no live toads inside her.

At much the same time there was living in Italy an illiterate Franciscan friar, one Joseph of Cupertino (born 1603), who according to some could fly.[20] Sometimes in church, said witnesses, he would fly down the nave, out into the open, and across the hills for miles. His ability is proved by "incontrovertible historical documents", as one reverent website tells us. Put on trial by the Inquisition, he flew over the inquisitors' heads (such is the first-hand evidence). Frederick Duke of Brunswick, Prince Casimir of Poland, and Urban VIII (who was pope from 1623 to 1644) all deposed that they had seen him flying around. His aeronautical ability was therefore generally accepted, and a century after he died in 1663 (did he crash?) he was made a saint in the Catholic Church.

10. Canine expert

In 1754 the *Norwich Mercury* told its readers that "THE LEARNED FRENCH DOG from Paris . . . is now to be seen at the Angel in the Market Place". The dog "reads, writes and casts accounts [does sums] by the means of typographical cards".[21] Newspaper standards of accuracy being what they are, we cannot doubt that the reporter had verified this personally. So here was documentary evidence – indisputable for those who think documents cannot lie – for a very accomplished animal indeed: it was such a clever canine that it had even (presumably, being French) mastered two languages, which is more than many human beings have done.

During the First World War, when the fighting in France was going badly for the Allies, Russia sent several brigades to fight alongside the British and French in other theatres of war. Reports of these reinforcements led to a popular belief that large contingents of Russian troops were travelling through England towards the south coast, en route to the Western Front, where (it was confidently expected) they would by sheer numbers swing the balance in favour of the Allies. Numerous eyewitnesses could testify that they had seen them, for example on trains going through Manchester (where, so family lore has it, my maternal grandfather, though he had not observed them himself, at least definitely knew someone who had). No one could doubt these stories, because the Russians "had snow on their boots". The archive of the head would have regarded the graphic detail of this impossibly persistent snow as disproving the whole narrative; but the desire to believe that the Allies would win – thus ending the heavy losses in France and Flanders – was so strong that many otherwise rational people accepted this fantasy.

On 1st April 1976 the astronomer Patrick Moore told his listeners on BBC radio that at exactly 9.47 a.m. Pluto would pass behind Jupiter, thus (he asserted) significantly lessening Earth's gravity: so listeners would experience a strange floating sensation. Hundreds of phone-calls from listeners confirmed that this completely fanciful buoyancy had in fact occurred. One listener, sitting round a table with eleven friends, had floated up into the air, along with the friends, and indeed the table. Another listener had risen so rapidly she had hit her head on the ceiling. This caller may have been meditating an action for damages against Pluto, or perhaps against the solar system generally; but altogether, the direct evidence was very strong.[22]

A mechanical acceptance that "first-hand is better than second-hand" would mean that one would have to believe in unbelievable events. For my own part I reject not only all the first-hand accounts of erudite dogs, rabbit-bearing women, flying friars, stomach-breeding toads, boots with unmeltable snow, reduced gravity, and people who (in Hamlet's words) "eat the air, promise-crammed" (and nothing else), but I would reject a million first-hand accounts if they asserted something which is not believable. In fact some say that more than three millions in Portugal during the first world war "saw" the sun stop in the sky and move backwards. (The sun also approached nearer to the earth; large crowds who had gathered, since the miracle had been foretold, had been soaked by heavy rain, but the sun's unusual nearness dried them all off in ten minutes.) Since it is not believable that the sun would behave in this way, (or, more precisely, that the earth would stop its regular daily rotation, thus presumably throwing off everything and everyone on its surface into outer space) the sceptic has to reject not one or two but millions of first-hand accounts.

11. Stroll in a minefield

I begin chapter one of this work with some remarks on the way in which different versions of history appear. Although I speak there of a "British" version of history as opposed to other countries', it would be a great mistake to suppose that home-grown historians always agree with each other. In fact, when one reads what historians say about other historians (even those in the same country), it appears that an outsider audaciously venturing into the world of historical research is rather like a thoughtless pedestrian taking a light-hearted stroll in a minefield. When many years ago I was reading history at Oxford a friend[23] took me along to All Souls to see A. L. Rowse, whom he had known in earlier years. Rowse saw himself as coming from Cornish tin-mining folk,[23] and since I had (when called up for National Service) chosen to work in the coalmines of South Wales for two years – not to mention the male members of my paternal family having all been coalminers in County Durham – he was very friendly. We talked over some of his historical theories and beliefs, and I was surprised to hear that not only were his fellow historians all, apparently, wrong, but they were reprehensible in almost every way. (It was the first time I had heard the word "heterosexual" used as a term of abuse.) These antagonistic feelings, it seems, were reciprocated. Hugh Trevor-Roper, Regius Professor of Modern History at Oxford, Master of Peterhouse at Cambridge, and Baron Dacre in the House of Lords, made the judicious assessment that Rowse, his fellow historian and fellow Oxford don, was "a Cornish peasant with the character of a mediaeval village usurer". In fact at about the time of my only meeting with Rowse, the Oxford history faculty was awash with rumours about what Trevor-Roper was going to do to Lawrence Stone, then a history tutor at University College (where I was an undergraduate): Stone had written about the Elizabethan gentry, claiming that many were in desperate financial straits. Trevor-Roper disagreed, alleging that Stone had simply misunderstood the documents, and had even got his sums wrong: the whisper was that Trevor-Roper showed people a file in his room at Christ Church marked chillingly "Death to Stone". The rumours had some foundation: in 1951 Trevor-Roper produced (in the words of the *D.N.B.*) an "essay demolishing Lawrence Stone's views on the Elizabethan aristocracy", the demolition being "a prime example of academic vituperation". Perhaps Stone "had it coming": at Christ Church earlier, Stone – said the *D.N.B.* – had gained "a reputation for arrogance during his post-war undergraduate year; on one occasion he stormed out of a revision class conducted by a newly appointed college tutor, Hugh Trevor-Roper". Afterwards Trevor-Roper called Stone "an utter charlatan" whom he had crushed – "I don't boast about it much", he added casually. So much for Trevor-Roper's views on Rowse and Stone. As for another Oxford historian at the time, A. J. P. Taylor – who was such a popular lecturer that despite his having been given the very unattractive time of nine o'clock on Monday morning for his lectures (in one of the largest halls in Oxford), one had to go early to get an adequate seat – as for Taylor, Trevor-Roper called him "an irresponsible left-wing demagogue, the Tom Paine of British television"; it says much about Trevor-Roper's intellectual approach that he thought "Tom Paine" was a kind of swear-word. A rancorous exchange between Trevor-Roper and Taylor took place in 1961. Trevor-Roper said, "I'm afraid that your book *The Origins of the Second World War* may damage your reputation as a historian"; Taylor replied, "Your criticism of me would damage your reputation as a historian, if you had one." Trevor-Roper cast his net more widely, in one case condemning a whole nation: the Portuguese, he thought, were (all of them, apparently) "slovenly". Many of these sagacious judgements were enshrined in Trevor-Roper's letters to Bernard Berenson. When the letters were printed in book form, Laura Cumming wrote in the *Observer*: "What's missing is compassion, proportion, an open mind, surely all virtues one would seek in a historian."24 True: but to seek is not necessarily to find. As for Stone, he survived Trevor-Roper's attacks, and became a professor at Princeton University in the U.S.A. – where, as the *D.N.B.* put it, "his directness in debate, a legacy of Oxford critical techniques, left many scars".

Years later Trevor-Roper, who had by then been made Lord Dacre, and also a director of *Times* newspapers, trustingly authenticated what were supposed to be Hitler's diaries, which *The Sunday Times* wished to publish, although it soon turned out that they were forgeries; fellows of Peterhouse, Cambridge, where Lord Dacre was then Master, and where numerous enmities had developed (in Dacre's own words, the college was "racked by civil war"), revenged themselves by calling him "Lord Faker".25

12. Proved incapable

These exchanges followed an established tradition. Passions run high in senior common rooms. G. R. Elton wrote of Lord Acton: "To study problems not periods was Lord Acton's much-quoted injunction, and those who cite him approvingly fail to note that it is now some seventy years since he uttered those gnomic words, and that in actual fact he proved incapable of studying either problems or periods to a practical conclusion."26 E. H. Carr said of Professor Butterfield's *Whig Interpretation of History*: "though it denounced the Whig Interpretation over some 130 pages, it did not (so far as I can discover without the help of an index) [i.e., the author was so unscholarly that he produced a book without an index] name a single Whig except Fox, who was no historian, or a single historian save Acton, who was no Whig. But anything the book lacked in detail and precision it made up for in sparkling invective." As for the great German historian Ranke, E. H. Carr wrote that Ranke's famous comment that he wanted "only to show what actually happened (wie es eigentlich gewesen)" (how it actually or essentially was) has since been intoned by historians "like an incantation – designed, like most incantations, to save them from the tiresome obligation to think for themselves".27

Scholarly clashes still continue. Tristram Hunt, the well-known historian (now Director of the Victoria and Albert Museum), said that his television rival David

Starkey was " 'a gossip columnist' who had turned history into 'soap opera'."[28] He also said (another account asserted) that Starkey was "dehumanizing history". So Starkey "labelled Hunt 'eye-candy', and said the new boy was jealous of his success".[29] Starkey also accused Elton of having "made Tudor history at Cambridge a desert",[30] and added perceptively that the collective noun for historians was "a malice".[31] Professor Richard Evans' 1997 book, *In Defence of History*[32] evoked a number of acid attacks from other historians. Lynn Hunt called it "a mishmash in which bald assertion substitutes for analysis". Michael Burleigh said of the book, "gossip involving Hugh Trevor-Roper figures more prominently than his major contributions to European history". Niall Ferguson accused Evans of "rudeness" towards "historians of broadly conservative inclinations". Evans had criticized some things Diane Purkiss had written: Purkiss accused Evans of not having read her book, or of not having read it accurately, and said, "any resemblance between my work and claims made about it by Evans is purely coincidental". In 2001, in a later edition of his book, Evans added an "Afterword", in which he defended himself, as well as history, by delivering some stinging ripostes. Ferguson, he affirmed, had made "a statement of . . . crass prejudice": he "wraps himself in contradictions". In fact "it would not seem unjustified to describe Ferguson's own remarks about gender history as deeply ignorant". Anthony Easthope had attacked Evans' book (said Evans) "by giving a deliberately false and distorted version of what it actually says"; he was guilty of "complete misrepresentation", which "quickly landed him in a predictably hopeless quagmire of self-contradiction". Evans accused him of "doctoring a sentence in a text to make it support the argument", and deplored "his distortion and misrepresentation of the book's contents". Peter Ghosh, thought Evans, had written "the most intellectually confused as well as the most aggressive of all the reviews of the book"; in fact "the confusions and contradictions" in the review, and "Ghosh's comprehensive misreading of *In Defence of History*" made it, said Evans, "hard to believe that Ghosh has read the book properly". Keith Jenkins had attacked Evans' work. Evans retorted that "the arguments Jenkins puts forward are based on an almost complete misunderstanding of what I wrote"; one of his claims, in particular, was "offensive as well as absurd". As for Diane Purkiss, she "not only gets herself tangled up in contradictions, but also attributes to me a whole series of propositions that I have never advanced"; one of her statements, said Evans, was "pure invention".[33]

13. Blustering and abusive

Two history professors, Professor Marwick (professor of history at the Open University) and Professor Munslow (professor of history at Staffordshire

INTRODUCTION

University), fought a flamboyant verbal duel[34] a few years ago in the scholastic press. Munslow attacked Marwick's latest work, and Marwick retorted, in diatribes which can be seen on the website of the Institute of Historical Research. Munslow thought Marwick had written a "blustering and abusive book", suffering from "many misconceptions" and indeed from "deep confusion"; he regretted Marwick's "descent to pretty low levels of misrepresentation", his "political narrow-mindedness", his "crude tub-thumping", and his "simple intellectual confusion". There were, Munslow alleged, "many descents into wanton professional abuse"; the book was written in a "mean-spirited and condescending tone". After exposing, as he claimed, one error, he said there were "many other regrettable/ludicrous/bizarre/funny/plainly wrong statements of this kind". After the bystander has considered the terms used in this debate, and has tried to decide whether history is a reconstruction, a replication, or a representation, and if the latter, whether it is a substitution representation or a resemblance representation, and whether it is best understood by "subjectivist a priorism", by an "empirical-analytical" approach, or as a "narrative-linguistic" enquiry – after all that, the bystander is relieved to read Professor Munslow's words: "Certainly we can choose to believe the past once existed (I choose to believe it did)." In his reply Professor Marwick gave as good as he got. Marwick's book had already called A. J. P. Taylor "ridiculous", and claimed that Elton had exposed the "nonsense spouted by philosophers (including Collingwood) and Marxists, particularly Carr". As for Munslow, Marwick asserted that he wrote "indigestible prose" and, further, that he "scarcely comprehends" his (Marwick's) material, and in fact "completely misrepresents" it. Marwick deplored Munslow's "ranting", and what he labelled "this nonsense". One of Munslow's comments was called "an astonishing and ignorant statement", while another was "a despicable inversion of the truth". In summary, Munslow's review evoked Marwick's retort: "Does he really have to go on boring the pants off us?"

The contest was so heated that standards of literacy slipped. In Munslow's piece "the historians thinking" lost its apostrophe, while "what historian's imagine" and "this initial list of historian's" illicitly gained that useful grammatical mark. Munslow said Marwick had accused a third historian of writing "nave drivel" (about churches?), while Marwick said historians might err because of "synchophancy towards a patron". (Perhaps this means several people engaging in servile flattery all at the same time.) Again, Marwick – as quoted by Munslow – warned against over-using the term "to construct", since that "simply evacuates from it of all significance". Munslow also economized on hyphens, as in "under theorized and weak arguments", "source based historical study", "data based methods", and "the history making enterprise as a whole".

In the particular field of enquiry which is dealt with by the present volumes, John Prebble's ground-breaking work on the Highland clearances – some parts of which I have, I hope politely, taken the liberty to disagree with – was described by Professor Donaldson, Historiographer Royal of Scotland (in more academically acceptable terms) as "utter rubbish".[35]

14. What hath been

Why should any – presumably sane – human being presume to set himself up against such forces as these, merely for the pleasure of spending a lifetime disinterring events which occurred very many years ago, and cannot now be changed? A general justification would perhaps quote Thomas Fuller: "He that would know what shall be must consider what hath been."[36] As to why I have spent time on this particular topic, I could only hesitatingly say that I felt an injustice had been done, and that I was endeavouring, however imperfectly, to make that injustice known. The Gaelic Highlanders, or so it seems to me, had been treated badly. Many religions, of course, offer the comforting thought that everything will be put right in a future world. Those who have been undeservedly penalized on earth will be favoured; those who have gained unfairly in this life will be made to suffer. All will receive their rightful reward – whether recompense or retribution – in due course: everyone will enjoy equity in the eye of eternity. But while awaiting this supernatural settling of scores, we must try as best we can, if not to correct injustice (a fate which is given to few), at least to let injustice be revealed. A past iniquity left obscure, or even worse vaunted as virtuous behaviour, is only laying the foundation for more injustices in the present and the future. It is of course obvious that many orthodox historians will not agree with what I have written, and that in the unlikely event of them reading or hearing of this work, I can expect some frosty rejoinders. But, as Byron said, in this world, a man – especially a writer – "should calculate upon his powers of resistance before he goes into the arena".[37]

Perhaps in the end the best justification would simply amend the words of George Mallory about Everest, and say merely that one writes about historical events because they occurred. At any rate there is some satisfaction to be gained from being able to conclude one's work by declaring that, so far as one person's honest attempts can make it so, – this is what really happened.

15. Envoi

What should be the send-off for a series of which the five volumes include over 1,600,000 words? Perhaps such prolixity justifies three of them.

INTRODUCTION

1. Robinson Crusoe, alone on his desert island, built himself a canoe that was too big and heavy for him to drag to the water, so in the end he had to leave it where it was, having wasted all his labour. "Now I saw, though too late, the folly of beginning a work before we count the cost, and before we judge rightly of our own strength to go through with it."[38] Crusoe constructing a craft that turned out to be too weighty for him to launch may well be compared to an unknown author writing a book so long that its length becomes a further reason for publishers to turn it down. Like Crusoe's canoe, the book was almost too heavy to drag to its intended destination.

2. Dr Johnson wrote in the Preface to his Dictionary in 1755: "I have protracted my work till most of those whom I wished to please, have sunk into the grave, and success and miscarriage are empty sounds: I therefore dismiss it with frigid tranquillity, having little to fear or hope from censure or from praise."[39] When Dr Johnson wrote that, he had attained the venerable age of forty-five; so the feelings of an author who is twice as old as that when his book is finally brought out may all too easily be imagined. Many friends who have over the years enquired, sometimes with a little smile, as to the progress of my work, have unhappily left the land of the living, so I will never be able to say to them – "You know that book I was writing? Well . . ." So I can only declare that I would like to offer, if it were possible, my belated apologies for such a delay to a large and increasing group of those who are no longer with us – Basil and Joy, Brian, Johnny and Sheila, David, Hans, Lol, John, Dennis, Jay, Ellis, Liz-Anne, Richard, Reg, Mike, Bill, Shirley, Gordon, Pen, Arthur and Phyllis, Edmund, Lionel, Pieter, Stan, Hardie, Gilmac and the others[40] – at the same time as I regret that my dilatoriness has deprived me of these small triumphs.

3. Huckleberry Finn, as transcribed by Mark Twain, was glad to bring his work to a close: "there ain't nothing more to write about, and I am rotten glad of it, because if I'd a knowed what trouble it is to make a book I wouldn't a tackled it and ain't a-going to no more."[41] Charles Dickens wrote about the sorrow with which an author finally lays down his pen; J. K. Rowling said she "howled" at the thought that her book was ending; in my more humble feelings at the moment, Huck Finn's sentiment beats the others' by several lengths.

ALWYN EDGAR

FOREWORD NOTES

1. *Ruined houses*
[1] Alexander MacKenzie, *History of the Highland Clearances*, A. & W. MacKenzie, Inverness, 1883; other editions, e.g. O'Callaghan, Glasgow, 1914; & Melven Press, Perth, 1986.
[2] MacKinnon 1961, 159: ". . . were gradually starved out. As the estates came on to the market they were sold to absentee landlords who knew nothing and cared less about their Highland tenants." These unhappy starving chiefs had already appeared three years earlier in another book by the same author (MacKinnon 1958). On page 9 he enumerated "the lands [of the MacKinnons] parted with after the unsuccessful attempt of 1745 . . . all of which, alas, were lost during these troublous times when chiefs, who could not easily be disposed of by other means, were starved out of existence".
[3] Gordon Donaldson, quoted by R. Gibson (Gibson 2006, 20), & by J. Prebble (Prebble 1986, 41). The remark was first printed in the Scottish *Sunday Standard*, 3rd May 1981. In 1985 the Post Office was thinking of issuing a special stamp to commemorate the passing of the Crofters' Act in 1886, but Donaldson, as the Historiographer Royal in Scotland, advised against it, and the idea was dropped. So Donaldson knew enough about the clearances, and the check to the landlords' power which was given by the Crofters' Act, to weigh in against any commemoration of the Act (A. D. Cameron, *Go Listen to the Crofters*, Acair, Stornoway (1986) 1990, 125-6.)

2. *The footprint on the sand*
[4] The Bible is often said to have 783,137 words – another computation is 774,746 words. I haven't counted them myself, so readers should not take my word for it.
[5] Conan Doyle 1986, 229.
[6] Historia Brittonum, c. 828, supposedly by Nennius: "Coacervavi omne quod inveni."

3. *What happened?*
[7] Smout, in foreword to MacKenzie 1989.
[8] Smout 1970, 353. The author says "at this date", which may refer to his earlier words "after 1800, and especially after 1820", on the same page, but it is not quite clear what "date" is referred to.

4. *Time to be in earnest*
[9] John MacLeod, author of *Highlanders* (1997), born in 1966. I began writing this book in 1963.

5. *Archive of the head*
[10] R. Kipling, *Jungle Book*, Macmillan, London, 1955, 71.

6. *Nothing personal*
[11] Richards 1999, 40, 36, 37; Richards 2005, 135 – in 1814 "the planners" tackled "the still densely populated parts of the great strath of Naver".
[12] Richards 1999, 389, quoting Bangor-Jones, *Assynt Clearances*, Dundee, 1998, 11.
[13] Richards 1999, 104, quoting letter from Young to Gower, 3rd May 1813, NLS dep. 313.
(The figures for Sutherland's thirteen parishes – ignoring the county's minor share of Reay parish – are these: Webster, 20774; 1801 census, 22252; increase,1478; percentage increase, 7.1% over half a century.)

7. *References*
[14] Lenman 1995, 221.
[15] Email to the author from Magnus Linklater, Old Etonian, journalist (working for the *Sunday Times*, he bought the forged "Hitler's Diaries"), historian, broadcaster, editor of Robert Maxwell's *London*

INTRODUCTION

Daily News, past chairman of the Scottish Arts Council; and husband of Veronica Baroness Linklater, a Liberal Democrat peer, the grand-daughter of Sir Archibald Sinclair of Ulbster, Viscount Thurso, owner of much land in Caithness, which had been cleared by his ancestors. (See volumes four and five of this work, which describe the clearances carried out by Sir John Sinclair, Sir George Sinclair, and Sir John Tollemache Sinclair, who were successively landlords of the Ulbster estates, & forebears of Sir Archibald.)

8. *Second-hand evidence*
[16] Charles Dickens, *Great Expectations*, Nelson, London, n.d., 338 (chapter forty).

9. *Fifteen rabbits*
[17] Bergen Evans, *Natural History of Nonsense*, Michael Joseph, London 1947, 112.
[18] *The Observer*, 2nd March 2003, & *Oxford D.N.B.*
[19] *Sunday Times*, 1st August 2004.
[20] *The Times*, 24th & 29th March 2003. Joseph also fasted, so we are told, for some 280 days in the year, leaving only eight-five, or eighty-six in a leap year – fewer than a quarter of them – on which to eat. This, no doubt, would have kept down Joseph's weight, which would be an aid to aviation. Since Joseph's aeronautics are proved by "incontrovertible historical documents", there is no point in an appeal to the archive of the head, since what is written cannot be gainsaid.

The devil also flies. He flew through Blythburgh church in Suffolk in 1577, and out through one of the doors (where his finger marks can still be seen) and across the countryside to Bungay. Lightning had struck Blythburgh church, bringing the steeple crashing down into the nave; Bungay church had trouble from the same storm, or (if preferred) from the same devil.

10. *Canine expert*
[21] As reported in the *Eastern Daily Press*, 24th March 2007.
[22] See website: museumofhoaxes.com.

11. *Stroll in a minefield*
[23] The friend was F. L. (Len) Stevens, whose son John M. Stevens I had known well at U.C.S. and at University College Oxford. Johnny Stevens was the wittiest man I have ever known: the only person of my acquaintance who made you laugh so much that you felt almost unwell. Both Johnny and his father are now dead.

A. L. Rowse remarked on "proletarians like myself" (Rowse, *Historians I have Known*, Duckworth, London, 1995, 108).

During the 1939-45 War the "Bevin Boy" system was introduced. Some of the young men who were called up as they reached the age of eighteen were chosen by lot to go and work in the coalmines instead of joining the army, navy, or air force. At the end of the war this system was abandoned, but instead young men when called up could choose to do their National Service in the coalmines; they were known as "optants". I was one of them. I took this path partly out of curiosity, since so many members of my paternal family had been coalminers. The curiosity was largely satisfied in the first hour or two, but I worked at Penallta Colliery for two years.

[24] *Letters from Oxford: Hugh Trevor-Roper to Bernard Berenson*, ed. Richard Davenport-Hines, Weidenfeld & Nicolson, London, 2006, 376. Oddly enough, Trevor-Roper (who had married the daughter of the Scottish Earl Haig, the First World War field-marshal, after her divorce from her first husband – an admiral – and who chose to buy his country house in Scotland), denounced Scotland – of whose pleasures he had thus twice availed himself – as "barbarian". He was not easy to please. He believed that the kind of history he wrote was the only legitimate kind, and famously claimed that Africa had no history, merely "the unrewarding gyrations of barbarous tribes in picturesque but irrelevant corners of the globe". Perhaps he thought that the Highlanders (and, indeed, even the Scots

Lowlanders) were merely "barbarous tribes" gyrating in irrelevant corners? Trevor-Roper saw himself as one of the upper class, or the elite, or whatever name one chooses for the governing stratum of society. So did his wife. On one occasion, two of her guests said they had spent the previous night at Birmingham. "Birmingham!", said Trevor-Roper's wife. "Whose place is that?" It reminds one of the (no doubt apocryphal) story of the grand châtelaine who said, "there are very few people round here. In fact, there's nobody between us and the Smythe-Johneses the other side of Sheffield." Trevor-Roper believed in free speech for himself, when he was (for example) attacking Scotland and the Highlanders; he was less concerned to defend free speech for others. He bleakly said of Salman Rushdie: "I would not shed a tear if some British Muslims, deploring his manners, should waylay him in a dark street and seek to improve them" (*The Independent*, 10th June 1989). An interesting example of fascism, as modulated in the respectable accents of an Oxford Senior Common Room.

[25] Adam Sisman, *Life of Hugh Trevor-Roper*, Weidenfeld & Nicolson, London, c. 2010. At Peterhouse Trevor-Roper retreated in high dudgeon to the Master's Lodgings: "But angry Dacre rather chose/ In his pavilion to repose."

12. Proved incapable

[26] Elton 1967, 161.

[27] E. H. Carr, *What is History?* G. M. Trevelyan lectures, Cambridge, Penguin, London, 1961. My minimal knowledge of German was shored up by my friend Dennis Armstrong.

[28] *The Times*, 16th August 2002. Hunt, a university lecturer who became an M.P., appears on the BBC, and writes scholarly articles in the newspapers, as well as books; he is now the Director of the Victoria and Albert Museum. (He is also a former U.C.S. pupil.)

[29] Also *The Times*, 16th August 2002.

[30] *The Times*, 21st October 2008.

[31] *Sunday Times*, 28th September 2008.

[32] Evans 1997.

[33] Evans 2001; all these quotations, from Evans and from his critics, are from Evans' "Afterword", pp. 254-316. Many readers will know of other similar academic disputes: for example that between the two historians G. Bowersock and T. Holland – not to mention the famous disagreements decades ago between C. P. Snow and F. R. Leavis and between Isaiah Berlin and Isaac Deutscher. As a postscript to the matters discussed here, one wonders if an outsider would be wise to risk involvement in the kind of controversies associated with the name of Professor Orlando Figes.

13. Blustering and abusive

[34] Website, history.ac.uk/discourse/munslow5.html, September 2001; the debate has now been moved to another website, history.ac.uk/ihr/Focus/Whatishistory/munslow5.html; and at least "nave" has been amended to "naive".

[35] Utter rubbish; quoted e.g. by Brian Wilson, *The Guardian*, 31st January 2001.

14. What hath been

[36] Thomas Fuller, *Gnomologia: Adagies [sic] and Proverbs*, n. p., London, 1732. If we took the advice of Miss Elizabeth Bennet in *Pride and Prejudice*, "Think only of the past as its remembrance gives you pleasure", it may be that not a great deal of history would survive. Jane Austen would be responsible for the wholesale destruction of history departments. And the lawyers, civil and criminal, would have no work if the accused, and the defendants, offered that plea in court.

[37] Lord Byron, in a letter to Shelley, 26th April 1821.

15. Envoi

[38] Daniel Defoe, *Robinson Crusoe*, Wordsworth Classics, London, (1719) 1993, 163.

INTRODUCTION

[39] Dr Johnson, *Dictionary*, preface.

[40] Basil Banks, Joy Banks, Max (Brian) Ettlinger, Johnny Stevens, Sheila Stevens, David Edgar (my brother), Hans (Imre) Strasser, Lol O'Keeffe, John Garrett, Dennis Armstrong, Jay Hobbs, Ellis Hillman, Liz-Anne Bawden, Richard Taylor, Josie Sutherland, Reg Littlefair, Mike Sharman, Bill Emmerich, Shirley Emmerich, Gordon Dixon, Pen Kent, Arthur George, Phyllis George, Edmund Grant, Lionel Selwyn, Pieter Lawrence, Stan Parker, Edgar Hardcastle, Gilbert MacLatchie – etc. It was Pen Kent who, deploring my procrastination, reminded me that the best is often the enemy of the good. And it was Edmund Grant who bought me a very useful book referring to the clearances – practical help much appreciated. (In Omar Khayyam's words, "For some we loved, the loveliest and best, That Time and Fate of all their Vintage prest, Have drunk their Cup a Round or two before, And one by one crept silently to rest.")

[41] Mark Twain, Huckleberry Finn, Wordsworth Classics, London, (1884) 1993, 435.

CHAPTER ONE

THE CLEARANCES IN HISTORY

1. To suit those in power

History is the handmaid of propaganda. Nothing is more false than the idea that history is a generally agreed narrative of days gone by. People disagree strenuously about what should be done in the future; they disagree even more strenuously about what was done in the past. Opera-writers are fond of claiming that woman is capricious: but no flirt was ever so fickle as Clio, the muse of history. In each country, history – that is to say orthodox, mainstream, academic history – is the account of former times that suits those currently in power. Most people would agree that if the Second World War had ended with a Nazi victory, then the account of what happened in Germany between 1933 and 1945 would be enormously different in our history books from what it is now. As George Orwell's *1984* party slogan put it, "who controls the present, controls the past".[1] In Samuel Butler's words, "It has been said that though God cannot alter the past, historians can."[2] Charles Dickens had an instructive exchange in David Copperfield. " 'I suppose history never lies, does it?' said Mr Dick, with a gleam of hope. 'Oh dear, no, sir!' I replied, most decisively. I was ingenuous and young, and I thought so."[3]

The history which is taught in the schools of each country in the world is almost always inconsistent with the history taught in the schools of other countries – even in adjacent countries: in fact, particularly in adjacent countries. Those who disbelieve this should look at the Chinese view of Tibet, the British opinion of Ireland, and the Turkish theories about the Kurds and the Armenians, as well as any "civilized" state's view of the primitive peoples whose countries they have taken over; and then contrast those perspectives with what the Tibetans, the Irish, the Armenians, the indigenous Americans and Australians, and the rest, believe.

In fact, these distinctions are seen even within the boundaries of a single state. Even now, the history taught in the schools of Northern Ireland, and of Glasgow, which are attended by Protestants, is not apparently the same as the history taught in the Catholic schools of those places. Many independent, though publicly-funded, religion-based schools are now being set up across the country, which will presumably perpetuate the divisions which now separate the various sections of the British populace: does anyone believe that the history taught in the Muslim schools, and the history taught in the Jewish schools, will be identical?

Not infrequently, acceptable history is amended before our very eyes: Japanese history was re-written by the Americans after the Allied victory in 1945, and it is now being re-written again by the present Japanese authorities. The emergence of the modern states of India, Pakistan, and Bangladesh, means that the previous picture of what loyal British historians always called the "Indian Mutiny" of 1857-8, a savage outbreak by a bestial band of criminal cut-throats and assassins, is now being challenged by local historians to whom the rebels were valiant freedom fighters in a noble war to expel the oppressors (and who now call the "mutiny" the "First War of Independence"). The Irishmen who staged the Easter Rising of 1916 against British rule were shot as treacherous dogs – no Geneva Convention for them; but to many Irish historians, they are heroic martyrs.[4] These revised opinions – of both 1857 and 1916 – are now seeping into official British history (for reasons which may be connected either with the immigration which has taken place into Britain from Ireland and from the Indian sub-continent, or with the fact that – most of – Ireland, and the countries which have replaced the Indian Empire, are now respectable independent states). Some British accounts of the Indian struggle of 1857 are becoming notably less strident; and when the last of the I.R.A. men from the 1920 conflict died early in the twenty-first century, even in some mainstream British reportage he had progressed from being a terrorist to being a nationalist hero. Either version of course may be right or partly right, but in both cases one would be unwise to forget the pressures that produced that particular portrait. The same is true of the Mau Mau risings of the 1950s in Kenya, described by the British propaganda machine at the time as a series of vile atrocities by people who were virtually subhuman, and punished (inter alia) by the hanging of many Africans, some apparently for the interesting fault of "associating with suspected persons",[5] and the torture of many others; but now there is an independent state of Kenya, the rebellion is regarded by some as part of a gallant struggle for freedom. Again, the sixteenth-century struggle between England and Spain meant that English propagandists needed to depict the Spanish as complete villains, which in turn led to sympathetic treatment of the despotic Aztec Empire with its mass human sacrifices, so that the Spaniards who overthrew it could be painted in blacker colours: different political imperatives now are leading to different historical approaches. In South Africa, the overthrow of the apartheid regime in the early 1990s transformed education; undergraduates at South African universities in those years found that the history they learned at the end of their courses was not the same as the history they learned at the beginning. In Russia, Tsarist history was toppled after the Bolshevik revolution, and some years later Stalin was presented as the all-conquering messiah; after Gorbachov's glasnost, history books began to give details of the millions massacred or starved to death under Stalinist rule. Now Putin, once an officer in the state security police under the Stalinist regime, has denounced this historical re-writing, and has ordered another re-writing himself. The man Putin appointed to produce a more acceptable history has made clear his perspective. "It is wrong to write a textbook that will fill children who learn from it with horror and disgust about their past and their people. A generally positive tone for the teaching of history will build optimism and self-assurance in the growing young generation and make them feel as if they are part of their country's bright future."[6] One would have thought the main aim in writing textbooks would be to tell the truth.

The versions of twentieth-century history offered by Israelis and by Palestinians are completely at odds; which interpretation will ultimately triumph no doubt depends on which of the competing armies and militias can kill most of their "enemies". So far the Israelis, bankrolled by the Americans, appear to be ahead of the Palestinians, bankrolled by various oil-rich Middle Eastern autocracies, in this particular race; but no doubt the Palestinians, if they get sufficient armaments, could overtake them and thus seize control of the present – and the past.

2. Conquest of the Highlands

These facts should help us to understand the way in which the Highlands of Scotland have been treated by historians. The Highlands (as will be shown at length later) can most accurately be regarded as a virtually independent country – or rather, as a series of small virtually independent mini-states, albeit heavily influenced by their powerful neighbour, Lowland Scotland – until the eighteenth century, despite the incessant and strenuous efforts of the Edinburgh authorities to conquer them. Then the armies of the Lowlands and England (which had become one, following the union of 1707) succeeded in subjugating the mountaineers after the Battle of Culloden in 1746, in a campaign of exceptional brutality; the result was the forcible incorporation of the Highland territories into the state of Great Britain. The history of people who have been overpowered is always written to suit the tastes of those who have overpowered them: and the history of the Highlands accordingly has been written to conform with the views of the Lowlanders and the English. The conquest of the Highlands after 1746 turned the chiefs (or petty princes) of these numerous clan countries into landlords, owning wide estates, and in due course they merged with the neighbouring upper class of the Lowlands and England. Not unnaturally this small group of prosperous Highlanders heartily welcomed its own accession to wealth: most people would regard the advent of affluence (to themselves) as its own vindication. Commentaries on the Highlands thereafter were almost entirely written by Lowland and English experts, and by representatives of this minor group of chiefs-cum-landlords, whose economic interests made them a kind of anglophone fifth column in the Highlands, and who like similar small factions elsewhere in the world have furthered their own prosperity by collaborating with foreign invaders.

Any writing on the history of the Highlands by Highlanders was often in Gaelic, which meant that it was all but inaccessible to the English-speakers who now ruled the Highlands.

One notable English expert was Dr Johnson. He gave no time to the study of the history or the current disposition of the Highlanders. He spent exactly two months in the Highlands – he reached what he claimed was "the verge of the Highlands" at Nairn on 26th August 1773, and left the Highlands again at the southern corner of Loch Lomond on 27th October in the same year. He had never been to the Highlands before, and never went to the Highlands again.[7] He could not speak or understand the Highlanders' language, Gaelic, and indeed regarded it as an obscure patois unworthy of engaging the attention of any serious scholar; he could therefore only communicate with those who spoke English, that is almost entirely the well-to-do Highlanders, and the Lowlanders, of course. His opinions (as might have been expected) are largely the same as the opinions of those who shared his language; yet he is considered as a major authority, and is frequently quoted in Highland histories. One Edinburgh academic thought Dr Johnson's account of his fleeting 1773 visit "contains probably the most profound analysis of the social changes taking place".[8] If an Englishman who had never thought about France or the French people, who could not speak French, and indeed regarded the language as an irrelevant dialect in which nothing had ever been written, were to spend two months on a single visit to a few districts of France, his subsequent peremptory pronouncements on French history and society, and in particular on the shortcomings of the entire French nation – would scarcely be regarded with much veneration. But the normal rules do not seem to apply when the Highlands are in question. Of course what Dr Johnson wrote is of great interest: but his impressions should only be accepted if they are approved by what was described in the Preface above as the archive of the head.

If an independent state of "the Scottish Highlands" were ever created, in the same way that numerous independent states (of all sizes) have appeared in many areas previously submerged in the British Empire, the clearances would be extensively depicted and energetically deplored by academics; but since there is no "Highland state", and owing to the dispersal of the Gaels there will presumably never now be one, the history of the Highlands will continue to be written from the standpoint of those Lowland and English state-authorities who viciously subjugated the Highlanders in the eighteenth century, and whose successors now shape our accepted cultural beliefs. Hence the established views about the Highland clearances, as they have been slowly developing over the last two centuries: firstly that (although in some respects distressing) they were unavoidable; secondly that when they were properly considered, they were not only unavoidable, but also praiseworthy; and thirdly (in the eyes of some avant-garde commentators) that they were not only unavoidable and praiseworthy, but also non-existent – they never happened.

3. Orthodox Highland history

These facts may help to explain some of the palpable inconsistencies that appear in the standard narratives of the Highlands. The account given by many orthodox historians of what has happened during the last dozen or so centuries in the Scottish Highlands is simple, and contains four basic propositions:

(a) The Scottish Highlands had a bleak climate and a poor unimprovable soil; the ground was so barren, and the weather so hostile, that even the most meagre supply of raw materials for food and clothing was produced only with great difficulty; adequate provisions for the natives often failed entirely.[9] The result was that the Highlands could clearly not support the Highlanders, who continually suffered – inevitably – from famine or near-famine conditions.

(b) During the second half of the eighteenth century the situation became even worse, since there was an "unparalleled",[10] a "prodigious",[10] a "torrential",[11] and indeed a "stupendous",[12] increase in the population of the Highlands. Since the Highlands had not even been able to support the smaller populace of earlier times, it could certainly not support these vastly increased numbers.

(c) Therefore many Highlanders had to leave; this was offered as the explanation of the emptiness of the Highlands.

(d) When they had gone, leaving only a remnant who had been transformed into semi-destitute small-holders in a few fringe areas, the Highlands were used to produce enormous quantities of food (e.g. meat, fish, game, and dairy products) and of wool (to make clothing), which were exported (producing, as the figures show, big profits for large farmers, and massive rents for landlords) to the Lowlands and England, where the progress of the Industrial Revolution was creating a larger and larger landless class which had to buy these things. In fact some observers contend that the clearances were justified precisely because they had made these gigantic Highland exports of food and wool possible.

When one examines these points, the fourth of them appears fatally to undermine the other three – especially as I could find no convincing evidence either of the alleged continuous near-famine conditions among the old clansfolk, or of the supposedly astounding increase in the eighteenth-century Highland population. The net result of the changes, on a prima facie view, was that the resources of the Highlands, which had previously gone to feed and clothe the Highlanders, now went to feed and clothe (at appropriate prices, of course) the inhabitants of the growing industrial cities of the Lowlands and England. When it appeared to me that the standard explanation for the emptiness of the Highlands was unpersuasive, I began to read everything I could find on the subject, and in due course it transpired that it was not all that difficult for a diligent and disinterested enquirer (both qualifications being necessary) to discover what had really happened. The following pages contain the story of, and the reasons for, the exodus of the Highlanders from the Highlands.

In order to avoid disappointment later, I should stress here and now that a large number of the confident opinions which are regularly set forth in the textbooks on Highland history will evoke no echo in this work. If the reader wishes to stay with the more regular versions of Highland history, which may be thought less demanding, he or she will find them in a great many of the numerous works that line the appropriate shelves in the bookshops and libraries. Since more of these standard books, with their standard narratives and their standard explanations, appear each year, perhaps it is reasonable to emphasize the unconventional approach of this work: particularly, no doubt, as it may be thought that in a work about the Highland clearances, it is felicitous to start with a clearance of some common misconceptions about events in the Highlands. Many of the stock sentiments in Highland history books almost seem to be a challenge to Lord Henry Wotton, in Wilde's *Dorian Gray* ("I can believe anything, provided that it is quite incredible")[13] or to Lewis Carroll's White Queen: "Why, sometimes I've believed as many as six impossible things before breakfast."[14] The White Queen would be the ideal reader of much contemporary Highland history-writing, except that to take on board all the orthodox assertions she would have to continue her exertions well into the afternoon.

To make my own position clear, I have indicated briefly below what I think (rightly or wrongly) are the flaws in the staple views. It will be seen that my views are so unorthodox that at least I am not running any risk of being accused of plagiarism (an imputation not completely unknown in the world of historiography). What appears to be a direct quotation in the list given below, designated by a Roman numeral, is not offered as a literal citation from any particular author, but is, I believe, a fair summary of what is stated, or what is strongly implied, in numerous texts. This is not to say that all commentators on Highland history unanimously embrace every one of the following opinions: but all these points are made repeatedly by historians (or they are inexorably entailed by their efforts).

4. Locating the Highlands

I. "The Highlands of Scotland is an area so obvious that it does not have to be defined."

When I first began to consider the history of the Highlands, I realized that I was working on a much more mundane level than many other observers, and one area where that soon became obvious was in the preliminary question which I thought would palpably have to be tackled first: where, to start with, are the Highlands? I found that commentators on Highland history often refrain from saying which exact part of Scotland they are talking about: a procedure that saves them much hard work. And, of course, the less you tie yourself down to definitions, the easier it is to soar off into airy generalizations without anyone being able to check the accuracy of what you say. Professor R. H. Campbell, of Stirling University, said nonchalantly that the Highlands were "easily identified",[15] and left it at that. Professor Youngson, of Edinburgh University, took his Highland population figures from (and only from) six counties, including the whole of Perthshire and Caithness, despite the fact that eastern Caithness, and southern Perthshire, were clearly part of the English-speaking Lowlands (and despite the fact that this approach resulted in many Highlanders, who lived in no fewer than ten other counties, being left out of the reckoning); and his uncertainty as to the location of the Highlands kept breaking through, in such phrases as "Caithness and the Black Isle (if these can be called Highland at all"; "if Caithness is to be regarded as part of the Highlands"; "districts [e.g. Brora and Blairgowrie] which are not easily regarded as belonging to the Highlands proper"; "marginally Highland districts such as Crieff and Blairgowrie"; and "it may be argued that the shores of the Cromarty and Moray Firths hardly belong to the Highlands proper".[16] It might be thought that if someone writes a whole book called *After the Forty-Five, The Economic Impact on the Scottish Highlands*, it would be advisable at the outset to decide where the Scottish Highlands are.

It would be helpful if it were true that the Highlands were "easily identified" – if there were a generally accepted Highland line, a clear boundary, whether by land or sea, round the Highlands; but in fact people who write about the Highlands must often be referring to different areas, since they frequently – for example – give bizarrely different estimates of the number of Highlanders in the middle of the eighteenth century, when the first serious attempt at a Scottish census was made. It is not unknown for one author to give two – or even three – different numbers as to the Highland population about 1750 in different books. (And there is seldom any acknowledgement that anyone else could give, or that many people have in fact given, dissimilar figures.) An early testimony was that of Robert Chambers, who (in 1827) said the Highlands "has never contained a large population. In numbers, the Highlanders did not now [in 1745] exceed 100,000, or a twelfth of the whole population of Scotland."[17] A few years before Chambers' book appeared, Dr Robertson, in his 1808 work on the agriculture of Inverness-shire, spoke of the number in the early nineteenth century as "a whole million of people, the supposed population of the Highlands of Scotland",[18] which might imply something not far short of a million in the 1750s. But both these estimates were (most people would now agree) wild and very inaccurate guesses, serving only to remind us that the Highlands until recently had been to all intents and purposes a foreign country, and was still a largely unknown land, populated by an alien and obscure people. What have modern authors decided?

Recent estimates, with each writer having defined the Highlands as seemed good to himself or herself, have given astonishingly divergent figures. Fixing a figure for the Highland population in 1750 has been treated almost as a round game, at which any number can play. And all the statistics, given by all the authors whom I have been able to find laying out their estimates for the Highland population in various years – all the figures, without exception, have exaggerated the rise in that population in the years after the failure of the '45. Why that extraordinary unanimity of judgement should have occurred is a question to which an answer may be supplied by the present volume. Let us see what observers have made of the "base number", so to speak, the Highland population in the middle of the eighteenth century; is it a hundred thousand, or is it nearly ten times that number, or is it somewhere in between? This is a necessary first step, before considering the remarkable claims made as to the escalation of that population (and before making any examination of the increased agricultural production during the same years, including the topic of how far the expansion of the food supply could have satisfied, or failed to satisfy, whatever expansion of the population may have occurred after the '45).

5. Numbers in 1750

Professor Rosalind Mitchison said that in the middle of the eighteenth century, when Dr Webster, an Edinburgh minister, tried to compute the numbers in Scotland, the "population of the areas geologically and geographically Highland"[19] (and I hope the reader understands what that means: I don't) was 115,000; Professor Michael Lynch (in a surprising coincidence) reached the same conclusion a year or two later – "the population of the Highlands [was] 115,000 in 1755";[20] John Home thought that the Highlands, as an area of land, embraced "nearly one half of Scotland", but "do not contain one-eighth part of the inhabitants of that kingdom",[21] a conclusion which would mean that there were fewer than 158,172 Highlanders (still 38% more than the Mitchison/Lynch figure); Sir Iain Moncreiffe thought that the numbers in what he considered to be the

Highlands were precisely 216,952, more again;[22] Frank Adam, as amplified by Sir Thomas Innes,[23] said "it has been estimated that in 1747 the population of the Highlands was about 230,000" (exactly twice as many as the Mitchison/Lynch figure); Michael Fry[24] said that in "Webster's census of 1755 the Highlands housed about 250,000 people"; and Professor Donaldson (displaying that finicky precision for which historiographers royal are famous) opined that in 1746 "the population of the Highlands must have been about a quarter of a million".[25] John Lister thought that in the "mid-eighteenth" century the number was 255,000;[26] Adam Collier felt it was "roughly 257,000";[26] Dr I. F. Grant said "the population of the Highlands . . . according to an estimate by a Dr Webster, made in 1755" was 257,153;[27] the *Oxford Companion to Scottish History*[28] said the 1755 population of the "Highlands and Islands, including Argyll and Bute" was 266,000; Michael Brander preferred "about 300,000" (out of a total Scottish population, he said mystifyingly and very inaccurately, of "some 3,000,000");[29] Professor Pryde put forward the figure of 314,823;[30] Dr J. S. Keltie preferred 332,332;[31] Dr I. F. Grant (who had apparently lost confidence in her earlier figure of 257,153), said that the "Rev. Dr Webster estimated the population of the Highland counties at 337,000 in 1755";[32] Michael Fry (some years after this calculation by Dr Grant) also turned against his earlier opinion that the Highlands had "housed about 250,000 people", and also wrote that the "Highland population" was "337,000 in Dr Alexander Webster's census of 1755".[33] Professor Youngson thought Webster's figures "cannot be far wrong", and said his figures showed "the population of the Highlands" was 337,038.[34] Caroline Bingham followed Youngson, and said, "in 1750 an unofficial but probably fairly accurate estimate gave a population of 337,038".[35] Professor Smout thought, somewhat imprecisely, that "between a third and a quarter of the Scottish population of 1,250,000 [Webster's figure for the whole of Scotland was in fact 1,265,380] lived in the Highlands around 1750"[36] – that is somewhere between 312,500 and 416,666. Dr I. F. Grant, in yet another stab at the figures, said "the population in the Highland counties" was "376,086 about 1755".[37] Dr William Ferguson[38] decided on one page that it was about 379,614, and on another that it was, perhaps, nearer to 420,000; James Halliday[39] wrote that "almost one-third of the total [population of Scotland] were natives and residents of the Highland, Gaelic area" – which must mean something of the order of 400,000; while John MacLeod[40] thought that "in 1745 . . . the Highlands held a full third of Scotland's population", – i.e. 421,000 or more. Professor Eric Richards[41] believed the Highlands had "supported practically half the population of Scotland", which has to denote a figure somewhere near 630,000; while Dr Grimble[42] affirmed that Gaelic was "the language of half the population of Scotland", thus indicating a similar number. John Prebble,[43] too, obviously thinking about the Webster count, said that "the Highland people were once the majority of Scotland's population", that is to say 633,000 or more. J. G. Kyd[44] maintained that in Webster's time the population of the "Highland area" was 652,000 (though he made clear that his area extended well beyond the mountains). One website gave a precise percentage: "in 1755, 51% of the Scottish population [or 645,344 people] lived in the Highlands and were Gaelic speakers":[45] this obviously relied on Kyd's computation for "the Highland area", and provided a figure which was more than double the actual number of Gaelic speakers then. Robert Mathieson quoted Kyd's figure, 652,000, as the population of "the Highland area . . . representing roughly the Highlands".[46] Henry Hamilton gave the same figure for the population of the "Highland region".[47] Jeff Fallow followed suit – of the Scots, he said, "652,000 were Highlanders".[48] Another website came equal first among modern competitors by claiming that before 1745 the Highlands was "home to three-fifths of the total Scottish population",[49] an assertion matched by a 2002 volume, which also alleged that "some three-fifths of the Scottish people" lived in the Highlands and Islands.[50] If these two sources were correct, it would mean there were 759,000 people in the Highlands. So the industrious reader can choose: in 1750 there may have been 115,000 Highlanders, or 759,000 Highlanders – or almost any number between. The highest modern computation, 759,000, is six and a half times as many as the Mitchison/Lynch total – and, indeed, seven and a half times as many as Robert Chambers' proposal of 100,000.

Not only the number, but the proportion, of Highlanders, was variously estimated. The correct fraction of the total Scottish population in the middle of the eighteenth century who were Highlanders (according to competing experts) is a twelfth (Robert Chambers), a tenth (Michael Brander), fewer than one eighth (John Home), just over a fifth (*Oxford Companion to Scottish History*), nearly a quarter (Professor Pryde), a quarter (Professor Youngson), between a quarter and a third (Dr Smout), almost a third (Dr Ferguson and James Halliday), a full third (John MacLeod), a half (Professor Richards, and Dr Grimble), just over a half (highlandclearances.info website), "the majority" (John Prebble), or three-fifths (planetware.com website, and Basil Davidson), according to the pundit you are consulting.

These writers surely cannot all have been referring to the same stretch of country.

6. Highland parishes

There are of course many schools of historiography, many views as to what can or cannot be said with certainty about times past. Some writers now appear to say that it is impossible to give an account of what has been, because (as I understand the argument) any attempted account of the past becomes merely an extended commentary on the present, coloured irremediably by the opinions of the commentator. Yet even a post-modernist would presumably accept that one should be allowed to indicate which bits of the earth's surface one was talking about, and which bits one was not. General observations, such as "I love the scenery in the Highlands", or "many clans used to live in the Highlands", may well be made without excessive delineation; it would be sad if anyone hearing Burns' line, "My heart's in the Highlands", should demand a map reference. But if one intends to come to convincing conclusions, or to claim that this or that happened in "the Highlands", and to assert or imply that people who allege the reverse are wrong, then an explicit definition is imperative. It is possible that disputes might arise simply because one person's Highlands does not cover the same extent of ground as another person's. Even more dangerously, it could happen that a writer mentioning the Highlands in 1750 does not refer to the same region when he goes on to talk of the Highlands in, say, 1850. If one takes (or estimates) population statistics from different areas in different years, one can of course show that the population figures are changing in any way one wants.

This train of thought, it seemed to me, was unarguable. Yet when one reads what experts on the Highlands have written, it is not unusual to find some of them making authoritative pronouncements without defining which area they are talking about. Of course, if an author mentions "Scotland", or "England", then normally one can feel fairly certain about which particular sector of the globe is meant, although there are uncertainties even here: without some clarifying phrase, "England" can and often does[51] indicate "Britain", while "Britain" can well mean "England". I remember seeing, in a popular history book, an illustration of what was described as a victorious "English" battle in the nineteenth century: the "English" soldiers illustrated all wore kilts and tartan plaids, and were being stimulated by the bagpipes.[52] The author, then, apparently thought that these kilted "Englishmen" were inspired by pipe music; perhaps he believed that Highlanders could only be roused by morris dancing.

Be that as it may, writers holding forth about events in "the Highlands", or "Buchan", or "East Anglia", or any other (in modern terms) nebulous region, need to define their subject-matter. (Some writers still discuss what is supposed to have happened in "the Highlands", without the least attempt to define them.) In the next chapter I go into some considerable detail about which parts of Scotland seem to me to be in the Highlands, and which not, and my reasons for thinking so. For now, I shall simply state that "the Highlands", as the term is understood in this work, consists of all the parishes in four of the old Scottish counties[53] – Sutherland (with thirteen parishes in most lists), Ross and Cromarty (thirty-three in the same lists), Inverness-shire (thirty-two), and Argyllshire (thirty-five), and some parishes in a further ten of those former Scottish counties – the shires of Bute (four parishes), Dumbarton (three), Stirling (two), Perth (twenty-two), Forfar (one), Aberdeen (three), Banff (four), Elgin (three), Nairn (two), and Caithness (five). That makes a total of 162 parishes. When I write of the Highlands in these pages, I mean those 162 parishes; when I write of the Lowlands, I mean the other 776 parishes of Scotland.[54]

The Highlands as thus defined has an area (so far as I can estimate) of about 16,300 square miles. Since Scotland as a whole contains about 29,800 square miles, that means that the Highland area is the greater part of Scotland. The non-Highland districts of Scotland cover about 13,500 square miles.

If this calculation is correct, "the Highlands" is larger than some independent European countries. Belgium has 11,755 square miles; the Netherlands 12,603; and Switzerland 15,940.

7. Documentary evidence

II. "Documents always tell the truth."

The question of the size and the situation of the Highlands is bound up with another matter: the treatment of documents. Nearly all accounts of history are based on documents: but they must be regarded as open to question, like all evidence, not as holy writ. Writers have sometimes taken words in a document to be so unchallengeable that, relying on the document, they have told their readers what is plainly incorrect. Some of the more distinct documentary delusions come to mind in relation to the geography of the Highlands. If a writer allows a document which contains incorrect information to lead him astray in the fields of social organization or popular diet or landownership, it may take a lengthy and involved argument to show that he is wrong; but if a writer has erred through naively accepting faulty geographical statistics given in a document, then sometimes the matter can be put right by simply consulting a map. Here are a few such cases.

In 1814 Sir Walter Scott sailed round Scotland in the yacht *Pharos*. In his diary of the voyage he wrote that he had visited "Lord Reay's estate, containing 150,000 square acres, and measuring eighty miles by sixty".[55] On the face of it, that is faulty: any estate measuring "eighty miles by sixty" would contain not 150,000 acres, but something much nearer to 3,000,000 acres, twenty times as many. More importantly, anyone possessing a map of Scotland and a ruler would see that Lord Reay's estate (the three Sutherland parishes of Tongue, Durness, and Eddrachillis) measured at most about thirty-one miles north to south, and no more than that from east to west. One persuasive estimate is that Lord Reay owned 625 square miles, or 400,000 acres[56] – many more acres, but many fewer square miles, than Scott alleged. Yet in 1951 Seton Gordon, one of the more knowledgeable writers on Highland affairs (he wrote no fewer than thirty books on the Highlands, and was connected with several leading Highland families), quoted Scott's figures[57] without the slightest hint that they were extremely inaccurate, no doubt because they had appeared in an actual document – Sir Walter Scott's diary.

In 1795 Sir John Sinclair said the Countess of Sutherland's estate must be "1755 square miles (739,000 English acres)", which is clearly mistaken, since it is easy to work out that 1755 square miles contain 1,123,200 English acres. (One could guess that Sinclair might have meant Scots acres; but not so – 1755 square miles is about 884,000 Scots acres.) Then Sinclair indicated that the county of Sutherland had an area approaching 3500 square miles. (Sinclair thought that the countess's estate was "at least one half of" Sutherland; in reality it covered nearly two-thirds.) Another contemporary writer, Captain John Henderson in 1812, said Sutherland contained 2925 square miles. So in 1976 David Forbes produced *The Sutherland Clearances*, calling it – perhaps significantly – "a documentary survey", and quoting both these estimates (without pointing out Sinclair's obvious error in arithmetic). He did not think it necessary to say that despite these claims of about 3500, or 2925, square miles, in fact Sutherland had 2028 square miles (and so was much smaller than either Sinclair or Henderson alleged), or that the countess's estate was about 1250 square miles (nearly twenty-nine per cent less than Sinclair's assertion).[58] It was more important to pass on the errors (without, of course, revealing them to be errors) in two contemporary documents than to give the actual size of Sutherland, or the Sutherland estate.

Robert MacKay wrote in 1829, in his *House and Clan of MacKay*, that the MacKay country, "from Drimholisten [Drumhollistan] which divides it from Caithness on the north-east [i.e. on the Caithness border], to Kylescow [Kylesku], an arm of the sea dividing it from Assint [Assynt] on the south-west, is about eighty miles in length".[59] Captain Ian Scobie, who came from Sutherland and knew the county well, quoted this passage verbatim, without the slightest misgiving, in his 1914 book about the Reay Fencibles.[60] Since there were now two documents to prove this "fact", the author and expert on clan history Sir Iain Moncreiffe of that Ilk, Albany Herald, Q.C., Ph.D. etc, repeated the information in 1969: the MacKay country was a tract "measuring eighty miles" in length.[61] However, any inexpensive map, even in the hands of a less educated reader, shows that it is under fifty miles from the Caithness border to Kylesku. Even to the further side of Handa Island, the MacKay country cannot be measured as more than fifty-four or fifty-five miles.

The Highland ministers writing in the two Statistical Accounts of Scotland (the first one published in 1791-9, and the second one in 1845) often gave exaggerated accounts of the size of their parishes: no doubt the aim was to magnify the amount of work they had to do, and the esteem owed to them for doing it. Kilmallie was alleged to be 589 square miles;[62] in fact, according to the *Gazetteer for Scotland*, it was only 444 square miles. Gairloch's minister claimed "about 600 square miles";[63] the *Gazetteer* said 356. Fortingall's report maintained its size was 448,000 imperial acres, or 700 square miles;[64] the *Gazetteer's* figure was less than half that, 319 square miles. Other ministers claimed mileage figures for the length of their parishes which would have suggested even larger areas; but the *Gazetteer* brings them back to sober reality. Kilmonivaig was said to be sixty miles long,[65] but it was really (said the *Gazetteer*) about forty. Kilmorack's minister (who said "there is not probably in Scotland a parish of greater extent") claimed that it was "upwards of sixty miles in length";[66] its length was really thirty-six miles. Ardchattan's minister maintained that it was "more than forty miles long"; it was really less than twenty-five.[67] The Farr report said it was "about forty English miles long"; the *Gazetteer* said the "utmost length" was thirty-two.[68] The Lochbroom reporter thought the parish might be thirty-six miles long; it was less than thirty.[69] "The extreme length" of Croy, according to the N.S.A., was "upwards of twenty miles";[70] it was really ten miles.

8. 400 square miles

It was presumably these inflated claims in the O.S.A. and the N.S.A., clearly wrong though some of them are, that led Professor M. Lynch, formerly Sir William Fraser Professor of Scottish History at the University of Edinburgh, to state that the Highland parishes "on average were 400 square miles in area".[71] Of course most Highland parishes are larger than most Lowland parishes; and admittedly matters are somewhat complicated by the fact that parish boundaries were subject to (mostly minor) changes over the years, for example in 1891, so it is not easy to be sure of the exact size of parishes as they were in, say, 1800. (However, where a Highland parish was enlarged, or diminished, it was almost always because another Highland parish was correspondingly diminished, or enlarged, thus leaving the average size of Highland parishes unchanged.) It does appear that, so far from it being the case that Highland parishes "on average were 400 square miles in area", there were in fact only a handful (perhaps only four) as big as that: Kilmonivaig, Kilmallie (both of which have been described as the largest parish in Scotland, as has Kilmorack), Lochbroom, and (after 1891, when it took over some of Reay) Farr. There were also a few Highland parishes over 300 square miles,[72] and a handful over 200;[73] but the *average* size of Highland parishes was much less than that.

If the Highlands had 16,300 square miles, and 162 parishes, then clearly the average parish was in area just over 100 square miles – only a quarter as big as Professor Lynch said. A defender of the "400 square miles average" theory might claim that the problem arises from my definition of the Highlands, and that if a different delineation of the Highlands were adopted, perhaps with fewer parishes, a different average size might be found. Let us then look at the four principal "Highland counties" – Argyllshire, Inverness-shire, Ross and Cromarty, and Sutherland – by themselves. However small an area a particular observer wished to demarcate as Highland, a definition of the Highlands which did not include these four counties would be less than convincing. The four named counties contained about 113 parishes.[74] Four authoritative modern surveys gave the total size of the four counties as being between 12,438 and 12,743 square miles, the average being 12,536 square miles.[75] (These numbers are only tentative, because some parishes had land in two counties, which meant that not every parish, and not every part of every parish, is always listed under the same county: see the footnote for some published figures.) If, however, we take this reckoning as being approximately accurate, it is easy to work out that the average parish size in the four main Highland counties was just under 111 square miles. As for the Hebrides, *Nelson's Gazetteer* and the *Gazetteer for Scotland* both said that the area of the Hebridean islands, from Lewis down to Islay and Gigha (all of them, of course, in the three counties of Ross-shire, Inverness-shire, or Argyllshire) was 2812 square miles; since there are 25 Hebridean parishes, that would make an average size for those parishes of 112.5 square miles.[76] It appears, therefore, that the average Highland parish, while certainly much larger than the average Lowland parish, was not nearly as large as an incautious reading of some of the O.S.A. and N.S.A. reports might suggest.

In 1994 Professor T. M. Devine, the Research Professor and Director of the Research Institute of Irish and Scottish Studies at the University of Aberdeen, and recipient of many honours (in his own words, "in 2001 I was presented by H. M. the Queen with the Royal Gold Medal, Scotland's supreme academic accolade"),[77] revealed a similar belief as to the size of Highland parishes; and he gave an example of what he meant. After warning his audience that Highland history "has long been shrouded in romance and myth through the ingenious efforts of Victorian writers who virtually invented a Gaelic past which fitted in with the assumptions and expectations of their readers", he said that now Highland history was "based on careful examination of contemporary documentary evidence"; and remarked that "there were few Highland parishes under 400 square miles in extent, a typical example being Harris which was forty-eight miles by twenty-four".[78] (Those asserted dimensions, if consistent, would of course mean that Harris contained over a thousand square miles.) In fact, as we have seen, there were very few Highland parishes (probably only four) as large as 400 square miles in extent: certainly Harris was nowhere near that size. Professor Devine gave no provenance for his statement about Harris, but it appears to be based on the

Harris minister's comment in the O.S.A. that his parish, "from the northern to the southern extremity, along the common track of travelling by land, and the course of navigation through the Sound, will be at least forty-eight miles long: its breadth varies much. Near the northern extremity it is 24 miles; from thence to the Sound, it may be at an average from 6 to 7; and, of the Sound, navigators calculate the breadth as well as length at 3 leagues [or 10 miles]."[79] The N.S.A. reporter thought the length of Harris was greater still: "its extent from north to south is fifty miles". The acceptance of these figures by an academic historian constitutes another case of over-reverence for a document, and indeed for an extreme interpretation of it: the width of "twenty-four miles" alleged for part of Harris by the O.S.A. minister only applies to a small section of the parish, as the minister himself made clear, while the "average of six to seven miles" is much nearer the truth. The atlas shows that though the greatest width of Harris (both the island and the parish) is indeed about twenty-four miles, the greatest length of Harris (the parish) is at the most twenty-six miles, from the northern point of Loch Resort to the southern end of Berneray (rather than the forty-eight miles claimed in the O.S.A., or the fifty alleged in the N.S.A.). Apart from that, the minister made it (and the map makes it) clear that most of the space inside these maximum measurements was occupied by extra-parochial water. Two authoritative calculations of the area of Harris are 193 square miles (the *Gazetteer for Scotland*); and 195 square miles (*Nelson's Gazetteer*). Whichever figure is correct, Harris – so far from being "typical" of parishes which were over 400 square miles, is less than half that size.

9. Sixty miles long

Professor T. C. Smout, the present Historiographer Royal in Scotland, and formerly professor of history at Edinburgh University and at St Andrews University, did not suggest an average size, or a minimum size, but he did claim that the "Highland parishes were of immense size", and gave four examples. The first was Kilmallie, where the O.S.A. minister had asserted that "the length . . . is about sixty miles in a straight line", a statement endorsed by the N.S.A. minister: "the length . . . is about sixty miles".[80] There were thus two documents giving the length of Kilmallie: and Professor Smout was presumably relying on them when he wrote firmly that "Kilmallie was sixty miles long".[81] It may be as we speculated earlier that the O.S.A. minister was tempted to over-estimate distances, and therefore his own hard work, as he journeyed round the local landscape, and it may also be that the N.S.A. minister found it the easiest option to copy his predecessor; but anyone writing now can look at a map and see that Kilmallie's length is about thirty miles, rather than sixty.[82] So where an allegation in a historical document, and the easily discernible fact, are at odds with each other, it is the fact that is rejected by academic orthodoxy. The document cannot be denied.

Dr Smout also claimed that Glenorchy was nearly as big: "Glenorchy was sixty miles long and twenty-four miles wide."[83] No doubt a document somewhere gave these "facts", though I have not found it yet (Dr Smout supplied no reference; and even the O.S.A. and N.S.A. only claimed a length of twenty-four or twenty-five miles).[84] However, the map shows clearly that Glenorchy was at the most only about thirty-one miles long and no more than fourteen wide (half the length, and not much more than half the breadth, given by Dr Smout).[85] Dr Smout's third example was Buchanan parish, which he claimed was nine miles across.[86] The *Gazetteer for Scotland* said that Buchanan was six miles across; the O.S.A. minister had claimed only six miles of breadth, and the N.S.A. report only five miles.[87] The fourth example was Drymen parish.[88] Here again Dr Smout cannot have been relying on the statistical accounts or on the *Gazette*; another document must have given the inaccurate figures. Smout said Drymen was "nine miles by seven", but the three other sources gave larger dimensions: the O.S.A. fifteen miles or more by nine, the N.S.A. fifteen miles by ten,[89] and the authoritative *Gazetteer for Scotland* eleven miles by just under eleven.[89] So in three of Dr Smout's examples he overstated the size, and in the fourth under-stated it.

The exact size of Highland parishes is perhaps not a matter of the greatest importance, though any statement is worth getting right; but accepting what a document says without investigation, and without using the archive of the head, can (and does) lead to great inaccuracy in much more significant matters, such as the idea that the old clan chiefs were tyrants, or that they owned their clans' land, or that the clansfolk (in dangerously large numbers) were merely crofters, fearfully fending off frequent famine by tilling a small patch of infertile ground for food.

10. Population "explosion"

III. "There was a population explosion in the Highlands in the second half of the eighteenth century."

The evidence which is available as to the numbers in the Highlands during the eighteenth century does not enable us to say whether the Highland population as a whole was at that time going up or going down; it certainly does not enable us to say that there was then a "population explosion" in the Highlands. In some Highland parishes, it is true, the population appears to have gone up sharply between 1750 and 1800; in other Highland parishes, it is equally true, the population appears to have gone down sharply between 1750 and 1800; in yet others, the figures increased or decreased more moderately. These changes in the parochial numbers naturally followed the population movements caused by the impact of what the landlords called "the improvements". Where a local landlord introduced sheep farms, for example, the population went down; where he told his factor to found a village or organize kelping or quarrying, for example, the numbers went up. However, the evidence at our disposal does not enable us to say that there was any certain increase at all in the Highland population as a whole between 1750 and 1800. It may even be the case that there were fewer people in the Highlands in 1800 than there were in 1750. (The number in the Highlands in 1800 would of course have been higher, but for those many Highlanders who had left in the previous half-century; the number in the Highlands in 1800 would also have been lower, but for those many Lowlanders who had arrived in the same years – a significant population movement often, strangely enough, ignored by the "overpopulated Highlands" enthusiasts, who prefer to ascribe any increase in numbers to the Highlanders' unrestrained procreation, as we see below.)

In 1743 the Rev. Dr Alexander Webster, an Edinburgh minister (and James Boswell's uncle), began – with the help of the parish ministers – to collect the Scottish parochial population figures, in connection with his scheme to provide payments for the widows and children of deceased ministers; in 1755 he was asked to make an official census. Some of the figures assembled years earlier were entered in the 1755 list with footnotes saying how much the place concerned had since grown. The population given for Perth was 9019; the footnote said it was now 12,000 (33% more). Dundee's stated population was 12,477, but the footnote said it was in fact 18,000 (44% more). Aberdeen's population was put at 10,785, but the footnote said it was now about 22,000 (twice as many). Paisley's population was 6799, but the footnote said it was now above 20,000 (three times as many). Glasgow's population had "increased to nearly double the number stated above". The Webster computation cannot therefore be regarded as too punctilious.[90] In the 1790s Sir John Sinclair published the Old Statistical Account of Scotland, which gave the then parish ministers' assessments of the current population figures.[91] If one took these two sets of figures at their face value, then one might conclude that there had been, overall, a mild increase in the Highland population between the 1750s and the 1790s. However, when one applies the archive of the head to the matter, it quickly becomes clear that the Webster figures were almost certainly an underestimate. This conclusion rests on a number of considerations. Firstly, most of the Webster figures are clearly exact representations of something (almost certainly the church membership figures, which ignored the smaller children: so the figure appearing in Webster's list would be lower than the real number). In contrast, many of the O.S.A. figures are clearly estimates, as shown by the large number of Sinclair's correspondents who sent in figures which ended in "0", or "00", or even "000"; the idea that the 1750s clerics were more up-to-date in their statistical thinking, and therefore used more accurate methods than their successors in the 1790s, may be dismissed. Secondly, one must examine what the O.S.A. ministers said about their local population figures – of those who gave their opinions of the earlier count, most thought that the Webster figure was too low. Thirdly, reference must be made to what contemporary observers generally thought about the expansion or contraction of Highland population in the eighteenth century; most of them were either amazed at how thin the population was, or gloomily forecast that the whole region might well become completely depopulated under the impact of the changes then being imposed. ("What is to be done to prevent the Highlands becoming a desert?" as the Rev. Dr Robertson, minister of Callander, asked in 1808.)[91] Fourthly, there are other pointers to the magnitude of the Highland population in the 1750s, such as estimates based on the number of soldiers the Highlands were supposed to be able to produce: these estimates would suggest a greater 1750s population than the Webster figures revealed. Fifthly, one should enquire whether the Webster ministers (and for that matter the O.S.A. ministers) were in fact concentrating their efforts on the true parishes "quoad civilia", that is to say within the formal and original parochial boundaries, as opposed to the parishes "quoad sacra", often with considerably adjusted borders, within which they actually officiated. Sixthly, it is necessary to decide whether any of the Highland ministers corresponding with Webster were trying to reach a population figure in the aftermath of Culloden, when many people from the parish – especially the younger men – may well still have been absent, either as supporters of the Hanoverian or the Jacobite cause; whether the local population had gone down after the murderous English/Lowland onslaught; or whether some of the parishioners were then hiding in the hills to escape Lowland/English attacks. All of these matters will be dealt with at length in volume two of this work. The conclusion there reached is that Webster's figures were probably an under-estimate, so that even the moderate increase suggested by comparing the Webster and the O.S.A. figures may well be illusory.

11. "Congestion" forced out the Highlanders

IV. "This alleged 'population explosion' of 1750-1800 led to overcrowding and congestion, which forced many Highlanders to leave."

This is an extraordinary claim, which has no basis in fact. A number of Highlanders certainly left the Highlands, but no-one went because of the non-existent "overpopulation". During the decades after 1746, the clan chiefs (and others), whose land charters had suddenly become enforceable, naturally began to implement their newly acquired rights, since by so doing they could – and did – make themselves large amounts of money. The small sums which the clansfolk had previously paid to their chiefs, which could most accurately be described as taxes paid to the ruler of the clan country to meet the expenses of government, were now transformed into the rent of privately-owned land. These rents shot upwards – in a few decades the old clan payments were multiplied many times – as each chief grasped the revolutionary (and delightful) concept that he was now a landlord, and could demand regular and substantial donations of money from the clansfolk in return for his kind permission to remain in their own clan land: or, alternatively, he now had the power simply to tell the clansfolk to leave (backing up his request if necessary by policemen and soldiers, sent up by the Lowland authorities), and then to let the land to big farmers for much higher returns. Details of the luxuriant mansion-houses that the landlords built with this new rental income, of the opulent fittings and embellishments which adorned them, of the splendid parks which surrounded these residences, and of the lavish landlordly life-style (particularly in "the season" in the autumn) will be given in volume two. As Dr Pryde accurately put it, events "from 1746 had the effect of transforming the clan chiefs from leaders of men into owners of land. Like landowners elsewhere, they developed a taste for luxurious living and craved French wines, imported fruits and spices, finery in dress, silverware and costly furnishings."[92] By raising the rents, by depriving the Highlanders of the right to take game, by confiscating their wide-ranging pasture lands, and by direct eviction and clearance, the charter owners drove many of the Highlanders out of their large farms on the good land; some of the evicted people took small holdings on poor soil, or crowded into villages, while others left the Highlands, or even Scotland, altogether.

Historians (except a few very impudent ones) cannot avoid admitting that there were clearances, poverty, and emigration, after 1746; and so, since landlords must apparently be held blameless, writers seize voraciously on the theory of "overpopulation". Hence the insistence that there was a dangerous and dramatic upsurge in the number of Highlanders, causing congestion: and the happy result is that all those unpleasant things – clearances, poverty, and emigration – can be put down as the inescapable consequences of an "explosive" escalation in numbers.

Even better, say some academics: this mythical "population explosion" was the fault of the Highlanders themselves! The naughty Gaels simply could not control their sexual urges. Fraser Darling said in 1955 that the Highlanders were congested because of their "remarkable fertility and fecundity".[93] Alexander Fulton agreed: "in the eighteenth century the [Highland] birthrate had increased so much that the land could no longer support the population."[94] Professor Smout said in 1970 that all the trouble was caused by "the high fertility of the Highlanders and their very conservative outlook, combined with the low fertility of their country".[95] (The "conservative outlook" accusation was presumably because they didn't like their land being taken off them; if someone crashed through my front door and told me to clear off out of my own house, no doubt the invader could claim that my reluctance to depart was because of my "conservative outlook".; The same happy contrast occurred to Professor Mitchison in 1993: "the basic problem here [in the Highlands] was that the people were much more fertile than the land."[96]

12. Population "doubled"

Professor Richards resolutely asserted that "the growth of the population of the Scottish Highlands stands at the centre of the story of the clearances", but he added, surprisingly (and incorrectly), "it is rarely accorded this status".[97] In fact the threadbare allegation about explosive growth is nearly always "accorded this status"; this bogus alibi about a vast population increase (since it can be used to exonerate the landlords) is an almost universal feature in current Highland and Scottish histories. Many historians obviously feel comfortable in repeating what others have said: they assume that repetition represents reality. As Daisy Buchanan remarked about a rumour in *The Great Gatsby*, "We heard it from three people, so it must be true".[98]

A few of these avowals may be mentioned here (though with the preliminary warning that the statistics confidently asserted begin and continue in a riot of inaccuracy). The supposed population increase in the Highlands, said Dr I. F. Grant, necessitated the "crowding of people" on to "even smaller portions" of land.[99] The Highlands, said M. Fry, suffered "the pressure on the land of the soaring population"; "at bottom lay the harsh fact that growth in the numbers of Highlanders would make social and economic transformation inevitable".[100] J. MacLeod insisted that emigration "was a necessity. A sustained time of heavy population growth, in many Highland districts, pressed hard on the land and its resources."[101] Earlier writers, D. Rixson felt, could not know that by 1761 the Highlands "were going to suffer from overpopulation",[102] while C. J. Withers thought it was in the late 1780s that the Highland population was "to reach crisis levels and lead to overseas emigration".[103] Professor Youngson fixed on 1775 as the year of doom: "pressure of population was already apparent in the last quarter of the eighteenth century. People increased, but resources did not, or at any rate not nearly as fast."[104] Feeding everyone, said Professor Mackie, "became impossible as the population increased"; the "root causes of emigration and clearances were overpopulation, land-hunger, near-starvation," etc.[105] "In relation to its resources that could utilized, the region had by the eighteenth century become overpopulated", opined J. Burke.[106] Alexander Fulton (to repeat) thought that in the eighteenth-century Highlands "the land could no longer support the population".[106] The Earl of Dundee claimed there was a "prodigious 'population explosion' which caused almost continuous famine accompanied by mass emigration".[107] Professor Donaldson affirmed (mistakenly) that the supposed population "upturn" meant that "observers were unanimous" in seeing that the Highlands "had more people than could be adequately supported".[108] One cause of the Highland exodus, said Professor Hamilton, was the "stupendous growth of population".[109] Sir Iain Moncreiffe asserted that there was an "unparalleled population explosion in the Highlands, that led inevitably to great hardship".[110] The Highland population, said E. Cregeen, "perhaps" doubled by the 1820s, resulting in "dire poverty, famine, and massive emigration"; "unless new resources were found progressive poverty was inevitable".[111] The Highland population, said Professor Mitchison, did in fact double, so the "standard of living" was "appallingly low".[112] She added that "most Highland areas had poor soil, and not much of it . . . overpopulation seems to have been the main cause of enhanced poverty"; admittedly crop yields increased, "but the increase in yield was not on the scale of that of the population".[113] The "primary cause of overall Highland emigration", wrote D. Hill, was the "inevitable pressure of population on severely restricted resources".[114] J. M. Bumsted said "the increase in population was undoubtedly the central demographic fact in the Highlands in the second half of the eighteenth century", and recorded the view of some historians that this "growth of population was (in Malthusian terms) outstripping the means of production".[114] Professor Richards, in all of his numerous works on the period, stresses this population "upsurge", thus himself giving the lie to his own statement that "the growth of the population of the Scottish Highlands" was rarely put at the centre of the story of the clearances. According to Professor Richards (for example), "the sheer size of the population expansion made structural transformation virtually inevitable".[115] The Highland economy, said C. Bingham, "was incapable of responding to rapid population growth such as this . . . the result was widespread misery and dislocation".[116] M. Flinn and his co-authors (trying to sound palpably reasonable and judicious) said it was not certain "when the pressure of Highland and Hebridean populations began to press against the limits of the capacity of their usable resources of land. But evidence, principally in the form of substantial emigration, begins to suggest that these limits were being approached after the middle of the eighteenth century."[117] (If mass emigration must be taken to show inadequate resources, perhaps it could be asserted that the flight of many thousands of Jews – and of other groups the Nazis persecuted – from Germany in the 1930s resulted from overpopulation. Or that the same reason could be given for the flight of the French settlers from Nova Scotia and New Brunswick when there was a hostile British occupation of their territory in the eighteenth century. In fact, wherever there is substantial enmity, there will be "substantial emigration": malignity means movement.) J. Gardiner and N.

Wenborn thought that "much of this [Highland] migration has been shown by subsequent research to have been the result of overpopulation in a marginal economy", and it was only after the Highlanders had gone that the "landowners used the vacant land to graze sheep and establish crofters";[118] this really is an astounding claim – that "the result of overpopulation" was that the landowners suddenly found their estates empty (though the result of overpopulation is usually more people, not none) and then had to cast round to find something to do with all this suddenly "vacant land". (This explanation of the appearance of sheep farms is as convincing as a burglar insisting that a householder had voluntarily brought all his valuables round to the burglar's hide-out). James Halliday thought that "feeding the rapidly rising population . . . was an increasing problem", since the output of food "could not keep pace with the growth in numbers".[119] One writer summed up the opinions of a number of historians: "In one view . . . the basic problem was population growth and pressure on the land . . . Congestion on the land inevitably led to the clearance of it."[120] As we see below, these alleged population figures, and purported population increases, are all without foundation. And if the foundation fails, the superstructure sinks.

(Another dozen or so historians who have convinced themselves that an increased population and a lack of food caused the emigrations are quoted below in subsection 32.)

13. Almost uninhabited

If one is talking of "harsh facts", one fact so harsh that it has had to be airbrushed out of history is that these sensational tales of overcrowding and congestion have no basis in reality. The sparse Highland population when Prince Charles was defeated grew at the most (if it grew at all: the figures before the official censuses began in 1801 are unreliable, but let us assume their most dramatic interpretation) only by two people per square mile in the next fifty years. So we are told that the alleged "exploding population, overcrowding of people, crisis levels, land-hunger, almost continuous famine, dire poverty, and widespread misery", were all caused by one more person appearing in each 320 acres after half a century.

The "overpopulation" excuse for the clearances is no more convincing if we consider the figures right up to the absolute zenith of the Highland population, in 1831/1841 (the census figures for the Highlands in 1831 and 1841 were virtually identical, at just under 406,000): after that it began persistently to decline (despite the continuing substantial Lowland immigration into the Highlands, which had started in the middle of the eighteenth century). Dr Webster's amateur census of Scotland began in 1743, and culminated – after the delay caused by the Jacobite rebellion – in 1755; some of his figures refer to years earlier in that period, some to later years, so his computation as a whole is often dated to 1750. In the 162 Gaelic parishes, Webster said he had found 295,566 people:[121] as I have just said, this figure was, for reasons that will be given at more length in a later volume, almost certainly an under-estimate. The O.S.A. ministers counted 325,355 people in those parishes. In 1801 the first official census was taken, and was followed by others every ten years. The official figures for these 162 parishes were as follows: 1801, 331,235; 1811, 347,359; 1821, 386,038; 1831, 405,773; 1841, 405,924. The 1851 figure was down to 400,979, five thousand less, and after that the numbers continually decreased. The largest population increase that could ever be persuasively alleged in the Highlands was in the ninety years (approximately) after Webster. The true figure at the time of Webster's enquiry, as we shall see later, was almost certainly well above 300,000, and may have been as high as 325,000, 330,000, or more. It is therefore possible that there was no population increase at all in the eighteenth century: it is quite feasible that there was a fall in the numbers between 1750 and 1800. But taking Webster's count at its face value, as 295,566, then it would appear that between 1750 and 1841 the numbers increased by 110,358 – 37.34% in ninety-one years, a figure which averages out at an undramatic 0.41% per year. In 1841, at the very highest point the Highland population has ever reached, there were more than twenty-five acres for each Highlander (or over 150 acres for each family of six). Since the population then went steadily down, the amount of land per Highlander steadily increased. In those ninety-one years, 1750-1841, as a number of ministers pointed out in the New Statistical Account in the 1840s, the production of food had often doubled, and in some places tripled, since Webster's time, with the aid of new methods, new crops, new implements, and new land-reclamation. (See below, in item XIX, and also in volume four.) The 37% increase in the population from 1750 to 1840 (if it was that high) was insignificant, compared with the 100% or 200% increase in food production. So any claim that the Highlanders had to leave because of "overpopulation", or because the growth in population overwhelmed the food supply, is patently absurd, despite the avowals of many historians.

These 16,300 square miles of ground were never at any time other than very thinly peopled – Adam Smith, writing in 1759, when this supposed "population explosion" was already under way, called the Highlands "almost uninhabited";[122] and in 1776, when the population had been (so we are told) prodigiously exploding for three decades, he referred to "the lone houses and very small villages which are scattered about in so desert [i.e., deserted] a country as the Highlands of Scotland".[123] In 1750, according to Webster, there were only about eighteen people per square mile – probably about three Highland families for each square mile of country. By the end of the century there were still only twenty people per square mile. In the next forty years this figure shot up to all of twenty-five people (perhaps four families) in each square mile – the highest figure there has ever been in the Highlands. To say that a population where there were at the very maximum only twenty-five people for every square mile is "congested" is surely to do violence to the English language.

The widespread currency of the idea that the eighteenth-century Highlands saw a vast population increase is one of the astonishing achievements of what I have called the "ipse dixit" – "he said it himself"[124] – school of history: in other words, if a clearing landlord (who desperately needed a plausible excuse for helping to drive overseas so many Highlanders, then showing themselves to be incomparably fine soldiers in Britain's constant European and colonial wars) – if a clearing landlord claimed there had been an enormous population increase, all succeeding generations have to take his word for it: only a confirmed cynic (such is the standard view) would think of looking at the actual figures. The exact numerical records are there, and always have been there, for those who wish to consult them, but a theory which justifies the actions of those in power does not die easily (as has been well said, a lie is halfway round the world before truth has got its boots on – and this is particularly the case when the lie is pleasing to the powerful); and as each new Scottish historian takes up and embroiders the assertions of his predecessors, it lives on in modern texts. In place of doing any arithmetic, authors spend their time thinking up dramatic new words meaning "large"; and as will be seen later, I have (in leisure moments) collected some fifty of the rousing synonyms used by various recent writers, ranging from "marked", "rapid", and "growing", to "prodigious", "torrential", and "stupendous" – to describe this imaginary Highland population increase after 1750. But however prodigious the number of historians alleging a population explosion, however torrential the barrage of books affirming it, however stupendous the commentators' indifference to the evidence, nothing can alter the facts of history.

14. The "kingdom of Scotland"

V. "There has been, for the last thousand years, a united kingdom called Scotland, including the Highlands as well as the Lowlands, and it was ruled from Edinburgh. It is true that the Highlanders (until the mid-eighteenth century) obstinately went their own way, ignoring all the orders and decrees and laws coming from Edinburgh – unless enforced by ferocious armed expeditions – but that merely showed how uncivilized they were."

The kings of the Scottish Lowlands, where they had as much authority as other European kings did in their countries in the same centuries, undeniably claimed to be the kings of the whole of Scotland, and there are stacks of original, well-attested and undeniably genuine documents to prove this pretence; but the duty of historians, one supposes, is to distinguish between the fiction and the fact, between the report and the reality. And the reality is that there is little evidence to support Edinburgh's claim to rule the Highlands as well as the Lowlands, compared with much evidence that they did not rule the Highlands. Certainly the kings of the Scottish Lowlands had aggressively boasted for a long time that they were really the rulers of the Highlands as well; it is of course common for heads of state to try to extend the territories which they control, particularly where the ruler of one country has a much less powerful country immediately neighbouring his own. The unhappy experiences – now or formerly – of Ireland, next door to England; of Poland, next door to Russia; and of Tibet, next door to China, are examples of this infelicitous proximity. Where a large and powerful state borders one or more small countries, the small countries are in constant danger of being sucked remorselessly into the dominance of the large one. In the secular world, when the wolf "shall dwell with the lamb . . .and a little child shall lead them",[125] the lamb becomes the dinner, and the wolf the diner; and the little child will be lucky to escape being the dessert. The ambition of the Lowland monarchs to rule the Highlands is indisputable; but despite that ambition, it seems clear that they did not succeed until the middle of the eighteenth century.

Of course the Edinburgh kings from time to time sent Lowland armies into the Highlands, slaughtering and ravaging as they went, and while there they indubitably acted as if they were rulers, holding courts and giving orders, and pretending to represent a central authority; but as soon as they withdrew, the Highlanders resumed control of their own lives. Similarly, the English (who would like to have ruled "Scotland", however that term is defined, and incessantly claimed that they did rule it) from time to time sent armies across the Anglo-Scottish border, armies which acted with just the same murderous brutality, and claimed the same sovereign power, until they withdrew; and the Lowlanders then resumed control of their own affairs. The Lowlanders invading the Highlands sometimes seized individuals, and took them to the Lowlands, and tried them and even executed them for insufficient submission; just as the English invading the Lowlands sometimes seized individuals, and took them to England, and tried and even executed them for insufficient submission (few Scotsmen can have forgotten the fate of Sir William Wallace, butchered as a traitor – i.e. a rebel against his lawful king – in 1305); but few Lowlanders would now concede that this meant that England ruled the Lowlands in the fourteenth century. It is interesting to see that some of those who are foremost in claiming that the Lowlanders ruled the Highlands in the centuries before the Battle of Culloden, 1746, are also foremost in denying that the English ruled the Lowlands in the centuries before the Act of Union, 1707; despite the fact that the kind of evidence put forward to support the

CLANS AND CLEARANCE

latter claim is much the same as the kind of evidence put forward to support the former claim.

15. The Highlands conquered

What had been for centuries an unfulfilled ambition became actuality after 1746. (Sometimes dreams "really do come true".) The Battle of Culloden marked the beginning of the coercive absorption of the Highlands – which had previously been a collection of effectively independent small states, though frequently much pressurized by their much large neighbour, the Lowlands – into Great Britain. This would probably (when one considers the history of the British Empire) have happened anyway, even if there had been no expulsion of the Stuart kings, and no Jacobite rebellions: the growing power of the Lowland/England union, based on the increase of mercantile wealth and the progress of industry (which led finally to the British possession of enormous territories thousands of miles away in every corner of the world), meant that almost inevitably the Highlands, at the other end of the same small island, would soon be taken over by the London/Edinburgh authorities. Indeed, as was remarked earlier, there is considerable evidence that this process was already beginning, even before Culloden. The Jacobite rebellion of 1745, and its defeat, meant that the complete take-over happened then, rather than perhaps a year or two later. The outbreak of the '45 rebellion enabled the southerners to depict the Highlanders even more emphatically as a barbarian menace, a savage threat to the stability of the ripening Lowland/English union (despite the fact that probably as many Highlanders fought for the Hanoverian George II as fought for the Stuart "James III and VIII": propaganda, one need hardly say, is not necessarily factually accurate). This served as the pretext to do what the anglophone powers of this island wanted to do anyway (and would before long surely have done even without the Jacobite excuse). The Highlands were forcibly incorporated into Scotland, and therefore into Great Britain, by a bloody campaign of exceptional savagery, during which the Lowland/English forces rampaged across the Highlands, murdering, molesting, raping, looting, burning, and destroying. Civilization had now arrived in the Highlands, and the previous Lowland theory had become reality. The victims included Highlanders who had supported the Hanoverians, as well as the Jacobites: the occupying army treated the whole Highland civilian population as enemies. Duncan Ban MacIntyre, a Highland bard who had fought for George II at Falkirk, said that if Prince Charles returned all the Highlanders would now fight for him, following their experiences at the hands of the Lowlanders and English after Cumberland's victory.[126]

The brutal anglophone invading armies after Culloden (now armed with the improved weapons produced by the growing coal-and-iron Lowland/English industrialization) were able to establish for the first time that the Highland land charters, which up till then had merely represented the chiefs' idle imaginings or their boastful bombast, were now legally enforceable documents. In the following decades the charter owners naturally took advantage of this transformation, which I have called the "landlord revolution", and began to establish large farms (mostly at first for cattle, then for sheep) rented to entrepreneurs in place of the centuries-old joint-farms of the Highlanders. These new ranches were the characteristic organization of an increasing number of Highland estates for a century or more. They produced food and wool for Lowland consumption, as well as prosperity for the reasonably prudent farming tenant, and high rents, leading to luxurious living for the reasonably prudent landlord; and the Highland landlords and big farmers were quick to claim that the clearances were justified, because they were doing the British people a good turn by helping to supply them with food and clothing.[126] However, by the late nineteenth century the produce of these new farms was largely priced out of the market by food and wool coming at a lower cost from overseas. Since sheep farming was no longer as profitable or rent-productive – partly through the deterioration of the land (the inevitable result of monoculture), partly through foreign competition – the powers-that-be forgot about their proclaimed altruistic duty to provide the rest of Britain with food and wool, and many estates were converted to deer forests and shooting moors: much of the Highlands became (and remains) merely a playground for those who now own the Highlands, and for rich Lowlanders, English people and other foreigners who pay those same landlords for permission to indulge in hunting, shooting, and fishing.

So far from the Highlands (before 1750) being part of a united kingdom of Scotland, contemporary accounts show that in their sparsely populated mountains and islands the Gaels existed for centuries in their own way, except for the intervals of armed aggression by the Lowlanders, just as the Lowlanders existed in their own way except for the intervals of armed aggression by the English.

16. A divided Scotland

VI. "The Lowlanders and the Highlanders were always really the same people."

A few writers have gone so far as to insist that there was never a distinction between the Saxons and the Gaels. "Medieval Scotland was racially homogeneous",[127] said one; "the whole concept of a distinctive Highland culture and tradition is a retrospective invention", said another;[128] "Highlanders and Lowlanders have not ceased to regard themselves as members of one nation",[129] said a third – while a fourth historian denounced "the 'fake' of a 'divided Scotland'".[130]

These assertions are well wide of the mark. Before the middle of the eighteenth century, the Highlanders and the Lowlanders (despite the current theory that they were all simply citizens of a single country) differed from each other much more than the inhabitants of many neighbouring – and hostile – European countries did. They diverged in language, dress, social and economic organization, attitudes of mind, day-to-day religion, and indeed in almost every possible way. Travellers crossing the Highland line said it seemed as if they had gone into a completely foreign country: so much was this the general impression, that a Lowlander would sometimes make his will before entering the Highlands. Many observers mentioned the contrast. The Lowlanders were farmers, getting most of their sustenance from tilling the fields; the Highlanders were hunters and herdsmen. The Lowlanders spoke the same language as the English, and dressed in the same way; in the seventeenth century, that meant that the men wore knee-breeches. The Highlanders, with their tartan plaids, were clad in a completely different fashion, and spoke only a wholly different language. The clan system, whether it is to be praised or pilloried, was totally unlike the Lowlanders' system of society. The main social and economic border in seventeenth-century Britain was not the one across the Cheviot hills from the Solway Firth to Berwick-on-Tweed, but the Highland/Lowland frontier known as the Highland line.

Yet several historians, past and present, have claimed that the Lowlanders and the Highlanders were (pretty much) identical, and moreover that anyone disagreeing with this judgement is acting from questionable motives. Perhaps the reason for this indefensible opinion is embarrassment at the years of slaughter and abuse which the Lowlanders, and the English, inflicted on the Highlanders when Scotland actually did become united after Culloden. And of course, the contention that the Highlanders and the Lowlanders were almost indistinguishable would help to bolster the other allegation that Scotland had always been one monolithic united country.

17. Petty tyrants

VII. "The chiefs were despots ruling the clansfolk tyrannically, and they punished their people at will or whim."[131]

This belief is erroneous. The clans had chiefs, and each chief ruled a clan country as its prince. It may well be that some of these rulers, like potentates elsewhere both then and now, might have had ambitions to become tyrannical dictators; but the machinery which has often unfortunately been used (in past and present times) to achieve such an aim – a skilful propaganda organization, total control of the contemporary "information" services (whether pulpits, official statements, newspapers, books, radio, television or all of them), formidable armed forces, overt and secret police, brain-washing security services, lawyers, courts, prisons, torture-chambers, gallows and so forth – did not exist in the Highlands. The only agents the chiefs had were the clansfolk; and people will not oppress themselves. We shall shortly see how the Highlanders were constantly acknowledged to be exceptionally sharp-witted and sagacious; perhaps they were the last people who could have been expected to practise any self-subjugation. Therefore the chiefs were under the necessity of ruling with the general consent of the governed, not because they were morally better than (or racially superior to) other rulers, or because they were devotees of democracy, but merely because in the then existing state of things in the Highlands it was not possible for them to do anything else. Observers should perhaps be just as pleased if people are good because they are not able to be bad, as they are when people are good through conscious effort, even though they could have been worse. The effect is the same.

The lack of any machinery of oppression meant that at any given time the Highlanders decided what they wanted to do, and then did it. If at a particular time it seemed a good idea to join a clan array, and go forth and do battle, then that is what they did; if subsequently it seemed a good idea to forget about the fighting and go home, then that is what happened. It is interesting to observe how often authors trot out the cliché that the chiefs were all-powerful tyrants, whose every order was and had to be obeyed without question by the clansfolk (any disobedience being instantaneously met with dungeons and judicial murder); and then – apparently blithely unaware of any inconsistency – go on in the same book (sometimes in the same chapters, or even in extreme cases in the self-same paragraphs) to rehearse the other cliché about the ungovernable and ill-disciplined behaviour of the Highlanders, since when they thought they had done enough fighting they simply ignored their chiefs and went home. The application of the archive of the head would save writers from saying on one page what amounts to a repudiation of what they have said on another.

The appearance of the "tyrant-chiefs" theory (as well as the "ungovernable Highlanders" theory) appears to derive from the pressure felt by the rulers of any new kind of society, which has overthrown and replaced an older form, to depict the older society in the most unflattering way. If the previous kind of society is believed to be deplorable, it helps to deflect any disparagement of the present regime. (A parallel process is apparent in our own era when any new government, of whatever complexion, takes power, and explains – by repeated angry condemnations of its predecessor's misdeeds – why the lavish times promised in the victorious party's manifesto have not yet actually materialized.) But criticisms are not convincing unless they are consistent.[132]

18. Crofters

VIII. "People living in the Highlands had always been crofters, that is to say very small peasant farmers or smallholders, who eked out a scanty living by subsistence agriculture."

In fact crofters first appeared in the Highlands as a result of the clearances. In the earlier mass evictions, the ejected people were often driven by this catastrophe to move out of the district entirely. This was a dangerous circumstance in the Highlands, which have never been other than very thinly populated. After a time the drawbacks of this development were increasingly felt by the landlords, who began to realize the perils of being left without a local subordinate caste – who would do the work? There cannot be an upper class without a lower class. As Voltaire said, "the comfort of the rich depends upon an abundant supply of the poor".   Adam Smith even essayed a kind of mathematical equation: "Wherever there is great property, there is great inequality.   For one very rich man there must be at least five hundred poor, and the affluence of the few supposes the indigence of the many."[133]

It seemed there was a danger of "the poor" being swept out of the Highlands entirely. In many later clearances, therefore, in the latter part of the eighteenth century, a new device was employed. Some of the evicted people were allowed to rent small plots of waste land so barren that the big farmers refused to take it on, in order to try to turn this worthless ground into arable. These diminutive pieces of terrain were intended from the first to be insufficient to keep a family; the objective was that while the crofting family was trying to reclaim its piece of stony moor or rocky coast, one or more family members would be compelled by economic necessity to become farmworkers on the new big farms, to take jobs as servants at the mansions where the landlords and the great graziers lived (unless they were virtually absentees, which many were), or to work in the various industries such as commercial fishing, kelp-making, forestry and logging, quarrying, or mining, which grew up in parts of the Highlands – in other words, to form part of a new proletariat. Although it is common for members of an upper class to hate and revile the local proletarians, without such people no modern state could exist.

These industrial enterprises were never successful enough to use up all the available labour – some after a time failed entirely. Besides that, any of these allotments which the crofters succeeded in improving into desirable possessions were taken off them in further clearances and rented out to big farmers.[133] The result was that the crofters had neither sufficient land nor sufficient employment to make an acceptable living, and they became a depressed populace, trying to exist on ever smaller segments of sterile ground, although surrounded by wide and much more fertile lands which used to be theirs; they were half-starving most of the time, and starving altogether in the potato famines of the 1830s and 1840s. A further drawback was that, since Highlanders knew their history (recitals of which formed an important part of their evening get-togethers), many of them never stopped grumbling about the loss of their land. However, this unhappy existence of the crofters served the ends of the landlords (who were more and more importing Lowlanders as farm-servants, as domestics and so on, and were therefore growing increasingly hostile to the idea of the native Highlanders being allowed to remain in the Highlands on any terms) in two ways. Firstly, said the proprietors, the crofters (who had been intentionally crammed together in small barren patches, after the productive parts of the estate had been rented out to the large farmers) were poor because they were "congested", the result of "overpopulation", and therefore most of them should emigrate. Secondly, any sympathy that might be felt for the expropriation of the Highlanders was clearly misplaced (so the landlords and their allies maintained), because they had always been what they were then – a wretched sub-class on the margins of society, people who must be better off if they were driven out of the Highlands altogether. This may be why so many histories of the Highlands, written from the landlords' point of view, so often refer to the old clansfolk, during the days of the clans before Culloden, as "crofters" – that is, penurious people on the verge of destitution: a usage that is of course extremely inaccurate.

19. Depended on their crops

IX. "Even before the clearances, the Highlanders depended on the crops they grew: their soil was poor, and the climate hostile, so they were often short of food."

This is another fairy story, which can only owe its longevity to the fact that historians often base their accounts on what earlier historians have written. The fact (easily discoverable) is that the Highlanders had very little reason to till the ground: their other food supplies made such labour unnecessary. They were firstly hunter-gatherers, and secondly herdsmen. They lived mainly off the products of snaring, shooting, angling, or otherwise catching, the numerous wild animals, birds, and fish, of the Highlands, and gathering nuts, berries, herbs, shellfish and so forth, supplemented by the produce of their throngs of cattle, sheep, goats, and poultry, and in a very small way by some minor and incidental crops of grain. This is not to say that arable farming is impossible in the Highlands. On a very small scale, some tillage was carried out in the Highlands in the days of the clans; and after the clearances, much more land was devoted to the growing of crops – potatoes and grain – for the simple reason that the Highlanders' immemorial way of life, based firstly on hunting and secondly on pasturage, had been made impossible by the landlords' confiscation of the clan lands. But there is much evidence, which will be set out later, to show that tillage during the clan system was of little importance.

To admit that the Highlanders gained most of their food-supplies from hunting, shooting, and fishing, and then from their flocks and herds, was perhaps thought to give too favourable a picture of clan society. Certainly the nineteenth-century Highlanders on their crofts, made out of what had been waste land, lived very largely on what they could grow on a small infertile patch, that is to say mainly on potatoes and perhaps a little grain; so many writers conclude that Highlanders must always have lived on their arable produce. It is known that the Highlanders took up the cultivation of the potato after the clan system was overthrown, and if one removes potatoes from a diet of oatmeal and potatoes, one is left with oatmeal: so that is what the old Highlanders must have eaten. (Two recent writers were not even able to accept the comparatively recent introduction of potatoes, so they asserted firmly that the *old* clansfolk used to eat them.)[134]

20. Land charters

X. "The Highland clan chiefs were really landlords, and had always been landlords ever since the clans were first formed."

This fanciful picture of the clan chiefs emerging from the dim mists of pre-history already clutching their certificates from the Land Registry does not correspond with the facts. Its prevalence may owe much to the propensity of commentators in one society to see events and institutions in a different society entirely in those terms with which they themselves are familiar. Besides that, many ancient documents, purporting to give private-property rights to land, still exist in the archives, and they are frequently invoked by those writers who believe documents cannot lie in order to "prove" this theory. These "land charters" in fact emerged because of the ambition of the Lowland kings. One way in which the rulers of the Lowlands tried to achieve their aim of ruling also over the Highlands (an ambition which was constant, though constantly failing until 1746) was to threaten, or cajole, or flatter, or suborn, the clan chiefs, who were of course princes like the Lowland monarchs, but who ruled over much smaller areas. One potent means of bribery was to give the chiefs (or chieftains, that is to say sub-chiefs) impressive pieces of penmanship-filled parchment called charters, which alleged that the person named thereon was the "owner" of a stretch of clan land. These gifts went particularly to those individuals who were prepared to play the obsequious courtier to the English-speaking ruler in Edinburgh (or, later, in London), and by blandishments or servility to try to procure such a benefaction.

The aim behind such grants (from the point of view of the authorities) was obvious; the lucky grantee would see clearly that if he helped to bring the Highlands under the rule of the Lowland state (in the same way that many prominent Lowlanders helped to bring the Lowlands under the rule of England in 1707), in fact as well as in the Edinburgh monarchs' fanciful theory, then he would be transformed from being merely an executive officer, having to please all or at any rate most of his high-spirited and uninhibited clansfolk, into a great landlord, who had to please nobody but himself, and could concentrate on making himself a fortune.

Besides that, the Lowland kings governed a society in which the private ownership of land was one of the cornerstones of the state, and so – like many rulers – they tried to impose their own views of what was "right" on all the lands over which they claimed to rule. (The British, conquering large areas of Africa, "knew" that all tribes have chiefs; so when they found a tribe that did not have a chief, they appointed one. Simple.) The fabrication of these charters alleging "ownership" occurred particularly when the Lowland monarchy (in the years before the union of the crowns in 1603) planned to go to war with England. The king would either grant a charter to a chief claiming to give him ownership of the land of his own clan, the aim being to make him grateful towards the king, and therefore less likely to help England by harassing the Lowlands while the Lowlanders were attacking England; or (in the case of less compliant clan princes) he would do exactly the opposite, and grant a charter to a chief claiming to give him ownership of the land of a neighbouring clan, the aim being to embroil the two clans in a quarrel which would absorb all their energies, and avoid the risk of either of them assailing the Lowlands while the Lowlanders were at war with England. In either case the objective of the Edinburgh king was to obviate any danger in the north while he pursued hostilities in the south. And in neither case (it will be seen) was there any attempt to make the charters conform to reality.

These charters had no effect at the time so far as "land-ownership" was concerned, although the charters that aimed at creating antagonism between clans sometimes did have that desired outcome. (Any conflicts between clans that resulted from this Lowland provocation were useful for Lowland propaganda, since such strife could be stigmatised by the Lowland authorities as being the result of innate Highland barbarism, or e.g. revenge for petty insults – and still is, by some anglophone historians.)[135] Each clan continued to own its own land whether or not an Edinburgh charter had purported to confer ownership on its own chief, or on another chief, or even (on some occasions) on Lowlanders, as can be shown repeatedly by successive incidents in each clan's history. (Once or twice the malign mischief-making of Edinburgh kings resulted in a clan being driven out of its lands by a rival chief – supported by *his* clan – as happened in Kintyre and in Ardnamurchan; and once or twice a clan had to accept being incorporated in another clan, as happened in Lewis and in Dundonnell; but the clansfolk existing in each area, as a matter of practical politics, owned their land, since the machinery to deprive them of it did not exist.) Many such episodes are detailed later in this work. Written documents such as these land charters, in other words (and this sadly is a challenge to accepted wisdom), do not necessarily tell the truth. However, at the Union of 1707 Lowland Scotland and England merged into one state, which with the rapid development of trading overseas and manufacturing expansion at home grew stronger year by year, to the point ultimately at which the combined power of England and the Lowlands controlled the greatest empire there had ever been in the entire history of the world – or, presumably, that there ever will be, since the power given by industrialization has now spread or is spreading across most of the globe. In contrast to the tremendous might of the British Empire, the scanty numbers of Highlanders were not even united among themselves, each clan considering that its own land was a separate country. So when the new state of Great Britain decided to conquer the Highlands after 1746, it was able to transform these Highland land charters – up to then only imaginative records of aspiration – into bitterly imposed reality. As Trevelyan quite correctly says, after Culloden "the chiefs were turned into landlords".[136]

21. Lawless and wild

XI. "The Highlands were in a state of barbarism, while civilization flourished in the Lowlands."

When writers have finished setting up the usual Aunt Sally effigy of the Highlands, they often seem to feel a compulsion to offer in contrast a much more favourable sketch of the Lowlands. Of course the history of the Lowlands is no secret. What happened in the counties from the Mull of Galloway to Dumbarton, from Berwick to the Pentland Firth and beyond, during all those centuries when clanship reigned supreme in the Highlands, can be read at length in many volumes – the tales of tyranny and brutal punishment, of internal butchery and external slaughter, of court convulsions and cross-border carnage, of religious intolerance and heartless cruelty – these records lie open to any enquirer. Yet not infrequently, when a writer has given the accepted, standard version of Highland history, he is overcome with the desire to point the contrast between what he has just alleged to be the sad state of the Highlanders, and what he would like his audience to believe was the happy life of the Lowlanders. Hence we have repeated assurances that while the Highlands were "lawless", the Lowlands were law-abiding; while the Highlanders were rough and abrasive, the Lowlanders were douce and gentle; while Highland society was merely a primitive structure dedicated to war,

Lowland society was sophisticated and peace-loving. Yet along with other facets of Highland history as it is presently written, it often requires merely comparing this picture with what the same writer has written on different pages to observe the yawning discrepancies.

And is the reader who is prepared to accept whatever a writer tells him free from all blame? Some victims invite trouble. Many would be tempted to think that anyone who is gullible enough to believe that the shady character who sidles up to him offering whispered bargains is really entitled to sell him the Tower of London at a remarkably low price, or who takes on trust the e-mail fraudster offering (in return for £10,000 paid up front) to share the ill-gotten riches of some deposed Third World dictator, is so ripe for victimhood that he almost deserves to be fleeced. And certainly those electors round the world who in many cases turn out in their millions to vote for someone who is clearly going to rule as a savage dictator, or for smooth-tongued politicians who promise an immediate impossible prosperity for all, must be held at least partly responsible for their own fate. In the same way readers who refrain from using the archive of the head, and who accept whatever a writer says to the extent that they find themselves believing in the unbelievable, can surely not escape all accountability.

This rubric must apply to those who study Highland history. For many of the genuine attributes of the actual historical Highlander have survived in existing accounts. The evidence is too strong to be ignored, and it is accepted that the Highlander was an incomparable soldier, that he normally went about heavily armed with both blade and gun, and that he was expert with these weapons from his youth. The difficulty arises when these characteristics have to be reconciled with the features of Highland existence constructed by the orthodox historians. The reader then has to try to accept a Highlander continually wasted by famine, and yet at the same a fearsome combatant. He has to give credit to a Highlander toiling all day at tedious subsistence farming, who is at the same time a crackshot and expert angler unaccountably ignoring the succulent wildlife all round him. He must believe in a brawny champion who quivers with dismay at his leader's slightest frown. He must have faith in a heavily armed warrior who immediately submits to his chief's harsh punishment, however unreasonable – humbly and submissively walking to the dungeon or the gallows in obedience to the chief's unwarranted edict.[137]

22. Popish clansfolk

XII. "The Highlanders were all, or nearly all, Catholic."

Not so many authors have started this hare as have subscribed to some of the fallacies above; but this fiction has appeared on a number of occasions during the past few years, in both books and newspapers. A selection of quotations will be given later about these supposedly ubiquitous "Catholic Highlanders", including some from commentators who believed that the Lowlanders' hostility to the Highlanders was the result of animosity towards the "Highland religion" (supposedly Catholicism), that Gaelic was the "Catholic tongue", and that the clearances themselves arose from anti-Catholic sentiment.[138] One author declared that "the Highlander was an unregenerate papist", and that "the Highlands . . . were Catholic";[139] another asserted that "loyalty to the Roman church . . . was assured in the Highlands";[140] and a third remarked on the Highlanders' "stubborn adherence to the Roman Catholic faith".[141] Here, as elsewhere, historians have often copied other historians,[142] instead of checking the figures or the facts. So the implacable reality must be revealed: the vast majority of Highlanders – ninety-five or ninety-six of them out of every hundred – were Protestant.

Webster's enumeration in 1743-55 found that 95.7% of the Highlanders were Protestant: only 4.3% of them were Catholic.[143] In 159 of the 162 Highland parishes the Protestants were in the majority, leaving only three parishes where most were Catholic. In 101 parishes, well over three-fifths of the total, there was not one single solitary Catholic, longing for a non-existent Mass. It may be objected that Webster's figures were supplied by the Protestant clergymen of the Highland parishes, who may have wished to obscure the true numbers of local "papists"; but two other calculations of the number of Highland Catholics, one before, and one after Webster, both of them from Catholic sources, came to much the same conclusion. No doubt it was convenient to try to tar the Highland clansfolk with the Catholic brush, in order to associate them with the autocracies of the European mainland which still held to Catholicism, and to depict them as a papist threat to the Presbyterian Lowlands: but propaganda cannot alter facts. (Admittedly propagandists are always trying to do just that.)

23. Whisky

XIII. "The old clansfolk drank enormous quantities of whisky, so the clearances were merely benign attempts to save the Highlanders from alcoholism."

After the chiefs-turned-landlords, and the British state, broke up the old society of the Highlanders, some of the latter sought consolation in a stringent form of religion, while others tried to find ephemeral escapes in the brief buoyancy offered by addictive alcohol. Writers ever since have been antedating these two forms of relief. One canny commentator put the two contrary easements in the same assessment, and alleged that, although the "primitive religion" of "the forgotten forefathers of the crofters" was "stern and savage", nevertheless they were never happy without their whisky. "In days gone by it must have run like water, and it was no uncommon thing for a man to drink a bottle of whisky daily."[144] So although the old clansfolk were "forgotten", one of their main characteristics was clearly remembered. Another historian discovered that "intemperance" was a "weakness of the Hebridean character"; and declared "there can be no doubt . . . that for centuries over-addiction to strong waters has been a curse of the Highlanders".[145] A third writer claimed that whisky was "long the staple liquor of the Hebrides".[145] Not long ago the writer Auberon Waugh procured a well-earned fee from the worthy Conrad Black (this was before the Americans convicted Black of fraud and put him in jail) by telling the readers of the *Daily Telegraph* (then owned by Black) that the Sutherland clearances were carried out because the Sutherlanders were "too drunk" to farm their land; that they lived in disgusting conditions, "drinking like fishes"; and that the eviction of these "drunken people" was motivated by "aesthetic" and "hygienic" concerns.[146]

These comments remind one that in some hands history is merely a branch of politics. The evidence shows that these propaganda attacks in the enduring anti-Highlander campaign were devoid of truth. Under the clan system, whisky had been virtually unknown in the Highlands, at least until the terminal years of that system. In 1582 George Buchanan said that the Highlanders "drink the juice of the boiled flesh [beef-tea]. At their feasts they sometimes use whey, after it has been kept for several years . . . but the greater part quench their thirst with water."[147] In 1703 a writer said they did not drink brandy or tea: "the purest water serves them."[148] In 1709 another author remarked on the Highlanders' "constant temperance . . . water being the ordinary drink of the vulgar [i.e., the common people]".[149] In the late 1720s, Edmund Burt's letters showed that the Highlanders knew about whisky by then, but he said that "the 'twopenny', as they call it [it was twopence a quart], was their common ale".[150] With the landlord revolution which followed Culloden, economic and social conditions were transformed, and so were food and drink. The minister of Halkirk, writing his O.S.A. report in 1792, said drinking habits had changed in the middle of the eighteenth century: "of late years . . . the use of whisky has almost superseded that of ale, which about forty years ago [i.e. about 1750] was the ordinary drink, both in taverns and private houses."[151] David Stewart was of the same opinion. Writing about 1820, he said: "It was not till the beginning, or rather the middle of last century [i.e. about 1750], that spirits of any kind were so much drank as ale, which was then the universal beverage . . . strong, frothing ale from the cask was the common beverage." Indeed, "till within the last thirty years [since 1790], whisky was less used in the Highlands than rum and brandy". Whisky, he said, was never mentioned in the old folk music, only "in the modern ballads and songs".[152] The gentry drank brandy or claret, and one account said that whisky did not "really take off until after 1780, when the tax on claret" made that drink more expensive.[153] Alexander

MacKay wrote about the closing years of the eighteenth century: "in those days, when rum and brandy were much more used than whisky, ale was also a common drink." [154] Joseph Mitchell wrote that "prior to 1745 . . . there does not seem to have been much whisky manufactured. Brandy appears to have been the more common spirituous drink in the Highlands."[155] P. Hume Brown, who edited the accounts of a number of travellers in the pre-Culloden days in the Highlands, said: "It is worth noting that by none of our travellers is whisky mentioned as a drink of the country."[156]

However, though it is clear that intemperate whisky-drinking was one of the delights brought in by the landlord revolution of the later eighteenth century, the accusation of over-indulgence in spirits is such a useful weapon with which to malign the Highlanders that perhaps one should not have expected conformist writers to allow themselves to be swayed by the evidence, however conclusive that seems to be.

24. Under the same roof

XIV. "The old Highlanders used to live in the same building as their cattle, until the kindly improvers rescued them from such insanitary conditions."

This misconception is parallel to the last one. In that blunder, orthodox history claims that the new society tried to rescue the Highlanders from excessive whisky-drinking, whereas the truth is exactly the opposite: the new society introduced excessive whisky-drinking into the Highlands. In the same way, orthodox history claims that the old Highlanders were rescued from living in the same house as their animals; the fact being precisely the reverse – it was the new society which forced the Highlanders to live in the same house as their animals. Those who spoke (and who speak) for the landlords have always stressed this supposed insanitary feature of clan society. James Loch, the commissioner of the Sutherland estate, and the person in charge of most of the Sutherland clearances, claimed that in the old days "under the same roof, and entering at the same door, were kept all the domestick animals belonging to the establishment"; in the new regime, however, "the cow and the pig begin no longer to inhabit the same dwelling with the family".[157] John Peter, the factor of the chief and landowner, Lord Lovat, told the Napier Commission that "in early times . . . frequently the cow was in one end of the house".[158] Professor Richards said the old Highlanders had as many sheep as cattle, and "it was common practice for the stock to be literally 'housed' overnight in the old economy".[159] Janet Glover said that in clanship days "the animals shared the dwellings with their owners".[160] Dr Gaskell described the Highlanders living in "hovels . . . the sole room shared all the winter through with starving cattle".[161]

Michael Fry gave a graphic picture of the old Highlanders "living through the winter under the same roof as their cattle".[162] (It must have been a big roof.)

The staple narratives such as these stand history on its head. Certainly the Highlanders *after* the landlord revolution, deprived of nearly all their virtually limitless grazing grounds and therefore of nearly all their flocks and herds, were often forced to share their dwellings with the few survivors (perhaps one cow and a couple of hens) which was all they had rescued from the disaster of the local clearance – space and materials for a separate cowshed, and henhouse, being impossible to acquire. But in the days of the clans the Highlanders were still in the pastoral stage of society, and we see elsewhere how observers unanimously remarked on the great flocks and herds which ranged everywhere in the Highlands; the Gaels still had many animals decades after the new society had begun to be imposed on the Highlands, at least in those districts least affected by the changes. As late as 1812, said Captain Henderson, in (uncleared) Strath Naver "at an average each family have about twelve head of cattle, six small horses, fifteen to twenty sheep, and a few goats". Formerly, they had more. In the old days, said Henderson, Sutherlanders had from twelve to a hundred Highland sheep, while "the Highlands of Scotland were formerly famous for flocks of goats: every farmer had from twenty to eighty of them wandering in the mountains".[163] Colin MacKenzie, the Countess of Sutherland's chief adviser, went through eleven townships in Assynt as late in the improvement era as 1799 and reported that there were 158 families there, with 1380 cattle, and 450 sheep – or some eight or nine cows per family, plus a few sheep, and no doubt some goats).[164] (We shall see later that David Stewart thought a Highland small tenant would have two to twenty milch cows plus followers, two to five horses, and twenty to two hundred sheep;[165] Hugh Miller thought six to ten cows, and a small flock of sheep;[166] Selkirk three to twenty cows, plus young cattle, and some horses and sheep;[167] the North Uist minister, in 1794, six cows, or their equivalent, six horses, and fifteen sheep.)[167] It would clearly have been impossible to cram all a Highlander's horses with their foals, and cattle with their calves, and sheep with their lambs, and goats with their kids, along with the accompanying various kinds of poultry, into one small Highland dwelling, even if there had been any need to do so. Any attempt of the kind would merely have been a forerunner of the scene in the Marx Brothers film *A Night at the Opera*, where more and more people forced their way into one small ship's cabin, until every last cubic inch appeared to be occupied by members of a noisy gesticulating mob, standing on the floor, the bed, and every other piece of furniture.

This conclusion – that the old Highlanders could not have lived "under the same roof as their cattle", unless they had each owned a stately mansion to give them enough room – a conclusion reached by using the archive of the head, turns out to be in tune (as one might have expected) with the evidence left for us by travellers in the Highlands. This point is dealt with more explicitly in the second volume, but a few quotations from what outside observers wrote may show the position. (In fact a few eighteenth-century authors, such as Burt and Walker – as we see below – criticized the Highlanders for leaving their animals always outside: they thought such treatment made it impossible to collect their dung for manure. It is interesting to see how some anglophone writers, such as Professor Richards, criticize the Highlanders for – as they assert – housing their animals, and others criticize them for not housing their animals. Perhaps so long as some way is found to criticize the Highlanders, the details are less important.)

How the animals lived in the old Highlands is made clear repeatedly by many reports, some of which are cited here. In 1549, in Lewis "there are many sheep, for it is very good for the same, for they lay forth ever [always] on moors and glens and enter never in a house".[168] In 1700, the Highlanders' "horses and flocks, which are very numerous, are outside all the winter exposed to the weather night and day".[169] In the 1720s, "in summer their cattle are dispersed about the shielings [the higher midsummer grazings], and almost all the rest of the year in other parts of the hills"; enclosures (this observer thought) would be a dearer way to graze their cattle "than letting them run as they do in the hills".[170] In the 1760s, in Coll "they do not house their cattle";[171] in Tiree, "the cattle of every kind range the fields here all the year round . . . they roam throughout the whole island";[172] in Skye, "the Highland cattle lie abroad all the year round" – in fact "it is commonly imagined in the Highlands, that the housing of cattle would enfeeble them, and render them less hardy".[173] In 1771, the Highlanders' black cattle "run wild all the winter, without any shelter or subsistence but what they can find among the heath".[174] In 1773, Boswell wrote about Coll: "The climate being very mild in winter, they never put their beasts in any house."[175] In 1794, Marshall's book on the central Highlands described where the farm animals ranged at different times; sheep, for example, were pastured on the communal holding in the winter, and on the surrounding moorland in summer.[176] In 1795, the cattle of Strath, in Skye, "lie out all winter in good pasture".[177] So much was this the case, that there was a Gaelic saying – "It is a big beast that cannot find enough room outside."[178] In 1811, Captain Henderson wrote that in Sutherland "the cattle are kept out night and day . . . which makes them very hardy".[179]

Burt deplored this practice, since it meant the animals' dung could not be collected: "as for manure . . . they have hardly any."[180] So did Walker: the Highland farmers "collect no dung", and therefore only used seaweed for manure.[181] The commissioners who ran the estates confiscated from the rebel chiefs who had joined in the '45 tried to stop the Highlanders keeping their herds in the open, and in 1762 they issued instructions to the tenants to "house and inclose . . . their Horse, Black Cattle, Sheep and all other Bestial", at least at night in the winter (orders which would obviously have been pointless if the tenants were already "housing and inclosing" their animals): the decrees met, it appears, with indifferent success.[182]

25. Milked in the field

By the time of the New Statistical Account, things were changing. The minister of Fortingall, in Perthshire, recalled the days when the cows were milked in the open air, but said in 1838, "the milk cows are now generally housed every night, summer and winter".[183] The improvements were slower to come to North Uist, however, and there in 1837 the minister still remarked on "the cattle being outliers, or not housed".[184] At the Napier Commission hearings in 1883, three witnesses recalled the earlier practice. Dr Martin said that in the old days "the people" had "folds [temporary enclosures] outside in the grazing where they kept their cattle at night . . . there is nothing of that kind now";[185] the Rev. Donald MacKinnon recalled how the people "used to turn their cows at night into these folds";[186] while Peter MacKinnon remembered that the cows were milked out in the field, "as no cattle were then allowed about the clustering hamlets".[187] In 1978 Dr D. F. MacDonald, speaking of the former Highland farms, said disapprovingly, "the cattle were seldom housed, but kept abroad all the year round".[188]

As first the shielings and then the other pastures were taken from the Highlanders, so it became unavoidable to bring the one or two remaining cows into the end of the cottage for part of the time, to prevent them spoiling by overgrazing the patches of poor grassland which was all that was left to the small farmers. By the end of the eighteenth century, in the Outer Hebrides, only the wealthy big farmers had enough land to keep their cattle outside in the winter. The Rev. J. L. Buchanan remarked (in his book *Travels in the Western Hebrides*, 1793) on the fact that "the gentlemen's cattle, who are seldom housed, but fed in good Winter grazing . . . are much stronger and bigger than the poor tenants' cows, which must be housed, as they have no Winter grass on the fields for them": as a result "the gentleman will sell a cow at four guineas, while the poor man will be glad of the half, and seldom draws so much from the drovers".[189] That was why the Strath minister, at much the same time, said the cattle "lie out all winter in good pasture". However, if a writer is determined to have the old Highlanders living cheek-by-jowl with their cattle, in order to assert that the new society saved them from such squalor, it must be a great temptation to dismiss all the reports showing that such wretched conditions only arrived after the clearances. The great flood of evidence is ignored, and all these accounts are stubbornly defied by received wisdom. If a writer is determined to defend the clearances, the facts are expendable.

26. Clan maps

XV. "The territories which each clan regarded as its own can be demarcated on a map with the same precision as one marks the boundaries between France and Germany, or the U.S.A. and Mexico, or Zambia and Malawi."[190]

The Gaels, whether this is to be applauded or deplored, regarded themselves not as Scots, nor primarily as Highlanders, but as members of a particular group of people called a clan, which looked upon a distinct area as its homeland. Sometimes the edge of a clan country was clearly marked by a high mountain ridge or a seashore, a loch-side or a riverbank. In other places, however, the dividing line between one group of hunter-gatherers and another, in a very thinly populated countryside much of which was rarely trodden by humans, was considerably more fluid. If one township's inhabitants considered themselves part of one clan, while the next township, miles away across the moorland, was part of another, at what point should the boundary be drawn? If there was a wide mountain range, several miles across, between territory where one clan hunted and herded, and territory where another clan did the same, where was the frontier? Sometimes only an approximate boundary can be suggested between the groups of roaming hunters and herdsmen who regarded themselves as MacDonalds and those who thought of themselves as Campbells, between the Menzies and the Robertsons, or between the Rosses and the Munros.

Even where more exact demarcation is possible, there are customary errors in most clan maps, which are carried on trustingly from one author to the next. Rum and Muck were MacLean territories, while Eigg and Canna belonged to the Clan Ranald; but all four Small Isles are consistently marked as inhabited by Clan Ranald. Again, much of the MacKinnon country in Skye is normally but mistakenly labelled MacDonald. The conventionally delineated Fraser-Chisholm frontiers do not carry conviction: Guisachan, for example, indubitably belonged to the Frasers, but is usually put down as being either in the Chisholm or the Grant country. Besides that, one has learned to be suspicious when a Mr MacX produces a clan map in which a "Clan MacX" either appears for the first time, or apparently occupies much more territory than anyone else has ever given it credit for.

Though the boundaries of the clan countries, in those days before modern states defined their frontiers to the nearest inch, were to our eyes somewhat nebulous, it is possible to make approximate estimates of their comparative sizes. Some of them were well under a hundred square miles in area; others were five times as large. That part of the MacKinnon clan country which was in northern Mull consisted of perhaps only ten square miles, although the same MacKinnon clan also inhabited well over a hundred square miles in Skye. The greater clan countries were larger than that, up to three or four hundred square miles, or even more. The clan countries were economically viable, as they showed by enduring for centuries: and they compared favourably in extent with many of the small Germanic states (about 160 of them) which existed in central Europe until the end of the eighteenth century, and, indeed, with some of the small independent states of Europe which have survived to the present day, such as Monaco (eight square miles), San Marino (thirty-eight square miles), Liechtenstein (sixty-five square miles), and Andorra (191 square miles). There were, and are, perhaps sixteen Highland *parishes* bigger than Andorra. Even Luxembourg, which appears to play a not inconsiderable part in the European Union, is only 998 square miles – not very much bigger than the biggest of the clan countries.

27. Scottish sentimentality

XVI. "The Highland landlords were ruined by the economic changes of the late eighteenth and the nineteenth centuries."

The income of the chiefs, which could best be described as rates or taxes to finance the necessary expenses of government during the clanship system, was transformed into the rent of land when the chiefs were converted into landlords by the triumphant British state authority in the middle years of the eighteenth century; and the amount of that income certainly increased enormously. There are some indications that the metamorphosis of the chiefs into landlords, and the corresponding magnification of the chiefs' tribute into landlords' rent, can be said to have begun in some areas of the southern and eastern border Highlands (where Lowland influence was particularly strong) as early as the 1720s and 1730s; it certainly became universal over the Highlands after the defeat of Prince Charles, and Cumberland's brutal conquest of the Highlands which followed. I have collected what evidence I can find as to the income of the chiefs/landlords during the century and half after the Highlands were forcibly subsumed into Great Britain. During that one hundred and fifty years, the income of many landlords appears to have enormously increased, up to fifty times as much as the amount of the tribute received by the chiefs in the days of clanship. In some areas, it increased even more. The rent of Eddrachillis appears to have become a hundred times greater in only one hundred years after Culloden. There can be no Highland estate whose rent did not go up to a figure at least twenty times higher during the century after the chiefs became landlords. The enthusiasm of the chiefs for this transformation can cause no surprise. The matter is dealt with later in this work, in volume two.

Of course, if somehow, by some astounding stroke of good luck, a large group of people were each given a million pounds, one would not be surprised to find after some years had passed that a handful of them had got through it all – either by breakneck spending, or by unwise investment, or by a particularly rash recipient handing on a virtually insolvent inheritance. All the others would still be very much better off. And if a commentator wished to gloss over the extraordinary good fortune of the great majority of the beneficiaries of this bounty, it could be done by ignoring that great majority, and instead harping on the misfortunes of the few.

It is interesting, too, to see in what an unbalanced way historians often approach the misfortunes (real or imagined) of the great, and of the not-so-great. Writers often sternly condemn "sentimentality" if anyone betrays any sympathy for the ordinary Highlanders. Tom Steel, dealing with the Sutherland clearances, denounced "the poets and writers who, at the time and since, have clouded economic reality with Scottish sentimentality".[191] Professor Smout thought "much Highland history of the period has been heavily charged with emotion".[192] D. McCloskey deplored the fact that "the ghosts of grasping capitalists, expropriated small farmers and exploited factory workers still haunt economics and politics", and J. Mokyr criticized "technophobic writers" who did not accept "the inexorable obsolescence that new techniques will bring about".[193] Malcolm Gray's history of the Highlands from 1750 to 1850, which almost ignored the clearances, earned praise from academics for its detached approach: Professor Smout applauded it as "scholarly" and "dispassionate",[194] Professor Richards as a "dispassionate" account, "without recourse to sentimentality", which eschewed "overheated prose",[195] and Professor Pryde as a "dispassionate study of a theme that has too often been charged with emotion in the past".[196] Dr Gaskell modestly claimed, on the first page of his book on Morvern, that he had tried "to avoid the customary over-emphasis on the misfortunes of the Highland peasantry [sic]"[197] (and he succeeded: one must give him that). Professor Youngson, too, said he had tried to write his book about the Highlands after 1745 "without that intense emotional involvement which characterizes so much that is written about the Highlands"[198] (and he, too, achieved the desired apathy). But this stern demand for "dispassionate" history only applies when writers are talking of ordinary Highlanders; when historians get on to the topic of the supposed sufferings of the landlords, emotion is suddenly to the fore – the tears start to trickle down, the violins to play. Suddenly it becomes acceptable to employ overheated prose, and to use Scottish sentimentality in order to cloud economic reality.

28. Became very poor

Here are a few of the comments made by historians about the estate-owners after the landlord revolution of the mid-eighteenth century sent the new landowners' rents rocketing upwards. Professor Mackie: "though some proprietors during the brief boom in kelp made large sums, others became very poor"; "some of the old proprietors incurred heavy debts", while many of them "had fallen into the hands of trustees or creditors".[199] Sir Thomas Innes: "the greater number of the chieftains [were] ruined . . . many of the old ancestral estates passed from the hands of the ruined chiefs into the possession of alien proprietors."[200] C. R. MacKinnon: "chiefs, who could not easily be disposed of by other means, were starved out of existence."[201] Dr Ferguson: "Most of the landlords indeed, unlike the wealthy Staffords, were relatively poor, and faced difficult, perhaps insoluble, problems."[202] (Relative to the crofters? Or relative to whom, exactly? If the Staffords are meant, then the wealthy were "relatively poor" compared with them – but they were still rich.) Professor Pryde: "Embarrassed beyond endurance, most of the Highland proprietors, between 1820 and 1846, had to sell their ancestral estates in whole or in part."[203] Professor Smout: in the Highlands, "particularly in the north and west", despite the improvements, "neither the peasants nor the landowners were better off than they had been before".[204] Chalmers Clapperton: after 1815, "many Highland and Island estates became bankrupt and were sold".[205] Douglas Hill: "On some estates sheep were introduced by impoverished landlords only after the tenants' departure ['to escape overcrowding'] had mostly emptied the land." (So some landlords, faced with empty estates after the tenants voluntarily departed, only brought in sheep to escape from their impoverishment.)[206] Eric Cregeen: "Many lairds" were "weaned away by their new interests. They accumulated debts and often became bankrupt . . . A new class of lairds, too, was rising, at the expense of the old landed families, many of whom had been ruined."[207] BBC website, History: "Respect for the traditional chiefs was fast disappearing, even where they remained on their lands. But many had as little benefit from the Clearances as their tenants did, and were forced to sell off land . . . to the nouveau riche of the industrialized south."[208] L. G. Pine: "The constant pressure of economic forces has compelled many chiefs to sell their ancestral property; those who remain are often in dire straits."[209] Andrew Newby: "The gradual bankruptcy of many native clan chiefs led inevitably" to sales of land, to "absentee speculators", etc.[210] Professor A. J. Youngson: It is a "gross distortion of history" to say that "a cash nexus" immediately replaced the old relations of the clan. "There was a struggle – for many landowners a long and saddening struggle – between feelings of social obligation on the one hand and mounting economic pressure on the other"; small tenants "were often . . . an absolute burden on an estate".[211] (To describe people who live and work on the land and have to pay rent as a "burden" does reveal an extraordinary attitude of mind: the main "burden" on any landed estate is the person who can claim "ownership", and to whom everyone else on the estate has to make repeated donations of money.) Ian Finlay: the landlords were hugely generous in famine times, "many a chief . . . well-nigh ruining himself in the attempt to keep his clanspeople alive".[212] Professor Mitchison: in and after 1846 "landowners went even further into debt".[213] Michael Fry: "Many chiefly houses entered the Victorian era with overwhelming burdens of debt, in some cases stretching back two centuries."[214] Professor Richards: "The ownership of Highland estates, despite clearances, was infrequently a lucrative business." In 1815-50, Richards claimed, "great pressure was now placed on the shrunken economic base of the region, resulting in bankruptcy for many landlords, especially in the west". "Landlords, where they survived, were saddled with difficulties vastly beyond their means." "Many Highland estates were in a financial stranglehold by the 1840s, gripped by the accumulation of debt and annuities." The landlords "tightened their own belts. Mostly they lived a life of excruciating financial anxiety. Some landlords, of whom there were several cases during the famine of the 1840s, crippled themselves in attempting to relieve poverty and destitution." "Much of the drama and tragedy of the Highlands is told in the negotiations between financially-racked landlords and their creditors, agents and trustees."[215]

(We will see later how Professor Richards – not surprisingly – championed the history that is based on the landowners' own records, and welcomed "the increasing availability of archives from the muniments of the descendants of clearing landlords" – muniments somehow preserved down the years in the comfortably-housed and well-tended archives of landlords despite their "excruciating financial anxiety".) Professor Richards' lament about "several landlords" crippling themselves in the 1840s was far too feeble for Sir Iain Moncreiffe, who bemoaned "the great financial sacrifices made" in 1847-8 "by many landlords".[216]

It may be briefly mentioned that as a question of unemotional fact, the money collected by charitable appeals and sent to the Highlands on "make-work" schemes when the Highlanders were suffering from the agonizing famine in and after 1846 actually had the effect of improving landlords' properties at no expense to themselves, with the gratuitous construction of roads, harbours, drains, fences and ditches, and so forth. Taxpayers' money was similarly beneficial to the proprietors: Professor Devine said the funds granted under the Drainage Act "amounted to an indirect subsidy from the state to the Highland landlord class".[217]

In this stern rejection of sentimentality (about the lower class), and this torrent of sentimentality (about the upper class), a few figures might be of interest. In volume four there is a survey of the average incomes received by various groups of Highlanders in 1840. The most destitute pauper would be lucky to receive two and a half pounds a year (most had less); a hard-working labourer might get an annual £25 (ten times as much as the most fortunate pauper); a minister £250 (ten times as much as a labourer); a middle-ranking landlord £2500 (ten times as much as a minister); while at least three landowners – Argyll, Breadalbane, and Sutherland – had £25,000 a year or more (ten times as much as many of their fellow landlords – in fact the Duke of Sutherland who died in 1833 was believed to have ten times as much as that). In other words, the average landlord was a hundred times as rich as a labourer, and a thousand times as wealthy as the luckiest pauper. The richest were ten thousand times as wealthy as the poorest (and the Duke of Sutherland was much richer even than that).

29. Biggest bonanza

The spurious theory that Highland heritors at this time were driven to the wall by inexorable economic developments (and that where a few owners got into financial difficulties, it had nothing to do with the gross over-spending by the landlord family of even a vastly increased income) is so far from the truth that it is difficult to see how even the most committed champions, the most blinkered supporters, of the landlords could bring themselves to repeat it. It is completely at variance with the facts, as we saw earlier.

Anyone who tries to find out what actually happened in the Highlands in past times is not infrequently dazed with astonishment at the vast gulf between what contemporaries experienced and wrote about then, and what many historians say now. In volume two a detailed examination, parish by parish, will be made of the position of landlords in the 1790s, and in volume four there will be a similar survey of proprietors in the 1840s. It will then be shown (assuming that anyone ever sees it), beyond any possibility of error, that the estate-owners in the clearance era were the beneficiaries of the biggest bonanza of unearned riches that the island of Great Britain has ever seen. The accounts left by people alive at the relevant time (after the landlord revolution of the mid-eighteenth century and the subsequent "improvements" produced enormously increased rents) are virtually unanimous; they show us the landlords building lavish new mansions, filling them with the latest desirable furnishings, purchasing expensive pictures and objets d'art, enclosing many acres round their residences to make stylish genteel parks, planting trees and bushes and creating lakes to achieve a fashionable residential ambience, establishing the lengthy vistas then required by trendy landscape gardening (while simultaneously claiming that the Highlanders had to leave the country because every last square yard of the Highlands was disastrously congested with crofters), bringing down troops of guests from England and the Lowlands, particularly in "the season", holding endless parties, and altogether living the life of Reilly. Some historians, as we have just seen, now prefer to dwell mournfully on the misfortunes of a very small unrepresentative group of island or coastal proprietors, who garnered immense amounts of money (the best kind, too, money-without-work) when the Napoleonic blockade made kelp soar in price, who proceeded to spend this wealth on sumptuous lifestyles as if there were no tomorrow, and who then lacked the self-control to accept that the triumph of free trade in the first half of the nineteenth century had made them merely very wealthy, instead of astoundingly rich. Again, there were landlords who succeeded to estates which had been mortgaged to the hilt by the previous owner, and which only came to them under wills which forced them to pay substantial annuities to various free-loading relatives; but that does not show that the estate was not productive of a large rental, merely that it had been very badly managed in the past. No one is compelled to accept the ownership of property; and it is significant that very few (if any) Highland landlords have ever voluntarily divested themselves of their estates.

Of course, even apart from the small number of kelp or ex-kelp landlords, not all the people who are lucky enough to gain possession of great riches are wise enough to keep them. There are not many fortunes which stupidity cannot disperse. A successful gambler might win millions of pounds on a football pool or a lottery, and then throw it away in mindless expenditure; such events are not unknown. But even when this kind of profligate madness is originated or exacerbated by the win itself, one would not be justified in talking of the winner's having been "ruined" by his good fortune. When someone gains great wealth and then squanders it, he is not ruined by extraneous circumstances; a fool is ruined by his folly. It is true that there were a few Highland landlords who devoted themselves to persistent monumental extravagance with such dedication that even the vastly augmented rents coming in from their cleared estates could not keep pace with their reckless spending; but the reasons for such disasters have little to do with economics. Lord Reay cleared his estate, and was able to draw (this was early in the clearance era) fifteen times – or more than fifteen times – as much income from it as it had yielded in the days of the clans only fifty years before (would you, dear reader, like to multiply your income that much? – and with no income tax); yet the expenses of his dissipated lifestyle increased even more, and he had to sell out. However, as we shall see shortly, historians still praise his (completely imaginary) "self-sacrifice". Some of them, indeed, go so far as to claim that he never carried out any clearances.[218] Many commentators appear to adopt a deferential cringe immediately they realize they are talking about a landlord.

It is interesting to observe how some anti-clearance writers gloated over any of these rare examples of spendthrift proprietors who finally went bankrupt: often such authors clearly believed – sometimes they even said in so many words – that it demonstrated the intervention of the Almighty who was enforcing heavenly justice, and executing divine punishment. However, the rarity of such events does not encourage one to believe in the inevitability of this supposed celestial squaring of accounts.

The exuberant expenditure of the estate owners made an uncomfortable contrast with the penny-pinching poverty of the Highland crofters, the two lifestyles being different sides of the same coin, having been caused by the same series of events – the clearances. Those who wish to blur this divergence, or who dare to deny the clearances, are naturally tempted to close their eyes to the luxurious lives of the landowners.

30. Transferred blame

XVII. "Admittedly there were some clearances, but the chiefs, who became landlords after Culloden, were not responsible for any of them."

The desire to exculpate clan chiefs from any guilt in connection with the clearances carried out on their estates leads to surprising allegations in the work of writers who feel they ought to shield the chiefs from any unmannerly criticism. One author said that the clearances occurred "essentially because former estates owned by clan chiefs were sold to the wealthy barons of the Industrial Revolution"; the new owners, rich industrialists who had taken over from the clan chiefs, wanted to grasp the profits offered by sheep, and since the people were in the way they "were forcibly removed from their homes".[219] At least this author acknowledges that there were many clearances, even though he is palpably mistaken as to the perpetrators. Often, however, any hint that there may have been clearances on a particular property meets simply with a blunt rebuttal: it never happened. (We shall shortly see some of these brave refutations, which demonstrate how often those who have power in our present society believe that they also have the power to transform the past, and to adjust history so that their predecessors are found guiltless.) However, where a propagandist feels that particular clearances are so well known that a flat denial is no longer possible, various mitigations are frequently offered. Sometimes we are told that it was not the chief who was to blame, but his wife; sometimes it was the chief's mother who merits reproof; sometimes the chief's advisers; and even sometimes, when the chief was a woman, it was her husband.[220] All these cases, as well as all the other customary fallacies, will be considered as they arise.

The subjugation of an entire people, the ruthless extermination of their whole society and way of life, and the resulting flight of a great number of them from their Highland homeland, all this happening within the last two or three hundred years in this comparatively small island of Great Britain, would (one would have thought) bulk largely in the published accounts of modern British history. But not so: sometimes it is ignored entirely, sometimes it is briefly dismissed in laughably inaccurate volumes. It is considered so unimportant that significant, and easily discoverable, dates within this story are often blatantly repudiated. One history professor claimed that the clearances only began after 1815. "Vast incomes had been made on the kelp shores . . ." (though not by the kelp workers, as the writer failed to make clear) ". . . when in 1815 peace destroyed the market . . . So came the 'clearances'."[221] (In fact they began as early as the 1740s.) Another historian said that in 1841 "the clearances were coming to an end", defying the reality, which was that there were probably more, and more calamitous, clearances in the 1840s and early 1850s than at any other time.[222] So these academics, between them, reduced the duration of the clearances, which actually lasted a century and a half, to not much more than twenty-five years.

The main clearances on the Countess of Sutherland's estate took place between 1807 and 1821, as anyone (whether a member of the educational establishment or not) can find out after the most cursory investigation. So it is difficult to see why one historian should say that they occurred "between 1799 and 1813",[223] or why another academic writing partnership should have asserted that they happened "between 1819 and . . . 1833".[224] Thus one account said they were over almost before they started, and the other claims they only started after they were nearly over. Another keen observer said that "the notorious Sutherland clearances" took place in "the late eighteenth century".[225]

31. Voluntary emigrations

XVIII. "Many Highlanders left the Highlands (and went to the Lowlands or to countries overseas) simply because they had a natural desire to better themselves, not because they were being driven out; the emigrations were all voluntary."

The idea behind this allegation is fairly clearly the defensive assertion that the Highlanders who left the Highlands were not going because of anything the landlords had done. Some of the enthusiasts for this belief seem to go close to a scenario in which clansfolk whose ancestors had lived in their glen for hundreds of years, who had lived there all their lives themselves, who knew the individual names of and the stories attached to every mountain and river, every hill and stream, every rock and rill in the landscape, who had always looked forward to seeing their children succeed them, whose fervent wish was to find graves at last in the sacred earth next to their forefathers, and whose almost fanatical devotion to their homeland was one of their most unmistakable characteristics, so much that one observer said, "their passion for staying at home . . . is predominant among the Highlanders",[226] nevertheless said – out of the blue – at breakfast one morning,

"I know! Let's all go and live in New Zealand!" So everyone immediately fell in with this idea, and that is how the emigration came to take place: and it was nothing to do with any clearance, or any other insufferably tyrannical behaviour on the part of the landlord. In fact the way in which this thesis (that the Highlanders all left voluntarily) is sometimes stated comes near to being merely an artificial kind of play on words, as in "I pointed a gun at his head, and he voluntarily gave me all his money". If a man's house is set on fire by an arson attack in the middle of the night, and he jumps out of his bedroom window, risking a fourteen-foot drop into the garden, is he acting of his own free will? Does it add anything to our comprehension to say that the man had a natural desire to better himself by going outside where there was plenty of fresh air to breathe, and where he would survive without being burned to death? – and that the "pull" of the desire to stay alive was stronger than any "push" which some might allege the burning house provided? It will be seen as we survey the history of the eighteenth and nineteenth centuries that over and over again a particular exodus from the Highlands followed immediately upon, and was manifestly motivated by, a clearance or some other intolerable action on the part of the landlord; so often that when in any given instance this cannot be immediately proved, any reasoned consideration of the move must make it seem overwhelmingly likely.

32. "No more cultivable land"

XIX. "It was not possible to increase the production of food in the Highlands, so the 'population explosion' meant that the Highlanders had to leave."

The constantly re-iterated – though unfortunately inaccurate – claims of a vast population increase in the hundred years after Culloden is usually followed up by an adamant assertion that nothing could be done to amplify the supplies of food (no doubt because if it is shown that the food supply did in fact expand more quickly than the population, then other reasons have to be found for the emigrations). Many examples of these claims were given above in subsection 12; many more could be given. Donnachie and Hewitt said that the Highlands "had experienced rapid population growth, pressure on available cultivable land, and acute poverty – resulting in enforced emigration".[227] John Lister said there was a "population explosion" between "the mid eighteenth century and the mid nineteenth century . . . and no land to till; there could be no further extension of cultivable land".[228] Marion Campbell said much the same: "the Highland population was increasing at a tremendous rate while the available sources of food hardly grew at all . . . every inch of workable ground was dug".[229] Fraser Darling thought the numbers of Highlanders had gone up "beyond the power of the land to feed them".[230] Malcolm Gray felt that there was "a population rapidly on the increase", so "land pressure was the basic problem".[231] Sir Thomas Innes (somewhat inelegantly) said that "since the productive capacity had not, nor could then be, doubled, there was bound to be poverty, and occasionally famine".[232] Professor Marwick thought the "rapid growth" of numbers meant that the "pressure of population on subsistence ... became acute".[233] Denis Rixson said the Highland population "rose steeply in the period 1751-1831", but "unfortunately population increase was not matched by a parallel increase in resources".[234] Jamie McGrigor, member of the Scottish Parliament, said that "in the latter half of the 18th century, there was an enormous population explosion ... Ever-expanding families tried to scrape a living from the land, but they failed. The little island of Inch Kenneth, off Mull, was ploughed from shore to shore, but still there was not enough food to keep the inhabitants alive."[235] Ian Finlay claimed that much of the Highland emigration "was inevitable", since "the population had almost doubled" by 1815, – "and this in a land without means of agricultural expansion".[236] Professor Richards maintained that "despite the explosive population growth of the late eighteenth century ... there was no concomitant and consistent growth of food supplies".[237]

The documentary evidence from the Highlands during this period shows that the opposite was true. As we have seen, between the 1750s and the 1790s it may well have been that there was no population increase at all; any increase in numbers cannot have been more than ten per cent at the most. If the reports are to be believed, any increase of population of that order could easily have been provided for. A score of reports spoke of waste land being reclaimed; half a dozen mused on how much more could be reclaimed. The Dunkeld report said "immense tracts" in the Highlands were recoverable for agriculture.[238] Dr John Smith in 1798 said 50,000 acres in mainland Argyllshire alone could be made into farmland,[239] and James MacDonald in 1811 said "many thousand acres in the Hebrides" could be reclaimed for food production.[240] Another thirty or more of the O.S.A. reports mentioned other farming advances – turnips and sown grass, lime or shell marl fertiliser, better ploughs, rotation of crops, and so on. The result of all that was a great increase in food production. The minister of Kingussie said that with better methods and reasonably long leases "there is little doubt but the soil could be brought to maintain double the number of its present inhabitants".[241] What was a forecast in Kingussie was elsewhere a fact. Dr Smith wrote about Argyllshire: "A few in our own county who have begun to raise green crops, and attend to a proper rotation, have already doubled their returns."[242] The minister of Dowally said that "per acre ... oats, which yielded formerly not more than four bolls, now yield eight";[243] in Fowlis Wester "superior skill and industry now raise a crop of double value" compared with twenty-years before,[244] while in Lochgoilhead "half the number of hands produce more than double the quantity of provisions".[245] Increased food production on this scale would obviously have more than compensated for the minimal (if any) increase in population during the second half of the eighteenth century.

33. More than tripled

We have seen that the Highland population rose by about a quarter between the 1790s and 1831/1841, when it reached its zenith: the highest possible increase that can be calculated in the century after Culloden was therefore thirty-seven per cent. So if the output of food was increased by the same – or a greater – percentage, there could not have been any shortages as a result of "over-population". The briefest reading of the N.S.A. reports (written between 1833 and 1844) shows that in fact the food production of the Highlands had shot up in the previous decades. Of the 162 reports, well over a hundred go into great detail about the strides made by agriculture in the relevant parish. The Luss minister talked of "the increased productiveness of the soil".[246] In Torosay they had better ploughs, harrows, etc.: "the consequence is, that a much greater productiveness is effected on the same extent of ground tilled." [247] In Kilninian, "there is a greater quantity of crop now produced".[248] In Ardnamurchan, there were better farm implements, "and crops are more abundant".[249] In Callander, "rich crops of oats, barley, turnips, and potatoes may be seen growing upon places, which, a few years ago, were covered with barren heath".[250] In Petty, "broom and whins" had been replaced by "fertile fields".[251] In Kingussie, "great part of the bleak and barren land . . . has been brought under cultivation", and "the wet swampy lands have nearly all given place to dry cultivated fields".[252] In Croy, agricultural advances had been "converting large tracts of barren moor into fields, yielding most luxuriant crops of wheat, oats, and barley, improving and adorning what had formerly been a useless waste".[253] In Fodderty, because of drainage improvements "what was formerly in a state of marsh and meadow now yields luxuriant crops of grain".[254] In Killearnan, compared with sixteen, or even twelve years before, "there are now many scores of acres yielding wheat and green crops, which were then useless, without any other cover than short heath and broom".[255] More than thirty parish reports say "a vast extent", or "a great quantity" (or some similar phrase) of waste had been reclaimed; thirty more give an exact number (or identify the increased proportion) of the hundreds or thousands of acres of unproductive land which had been turned into farmland in their parishes. Patrick Sellar affirmed: "I have increased Culmaily farm 100 acres . . . I have added sixty tillage acres to Morvich."[255] Urquhart and Logie Wester boasted of "modern improvements in husbandry", such as rotation of crops and fertilizers, while "many a valuable acre has been brought under the plough"; "the result is a great increase of produce, amounting to double what it was twenty years ago".[256] In Kilchoman, although "the improvements may be said to be only in their infancy . . . the produce has, in many instances, been more than doubled".[257] In Moulin, "farms are now known to yield double the crops they were wont to bear".[258] In South Uist, "the produce has been more than tripled since 1796".[259] I have often read in history books that the population of South Uist in the 1840s had more than doubled since the O.S.A.; I cannot remember ever reading in a history book that the produce of South Uist had "more than tripled", so that (other things being equal) everyone there must have had over fifty per cent more food. It is uncanny that the one fact should be ubiquitous, and the other unmentionable.

This subject is dealt with at length in volume four of this series; but it should be said now that no one reading the N.S.A. and the other contemporary evidence can have any doubt that the expanded agricultural production in the century after 1750 had greatly outstripped any growth in population: and these reports were written by men who were farmers themselves, not by desk-bound academics. It is surprising to see some writers ignoring this mountain of evidence, and claiming that "the productive capacity" of the Highlands could not be augmented, that "the available sources of food hardly grew at all"; that "there could be no further extension of cultivable land"; that there was no "increase in resources"; that there was "no consistent growth of food supplies"; and that the Highland area was "without means of agricultural expansion". It is not obvious what explanation there can be for these palpable mis-statements, other than the ubiquity of that popular labour-saving device – the pervasive propensity of historians to copy other historians.

34. Massacre of Glen Coe

XX. "Glen Coe is now empty not because of the clearances, but because of the 1692 massacre."

Several writers have claimed that the people of Glen Coe were driven away by the Lowland plot to exterminate them in 1692, and therefore not (as other Highlanders were) by the improvements. More than one website has (while deploring the present desolation of the glen) managed to blame not only the 1692 massacre, but also "the English King", or "the English government". The phrase "English King" may mean either that William III was the King of England, or that he was English: whichever meaning was intended is misleading. William was a Dutchman, not an Englishman, and he was then giving orders as the King of Scotland (which he had been for the past three years), on the advice of the various Lowlander grandees, or Highland dignitaries turned Lowland politicians, who directed matters in Scotland, principally John Dalrymple (the Master of Stair, who was Secretary of State for Scotland), the Earl of Argyll, and the Earl of

Breadalbane: the orders for the massacre, having been hatched by these Scottish worthies, were transmitted by Sir Thomas Livingstone, Lieutenant-Colonel Hamilton, Major Duncanson, and Captain Drummond, and were carried out by Captain Robert Campbell of Glenlyon and the soldiers under his command – all of whom, from Dalrymple onwards, were Scottish. "The English" were notable absentees. It is, however, always useful to be able to reproach foreigners for anything disreputable. *The Scotsman* recently quoted, apparently with approval, an assertion that "the Campbells" had been guilty of the massacre at Glen Coe, having been sent there to "do the bidding of their English masters".[260]

A television programme about the massacre, broadcast in the 1990s, ended with the presenter mournfully telling us, "the pitiful ruins of their homes can still be seen", obviously believing that the glen had been empty since 1692. One (otherwise very perceptive) author in 1993 made it still clearer: "for the MacDonalds it [the massacre] was the end ... they never reclaimed their old lands in Glen Coe." Seton Gordon wrote that "Glen Coe is still a desolate glen; it has never recovered from that night's work of long ago"; "before the massacre Glen Coe was the home of a virile race", but since that event "the summer shielings in the corries have crumbled into ruin".[261] George Eyre-Todd wrote: "In many a spot above the sunny little clachan of Invercoe are still to be seen the ruins of the houses associated with the tragedy of that terrible February morning in 1692."[262] A. Wainwright said that the attack resulted in "the annihilation of the MacDonalds".[263] Other authors have said the same, and no doubt still further experts will copy them.

The reality is otherwise. The murderous (though bungled) assault on the people of Glen Coe did not "clear" Glen Coe. The soldiers killed directly "only" about forty people, though others died, fleeing on the snow-covered mountains through difficult passes which had not yet been sealed off. (We must all be grateful that autocracies are so often inefficient.) The fact that no more people were killed, in an attack out of the blue by some 130 soldiers on scattered civilians fast asleep at five o'clock on a February morning, strongly suggests that some of the attackers were reluctant; in fact two lieutenants refused the outrageous order, and were arrested (though later vindicated). The MacDonalds returned to Glen Coe when the soldiers left, and resumed their traditional way of life there; the clearance of the glen was carried out by the MacDonalds' own chief at some point in the late eighteenth century, as we shall see in volume two. However, the enormous propaganda effort which has been, and still is, carried out to clear the chiefs/landlords from any blame for the clearances, must tempt writers to point to the 1692 massacre as the cause of the desolation of the glen.

35. Clearance of Glen Coe

A possible date for the actual clearance may be suggested (for the benefit of those who prefer reality to romance). Travellers in the nineteenth century all agreed that at that time there was almost no human life in Glen Coe, so the glen must have been cleared before then. Dorothy Wordsworth in 1803 found only traces of "former habitation";[264] Sarah Murray, in a book published the same year, said there were fewer than thirty human beings in the entire glen.[265] The MacDonalds were certainly still there in 1745, when the memo about the clans said the Glen Coe people could raise 150 fighting men. (120 men went to join Prince Charles in that year.) The clansfolk were still there in 1778, when the 76th regiment, MacDonald's Highlanders, was embodied. Stewart of Garth said one of the chiefly family of the Glen Coe MacDonalds became an officer in the regiment: the way that Highland regiments were then recruited meant that he would have had to bring a number of soldiers along with him to justify his commission, and that would only have been possible if the people were still in the glen.[266] The War of American Independence ended in 1783, and with it the immediate usefulness of a population to supply any necessary recruits. If that is the case, something must have happened soon afterwards. William Thomson travelled through the glen only two years later, in 1785. "After getting out of Glen Coe, which is ten miles long, you may see the King's House, at the distance of three miles . . . Around this lonely hut, for twenty miles in each direction, there seems to be no habitation, nor food for man or beast."[267] Twenty miles from the King's House inn would cover the whole of Glen Coe; so the clearance of Glen Coe must have taken place by then – possibly between 1783 and 1785. In 1792 another traveller, Kerr Richardson, said he "went to Glen Coe, where I met with Mr MacDonald of Achdrichtan, who was among the first who introduced sheep into that part of the country". This trailblazer was probably MacDonald of Achtriochtan: he was one of the old clan tacksmen or sub-chiefs (his ancestor was killed in the 1692 massacre), but he had, like other tacksmen, accepted the new order and become a sheep farmer. In 1792 he had 8000 sheep.[268] So it seems that the clansfolk of Glen Coe had by then been replaced by sheep, brought in by the pioneer sheep farmer, Achtriochtan. Which chief was responsible? Alasdair, 12th of Glencoe, was murdered in the Lowland plot of 1692; his great-grandson John, 15th of Glencoe, flourished in 1785.[269] (It was apparently in the same year, 1785, that the first road was built through the glen; a transport improvement often associated with the first arrival of the large graziers.) If all these probabilities are correct, it was John MacDonald, 15th chief of Glencoe, who cleared the glen, perhaps at some time soon after 1783. John's son Alexander, 16th of Glencoe, became a sheep farmer himself – Fraser-Mackintosh said he was "a great monopolist" on the estates of Cameron of Lochiel and others in the early nineteenth century.[270] At one time he held the Keppoch sheep farm;

and when he died in 1814 he was described as "the greatest and most extensive sheep farmer in the Highlands".

We may as well round off the story. The son of Alexander the sheep farmer was Ewen. When he was a young man he went out shooting with a friend in Glen Roy, and they saw a herd-boy, John MacIntosh, in the hills above Bohenie. Ewen thought it would be fun to take a pot-shot at him, and he succeeded in hitting him, said Stuart MacDonald. "Though the wound inflicted was 'to the danger of life', Ewen was not imprisoned. His father was a landlord."[270]

Ewen became a surgeon with the army in India; he, and an Indian woman, had a "natural", i.e. "illegitimate", daughter, Ellen. Ellen inherited Glen Coe; she married Archibald Burns in Ceylon in 1888. Burns changed his name to MacDonald, and they had two children. The elder, Archibald, 19th of Glencoe, died unmarried; his younger brother Duncan, 20th, inherited Glen Coe, and sold off the glen, once belonging to the local MacDonald clan, in 1894. According to some authorities, his son William, 21st of Glencoe, died unmarried. William's brother Roy, 22nd, was an aircraftsman in the R.A.F. in the second world war, but has not been traced since. Various other claimants to the chiefship have come forth, but since there is now no question of landownership involved, perhaps there is less urgency to arrive at a decision.

So much for a score of the standard vindications or mitigations of the clearances. It must, however, be conceded at the outset that if the archive of the head is consistently employed, it will reveal discordant elements not only in the work of those who defend (or deny) the clearances, but also in what anti-clearance writers have sometimes asserted. Some of these allegations will now be listed, for, as Richard Porson realized, "He does the best service to truth, who hinders it from being supported by falsehood."[271]

36. The English were responsible

XXI. "The native chiefs were either expelled after Culloden, or were driven out subsequently by economic stress: the English bought up the Highland estates, and they then proceeded to clear out the Highlanders."

Many of those who denounced the clearances, whether they were Highlanders or sympathizers from outside the Highlands, blamed "the English" for these tragic events, rather than the Highland chiefs. It is true that a few of the chiefs were denuded of their land charters after the failure of the '45 – a dozen of them out of some hundreds: the estates confiscated in this way can scarcely have amounted to more than one-twentieth part of the land of the Highlands. Even these properties were restored to the heirs of the expropriated families in 1784; and while they were subject to confiscation, they were run, not by "the English", but by a state-appointed body of Scotsmen, the commissioners on the forfeited estates (who in fact managed them so well – from a landlord's point of view – that they were in much better condition, from that same point of view, when they were handed back than when they were taken over).

Robert Mathieson said that "by the eighteenth century" in the Highlands, the class of proprietors included "landowners with no genealogical claim to former clan lands . . . Many were not even Scots."[272] The Amazon website some time ago had a page which advertised books on Highland history: it defined "the clearances" as the "wholesale eviction of Highland sub-tenants and small farmers by English landlords", a remarkable example of an assertion which the least acquaintance with its subject would show to be untrue. Another website said that when wool and mutton increased in price, "the English lords of the Highlands began a campaign now known as 'The Clearances'."[272] In fact the great majority of those who cleared their estates, particularly in the earlier stages of the new development, were the native Highland chiefs. Later (in volume two) there will be a comprehensive survey of the Highlands in the 1790s, which will show that nearly all the landowners at that time were those (or more usually the immediate heirs of those) who had been chiefs in the days of the clans; even fifty years later, in the 1840s, a further survey (in volume four) will show that after nearly a century during which the northern mountains had become part of the general British real-property market, so that members of the Highland upper class began to buy land elsewhere in Great Britain, while wealthy people from the Lowlands and England had begun to buy land in the Highlands, it was still the case that the great majority of Highland landlords were even then Gaels, or at any rate owed their landownership to their family descent from forebears who were clan chiefs.

It is of course easier to censure "foreigners" for things which have gone wrong: the twentieth century showed many times how useful this device was for rulers, and how easily otherwise mild citizens can be dragooned into war against "foreign" enemies. But history cannot be altered to fit nationalist prejudices.

37. *The sheep farmers were Lowlanders*

XXII. "Most of the new big farmers were Lowland Scots or English."

Very many of the great farmers who took over the cleared land were Highlanders, quite often men who had been clan tacksmen or sub-chiefs during the clan system. Some were Lowlanders; a tiny number had come from England. The clan tacksmen were on the spot when the clearances occurred, and being gentry they either had money or could borrow it: so they knew about the modern large farms, they knew about people much like themselves who were making fortunes as graziers, and they knew how to obtain the finance to support a bid for ranches on the cleared land.

Of course, wherever in any society a group of people becomes unpopular, any apparently exotic quality (or even any apparently harmless characteristic) possessed by one or two of the new group will often – in the popular estimation – spread miraculously to cover the whole company. When bankers become detested in any particular economic predicament (it can happen), and one per cent of them happen to be Jews, then it is easy to inveigh against "Jewish bankers", ignoring the fact that ninety-nine per cent of them are not Jewish at all. If a large immigration takes place into any country, and – as could be expected – a handful of the newcomers (like a handful of the older inhabitants) are criminals, then such a minority quickly becomes the majority in the prevailing opinion. It will soon be believed that now all the immigrants are criminals, or that now all the criminals are immigrants. (There are people in Britain at this moment – as well as in the U.S.A. – who would go near to upholding both of those propositions.)

Some of the new sheep farmers, it is quite true, were Lowland immigrants – a very few were even English; so, since the new graziers were, not surprisingly, very unpopular among the Highlanders, that unpopularity soon encouraged a conventional belief that they were "all" Lowlanders (or even "all" English), i.e. outsiders. One historian said that "from the 1760s sheep farmers from the Lowlands introduced new breeds of sheep";[273] a second, that when sheep-farming was introduced, "those who carried it on were almost always outsiders . . . normally wealthy Lowland tenants";[274] another, "the sheep-masters commonly came from the Lowlands";[275] a fourth, the new sheep farmers "were mostly Lowland Scots or Englishmen";[276] a fifth, "great tracts of the hills were turned into sheep runs and rented to Lowland farmers";[277] a sixth, "the big Lowland farmers continued to add sheep-walk to sheep-walk in the Highlands", while "the landlords accepted the gold of the southern graziers at the price of deforcing, sometimes under circumstances of revolting cruelty, their unfortunate tenantry";[278] a seventh, when the "Lowland farmers" came in, "the inhabitants of the straths and glens" were "more or less forcibly removed to barren tracts and coastlands, in order to make room for a few Lowland shepherds";[279] and an eighth, "Lowland-run sheep farms cleared the higher straths".[280] John Prebble said the Sutherland glens "were let or leased to Lowlanders";[281] John MacLeod claimed that in Sutherland "hundreds of families were evicted from their homes" so the land "could be rented to Lowland sheep-farmers".[282] J. M. Bumsted said the Staffords were renting their Sutherland estate "to experienced sheep farmers from outside the region".[282] (As to this last revelation, of the thirty great sheep farmers in Sutherland after the clearances, at least half were Highlanders, from the class of Sutherland tacksmen.) Sheep farming, said Professor R. H. Campbell "required new men. The Highlanders had neither the capital nor the requisite technical skill."[283] In fact firstly the Highlanders had been raising sheep for centuries – their numerous herds of cattle and sheep formed one of their main sources of food. Secondly some of the Highlanders – the chiefs and the tacksmen – had the capital or could get it: that is why a few of the chieftains, and not a few of the tacksmen, actually became sheep farmers. John Lister explained the necessity for Lowlanders to operate the new sheep farms: "the Highlanders were not skilled shepherds" – despite the long history of sheep-herding in the Highlands, and the fact that a number of Highlanders actually became shepherds on the new sheep farms.[284] Again we see how useful is the cry of "Blame the foreigners!" When in early 1817 a meeting was held at which it was decided to hold the first annual "Inverness Great Sheep and Wool Fair", which was going to provide a market for the products of the newly-cleared large farms, twenty-three people were present: six from Inverness (town-officials etc.), three Lowlanders, and fourteen Highlanders; thirty-four others sent messages of support, twenty-seven of them Highlanders.[285] So three-quarters of those who declared their interest were Highlanders.

Later we will examine the evidence which can be collected from contemporary sources as to the origins of this class of sheep farmers: but it can be said now that very many of them were Highlanders.

It is quite true, of course, that most of those who were bringing in the changes were English-speakers, whether landlords or the new big tenants, and it is equally true that they were introducing the economic and social system which flourished in the anglophone parts of Great Britain – that is, in the Lowlands and England. That is not the same thing as the claim that the clearing landlords and the new big farmers were all, or mainly, Lowlanders, or English.

38. 2000 families at a time

XXIII. "Evictions at the rate of 2,000 families in one day were not uncommon."[286]

"Estate records show", said one website, that "as many as 2000 families a day were forced from their homes".[287] Another website gives even more dramatic detail. "At the height of the Highland clearances, it was not uncommon for 2000 houses to be burned in a single day." Not only did this not happen repeatedly, as these websites allege or imply, the evidence shows it did not happen at all. It could not have happened. It is not all that easy to burn a house down, even a Highland cottage; and to burn down in one day 2000 of them, scattered across miles of countryside, an army of incendiaries would have to be imported. A consideration of the number of people who actually lived in the Highlands also indicates that this was, in practical terms, impossible. Trying to work out where this idea originated, I remembered that the number 2000 did occur in Donald MacLeod's

Gloomy Memories. MacLeod said that in the Sutherland clearances almost all the inhabitants of Kildonan, "amounting to near 2000 souls", were driven out:[288] but firstly MacLeod gave that number as the total of the whole population (somewhat exaggerating it), not the number of families, and secondly they were not evicted "in a single day", but in at least half a dozen successive clearances, spread out over fifteen years, between 1807 and 1821. Again, in 1814, in the north of Sutherland, it may well be that 2000 *people* were evicted in one day: William Young, the factor, said in May of that year that he then had "at least 430 familys to arrange in different allotments . . . in Straths Naver and Brora"[289] – probably some 2000 people: but, again, not 2000 families. In 1819 the Sutherland estate as a whole, partly because it was the largest Highland property, must have seen the greatest number of families evicted in any one single simultaneous clearance. At Whitsun in that year, in a clearance spread over eight parishes, the Sutherland management cheerfully reported ejecting 706 families, which numbered 3331 individuals. At Whitsun in 1820, as the official estate papers also amiably reveal, a further 401 families, with 1892 members, were thrown out of their homes, making (in two years) a total of 1107 families, probably containing altogether some 5223 people.[290] These clearances were certainly cataclysmic events; but even 1107 families at two successive Whitsundays still falls well short of the claimed "2000 families in one day".

There were not enough Highlanders to bring this assertion within the realm of the possible. 2000 families, in those times in the Highlands, would probably have had between 8000 and 9000 members. The very highest numbers who ever lived in the Highlands were found at the 1831 and the 1841 censuses – 405,000. This figure of the total Highland population of course included resident landlords, factors, sheep-farmers, shepherds, ministers, villagers, townsfolk, private and public officials, servants at the big houses, tradesmen, quarriers, foresters, and so on (a roster which included thousands of Lowland immigrants); the number of Highland small tenants and their families never reached anything like that height. The clearances took place fairly continuously, in one district or another, over at least a century and a half; so it will be seen that the Highland population was never numerous enough to make it possible for evictions of 8000 or more people in a day to be "not uncommon" during an era stretching over more than 150 years. However, possible or not, such an enormous clearance never happened.

39. Glenorchy clearances

XXIV. "The clearances in Glenorchy were so sweeping that the parish lost nearly a thousand people in ten years. In 1831 there were 1806 people; in 1841 only 831."

This allegation was made by Alexander Robertson, author of *Barriers to the National Prosperity of Scotland*, in a letter he wrote to the Marquis of Breadalbane in 1853. Robertson's assertion was quoted by Alexander MacKenzie in his *History of the Highland Clearances*, which first appeared in 1883: a later edition, with a foreword by John Prebble, and still with the same figures, came out in 1986.[291] It has regularly re-appeared in other texts: no one seems to like examining critically statements which support one's own convictions. It is, however, incorrect. Like over half of the Argyllshire parishes, Glenorchy was in fact part of a joint-parish, called Glenorchy and Inishail. So Glenorchy can be taken to mean either the single parish of that name, or the joint-parish, coupled with Inishail. In 1831 Glenorchy had 971 people; Glenorchy-Inishail had 1806. In 1841 Glenorchy had 831 people; Glenorchy-Inishail had 1644. The single parish of Glenorchy lost 140 people in those ten years; since Inishail lost 22 people in the same decade, the joint-parish lost in total 162. The dramatic loss alleged by MacKenzie and others only appears when like is compared with unlike, when the joint-parish in 1831 is contrasted with the single parish in 1841.

This is not to say that population movements of that magnitude did not occur during the clearance years. From time to time it happened that in the course of a decade as many as a thousand (or more) people in a single parish, perhaps 200 families, would be driven off their large farms on the good land, into small crofts on the bad; but since very often this transfer was within one single parish, the total population of the parish would remain much the same. Sometimes it did come about that people after a clearance would cross a parish boundary. After the clearances in the Sutherland parish of Kildonan, around the second decade of the nineteenth century, many of the evicted had to accept crofts at the coast nearby: but, unusually, this coastal destination was in Loth, the next parish. The result was that the Kildonan population figure was 1574 in 1811, and only 565 in 1821 – a reduction of 64%. Indeed, after further clearances in the 1820s, the Kildonan population in 1831 was down to 257 (and even of that 257, quite a number would, of course, have been the new big farmers, their families, their farmworkers, and their servants). The figures as they stand, however, show a loss over twenty years of no less than 84%. These embarrassing (from the landlords' point of view) census figures led to an alteration in the parish boundaries, Kildonan parish being expanded to incorporate part of Loth; this boosted the population of Kildonan, and made the upheaval resulting from the clearance less obvious from the parochial population figures.

However, all this does not alter the position in Glenorchy. History does not consist of what might well have happened, or could have happened, or perhaps happened, but of what did happen. It is not the only task of the historian, of course, to produce correct figures; but unless the figures he produces are correct, any conclusions drawn from them will be worthless.

40. Forbidden to speak Gaelic

XXV. "During the repression after the defeat of the Jacobite rebellion of '45, the Highlanders were forbidden to speak Gaelic."

Half-a-dozen recent popular histories of Britain (as well as several websites) have repeated this assertion. Professor Simon Schama said that after the Jacobite defeat at Culloden, "speaking Gaelic was forbidden",[292] P. and F. Somerset Fry said that "Gaelic was prohibited",[293] and J. Fallow (with exemplary precision) revealed that "the speaking of the Gaelic language . . . was barred for ten years".[294] Wikipedia,[295] and J. Sharkey ("the native tongue was forbidden by law"),[296] also alleged that no one was allowed to speak Gaelic. HarperCollins' *Scottish Clan and Family Encyclopaedia* included *Clanship: A Historical Perspective*, by Professor Allan Macinnes, who said that after 1746 "speaking Gaelic was proscribed".[297] So did David Ross – "Gaelic was now outlawed".[298]

Firstly, no one has ever given any details as to when, or by whom, this ban was supposed to have been promulgated. Secondly, using the archive of the head, one can see that such an edict could never have been made, because it would be tantamount to prohibiting every Gael communicating with every other Gael (very few Highlanders had any language but Gaelic in 1746, or even in 1846) – an impossible decree to impose, when applied to perhaps 300,000 people inhabiting over 16,000 square miles of mountainous country. In places where nearly everyone knew two languages, some despots have tried to abolish one of them – that has certainly happened on a number of occasions: but the most savagely tyrannical dictator in history has never gone so far as to ban all human speech – a prohibition which could never be enforced, and if it could ever be enforced, would clearly make any human society impossible. No doubt the reason for such restraint is that taxes, which are esteemed and extorted equally by every executive, democratic and dictatorial, can only be paid out of activities which the prohibition of all human language would make impossible.

It is quite true that Gaelic was officially scorned and sneered at and discouraged by the Lowland authorities in the years following Culloden, just as it had been scorned and sneered at and discouraged for centuries before that battle and for centuries after it; but to issue a command forbidding people to speak to each other in the only tongue they knew would be as self-defeating as to order everyone to walk on their hands instead of their feet.

Professor Schama, who said that "speaking Gaelic was forbidden" after Culloden, added on the same page the assertion that after Culloden "thousands of crofters were turned off their land;"[299] in fact, there were no crofters at that time – they appeared at the earliest several decades after Culloden.

41. No mass graves

XXVI. "The potato famines either did not occur at all, or (conversely) were much more devastating than has been thought."

Some of the Highlanders cleared off the good land, which the proprietors instead consolidated into large farms for wealthy graziers, were allotted small segments of poor land, with permission to make it as fertile as they could. On such barren strips these new lotters or crofters were able to keep themselves and their families alive only with the help of the potato, an almost miraculous crop which yielded more food per acre than any other produce, which could be grown year after year even on poor ground, and which constituted by itself a diet almost adequate to sustain human life. When therefore the potato blight arrived, firstly in 1837 and then even more fiercely in 1846 and the following years, the crofting families, deprived of the only crop which could go near to providing enough food from a limited piece of inferior land, were kept alive only by charitable donations from elsewhere in Great Britain and the colonies.

This "potato famine" has led some contributors to both sides of the dispute about the clearances into misconceptions. One commentator says there was no famine, because "no mass graves . . . full of skeletons"[300] have been found – thus casually rejecting the standard definition of "famine" (a word derived from the Latin "fames", meaning hunger) as being a widespread shortage of food.[301] Another contributor to the discussion has spoken, with equal confidence and equal inaccuracy, of "untold millions" having died.[302] That opinions can be so boldly stated (though on opposite sides of a dispute) which have so little to do with the facts of history must remind us of the necessity of the basic requirement of all research – to find out what really happened.

Other misapprehensions regularly appear. Many writers have entertained themselves and their readers by constructing a fictional "Lowlands", a peaceful, civilized and law-abiding area where all was governed by high-minded Lowland ethics and morality, and which was so eminently virtuous that the Lowland subjugation of the Highlands was merely a question of right triumphing over wrong.[303] Later in this work there will be an attempt to see whether this fabricated fantasy has any factual foundation at all.[304]

Another interesting modern belief is seen in the present usage of the word "Sassenach", the Gaelic word for "Saxon", which is what the Highlanders called the Lowlanders and, secondarily, other English speakers. Now the Lowlanders (the original Sassenachs) have appropriated it, and use it to mean exclusively people who live in England.

42. The duke did it

XXVII. "The Duke of Sutherland was responsible for the clearances on the Sutherland estate between 1807 and 1821."

To begin with, there was no Duke of Sutherland then. The Sutherland estate, in 1807 about 1250 square miles (just over three-fifths of the county of Sutherland), had been inherited (after a five-year legal battle) by the Countess of Sutherland, along with the comital title, from her father, the last Earl of Sutherland, who died in 1766. She married Viscount Trentham, later Earl Gower, who subsequently succeeded his father (and his uncle) as the owner of great estates in the north and midlands of England, along with his father's title as the Marquess of Stafford. In those days of masculine supremacy, the Sutherland estate was formally considered as belonging to the marquess. However, the countess was acknowledged by all concerned as the real owner, and the surviving correspondence shows clearly that she was the person who decided what should be done on the estate, how it should be done, who should do it, and who would benefit: the revolution of 1807-21 was her scheme.

Her husband was depicted by the people who knew him as a kind of amiable nonentity. No doubt he went along with his wife's schemes, and supported the idea of the clearances, especially the idea of the much greater sheep farm rents which were going to replace, and did replace, the much lower rents paid by the Sutherland joint farmers; but he was slow at school, and his wife treated him almost as if he were backward. His grandson wrote: "For that he was dull I think there can be little doubt . . . Neither have I heard that he ever said anything that was worth remembering; if he did, it has been forgotten long ago."[305] Subsequent commentators have respectfully carved out a much greater role for him than he ever occupied in real life. One said that the marquess "had conceived the idea of removing the tenants" from the interior to the coast.[306] Another said that the marquess "conceived a wonderful plan for the improvement – his word – of the Sutherland estates"[307] (this author was able to remember "his word", despite his grandson's confession that all his words had been forgotten). A third claimed "the duke . . . was the Great Improver".[308] A fourth criticized "such disciples of progress as the Duke of Sutherland".[309] A history professor said, "the intention of the Duke of Sutherland was to get the population on to the coasts for industry or fishing"[310] (to which one can only say: no intention, no duke). The name of the Marquess of Stafford was sometimes entered into the records of the Sutherland estate as being the tenant of some farms which the managers wished to retain for themselves; and one cannot be the owner and the tenant at the same time.[311]

It may be that these stern condemnations have a hidden purpose; since to blame "the duke" for the Sutherland clearances is to help in shifting the blame from the Highland chiefs, who were the main clearers, on to other shoulders. Eric Evans wrote (inaccurately): "many landowners most associated with wholesale clearances were either Lowland Scots or, like the Duke of Sutherland, English."[312] Sir Iain Moncreiffe asserted that the Sutherland clearances were ordained "by an English liberal 'planner', the Marquess of Stafford".[312] A. G. MacDonell said that the Countess of Sutherland "married a young Englishman, Leveson-Gower, the Marquess of Stafford, and it was he who hit upon the device of converting the greater part of Sutherlandshire into a sheep farm . . . he was an Englishman."[313] (As to which one can only say – yes, we get the point.) Concerning the rest of MacDonell's contribution, it should have been sheep farms, in the plural, of course; and this "device", which Leveson-Gower was said to have cleverly "hit upon", had been common in the Highlands for half a century or more.

In reality, of course, the sad fact is that despite these and many other attempts to incriminate outsiders, most clearers indisputably were Highlanders, or of Highland descent.

Contemporaries, or people who wrote within a decade or two of the upheavals, all named the countess as their author: for example, among those who defended the clearances, Alexander Sutherland, Robert Chambers, Beriah Botfield, Sheriff Gordon, Sir William Fraser, the *Scotsman* newspaper, and a *Quarterly Review* writer; and among those who attacked the clearances, Donald MacLeod, Thomas Bakewell, Hugh Miller, an *Edinburgh Star* letter-writer, the *Times* correspondent, Simone de Sismondi, and F. W. Newman. The more recent an author is, the more likely he is to say that the Duke of Sutherland was the clearer of Sutherland.

Does it matter? Surely it must. If one is writing history (or any other non-fiction), then every fact which is put into one's work should be as accurate as it is possible to make it.[314]

43. Common blood and speech

Other experts go near to ignoring the Highland clearances altogether. *Scotland, The Story of a Nation*, written by Magnus Magnusson, and published by HarperCollins in 2000, is not unusual in this respect. It has 734 pages, and it mentions the Highland clearances twice;[315] there are two references, in two separate sentences, admittedly on two different pages. One hesitates to criticize anyone for what he did not write – one can soon find oneself complaining that the author ought to have written a different book – but the title does imply that it deals with all of Scotland. (No one could have objected if the book had been called, for example, *Lowland Scotland, the Story of the Scots Lowlanders*.) The stretch of territory which is now called Scotland has contained for much of its history two separate peoples. The culture, the language, the way of life, the beliefs, the habits, the dress, the traditions, and even the very separate existence, of one of these two peoples, have all now been virtually ended. If from the eighteenth to the twentieth centuries the English language as spoken in the Lowlands had been in effect killed off, so that by this time only a few thousands in remote corners still spoke any English at all, if the Lowland way of life had been destroyed, and if most of the Lowlanders had been driven out of the Lowlands, many of them overseas, leaving vast areas of the Lowlands almost unpopulated, while the Gaelic language, along with the Highlanders' culture, dress and social system had been forcibly established in its place from Elgin to Edinburgh, and from Glasgow to Gretna, one wonders if the fate of the Lowlanders would have merited only two sentences in a history of Scotland.

The Highlanders have often been treated as non-existent – Scotland has frequently been regarded as consisting of the Lowlands. J. R. Green's classic work, *A Short History of the English People*, written in 1874, praised the 1707 Act of Union, which joined together England and Scotland, since it united "two peoples whom a common blood and common speech proclaimed to be one".[316] The Highlanders, who clearly had neither common blood nor common speech with the other inhabitants of Britain, and who occupied most of what is now called Scotland, were consigned to oblivion, in the same way that the clearances themselves have now been erased from the record by subservient commentators.

The whole historical existence of the Highlanders is currently under attack. We have already seen how some historians have insisted that the Highlanders were really just the same as the Lowlanders. And in a 320-page *Atlas of British and Irish History*, published in 2001 by Penguin, the editors did not feel it necessary to use even one of their 320 pages to put in one solitary map showing where the Gaelic clans used to live. There was one small part of a single map[317] illustrating the progress of the Jacobite rebellions, in which there were eleven clan names on the Highlands – at least two of them wrongly placed; but not a single map to show where lived the Highland clans who occupied most of Scotland for centuries. The Gaelic Highlanders have almost been wiped out of the present; historians may succeed in wiping them out of the past as well. Some writers act almost as if their task is to make the past conform to the present. It reminds one of Dorian Gray, who said: "If one doesn't talk about a thing, it has never happened. It is simply expression . . . that gives reality to things."[318] The Dorian Gray school of history is still alive and flourishing.

To adapt the language of George Orwell in *Animal Farm*, perhaps one should say that everything in history is historical; but, clearly, some things are more historical than others.[319]

44. Illuminating the present

It is strange, but true, that where a historian is complying with the received wisdom of his subject, what he says is not closely examined by other historians. Apparently commentators do not consider critically articles or books that come to the politically correct conclusions. The result is that numbers of writers have published work on Highland history that contains clear inaccuracies, but these are ignored by their colleagues and successors, even though they are obvious to anyone who makes any effort to employ the archive of the head. It may be that some writers can be understood more clearly if one thinks not only of the period to which their work apparently refers, but also of the period when it was written. Indeed, some ostensibly historical work tells one more about the historian than about the subject theoretically under discussion; it is more perceptive about the present than the past, and more revealing about the writer than the written.

Margaret Adam wrote a series of articles in a historical journal in 1919-22,[320] about what she alleged had happened in the Highlands during the later eighteenth century (these articles are dealt with in volume two); and one is puzzled about some of the plainly erroneous conclusions she claimed to have reached, and the even more astonishing fact that none of her fellow academic historians ever challenged her manifest mistakes (some of them, indeed, still go out of their way to recommend or endorse her work),[321] until one considers not what may or may not have happened a hundred years or two hundred years earlier, but what was undeniably happening in the Highlands at the time she was writing. (The background to Adam's articles, and doubtless what prompted them, was a swelling chorus of demands for the authorities to keep their promise, made during the first world war, to "return the Highlands to the Highlanders" – who had contributed, in proportion to their numbers, more men to the armed forces in 1914-18 than had the Lowlanders or the English: an agitation rounded off by an official report in 1919, which said, "in the cold light of history it is clear that the power of wholesale eviction by private persons was one which ought never to have been permitted").[322] Furthermore, the Napier Commission's findings in 1884 are often clearly very wide of the mark (as can easily be shown, and will be shown in volume five of this work), and again no historian so far as I know has ever pointed this out; but the commission's views on history become much more understandable when one remembers what was happening, not during the clearances which began many years before, but in the disturbances (known as the "Crofters' War") in the very decade during which the commission sat.

The same could be said about some present-day commentators. Michael Fry alleges that "there is a contemporary resentment against people who own land, and the idea terrible things happened to force people to leave fits in with the socialist agenda in Scotland":[323] an assertion which is on the face of it more concerned with current controversies than with historical accuracy. Presumably, if one doesn't want to be accused of taking a particular position in present-day politics, one has to adjust one's beliefs about the past. No doubt Mr Fry's views of history are not coloured at all by his fortunate freedom from what he calls the "contemporary resentment against people who own land".

When one reads Mr Fry's repeated assertions that there were hardly any clearances, the theory seems to depend on a very narrow interpretation of the word "clearances". If people were deprived of the hunting and the herding which gave them their food, and were evicted from their long-standing fertile joint farms, which formed their third (historically much less important) food-source, but at the same time were (some of them) allowed an acre of two of barren soil to try to make productive, as happened in the Sutherland clearances, it seems that the evictions cannot be ranked as "clearances". " 'When *I* use a word', Humpty-Dumpty said in rather a scornful tone, 'it means just what I choose it to mean – neither more nor less.' 'The question is', said Alice, 'whether you can make words mean so many different things.' 'The question is', said Humpty Dumpty, 'which is to be Master – that's all.' " On that basis, Mr Fry has certainly shown himself to be "Master".[324] Indeed, Mr Fry's strident insistence that he is unaware of any clearances of any importance must rank as the most surprising declaration of oblivion since Trabb's boy, in Dickens' *Great Expectations*, severely mortified the newly enriched Pip by cheekily mimicking his garb and gait while drawling "Don't know yah, don't know yah, 'pon my soul don't know yah!" This is exactly Mr Fry's reaction when faced with the unfortunately quite conclusive evidence of the clearances: " 'Pon my soul don't know yah!"[325]

45. Out of all proportion

Mr Fry has in doctrinaire fashion re-written history entirely: "I believe that the Clearances did not happen, except very occasionally on a small and local scale . . . I think the Clearances are one with the poems of Sorley MacLean in being great works of the imagination."[326] Joseph Stalin himself, who was a pastmaster at historical revision, would have been astounded by such bombast.[327] While a foolhardy pretence like this may merely cause merriment – as if a misguided individual had somehow persuaded all his journalist friends to give free publicity to his dramatic claims that the sun rises in the west, or that grass is really coloured pink – he is only (so far) the foremost in a field of many runners. I have collected a number of interesting statements on the question of the reality of the clearances. All the following quotations are taken either from published work, which is therefore addressed to "the public", that is to everyone; or from unpublished material addressed to me personally (by people who knew I was writing a book on the clearances, and who were in touch with me for that very reason), being written either by various landlords – or by people very close to them, almost always in their families, or their employees, speaking for them. The words cited between each pair of quotation marks are from one writer; subsequent pairs of quotation marks enclose observations from different commentators. If more than one brief quotation, or one limited set of quotations, from each individual observer had been given, this section would have been too long. The evidence unhappily refutes not only Mr Fry's astonishing claims, but also all of the assurances appended below, as these volumes will demonstrate.

Dr Gordon Donaldson, the Sir William Fraser Professor of Scottish History and Palaeography in the University of Edinburgh, and Historiographer Royal of Scotland from 1979 to 1993 (that is to say, the leading member of the Scottish historiographical profession), said in 1981: "I am 68 now and until recently I had hardly heard of the Highland Clearances. The thing has been blown up out of all proportion."[328] Magnus Linklater, former editor of *The Scotsman* and former chairman of the Scottish Arts Council (which by its ability to give or to withhold grants to publishers was able to exercise a strong influence over what was or was not printed, and therefore what was or was not generally disseminated, about Scottish history – the present work, one need hardly say, was refused a grant by the council) – Magnus Linklater referred in his column in *The Times* newspaper to the "so-called . . . nineteenth century 'Highland Clearances', when crofters were allegedly driven off their land by rapacious landowners, in order to turn it over to more profitable sheep", and then briskly demolished the distasteful rumour: "this is largely myth".[329] Two years later he repeated his startling assertion, though perhaps not wishing to be accused of being paid a second time for the same material, he put in an intrusive indefinite article and said it was "largely a myth".[330] Linklater's second column gave valuable free limelight to Michael Fry, to Fry's clearance-denial theories, and to Fry's vigorous assertion that writers who dared to mention the clearances were merely peddling "lazy and emotional versions of Scottish history". Such a public boost as Linklater gave Fry would be very expensive if an advertisement had to be paid for: fortunate are those who are given gratuitous publicity by their journalist friends, who luckily have the same politically correct opinions. Another commentator derided "the Highland Clearance Myth Preservation society".[331] Some observers, though not so rash as to repudiate completely such a large part of recent Highland history, still maintained

THE CLEARANCES IN HISTORY

that at least some regions of the Highlands could be absolved from these unhappy slanders. A Highland proprietor claimed that "only a small part" of the Highlands "was involved" in the clearances.[332] Evander MacIver, a Sutherland factor, maintained there were in the Highlands "districts from which no removals were made".[333] Professor Richards wrote repeatedly of the "uncleared parts of the Highlands . . . [of the] uncleared areas within the Highlands . . . [and of the] uncleared zones within the Highlands",[334] and demanded emotionally: can the landlords be "condemned both when they cleared their lands, and when they did not clear?"[335] (Thus clearly reiterating that there were estates where there were no clearances.) Others have written about "the Highland regions in which no clearances ever took place",[336] the Highland "areas where clearances did not take place",[337] and the "estates that never cleared[338] . . . [and] the numerous Highland estates where no clearances took place[339] . . . [owned by the] many reactionary chiefs and chieftains [who] were horrified altogether by the Clearances[340] . . . [and by] the relentless clearances that shocked reactionary old-fashioned chiefs".[341] These generalized assurances, both as to estates and chieftains, were unfortunately given without adequate details, so they cannot immediately be rebutted, except in equally general terms.

46. Areas exonerated

Other writers, however, were prepared to come closer to a definition of these favoured districts. "The eastern side of the Highlands . . . did not see many landlords involved in clearing people", said one commentator,[342] while another declared, "it should be said here that the Central Highlands suffered much less [from clearances] than the west and north".[343] As far as the north was concerned, it would be difficult for a commentator to shrug off the Countess of Sutherland's operations, but Adam Collier spoke up for Caithness, where, he believed, there had been only slight incidence of clearance;[344] and as for the west, others have made it their business to acquit the landlords there, e.g. in the western islands. In the Hebrides, said Professor Smout (as we have already seen), "there is little hint (except on Rum and Jura in 1826 and on Arran in 1828) of men at this date [the fifteen years after Waterloo] being turned out to make room for sheep".[345] Another author concurred, citing "the Hebrides, where ['in the last years of the eighteenth century and the first years of the nineteenth'] tenants were hardly ever turned out for the sake of sheep (except in a limited way on Rum and Arran in the 1820s)".[346] Even this reluctant partial admission as to Rum was too much for Professor Henry Hamilton, who denied that Rum was cleared for sheep: "large numbers emigrated from parts of the Highlands which were practically unaffected by sheep farming. For example, in 1826, 400 left Rum . . ."[347] (In fact, of course,

Rum was cleared by its landlord of virtually the whole population in order to turn the entire island into a ranch for a sheep farmer, who came in with his flock as the Rum people were being deported.) A fourth author thought "the Hebrides had escaped very lightly during the peak clearance years",[348] a fifth brooded over "the uncleared parts of the Outer Hebrides",[349] and a sixth asserted that in the early nineteenth century "the Isles were still in the hands of the chiefs' families, who were revolted at the very notion of such methods" as the clearances.[350] Another writer (though having to admit that when sheep farming came, it produced "a large rent to the owners", the result being that clearances "on a large scale were resorted to; whole glens were depopulated") still did his best to exempt "Skye, where it is doubtful how far clearances were resorted to".[351] John Prebble, who wrote a whole book deploring the clearances, included a map (said to be of "the Highlands") to illustrate the areas affected: on that map the districts below the Great Glen were left almost entirely blank,[352] thus seemingly intimating that there were no clearances in the south, the south-west, and the south-east of the Highlands – which together amount to at least a third of the whole Gaelic area. Another author spoke up for at last one south-western county, Argyllshire, "where there were in the period before 1830 few large clearances".[353] Yet another historian, though saying quite correctly that there had been "major removals" in many Argyllshire parishes, nevertheless was able to exonerate the landlords of six Argyllshire parishes, at least so far as the New Statistical Account was concerned. "In six parishes, Kilbrandon, Tiree and Coll, Kilchoman, Kildalton, Kilarrow, Kilmodan (the latter four in Islay [though Kilmodan is really in Cowal]) there was clear evidence [in the N.S.A.] that few removals had occurred"; and he hinted that the same might be true of a number of other Argyll parishes, since in "Craignish, Kilninver, South Knapdale, Torosay, Kilninian, Kilfinan, Kilchrenan, Kilcalmonell, Campbeltown, Muckairn, Kilmore, Dunoon, North Knapdale, Glassary, [and] Lochgoilhead, information is too sparse to permit generalization." In fact, as these pages will show, the evidence (whether in the N.S.A. or elsewhere) demonstrates that the clearances in Argyllshire were early and ubiquitous.[354] The information about the clearances is the opposite of sparse.

The Romans said, "Everything unknown is taken to be on a great scale"; the moderns seem to say, "Everything unknown (to me) didn't happen."[355]

47. No evictions on this estate

Other commentators were brave enough to eschew generalities, and the exoneration of unspecific areas: and they named names. Particular estates and particular landowners all had (and have) their champions. The Duke of Argyll's property? "There were *no* evictions on this estate" (original emphasis).[356] And again, "Argyll, for example, bringing in sheep in abundance, performed no clearances".[357] Furthermore, "not all landowners . . .submitted immediately to the temptation. The Duke of Argyll . . . was no friend to the wealthy Lowland farmers . . . but with his wealth he could afford to stand aloof."[358]

Fraser of Lovat? Even more testimonials. "The Frasers have a good record in the clearances which has kept the clan united."[359] Lovat "disapproved of the clearances";[360] Lovat "not only did not clear, but sheltered many refugees who had been evicted elsewhere".[361] Lovat "not only refused to clear but gave shelter to the victims of neighbouring clearances".[362] The Lovats "were more humane for much of the clearance period".[363] "I don't know [about any Lovat evictions]. I never heard of them[364] . . . There never were any crofters [small tenants] in Strath Farrar"[365] – on the Lovat estate, so they could never have been cleared from it.

Grant of Grant? "There were no infamous 'clearances' on the Grant estates."[366] "Neither in his time [the time of Sir James Grant, 1738-1811] nor in those of his successors was there any 'clearing' of the tenantry on the Grant estates."[367] "I have never heard that . . . the Grants were major offenders . . . [though] it seemed to have been a general landowners' practice at one time."[368] "Grant lairds largely avoided the cruelty of clearances so widely practised elsewhere."[369] And like the Lovats, "the Seafields [as the Grant chiefs became] were more humane for much of the [clearance] period . . . [the area benefited from] the policy of the Seafield estate not to clear their small tenantry[370] . . . [the Seafields decided] not to clear their small tenantry".[371] A radio talk alleged that "no family of chiefs who kept their lands in 1746 or had them restored in 1782 were innocent of clearances except the Grants of Glen Urquhart [i.e. the family of Grant of Grant] and Glen Moriston".[372] So not only Grant of Grant, but also Grant of Glenmoriston, were "innocent of clearances". Grant of Rothiemurchus? "So far as I am aware, there were no clearances of crofters from this estate"; the landlord family "did not go in for sheep farming, which was the usual reason given for the clearances".[373]

48. Choosing poverty

MacKay, Lord Reay? "Other chiefs having resisted the urge to put their lands to the most profitable uses were [wrote Professor Smout] compelled by the remorseless logic of debt or bankruptcy to sell out to others with less fine feelings, as Lord Reay was forced to sell to the Duke of Sutherland in 1829."[374] "In many cases a laird might resist that process [of clearance] as long as possible, choosing poverty in preference to evictions", echoed Douglas Hill; "but then his heir . . . might be forced by debts and the threat of legal action to sell lands to other lairds with fewer scruples, as Lord Reay sold his estates to the Duke of Sutherland in 1829."[375] (Despite the assertions of these two writers it was the Marquess of

Stafford who bought the Reay estates in 1829; by which time Lord Reay – such is the stubborn reality, rejected by many commentators – had cleared them in order to make ten large and highly-rented sheep-farms. There were few scruples, and fewer urges resisted, on either side of the Reay-Stafford bargain.)

In fact a number of historians have assured us that Lord Reay never evicted anyone, and that the Reay country was only cleared after Lord Reay sold it. Seton Gordon claimed that it was "fortunate for the name and honour of MacKay" that Lord Reay sold his estate to "the Earl of Sutherland" (in fact to the Marquess of Stafford) – and it was this (otherwise unknown) "Earl of Sutherland" who "ordered the great Sutherland Clearance": so Lord Reay had nothing to do with it.[376] Professor Richards appears to sit on the fence. In one book he agreed that the Reay estate was cleared (in "1810 to 1815";)[377] but in another he wrote that "the Lords Reay in Sutherland – were incapable of . . . improving their estates, or supporting their people";[378] though in fact Eric Lord Reay (in order of course to force "his people" to support him) had improved his clansfolk out of their good farms on to barren crofts, in order vastly to improve his own income with the sheep-farm rents. Michael Fry was under the impression that "the Reays had long forsaken their precipices for the Netherlands" (a mistaken idea: it was a junior branch of the family who went to Holland)[379] and that therefore, it seems, they had nothing do with any clearances. (Though since Fry denounces any suspicion that *any* landlord ever cleared his estate, it may seem futile to mention this misapprehension. Other historians have their favourite Highland landlord family or families, whose good names they are zealous to protect: Fry fondly cherishes them all, without exception, so, naturally, none of them ever cleared.) John Prebble, too, thought Lord Reay was innocent of clearances; when the Staffords bought the Reay estate in 1830, he wrote, their manager "was busy with plans for . . . its transformation into sheep-walks" – but it was already in sheep-walks.[380] Ian Grimble said the MacKay chief sold "the clan lands to one who would evict them from their homes"; there had to be "a change of ownership" before sheep could come to the Reay country. But of course sheep had already come to the Reay country under the existing ownership, and the Reay clan lands had been cleared before the Staffords bought them.[381] (Neither Prebble nor Grimble could be accused of being unduly favourable to landlords, since both of them were notable for having written books attacking the clearances: yet both of them were taken in by the customary deferential stories in the case of Lord Reay, and therefore held him blameless. And if two strongly anti-clearance writers were deceived by the orthodox propaganda which has obsequiously defended Lord Reay down the years, it is the less surprising to see how many other people have been similarly fooled.)

Sometimes the very earth underfoot provided a clue to the benevolence of the local landlord, as when Tom Atkinson talked of "the great outcrop of Durness limestone, which provides a much kindlier soil . . . there were no clearances here"[382] – "here" was Durness, Eddrachillis, and Tongue, which composed the Reay country, owned by Lord Reay, who (in obdurate truth) cleared it.

49. Never heard of them

Munro of Poyntzfield, at Gruids in the south of Sutherland? When the Napier commissioners of 1883 enquired about the notorious Gruids clearances (three successive mass evictions in 1808, 1820, and 1821, had led to riots reported in the newspapers, the calling in of troops, and prison sentences imposed on the Highlanders who resisted), the Gruids factor (whose father had actually held a sheep farm on the Gruids estate) had the audacity to say solemnly to the Napier commissioners, when asked about the Gruids clearances, "I never heard of them".[383] Innes Munro of Poyntzfield, the landlord who carried out all these evictions, was celebrated enough to get a 200-word entry in the *Oxford Dictionary of National Biography*, but the author of the biographical tribute was too polite to allude to the sensational events at Gruids. Perhaps in respectable circles it is considered rude to mention such occurrences.

MacKenzie, Earl of Cromartie? "MacKenzie of Cromartie . . . refused to evict anyone."[384] "So far as the Cromartie estates were concerned I am as certain, as it is possible to be in these matters, that there were no evictions."[385] Like Lovat, "MacKenzie of Cromartie not only refused to clear but gave shelter to the victims of neighbouring clearances".[386] There was no "record of clearances on the Cromartie estates before [the middle of the nineteenth century] – far from" it.[387]

MacKenzie of Gairloch? "There were no clearances in Gairloch in the 19th century."[388] "There have never been clearances on the lands owned by the MacKenzies of Gairloch."[389] "The MacKenzies fought to keep clearances off their land . . . There were no clearances in Gairloch."[390] "This part [Wester Ross, around Gairloch] suffered little during the clearances of the nineteenth century."[391] "This extensive parish [Gairloch] escaped the worst clearances . . . The MacKenzie lairds prided themselves on their fair treatment of the tenantry . . ."[392]

50. No tenants removed

The Isle of Lewis, owned first by the Seaforth family, and then by Sir James Matheson? "The clearances" fortunately did not extend "to Lewis where the Seaforth family, impoverished though it was, refused to evict".[393] "Some [Highland] districts, for example Lewis under the Seaforths, which were not cleared . . ."[394] "There had been practically no evictions in Lewis."[395] "No one was evicted from the Isle of Lews, in the strict sense of the term . . ."[396] "There had been no earlier clearances like those of Uist and Barra – Lewis was fortunate in its owners."[397] Lewis was bought by Sir James Matheson, but still "there were no evictions".[398] During the Matheson regime in Lewis, "there were no removals", and there was "no pressure on them [the Lewis people] to leave".[399] If all Highland landlords had "behaved so humanely to their tenants" as Sir James, all would have been well.[400] "There were no tenants removed from any place [in Lewis] in Sir James Matheson's day, or for many a year before then."[401]

This last avowal was made by William MacKay, Sir James Matheson's factor, when he gave evidence soon after the Napier Commission had begun its first hearing in Lewis, early in June 1883. MacKay was the fourth witness to appear on the stand, and presumably felt at that early date that loyalty to his employers demanded his solemn testimony that no clearances had ever occurred. But as a procession of witnesses, one after another during the four successive hearings in Lewis, described the Lewis clearances, MacKay must gloomily have seen he would not be able to get away with this whitewash. Accordingly he changed his tune, and when he sent in a written submission only three months later, he said: "with regard to the clearances that took place since Sir James Matheson purchased the island, I may mention it was not for the sake of profit that any one township was cleared" – the real reason (he asserted firmly) was that, "in consequence of the potato failure and other causes",[402] the crofters could no longer make a living there. So the clearances were carried out to benefit the crofters. This was a complete somersault since he told the commission "there were no tenants removed" in Lewis. In June he affirmed that no tenants had been removed; in September he shamelessly came up with excuses why the tenants had been removed. MacKay made no apology for having told the commissioners that "there were no tenants removed from any place in Sir James Matheson's day, or for many a year before then", but since he was supporting the landlords, he could be confident that no one, certainly no orthodox historian, was going to reproach him either then or later for so obviously telling lies.

The MacKenzies of Seaforth, owners of Lewis until 1844, also owned Kintail and other land on the mainland, but their record there, we are assured, was equally spotless. John Knox, who toured the Highlands in 1786, said that "south country sheep farmers" had offered Seaforth "double the present rent" for some land in Wester Ross; but he replied "he would neither let his lands for sheep pasture, nor turn out his people, upon any consideration, or for any rent that could be offered".[403] A twentieth-century author agreed. "All of this land [around Loch Duich] was once owned by the MacKenzies of Seaforth, and to give them their due, they stoutly resisted all temptations to clear the people off their lands, in spite of the high rents offered for sheep farms."[404] One author was able to write a 9,000-word account of "The Clan MacKenzie" without mentioning a single eviction, although apparently "many MacKenzies [for some extraordinary unexplained reason] found their way overseas at this time".[405] Another writer discovered that "a few Highland landowners", of whom Seaforth was "a prime example", made "a genuine attempt to help their people, sometimes at the cost of their personal fortunes . . . MacKenzie of Seaforth, who resisted the new economics of estate management [i.e. the clearances] . . . not surprisingly"[406] went bankrupt as a result. This heart-rending tale of self-sacrifice leading to disaster is, in sober truth, simply false. The record is clear: the then MacKenzie of Seaforth, Francis Humberstone MacKenzie, who held the estate from 1783 to 1815, in fact enthusiastically embraced "the new economics of estate management", and avidly accepted "the high rents offered for sheep farms" (whatever he was supposed to have alleged at the time Knox in his 1786 book quoted him – or perhaps a predecessor). He drove off the MacRaes and MacLennans of Kintail in the first half-dozen years of the nineteenth century (as well as clearing many MacLeods and MacKenzies from their Lewis townships). The Seaforths could not have "gone bankrupt" as a result of holding aloof from clearances, because they did not "hold aloof" – they did clear. Like a number of other proprietors, they went bankrupt simply by squandering a greatly increased income (Seaforth was in the Prince Regent's circle of high-spending and gambling friends), which they had obtained by means of clearances on their estates: a boring and typical fact with no appeal to the emotional historians who like a romantic story.

This is one of those occasions where ipse dixit history comes in so useful; if a landlord said he was not guilty of clearances, then he was not guilty, whatever the humdrum historical record says.

51. Never sullied

MacLeod of MacLeod? "The MacLeod estates were never sullied by the blot of 'clearing' the people from their holdings."[407] "There were no clearances on the MacLeod estate."[408] MacLeod of MacLeod "resisted the idea of clearances".[409] "The family name was never sullied by the clearances."[410] Numerous commentators declared that so far from evicting anyone, the MacLeod chief at the time of the 1846 famine pauperized himself by his quixotic generosity.[411] One author claimed, "Duirinish did not experience the Clearances to which other parts of Skye were subjected, largely because it was MacLeod-controlled rather than part of Lord Macdonald's land".[412] Those who denied there were any clearances on the MacLeod estate were following the lead of John MacKenzie, the factor of Norman MacLeod, 25th of MacLeod, who assured the Brand Commission in the 1890s that the MacLeod land had always been organized in large individually-tenanted farms: the only people in the MacLeod country besides the large farmers had always been simply small colonies of "squatters or cotters", who were there merely to do wage-work on the large farms. MacLeod himself gave similar evidence: he rebuked a member of the commission who talked of "re-settling" the people on the land, because, MacLeod brazenly said, they had never been settled on the land at all. So easy is it for important people to sweep away any history they are unhappy with.[413]

While one observer defended MacLeod by attacking Lord Macdonald, the latter also has his supporters. One writer meditated on "the parish of Kilmuir in the north-west [of Skye, owned by MacDonald], which largely escaped the clearances".[414] In reality Lord Macdonald (among a large number of other improvements) evicted many of his small tenants in Skye in – for example – 1801-3, offering them instead only small crofts of poor coastal land, with the result that several hundreds of them emigrated: but one historian surprisingly felt able to assure his readers that these emigrants "were in no sense victims of clearance".[415] Another commentator assured us that "Lord Macdonald . . . literally ruined" himself helping his tenants[416] – an assertion echoed by a number of other respectful writers.

The Greshornish and Skeabost estates of northern central Skye, owned after the mid-nineteenth-century by an inter-related family of MacLeods and MacDonalds? The landlords there were so far from evicting anyone that they apparently basked in the admiration of their tenants, "at a time when Clearances were going on elsewhere".[417] The 1852 clearance of the native MacKinnons in Strathaird by MacAlister of Torrisdale? (After the clearance, of Strathaird's twenty-eight square miles, two Lowland farmers had twenty-seven square miles, and the remaining 400 Highlanders had one square mile, which meant they were congested "as a result of over-population" and ought to emigrate, according to proprietorial thinking.)[418] Any account of this clearance "may be . . . inaccurate", according to a letter to the author from a member of Torrisdale's family.[419] The minister of the parish, Rev. Donald MacKinnon, was more positive (that is to say, he was brave enough to be more positive when he could no longer be contradicted). After he listened in silence to the account of the clearance given by a crofter witness to the Napier Commission in 1883 during the local hearing, in the presence of the Skye people who would all know about the clearance – and he could have spoken up: he intervened and gave evidence himself about a minor point of the crofter's testimony – he later wrote to the commissioners (when it was too late for the people to protest, since the public hearings, and the public testimonies, were finished) to say that it had never happened; the account of the clearance, he boldly asserted, was owing to the "fertile imagination" of the crofter witness. (The minister's views may have been coloured by the fact that he also had a large sheep farm, on land which had, naturally, been cleared of its small-tenant townships a few years before.) In fact the crofter witness – despite the minister's slanderous attack – was merely stating the facts of the matter, as much contemporary evidence (for and against the clearance) shows.[420]

52. Firmly opposed

Robertson of Struan? The clearances in Sutherland had "shocked reactionary old-fashioned chiefs like Robertson of Struan[421] . . . The Robertson chiefs evicted no one, and in 1854 the 18th Chief had to sell Struan in his efforts to look after his Rannoch folk[422] . . . Struan Robertson refused to clear: now his heir has no land in Scotland and has to live in Jamaica."[423] (I know of a large number of Scotsmen who own "no land in Scotland"; at the moment none of them has decided that this means he "has to live in Jamaica". On the other hand some Jamaicans, who own no land in Jamaica, have gone to live in Scotland, because more jobs were available there: perhaps they passed the Robertson chief on the way.)

MacNeill of Barra? The MacNeill chiefs were "in the unique position of being firmly opposed to 'the clearances' and emigration of all kinds . . . *all emigration* of Barra folk has been wholly voluntary" (original emphasis);[424] "MacNeill of Barra was said to have pleaded with his tenants, whose emigration was voluntary, to stay."[425] The Earl of Moray? The nearest the family got to any evictions were some instances "where a few were moved from very poor land which was more suitable for tree growing than farming, but in each case were given alternative land far more suited for agriculture or stock raising".[426]

The Duke of Gordon? There appear to be "no records of any part having been played by" the dukes "in the Scottish Highland Clearances".[427] In fact "the Gordons suffered from no wholesale evictions and clearances such as were only too common elsewhere, and there was little voluntary emigration among the clansmen".[428] The author of this tribute to the absence of clearances among the Gordons, despite referring to the "too common" clearances "elsewhere", was also able to absolve the MacIntosh chiefs from any such calumny. Indeed three authorities praised the record of the chiefs of Clan Chattan. "There is no tradition in the Inverness area of any discreditable 'clearances' by" the MacIntosh chiefs[429] (or perhaps it would be truer to say that, understandably, no such tradition was preserved in the chief's family). "There were no evictions from the MacIntosh estates."[430] The Strath Nairn lands of the MacIntoshes? "No clearances took place there."[431]

53. Certainly no clearances

So the praises proliferate. Colquhoun of Luss? "There were certainly no clearances here."[432] The Duke of Montrose? "The Montroses had a clean bill of health on this score."[433] Farquharson of Invercauld? "There is nowhere any hint of any 'eviction' " on the Invercauld estate – "quite the reverse".[434] Malcolm of Poltalloch? The family "never had anything to do with the clearances in this part of Argyll".[435] MacLean of Ardgour? "There were no very drastic clearances at Ardgour";[436] in fact "there were no evictions"[437] on the Ardgour estate. MacLean of Coll? "He [Hugh MacLean] was one of the landowners who refused to evict his crofters",[438] while, as we saw earlier (and there will be more details in volume four) MacLean's expulsion in 1826 of the entire population of Rum, to turn the island into a sheep farm, clearly showed (in the opinion of one sagacious history professor) that some people emigrated though they were "practically unaffected by sheep farming".[439] Campbell of Glendaruel? The "estate papers of the period contain no entries bearing on this matter" (perhaps not surprisingly).[440] Campbell of Strachur? The 700-year family history contains "no mention of the 'clearances' " (an omission equally unsurprising).[441] MacLeod of Raasay? The Raasay chiefs were "one of the very few old Highland aristocratic families unstained by clearances";[442] indeed MacLeod of Raasay "ruined himself through an attempt to save his people".[443] (MacLeod in reality began the clearance of Raasay.) And George Rainy, who bought Raasay from the MacLeod chieftains? We are authoritatively told that Rainy "personally resisted all factorial advice to remove the people despite the financial sacrifice such an attitude required".[444] (Rainy was in fact the main clearer of Raasay, as may be seen in volume five of this series.)

MacNeil of Colonsay? Colonsay "was one of the few Hebridean islands which was fortunate enough to escape the nineteenth-century clearances as the laird at the time, John MacNeil, had a liberal approach".[445] Moray of Abercairney? "There were no forcible evictions"[446] on this estate. Munro of Foulis? "No Munro of Foulis thrust emigration upon a reluctant tenantry."[447] Sinclair of Ulbster? The Sinclair family "were opposed to the method of the clearances";[448] in fact Sir John Sinclair was an "honourable exception" to the "native landlord policy" of clearance.[449] Stewart of Appin? "There do not seem to have been any clearances in Appin for sheep."[450]

Cameron of Lochiel? One writer,[451] backed up by another,[452] said that what some deluded people had alleged were Lochiel's main clearances, in 1801 and 1802, were really paternalistic "removals", carried out in order "to enable the people to obtain constant employment" building the Caledonian Canal (the construction of which only began in 1803, a year after the second clearance was completed, apart from the fact that the work of digging a canal can scarcely be "constant", since it can only last until the canal is dug, not to mention the obvious point that if people were better off digging the canal they would have gone to do it without a clearance; but writers in the great mainstream of history, defending the clearances, have never had to be logical or rational, since they know the pliant history schools are never going to question the orthodox narrative). The Duke of Atholl? "Blair Atholl" was "well away from where the Highland Clearances took place."[453] The Perthshire Highlands generally? "I do not think that any one was forcibly turned out in this part of the world."[454] (This would exonerate several landlords who owned land in the Perthshire Highlands.) The Drummonds of Perth? According to one authority the Perth family were not concerned, because "the Lord Perths of the nineteenth century owned no property in the Highlands".[455] (In fact the two statistical accounts of Scotland show that the Perth family owned property in six Highland parishes – Balquidder, Killin, Comrie, Callander, Muthill, and Monzievaird.) Sir Alexander Matheson, in Lochalsh? The clearances had come to Lochalsh "to no extent at all. [Any talk of clearances] certainly does not apply to this estate", said Matheson's factor.[456] There had been "not one . . . case of eviction on this property since Sir Alexander acquired it"; even when the rent is not paid, Sir Alexander "writes off the arrears".[457]

MacDonald of Clanranald? He "has rather unfairly been accused of 'clearing' when in fact" he was only "landscape gardening".[458]

One cannot help the feeling that the behaviour of so many academic historians in accepting these exculpations, and producing accounts of what happened in the Highlands in conformity with the landlords' excuses, must constitute a modern "trahison des clercs".

It is interesting that several of those, particularly in the southern Highlands, who were exonerating particular landlords from any blame for the clearances, said that they believed such events had occurred only, or principally, in Sutherland, or in "the north". One said that the clearances he "always understood took place in Sutherland"; another, that "the main culprit was the Duke of Sutherland"; a third, that the clearances occurred "in Inverness-shire and Sutherland"; a fourth, that the term clearances "applied to the north"; a fifth, that the clearances "were mostly further north".[459] The Sutherland clearances had become so notorious that the events there became useful to divert attention from evictions in other parts of the Highlands. The ducal family of Sutherland, however, one professor tells us, "abhorred the many examples of wholesale eviction in the Highlands" – where the ejected Highlanders were not even offered crofts of poor land to retreat to.[460] Joseph Mitchell, too, said that William Young, who as the proprietor's agent carried through many of the Sutherland clearances, insisted that the Sutherland managers had done their best to provide for those evicted, instead of just "ruthlessly clearing the people off their lands, as had been done in the southern Highlands".[461] While some southern landlords were pointing accusing fingers northwards, the Sutherland grandees were pointing accusing fingers southwards. To accuse someone else, of course, is always serviceable as a defence.

54. Facts are facts

There are listed here comments which exonerate from any blame in the clearances perhaps forty chiefly families – apart from the more generalized assertions about the rarity of clearances in the Hebrides, or Skye, or the central Highlands, or the eastern Highlands, or the southern Highlands, or observations about the "numerous Highland estates" which never saw any clearances, and so on. The lands owned by these individually exculpated families must amount to much more than half of the Highlands. I have been researching the history of the Highlands for only sixty years or so, so I cannot claim to have read everything which has been written on the subject; it is likely that other chiefly families have also been absolved by friendly authors (or by themselves, or by their employees). And yet not a single one of these vindications I have recounted appears to be justified by the unforgiving facts of history.

It is slightly awkward (from the point of view of those who seek to play down the clearances) that so many writers, while rushing to protect the particular proprietorial family they are putting on a pedestal, then proceed to highlight their plea by admitting or even emphasizing that many other clearances did take place contemporaneously: as we saw, the Sutherland factor (and the Sutherland family) deplored the "ruthless" evictions in the south Highlands, while southern landlords condemned the clearances in the north. One Highland landlord, though of the opinion that there were no local clearances, nevertheless was sure the clearances were of enormous significance; he said, "the clearances have left their mark on Scottish history, the effects in one way or another lasting to the present day".[462] The champion who vindicated the Gordons did so by contrasting their record with that of many other proprietors, talking of "clearances such as were only too common *elsewhere*" [my emphasis]. The commentator who exonerated one Skye landlord family from clearances said it was "at a time when clearances were going on *elsewhere*". The Lovat apologist talked of "refugees who had been evicted *elsewhere*". One observer speaking up for the Grant family said "it seemed to have been a general landowners' practice at one time", while another said the Grant chiefs "largely avoided the cruelty of clearances so widely practised *elsewhere*". (One begins to wonder whether the only place that actually did have clearances was "elsewhere".)[463] One correspondent referred to "sheep farming, which was the usual reason given for the clearances", which made it sound as if clearances were not exceptional occurrences. Lewis – in one view – had no clearances "like those of Uist and Barra"; while the Barra owners – said another writer – were "in the *unique* position of being firmly opposed to 'the clearances' " (if the Barra landlords were really "unique" in their opposition, then all the other Highland landlords, including those in Lewis, must have been in favour of clearances), and the owner of South Uist was really only landscape gardening. Again, the owner of Duirinish was declared faultless, but only in contrast to "the clearances to which other parts of Skye were subjected". Another writer, absolving the Gairloch family, could not avoid referring to "the clearances of the nineteenth century". Malcolm of Poltalloch referred explicitly to "the clearances in this part of Argyll", though denying that his family had anything to do with them.

At least two landlords (Cromartie and Lovat) are credited with giving "shelter" to the victims of, or refugees from, "neighbouring clearances" – so some clearances must have occurred, to produce these victims. (In fact, of course, they were profiting by these neighbouring clearances, since the refugees from the evictions jumped at the chance of staying in their beloved Highlands by taking on an acre or two of barren ground – on the Cromartie or the Lovat estates – to make it by laborious toil into valuable agricultural land, for the benefit of the landowner.) Again, MacLean of Coll was said to be "one of the landowners who refused to evict his crofters" (so others did "evict their crofters"), while the MacLeods of Raasay were "one of very few old Highland aristocratic families unstained by clearances" (so most other families were "stained"), and Colonsay was "one of the few Hebridean islands which was fortunate enough to escape the nineteenth-century clearances" (meaning that most Hebridean islands did not escape). MacKenzie of Seaforth (we are told) refused to accept "the new economics of estate management", which indicates clearly that others had accepted "the new economics", i.e. the clearances. Sir John Sinclair was an "honourable exception" to the "native landlord policy" of clearance. (If it was the "native landlord policy", then most landlords must have been involved: if there is no general rule, there can hardly be an "exception" to it, honourable or otherwise.) In the same way, if some landlords "were horrified altogether by the clearances", or "were revolted at the very notion" of evictions, or were "shocked" by the "relentless clearances", or "abhorred . . . the wholesale evictions", then obviously clearances and evictions existed: otherwise, what was making these landlords "horrified", or "revolted", or "shocked"? What were they "abhorring"? Yet the sum total of what many of these writers say – sometimes implicitly, sometimes explicitly – is that across the Highlands there were hardly any clearances.

There was certainly no collusion among those who defended the landlords. Sir Iain Moncreiffe maintained that there were "many reactionary chiefs" who were "horrified" and "shocked" by the "relentless clearances", only to have Michael Fry arrive on the scene with his assurances that since the clearances virtually never happened, the chiefs were being horrified and shocked about nothing.

55. Why the denials?

Assuming that all these partial or wholesale denials of clearances were not in accordance with the facts – and a brief scan through the rest of these volumes would soon decide the matter – how could this have occurred? How could so many people whose job it is to tell us what happened in the Highlands during the last three hundred years have been betrayed into inaccuracy? It may be that part of the answer lies in the structure of academic life.

What I say now is based upon my study of Highland history, and Highland historians. (My knowledge of history which deals with other times and places, such as it is, is merely what anyone may discover from the standard textbooks.) So far as orthodox Highland history is concerned, it does appear to an outsider like myself that academic advancement depends very much on conformity.[464] When the eager young research fellow has an interview for a better job, or even for the prolongation of his present one, and he has to face a particular professor on the appointments panel, or friends of that professor, he would be very brave, and no doubt many would think he would also be very unwise, to announce that the professor has got his facts wrong: in the real world the way to keep friendly with your superior, and to make sure he helps to forward your career, is to be careful that your opinions are the same as his. The same applies to the regular tests which academics apparently now face – the "quality assurance audits", the "research assessment exercises", the "research excellence framework": an aspiring historian would be asking for trouble if he allowed it to be understood that he considered the work of his seniors (who are going to judge him) to be faulty. There are similar pressures when the young academic produces scholarly papers or books. Is his paper going to denounce the work of the editor of the academic journal, who can accept or reject his article? Is his book going to call into question the accuracy, or even the research skills, of those leaders of the profession who can help on his career, or (on the contrary) impede his progress? When he sends his manuscript to a publisher (and publication is increasingly a sine qua non for academics who wish to prosper), he knows that the publisher will almost certainly (to help him decide on acceptance or rejection) send his effort to an older, established historian – who is not going to recommend publication of a work that reveals he himself is incompetent.

A further point is this. Not many authors hope that their books will remain unsold. Sales can be helped, or hindered, by the recommendations of other academics, who write reviews in the more intellectual papers, praising or condemning new publications, and who tell their university students that this or that book will be useful (or useless) to them in their studies. And, human behaviour being what it is, what professor is going to boost the sale of a book which says or implies that he has been doing his work inadequately for years past?

The result of these constraints appears to be that many books about the Highlands (or Scotland) keep closely to the opinions given in the last histories of the Highlands (or Scotland); not only is it very advisable from the point of view of an author's career, but it is obvious that to duplicate in slightly different words what has already often been said is a much quicker way to get material ready for publication when a deadline has been passed, and a publisher has begun to hint about the return of an advance. As Dr Johnson remarked, if a writer "is content to take his information from others, he may get through his book with little trouble, and without much endangering his reputation"[465] (at least so far as respectable critics are concerned). In this way inaccuracies are carried on from book to book. It is not only Lewis Carroll's snark-hunter who believes that "what I tell you three times is true". If one is thinking of the Highland clearances, the claim that a new piece of work is "peer-reviewed" is not a greatly impressive recommendation, because it means that the writer will have had to accept the opinions of those "peers" who are "reviewing" him.[466]

56. Wealth smells good

It is also the case that many universities, perhaps all, want more money than they have; and more than one Scottish university has been grateful to receive donations from Highland landlords. Will the history department of such a university regard with favour the proposal of one of its members to write a book drawing attention to the Highland clearances, some of which may have been carried out by its benefactors' forebears? That is not the way to solicit further gifts. Few people have ever achieved prosperity by speaking up for the underdog. Financial good fortune, as well as professional preferment, is procured by pleasing the powerful. No poor people have ever paid for new buildings at a university, or funded the expansion of a history department. On the other hand not many rich people, wishing to contribute to university funds, have ever been turned down, however dubious the source of their wealth. Recipients seldom look a gift horse in the mouth. One could take more than one example from the history of Oxford University during the twentieth century; and in this present century, to take a recent conspicuous case, the connections between the London School of Economics and the now defunct Libyan dictatorship have caused embarrassments. When the son of the Roman Emperor Vespasian objected to his father's proposal to tax malodorous public urinals, Vespasian showed him a coin, and said, "money doesn't smell".[467] Juvenal went further and insisted: "wealth smells good wherever it comes from."[468] So when the head of a history department at a university, in Scotland or England, is negotiating with the Duke of Z, or the Earl of Y, or MacX of MacX, who are large Highland landowners, for a weighty subvention which will pay for funding another fellow or erecting a new extension, does he encourage the junior members of his department to write about the Highland clearances, and criticize the way the donor's ancestors got his estates? There are thousands of other subjects to investigate in the history of Scotland which are not going to annoy potential philanthropists. One cannot expect these facts to have no bearing on the activities of university scholars. Few ivory towers are that remote. Doubly relevant, when one is considering the clearances in the land of the bagpipes, is the saying, "He who pays the piper calls the tune."

Even if some independent-minded academic decides to ignore all these considerations, and to risk his or her career by finding out what actually happened, despite the potential annoyance to others, there are further obstacles to accuracy. Many of the former Highland landlords have descendants who now own part or all of the estates that their forefathers cleared. When the enquiring historian arrives on the scene, therefore, the landowner is able to assure him that although admittedly there were frequent clearances "elsewhere" in the Highlands, in this particular favoured locality nothing untoward had ever happened. I myself, though embarking on this history with no academic accreditation or university endorsement, that is to say as someone who might safely be (and indeed expected to be) completely ignored, was freely assured by landlords all over the Highlands, in personal hand-written letters, that there were no local clearances. In many of the Highland parishes there are few or no native Gaels left to give their interpretation of events (and even if such individuals exist, very few of them come from families rich enough to have kept accounts and documents from long ago detailing events as seen in the eyes of the evicted), while in every Highland parish there are one or more landlords (or their representatives) to give the landlord version; and the estate papers in the proprietorial archives cannot be expected to do anything other than support the proprietor's version of events.[469] This may account for some of the frequent authorial testimonies to the unblemished record of particular landowning families, which otherwise might be hard to explain.

57. The power of the pen

Many years ago I wrote to all the descendants of the eighteenth and nineteenth century Highland landlords whom I could trace (over ninety of them), saying in a studiously polite and non-committal way that I was writing a history of the Highland clearances, and would be grateful for any assistance they might be able to give. I sent the letters half-hoping I might actually get some help, but mainly so as to avoid any clearing landlord's descendant being able to say, after the book appeared (assuming optimistically that it might ever get published), that if I had asked him he could have told me what in fact had happened on his estate. I did not really expect any replies. I imagined the letters, from a completely unknown person, would probably end up in the waste-paper basket with the rest of that morning's junk mail; but at any rate I would be able to defend myself against any subsequent accusation that the heirs of former Highland proprietors had not been asked for their opinion. To my amazement all ninety-odd of them took the trouble to reply (with only one single exception – the seventh Lord Macdonald, who as it happened died suddenly in 1970, soon after I had written to him: I trust it was only post hoc, not propter hoc). It was an extraordinary testimony to the power of the pen. The replies fell roughly into two categories. Most of those to whom I wrote still owned land in the Highlands, and they almost all said there had been no clearances there, or at any rate they had never heard of any, and felt sure that none had occurred; a smaller group, those who no longer owned land in the Highlands, tended to be more moderate in their replies, and were in fact much more likely to say they could offer no defence for their ancestors' operations (and, of course, the reality is that since they no longer figured among Highland landlords, they could disregard any possible repercussions).

Incidentally, some of the replies I received were couched in unexpectedly friendly terms, and invited me to meet the writers, and to look through their records. So the opportunity was presented to me to go and see a number of people, all well-to-do and many well-known; some of them were even members of the aristocracy. No one is worse off for having prominent acquaintances: and encounters of this kind would have sounded very well, mentioned casually during subsequent conversations with friends. I like to boast as much as the next man, so I felt the attraction of such overtures, which might perhaps have led to a different approach to the clearances; and I can well understand how some aspiring authors might have gone along this route. By that time, however, my researches had led me to form certain opinions, and I reluctantly felt unable to follow up these amicable proposals.

These are merely random thoughts, which other writers may wish to challenge. As to the inaccuracies with which the current standard representations of Highland history are riddled, however, there can now be no dispute. These will be dealt with as they arise during the course of this work, but it is a temptation too great to be resisted to give one or two outstanding examples here. Sir James Matheson "owned the entire island of Harris . . .", said the *Oxford Companion to Scottish History*:[470] In fact Sir James never owned Harris, or any part of it. MacDonald of Clanranald (say two sympathetic authors) bankrupted himself helping his small tenants during the 1846 famine:[471] in fact he had no small tenants by then – having sold off all his land years before. MacLeod of Harris also "did all he could" to help his small tenants in the 1846 famine:[472] in fact he too had sold off his land years before. We shall see later Professor Mitchison's opinion that "in the eighteenth century, very little of Caithness was reported as Gaelic speaking";[473] in fact half of the Caithness people, or probably over half, spoke Gaelic. The Duke of Sutherland in 1847 "had no property" in Clyne parish, Sutherland,[474] and therefore could be cleared of responsibility for anything unseemly which had occurred there, said one writer – Michael Fry, who tells us he only deals in "distinct facts"; in reality one unfortunately "distinct fact" is that the Duke of Sutherland in 1847 not only had property in Clyne, but he owned the entire parish, every last square yard of it. Again, Michael Fry, when talking of "the old Sutherland" and of the plans to improve it, informed us that "the Reays had long forsaken their precipices for the Netherlands"[475] (it's embarrassing to have to mention such an obviously incorrect statement again); clearly the idea behind the allegation was to show that "the Reays" were too far away to do any evicting. No doubt the MacKay clansfolk earnestly wished that Eric, Lord Reay, had indeed "long forsaken" any interest in their clan country, but in fact he ordered its clearance – though usually himself preferring to frequent the drinking-houses and bordellos of London, spending the money he had gained by expelling his MacKay clansfolk from the good farms which they and their fathers had inhabited for centuries, and letting the land instead to sheep farmers. To find a further reason to criticize an author who has dismissed as non-existent such a momentous part of the history of Scotland in the eighteenth and nineteenth centuries (i.e. the Highland clearances), may seem analogous to censuring Attila the Hun on the ground that he should have collected more dandelions for his pet rabbit; but facts are facts, and they will come out.

58. The Scottish story

I have suggested that some of the writers who have produced histories of Scotland seem to have done little more than follow in the well-trodden paths of their predecessors. There is no evidence that Scottish history is particularly prone to this kind of duplication. Those who have read John Wiener's book, *Historians in Trouble*, will know of a number of cases concerning historians in other fields.[476] And *The Times* not long ago carried an obituary of what it called an "unworldly eccentric and clubman who wrote some well-respected books on historical subjects"; his first book was "a scholarly survey" of the Ionian Islands.[477] Four days later the same newspaper published an indignant contribution from a third party, which said that this work, so far from being "scholarly", was in fact "a work of flagrant plagiarism": it was "deeply indebted" to an unpublished doctoral thesis in the Cambridge University library. The deceased had "plundered the thesis unscrupulously, even including passages verbatim as his own". The author of the doctoral thesis had planned to expose the plagiarism, but he died, and his "widow and literary executor" decided not to pursue the matter. Whatever the writer's other virtues, said this second contributor, "scholarly honesty was not one of them".[478] "Unworldly", in the original obituary, appears to have been an ill-chosen adjective. The reader will doubtless remember similar cases, not only in history but, for example, in the allied discipline of archaeology (where on rare occasions a revered practitioner has been observed in the dusk quietly burying significant artefacts to be expertly discovered the next day): so it is not necessary to discuss them further.

So far as books on Scottish history are concerned, though, the persistent reader of such texts may sometimes make a shrewd guess as to which antecedent volume a particular writer had open on his desk when he was seeking inspiration for his own account. It may be of interest to compare some excerpts from two such histories, one published in 1960, called *The Story of Scotland*,[479] and one in 1984, entitled *Scotland's Story*.[480] (The latter was a great success: the hardback edition of 1984 was followed by a paperback edition in 1985, which was "reprinted five times", and then by a second paperback edition in 1994.)

1960: "During the sixty years of these two brothers [King Malcolm and King William] . . . it was a time of peace and promise." 1984: "During the sixty years that these two brothers ruled, Scotland was a land of peace and promise."

1960: "Almost immediately, Edward I of England suggested the little girl's betrothal to his own young son, and in 1290 a marriage treaty was signed . . ." 1984: Edward I "immediately suggested a marriage between the Maid and his own son, and in 1290, a treaty was signed . . ."

1960: "Thirteen lords forthwith put forward claims to the Scottish throne. The two strongest were those of John Balliol and Robert Bruce . . . Both were powerful men." 1984: "immediately thirteen Scottish lords laid claim to the throne, including John Balliol and Robert Bruce. Both were powerful men . . ."

1960: "Twenty-four English and 80 Scottish auditors were appointed to scrutinize the claims . . . Edward announced the award to Balliol." 1984: "Twenty-four bishops and barons from England, together with eighty Scottish representatives, spent six months scrutinizing the evidence. Edward awarded the throne to John Balliol."

1960: Edward aimed at "reducing Scotland to the condition of an English shire . . . Perhaps he was corrupted by power . . . possibly his bloody conquest of Wales" encouraged him. (The tentative terms "perhaps" and "possibly" were clearly too feeble for the second author.) 1984: "Edward made clear his intention to reduce Scotland to the status of an English shire. He had just completed his bloody conquest of Wales, and, corrupted by power, wanted Scotland too."

1960: Balliol "renounced his allegiance to Edward and in 1295 negotiated an alliance with France . . . England's fiercest enemy." 1984: Balliol "renounced his allegiance to Edward and negotiated an alliance with France . . . England's fiercest enemy."

1960: Balliol "confiscated all the Bruce properties in Scotland and conferred them upon his brother-in-law, John Comyn. From this moment onwards, the struggle in Scotland became a three-cornered one." 1984: Balliol "confiscated all the Bruce lands in Scotland and gave them to his brother-in-law, John Comyn. The struggle for the mastery of Scotland thus became three-cornered."

1960: The English took Berwick-upon-Tweed. "Many hundreds of people were slaughtered, including almost the entire Flemish colony, buildings were sacked . . ." 1984: "English troops slaughtered hundreds, and the hardworking colony of Flemish craftsmen and traders were killed to a man. Every building was sacked." (It will be noted that the indeterminate "buildings" in the first account became "every building" in the second; and that "almost the entire Flemish colony" in the first book became "to a man" in the second.)

1960: "The horror of the whole affair made the deepest impression on Scotland . . . that bitter hatred for all things English which was to be nourished so consistently by English policy during the next three hundred years . . . Its commercial status was never recovered." 1984: "The Scots were horrified by the brutality. The town was never to recover its commercial status, and the seeds were sown in Scotland for a hatred of the English that was to last 300 years."

59. A broken, forgotten failure

1960: Edward advanced, "taking possession of castles all the way from Roxburgh to Elgin and even further north". 1984: Edward "took every castle from Roxburgh in the south to Elgin in the north".

1960: "In August 1296, he returned to Berwick, where a massed act of allegiance was staged . . ." 1984: "In August 1296, he staged a mammoth act of Scottish allegiance at Berwick . . ."

1960: "Quantities of charters and official records were confiscated and either destroyed or taken to London, along with what was believed to be the Stone of Destiny . . ." 1984: "The official records of Scotland were confiscated and burnt or else taken to London. The Stone of Scone, Scotland's symbolic Coronation stone, was taken to Westminster Abbey . . ."

1960: "English officials were left to govern Scotland in Edward's name. English garrisons held every castle of importance . . . the barbarity of the English garrisons . . . hardened Scottish national feeling." 1984: "English officials now

THE CLEARANCES IN HISTORY

governed Scotland. English garrisons manned every strategic castle and their barbarity bred and hardened Scottish national feeling."

1960: "John Balliol gave up his crown, and after three years in the Tower of London, retired to his family estates in France and died in 1313, a broken, forgotten failure." 1984: Balliol "was imprisoned in the Tower of London for three years. He subsequently retired to his family's estates in France and died in 1313, a broken, forgotten failure."

1960: "Wallace's army had included men from every part of the country, Galwegians, Highlanders, contingents from the north-east, and from central Scotland." 1984: Wallace's "army included men from all over Scotland, from Galloway, Aberdeen and the Highlands as well as central Scotland." (Both these writers perpetuate the myth that in 1300 the Highlands were already part of a united country of Scotland: in fact these Highlanders – who were hardy fighters, despite having supposedly been, as the orthodox historians desperately try to convince us, semi-starved in regular famines for years – were tough mercenaries going abroad for pay. Swiss mercenaries manned the Pope's Swiss Guard for centuries, but the Pope did not therefore claim to rule Switzerland. The Doge of Venice traditionally had a Slav bodyguard, though having no Slav domains. Many Gurkhas from Nepal served and serve in the British army, but Nepal was and is not ruled by the British. The medieval French kings were often served by Scots soldiers of fortune, without making any claim to Scottish suzerainty. This subject is dealt with later.)

1960: "The eighth Robert Bruce served him [Edward] both as Governor of Carlisle and as Sheriff of Lanark . . . he was in secret league with the Bishop of St Andrews and others, waiting for the time when he could . . . assume the crown which he believed should be his." 1984: "Robert Bruce, the eighth in the family to bear the name, became restless. Governor of Carlisle and Sheriff of Lanark in the service of Edward I, he was in secret league with the Bishop of St Andrews and others, waiting for the time he could assume the crown of Scotland which he believed was rightly his."

1960: After killing John Comyn, Bruce "went to Scone and there arranged the strangest coronation ceremony in recorded Scottish history". 1984: After the death of Comyn, Bruce "went to Scone, where the strangest coronation in Scottish history took place".

1960: "Early in 1307, the tide turned. In the spring of that year a great band of Yorkshiremen and Borderers were slaughtered by Bruce's men in Glentrool." 1984: "In April 1307 the tide turned. At Glentrool in Wigtownshire an English army of Yorkshiremen and Borderers was slaughtered by Bruce's men." (Other historians describe this encounter less dramatically as a minor skirmish, but our second author followed faithfully after the first.)

1960: Bruce "first planned a campaign north of the Forth and Clyde . . . By summer 1309, only Dundee and Banff remained in English hands north of the Tay . . ." 1984: "Bruce took his campaign north of the Forth and Clyde . . . By the summer of 1309 Dundee and Banff were the only strongholds north of the Tay still in English hands."[481]

60. Prolonged and bloody wars

1960: Robert summoned another gathering, "the Parliament he held at Cambuskenneth in 1326. This is the first recorded occasion on which a Scottish king summoned clergy, barons and also representatives of the burghs to a Parliament." 1984: "When King Robert the Bruce held a parliament at Cambuskenneth in 1326 he summoned not only barons and representatives of the clergy, but also representatives from Scotland's burghs. It was the first time their presence had been officially requested."

1960: At Cambuskenneth, "Two important matters were dealt with, one financial, the other political. A contribution of one-tenth of all rents was decided upon for Robert, to defray the expenses of Government." 1984: "The two main topics of discussion were the succession and money. The parliament agreed that henceforth a tenth of all rents were to be paid directly to the King to help defray the expense of government."

1960: A Highland clan was ruled by ". . . a chieftain whose authority was unassailable . . . They dealt summarily with criminal and civil cases, without reference to Sheriffs . . ." 1984: "The chief's authority was absolute . . . Criminal and civil cases were tried without any reference to the Royal Sheriff." (This myth about "despotic" chiefs is dealt with elsewhere. This example may show how assertions are passed down from one writer to the next, without much apparent effort to verify them. Other stale myths will be seen in the next examples, handed on without reflection in the book-making relay race; if the material is altered at all, it is only in order to strengthen it; e.g. in Berwick "buildings were sacked" and "every building was sacked" above, and "sour, thin *and* water-logged soil" below.)

1960: "But the chieftains maintained interminable vendettas against each other, in the interests of which they called out their clans for prolonged and bloody wars. Organized cattle-raiding and wife-stealing were accompanied by murder, betrayal and cruelty." 1984: "The chiefs frequently called upon their followers to fight vendettas. Often these were prolonged and bloody wars. They were frequently the consequence of the theft of wives or cattle; and murder and pillage were commonplace."

1960: In the Highlands, "autumn gales destroyed on average every fourth harvest, the soil was either sour and thin, or else water-logged".[482] 1984: (The 1984 author disdained his 1960 predecessor's diffident "or else".) "The soil north of the Highland Line was sour, thin and water-logged. Autumn gales ruined one harvest in four."

1960: "The scraggy cattle were always in danger of being stolen." 1984: "The scraggy cattle were also plundered by neighbours."

1960: "Families lived in long, low-built huts . . . the walls were piled up with stones and pebbles held together by mud, the roofs were heather thatch, there were neither windows nor chimneys, so the peat-smoke hung about . . . damp and filth were unavoidable". 1984: "The ordinary home was a long, low hovel of stone and pebble, held together by mud and roofed with heather thatch . . . they had neither windows nor chimney. Smoke, damp and filth were unavoidable." (These descriptions could well have been applied – even more fittingly – to mediaeval Lowland houses; but that wouldn't have satisfied the standard anglophone approach to the Highlands. All this is dealt with later.)

61. The Uists

It may be of interest to give some further examples of the way inaccurate information is happily passed on, once it has achieved the unchallengeable certainty of publication. (It reminds me of arguments in the school playground when I was a boy, when the triumphant claim "I've seen it in print!" meant that it must be true.) Of course it could be argued that much of this is innocuous. If it is true that the British Parliament passed the famous Reform Bill in 1832, it can be maintained that it does no harm to repeat the information, and even to use much the same language as another author in doing so. (Writers, however, would be wise to ignore Tom Lehrer's sardonic exhortation to "Plagiarize, plagiarize! That's why God made your eyes!") Harm does occur when the information is not true in the first place, as in the passages above about the Highland chiefs' authority, the "prolonged and bloody wars" (with the startling implication that the Lowlands, and England, enjoyed unbroken peace), the frequent failure of harvests (with the quite false inference that tillage supplied most of the Highlanders' food), and the rest of the Lowlanders' misconceptions. Certainly the language used does suggest that the second author derived not a little of his inspiration from the first. In the next parallel the second writer made it clear he was following an earlier one.

Professor Richards quoted a statement consisting of "the words of Sir John MacDonald of Sleat in 1763";[483] six years later Professor Lynch (who was quite open in saying that his information came from Professor Richards' book – he had a footnote giving the Richards reference which I have just provided)[484] used the same quotation, which he too said were the words of "Sir John MacDonald of Sleat". All writers borrow from other histories and other historians: I certainly do, as anyone reading this book will often have observed (though the careful reader will have perceived that I often disagree with what I have borrowed). But it would be wise to check that what is borrowed is true. In this case, the words quoted were those of Sir James MacDonald. Not only was there no "Sir John MacDonald of Sleat" in 1763, there never was a "Sir John MacDonald of Sleat", since the Sleat family tree (with which, surely, historians of the Highlands should be at least vaguely familiar?) shows that the chiefs kept to the first names Donald, James, Alexander, and Archibald, from the sixteenth century until well into the nineteenth (by which time the baronets had become barons: Sir Alexander MacDonald became Lord Macdonald in 1776).

There are many other interesting coincidences to be observed in literature about the Highlands. Dr Anne Marie Tindley, of Glasgow Caledonian University, wrote a "Short History of the Sutherland Estate", in which she assured her readers that the clearances were "admirable in intention"; the proprietorial aim in the Sutherland clearances (she asserted) was firstly to increase the value of the estate, and "secondly, to improve the economic and social position of the many small tenants". Not surprisingly, this enthusiastic academic approval has been quoted on the noble family's website.[485] (Aristocratic patronage goes to those who echo aristocratic propaganda.) The author's respectful standpoint may perhaps be indicated by her description of the oily and obsequious account of the Sutherland changes by Sir William Fraser (whose book was being paid for by the Sutherland estate owners, and naturally therefore simply regurgitated the implausible excuses made by them: for example, Fraser blandly alleged that the clearances produced "increased wealth and prosperity among the people") – Dr Tindley called Fraser's book "a beautiful piece of work" and "a good overview" of "the early and modern history of the Sutherlands". She then said that Sellar's trial was "in 1818". It was, of course, in 1816. I was surprised that anyone who had spent any time thinking about the Sutherland clearances – to the extent, indeed, of being confident enough to assure her readers that Fraser's revolting toadyism was "a good overview" – could have made such an elementary mistake, until I remembered that Francis Thompson some years ago made exactly same error: "in 1818 Sellar went on trial."[486]

There is no shortage of other coincidences. Professor R. H. Campbell wrote in 1965 about "Clanranald, who owned the Uists . . ."[487] This, of course, was an obvious blunder. South Uist, certainly, was Clan Ranald territory, and when the chiefs became landlords it was therefore largely owned by the chief, Clanranald (though he did not own even the whole of South Uist: in 1800 a junior branch of the family, "of Boisdale", owned part of it); but North Uist was and always had been Clan Donald country, and was therefore owned by Lord Macdonald when the British state power overthrew the old Highland system in the middle of the eighteenth century, and handed vast landed estates to the Highland chiefs. However, palpable though the mistake was, Professor Smout followed Professor Campbell down the blind alley, and in 1969 Smout wrote sympathetically of the difficulties of "MacDonald of Clanranald in the Uists", although he thought he could have done more for the islands: "Clanranald [though rich from kelp] never ploughed anything back into the Uists."[488] (This was not quite a statement of ownership in so many words, but if Clanranald had difficulties in "the Uists", and was considered capable of "ploughing anything back into the Uists" he must have owned both islands.) These two authors were both professors of Scottish history at Scottish Universities, writing about the Scottish Highlands, but neither was apparently aware that North Uist was Clan Donald territory, which after 1746 was owned by Lord Macdonald.

62. Less fine feelings

Professor Smout also figures in the next example, since in 1969, as we saw earlier, he also wrote: "Other chiefs having resisted the urge to put their lands to the most profitable uses were compelled by the remorseless logic of debt or bankruptcy to sell out to others, with less fine feelings, as Lord Reay was forced to sell to the Duke of Sutherland [i.e. to the Marquess of Stafford] in 1829",[489] so clearly the saint-like Lord Reay, having nobly renounced "the most profitable uses" of his estate, had nothing to do with any clearances. Three years later Douglas Hill (who thanked "the Canada Council for a generous research grant", part of which he must have spent on buying Professor Smout's book – it is hard to see where there was any independent "research") wrote that some lairds resisted the temptation to "move tenants off . . . as long as possible, choosing poverty in preference to evictions, [but were then] forced by debt and the threat of legal action to sell lands to other lairds with fewer scruples, as Lord Reay sold his estates to the Duke of Sutherland [i.e., to the Marquess of Stafford] in 1829".[490] (We see elsewhere that both these observers were in that not inconsiderable band of historians who have not heard about Lord Reay's clearances, or about the correct date of the marquess's elevation.)

Other parts of the same two books are equally interesting. Professor Smout (to repeat) wrote that in the Western Isles "there is little hint (except on Rum and Jura in 1826 and on Arran in 1828) of men at this date being turned out to make room for sheep."[491] Douglas Hill more or less followed suit, though with his own intuitive insights. "In the Hebrides tenants were hardly ever turned out for the sake of sheep (except in a limited way on Rum and Arran in the 1820s)."[492] So the first author's claim that there was "little hint" of clearances except on three islands, becomes clearances in "a limited way" on two islands: the second author could not even make an accurate copy. There was nothing "limited" in the Rum clearance – the island was emptied. (And Professor Hamilton, as we saw, would have been more correct if he had done a bit of borrowing: the Rum clansfolk, he said mistakenly, had simply decided to go to America – though Rum was "practically unaffected by sheep farming".)[493] In reality, as is shown elsewhere, during those years almost every Hebridean parish had seen "men turned out to make room for sheep".

Professor Smout evidently considered the Highlands to be a hopeless case, and mused that "it is possible" there was no "alternative to congestion or clearance". He chided (de haut en bas) those who thought otherwise: "perhaps it is all to the good that they do not allow themselves to be diverted from their vision by the study of so dismaying a subject as history." As to that, it may be that the more we can find out what actually happened in history, the less we merely copy previous texts and persuade ourselves that twenty-five people *per square mile* amounts to "congestion", the less "dismaying" it would become.[494]

A further example of an error occurring in one historical textbook, and then reappearing in another, came in Dr I. F. Grant's allegation that "by the middle of the seventeenth century" MacDonald of Keppoch "had obtained sole and legal possession" of the Keppoch lands[495] (i.e. a Lowland charter) which of course is not the case: Keppoch never acquired a Lowland charter to his clan's land. The same mistake, that Keppoch was the "owner" of the Keppoch clan land, was later made by Professor George Pryde.[496]

In 1989 Dr Donnachie and Dr Hewitt wrote, under the heading "Clans" (so they were talking about the Highlands) that some of the estates forfeited after Culloden by "Jacobite chiefs" were "sold off".[497] This was inaccurate: a dozen Highland chieftains lost their estates, but they were all carefully managed and restored to the chiefs' heirs less than forty years later. In 1990 (one year after the first book) John Burke wrote, equally inaccurately, that after Culloden "London speculators" bought up the "forfeited lands" in the Highlands.[498] (This matter is looked at later.)

63. 400 square miles

We saw earlier that Professor Mitchison said that in Webster's census the population of what she considered to be "the Highlands" was 115,000 – an inexplicable figure well below the true number; the book in which this statement appeared was first published in 1990.[499] The next year, 1991, Professor Lynch's book was published with the same figure – "the population of the Highlands [was] 115,000 in 1755".[500]

In the same 1991 book Professor Lynch said mistakenly that the Highland parishes "on average were 400 square miles in area".[501] In 1994 Professor Devine gave a similar and equally mistaken assessment – "there were few Highland parishes under 400 square miles in extent"[502] As we have seen, the Highland parishes were in fact about 100 square miles on average – a quarter as much.

Yet another curious coincidence occurred when Dr I. F. Grant, ignoring her two earlier estimates of the Highland population in 1755 as 376,086[503] and then as 257,153,[504] gave the figure of 337,000 as the true total;[505] a year or two later Michael Fry, who was also ignoring another estimate of his as "about 250,000",[506] also plumped for 337,000[507] (which is thirty-five per cent higher than his earlier figure) as the 1755 Webster estimate of the Highland population. (Soon afterwards Fry went back to alleging that the Highland population in 1750 was 250,000.)[508]

A parallel instance was this. In 1989 Dr Donnachie and Dr Hewitt, when discussing "the eviction of the Highlanders from their traditional lands", said that "the term 'clearance' was never actually applied at the time".[509] In 2005 Michael Fry echoed this opinion, in questioning whether some development "can be called 'clearance' at all. The term was never used at the time . . ."[510] It *was* used, of course. Here are a few examples.

In 1804 an agent wrote to Campbell of Combie about an offer to pay £90 a year for Killin sheep farm "upon having the farm cleared of any followers (as is now the Case)".[511] In 1806 William MacKenzie, acting on behalf of the countess, told Combie: "the Farms of Culgower will be cleared for Mr Pope by a proper warning and Removing".[512] In 1817 Patrick Sellar told Loch that the Sutherland population should be reduced "by clearing a certain district annually and laying it under stock", thus producing "cleared districts".[513] In 1818 Patrick Sellar wrote to James Loch, exulting that the forthcoming ejectment of "these animals", as he genially called the Highlanders, "shall make our clearance of the hills . . . once and for all".[514] And Sellar, the hero of the improvers (and of some modern historians), cannot be denied. Also in 1818 the Rev. David MacKenzie told Loch that "the lands on the coast" were already over-crowded, "since so many were sent down from the heights to clear Sellar's farm".[515] In 1819 Francis Suther, then the Sutherland factor, gave Loch details of that year's operations: "To give you some idea of the extent cleared I subjoin a list of the numbers removed in the different parishes."[516] In 1821 Loch wrote a letter about "the policy of clearing the hills of people, in order to make sheep walks".[517] In 1825 Duncan Shaw, Clanranald's factor, said the landlord would have "to clear particular districts particularly well calculated for pasture, where the poorest of the people and most of the subtenants reside".[518]

So the terms "clearance", "clearing", "clear", and "cleared" were all being used contemporaneously.   It does make one wonder how an observer can avoid reading about so many documents.

64. Variously calculated

Another interesting case came in the reporting of the conclusions reached by a Select Committee of the House of Commons in 1841. This committee (consisting of course of a cabal of Highland landlords) claimed there was in the Highlands a surplus "variously calculated at from 45,000 to 80,000 souls",[519] whom the Government should help to emigrate. Professor Richards in 1985 said erroneously that the figures specified by the committee were "between 45,000 and 60,000 people";[520] in 1991 Professor Lynch thought the same – "between 45,000 and 60,000 people";[521] and so did Professor Devine in 1994 – "45,000 to 60,000 people".[522] Presumably the latter two errors were the result of historians copying another writer instead of going to the original source.

There is a further possible case, mentioned elsewhere. Trevelyan claimed that the old Highland clansfolk paid "most oppressive . . . rack-rent terms" to tacksmen.[523] All the other evidence said that the clansfolk paid extremely low sums to the chiefs and chieftains: not infrequently this fact, the inadequacy of the income going to the chiefs, now landlords, was used as an unanswerable argument by supporters of the landlords to show that the old system could not be allowed to endure in the brave new proprietorial world – that it was not fair to the chiefs, now landowners, for the clansfolk to continue paying such very low "rents". However, I have found one other author, J. A. MacCulloch, who in 1905 made the same erroneous claim about very high "rents" in the days of the clans;[524] so it is possible that that is where Trevelyan got the idea, and that Trevelyan's "rack-rent terms" demanded by the tacksmen were merely the echo of MacCulloch's "exorbitant rates" demanded by the tacksmen. It is very hard to think of anywhere else Trevelyan could have discovered this drama, since like so much of the established narrative of these years in the Highlands it is in direct conflict with reality. (This topic is discussed below, in chapter three, subsections 41 and 45 to 51.)

I have mentioned here some of the more striking coincidences which appear in the books on Highland history. There must be others. It seems likely, for instance, that those who excitedly tell us that the Highlanders were all, or nearly all, Roman Catholics, when in fact nineteen out of twenty of them were Protestants, were in fact allowing themselves to be inspired simply by modern textbooks. The same thought applies to those who claim that the Highlanders were forbidden to speak Gaelic after 1746; or that there was a great increase in the eighteenth-century Highland population; or that the Highlanders and Lowlanders were really the same people, in one united country; or that the clan chiefs were despotic landlords, ruling over cowering minions; or that the old Highlanders drank vast quantities of whisky; or that the clansfolk lived under the same roof as their animals; or that most of the Highland landlords led impoverished lives, many going bankrupt; or that "the English" carried out the clearances; or that the new big farmers were all Lowlanders; or that 2000 families were often driven out in one day (none of which confident assertions has any foundation in reality).

The emphatic words of Sir Richard Evans, Regius Professor of History at Cambridge University, that history "among other things" is "about interrogating and questioning myths, not uncritically repeating them", are unfortunately often ignored.[525]

65. The first Sutherland clearance

Anyone who may read the volume about the Sutherland clearances in this series will come across a further case. The first Sutherland clearance took place in 1807, to set up the Great Sheep Tenement. There is no doubt about the date. Those who are interested can examine many references from various sources (supportive and hostile); they can watch the development of the idea month by month, beginning with the discussions among the owners and the managers in 1805 and 1806; they can observe the drawing up of the exact boundaries of the farm in the summer of 1806, along with the preparation of the lists naming those to be evicted, the exploratory visit of the projected new sheep farming tenants, and the signing of the lease, followed in May 1807 by the triumphant inauguration of the new ranch and the inevitable evictions, attempted re-settlements, emigrations, and deaths, which accompanied it. But some years later Captain Henderson, one of the Caithness landed gentry, visited the county to produce his book *The General View of the Agriculture of Sutherland*, and he mistakenly wrote about the families who "were removed . . . in 1806 to form a sheep farm",[526] and also erroneously alleged that "in 1806 Messrs Atcheson & Co took the sheep walk from the Marquess of Stafford".[527] Henderson was not always accurate with his details – the reader has just observed that he thought Atkinson, one of the new sheep-farming partnership, was called Atcheson (as well as forgetting Marshall's name); but there was now a respectable document (Henderson's book) naming 1806 – twice – as the date of the first Sutherland clearance. From then on the document took priority over the deed, the affirmation over the fact. James Loch mistakenly told the Earl of Shaftesbury in 1854 that "the first farm that was so formed on the Sutherland estate was in 1806";[528] and writers still fall into line. Richards in 1973 said "the Sutherland clearances occurred mainly between 1806 and 1820"[529] (in fact they were between 1807 and 1821), while "the first clearance of the Sutherland estate seems to have occurred in 1806".[530] Forbes, in his 1976 book, said the evictions in Sutherland "began on the Marquess of Stafford's estate in 1806".[531] Richards in 1982 quoted Loch's letter with its 1806 date (as he had done in 1973) without mentioning that Loch was mistaken.[532] Clapperton in 1983 said "the first

Sutherland clearance took place in 1806".[533] Richards in 1985 talked of "the early clearances in Sutherland (in 1806)".[534]

In fact 1806 is not the only blessed year which was supposed to have launched the brave new world in the far north. Atkinson & Marshall, if we make the effort to believe what some modern chronicles seem to say, apparently first brought their sheep to Sutherland – after the inaugural great clearance – in 1800 (Prebble 1973, 322). And in 1805 (Richards 1999, 42). And in 1806 (Henderson 1812, 24 & 104; Richards 1973, 158, 170 & 277; Richards 1982, 184; Richards 1985, 202; Forbes 1976, 24). And in 1808 (Mitchison 1993, 191). And in 1810 (Youngson 1973, 170, and Clapperton 1983, 140). And in 1812 (Prebble 1971, 103) – as well as in 1807, the date they actually arrived. (We saw earlier that a further expert told us that the Sutherland clearances began in 1799;[535] yet another knowledgeable partnership said it was in 1819 – so that gives us two more dates for the arrival of Atkinson and Marshall.)[536]

Some people may say, "So what? 1799, 1809, 1819, what's the difference?" But there is a difference. Those who write history books, or any books (to repeat what was said earlier) should make every effort to ensure that every fact, every date, every assertion that appears in their work should be as accurate as it is possible to make it. Secondly – and this is crucially significant – to accept without question what a document (or a history book) says can and does lead to further much more important errors, such as the belief that the clan chiefs were virtual dictators, as well as being the owners of their clans' land, and that the clansfolk were merely downtrodden half-starved peasants, along with all the other misconceptions cited earlier in this chapter.

THE CLEARANCES IN HISTORY

CHAPTER ONE NOTES

1. To suit those in power
[1] George Orwell, *1984*, Penguin, London, (1949) 1979, 199: "Who controls the past, controls the future: who controls the present, controls the past." O'Brien explains to Winston Smith that when he holds four fingers up, if the Party says they are five, then they are five. In the same way, if historians say there were no Highland clearances, then there were no Highland clearances.
[2] Samuel Butler, *Erewhon & Erewhon Revisited*, Dent, London, (1901) 1947, 293: "It has been said that though God cannot alter the past, historians can; it is perhaps because they can be useful to him in this respect that he tolerates their existence."
[3] Charles Dickens, *David Copperfield*, Dent, London, (1849) 1950, 237.
[4] James Connolly, one of the leaders, was too badly injured to stand, so he was tied to a chair and shot. The executions were carried out by the soldiers of the state which proclaimed that it was fighting the bloody and destructive 1914-18 War in order to "protect the rights of small nations", such as Serbia and Belgium, against the neighbouring countries (Austria-Hungary and Germany) which had invaded them. It is not clear what "the rights of small nations" are, or how they would benefit ordinary people, but whatever they are or were, they did not apparently apply to Ireland. There are endless examples of inconsistent versions of history, as portrayed in the history books of neighbouring countries. Waterloo, in 1815, was won by the British, in British history books; the Germans know that it was the arrival of Blucher with the Prussian army which brought about the victory. Similarly the Battle of Agincourt, 1415, four centuries earlier, is celebrated in England as a heroic victory, gained against overwhelming odds by a small army – "we few, we happy few, we band of brothers". In French history books it is the story of an English war-crime, because of the deliberate cold-blooded slaughter of "many hundreds" (in Sir Charles Oman's words – *History of England 1377-1485*, Longmans, London, 1918, 257) of unarmed French prisoners. (Even Shakespeare mentioned it.)
[5] Many people would feel aggrieved if they were hanged for the "crime" of actually being "a suspected person"; but the hanging of someone for having been in the company of "a suspected person" seems hard to justify. The British government now admits (*The Times*, 18th & 20th July 2012) that torture, including castration, was used against Mau Mau *suspects* during the rebellion, thus showing how "history" – that is, the official version of events – can change with the passage of time. When I wrote articles in the 1950s on the subject of the brutality used by the British against the Africans (articles which must have been read by at least five people), the official answer to any criticisms was that nothing untoward had occurred, and that only dubious characters would suspect such things.
[6] *The Times*, 1st December 2009. And see *The Times*, 7th September 2012, which quoted Putin: "anyone who doesn't regret the passing of the Soviet Union has no heart." As one of the "heartless" majority, Ben Macintyre wrote: "At times of international uncertainty, history is up for grabs, another natural resource to be seized and exploited for political ends." An undeniable sentiment, especially allowing for the fact that "international uncertainty" is permanent.

2. Conquest of the Highlands
[7] Johnson & Boswell 1930, 22 & 145.
[8] Cregeen 1970, 10. Dr Johnson (like other people) was often wrong, of course: he was wrong about *Tristram Shandy*, about the number of trees in Scotland, about how colds spread in St Kilda when outsiders arrived, and about the character of the clans near the Lowland border (to give four examples).

3. Orthodox Highland history

[9] A bleak climate and a poor unimprovable soil: this is the standard view. But there is evidence that this opinion is quite wrong. Arable farming experiments were carried out in the 1870s at Lairg, Uppat, and Kildonan, in Sutherland, under the aegis of the third Duke of Sutherland, and when a deputation from the Scottish Chamber of Agriculture visited in July 1878 they concluded that "there was nothing in the climate which prejudicially affected vegetable growth in this county" (Mitchell 1971, II 100-1). See volume three of this work.

[10] Moncreiffe 1967, 35, "unparalleled"; Moncreiffe 1967, 251, quoting Dundee 1965, "prodigious".

[11] Muir 1985, 161. In the eighteenth century, there was "a torrential growth in the Highland population".

[12] Hamilton 1966, 73. One cause of the eighteen century emigrations from the Highlands was "the stupendous growth of population". Orthodox historians have used not only these four adjectives, but also many others, often equally melodramatic, to describe what they claim was a great increase in the Highland population after 1750. (This subject is dealt with briefly below, and more fully in volume two.)

[13] Oscar Wilde, *The Works of Oscar Wilde*, Collins, London, (1948) 1960, 21 (*Dorian Gray*). Lord Henry was apparently based partly on Wilde's friend Lord Ronald Sutherland Gower (son of the 2nd Duke of Sutherland, and grandson of the clearing Countess of Sutherland); Lord Ronald's defiant defence of the Sutherland clearances is mentioned in volume three of this work. The friendship cannot have been based on any similarity of views on affairs of state, since their writings show them to have been at opposite ends of the political spectrum: it may simply have been that they were both men about town, and homosexuals. Appropriately enough, Lord Ronald's opinions on the Sutherland clearances showed clearly that he could easily believe in what was incredible. Wilde may even have been hinting at this fact in what he said about Lord Henry. It is also tempting to think that perhaps Lord Ronald, whose family surname "Leveson-Gower" was pronounced "Looson-Gor", may perhaps also have been the model for "Lord Goring" in *An Ideal Husband*.

[14] Lewis Carroll, *Through the Looking Glass*, Macmillan, London, 1940, 101.

4. *Locating the Highlands*

[15] R. H. Campbell, preface to Gaskell 1980, ix.

[16] Youngson 1973, 7, 130, 140, 167, 200. This uncertainty as to where the Highlands were may have led to further ambiguity. Professor Youngson (Youngson 1973, 134) said the population of the Highlands was 300,000 (apparently in the middle of the 19th century) and also (p. 177) 470,000 (apparently at the same time).

[17] Chambers 1869, 30.

[18] Robertson 1808, x.

5. *Numbers in 1750*

[19] Mitchison 1993, 180. If writers use perplexing phrases like "the areas geologically and geographically Highland", would it not be a good idea to put in some explanation? Mitchison said in an article in the journal *Scottish Economic and Social History*, 1981, I 4, that "In the region as defined by F. Fraser Darling's *West Highland Survey*, [the population] rose from 115 thousand to 154 thousand in 1801 and 201 thousand in 1831." But it appears from an article by T. M. Devine in the *Scottish Historical Review*, LXII 2, October 1983, that Fraser Darling was talking only about "the north-west and outer isles" where, of course, the landlords had been at great pains to expand the population as far as possible in order to have more kelp-workers, and therefore more kelp-profits.

[20] Lynch 1996, 367. This figure of 115,000, given by both Mitchison and Lynch, seems to have originated in the way suggested above. It may be significant that Professor Lynch later seemingly changed his mind, and edited a volume which gave a much larger figure for the 1755 population. According to the Webster figures, the four main Highland counties alone had many more people than that. Webster said that Argyllshire had 62,348 people, Inverness-shire 64,321, Ross and Cromarty

47,656, and Sutherland 20,774, a total of 195,099. So Mitchison's calculation presumably left out some two-fifths even of these four counties, not to mention the ten counties which were also partly Highland (Buteshire, Dumbartonshire, Stirlingshire, Perthshire, Angus, Aberdeenshire, Banffshire, Morayshire, Nairnshire, and Caithness). Other writers, in contrast, include not only the main four Highland counties, but also the whole of some or all of the ten part-Highland counties. Some observers include the populations of Orkney and Shetland (which have never had Gaelic inhabitants). Only a few of them appear to have applied themselves to the hard work of trying to decide where the Highlands actually are, with the resulting arduous computation of the total population of a large number of parishes. But anyone reluctant to engage in laborious toil should not be writing history.

[21] John Home, *History of the Rebellion in Scotland in 1745*, Brown, Edinburgh, (1802) 1822, 9. Home began writing this in 1746, & his estimate of the Highland population apparently refers to the mid-eighteenth century.

[22] Moncreiffe 1967, 35.

[23] Adam/Innes 1965, 77.

[24] M. Fry, *The Scotsman*, 7th March 2005; Fry gave the same estimate, "about 250,000", in the *Scottish Review of Books*, 28th October 2005. In the same year, 2005, he gave another figure, 337,000, (which is thirty-five per cent higher) as the amount of the "Highland population" at the time of Webster's enumeration – Fry 2005, 135. So his three estimates, in the one year, were 250,000, 337,000, and 250,000. Mr Fry claimed that he only dealt in "distinct facts", but this fact appears to have been something less than distinct.

[25] Donaldson 1993, 166.

[26] Lister 1978, 19; Collier 1953, 46.

[27] Grant 1980, 53. "According to an estimate by a Dr Webster, made in 1755, it was 257,153. From 1801 census returns are available and by 1811 the population was 362,000. By 1841, when the clearances were coming to an end [!], it was 396,000."

[28] *Oxford Companion to Scottish History*, 2001, 489. This volume was edited by Professor Lynch, who as we saw had earlier given the figure of 115,000.

[29] Brander 1980, 126.

[30] Pryde 1962, 150 fn.

[31] J. S. Keltie, as quoted in Adam/Innes 1965, 89.

[32] Grant & Cheape 2000, 209.

[33] Fry 2005, 135.

[34] Youngson 1973, 161 (& 44, "one quarter").

[35] Bingham 1991, 162.

[36] Smout 1970, 501.

[37] Grant 1934, 213.

[38] Ferguson 1994. On page 175, "something of the order of 30% can safely be assigned to the Gaelic-speaking Highlands and Islands", or 379,614; while on page 90, "the Gaels possibly numbered almost a third of the total population" or almost 421,793.

[39] Halliday 1996, 115.

[40] MacLeod 1997, 4.

[41] Richards 1985, 6 (see volume two).

[42] Grimble 1973, 83 (see volume two).

[43] Prebble 1970, 9.

[44] Kyd 1952, xviii.

[45] Website highlandclearances.info.

[46] Mathieson 2000, 74.

[47] H. Hamilton, *Economic History of Scotland in the 18th century*, Clarendon Press, Oxford, 1963, 4.

[48] Fallow 1999, 89.

[49] Website planetware.com.

⁵⁰ Paul Strand and Basil Davidson, *Tir A'Mhurain*, Aperture, New York (1962) 2002, 96.

Hopkins 1998, 11, mentioned the Highlands in 1660, "where perhaps nearly a third of the Scottish population lived".

6. Highland parishes

⁵¹ Wilkie Collins, in *The Moonstone*, 1868, Prologue III, tells of "the English army" which attacked Seringapatam in 1799, and planted "the English flag" there. The assault force consisted of two columns, one admittedly led by an Englishman, one led by a Highlander; the whole onslaught was commanded by a Scots Lowlander. The total offensive force was about 50,000, of which 46,000 were Indians; of the thirteen European regiments, four were Highland, one Lowland, and one Swiss. The English soldiers involved can scarcely have numbered as many as 2,500, or five per cent of the total force which was described as an "English army". In the same author's *Armadale*, Penguin, London, (1864) 2004, one character is described as "every inch a Scotchman" on page 11, and "the only Englishman in Wildbad" on page 19. Which was he? Collins, of course, was English, but Robert Louis Stevenson, a Scotsman if ever there was one, went along the same path. In 1888 he described his uncle, Dr Balfour, son of an Edinburgh manse, as "the last Englishman in Delhi" during the so-called Indian Mutiny (R. L. Stevenson, *Stevenson & the Highlands & Islands*, Creag Darach Publications, Stirling, 1992, 11).

⁵² "A popular history book": a Scottish friend, Peter Cumming from Glasgow, showed me this interesting volume.

⁵³ Some Scottish parishes were partly in one county, partly in another, so in official lists at different times some of these border parishes were said to be in different counties. Sutherland was usually credited with thirteen parishes, though it also contained part of a fourteenth (Reay); and some parishes, e.g. on the Inverness-Moray border, or the Inverness-Argyll border, appeared at different times in different county lists. In this work I have kept to the tally that was used in the Old Statistical Account of Scotland, which appeared in the 1790s. This subject is also discussed in volume two. The uncertainty as to which county contains which parishes means that different totals of the county populations are given by different authorities even as to the same year.

⁵⁴ Scotland in the 1790s had 938 parishes according to one calculation (Pryde 1962, 162 fn). Another estimate is that Scotland had 892 parishes. Trevelyan thought there were "some 900 parishes in Scotland" (Trevelyan 1946, 443), and Wikipedia said there were "871 civil parishes". Whatever is the correct figure for the total of Scottish parishes, the Highlands certainly (in my view) had 162 parishes.

7. Documentary evidence

⁵⁵ Sir Walter Scott, *Voyage of the Pharos*, Scottish Library Association, Edinburgh, (1837) 1998, 71. In volume three of this series, dealing with the Sutherland clearances, I wrote about the Reay country: "Its extreme dimensions, as near as I can calculate, were some thirty-one miles north to south, thirty-six miles west-south-west to north-east, and twenty-six miles north-west to south-east."

⁵⁶ Mitchell 1971, 79; Richards 1973, 236, & 1999, 270. James Barron, 1903-13, also thought Lord Reay owned 400,000 acres – 625 square miles. According to the *Gazetteer*, of the three parishes which made up the Reay country, Tongue had 136 square miles, Durness 230, and Eddrachillis 226 - a total of 592 square miles.

⁵⁷ Seton Gordon 1951, 288.

⁵⁸ Sinclair and Henderson, both quoted by Forbes 1976, 3.

⁵⁹ R. MacKay, *History of House & Clan of MacKay*, printed for author, A. Jack, Edinburgh 1829, 1.

⁶⁰ Scobie 1914, 8.

⁶¹ Moncreiffe 1967, 175.

⁶² O.S.A. VIII 47, Kilmallie Inv.

⁶³ N.S.A. XIV 90, Gairloch Ross.

⁶⁴ N.S.A. X 527, Fortingall Perth.

⁶⁵ O.S.A. XVII 543, & N.S.A. XIV 503, both Kilmonivaig Inv.

THE CLEARANCES IN HISTORY

[66] O.S.A. XX 401, 402, Kilmorack Inv.
[67] N.S.A. VII 469, Ardchattan Arg.
[68] N.S.A. XV 69, Farr Suth.
[69] O.S.A. X 461, Lochbroom Ross.
[70] N.S.A. XIV 445, Croy Inv.

8. *400 square miles*
[71] Lynch 1996, 364.
[72] E.g. Ardchattan ("nearly 400 square miles" – *Gazetteer*), Gairloch, Fortingall, Contin, Ardnamurchan.
[73] E.g. Glenelg, Glenorchy, Laggan, Blair Atholl.
[74] I explain elsewhere that I have taken Argyllshire to have 35 parishes, Inverness-shire 32, Ross-shire 33, and Sutherland 13 (as in the O.S.A.) – a total of 113.
[75] Here are the figures given for the number of square miles in each of the four main Highland counties by four authorities, each one offering slightly different statistics – *Nelson's Gazetteer* of 1941, the U. K. census of 1951, the *Reader's Digest Atlas* of 1965, and www.scottish-places.info. Inverness-shire and Sutherland have two different sizes; Ross & Cromarty, and Argyllshire, have three.

	Nelson 1941	Census 1951	Reader's Digest 1965	www.scottish-places.info
Argyllshire	3165 square miles	3110	3110	3255
Inverness-shire	4211	4211	4211	4232
Ross & Cromarty	3089	3089	3121	3130
Sutherland	2028	2028	2028	2126
total size of the four counties	12493	12438	12470	12743
so the average parish size, in square miles	110.56	110.07	110.35	112.77

[76] The Hebrides – that is, Lewis, Harris, the Uists, Benbecula, Barra, Skye, the Small Isles, Coll & Tiree, Mull, Colonsay & Oronsay, Jura, Islay, Gigha & Cara, plus the neighbouring islets.
[77] Website ed.ac.uk/schools-departments/history etc.
[78] Devine 1998, preface & 100.
[79] O.S.A. X 343, N.S.A. XIV 155, both Harris Inv.

9. *Sixty miles long*
[80] O.S.A. VIII 407, & N.S.A. XIV 117, both Kilmallie Inv.
[81] Smout 1970, 461.
[82] The *Gazetteer for Scotland* 2002-13 said that Kilmallie's greatest length was 29 1/8 miles, and its greatest breadth 30¼ miles.
[83] Smout 1970, 461.
[84] O.S.A. VIII 336, N.S.A. VII 83, both Glenorchy Arg.
[85] The *Gazetteer for Scotland* 2002-13 said Glenorchy's "utmost length . . . is 31½ miles", and its greatest "breadth 13 5/8 miles".
[86] Smout 1970, 461.

[87] O.S.A. IX 13, & N.S.A. VIII 89, both Buchanan Stir.
[88] Smout 1970, 461.
[89] O.S.A. VIII 547, & N.S.A. VIII 99, both Drymen Stir.

10. *Population "explosion"*
[90] Kyd 1952, 45, 47, 51, 32, & 29 fn.
[91] Sinclair 1791-9, passim; Robertson 1808, xi. If a census covered 1000 parishes, one might expect one parish to return a figure ending in 000, and ten in 00; but in the O.S.A. count of only 162 parishes, eight parish figures ended in 000, and a further twenty-two in 00. In other cases, the cumulative parish total disguised what was obviously an estimate of a significant part of the parish. In Webster's count, two parish figures ended in 000, and three in 00.

11. *"Congestion" forced out the Highlanders*
[92] Pryde 1962, 151.
[93] Fraser Darling, quoted in Richards 1985, 123.
[94] Fulton 1991, 35.
[95] Smout 1970, 358.
[96] Mitchison 1993, 180. Some writers have shown (at least in this particular) more independence of mind, and have not joined in the "population explosion" theory, e.g. P. Hume Brown in 1908, Janet Glover in 1960, Michael Brander in 1980, and P. & F. Somerset Fry in 1982. If this astonishing "population explosion" in the Highlands had ever taken place, it would be surprising that any writer could produce a history of Scotland without mentioning it.

12. *Population "doubled"*
[97] Richards 2005, 45.
[98] F. Scott Fitzgerald, *The Great Gatsby*, Penguin, London (1926) 1974, 26.
[99] Grant 1980, 33.
[100] Fry in *The Scotsman*, 7th March 2005; Fry 2001, 64.
[101] MacLeod 1996, 9.
[102] Rixson 2004, 21.
[103] Withers 2005, vii.
[104] Youngson 1973, 179.
[105] Mackie 1964, 320-1.
[106] Burke 1990, 178; Fulton 1991, 35.
[107] Dundee 1965, in Moncreiffe 1967, 251.
[108] Donaldson 1966, 48.
[109] Hamilton 1966, 73.
[110] Moncreiffe 1967, 35.
[111] Cregeen 1970, 13 & 22, & Cregeen 1964, xxviii-xxix.
[112] Mitchison 1971, 376 & 378; "The Highland population grew by over 30 per cent between 1755 and 1801", and added "50 per cent in the next forty years" (Mitchison 1971, 376); I trust any mathematicians among my readers will agree that this assertion (though, as it happens, erroneous) means the Highland population at least doubled between 1755 and 1841 (assuming that "over 30 per cent" means 33.4% or more). Elsewhere figures given by Mitchison for the "increased population" claimed between 1755 and 1801 do show a 33.9% increase.
[113] Mitchison 1990, 180, 181; Mitchison 1971, 376.
[114] Hill 1972, 51; Bumsted 1982, x, 43.
[115] Richards 1982, 34; Skye suffered from "the undeniable symptoms of overpopulation", ditto 389.
[116] Bingham 1991, 162.
[117] M. Flinn & others, editors, *Scottish Population History*, University Press, Cambridge, 1977, 30.

[118] Gardiner & Wenborn 1995, 172-3.
[119] Halliday 1996, 115.
[120] Lynch 1996, 367. See Appendix A.

13. *Almost uninhabited*
[121] Kyd 1952, passim.
[122] Richards 1985, 16, quoting Adam Smith's letter to Lord Shelburne.
[123] Adam Smith 1895, 13. Anyone talking of a "population explosion" should take account not merely of the rate of increase, but of the numbers there before the increase. If one person is living in a ten-bedroom house, and then another person also comes to live there, it could be described melodramatically as a "population explosion" of 100%; but no one could convincingly describe the house after the second person's arrival as "congested".

To put the matter briefly, the landlords cleared the Highlanders off all the wide expanse of their clan lands, allowing a few of them to become crofters in odd corners of poor land; then, having made them "congested", they blamed them for the "congestion". In later volumes the story of Strath Conon will be told; in 1802 the chief, MacKenzie of Fairburn, cleared his estate and let it to sheep farmers, with a small area left for a few of the original MacKenzies; in the 1830s half of those were driven out; in the 1840s and later, still more were ejected by the Balfours, who had bought the strath; the Balfours, naturally, copied by compliant journalists, said this was necessary because of "congestion". The story is there, at length, in volumes two and four.

[124] Henry Fielding touched on the theory behind ipse dixit history, in the process of exonerating one of his own characters in *Joseph Andrews* (O.U.P., London, [1742] 1949, 69): "I am sufficiently convinced of his innocence, having been positively assured of it, by those who received their informations from his own mouth; which, in the opinion of some moderns, is the best and indeed the only evidence." "In the opinion of some moderns", Fielding said in 1742, and it seems in the opinion of some historians in the twenty-first century.

14. *The "kingdom of Scotland"*
[125] Isaiah, xi, 6. It may be difficult for some readers, who happen to be (like the present writer) English, to accept the idea that in Scotland (and, indeed, anywhere outside England) the English are foreigners. George Mikes, in his classic work *How to be an Alien*, on pages 7 & 8, tells the story of how when he was young, in his native Hungary, he had to explain to an English girl that he could not marry her because she was a foreigner. She was indignant: she was English, she said, and he was the foreigner. "In Budapest?" said Mikes. "Certainly," she said. "Truth does not depend upon geography. If it is true in England, it is true everywhere."

15. *The Highlands conquered*
[126] Website electricscotland.com/poetry, *Song to the Breeches*.

16. *A divided Scotland*
[127] Adam/Innes 1965, 130, quoting Sir Robert Rait, former Historiographer Royal in Scotland.
[128] Trevor-Roper 1983, 15.
[129] Fry 2005, 323.
[130] Adam/Innes 1965, 130.

17. *Petty tyrants*
[131] For example Scott 1925, 39, 170, 201; Glover 1966, 93, 209; Steel 1994, 61, 120-1. Burt 2005, 191-3, said the "ordinary Highlanders" paid their chief "a blind obedience"; "they say they ought to do whatever he commands without inquiry"; "the chief exercises an arbitrary authority over his vassals"; in fact there is "an unlimited love and obedience of the Highlanders to their chiefs". Then (in the same

book, p. 112), he said he had been told that in 1715, "the then Earl of Mar [at that time a clan chief in Braemar, trying to rally his clansmen] continued here for near two months together before he could muster two hundred Highlanders, so unwilling were these poor people to leave their little houses and their families to go a king-making". So was there a "blind obedience", an "arbitrary authority", an "unlimited . . . obedience" or not? Again, Burt described how one chief had complained to him about Burt's being too generous when he paid some Highlanders for work they did for him (Burt), since when the chief was going to pay them less for some work, the clansmen had "remonstrated" with the chief, and "said he injured them" (Burt 2005, 200). So what happened to the "blind obedience"? On this point, see below, chapter three, subsection 26, *In all things subservient*. For Burt, see Appendix B.

[132] Stewart 1822, I 24, described the Highland polity: "with very few laws, and no controlling power to enforce the execution of the few they had" – except public opinion, a potent force.

18. *Crofters*
[133] Smith 1895, book five, chapter one, part two. These thoughts remind one of what Honoré de Balzac said: "The secret of great fortunes without apparent cause is a crime forgotten" (*Le Père Goriot*).

See MacKenzie 1810, 301-2: if evicted Highlanders (said MacKenzie) were allowed to break in waste ground, it would then have to be put into big farms – "For at last the rent of the land will come into view, and must be got; and it cannot be obtained but from a farmer of skill and capital." MacKenzie insisted that the very highest rent for land "must be got" – landlords had no choice in the matter. It was, apparently, a natural law, like the law of gravity, the only difference being that while gravity always operates downwards, the law of rent (at least from the point of view of the tenant) always appears to operate upwards. Michael Fry even suspects the intervention of supernatural forces: what happened in the 18th century Highlands was, it seems, the result of some spectral non-human agency, "the spontaneous emergence of a new agrarian order", and it's all the result, thinks Fry, of Adam Smith's "invisible hand". It is foolish (Fry thinks) to ascribe it to any voluntary actions of the landlords, since it was all apparently the work of some unstoppable ghostly impulse, an "invisible hand" – "landowners were no more able to resist the motions of the invisible hand than anybody else" (Fry 2005, 135). This slick supposition of a supernatural source does relieve an author of the dull drudgery needed to discover what really happened.

19. *Depended on their crops*
[134] Muir 1985, 161; Lister 1978, 20. This topic is more fully explored below, in chapter five.

20. *Land charters*
[135] Fulton 1991, 14.
[136] Trevelyan 1946, 453. N.S.A. VI 637, North Knapdale Arg., describes how the Lowland charter right was transferred from one self-important notable to another over many years without the actual possessors being disturbed – or even being aware that these lawyerly transfers were even happening.

21. *Lawless and wild*
[137] See, e.g., John Major, *Historia Majoris Britanniae*, 1521, passim.

22. *Popish clansfolk*
[138] See below, chapter seven, subsection 30, *Catholic clans*.
[139] McMillan 1969, 187, 183.
[140] Glover 1966, 193.
[141] Somerset Fry 1985, 197.
[142] See below, chapter one, subsection 58, *Less fine feelings*.
[143] Kyd 1952, passim.

23. Whisky

[144] MacCulloch 1948, 173.
[145] Simpson 1975, 23; MacLeod 1996, 188. These writers do not adduce any evidence to support their statements that the Highlanders always drank whisky. Apparently if "everybody knows" something, reportage and reasoning are both redundant.
[146] Gibson 2006, 25.
[147] George Buchanan, *History of Scotland*, 1582, I 440.
[148] Martin 1703, 202.
[149] Stewart 1822, II xiii, quoting Toland 1709, 221.
[150] Burt 2005, 86.
[151] O.S.A. XIX 29, Halkirk Caith.
[152] Stewart 1822, I 196-7 fn.
[153] *The Observer*, 20th January 2007, quoting Ranald MacDonald, who was then, the paper said, "the son of the 23rd Captain and Chief of Clan Ranald".
[154] MacKay 1889, 232.
[155] Mitchell 1971, 60.
[156] Hume Brown 1891, 264 fn.

24. Under the same roof

[157] *Farmer's Magazine*, 12th February 1815, no. LXV, Constable, Edinburgh, 1816, 46; Loch 1820, 52.
[158] Napier 1884, IV 2878, qu. 42561, John Peter.
[159] Richards 1982, 174. At the beginning of Professor Richards' paragraph, he was quoting Malcolm Gray, and it is not clear whether this thought was Gray's or Richards'; the same observation might be made as to other parts of Richards' work. These sheep, said Richards, "were not produced for the market". In view of the emphasis placed by Richards and others on the fact that the old Highlanders' staple diet was oatmeal, the reader begins to wonder what on earth the sheep were for (if they were not milked, nor eaten, nor sold). And if a Highlander had fifteen, or twenty, or a hundred sheep, how was he supposed to build a structure big enough to "house" them every night? (The question only arises if one attempts to imitate the orthodox historians, and ignore all the manifold contemporary evidence that the sheep were never housed.)
[160] Glover 1996, 94.
[161] Gaskell 1980, 9.
[162] Fry 2005, 154.
[163] Henderson 1812, 26, 103, 106.
[164] Adam 1972, II 2.
[165] Stewart 1822, I 210 fn.
[166] Miller 1854, 301-2.
[167] Selkirk 2010, 17; O.S.A. XIII 307-11, North Uist Inv.
[168] Dean Monro, *Description of the Western Isles of Scotland in 1549*, published 1582, no. 207.
[169] Odo Blundell 1909, 123, quoting Bishop Nicolson.
[170] Burt 2005, 213, 215, & 206.
[171] Walker 1980, 172.
[172] Walker 1980, 186.
[173] Walker 1808, 60.
[174] Smollett 1967, 20-1.
[175] Johnson & Boswell 1930, 361-2.
[176] Marshall 1794, 30-1 (see Youngson 1973, 16).
[177] O.S.A. XVI 229, Strath Inv.
[178] *Highlands & Highlanders*, Empire Exhibition, Glasgow, 1938, 87.
[179] Henderson 1812, 103.

[180] Burt 1998, 213.
[181] Walker 1980, 185.
[182] Youngson 1973, 29.

25. *Milked in the field*
[183] N.S.A. X 557, Fortingall Perth.
[184] N.S.A. XIV 161, North Uist Inv.
[185] Napier 1884, I 434, qu. 7565, Dr Nicol Martin.
[186] Napier 1884, I 250, qu. 4706, Rev. Donald MacKinnon.
[187] Napier 1884, I 395, qu. 6954, Peter MacKinnon. Despite these (and other) witnesses who said that the Highlanders no longer had folds in the open air to keep their cattle overnight, in a few areas the folds had not completely disappeared. The Long Island was so far from the Lowland markets for meat and wool, with the added disadvantage of a lengthy sea crossing, that the people there were not quite so much overwhelmed by the new society. It was true they were much worse off: as Alexander Carmichael told the Napier Commission, the fathers of the then Long Island generation "had more land and of better quality; they had more horses, sheep and cattle", and so on (Napier 1884, V 473); but even in the 1880s, it seems, they still had too many cattle to keep them housed. Folds were still a necessity. "Every townland has a cattle fold on the machair [pasturage, usually near the beach], and another on the gearraidh [the home pasture]" (Napier 1884, V 454), while, Carmichael added, a milkmaid with "no music in her soul", would perform "but indifferently among a fold of Highland cows" (Napier 1884, V 454).
[188] Dr D. F. MacDonald, *Scotland's Shifting Population 1770-1850*, Porcupine, Philadelphia, 1978, 35.
[189] Buchanan 1997, 67.

26. *Clan maps*
[190] See, e.g., Johnston's *Clan Map*, Johnston & Bacon, Edinburgh, 1958, and *Scotland of Old*, a clan map by Sir Iain Moncreiffe of that Ilk & Don Pottinger, John Bartholomew, Edinburgh, 1960. Other errors on clan maps appear to have been thought up with less external aid. One clan map (MacKenzie 1906, 16) gave half of the Keppoch clan territory to "Clan Ranald of Lochaber", which is, of course, simply another name for the MacDonalds of Keppoch; and it ignored the Glengarry MacDonald clan completely. And I have seen a clan map which gave the Clan Donald territory of Sleat to the MacIntyres.

27. *Scottish sentimentality*
[191] Steel 1994, 243.
[192] Smout 1970, 541.
[193] Richards 1999, 376 & 379, quoting D. McCloskey & J. Mokyr.
[194] Smout 1970, 541.
[195] Richards 1985, 128, 129, & 132.
[196] Pryde 1962, 156 fn.
[197] Gaskell 1980, v.
[198] Youngson 1973, v.

28. *Became very poor*
[199] Mackie 1978, 321.
[200] Adam/Innes 1965, 89 & 87.
[201] MacKinnon 1958, 9.
[202] Ferguson 1994, 277.
[203] Pryde 1962, 160.
[204] Smout 1970, 347.

[205] Clapperton 1983, 139.
[206] Hill 1972, 51.
[207] Cregeen 1993, 141-2.
[208] BBC website, History, *Highland Clearances*, Ross Noble.
[209] *Genealogists' Encyclopaedia*, David & Charles, Newton Abbott, 1969, 297.
[210] Andrew Newby, lecturer at the University of Aberdeen, *International Review of Scottish Studies*, volume thirty-five, 2010, 10.
[211] Youngson 1973, 181.
[212] Fry 2005, 212.
[213] Finlay 1966, 39.
[214] Mitchison 1971, 378.
[215] Richards 1982, 359; Richards 1985, 130; ditto; Richards 1985, 454; Richards 1985, 455; Richards 2005, 321-2.
[216] Richards 1985, 167, quoting Sir Iain Moncreiffe, *Scotsman*, 31st January 1977.
[217] Devine 2004, 102.

29. *Biggest bonanza*
[218] For Lord Reay, see chapter one, subsections 7, 39, 46, & 50; & chapter three, subsection 7.

30. *Transferred blame*
[219] Francis Thompson, *The Western Isles*, Batsford, London, 1988, 144.
[220] See e.g., Moncreiffe 1967, passim. Moncreiffe was not able to deny that a number of clearances did take place (he was too knowledgeable to be able to join in the present genteel theory that there never were any clearances); but he did his best to defend the landlords – he ingeniously explained each mass eviction in such a way that the chief was never at fault – the blame always rested on other shoulders.
[221] Mitchison 1971, 377.
[222] Grant 1980, 53. Two other observers claimed inaccurately that the clearances had ended by about 1850. Sir Iain Moncreiffe wrote that 1851 was "*after* the clearances" (his emphasis, Moncreiffe 1967, 35); and the Earl of Dundee wrote that in "the middle of the nineteenth century ... the 'clearances' had terminated" (letter to author, 8th April 1972). In fact some of the worst clearances took place in the 1850s, and there were further mass evictions at intervals during the rest of the century.
[223] Halliday 1996, 119.
[224] Houston & Knox 2001, 375.
[225] Neil Grant, *Scottish Clans & Tartans*, Hamlyn, 2000, 265.

31. *Voluntary emigrations*
[226] Anon. 1747, 29.

32. *"No more cultivable land"*
[227] Donnachie & Hewitt 1989, 43.
[228] Lister 1978, 19.
[229] Campbell 1977, 180.
[230] Richards 1985, 123, quoting Fraser Darling, *West Highland Survey*, 1955, 1-13.
[231] Gray 1957 (1), 60.
[232] Adam/Innes 1965, 77.
[233] Marwick 1964, 33.
[234] Rixson 2002, 109-110.
[235] Website his.com/~rory/hlndclr.html, Jamie McGrigor (Highlands and Islands, Con.). This was during a debate in the Scottish Parliament, 27th September 2000. No other member intervened to put the record straight.

[236] Finlay 1966, 38; Halliday 1996, 115.
[237] Richards 2005, 46 & 47.
[238] O.S.A. XX 481, Dunkeld Perth.
[239] Smith 1798, 182.
[240] MacDonald 1811, 259.
[241] O.S.A. III 37, Kingussie Inv.
[242] Smith 1798, 84.
[243] O.S.A. XX 476, Dowally Perth.
[244] O.S.A. XV 604, Fowlis Wester Perth.
[245] O.S.A. III 183, Lochgoilhead Arg.

33. *More than tripled*
[246] N.S.A. VIII 162-3, Luss Dumb.
[247] N.S.A. VII 295-6, Torosay Arg.
[248] N.S.A. VII 344, Kilninian Arg.
[249] N.S.A. VII 118, Ardnamurchan Arg.
[250] N.S.A. X 353, Callander Perth.
[251] N.S.A. XIV 415, Petty Inv.
[252] N.S.A. XIV 79, Kingussie Inv.
[253] N.S.A. XIV 455, Croy Inv.
[254] N.S.A. XIV 248, Fodderty Ross.
[255] N.S.A. XIV 68, Killearnan Ross; Loch 1820, appendix VII, 67.
[256] N.S.A. XIV 376, Urquhart & Logie Wester Ross.
[257] N.S.A. VII 653, Kilchoman Arg.
[258] N.S.A. X 642, Moulin Perth.
[259] N.S.A. XIV 197, South Uist Inv.

34. *Massacre of Glen Coe*
[260] *The Scotsman*, 9th October 2013. The only Englishman who might be given a place among this otherwise homogeneous group of Scotsmen was Colonel Hill, governor of Fort William: he was old, ill, and thought to be not very keen on the plan (Linklater 1982, 106).
[261] Seton Gordon 1951, 53; Seton Gordon 1963, 230-1.
[262] George Eyre-Todd, *The Highland Clans of Scotland*, Appleton, New York, 1923, I 259.
[263] A. Wainwright, *Wainwright in Scotland*, Michael Joseph & BBC, London, 1988, 135.

35. *Clearance of Glen Coe*
[264] Wordsworth 1894, 173.
[265] Sarah Murray, *Companion to Scotland*, 2nd edition, 1803. Despite the clear evidence that Glen Coe was empty before the turn of the century, the continual talk of congestion and overcrowding makes some writers reluctant to accept that this was the case. One author wrote inaccurately that despite the massacre, "the population of the Glen actually increased and by the end of the eighteenth century there was a problem of over-population" (T. Hunter, *Guide to the West Highland Way*, Constable, London, 1979, 114). In fact, by then the glen was almost empty; the humans had been replaced by sheep.
[266] Stewart 1822, II 116.
[267] Thomson 1788, 134; Thomson 2010, 40.
[268] Arthur Young, *Annals of Agriculture*, London, XX 314, article by Kerr Richardson.
[269] Linklater 1982, 154.
[270] Fraser-Mackintosh 1897, 214; MacDonald 1994, 237. This whole topic is canvassed fully in *Glencoe and Beyond*, by Iain S. Macdonald, 2005, e.g. 104.

[271] Richard Porson, article in the *Oxford D.N.B.* Porson (1759-1808) was a poor boy from the village of East Ruston in Norfolk, not far from where this account is being written, who became probably the greatest classical scholar of his time. He was prominent enough to be mentioned by Dickens, in *Nicholas Nickleby*, chapter four – "Porson was an odd-looking man, and so was Doctor Johnson; all these bookworms are"; and by George Eliot in *Middlemarch*, chapter fifty-seven, where a character wanted to be "a regenerate Porson".

36. *The English were responsible*
[272] Website, islesproject.wordpress.com/2007/11/22/1746-onward-the-highland-clearances; Mathieson 2000, 4; website tlio.org.uk/the-cries-of-the-never-born-the-highland-clearances.

37. *The sheep farmers were Lowlanders*
[273] Donaldson 1993, 168.
[274] Smout 1970, 350.
[275] Youngson 1974, 29.
[276] Halliday 1996, 117.
[277] Finlay 1966, 38.
[278] MacKenzie 1908, 311, & MacKenzie 1949, 273-4.
[279] Adam/Innes 1965, 78.
[280] Moncreiffe 1967, 35.
[281] Prebble 1971, 57-8.
[282] MacLeod 1996, 8; Bumsted 1982, 209.
[283] Campbell 1985, 133.
[284] Lister 1978, 20; Andrew Kerr, a Lowland expert, visited Sutherland in 1791, and said the Sutherlanders "know nothing about sheep, or the management of them", Richards 2005, 124. This was untrue, since the Highlanders had always kept sheep. Perhaps he meant that the Sutherlanders knew nothing about making money from a commercial sheep farm, a much severer criticism.
[285] Fraser-Mackintosh 1865, 299. Iain MacDonald (MacDonald 2005, 4) adjudged that "in the late eighteenth and early nineteenth centuries most commercial sheep farming in the Highlands was undertaken by Highlanders".

38. *2000 families at a time*
[286] This quotation is word for word from *The Scotsman*, 13th September 2005; the same wording also appeared on the *Earth Changes* website in 2007.
[287] Websites: highlandclearances.info/clearances; members.aol.com/Skyewrites; rfs.scotshome.com; & tartansauthority.com.
[288] MacLeod 1892, 20.
[289] Adam 1972, II 213.
[290] Richards 1982, 330, 342.

39. *Glenorchy clearances*
[291] MacKenzie 1986, 348, 361.

40. *Forbidden to speak Gaelic*
[292] Schama 2001, 386. When minority populations (and almost every European country has one or more minorities) can almost all speak the majority language nearly as well as their own, then certainly the state can and does display hostility towards the minority language (cf. Welsh and of course Gaelic in Britain, Breton and Basque in France, Basque and Catalan in Spain, Austrian in Italy, Greek in Albania, Turkish in Greece and Bulgaria, Hungarian in Romania, and so on); but that was not the position in 1750 in the Highlands, since at that time very few Gaels could speak any English at all (as

Dr Johnson found in 1773). So it would appear impossible to "forbid the speaking of Gaelic". Professor Schama is, of course, an eminent historian at a leading American university, a successful journalist, a well-known broadcaster, and the author of many authoritative tomes, so I thought it not improbable that he had found material inaccessible to me (that would be not at all surprising); I therefore sent him an e-mail at Columbia University, on 2nd September 2010, asking why he had said Gaelic was forbidden. Having received no reply, I sent a further e-mail in case the first one had not arrived. I have still not received any answer. Of course we must all take many facts on trust, as it were; that could be argued as a perfectly justifiable proceeding when the "fact" is not improbable on the face of it – such as Parliament passing an Act, or two states going to war. But the allegation that all speech, all communication, was (apparently successfully) forbidden among perhaps three hundred thousand people across half of Scotland, is prima facie so unlikely that one is surprised to find the idea being accepted without further investigation. According to *The Times* of 7th September 2013, "Simon Schama has never lacked chutzpah: he admits that he began his *History of Britain* knowing next to nothing about it." If that were the case, it would surely be advisable to employ the archive of the head to test all the allegations that this or that happened at a certain time in the past (however often such allegations appeared in successive history books); if that had been done, it would have been seen that no regime, however harsh, would ever injure itself by trying to forbid all human speech.

[293] Somerset Fry 1985, 197.

[294] Fallow 1999, 86.

[295] The Wikipedia entry for "History of Scotland" said that after Culloden "all aspects of Highland culture including the language were forbidden on pain of death". Does this mean that Highlanders were forbidden to tell any of the host of Gaelic stories? – or sing any Gaelic song? – or join in any Highland dance? And if so, how was it supposed to be enforced? An army of Edinburgh spies pretending to play the fiddle at every Highland ceilidh? Observers should really learn to use the archive of the head.

[296] J. Sharkey, *Road Through the Isles*, Wildwood, Aldershot, 1986, 59.

[297] Way & Squire 1994, 20.

[298] Ross 1998, 237.

[299] Schama 2001, 386.

41. *No mass graves*

[300] Fry 2005 (2).

[301] Some definitions of famine: Chambers Dictionary, 1993, "extreme general scarcity of food"; Oxford Modern English Dictionary, 1992, "extreme scarcity of food"; Thorndike English Dictionary, 1948, "lack of food in a place"; New English Dictionary, 1932, "distressing scarcity of food"; Modern English Illustrated Dictionary, 1920, "an extreme dearth"; The Russell English Dictionary, n.d., "extreme dearth; great scarcity". (No mention of skeletons.) Any commentator will have a hard task on hand if he seeks to make so many dictionary-makers change their definitions.

[302] Christine O'Keeffe's *Tartan History* website: as a result of the famine, "by 1847 . . . untold millions of Highlanders were dead". Another thought from the same website: "Sir Walter Scott's propaganda on Highland culture . . . is called Balmoralism after King George IV's coronation at Balmoral Castle in 1822." And, equally inaccurate: in 1746, "land was taken away again from the Highland chiefs who did not give allegiance to the crown and given to new owners under Heritable Jurisdictions Act. The few remaining Highland landlords had no option but to accede to English domination."

[303] *The Scotsman*, 12th August 2013, 304. This belief has served some Scotsmen well. The author knew a man who left Glasgow at fifteen to go to sea – though he kept his accent unadulterated till he died. He became in due course, among other things, a shantyman on some of the old sailing vessels before the First World War (his version of "In Plymouth Town there lived a maid" differed in some respects from that sung in a thousand primary schools). Down on his luck in New York in the Great Depression of the early 1930s, he was lining up for a free handout of soup and bread, and by chance chatting to the

man next to him, when a passer-by turned back and spoke to him. "D'you wanna job?" The passer-by had heard his Scottish accent, and under the impression that anyone from Scotland must be of irreproachable rectitude, he (being a banker) made my friend a bank-messenger, carrying around thousands of dollars between branches of the bank, as demand rose and fell. Fortunately my acquaintance (Jack Kilgour) was rigidly honest, and stayed working for the bank till he retired. "Ah didnae tell him aboot the Glasgae race-course gangs", Kilgour remarked when recounting the story.

[304] See below, chapter six, subsection 34.

42. *The duke did it*

[305] Lord Ronald Gower, *Reminiscences*, Kegan Paul, London, 1883, 65-6.

[306] Youngson 1973, 178.

[307] MacLeod 1996, 191.

[308] Prebble 1971, 57.

[309] Finlay 1966, 39.

[310] Mitchison 1971, 377.

[311] Adam 1972, I 226, & I 227.

[312] Eric Evans, *British History Handbook*, Hodder & Stoughton, London, 1998, 191; Moncreiffe 1967, 35.

[313] MacDonell 1937, 41 (line 5-6, line 10).

[314] This is an open invitation to readers to find mistakes in my work, of course. But as I said earlier, the disagreements I have expressed with many other authors make it certain that any errors in what I have written will doubtless soon be revealed in rapid retaliation.

43. *Common blood and speech*

[315] Magnusson 2000, which has 734 pages. See also, for example, Fisher 2002 (another book supposedly giving the "history of Scotland") in which the clearances are mentioned once, (on page 180) – "the Highlands, where the clearances, with their emphasis on sheep farming and the removal of tenants, were now having a profound effect"; the only mention of the final fate of the people who once occupied more than half of Scotland's land-area.

[316] Green 1945, 673-4.

[317] *Atlas of British and Irish History*, Penguin, London, 2001, 149.

[318] Oscar Wilde, *The Works*, Collins, London, (1948) 1960, 89.

[319] George Orwell, *Animal Farm*, Penguin, London, (1945) 1982, 114. "All animals are equal, but some animals are more equal than others" – the slogan produced by the pigs when they seized power as a new ruling class, and took over what had been Animal Farm, at the end of the book. With this slogan, was Orwell pointing out that in our system of politics and economics, everyone is theoretically equal at the ballot box, but that in routine reality some of us are more equal than others? If Orwell was alive today, he might have been tempted to produce a new slogan; "We are all in this together, but some of us are more in it than others."

Orwell wrote *Animal Farm* in 1943-4, during the second World War, when he lived at 10A Mortimer Crescent, London NW6, just south of the railway line from South Hampstead to Queens Park. At that time I lived just north of it, at 13A Priory Terrace, London NW6; during air-raids a mobile cannon, "a naval gun" as it was described locally, used to fire at enemy aircraft from this railway line – the noise of the gun was even more terrifying to me than the sound of the bombs. In June 1944 a flying bomb wrecked Orwell's house (he had to dig about among the rubble to find the manuscript of *Animal Farm* – luckily he succeeded); it also blew out all the windows at the front of our house. (Another flying-bomb later blew out all our windows at the back.) That one of "our" flying-bombs, the Mortimer Crescent one, had "bombed out" George Orwell, was a fact I only found out about many years afterwards, of course.

44. *Illuminating the present*
[320] Articles by Margaret I. Adam in the *Scottish Historical Review*: *The Highland Emigration of 1770*, volume sixteen, 1919, 280; *The Causes of the Highland Emigrations of 1783-1803*, volume seventeen, 1920, 73; *The Eighteenth-Century Highland Landlords and the Poverty Problem*, volume nineteen, 1921-2, 1 & 161.
[321] Such as Smout 1969, 541; Richards 1982, 141, & 1985, 105-11; Hill 1972, 51; Hamilton 1966, 73 note 1; Professor Marwick, *Economic Developments in Victorian Scotland*, Allen & Unwin, London, 1936, 135, & *Scotland in Modern Times*, Frank Cass, London, 1964, 32; Dr Harper, *Canadian Migration Patterns*, ed. B. J. Messamore, University Press, Ottawa, 2004, 17. In the *Journal of Scottish Historical Studies*, May 1984, Professor Richards reviewed Professor Bumsted's *People's Clearance*, University Press, Edinburgh, 1982. He praised Bumsted's conclusions that "Highland emigration pre-dated the sheep clearances". "Nor . . . were the emigrants the hapless prey of landlord pressures or sheep evictions." Bumsted's work "extends the thesis long ago constructed by Margaret Adam (and never fully confronted in the literature)"; but Richards did not examine the interesting question why Adam was "never fully confronted", or why he himself (for example) "never fully confronted" her.
[322] J. G. Leith, *Man who went to Farr*, Baseline Research, Aberdeen, 2010, 138; also in Richards 1985, 119.
[323] M. Fry, article in *The Herald*, Glasgow, 16th May 2000.
[324] Lewis Carroll, *Through the Looking Glass*, Macmillan, London (1871) 1940, 125.
[325] Charles Dickens, *Great Expectations*, Nelson, London, (1861) n.d., 248.

45. *Out of all proportion*
[326] *The Herald*, Glasgow, 16th May 2000.
[327] See the *History of the C.P.S.U.(B.)*, Cobbett, London, (1939) 1943, said to be the work of Stalin, in which history is re-written wholesale.
[328] Gordon Donaldson, quoted by Gibson 2006, 20, & Prebble 1986, 41. Originally in the *Sunday Standard*, 3rd May 1981.
[329] M. Linklater, *The Times*, 23rd January 2003.
[330] M. Linklater, *The Times*, 9th March 2005. I should make it clear that Mr Linklater was not the chairman of the Scottish Arts Council when it refused a grant to this work. The council was able to keep a tight grip on what is allowed to be known about Scottish history without the aid of Mr Linklater. But the fact that someone who thinks that the idea that there were any Highland clearances is "largely a myth" could actually be made chairman of the Scottish Arts Council perhaps conveys all that anyone needs to know about the present Scottish arts establishment. Liberty of opinion is invaluable; but how far would the Scottish Arts Council, or its successor, Creative Scotland, go? Would it appoint someone as chairman who seriously thought that St Giles was a Roman Catholic oratory, or that Swindon was the capital of Scotland? It would be interesting to know how far freedom of thought is allowed to override all other considerations. Would an atheist expect to be made Archbishop of Canterbury?
[331] An article in *The Scotsman*, 27th January 2003.
[332] Major C. J. Shaw of Tordarroch, letter to the author, 14th December 1968: "I often think that the horrors of these happenings are overstressed for only a small part [of the Highlands] was involved."
[333] Evander MacIver, quoted in Richards 1973, 279. MacIver said that it was not only in Sutherland that recruiting was difficult in the Crimean War: "the same aversion exists all over the North and in Districts from which no removals were made."
[334] Richards 1985, "parts" 111, "areas" 132, "zones" 172. See also Richards 1973, 254, where the author regretted the absence of "studies of cleared and uncleared areas", invoking, of course, the obvious question – why doesn't he do it, since he clearly knows where they are?
[335] Richards 1985, 173. Richards also quoted Moncreiffe to the effect that there were "numerous Highland estates where no clearances took place". Unfortunately Richards spelled his name "Moncrieff" – which probably pained that gentleman, who made a career out of the reverent treatment

of armorial exactitudes, as much as Richards' support for the "estates which never cleared" theory pleased him (Richards 1985, 167-8). So rare is unalloyed pleasure in this world.

[336] Earl of Dundee, letter to the author, 8th April 1972.

[337] Hon. R. M. Sinclair, son of Lord Thurso, letter to the author, 5th December 1968.

[338] Moncreiffe 1967, 36.

[339] Moncreiffe, *The Scotsman*, 31st January 1977; quoted in Richards 1985, 168.

[340] Moncreiffe 1967, 36.

[341] Moncreiffe 1967, 172. Moncreiffe complained (Richards 1985, 168) that "nobody has yet bothered to publish a study of the numerous Highland estates where no clearances took place"; again, the complaint invites the response that surely Moncreiffe himself, with his specialized knowledge of these otherwise unidentified districts, should have attempted the study. The way this particular grievance is phrased takes us at once into the effortless world of the celebrities, where a well-known "name" has only to write a study for a number of publishers to compete with each other in offering to bring it out – a world as alien to most of us as that other sphere of orthodox history where no clearances ever took place (according to some of the same celebrities).

One writer has claimed that so far from landlords having cleared every part of the Highlands, some areas "cleared themselves" – "the districts not cleared have since largely cleared themselves", said an editorial in *The Scotsman*, 8th January 1977 (Richards 1985, 168). (It takes a considerable degree of effrontery to claim that a "district" can "clear itself"; it would be a particularly brazen burglar who would dare to assert at his trial, "the houses I did not burgle have since largely burgled themselves", or a particularly impudent S.S. man who claimed, "the gypsies we did not kill have since largely killed themselves".) This editorial was, it seems, written by Michael Fry (Fry 2005, xii), who had been given while still very young a prominent journalistic position on one of Scotland's leading papers: his fervent devotion to Highland landlordism had clearly been no hindrance to his progress – perhaps, indeed, it helped to prove his suitability to write regular articles in the newspapers telling their readers what to think. Later Fry's theories moved still further forward. In the 1977 editorial he had tried to give a sympathetic explanation as to why the Highland landlords carried out clearances ("the main motive of the Sutherlands", and "of the many other landlords who followed the same course", that is, who also cleared their lands, "was to improve the wretched condition of the people on their estates"); subsequently, he apparently persuaded himself (and tried to persuade the rest of us) that the clearances – practically – never happened. If he had come to this pleasing conclusion earlier, he could simply have said that as far as "the Sutherlands" and "the many other landlords who followed the same course" were concerned, there was nothing that needed explaining away.

46. Areas exonerated

[342] Dr Marjory Harper, senior lecturer, Aberdeen University, *Scotland on Sunday*, 12th January 2003. Thus easily were the MacIntosh, the Grant, the Gordon, the Farquharson, the Ogilvy, the eastern Perthshire, and other, clearances disposed of.

[343] Finlay 1976, 24: "the miserable remnants of many a clan were driven off with extreme cruelty by the agents in those clearances, although it should be said here that the Central Highlands suffered much less than the west and north." The details of the Fraser, Chisholm, MacPherson, Keppoch, Cameron (and so on) clearances will be given in due course, and the reader will then be able to see whether this statement is justified.

[344] Collier 1953, 38. Collier felt that Caithness was "practically unaffected by the collapse of the clan system", and thought that in the Highlands generally there had been an "excess of attention paid to the Highland clearances of the late eighteenth and early nineteenth centuries". Many authors have manfully attempted to remedy this so-called "excess of attention".

However, Collier was surprisingly honest in his definition of the clearances as "the expropriation of the greater part of the original possessors of the land". (Collier 1953, 38).

Mitchison 1971, 377, admitted there had been clearances in Caithness, but said they were done "with consideration and skill", and "little real hardship was caused". So Professor Mitchison asks us to visualize people being driven from their homes and farms with "consideration and skill", in such a way as to cause "little real hardship". This view was shared by Lord Burton (i.e., the then Baillie of Dochfour) who wrote: "I believe that there were instances when the Clearances could have been shown to be beneficially and humanely executed" (letter to author, 9th December 1968). One can only conclude that some of those who have given us their opinions on the clearances appear to have no imagination. As Bernard Shaw said, in the epilogue to *St Joan*, "Must then a Christ perish in torment in every age to save those that have no imagination?"

[345] Smout 1970, 353. In fact, in the 1820s alone there were probably clearances in every last parish in the Hebrides, apart of course from the many Hebridean clearances before and after that date. Volume four of this work gives ample details. It is a fact those who deny or minimize the clearances have naturally more influence in the academic and publishing spheres than I have, and therefore find it easier to disseminate their views, however groundless they may be.

[346] Hill 1972, 51. It seems likely that Hill was taking his information from Smout, whom he quotes occasionally: Smout's book (see above) was published three years earlier. Hill was a Canadian, born in Manitoba and brought up in Saskatchewan (I was born, to English parents, in Saskatchewan, and my family moved thereafter to Manitoba – and thence to England, whose shores I reached at the mature age of nearly four). Hill lived as an adult in England, where in a writing career of some forty-two years, he wrote about sixty books (or three books every two years). This showed tremendous industry; but of course when he wrote about Highland history he could scarcely have been expected to have the time for much extensive research. So it may be that he took Professor Smout's word (in fact improving on it) for what had happened in the Hebrides after 1815, and that Smout's "there is little hint" of any clearance during about fifteen years except on three islands, became Hill's clearances "in a limited way" on only two islands over a much longer period. It does appear to show that a "fact" may gain approval, and may as it were be strengthened, by simple repetition. It seems that truth, as generally understood, could be defined as any statement which is repeated many times.

[347] Hamilton 1966, 72. Professor Richards said Professor Hamilton "devoted half a century to the study of Scottish economic history" (Richards 1985, 111), but it is hard to see how Hamilton can have failed to observe the evidence as to the clearing of Rum for a sheep farmer, even in the briefest glance at the subject. It does appear that occasionally historians praise each other on inadequate grounds (a practice apparently known in the trade as "log-rolling"). Still, it makes a welcome change from them praising the Highland landlords.

[348] Muir 1985, 158.
[349] Richards 1985, 499.
[350] Murray 1973, 221.
[351] MacCulloch 1905, 219 fn.
[352] Prebble 1971, 198.
[353] Smout 1970, 466.
[354] Devine 2004, 316.
[355] "Atque omne ignotum pro magnifico est": Tacitus, *Agricola*, 30.

47. *No evictions on this estate*
[356] 11th Duke of Argyll, letter to author, 16th March 1969.
[357] Hill 1972, 49.
[358] Smout 1970, 357.
[359] Simon Fraser, 15th Lord Lovat, letter to author, 30th November 1968.
[360] Moncreiffe 1967, 36.
[361] Moncreiffe, *The Scotsman* 31st January 1977, quoted Richards 1985, 168.
[362] MacLean 1995, 229.

THE CLEARANCES IN HISTORY

[363] Gibson 1985, 10.
[364] Napier 1884, IV 2887, qu. 42703, John Peter. (Fraser-Mackintosh, "There were a good many evictions in the old times?" John Peter: "I don't know. I never heard of them.")
[365] Brand Commission, P.P. 1895, XXXVIII, John Peter, Lovat's factor.
[366] Moncreiffe 1967, 125.
[367] Grant 1984, 25.
[368] Lord Strathspey, letter to the author, 3rd December 1968. He said, referring to the clearances – "It seemed to have been a general landowners' practice at one time. But I cannot be convinced that the Grants were major offenders. I have never heard that they were."
[369] Website clangrant.org.
[370] Gibson 1985, 10.
[371] Gibson 2006, 55.
[372] Neil Gunn, quoted by Sorley MacLean, MacLean & Carrell 1986, 10.
[373] J. P. Grant of Rothiemurchus, letter to the author, 28th November 1968: "So far as I am aware, there were no clearances of crofters from this Estate, and this may to some extent be corroborated by the fact that my family did not go in for sheep farming, which was the usual reason given for the clearances."

48. *Choosing poverty*
[374] Smout 1970, 357.
[375] Hill 1972, 49.
[376] Seton Gordon 1951, 288.
[377] Richards 1982, 287.
[378] Richards 1985, 455. It is extraordinary (and it tells us much of his mindset) to see how Professor Richards talks of landlords "supporting their people", when in the real world it is manifestly "the people" – the tenants – who support their landlords. Who pays rent, and who receives it? Who gets an income from working on the land, and who gets an income from merely owning it?
[379] Fry 2005, 170.
[380] Prebble 1971, 161.
[381] Grimble 1962, 25, & see 152; Grimble 1980, 242, & see 254-5, 256.
[382] Atkinson 1987, 143 & 145; Atkinson 1999, 52 & 53. Atkinson 1999 was the 12th edition since 1986; so presumably everyone who read the book agreed that Lord Reay did not clear his estate; or if they did know they did not tell the publisher; or if they did tell the publisher the information was ignored. One of these three possible conclusions must be true.

The same reasoning applies to Professor Smout's book, *A History of the Scottish People*, 1560-1830, in which he alleges that Lord Reay "resisted the urge" to clear his lands, but finally was forced to sell to the Sutherland family, who had "less fine feelings"; so obviously Lord Reay was never guilty of evictions. From the various copies of this book in my possession, I observe that there were at least two hardback editions, 1979 and 1980; that it appeared in paperback in 1985, and was then "reprinted six times" up to 1998 – which means apparently nine editions at that point. Lord Reay's clearance of the Reay country is no secret, except perhaps in deferential academic circles, but (as with the Atkinson book) either the readers of Professor Smout's book (like Professor Smout) had not heard of the Reay clearances, or none of them told the publisher, or the publisher took no notice. The thoughtful seeker after truth can choose his or her most probable explanation.

If anyone wishes to know what happened in the Reay country at this time, volume three in this series (when – or I should say if – it is ever published) has about 10,000 words on the subject, including a detailed account of Lord Reay's activities, and the observations made by the supporters, and by the opponents, of Lord Reay. For the serious researcher, there is no difficulty in finding out the fate of the MacKays in the Reay country.

49. *Never heard of them*

[383] Napier 1884, III 2537-2540, evidence of William Sutherland Fraser (82), factor of Lady Matheson, then the proprietor of Gruids, the estate formerly owned by Colonel Innes Munro of Poyntzfield. Poyntzfield had ordered clearances on the estate in 1808, 1820, and 1821; the 1820 and 1821 evictions had resulted in riots; in 1821 the army had to be brought to complete the clearance, leading to arrests and prison sentences. William Fraser said he had known the estate since 1823, only two years after the final riotous clearance, when many of those ejected must still have been in the district (p. 2539, qu. 39456); and he had actually been the factor of the estate since 1833; but claimed he had "never heard" of any evictions. His father had indeed been a sheep farmer on the Gruids estate, and so was in occupation of the land from which the small tenants had been removed. As factor, Fraser had all the estate papers under his hand, in which the changes in tenantry in the three successive clearances must have been clearly itemized and located; the clearances must have been (and were) the talk of the neighbourhood for many years – when David Craig went there in the 1980s (160 years or more after the sensational events), researching for his book *On the Crofters' Trail*, the locals told him what had happened: yet the factor of the Gruids estate, in the 1880s, a century earlier, when question about the Gruids evictions, said firmly, "I never heard of them. There may have been, but I never heard of them" (p. 2539, qu. 39462.) As with many other factorial (and landlordly) pronouncements, both to the Napier Commission and to the world at large, the reader must decide what language would best describe Fraser's veracity. The everyday phrase which first springs to mind is "bare-faced lying". It is strange that any historian could deal with the Napier Commission evidence without expressing surprise at (e.g.) the solemn testimony of William Sutherland Fraser, who held a highly responsible position not only in estate management but in the public law-enforcement regime – he was the local procurator-fiscal (i.e., the public prosecutor). One wonders what his attitude would have been towards people who told blatant falsehoods during official investigations. No doubt Fraser would have enjoyed reading articles boldly entitled "Clearances? What Clearances?" written by modern experts.

[384] Moncreiffe 1967, 36.

[385] Earl of Cromartie, letter to author, 2nd December 1968.

[386] MacLean 1995, 229.

[387] Richards 1973 (2), 150.

[388] Murray 1968, 305.

[389] W. C. MacKenzie of Gairloch, letter to author, no date (probably 1968): "To the best of my knowledge there have never been clearances on the lands owned [!] by the MacKenzies of Gairloch from 1494 to the present day."

[390] Atkinson 1987, 106.

[391] Strang 1975, 85.

[392] Gibson 2006, 46.

50. *No tenants removed*

[393] Ferguson 1994, 277.

[394] Richards 1985, 137. Professor Richards was able to bolster his tribute to the Seaforths by quoting Dr Ferguson, who (Richards wrote) "drew attention to the poor condition of some districts, for example Lewis under the Seaforths, which were not cleared"; so both Richards and Ferguson ignored the voluminous evidence of the Seaforth evictions in Lewis.

[395] J. P. Day (Day 1918, 182) wrote, "The trouble [in the 1880s] was most serious in Lewis and Skye, and, in one respect, this is rather curious, since there had been practically no evictions in Lewis . . ." Like many other "curious" problems in history, this one becomes "curious" only if the full facts are not known or ignored. Admittedly, in those parts of the Highlands where the native Highlanders had been cleared out completely, there were no disturbances in the 1880s. Where there was no one left to complain, there were no complaints: a most satisfactory termination. From that point of view, the proprietors of many districts in the central and eastern Highlands had done a more efficient job, since

they had driven out the Highlanders more thoroughly (having no kelp shores to tempt them to retain some of the aboriginal inhabitants).
[396] MacKenzie 1986, 312.
[397] Murray 1969, 186.
[308] Murray 1973, 226.
[399] Smout 1997, 70.
[400] Adam/Innes 1965, 87.
[401] Napier 1884, II 893, qu. 13942, William MacKay.
[402] Napier 1884, V 161.
[403] John Knox, *A Tour through the Highlands & Hebrides in 1786*, J. Walter, London, 1787, 125.
[404] Atkinson 1987, 48.
[405] Dunlop 1987, 24.
[406] Mathieson 2000, 9-10. Francis' elder brother, Thomas, held the estate as a young man for two years, 1781-83; he was an army officer, and became colonel of the Seaforth Highlanders in 1781 (succeeding his cousin as chief, as landlord, and as colonel) before being killed in a sea battle near Bombay in 1783. Perhaps Thomas is the elusive "Seaforth" who is credited with having been against clearances; but in his brief reign he had little opportunity to show whether he was for or against them. During the short time that Thomas owned the estate he was never in Scotland, or even in Great Britain; when he succeeded his cousin he was already en route to India with the Seaforth Highlanders (the voyage across the Atlantic and Indian Oceans took eleven months, May 1781 to April 1782), and then on active service in India. The fact that he never got around to ordering any clearances, unlike other landlords at the time, and unlike his own successors, may have led his clansfolk blissfully to conclude that he opposed them: the ordinary clanspeople were always willing to think the best of their chief. (We may think they were foolish to do so: but in fact they were only guilty of applying ways of thinking – which had grown up in clan society – to situations which arose out of the new individualistic procedures which had come to the Highlands after 1746, and which therefore were, to say the least, no longer appropriate.)

51. *Never sullied*
[407] Grant 1953, 29. Dr Grant's absolution was naturally quoted by Moncreiffe (Moncreiffe 1967, 69) to prove that there had never been any clearances on the lands owned by MacLeod of MacLeod. In Dr Grant's book, *The Clan MacLeod*, she told her readers all about the flag which the elfin folk conferred upon the MacLeod chief, but nothing about any evictions. The arrival of the fairy flag was more important than the departure of the MacLeod clanspeople. Professor Richards (in another bout of log-rolling) said that Dr Grant "brought to the study of change in the Highlands a convincing measure of realism" (Richards 1985, 112). "Realism" here may mean "political correctness", or perhaps "history acceptable to landlords". It seems that the fairies were more "real" than the clearances.
[408] Joan Wolrige Gordon, daughter of (& p.p.) Dame Flora MacLeod of MacLeod, letter to author, 2nd December 1968: "We have always been very proud of the fact that there were no Clearances on the MacLeod Estate – though of course there was emigration."
[409] Richards 1985, 471.
[410] *The Independent*, 17th March 2007, obituary of John MacLeod, 29th of MacLeod. This significantly used Dr Grant's phrase, "never sullied", to describe the history of the MacLeod estates and the claimed absence of clearances. It may well be that the writer of the obituary looked up, and repeated, the opinions of the "experts". (Whether this redounds more to the credit of the obituary-writer or to that of the "experts" is a moot point.) So do myths persist.
[411] Napier 1884, V 28, Appendix A; Donaldson 1920, quoted by Cooper 1970, 15; Swire 1952, 118; Grant 1953, 27, 29; Darling 1955, 8; Glover 1966, 226; Dundee 1965, quoted by Moncreiffe 1967, 251; Murray 1966, 19; Moncreiffe 1967, 37; Sillar & Meyler 1973, 109; Murray 1973, 224; Donaldson 1993, 170; Devine 1980, 86; Grimble 1980, 255; Richards 1982, 385; Steel 1985, 299; Smout 1986, 62; Halliday 1996, 119; Keay & Keay 1994, 785; MacLean 1995, 229; MacLeod 1996, 201, 198; Fry 2005, 211;

Linklater 2007, email to author; website dunvegancastle.com; website castlegatewebdesign.com; website Clan MacLeod Society of Scotland.

[412] Duirinish was MacLeod-controlled, so "it escaped the clearances of other parts of Skye": website theclearances.org (which otherwise is full of invaluable information about Highland history).

[413] P.P. 1895, XXXVIII 49, & ditto 134.

[414] MacLeod 1997, 12.

[415] Richards 1985, 206 & 216.

[416] MacLean 1995, 229 et al. The difference of opinion as to which landlord family was most blameless or most culpable, the MacLeods or the MacDonalds, may be settled by Dr James Hunter's comment (Hunter 2000, 291): between these two families "there is little to choose as far as numbers of evictions are concerned".

[417] Ruaraidh Hilleary, letter in *West Highland Free Press*, undated.

[418] Napier 1884, I 223, qu. 4226, & I 226, qu. 4277.

[419] Letter to author from R. M. B. MacAlister of Glenbarr, 6th December 1968.

[420] Napier 1844, I 223, qu. 4225, Donald MacKinnon; Napier 1884, V 44, Appendix A XIII, Rev. D. MacKinnon.

52. *Firmly opposed*

[421] Moncreiffe 1967, 172.

[422] Moncreiffe 1954, 21.

[423] Moncreiffe 1967, 36.

[424] Robert MacNeill of Barra, letter to author, 28th December 1968: "From all that I have gleaned in our clan history, my predecessors were in the unique position of being firmly opposed to 'the clearances' and emigration of all kinds . . . I feel quite safe in stating that *all emigration* of Barra folk has been wholly voluntary" (original emphasis).

[425] Muir 1985, 175.

[426] Earl of Moray, letter to author, 1st Jan 1969: "Undoubtedly there were hardships, often severe, caused to a number of crofters or farmers or whatever one may call them but I get the impression that the majority had their conditions and position improved in the end . . . I believe there were cases here where a few were moved from very poor land . . ." etc. The clearance (for example) of the MacIntoshes by the then Earl of Moray in 1819 is, however, well known.

[427] Letter to author from the secretary of the Duke of Richmond & Gordon, 2nd December 1968: "I am afraid that we appear to have no records of any part having been played by the Duke's ancestors in the Scottish Highland Clearances and regret that we are therefore unable to assist you."

[428] Dunlop 1955, 27.

[429] L. Mackintosh of Mackintosh, letter to author, 8th December 1968: "I can say that there is no tradition in the Inverness area of any discreditable 'clearances' by my predecessors. Having always believed this lack of tradition to be correct, nevertheless, since getting your letter I have checked it from three quite separate living local historical sources as well as reference books."

[430] Dunlop 1960, 30.

[431] C. J. Shaw of Tordarroch, letter to author, 14th December 1968: "In Inverness-shire, our Strathnairn lands of Tordarroch had been taken over by our cousins, The Mackintosh, to be again regained recently. No clearances took place there."

53. *Certainly no clearances*

[432] Sir Ivar Colquhoun of Luss, letter to author, 29th November 1968: "There is no record of my forebears having much to do with the clearances. There were certainly no clearances here as it was never a crofting county and Glasgow, being only 25 miles away, absorbed any surplus population." (This letter could be interpreted to mean that the only Highlanders who were cleared were crofters; in fact it was the original Highland joint-farmers who suffered in the primary evictions. It also seems to

indicate a belief that in Luss any Highlanders who felt they formed a "surplus population" left voluntarily to wallow in the delights of the Glasgow slums.)

[433] 7th Duke of Montrose, letter to author 17th February 1969: "I am not aware that my predecessors had any part in the Highland clearances, in fact, my many Highland friends have always been at pains to assure [me] that the Montroses had a clean bill of health on this score. I would imagine this to be true as I don't think the family lands, with a possible exception of the bare slopes of Ben Lomond, encompassed Highland Territory." An interesting example of the fact that prominent people often have "many" friends who tell them what they want to hear. And, of course, the Montrose lands certainly "encompassed Highland territory". The Duke of Montrose owned the whole of Aberfoyle (O.S.A., X 125); he owned virtually the whole of Buchanan (O.S.A., IX 21); he was one of the two "principal proprietors" of Drymen (O.S.A., VIII 551); he was given third of the eight named landlords in the N.S.A. report on Port of Menteith (N.S.A., X 1108); and he probably had an estate in Callander. The 1746 memorial on the Highlands lists the Duke of Montrose as a clan chief in the Highlands (Stewart 1822, II vii).

[434] Alwyne Farquharson of Invercauld, letter to author, 4th December 1968: "I am unaware of any evidence that my predecessors, by which I assume you mean Farquharsons of Invercauld, played any direct part in the Clearances... There is nowhere any hint of any 'eviction'; quite the reverse."

[435] Lt.-Col. G. I. Malcolm of Poltalloch, letter to author, 29th November 1968: "As far as I know, my family never had anything to do with the Clearances in this part of Argyll." As it happens, the clearances carried out by the Poltalloch chieftains are better documented than many of the other Argyllshire clearances.

[436] Sir Fitzroy MacLean, descendant of the MacLeans of Ardgour, letter to author, 3rd April 1969: "As far as I know, there were no very drastic clearances at Ardgour and my great-great-grandfather, Alexander MacLean of Ardgour, seems to have provided alternative accommodation on the coast for any crofters who left the glens." The provision of "alternate accommodation [or crofts] on the coast" was of course standard practice where landlords cleared "the glens" for sheep, but still hoped to make money from kelp. It is interesting to see this process described almost as an instance of benevolence. (The Highlanders "in the glens" were joint-farmers, not crofters.)

[437] MacLean 1889, 368. Dr J. P. MacLean, whose history of the Clan MacLean was published in 1889, asked the then MacLean of Ardgour about some disturbing reports concerning the Ardgour estate; and the then MacLean of Ardgour was able to exonerate his family, because his aunt had old him "there were no evictions"; and his "old gamekeeper" said the same. No doubt orthodox commentators would take both of these individuals to be impartial observers, with nothing to gain by flattering the powerful local landlord.

[438] Finlay 1959, 26.

[439] Hamilton 1966, 72. The 1826 ejection from Rum was treated differently by different history professors. Professor Smout thought it was a case of turning out men for sheep; Professor Hamilton thought it had nothing to do with sheep; while it gave Professor Richards another opportunity to praise the landlord. The clearance, he said, proved how exceptionally kind the landlord was, for (he said) it was an example of "the extraordinary humanity of many Highland proprietors who made financial sacrifices of this sort on behalf of their people" (Richards 1982, 367). The enforced expulsion of almost all the human race from an island where they had lived for at least 9000 years, so that the man who had obtained a piece of paper giving him "ownership" of the island could increase the rent payable to him from £300 per annum to £800, much more than doubling it, may not seem a case of "extraordinary humanity", or indeed much of an example of a "financial sacrifice"; but Professor Richards reached this conclusion because the landlord actually paid good money to the shipowner who transported the Rum people to America.

It may seem a minor point that the landlord who swept the humans from the island was actually Alexander MacLean of Coll, not MacNeill of Canna, as Professor Richards thought. Apparently no reader of Professor Richards' 1982 book informed him of the error, so there it was again twenty years later (along with Richards' lament over "the common vilification of the Highland landlords in the Age of the Clearances", Richards 2002, 191). But, clearly, if Professor Richards had read all the material which is available about the clearance of Rum, instead of merely a brief exculpation of the landlord, he could not have made so egregious a mistake as to which proprietor he felt it necessary to eulogize. As for the "extraordinary humanity" of the landlord in paying for the deportation of the Rum people across the Atlantic, perhaps if one was so disposed one could praise the kindness of the Nazi authorities in the early 1940s, since they no doubt paid many genuine reichsmarks to the German railways to transport many thousands of unwanted human beings from various European cities to the concentration camps and the gas chambers.

The clearance of Rum, and the neighbouring islands, is dealt with in volume four of this series.

[440] A. H. Campbell of Glendaruel, letter to author, 29th November 1968: "I do not remember having heard that Glendaruel was directly in the Clearances and our Estate papers of the period contain no entries bearing on this matter."

[441] Niall Campbell of Strachur, letter to author, 30th November 1968: "My father who died in '65 wrote a short history of my family covering some seven hundred years . . . I'm afraid there is no mention of the 'Clearances', which I always understood took place in Sutherland, and fired by the Countess of Sutherland."

[442] Sorley MacLean, *Gaelic Society of Inverness* XXXVIII 308.

[443] McLaren 1977, 56.

[444] Richards 1982, 484.

[445] Haswell-Smith 1996, 45.

[446] John Drummond-Moray of Abercairney, letter to author, 11th January 1969: "The [Abercairney] properties were however in the marginal Highland/Lowland area, and accordingly as far as we are aware, there were no forcible evictions . . . Moreover it would seem that the landlords were rather philanthropic towards their tenants."

[447] Munro of Foulis: Fraser 1954, 30.

[448] Hon. R. M. Sinclair, son of Lord Thurso, letter to author, 5th December 1968: "Our family were opposed to the method of the clearances and the social, economic and agricultural set up being aimed for by those who were carrying them out."

[449] McLaren 1977, 56.

[450] Brig. I. MacA. Stewart of Achnacone, letter to author, 5th November 1968; "There do not seem to have been any 'clearances' in Appin for sheep in the way that word is understood. There was however very considerable emigration due to the pressure of a rapidly increasing population and the relative attraction of a new country with the opportunities it offered."

[451] Donald Cameron, 24th of Lochiel, in a letter in the *Celtic Magazine*, November 1884.

[452] John Cameron (Cameron 1894, 17): "I am assured, on excellent authority, that this was one of the wisest and best things that ever was done in the interest of the people themselves."

[453] Sir Kenneth D. Stewart of Strathgarry, letter to author, 4th December 1968: "This [Strathgarry] is in Blair Atholl, and well away from where the Highland clearances took place."

[454] Major Sir David Butter of Pitlochry, letter to author, 16th December 1968: "To my knowledge, in Perthshire, the sort of clearances I presume you mean, as applied to the north, did not occur . . . I do not think that anyone was forcibly turned out in this part of the world."

[455] 8th Earl of Perth, letter to author, 4th December 1968: "I am puzzled on how to reply because as far as I know the Lord Perths of the nineteenth century had no property in the Highlands." The Perth family of the nineteenth century (in fact it was "Lady Perth" who held the family estates for two-thirds of the nineteenth century, from 1800 to 1865) owned land in six Highland parishes, Balquhidder (O.S.A., VI 90), Killin (O.S.A., XVII 374), Comrie (N.S.A., X 581 & 584), Monzievaird (N.S.A., X 739), Callander (N.S.A., X 350), and Muthill (N.S.A, X 314, 317, 320, & 327). The 1746 memorial on the Highlands said Drummond of Perth was a clan chief "in Glen Artney and other glens in the county of Perth" (Stewart 1822, II vii). It is interesting, and perhaps surprising, that both the Earl of Perth and the

Duke of Montrose said they had no knowledge of any Highland estates owned by their ancestors, and apparently disclaimed the important roles in the Highlands played by their forebears. (Sometimes one feels that some great people don't deserve to have any ancestors.)

[456] Sir H. C. MacAndrew, head of Lochalsh management, to the Brand Commission.

[457] Roderick MacLean, Sir Alexander Matheson's factor, was asked about evictions by Lord Napier. "Has there been any case of eviction on this property since Sir Alexander acquired it?" – "Not one." "Not even in the case of non-payment of rent?" – "No, when the case becomes extreme, Sir Alexander Matheson writes off the arrears." So the factor MacLean, giving evidence to a Parliamentary commission, described a small-tenant paradise, where small tenants could fail to pay the rent, which was then written off, with no eviction, "not one", ever occurring. It would take a commission of landlords, earnestly upholding landlordism, to swallow that one. (Napier 1884, III 1976, qu. 31001 & 31002.)

[458] Moncreiffe 1967, 37.

[459] I received five letters from landlords in the more southern parts of the Highlands which indicated a belief that the clearances had been confined to the northern Highlands. " 'Clearances', which I always understood took place in Sutherland, and fired by the Countess of Sutherland" – N. Campbell of Strachur, letter to the author, 30th November 1968. "As far as I know there were no 'clearances' of the type that took place in Inverness-shire and Sutherland" – I. Campbell of Succoth, letter to the author, 7th December 1968. "The main culprit was the Duke of Sutherland at that time or so I have always been led to believe" – Sir Ewan MacPherson Grant of Ballindalloch, letter to the author, 11th December 1968 (this letter was particularly interesting: the "main culprit", to use this writer's phrase, in the Sutherland clearances was of course the Countess of Sutherland, and one of her principal advisers at that time, although the letter-writer modestly omitted to mention it, was the then MacPherson Grant of Ballindalloch – in fact he was the man who advised the countess to bring to Sutherland two men he knew from his part of Scotland, namely William Young and Patrick Sellar). "To my knowledge, in Perthshire, the sort of clearances I presume you mean, as applied to the north, did not occur" – Sir David Butter of Pitlochry, letter to the author, 16th December 1968. "I don't think you will find that my forebears had anything whatever to do with the clearances, which were mostly further north anyhow" – J. L. Fergusson of Baledmund, letter to the author, 2nd January 1969.

[460] Richards 1973, 284.

[461] Mitchell 1971, II 85.

54. *Facts are facts*

[462] I. Campbell of Succoth, letter to the author, 7th December 1968; he hoped for "a more balanced view than Prebble's almost hysterical outpourings on the subject! . . . There is no doubt that the clearances have left their mark on Scottish history, the effects in one way or another lasting even to the present day . . . As far as I know there were no 'clearances' [in Argyll] of the type that took place in Inverness-shire and Sutherland, though obviously towards the end of the 18th and the beginning of the 19th centuries people were leaving the area and the agrarian policy was changing."

[463] See footnotes 361, 369, 417, 428.

55. *Why the denials?*

[464] A letter in *The Times*, 25th February 2009, said a study "found that the brain releases more of the reward chemical dopamine when we fall in line with the group consensus". Perhaps dopamine is to blame for the surprising group consensus of opinion on so many features of Highland history. To follow up the thoughts above, I may say that one publisher was seriously considering accepting my work on the clearances; and he sent it to an academic historian (who was then in residence at the Huntingdon Library, in the U.S.) for his opinion. The publisher showed me the advice he received: it was an expertly crafted text, which described my work in such terms (praising it with faint damns) that

no publisher would have been prepared to take it on. So it is that the accepted opinions about the clearances continue without challenge.

[465] Boswell 1928, I 467, 29th April 1773.

[466] There was another interesting letter in *The Times*, 10th December 2009. "The implication of the University of East Anglia e-mail affair that not only might scientific evidence be manipulated to fit the preferred outcome but that dubious tactics might be deployed to discredit or suppress contrary evidence, will hardly occasion surprise among seasoned academics. The much vaunted peer review system is predisposed to favour research and opinion that is acceptable to the academic establishment, and in the pursuit of research funding or the publicity of publication there is no reason to suppose that scientists or academics will conduct themselves with any greater integrity than we might expect of bankers or politicians. Academic cabalism has been around for a very long time, and is responsible for driving many young researchers with original and challenging ideas out of the academic profession. *Quis custodiet ipsos custodes*?" – D. W. Harding, Gullane, East Lothian.

At Oxford, one could – perhaps when having coffee mid-morning in one of the local cafes – see (taking similar refreshment) the eminent professor with a group of reverential acolytes, competing to hand him his cup, and one might hear rumours that he was writing much of the forthcoming lengthy tome supposedly written by the great politician (who certainly did not have time to write it all himself – merely contributing the purple passages), while the acolytes, said the gossip, wrote much of what appeared under the professor's own name, as well as seeing to the footnotes and other ancillary matter. Whether these peculiar rumours were accurate I have no means of knowing: but it is certain that the junior members of such a group, aiming at an academic career, would not improve their chances of clambering on to the first rung of the scholastic ladder by disagreeing with their mentor.

56. Wealth smells good

[467] *The Times*, 8th August 2013: "pecunia non olet."

[468] Juvenal, *Satires* xiv, lines 204-5: "lucri bonus est odor ex re qualibet."

[469] I should confess here that what I wrote in this subsection as if it were too obvious to admit dissent – i.e., that documents preserved in proprietorial archives must be expected to give the proprietorial view – is not universally accepted. Professor Richards spoke eloquently of the excellence of the history which can be written with the help of the material preserved in the landlords' archives. He welcomed the Countess of Sutherland's promise "to open to scholarship one of the greatest extant resources on Highland history, the Dunrobin Muniments", that is to say, the documents that the successive landlords (and managers) of the Sutherland estate saw fit to preserve. Richards was also pleased by "the increasing availability of archives from the muniments of the descendants of clearing landlords". (At last, we are perhaps supposed to feel, the landlords' side of the story can be heard!) Generally, Richards praised history based on the landlords' papers. "As for estate records, they are the finest single source of evidence relating to the agricultural world of the nineteenth century and contain the richest material not only about the structure and finances of landed power, but also about the conditions of the people and the relations of the clan. Alone they are an inadequate source of social realities, but so long as their provenance is kept centrally in mind, they are a vital treasury of the Highland past. It would be absurd to say that history from estate papers is landlords' history: this would be a negation of historical method." Estate records no doubt are the best source of information about the organization of "the agricultural world of the nineteenth century": which areas were currently devoted to sheep farms, and what were the boundaries of the ranches, their rents, their current leaseholders, and so forth. However, anyone hoping to find accurate information about "the conditions of the people and the relations of the clan" would look for a long time before he found landlords or factors producing long screeds about the injustice of the confiscation of the lands that used to belong to the clan, or about how inequitable it was that the people who had once been able to range over the whole of their clan land hunting, shooting, and fishing, and tending their vast herds and flocks, were now confined to small scraps of the worst land; and that each of these barren scraps, or crofts as they were called, had been intentionally cut

down to a size which would not support the family on it, thus forcing one or more family members to grovel as cringing proletarians to the wealthy estate-owners, in the hope of being allowed to work on the great new farms, or servicing the impressive new landlords' or sheep-farmers' residences, or labouring in the developing industries owned by their betters. But perhaps we should welcome Professor Richards' frankness as to his preferred sources: no doubt it helps to explain why he says some of the things which he does say, which otherwise might be hard to understand (Richards 1985, 171, 127, 146-7).

57. *The power of the pen*
[470] *Oxford Companion to Scottish History*, ed. Lynch, 2001, 376.
[471] Richards 1982, 385, & MacLeod 1996, 198.
[472] MacLeod 1996, 198.
[473] Mitchison 1962, 6.
[474] M. Fry, *Scottish Review of Books*, volume one, issue 2, 2005, para. 16. Surely anyone who is going to make authoritative pronouncements about the reality or otherwise of the Highland clearances should first make the effort to find out about such basic facts as the extent of the Sutherland estate's land-ownership in Sutherland?
[475] Fry 2005, 170.

58. *The Scottish story*
[476] J. Wiener, *Historians in Trouble*, New Press, New York, 2005, passim.
[477] *The Times*, 17th September 2007.
[478] *The Times*, 21st September 2007. Those who follow the news will realize that it is not only in this country that people have gained academic honours by submitting work which is later found to be less than original.
[479] *Story of Scotland*: Glover 1966, 68-94.
[480] *Scotland's Story*: Steel 1994, 38-51, 60-1.

59. *A broken, forgotten failure*
[481] Both these writers appear to accept the myth that in 1300 the Highlands were already part of a united country of Scotland, compelled to obey the rulers in Edinburgh. This legend is dealt with later.

60. *Prolonged and bloody wars*
[482] Professor Mitchison joined in this dismal jeremiad: the Highlanders, she said, had to live on "a thin, poor soil, soured by cold and wet" (Mitchison 1971, 376). Although I have given here examples of how the author of *Scotland's Story* appears to have been closely inspired by another history, some of his work leads one to wish that he could have copied some details more accurately. Within three pages (Steel 1994, 251-3) Strath Naver became Strathnavar (twice), MacKid became MacKidd, Sutherland of Forse became Sutherland of Forth, and Viscount Trentham became Viscount Trenton.

61. *The Uists*
[483] Richards 1985, 197.
[484] Lynch 1991, 368.
[485] Website sutherlandestates.com, pp. 2, 3, 4.
[486] Thompson 1974, 61.
[487] Campbell 1965, 131. Was Professor Campbell led astray by the 1746 memorial, which claimed that Clanranald had "a very handsome estate", e.g. in "the isles of Uist" (Stewart 1822, II vi)?
[488] Smout 1970, 352, 349. On page 349 Smout mentioned "MacDonald of Clanranald, who owned South Uist" (more accurately, he owned a large part of it); but twice Smout spoke of what Clanranald

had done or might have done in "the Uists", carrying the necessary implication that he also owned North Uist.

62. *Less fine feelings*
[489] Smout 1970, 357.
[490] Hill 1972, v, 49.
[491] Smout 1970, 353.
[492] Hill 1972, 51.
[493] Hamilton 1966, 72.
[494] Smout 1970, 360.
[495] Grant 1934, 146.
[496] Pryde 1962, 153.
[497] Donnachie & Hewitt 1989, 43.
[498] Burke 1990, 178.

63. *400 square miles*
[499] Mitchison 1993, 180.
[500] Lynch 1991, 367.
[501] Lynch 1991, 364.
[502] Devine 1994, 100.
[503] Grant 1934, 213.
[504] Grant 1980, 53.
[505] Grant & Cheape 2000, 209.
[506] *The Scotsman*, 7th March 2005.
[507] Fry 2005 (1), 135.
[508] Fry 2005 (2).
[509] Donnachie & Hewitt 1989, 43.
[510] Fry 2005 (1), 158.
[511] Adam 1972, II 30.
[512] Adam 1972, I 10.
[513] Richards 1999, 235.
[514] Richards 1985, 399.
[515] MacKay 1889, 208.
[516] Richards 1982, 5.
[517] Richards 1982, 5.
[518] Richards 1982, 5-6.

64. *Variously calculated*
[519] Sessional Papers, order of the House of Lords, 24th May 1841, website books.google.co.uk.
[520] Richards 1985, 250.
[521] Lynch 1991, 371.
[522] Devine 1994, 185. (The Wikipedia article *Highland Clearances* gives the same figures, citing Devine.)
[523] Trevelyan 1946, 447.
[524] MacCulloch 1948, 184.
[525] *The Times*, 1st March 2013.

65. *The first Sutherland clearance*
[526] Henderson 1812, 24.
[527] Henderson 1812, 104.

THE CLEARANCES IN HISTORY

[528] Richards 1973, 277.
[529] Richards 1973, 158.
[530] Richards 1973, 170.
[531] Forbes 1976, 24.
[532] Richards 1982, 184.
[533] Clapperton 1983, 139.
[534] Richards 1985, 202.
[535] Halliday 1996, 119.
[536] Houston & Knox 2001, 375.

CHAPTER TWO

THE HIGHLANDS AND ISLANDS

1. The Highlands

Sometimes it appears that the Highlands are regarded as being far away towards the Arctic regions, well to the north of England, Ireland, and Lowland Scotland. Yet the most southerly points of the Highlands and Islands, the Mull of Kintyre and the Isle of Sanda, are further south than the most northerly point of Ireland (which is of course part of the Irish Republic, not of "Northern Ireland"); they are further south than the greater part of the Lowlands (further south, that is, than Jedburgh, Hawick, and Ayr, and much further south than Glasgow and Edinburgh); and they are even further south than a sizeable triangle of English soil: Bamburgh, the Farne Islands, and Alnwick, are all further north than the southernmost point of the Highlands. Berwick-on-Tweed – whether the reader considers it should be placed in England or Scotland politically – is geographically further north than the whole of the Isle of Arran, once a Gaelic stronghold, and is thirty miles north of the Mull of Kintyre. As for Scotland itself, the non-Gaelic part of the country – in this case Orkney and Shetland – extends much further north than Cape Wrath and Holborn Head, the most northerly outposts of what used to be Gaelic Scotland.

These errors have a long ancestry. Dr Johnson, who took his famous journey to the Hebrides in 1773, was not sure of the geographical location of the Highlands. When he and his fellow-traveller James Boswell reached Armadale in Skye, to stay with the chief of the MacDonalds, they were both (wrote Boswell, in his *Tour to the Hebrides*) "dissatisfied at hearing of the racked rents and emigration; and finding a chief not surrounded by his clan. Dr Johnson said: 'Sir, the Highland chiefs should not be allowed to go farther south than Aberdeen'."[1] Neither Johnson nor Boswell apparently realized that, even though they were in the heart of the MacDonald country, and staying at the residence of the MacDonald chief, they were at that moment south of Aberdeen. Dr Johnson, however, had the excuse that the extent and position of the Highlands were at that time little known.

If compass-point directions are required, it makes more sense (as we see below) to think of Gaeldom as being to the west, and the rest of Scotland to the east, rather than to regard them as being to the north, and south, of each other.

2. Natural defences

For many centuries the outer boundary of the mountains, as well as the terrain in the interior of the mountainous area, was so formidable – especially to those unused to it – that it was no easy matter for even a peaceful traveller to journey into the Highlands; for hostile forces, it was very difficult indeed. Colonel David Stewart of Garth, who afterwards became General Stewart, remarked that along the Highland line – as the brink of the Highlands is usually called – there were many "glens and valleys, whose lower entrances are so rugged and contracted, as to be almost impassable, till opened by art. These are known by the name of passes, and are situated both on the verge of the outward line, and in the interior of the range. The most remarkable are Balmaha upon Loch Lomond, Aberfoyle and Leny in Menteith, the pass of Glen Almond above Crieff, the entrance into Atholl at Dunkeld, and those formed by the rivers Ardle, Isla, and South and North Esk . . . Immediately within the external boundary are also many strong and defensible passes, such as Killiecrankie, the entrances into Glen Lyon, Glen Lochy, Glen Ogle, etc. . . . These boundaries constituted one of the principal causes which preserved the Highlanders a distinct race from the inhabitants of the plains. For seven centuries, Birnam Hill, at the entrance into Atholl, has formed the boundary between the Lowlands and the Highlands, and between the Saxon and Gaelic languages. On the south and east sides of the hill, breeches are worn, and the Scotch Lowland dialect spoken, with as broad an accent as in Midlothian. On the north and west sides are found the Gaelic, the kilt, and the plaid, with all the peculiarities of the Highland character. The Gaelic is universal, as the dialect in common use among the people on the Highland side of the boundary. This applies to the whole range of the Grampians; as, for example, at General Campbell's gate, at Monzie, nothing but Scotch is spoken, while at less than a mile distant, on the hill to the northward, we meet with the Gaelic."[2]

Other writers said much the same about what Stewart called this "line of demarcation between the two distinct parts of the kingdom" of Scotland.[3] In the Old Statistical Account of Scotland, the reporter from the joint parishes of Dunkeld and Dowally wrote in 1798 that the hills of King's Seat and Craigie Barns, at the southern boundary of Dowally parish, marked also the boundary between the languages. "In the first house below them, the English is, and has been, spoken; and the Gaelic in the first house, (not above a mile distant) above them."[4] James Hogg, the Ettrick Shepherd, crossed this boundary in July 1802. He wrote to Sir Walter Scott: "I passed the hill called King's Seat . . . This hill they reckon the march between the Highlands and the Lowlands of Perthshire; yea, so exactly does it separate them, that the family below it talk English and the one above it, Gaelic – which is the prevailing language all beyond it."[5]

3. The old counties

Perthshire was one of the old counties – there were thirty-four of them (or thirty-three after 1890, when Ross-shire and Cromarty were merged) – into which Scotland was divided for centuries; this system persisted until 1975, so it had at least earned whatever legitimacy derives from longevity. These counties will often be referred to in this work. The people who replaced the old counties with newly delineated sectors went out of their way to defy both geography and history. Among the new divisions were entities called "Strathclyde", which included (southwards) Ballantrae, in Ayrshire, and Biggar, in Lanarkshire (in fact it reached down to within thirty miles of the English border) and also (northwards) Coll and Tiree, in the distant Hebrides; "Central", which stretched from Falkirk in the Lowlands to Tyndrum in the Highlands; "Tayside", from Lowland Montrose to Highland Rannoch; and "Grampian", from Fraserburgh on the Buchan coast to the Cairngorms and their Highland summits. In 1996 the whole system was changed again, these ten regions being replaced by thirty-two unitary authorities. The old counties were probably equally irrational, but they did last for hundreds of years, including the whole period with which this work is concerned. The former counties, then, will often be mentioned, if only because the present fashion is so strong for pointless change and novelty that the new divisions might well be altered again in the not-too-distant future, rendering the present zones equally obsolete. Clearly, many things in our society need to be changed: so our rulers show they are alive to the problem by changing things that do not need to be changed. They overcome the arguably arbitrary by introducing the incontestably illogical.

Beyond the Highland line lived the Highlanders. Edmund Burt said, "they are exceedingly proud to be thought an unmixed people";[6] Alexander Sutherland said the Highlanders were proud of their "uncontaminated descent;[7] and R. Jamieson described their pride in "the unmixed purity of their Celtic blood and language".[8] In fact, of course, the Highlanders were in origin racially mixed, as we all are. Many of the ancestors of the Gaelic Highlanders were called Scots, and they came originally from Ireland. In the early nineteenth century their language was still being described as Irish or Erse; Scots Gaelic and Irish Gaelic are still mutually intelligible. These original Scots landed in what is now Argyllshire, and spread throughout the mountainous districts. It seems likely that they absorbed the Pictish people, who had lived in much of the same area. Among other contributors to the mix were some Normans in the south and east, Norsemen in the north and west, and Britons (or Welsh) in Dumbartonshire and Gigha: but for centuries the mountaineers regarded themselves as one homogeneous people – they spoke Gaelic, and called themselves Gaels.

The ancestors of the Lowlanders included some Britons, who inhabited southwest Scotland as well as Cumberland in England, some English people, originally Anglians (like the Northumbrians in the north of England), particularly in the east, as well as some Norsemen, some Normans, and others. (Sir Walter Scott said the Lowlanders were "of twenty different races".)[9] The Scottish Gaels extended their power over much of the Lowlands as well as the Highlands, and Gaelic was for some time spoken well beyond the boundaries of the mountainous area: language always follows authority. Then in the ninth century came a move pregnant with future significance: the capital, the main stronghold of the king, moved south from Highland Argyllshire to the Lowland part of Perthshire. In the course of time English prevailed as the language of the Lowlands; but for another millennium Gaelic remained the language of the Highlands. The endurance of Gaelic in the Highlands is another indication that the Lowlands were not yet able to assert their domination over the Highlands; as soon as the Highlands were conquered by the Lowland/English state of Great Britain in the middle of the eighteenth century, Gaelic was doomed, and was progressively extinguished. It is now spoken only by a small, and progressively smaller, minority of people in the farthest corners of the Highlands and Islands.

4. An impregnable fortress

The mountains surrounding the Highlands as a whole, and separating the clan countries from each other, performed for them the same invaluable office of keeping out enemies that the sea did for England. The narrow passes in the mountain walls, both on the Highland-Lowland border and internally, were, as Stewart declared, "almost impassable" in the days of the clans.[10] The Chevalier de Johnstone said that "the Highlands are full of precipices and passes through mountains, where only one person can proceed at a time and where a thousand men can defend themselves against a hundred thousand for years" (and where, moreover, the defenders had plenty of provisions, since the Highland territory in Johnstone's words "abounds with horned cattle").[11] Dr Johnson said, "mountainous countries . . . are not easily conquered, because they must be entered by narrow ways, exposed to every power of mischief from those that occupy the heights; and every new ridge is a new fortress".[12] The same analogy occurred to William Thomson, who toured the Highlands in 1785; he thought that the Highlands had been "formed by nature into an impregnable fortress", which had kept the "Caledonians" as "an unconquered and independent nation" till then.[13] A year or two later, the O.S.A. reporter on Moy parish wrote: "The ancient name is Starsach-na-gal, i.e. the threshold of the Gaels, or Highlanders, being the pass, by which the Highlanders enter to the low country, so narrow between high mountains, that a few men could defend it against numbers."[14] John Bristed travelled through the pass of Killiecrankie in 1801, and said that before General Wade built the road, "half a dozen Highlanders with a few loose stones might have defended the pass against a whole army of assailants".[15] The Dunkeld report in the New Statistical Account of Scotland, 1845, remarked that the Romans had "approached near to the place [the Highlands]; but, from the many passes and dangerous defiles with which it abounds, they never could successfully invade it".[16] (The Romans had conquered much of southern and western Europe, much of Asia Minor, and much of northern Africa, but the Highlands were beyond them.) The minister of Kintail wrote in the same publication that formerly access to his district had been "an arduous undertaking – the country being entirely without roads, and the principal approaches being through extremely narrow glens, where a few individuals might defend the country against an invading army of many hundreds".[17]

These passes look forbidding enough now, after powerful machinery has bulldozed roads along the mountain sides: in the days of the clans, they appeared to be totally impenetrable. James Hogg wrote that "in the year 1746 a body of auxiliary Germans, who were marching north against the rebels, made a full stop [at Killiecrankie], refusing to proceed a step further, and expostulated with their leaders on the unreasonableness of carrying them beyond the boundaries of human existence".[18]

5. As if by magic

Sometimes the actual boundary between the Gaels and the English-speakers was merely a stream, or a hillock, or some other apparently insignificant topographical feature; but the people on either side of it were palpably different. David Stewart returned in his book to the subject of the contrast in character between the Highlanders and the Lowlanders, which, he said, "though so distinctly marked, was divided by so slight a line, as the small stream or burn of Inch Ewan below the bridge of Dunkeld, the inhabitants on each side of which present perfect characteristics of the Saxons and Celts".[19] Similarly, on the south-eastern coast of Caithness the boundary between the two peoples was the burn of Easter Clyth, about eight miles south of Wick. Of this brook the minister of Latheron wrote in 1840: "on the east side of it, scarcely a word of Gaelic was either spoken or understood, and on the west side the English shared the same fate."[20] A third example was given by a traveller in the Highlands in 1818, who wrote that on the way to Kirkmichael in Perthshire "a hill-stream about three or four miles above the bridge of Cally constituted . . . the boundary between the Highland and Lowland languages, notions, manners, customs, and habits . . . On passing the bridge of Cally to the north, or the stream already mentioned to the west, the people seemed to be in language, dress, and manners, entirely different from those behind in their immediate vicinity; and the traveller, from everything he then saw and heard, appeared to be transported at once, as if by magic, into some remote foreign region."[21]

Tobias Smollett's fictional characters in *Humphry Clinker*, published in 1771, travelled north on the west side of Loch Lomond (an area Smollett knew well, having been born nearby): "This country appears more and more wild and savage the further we advance; and the people are as different from the Low-land Scots, in their looks, garb, and language, as the mountaineers of Brecknock are from the inhabitants of Herefordshire."[22] Dorothy Wordsworth went the same way in 1803, with her brother William and his fellow-poet Coleridge. She put the border about a mile and a half south of Luss village, where the island of Inch-ta-vannach off the shore encloses a patch of water, making almost a separate lake: "it was like a new region. The huts were after the Highland fashion, and the boys who were playing wore the Highland dress and philabeg" (the kilt). When the travellers spoke English at Tarbet, only eight miles further north, they found that Gaelic was so much the prevailing language that people "did not understand us at once".[22]

The language boundary was quite abrupt. Duncan Forbes was born in 1798 to a family of Highlanders which was then living at Kinnaird, which is in the Lowlands, halfway between Perth and Dundee, but according to the *D.N.B.* he was brought up from the age of three in "Glenfernate", some seven or eight miles north of the hill-stream "above the bridge of Cally", which was the language border. In 1837 he became Professor of Oriental Languages at King's College, London, but until he was some thirteen years old (that is, into the second decade of the nineteenth century, living no more than eight miles from the English-speaking frontier) he knew no language but Gaelic.[23] David Stewart remarked on how sharp the change was at the boundary; he instanced the great fiddler "Neil Gow, whose genius has added fresh spirit to the cheerful and exhilarating music of Caledonia, and who, although he was born, and, during the period of a long life [1727-1807], lived within a mile of the Lowland border [at Inver, near Dunkeld], exhibited a perfect specimen of the genuine Highlander in person, garb, principles, and character".[24] It is interesting that none of these Highland/Lowland borders, however clear on the ground and however historically significant, now bear (so far as the author knows) any sign to show how momentous they once were. Inconvenient history is easily ignored.

Lowland Scotland had been put together as a single country through the chances of war, as a result of the competing ambitions of the rulers who reigned over the various kingdoms that appeared in the island of Britain in the centuries between the departure of the Romans and the coming of the Normans. There was, as it happened, much similarity in the traditions, habits, and language of the people in large districts of what became the south of Scotland and those in large districts of what became the north of England: in fact for a long time it was not certain where the Anglo-Scottish border would lie in that part of the world – successive Scots kings for many years pursued an aggressive claim to Northumberland, Durham, and Cumberland, while the English monarchs claimed suzerainty over the whole of "Scotland", sometimes occupying much of the Lowlands, and even annexing the Scottish town of Berwick-upon-Tweed.[25] King Athelstan of England, when the Scots disputed his overlordship in 934, took an army and a navy into Scotland and harried the east coast as far as Caithness.[26]

Without question the Scots Lowlanders and the northern English had much more in common than did the Lowlanders and the Highlanders; but potentates bent on extending their domains are indifferent to considerations of that kind.

6. Highlander and Sassenach

So dissimilar were the two peoples that sometimes Lowlanders were apparently not disposed to allow that the Highlands were part of Scotland at all. In 1825 Alexander Sutherland, then touring the Highlands, found that the innkeeper at Brora, in Sutherlandshire, was from Morayshire. The innkeeper's daughter said: "We do not belong to this country, we come from Scotland, yonder", and pointed towards the Moray coast.[27]

On the other hand, it seems that some Highlanders regarded themselves as the Scotsmen, and the Lowlanders as the outsiders. One of the witnesses before the 1883 Napier Commission claimed that the Black Watch had gone downhill since non-Highlanders were admitted; now it was a mixture of "Irish, Scotch, and Lowlanders".[28]

David Stewart at one point maintained that these terms were used only when English was being spoken. "The epithets England and Scotland, or Scots and English, are totally unknown in Gaelic. The English are Sassenachs, the Lowland Scots are Guals, the low country is Gualdach (the Country of Strangers), the Highlanders are Gael and Albanich, and the Highlands Gaeldach."[29] Stewart himself, however, often did not follow this rule. As we have already seen, he called the Lowlanders' English the "Saxon" (i.e. Sassenach) language;[30] he described the anglophone inhabitants of these islands as "Saxon invaders";[31] he referred to the border near Dunkeld as separating "the Saxons and the Celts";[32] and as we shall see later, he wrote (twice) of "the Saxons of the Lowlands".[33] Other writers made it equally clear that the Highlanders called the Lowlanders Sassenachs. In about 1771 Tobias Smollett, who was born close to the Highland border in Dumbartonshire, wrote that "the Highlanders have no other name for the people of the Low-country, but Sassenagh, or Saxons."[34] The Rev. James MacKenzie, giving a Lowland view (despite his Highland surname) of events in his *History of Scotland*, 1911, had the same opinion as Smollett: he said that the "half savage" Highlanders hated "with an ancient grudge the 'Sassenach', or Lowlanders."[35] The Rev. Norman MacLeod referred in 1867 to "rare" visitors to the Highlands – "some foreign 'Sassanach' from the Lowlands of Scotland or England".[36] Principal J. C. Shairp, a Scottish academic whose mother was a Highlander, said the general belief was that "Scott was the first 'Sassenach' who discovered the Trossachs", whereas, he said, there had been at least three publications drawing attention to the district before *The Lady of the Lake* came out.[37] Sir Walter Scott, then, the champion of all things Scottish, was considered to be a "Sassenach". Scott himself confirmed the usage. In *A Legend of Montrose*, Scott said that the sister of Sergeant Mor MacAlpin had stayed in her native glen when it was cleared for sheep by taking service with "the intruding Lowlander, who, though a Saxon . . . had proved a kind man to her".[38] In *The Fair Maid of Perth*, Scott said "the Saxons of the plain [clearly the Lowlanders] and the Gael of the mountains" often battled in the vales of Perthshire.[39] The term, once used (according to Smollett, MacKenzie, MacLeod, Shairp, Scott, and Stewart) by Highlanders to denote the Lowlanders, is now used by Lowlanders to denote the English.

People might be surprised sometimes if they knew the history of the words they employ.

7. The fringe

Since the seat of government in Scotland was in Edinburgh, the Highlands came to be thought of as lying in the north; if the capital had been at Thurso or Kirkwall, no doubt they would have been thought of as lying in the south. That would have been more accurate, for non-Gaelic Scotland (as represented by north-east Caithness, Orkney and Shetland) stretches more than three times as far to the north of Gaelic Scotland as it does to the south. What used to be the Gaelic and non-Gaelic parts of Scotland do not lie north and south of each other; it would be closer to the truth (as was remarked earlier) to say that they lie east and west.

The whole of Scotland lying south of the Firths of Clyde and Forth, all the thirteen old counties, covers only 7207 square miles.[40] The Border lies almost as near to Edinburgh as it does to Newcastle. What used to be known as Yorkshire alone is 6071 square miles, and Yorkshire and Lincolnshire together are 8717 square miles. Even taking in all the non-Gaelic areas lying along the east coast of Scotland, and Orkney and Shetland, the total non-Gaelic part of Scotland only amounts to some 13,500 square miles, very little more than the four largest English counties combined. The Highlands, on the other hand, cover some 16,300 square miles. One historian defined the Highlands as merely "the high north-western third of Scotland", but the Highlands as here defined constitute more than half of Scotland – just under fifty-five per cent of it. (The area of Scotland as a whole is about 29,800 square miles.)[41] Although the Highlands and Islands are in some English eyes simply a romantic tourist area lying beyond the "real" Scotland, in fact from the point of view of size the once-Gaelic area preponderates.

Seen from London or Birmingham, the formerly (or currently) Celtic-speaking areas of the British Isles appear to form a kind of fringe, away to the west. It is not unknown for Lowland Scots to refer to Scotland's previously Gaelic areas as a fringe. Professor Pryde, for example, in his *Scotland from 1603 to the Present Day*, 1962, referred to the natives of the "northern regions" forming a "Celtic fringe".[42] But clearly, if there is a fringe in Scotland, it is not Celtic: it is non-Celtic. A recent work said that because their ancestors came originally from Ireland, the Highlanders "were outsiders in their own country"; but, of course, the various peoples who came to live in the Lowlands were also originally from outside what is now Scotland.[43] (The English also came from abroad.) The Gaels were the original Scots, and it was they who gave the name to the country; they occupied the larger area; and even in the strictly literal sense, a glance at the map of Scotland will show that geographically what used to be Gaeldom is the heart of the land mass, while the non-Gaelic part stretches tenuously from the northern islands down the east side and across the south from Shetland to Wigtownshire, forming, in fact, the non-Gaelic (or perhaps Anglo-Welsh-Norse) fringe.

8. The weather

No doubt because of the idea that the Highlands are a distant land, far to the north, there is also occasionally a feeling in the south of Great Britain that the Highlands and Islands have an almost glacial climate. The Highlands are not so remote from England: it is about 600 miles from Cornwall to Cape Wrath, which is no further than from the north of France to the south, and is less than the distance from Warsaw to Moscow, or from Adelaide to Sydney, or from one end of Texas to the other. The degrees of latitude – something under nine – from the Lizard (the most southerly point of Great Britain) to Dunnet Head (the most northerly) are not sufficient in themselves to produce a great difference in climate, especially since the warm North Atlantic Drift washes all the British Isles impartially. Yet some English and Lowland people seem to have been always convinced that the Highland line and the Arctic Circle are practically synonymous. Edmund Burt, who was in the Highlands in the 1720s and later (collecting rents on the forfeited estates of Glenmoriston and Seaforth), said in his *Letters from a Gentleman in the North of Scotland* that the year in that part of the country was nine months' winter and three months' bad weather.[44] Writing of a plan to build a town at Fort Augustus, he said, "I verily believe there is not an Englishman, when he knew the country, but would think of a settlement there with more horror than any Russian would do of banishment to Siberia".[45] An English servant who went with a MacLeod to Skye in 1782 confided to his journal his belief that "it is constantly raining" in the Hebrides.[46] A 1791 report on the Highlands by the Society for the Promotion of Christian Knowledge said, "rains prevail through a great part of the year".

It does in fact rain more in the Highlands than in most parts of England. One must, however, compare like with like. The western coasts of the British Isles are wetter than the eastern coasts, and it is misleading to compare the west coast of Scotland with the east coast of England. On the west coast, Fort William has as much as seventy-eight inches of rain a year; although even that must seem like a drought to the English inhabitants of Seathwaite in Cumbria, which has 130 inches, two-thirds as much again. Fort William's heavy rainfall is due not to its being further north than England, but to its surrounding mountains. If Plymouth had Ben Nevis as a near neighbour, it would probably have as much rain as Fort William. On the east side of the Highland mass, the position is very different. The rainfall at Nairn, lying at the eastern edge of the old Gaelic area, is twenty-five inches, virtually the same as London, and less than Eastbourne and Tunbridge Wells, which have thirty-one inches each. The further west one goes, the more rain one gets. Buxton in Derbyshire has forty-eight inches, and Ashburton in Devon fifty-two.[47]

9. Inured to the weather

Since, owing to the prevailing westerly winds, places on the west coast of Britain have more rain than those on the east, and since mountains bring down more rain than lower country does, Gaelic Scotland – much of it being on the west side of the country, and having more mountains – has on the average more rain than the Lowlands and England. But the Highlanders of old, a hardy, out-of-doors race inured to the vagaries of the weather, liked their climate as it was. Burt wrote that the Highlanders were accustomed from their infancy to be often wet; rain "can scarcely be called a hardship to them, insomuch that I used to say, they seemed to be of the duck kind, and to love the water as well". Sometimes, Burt was told, they dipped their dry plaids in the burn and slept in them wet, even in dry weather, because, they said, it kept them warm.[48] Later in the century, Lieutenant Patrick Campbell went to North America to visit the Highland emigrants there, and wrote a book on his journey, *Travels in North America, 1791-2*. One of the emigrants he met was a Cameron, who thirty years before had been his servant and fellow deerstalker when he was ranger of the forest of Mamore. Cameron lamented the lack of rain; when "a plump shower happened to fall, he would run out of the house, stand under it until he would get drenched to the skin, and say what a pleasant thing rain was".[49] Sir Archibald Geikie said that Highlanders did not mind the rain: "on any wet day you may see these men standing together in pouring rain, although a shed or other shelter may be close at hand . . . they say themselves that the wet thickens the cloth of their raiment and keeps them warm."[50]

As for temperature, it is a little colder in the Highlands than it is in England – at sea level. At two or three thousand feet above sea level, in England or Scotland, it is colder than in the valleys: that is a question of elevation, not of latitude. On the eastern side of the Gaelic area, Nairn has a mean monthly temperature range over the year of 0-18 degrees Celsius, which compares with 2-18 at Tynemouth, 0-21 at Tunbridge Wells, and 3-20 at Eastbourne. On the west, Fort William's range of 1-18 degrees compares with 1-19 at Dumfries, 4-17 at Holyhead, 3-19 at Plymouth, and 6-18 in the Scilly Isles.[51] A summer day in some of the sheltered valleys of the Highlands can be very warm indeed. Burt himself remarked on the heat given off by the reflection of the sun on the rocks; one August day in the Highlands, Burt said, "was the hottest I think I ever felt in my life".[52] The minister of Fortingall wrote in the N.S.A. of the effect of the mountains on the weather in summer. "Their steep fronts, reflecting the solar rays, occasion a greater degree of warmth in our narrow glens than is felt in lower and more southern situations; and during the continuance of this warmth, vegetation is very rapid."[53]

The mean annual temperature of the island of Islay, off the west coast of the Highlands, is the same as that of the Isle of Wight, off the south coast of England. In sum, as could be expected in such a small island as Great Britain, the climate does not vary greatly from one end to the other, except where high hills – whether in England or Scotland – precipitate more rain. Any implication, therefore, that the Highlanders abandoned their homeland merely for climatic considerations would not be justified.

10. The Highland line

It occasionally seems that some of the disagreements over Highland history could be resolved immediately if all the participants had to say which area they meant by "the Highlands". In 1761, when the age of clearances was still in its infancy, Laurence Sterne (in the person of Tristram Shandy) said that in authorship "what you have to do, before you set out" is "to give the world a good definition, and stand to it, of the main word you have most occasion for", and then both writer and reader can defy "the father of confusion" to confound the issue.[54]

THE HIGHLANDS AND ISLANDS

If "Highlands" is the main word which historians of the Highlands "have most occasion for", then many of them have ignored Sterne's advice, and the issue has certainly been confounded, though whether "the father of confusion" had a hand in it is a question that must be left to theologians. As we saw, widely differing modern estimates have been made of the Highland population in 1755: some as low as 115,000,[55] at last one other as high as three-quarters of a million.[56] Writers are not necessarily numerate (as many examples in this work will show) but presumably these discrepant estimates cannot be based on the same area of land. To avoid uncertainty, a definition applicable at any rate to this work will shortly be attempted.

Where commentators have attempted to define the Highlands, the definitions which have been produced may sometimes have obscured the reality even further; though Edmund Burt, in the 1720s, was surprisingly accurate. He said, "The Highlands take up more than one-half of Scotland; they extend from Dumbarton, near the mouth of the River Clyde, to the northernmost part of the island, which is above two hundred miles, and their breadth is from fifty to above a hundred."[57] Burt was not far out. From Dumbarton to Thurso is about 190 miles; from Cape Wrath to the southern end of Loch Lomond is about 180 miles; from Thurso in the north-east, or more exactly from Holborn Head, about two miles further north, to the Mull of Kintyre in the south-west, it is some 250 miles. The Highland mainland at its broadest, say from Ballater to Ardnamurchan Point, is about 125 miles. From Ballater to Barra Head, it is about 180 miles; from Ballater to St Kilda the distance is over 200 miles.

W. F. Skene is perhaps the most persuasive of those who have delineated the Highlands. According to him the Highland line ran from Balmaha, near the south-eastern corner of Loch Lomond, through Callander, Crieff, Dunkeld, and Blairgowrie, then up the east side of Glen Isla to Lochnagar, across the Dee at Ballater and the Spey at Craigellachie, and so to the coast at Nairn.[58] To complete Skene's demarcation, many writers say that at the south-western end of this line the division between Gaelic and non-Gaelic Scotland was the Firth of Clyde, going up to Ardmore, south of Helensburgh, and thence to Balloch at the southern tip of Loch Lomond; and at the northern end, the division ran through Caithness, from the Easter Clyth burn already mentioned to Thurso. A. Fullerton, in his *Gazetteer of Scotland*, 1836, gave a similar route. "The line commences at the mouth of the river Nairn [at Nairn town]; it then, with the exception of a slight north-eastward or outward curve, the central point of which is on the river Spey, runs due south-east until it strikes the river Dee at Tullach [i.e. Milton of Tullich, a mile east of Ballater], nearly on the third degree of longitude west of Greenwich; it then runs generally south until it falls upon the West-water, or the southern large head-water of the North Esk; it thence, over a long stretch, runs almost due south-west, and with scarcely a deviation, until it falls upon the Clyde on Ardmore in the parish of Cardross; and now onward to the Atlantic Ocean, it moves along the frith [firth] of Clyde, keeping near to the continent, and excluding none of the Clyde islands except the comparatively unimportant Cumbraes."[59] A few years later, in 1852, John Hill Burton put "the Highland line near Doune or the Leven"[60] – Doune which is seven miles south-east of Callendar, and the River Leven which runs southward from the southern end of Loch Lomond to Dumbarton. Similarly the Rev. Norman MacLeod said in 1867 that "the Highlands proper were entered upon at Dumbarton or Callander".[61]

In 1784 an Act of Parliament gave another definition of the Highland line, for the purposes of a tax on distilleries. "A certain line or boundary beginning at the east point of Loch Crinan, and proceeding thence to Loch Gilpin [Lochgilphead]; from thence . . . along the west side of Loch Fyne to Inveraray and to the head of Loch Fyne; from thence . . . to Arrochar . . . [and] to Tarbet; from Tarbet on a supposed line eastward on the north side of Ben Lomond, to . . . Callander . . . from thence north eastward to Crieff . . . to Ambleree [Amulree] and Inver to Dunkeld; from thence along the foot and side of the Grampian Hills to Fettercairn . . . and from thence northward . . . to . . . Kincardine O'Neil, Clatt, Huntly and Keith to Fochabers; and from thence westward by Elgin and Forres, to the boat on the river Findhorn, and from thence down the said river to the sea at Findhorn, and any place in or any part of the county of Elgin which lies southward of the said line from Fochabers to the sea at Findhorn."[62] This variant would apparently exclude from the Highlands Colonsay, Jura, and Islay; and would certainly exclude Knapdale and Kintyre, Cowal, Bute, and Arran, as well as the MacAulay, Colquhoun, and Buchanan countries, and part of the MacFarlane country, but would include large areas in the eastern foothills of the mountainous region which have not been Gaelic-speaking since well before the eighteenth century. Tom Steel's Highland line, on the other hand, begins at Glasgow: so by that demarcation the north bank of the Clyde west of Glasgow, along with the Kilpatrick Hills, the Campsie Fells, Strath Allan, and Blairgowrie would be considered as part of the Highlands.[63] Much of this territory, from the Clyde to Blairgowrie, has been English-speaking for centuries.

11. The Gaelic-speaking Highlands

David Stewart also attempted a definition of the Gaelic-speaking area. "The space which the Gaelic population occupied within the mountains, includes the counties of Sutherland, Caithness, Ross, Inverness, Cromarty, Nairn, Argyll, Bute, the Hebrides [all of which islands are or were within the counties of Ross, Inverness, and Argyll, of course], and part of the counties of Moray, Banff, Stirling,

Perth, Dumbarton, Aberdeen, and Angus. It may be defined by a line drawn from the western opening of the Pentland Frith [between Caithness and Orkney], sweeping round St Kilda, so as to include the whole cluster of islands to the east and south [of that line], as far as Arran; then stretching to the Mull of Kintyre, re-entering the mainland at Ardmore in Dumbartonshire, following the southern verge of the Grampians to Aberdeenshire, cutting off the Lowland districts in that country, and in Banff and Elgin, and ending on the north-east point of Caithness. Throughout its whole extent this country displays nearly the same features."[64] Stewart's demarcation, since it includes the whole of Caithness, Nairnshire, and Buteshire, is broader than the definition attempted below.

Dr I. F. Grant, in 1934, took "the Highland counties" to be Inverness, Ross and Cromarty, and Sutherland (remarkably leaving out Argyllshire); plus Perthshire and Caithness (both part Lowland), and Orkney and Shetland (which have never been in the Gaelic area).[65] A 1946 Philips map surprisingly includes in the Highlands both Dumbarton in the south and Nairn in the north; yet further north still (even more surprisingly) it excludes both Helmsdale village and Reay village from the Highlands.[66] In 1963 Ian Finlay apparently considered the Highlands as everything north of a line drawn from the River Clyde, above Dumbarton, across to the Firth of Tay, below Perth.[67] More recently John MacLeod said that the Highlands comprehended the whole of Caithness, along with Sutherland, Ross and Cromarty, Inverness-shire, Argyllshire, and Highland Perthshire (a smaller area than others'; his line ran west from Dunkeld to a point some miles north of Loch Lomond, leaving out e.g. Killin parish, then south to Tarbet, Arrochar, and Loch Long).[68] The *Companion to Gaelic Scotland* took the Highlands to be the counties of Argyll (though for some reason omitting the parish of Gigha and Cara), Inverness, Ross and Cromarty, and Sutherland, with only nine parishes in north-west Perthshire, together with the whole of Caithness, but not including any parishes of the eight other part-Highland counties from Buteshire to Nairnshire: this would put Killin parish, the Braes of Balquhidder, Glen Gyle and Loch Katrine, and the Trossachs, in the Lowlands, and would produce a total of 132 Highland parishes.[69] Charles Withers wrote in 1998 that "the Highlands have been defined here as the pre-1974 counties of Argyll, Bute, Inverness, Ross and Cromarty and Sutherland together with those parishes elsewhere in Scotland where, by 1891, Gaelic was spoken by more than 25 per cent of the parish population". From his definition, and his map, it seems that he included only four parishes (out of five) in Buteshire, as well as twelve in Perthshire, one in Moray, one in Nairnshire, and two in Caithness. This gives a total of 133 Highland parishes.[70] (My own definition, below, gives 162.) Withers took 1891 as the date to designate the Gaelic-speaking area of Scotland: I take the middle of the eighteenth century. The later the date, of course, the smaller the Gaelic area. If one defined the

Highlands now as the area where significant numbers of the people still speak Gaelic, then the Highlands would consist only of a few of the north-western coastal parishes, and some of the further Hebrides: a definition which ought to satisfy few.

In the 1890s Dr Geikie, in Groome's *Gazetteer*, said firmly that "an approximately straight or gently undulating line from Stonehaven, in a south-west direction, along the northern outskirts of Strathmore to Glen Artney, and thence through the lower reaches of Loch Lomond to the Firth of Clyde at Kilcreggan [at the southernmost point of the Rosneath peninsula], marks out with precision the southern limits of the Highland area".[71]

Professor Pryde said the "Highland line" was "the geological fault which runs from the vicinity of Dumbarton in the south-west to that of Stonehaven in the north-east", while insisting that much territory north of that line must be "distinguished from the main mountainous mass"; and when he boldly asserted that "the Highlands" were "already over-populated" before the improvements, he relied on the population statistics from the whole of Perthshire, as well as from the four main Highland counties.[72] If figures are taken only from those five counties, it means that twenty-seven Highland parishes, from Caithness down to Buteshire, are ignored, while fifty-one Lowland parishes – in the low country of southern Perthshire – are wrongly brought into the equation. This cannot lead to convincing conclusions.

Professor Smout's Highland line begins on the north Sutherland coast, far enough to the west to exclude from the Highlands not only Thurso but even Reay and Melvich. It also excludes the lower part of Kildonan strath, as well as all the south-eastern part of Sutherland, the whole peninsula between the Dornoch Firth and the Cromarty Firth, the Black Isle, much of the Munro country, lower Strath Conon, the Aird, and the north-western third of Loch Ness (Urquhart Castle being on Dr Smout's border). The line then goes east, including much of central Aberdeenshire and perhaps a small part of Kincardineshire (areas more usually considered as part of the Lowlands), before heading south-east in a more expected direction to reach the River Clyde north of Dumbarton.[73]

12. "Eight Highland counties"

James Hunter, in his 1999 history of the Highlands, *Last of the Free*, says very truly that the physical extent of the Highlands and Islands is "a matter of dispute". But "mostly I stick with Shetland, Orkney, the Hebrides and those parts of the mainland to the west and north of a line drawn from Loch Fyne, by way of the Drumochter Pass, to Forres" on the Moray coast.[74] This delineation leaves out, it will be seen, the whole of the once-Gaelic districts in Buteshire, Dumbartonshire,

Stirlingshire, Perthshire, Angus, Aberdeenshire, and Banffshire, as well as parts of Highland Morayshire and of Argyllshire (for example part of the clan country of the Campbells of Argyll, much of the clan country of the Campbells of Breadalbane, and the whole of the countries of the Atholl clan, the Farquharsons, the clansfolk acknowledging the Duke of Gordon as chief, and many more), but would include much non-Gaelic country further north. Other writers have included either the whole of Perthshire, or the whole of Caithness (or, on the contrary, no part of those two counties) in the Highlands. Others again embrace the distant, formerly Norse, Orkney and Shetland in the Highlands. Professor Eric Richards said there were "eight Highland counties": Argyll, Inverness, Ross and Cromarty, and Sutherland (which were in the Gaelic Highlands), Perth and Caithness (which were only partly in the Gaelic Highlands) and Orkney and Shetland (which have never been in the Gaelic Highlands).[75] In 1851 Sir John MacNeill satisfied himself, and defended the caste of Highland landlords to which he belonged, by asserting that "any fear of the depopulation of the Highlands is totally unfounded", because, he said, the numbers in "the Highlands" had increased in the century following 1755; a comforting conclusion he was able to reach by including in "the Highlands" the whole of the Lowlands of Perthshire and the Lowlands of Caithness, with their quickly growing Lowland towns and villages.[76] Others have apparently taken the Highlands to consist only of the four main Highland counties, for example Professor T. M. Devine, in his *Great Highland Famine*, so that (as he lists them) the Highlands have only 106 parishes (in one appendix) and 114 (in another), instead of the 162 which I have calculated.[77] On the other hand, Professor Devine's *Clanship to Crofters' War* gives a Highland line stretching fairly directly from just north of Helensburgh to Stonehaven, thus embodying in the Highlands not only the ten part-counties which I have included, but also most of Kincardineshire, plus the Lowland parts of the shires of Aberdeen, Banff, Moray, Nairn, and Caithness.[78]

However, the most important thing is not so much the actual area, about which different observers may well come to different conclusions (or even the same observer on different occasions); the essential thing is to know what an author means by "the Highlands". Problems occur when the area under discussion is left undefined, so that disagreements may arise between writers simply because each writer has a different "Highlands" in mind.

13. Highlands and Lowlands

Since there is so little agreement as to where the Highlands actually are, it is necessary to state what is meant by "the Highlands" in this work. The division between "the Highlands and Islands" on the one hand, and the rest of Scotland on the other, is taken to begin in the Firth of Clyde. This neatly separates the mountains and islands where (in 1750, and indeed much later) Gaelic was spoken, from the lower country where only English was heard. The dividing line runs northwards, with Ayrshire and the other Lowland counties to the east, and Kintyre, Arran, and the Highlands and Islands generally, to the west. The isle of Arran, the isle of Bute, and the two small islands of Cumbrae off the Ayrshire coast, formed the old county of Buteshire. Of these, Arran and Bute are in the Highlands, while the Cumbraes are in the Lowlands. The dividing line continues, between Renfrewshire to the east, and Cowal and the rest of Argyllshire to the west.

The Highland line, going upriver along the Firth of Clyde, now turns east. To the north of the firth and of the River Clyde which feeds it is Dumbartonshire, behind which are Stirlingshire and Perthshire, all three counties partly Highland and partly Lowland. It is significant that the Highland line (however it is defined) is never used as a county boundary. Those who drew up the borders of the shires clearly intended to ignore, and perhaps hoped to obscure, the natural frontier between the two strongly contrasting peoples who inhabited "Scotland", even in areas where, it seems, it would be easier to follow the natural Highland line than to invent boundaries elsewhere.

After the sharp turn to the east in the Firth of Clyde, there is no equally clear line of demarcation. One difficulty is that the Highland border is not only never a county boundary, it seldom even marks accurately the edge of a parish; so not only counties, but even individual parishes, contain both Highland and Lowland areas. Drymen in Stirlingshire, and Port of Menteith in Perthshire, for example, are two parishes that clearly stretch both north and south of the Highland border. Those parishes straddling the border, yet containing important amounts of Highland territory (that is, apparently over half the parish), have all been counted as Highland; conversely, parishes containing (so far as can be estimated) only smaller amounts of Highland territory have been counted as Lowland.

A more fundamental problem still is that the Highland boundary itself is hard to find in many cases. Three tests have been applied in this work. Firstly, was a district normally thought of as "Highland"? – and here Skene's Highland line, for the greater part of its length, has been taken as being the most seemingly plausible attempt to define the border. Secondly, is the district physically within the mountainous area – would the locality be thought of as, at least, in the hill country? Thirdly, was Gaelic spoken in the district by natives in the middle of the eighteenth century? Before that, Gaelic was known more widely; apparently it was spoken in Galloway into the seventeenth century (whether it had been introduced there from the north or from the west) and in Fife even into the eighteenth century. However, according to Edmund Burt, writing about Inverness in the

1720s, language was then the deciding factor in distinguishing the Highlanders from the Lowlanders. This was the rule, said Burt, applied by the Church of Scotland: Highlanders were those who spoke Gaelic, and Lowlanders those who spoke English.[79] So far as the boundaries of Gaelic are concerned here, the middle part of the eighteenth century, which was the closing era of the Gaelic clan society, and the opening era of the subsequent transformation, has been taken as the operative period.

As a general rule, where a district qualifies when measured against at least two of these three yardsticks, it has been considered within the Highland boundary.

14. Southern boundary of the Highlands

In Dumbartonshire, Arrochar parish was both entirely within the mountainous area and entirely Gaelic-speaking, while nearly the whole of Rhu and Luss were within the Highlands on both counts. The reporter on Luss parish in the O.S.A. said, "south from Luss English, and north from it the Gaelic, is the prevailing language":[80] regrettably he did not say whether he meant Luss village or Luss parish, nor whether he thought Luss village was north or south of the Highland/Lowland border; but as we saw Dorothy Wordsworth affirmed that in 1803 the border, that is to say the English/Gaelic boundary, was a mile or two south of the village.[81] The other parishes of Dumbartonshire have been considered as Lowland. Ardmore, a promontory on the Dumbartonshire bank of the Clyde, was often considered (for example by Skene, Fullerton, and Stewart) as marking the Highland-Lowland boundary in that area. Indeed Daniel Defoe (like Burt, Norman MacLeod, Pryde, and the Philips cartographer) thought that Dumbarton, five miles still further south-east, marked the border: Dumbarton Castle, wrote Defoe, was "the gate, as 'tis called, of the Highlands".[82] If the Highland line began at Ardmore (and even more certainly if it began at Dumbarton), part of Cardross parish would be in the Highlands; but the Cardross New Statistical Account reporter said "no Gaelic has been spoken in the parish for some generations past",[83] and the highest hill in the parish was only 1028 feet, or 313 metres. Cardross therefore has been counted as Lowland. The Highland line of 1750 (the date chosen for this work) should more realistically be drawn from Helensburgh, three miles north of Ardmore, due east to the southern extremity of Loch Lomond.

The peninsula of Rosneath, between the Gare Loch and Loch Long, is a marginal case, but it is not mountainous (it rises to only 717 feet, or 219 metres), and Gaelic seems to have died out there before 1750. The N.S.A. reporter said that Gaelic disappeared in Rosneath because of "immigration and settlement from the Lowlands" by Covenanters. "There were Gaelic services at communions in the neighbouring church of Rhu, although not half a mile across the Gare Loch, for 50 years after they had been laid aside at Rosneath."[84] For our purposes, therefore, Rosneath has been taken as Lowland.

In Stirlingshire, on the other side of Loch Lomond, two parishes pass the tests: Buchanan is nearly all Highland in character, and so is a considerable part of Drymen.

In Perthshire, Aberfoyle was wholly within Skene's Highland line, and most of it was both in the mountains and Gaelic-speaking. The northern part of Port of Menteith was in the mountainous area, and also inside the Skene line; and at least that part seems to have been Gaelic-speaking in 1750. Callander, Comrie, Monzievaird, and Monzie, must all be ranked as Highland, though each includes a Lowland area. Muthill is another borderline case; but much of it is mountainous, at least part of it is within Skene's line, and some Gaelic must have been spoken in its north-western part as late as 1750: so it is counted as Highland. Fowlis Wester, Clunie, and Alyth, each had a large enough Highland area to be counted as Highland. The Gaelic spoken in the northern parts of Fowlis Wester[85] and Clunie[86] is mentioned in their O.S.A. reports, and that in the north of Alyth[87] in its N.S.A. report. Little Dunkeld was largely Highland. The joint parish of Dunkeld and Dowally presents difficulties; the Dunkeld part of the parish, consisting only of the town, was in the Lowlands, though on the edge of the Highlands, and was English-speaking, while Dowally was both in the mountains and Gaelic-speaking.[88] The census-takers from the O.S.A. onwards gave separate population totals for Dunkeld and for Dowally; but the figures given in Dr Webster's enumeration of 1743-55 are undifferentiated, so the joint parish has had to be counted as Highland.

It is a curious fact that the River Tay, where for about a mile and half it flows from west to east past Dunkeld, was in the eighteenth century the language border – but English was spoken on the north bank, and Gaelic on the southern. Dunkeld was north of the Tay, while the Inch Ewan burn joined the Tay from the south. The south bank also saw the confluence of the River Bran, coming out of Strath Bran, which was part of Gaeldom. So the south bank, from the Inch Ewan burn (and the adjacent Birnam Hill) westwards, was Gaelic-speaking, while the north side, westwards as far as the King's Seat hill, was English-speaking. Of the three hills which marked the dividing line between the languages, King's Seat, and Craigie Barns behind it, are two miles north-westward of Birnam Hill, and on the other side of the Tay.

15. Highlanders in other Perthshire parishes

The Perthshire parishes named above, and the other Perthshire Highland parishes to the north and west of them, did not include quite all the Gaelic speakers of the county in the latter part of the eighteenth century. There were several parishes of Lowland Perthshire, such as Kincardine in Menteith[89], Caputh[90], and Perth itself,[91] where Gaelic was spoken by refugee Highlanders (though less and less of it as the years went by, and the original fugitives died out); these parishes, however, were none the less Lowland even though they served as an asylum for Highlanders expelled from their homes. Apart from these, there were a number of parishes that touched on the Gaelic-speaking area, and therefore included some native Gaelic-speakers. There is evidence, either in the O.S.A. or the N.S.A., of Gaelic being spoken in 1750 – and indeed much later – in the north-western part of Kilmadock;[92] in a detached part of Crieff (in Glen Almond);[93] at the western end of Auchtergaven (in the heights of Strath Bran);[94] and in a detached part of Blairgowrie (some of which was in the Forest of Clunie, and some in Strath Ardle), as well as in an outlying district (in western Glen Ericht) of the main part of the parish.[95] (There, said the minister as late as the 1840s, "in the upper district of the parish the Gaelic language is still partially spoken by the common people", but it was "gradually disappearing".) Some Gaelic may have been spoken in 1750 and later in a detached part of Bendochy, situated in Glen Shee, and also in the extreme north-west of Methven and of Moneydie.

Some of these parishes could be claimed to extend across the Highland line, or included detached districts that were in the mountainous, Gaelic-speaking area. Crieff parish encompassed Glen Almond, which had 500 people in the 1790s, and (after the introduction of the large-farm system) only 230 in the 1840s; but the glen was merely an appendage of Crieff parish, which was largely in the Lowlands and largely English-speaking. Other parishes with some Gaelic speakers would appear to be altogether in the lower country.

It is not always easy to determine where the language frontier lay. Kilmadock is a case in point. According to the O.S.A., some parishioners spoke Gaelic in the 1790s: "in the quarter towards Callander", that is, the north-western end of the parish, "the generality of the inhabitants speak Gaelic". The N.S.A. reporter in 1844 said "a few families" spoke Gaelic; then he quoted his predecessor's words about the people near Callander speaking Gaelic, and added, "as some of them do to this day". From that one would conclude that the language border was at the most a mile or two below Callander. But John Murdoch said that when in 1838 he went to Doune, which was at the opposite or south-eastern end of Kilmadock parish, some seven miles from Callander, Gaelic was still not unknown: "the old knew Gaelic, the middle-aged knew some and despised the language – and the young ignored it".[96] Much of Kilmadock, however, is low-lying, as well as being outside Skene's Highland line, and for the purposes of this work it has been considered to be Lowland.

These marginal parishes probably contained a few hundred Gaelic speakers at the most; in Auchtergaven at the time of the N.S.A. the native Gaelic population – as opposed to the Highland immigrants – numbered only four families. The parishes mentioned in this section have for these reasons not been included in the area of the Highlands of Perthshire for the purposes of this work.

16. Eastern boundary of the Highlands

Across the county border in Angus, Glenisla parish is almost entirely both mountainous and within Skene's Highland line,[97] and it seems unlikely that no Gaelic at all was spoken in 1750 in at least the upper parts of Glen Isla. It has therefore been included among the Highland parishes.

Even with the help of these three criteria, however, the Highland-Lowland border is particularly difficult to define in Angus, apart from Glenisla parish. Physically, the mountainous area there includes not only Glen Isla, but also Glen Prosen, Glen Clova, and Glen Esk, and several similar smaller valleys. Furthermore, David Stewart described the passes formed by the North and South Esk (the valley of the South Esk is Glen Clova) as being on the boundary of the Highlands, and in his map of the Highlands he included the hilly district of Angus, which – apart from the Ogilvy country of Glen Isla – was marked as being Lindsay territory.[98] But Skene put the Highland line on the eastern side of Glen Isla, leaving out the rest of Angus, and there seems to be no trace of Gaelic being spoken as late as the middle of the eighteenth century in Glen Prosen, Glen Clova, and Glen Esk. They have therefore been excluded from the area now under consideration.

Aberdeenshire also presents problems. The mountainous area there ends less abruptly, descending more gradually to the plain. The Gaelic test gives more help. In 1791 Robert Heron said that in Aberdeenshire Gaelic was spoken from six or seven miles to the west of Cromar:[99] that would put the language boundary at or very near Ballater, a conclusion which is supported by the O.S.A. evidence. Skene, too, said that Ballater was where the Highland line crossed the River Dee;[100] and Thomas Pennant said that "the Pass of Bollitir" was "the eastern entrance into the Highlands".[101] From Ballater Skene's Highland line ran northwards to Craigellachie, where the Spey leaves the hills for the lower ground; and the Gaelic-English language border seems to have followed much the same path. Three parishes, therefore, have been taken as being entirely or mainly in the Highlands – Crathie and Braemar, Glenmuick Tullich and Glengairn, and Strathdon. Of these,

Gaelic was the general language in Crathie,[102] and was still spoken in parts of Glenmuick[103] and of Strathdon.[104]

Of the four Banffshire parishes which Skene's definition would put (in whole or in part) within the Highlands, Kirkmichael was Gaelic-speaking in the 1790s (though English was beginning to make inroads),[105] and at that time Gaelic had not entirely died out in part of Mortlach:[106] and although the O.S.A. reports on Inveravon and Aberlour do not mention Gaelic, since Mortlach to the east, Kirkmichael to the south, and Cromdale[107] and Knockando[108] to the north-west, were all – wholly or partly – Gaelic-speaking in 1750, it seems very likely that Inveravon and Aberlour were still part of the Gaelic area at that time. (In Inveravon, indeed, Gaelic had still not completely disappeared even in 1836, according to the N.S.A.)[109]

From Craigellachie, said Skene, the Highland line went west-north-west, reaching the Moray Forth to the east of Nairn. Stewart, like Skene, included the whole of Nairnshire in the Highlands: but that would bring in too much territory for the Highlands as they are now being defined. From the evidence in the O.S.A. and the N.S.A., only three parishes in Morayshire – Cromdale, Knockando, and Edinkillie[110] – were wholly or partly Gaelic-speaking about 1750, and in Nairnshire, from that evidence, only one, Cawdor.[111] In a second Nairnshire parish, Ardclach, neither of the statistical reports, old or new, mentioned language (both accounts were written by the same minister, Donald Mitchell); but from its position between Cawdor and Edinkillie, both wholly or partly Gaelic-speaking, it must have been to a certain extent within the Gaelic area. Apart from that, John Murdoch was born in Ardclach in 1818, and John Hunter wrote that even at that late date Ardclach was "a Gaelic-speaking locality", so Murdoch grew up in a Gaelic household.[112] (There is just a possibility that Dallas, too, of the Moray parishes, had some native Gaelic speakers in 1750, but there does not seem to be enough evidence to make us accept Dallas as within the Highland line.) Further north in Morayshire and Nairnshire, the land (though partly still within Skene's Highland line) was not mountainous, nor was Gaelic spoken. (In the counties of Nairn, Moray, and Banff, the Lowlands were to the north, and the Highlands to the south.)

Nairn parish itself is hard to classify. James VI of Scotland and I of England (who died in 1625) is supposed to have boasted that he had a town in his dominions which was so large that the people at one end of it could not understand the people at the other. This was the town of Nairn, where at that time the English speakers (who were fishermen) lived at the north side of the town, on the coast, and the Gaelic speakers lived inland on their farms to the south of the town. Skene said that the Highland line "terminates at the mouth of the River Nairn, which flows through the town of Nairn, and formerly separated the Gaelic-speaking people on its left bank from the Lowland population on its right". Dr Johnson, a century and a half later, considered it to be on the Highland border. "At Nairn we may fix the verge of the Highlands; for here I first saw peat fires, and first heard the Erse [that is, the Irish or Gaelic] language."[113] Peat fires alone would not put Nairn in the Highlands; and as for "the Erse language", Johnson did not say whether the Erse he heard was spoken by a Nairn native, by a Gael who had come to live in the town, or even by a Highlander who happened to be passing through. Gaelic as a local language is not mentioned in the Nairn reports in the O.S.A. or the N.S.A., so presumably it had died out there since King James's boast early in the previous century; and in Skene's comment that Nairn was "formerly" the language frontier, "formerly" must mean before the eighteenth century. Nairn is outside the mountainous area; and the majority of the most convincing versions of the Highland line (as it was understood after the '45) seem to leave Nairn outside. Therefore, for the purposes of this survey, Nairn parish has not been considered as part of the Highlands.

The whole of Inverness-shire, however, has been embraced in the area to be considered, including the strip of country bordering the Moray Firth (largely the parishes of Inverness itself, Petty, and Ardersier) for although there were no mountains in that margin of Inverness-shire, it was within Skene's Highland line, and the people spoke Gaelic.

17. Ross-shire and Sutherland

The peninsula on the east of Ross-shire, between the Beauly Firth and the Cromarty Firth, is called Ardmeanach in Gaelic and the Black Isle in English (the latter being a triumph of inaccuracy, since it is neither black nor an island). Should it be considered as Highland or Lowland? Or should it be divided between the two, and if so where is the division? It is not mountainous, no part of it reaching as high as 900 feet (275 metres); but it is often considered as being within the Highland line. Yet Lowland influence was so strong in the easterly part of the Black Isle that in the middle of the eighteenth century (which earlier was taken as the operative period) very little Gaelic, apparently, was spoken in the two parishes of Cromarty and Rosemarkie, and not much of it in Avoch. It seems that Gaelic had been spoken there at an earlier date (the Avoch minister said that no Gaelic had "been preached in this parish since the beginning of this [eighteenth] century"):[114] and later in that century so many Highlanders had come to the Black Isle as refugees from clearances further west that Gaelic was spoken widely in those two and a half parishes as well as in the four and a half where it had always prevailed. Without any claim that the decision is defensible in strict logic, the whole of the Black Isle will be taken as part of the Highlands for the purpose of this work.

English was then, and was to become even more, the dominant language of these islands and indeed of many parts of the world overseas; so a smaller amount of English will in some eyes outweigh a greater amount of Gaelic. Of the seven Ardmeanach parishes, in 1750 four and part of another spoke Gaelic, while two and part of another spoke English – the Gaelic area of Ardmeanach covered at least two-thirds of the peninsula, if not three-quarters: but one commentator wrote that "the inhabitants of the Black Isle . . . spoke English" – they were "Sassenachs",[115] while another thought that on the Black Isle "the people are Teutonic".[116] In the same way, the English "Black Isle", inaccurate though it is, has been allowed to oust the Gaelic name.

The remaining Ross-shire parishes are all clearly Highland whatever rubric is applied. The same is true of the parishes of Sutherland. (Professor Smout's surprising decision to exclude parts of northern and eastern Sutherland – such as Reay village, Melvich, and much of Strath Halladale, of Easter Ross, and of eastern Inverness-shire, from the Highlands, has not been followed here.)

18. The border in Caithness

Caithness at the time of the O.S.A. had ten parishes in all (including Reay, which was mainly in Caithness, but partly in Sutherland). The opinions of experts differ remarkably as to whether Caithness was in the Gaelic Highlands, or the anglophone Lowlands. Professor Rosalind Mitchison (writing a whole book about a leading Caithness landowner) said that there was scarcely any Gaelic in Caithness: "typically, in the eighteenth century, very little of Caithness was reported as Gaelic speaking." [117] Sir Archibald Geikie asserted that "Caithness . . . belongs not to the mountains, but to the Lowlands, and has been for many centuries in possession of the Scandinavian stock"[118] – i.e., Lowlanders. Lord Napier apparently believed that Caithness was "not inhabited by the Celtic race".[119] Dr Grimble remarked of the county as it was in the early 1600s: "it so happened that Caithness . . . was not a Gaelic region and never had been."[120] Seton Gordon wrote: "Caithness is generally considered without [outside] the Highland boundary."[121] R. C. MacKenzie said: "Caithness . . . is a lowland shire."[122] Allan W. MacColl maintained that "Caithness was different [from the rest of the Highlands], agriculturally, socially, and linguistically".[123] (This presumably means that Caithness was English-speaking.) Others, in contrast, affirmed that Caithness was definitely part of the Highlands. John MacLeod asserted that "the North Highlands are two counties: Sutherland and Caithness", although he thought "Gaelic vanished from Caithness very many years ago".[124] James Kyd not only considered Caithness to be in the Highlands, but called it a "typical Highland county",[125] while David Stewart maintained that the "Gaelic population" occupied the entire county up to the Pentland Firth and "the north-east point of Caithness", although accepting that "there has always been more of the Lowland costume, and of the Saxon or Scotch language, in that than in any other Highland county".[126] Professor Richards (as we saw earlier) regarded Caithness as a Highland county, and so did the *Companion to Gaelic Scotland*. It is curious that all these writers thought that the boundary artificially drawn round the north-east projection of Great Britain (i.e. Caithness), that is to say the shire-border as defined by the Lowland authority, was so sacrosanct that the whole of the county had to be either in the Highlands or out of the Highlands: seven writers put Caithness in the Lowlands, and five in the Highlands. That all these diametrically opposed views could be asserted without any of the commentators trying to deal with what other writers had written, does perhaps show us how little importance was placed by academe on the achievement of accuracy in matters of Highland history.

The truth was somewhere between the two extremes championed above: in reality half of the ten Caithness parishes, the western, hillier ones, were mainly Gaelic speaking during the eighteenth century, and half of them, the eastern, flatter ones, were English speaking: so Caithness should be considered as part Highland, part Lowland.

Donald Omand quoted a document in MacFarlane's *Geographical Collections* to the effect that "in the parishes of Latheron, Watten, Halkirk, Thurso, and Reay, 'at least the greater part of the common people' spoke 'the Irish tongue' – Gaelic", in the 1720s.[127] (Earlier, in 1706, a report on the Caithness parishes said some Gaelic was spoken even in Wick; but this apparently died out later.)[128] Earlier still, in the 1680s, Sir Robert Sibbald had said of Caithness, "the people for the most part, speak both Irish and English" – but English was the main tongue in the east, and Gaelic in the west.[129] The anonymous author of the description of the Highlands in the 1750s said that of the Caithness parishes, five spoke English, and five "Irish".[130] Dr Richard Pococke, travelling in 1760, said there were nine parishes in Caithness (presumably he was counting Reay as a Sutherland parish); "the three eastern parishes [which are Canisbay, Bower, and Wick] talk English and no Eirshe, and also two others in this part"[131] (which must be Dunnet and Olrig). That would leave the other four (or five, including Reay) parishes as Gaelic speaking. The two Statistical Accounts lead one to the same conclusion. The O.S.A. shows that Gaelic was spoken both in the middle and at the end of the eighteenth century in three parishes – Reay,[132] Thurso,[133] and Halkirk,[134] and the N.S.A. shows the same as to Latheron.[135] The O.S.A. report on Watten (like the O.S.A. report on Latheron) did not mention language, but the N.S.A. Watten reporter boasted (in 1840) that "a remarkable improvement has taken place in the last forty years" in various ways, one of them being "in the language generally spoken".[136] This was the attitude of many apostles of improvement to the extirpation of Gaelic by English; and we may take this as a confirmation that Gaelic was still "the language generally spoken" in Watten at the end of the eighteenth century, before it was "remarkably improved" out of the parish.

In 1779 some Highlanders who had been recruited for two Highland regiments were told, on arriving at Leith, that they had to join Lowland regiments instead. Naturally they resisted, being independent-minded Highlanders (the feeble and submissive clansmen pictured for us by Lowland writers would of course have made no trouble); so much did they stand up for themselves that they killed ten and injured thirty-one of the soldiers sent to arrest them. Those put on trial for this mutiny included Robert Budge, who told the court "he was a native of the upper parts of Caithness, and being ignorant of the English language, and accustomed to wear the Highland garb", he had enlisted in a Highland regiment.[137] (He and the other accused were sentenced to be shot, but were then pardoned, and joined the Black Watch.) So Budge not only spoke Gaelic, but (despite having an apparently Sassenach name) he had – he said – no English.

In 1750 the Gaelic-speaking region, including the greater part of the parishes of Watten and Thurso, occupied about two-thirds of the land area of Caithness. It seems likely that half, at least, of the Caithness people were Gaelic speakers, since the five parishes where Gaelic could be heard contained just over sixty per cent of the population of the ten parishes, while the five other parishes had just under forty per cent. The Highland line of the mid-eighteenth century is often drawn from the town of Thurso to the burn of Easter Clyth, in the east of Latheron, and that demarcation was the boundary between Gaelic and English. The five Caithness parishes here defined as Highland bring the total of Highland parishes to 162.

19. The Highlands and Islands

The Highlands, then, as that term is used in this work, includes the whole of four of the old Scottish counties, and part of ten others. It covers Sutherland (with thirteen parishes), Ross-shire (with thirty-three), Inverness-shire (with thirty-two), and Argyllshire (with thirty-five). Added to these are four parishes in Buteshire; three in Dumbartonshire; two in Stirlingshire; twenty-two in Perthshire; one in Angus; three in Aberdeenshire; four in Banffshire; three in Morayshire; two in Nairnshire; and five in Caithness. (Where parishes cross, or crossed, county boundaries, they have been included in that county where, so far as one can tell, most of their acreage lies; but as many as a dozen parishes are switched from one county to another in various lists.) If the tally given here is accepted, it will be seen that the four counties (of Argyll, Inverness, Ross and Cromarty, and Sutherland) which are sometimes taken to comprehend the whole of the Highlands, in fact contain only 113 parishes, leaving forty-nine parishes, nearly a third of the total, out of the picture.[138]

The 162 parishes which are counted as Highland in this work are as follows:

Sutherland (thirteen parishes): Assynt, Clyne, Creich, Dornoch, Durness, Eddrachillis, Farr, Golspie, Kildonan, Lairg, Loth, Rogart, Tongue.

Ross-shire (thirty-three): Alness, Applecross, Avoch, Contin, Cromarty, Dingwall, Edderton, Fearn, Fodderty, Gairloch, Glenshiel, Killearnan, Kilmuir Easter, Kiltearn, Kincardine, Kintail, Knockbain (or Kilmuir Wester & Suddie), Lochalsh, Lochbroom, Lochcarron, Logie Easter, Nigg, Resolis (or Kirkmichael), Rosemarkie, Rosskeen, Tain, Tarbat, Urquhart (or Logie Wester), Urray, Barvas, Lochs, Stornoway, Uig. (In other words, twenty-nine mainland parishes, and four island ones.)

Inverness-shire (thirty-two): Abernethy & Kincardine, Alvie, Ardersier, Boleskine & Abertarff, Croy & Dalcross, Daviot & Dunlichity, Dores, Duthil & Rothiemurchus, Glenelg, Inverness, Kilmallie, Kilmonivaig, Kilmorack, Kiltarlity, Kingussie & Inch, Kirkhill, Laggan, Moy & Dalarossie, Petty, Urquhart & Glenmoriston, Barra, Bracadale, Duirinish, Harris, Kilmuir, North Uist, Portree, Sleat, Small Isles, Snizort, South Uist, Strath. (Twenty mainland parishes, and twelve insular ones.)

Argyllshire (thirty-five): Ardchattan & Muckairn, Ardnamurchan, Campbeltown, Craignish, Dunoon & Kilmun, Glassary (or Kilmichael), Glenorchy & Inishail, Inveraray, Inverchaolain, Kilbrandon & Kilchattan, Kilcalmonell & Kilberry, Kilchrenan & Dalavich, Kilfinan, Killean & Kilchenzie, Kilmartin, Kilmodan, Kilmore & Kilbride, Kilninver & Kilmelfort, North Knapdale, South Knapdale, Lismore & Appin, Lochgoilhead & Kilmorich, Morvern, Saddell & Skipness, Southend, Strachur & Strathlachlan, Gigha & Cara, Jura & Colonsay, Kilarrow & Kilmeny, Kilchoman, Kildalton, Kilfinichen & Kilvickeon, Kilninian & Kilmore, Tiree & Coll, Torosay. (Twenty-six – mainly – mainland parishes, and nine insular ones. Kilbrandon, and Lismore, are part mainland, part island, and have been considered mainland parishes in this list, since that is where most of their acreage lay.)

Buteshire (four): Kilbride, Kilmory, Kingarth, Rothesay. (The first two parishes formed the island of Arran, and the second two the island of Bute.)

Dumbartonshire (three): Arrochar, Luss, Rhu.

Stirlingshire (two): Buchanan, Drymen.

Perthshire (twenty-two): Aberfoyle, Alyth, Balquhidder, Blair Atholl, Callander, Clunie, Comrie, Dull, Dunkeld & Dowally, Fortingall, Fowlis Wester, Kenmore,

Killin, Kirkmichael, Little Dunkeld, Logierait, Monzie, Monzievaird & Strowan, Moulin, Muthill, Port of Menteith, Weem.

Angus (one): Glenisla.

Aberdeenshire (three): Crathie & Braemar, Glenmuick Tullich & Glengairn, Strathdon.

Banffshire (four): Aberlour, Inveravon, Kirkmichael, Mortlach.

Morayshire (three): Cromdale, Edinkillie, Knockando.

Nairnshire (two): Ardclach, Cawdor.

Caithness (five): Halkirk, Latheron, Reay, Thurso, Watten. (All the parishes listed from Dumbartonshire to Sutherland and Caithness are of course on the mainland.)

These 162 parishes will be taken in the present work to mark out the Highlands and Islands of Scotland. This definition will certainly not satisfy everyone; many people will disagree in part or whole with my conclusions. However, at least the reader will now know what is meant by my use of the term "the Highlands".[139]

The Highland parishes were much larger on the average than the parishes of the Lowlands. In the whole of Scotland, according to one calculation, there were 938 parishes, which covered about 29,800 square miles. The 162 Highland parishes contained about 16,300 square miles (nearly 55 per cent of the area of Scotland), while the 776 Scottish parishes outside the Highlands – assuming that Scotland as a whole did have 938 parishes – contained about 13,500 square miles (just over 45 per cent). It follows that the 162 Highland parishes averaged about 100 square miles (more exactly, 100.6) each, while the 776 non-Highland parishes averaged only about seventeen square miles (or 17.4) each.[140]

20. What is a clearance?

Having now complied with Sterne's injunction by offering my definition of "the Highlands", it seems only reasonable (in a book about the Highland clearances) to round the matter off by defining "clearances". In this work, therefore, a "clearance" will signify any episode where a number of small tenants, and of course their families, were evicted by their landlord, in order to make the land they had occupied available for another purpose. That other purpose was normally the creation of a large farm, whether mainly arable, or mainly for cattle or for sheep; usually the cleared farm was run by a large tenant, occasionally by the landlord himself. Sometimes the other purpose was the establishment of a game preserve. (This development is examined in volume four.) By extension, I have thought it reasonable to use the term "clearance" also for occasions where a landlord imposed such great rent increases, or such onerous tenancy terms, that the result was the departure of a number of small tenants (even consecutively over a brief period of time, rather than simultaneously), in such a way that a reasonable person would consider that outcome to be the main aim of the landlord, or alternatively that it was the inevitable result of his measures.

Sometimes the families ejected in these mass evictions were given small pieces of waste land to bring into cultivation; sometimes they found a refuge in a nearby Highland village, or in one of the growing Highland towns; sometimes they left the Highlands altogether, and moved to the Lowlands or even further afield, to one of a number of destinations overseas. What happened to the small tenants after such an episode does not affect the use of the term "clearance". It is necessary to make this point – that a clearance consisted in the expulsion of the small tenants, not in the destination of the expellees – because of the terminology employed by one enterprising writer, who has in recent years gained much publicity for himself and his books by making widely reported claims that there were no clearances, or that at the most there were only a few unimportant ones.[141] Such a sensational departure from reality, equal perhaps to claiming that no one was killed in the Second World War, or that the Spanish Inquisition was staffed exclusively by Plymouth Brethren, certainly gained him attention; and this is especially curious, because one finds that the events described as clearances by everyone else are mentioned in his published works. Sometimes in this author's output the assumption appears to be made that multiple simultaneous evictions did not count as a clearance unless police and soldiers were called out in force to eject the small tenants in a violent confrontation, and then to drive them immediately on to ships bound for foreign parts. In fact events of this kind formed only one segment of the long history of the clearances, and took place mainly in the mid-nineteenth century, when the imposition of a Scottish Poor Law, and two successive famines among the evicted Highlanders, meant that the landlords were terrified of being taxed to pay for the paupers they had themselves created, resulting in an almost hysterical hostility on the part of the proprietors to any last stray native Highlander being allowed to remain on their estates.

So it appears that the "clearance-denial" school, consisting of this writer and his allies, attempts to justify its assertions by restricting the use of the term "clearances" to one particular subdivision of the mass evictions. It is, of course, not difficult to make a sensation by re-defining accepted terms. If one insisted that the term "chairs" really meant cheetahs, then it would be easy to prove (especially if you have a number of journalist friends willing to give you free publicity) that few houses contained chairs (as then interpreted), and to produce the eye-catching headlines, "writer claims very few houses have chairs", or "chairs almost unknown in houses". And if one re-defined clearances as lollipops, one could soon "prove" there were not very many of them in the Highlands. Hence the need to make clear the meaning of one's terms.

THE HIGHLANDS AND ISLANDS

21. Two countries

In the area covered by these 162 parishes the Gaelic-speaking clans flourished for hundreds of years. During that time the prevailing language, dress, social and economic organization, standards of conduct, customs and habits, all differed sharply from those obtaining outside the Highland line. For centuries the Lowlands and the Highlands were, in effect, two separate countries, one of which claimed to rule the other: or rather, though the Lowlands was one country, the Highlands consisted of a number of distinct small countries, all of which the Lowlands claimed to rule. In the same way, England claimed to rule France for many years after that particular dream was ended with the English defeat at Castillon in 1453; in fact each English (or British) monarch for the next *three and a half centuries* claimed vociferously to be also the current king of France, until the claim was abandoned in 1800, in the reign of George III (perhaps because in 1800 even the king of France wasn't the king of France). At every coronation the new English monarch, despite Castillon, was crowned also king of France. After 1603, when the thrones of England and Scotland were united, each sovereign in turn was hailed as "King of England, Scotland, *France*, and Ireland".[142] But a claim is not the same as an accomplishment. Few people now would say that George III of England *was* king of France for forty years, and that his predecessors on the throne of England since Castillon (about twenty of them) had also been monarchs of France, even though the documents are there to "prove" the title. Fewer still would claim that the English kings' inability to influence events in France – short of invading the country with an English army (which of course they did from time to time) – was due solely to the barbaric lawlessness of the French; but many writers make exactly parallel allegations about the Lowland authorities' pretension to rule the Highlands. In the same way, if I claimed to be the king of Bolivia, then it would be easy to prove conclusively (at least to all who were prepared to accept empty assertions) that all Bolivians must be barbarians outside the law, since it can be shown irrefutably that they have always ignored all my orders and decrees.

Of course, if the English monarchs had been able in reality to conquer France – say in the middle of the eighteenth century – then it is probable that conventional historians would have regarded this conquest as confirming all the documentary evidence that the kings of England in the fifteenth, sixteenth and seventeenth centuries were in fact kings of France also, and to declare that the scandalous failure of the French people in those centuries to behave as if they were subjects of the London king was proof of their deplorable savagery.

The clear distinction between the Highlands and the Lowlands was, admittedly, blurred by the self-interest of those Highland chiefs who had obtained impressive documents from Lowland officials naming them as the owners of their clans' land, or, often (equally fictitiously), of the land belonging to other clans. The charters were in effect valueless for any significant purpose while the Lowlanders could be kept at bay: but since it was more and more obvious that a Lowland conquest of the Highlands would enormously increase the power and opulence of the Highland chiefs who had these charters, many of those chiefs, not surprisingly, acted almost as a fifth column, working for the Lowland authorities in the mountains, and hankering after that Edinburgh supremacy which would (as in fact it did after 1746) transform the charter holders into wealthy landlords, owning many thousands of acres, and with a great rental income able to mix with the English and Lowland upper class on practically equal terms.[143]

22. Racially homogeneous

Some of those who were either landlords or their natural allies in the new system believed that they were not only putting an end to the separate society of the Highlanders, but that even any memory of such a society would be lost. James Loch boasted: "The children of those who are removed from the hills will lose all recollection of the habits and customs of their fathers."[144] The minister of Strachur and Strathlachlan, reporting on his parish for the O.S.A. in 1792, said that the clan "system is exploded, and in a short time the existence of it will be totally forgotten".[144] Some later Lowland or English commentators wrote as if that had in fact happened: they tried (as we saw earlier) to legitimize the Lowland/English conquest of the Highlands by asserting that the Highlanders and the Lowlanders were really just the same people. Professor Sir Robert Rait, Historiographer Royal for Scotland in the 1920s, said that "mediaeval Scotland was racially homogeneous and conscious of its unity", and that "centuries had to pass before the Scottish Highlanders were taught [by some unknown troublemakers, whose identity Sir Robert sadly left obscure] to speak of their Lowland countrymen as Saxons".[145] Another historian, Professor Hugh Trevor-Roper, so eminent in the profession that he was elevated to the House of Lords as Baron Dacre, said (in the words quoted above) that "the whole concept of a distinctive Highland culture and tradition is a retrospective invention".[146] Sir Thomas Innes of Learney (Lord Lyon King of Arms in Edinburgh) asserted that "the 'fake' of a 'divided Scotland' . . . which caught the imagination of uncritical writers of the past generation or two, is something much more sinister" – it was merely "propaganda for dividing Scotland against itself".[147] Michael Fry boldly claimed that there was never any "antagonism of Highlanders and Lowlanders as such . . . On the contrary, through all their troubled relations over 400 years [1600 to 2000], Highlanders and Lowlanders have not ceased to regard themselves as members of one nation."[148] (In fact, of course, most Highlanders not only did not regard themselves as "Scotsmen or Scotswomen"; they did not even regard themselves primarily as Highlanders, but as members of a specific clan, and citizens of a specific clan country.)

While some Lowland or English writers thus bravely insisted that the Gaelic-speaking Highland hunters and herdsmen (many of whose ancestors had come originally from Ireland, the sister island to the west) were really just the same people as the bitterly hostile English-speaking Lowland townsfolk and husbandmen (most of whose ancestors had come originally from the southern parts of Britain, and before that from the Continent), others were audacious enough to ignore the Gaels entirely. As we saw above, J. R. Green said the people of England and of Scotland had "a common blood and common speech",[149] thus firmly rejecting any suspicions some might hold that the Gaels, who occupied most of Scotland – not to mention the Welsh and the Cornish – were equally legitimate inhabitants of the new kingdom of Great Britain.

It might be thought that the final blow, when a whole way of life has been deliberately destroyed, is to claim that it never existed. There is, however, much evidence, as we shall see, that there was a "distinctive Highland culture and tradition". As we saw earlier, the traveller who crossed the Highland line in Perthshire in 1818 asserted (in words already quoted) that "the people seemed to be in language, dress, and manners, entirely different"; it appeared to him that he had been "transported at once, as if by magic, into some remote foreign region".[150]

The Highlanders and Lowlanders were in fact so different from each other, in their speech, their social attitudes, and their whole way of life, and each people found it so difficult to empathize with the other, that for centuries they lived in unremitting mutual malevolence. In modern times the Lowlanders have zealously appropriated the tartan, the bagpipes, and the other outward symbols of the old Highland society; as soon as a visitor crosses the border from England into Lowland Scotland, he may well see fully-accoutred "Highlanders" playing the bagpipes as a bait for his camera, and his wallet. For centuries, however, the Scots Lowlanders regarded these Highland emblems with horror. Macaulay said that after the Highlands had become fashionable, "by most Englishmen, Scotchman and Highlander were regarded as synonymous words. Few people seemed to be aware that, at no remote period, a MacDonald or MacGregor in his tartan was to a citizen of Edinburgh or Glasgow what an Indian hunter in his war paint is to an inhabitant of Philadelphia or Boston." The Highland garb, "before the Union, was considered by nine Scotchmen out of ten [i.e., nine Lowlanders out of ten] as the dress of a thief".[151] At least Macaulay realized the great gulf between Highlander and Lowlander.

23. Most murderous commanders

We shall see later that the Lowland kings, and the Lowland authorities, routinely described the Highlanders as "all utterly barbarous", like "wolves and wild boars", a "bloody people" who were "trained up in all manner of cruel barbarity and wickedness", mere depositories of "barbarity and incivility", fit only for extirpation,[152] so that they could be replaced by civilized people from the Lowlands. Those who held these opinions clearly did not believe that Scotland was "racially homogeneous", and that any talk of the differences between the Highlanders and the Lowlanders was merely "a retrospective invention" of "sinister" origins.

The defeat of Prince Charles was followed by a long campaign of continuous atrocity against the Highlanders and all that belonged to them. Professor T. C. Smout said the '45 rebellion led to "the utter disaster of those who took up arms against the king";[153] but that understates the case. In the Lowlands, certainly, those who had been active Jacobites were relentlessly pursued as individuals, but in the Highlands the quarry was virtually all the Gaels, together with their possessions, their habitations, and their flocks and herds. The horrors of the Hanoverian revenge were perpetrated not merely upon those who had supported Prince Charles, but upon all the Highlanders. The savagery was racial, in intent and in execution: those who had supported the Government, and those who had opposed it, suffered equally if they were within reach of the conquering army. As Professor Lenman put it, "Cumberland's troops swept down [in the Highlands] and burned all the houses and stole all the cattle and effects, with absolutely no distinction between rebels and non-rebels".[154] Walter Scott said that after Culloden the Hanoverian regiments were "laying waste what it was the fashion to call 'the country of the enemy'."[155] The watchword was certainly vae victis – woe to the vanquished; but so far as the British authorities were concerned the vanquished in 1746 were the whole race of Highlanders. The centuries-long belligerence between the Gael and the Sassenach was settled once and for all by the complete victory of the Lowlanders, now made very much stronger by their union forty years before with England, and by the wealth which accrued to the rulers of the united Great Britain from Lowland/English trade abroad and developing industries at home.

Duncan Ban MacIntyre, who like many other Highlanders had supported the Hanoverians, and had in fact fought for them at Falkirk, realized afterwards (to repeat) that the target of the Lowlanders and the English after Culloden was all the Highlanders. "We are made the Saxon's jest. To us victory has proved an evil. Should Charles return, we are ready to stand by him: then up with the carmine plaid! – then up with the rifle!"[156] The excuse for the atrocities was the necessity to stamp out Jacobitism, but the real aim was to clamp down on the Highlanders, to extirpate their independence once and for all. Even the ultra-loyal Duke of Argyll protested at the punitive expedition against Morvern on the west coast, to much of which he held the charter-right, and said that Jacobite Lowlanders were not treated so harshly: "I don't find any houses have been burned by the army on the east side of Scotland" – that is, in the Lowlands. In this onslaught on all the Highlanders, Argyll said he was afraid he might see "the well affected suffer as much and even more than the rebels".[157]

Some commentators have ascribed the outrages merely to "the English",[158] and certainly English soldiers did their share; Captain Loftus of the Royal East Kent Regiment showed himself to be an enthusiastic plunderer,[159] while Lord George Sackville's men, the East Devonshires, committed rape and murder.[160] The basic cause of the barbarity, however, was the enmity long felt, and now in the hour of triumph able to be fully expressed, of the Lowlanders for the Highlanders. Stuart MacDonald (descended from the Keppoch MacDonalds) wrote that Cumberland's "most murderous commanders, those renowned for their atrocities against captive or wounded Highland men, women and children, were Scots. Major Lockhart of Cholmondeley's, Captain Caroline Scott of Guise's, Captain Dunlop of Blakeney's and Captain Ferguson RN top the roll of shame. It was Scots of the Royals who bound and shot nineteen badly wounded Jacobite officers on Culloden Moor two days after the battle."[161] It was the same Lowland regiment, the Royal Scots, which, on the day following the battle, collected the Highland wounded into two heaps, and then showed the barbarians how civilized soldiers behaved by firing a six-pounder cannon into each pile.[162] Captain Robert Duff RN, and Captain John Hay RN (Lowland naval men), commanded the forces of devastation in Morvern, where every boat found was smashed, and "near 400 houses", together with "several barns well fill'd with corn, horses, cows, meal and other provisions were distroy'd by fire and fire-arms".[163]

24. Very distinct species

It must be rare that two such dissimilar and hostile national groups have together inhabited for so long a region that was claimed (by one group's authorities) to be a single country. As T. M. Devine said, "there is a long tradition of anti-Highland satire in both Lowland poetry and song which can be traced back to the Middle Ages, and references in satiric works by such poets as William Dunbar and Sir Richard Holland caricatured the Gael as stupid, violent, comic, feckless, and filthy".[164] Early in the seventeenth century, an Irish Franciscan missionary reported that "there is a lasting and mutual enmity between the Anglo-Scots and Gaelic-speaking Scots . . . there is as much difference in mode of life and in outlook between the Anglo-Scots and the Gaelic-speaking Scots as there is between the Scots and the Greeks".[165] In 1689 Thomas Morer wrote: "We take the

Lowlanders to be a Medley of Picts, Scots, French, Saxons and English, as their language and habit insinuate, which is the reason why the Highlanders, who look on themselves to be a purer race, cannot affect 'em; but on the contrary deal with 'em as a spurious, degenerate people."[166] An inhabitant of Derby, who in December 1745 had some of the Highlanders in Prince Charles' army quartered on him after their advance south, agreed with the Lowlanders; he temperately described the Gaels as "fiends turn'd out of hell", "vagrant gypsies", a "herd of Hottentots", and "a set of banditti", whose strange language was merely "jabbering, screaming, and howling together"[166]. The Highlanders had an equally low opinion of those who lived outside the mountains, and of their language. John MacLachlan, the bard of Rahoy, described English as an "unpleasant noise",[167] while Allan MacDougall, the Glengarry bard, said the incoming Lowland shepherds, talking English, were merely "harshly screeching" (and followed up this stricture by the amiable thought – this was in the French wars around 1800 – that "we would love the French to come and chop the heads off the Lowlanders").[168] The hostility between the two communities may be reflected in the fact that the speech of the Lowlanders had borrowed many more words from the language of France (even Hogmanay was probably taken from a French dialect word meaning a gift at New Year), which was spoken at the nearest 360 miles away, than it had from Gaelic, though the people of the Lowlands had a common border – the Highland line – with the Highlanders not far short of 200 miles long, and were supposed to live in the same country.[169]

The contemporary witnesses, whether in the eighteenth or the early nineteenth centuries – the Highlanders David Stewart and Anne Grant of Laggan, the Lowlanders Tobias Smollett and Sir Walter Scott (later backed up by Eric Linklater), and the Englishmen Edmund Burt and Dr Johnson – all spoke of the intense hatred and hostility between the Highlanders and the Lowlanders. David Stewart said of the Highlanders, "distinguished by their language, manners, and dress, they considered themselves the original possessors of the country, and regarded the Saxons of the Lowlands as strangers and intruders". In fact, "the demure solemnity and fanaticism of the plains unluckily afforded a ceaseless subject of ridicule and satire to the poetical imaginations of the mountaineers. The truth is, that no two classes of people of the same country [as if the Highlanders had ever regarded themselves as being in the same country as the Lowlanders], and in such close neighbourhood, could possibly present a greater contrast . . . Differing so widely in their manners, they heartily despised and hated each other."[170] Sir Walter Scott wrote that the Lowlanders were ill-disposed towards "the Highlanders, who, as totally differing in laws, language, and dress, they were induced to regard as a nation of savages".[171] The Lowlanders, Scott said (to repeat an earlier reference) "were of twenty different races and almost all distinctly different from the Scots Irish, who are the proper Scots".[172] Tobias Smollett, after saying that the Highlanders were "as different from the Low-land Scots, in their looks, garb, and language", as the Welsh hill-dwellers were from the people of Herefordshire, repeated that "they are undoubtedly a very distinct species from their fellow-subjects of the Lowlands, against whom they indulge an ancient spirit of animosity . . ."[173] Edmund Burt agreed there was "a difference in the other part of this island between the English and the Welsh", but the contrast between the Lowlanders and the Highlanders was "hardly in any degree to be compared with the above-mentioned distinction", since "the Highlanders differ from the people of the low county in almost every circumstance of life. Their language, customs, manners, dress, etc., are unlike, and neither of them would be contented to be taken for the other." The result was "that coldness, to say no more, which subsists, at present", between them, "as if they bore no relation one to another".[174] Dr Johnson referred to the dislike felt by the Highlanders for the Lowlanders – "they have long considered them as a mean and degenerate race".[175] Anne Grant of Laggan thought the two groups were completely dissimilar. "No two nations ever were more distinct, or differed more completely from each other, than the Highlanders and Lowlanders; and the sentiment with which they regarded each other, was at best a kind of smothered animosity. The Lowlander considered the Highlander as a fierce and savage depredator, speaking a barbarous language, and inhabiting a gloomy and barren region, which fear and prudence forbade all strangers to explore. The attractions of his social habits, strong attachment, and courteous manners, were confined to his glens and kindred. All the pathetic and sublime charms of his poetry, and all the wild wonders of his records, were concealed in a language difficult to acquire, and utterly despised as the jargon of barbarians by their southern neighbours. If such were the light in which the cultivators of the soil regarded the hunters, graziers, and warriors of the mountains, their contempt was amply repaid by their high-spirited neighbours. They again regarded the Lowlanders as a very inferior mongrel race of intruders, sons of little men, without heroism, ancestry, or genius; mechanical drudges, who could neither sleep on the snow, compose extempore songs, recite long tales of wonder or of woe, or live without bread and without shelter for weeks together, following the chase. Whatever was mean or effeminate, whatever was dull, slow, mechanical, or torpid, was in the Highlands imputed to the Lowlanders, and exemplified by allusions to them; while, in the low country, every thing ferocious or unprincipled, every species of awkwardness or ignorance – of pride, or of insolence, was imputed to the Highlanders. No two communities, generally speaking, could hate each other more cordially, or despise each other more heartily."[176]

Much later, Eric Linklater observed: "Even so late as the beginning of the nineteenth century, Scotland was inhabited by two quite different sorts of people. There have been those, within our own time, who have tried to diminish this difference..."[177]

25. Only nominally subjected

The Highlands and the Lowlands, as was remarked earlier, were virtually independent countries before the middle of the eighteenth century: or rather, the Lowlands was an independent country, while the Highlands consisted of perhaps half a hundred independent little states. They were then aggressively and brutally united into one country, Scotland: and the Lowlanders were able to impose their social system, their language, their dress, and their political procedures on the Highlands. The fact that the Lowlanders only inflicted their social and economic structures on the Highlands after the mid-eighteenth century is yet another proof that it was only then that the two areas were forcibly fused, and that Edinburgh really began to rule the Highlands. The Lowlanders hated the Highlanders and their society so much, as we have just seen (and will see later at more length), that if the Lowlanders could have enforced their way of living upon the Highlanders earlier, they would certainly have done so. The survival of the clan system until halfway through the eighteenth century shows that in reality the Highlanders were not ruled by the Lowlanders until then.

Commentators on these matters, even though many of them ritualistically insisted that Scotland was always a single kingdom, have often made comments showing that inwardly they came very near to confessing the reality. Simon Lord Lovat (well known for his steadfast support for lawful and decorous behaviour) said in 1724, "the law [i.e. the Lowland law] has never had its due course and authority in many parts of the Highlands, neither in criminal nor civil matters".[178] Duncan Forbes observed in 1746 that because the clans "live by themselves, and possess different straths, glens, or districts, without any considerable intermixture of strangers, it has been for a great many years impracticable (and hardly thought safe to try it) to give the Law [i.e. the Lowland law] its course among the mountains", which has "left the Highlanders in possession of their own idle customs and extravagant maxims".[179] Dr James Anderson wrote in 1785 that until recently the Highlands had been "under such peculiar circumstances with regard to civil government, as to be only nominally subjected even to the Crown of Scotland".[180] William Thomson toured the Highlands in the same year, and wrote (as we saw above) that the mountains were "formed by nature into an impregnable fortress . . . which has enabled the natural hardiness and valour of the ancient Caledonians to transmit, from the earliest records in their history, the dignity of an unconquered and independent nation to their latest posterity".[181] Dr John Smith, minister of Campbeltown, said, "in the course of ages, the influence of no regular government reached these remote corners, which the Scottish sovereigns had totally abandoned".[182] (Perhaps it is possible to abandon what you never had; no doubt someone who does not own – and never has owned – luxury yachts could be said to have "totally abandoned" luxury yachts.) The Earl of Selkirk said that the change in the Highlands after the '45 rebellion "was great and sudden. The final issue of that contest annihilated the independence of the chieftains; and the vigorous measures [!], by which the victory of Culloden was followed, gave to regular government an authority which it had never before possessed in that part of the kingdom."[183] A. J. Youngson ran through the earlier history of the Highlands, and concluded: "thus it was that the Highlands were ruled, or not ruled, in the middle ages."[184] Janet Glover said: "The Highlands were too inaccessible for any mediaeval King to bring them under control. The Highland line continued, therefore, as a frontier between two peoples who lived completely apart from each other and who developed quite different traditions. James IV has been criticized as 'ineffective' because he failed to make his writ run permanently in the Highlands and Islands. This seems hard criticism, as no Government really succeeded in this difficult assignment until the second half of the eighteenth century." (In other words, surely, the Lowlands did not really rule the Highlands until then). Glover also wrote that in the eighteenth century "to cross the Highland line was like entering another country".[185] Otta Swire said, "the king's writ sat very lightly on Skye in those days".[186] Professor Smout called the Highlands "a region of largely Gaelic culture where the king's writ did not run", and acclaimed "the conquest of the Highlands" by "the central government in the eighteenth century".[187] (You don't have to "conquer" what you already rule.) Ian Grimble said that neither James I (of Scotland) "nor his officials could even understand the language of the Gaelic west, and the central government had never administered the region beyond mounting occasional punitive expeditions into it".[188] Tom Steel wrote that in the twelfth century "the Scots monarchs, however, could do little to bring order and firm government to those who lived north of the Highland line" (though an impartial observer might confess that "order and firm government" were not in great supply even in the Lowlands), while about the year 1500 James IV was vainly "hoping to extend his authority beyond the Highland line".[189] According to L. G. Pine, "for many centuries the condition of the Highlands had been that of an area where the law of Scotland had been very imperfectly obeyed"; even after the union of the crowns in 1603 "the Highlands were not reduced to order".[190] Paul Hopkins admitted that the Lowland authorities were powerless to prevent the clans running their own affairs, and that the Highlanders ignored both the Lowland government and the Lowland rules of succession: "the passing over [as the next chief] of the 'rightful' branch among the Glengarry MacDonalds was accepted without comment as late as 1680."[191] Professor T. M. Devine said "the '45 put the Highlands on the map within the United Kingdom":[192] an apparent acceptance of the fact that the Highlands had not been "within the United Kingdom" until then. Professor Eric Richards, after referring to the "wild independence" of the Highlands, said they were "subject, in the eighteenth century, to conquest and improvement by forces from the south".[193] (Again, rulers do not have to conquer their own countries.) Dr Johnson himself said the Highlanders had been crushed "by the heavy hand of a vindictive conqueror", after Culloden, and talked of "the final conquest of the Highlands" in the middle of the eighteenth century.[194] Prince Charles landed where he did in 1745 for this very reason: the Highlands not being ruled (in reality) by Edinburgh, he was able to travel round, gather an army, and begin his bid for the British throne without interference from the Lowlanders.

26. Appearance and reality

The gap between the two beliefs, often put down in the same book or even on the same page – that the Highlands were part of Scotland, ruled from Edinburgh, and also that in fact they were not part of Scotland, ruled from Edinburgh – has to be filled somehow, and the charge of lawlessness lies conveniently to hand: the Highlands were "part of Scotland", say the orthodox commentators, and the fact that the Highlanders were clearly not behaving as if they were part of Scotland is explained by the Highlanders' depravity.[195] Dr William Ferguson, for example, said "lawlessness was endemic" in the Highlands, and that "many Highlanders thrived on disorder".[196] Dr T. C. Smout deplored "the lawlessness which was native to the hills".[197] It is as if a tramp, sitting on the pavement outside the railings of Buckingham Palace, loudly proclaimed that the palace was really his property, and then when anyone retorted that other people had been in undisturbed possession for many years, the tramp explained matters by saying he had been kept out by the "lawlessness" and "disorder" which was "endemic" and "native" to the House of Windsor.

Writers are often tempted to antedate historical developments, but it is a temptation that historians in particular must always resist. For example, the exploits of the 93rd Regiment, the Sutherland Highlanders, during the first eighty years of the nineteenth century, are sometimes now ascribed to "the Argyll and Sutherland Highlanders", since the old Sutherland regiment (after eight dauntless decades) was amalgamated into that new creation in 1881.[198] In the same way, crofts and crofters first made a significant appearance in the Highlands only in the 1780s (and in many districts, several decades later still),[199] but historians regularly call the old Highland joint-farmers of the seventeenth or sixteenth centuries "crofters". In another parallel process, as we shall shortly see, since the Highlanders became merely tenants of the land after the tenurial revolution of the mid-eighteenth century, even the Highlanders before that change are still called "tenants" – sometimes by writers who say, self-contradictingly, that the so-called "tenants" could not be moved from their possessions. Similarly, since the Lowlanders and the English conquered the Highlands after the Jacobite defeat in 1746, commentators often antedate this process, and regard that conquest as having taken place centuries earlier. Certainly there are many documents still extant in which the Lowland kings and the Lowland authorities claimed to be ruling over the Highlands as well as over their own country, just as there are many documents in the archives declaring that the kings of England were also the kings of France until the end of the eighteenth century (not to mention the claim of the kings of England that they also ruled Scotland in the centuries before 1603): but no one who has lived through many years of the modern era can be unaware that official pronouncements are not always true, and that in governmental declarations (whether as to home or foreign affairs), appearances and reality do not always coincide.

27. Union and Industrial Revolution

The actual takeover of the Highlands by the authorities in Edinburgh and London was made possible by two important developments, one political and one economic. The political development was the Act of Union of 1707, which claimed to be uniting the two kingdoms of England and "Scotland". In fact it united England with the Lowlands. Strangely, the way some historians have treated this union reveals that, perhaps subconsciously, they are acknowledging the facts of the matter. As we saw earlier, J. R. Green's remark that the 1707 Union joined peoples with "a common blood and common speech" shows that he was thinking only of a union between England and the Lowlands.[200] But the Union of 1707 did mark a dramatic change in the balance of power. Previously it had been the Lowlands against the Highlands: from now on it was the Lowlands plus England – a very much more substantial entity – against the Highlands.

The other change that made the conquest of the Highlands possible was the increasing (coal, iron, and cloth) industrialization of both the Lowlands and England, already under way in the early eighteenth century, and increasing until it came to full flower in the epoch-making Industrial Revolution. This economic upheaval transformed society in the British state which after 1707 stretched (in fact) from Cornwall and Kent to Glasgow, Edinburgh, Aberdeen, and indeed to Wick, Kirkwall, and Lerwick; and it gave so much power to Great Britain (as the state created by the union of 1707 was called) that it was able to conquer the greatest empire that the world has ever seen, or probably ever will see, ruling extensive territories in faraway America, Asia, Africa, and Australasia – amounting to a quarter of the entire globe – not to mention dominating the planet's seas and oceans. The new British world power, which was in due course able to dictate events in the farthest reaches of the Pacific and the Himalayas, up to 12,000 miles away on the other side of the world, could not be withstood by a small population of hill-folk, divided among themselves, in the home island – the furthest of them less than 700 miles from London – however much they tried to resist. The fusion of the Lowlands and England helped to make all this possible. Whatever arithmetic ordains, in the political sphere one and one sometimes make more than two.[201]

28. Invasion or conquest

From time to time the Lowlanders, well before Culloden, sent soldiers into the Highlands, and even left them there for months at a time, "billeting them upon" – that is, occupying – particular glens or islands, and sometimes holding "courts" which decided matters according to Lowland law, and issuing documents in what some called English, and others Scots – that is, the Lowland language.[202] But before the middle of the eighteenth century, such soldiers had at length to withdraw, leaving Highland affairs just what they had been before the incursion. In the same way, Lowland armies sometimes invaded England, and even remained there for some time; but no one would claim that therefore the Lowlanders ruled England. The English, too, sent armies into the Lowlands, and strenuously claimed from time to time that they were ruling that country; but for all that, the Edinburgh regime remained independent. Besides that, every so often the English invaded France; and if France had been divided into forty or more statelets, none of which saw any need to cooperate with the others, no doubt England would have sent armies across the Channel even more often, holding "courts" and issuing English-language documents which purported to settle matters there as the English would like them to be settled. But before the Industrial Revolution English armies, whether in Scotland or France, found it difficult to stay long in the invaded country, and when they withdrew matters reverted to what they had been before the incursion. It was exactly the same when the Lowlanders (or even the English) sent armies into the Highlands; they could dictate matters while they remained there, but when they went home the Highlanders necessarily resumed control of their own affairs.

It is also quite true that from time to time the Edinburgh authorities recruited Highlanders to serve in their armies (an inexplicable proceeding, presumably, in the minds of those who tell us that the clansmen were weaklings, enfeebled by frequent famines), but that did not alter the de facto independence of the clan countries. There were parallel cases elsewhere, as we saw earlier: the Pope recruited Swiss guardsmen, the Doge of Venice Slav soldiers, the British Gurkhas from Nepal, and the French kings Scots mercenaries, without any claim to sovereignty over the countries which produced these soldiers of fortune.

A. G. MacDonell insisted that the Highlands were ruled from Edinburgh, and then used the existence of this imaginary unified Scottish state to criticize the Highlanders for not helping the Lowlanders more in their battles against the English. They were not there, he claimed, at "Dupplin, Halidon, Homildon" and so on, and they could "claim only a small part of the credit of the maintenance of Scottish independence after Bannockburn". This is like criticizing the French for not being in the German armies fighting for a united Germany, or the Spanish for failing to join the Italian forces struggling for Italian independence. The Lowlands, and each of the Highland clan countries, were all separate entities, and can only be understood as such.[203]

29. Number of clans

How many clans were there? That is a very difficult question to answer. The point has already been made that just as the Highland line itself was often obscure, and not easy to define, so also the boundaries of the clan countries were hazy and imprecise. Apart from that, it might not be absolutely clear at all times which groups of people belonged to which clan. In the days before formal customs barriers and military frontier posts, it could almost be maintained that a clan would re-define itself every time a clan chief proposed a certain course of action. Those who rallied to the chief would be in the clan; those who did not might consider themselves (and might be considered by others) to be out of it. Those of us who live in the days of exact boundaries, where the end of one country and the beginning of the next is known (and insisted on, by devastating armaments) to a precise scratch upon the ground, may find it difficult to accept the more flexible arrangements of the Highlands of yesteryear, before each state apparatus of modern times with its armed forces, its police and civil servants, its courts and judges, its lawyers and prisons, its jailers and hangmen, its Acts of Parliament and its store-rooms full of charters and decrees, could and did insist on defining the exact "nationality" of every blade of grass and lump of mud.

It is also necessary to decide how precisely a "clan" is to be defined. For example, there were many MacDonalds. One section of them (or branches of that section) lived in North Uist, as well as in the north of Skye, and also some miles away in the south of Skye; another section (or, equally, branches of that section) lived in

Morar, Arisaig and Moidart on the mainland, in the Inner Hebrides on Eigg and Canna, and in the Outer Hebrides on South Uist; another section lived in Knoydart and Glengarry; another in Glen Spean and Glen Roy; another in Glen Coe. (In ancient times there had been other sections of the clan in Ardnamurchan, Islay, south Jura, and Kintyre.) Sometimes the sections would act together, sometimes independently. Were the MacDonalds one clan, or five? Similarly the Campbells lived over a great stretch of territory in Argyll and Perthshire (and elsewhere), and included a number of different sections. Some Campbells belonged to the Argyll clan, and some to the Breadalbane clan, while others saw themselves as being in the Lochnell, Ardkinglass, Strachur, Inverawe, Calder, or several other, Campbell groupings; was it one clan, or was it half-a-dozen or more? The same question could be asked about the other most numerous names of the Highlands. The Campbells were supposed to be able to muster 5000 men in the field if they all acted together; the Atholl clan (some Stewarts, some Robertsons, and some others) 3000; the MacKenzies 2500; the MacDonalds well over 2000; the Sutherland clan 2000; the Clan Chattan in all its branches nearly 2000; the Sinclairs 1000; the Grants 1000; and the Frasers, the Reay MacKays, the Camerons, the MacLeods, and the MacGregors, nearly as many. If all these extensive names are to be considered as single clans, then altogether there were probably about forty clans in the Highlands. If, however, some of these names are thought of as covering a number of clans; if wherever there was a group of clansfolk who regarded themselves as a recognisably separate formation, with a chief rather than a chieftain, so that one could list five MacDonald clans, even more numerous Campbell clans, and so on, then it would be possible to enumerate upwards of sixty Highland clans. The memorial about the Highland clans, drawn up in 1746, has forty-three separate entries. In the memorial the five MacDonald clans are given separately; the main Grant clan, and the Grants of Glenmoriston, are also listed separately; and the Stewarts of Appin, and the Stewarts of Grandtully, are entered as separate groups. The Atholl clan, of which Stewarts were leading members, is also given separately, but that clan encompassed many other names, so it must be regarded as an autonomous body. In contrast, the Campbells, the MacKenzies, the Sutherland clan and the rest, are treated as single entities by the memo.[204]

If the MacDonalds, and the Grants, and the Stewarts of Appin and of Grandtully, were also to be considered as single clans, then the total number of clans in the memorial would be only thirty-seven. (And if three other clans which, as we shall see later, the 1746 memorial – for whatever reason – omitted were to be added, that would give a total of forty clans.) Robert Chambers reached the same conclusion: he wrote in 1827 that in the Highlands there were "about forty different tribes, denominated *clans*".[205]

THE HIGHLANDS AND ISLANDS

As with many other questions, the aptness of the answer depends upon the elucidation of the enquiry.

CHAPTER TWO NOTES

1. *The Highlands*
[1] Johnson & Boswell 1930, 255.

2. *Natural defences*
[2] Stewart 1822, I 5 & I 5fn.
[3] Stewart 1822, I 3-4.
[4] O.S.A. II 490, Dunkeld Perth.
[5] Hogg 1981, 35.

3. *The old counties*
[6] Burt 2005, 182.
[7] Sutherland 1825, 87.
[8] Jamieson 2005, xxi.
[9] Pine 1972, 172, quoting Sir Walter Scott.

4. *An impregnable fortress*
[10] Stewart 1822, I 5 fn.
[11] MacLean 1988, 226, quoting Chevalier de Johnstone.
[12] Johnson & Boswell 1930, 38.
[13] Thomson 1788, 104; Thomson 2010, 31.
[14] O.S.A. VIII 499, Moy Inv.
[15] Bristed 1803, 121.
[16] N.S.A. XX 968, Dunkeld Perth.
[17] N.S.A. XIV 171, Kintail Ross.
[18] Hogg 1981, 38.

5. *As if by magic*
[19] Stewart 1822, I 108-9.
[20] N.S.A. XV 93, Latheron Caith.
[21] Larkin 2010, 13-14.
[22] Smollett 1967, 275; Wordsworth 1894, 67, 79.
[23] *Oxford D.N.B.*, article Duncan Forbes, 1798-1868. The O.S.A. report on Moulin, written about 1791, said that Glen Fernat (among other places) had been "denuded of [its] inhabitants, and converted into sheep-walks and grazings"; that no doubt explains why Forbes was born in the Lowlands. Forbes later returned to Straloch, at the foot of the glen, where he became village schoolmaster at the age of seventeen.
[24] Stewart 1822, I 108-9.
[25] Hume Brown 1955, 28. It appears that the D.N.A. of Lowland Scots and of northern English people is remarkably similar (*Sunday Times*, 17th June 2012). In fact it seems that if Great Britain had been divided up so as to put similar inhabitants in each division, then three of the largest divisions would have been firstly the Highlands, secondly the Scots Lowlands and northern England, from the Highland line down to a border perhaps from say Chester to Skegness, and thirdly the rest of England below that line.
[26] F. M. Stenton, *Anglo-Saxon England*, (1943) 1950, 338.

THE HIGHLANDS AND ISLANDS

6. *Highlander and Sassenach*
[27] Sutherland 1825, 105.
[28] Napier 1884, I 64, qu. 1136, John Nicolson.
[29] Stewart 1822, I 15 fn.
[30] Stewart 1822, I 5 fn.
[31] Stewart 1822, I 23 fn.
[32] Stewart 1822, I 108.
[33] Stewart 1822, I 8, I 100.
[34] Smollett 1967, 277.
[35] MacKenzie 1911, 608.
[36] MacLeod 1910, 31.
[37] J. C. Shairp, in notes to Wordsworth 1894, 313. John Campbell Shairp, 1819-85, was the principal of the United College of St Andrews. His mother Elizabeth was the daughter of John Campbell of Kildalloig, Argyllshire.
[38] Scott 1925, xxiii.
[39] Scott, *Fair Maid of Perth*, MacMillan, London, (1828) 1905, 16.

7. *The fringe*
[40] The former shires of West Lothian, Midlothian, East Lothian, Berwick, Roxburgh, Selkirk, Peebles, Lanark, Renfrew, Ayr, Wigtown, Kirkcudbright, and Dumfries.
[41] It might be assumed that the size of Scotland, the homeland of statistics, would be generally agreed by now, but reference books differ.

Groome's *Gazetteer*, 1892-6, said Scotland was 30,902 square miles (29,786 square miles of land, 631 square miles of water, and 485 square miles of foreshore). *Nelson's World Gazetteer*, 1941, 29,796 square miles. Kyd 1952, xviii, gave 29,795 square miles (virtually the same as Nelson; perhaps a few acres fell off a cliff somewhere between 1941 and 1952). Pryde 1962, 150 fn, also said 29,795. *Reader's Digest World Atlas*, 1965, 30,411 square miles (615 more than Nelson). Bartholomew *Gazetteer of Great Britain*, 1977, 29,801 square miles (or 77,205.27 square kilometres); very near to the Nelson & Kyd figures. Macmillan *World Almanac*, 1994, 30,987 square miles. (So Scotland appears to be growing: this is nearly 1,100 square miles more than the Nelson figure.) *Wikipedia*, the internet encyclopaedia, 2007, 30,414 square miles. (So between Nelson and MacMillan, but nearer the latter.) I have taken the area as 29,800 square miles, to conform – almost – with Nelson, Kyd, Pryde, and Bartholomew.

The division of Scotland into the 162-parish Highlands' 16,300 square miles, and the Lowlands' 13,500 square miles, is the best calculation that I can make, and is subject to correction by more expert geographers (a numerous group). James Kyd's northernmost area, "representing roughly the Highlands", had (he said) 21,330 square miles: but that area included all of Buteshire and Perthshire, as well as the county of Kinross and the county of Angus except Dundee, plus everything to the north of that – i.e. all of the counties of Aberdeen, Banff, Moray, Nairn and Caithness. This was obviously a considerably larger area than the one I am suggesting.
[42] Pryde 1962, 150.
[43] R. McCrum, W. Cran, & R. MacNeil, *Story of English*, Faber, London, 1986, 141. The English, of course, were also originally "outsiders in their own country", many of their predecessors having arrived from northern Europe at much the same time as many of the Highlanders' ancestors were coming from Ireland.

8. *The weather*
[44] Burt 2005, 301.
[45] Burt 2005, 101.
[46] Barron 1903-13, III, see 386-94.

⁴⁷ Goodall 1952, vi, vii.

9. *Inured to the weather*
⁴⁸ Burt 2005, 198.
⁴⁹ Campbell 1968, 229.
⁵⁰ Geikie 1908, 428.
⁵¹ Goodall 1952, vi & vii.
⁵² Burt 2005, 184, 203, 237.
⁵³ N.S.A. XX 537, Fortingall Perth.

10. *The Highland line*
⁵⁴ Sterne, *Tristram Shandy*, Penguin, London (1759-67) 2003, 196.
⁵⁵ Mitchison 1990, 180, & Lynch 1991, 367.
⁵⁶ Strand & Davidson 2002, 96.
⁵⁷ Burt 2005, 154.
⁵⁸ Skene 1890, III 285-6.
⁵⁹ A. Fullerton, *Gazetteer of Scotland*, 1836, quoted in Keay 1994, 540.
⁶⁰ J. Hill Burton, *Criminal Trials in Scotland*, quoted in Ian Henderson, *Scottish Kirk & People*, Lutterworth, London, 1969, 66.
⁶¹ MacLeod 1910, 241.
⁶² Brander 1980, 133.
⁶³ Steel 1994, 248-9.

11. *The Gaelic-speaking Highlands*
⁶⁴ Stewart 1822, I 6.
⁶⁵ Grant 1934, 213 fn.
⁶⁶ Philip 1946, 38a.
⁶⁷ Finlay 1966, 13.
⁶⁸ MacLeod 1997, 26 & map in prelims, p. xii.
⁶⁹ Thomson 1983, 129.
⁷⁰ Withers 1998, 17.
⁷¹ Groome 1892-6.
⁷² Pryde 1962, 150.
⁷³ Smout 1970, 552.

12. *"Eight Highland counties"*
⁷⁴ Hunter 1999, 14-15.
⁷⁵ Richards 1985, 275.
⁷⁶ MacNeill 1851, xxvi.
⁷⁷ Devine 2004: Appendix 7, p. 314, 114 parishes; Appendix 8, p. 317, 106 parishes. As is remarked elsewhere, a number of Highland parishes included land in two counties, and therefore the number of parishes in each county can differ from one list to the next, depending on how the writer chooses to allot each parish in the county lists. In Devine's *The Great Highland Famine* two appendices give lists of the parishes in the four main Highland counties (Appendix 7, on p. 314, "Removals and Land Consolidation, Highland Parishes, before 1845 [from New Statistical Account]", and Appendix 8, on p. 317, "Numbers 'Temporarily Absent' at Census, Highland Parishes, 1841-61"). The number of parishes given in each of the four counties, compared with my own calculation and that of the *Companion to Gaelic Scotland* (1987), is –

THE HIGHLANDS AND ISLANDS

	Argyllshire	Inverness-shire	Ross & Cromarty	Sutherland	total
Appendix 7, total stated	37	31	33	13	114
Parishes specified	34	29	33	13	109
Appendix 8, parishes specified	35	29	29	13	106
My calculation	35	32	33	13	113
Companion to Gaelic Scotland	38	33	33	13	117

Notes on the county lists:– in Argyllshire, my total is 35. The Appendix 7 total is given as 37; however, only 35 parishes are specified, and since Ardchattan and Muckairn (which formed an O.S.A. joint-parish) are given separately, the real total is only 34. The discrepancy is explained by the omission of Jura, which would bring the total up to 35. (The note after the table says Islay has four parishes – Kilchoman, Kildalton, Kilarrow, and Kilmodan. In fact Islay has three parishes – Kilmodan, to repeat, is in Cowal.) The Appendix 8 total appears to be 36 only because Ardchattan and Muckairn are again given separately, so the real Appendix 8 total is 35. Inverness-shire: my total is 32. The Appendix 7 total is given as 31, but in fact 29 parishes are enumerated. Compared with my list, Abernethy, Duthil, Ardersier and Croy are omitted, but Cromdale (which I have listed under Moray) is included. The Appendix 8 total is 29, since Abernethy, Duthil and Kilmallie were omitted. Abernethy and Duthil (both of which were considered as Inverness-shire parishes in the O.S.A.) were put into Elginshire – i.e. Moray – in the N.S.A. (XIII, 92, 123): my total is 33. The Appendix 7 total is 33, apparently the same. The Appendix 8 total is 29, since Alness, Knockbain, Resolis, and Urquhart are omitted. In the *Companion*, Argyllshire was said to have 38 parishes. Compared with my list, Tiree and Coll were entered separately instead of as part of a joint parish: the same applied to Jura and Colonsay, and to Strachur and Strathlachlan. Ardgour was put down as a separate parish, whereas in my list it formed part of the parish of Ardnamurchan. Conversely, Gigha and Cara was omitted from the *Companion* list. This explains why my list was 35. The *Companion* lists 33 parishes in Inverness-shire; I have 32. The discrepancy arises because the *Companion* included Arisaig and Moidart jointly as a separate parish in Inverness-shire, whereas my list has them as part of the parish of Ardnamurchan, in Argyllshire (following the lists in the O.S.A.).
[78] Devine 1998, map on p. xiii.

13. *Highlands and Lowlands*
[79] Burt 2005, 19.

14. *Southern boundary of the Highlands*
[80] O.S.A. XVII 266, Luss Dumb.
[81] Wordsworth 1894, 67.
[82] Defoe 1974, II 428.
[83] N.S.A. VIII 88, Cardross Dumb.
[84] N.S.A. VIII 116, Rosneath Dumb.
[85] O.S.A. XV 608, Fowlis Wester Perth.

[86] O.S.A. IX 226, Clunie Perth.
[87] N.S.A. X 1122, Alyth Perth.
[88] O.S.A. XX 490, Dunkeld Perth.

15. *Highlanders in other Perthshire parishes*
[89] O.S.A. VI 487-8, Kincardine Perth.
[90] O.S.A. XXXIII 485, Caputh Perth.
[91] O.S.A. IX 602, Perth Perth.
[92] O.S.A. XX 53, & N.S.A. XX 1232, (both) Kilmadock Perth.
[93] N.S.A. X 488, Crieff Perth.
[94] N.S.A. X 436, Auchtergaven Perth.
[95] N.S.A. X 917, Blairgowrie Perth.
[96] Murdoch 1986, 63.

16. *Eastern boundary of the Highlands*
[97] Skene 1890, III 285-6.
[98] Stewart 1822, I 5 (North & South Esk), & in II the map before page one. The mountains of north Angus were not completely divorced from Highland matters. The enmity between MacIntosh and the MacDonalds of Keppoch over the former's attempt to establish private-property rights over the Keppoch lands meant that Lindsay of Edzell, a chieftain in Glen Esk, was drawn into the quarrel when MacIntosh married his daughter; and a party of Keppoch men entered Glen Esk and plundered a spreagh of cattle from him (Shaw 1880, 388).
[99] R. Heron, *Scotland Delineated*, James Neill, Edinburgh, 1791, 143.
[100] Skene 1890, III 286.
[101] Pennant 2000, 85.
[102] O.S.A. XIV 343, N.S.A. XII 651, (both) Crathie & Braemar Aberd.
[103] O.S.A. XII 219, Glenmuick etc. Aberd.
[104] O.S.A. XIII 171, Strathdon Aberd.
[105] O.S.A. XII 454 & 456 fn, Kirkmichael Banff.
[106] O.S.A. XVII 426, Mortlach Banff.
[107] O.S.A. VIII 256, Cromdale Moray.
[108] O.S.A. IV 304, N.S.A. XIII 72, (both) Knockando Moray.
[109] N.S.A. XIII 135, Inveravon Banff.
[110] O.S.A. VIII 566, Edinkillie Moray.
[111] O.S.A. IV 355, N.S.A. XIII 23, (both) Cawdor Nairn.
[112] Murdoch 1986, 12.
[113] Johnson & Boswell 1930, 22.

17. *Ross-shire and Sutherland*
[114] O.S.A. XV 632, Avoch Ross.
[115] Finlay 1966, 30.
[116] Geikie 1908, 414.

18. *The border in Caithness*
[117] Mitchison 1962, 6.
[118] Geikie 1908, 415.
[119] *Wikipedia*, article Napier Commission; www.revolvy.com/page/Napier-Commission.
[120] Grimble 1980, 145.
[121] Seton Gordon 1951, 11; cf 315, "Caithness not being generally considered a Highland county".
[122] MacKenzie 1989, 222.

[123] Allan W. MacColl, *Land, Faith and the Crofting Community*, University Press, Edinburgh, 2006, 1.
[124] MacLeod 1997, 13.
[125] Kyd 1952, xxv.
[126] Stewart 1822, I 6.
[127] Omand 1989, 98.
[128] *Am Bratach* No 200, June 2008, Dr Domhnall Uilleam Stiubhart.
[129] Ferguson 1994, 91 fn.
[130] Lang 1898, 8: "Caithness contains Ten Parishes, Five whereof speak English, after the Scottish dialect; and the other Five a Corrupt Kind of Irish, tho' the English is daily gaining ground."
[131] Kemp/Pococke 1888, 29.
[132] O.S.A. VII 579, Reay Caith.
[133] O.S.A. XX 508, Thurso Caith. "Though almost all the parishioners understand English, a sermon is preached every Sunday in the Erse or Irish." Some writers say that the language border was the Forss Water, about four miles west of the town of Thurso, while Skene said that "Brinsness [or Brimsness?] on the west side of Thurso Bay" (Skene 1890, III 286) divided the Gaels from the Lowlanders: this was about a mile east of the Forss Water. Part of Thurso parish was anglophone, but there is much evidence, as we have seen, that part of it was Gaelic-speaking.
[134] O.S.A. XIX 62, Halkirk Caith.
[135] N.S.A. XV 93, Latheron Caith.
[136] N.S.A. XV 43, Watten Caith. Thomas Pennant said: "Of the ten parishes in Caithness, only the four that lie south-east speak Erse; all the others speak English . . ." (Pennant 2000, 121). The Gaelic-speaking part of Caithness is of course in the west and south-west of the county; Pennant's claim that the "south-east" was the Gaelic part must make the reader dubious as to how much he really knew about Caithness. It is just possible that he was not counting Reay (as a Caithness parish) when he reckoned up the parishes that spoke Gaelic, and that he did count it when reckoning up the total number of Caithness parishes. However, all the other evidence makes it clear that Gaelic was spoken in five Caithness parishes. A further small point: when a contemporary account of the Highlands is re-published in modern times, and it happens to include what is clearly inaccurate information, would it not be a good idea to insert a footnote making this clear?
[137] Stewart 1822, II 411.

19. *The Highlands and Islands*

[138] Even where the four main Highland counties are taken to represent the Highlands, since the number of parishes listed in each county differs in different authorities, the total parishes given for those four counties is not always the same. For example, in Devine 2004 (188, 314-19, 327-32) Appendix 7 specified 109 Highland parishes in the main four Highland counties: that total would leave 53 parishes in the south and east of the Highlands (almost a third of the whole) out of the reckoning.

[139] Dr John Walker (Walker 1808, I 20) also said that "the Gaelic part of Scotland", that is to say where "the Gaelic language is either preached or spoken by the natives", had 162 parishes, but there were differences between his list and mine. His reckoning left out the parishes of Rhu, Fowlis Wester, Monzievaird, Clunie, Cromarty, Aberlour, Mortlach, Edinkillie, and Watten (all of which my list embraced); but he included the parishes of Cumbrae, Rosneath, Crieff, Kincardine O'Neil, Coldstone, and Nairn (none of which appeared on my list). Of these latter six parishes, none of the parish reports on Cumbrae, Kincardine O'Neil, Coldstone, and Nairn, in either the O.S.A. or the N.S.A., mention Gaelic; the O.S.A. report on Rosneath seems to show clearly that Gaelic was no longer spoken there; while as for Crieff, the Gaelic that could be heard in the main part of the parish was spoken by refugee Highlanders, fleeing from the improvements – many Lowland towns at that time had numbers of these fugitive families, but (without some specific local consideration) that does not in my opinion justify us treating them as part of the original Gaelic area. Dr Walker treated Tiree and Coll as two separate parishes; and he counted Kilbrandon, and Lismore and Appin, twice, since both of them appeared both

in his island and his mainland lists. His "Islay" had only two parishes. (I have assumed that Dr Walker's "Skipness" was Saddell and Skipness, his "Abertarff" was Boleskine and Abertarff, and his "Rothiemurchus" was Duthil and Rothiemurchus.)

[140] Different totals are given for the number of Scotland's parishes, but the various numbers suggested are fairly close together, and most of them would give an average size for Lowland parishes not much different from that given here.

20. *What is a clearance?*
[141] M. Fry, e.g. article in *The Herald*, Glasgow, 16th May 2000.

21. *Two countries*
[142] E.g. Steel 1994, 108. Such empty boasts were not exclusive to England. When Henry II of France died in 1559, his son Francis II claimed to be king of France, Scotland, and England (Glover 1960, 138).
[143] Though the Highland chiefs, by becoming landlords, were able to join the British upper class, it was some time before they were considered to be anything other than outsiders. The meeting of the "Bollinger" club at Oxford, which opens Evelyn Waugh's *Decline and Fall*, admittedly included some of these newcomers, but as late as the early twentieth century they were described snobbishly as "illiterate lairds from wet granite hovels in the Highlands": *Decline and Fall*, Penguin, London, (1928) 1953, 9. "Lumsden of Strathdrummond" was portrayed as not very bright, being unable to distinguish between two ties, both of them being pale blue and white (p. 10).

22. *Racially homogeneous*
[144] James Loch, quoted in Grimble 1962, 109; O.S.A. IV 568, Strachur Arg.
[145] Sir Robert Rait, Historiographer Royal of Scotland 1919-29, quoted in Adam/Innes 1965, 130.
[146] Trevor-Roper 1983, 15-16. Trevor-Roper said that there was no "distinct Highland culture and tradition" because the Highlanders had come originally from Ireland, and still maintained some connection with that country: the Highlanders "were simply the overflow of Ireland", and Gaelic "was regularly described, in the eighteenth century, as Irish". It is true that one of the main elements in the racial mix that formed the Highlanders had come originally from Ireland, beginning in the sixth century, and that the language spoken by the Gaels was described as "Irish" up to the eighteenth century and even later; just as it was true that one of the main elements in the racial mix that formed the Lowlanders had come originally from the south of Britain, and before that from northern Germany and neighbouring lands, beginning in the sixth century, and that the language spoken by the Lowlanders is regularly described (not only in the eighteenth century, but now) as "English". But that is not to say that there is no "distinct Lowland culture and tradition".
[147] Adam/Innes 1965, 130.
[148] Fry 2005, 323. In view of the unanimous contemporary opinions, which are quoted a few pages further on, as to the heartfelt millennium-long hatred between the Highlanders and the Lowlanders, it is difficult to see how any modern writer could deny there was any hostility between them, or claim that these two distinct and inimical peoples "have not ceased to regard themselves as members of one nation". Seldom can so much evidence have been so lightly swept aside. But such an achievement must come easily to one who claims the clearances virtually never happened.
[149] Green 1915, 673-4.
[150] Larkin 2010, 14.
[151] Macaulay 1907, 424; and see Scott, *Redgauntlet*, Collins, London, n.d., 66 (Letter V), where Alan Fairford defends his father's retreat at the Battle of Falkirk by saying anyone would retreat "when three or four mountain knaves, with naked claymores, and heels as light as their fingers, were scampering after him" – i.e. Highlanders as such were "light-fingered", that is to say, were thieves. One author quoted Macaulay as saying that nine Scotchmen out of ten regarded the Highland garb as the dress of "a chief" – much more acceptable (Devine 1998, 88).

23. Most murderous commanders

[152] E.g. MacLeod 1996, 122-5.
[153] Smout 1970, 342.
[154] Lenman 1995, 172-3.
[155] Scott 1900, 44; & *Oxford D.N.B.*, article "Duke of Cumberland".
[156] Duncan Ban MacIntyre, quoted in Macdonald 1994, 183-4. Duncan Ban's use of the phrase "carmine plaid" may mean that he was thinking of the dress of some of the clans who took part in the '45 rebellion, most of whom seem to have had predominantly red (or carmine) tartans, as against (for example) the Campbells (and the MacIntyres) whose tartan was predominantly green.
[157] Gaskell 1980, 4.
[158] MacLean 1889, 365: Dr MacLean described the events after Culloden as "the butchery of unarmed, defenceless, and wounded men, the burning of houses, the slaughter of cattle, and the raping of inoffensive women by the brutal English soldiery . . ." It would have been more accurate had he said, "brutal Lowland and English soldiery . . ."
[159] Lenman 1995, 173.
[160] MacLean 1988, 285. The exploits of Sackville's 20th Regiment of foot, the East Devonshires, were still being boasted about a hundred years afterwards. The official history of the regiment said that after Culloden the regiment was stationed at Perth, and "was employed in searching for arms, and in executing necessary measures of severity against the clans which had been guilty of rebellion" (*Historical Record of the Twentieth*, Richard Cannon, Parker Furnival & Parker, London, 1848, 14; a record produced following William IV's call in 1836 for a history to be written of each regiment).
[161] MacDonald 1994, 177. The scoundrel Major Lockhart was commemorated in the song "You're welcome, Charlie Stewart": "Hadst thou Culloden's battle won/ Poor Scotland had not been undone/ Nor butchered been with sword and gun/ By Lockhart and such cowards."

In 1928 the title of Baron Culloden was created for Prince Henry, Duke of Gloucester, the son of George V; the title is now held by the second duke. It is strange, and indeed uncomfortably significant, that the British establishment chose to commemorate a battle which was the setting for a number of British war crimes.

[162] N.S.A. XIV 452, Croy Inv.
[163] Gaskell 1980, 3, 4.

24. Very distinct species

[164] Devine 1998, 85, 21.
[165] Rixson 2004, 151, quoting Giblin, *Irish Franciscan Mission to Scotland 1619-46*, Assisi Press, Dublin, 1964.
[166] Rixson 2004, 68, quoting Hume Brown, *Early travellers in Scotland;* Devine 1998, 21-2.
[167] John MacLachlan (Rahoy), quoted in Prebble 1986, 110-1.
[168] Allan MacDougall, in Meek 1995, Poem 1, verses 2 & 10, & verse 5.
[169] See the *Concise Scots Dictionary*, 1991, xv. Examples are ashet (assiette), douce (feminine of doux), dour (dur), disjune (déjeuner), gardy-loo (garde à l'eau), fash (fâcher), vivers (vivres – food), cockalane (du coq à l'âne, a cock and bull story), tassie (tasse), probably Hogmanay (hoguinane, a new year's gift), and (surely) bonnie, etc. Burt (Burt 2005, 37-8) said that in the Lowlands "many things are aggrandized, in imitation of their ancient allies (as they call them), the French. A pedling shopkeeper, that sells a pennyworth of thread, is a 'merchant'; the person who is sent for that thread has received a 'commission'; and, bringing it to the sender, is making 'report'. A bill to let you know there is a single room to be let, is called a 'placard'; the doors are 'ports'; an enclosed field of two acres is a 'park' " . . . and so on. All the words that Burt complained of in this passage were borrowed from the French: "marchand", shopkeeper; "commission", errand; "rapport", report; "placard", poster; "porte", door; "parc", paddock.

[170] Stewart 1822, I 8 & I 106.
[171] Scott 1925, 168.
[172] Pine 1972, 172, quoting Sir W. Scott, letter 5th June 1829.
[173] Smollett 1967, 275 & 291.
[174] Burt 2005, 153, 247.
[175] Johnson & Boswell 1930, 31.
[176] Grant 1811, I 27-9; & quoted Stewart 1822, I 106-7.
[177] Linklater 1962, xi.

25. *Only nominally subjected*
[178] Lovat, *Edinburgh Magazine*, July 1817, 399.
[179] Youngson 1773, 23-4, quoting Duncan Forbes.
[180] Anderson 1785, v.
[181] Thomson 2010, 31.
[182] O.S.A. X 533, Campbeltown Arg.
[183] Selkirk 2010, 7.
[184] Youngson 1973, 11.
[185] Glover 1966, 117-118, & 221.
[186] Swire 1961, 174.
[187] Smout 1970, 30, 209.
[188] Grimble 1980, 86.
[189] Steel 1994, 40 & 63.
[190] Pine 1972, 11.
[191] Hopkins 1998, 14.
[192] T. M. Devine, *Scotland's Empire 1600-1815*, Penguin, London, 2004, 360.
[193] Richards 1982, 41.
[194] Johnson & Boswell 1930, 81, 41.

26. *Appearance and reality*
[195] The present corps d'elite of the Highlands accepts and repeats the story that the old Highlands were lawless, perhaps because it gives an excuse for the former chiefs having carried out the clearances. In *The Observer*, 20th January 2007 (in an article which has been cited above), "Ranald MacDonald . . . the son of the 23rd Captain and Chief of Clan Ranald" was quoted as saying that in 1616 his family was limited by James VI and I to "one hogshead of claret a year because he believed that the barbaric behaviour of the clans of the west coast was all down to our inordinate love of red wine". There is also the pleasure of boasting about how wild one's ancestors were (and the reader will have observed the use of "our" instead of "their"). The opinions given in this newspaper article are based on the idea that the Highlands had already been conquered by the Lowlands in 1616, whereas in fact the Lowland authorities were unable at that time to exercise any authority over the Highlanders – short of invading the Highlands in a military expedition: much less were they able to control what the Highlanders ate and drank.
[196] Ferguson 1994, 15.
[197] Smout 1970, 207.
[198] Argyll and Sutherland Highlanders. Another example of the ante-dating of historical occurrences can be seen in the history of Germany from 1933 to 1945. As soon as the Nazis took power in Germany they began to treat the Jewish minority, as well as trade unionists, political opponents, gipsies, and so on, with great cruelty. There is nothing surprising about that; dictatorial regimes then often treated minorities (racial, political, or other), and of course often treat minorities now, with great cruelty. In fact anti-semitism in autocratic Poland during the same years (1933-39) was leading to much the same kind of state brutality towards the Jews. A. J. P. Taylor wrote (in *English History, 1914-45*, O.U.P., 1965,

419) that "Englishmen . . . were offended by the Nazi treatment of the Jews. Here again, Jews were treated as badly in other countries, and often worse – in Poland, for example, with whom, nevertheless, Great Britain remained on friendly terms." Some people later claimed that Britain had gone to war in 1939 out of sympathy for the Jews: but if Britain had been motivated by repugnance towards anti-semitism, Poland was perhaps the last country with which it would have chosen to ally itself. When the war broke out in 1939, the Nazis began to use what they sneeringly called the "untermenschen" as forced labour in factories (at the same time confiscating any remaining property they had), thus releasing so-called "Aryans" for military service. In June 1941 Germany invaded Russia, bringing that country and its sympathizers into the alliance against them; then in December Japan entered the war, with the result that America joined the Allies. Against what were at that time the three greatest world powers, the British Empire, the Soviet Union, and the United States of America, Germany now faced a titanic struggle. As a result of the Nazis' horrific treatment of various minorities, there were now many millions of Jews and others within Germany (and the countries it had occupied) who would be desperately hoping for an Allied victory, who – the German rulers feared – might therefore form themselves into a "fifth column" within the German lines, and who would enthusiastically support any Allied military invasion of Germany. In January 1942 (a matter of weeks after the U.S.A. entered the war, and Germany's critical position became obvious) the decision was taken to murder all these potential enemy fighters or supporters, so far as that could be done – and many millions were in fact slaughtered in (and out of) concentration camps: a few survived, only because they were used as forced labour in the factories supporting the German war effort. This gigantic atrocity was so appalling that many observers now antedate it, and claim the Nazis began a deliberate state campaign of murdering the "untermenschen" as soon as they seized power in January 1933. (See the *Sunday Times*, 25th August 2013, which gave some dates from the history of the Jews, including "1933, beginning of Nazi era and the Holocaust".) The Nazis were bad enough to have begun the Holocaust in 1933, no doubt about it, but facts are facts. It is curious that the Holocaust was a monstrosity so dreadful that it has led some to antedate it, and others to deny it.

[199] One writer said that as late as 1800 there were crofts only in Mull and some parts of western Inverness-shire. (The term "croft" was used for any odd piece of land not built on, when I was a small boy in the urban north of England, and Lowland writers also seem to have used the term with much the same meaning: but "crofters" only emerged towards the end of the eighteenth century.)

27. Union and Industrial Revolution
[200] J. R. Green, *Short History of the English People*, Dent Everyman, London, 1915, 673-4.
[201] Some writers reproach the Highlanders for not mounting a successful resistance. Hugh Trevor-Roper (Hobsbawm and Ranger 2008, 25) said the Highlanders benefited from "the romantic movement, the cult of the noble savage . . . after 1746, when their distinct society crumbled so easily" (although elsewhere, as we have seen, he appeared to think that the Highlanders did not have a "distinct society" – it was a "retrospective invention"); but when one considers the enormous power of Great Britain and the British Empire, the defeat of the small Gaelic minority (and the similar defeat of many other small racial minorities in every part of the world) was inevitable, living as they did on one minor part of the small island which had become the centre of this new world power.

28. Invasion or conquest
[202] *Concise Scots Dictionary*, (1985) 1991, ed. Mairi Robinson, x-xi.
[203] MacDonell 1937, 18, 10-11.

29. Number of clans
[204] Stewart 1822, II v. One website (planetware.com) said there were "almost 180 clans"; the writer could only have reached that figure by including very many groups usually described as septs. Stewart (II iii fn) said that "although the chieftains of the MacDonalds are separately numbered, agreeably to

the President's Memorial, they form only one clan. The branches of the Stewart family are likewise numbered separately, although they are but one clan. This applies to other clans when the name is repeated."

[205] Chambers 1869, 30. The Duke of Montrose wrote in 1947: "there would be about forty different clans originally" (Bain 1947, 8). He probably took his information from Chambers.

CHAPTER THREE

POWER WITHIN THE CLAN

1. Lowland fiction

It is impossible fully to understand the impact of the clearances without knowing something of the state of Highland society in the centuries that preceded them. Of course it is easy to find narratives purporting to describe the manners of the mountaineers; it is harder to decide on their trustworthiness. Many writers seem to base their opinion of the old Highlanders and their way of life very largely on the accounts that have come down to us from English or Lowland travellers, or even from English or Lowland novelists. Much of this evidence may well be true, of course; nothing should be rejected out of hand; but it is possible that the English speakers carried with them into the Highlands (or even more into their novels) the prejudices that were rife in their home countries. One recent *history*, for example, described the state of affairs in the early eighteenth-century Highlands by quoting half a page from a Lowland novel which appeared in the next century, in 1817, introducing it by the sentence: "Scott in *Rob Roy*, through the mouth of Bailie Nicol Jarvie, summarized the position."[1] It would be surprising to see the position of affairs in the early eighteenth-century Lowlands "summarized" by quoting a fictional Highlander who appeared in a Gaelic novel a hundred years afterwards.

One might construct a philosophical case that if an attempt is made to draw a picture of a particular society, with only the evidence of strangers to go on, a commentator who has a wide understanding of how human beings behave, and in particular how ruling groups operate, could by making due allowance for all the foibles to be expected of outsiders, and hostile outsiders at that, arrive at something like the truth. But perhaps it would be safer to assume that if one comes upon a history of the Highlands based mainly on external, and almost always unfriendly, sources, then one could well suspect that it might not be wholly accurate. For these reasons, while of course not rejecting the opinions of Lowlanders and English people about the Highlands, I have done my best to keep close to what Highlanders have said about the Highlands, particularly those Highlanders who were still part and parcel of their own local communities. I am not a Gaelic-speaker, sadly; but the lack of Gaelic has never been considered as a barrier by all the Lowland and English historians who have given us their opinions of the Highlands. If ignorance of Gaelic were to be regarded as a disqualification for writing about the Highlands, then more than ninety-nine per cent of our history books dealing with the Highlands could be thrown into the waste-paper basket immediately. (Incidentally, it would be astounding if nearly all our histories of France were written by people who could not speak French; or if nearly all our histories of England were written by people who could not speak English.) It is the fact that what is written by English monoglots, whether sympathetic or unsympathetic to the Highlanders, will almost inevitably largely reflect the Highlands as seen through Sassenach eyes.

2. Campbell of Canna

Dr J. L. Campbell, who owned Canna, made much the same point in the preface to his history of the island. (Campbell, though a landowner himself, could not accept the standard accounts of Highland history.) The landlords, he said, had the power "in the nineteenth century to clear their lands of tenants-at-will without any kind of financial compensation, in order to improve their own financial position": Canna had "ample experience" of that. Dr Campbell had decided that his account "should be written from what I would call the Gaelic point of view, which meant regarding official records with a good deal of cynical scepticism. In the matter of Highland history, in the absence of the lost records of the Benedictine Monastery of Iona, and of the Lordship of the Isles . . . the bulk of the written material available to historians lies in official Scottish records such as the Acts of Parliament of Scotland, the reports of the Scottish Privy Council, and so on, and these are consistently hostile to the Highlanders and Islanders and to the Gaelic language and institutions; but they occupy the great part of the available written record, and unless a historian possesses some knowledge of the Gaelic language and its written and oral literature, and has the insights that that knowledge bestows, it is very difficult not to be borne down by the accumulating weight of official assertions and propaganda, and to arrive at the mental state of accepting them without question. But now we are better acquainted with ideological politics than the Victorians, questions have become inevitable."

Dr Campbell felt he had to warn his readership that this attitude might lead to unorthodox conclusions. "It follows that some readers may find this book not what they are accustomed to, something that used to be a considerable obstacle to book publication in Scotland [and still is, of course]. If so, I hope it will help to acquaint them with a new point of view. Far too long have the Scottish Gaels been treated by historians as non-persons with no legitimate point of view. Barbarous things certainly happened in the Highlands and Islands of Scotland, but they equally certainly happened in other parts of Scotland as well, and in England too for that matter . . . I see the history of the Hebrides as a sustained attempt to retain the semi-independence of the Lordship or Kingdom of the Isles, and its institutions, and a determination to restore the Lordship after it had been brought down . . . It is indeed regrettable that the Lordship of the Isles did not survive to develop into something like the local independence now enjoyed by the Channel Islands and the Isle of Man."[2]

3. Hereditary right to their farms

In the old Gaelic society, to all intents and purposes, the basic means of production was land, and the people's needs were met by what lived or grew upon the land. The Highlanders' physical necessities, their food, their clothing, and their shelter, as well as their mental embellishments, their culture and their pastimes, came in a direct and visible way from the land. In such a society, power would go with the ownership of the land. And there can be no doubt that the clan as a whole owned the land on which it lived. Undeniably the clansfolk believed that the land was theirs. Indeed, that even continued to be their conviction for many decades after the fight on Culloden Moor had set under clan society a mine whose explosion would destroy it. The survival over many centuries of a belief in such a fundamental practical matter, which the experience of every year, every month, every day, would show to be either right or wrong, is strong evidence that this widespread opinion was correct.

Edmund Burt said in the 1720s, "strangers will not be admitted among the clans" – that is, to live: the Highlanders' hospitality to visitors and travellers was legendary. "The tribes will not suffer strangers to settle within their precinct, or even those of another clan to enjoy any possession among them; but will soon constrain them to quit their pretensions, by cruelty to their persons, or mischief to their cattle or other property."[3] (In other words, the clansfolk enforced their exclusive right to their land by whatever means lay at hand, just as after 1746 the landowners enforced their exclusive possession of the land by the any means available to them, however much "cruelty" or "mischief" was involved.) These statements, by an often acute (though an alien and unfriendly) observer, indicate not only the clansfolk's belief as to their rights of ownership, but their exercise of them. (If the charter holders had really owned the Highlands in the 1720s, when Burt was writing, then of course they would have "admitted strangers": as soon as their fanciful charters became real titles to ownership, in the years after Culloden, they not only passively "admitted strangers" but eagerly brought in many thousands of them across the Highlands, as big farmers, factors, farmworkers, artisans, lawyers, surveyors, and so forth.) Burt gave two examples (which will be detailed later) of the resistance of a clan to intruders whom the chiefs attempted to admit into the clan land; and said that he thought this resistance arose "from their dread of innovations, and the notion they entertain, that they have a kind of hereditary right to their farms; and that none of them are to be dispossessed, unless for some great transgression against their chief, in which case every individual would consent to their expulsion".[4] In passing, it may be said that this picture of "every individual consenting" is an accurate indication of the self-governing way in which of necessity the clans conducted their affairs.

4. In full possession of their holdings

The old order was overturned by the victory of the Hanoverian government in 1746; but it took many years before the new system was completely accepted by the clansfolk, who were going to lose by it – or, for that matter, by many of the chiefs, who were going to gain by it. At the trial in 1752 of James Stewart of the Glen, then accused (almost certainly erroneously) of the murder of Colin Campbell of Glenure, who was about to turn out some Stewart small tenants, the Lord Advocate told the jury that the Highlanders held it "to be a cause of mortal enmity than a man should be removed by another from his farm or possession"; this was a "prejudice or delusion" that "seems to be in a particular manner prevalent in the Highlands".[5]

The author of *A Candid Enquiry into the Migrations*, 1771, said of the Highlands, "there was formerly a general or national belief, that tenants, while they were industrious and paid their rents, had a sort of right to continue in possession of their respective farms".[6] (The small sums paid to the chief by the joint-farmers, though naturally called "rents" by the proprietors after the landlord revolution of the mid-eighteenth century, and even by over-optimistic chiefs before that revolution, were in fact – as we see elsewhere – taxes, sums paid to the executive to carry on the public business of the small state which was the clan country.) This belief in a "right to continue in possession" could have been tested at every returning term day, and yet it was still firmly held into the second half of the eighteenth century. Even when, after 1716 and still more after 1746, the military forces of the Lowlands and England began to penetrate the Highlands on a more regular basis, in order to try to establish that coercive power which later would enable the chiefs to turn out their clansfolk, the chiefs did not think it wise to attempt evictions without first trying their best to convince the clansfolk that the old system had been turned upside down, and that now the chiefs owned the land. As the anonymous author of 1771 said, for half a century and more past, the landlords had been at great pains to explode the belief that the clansfolk had any rights to their land: and they had, he explained, enlisted some of the clergy to help them. No one, of course, has to go to great pains to explode a belief that does not exist. In 1774 Pennant said the old Highlanders "held their farms at a small rent, from father to son, by a kind of prescribed right, which the Highlanders called duchàs. This nature, in the feudal times, was deemed sacred and inviolable."⁷ This was the somewhat awkward attempt of Pennant, a landowner in a part of Britain where the private ownership of land was old-established, to explain that the clansfolk owned their own land – that their claim to it was "sacred and inviolable".

William Marshall, who wrote about the *Central Highlands of Scotland* in 1794, was completely in tune with the new order: for example, like the 1771 author quoted above, he accepted the landlords' claims as to their pre-Culloden rights by calling the old clansfolk "tenants". Even he, however, admitted that the right of ownership claimed by the chiefs' charters before Culloden was merely a chimera. Under the "feudal system", he wrote (at that time writers often called the pre-1745 structure the "feudal system") – under that system, he wrote, "the tenants [sic] might be said to be in full possession of their respective holdings; neither the chieftain nor his chamberlain dared to remove them . . ."⁸ Strange powers for "tenants" to have! How could someone who could not be put out of his holding be called a "tenant"? A "tenant" who cannot be removed must be accounted the owner, or as part of a group of owners, if words are to have meaning. A person in England who occupies land unchallenged for a certain number of years cannot thereafter be removed, and is therefore, in fact and in law, admitted to be the owner. The same reasoning must apply to the question of proprietary rights in the old Highlands.

5. Their property

The Earl of Selkirk, whose *Observations on the Present State of the Highlands* was published in 1806, thought that the clearances were inevitable and that emigration was the only answer to the problems of the Highlanders: he himself organized a number of large emigrations. He was also a member of that landlord class many members of which were making large fortunes out of the clearances; but though he was a hostile witness, he could not deny the Highland reality before 1745. "Accustomed to transmit their possessions from father to son, as if they had been their property, the people seem to have thought, that as long as they paid the old and accustomed rent [sic], and performed the usual services, their possessions were their own by legal right."⁹ Selkirk in fact was aware that in reality there was no "as if" about it, nor did the people do this merely on account of what they "thought"; because he wrote himself that the unrest which was then to be seen among the Highlanders arose from the remembrance of "the permanent possession which they had always retained of their paternal farms". The Highlanders knew, he said, that claims based merely on "a piece of parchment and a lump of wax", which was the significantly dismissive way in which he described an Edinburgh charter, were of no use in the old system.[10] Eight years later Selkirk became involved in Sutherland affairs, and he wrote again that the people of Sutherland had "so much of the Old Highland Spirit as to think their land their own . . . According to the ideas handed down to them from their ancestors, and long prevalent among high and low throughout the Highlands, they were only defending their rights and resisting a ruinous, unjust, and tyrannical encroachment on *their property*" (my italics).[11]

An even greater enthusiast for the landlord revolution, Sir George Steuart MacKenzie of Coul, boasted in 1808 of the progress of the clearances, and urged his fellow landlords on to greater efforts in that direction; but at the same time his account of the improvements could not avoid mentioning the odd beliefs of the Highlanders – "it has been found necessary to remove a very great number of people from possessions to which they were strongly attached, and to which they considered themselves, in great measure, the rightful heirs."[12]

Sir John MacNeill, who heard many Highland witnesses during his enquiry into the supposed necessity for Highland emigration in 1851, belonged to a family whose prosperity was based on its ownership of Colonsay, and was therefore as much opposed to such beliefs as any other family of Highland landlords, but he could not deny they existed: "They [the Highlanders] had very generally formed or imbibed erroneous and exaggerated notions of their rights, and especially with reference to the occupation of land."[13] James Loch, the Sutherland commissioner, was naturally also sceptical, but in 1855 he wrote that there was "a feeling among the people that they would all resume possession of what they conceived to be the possessions of their fathers".[14] Philip Gaskell wrote that the Morvern Highlanders were "established on ground which they considered (however mistakenly) they had a right to occupy".[15]

In 1883 the Marquess of Bute, although he was the owner of great estates in the Highlands and elsewhere in Great Britain (indeed his ownership of the coal-exporting Cardiff docks meant he was credited with being the richest man in the world) gave a lecture in Edinburgh, in which he said that in the days of the clans, "the land belongs not to individuals in proprietorship, but to the inhabitants of the district in common". Originally "the office of chief was elective every time, with the choice confined to the members of a certain family; but even were it strictly hereditary when the chief's ancestor was chosen by his fellow-tribesmen, they intended to invest him with certain well-defined political rights, but certainly not with the power of turning themselves out of the common tribe territory. The change into proprietorship [was] chiefly the consequence of the '45 . . . Our indignation is invoked to reprobate such acts as what are called the Sutherland clearings, for instance, and more recent cases of the same kind."[16] Also in 1883, the *Athenaeum* carried a review of MacKenzie's *Highland Clearances*, in which the writer said the Sutherlanders had been "turned out of the homes to which they had a better claim than those who expelled them".[17] In the following year, the Napier enquiry reported that the Highlanders all believed they had an "inherited inalienable title to security of tenure in their possessions while rent [sic] and service" were duly paid.[18] And in 1885, the Liberal Unionist leader Joseph Chamberlain said that in the clearances thousands of people "were driven from the lands which had *belonged to* their ancestors" (my italics).[19]

6. No better title

As for the Highlanders themselves, they knew that they had owned their own land, and continuously insisted on this fact. John MacDonald (or Iain MacCodrum in the familiar Gaelic) deplored the North Uist emigration caused by Sir Alexander MacDonald's rent-raising; Sorley MacLean called MacCodrum's poem "a very clear statement of the old view of the clan's right to the territory".[20] Alexander Sutherland visited Sutherland in 1825 (as we shall see later), and talked to the Kildonan people. "They argued that they had a prescriptive claim to the soil: that they did their lady [the Countess of Sutherland] justice if they farmed it as their fathers had done; and that, chieftainess though she were, she had no better title to eject them from their humble tenements than they had to drive her from her castle." Sutherland made clear his own distaste for such obnoxious views: anywhere else, he said, these arguments "would not be listened to". But in the Highlands "they were not merely heard with indulgence, but warmly advocated".[21] A poem written by Elizabeth MacKay in 1889 deplored the effects of the clearance:

"The sportsman now roams o'er the Sutherland hills
  And down where the Naver runs clear
  And the land a brave race had for centuries *owned* [my emphasis]
  Is now trod by the sheep and the deer."[22]

The people of Sutherland had exactly the same views thirty or more years earlier. When the Crimean War broke out, few recruits were obtained in the county, and at a public meeting the Sutherlanders said they did not see that they had anything to fight for, since "our lands have been taken from us".[23] In 1886 John MacLean, from Balemartin in Tiree, wrote a song including the verse of which this is a translation:

"Before a duke came or any of his men
  Or the first of the Georges from Hanover did sail,
  This low-lying isle, with shielings a-plenty

Belonged as a home to the children of the Gael."[24]

In other words, the people of Tiree owned Tiree, not the Duke of Argyll, nor the Argyll management, nor the Hanoverian monarchs. Dr I. F. Grant, who naturally, coming from a family of Highland chieftains, cherished the chieftains' claims to own the Highlands, was constrained to admit this universal conviction of the Gaels in her book *Periods in Highland History*, 1987, when she mentioned the "beliefs in natural rights, doctrines which had surfaced frequently in seventeenth and eighteenth century Britain, and which were given a thorough airing in the Highlands in this period [after 1745]. The main elements of this stated that the land belonged to the people, though there was nothing in law to bear this out."[25] The law of the Lowlands and England, created by the Scottish and English landlords, naturally supported the landlords' pretensions: any other outcome would have been strange. Legislators naturally give themselves the best position under their legislation. The man who makes the law is always the law's main beneficiary.

It is interesting to see how often those writers who adhere to the accepted version of Highland history – that the clansfolk were merely abject serfs, trembling before the untrammelled authority of the tyrannical chief, who had the complete private-property right to the clan land – then go on, as a further demonstration as to why the clan system had to be ended, to complain that in the old days the clansfolk paid no (or very little) "rent". Such writers do not pause to consider how far the various sections of their narrative are consistent with each other; otherwise they would realize that private property owners, particularly private property owners with autocratic powers over all the others in their community, would inevitably be exacting a very large rent indeed from those who were living on "their" land. Writers who deplore the derisory amounts paid as "rent" in the old days are in fact showing yet again that the clans owned their land, and that the negligible sums called "rent" by the chiefs were in reality no more than taxes, paid to the chief in order to enable him to fulfil his function as the chief executive of the clan.

7. Owners in common

Mere assertion, however repetitive, clearly does not prove a point (though many dictatorial regimes have done their best to demonstrate the opposite); but it is interesting that so many of the commentators who have studied Highland history in detail (even though they have all lived, moved, and had their being in a society where private property, in land and most other things, is the ark of the covenant) have concluded that in the old society, as a matter of historical fact, the clans owned their land. The Rev. Angus MacDonald and the Rev. Archibald MacDonald wrote in their book, *The Clan Donald*: "The land belonged originally to the tribe, or clan, and though the chief came in course of time to hold by feudal right, yet the clan had not lost their interest in the soil. The chief exercised a certain superiority, or lordship, over the clan territory, not in his individual or private capacity, but as head and in name of the clan." The change that came to the Highlands after Culloden "was the result of transforming the chief into a landlord, without conserving the tenants' [sic] rights under the immemorial, though unwritten, contract which gave the people, as well as the heads, a right upon their native soil".[26] The Rev. Angus MacKay deplored in his *Book of MacKay* the sale by "a degenerate son" (Eric, the seventh Lord Reay) of "what the MacKays held through sunshine and through storm for about twenty generations".[27] Duncan MacLaren said that "under the old Celtic tenure . . . the land was really the property of the clan".[28] John Murdoch wrote that in Gaelic society there was "a distinct recognition of the fact that the land in the Highlands belonged to the clans as such and not the chiefs" – a chieftain "was head of the clan or family, not owner of the great tract of land which that clan occupied"; since those days, "the landlord class in the Highlands have been but the usurpers of the rights which the people there once possessed in the soil".[29] Mrs M. Gunn (in *The Caithness Book*, edited by Donald Omand) wrote of the same process more severely: "the conversion of the clan chiefs into landowners who held the land as their personal property opened the way to the fearful abuses that followed."[30] Hugh Miller wrote in *Sutherland as It Was and Is*, "under the old Celtic tenures, the only tenures, be it remembered, through which the lords of Sutherland derive their rights to their lands, the Klaan, or children of the soil, were the proprietors of the soil".[31] Sismondi, talking of the same county, said that in the days of clanship "the whole of Sutherland belongs to the men of Sutherland, the head of the clan was a chief, not appropriator".[32] Robert Mathieson said that in the pre-1745 Highlands, the "land belonged to the clan".[33]

Dr J. P. MacLean expressed the same opinion in his *History of the Clan MacLean*. "The history of the Highlands proves conclusively that the clans were the owners, in common, of the soil of their native districts, and elected their own clan or local rulers."[34] Dr Fraser Darling, in his *West Highland Survey*, adhered strongly to the landlords' view of events, but he could not accept their view of Highland landownership: "The land upon which the clan lived was not the property of the chief; it belonged to the tribe . . ."[35] Sheriff J. MacMaster Campbell, in the collection of essays called *The Home Life of the Highlanders, 1400-1746*, underlined the fact: "The outstanding characteristic of Celtic tribal law was the communal ownership of the land."[36] Even Frank Adam, a fervent defender of the actions of the Highland chiefs, wrote: "the people had a right to live the life they loved, and from which, under the old feudo-clan law, they could not have been evicted."[37]

Angus MacLeod (from Calbost township in Lewis) stated the matter succinctly in his account of his people's history which can be consulted at the *Angus MacLeod Archive*: "Under the clan system of land tenure, the land within the area occupied by a clan belonged to the clan as a whole collectively, and it was defended by the sword of the clan . . . by the eighteenth century there were political and economic forces at work in the Highlands, over which the common people had no control because their voice was never heard in Parliament, and the principle of common ownership of the land in the Highlands and Islands was gradually eroded over a long period . . . the clan chiefs were encouraged to assume control of the clan lands as private landowners."[38]

8. Charters of possession

Dr J. J. Galbraith pointed out that the Scottish kings encouraged the chiefs to acquire land charters, since the king had a hold over a chief who owned such a charter. Before the charters, there was no link whatever between the king on the one hand, and on the other hand the clans and the great extent of land they occupied and controlled. In the Highlands, said Galbraith, "the ownership of land did not exist" – i.e., private ownership. So the Edinburgh authorities tried to impose it. "The simplest way out of the impasse was to make the chiefs take out charters of possession for the lands which they never possessed in the sense of personal property."[39] A. G. MacDonell, whose *My Scotland* – despite the author's surname – is a continuous hymn of praise for the Lowlanders, and denigration of the Highlanders (the recalcitrant clans were, he thought, pent-up, baffled, sulky, romantic, muddle-headed, and childish: they were certainly not short of adjectives) – even MacDonell called the changeover "the abolition of the clan system of land tenure and the substitution of the proprietary system".[40] As James Shaw Grant phrased it, "a society based on human relationships was replaced by one based on the sanctity of private property".[41] Highly respectable Highlanders found it hard to accept the chiefs' pretensions. Dr Roderick Ross, of Lewis (or the Lews) gave evidence to the Napier Commission: "How did the MacKenzies of Seaforth acquire their right to the Lews? . . . We know they got it by a process that cannot bear investigation, and cannot bear daylight; and we know the right they got to the Lews is certainly more questionable than the right the Lewismen have to their share of it." Dr Ross's grandson was Iain MacLeod, who became Conservative Chancellor of the Exchequer in 1970.[42]

J. B. Caird, writing in 1951 about the clearance of Harris, said that the land there was "at one time the people's through clan ownership".[43] Eric Linklater said in

1962 that the chiefs or landlords expelled the clansfolk "from the lands which immemorially were theirs".[44] About the same time Farquhar Gillanders said that after Culloden "the widespread belief that clan lands belonged to the clansfolk gave way to an imposed system of landlord and tenant. Clansmen now had to pay a rent to farm their land." This was, he continued, a "violation of the fundamental Highland belief that land is the property of the community".[45] L. G. Pine (the editor of *Burke's Peerage*) affirmed in 1972 that "the land had belonged to the whole clan and was merely administered by the chief".[46] Tom Weir said in 1973 in his *Western Highlands* that "a clan was a tribe which owned tribal land, and all rights were common rights": in fact, "for the clansmen, property ownership was a new concept, dating only from Culloden and the break-up of the old order".[47] Malcolm MacLean and Christopher Carrell, in *As an Fhearann* (1986), gave 1760 as the approximate date of "the final transition from the concept of clan lands to the private ownership of land by the clan chiefs".[48] Also in 1986 Tom Atkinson referred to "the clan lands, lands which the English [or rather Scottish] law now declared to belong to the chiefs".[49] A third book appearing in 1986 was *Skye the Island*, in which James Hunter said that the clansfolk of Skye in the old days had no notion of private landownership: "the entire concept of private property in land would have made no more sense to them than the idea that a man might own the clouds or take out a financial interest in the ocean."[50] In 1991 Grant Jarvie wrote: "Unlike feudal forms of land ownership, the land of the Highland clan was not the private property of the chief, but the public property of the clansfolk."[51] Alastair Scott wrote in 1995: "One essential aspect of this period is frequently overlooked: the land of the Highland clans was *not* [his emphasis] the private property of their chiefs but the public property of the clansfolk", although after 1746 the chiefs "assumed ownership of the land once held in common by their people, and adopted the lifestyles and roles of southern, commercial landlords".[52]

Robert Bain, in his *Clans and Tartans of Scotland* (1938), had no doubt about the clan ownership of the land. Clanship, he said, "was an ideal system in so far as it recognized that land, the basis of life, was not an individual possession, but belonged to the people in common ... The land belonged to the clan."[53]

Of course the Highlanders themselves knew that their forefathers had owned their land, and they used every opportunity to state this (to them, fundamental and obvious) truth. The Napier Commission had to listen frequently (as we shall see later) to crofters who claimed that the only solution to poverty was to give them back the land which their ancestors had owned. The Rev. John MacTavish, a minister of the Free Church (to which virtually all the crofters belonged) summed it up in his evidence: "the Crown should never have given to the chiefs the property which belonged to their clan or tribe."[54]

9. No known concept

Naturally the Highland landlords rejected this idea completely, and claimed that the land in the Highlands had always (presumably since Adam) been owned privately. And just as naturally, many orthodox historians, who write their histories from the point of view of the landlords, have fallen into line.

Dr T. C. Smout, Professor of Scottish History at the University of St Andrews, put forward a theory more in tune with the landlords' claims, as we shall see (at more length) later. He said that "there was in the medieval Highlands no known concept of clan lands".[55] Malcolm Gray claimed that "the ownership of land within the Highlands has always been aristocratic and highly concentrated".[56] Professor T. M. Devine said that the MacDonald clan of Keppoch and the MacDonald clan of Glen Coe were "landless or possessed only marginal property".[57] (From the point of view of the Lowland authorities, clans were not even recognized as legal bodies; much less could they possess property, marginal or other. In other words, so far as the Lowland authorities were concerned, every clan was "landless". From the Highland – or factual – point of view, the first clan owned Keppoch, in that they possessed and occupied it without intermission for centuries, while the second clan owned Glen Coe, for the same reason.) Sir Iain Moncreiffe of Moncreiffe, who was a laird himself, and a strong advocate of the Highland landlords' point of view, of course supported (like these three orthodox historians) the proprietorial position in his *Highland Clans*, 1967. "Contrary", he wrote, "to much woolly thought in modern times, the land was always theoretically the chief's or laird's, subject to customary obligations . . ."[58] Perhaps even Moncreiffe himself did not feel too sure of his ground, for in a different part *of the same book* he incorporated a long memorandum written in 1965 by the Earl of Dundee, formerly Under-Secretary of State for Scotland. Not surprisingly, the earl was a firm supporter of his fellow-landlords, but his memorandum included the following woolly thought: "The compulsory clearances, and the harsh manner in which they were sometimes enforced, were all the more bitterly resented in Highland memory, because under the ancient Highland customary law, the land had been the property of the clansmen, and it had been the duty of the chief to protect each clansman's right to his own holding."[59] Woolly or not, the idea that a clan owned its land is, as we have seen, scarcely modern; and after considering all the evidence, it is difficult to disagree with Donald Campbell's verdict in his *Caledonians and Scots*, written in 1861 – over a century before Moncreiffe's strictures about modern errors – when he called the Highlanders "a virtuous and warlike people defrauded of their undoubted right to the soil of their native land, and expatriated".[60]

10. Origin of the chiefs

The clans, which were small nation-states, sometimes went to war with each other, just as our own modern nation-states do. (It should be said immediately, though, that in historical times these disagreements were frequently the result of malicious interventions in Highland affairs by the Lowland authorities, whose intention, and achievement, was simply to stir up trouble: this will be shown later.) In times of warfare, a clansman who showed himself to be expert in the gruesome arts of war would come into prominence; and these qualities, though many might think them not particularly admirable ones, would be valuable to the clan when battles had to be fought. The clansfolk might well agree to accept the advice and direction of such a man when a dispute arose with a neighbouring clan. The successful warrior might come to have a special standing within the clan or the sept (a sept was a small clan, or part of a clan). Even in times of peace, if disputes arose within the clan, it would be useful to have someone of sufficient eminence to adjudicate on any disagreements, lest they should fester and endanger the unity of the clan; and in such circumstances the war-leader might be called upon to decide who was in the right. The office of leader in war and judge in peace having been combined in the person of one man, his position would be still further enhanced; and on the death of this man, to prevent any dissension as to who should take over his office, the clan might well choose one of his family – his son, or another male relative – to succeed him. Seton Gordon wrote: "The title of Highland chief usually passes from father to son, although there are instances when a person not of the direct line has been appointed by the people."[61] Some of these (not infrequent) instances will be mentioned later. Usually the chief would be, or would be considered as, the eldest of the lineage, carrying the right of primogeniture down from the man who was considered to be the first to bear the common clan surname, and the common ancestor of all the clansfolk.

People living in clans or septs do not necessarily have chiefs; some tribes, when first revealed to the gaze of the outside world, had no chiefs or leading men. The *Journal* of the MacColl society quoted from a letter written by a Hugh MacColl in 1879: "My grandfather, who was known far and wide as a shrewd, quiet man, often told me that for many generations we had no ruling family who were the chiefs of the tribe by hereditary descent. They were ruled by elders in time of peace, but in war the fittest and wealthiest to maintain the men in arms were elected till troublous times had passed away, when they fell back into their places maintaining their families like the rest of a clan."

In many clans, however, the office became more or less hereditary. Further, the man who was the wartime leader and peacetime judge sometimes came to be regarded as the living embodiment of the clan. The chief of the MacLachlans was, simply, MacLachlan; the chief of the MacAulay clan was, simply, MacAulay. He and his family were supported by the tributes, willingly paid, of the clansfolk. His ancestry, and the feats of his progenitors, were recited by the bards and seannachies of the clan. He lived in a house, or a hut, somewhat grander than the rank-and-file habitation; and some of the young men of the clan acted as his personal attendants.

Although most of the clansfolk, like ordinary people in any society, seem to have married partners coming from the locality, the chief would sometimes marry outside the clan, outside the name. Some clans prospered and grew, and came to extend over more territory than could cohere as a single clan "country", as it was called, under the old Highland system. These – the Sinclairs, the MacKenzies, the Campbells, the MacDonalds, the MacLeods, the MacLeans, for example – split up into several separate clans, although they still seem to have regarded themselves as associated in a loose confederacy of all their name. The chieftains of the newer, smaller, clans might marry women within the confederacy. Alexander MacKenzie, seventh of Gairloch, who flourished in the second half of the seventeenth century, for example, married a daughter of MacKenzie of Tarbat; their son, the next chief, married a daughter of MacKenzie of Findon; the next chief married a daughter of MacKenzie of Scatwell; and the next a daughter of MacKenzie of Redcastle. This marriage was in 1755, by which time the clan system was under heavy attack; but even this fourth chief's two daughters married MacKenzies, as did two of his grandchildren.[62]

11. The chief's name

Among the Highlanders the chief's name was his Gaelic patronymic: the chief of the Clan Gunn was Mac Sheumais Chataich, the chief of the Campbells was Mac Cailein Mor, MacLean of Coll was Mac Iain Abraich, Fraser of Lovat was Mac Shimidh, Grant of Glenmoriston was Mac Phadrig, and MacDonald of Clanranald was Mac Mhic Ailein. More formally, the chief was called by the clan surname, without forename or title – MacKinnon, MacNaughton, Menzies, MacKay. This was sometimes expanded, either by repeating the clan name (Grant of Grant, MacGregor of MacGregor, MacDougall of MacDougall); or by adding the words "of that ilk" – literally of that same, or of that same clan (Lamont of that ilk, Buchanan of that ilk).[63] In some cases, for example where several clans shared the same surname, the chief might have a territorial designation. Examples include the Campbells of Argyll, of Breadalbane, of Ardkinglass, of Lochnell, of Strachur, and of Calder; the MacDonalds of Sleat, of Glengarry, of Keppoch, of Ardnamurchan, and of Glencoe; the MacKenzies of Seaforth, of Cromartie, of Gairloch, and of Scatwell; the Camerons of Lochiel, of Fassfern, and of Glennevis; the MacLeans of Duart, of Lochbuie, and of Ardgour; the Sinclairs of Ulbster, of Forss, and of

Murkle; the MacKays of Reay, of Strathy, and of Strath Halladale; and the Stewarts of Appin, of Ardshiel, and of Grandtully. Sometimes a strong point within the clan territory, where the chief would usually reside, would be part of the chief's title: MacPherson of Cluny, MacLean of Duart, Munro of Foulis. These various forms were not necessarily mutually exclusive; MacLeod of MacLeod was also called MacLeod of Dunvegan, and Colquhoun of Luss was also known as Colquhoun of Colquhoun. A territorial designation could be used by itself to indicate a chief: Ross of Balnagown, MacCallum of Poltalloch, and Farquharson of Invercauld were also called simply Balnagown, Poltalloch, and Invercauld. In two cases the chief's designation was used as a kind of generic forename. Successive chiefs of the MacPhersons were called Cluny MacPherson, while each Robertson chief in turn was known as Struan Robertson. No doubt this was because there were other chieftains who could be called Cluny, and other chieftains who could be called Struan or Strowan.

The only clan chief whose name was prefixed by "the" was the Chisholm. This led to the saying that the only three people entitled to put "the" before their names were the Chisholm, the Pope, and the Devil.[64] Robert Lister Macneil, the American descendant of the old chiefs of Barra who bought back Kisimul Castle, and claimed the chiefship of the MacNeills by tanistry (i.e., a choice made by the clansfolk among the members of one family), was sometimes referred to as "the MacNeill of Barra"; a recent writer alluded to "the clan chief, the Gregor MacGregor"; and chiefs of the MacIntoshes in the nineteenth century were sometimes called "the MacIntosh" (more recently Sir Iain Moncreiffe wrote of "the Mackintosh" in his *Highland Clans*).[65] But there seems to be no authentic example of this usage before 1745 in any case other than that of the Chisholm. The chief of the MacFarlanes corrected General Wade (who had called him Mr MacFarlane) and told him that he was, simply, "MacFarlane" – not "the MacFarlane".[66] The innovation may have arisen from such expressions as "the MacNab who died in 1816 was Francis MacNab, 12th of MacNab", or "the MacLachlan who was killed at Culloden was Lachlan MacLachlan, 17th of Strathlachlan"; but this would no more justify the normal use of the definite article than a statement such as "the London in Canada is 100 miles from Toronto" would justify a reference to "the London, Ontario". Seton Gordon protested against this use of the definite article in the name of a chief; he said this "innovation . . . in the press of recent years is entirely wrong".[67]

If chiefs called by the clan name did not preface their names with "the", much less did chiefs who had territorial designations. A document of 1862 refers to the then Robertson of Struan as "the Struan"; and in a recent book MacKenzie of Kintail or Seaforth, the Earl of Seaforth, is described as "the Seaforth"; but for this there is no historical justification whatever. One might as well talk of "the Glengarry" or "the Sutherland".

When the head of the Bosville family successfully claimed the MacDonald of Sleat baronetcy in 1910, his wife and children assumed the surname "MacDonald of the Isles"; and the children of Lord Strathspey, descendant of the chiefs of Clan Grant, have taken the name "Grant of Grant". Roderick MacLeod, young brother of two MacLeod chiefs in the nineteenth century, was sometimes described as R. C. MacLeod of MacLeod.[67] This kind of designation is a recent, and many would think an unwarranted, development. Under the clan system a title such as this was restricted to one person – the head of the clan. The only apparent exception was that when the chief was too old to exercise the chiefly functions, perhaps in time of war, the man who was agreed to be the next chief, usually the old chief's eldest son, would act as regent for his father; and he would take the chiefly title, with the addition of the word "younger". The effective chief of the Camerons in the 1745 rebellion, for example, was not John, 18th of Lochiel, who was too old, but his son, who was known as "Donald Cameron, younger of Lochiel". (Donald was strictly chief only briefly, after his father died late in 1747 or early in 1748, and before he himself died in the latter year. He had not "succeeded to [the] chieftaincy" in 1719, as the *Oxford D.N.B.* inaccurately asserts; 1719 was when his father, John, succeeded his grandfather, Sir Ewen.)

12. King and country

A clan chief was, in fact, a ruler – a prince over a small country. The clan land can best be understood as an independent state, a separate political entity. The inland boundaries of the clan lands were often ranges of mountains. The Aboyne reporter in the O.S.A. remarked that the Highlanders "uniformly call all that extent of ground which is bounded by the sensible horizon by the name of *a country*".[68] Mrs Grant of Laggan wrote: "a country in the Highlands is understood to mean a habitable tract, divided by rocks, mountains, and narrow passes, from the adjacent countries, and inhabited by a particular clan."[69] James Hogg explained in 1803 "what is meant by *a country* in the Highlands. In all the inland glens the boundaries of a country are invariably marked out by the skirts of the visible horizon as viewed from the bottom of the valley. All beyond that is denominated *another country*, and is called by another name." Among the peninsulas of the west coast of Argyllshire and Inverness-shire, he continued, "the bounds of the country [are] marked out by the sea coast"; but in Wester Ross the former system is followed, and so "the country of Kintail, the country of Loch Carron, the country of Torridon, the straths of Loch Broom, etc., comprehend both sides of their respective firths, with all the waters that descend into them".[70]

The habit of calling a clan territory a "country" long survived the clan system itself. One of the witnesses before the Napier Commission in 1883 was questioned at Stenscholl, in Skye, which had been in the Clan Donald country:

"Was your family a crofting family? – Yes, but not in this country."

"From what country do you come? – MacLeod's [or MacLeods'?] country – Colbost."

Stenscholl was in Trotternish, in north Skye, the country of Clan Donald, while Colbost was in Duirinish, in west Skye – in Clan Leod country: Stenscholl and Colbost were only a score of miles apart as the crow flew, and in the same island, and of course the same county, but they were in different "countries".[71]

How many "clan countries" were there at the end of the clan era? Each clan had its own clan country, so the number of clan countries was the same as the number of clans. Since (as we saw earlier) there were about forty clans – or perhaps as many as sixty, if a more expansive definition is given to the term "clan" – then there were the same number of clan countries.

Of a clan country, the chief was king. Defoe considered the chiefs to be "little monarchs, reigning in their own dominions".[72] Johnson agreed: "Every chieftain is a monarch."[73] Burt said: "The chiefs, like princes upon the continent whose dominions lie contiguous, do not invade each other's boundaries while they are at peace and friendship with one another, but demand redress of wrongs."[74] Pennant called the chiefs of the clan days "the little kings of the country".[75] Before 1745, wrote the O.S.A. minister of Kirkhill, "every chief considered himself as an independent prince"; the clansfolk were "like the subjects of independent states".[76] The minister of Kiltearn said that "in ancient times, those tribes or clans who inhabited different districts of the country, looked upon themselves as a distinct people or nation, united together under their respective chiefs or leaders, who exercised a sovereign, and at the same time a parental, authority over them". The clans made war, and then entered into bonds of peace, "with all the solemnity of treaties entered into between two sovereign powers": he instanced a treaty at the end of the seventeenth century between Kenneth Earl of Seaforth and John Munro younger of Foulis.[77] The Earl of Selkirk made the same point: "The clans were little separate nations, and acted on a small scale, on the same principles on which we see the great kingdoms of Europe conduct themselves. MacIain, when he stole the cow for which he was hanged, was no more ashamed of what he had done, than a captain in the British navy would be of having taken a Spanish galleon loaded with dollars. The circumstance of the clans being separate and distinct political communities, and the chiefs, in effect, petty independent princes, is the fundamental principle on which the whole of the ancient state of the country essentially depended."[78] Selkirk compared the clan countries with "the great kingdoms of Europe"; but he could have made an even closer comparison with some of the continent's smaller realms. Before the French revolutionary wars the largely German-speaking tract of Middle Europe (the so-called Holy Roman Empire, which, as has often been pointed out, was neither an empire, nor Roman, nor holy) was divided up into some 160 separate principalities. Many of these were no larger than the clan countries in the Highlands of Scotland: some of them consisted only of a few neighbouring villages.

13. Many miniature courts

Thomas Babington Macaulay, Lord Macaulay, described the Highland system in his *History of England*. Macaulay himself was descended from the MacAulays who lived in Lewis; his great-grandfather became minister of Harris, his grandfather was minister successively of South Uist, Lismore, and Inveraray (all in the Highlands), and then Cardross (in the Lowlands), and his father was Zachary Macaulay the anti-slavery agitator, who made his career in the colonies and in England; in fact by then this branch of the MacAulays had become virtually an English family. Lord Macaulay's uncles were General Colin Macaulay, a leading light in the British army, and the Rev. Aulay Macaulay, a prominent Anglican clergyman and writer. T. B. Macaulay himself was born and brought up in England. He wrote of the Highland polity as it existed in 1689: "Within the four seas, and at the distance of less than five hundred miles from London, were many miniature courts, in each of which a petty prince, attended by guards, by armour-bearers, by musicians, by a hereditary orator, by a hereditary poet laureate, kept a rude state, dispensed a rude justice, waged wars, and concluded treaties . . . There was a commonwealth of clans, the image, on a reduced scale, of the great commonwealth of European nations. In the smaller of these two commonwealths, as in the larger, there were wars, treaties, alliances, disputes about territory and precedence, a system of public law, a balance of power."[79] Macaulay said that all this was less than five hundred miles from London: in fact the nearest part of this Highland clan territory was – in a direct line – something under four hundred miles from London.

The chiefs, the kings of these clan countries, were like kings elsewhere in that the prevailing rules of sexual morality were not considered to apply to them. Liaisons between chiefs and young women, wrote Thomson, were not thought shameful, much as a woman in larger kingdoms was (and is) not discredited by becoming the mistress of a king or prince.[80] As we shall see, though, this regard for the chief depended on his acting as a just ruler; if the members of a clan began to consider their chief as unjust, then he ran a great risk (and knew he ran a great risk) of being deposed.

14. Fidelity of the clansfolk

The chief being both the principal executive of the clan and its figurehead, the holder before all others of the clan name, his honour and safety came to be bound up with the honour and safety of the clan itself. Even when the chiefs who took part in the rebellion of 1745 had been deprived of the charters which spuriously named most of them as "owners" of large stretches of clan land, this loyalty was just as strong – perhaps stronger: it was given to the chief as chief, not to the position he was being encouraged to claim under Lowland law as landlord. Sir Walter Scott wrote that even after the ending of the hereditary jurisdictions and the confiscation of some of the charters, clanship continued to exist "as a law of love": it had never been anything else, of course. "The Highlanders maintained, in many instances, their chiefs at their own expense; and they embodied themselves in regiments, that the head of the family might obtain military preferment."[81] An anonymous friend of Lord Chatham wrote of this process. "Frasers, MacDonalds, Camerons, MacLeans, MacPhersons, and others of disaffected names and clans were enrolled; their chiefs or connections obtained commissions, the lower class always ready to follow, they with eagerness endeavoured who should be first enlisted."[82]

Many examples of the clansfolk's fidelity will be given later: two instances, given by David Stewart, may be mentioned now.

"A gentleman possessing a considerable Highland property, and descended from a warlike and honourable line of ancestors, long held in respect by the Highlanders, fell into difficulties some years ago. In this state, he felt his misfortune the more, as his estate was very improvable. In fact, he attempted some improvements, but employed more labourers than he could easily afford to pay. Notwithstanding this prospect of irregular payments, such was the attachment of the people to the representative of this respectable house, that they were ready at his call, and often left the employment of others, who paid regularly, to carry on his operations." This was the more remarkable in that the chief concerned had learned that in the new commercial society a civilized gentleman should disdain those he considered his inferiors. In the Highlands, said Stewart, "if a gentleman pass a countryman without returning his salute, it furnishes matter of observation to a whole district. The gentleman now in question was educated in the south, and, ignorant of the language and character of the people, and of their peculiar way of thinking, paid little regard to their feelings, and although a countryman pulled off his bonnet almost as soon as he appeared in sight, the respectful salute generally passed unnoticed; yet this was overlooked in remembrance of his family, in the same manner that generous minds extend to the children the gratitude due to the parents."[83]

The second episode occurred at about the same period. "A few years ago, a gentleman of an ancient and honourable family got so much involved in debt, that he was obliged to sell his estate. One-third of the debt consisted of money borrowed in small sums from his tenants, and from the country people in the neighbourhood. The interest of these sums was paid very irregularly. Instead of complaining of this inconvenience, these people kept at a distance, lest their demands might add to the difficulties of the man whose misfortunes they so much lamented; and many declared that, if their money could contribute to save the estate of an honourable family, they would never ask for principal or interest."[34]

The Rev. Canon Roderick C. MacLeod (youngest son of Norman, 25th of MacLeod, who was chief for sixty years in the nineteenth century) drew attention to an incident in 1777. Norman MacLeod, 23rd of MacLeod, who was then chief, was in desperate financial straits, so his tenants voluntarily paid more rent: by that time, of course, "rent" was the correct term, since the payments were being made to a landlord. A document in the Dunvegan muniment room, wrote Canon MacLeod, runs as follows: "We, the undersigned tacksmen, tenants and possessors on the estate of Norman MacLeod, Esq., wishing to shew our attachment to the family, and our desire to contribute, as far as our ability will admit, towards the support of their interest, and preservation of their estate, do hereby, in the hope that it may enable MacLeod and his Trustees to re-establish his affairs, and preserve the ancient possessions of the family, bind ourselves and our successors for the space of three years to pay an additional rent of one shilling and sixpence in the pound [7½% more] than the rent now payable on condition that, as our principal motive for coming under this voluntary burden is our attachment to the present MacLeod, to the standing of the family, and our desire of their estate being preserved entire, that we shall be freed therefrom if we should have the misfortune to lose him by death, or if any part of the estate should be sold within the aforementioned time." There were thirty-six signatories – nineteen of them MacLeods, and five MacAskills or MacSweynes, who were septs of the clan.[85]

15. Cat o' nine tails

The chiefs and chieftains who took part in the rebellions of 1715 and 1745 had to flee for their lives when the Hanoverian forces triumphed; and a number of them, particularly after the '45, returned to their own clan countries and lay concealed there for years. Their clansfolk of course knew of their whereabouts; but none of them were ever betrayed, despite the large rewards offered to anyone who would inform on one of these hunted rebels. Ewen MacPherson, 12th of Cluny, for example, returned to the MacPherson clan country in Badenoch, and hid there for nine years. The clansfolk excavated a cave for him, part of the way up a precipice;

they dug it out at night, and laboriously carried the earth and stones to throw into a neighbouring lake, so no trace should be left to reveal the project. The front of this artificial cave was entirely obscured by trees and rocks, and its position was planned so that the smoke from Cluny's fire rose against a grey cliff above, making it virtually invisible. Here he was supplied with food and necessaries by his clanspeople. A detachment of eighty Government soldiers was stationed in the area, because it was known that he was hiding there, and further troops marched into the neighbourhood from time to time; the local MacPhersons knew exactly where he was, but the soldiers never found him. At length, in 1755, he gave up hope of pardon, and escaped to France, where he died a year later.[86]

Any captured Highlander who was suspected of knowing the whereabouts of any of these Jacobite fugitives was mercilessly flogged to make him talk. We shall see later how John MacInnes, who in July 1746 helped to row Prince Charles from Skye to the mainland, was a little later caught by Captain Ferguson, and sentenced by the brave captain to 500 lashes with the cat o' nine tails, in instalments of fifty at a time; but he refused to give any information, though "the blood gushed out at both his sides".[87] We shall also see how Ewen MacPhee, from the Cameron country, was caught in October 1746 carrying letters written in French. He refused to make any explanation, so he was given 500 lashes, and another 500 some days later; remaining silent, he was finally killed by a beating with musket butts and bayonets.[88]

One trusts that MacInnes and MacPhee would have been happier with their treatment if they had realized it was simply part of what conventional historians now comfortably describe as the arrival of Lowland civilization and morality, and the conquest of "lawlessness", in the Highlands. Perhaps in due course it will become acceptable to excuse the behaviour of other savagely dictatorial regimes in the same forgiving way.

16. Authority of the chiefs

Many writers consider the old clan chiefs, before 1745, to have been complete tyrants, and the clansfolk mere helots, quaking minions sunk in thraldom. The orthodox belief is that anyone bold enough to offer the most trivial opposition to a chief's slightest caprice was immediately held in durance vile, or worse, slaughtered on the spot. This view has been given emotional expression by many authors. In 1773 Dr Johnson wrote, "not many years have passed since the clans knew no law but the Laird's will".[89] In 1898 Andrew Lang (grandson of Patrick Sellar, and therefore eager to divert criticism) deplored the "arbitrary power" of the chiefs, who were "tyrannically severe" towards the "enslaved" commons.[90] More recently James Halliday said that the clansfolk "had never combined against their chiefs; the very concept was beyond them"[91] (despite all the many instances detailed below when the clansfolk did exactly that: perhaps the very concept of looking at the evidence is beyond this writer). E. R. Cregeen said that the "chiefs had virtually absolute power over their people".[92] J. Glover said that the clans were ruled by chiefs "whose authority was unassailable".[93] T. Steel said "the chief's authority was absolute"[94] (not even "virtually absolute"). H. Trevor-Roper, referring to the MacDonald chiefs of Glengarry, said, "the clansmen, as always, obediently followed their chief".[95] (One is tempted to amend this to: "the historian, as always, obediently followed other historians.") A. J. Youngson said the clansfolk thought their chief was all-important: "they were bound to regard his will as law, and to lay down their lives at his command."[96] Dr R. Muir claimed the chief was an "undisputed despot";[97] and dozens of other commentators joined in, and said, no doubt shivering delightedly, that the chiefs could at the drop of a hat consign any clansman to "pit and gallows".

Dr George Macaulay Trevelyan, who was perhaps the most prominent historian of his generation, said the same in one of the most widely read history books of the twentieth century, *English Social History*. (Published in Britain in 1944, in the first five years it sold 392,000 copies.)[98] Dr Trevelyan, as we saw, was Regius Professor of Modern History at Cambridge University, and then Master of Trinity College in the same university; his work was praised by many other historians.[99] Though the title *English Social History* did not seem to justify the digression (unless, like many English writers, he assumed that "English", rightfully considered, ought to comprehend the whole island), Trevelyan felt unable to deny his readers his opinions as to the horrors of Highland life. "The Chief had the power of life and death, and exercised it to the full, keeping his clan in awe", Trevelyan proclaimed: the chief had "been able, at will or whim, to imprison the disobedient in fetid dungeons, without appeal lying to the King's tribunals".[100] (Dungeons would have been bad enough; but "fetid" dungeons – having a strong, offensive smell – were even worse. Being imprisoned in "fragrant" dungeons would not be quite so melodramatic.) Historians seem to love this exciting portrayal, and Highland chiefs stamp tyrannically across their pages, shouting "Off with his head!" like hybrid offspring of Shakespeare's Richard III and Lewis Carroll's Queen of Hearts. Unfortunately, the prosaic facts of the matter give no support to this rousing but romanticized unreality.

In some ways, the chief of reality was like a petty king; in others, he was more like an elective president. This can be shown in various ways, by applying what I have called the archive of the head: that is to say, by considering the question in the light of what one knows about the activities of human beings generally, along with the material conditions of those humans at the relevant time. For example, one can sometimes tell that a particular tale from a specific epoch in history is inaccurate because the necessary apparatus was not at that time in existence. If someone should come up with a story that in 1066 William the Conqueror brought his army across the Channel by jumbo jet, one could immediately dismiss the tale because human beings had not then learned how to make flying machines. Years of painstaking research in remote archives would not be needed before one could say that the story was inaccurate. In the same way, anyone claiming that Francis Drake on Plymouth Hoe was informed of the approach of the Spanish Armada by radio would not find many to believe him, because it is generally known that wireless communication had not then been invented. This kind of reasoning enables one to come to a conclusion on the "will or whim" theory immediately. Just as William I had no jet-planes, and Drake no radio, in the same way there was no apparatus in the Highlands during the days of the clans to enable a chief to achieve any ambition he might have had to become a tyrant. That machinery began to be introduced only tentatively after the Jacobite Rising of 1715, and came into full operation only in the years after 1746, when Lowland and English soldiers forced their way into the mountains – murdering, raping, plundering, and destroying, in their zeal to enforce what Dr Smout calls "the triumph of order and of Lowland ethics", and a "moral reformation"[101] – and then in the following years stood ready at the beck and call of the chiefs to execute their eviction orders. In the clan system, the chiefs had no policemen, no standing armies, no courts or lawyers. Their only soldiers were the rank-and-file clansmen – the very people against whom, had they been tyrants, their tyranny must have been exercised. The tribute given to the chiefs by their clansfolk was enough to support themselves, their families, a piper and a bard and perhaps one or two other attendants; it was never enough to support an autocracy. Dictatorship is expensive, as well as execrable.

E. R. Cregeen neatly sidestepped the issue by saying that the "chiefs had virtually absolute power over their people and a private army of kinsmen and followers at their backs", as if these two groups were in some way different. If he had said the "chiefs had virtually absolute power over their kinsmen and followers, and a private army of kinsmen and followers at their backs", or, conversely, if he had said they had "absolute power over their people, enforced by a private army of their people", it would have been apparent that his allegation amounted to saying simply that the clansfolk had absolute power over themselves.[102]

17. Ad vitam aut culpam

The fact that the chief was not able to play the despot in Highland society as it existed before the '45 is no startling new discovery: many commentators (those who knew the Highlands well, or who used the archive of the head) have made the same point. Agnes Mure MacKenzie remarked, in *Scotland in Modern Times*, that a chief whose "life and property depended on the willing service of his followers, and whose only police were those same followers, had to behave himself reasonably well so far as they, at any rate, were concerned".[103] R. Jamieson said, in his introduction to Burt's *Letters*, that there was no slavish submission to the chiefs: "we believe the Highlands of Scotland to be the only country in Europe where the very name of slavery was unknown." If a chief proved unworthy of his rank, he was deposed, and "the next in order was constituted in his room". The deposition was usually enough; for the ex-chief, "having none among them [the clansfolk] to take his part, was no longer dangerous". A chief, Jamieson affirmed, was "considered as such only *ad vitam aut culpam*" – for life, or until he misbehaved.[104] Burt wrote, "the power of the chiefs is not supported by interest, as they are landlords, but as lineally descended from the old patriarchs, or fathers of their families". Burt defined the duties of the chief as to protect his clansfolk, to lead in clan quarrels, to free the necessitous from arrears of "rent", and to maintain such as fell into total decay; if the tribe increased (he said), the farms were subdivided, for all had to be provided for. Indeed, said Burt, on the average, the "landlord" frees the "tenant" from his "rent" arrears "about one year in five". (Very generous behaviour on the part of a "landlord" who could at any moment send any defaulting "tenant" to the gallows.) Landlords (for that is what the chiefs later claimed that their forebears were) would read this list of duties with no little astonishment.[105]

D. J. MacDonald of Castleton, in his book on the Clan Donald, made the point that "the chief who abused his power and became oppressive was apt to find himself in trouble with his clan".[106] The Rev. Donald MacNicol, in his *Remarks on Dr Johnson's Journey*, 1779, scouted the idea that the chiefs were despotic. "They were", he wrote, "under a necessity of acting in a much more humane and mild manner towards their clans, or people, as they knew that their own security and importance depended on their attachment; and that, without that, their power and influence would be nothing."[107] David Stewart called attention to the fact that many of the Highland chiefs when the clan system began to be destroyed in the middle of the eighteenth century had ancestors who had fought at the head of their clans at the Battle of Bannockburn in 1314, over four centuries earlier. "The long unbroken line of chiefs is as great a proof of the general mildness of their sway as of the fidelity of their followers; for the independent spirit displayed on various occasions by the people, proves that they would not have brooked oppression, where they looked for kindness and protection."[108] In fact, "it required much kindness and condescension on the part of the chief in order to maintain his influence with his clan, who all expected to be treated with the affability and courtesy due to gentlemen".[109] Stewart later returned to the topic. "Nothing can be more erroneous than an opinion, often repeated, and therefore sometimes believed, that whatever side the feudal superior took in any great political question or contest, he was invariably followed by his subservient adherents. Many instances to the contrary have been stated, and I could produce many more, all highly creditable to the spirit of independence which long distinguished the clansmen."[110] He gave various examples (which are quoted elsewhere in this work) of clansfolk holding to their own opinion in defiance of their chiefs, and said that such circumstances were "sufficient to prove, that the Highlanders were not those slaves to the caprice and power of their chiefs they have been supposed; and that, on the contrary, as I have already noticed, the latter were obliged to pay court, and yield to the will and independent spirit of their clans".[111]

One story from the days of clanship is significant. A chief – MacDonell from Lochaber, that is, no doubt, MacDonell or MacDonald of Keppoch – accepted the cattle of Forbes of Culloden to pasture them through the winter. Then he dishonestly decided to keep the cattle for himself, and sent a man to Culloden to say they had been stolen. Culloden suspected the truth, and treated the man with great hospitality, plying him with food and drink. As Culloden hoped, the messenger was so impressed by this treatment, that he returned to his chief, MacDonell, and told him Culloden had to have his cattle back! The commonalty having spoken – although in this case, apparently, only one of them – MacDonell had to agree, and returned the cattle. Ivan the Terrible would not have given in so easily.

18. Good will of the tribe

Cosmo Innes said, in his *Scotch Legal Antiquities*, that the clans originally lived in patriarchal fashion.[112] The clansfolk looked to the chief as their father and leader, but the common people of the clan held their farms from father to son, generation to generation, by a right as indefeasible as the chief's. "The power of the chief", wrote Innes, "from its very nature, depended on the good will of the whole tribe – for who was to enforce a tyrannical order?"[113]

Burt told the story of a ship which was stranded on Barra, the country of the MacNeills. MacNeill, instead of resolving himself what was to be done, called a council of about fifty of the clansfolk to decide.[114] And these "elders" of the clan had the last word. Mrs Grant of Laggan wrote: "Nothing can be more erroneous than the prevalent idea that a Highland chief was an ignorant and unprincipled tyrant, who rewarded the abject submission of his followers with relentless cruelty and rigorous oppression. He was, on the contrary, the father of his people: gracious, condescending, and beloved, far from being ruled by arbitrary caprice. He was taught from the cradle to consider the meanest individual of his clan as his kinsman and his friend, whom he was born to protect, and bound to regard. He was taught, too, to venerate old age, to respect genius, and to place an almost implicit dependence on the counsel of the elders of his clan . . . There is no instance of a chieftain's taking any step of importance without the consent of the elders of his tribe." In fact, she wrote, if the clan chief was "ferocious in disposition, or weak in understanding, he was curbed and directed by the elders of his tribe, who, by inviolable custom, were his standing counsellors, without whose advice no measure of any kind was decided upon".[115] This council of elders often had a regular meeting place. In Islay, for example, according to the N.S.A. report on Kilarrow, "the MacDonald council held their meetings" on an islet in Loch Finlaggan.[116] The Atholl council met at Logierait.[117] David Stewart had discussed the matter with "several old gentlemen", all very knowledgeable about "what to them was of the greatest importance, the history, the policy, the biography, and the character of their ancestors and contemporaries", and they told him of "the control of the Elders, and the firmness and independence of sagacious peasants [sic], in setting effective limits to arbitrary power".[118] The Rev. Lachlan Shaw, a Highlander from Rothiemurchus, wrote (in his *History of Moray*, published in 1775) that "anciently every chief of a clan was by his dependants considered as a little Prince, not absolute, but directed by the Gentleman of his Clan". As the Grand Council was to the king, "so the Gentlemen and Heads of Families were to the Chief, by whose advice all things that regarded the Clan in common, or particular Families, were determined".[119]

Alexander Nicolson outlined the same fact. "Far from being an irresponsible autocrat, the chief was at all times expected to seek counsel from the cadets of the tribe, and he was invariably guided by their advice. His conduct was closely watched by these elders; and should he commit any action that might be construed as being derogatory to the good name of the clan, or unworthy of his own high office, his people had no compunction in bringing him to book, and even threatening him with deposition." Earlier in his *History of Skye* Nicholson had given an example. Sir James Mor MacDonald, tenth chief of Clan Donald, "began to frequent the cities of the south, and there he entertained on a lavish scale. Numerous guests visited also at Duntulm and at Armadale [Sir James' homes in Skye], where all was gaiety and unfailing generosity." Before long he was deep in debt, and also at odds with his eldest son. These "domestic troubles . . . caused much anxiety to the clan". So "the leaders of the clan met in conclave, and, in no uncertain voice, informed the disputants [the chief and his son] that, unless they composed their differences, the chief would be summarily deposed, and the heir would be prevented from the succession". Only Sir James' death in 1678 saved him from further sanctions.[120]

POWER WITHIN THE CLAN

In the sixteenth century Campbell of Glenorchy decided to build a castle on a hill above Loch Tay, and laid the foundations. But his clan did not approve of this site: they wanted him to build it instead at Balloch, or Taymouth, on the low ground. The chief had to agree, and accordingly he built the castle at Taymouth. Similarly, in the early eighteenth century the Earl of Seaforth, chief of the MacKenzies, decided to demolish Brahan Castle, the principal seat of the family. But the MacKenzies wanted it to be left standing; and Seaforth had to give way.[121] Even the chief's domestic arrangements were decided by the clan. Tobias Smollett related how Dougal Campbell, hereditary captain of one of Argyll's castles, probably Dunstaffnage, wanted to silence his bagpiper, who played for an hour in the hall every morning, as custom required him to do. (David Stewart insisted that piping was outdoor music; the bagpipe, he said, "was no more intended for a house, than a round of six-pounders" – artillery fire.[122] Dougal Campbell seems to have agreed with him.) But the chieftain's proposal was unavailing. "A consultation of the clan being held on this occasion, it was unanimously agreed, that the laird's request could not be granted without a dangerous encroachment upon the customs of the family"[123] – and Campbell had to endure, with as good a grace as he could muster, an hour's piping serenade each morning. So far from the Campbell chieftain being able to order immediate executions, he could not even get any peace and quiet to digest his breakfast.

19. Twelve men fully armed

James VII and II having fled from London at the end of 1688, he was declared to have abdicated. In 1689 William and Mary were proclaimed King and Queen of Scotland (a more accurate title would been King and Queen of the Lowlands, of course), and the Edinburgh authorities ordered the dismissal of Episcopalian clergy throughout Scotland. This was formally ratified the next year by the Scots Parliament, which in 1690 abolished the Scottish bishops and ordained that the Scots church should "purge out . . . erroneous", i.e. Episcopalian, ministers and settle Presbyterians in their place.[124] The first General Assembly of the re-established Presbyterian Church took place in the same year. It claimed to represent Scotland, but as usual when that claim was made it really represented the Lowlands. Of the 182 representatives who appeared, scarcely any came from the Highlands. Those few Highlanders who did come were mainly from Argyllshire. The Duke of Argyll, like some other Highland charter holders, was a strong ally of the Lowlanders in their attempts to take over the Highlands, since if they succeeded the chiefs would be able to transform themselves into landlords: so Argyll, as a leading player in Lowland politics, would have been able to contrive that at least a few of his cronies attended the General Assembly. What occurred in the Highlands as a result of this religious settlement is instructive, since it demonstrates the difference between the picture painted by the official contemporary documents (followed by modern accounts) and what actually happened – the contrast between fiction and fact, the distinction between historians and history.

The head of the house of Argyll was perhaps the most potent chief in the Highlands; he was also the most powerful politician in Scotland; and he was one of the most prominent statesmen in the affairs of Britain as a whole. John, the first Duke of Argyll (who died in 1703), took a prominent part in setting William and Mary on the British throne in 1689, and his son the second duke (who died in 1743) took the foremost role in forging the 1707 union with England, and later in making George I king in 1714. But though they helped to dictate these great matters of state in London and Edinburgh, and exercised immense influence in making or unmaking the sovereigns of the whole new combined country of England and the Scottish Lowlands, neither of them could prevail as against the handful of ordinary clansfolk who lived in the Highland parish of Glenorchy. David Stewart recorded the events. "The last Episcopal clergyman of the parish of Glenorchy, Mr David Lindsay, was ordered [after the decision of the Scots Parliament in 1690] to surrender his charge to a Presbyterian minister then appointed by the Duke of Argyll. When the new clergyman reached the parish to take possession of his living, not an individual would speak to him, and every door was shut against him, except Mr Lindsay's, who received him kindly. On Sunday the new clergyman went to church, accompanied by his predecessor. The whole population of the district was assembled, but they would not enter the church. No person spoke to the new minister, nor was there the least noise or violence, till he attempted to enter the church, when he was surrounded by twelve men fully armed, who told him he must accompany them; and, disregarding all Mr Lindsay's prayers and entreaties, they ordered the piper to play the march of death, and marched away with the minister to the confines of the parish. Here they made him swear on the Bible that he would never return, or attempt to disturb Mr Lindsay. He kept his oath."[125] Stewart's is not the only account of the matter. A subsequent Presbyterian minister of Glenorchy (who would not have enjoyed having to tell of this repulse of the Presbyterian minister) related the same affair in the O.S.A., and said that Mr Lindsay was not troubled till his death over thirty years later (that is, in the 1720s).[126] Another writer, John MacKay, in his *The Church in the Highlands*, said that Lindsay "retained the benefice" until he died, in 1723 – thirty-four years after the most powerful chief in the Highlands (armed with the irresistible "power of life and death", as Trevelyan has it, and "whose authority was unassailable", in Janet Glover's words, who was "tyrannically severe", in Andrew Lang's phrase, who was possessed of "absolute authority", as Tom Steel put it, whose despotism was backed by "pit and gallows", as a hundred historians hammer home) had decided to depose him.[127]

The Presbyterian minister sent to Glenorchy had, in fact, no alternative to keeping his promise to forget about his presentation to the parish by the all-powerful Duke of Argyll, for in those simple times in the Highlands, if the people wanted one minister neither the chief – nor, for that matter, the entire might of the British Government – could force them to accept another. (It is for the sages of the present day to tell us if that system is less, or more, democratic than our modern arrangements.) The Duke of Argyll took the affront, as he had to, without attempting to contest it. G. M. Trevelyan alleged that the clans were "in awe" of their chiefs: the fact was, as this and many similar incidents show, that it was the chiefs who were "in awe" of their clans. If the Duke of Argyll, with all the enormous Lowland and indeed British authority at his disposal, could do nothing with a few hundreds of "disobedient" clansfolk even at this late date, what could be done by less eminent chiefs, either then or in earlier times?

20. Ignored the sentence

This was very far from being an isolated case. What happened in each Highland parish, when (on the flight of James VII and II, and his replacement by William and Mary) Presbyterianism triumphed in the Lowlands, depended on the will of the local Highlanders. If they wanted the new minister, or were indifferent as to the occupant of the manse, then the Presbyterian parson came in without trouble. But where the local clansfolk decided that they preferred to keep the existing incumbent, they kept him; and attempts to replace him were, and in the nature of things had to be, unsuccessful. The Episcopalian minister retained his position in Moy until about 1727 (throughout the reigns of Mary II, 1689-1695, William III, 1689-1702, Queen Anne, 1702-14, and George I, 1714-27).[128] In the parish of Petty the Episcopalian minister, the Rev. Alexander Dunoon, officiated from 1684 until 1718.[129] In the parish of Rosskeen the Episcopalian minister kept his place for many years after the official establishment of the new state religion – the first Presbyterian minister was Daniel Bethune, who arrived in 1717 (no less than twenty-eight years after the Revolution settlement).[130] The Lochcarron report in the N.S.A. told how the people in that parish, who had become not for religious reasons (the minister said) "but from political considerations, attached to Episcopacy, conceived a rooted dislike to the Presbyterian system, which all the prudence of the clergy was for some time unable to eradicate". So much so that the presbytery (the local church ruling body) was put to flight when it tried to meet in Lochcarron in September 1724 (thirty-five years after Presbyterianism had triumphed – in the Lowlands), and the meeting had to be held across the mountains in Kilmorack six months later.[131] A similar attempt to replace the Episcopalian incumbent in Gairloch also met successful resistance. The writer John MacLeod (son of a Presbyterian manse) said disapprovingly: "When the induction of a lawful minister was attempted in the parish of Gairloch, the district was convulsed in riot", and the minister "fled the district".[132] According to John MacKay in his work on the Highland Church, the Rev. Angus MacQueen of Sleat, in Skye, "was deposed" (a meaningless verb in this context) by the incoming Presbyterian authorities: "but he ignored the sentence, and held his position till he died."[133] Another Skye minister, Donald MacQueen of Snizort, was also "deprived" for non-jurancy; "but he followed the example of his namesake in Sleat, and defied the Church authorities" – or rather, the ordinary clansfolk of Snizort, like those of Sleat, defied the Church (and state) authorities.[134] Of the Ross-shire ministers, according to John MacKay "nineteen held their benefices without submission till their removal by death".[135] The last of them died in 1727 (like the unauthorized minister of the Inverness-shire parish of Moy). Donald Sage wrote that among these Ross-shire parishes were Alness, Kilmuir Wester, and Avoch; Sage (an Evangelical Presbyterian) thought that the successful defiance of the state and church decision to put in Presbyterian ministers owed much to "the heritors, rigid Episcopalians",[136] but we have seen – from the events in Glenorchy and elsewhere – that the charter holders (however enthusiastically Presbyterian) were powerless when the people had decided what to do. If the Duke of Argyll could do nothing, neither could lesser chiefs.

In Sutherland, John Dempster, minister of Lairg, "was deprived by the Privy Council on 7th November 1689", wrote John MacKay, for ignoring the Edinburgh decisions about religion, "and for praying for the late king, in disregard of the law, yet he continued in his charge till he died about 1705" – sixteen years after the Privy Council had "deprived" him.[137] Dempster's neighbour, Walter Ross, the minister of Rogart, was summoned by the Privy Council for similar offences, but the prosecution was not followed through, "and he retained his position as Episcopal parish minister of Rogart for thirty-one years".[138] In fact "all the incumbents in the county [of Sutherland] refused to conform to Presbyterianism", but they all "retained their benefices".[139] The official documents, carefully archived in Edinburgh until keen historians come to disinter them, say one thing; reality says another. It is clear that the contemporary Privy Council, and the other Edinburgh authorities, had to accept the mundane truth of the matter – that the Highlands were de facto a collection of foreign countries – more readily than some modern commentators.

21. Edinburgh intrusions

The power of the people under the clan system was shown not only in the far north, or in the Highland hinterland. At the time of the O.S.A. the minister of Muthill, a parish at the very southern edge of the Highlands in Perthshire, was the Rev. John Scott. He wrote in his parish report that he had succeeded his father in 1767; his father's "predecessor was Mr William Hally, the first Presbyterian minister after the Revolution, and who, for several years after his ordination, was obliged to preach from a tent in the churchyard, while the Episcopal incumbent kept possession of the church".[140] Another parish at the southern boundary of the Highlands was Callander: the O.S.A. report there said that "Mr James Menzies was the last Episcopal minister, and continued to officiate long after the Revolution".[141] Although Presbyterianism was by Lowland enactment the official religion of the whole of Scotland from 1689, in many Highland parishes, as Stewart says, "the Presbyterian clergy were not established till the reigns of George I and II"[142] – George I who began ruling in 1714, and George II who came to the throne in 1727. In those days, of course, there was no coercive force available to make the Highlanders accept a system, economic or religious, that they did not want – nor could anyone compel them to accept such a system's office-holders.

The ending about the middle of the eighteenth century of the old system where the will of the people prevailed had its inevitable consequence in religious affairs. The minister of Kiltearn said in the N.S.A., "all the ministers were settled by a popular call until 1770. Mr George Watson was, soon thereafter, settled by a Crown presentation, as were also his two successors."[143] Before the Lowland takeover, the clansfolk decided who should be their minister: now, the Edinburgh authorities were able to intrude their own candidate. The facile orthodox view, that Culloden marked the arrival of popular freedoms in the Highlands, turns history on its head; Culloden marked the end of these popular freedoms.

The will of the clan prevailed in secular as in ecclesiastical matters. A son of the chief of the Grants, called Laird Humphry, lived a riotous youth, and became an annoyance and an offence to the members of the clan. He was the eldest son, and would normally have become chief. But the clansfolk (not realizing that Trevelyan would later assert that they were in terror of the chief's merest "will or whim") knew how to deal with him. "Laird Humphry", wrote David Stewart, "had, in the meantime, incurred many heavy debts. The elders of the clan bought up these debts, which gave them full power over him; then they put him in prison in Elgin, and kept him there during the remainder of his life, leaving the management of the estate in the hands of his younger brother. The debts were made a pretext for confining him, the elders not choosing to accuse him of various crimes of which he had been guilty, and the consciousness of which made him submit more quietly to the restraint."[144] Sir Iain Moncreiffe mentioned the same incident.[145] Humphry

Grant died unmarried in 1732 (that is, only fourteen years before Culloden), and his younger brother Ludovic in due course succeeded their father in the chiefship.

Stewart also described what had happened to one of his own ancestors, who was chieftain of Garth. Because of his "ungovernable passions and ferocious disposition", he was not considered a suitable chieftain. In about 1520 he was deposed, and imprisoned for the rest of his life in a cell in the castle of Garth, "by his friends and kindred" – that is, the clansfolk of the Stewarts of Garth clan.[146]

22. Many voices against one

When James Boswell and Dr Johnson made their tour to the Hebrides in 1773, they met a number of people, for example Flora MacDonald, who had helped Prince Charles when he had been hiding in the Highlands after the failure of the 1745 rebellion. One of the episodes which Boswell heard about at this time was significant, like the incidents mentioned above, in its bearing on the question of authority in the Highlands. Prince Charles and three companions from the MacLeod clan, fleeing from the reign of terror inflicted by Cumberland's vicious marauders, had been rowed from Skye to Raasay by two Highlanders, John MacKenzie and Donald MacFriar. In Raasay the prince and the MacLeods took cover in a hut, wrote Boswell. "While they were in the hut, MacKenzie and MacFriar, the two boatmen, were placed as sentinels upon different eminences . . . There was a man wandering about the island, selling tobacco. Nobody knew him, and he was suspected to be a spy. MacKenzie came running to the hut, and told the fugitives that this suspected person was approaching. Upon which the three gentlemen, young [MacLeod of] Raasay, Dr MacLeod, and Malcolm [MacLeod], held a council of war upon him, and were unanimously of the opinion that he should be instantly put to death. Prince Charles, at once assuming a grave and even severe countenance, said, 'God forbid that we should take away a man's life, who may be innocent, while we can preserve our own.' The gentlemen however persisted in their resolution, while he as strenuously continued to take the merciful side. John MacKenzie, who sat watching at the door of the hut, and overheard the debate, said in Erse [Gaelic], 'Well, well; he must be shot. You are the king, but we are the parliament, and will do what we choose.'" Prince Charles laughed loudly when MacKenzie's comments were translated into English for him. The unknown man, fortunately for himself, walked past the hut without stopping. They found later he was a former rebel, on the run after Culloden like themselves. When twenty-seven years later Malcolm MacLeod met Boswell he told him that "in such a situation, I would have shot my brother, if I had not been sure of him"; and certainly Prince Charles and the three MacLeods would not long have survived discovery.[147]

The noteworthy point here is the frankness with which MacKenzie, an ordinary Highlander, spoke to the man he believed to be the son of the rightful king. In Lowland eyes MacKenzie was a mere underling: no one had asked for his opinion, but he gave it – a very forthright one, at that – nonetheless. It hardly accords with the orthodox view of the relations between the clansfolk and their supposed superiors.

Even more interesting was what MacKenzie said later. When Boswell met the former sentinel during his "Highland jaunt" of 1773, he was curious to know if the Highlander had been influenced in his conduct by anything he might have heard of the British constitution. "Why, John," said Boswell, "did you think the king should be controlled by a parliament?" MacKenzie answered, "I thought, sir, there were many voices against one."[148] This reply breathes the very spirit of the old Highland polity. The majority, the many voices, decided the course of action: the chief, even royalty itself, had only one voice in the council. It also tells us much about the comparative degrees of social stratification in the old and the new societies that when MacKenzie was speaking in English, he called Boswell, a Lowland tourist, "Sir"; when speaking in Gaelic, he had addressed Prince Charles, whom be held to be the heir of his legitimate sovereign, as "You".

It was the same when the Chevalier, at another point in his flight after Culloden, was being looked after by the seven (or eight) men of Glen Moriston. These men were all former rebels, existing as fugitives: yet all of them, in Bishop Forbes' words, had "the superlative honour to despise £30,000" (equalling in modern terms the biggest win on the National Lottery) which they could have got immediately by betraying Prince Charles. All these men profoundly believed Charles to be the rightful heir to the throne, to the extent of having given up everything for him, and living as hunted outlaws, with a price on their heads. But there were eight voices against one, and when he said he might leave against their judgement, they threatened to tie him up. Charles said ruefully: "Kings and Princes must be ruled by their privy council, but I believe there is not in all the world a more absolute privy council than what I have at present."[149] It seems unlikely that the Highlanders would have allowed more authority to a mere chief than they were prepared to concede to the (as they were convinced, to their own great detriment) heir of the rightful wielder of sovereign power in Edinburgh and London.

23. Chiefs as war-leaders

The original, and always the most important, duty of the chief was to lead the clan in war, to command the clan against its enemies. Here, surely, if anywhere, the stories of chiefs having paramount authority, never to be questioned, must have some reality: for a military leader, in the very nature of the case, must be more of a despot than a civil executive. (It is difficult to have a calm debate in the middle of a battle.) But even here, at the very core and centre of the chief's power, we find the clansfolk as independent as in any other area of the clan's life. This fact was hard for Lowland historians to accept. Patrick Fraser Tytler, a leading Lowland historian, used dramatic terms to describe the rallying of the clans by the croishtarich (a stick, sometimes with a cross piece, dipped in blood at one end and burnt at the other, and called "the fiery cross"): "it is certain that, throughout the Highland districts of the country, its summons, wherever it was carried, was regarded with awe, and obeyed without hesitation."[150] Professor Mitchison said emotionally, "in both rebellions [1715 and 1745] the ordinary Highlander only fought because he was forced 'out'; his own political opinions did not matter a damn".[151]

In fact the ordinary Highlander's opinion mattered a great deal (it mattered very much more, in fact, than the opinions of the ordinary Lowlander, or the ordinary English person). The response to the summons of the croishtarich depended entirely on the judgement of the clansfolk. Three pertinent incidents were mentioned by David Stewart. At the Revolution of 1689, when King James was replaced by King William, the Marquis of Atholl had been chief of the Atholl clan for nearly half a century, and was too old for soldiering. So his eldest son, Lord Tullibardine, became the acting chief, with the chief's powers, and he summoned together "a numerous body of Atholl Highlanders": his brother-in-law, Hugh Lord Lovat, brought three hundred Frasers along. The clansmen thought that they were going to support the recently deposed sovereign, James VII of Scotland (and II of England); but when the assembly was complete in front of Blair Castle, Lord Tullibardine (who was then wielding the powers of the chief, before whom, we are assured, the clansfolk were compelled to grovel) revealed that he intended to side with William, the new monarch. Immediately his putative regiment (all trembling serfs, in the orthodox view) broke away and, running to a nearby stream, "drank to the health of King James". Then they put themselves under the command of the Jacobite chieftain, Stewart of Ballechin, and with colours flying and pipes playing they marched off to join Lord Dundee, King James's commander.[152] If Lord Tullibardine, left trying to command the empty air, had known how Lowland and English historians were later going to describe the powers of the chief, he might have wished that the Atholl clansmen could have read the assertions of the English-speaking experts.

In 1745, 1100 men of the Clan Grant came forward and offered to fight under their chief for Prince Charles. But the chief had decided to embrace the opposite side; and, later, he tried to summon his followers to attend him to Aberdeen to complement the successful Hanoverian forces. Only ninety-five could be persuaded to join him, even though (Stewart said) the chief was much loved by his people.[153] The 1750 report on the Highlands, edited by Andrew Lang, mentioned the stubborn independence of the Grant clansmen during the '45; the members of the Clan Grant, he said, "made also, in opposition to their Chief's desire, a separate treaty of neutrality with the Highland army".[154] Despite the wish of Grant of Grant, who supported the Hanoverians, that the Grants should stay at home, the western Grants in Glen Urquhart and Glen Corrimony went off to join the Chevalier.[155]

Also in 1745 (said Stewart), more than 1000 men gathered at Dunvegan Castle to support MacLeod, under the impression that he was for Prince Charles. When they found he was going to support the Hanoverians, only 200 men (no more than one in five) would stay with him.[156]

John MacDonald of Glengarry, too, tried in the same crisis to get his clan to stay at home; instead, the clansmen not only joined the Jacobites but "threatened to take himself Prisoner if he did not likewise join them".[157] (True, that was Glengarry's own account of the affair; but since the great part of the Lowland-written history of these years in the Highlands is based upon the chiefs' testimony to their own good deeds, it would seem perverse to reject Glengarry's story.)

24. View of the clan

In each clan, the success of recruitment depended on the feelings of the clansfolk. Where the members of the clan shared the opinion of the chief, whether the latter in 1745 supported Prince Charles or King George, there was no difficulty in mobilising the clan. Stewart said that "in the county of Ross, Munro of Culcairn, and other gentlemen of that loyal [i.e., Hanoverian] clan, were very successful, and armed a considerable body of men [to fight for George II]. The Earl of Sutherland raised and appointed a brigade of 2,400 men at his own expense"[158] – to fight on the same side. Everything was determined by the view taken by the clan of the coming conflict; and usually one view would be shared by the clansfolk generally, which is not surprising, since the social and economic organization of the clan gave its members something close to an identity of interest.

David Stewart emphasized the importance of this general clan opinion in the contrasting response to the various chiefs' appeals in 1745. For example, the Athollmen (that is to say some of the Stewarts, some of the Robertsons, and many others) were as fervent for the Stuart family as they and their forebears had been in 1689 (when in opposition to their chief's wishes they marched off to fight for King James). "In Perthshire the influence of the loyal [i.e., pro-George II] proprietors [sic] completely failed. The Duke of Atholl and the Earl of Breadalbane could not bring out a man in arms. Powerful as the Duke of Atholl was by feudal rights and privileges, popular in his personal character, and attracting the notice of the people, in a peculiar manner, by his affability and graceful majestic appearance, he could not raise a man, as his principles and opinions were contrary to those of his people; while his [Jacobite] brother, Lord George Murray, found himself in a few days at the head of a brigade of 1,400 men of Atholl, anxious to be led to the field: so little did the people regard feudal authority, and so independent were they when submission to their superiors interfered with what they called their loyalty; and yet these people are generally believed to have been such slaves to the caprice and will of their imperious chiefs, that whichever side they [the chiefs] took their vassals followed. The Duke of Atholl's agents were particularly active in the service of Government; the clergy also, with one exception, were zealous in their exhortations, and exerted themselves in support of the Duke's authority, but to no effect. The Earl of Breadalbane was equally unsuccessful, although highly respected as an honourable, humane, and indulgent landlord [sic]. While such was the case in Perthshire, in Argyllshire it was different; two battalions, or a brigade of 1,200 men, were raised [for the Government – the Campbells of the Argyll clan supported the Hanoverian dynasty], and were actively employed during the whole of the troubles of that unfortunate period."[159] A. G. MacDonell inaccurately said that "the Clan Campbell came out strong and solid" for the Hanoverians, but his admiration for the Duke of Argyll and his assaults on the clans unfortunate enough to live near the lands to which Argyll had got hold of an Edinburgh charter-right led him to ignore all the many other Campbells.[160] As Stewart pointed out, there was a strong Jacobite feeling among, for example, the Breadalbane Campbells.

As it was in 1689 and 1745, so it was in 1715. A list drawn up by the authorities to show which clans had revolted in 1715 revealed that the Atholl clan had joined the Jacobite rebellion with 1500 men, and the Breadalbane clan had done the same with 1000. There was a footnote. "N.B., the Duke of Atholl's and Breadalbane's men went into the Rebellion without their Superiors."[161] Professor Mitchison believed that the Highlanders had been "forced 'out' " by the chiefs, and that their "opinions did not matter a damn"; these were curiously paradoxical assertions, since the evidence shows that it was the chiefs' opinions that "did not matter a damn" – the stubbornly independent Highlanders took their own decisions. In the work of some orthodox historians, it seems to be the evidence that "does not matter a damn".

25. Chose their commanders

The chief of the MacLeans, Sir Hector MacLean of Duart, had been imprisoned as a Jacobite in London when the rebellion broke out in 1745, so one of the

MacLean chieftains, MacLean of Drimnin, deputized for him and commanded the MacLean contingent at Culloden.[162] Some of the MacLeans, however, put themselves under the chief of a neighbouring clan, the MacLachlans, and fought with the MacLachlans at Culloden. Colonel MacLachlan of that ilk commanded his own clan at Culloden and also 182 MacLeans, "who chose to be under his command, seeing their chief was not there" (according to a letter written in 1748 by the Rev. John MacLachlan, of Kilchoan).[163] In all these cases, the Highlanders chose which side they would fight for, and under which commander.

In 1675, Cameron of Lochiel complained that "the Camerons refused to serve him on the terms he had granted",[164] evoking the strange picture of clansmen bargaining with a man who could send them all to the gallows on a whim. After the flight of James VII and II in 1688, the Duke of Gordon tried to raise his Highland clan to fight for James, and chose a force of 300 men: but unfortunately, according to one account of those years, they "refused to leave the area".[165] The same writer told how ten years earlier MacIntosh had tried to raise his clansmen to pursue his claim to the Keppoch lands; but MacIntosh could not get a "commission of fire and sword" from Edinburgh to justify his onslaught, and "without it not enough of MacIntosh's men would join him".[166] In other words, the Clan Chattan men decided not to support their chief, and gave that as an excuse. (The idea that clansmen who had decided not to follow their own chief in their own clan country would change their minds because of an order from distant Edinburgh, in the alien English-speaking Lowlands, is as we have seen absurd.)

So much for the powers of the chief, even when acting in the very role that had first brought him into existence. So much for the belief of Professor Mitchison and many other anglophone experts that these powers helped Jacobite chiefs to "call out" their clansmen in 1745. It is difficult to disagree with David Stewart that a study of what actually happened in 1689, 1715, and 1745, is sufficient to "refute a general opinion, that those who engaged in the Rebellion were forced out by their Chiefs and Lairds".[167] No evidence, however, was sufficient to convince Trevelyan, who wrote that the "powers" of the chief, "it was believed, helped Jacobite lairds and chiefs to 'call out their men' in 1745".[168]

The more one looks at the history of the Highlands, the less persuasive is the theory that the chiefs were all tyrants. In 1664 MacIntosh wanted to lead his clan against the Camerons, to enforce his Lowland-granted charter to the Camerons' land; but two-thirds of his clan refused to follow him.[169] So two-thirds of the MacIntoshes did not realize that the authority of the clan chief was absolute, and that any refusal to obey him was met immediately by dungeons and gallows. How did they survive? In 1670 the Scottish Privy Council recommended that MacIntosh should accept some small monetary compensation, and give up his claim to the Camerons' land, because "it was believed the Clan Cameron, whatever their chief might do, would never allow any but themselves to inhabit these lands in peace".[170] So clearly the Privy Council did not believe that the clansfolk always obeyed their chiefs: and their evidence may be thought more significant than the opinion of modern writers.

One comment made by A. M. Shaw – "delay being at any time disastrous to a Highland force"[171] – is inexplicable to anyone who accepts the orthodox assumption, since according to that supposition any Highland force could be kept together simply by the chief ordering it to keep together.

26. In all things subservient

English-speaking commentators, like so many facsimiles of the fat boy of Dingley Dell, loved – and love – to make their readers' flesh creep by allegations of the despotism of the chiefs and the servility of the clansfolk, by avowals that the chieftains' slightest fad or fancy was accepted by their humble followers as the law of the Medes and the Persians, which altereth not, and by spine-chilling assertions that any dissent was immediately silenced by the summary execution of the offender. In the same books, sometimes on the same few pages, these identical commentators lament the unreliability of the clansfolk, who joined in a war only if they felt like it, and who as soon as they decided that enough was enough, simply went home!

Alexander Cunningham said the clansfolk thought "nothing more shameful than to refuse anything to their chief", and they deemed it "an honour to be in all things subservient to his will"; yet Cunningham was not able to resist repeating the sneer that in battle all the Highlanders wanted was to loot the enemy's baggage, and if they got their hands on that, then "disregarding all discipline and oaths, and leaving their colours, home they run". So they refused nothing to their chief, and were always "subservient to his will", and at the same time they spurned their chief, and were completely antagonistic to his will, "disregarding all discipline and oaths", even at such critical times as open warfare.[172] These allegations cannot all be valid. If a writer wishes to attack a person or a group of people, he must remember always to be consistent: if one of his criticisms means that another of his criticisms cannot be true, then the rational reader will reject both of his strictures.

Sir Walter Scott, in *A Legend of Montrose*, insisted that the Highlanders gave "implicit obedience to their own patriarch", and he made one character say, "not one of these men [clansmen] knows any law but their chief's command". But Scott himself, in that very novel, described how these same Highlanders went home from campaigns when they felt like it, since "they had their cattle to look after, and their harvests to sow and reap", the result being, said Scott, that they could not make any "permanent conquest" – which undeniably meant that they did not give "implicit obedience to their own patriarch".[173]

As we saw, Janet Glover said that in the days of the clans the chieftain's "authority was unassailable"; she also said, in the same book, that in the '15, after Sheriffmuir, "the Highlanders began to go home. Desertion depleted the Pretender's armies"; while in the '45, after the retreat from Derby, "discipline weakened and desertion increased".[174] So was the chiefly authority "unassailable", or did the clansmen desert? The author cannot have it both ways. As we also saw, Tom Steel wrote that "the chief's authority was absolute. He practised his own law in his own court . . . Punishment was harsh and normally swift." Steel went on to say (in the self-same book) that in Montrose's campaign of 1644-5, the royal commander was never certain what his Highlanders would do. At various times "they drifted off to their mountainous homes"; the royal army was "plagued by desertion"; and again, the Highlanders "retired to the hills".[175] So was the chief's authority "absolute" or not? Authors should first convince themselves, if they hope to convince their readers.

Many other commentators on the '45 rebellion repeat the fairytale that the Highlanders were quivering serfs, whose slightest disobedience was met with a dungeon or a gallows, and then – faced with the overwhelming evidence of the Highlanders' sturdy independence – take refuge from their embarrassment at having alleged what could not possibly be true by denouncing the Highlanders' indiscipline. In reality, the clansmen frequently showed their self-rule, and freedom of action. For example, Prince Charles, having landed from the *Doutelle* at Moidart in 1745, wanted the supplies he had brought to be unloaded; but the Highlanders declined the task, since menial work was below them. Lowlanders, they felt, who regularly humbled themselves to work for somebody else, could do that kind of thing. (This refusal, said Clennell Wilkinson sadly, revealed one of "the weaker points in the Highland character";[176] if they had agreed to lug the supplies ashore like hired labourers, it would no doubt have "revealed" the tyrannical nature of the clan system – while the refusal to do the donkey work still made it possible to criticize "the Highland character". If you are hostile to people, you can manufacture a criticism out of anything they do.) It was the same when the Prince's army captured Stirling in January 1746; the engineer in charge of the defences decided to throw up ramparts, but the Highlanders stood aloof, "considering the spadework involved beneath their dignity".[177] The clansmen decided what they would do, or would not do, and the boasted mastery of the chief, who "had the power of life and death, and exercised it to the full, keeping his clan in awe" (in Trevelyan's baleful words), made not the slightest difference.

There is a plethora of evidence to show that the Highlanders were strongly independent, in thought and action: therefore the theory that the chiefs were able to act as so many petty tyrants cannot be sustained. As Hercule Poirot astutely said, "If the fact will not fit the theory, let the theory go".[178]

To sum up the orthodox teaching, the Highlanders had to do whatever they were told, because their "chief's authority was absolute", while at the same time the Highlanders often did not do what they were told: a conclusion which would be recognized as inconsistent by anyone but a historian dealing with the Highlands. (Do writers never read their own books, to eliminate such discrepancies?) Nor, so far as this author knows, has any observer yet pointed out this ubiquitous incongruity. In fact it is clear that if the chiefs' orders had to be obeyed without question by the clansfolk, keeping a clan array together would have been very easy: the chief would only have had to issue his instructions, and that would have settled the matter. Writers (or if not the writers, then at least their publishers' editors) should repeat every day: nothing is convincing if it is not consistent.

27. A private quarrel

Throughout Prince Charles' campaign, the Jacobite leaders were never quite sure at any given moment how many men they had, because the Highlanders frequently departed to their native glens to see their families, and then either returned to join the chief (whose "authority was absolute"), or did not return, according to how they felt at the time. The Keppoch MacDonalds and their chief, for example, arrived to support the Chevalier as soon as he unfurled his standard at Glen Finnan in 1745. Only a week later, the rebels (including the Keppoch MacDonalds) were passing through the Keppoch country on their way to attack General Cope, and Murray of Broughton wrote that "the most of them [the Keppoch men] having had liberty granted to be absent for one day as they pass'd by their own homes, numbers of them deserted, not from any reluctancy they had to the undertaking but on account of a private quarrel they had with their Chief".[179] (Brave men, to have "a private quarrel" with the tyrant who could have them slaughtered at any moment!) The Keppoch clansmen were Catholics, and apparently wished to have their priest with them, while the chief thought it would be too dangerous for him to come; but whatever the cause of the disagreement, a "private quarrel" there was, impossible though that would have been in the clan system as many historians now describe it.

Again, after the battle at Prestonpans, a thousand men in the Highland army went back to their clan lands to see their wives and children. Hugh Douglas chided the Highlanders, who, he wrote, "were ill-disciplined and considered themselves free to go home whenever they wished, to harvest their crops, to deliver the spoils of war to the clan, or simply to see their families".[180] The author intended his account as a condemnation, but it actually comes over (in the eyes of any reasonable reader) as a compliment. It hit the nail squarely on the head: under the clan system the Highlanders *were* "free to go home whenever they wished". It was the same after the return from Derby in December 1745: the Prince's advisers told him that "a vast number of the soldiers of your Royal Highness's army are gone home". In March 1746, wrote Fitzroy MacLean, "more and more men who had gone home to see their families or sow their land somehow failed to return"; though other Highlanders, who had at first joined the loyalist ranks under the Hanoverian Lord Loudoun, now further showed their independence by leaving the government forces and enlisting with the Jacobites.[181] According to Clennell Wilkinson, Lord Elcho (a Jacobite officer) said the Highlanders "very often mutinied"; indeed a good many "threw down their arms and went home".[182] At the same time the Lowland and English soldiers, though fortunately (so the approved story runs) free from the trammels of such a barbarous form of society, and rejoicing in the "liberties of free-born Britons", could do nothing except obey their officers' commands, however unreasonable, on pain of a flogging for disobedience, or immediate execution as deserters. For example, after his defeat at the Battle of Falkirk in 1746, the despicable Hanoverian commander General Hawley (to excuse his own gross incompetence, which had lost the battle, and presumably to demonstrate to the Highlanders what exactly the Lowlanders' valuable "constitutional rights and liberties" amounted to) hanged thirty-one of his soldiers for "desertion" on gallows specially erected in Edinburgh to strangle Jacobites – and then, going one better, shot thirty-two for "cowardice".[183] The Highland soldiers, however, were still their own men: they fought if they felt like fighting, but if they thought that the cause was unworthy of them, or that they had done enough, they went away and got on with their own affairs.

It is not difficult to decide which group was suffering under "despotism".

(This topic is also dealt with later in the second and subsequent subsections of chapter six; the illusory idea that the chief was a tyrant is so pervasive in modern history books that it needs to be thoroughly scrutinized.)

28. Clan recruitment

The Stuart succession became a hopeless cause after the defeat on Drummossie Muir, followed by Prince Charles's final order, "Let every man seek his own safety the best way he can". As the years passed it became clear that there was now only one, generally accepted Government. Again it became the case that Highlanders, both those who had supported the Stuarts, and those who had supported the Hanoverians, would sometimes join regiments when their chiefs asked them to – even in the service of the established Government. The fundamental reason for this was what it had always been: it was a matter of loyalty to the clan ideal. The clan held its lands because it was prepared to defend them, and the land gave the clansfolk their livelihood. The Highlanders in their clan countries were able peacefully to enjoy the bounties of nature on their land – that was one side of the coin; the other side of the coin was a readiness to defend that land. A member of a clan lived in the clan country, enjoyed food, clothing, and shelter from it and on it, and so considered that it was only fair to defend it when the request was made. If the Highlanders were to be seen as ready soldiers for the defence of the realm, however, that would present them in a good light, which would make the clearances all the more difficult to defend. Therefore that view was unacceptable to many commentators. Another view was substituted. The Highlands were good recruiting country, said one authorial partnership, "not because the people there were inclined to fight and die for king and country, but because the area was over-populated [this completely fanciful over-population theory is dealt with elsewhere] and landowners were able to use the threat of eviction to force tenants to join up".[184]

How accurate this theory was – that the Highlanders joined the colours because the Highlands were "over-populated", and because of the landlords' "threat of eviction" – may be discovered by using the archive of the head (that is, by applying ordinary common sense), and by comparing the situation in say the 1750s, with what occurred in the 1850s. After the widespread "improvements", the Highlanders became increasingly reluctant to defend what the clearances had forcibly shown them was no longer their country. Later in the nineteenth century, when the Crimean War (1854-6) and the Indian Mutiny (1857-8) broke out, the population of the Highlands was greater than it had been in the eighteenth century, and the amount of land still in the possession of the Highlanders was much less than it had been a century earlier (so if there was "over-population" in the 1750s – that is, an excess of population compared with the land available – there was much more of it in the 1850s); and the ability of landlords to apply "the threat of eviction" or other pressure was not only just as great, it was indeed much greater – the power of the landlords had grown by the 1850s, not diminished, and yet (strange to say) the supply of recruits dried up. That shows that the recruitment in the second half of the eighteenth, and early in the nineteenth, centuries must have been substantially voluntary. If recruits for the Highland regiments were found in the latter part of the eighteenth century only because of the landlords' threats of eviction, allied with a supposed "over-population", then the same factors must have ensured an equal (or greater, because of the greater population, and the greater dominance of the landlords) supply of recruits in the later parts of the nineteenth century. The fact that Highland recruits could no longer be found for the Crimean and Indian conflicts shows that the attempted explanation of why the eighteenth-century Highlanders rallied to the colours is a false one.

As usual, the archive of the head is able to help the process of discovering what, and why, things really happened. Strangely, it is often ignored.

29. Not used to subjection

Alexander Cunningham wrote of the Highlanders: "Most of them are tall, and produce tall children, not being accustomed to hard labour or discipline, and seldom used to harsh treatment, or any kind of subjection."[185] Not being used to subjection, the Highlanders as soldiers presented some unusual problems to their officers. The author of the *History of Scotland in 1750* told how one of the Glengarry MacDonalds in the Prince's army on the way back from Derby took some shoes from a countryman in a field. When MacDonald came back to the road Lord George Murray, the Prince's most capable general, who to his credit was opposed to any form of looting (wholesale robbery, rape, murder, and devastation, was then, of course, the normal and accepted behaviour of a civilized European army on the march, as the British regiments showed in the Highlands after Culloden) – Murray struck him with a whip. MacDonald (who had not had the advantage of reading later historians, who stated clearly that the Highlanders were all obsequious serfs) aimed his gun at Murray, threatening to kill him. Murray's men disarmed him and took him prisoner, and he was court-martialled the next morning: but five hundred MacDonalds, a daunting array, came and demanded the prisoner, threatening to slay Murray or any other officer who should sentence their fellow-clansman. Prince Charles had to approach Murray personally to ask him to forget the incident, and Murray, to restore good feeling in the ranks, had to make himself agreeable afterwards to the accused man.[186]

When the Lowland and English authorities began to set up the matchless Highland regiments, they had to accept that the Highlanders were not as other soldiers. Barnes and Allen, in their *Uniform and History of the Scottish Regiments*, remarked that "according to the clan system, every private soldier was the social equal of his commanding officer . . . thus the discipline was a matter of choice and clan loyalty rather than of King's Regulations".[187]

Highlanders after the '45 found it difficult to understand how oppression, once impossible in the Highlands, could now have established itself there. In *Kidnapped* R. L. Stevenson makes Allan Breac Stewart lament the exile of Stewart of Ardshiel (the acting chief of the Stewart clan), and the harshness of Red Colin Campbell of Glenure, the Government factor who managed the forfeited lands of the Appin Stewarts. Allan Breac (in Stevenson's story) bemoaned the fact that there were "men like Ardshiel in exile and men like the Red Fox sitting birling [pouring out] the wine and oppressing the poor at home. But it's a kittle [puzzling] thing to decide what folk'll bear and what they will not. Or why would Red Colin be riding his horse all over my poor country of Appin, and never a pretty lad to put a bullet in him?"[188] This was written as a work of fiction, of course, but clearly this is what the Highlanders were thinking, for in plain fact Campbell of Glenure found that Highland intolerance of oppression (even after Culloden) was not quite dead. The day before he was planning to evict some Stewart clansfolk, Glenure was killed by two successive shots from the mountainside.[189]

30. Highlanders' arms

Apart from all the direct evidence, one reason for doubting the stories of the "despotism" of the chiefs and the "serfdom" of the clansfolk is that weakling serfs do not normally walk abroad heavily armed. The clansmen, however, were never without their weapons. They needed them both for hunting, and because of the constant danger from the Lowlanders' relentless ambition to rule the Highlands. In early times, they often had bows and arrows, a short-handled axe (tuagh) like a tomahawk, a one-sided dagger (one edge sharpened, and the other edge serrated), a sword, and the Lochaber axe (tuagh-chatha) – a pike, with a kind of hatchet at the end of it. When guns became available, they were immediately part of the Highlander's armoury. His weapons then consisted of two kinds of blade – a sword and a dagger – and two kinds of firearms, a long gun and a pistol (or a pair of pistols). Besides these four or five weapons, he carried a defensive shield, a frame made of a double layer of oak and covered with bull's hide and brazen-studded nails; this shield was called a targe, or target (the latter meaning, of course, a little targe).[190]

One author, writing (in Latin) about 1500, said of the Highlanders: "Their arms are bow and arrows with in addition a sword, somewhat broad, and a dagger, sharp only on one side."[191] An account in 1512, also translated from the original Latin, said of the clansmen: "They always carry a bow and arrows, a very broad sword with a small halbert [combined spear and battle-axe], a large dagger, sharpened on one side only, but very sharp, under the belt."[192] At the Battle of Pinkie in 1547, the Highlanders were "armed with broad swords, large bows, and targets"[193] (the spelling is modernized, as it is in the following quotations). A 1583 commentator wrote: "Their arms are the bow and arrow and some darts, which they throw with great dexterity, and a large sword, with a single-edged dagger."[194] (Forty years earlier a Highland priest had said that the Highlanders loved "running, leaping, swimming, shooting, and throwing of darts".)[195] In the same year of 1583 the MacDonalds of Keppoch were accused of having been armed "with bow, darloch [quiver] and other weapons invasive". In 1597 an observer said their weapons were "bows and arrows ... broadswords and axes". In 1608 an Act of Parliament purported to prohibit the clansfolk from using any guns, bows, or two-handed swords;[196] but since the Lowlanders had not yet conquered the Highlands, the Act was of course futile. The Statutes of Iona, the next year, included the same stern prohibition: no firearms of any kind were to be used, even to kill game.[197] Those who claim that "Scotland" was one "homogeneous" whole during the days of Highland clanship will have to explain why the laws passed with such pious solemnity in Edinburgh (the prohibition of arms was only one example out of many) were completely ignored only forty miles away.

31. Muskets and pistols

In 1616 the Highlanders still had bows (an enormous yew-tree in Fortingall churchyard traditionally supplied wood for bows, and also for dirk handles – it is there now, and is thought to be the oldest tree in Britain),[198] but in addition (despite the enactments of the English/Lowland king and Parliament in 1608 and 1609, which were, and could only be, completely impotent) they had firearms. In 1617 200 Camerons were said to have assembled "with bows, dorlochais [quivers], dirks, Lochaber axes", and also with "muskets [smoothbore guns fired from the shoulder] and hagbuts [smoothbores supported by upright rests] . . . and pistols".[199] A similar account comes from Braemar in 1618: "Now their weapons are long bows and forked arrows, swords, and targets, harquebusses [or hagbuts], muskets, dirks, and Lochaber-axes."[200] In the 1620s John Spalding described the weapons of the MacIntosh clan: "swords, bows, arrows, targets, hagbuts, pistols, and other Highland armour."[201] One observer said of MacKay's Regiment in Germany in 1631: "besides muskets, they have their bows and arrows and long knives."[202] Highlanders, and others, still had bows and arrows from time to time, it seems, as late as the civil wars of the 1640s (the Highlanders in Montrose's army used them when winning the battle at Tippermuir in 1644).[203]

Somewhere about the middle of the seventeenth century, however, most Highlanders seem to have abandoned the bow as a standard weapon (though there is one mention of them at the end of the century, as we see below), but they were still formidably armed. A description of the Highlanders in 1677 had this: "On their right side they wear a dagger about a foot, or half-a-yard, long, the back filed like a saw, and several kinnes [sgians, or knives] stuck in the sheath of it, in either pocket a case of iron or brass pistols, a sword about a handful broad, and five feet long, on the other side, and perhaps a gun on one shoulder . . . Thus accoutred, with a plaid over the left shoulder and under the right arm, and, cap a-cock, he [the Highlander] struts like a peacock."[204] A document describing (as we shall see later) the MacLeans' resistance when the Marquis of Argyll attacked them in the mid-1670s said they were armed with "swords, hagbuts, pistols, dirks, and other weapons invasive".[205] At the Battle of Mulroy in 1688, the MacDonalds of Keppoch successfully resisted with "sword and target and Lochaber axes"[206] an attempt to turn them out of their clan country. In 1689, when the same clansfolk rallied to Dundee, they were described as "bristling with swords, spears, Lochaber-axes, targes, javelins, knotted clubs and brass-bound muskets".[207] About the same time, an observer described the Highlanders: " 'What should be concealed' is hid by a large shot-pouch, on each side of which hangs a pistol and dagger, as if they found it necessary to keep these parts well guarded. A round target on their backs, a blew bonnet on their heads, in one hand a broadsword, and a musket in the other; perhaps no nation goes better armed, and I assure you they will handle them with bravery and dexterity, especially the sword and target, as our veteran regiments found to their cost at Gille Crankee"[208] (the Highlanders' victory at Killiecrankie had been gained some months earlier). Sir Walter Scott, we can see, was perfectly accurate in his description of a Highlander's arms in *Waverley*, when he said that a "goat-skin purse, flanked by the usual defences, a dirk and steel-wrought pistol, hung before him", while "a broadsword dangled by his side, a target hung upon his shoulder, and a long Spanish fowling-piece occupied one of his hands".[209] (A broadsword was sharpened on both edges.)

32. Armed wherever they go

The Catholic Bishop Nicholson said in his report on his visitation to the Highlands in 1700 that "there is not the humblest peasant but has his sword, his musket, his targe and a large dirk, which is always to be seen hanging at his side".[210] (One reason for this formidable personal armoury was, of course, the fact that the Highlander was not a "peasant", and he was certainly not "humble", despite Nicholson's terminology – as we shall see shortly. The "humblest peasant" would not have been allowed to go about habitually heavily armed.) Writing about 1695 (the work was published in 1703), Martin Martin observed that "for arms some had broad two-handed swords and head-pieces, and others bows and arrows . . . Since the invention of guns they are very early accustomed to use them, and carry their pieces [firearms] with them wherever they go. They likewise learn to handle the broadsword and target." By their skill in battle, said Martin, they achieved "aut mors cito aut victoria laeta"[211] – either a quick death, or joyful victory. These weapons were worn even when the Highlander was pursuing a peaceful avocation. Daniel Defoe was loftily amused in 1706 to see a Highlander driving a cow in Edinburgh, "armed with a broadsword, target, pistol, at his girdle a dagger".[212]

Rae, in his *History of the Rebellion of 1715*, described the appearance of Sir Humphrey Colquhoun of Luss and his son-in-law James Grant of Pluscardine, "followed by forty or fifty stately fellows in their hose and belted plaids, armed each of them with a well-fixed gun on their shoulders, a strong handsome target, with a sharp pointed steel, of about half an ell [perhaps a foot, or thirty centimetres] in length, screwed into the navel of it, on his arm, a sturdy claymore by his side, and a pistol or two, with a dirk and knife, in his belt".[213] (The "sharp pointed steel" of the target carried the clear message – "keep your distance": it defined the Highlander's "personal space", into which others would be unwise to intrude.) This, admittedly, was during wartime; but, as we have seen, in this respect there was little distinction between war and peace. Daniel Defoe, some twenty years after his amusement in Edinburgh, observed that the Highlanders "wear the dirk and the pistol at their girdle, and the targe or target at their shoulder". He added that "the Highlanders not only have all of them fire-arms, but they are all excellent marksmen".[214] In 1724 Lord Lovat said the Highlanders were "in constant use of wearing arms . . . they constantly practise their use of arms".[215] General Wade, writing in 1727, said that it was "seen to be a reproach to a Highlander to be seen without his Musket, Broadsword, Pistol and Dirk. These by a long custom were esteem'd part of their dress"; these arms "were worn by the Meanest of the Inhabitants, even in their churches, fairs and markets, which looked more like places of parade for soldiers, than assemblies for devotion or other meetings of civil societies".[216] Wade tried to disarm the Highlanders, but his efforts were naturally ineffectual, and Burt wrote: "when any one of them is armed at all points, he is loaded with a target, a firelock, a heavy broadsword, a pistol, stock and lock of iron [i.e., all-metal], a dirk; and besides all these, some of them carry a sort of knife, which they call a skeenochles [sgian achlais, or armpit knife] from its being concealed in the sleeve near the armpit".[217] The Earl of Islay (later the Duke of Argyll), writing of the Jacobite threat in the early 1740s, asserted that "the only source of any real danger" to King George lay in the fact that the Highlanders were "armed and used to arms".[218]

The author of *Remarks on . . . the Highlanders*, published in 1747, said of the Highlander: "as for his arms they consist in a fuzil [a flint-lock musket], a broadsword, a dirk or dagger, an Highland pistol all of steel, hung on the other side of his belt, opposite to the dirk, and a target. The use of these arms they learn from their infancy and are extremely adroit in them. The nature of their country, their manner of living, and their continual exercise in hunting, fishing, and fowling, render them hardy, robust, enterprising, and equally capable of long marches, and of sustaining patiently the want of food or rest . . . The Highlanders, whenever they were in arms, by their agility and perfect knowledge of the country, had been always too many for the regular troops."[219] Duncan Forbes of Culloden observed that "arms in the hands of men accustomed to the use of them", that is, in the hands of the Highlanders, were "dangerous to the public peace".[220] John

MacCodrum, the North Uist bard who flourished in the eighteenth century, described "the Gael of finest presence" as wearing "pleated tartan, with his sword behind his buckler [or target], and his pistols so well primed that they wait not for the spark; a shield on the champion's shoulder, a slender gun beneath his arm".[221]

John Campbell wrote in 1752: "They are a warlike people, delighting much in the use of arms even from their infancies, and a broad sword, target, pistols, dirk and powder horn, are a part of their paternal heritage, and without these accoutrements they seldom or never stir abroad."[222] Campbell's affirmation that the Highlanders were always armed whenever they went out echoes both Bishop Nicholson and Martin Martin half a century earlier, and General Wade twenty-five years before. Dr Johnson agreed: "the Highlanders, till lately, always went armed, and carried their weapons to visits, and to church."[223]

33. Every man bore arms

William Gilpin in 1776 quoted the report of about 1500 given above (which said the Highlanders were armed with bow and arrows, sword, and dagger), and went on: "If we take away his bow and arrows and stick a couple of pistols in his belt, the Highlander of those days is the very Highlander of these."[224] Gilpin went on to describe a Breadalbane emigration of 1775, in which, he said, "the men were armed in the Highland fashion".[225] David Stewart said that the clansmen's weapons "consisted of a broadsword girded on the left side, and a dirk, or short thick dagger, on the right, used only when the combat was so close that the swords could be of no service . . . A gun, a pair of pistols, and a target, completed their armour." In the Highlands, "men were accustomed to go continually armed".[226]

Sir John Dalrymple, referring to the Highlanders' habitual use of arms at the end of the seventeenth century, said it was "a fashion which, by accustoming them to the instruments of death, removes the fear of death itself; and which, from the danger of provocation, made the common people as polite and as guarded in their behaviour as the gentry of other countries".[227] Sir Walter Scott said much the same, in a footnote to *Waverley*: the Highlander's "language abounded in the phrases of courtesy and compliment; and the habit of carrying arms, and mixing with those who did so, made it particularly desirable they should use cautious politeness in their intercourse with each other".[228]

John Hume, who was captured by the Highlanders at the Battle of Falkirk in 1746, wrote later that "fierceness of heart, prompt to attack or defend, at all times and places, became the characteristic of the Highlanders. Proud of this prime quality, they always appeared like warriors; as if their arms had been limbs and members of their bodies, they were never seen without them: they travelled, they attended fairs and markets, nay they went to church with their broadswords and dirks; and in later times, with their muskets and pistols."[229] The writer of the Fortingall report in the O.S.A. said, when discussing conditions before 1745: "every man then bore arms",[230] while the writer of the Killin report said disapprovingly, "the man who could best handle his sword and his gun was deemed the prettiest fellow".[231] William Thomson remarked in 1788 on the Highlanders' "passionate love and genius for music", and for poetry, and continued: "their compositions, whether of music or poetry, were the natural productions, and perfectly suited to the taste of a country, where, within the memory of man, every male, without exception, was trained to arms."[232] The practice of sending round the croishtarich, the fiery cross, by which the fighting strength of a clan could be asked to mobilize in a matter of hours, was based on the assumption that each clansman had his arms always by him – and, for that matter, was ready to use them if he deemed the cause was worthy.

There are a number of references, elsewhere in this work, to the fact that the Highlander and his weapons were closely acquainted. In the reign of Charles II, "fully armed" MacLeans descended on the Garvellach islands to dispute the attempted take-over by Argyll.[233] A little later, Lochiel and "400 armed Camerons" foiled an attempt to hold a Lowland court in Lochaber.[234] About 1689, twelve Campbell clansmen, fully armed, and acting on behalf of the parishioners generally, saw off a minister whom Argyll had attempted to impose on the parish of Glenorchy.[235] In 1696, the Frasers having decided that the Beaufort branch of Lovat was to provide the next chief, sixty armed men captured and expelled a band coming to attempt the installation of a rival claimant.[236] And in both 1715 and 1745, the clansmen were already furnished with weapons, whether they decided to support the existing monarch or the Stuarts.

Originally the clansman's sword was the claidheamh mór, or claymore, which was a big, two-handed sword with a cross hilt: a fearsome weapon. The Wardlaw Manuscript has a story about a man who was cut in half "by one slash" of a claymore, "which they [the Highlanders] mostly used".[237] During the seventeenth century this weapon was gradually replaced by a lighter sword with a basket hilt; the claymore was still seen, but it had become more of a status symbol.[238] Perhaps as the Highlanders equipped themselves with firearms, a slimmer blade was considered sufficient. One of the most famous makers of these lighter swords was called Andrea Ferrara: so famous that other makers sometimes forged his name on their products. William Gilpin, who as we saw toured the Highlands in 1776, referred to the Highlander "armed with his pistols and Ferrara".[239] Ferrara was an Italian by birth, who flourished in the early sixteenth century. Presumably he came from somewhere near the town of the same name, which was renowned for its steel blades. He settled in Spain, where he became famous as a sword-maker; and then was invited to Scotland to teach the locals his skill in tempering steel. A biographical dictionary says "his name is found on great numbers of Highland claymores [perhaps "claymores" is used here simply as a synonym for swords], which . . . as weapons of admirable quality, are highly prized"; specimens can still be seen in armouries.[240] In *Waverley*, Scott made Prince Charles give a broadsword, "a genuine Andrea Ferrara", to an adherent;[241] and in *A Legend of Montrose*, the same author used the phrase "taking to Andrew Ferrara" to mean resorting to sword-play.[242]

34. Named fire-arms

The Highlander cherished all his private arsenal, swords and guns, which were necessary firstly for the hunting which provided the Highlanders' food, and secondly for repelling the constant Lowland attempts to subjugate the clansfolk. The bards often mentioned the "lannan Spàinnteach" – Spanish or Toledo blades or swords.[243] Ninety years after the Government took advantage of Culloden to order that all arms in the Highlands should be handed over to the authorities, a decree that was often ignored despite the Lowland conquest of the Highlands in those years, the old guns were still treasured. "Some of the old Spanish rifles", wrote the minister of Kintail in 1836, "once so celebrated and so common in this country, are still extant, and are highly valued, if not venerated, by the possessors. They receive certain names, indicative of certain properties or deeds. Such as Maighdeann (maiden), Surgadh-Caoradh (sheepshank), Nighean Ewan (Evan's daughter), etc."[244] Duncan Ban MacIntyre wrote a poem to his own gun, *Song to the Gun named Nic Coiseim*: "By means of thee I oft laid low/ The stags and the red young hinds".[245] The weapon which killed Campbell of Glenure was a long Spanish gun called "an t-Slinneanach", or the broad-shouldered: after that event, and the grim reprisals which followed, it was also dubbed "gunne dubh a mhi-fhortain" – black gun of the misfortune.[246]

Even in the immediate aftermath of Culloden, when trigger-happy Lowland and English troops (brainwashed into the belief that all Highlanders were barbarians and scoundrels) were roaming the Highlands hunting down any local inhabitants, the Highlanders could not accept complete disarmament; a clansman would not go out without at least a knife, which he put down his stocking.[247] The Highlander's custom of carrying his sgian dubh or dagger in that way perhaps originated at this time, since it does not seem to be referred to by any of the authors who discuss the Highlander's weapons before the defeat of Prince Charles: those who mention the position of the dagger always say it was under his belt, or hanging from his belt, either in front or at the right side (apart from Burt's mention of the sgian achlais, the "armpit knife").[248]

Just as each clan had its own bards, pipers, and storytellers, so it had its own armourers, who made swords and guns. In Skye, for example, the MacLeods of Suardal were armourers to the MacLeod clan centred on Dunvegan (the well-known clerical family of MacLeods, several generations of whom were ministers of Morvern, was descended from these MacLeod armourers).[249] In Harris, the hereditary armourers were Morrisons: one of their descendants, John Morrison, musician, bard, and blacksmith – Gobh'na Hearradh (or the Harris smith) – was an evangelical catechist in the 1830s and 1840s.[250] The MacRory (or MacRury) family of Baile Ghobhain (or smiths' town) in Kilmuir made weapons for the Skye MacDonalds. Another branch of the family pursued the same trade in North Uist.[251] J. E. Bowman, a traveller in 1825, referred to "the MacNabs, a family of blacksmiths who have been resident in Glen Orchy for nearly four hundred years, each successive generation having followed their hereditary trade. Its present representative does not degenerate, and has the reputation of making excellent Highland dirks."[252] Thomas Garnett, touring the Highlands in 1798, mentioned the same family, who, he said, lived at Barr nan Caistealain by Dalmally.[253] A family called MacEachan or MacEachern, who were smiths in Islay, made a particular kind of sword called the ceann-Ileach (an Islay-head, or Islay-point).[254] There are some indications that the hereditary blacksmiths to the MacDonald clan of Keppoch were a family called Kennedy.[255] Around 1675 one William Smith was making guns at Duthil, in Grant country.[256]

Apart from these clan gunsmiths, there were a number of pistol-makers in Doune, a village seven miles south-east of Callander which was at the southern extremity of the Gaelic-speaking area; it had a regular fair to which Highlanders brought their cattle. "For a long time", said Ian Finlay, "Doune played a very special part in the Highland economy, for it made some of the finest of the weapons and accoutrements in which the clansman's heart delighted. It was especially celebrated for its pistols, and this over a period of something like two centuries."[257] The Doune pistol was "all-metal, butt, stock and barrel" (a phrase recalling the 1747 author's words – "an Highland pistol all of steel", as well as Scott's "steel-wrought pistol"),[258] and specimens of the work of the "great Doune pistol-smiths, Campbell and Caddell, Murdoch and Christie", found ready buyers both in the Highlands and abroad, and are now treasured in museums. Several successive Caddells made pistols in Doune from about 1640 to about 1780. John Murdoch was still working there towards 1800. Dunvegan Castle preserves the Doune pistols worn by John MacLeod of MacLeod at Edinburgh in 1822.[259]

35. A constant firing

The Highlanders' firearms helped to make a cheerful, noisy procession when weddings were taking place. David Stewart wrote: "On the wedding-morning, the bridegroom, escorted by a party of friends, and preceded by pipers, commenced a round of morning calls, to remind their invited friends of their engagements. This circuit sometimes occupied several hours, and as many joined the party, it might perhaps be increased to some hundreds, when they returned to the bridegroom's house. The bride went a similar round among her friends. The bridegroom gave a dinner to his friends, the bride to hers. During the whole day, the fiddlers and pipers were in constant employment. The fiddlers played to the dancers in the house, and the pipers to those in the field. The ceremony was generally performed after dinner [dinner would normally be taken about mid-day]. Sometimes the clergyman attended, sometimes they waited on him: the latter was preferred, as the walk to his house with such a numerous attendance added to the éclat of the day. On these occasions the young men supplied themselves with guns and pistols, with which they kept up a constant firing. This was answered [with more firing] from every hamlet as they passed along, so that, with streamers flying, pipers playing, the constant firing from all sides, and the shouts of the young men, the whole had the appearance of a military array passing, with all the noise of warfare, through a hostile country ... As all these ceremonies, which were very numerous and very innocent, added much to the cheerfulness and happiness of the young people, I cannot avoid regretting their partial disuse. Nor can I help preferring a Highland wedding, where I have myself been so happy, and seen so many blithe countenances and eyes sparkling with delight," to the gloomy rituals of the Lowlands, where music and dancing were often replaced, said Stewart, merely by alcohol and tobacco.[260]

36. Dougal Roy Cameron

The Highlanders were practised in the use of these weapons: as hunters, their livelihood (and their dinner) depended on their skill. In 1752, the man who killed Colin Campbell of Glenure fired two bullets from the hillside at a moving target – from a position far enough away to enable him to escape if pursuit should be made; yet both bullets hit their mark. A year or two earlier, when the Hanoverian army descended on the Highlands to ravage the inhabitants after Culloden, they reached Lochaber in due course. "About 400 of the royal army", said the N.S.A. report on Kilmallie, "passing up Locharkaigside, found a young man of the name of Cameron, having a gun in his possession. Without civil or military trial, the unfortunate youth was posted up and shot, by an order from Grant of Knocceanach, who commanded a party of the Ross-shire militia." The boy's father,

Dougal Roy Cameron, reacted to this atrocity just as any clansman would have reacted had a chief tried to turn oppressor – and this despite the fact that the whole area was controlled by an army of occupation. Dougal Roy "watched the party as they were returning with their plunder. Grant of Knoc-ceanach, whether designedly or not, gave his horse to Major Munro of Culcairn; and Dougal, mistaking his man, shot [and, firing accurately, killed] the amiable major." Dougal Roy slipped away, and then again (no doubt hearing that his target had escaped) took up a position on the road the party had to travel, to wreak more revenge. In the event the Hanoverians were detained, and so "they escaped without meeting their incensed enemy again; – but he taught them not to come back on a similar expedition. There was no more burning or plundering in Lochaber, though a party of the royal army were quartered for years at the head of Loch Arkaig."[261]

According to David Stewart, the young Cameron had done more than merely possess a gun. The Government troops had burned the family's home, and plundered their cattle, and the young man had tried to resist; that was why he was "posted up and shot". The man slain by Dougal Roy in revenge was George Munro of Culcairn, the brother of Colonel Munro of Foulis, who had been killed earlier the same year at Falkirk fighting for King George. The authorities, according to the Kilmallie N.S.A. report, never found out who shot Munro, although Dougal Roy continued to live in Lochaber for many years. On the other hand, Stewart wrote: "The man who shot Culcairn was known; but, through some unexplained cause, he was not apprehended."[262] It may be that the Government forces had come to a realistic appraisal of what was, and was not, possible at that time in Cameron country. At any rate they desisted from oppression because of the resistance they encountered, and it hardly seems likely that a chief, who was only one man, could have been more successfully tyrannical than 400 soldiers, backed as they were by the whole power of the British Government. Only a few years later, when the chiefs and the state forces combined against the clansfolk, a different story was unfolded; and the destruction of people's houses, and the turning out of families in all weathers, became not an extraordinary isolated incident incurring dire retribution, but a normal feature of the prudent and praiseworthy superintendence of properties.

37. Well qualified for war

The clansman had all the qualities that, if the occasion arose, would make him an excellent soldier. He was (we shall see the evidence for all this later) physically fit; as a hunter and herdsman, he was practised in his weapons; he was self-reliant; he was intelligent and ingenious; and (as he hunted, or herded, or co-operated on township matters) he often worked together with his fellow-clansmen for their joint purposes. The Highlander, Macaulay wrote, was "well qualified for war, and especially for . . . war in so wild and rugged a country as his own. He was intrepid, strong, fleet, patient of cold, of hunger, and of fatigue. Up steep crags, and over treacherous morasses, he moved as easily as the French household troops paced along the great road from Versailles to Marli. He was accustomed to the use of weapons and to the sight of blood; he was a fencer; he was a marksman; and, before he had ever stood in the ranks, he was already more than half a soldier."[263] Hugh Miller, writing in 1854 about Donald Roy Ross, a relative of his own several generations back, said that in the seventeenth century "the Highlander still retained his weapons, and knew how to use them".[264] Ramsay of Ochtertyre said that in the Highlands "every person wished to be thought a soldier".[264] Dr Johnson was more emphatic still in his portrayal of Highland society: "in the beginning of the present [eighteenth] century . . . every man was a soldier." The contemplation of the former practice of the clans, and the way in which the Highlanders were willing and able to defend themselves, pleased Dr Johnson. "It affords a generous and manly pleasure, to conceive a little nation gathering its fruits and tending its herds, with fearless confidence, though it is open on every side to invasion; where, in contempt of walls and trenches, every man sleeps securely with his sword beside him, and where all, on the first approach to hostility, come together at the call to battle . . ."[265]

Not only was the clansman a natural soldier: the Highlander was so used to co-operating with others for a common end in his ordinary life that if it became necessary the clan was a natural military formation. Barnes and Allen, in their history of the Scottish regiments, said: "These brawny and purposeful hill-men, once they were let loose, could put the fear of God into any but exceptionally highly disciplined troops."[266] In the 1720s Daniel Defoe visited the field where the indecisive battle of Sheriffmuir had been fought in 1715, and wondered "how it was possible, that a rabble of Highlanders arm'd in haste, appearing in rebellion, and headed by a person never in arms before [the Earl of Mar], nor of the least experience, should come so near to the overthrowing an army of regular disciplin'd troops, and led on by experienc'd officers, and so great a general [the Duke of Argyll]". Defoe would have been less astonished if he had realized that the rebels had not been "arm'd in haste", but had brought along their usual weapons, with which they had been familiar since childhood; and that, far from being a rabble, the ingrained and habitual co-operation and camaraderie of the clansfolk in their daily lives made easy a similar co-ordination in war. Defoe himself indeed, in the same *Tour through Great Britain*, affirmed that most of the victories said to have been won by the "Irish" in the service of France in the late wars were really the work of Highlanders: "most of those they call Irish in the armies of France and Spain, and to whom so many glorious actions have been justly ascrib'd, are to this day Scots Highlanders [who of course spoke Gaelic, or 'Irish'], or at least most of them are so."[267]

This ability of the clansmen to defend themselves when necessary was called into play chiefly when the Lowland rulers, or their puppet chiefs (incited by Lowland charters), were making trouble in the Highlands. Some commentators have alleged that the clansmen were so efficient as soldiers because their whole society was organized to that end. Trevelyan called the Highlanders "a population that had always lived for and by war".[268] Eric Linklater said they were "a people to whom war was a natural exercise".[269] This allegation is made partly to overcome the glaring inconsistency between the assertion that the Highlanders were merely quaking serfs, tyrannized over by despots, unable to take any action for themselves, and the inescapable fact of their pre-eminence as independent and resourceful fighters; and partly because it painted a (fictitious) picture of the Highlands as a chaotic region which justified the Lowlanders stepping in to restore order. The Lowland conquest of the Highlands, Trevelyan continued, meant that the Highlanders were "at last effectively disarmed".

38. Secrecy, dispatch, and address

The Highlanders showed their ability to combine as a military force in other than official army formations. In 1746 Atholl was garrisoned by three Government regiments, with detachments in a number of mansion houses and other strong points. David Stewart wrote that Lord George Murray, who was of course from Atholl, "wishing to dislodge those troops, and relieve his native district from their pillage and oppressions, marched from Inverness-shire into Atholl with a battalion of the Atholl brigade, and, as they passed through Badenoch, took along with him 300 MacPhersons, under their chief, the Laird of Cluny". He divided up this improvised armed force, and sent a party against each post occupied by the Hanoverian troops. In the space of two hours, between three o'clock and five the next morning, the rebels attacked (said Stewart) no fewer than twenty Government posts, and captured all of them. Stewart wrote: "Here we have a body of men taken from their ploughs, or from tending their sheep and cattle, and commanded by a few country gentlemen, without the least military experience; with nothing but the natural genius for war which marked the Highland character of that age, planning and successfully executing a combination of attacks and surprises of posts, several of which were strong and defensible, being ancient houses of gentlemen, having thick walls, small windows, and loop-holes, and being defended by disciplined troops. Their operations were conducted with such secrecy, dispatch, and address, and each party marched with such precision to the different points of attack, that the whole were carried within the hours appointed, although they had to cross rapid rivers, high mountains, and deep glens, and although several of the posts were many miles asunder."

After sending off these attacking parties, Lord George Murray continued his march to the Bridge of Bruar, two miles west of Blair Castle, which had been arranged as the rendezvous for the returning Jacobite Highlanders after their attacks on the Hanoverian strongholds. Blair Castle had at that time been occupied by Sir Andrew Agnew, the Hanoverian commander, as his headquarters. When he had taken up his position at the Bridge of Bruar, Murray was informed that Agnew had been alerted to these movements, and was bringing an armed force to attack him. Stewart wrote, "when Lord George and Cluny [the MacPherson chief] received this notice, they had along with them only twenty-five private men, and some elderly gentlemen". Murray refused to abandon his position, since that would mean that each party of Jacobites returning to the rendezvous would fall piecemeal into the hands of the enemy. Nearby Murray saw a fold dike, a turf wall to keep in cattle; so he ordered his handful of men to disperse themselves behind the dike, well apart, with the colours of both rebel regiments (the Athollmen's, and the MacPhersons') flying above. The Atholl and the MacPherson pipers had all been kept back when the Jacobite attacking parties went off, since the Government posts were to be surprised without warning. These too were scattered at wide intervals along the wall, and when Agnew's force appeared, just as the sun rose, "that instant the pipers began to play one of their most noisy pibrochs", while the sprinkling of Jacobites, officers and men, all drew their swords and brandished them over their heads. Agnew, seeing this martial display from an apparently large force, ordered a retreat to Blair Castle. Murray waited until his men returned from their attacks, and then marched after the Government troops and laid siege to the castle.[270]

39. Kingdom in confusion

Smollett wrote of the Highlanders (in *Humphry Clinker*, 1771) that "we have lived to see four thousand of them, without discipline, throw the whole kingdom of Great Britain into confusion. They attacked and defeated two armies of regular troops accustomed to service. They penetrated into the centre of England; and afterwards marched back with deliberation, in the face of two other armies, through an enemy's country, where every precaution was taken to cut off their retreat. I know not any other people in Europe, who, without the use or knowledge of arms, will attack regular forces sword in hand, if their chief will head them in battle" – though, of course, the Highlanders did have the "use or knowledge of arms", since they lived mainly by hunting; furthermore, they would fight for what they believed just whether the chief was there or not, and as for "discipline", they had their own accepted and routine self-control, which is the best discipline of all.[271] Thomas Pennant, too, in his *Tour in Scotland*, remarked of the 1745-6 campaign: "In future times posterity will almost doubt the fact, when they read that an inconsiderable band of mountaineers, undisciplined, unofficered, and half-armed, had penetrated into the centre of an unfriendly country, with one army behind them, and another in their front; that they rested at Derby a few days; and that they retreated above three hundred miles, with scarcely any loss, continually pressed by a foe supplied with every advantage that loyalty could afford."[272] This kind of campaign would in fact have been unthinkable for a population of half-starved peasants, tilling an acre or two for subsistence crops, and cowering under the absolutism of despotic rulers: all the evidence combines to show that this now standard picture of the Highlanders, set down in a thousand history books, must simply be untrue.

The British Government, as we shall see below, was later very glad to take advantage of the exemplary physical, mental and social abilities of the Highlanders, when they enlisted them in the Highland regiments; and indeed, where the clansmen's services were required immediately, the recruits needed no parade-ground discipline or tuition. Both Keith's and Campbell's Highlanders, in Germany in 1759, and Fraser's Highlanders, in America in 1776 (all newly recruited), were thrown into battle as soon as they arrived at the theatre of operations, and performed victoriously against well-drilled armies, virtually without military training or instruction.[273]

Orthodox Lowland writers describe the clansfolk as wild and ungovernable, and as so brutal and ferocious that they were liable to lash out viciously on the least excuse, or no excuse at all; and at the same time as so pathetically feeble that they meekly accepted the domination of a single man who (without the slightest vestige of state machinery to support him) tyrannized over hundreds or thousands of clansfolk, the latter being so docile and submissive that they accepted whatever barbarous punishments he decreed. The genesis of these two widespread but completely incompatible caricatures is of course their utility (in totally opposite ways) in justifying the dispersal of the Highlanders. If they were irredeemably savage, then they deserved to be driven out of their glens, thereafter to be tamed by many years of arduous toil in Lowland factories or colonial outposts; if they were so humble and enervated that they submitted compliantly to harsh oppression, then they deserved to be rescued and enrolled in the ranks of a modern industrial state, or as imperial pioneers. But, useful though both of these fantasies have been in the conventional chronicles, it is clearly not possible for them both to be true of the same people at the same time; and as we have seen, neither is in fact accurate.

To sum up, it would have been difficult, even had the other conditions for despotism been present, to tyrannize over men who were always armed, who constantly used their blades and their firearms in their normal daily lives, and who were natural soldiers able to combine and defeat even regular army units. As was remarked earlier, Trevelyan and his followers forget the basic requirement of historiography: for an account to be credible, it must be consistent.

40. Tribute to the chiefs

No despotism could ever have grown up naturally in the Highlands of Scotland – as opposed to being inflicted from outside. The classic grounds of tyranny were the fertile river valleys of Egypt, Mesopotamia, India, and China, where one family working all the year could produce enough for several families to live on: or where the mass of the population, constantly labouring, could produce enough of a surplus to keep a small upper class in luxury. (The same useful system is still familiar in these – and other – areas today.) Nature was not so bountiful in the Grampians as in the valleys of the Nile or the Ganges: still, a Highland family, strongly exerting themselves when the season or the hour demanded it (though Highlanders then, like tycoons now, may not have considered hunting, shooting, and fishing to be "work"), and enjoying their leisure for the rest of the time, could and did produce enough for themselves and a small surplus. The mountains, too, bred – as they always have done – a hardy race of people; and the walls of rock were ramparts to keep out those who would have introduced despotism. Mountain air has always been the breath of freedom: and so it was in the Highlands.

St Paul went so far as to tell Timothy that "the love of money is the root of all evil", and certainly the amassing of money is the root of much tyranny.[274] It is on the flat and fruitful lands that trade springs up and money is accumulated; it is the peasant of the plain who is ground down into serfdom by the demands of a united upper class against whom he cannot defend himself. An alliance of chiefs or war-leaders can certainly grow into a tyrannical upper class when economic and geographical conditions are favourable. But in the Highlands, each valley, each lochside was virtually a separate country; and until the eighteenth century there was never sufficiently easy communication or traffic between the clan countries to allow the chiefs to unite against the people. Even after roads were built, the chiefs were able to develop into local tyrants only with the help of the state-power of the Lowlanders and the English, and the strength given to these alien invaders by the burgeoning Industrial Revolution in England and the Lowlands.

41. Appearance of crofters

In the clan countries there was never enough tribute levied, even if there had been sufficient currency in which to pay it, to support the apparatus of despotism.

Trevelyan, it is true, said that "a crofter of Queen Anne's reign was fain to hire a patch of ground from the 'tacksman' or leaseholder of the chief, who sublet it on rack-rent terms that were usually most oppressive".[275] This comment is misleading on two points. Firstly, there were no crofters when Queen Anne was reigning, from 1702 to 1714: sub-tenants were either joint-farmers, like the majority of the clansfolk, or cotters. (Cotters, in their turn, were usually either widows or widowers in their declining years, or single women of no family, or the physically handicapped, or very occasionally tradesmen – tailors, shoemakers, smiths, etc. – whose appearance as something like dedicated artisans very late in clan history may be seen as marking the beginning of a division of labour, and thus to have heralded the approaching dissolution of clan society.)[276] Secondly, there was no rack-rent in Queen Anne's day either.[277]

As to the first point, crofters (as we saw in chapter one, subsection eight) emerged only some decades after Culloden, when the clan chiefs were able to begin treating the clan lands as their own personal property. What the landlords insisted on calling "the improvements" began in some areas of the southern Highlands in the 1740s, or even earlier, and had reached some estates in the furthest north in or before the 1780s. These "improvements" – the levying of massive rents,[278] the prohibition of hunting, shooting, and fishing (which activities together produced most of the Highlanders' food), the diminution or complete deprivation of the pasture lands (the second most important source of the Highlanders' food), and outright evictions – meant that more and more Highlanders were being driven out of their old quarters. For some decades parties of well-to-do joint-farmers reacted to this attack by leaving the Highlands altogether in well-planned migrations, either to the Lowlands or across the Atlantic. This first stage of the improvements was therefore often accompanied by depopulation. When, however, the Highlanders had been further impoverished by decades of rocketing rents and similar unremitting economic pressure from the landlords, subsequent clearances often involved small tenants who could no longer afford to emigrate to America, who by then knew of the risks and dangers incurred by emigrants on the Atlantic crossing, and of the hardships faced by the first settlers in the American wilderness, and who had also become painfully aware of the destitution and factory serfdom into which earlier Highland migrants to the Lowlands had been plunged. At the same time the regular Continental and imperial wars which Britain fought (e.g. 1739-48, 1756-63, 1775-83, and then 1793 onwards), along with frequent colonial conflicts during these wars and between them, made the ruling class reluctant to lose so many first-class recruits for the British armed forces. So after decades of emigration the landlords tried to stem the flow outwards by offering those whom they had evicted small plots of waste ground to make fertile (which, of course, had the added advantage of turning valueless moor into ground which might then attract a big farmer) and at the same time the Highlanders, made increasingly penurious by the improvements, were increasingly ready to accept such offers. Hence the appearance of crofts, and of crofters, late in the eighteenth century. These new-fangled crofters or their children, since their plots of ground were so small, were also available as day-labourers: valuable recruits to that new class of wage-workers, now essential if the improvements were to succeed.

42. Small farmers dispossessed

A few contemporary references to this innovation, seven from the parochial reports in the Old Statistical Account of the 1790s, two from landlords, and three from other sources, may be sufficient to demonstrate the novelty of this development. The minister of Petty said that the farms there were larger than they had been, and that there was in the parish "a great number of crofters"; he felt he had to explain this word by adding that they had been "planted by the proprietors in waste ground to improve it".[279] The Kiltarlity O.S.A. reporter introduced this novel term, "a croft", to his readers by remarking that "the small farmers that have been dispossessed have remained as cottagers in the parish, or have built houses for themselves in the moors, and improved a small portion of ground called a croft, around their houses".[280] The minister of Gigha, too, felt that he had to define the term "crofter" – "a crofter has a plot of ground, for rearing a small crop and keeping a milk cow, and pays a yearly rent . . ."[281] The minister of Urray, the parish just west of the Black Isle, also thought he should explain who mailers were (mailer, or mealler, was a synonym for crofter). "The mailers are those poor people who build huts on barren ground, and improve spots around them, for which they pay nothing for a stipulated number of years"; after that time they paid from three shillings to forty shillings. They usually had one cow.[282] In Rosskeen, "the number of inhabitants has of late been much increased, by a species of cottagers, here called meallers, who build a small house for themselves on a waste spot of ground, with the consent of the proprietor, and there, are ready to hire themselves out as day labourers".[283] In Kilfinan, there were some separate holdings in odd corners: "these small farms, so cut off, are called butts; in other places, they are termed crofts."[284] In Kilmartin, "the crofter" was defined as having one, two, or three acres, and grass for one or two cattle.[285]

The proprietor Sir John Sinclair explained in his *General View of the Northern Counties* (1795) that the "mailers" of the Black Isle were handicraftsmen or day-labourers, who were given patches of "barren wastes and moors" to bring into cultivation. Sir George Steuart MacKenzie of Coul, himself an evicting landlord, said in his *General View of Ross and Cromarty* (1810) that "crofters" were those "removed from other places" who did not have "the means of transporting themselves to America"; instead, said MacKenzie, they broke in waste ground.[286] Dorothy Wordsworth, on her 1803 tour with her brother, also regarded "croft" as a new term to be explained to her readers: she said that when they saw some settlers' cottages near Dalmally, a fellow traveller told them that the cottages "belonged to Lord Breadalbane, and were attached to little farms, or 'crofts', as he called them".[287] David Stewart (in 1820) mentioned this modern development; when the "old occupiers" were in "many cases removed from the fertile and cultivated farms", he said, some of them were "offered limited portions of land on uncultivated moors".[288] Elsewhere, he said some of the evicted were placed "on paltry lots of land . . . perhaps not one-tenth of the extent of the farms from which they were removed, on the ground that they [their previous farms] were too small".[289] As late as 1835, Lord Teignmouth (describing a Highland tour) realized that this phenomenon was even then so new that a definition was required for an English audience: "The houses belong to *crofters*, there being attached to each a small piece of ground, called a *croft*, on which vegetables are raised for the use of the family" (his italics), while each "crofter" had a cow or two.[290]

43. Designedly inadequate

The landlords had several bites at the cherry. They let the cleared ground to sheep farmers for a greatly increased rent: they placed many of the evicted people on waste ground, for which no incoming speculator would give any money, so that they would improve it to the point where (as remarked earlier) a big farmer would be prepared to pay rent for it; and they made the new "crofts" so small that the crofters had to take up wage work in the new industries which the landlords were trying to introduce to the Highlands. The landowners made sure that the croft was always too small for the hardest-working family occupying it to be able to live from its produce – and at the same time pay rent.[291] Thus the evicted Highlanders had to work outside the croft in one of three ways, all of them lucrative – to the landlord, that is. They either had to go fishing, so that the very fish in the sea would swell the landlord's income, or they had to collect and burn kelp to produce industrial alkali, and thereby boost the landlord's kelp-profits (thus making even the seaweed pay tribute to the proprietor), or they had to take other wage-work for the big farmers or the landlords, in that way overcoming the shortage of day-labourers in such a sparsely-populated country (which would otherwise discourage potential entrepreneurs, and cause inconvenience to landowners).

The fishing was always uncertain, since the shoals became fitful; the kelping failed almost entirely after the Canningite Tories brought in free trade in the 1820s, thus admitting cheaper competing products from overseas; and there was seldom sufficient other wage-work (though again this was not displeasing to the landlords and the great farmers, since a surplus of labourers always keeps wages down). The result was that the crofters, on their patches of ground that had been specifically designed to be inadequate for their support, grew poorer and poorer. The crofters became a population of rural paupers: they said it themselves, outsiders said it, the landlords said it. It was an accepted starting-point in any discussion about the Highlands. And before long this rustic misery became a valuable propaganda tool for the proprietors. Look at the crofters (said the landlords and their supporters) – perpetually half-starving or distressed, and sometimes reduced to appealing for Lowlanders' charity: that (they insisted) is what the Highlanders have always been. In fact (they continued) that is exactly what all the improvements of the eighteenth and nineteenth centuries were aimed at eradicating. So when Highlanders say they want to go back to the old days, that is what they are talking about: obviously we have to save them from themselves. The regular hunting and herding of the authentic clansfolk, which provided nearly all their food, were quietly ignored (along with their sizeable joint-farms on the good land) and therefore forgotten about: and a cascade of books about the Highlands pounded home the message – the Highlanders had always been crofters, that is, rural mendicants. The contented, self-sufficient hunters and herdsmen of the clan days were airbrushed out of history; and the clansfolk, throughout the centuries of clanship, were frequently referred to by historians as "crofters"[292] – in other words, people who were accepted on all hands as being a permanently impoverished marginal population. So much was this the case that when one author, even one who accepted many of the orthodox fictions about the old Highlanders, was unable to swallow this particular concoction – that the Highlanders were "crofters" before the clearances – she had to apologize for it: "most 'crofters' are later than most 'clearances' (yes, I hear the snorts of disbelief; I must go a long way round to explain)."[293]

W. Douglas Simpson's book *Skye and the Outer Hebrides* may fairly be taken to represent this torrent of literature written either by Lowlanders, or by that Highland fifth column, the landlords and their supporters. It was published in 1967, and reprinted (at least) in 1968, 1973, and 1975. Simpson was by no means the worst of the army of anglophone experts who have told us what to think about the Gaelic Highlanders. He even admitted that there were clearances in Lewis – when Sir James Matheson was landlord, he said, Lewis people "were evicted to make way for sheep and deer" – although the orthodox view of Lewis now is that there never were any evictions there (as we saw earlier). However, on the question of crofters, Simpson sedulously propagated the official view. Discussing the Hebrides, Simpson claimed that "crofting has been for ages the chief occupation of the islanders", and quoted Dr Johnson who, he asserted, was "writing about the crofters of Skye". In fact neither Dr Johnson nor Boswell mentioned crofters, for the simple reason that they had not yet been invented. They spoke of small tenants, certainly. They mentioned both the joint-tenants of the old Highland farms, and also the cotters or sub-tenants of the joint-farmers, who shared in the communal labours of the farm – these latter had appeared by 1773, in the changed circumstances after Culloden. They would have had to have a fruitful session with a crystal ball to be able to speak of crofters. Ignoring the intractable reality, Simpson said that the Skye tacksmen at the time of the visit by Johnson and Boswell "lived in intimate personal contact with their crofters"; that the MacKenzie tacksmen established in Lewis in the early seventeenth century "tended to live a life apart from the native crofters" (that is, a century and a half before there were any crofters, native or other); and that Dean Munro, who mentioned ploughing in Lewis *in 1549* (a quarter of a millennium before crofters appeared), was in fact describing "a combined operation by a crofting team".[294]

44. A patch of ground

The same kind of reference can be found in dozens of history books. Malcolm Gray wrote in 1957 that in "the Highlands of Scotland . . . there persists, in the form of the crofting system, a society cast in the mould of the early eighteenth century".[295] In 1985 Peter & Fiona Somerset Fry, writing of the days just after 1745, mentioned "tenants (in the Highlands they were known as crofters) . . ."[296] In 1991 Professor Lynch said: "Both before the Clearances and after them, the basic health of the Western Highlands and Islands depended, not on the inherent productivity of crofts, but on the wider Highland economy and the availability of seasonal work in the Lowlands."[297] So there were crofts before the clearances, and the well-being of the Highland hunters and herdsmen in the 1600s and earlier depended on "seasonal work in the Lowlands" – neither of which extraordinary concepts finds much support in the historical evidence. (Before the new regime came to the Highlands, the main contacts between the Highlanders and the Lowlanders were destructive, plundering attacks by each group on the other group.) Way and Squire thought that "crofters and cotters" were there in the sixteenth century and earlier.[298] C. V. Wedgwood, writing of Montrose's flight after the Battle of Carbisdale, said he hid in some hay after having "reached a croft" – in 1650.[299] Sir Iain Moncreiffe would not be behindhand in such work, and he, too, repeatedly described the clansfolk before 1745 as "crofters", who lived on "crofts".[300] As we saw earlier, Professor Schama asserted that thousands of crofters were evicted as part of the Hanoverian revenge after Culloden.[301] Margaret Adam asserted that in the old Highland society the tacksmen "had the pleasing appearance of bridging the social gulf [sic] between owner [sic] and crofter [sic]",[302] thus propounding a "social gulf", which did not exist, between "owners", who did not exist, and "crofters", who did not exist – three delusions in six words.[303] Could a writer travel further into fairyland? Adam's mythological excursions were of course welcomed by the Bible of the orthodox Lowland historians, the *Scottish Historical Review*, which published no fewer than four chimerical contributions by her over a period of four years. Doctrinally sound historians (as we saw above) still praise the palpable fictions with which she defended the landlords.

Trevelyan gave vigorous support to this theory. He asserted that "the crofter of Queen Anne's reign" existed on "a patch of ground": thus the hunting, shooting, and fishing which brought in the main part of the Highlanders' food supplies, as well as the flocks and herds which formed his secondary source of subsistence, were swept into oblivion. Warming to his task, Trevelyan dramatically denounced even the imaginary crofter's imaginary "patch of ground": for "the soil on the mountain-side was thin and stony, denuded by torrents, unimproved by manure".[304] Why the clansfolk, even in the minor crop-raising which was the least of their food sources, should have ignored the good soil in the valley bottom, extensively manured not only by wild life but also by the abundant roaming herds of the Highlanders' cattle, sheep, and goats, in favour of "patches of ground", on "the mountain-side . . . thin and stony . . . unimproved by manure", Trevelyan did not try to explain. It is clear that Trevelyan had taken the indigent post-clearance Highlander of the mid-nineteenth century, who had in fact been forbidden to hunt on the mountains, or shoot on the moors, or fish in the rivers and lochs, whose pasture land had been taken from him, who had lost all the good land to the new big farmers, and who had indeed been forced to exist on a "thin and stony . . . patch of ground" on the "mountain-side" – Trevelyan had taken this impoverished Highland crofter of 1850 and unblushingly presented him as the authentic clan-member existing centuries earlier. It may be thought strange to find a historian behaving in such an unhistorical way.

These references, by Trevelyan and his imitators to "crofters" – existing centuries before there were any – played a large part in establishing the old clansfolk in the general mind as famished, often destitute, peasants.

45. Lochiel's tribute

The other contention in Trevelyan's comment – that Highlanders paid "most oppressive" rack-rents – is equally divorced from reality. For it is established beyond question that in the old Highlands the clan tribute, called "rent" by the chiefs, was very low indeed: indeed, one of the main excuses advanced by the chiefs when they were reproached for their clearances was that their income in the old days was so painfully low that they could not have been expected to turn down the much higher rents of the new system. Selkirk, for example, says that the total income of all the Highland chiefs who took part in the '45 was no more than five or six thousand pounds.[305] (After the clearances, one single grazing ranch on one single Highland estate – Lairg sheep farm, in Sutherland – was rented at £1500, a quarter or more of that amount.)[306]

One of the leading Jacobite chiefs was Cameron of Lochiel. He is supposed to have taken some 800 men with him, either Camerons or members of the clan septs, to join Prince Charles.[307] When one allows for all those among the males of the clan who were too young, or too old, or for some other reason unfit, to be soldiers, and then for all the women and girls, there must have been at the very least several thousands in the Clan Cameron. One common calculation was that the men of the right age and fitness to be soldiers, if they were expected to be taken off on an external expedition, formed some ten per cent of the whole population: on that reckoning, there must have been perhaps 8000 Camerons. The parish of Kilmallie, sometimes considered to be conterminous with the original Cameron country, had 3093 people in the 1750s according to the assessment made for Dr Webster; but besides these Camerons of Lochaber, the clan had spread into Morvern ("whose inhabitants were mainly Camerons", said Paul Hopkins),[308] into Ardnamurchan, and into Rannoch Moor in Fortingall parish (a hundred Cameron men went from Rannoch alone to join Lochiel in the '45 rebellion – which, on the calculation above, would indicate perhaps a thousand Camerons in Rannoch). So it appears that the figure of 8000 may be somewhere near the truth.

Lochiel's tribute or "rent" was about £500 per year.[309] At an average of five per family (including couples just married, or with only their first child or children, as "families"), 8000 people would make about 1600 families; which would mean that just over six shillings (thirty-one of today's pence, or less than a third of one pound) per year reached Lochiel as tribute from each family in the Cameron country, either directly or via the tacksman. Other evidence shows that even this figure may be too high. Adam Smith, in his *Wealth of Nations*, 1776, wrote: "A crown [five shillings, or 25p – a quarter of a pound], half-a-crown [two shillings and sixpence, or 12½p, an eighth of a pound], a sheep [in 1745 worth half-a-crown], a lamb, was some years ago in the Highlands of Scotland a common rent for lands which maintained a family. In some places it is so at this day; nor will money at present purchase a greater quantity of commodities there than in other places."[310] David Stewart, writing in 1822, said "five shillings was of some value seventy years ago [i.e., in 1750], and would have bought two sheep in the Highlands".[311] So what Adam Smith was saying was that "in the Highlands . . . a common [annual] rent for lands which maintained a family" was five shillings, two and a half shillings (i.e. a quarter or an eighth of a pound), or even less than that.

46. Violence in Scalpay

Even this microscopic amount, which from its very size would suggest a public tax rather than a private "rent", seems to have been regarded by the clansfolk just as taxes are often regarded today: as something one should pay if one has to, but which one is justified in avoiding where one can. It was certainly not regarded as something to be paid at all costs, for example in a case of personal misfortune or a bad crop. Quite often it was not paid. Burt has already been quoted as saying that part of a chief's duty was to free the necessitous from arrears of "rent".[312] The minister of Killin wrote in the O.S.A. that "towards the beginning of the present century" (that is to say, in the time of Queen Anne, 1702-14, who reigned over what Trevelyan alleged to be "oppressive . . . rack-rents") "rents were ill paid, and sometimes not at all".[313] In 1698 (only four years before Anne ascended the throne) the Marquis of Atholl grumbled, in a letter to his eldest son, "'Tis well know I have got noe Rent these two years by past, not soe much as payment for meale and seed I gave my tenants, and this year is like to prove worse than ever"[314] (the marquis naturally upheld the fiction that the Atholl clansfolk were his "tenants"). Not only were the clansfolk often accused of paying very low rents, sometimes they were condemned for paying no rent at all. Patrick Sellar, one of the most notorious of the sheep farmers who took over the cleared land in Sutherland, denounced the Highlanders of the old days as "merely a nest of outlaws who paid no rent".[315] On the same estate, Colin Campbell, one of the countess's managers, complained that no progress could be made while the small tenants paid such "low rents",[316] and James Loch, another of the managers, was infuriated (like Sellar) to find that many Sutherlanders – even worse than paying low rents – were not paying "any rent whatever".[317] In the central Highlands, the minister of Kilmallie said that before the new improvements, "the rents were low".[318] The minister of Halkirk also remarked on "the rent being formerly very low".[319] Pennant made the same point – the old Highlanders, he said, "held their farms at a low rent".[320] The minister of Kilmartin said in about 1791 that forty years before the "hill land" was "very low rented".[321] The Boleskine O.S.A. report said that in the old days the Highlanders paid a "pittance of rents".[322] The minister of Eddrachillis reported that in the old days the people of his parish "paid no rent, and acknowledged no landlord or superior".[323] Dozens of observers agreed that in the days of the clans the "rent" was either negligible or non-existent.

So while some orthodox commentators said that the old Highlanders were lawless ne'er-do-wells who paid such a small amount of "rent" – or even none at all – to their betters that they had to be cleared out of the Highlands to be fair to the landlords, in order to make room for profitable sheep farms or deer forests, others (such as Trevelyan) asserted that they were suffering under rack-rents, and had to be cleared out of the Highlands to rescue them from such intolerable conditions. (The phrase "crocodile tears" springs to mind.) So long as the desired conclusion – that the Highlanders had to be driven from the Highlands – was reached, the route taken to get there was of minor importance: consistency was as expendable as fact. What is written depends on whether the writer feels it necessary to produce propaganda to support the landlords and their clearances, or is merely putting down what actually happened.

If it be objected that Trevelyan only accused the tacksmen (not the clan chiefs) of sub-letting land "on rack-rent terms that were usually most oppressive", then one has to try and imagine a clan society where the clan chief was receiving only a minimal tribute each year, while at the same time the tacksmen, sub-chiefs of a small part of the clan, were living high on the hog from their rack-rents, and were therefore better off than the chief; not only is there no evidence whatever for such conditions, but clearly no clan chief would ever have passively accepted such a state of affairs.

Again we return to the question: who was to enforce compliance with a demand that the clansfolk considered unreasonable? After the mid-eighteenth-century transformation, certainly, the chiefs could begin to play the tyrant as much as they liked, and, with the help of the forces of the Lowland law, did play the tyrant, rack-renting (and evicting) without remorse. Dr Johnson mentioned an episode which shows concisely what the attitude of the clansfolk to Trevelyan's supposed "rack-rent terms" would have been: "The tenant of Scalpa [Scalpay, off the coast of Skye], an island belonging to MacDonald, took no care to bring his rent; when the landlord talked of exacting payment, he declared his resolution to keep his ground, and drive all intruders from the island, and continued to feed his cattle as on his own land, till it became necessary for the sheriff to dislodge him by violence."[324] (Scalpay was in MacKinnon country, and had been sold in 1765 by the MacKinnon chief's trustees to the chief of Clan Donald; this incident appears to have been the Scalpay occupant's reaction to this disloyal surrender of MacKinnon land.) The Scalpay tenant (the correct word in the new dispensation) had to be dislodged "by violence": but what had happened when there was no effective sheriff, able to evict defiant occupiers "by violence"? Before 1745 the Lowland state authorities had virtually no power beyond the Highland line, unless they launched a military invasion; and a chief by himself (whatever he might have privately hankered after) could not successfully resort to violence, because the sturdy and heavily armed Highlanders were still able to defend themselves.

47. "Rent-collecting" in Kintail

After the subjugation of the Gaels following Culloden, in Scalpay and elsewhere in the Highlands the policies of the Lowland authorities and the newfound rights of Highland chiefs were, it is all too obvious, imposed "by violence". Before that, such attempts were thrown off by the popular will. For example, after the Battle of Glenshiel in 1719, when the Jacobites' second rising failed, the Government confiscated the charters of the Jacobite MacKenzie of Seaforth (the chief acknowledged by the MacRaes of Kintail), who took part in the rebellion; so whatever powers the charters had given to Seaforth in Kintail – and, according to the present orthodox belief, they were very extensive indeed – now belonged to the Government. As we have seen, and will see in more detail later, there is a widespread belief among historians that a chief had "virtually absolute control" over his clan land. So since the Government now held the chief's charter, which had conferred on him this "virtually absolute control", it was now in possession of these tremendous powers of the chief. The Government claimed to believe this as firmly as a modern academic, and it naturally wanted its "rents", so it sent its agent, Ross of Easter Fearn, accompanied by an armed force, to Kintail to collect them. This was already five years after the death of Queen Anne, but the news – as subsequently discovered by Trevelyan – that Highlanders could now be rack-rented by their betters had not yet reached Kintail. This, indeed, was a case where it was not a mere chief – one single man, supported only by an ingratiating simper – trying to collect "rents", but the Government of the country, with all the forces of Great Britain at its disposal: and it was not trying to collect rack-rents, but merely the very modest sums which the MacRaes had been in the habit of paying to Seaforth to support his chiefly state. The fact that a warlike expedition was thought necessary by the Government to do something so mundane as collect "rents" in peacetime perhaps needs explanation from those many historians who claim that the chiefs' charters had any validity in the real world, and that landlordism was already as firmly established in the Highlands as it had been for centuries in the Lowlands and England, because the charters said so.

This bellicose mission under Ross of Easter Fearn was a fiasco, as was inevitable in the current Highland social structure. The Government, so far from being able to rack-rent the clansfolk, was not able to obtain any money at all: since the Government authorities palpably did not have "virtually absolute control" of the MacRaes' land, their expedition was a more than "virtually absolute" failure. The Kintail clansmen gathered, the belligerent incursion collapsed, and Ross and his strong-arm men were quickly sent on an immediate return journey to the Lowlands. The great "rent"-collecting armed expedition, sent by the Government of a powerful country against a handful of country folk quaking in fear of the "will or whim" of their superiors, had amassed – not so much as a single bawbee.[325] The

Government despatched Captain MacNeill the next year on the same errand, but he too was given a free lesson by the MacRaes on the realities of power under the clan system, and he also returned having collected blows instead of ha'pence. Further attempts were made subsequently, but all with the same unprofitable result – a zero sum on one side of the ledger, and injuries, even some fatalities, on the other. The MacRaes had decided not to pay, so they did not pay, and the whole power of the state failed to make them pay – since there was no societal structure in the Highlands which could have made them pay.[326]

48. Safely lodged in the bank

The MacRaes, however, as sensible and autonomous clansfolk, continued to do what they considered reasonable. Having refused to concede anything to the forceful "sovereign power" of the Lowland/English state, they kept on paying their tribute to Seaforth, then exiled in France. Indeed, wrote Stewart, on one occasion 400 MacRaes "escorted the money to Edinburgh to see it safely lodged in the bank. Their first appearance there on this errand caused no small surprise."[327] It will be seen that the chief was not able to enforce the payment of his tribute – he was outside the country, and if he had returned to Scotland, he risked execution. In fact, the MacRaes could only send their tribute to the chief by defying the powerful Lowland government. The voluntary nature of the tribute could hardly be demonstrated more clearly. This episode is surely enough by itself to give the lie to Trevelyan's romanticized picture of subjugated clansfolk, oppressive rents, and tyrannical chiefs.

James Hogg, writing from the Highlands on his 1803 tour, was naive enough to conclude that the episode demonstrated the kind-heartedness of the Government. After Seaforth was forfeited, he said, "the bold and tenacious inhabitants [of Kintail] absolutely refused paying rents [sic] to any man excepting their absent chief, and all endeavours of Government to collect them were baffled with disgrace. Their agents were repelled and some of them slain, while the rents [sic] were regularly transmitted to the earl, and it showed the great lenity of our Government that they were not made examples of."[328] In fact, it was not forbearance, but feebleness, that made that Government abandon their repeated onslaughts; not indulgence, but impotence to decree events beyond the Highland line, that dictated the authorities' acceptance of this rebuff. As for the Government's "great lenity", the foolishness of the phrase was shown only twenty-five years later, in the bloodthirsty reign of terror that the "lenient" Lowland/English Government imposed throughout the Highlands after Culloden.

Similarly, the Cameron clansfolk sent money to Lochiel when he was in exile after the '45, as did the Appin Stewart clansfolk to the exiled Ardshiel, their acting chief.[329]

The same attitude to the payment of "rents" persisted even in the immediate aftermath of the British state's triumph at Culloden. Colin Campbell of Glenure, who had been made the Government factor on the lands to which Stewart of Ardshiel and Cameron of Lochiel had the charter right, complained bitterly of the Highlanders' obstruction. Again, as in the attempt to collect the "rents" of the MacRaes of Kintail after the Battle of Glenshiel, it was no longer a single man, the chief, trying to get money out of the Highlanders, but an agent of the central power, backed by all the authority of the British Government. Yet Glenure was constrained to write in a 1749 letter, after three years of official punitive murder and destruction across the Highlands, "the law or the Crown's factor is no more regarded by these barbarians than if there were no law or government in Great Britain. They told the baron-bailie officer and other servants I sent with him – and that in my own presence – that if they dared touch any part of their effects [possessions] for payment of His Majesty's rents, they would beat out their brains. Nothing will do with these ruffians without the concurrence of the troops."[330] No doubt in the changed circumstances after Culloden, troops would have been called in to enforce payment of the rents (which was now the accurate word, after the post-Culloden conquest of the Highlands); but what would have happened, and what must have happened, before such troops were readily available? It is to be regretted that Trevelyan did not, and his followers do not, address such questions.

49. Rob Roy MacGregor

About the same time, Rob Roy MacGregor was beginning the feud with the Duke of Montrose that made him famous. This duke was James, originally the fourth Marquis of Montrose, whose standing had been mysteriously improved just after the Act of Union with England. In January 1707 the Scots Parliament (with Montrose's disinterested support) agreed to the union; in March 1707 the English Parliament agreed to it; and in April 1707 the fourth marquis was able to shine forth as the first Duke of Montrose. Montrose also hoped to benefit personally in other ways from the union of 1707, since that fusion resulted in the opening of the Scottish-English border, which had previously – as a frontier between two countries that were still distinct, even though the same monarch ruled both – been a barrier to commerce. One result was that Highland cattle could now be more easily driven down into England for sale, and according to one account Montrose went into partnership with Rob Roy, each of them putting 10,000 merks into the venture: merks were Scottish marks, and 10,000 of them made about £556 sterling.

Rob Roy was to buy cattle (a good cow was £1 sterling or less), drive them into England and sell them. The partnership was profitable at first, but then one of the drovers employed by the partnership absconded with a lot of money. Montrose refused to accept that this was a partnership loss, and instead demanded the full amount he had invested, plus interest. Having sold the independence of his country for a step up in the peerage, Montrose was not the man tamely to accept any financial setback. His idea of partnership was to share the profits, when there were any; but if there was a loss, to let his partner bear it all. Rob Roy therefore is supposed to have said, "In that case, my Lord, if these be your principles, I shall not make it my principle to pay the interest, nor my interest to pay the principal; so if your Grace do not stand your share of the loss, you shall have no money from me."[331] Montrose went to law (in the Lowlands, of course), and had Rob declared bankrupt; then, equipped with this Lowland justification, he sent an armed expedition which, in MacGregor's absence, turned out Rob Roy's family, burned down his house, and cruelly ill-treated his wife for good measure.

Later, when the Highlands had been civilized, the destruction of houses and the expulsion and ill-treatment of families became normal and commendable landlord routine (indeed, most books on the history of the Highlands now explain how excellent this new system was): then, in the sad dark days of barbarism, such villainy incurred condign punishment. Rob Roy took his revenge by carrying on a kind of guerrilla warfare against Montrose, collecting Montrose's "rents" from his "tenants" – and giving a full receipt for them – before Montrose's agents arrived. Significantly, Montrose was not able to force his clansfolk to pay a second time (despite the fact that all this began in the remorseless reign of Trevelyan's Queen Anne). All the powers of London and Edinburgh could do nothing to stop Rob Roy, even though these events were happening, not behind vast mountain ranges, but within thirty miles of the garrisons of Stirling and Dumbarton, and within the same distance of the rapidly-growing city of Glasgow – one of Rob's raids, indeed, was at Duntreath, only ten miles from Glasgow (and several miles beyond what might be called the nearest point of the Highlands proper). There was even a Lowland garrison stationed at Inversnaid, in the heart of the MacGregor country, only a few hundred yards from Rob Roy's ruined house, for the express purpose of catching Rob Roy: but without success. The ordinary Highlanders, of course, sympathized with Rob Roy, since Montrose had broken not only the Highland laws of conduct but any reasonable standard of behaviour by going back on his word; otherwise Rob would never have been able to continue his depredations in the midst of a people so eminently able to defend themselves. But if the great Duke of Montrose was unable to collect the small sums which he called his "rents", and this on the verge of the Lowlands, and indeed even in the debatable country on the Highland-Lowland border, what chance had landlords of less power, either there or further into the Highlands, to rack-rent their tenants (as the modern orthodoxy would have it)?

The tribute to the chiefs being so small, it followed that in comparison with the Lowland landlords the Highland chiefs (despite their charter-based claims to be owners of their clans' land) seemed poor indeed. Hence Stevenson's remark in *Kidnapped*: "A Highlander is used to see great gentlefolk in great poverty."[332] Dr Johnson thought that the comparatively small sums of money paid to the chiefs for the loss of their heritable jurisdictions in 1747 was "perhaps a sum greater than most of them had ever possessed, which excited a thirst for riches, of which it shewed them the use". Johnson also used a significant phrase in his description of a typical eviction of his time (he was writing in 1773). The landlord, he said, puts up the rent; the tenant refuses to pay, "and is ejected". The land is then let to "a stranger", who, "taking the land at its full price, treats with the Laird upon equal terms, and considers him not as a Chief, but as a trafficker in land".[333] It was only after the new age came to the Highlands that the land was let "at its full price".

Neither Stevenson nor Dr Johnson, of course, had had the advantage of being able to read about Trevelyan's discoveries, and to learn of the oppressive rack-rents supposed to be standard practice in the Highlands all of sixty or seventy years before Dr Johnson's journey.

50. Keppoch and Glengarry

Where an outsider, rather than the clan chief, had procured a Lowland charter to the clan land, the clan was not surprisingly even more cavalier in its attitude to the charter holder's demand for "rent". In earlier days, no money at all would have been forthcoming; by the middle of the eighteenth century, after Culloden, the pressure of the new society (and its state apparatus) was becoming much less easy to evade. At that time, or even shortly before, the clansfolk would sometimes pay small sums - a few Scots pounds (worth only a twelfth of English pounds), or a few sheep or hens - if only to avoid the charter holder's attempts to stir up trouble; but there was no certainty or regularity about it. Nor could these payments accurately be called rent. Such sums were really a kind of blackmail - handed over because the payer felt it was less trouble to pay the insignificant amounts asked than to risk the charter holder coming with his own clansmen, or with a Government regiment, and making a destructive assault on some townships. In the second half of the twentieth century numbers of London shopkeepers used to give the gang led by the Kray twins regular sums in cash, but no one could call the payments "rent" - they were merely protection money. The author of the 1818 *Sketch of a Tour* said that the Keppoch MacDonalds who lived on the land to much of which MacIntosh had got hold of a charter paid him no "rent" at all until after the '45.[334] Even after the Lowland conquest following Culloden, the newly triumphant system of private landlordism was being imposed on Keppoch only slowly: the author of the *History of Scotland in 1750* said that though MacIntosh and the Duke of Gordon were the "owners" (according to the new regime, that is, four years after Culloden) of the land where the Keppoch MacDonalds lived, "the Rent they pay is rather an Acknowledgement than the Real Value, and even that they pay but as they are in Humour".[335] Other chiefs who found that outsiders had obtained a charter to the clan land sometimes agreed to pay a minimal sum as a feu-duty (a feu was a kind of permanent lease) to the charter holder to give themselves some kind of position under Lowland law, and then found that they were halfway towards being able to claim full private ownership after Culloden; the chiefs of Keppoch refused to pay anything, or to wangle any kind of Lowland charter, so their descendant found that after 1746, when Lowland law was clamped down over the newly conquered and now defenceless Highlands, he had in the new Lowland dispensation as little enforceable claim to the Keppoch lands as the Keppoch MacDonald clansfolk themselves.

The tribute that a clan gave to its own chief was paid only during good behaviour on the chief's part. Andrew Lang, in his introduction to the *Highlands of Scotland in 1750*, said that MacDonald of Barrisdale (a Glengarry chieftain) and others had accused MacDonald of Glengarry of fraud; they denounced him "for having received the Prince's money to raise the clan, kept the gold, and sent out the clan at their own expense. Old Glengarry was therefore consigned to Edinburgh Castle, where, as we learn from a letter in Sir William Fraser's *Book of Grant*, he was totally destitute, the tenants paying no rent [and this was after Culloden, which marked – so far as any single event did – the arrival of the new rent-paying society]. Released in 1749, he died at Edinburgh in September 1754."[336]

Referring to earlier centuries, the minister of North Knapdale wrote in the O.S.A. that "rent" consisted of feasts at clansfolk's houses. "The men who provided these entertainments partook of them; they all lived friends together; and the departures of the chief and his retinue never failed to occasion regret."[337] The minister of Campbeltown wrote (also in the O.S.A.) that when the MacDonalds had Kintyre, before the Campbells replaced them in a piece of Lowland-inspired aggression, the "rent" of the whole of Kintyre, together with that of Islay, was no more than £139. "It was principally paid in kind, and generally spent where it was paid, in entertaining their followers. In those rude ages, no other use could be made of any revenue. Luxury was unknown; and, of the gross produce of the earth, the lord could consume no more than his vassal, or meanest follower."[338]

Among the luxuries that the chief did not know and could not afford was tyranny. It would have taken more than £139 per annum to support a dictator, ancient or modern. The chiefs themselves of course knew what their position was vis-à-vis their clans, and showed it in their demeanour.

51. Most cordial manner

The bearing of the chiefs towards their clans was propitiatory and ingratiating to a degree that can now only be compared to a parliamentary candidate's approach to his voters – at election time, that is; perhaps it may be slightly less effusive after the polling-stations have closed. Some comments on this subject were quoted earlier; others can be cited. Jamieson, writing in 1818 of the old clan society, said that "the gentry . . . conversed with the lower classes, in the most kindly and cordial manner, on all occasions".[339] The Rev. Donald MacQueen, minister of Kilmuir in Skye, said in 1774 that in the attitude of the chiefs towards their clans, "no art of affability, generosity, or friendship, which could inspire love or esteem, was left untried".[340] Burt, writing in the 1720s, said that the "meanest" among the clansfolk "insist upon the privilege of taking him [the chief] by the hand whenever they meet him", as being his relations.[341] Dr Johnson, in 1773, described the friendship between Donald MacLean, younger of Coll, and his clansfolk: "He did not endeavour to dazzle them by any magnificence of dress: his only distinction was a feather in his bonnet; but as soon as he appeared they forsook their work, and clustered round him; he took them by the hand, and they were mutually delighted."[342] Patterns of behaviour arise from the social and economic circumstances existing in any society; but they often continue to a diminishing degree (since human behaviour does not usually change overnight) when that society is under heavy attack from outside, or is even on its deathbed. Some chiefs and clansfolk continued to comport themselves in much the same way years after clan society had received what turned out to be its fatal blow. Sixty years after Dr Johnson's journey, another traveller in the Highlands, Chauncy H. Townshend, encountered Donald MacLean's nephew, Hugh, 15th of Coll. Townshend and his companion were rowed across the bay at Tobermory to see Hugh's new house at Drumfin. The boatman was a MacLean, and the travellers – who were English, and had a proper regard for class distinctions, and in particular a suitable reverence for landlords – were astonished to hear him speak freely about Coll. "He blamed or praised the laird's conduct, too, like one that had a right to do so", said Townshend, who was an old Etonian, and had come from a society where the rank-and-file did not presume to criticize their superiors (at least openly). The tourists came across MacLean of Coll himself, and to their surprise "our boatman advanced to meet and to shake hands with him, with all the independent airs of an equal. He then beckoned us to come forward; and, when we modestly hung back, downright pulled us into the presence, and took upon himself to perform the ceremony of mutual introduction with a great deal of modest impudence. 'The Laird, twa jontlemen frae England.' The Laird, apparently used to his clansman's ways, seemed nothing fashed, but received and shook hands with us with a pleasant cordiality."[343]

A relevant narrative occurs in the Duthil report in the N.S.A. At the beginning of the eighteenth century a wolf was at large in Moy parish – MacIntosh country. When it killed a woman and her child, the chief of MacIntosh carried out his clan function, and summoned the active males of the clan to gather and destroy the animal. As it happened, one of the clansmen came across the wolf on his way to the gathering, and managed to slay it. "With his dirk he cut off the animal's head, and carried it as a trophy of his victory to the place of meeting. On his arrival, the laird reproached him for his tardiness; when the man with affected contempt replied, that he believed he came sufficiently soon for all that was to do. As the laird was about to reproach him in somewhat more bitter terms, he drew the wolf's bleeding head from under his plaid, and threw it at his chieftain's feet." The chief's office was to rally the clan for a joint effort when it was necessary; but this did not mean that he was considered above a clansman's addressing him "with affected contempt".[344]

The Earl of Selkirk made the same point. The authority of the chief was, he said, "not of that absolute kind which has sometimes been imagined". It could not be maintained "without an unremitting attention to all the arts of popularity. Condescending manners were necessary in every individual, of whatever rank; the meanest expected to be treated as a gentleman, and almost as an equal." If any of the chiefs or chieftains did not really feel this affability, Selkirk went on, they concealed the fact.[345]

Despots of any age – whether the ancient Pharaohs, or medieval monarchs, or the twentieth-century breed such as Hitler and Stalin – never had to be as careful as that. A tyrant does not usually find it "necessary" to treat his serf "almost as an equal", nor does a member of the rank-and-file talk to a tyrant "with affected contempt" (not after the first time, anyway).

52. Fostering of the chief's heir

It is perhaps unfair to put down the chief's invariable informality and friendliness towards the members of his clan as inspired in every case by self-interest. Many a chief must have been extremely proud of the stalwart Highlandmen who surrounded and protected him, and who would indeed while relations were harmonious defend him to the death; just as the clansfolk were proud of their chief. From mutual respect, affability naturally flows. The chiefs, moreover, while the clan system flourished, were not usually brought up separately and apart from their fellow clansfolk. A chief who had experienced such an isolated upbringing might have been more tempted to try to establish an autocracy, although in the conditions of clan society he could not have succeeded. In fact it was the custom for the son of the chief to be brought up by foster-parents, who belonged to the clan. He would live the ordinary life of a boy and a youth within the clan; he would grow up among those with reference to whom, given good behaviour on his part, he would later exercise the chiefly powers. If the idea behind this traditional way of educating the heir to the chiefship was to prevent him thinking that he was more important than he was, better means could scarcely have been chosen. It is as if, in modern times, the son of a duke or a billionaire was brought up in a council house by a couple who spent long hours at boring, ill-paid jobs, and gained his education at the local comprehensive; it would, at least, give the child a view of life not normally experienced by a member of the upper class.

As could be expected, the chief and the family who had brought him up remained very close throughout his life. Colonel Cameron of Fassfern had a foster brother called Ewen MacMillan (the MacMillans were a Cameron sept). At Quatre Bras, the preliminary battle before Waterloo, where Fassfern was commanding the 92nd Regiment, the Gordon Highlanders, he had become isolated when his horse was shot under him: "he was so entangled by the fall", wrote the Rev. Dr Norman MacLeod, "as to be utterly unable to resist a French soldier, who would have transfixed him but for the fact that the foster-brother transfixed the Frenchman." MacMillan got Colonel Cameron back to his regiment, and then returned under heavy fire "to retrieve Fassfern's saddle". Later, when Fassfern was mortally wounded, MacMillan carried him out of the battle and took him to a deserted house; and then, when he died, performed the last duty of a comrade – decent and reverent burial.[346]

In modern society there is as little contact between rich and poor, other than the strictly business transaction of work performed on one side and wages paid out on the other, as there is between a Cockney and a Papuan islander; it is therefore perhaps difficult for us to comprehend the amiability which existed in this quite different state of society between the chief and his clansfolk. Yet the evidence that it did exist is quite overwhelming. Late in the eighteenth century, David Stewart of Garth, a chieftain from Perthshire who afterwards became a major-general, was as a young officer in a Highland regiment assigned a private as a personal servant; and this Highlander, speaking Gaelic, naturally addressed Stewart – without intending, or giving, the least offence – by his Christian name.[347] It is not easy to imagine the equivalent in our society (whether in the eighteenth or the twenty-first centuries) – a rich young Guards officer addressed as "Tom" or "Jack" by his batman.

Another incident recalled by Stewart touched on the same theme. In 1775 Colonel Simon Fraser of Lovat raised a regiment (the 71st, Fraser's Highlanders). He addressed the newly formed regiment, naturally speaking in Gaelic. An old Highlander, the father of one of the soldiers, listened to him attentively. "When he had finished, the old man walked up to him, and with that easy familiar intercourse which in those days subsisted between" the chiefs and the clansfolk "shook him by the hand, exclaiming, 'Simon, you are a good soldier, and speak like a man; so long as you live, Simon of Lovat will never die'."[348] This was allusion to the colonel's father, Lord Lovat. As a matter of course, the Highlander, speaking in Gaelic, used the chief's Christian name. (This old Highlander, unfortunately, was mistaken; as we shall see later, this Fraser of Lovat, like his father, was an iniquitous character. But though the clansman's opinion was erroneous, he gave it – and was expected to give it – freely.)

Arthur Geddes said that "playful rhyming, chaffing contests" were recorded between the chief of the MacKenzies, the great Earl of Seaforth, on the one hand, and a rank-and-file clansman – a small tenant paying perhaps two or three pounds a year tribute – on the other. One can hardly imagine such familiarity existing between two men of what might have been considered corresponding social strata in Wiltshire in the eighteenth century – or for that matter now.[349]

It seems possible that the Highlanders' habit, rooted in clanship but continuing even when clanship was being destroyed, of treating a person as he or she was rather than with the exaggerated deference due to the holder of a certain position in society, may explain why Queen Victoria was always so eager to escape from the court life of England and the Lowlands, and to return to the Highlands and the Highlanders.

53. Stories of despotism

Stories purporting to demonstrate how despotically the old chiefs behaved are still the standard fare. Writers of history books no doubt find that they add a spurious excitement to what without them might be a somewhat tedious account: perhaps the tales are (in W. S. Gilbert's words in *The Mikado*) "merely corroborative detail, intended to give artistic verisimilitude to an otherwise bald and unconvincing narrative". Certainly those acting as guides in Highland castles or mansions, whether the owners or their employees, seem to find that such stories liven up what could be a dull recital of dates and descents and building work, and give pleasurable shocks to the tourists – besides which, someone boasting about an ancestor's great power in the days of the clans gets some reflected distinction for himself. We know that the conditions of Highland society before Culloden mean that such melodramas can only be fictitious: not infrequently the stories themselves are such that only the very credulous would accept them. One chronicle, for example, has a Highland chief condemning a woman to death because she owed him money; the rarity of such fiscal transactions among the ordinary clansfolk already makes one suspicious. (Did the debt arise through an overdraft, or a mortgage, or a credit card?) The chief is supposed to have ordered the woman to be tied by her hair to the seaweed on the shore, so that when the tide came in she was drowned. The originator of this fantasy cannot have seen much seaweed; and to make the victim a Highlander, who dies because she cannot pull apart a few strands of wrack, when thousands of Highlanders later spent months of each year detaching and dragging ashore many tons of seaweed to make kelp, does make one wonder how such stories can be believed. Another tale, told by Adam Collier, has the chief Clanranald trying to introduce the potato to South Uist, and having to "throw some of his tenants into prison before they would plant the new root". Prison? In South Uist?[350] This does not mean, of course, that chiefs did not sometimes hand out extreme punishment to erring clansfolk, with the consent of their clans, since a chief was also a judge – but that does not mean that he was a despot. The modern British state sometimes imposes sentences of many years' imprisonment, or even lifelong confinement (and until recently it could decree death), on those who have earned – or are thought to have earned – universal condemnation, but that fact alone does not make Britain a despotism.

This remains true despite the fact that in our society judges are specifically selected, whereas in clan society the chief was also the judge. Our judges are not raised to the bench by any electoral or representative process; the chief could claim a much stronger mandate from the point of view of popular consent (which may be thought to be the basis of democracy), since no chief held that position long without the whole-hearted approval of his clansfolk.

There may be a further reason for the inception of such legends. It is possible that the abuses of Lowland feudalism (and even rack-renting) may have crept into parts of the extreme eastern Highlands which had previously known something akin to clan society. It is significant that in the O.S.A., some reports on parishes in what might be called the eastern foothills of the Highlands, between Moray and Angus, say or give hints that Gaelic was once spoken there, but was now spoken no longer: for example Botriphnie and Boharm in Banffshire, Cushnie in Aberdeenshire, and Lintrathen in Angus. In other parts of the Highlands, the extinction of Gaelic followed the extinction of clan society, although there was usually a time-lag; and it may have been so here. Yet the ministers of these border parishes seem to have thought of their people as Highlanders. The minister of Aboyne, in Aberdeenshire, described (as we saw) how the Highlanders thought of a stretch of land surrounded by mountains as a "country", and obviously thought of his own parishioners as being Highlanders.[350] The incumbent of Rhynie, in the same county, said that his parish had been the seat of many of the Gordons "during the feuds of the clans"[351] – in spite of the 1746 memorial on the Highland clans, which said succinctly, "the Gordons is no clan family, although the Duke is chief of a very powerful name in the Lowlands".[352] These foothill parishes are outside the Highland line as it was determined above, but inside it according to the 1796 Act of Parliament mentioned earlier. So it may be that in these border parishes, where the people were thought of by some as Highlanders and where a few either spoke Gaelic or had comparatively recently abandoned it, and yet where the configuration of the ground did not afford the same protection against Lowland influences that the higher hills did, it may be that here the local lairds tried to play the despot and thus gave rise to stories that in the Highlands proper the chiefs of the clans were tyrants. It is also possible that the same is true of some areas on the fringe of the southern Highlands, where the hills were lower and therefore less of an obstacle, such as the island of Bute, or in one or two parishes on the Highland-Lowland border in Perthshire: and especially where those chiefs who were also Lowland grandees, such as the Duke of Atholl, held sway. It is of interest that what complaints of "feudal oppression" in former days did appear in the O.S.A. were almost entirely in the reports from these two border areas.

The eastern fringes of Inverness-shire, Ross-shire, and Sutherlandshire were also susceptible to some Lowland influence even in the days of the clans. The village of Golspie, for example, on the eastern shore of Sutherland, apparently takes its name from the Gaelic Gaulsbith, meaning Lowlanders' village.

Stories of the dreadful state of affairs in the Highlands would no doubt be given more credence in the Lowlands, since the Lowlanders knew nothing of the clans except in so far as they feared and hated them. The compound of ignorance and animosity has always been a forcing-ground of error.

54. Despotism in a former age

Another, perhaps more prolific, source of the "despotic chiefs" theory was the self-defence mechanism of the "improvers" themselves. When they were attacked – as they increasingly were during the nineteenth century – for the misery they were causing the clansfolk whom they were evicting, it was a temptation not often resisted for them to allege that the Highlanders had been even worse off during the bad old days. The men of a new order always decry the old: to draw attention to the malpractice of others has always been an excellent way to divert scrutiny from one's own shortcomings, even when the former may be fallacious, while the latter are all too authentic. (Every British general election, as was remarked earlier, displays a parallel phenomenon.) When the new mercantile system was introduced in England, the bad features of feudalism were naturally emphasized, and what good features it had were ignored. It is possible that our picture of Richard III is still biased because most of our knowledge of him is derived from writers who lived under the imperious Tudors, monarchs who could only assert their own right to the throne by denying Richard's. Ambitious people who lived under any of the five Tudors, between 1485 and 1603, would not have prospered (to say the least of it) if they had alleged that those autocratic rulers were merely usurpers. In the same way, the writings of the "improvers" and their friends are not the best guide to the old clan society which they were in the process of destroying.

Among these "improvers" must be counted not only immigrant Lowlanders and Englishmen, but also many of the Highland chiefs and tacksmen. As soon as the first tentative efforts at change began, early in the eighteenth century, the chiefs felt the need to excuse their innovations by spreading stories about a former system of despotism (partly to boast about how powerful their ancestors were – always a temptation – and partly to assert that the new system was an improvement on the old). The writers of the later eighteenth and nineteenth (and subsequent) centuries referred (and refer) to this despotism as having existed in the early eighteenth century. When one goes back to the early eighteenth century, one still finds the same stories – except that then they were dated still earlier, in some unspecified "former times". In the 1770s, Dr Johnson was told by the English-speakers he met (he had no other source of information, being ignorant of the Highland language) of the "outrages and oppressions" committed previously, for example some thirty or forty years before. And fifty years before Johnson's visit, in the 1720s, Burt was frequently told of the enormous powers exercised by the chiefs – formerly. A chief (to refer to a story give earlier) wanted his clansmen to work for him for sixpence a day, instead of the sixteen pence a day which Burt was paying them; the clansmen told the chief in no uncertain terms what they thought of such a miserly offer, and the chief assured Burt if they "had *formerly* said as much to their chief", (my italics) they would have been thrown off the nearest precipice. On another occasion, a chief said he would behead any clansman guilty of acting towards Burt without due civility, and another chief present made no objection to this braggadocio: Burt thought they were merely imagining they had kept "that exorbitant power they had *formerly* exercised over the lives" (my italics) of their clansmen. Again, Burt was told that only a few years before, a chief was going to hang two officials who had come to enquire about the local timber. All these stories depict the chiefs as having had this power "formerly". Burt was convinced by this vainglorious bluster: "*formerly* the power assumed by the chief in remote parts was perfectly despotic" (my italics).

The cause of this empty boasting is not hard to find. At this date the chiefs were spending more and more time in Edinburgh and even in London. There they liked to fancy themselves the equals of the wealthy Scots Lowland and English landlords, and to brag about their own broad acres in the Highlands, which, they boasted (and they had the charters to "prove" it), were their own private property. They saw, no doubt with envy, the subservience of the beaten-down Lowland and English farm labourers and town shopkeepers and workmen. They were already put out of countenance by the shallowness of their purses, the result of the fact that they only received the modest clan tributes from their clansfolk in place of the full rental value which the Lowland and English proprietors exacted from their estates. When, on their return to the Highlands, they were confronted with their own proud and independent-spirited clansfolk, in place of the forelock-pulling English or Lowland lower orders, it is not surprising that they tried to compensate themselves by inventing past glories. No wonder the discomfited chief, who was seen by Burt being reprimanded to his face by ordinary Highlanders, took refuge in fabricating a golden age in the past, when no one would dare to contradict him.

Another experience of Burt's confirms this view. Referring to the custom of the clansfolk taking the chief by the hand, as being his social equals, whenever they met him, Burt says: "concerning this last I once saw a number of very discontented countenances when a certain lord, one of the chiefs, endeavoured to evade this ceremony. It was in the presence of an English gentleman, of high station, from whom he would willingly have concealed the knowledge of such seeming familiarity" with rank-and-file Highlanders; "and thinking it, I suppose, a kind of contradiction to what he had often boasted at other times, viz. his despotic power in his clan".[353]

These actual exchanges between chiefs and their clansfolk which Burt witnessed are surely better evidence as to the state of the relations between the two parties than the chiefs' allegations about what had been the case in former centuries. Usually, however, when modern writers refer to Burt, it is not the incidents that Burt himself saw and reported (that is, the direct evidence) which they quote, but the chiefs' hollow braggadocio about what they alleged was their power *formerly*, at some vague earlier date (that is, hearsay). Adam Collier, for example, claimed the chiefs had enormous power over their clansfolk, which "reached the pitch of despotism on the one side and subjection on the other pictured for us in the pages of... Burt even so late as the first quarter of the 18th century".[353] As we have seen, what Burt really "pictured for us" was the sturdy independence of the Highlanders. This direct evidence of what was actually happening then was overwhelmed in Collier's estimation by the empty boasting of the chiefs about the power they had had "formerly". Since this bluster conformed to the orthodox beliefs about the clan system, Collier's account of what Burt had said was the opposite of the facts, and anyone taking Collier's report to be accurate would be completely misled.

In fact, as we shall now see, when serious disagreements did occur during the days of the clans between a chief and his people, it was not the clansfolk who risked being killed: it was the chief.

55. Lowland education

There were a number of such disagreements; at some time or other they seem to have occurred in almost every clan. Often the cause was the interference of the Lowland authorities. We saw above how a chief's eldest son, traditionally, was brought up in the clan. This did not please officialdom in Edinburgh and London, and attempts were made to force the chiefs to give their likely heirs a Lowland upbringing. Young people brought up in the Lowlands would no doubt accept Lowland opinions, and imbibe Lowland prejudices, and would therefore be valuable allies of the Edinburgh government after they had returned to the Highlands. The Statutes of Iona, in 1609, to which a number of the chiefs were compelled to subscribe (even though they then ignored them), ordained that (for example) anyone possessed of more than sixty head of cattle had to send his eldest son to the Lowlands to be educated.[354]

As we have seen, what the Edinburgh writing said, and what actually occurred in the Highlands, were two different things. The Statutes of Iona also tried to forbid firearms, and to silence the bards; but all these edicts represented what the Edinburgh authorities would have liked to happen – they give us no information as to what actually did happen. However, increasingly some of the men who became chiefs had spent time in the low country, and had there absorbed theories about the powers of the chiefs which later brought them into collision with the realities of life in the Highlands. As with a number of other adverse aspects of clan life, however, the blame clearly lies not with the clan system as such, but with the attempts of the Lowland authorities to subvert it.

56. Clan Ranald chiefs

The descent of the chiefship in the Clan Ranald branch of the MacDonalds in the sixteenth century is instructive in this connection. When Allan Mac Ruari, the fourth chief, died, his son Ranald Ban became fifth chief; but Ranald's ideas of his powers differed from the clan's ideas, so the clansfolk rose against him and put him to death. His son Dugald MacRanald succeeded as sixth chief, but he had apparently learned nothing of the realities of power within the clan from this gruesome example; and when he was guilty of cruelty to some of the clanspeople, he too was killed, and his sons excluded from the succession. Instead the brother of Ranald Ban, Alistair MacAllan (who was Dugald's uncle), was made chief, and when he died the clan chose Iain Mudartach, or Moydartach (John of Moidart), who was the son of Alistair MacAllan (and grandson of Allan MacRuari) outside wedlock, to succeed as the eighth chief. This was despite the fact that Ranald Ban's grandsons, of whom there were a number, had a prior claim by ordinary hereditary descent, as did Mudartach's uncle, Ranald Gallda (brother of Ranald Ban and Alistair MacAllan) whose birth was "legitimate". Mudartach having been made chief, the king, James V, gave him a charter to the clan lands. But in 1540 Mudartach lost favour at court: James V imprisoned him, and gave a charter to Ranald Gallda. (Ranald Gallda means Ranald the Stranger, an epithet given him because he had been brought up by his mother's people, the Frasers.) Gallda, with the help of the Frasers, established himself in the clan country; but, as A. M. Shaw wrote, "Ranald was unable to obtain the goodwill of the clansmen, who remained obstinately faithful to the chief they themselves had chosen".[355] On Mudartach's return from his imprisonment in 1544, the clan rose in his favour, and Ranald Gallda had to flee. Obtaining the help of the Frasers again, Ranald Gallda attempted to re-assert his claim to the chiefship. There was a battle at the head of Loch Lochy in that year between Clan Ranald, supported by their MacDonald allies of Keppoch and Glen Coe, and Ranald Gallda, supported by the Frasers. The day was so hot that the two armies threw off their outer garments, and fought in their shirts: hence the battle was called Blar na Léine, or Field of Shirts. The men of Clan Ranald were victorious, and thus kept the chief of their choice.

The battle at Blar na Léine was the direct result of the Lowland king imprisoning the chosen chief of Clan Ranald, and attempting to impose a substitute. Some modern authors, however, are happy to imply that the old Highlanders were simply barbarians, fighting almost for the pleasure of it: one writer has claimed that this engagement, Blar na Léine, "was ignited merely by a MacDonald chieftain's complaint that he had been insulted".[356] In fact, like other clan battles, it was the clear and foreseeable consequence of the Edinburgh authorities interfering in the Highlands and intentionally creating disputes.

The descendants of Iain Mudartach, who had gained the chiefship only by the decision of the clansfolk, later claimed that they personally owned all the Clan Ranald lands, and evicted many of the clan's members.

The rules of landownership, as operated in the Lowlands and in England, restricted succession to estates to the "legitimate" heirs of the last owner. But a chief was not a landowner, and so the Clan Ranald was able to choose the "illegitimate" Iain Mudartach as chief. Other examples of men made chiefs by their clans even though they were "illegitimate" are Angus Og, who succeeded his father John as Lord of the Isles and chief of Clan Donald; Lachlan Cattanach MacLean, acknowledged as chief by the MacLeans, and from whom the MacLeans of Duart were descended; and John of Killin, who became chief of the Clan

Kenneth – the MacKenzies. All three, according to the Rev. Angus and the Rev. Archibald MacDonald, were born out of wedlock.[357]

It is surely impossible to understand these events by regarding the chief merely as a landlord, and his clansfolk merely as his tenants, as many orthodox writers maintain.

57. MacLeods of Harris

Similar examples can be taken from the history of the MacLeod clan. William, the ninth chief of the Harris branch of the clan, the Tormod MacLeods, had a daughter, Mary, whom he tried to persuade the clan to accept as a chief. But a woman, although she would have been perfectly satisfactory as a mere landlord and rent-collector, was not considered suitable to fill the office of chief, whose role was not to own the clan land, but to lead the clan in conflicts (such as those in which the Lowland authorities were then trying to entrap the MacLeods). When William died in 1551, the clan refused to elect his daughter as their chief. At this date even England, which claimed to be at a much more sophisticated stage of civilization, had not yet accepted a woman as its monarch; the first woman to be acknowledged as the sovereign of England was Mary Tudor, who came to the throne in 1553. (John Knox published his *Monstrous Regiment of Women*, arguing that a woman being a crowned monarch was forbidden by the Bible, in 1558.)

Having rejected William's daughter, the clan also passed over William's younger brothers, and instead chose as their new chief Iain-a-Chuail Ban, the representative of a junior branch of the family. But after the death of Iain-a-Chuail Ban, one of his sons killed a brother and a nephew in an attempt to impose himself on the clan as chief. The attempt did not succeed. The clan threw out Iain-a-Chuail Ban's posterity as they had thrown out Mary, and when Tormod, a younger brother of William (and thus Mary's uncle), returned from France in 1559 the clan chose him as chief.

Canon R. C. MacLeod, son of the twenty-fifth chief, realized that according to Lowland land law Mary was the rightful heir. After the death of William MacLeod, he wrote, "the family estates passed, legally speaking, to his daughter Mary, who was thus one of the greatest heiresses in Scotland . . . But though Mary was the undoubted owner of the estates in the eyes of the law, her uncle [Tormod], the male heir, took possession of them and held them in spite of her legal rights, and at length, about 1570, she recognized the futility of persisting in her claims, and resigned all rights to the property, receiving a dowry of £1000. Her descendants were constantly endeavouring to substantiate their claims, alleging some flaw in her resignation, but they never succeeded in doing so."[358]

All this is written from the point of view of the family (including Canon MacLeod himself) that took advantage of the landlord revolution to turn the MacLeod clan land into its own private property. The members of that family were still in the Highlands, clothed with their new legal powers after the upheaval of the mid eighteenth century, and were able to impose their own views even on accounts of events before that cataclysm; many of the MacLeod clansfolk had been pushed out into the Lowlands, or overseas, and the orthodox historians had produced accounts of the past which claimed that the chiefs had always been landlords. So Canon MacLeod, naturally, made no mention at all of the decisive part taken by the clansfolk. (If it was so easy for Tormod to "take possession" of the estates, and the clan had nothing to do with it, why did not Mary and her friends "take possession" of them? And why in this account are Iain-a-Chuail Ban and his sons ignored?) But the descent of the chiefship, and thus the chief's land charters, quite contrary to the rules of Lowland landownership, is clearly admitted, since it can scarcely be denied.

It was from Tormod, who had thus gained the chiefship and the charters, that the MacLeod chiefs of the eighteenth and nineteenth centuries descended. This was the family which, despite the fact that (as they knew) the chiefship only came to them by the decision of the clan, and after the rejection of the legitimate line, claimed to be the owners of the land of Clan Leod, and cleared out their clansfolk.

58. MacPhersons and Clan Chattan

A similar case of a refusal to accept a woman as chief, because of her obvious disadvantages as a leader in war, occurred in Badenoch much later. Duncan MacPherson, 10th of Cluny, had no surviving son; but he had a daughter, who became the wife of Archibald, the second son of Campbell of Calder. "In 1689", wrote A. M. Shaw in his *Historical Memoirs of Mackintosh and Clan Chattan*, "Duncan attempted to nominate his son-in-law as his successor both in his estates [i.e., his charters] and in the headship of the clan. His attempt was frustrated by the energetic action of his indignant clansmen, who subscribed a band [a formal alliance or bond] declaring the rightful successor to be the heir-male, William MacPherson of Nuid."[359]

If Duncan MacPherson, 10th of Cluny, had been the owner of the MacPherson lands, then of course his desires would have prevailed. If you own something, you can leave it to whomever you like. But, as a matter of obstinate fact, Duncan MacPherson was not the owner of the clan lands: the Clan MacPherson owned the MacPherson country. And so, when Duncan died in 1722, the chiefship (and the charters to the MacPherson clan lands) went by the clansfolk's decision to Lachlan, the son of William MacPherson of Nuid (William having died), who was Duncan's second cousin, instead of to Duncan's daughter and son-in-law. It was the grandson of this Lachlan who claimed to be merely a private property-owning landlord, and began the expulsion of the Clan Mhuirich from its ancestral possessions.

Although on this occasion the MacPhersons chose a male heir, on other occasions a daughter – and son-in-law – of the last chief was preferred. At the end of the thirteenth century, when Dougal Dall, chief of the Clan Chattan confederation, died, the clansfolk chose as their chief Dougal's son-in-law, Angus, sixth chief of MacIntosh. This was despite the fact that there were a number of male heirs of the old chiefly line still alive, Dougal's cousin Kenneth, ancestor of the MacPhersons of Cluny, being the senior. The Cluny MacPhersons, at least from 1591 onwards, claimed the chiefship of Clan Chattan on the grounds that they were the eldest male heirs, as they were. But the clan having chosen Angus, the de facto chief of Clan Chattan was always, while the clan system lasted, the chief of MacIntosh.

59. Stewart of Appin; Cameron of Lochiel

In 1463 Iain Stewart, the chief of the Stewarts of Appin, was a widower, who had three "legitimate" daughters, and one "illegitimate" son (and "illegitimate" children do not inherit land). The daughters had all married Campbells: the eldest the Earl of Argyll, the second Campbell of Glenorchy, and the third Campbell of Otter. (Nothing made a Campbell chieftain as amorous as the thought of getting his hands on a land-charter.) When Iain Stewart of Appin died, the Campbells claimed the land of Appin, but the Stewarts chose the "illegitimate" son, Dugald, as their chief. Dugald summoned the help of his mother's clan, the MacLarens of Balquhidder. The Campbells arrived in force to prosecute their claim, but the Stewarts and MacLarens defeated them at the foot of Ben Dorain[360] in another pitched battle between (as it might be thought) landlord right and clan right. It would be more accurate to say a pitched battle between one clan and another: for even had the Campbells won and conquered Appin, and either driven out the Stewarts or allowed them to stay on as lieges of Mac Cailein Mor, it would still have been not a victory for landlord right but a victory for the Clan Campbell. Landlord right was a conception that had no existence inside the Highland line, and did not have any existence until the Lowland soldiers and police garrisoned the clan countries after Culloden, and forcibly introduced the Lowland system.

One version of this incident says that Iain Stewart of Appin married his "illegitimate" son's mother, and thus tried to "legitimize" him. On the way to the church before the wedding, he was attacked by an anonymous gang and mortally wounded (an attack which could surprise only those who did not know how keen the clan chiefs were to seize land-charters); but before he died he managed to go through with the ceremony. The chiefs always liked to have a veneer of Lowland legality to cover their encroachments; so the subsequent Stewarts of Appin would have preferred to be able to trace their descent through a legitimate line – a fact which may account for the story of how Iain Stewart of Appin successfully married his son's mother. However, so far as the clansfolk were concerned, as we have seen from the events described above, the question of "legitimacy" was immaterial. If the clan wanted a particular person as chief, the question of what religious ceremonies his parents happened to have gone through did not arise.

The land of the Appin Stewarts, which they had thus successfully defended against outside attack, was lost to an enemy within. One of the Stewarts' own chiefs, whose claim arose only because he was descended from Dugald Mac Iain, whom the clan had chosen as chief, sold their land, lock, stock, and barrel, in 1765.

There are numerous other incidents to show that the chief was very far from being a landlord, who would succeed under the normal rules for the inheritance of land. It is probable that the MacMartins of Letterfinlay were originally the chiefs of Clan Cameron, and that by the wish of the clan's members they were superseded as chiefs by the family of Lochiel, a younger branch of the same stock, at some time between 1396 and 1430. Later Allan Cameron of Lochiel, a chief in the sixteenth century, was responsible for the death of one of the clansmen, Donald Mac Eoghainn; and the Camerons expelled him. Subsequently the clan changed its mind and invited him back to resume the chiefship, but what the clan had done once it could do again. Although the Camerons of Lochiel were demonstrated thus clearly to owe their position simply to the choice of the clan, they later claimed to be hereditary landowners, and evicted their clansfolk.

60. Keppoch, Glengarry, Lewis

The history of the MacDonalds of Keppoch alone should be enough to demonstrate the true nature of the relations between a clan and its chiefs. Donald, 3rd of Keppoch, died in 1496, and was succeeded by his son John, or Iain Aluinn, 4th of Keppoch. This chief was (in the words of *Burke's Landed Gentry*) "deposed by the clan for his unwarlike disposition" in 1497. (Has a landlord, however "unwarlike", ever been "deposed" by his tenants?) One of his descendants was Iain Lom, the Keppoch bard who lived from about 1620 to about 1716. Others of Iain Aluinn's descendants were alive in the nineteenth century (so the Iain Aluinn family did not lose the chiefship through lack of heirs). After this deposition, the clan went to Alistair, Iain Aluinn's uncle, for its next chief. He was followed in turn by his son, his grandson, and his great-grandson, Alexander, 8th of Keppoch. Alexander was succeeded on his death in 1549 by his brother Ranald Og, the ninth chief. The genealogists do not say whether Alexander had any children, nor that he died without any: so this may be another case of an elder line (against all the rules of landlordism) being rejected for a younger. Ranald Og was followed by his son Alexander, 10th of Keppoch, who had three sons. The eldest, another Ranald Og, was passed over by the clan for reasons unspecified, as was his son, Angus Og. Alexander's second son, Donald Glas (Ranald Og's younger brother), became chief as 11th of Keppoch, but he died early, in 1657, leaving his wife with two young sons. She was a Lowlander, according to the *History of Scotland in 1750*, and she brought the two boys up in the Lowlands, instead of having them brought up in the usual way by foster-parents within the clan. After some years the two boys returned to Lochaber, resolved "to Reform and Civilize their Clan".[361] But the MacDonalds did not wish to be "Reformed and Civilized" if it meant accepting Lowland ways, and in September 1663 they rose under Donald Glas's two brothers, Ranald Og (who was older) and Alistair Buidhe (who was younger). In the fighting that followed the two would-be reformers, Alistair, 12th of Keppoch, and his brother Ranald, were both killed by the clansfolk. This involved the Keppoch MacDonalds in a battle with MacDonald of Sleat, who – whether because he wanted to fish in troubled waters, or because he genuinely regretted the brothers' death – came with his followers to take revenge for the killings. However, the will of the Keppoch clan prevailed; and Donald Glas's younger brother, Alistair Buidhe (not the elder brother), became the thirteenth chief. He was the grandfather of Coll, 15th of Keppoch, who fought at Mulroy in 1688 and led the clan in the '15, and the great-grandfather of Alistair, 16th of Keppoch, who was killed at Culloden.

Thus the Keppoch MacDonald clansfolk defied the rules of primogeniture three or perhaps four times in less than 200 years, and thus demonstrated that it was with them, and not with their chiefs, that the real power lay.

The author of the *History of Scotland in 1750* referred to a similar episode in the history of the MacDonalds of Glengarry. The chief of Glengarry at the time of the restoration of Charles II in 1660 was made Lord Macdonald, wrote this author, but he left no heir. "Alexander MacDonald, Father to the present Glengarry, succeeded him, tho' 'tis said that others stood nearer related to the Family, but he being a Bold resolute man, of Greater Natural Parts tho' no Education, *got the Clan of his Side* and became their chief" (my italics).[362] This occurred in 1680. Getting the clan "of his side" was the route to the chiefship; no landlord's heir, or claimant to that position, ever had to get the tenants of an estate "of his side" before he could succeed. Alexander became eleventh chief of Glengarry. It was Duncan, 14th of Glengarry, the great-grandson of the man who "got the Clan of his Side" and thus pocketed the charters, who claimed to be the private and personal owner of the clan lands, and began clearing out the Glengarry MacDonalds.

POWER WITHIN THE CLAN

In the reign of James VI (and I), the chief of the Torquil MacLeods of Lewis died, leaving no legitimate issue, but many natural sons. The eldest son was "not popular among the name" (as one account has it), so he had to leave Lewis, and the clan chose one of his brothers as chief. Being "not popular among the name" meant the loss of the chiefship (and the charters); an aspirant would know that getting the clan "of his side" meant gaining the chiefship – and the charters.

Further examples could be given from the history of every Highland clan, but perhaps the point has already been proved.

61. Chief and tacksmen

W. C. MacKenzie, in his *Short History of the Scottish Highlands and Islands*, said: "There is cumulative evidence of the patriarchal character of the Gaelic polity. The chief was the ceann-cinnidh, or head of the lineage (the Pen-cenedyl of the Cymri [the Welsh]), kinship forming the basis of the system; and the administration of the tribal lands was in his hands for the common welfare."

The right of the clansfolk to the clan land was not the right of an individual landowner to one piece of land: that would have been indistinguishable from a private-property title. The birthright of the clan member was a claim to some share in the land of the clan, the right to a stake in the "country" of the clan to which he belonged. The welfare of the clan as a whole might well require that a member of the clan should take this piece of land instead of that; if the numbers in the clan increased, for example, farms might have to be re-arranged, or some waste land broken in, to accommodate all the rising generation. And the administrative duty to make these re-arrangements, subject to the general approval of the clan, would lie in the hands of the chief. As W. C. MacKenzie put it, where the occupiers of lands were removed by the chief, "he was bound to provide them with other lands on the tribal territory".[363] This kind of re-disposition of land within the clan must be sharply distinguished from the evictions of the eighteenth and nineteenth centuries, when the clansfolk were thrust out from any share whatever in the clan land.

It was remarked earlier that when a clan prospered and increased in numbers, it often separated into several clans, since the unsophisticated Gaelic system of society was not able to provide an adequate framework to hold together more than a certain number of clansfolk. At an early stage of this development, a clan might have only a chief and the body of the clansfolk; other names were so numerous that they had broken up into two or three separate clans; others again were at the intermediate stage, a stage marked by the existence of tacksmen.

When a clan grew beyond a certain point, it became too large for the chief to handle the executive power personally – to act as the sole leader of the clan in time of war, for example – and at the same time it gave the chief an opportunity to create a position for his younger sons as well as his eldest. Part of the clan land, called a tack, would be hived off to become a kind of incipient clan on its own. The tack would be leased, in return for a small amount of annual tribute, to a tacksman, usually one of the chief's relatives. The clansfolk would pay the tribute they had formerly given to the chief to the tacksman. This kind of progression would be encouraged, at an earlier date when most or all of the tribute was still paid in kind, by the fact that beyond a certain point, food is useless. One family, even if it were the chief's, could only eat a certain number of wildfowl, a certain amount of venison. Money might be amassed; but not dead hens.

An alternative way of consuming the additional tribute that would come from an expanding clan would have been for the chief to enlarge his retinue. But these matters were governed by precedent. And the history of his own and of the neighbouring clans – which every Highlander was perfectly conversant with – would afford examples of the dangers of a chief's becoming infected with ideas of personal aggrandizement. This, too, would not have solved the organizational problem.

The chief did not lease the whole of the clan land out to tacksmen; he kept part for those clansfolk who paid their tribute to himself. But whether the clansfolk paid their tribute to the chief, or to the tacksman, they still owned the clan's land. The tacksman, nevertheless, had his recognized place in clan society, somewhere between the chief himself and the ordinary clansfolk; and when in the eighteenth century the tacksmen began to be ejected by the chiefs, they were just as astounded by this turn of affairs as the clansfolk were when they were evicted. The tacksmen, indeed, were often the first to suffer from the new methods. The chief, having claimed that the clan land was his own personal property, and having raised the rents, was reluctant to share his newly obtained ownership and his new-found wealth with anyone else, and often drove out the tacksmen even before he drove out the rank-and-file Highlanders.

62. Tacksmen with charters

Since the terms landlord and tenant had no meaning in the old Highland society, it is impossible to answer and therefore useless to ask whether the younger sons who became tacksmen, or sub-chiefs, were regarded as "landlords" or "tenants". What the Lowland law regarded them as when the new system was imposed at the middle of the eighteenth century depended in each case on whether the main chief or the sub-chief had been self-seeking or servile enough in his Edinburgh schemings to obtain a Lowland charter to the clan land.

The history of the Clan Leod is instructive in this connection. One of the chiefs of the MacLeods of Harris – Malcolm MacLeod, 3rd of MacLeod, who died in about 1360 – established his second son Tormod as a sub-chief, or tacksman, in Berneray. Tormod fathered a line of MacLeods of Berneray which died out in the seventeenth century, when Rory Mor, or Sir Roderick MacLeod, 16th of MacLeod, was chief. So Rory Mor set up his third son, Sir Norman MacLeod (who commanded the regiment of MacLeods at the Battle of Worcester in 1651) as sub-chief in Berneray; and a new line of MacLeods of Berneray began. The same Rory Mor established his second son, also called Sir Roderick, as sub-chief of Talisker, a MacLeod district in western Skye. When the old society was demolished, Talisker was regarded as the private property of the then chief of MacLeod, although the sub-chiefs were allowed to take a lease of it. Donald MacLeod, 6th of Talisker, "sold the remainder of the lease of Talisker and emigrated to Tasmania in 1820", said *Burke's Landed Gentry*. The MacLeods of Harris had obtained charters to Talisker, and also, apparently, to Berneray, as well as to the rest of the MacLeod lands, and were therefore able after Culloden to treat these lands as their private property.[364]

The history of the Torquil MacLeods shows an example of the opposite process. Malcolm MacLeod, 9th of Lewis, who became chief of that branch of the MacLeods in 1511, instituted his second son, Malcolm Garbh, as sub-chief of Raasay. His third son, Norman, he made sub-chief of Eddrachillis. The Eddrachillis arrangement did not last long, for early in the sixteenth century the MacKays conquered the MacLeods there. But the Raasay line survived, and ultimately obtained charters to Raasay; so they were able to establish themselves as landlords after the '45. John MacLeod, 11th of Raasay, was therefore able to treat the island as his own personal property, and to begin evicting the MacLeod clansfolk in the early 1800s.

Among the Glengarry tacksmen – of whom details will be given later – MacDonald of Scottas had obtained a charter and was apparently able (when the changeover to private property occurred) to do some evicting on his own account, while MacDonald of Barrisdale, equally or more eminent as the head of a sept which could produce 150 men under arms, had no charter, and so was himself numbered among those on the receiving end of the new landlord methods.

63. Other names in the clan

Surnames appeared in England about the middle of the fourteenth century, but they were not customary in the Highlands until the last part of the seventeenth century, or even later. Before that time, a Highlander would be known by his or her given name, plus either a patronymic (which incorporated the father's name) or a by-name (having to do with some personal quality or peculiarity, some achievement, or some past incident).

After the emergence of surnames, most of the clansfolk would assume the common clan surname, but not all of them. When a number of Highlanders were being driven (directly or indirectly) out of their clan country, it was often the case that some of them would have a surname different from the main local name; but they would still have regarded themselves as full members of the clan which occupied that clan country. Over the centuries during which Gaelic society flourished, there was bound to be a certain amount of coming and going. This might be caused by several factors. When a chief married a woman from another clan, she would often bring some of her original clansmen and clanswomen with her; and these might stay on in the new country and settle there. As the Rev. Dr Norman MacLeod wrote: "It was customary of old, when a lady [that is, from a chief's or chieftain's family] married beyond her father's clan, as was generally the case, that she took with her two or more of her family followers, who always formed a sort of bodyguard to her, considering themselves entirely at her disposal."[365] (There are marriages now where the bride might benefit from some similar arrangement.) It must be remembered that although later on there were many writers who defended the landlords from the accusation that they were expelling the Highlanders by claiming that the dispersal was the result of the Highlands being "congested", in fact the Highlands were always very thinly populated. Newcomers who would help the existing inhabitants in their hunting and herding would always be welcome, and in such a sparsely peopled country there was always room for them. And while the rulers of the powerful neighbouring Lowlands were industriously stirring up trouble among the Gaels whenever they had a chance, no sept or group was likely to reject an accession of new blood.

Somerled MacMillan described how at different times in the history of the Keppoch MacDonalds they had been joined for various reasons by some Campbells (who then were called Glasserich, having come from Glassary parish), some MacGlashans (also Campbells originally; one of them became Keppoch's piper), some Stewarts (one Stewart became hereditary standard-bearer to Keppoch), some MacArthurs, some Kennedies, and even some Burkes and Boyles from Ireland. The latter had come when Alastair nan Cleas, 10th of Keppoch, married an Irish lady; the Boyles kept their name, but some of the Burkes took the name MacDonald.[366] (Dr MacLeod also mentioned having come across these Boyles and Burkes "in the very centre of Lochaber".)[367]

There were other Highlanders called Burke in the Outer Hebrides. The Gaels of the Highlands, not surprisingly, had in many ways a closer relationship with their fellow-Gaels in Ireland than they had with the Sassenach in the Lowlands. Among the half-dozen men who rode off the field of Culloden with Prince Charles in 1746 was Ned Burke, who had been born in North Uist.[368]

An earlier chief, Ronald MacDonald, 7th of Keppoch, married a daughter of MacIntosh of Kyllachy; some MacIntoshes came with her, and took up their residence in Lochaber.[349] When the clearances came, among those evicted were the descendants of all these incomers to the Keppoch clan.[370]

Somerled MacMillan also said that some MacIains of Ardnamurchan had "sought asylum in Lochaber and had changed their name to Cameron"; other recruits to the Cameron clan, he added, were "a few MacGregors from Balhaldie, Perthshire, who were then known as MacOilvan or White".[371] Yet further incomers were some MacKenzies, who took up their residence at North Ballachulish.[372] In contrast, when Janet Cameron, the daughter of Sir Ewen of Lochiel, married John Grant of Glenmoriston, she took some young men with her, including Donald MacSorlie, member of a Cameron sept. Outside Cameron territory, as usually happened, he took the main surname of his clan, and became known as Cameron; his son Alexander emigrated with his family to New York and then (when the American war broke out in 1775) to Canada, where *his* son Duncan, who had been born in Glen Moriston in 1764, became one of the founders of the North-West Trading Company, and ironically was involved in the struggle (as we shall see later in this work) against those other Gaelic immigrants, the Selkirk settlers, in what is now Manitoba.[373] Another daughter of the house of Lochiel married a Stewart of Kincardine; twelve young Cameron men, according to the tradition, went with her; and from them descended the Camerons who dwelt in the parishes of Abernethy and Kincardine.[374]

64. Newcomers to the clan

Another instance of Highlanders changing clans occurred when a sept of MacDonalds, known as the Clann Iain Uidhir, who originated in Ross-shire, settled among the Chisholms in Strathglass.[375] Again, when one of the Chisholm chiefs became enamoured of a Mrs MacRae in the neighbouring land of Kintail, the lady, accompanied by her son, came to Strathglass to live with the chief. From these descended the MacRaes of Strathglass, who lived and worked together with the Chisholms and considered themselves part of the Chisholm clan. When Donald Chisholm gave evidence to the Brand Commission in 1893 he recounted the names of the small tenants he remembered before the clearance in Glen Cannich, part of the Chisholm country. Of fifty tenants, twenty-nine were called Chisholm, eight MacRae, five MacKenzie, and four MacDonald or MacDonell; the four others were named MacGregor, MacLean, Fraser, and MacPherson. (The Chisholms' neighbours to the north were MacKenzies and Frasers, to the west

MacRaes, and to the south MacDonalds.) Nearly three-fifths of these Glen Cannich tenants bore the main clan surname, Chisholm, and the Chisholms and MacRaes together made up three-quarters of the number.[376]

When Mora Nian Ranald, the daughter of MacDonald of Moidart, married Malcolm Beg MacIntosh, chief of Clan Chattan, one of the men who went with her was called Revan, alias Roderic Mac Milmoir Vic Swen; his posterity, called Clan Revan or the MacQueens, came to regard themselves as part of Clan Chattan. Another who came with Mora was Donald Mac Gillandrish; from him descended the Clan Andrish – individually known as MacAndrew or Gillanders – who were also a sept of Clan Chattan.[377]

Another Highlander who moved was a MacDonald from Glengarry, who went to live in the country of the main Grant clan. When England and the Lowlands were at daggers drawn over the rival claims of James VII and II, and William of Orange, to the British throne, and each side tried to stir up the Highlanders to take part in the quarrel, the Jacobites attacked the Grant clan, who supported William. One of those killed in the fighting, T. B. Macaulay wrote, "was a MacDonald of the Glengarry branch, who had long resided among the Grants, [and] had become in feelings and opinions a Grant"; and who had therefore stayed with his adoptive clan, instead of joining the muster of the Glengarry MacDonalds, who were in arms for James.[378] Even so, Glengarry protested about his clansman having been killed. It will be noted that this MacDonald, now allied with the Grants, was showing yet again that the Highlanders, unlike the Lowland or English soldiers, had the liberty to decide for themselves whether (and for whom) to fight.

There were MacKinnons who lived in Lochaber. Mary MacKellar, the Lochaber poetess, wrote that "the ancestor of these MacKinnons had come from Skye" as one of the entourage of "a lady who married into the Lochiel family". This MacKinnon ancestor also married, and lived in the great forest, the Coille a' Ghiubhais bordering Loch Arkaig, though later the family had a place at Easter Moy: "to this day they are known in Lochaber as 'Sliochd Iain Maidh na Giubhsaich' " – from their first habitation.

Some Highlanders crossed the usual clan boundaries in other ways. Allan MacDonald, the heir of the chieftain of Moidart, was living at Locharkaigside in Cameron country when his father died; and a party of MacMillans, another of the Cameron septs, went back to Moidart with him. They were the origin of the MacMillans who from that time were part of the Clan Ranald, both on the mainland and in South Uist.[379] One of the fifteenth-century Shaws of Rothiemurchus, wrote A. M. Shaw in 1880, had a son Iver, whose "posterity settled in Harris and the Western Isles": a document of 1625 mentioned Donald Shaw of Harlosh and John Shaw of Trumpan, both in Skye, while "the posterity of Iver are still to be met with in Harris, where they are known as 'Clann Dhom'l 'ic Iomhair' or Iver".[380]

65. Movement within the Highlands

A colony of Shaws was settled in the Black Isle from the seventeenth century; they were called MacKays, after a Shaw whose first name was Aoidh.[381] Similarly, among the MacNachtans, or MacNaughtons, who lived in Argyllshire around the head of Loch Fyne, there were many MacKays, again taking their name after an ancestor named Aoidh. Though the main MacKay country was in northern Sutherland, there was another sept of MacKays, called Siol Thornais, in the south of Sutherland and in Ross-shire. The MacLeans were not all in the great MacLean lands, Mull, Morvern, Ardgour and so on; there were MacLeans at Dochgarroch, who belonged to Clan Chattan. A colony of MacIntoshes who were descended from a natural son of the seventh chief of MacIntosh settled in Strath Ardle and in Glen Shee.[382] There were other MacIntoshes in Glen Tilt, who later moved to Dalmunzie. Numbers of MacFarlanes settled in Aberdeenshire and Banffshire, where they were known as Allan or MacAllan, after their precursor Allan MacFarlane, younger son of a chief.[383] Some of the MacLeods of Assynt, known as the Sliochd Iain-mhoir, had moved two parishes northwards, and lived in Durness.[384] There were Camerons as far away from Lochaber as Cowal, and MacIntyres as far from Loch Etive as Badenoch. In Glendaruel, in Campbell country, there was a sept of Buchanans, not apparently related to the Lochlomondside Buchanans, and also a sept of MacGibbons or Gibsons. There seems to have been a sept in Islay called Keith, or Mac-cich – a long way from the main body of Keiths, in Caithness.

As we have seen, an individual, or a sept, might become transplanted in several different ways. A clan chief, on an expedition, might take under his protection a wandering bard, whose descendants would become part of the clan. Or there might be an affray which resulted in the death of one of the combatants: the man responsible, whether or not he had intended the death, might well flee to escape any repercussions, and would seek shelter in a distant clan, into which his progeny would become incorporated. For example, John Murray, writing in *An as Fhearann*, said that his ancestor, William Murray, a bow-maker, was (as might be expected from his surname) a Sutherland man; in 1607 William and two others became involved in an altercation with three local ministers called Pape (or, perhaps, Pope – a Sutherland family of ministers and tacksmen who had come originally from the Black Isle).[385] There was a struggle in Dornoch churchyard: in the fight Charles Pape wounded Murray in the face, and Murray retaliated with a blow that killed his opponent. Murray (to avoid any unpleasant consequences) fled to Lewis, where he became a blacksmith, and his descendant John Murray grew up in Barvas. The Murray family would quickly have become incorporated with the MacLeods of Lewis, and would soon have regarded themselves as members of that clan, though retaining their ancestral surname.

Another example of the same kind of transfer is recorded in a letter of which Boswell took a copy when he and Dr Johnson were staying with MacLean of Coll. The letter, which Boswell "found in Coll's cabinet", was from four men, all called Dougal Cameron (respectively of Strone, Barr, Inveriskvouilline, and Invinvalie). It was written in March 1737, and was addressed to their friend "the Laird of Coll", asking him to give shelter to "the bearer, Ewen Cameron, our cousin, son to the deceased Dougal MacConnill of Innermaillie, sometime in Glen Pean" – Dougal MacConnill being yet another Dougal Cameron (he was a MacLonich, which was a Cameron sept). Ewen was "alleged to have been accessory to the killing of one of MacMartin's family about fourteen years ago". He had gone "at Lochiel's desire to France, to gratify the MacMartins", but had now returned to Lochaber, where he had married. The MacMartins, however, were still intent on getting their revenge; so the letter asked if MacLean could harbour Ewen in Coll. He did harbour him, and his son (Boswell added) now had a farm from MacLean of Coll in Mull (where some of the Coll MacLeans lived).[386] Ewen's son would no doubt have by that time have regarded himself as part of the MacLean of Coll clan, though still keeping his ancestral name.

There were many eventualities that would lead to a man who was in every way a member of one clan, with his natural claim upon the land of that clan, having the surname more appropriate to another clan. This is a point to be remembered when in a clearance, say, of a MacDonald country, it is found that only three-quarters, or one-half, of those evicted actually bore the surname of MacDonald. The forebears of the others might have become members of the clan in the ways described above. Still others, of course, would be members of septs within the clan, families who traced their descent from some minor hero, perhaps the son or grandson of the founder of the clan, and still bore his name. The MacDonalds of Islay, for example, had septs with the names MacBeath, MacLaverty, and Darroch. Others, again, would be descended from small clans or septs which had become absorbed in larger clans, and which in every way were part of the larger clan.

66. Clan and name

To help differentiate between the possessors of the same name, "many families of the same descent", wrote Stewart, "had two names, one common to the whole clan, as MacDonald, MacLeod, etc., the other to distinguish a branch, which last was called the bun sloine, or genealogical surname, taken from the Christian name, or whatever designation marked the first man who branched off from the original family". Thus Campbell of Strachur was also called MacArthur, while the more familiar name of Campbell of Asknish was MacIvor. There were also MacIvors descended from Struan Robertson; the Clan Duilach, and the Camachas, were both septs within the Stewart of Garth clan; while some of the Stewarts of Appin were called Combich. It was the same "through nearly all the clans, tribes, and families, in the Highlands; never, at the same time, forgetting the proper surname of their chief, or stem of their family. Thus, all the MacArthurs of Strachur are Campbells, as are all the MacIvors of Argyllshire; while the MacIvors of Atholl and Breadalbane are Robertsons, and the Duilach, Camachas, and Combich, are Stewarts, and so sign their names, and are designated in all writings, while in common conversation the bun sloine, or genealogical surname, is their usual appellation."[387] The Jacobite from the Clan Ranald country of South Uist who escaped to France after the failure of the '45 was called Neil MacEachan; but outside the Highlands he went back to using the common clan surname, and so his son, who rose to high rank in Napoleon's army, appears in history as Marshal MacDonald.[388] The marshal's first cousin, Ranald MacEachan, was a Catholic priest in South Uist from 1782 to 1803;[389] two other Catholic priests from South Uist, about the same time, were known either as "MacEachan or MacDonald" (the Rev. Angus and the Rev. John).[390]

Others within the clan would be known by a patronymic, that is, by a designation including the father's name: Roderick, son of Lachlan, would be called Ruairidh Mac Lachlann. Sometimes the patronymic would include three or four generations. Smollett mentioned a hereditary captain of one of Argyll's castles, who was formally (or, no doubt, when in the Lowlands) known as Dougal Campbell: but more familiarly (to give Smollett's spelling) he was "Dou'l mac-amish mac-'oul ich-ian, signifying Dougal, the son of James, the son of Dougal, the son of John".[391] The N.S.A. report on Kilmuir mentioned the same point: a man's name might be (in the N.S.A. spelling) "Aonghas mac Alasdair, mhic Raonuill, mhic Uistein, mhic Cholla", that is to say Angus, son of Alexander, son of Ranald, son of Hugh, son of Coll.[392] Burt spelled out the patronymic of Donald Grant in this way: "Donald Bane Mac oil Vane Vic oil roi Vic ean", or "White-haired Donald Son of grey-haired Donald Grandson of red-haired Donald Great-grandson to John".[393] The Rosskeen parish reporter in the N.S.A. also remarked on the local use of patronymics, which helped to make a distinction among the many inhabitants called Donald Munro or John Ross. But the main clan surname (he said) was kept for all formal or official matters.[394] Another example was seen in the letter quoted above: Dougal Cameron of Innermaillie was also called MacConnill.

67. Identity of name

One author rejected the idea that a chief and his clansfolk shared the same surname, calling it a "quite untenable" view. Elsewhere in this work are mentioned the not uncommon cases where the members of a clan or sub-clan accepted as chief a man not of their own blood or name. But over most of the Highlands, despite all the examples given above, the evidence shows the clan surname was often common to the chief and to the majority of the clansfolk. "Many members of the clan", wrote David Stewart, "bore the same name with the chief",[395] and he gave a number of instances from his own day, or within what was then the recent past, even though the clan system had been under attack for the better part of a century. "On the estates of many noblemen and gentlemen, the number of their own surnames is often beyond all proportion greater than any others. On a part of the estate of the Laird of Menzies, running four miles along one side of a valley, on the banks of Tay, there are 502 of his name, descended of his family. Many similar instances are still to be met, where gentlemen have retained their ancient tenantry. In Atholl, an extensive district of Perthshire, there were, not many years ago, thirty-six land-holders of the name of Stewart; there are still twenty-three; and in Atholl, Strath Earn, and Menteith, there are nearly 4000 people of that name."[396]

Daniel Defoe, in his *Memoirs of a Cavalier*, wrote of the Highlanders in the Scots army in 1640: "they are in companies all of a name, and therefore call one another by his Christian name, as James, John, Rob, and Alister, that is Alexander, and the like."[397] It was much the same 150 years later. In the Sutherland Fencible Regiment of 1793, there had been, David Stewart wrote, 104 William MacKays – seventeen of them in one company (Captain Sackville Sutherland's).[398] When the second battalion of the 78th Ross-shire Highlanders was raised, in 1804, one ensign called Christopher MacRae brought twenty men with him, eighteen of them MacRaes.[399] Major Ross, of the 1778 Aberdeenshire Highland Regiment, said David Stewart, "was followed by so many of his own clan and name, that he had nine men of the name of John Ross".[400] In fact "name" was a common synonym for "clan". As we saw above, the eldest son of the chief of the MacLeods of Lewis was not chosen chief himself because he was "not popular among the name". In 1786 Norman MacLeod of MacLeod wrote to his superior officers, "My own company are all of my own name and clan . . ."[401] Burt said that among Highlanders "the whole clan, or name", would assist each other against enemies.[402] Simon Fraser, younger of Beaufort, later of Lovat, in a letter of 1696 to the Governor of Fort William, called the Fraser clan "the whole name of Fraser", three times wrote "the name" as synonymous with the clan, and then pointed out that "the whole name . . . have unanimouslie joyned with me".[403] Alexander Cunningham used the phrase "sameness of name" to denote clanship.[404] Campbell of Stonefield, touring the

Argyll estates in 1732, criticized a farm held by a MacLean tacksman and a "swarm of poor people of his own name".[405]

It seems, therefore, after making due allowance for all the exceptions and qualifications, that the common opinion as to the identity of name between a Highland chief and his clan is also, in the majority of cases, substantially the correct one.

Each clan believed that it was simply a large family, descended from one ancestor. The very word clan is taken from the Gaelic term for children. In the MacLeod clan, for example, a man was called Mac Leoid, son of Leoid; a woman Nic Leoid, daughter of Leoid;[406] and the whole body of people Clann Leoid, children of Leoid. Thus the clan was believed to be formed of the descendants of Leod, and bore his name. Septs of the clan, that is smaller tribes within the clan, would sometimes trace their descent from a more recent clan celebrity, but all descended ultimately from this one progenitor. Even when the improvements had brought poverty to many of the clansfolk, they still took comfort in their knowledge of their ancestors. As the minister of Greenock wrote in the O.S.A.: "It is not uncommon with the poorest people from the Highlands to boast of their descent from some great family or other", which helped to make up for their poverty.[407] Dr Robertson remarked in 1808 that the Highlanders counted themselves as descended from some renowned chief, and kindred of their own chieftain. "It inspires them with a certain elevation of mind"; this gave them "consequence in their own eyes, and they aspire to obtain the same consequence in the opinion of others".[408]

There was a drawback, however, Robertson thought; this attitude was "perhaps unfriendly to the drudgery of continued labour", and since this same "drudgery of continued labour" was the destiny which their betters had decided on for most of the Highlanders, this pride of family had to be (and was) extinguished in due course among the congested tenements of the big cities.

68. Twelve generations

Even in the twentieth century, Alastair Alpin MacGregor wrote that among that minority of the Highlanders who managed to stay in the Highlands "the verbal repetition of entire genealogical tables dating back several centuries, was looked upon not as an unusual feat of memory, but as a piece of everyday knowledge. All clansmen worthy of the name strove to acquaint themselves with the lineage of their chieftain, as also their own descent; and shame upon him who exhibited uncertainty on matters of clan genealogy . . . I know a number of old people in Lewis who can trace descent back ten or twelve generations with the utmost ease and assurance."[409] David Livingstone was born in the Lowlands, but his grandfather, from Ulva, "could rehearse the traditions of the family for six generations before him".[410] James Shaw Grant in 1977 wrote of meeting two crofters. One of them said his family had been on the same spot "in the village of Aird since they first came to Benbecula from Ardgour in 1631. His companion could not be so specific in regard to the location of the family residence because his croft in the village of Kyles Paible is one of those constituted in modern times, following the breaking up of the farms, but he knew that his ancestors had been in Uist since 1400, and was able to give me his genealogy back to that date, naming the members of his family who had fought at Sheriffmuir, and those who had taken part in an even earlier historic raid on Orkney."[411] In 2004 was published *Roots of Stone*, in which a Highlander casually followed his family back some 1800 years, to Conn of the Hundred Battles, who ruled Ireland in the second century A.D.[412] (It would be a very rare Lowlander, or English person, who could match that; in modern society the ability to know, or to find out, one's family history, is, like many other desirable things, mainly restricted to the more affluent.)

Such was the accepted theory of the origin of the clan, although naturally in the course of time all clans received accessions of the kind mentioned above. A clan member could usually recite the whole lineage of the chief reaching back to the founder of the clan, and more important, could recite his or her own lineage back to the chiefly line, or back to the time when his or her ancestor came into the clan. "They have a pride in their family", said Burt; "almost everyone is a genealogist."[413] They were familiar from the cradle with the stories of the deeds of the generations who were the common ancestors of the chief and themselves. According to this theory, the chief and the clansfolk shared a common heritage. The chief might be the first-born, but all the members of the clan were brothers and sisters.

69. No foundation

Those who destroyed the clan society, especially the clan chiefs among them, scouted the whole idea. The belief in blood relationship, said the eighth Duke of Argyll, "in nine cases out of ten had no foundation whatever". Argyll ridiculed the theory, and told a story about a gamekeeper who called himself Grant when he lived in the Grant country, and MacPherson when he moved over the border to the MacPherson country.[414] This derision did not extend to landlords, such as the proprietor in the early nineteenth century who was a MacPherson – of Invereshie – on his father's side, and a Grant – of Ballindalloch – on his mother's, and who inherited estates from both sides; and then called himself by both names – choosing to be known as MacPherson Grant, not Grant MacPherson, because the Grant estate was the larger one, thus ignoring the fact that he had been born a MacPherson.[415] In effect he was calling himself Grant in the Grant country, being a landlord there, and MacPherson in the MacPherson country, being a landlord *there*: but since he was a landowner, no one felt that this was a subject for jest. Nor did anyone in the twenty-first century criticize John MacLeod of MacLeod for having assumed that name; his father's name was Wolrige Gordon, and his mother's maiden name was Walter – he had had to go back to his grandmother's maiden name to re-christen himself satisfactorily. And, of course, some people do change their names. Numbers of people are known to contemporaries and to history by names which are not really theirs, if everyone had to be called by the surname of their direct male ancestors.[416] But if chiefs and landlords are to be allowed the licence to amend their names, why should that liberty be denied to clansfolk?

The important thing about the blood-relationship theory is not whether it was correct or not – but that it was commonly believed. For a theory to have endured so long, and to have gained such widespread and unquestioned acceptance, it must have corresponded – and did correspond – to the actual attitude of the Highlanders towards the other members of their clans, and to their way of living within the clan. For within the clan, all men and women *were* brothers and sisters. The Gaelic clansfolk's watchwords were fellowship, fairness and freedom;[417] and the standards set by those watchwords were the actual standards of clan society. There was a marked degree of equality among the members of the clan in their relationship to the land. The clanspeople worked together on the tasks of the day, and helped each other in times of adversity, not because they were morally – or racially – better than the citizens of modern societies, or had a different kind of "human nature" (if there are different kinds of "human nature", mutually exclusive, then the phrase is clearly meaningless), but because that was the way in which their society was organized. Fraternity was then not merely the catch phrase of an otherwise bankrupt politician: it was a way of life. And fraternity or fellowship, camaraderie or comradeship, was the keynote of the Highlanders' beliefs in their origins.

In the same way, the theory of blood relationship ran so counter to the behaviour of the chiefs towards their clans in the eighteenth and nineteenth centuries that the chiefs had to reject it. It no longer corresponded to the kind of society which was then coming into existence in the Highlands; therefore it had to be denounced as false. This is one of those cases where a theory is found acceptable or otherwise not because of its intrinsic strength or weakness, but because of extraneous factual developments.

In the case of most or all of the clans, it is probably no longer possible to determine whether the theory of the common origin of the clan is true or not. One can only say that while oral tradition is by no means invariably true, it is true – or contains important elements of the truth – far more often than modern man, who relies so heavily on paper documents or electronic records, would think possible. The oral traditions and the genealogies that were possessed by every clan, together with the Gaelic meaning of the very word clan, seem strong presumptive evidence. More than that one cannot say.

CHAPTER THREE NOTES

1. *Lowland fiction*
[1] Grant & Cheape 2000, 156. What Scott wrote here must be rejected, because it fails the test of the archive of the head; but that is not to say that everything Scott wrote about the Highlands must be dismissed. Where any written document passes that essential test it is entitled to be considered in the same way as any other source.

2. *Campbell of Canna*
[2] Campbell 1994, viii-ix.

3. *Hereditary right to their farms*
[3] Burt 2005, 225-6.
[4] Burt 2005, 301.

4. *In full possession of their holdings*
[5] Lord Advocate prosecuting James Stewart of the Glen, 22nd Sept 1752. George Malcolm Thomson (Thomson 1970, 170) mentioned the same point in the Lord Advocate's speech: "in the Highlands, there was a particular prejudice against evicting a man from land which, however wrongly, he believed to be his." (Brian Ettlinger, mentioned in the Foreword, was G. M. Thomson's son-in-law.)
[6] Anon. 1771.
[7] Pennant 1998, 366 fn.
[8] Marshall 1794, 24. In former times, Marshall said, possession depended "on force of arms, rather than on legal right [i.e., according to Lowland law] . . . Under these circumstances, and more particularly in the times of disturbance, the tenants might be said to be in full possession of their respective holdings; neither the chieftain nor his chamberlain dared to remove them . . ."

5. *Their property*
[9] Selkirk 2010, 8; Selkirk 1806, 14.
[10] Selkirk 2010, 36; Selkirk 1806, 123.
[11] Richards 1973, 181, quoting Selkirk in a letter of 12th June 1813.
[12] MacKenzie 1810, 294.
[13] MacNeill 1851, xxvi, 902.
[14] Richards 1973, 275, quoting James Loch.
[15] Gaskell 1980, 1.
[16] Celtic Magazine VIII 156 (February 1883).
[17] Richards 1999, 365.
[18] Napier 1884, V 8.
[19] Joseph Chamberlain, quoted in Thompson 1974, 62; & in *Highland Clearances*, A. MacKenzie, 2nd edition, O'Callaghan, Glasgow, 1914, 263; & in Brander 1980, 195-6. (Joseph Chamberlain came from a London family – he went to U.C.S. – though now he is always associated with Birmingham.)

6. *No better title*
[20] Sorley MacLean, *Gaelic Society of Inverness* XXXVIII, *Poetry of Clearances*, 299.
[21] Sutherland 1825, 102.
[22] Website chebucto.ns.co/heritage.
[23] Quoted in Prebble 1971, 322.

[24] Grant & Cheape 2000, 252.
[25] Grant & Cheape 2000, 252.

7. *Owners in common*
[26] MacDonald 1904, III 155.
[27] Rev. Angus MacKay, *Book of MacKay*, Norman MacLeod, Edinburgh, 1906, 232-3.
[28] Duncan MacLaren, 1800-86, Lord Provost of Edinburgh 1851-4, MP for Edinburgh 1865-81, brother-in-law of John Bright.
[29] Murdoch 1986, 21.
[30] Omand 1973, 137.
[31] Hugh Miller, *Leading Articles*, Nimmo, Edinburgh 1870, Filiquarian reprint 2011, 235-6.
[32] MacLeod 1892, 173, quoting Sismondi.
[33] Mathieson 2000, 50.
[34] MacLean 1889, 365.
[35] Darling 1955, 1 (& quoted Richards 1985, 122).
[36] J. MacMaster Campbell, *Home Life of the Highlanders*, chapter on Organization & Tenures, website electricscotland.
[37] Adam/Innes 1965, 86.
[38] Website angusmacleodarchive.org.uk.

8. *Charters of possession*
[39] J. J. Galbraith, *Gaelic Society of Inverness* XXXVIII, *Parish in the Highlands*, 465.
[40] MacDonell 1937, 14, 26.
[41] Grant 1987, 126, 129.
[42] Napier 1884, II 1163, qu. 17708, Dr Roderick Ross; & Grant 1987, 135.
[43] J. B. Caird, 1919-89, Inspector of Schools for Ross & Cromarty; professor of Dundee University.
[44] Linklater 1962, xv-xvi.
[45] F. Gillanders, *West Highland Economy*, Transactions of Gaelic Society of Inverness, XLIII 255.
[46] Pine 1972, 13.
[47] Tom Weir, *Western Highlands*, Batsford, London, 1973, 102, 170.
[48] MacLean & Carrell 1986, 104.
[49] Atkinson 1987, 7.
[50] J. Hunter, *Skye the Island*, Mainstream, Edinburgh, 1986, 147.
[51] G. Jarvie, *Highland Games, the Making of the Myth*, University Press, Edinburgh, 1991, 45.
[52] A. Scott, *Native Stranger*, Little Brown, London, 1995, 93.
[53] Bain 1960, 24, 21. Bain's book was very successful. First published in 1938, by 1960 there had been fifteen new editions or reprints. I have two of them, and it is interesting to see that the 1947 edition had a foreword by the Duke of Montrose, and the 1960 edition had a foreword by the Countess of Erroll. Does this mean that these two leading members of the present bodies representing the Scottish chiefs agreed that before 1745 the clans, not the chiefs, owned the land? Or does it mean that they had not read the book to which they were contributing a foreword?
[54] Napier 1884, IV 2798, qu. 42017, Rev. John MacTavish.

9. *No known concept*
[55] Smout 1970, 45.
[56] Gray 1957 (2), 31.
[57] Devine 1998, 26.
[58] Moncreiffe 1967, 27.
[59] Moncreiffe 1967, 251, quoting Dundee 1965.
[60] Donald Campbell, *Caledonians and Scots*, Nimmo, Edinburgh, 1861, 37.

10. *Origin of the chiefs*
[61] Seton Gordon 1951, 12.
[62] Burke 1891, article on MacKenzie of Gairloch.

11. *The chief's name*
[63] "Ilk" meant originally "same", but because of this usage in the name of Highland chiefs it has come to mean "kind" or "sort".
[64] Seton Gordon 1951, 15.
[65] Moncreiffe 1967, 153.
[66] E.g. in Johnson & Boswell 1930, 139.
[67] Seton Gordon 1951, 14; Adam/Innes 1965, 583 fn.

12. *King and country*
[68] O.S.A. XIX 297, Aboyne Aberd.
[69] Grant of Laggan 1806, I 221.
[70] Hogg 1981, 93-4.
[71] Napier 1884, I 147, qu. 2808, Norman Munro.
[72] Defoe 1974, 411.
[73] Johnson & Boswell 1930, 25.
[74] Burt 2005, 227.
[75] Pennant 2000, 82.
[76] O.S.A. IV 119, Kirkhill Inv.
[77] O.S.A. I 267, Kiltearn Ross.
[78] Selkirk 2010, Appendix A.

13. *Many miniature courts*
[79] Macaulay 1907, 422, 425. Zachary Macaulay's sister Jean married Thomas Babington of "Rothley Temple", now Rothley Court, in Leicestershire; Zachary himself married Serena Mills, and their son Thomas was born at Rothley (and was called Thomas Babington Macaulay). When Macaulay received a peerage, he called himself Lord Macaulay of Rothley. Rothley Court, birthplace of Macaulay, is now a hotel; I have stayed there.
[80] Thomson 1788, 219 fn.

14. *Fidelity of the clans*
[81] Sir Walter Scott, *Miscellaneous Prose Works*, Baudry, Paris, 1838, VII 192.
[82] Stewart 1822, II 19.
[83] Stewart 1822, I 126 fn.
[84] Stewart 1822, I 147 fn.
[85] MacLeod 1905, 356-62.

15. *Cat o' nine tails*
[86] Stewart 1822, I 60-1; & II xxxix-xl.
[87] N.S.A. XIV 316, Strath Inv, & Nicolson 1930, 251.
[88] Fraser 1987, 27, & MacLean 1988, 294.

16. *Authority of the chiefs*
[89] Johnson & Boswell 1930, 77.
[90] Lang 1898, ix, xi.
[91] Halliday 1996, 120.

[92] Cregeen 1993, 140.
[93] Glover 1966, 93.
[94] Steel 1994, 61.
[95] Trevor-Roper 1983, 22.
[96] Youngson 1974, 17.
[97] Muir 1985, 159.
[98] Trevelyan 1949, 49.
[99] He was O.M., C.B.E., F.R.S., & F.B.A.; and had honorary doctorates from many universities. He turned down a knighthood, and probably turned down a peerage.
[100] Trevelyan 1946, 448, 453. Trevelyan was conscious of his position as a member of Britain's upper class. His elder brother Charles inherited the family baronetcy, its three houses, and its 22,000 acres. George wrote to him, "the world [or rather, the current economic system] has given us money enough to enable us to do what we think right: we thank it for that, and ask no more of it, but to be allowed to serve." G. M. Trevelyan's "service" included confirming and propagating the orthodox view of Highland history. He demonstrated his grasp of political rectitude, and displayed his credentials for criticizing civic structures, by describing Mussolini, the brutal fascist dictator of Italy, as "a man of genius", and "a very sincere patriot" (David Cannadine, *G. M. Trevelyan*, Fontana London 1993, 83).
[101] Smout 1970, 344, 345, 347.
[102] Cregeen 1993, 140.

17. *Ad vitam aut culpam*
[103] Agnes Mure MacKenzie, 1941, 42.
[104] Jamieson 2005, xl, xli, xli fn.
[105] Burt 2005, 193, 219.
[106] MacDonald 1978, 152.
[107] MacNicol 1779, 103.
[108] Stewart 1822, I 28 & 28 fn.
[109] Stewart 1822, I 58.
[110] Stewart 1822, II i fn.
[111] Stewart 1822, II 2 xxxvii.

18. *Good will of the tribe*
[112] Cosmo Innes, 1798-1874; antiquary, sheriff, and professor. The life of Innes is evidence that even very successful people do not have to be blind to society's injustices.
[113] Innes 1872, 156-7.
[114] Burt 2005, 272.
[115] Grant of Laggan 1811, I 207 & 208.
[116] N.S.A. VII 669, Kilarrow Arg.
[117] Stewart 1822, I 50-1 fn.
[118] Stewart 1822, I 51 fn.
[119] Rev. L. Shaw, *History of the Province of Moray*, Grant, Elgin, (1775) 1827, 274.
[120] Nicolson 1930, 267, 150, 178.
[121] Stewart 1822, I 57, & II xl fn.
[122] Stewart 1822, II xxv fn.
[123] Smollett 1967, 278.

19. *Twelve men fully armed*
[124] MacKay 1914, 158-9.
[125] Stewart 1822, I 101-2 fn.
[126] O.S.A. III 354-5 fn, Glenorchy Arg.

[127] MacKay 1914, 164. MacKay gave Lindsay's Christian name as Dugald; so did MacIntyre.

20. *Ignored the sentence*
[128] N.S.A. XIV 104, Moy Inv.
[129] The O.S.A. minister of Petty said Dunoon officiated from 1684 until 1718 (O.S.A. III 32); the N.S.A. minister agreed that Dunoon arrived in 1684, but claimed he died in 1709 – an obvious misprint, because he had just told of further official efforts to get rid of him in 1711 and perhaps in 1712 (N.S.A. XIV 408-9). So Dunoon remained in his parish for twenty-nine years after the Lowland authorities told him to go.
[130] N.S.A. XIV 277, Rosskeen Ross.
[131] N.S.A. XIV 119, Lochcarron Ross.
[132] MacLeod 1997, 146, 213.
[133] MacKay 1914, 165.
[134] MacKay 1914, 165.
[135] MacKay 1914, 167.
[136] Sage 1975, 2.
[137] MacKay 1914, 181.
[138] MacKay 1914, 181.
[139] MacKay 1914, 166.

21. *Edinburgh intrusions*
[140] O.S.A. VIII 491 fn, Muthill Perth.
[141] O.S.A. XI 596 fn, Callander Perth.
[142] Stewart 1822, I 134.
[143] N.S.A. XIV 328, Kiltearn Ross.
[144] Stewart 1822, I 56-7 fn.
[145] Moncreiffe 1967, 125.
[146] Stewart 1822, I 57.

22. *Many voices against one*
[147] Johnson & Boswell 1930, 286. Incidentally, this is the only example I have come across of the surname "MacFriar", in over half a century of studying Highland records.
[148] Johnson & Boswell 1930, 287.
[149] Douglas 1975, 194. The "Seven Men of Glen Moriston" were Patrick Grant; John MacDonald; Alexander MacDonald; Alexander, Donald, and Hugh Chisholm (brothers); and Gregor MacGregor. Hugh MacMillan joined them a little later (Linklater 1976, 114).

23. *Chiefs as war-leaders*
[150] Tytler 1874, 125.
[151] Mitchison 1970, 30.
[152] Stewart 1822, I 65.
[153] Stewart 1822, II xxxvii.
[154] Lang 1898, xl.
[155] Lenman 1995, 122.
[156] Stewart 1822, II xxxvii.
[157] Lenman 1995, 172.

24. *View of the clan*
[158] Stewart 1822, II 294-5.
[159] Stewart 1822, II 295.

[160] MacDonell 1937, 17.
[161] Hunter 2006, 83.

25. *Chose their commanders*
[162] J. MacKechnie, *Clan MacLean*, Johnston & Bacon, Edinburgh, n.d., 21.
[163] R. Forbes, *Lyon in Mourning*, University Press, Edinburgh, 1895, II 209.
[164] Hopkins 1998, 59.
[165] Hopkins 1998, 138.
[166] Hopkins 1998, 64.
[167] Stewart 1822, II xxxvii.
[168] Trevelyan 1946, 453.
[169] Shaw 1880, 361.
[170] Shaw 1880, 369.
[171] Shaw 1880, 376.

26. *In all things subservient*
[172] Thomson 2010, 62, 63, 64, quoting Cunningham 1787.
[173] Scott 1925, 39, 170, 201. To repeat what was said earlier, much of what Scott says is valuable confirmation of contemporary evidence, since it is accepted by the archive of the head; but where that archive cannot accept it, Scott's words – and anyone else's, of which the same is true – must be rejected.
[174] Glover 1966, 93, 209.
[175] Steel 1994, 61, 120-1.
[176] Wilkinson 1936, 78.
[177] MacLean 1988, 146.
[178] Agatha Christie, *The Mysterious Affair at Styles*, Diamond, London, (1920) 1993, 69 (chapter five).

27. *A private quarrel*
[179] MacDonald 1994, 46.
[180] Douglas 1975, 111.
[181] MacLean 1988, 169, 188.
[182] Wilkinson 1936, 193-4.
[183] MacLean 1988, 165.

28. *Clan recruitment*
[184] E. J. Cowan & R. Finlay, *Scotland since 1688*, Cima, London, 2000, 65. These authors, indeed, had a brisk entry in their index (p. 191), "famine/clearances"; if each clearance was the result of famine, as this entry strongly implies, then no further defence is required.

29. *Not used to subjection*
[185] Thomson 2010, 62-3, quoting Cunningham 1787.
[186] Lang 1898, 65.
[187] Barnes & Allen 1956, 151.
[188] Stevenson 1954, 77.
[189] Stewart 1822, II xl.

30. *Highlanders' arms*
[190] Grant & Cheape 2000, 199.
[191] Adam/Innes 1965, 374.
[192] Adam/Innes 1965, 352.
[193] Stewart 1822, II xxi.

[194] Adam/Innes 1965, 354.
[195] Adam/Innes 1965, 353.
[196] Adam/Innes 1965, 55; cf. Smout 1970, 112.
[197] Adam/Innes 1965, 56. In 1616 a further Act specifically forbade the carrying of hagbuts and pistols, except in the king's service (Shaw 1880, 300 fn); it was also ignored in the Highlands.

31. *Muskets and pistols*
[198] Stewart 1822, II xxiii.
[199] Shaw 1880, 299-300.
[200] John Taylor, Water-Poet, quoted in Hume Brown 1891, 121, Seton Gordon 1949, 381, Rixson 2004, 224.
[201] Shaw 1880, 314.
[202] Grimble 1973, 82.
[203] Scott 1925, 179, 179 fn.
[204] Thomas Kirk, *Travels in Scotland 1677 & 1681*, ed. Hume Brown, Douglas, Edinburgh, 1892, 29.
[205] Moncreiffe 1967, 73.
[206] Shaw 1880, 397.
[207] MacDonald 1994, 148.
[208] Sacheverell 1859, 99. William Sacheverell, Governor of the Isle of Man, visited Mull in 1688; the first edition of his book was published in 1702, the second in 1859. So it was in the seventeenth century that Sacheverell made his observation about the Highlanders having "a large shot-pouch", strategically placed below the front of the waist; this is surely the sporran (sporan bring the Gaelic word for a purse or pouch), though Michael Fry claims – no doubt in order to try to disallow as far as possible any "distinct Highland culture and tradition" – that the sporran was "invented about 1770" (Fry 2005, 183).
[209] Scott 1900, 142.

32. *Armed wherever they go*
[210] Bishop Nicholson, quoted in Blundell 1909, 122.
[211] Martin 1703, 210.
[212] G. H. Healey, *Letters of Daniel Defoe*, O.U.P., London, 1955, 147.
[213] Rae, *History of Rebellion of 1715*, quoted Stewart 1822, I 69 fn.
[214] Defoe 1974, II 426.
[215] Lovat, *Edinburgh Magazine*, July 1817, 399 & 400.
[216] Grant & Cheape 2000, 197; & Dodgshon, *Age of the Clans*, Birlinn, Edinburgh, 2002, 43.
[217] Burt 2005, 249.
[218] Mitchison 1970, 31; & Devine 1998, 21.
[219] Anon. 1747, 20, 18.
[220] H. R. Duff, editor, *Culloden Papers*, Cadell & Davies, London, 1815, 299.
[221] John Lorne Campbell, *Highland Songs of the Forty-Five*, (1933) 1979, Arno Press, New York, 251, has the full chauvinistic verse of MacCodrum's *A Song Against the Lowland Garb*:
Not a mother's son you saw on street or on parade-ground,
Finer than the Gael, of truly splendid presence;
Kilted tartan wearing, his sword behind his buckler,
His pistols so well oiled the flint straightway fires the priming;
His shield upon his shoulder, his slim gun beneath his armpit,
No foreigner alive but would expire before the vision.
[222] John Campbell, *Full Description of the Highlands of Scotland*, printed for the author, London, 1752, 17.
[223] Johnson & Boswell 1930, 40.

33. *Every man bore arms*
[224] Gilpin 1789, II 139.
[225] Gilpin 1808, I 169-70.
[226] Stewart 1822, I, 69 & 242.
[227] Stewart 1822, I 98, quoting Dalrymple 1771.
[228] Scott 1900, 228 fn.
[229] John Home, *History of the Rebellion in Scotland in 1745*, Brown, Edinburgh, (1802) 1822, 8.
[230] O.S.A. II 457, Fortingall Perth.
[231] O.S.A. XVII 383, Killin Perth.
[232] Thomson 1788, 215 (Thomson 2010, 64).
[233] Cregeen 1970, 8.
[234] Macaulay 1907, 427.
[235] Stewart 1822, I 101-2 fn.
[236] Atholl 1908, I 389.
[237] Grant & Cheape 2000, 197, quoting the Wardlaw Manuscript.
[238] Grant & Cheape 2000, 87, 196.
[239] Gilpin 1799, II 137.
[240] *Imperial Dictionary of Universal Biography*, MacKenzie, Glasgow, 1857-63, article Ferrara.
[241] Scott 1900, 292.
[242] Scott 1925, 38, 148.

34. *Named fire-arms*
[243] Grant & Cheape 2000, 197.
[244] N.S.A. XIV 176 fn, Kintail Ross.
[245] A. MacLeod, editor, *Songs of Duncan Ban MacIntyre*, Oliver & Boyd, Edinburgh, 1952, 226.
[246] Grant & Cheape 2000, 200-1; & G. F. Maine, ed., *Book of Scotland,* Collins, London, 1959, 146.
[247] Stewart 1822, I 118.
[248] Grant & Cheape 2000, 199.
[249] See, e.g., the website ncgenweb.us/cumberland/doncamscalpay.html.
[250] MacKay 1914, 245-6 ("Godh'na", on p. 246, should be "Gobh'na").
[251] Grant & Cheape 2000, 197.
[252] Bowman 1986, 64.
[253] Garnett 1811, I 114.
[254] See, e.g., the website weebly.com, McKeegan and MacEachan; & Grant & Cheape 2000, 82, 93.
[255] MacMillan 1971, 160.
[256] Grant & Cheape 2000, 201-2.
[257] Finlay 1966, 44-5.
[258] When the Black Watch was ordered to America, "new arms and accoutrements were supplied to the men, together with broadswords and pistols, iron-stocked" (Stewart 1822, I 367; & see I 399); and Stewart said "a dirk . . . together with a pair of steel pistols, were essential accompaniments" to Highland dress (ditto, I 78).
[259] W. Douglas Simpson, *Dunvegan Castle*, University Press, Aberdeen, 1968, 24.

35. *A constant firing*
[260] Stewart 1822, II xxv.

36. *Dougal Roy Cameron*
[261] N.S.A. XIV 121, Kilmallie Inv (the reporter spelled it Dugal); Stewart 1822, II xl.
[262] Stewart 1822, I 272, & II xl.

37. Well qualified for war
[263] Macaulay 1907, 430.
[264] Miller 1854, 40; Youngson 1973, 13.
[265] Johnson & Boswell 1930, 82-3.
[266] Barnes & Allen 1956, 60.
[267] Defoe 1974, 389, 427.
[268] Trevelyan 1946, 453.
[269] Linklater 1962, xi.

38. Secrecy, despatch, and address
[270] Stewart 1822, II liv-lv.

39. Kingdom in confusion
[271] Smollett 1967, 291.
[272] Mawman 1805, 160.
[273] Stewart 1822, II 23, & II 49-50.

40. Tribute to the chiefs
[274] St Paul, *First Epistle to Timothy*, chapter six verse 10.

41. Appearance of crofters
[275] Trevelyan 1946, 447. On the question of high or low rents in the old days, see chapter three, subsection 45, *Lochiel's tribute*, and subsection 46, *Violence in Scalpay*. Perhaps Trevelyan was relying on J. A. MacCulloch, who gave an inaccurate description of clan society (MacCulloch 1905, 217): "The tacksman frequently kept the best part of the land for himself, and rented out the worst parts to the subtenants at exorbitant rates out of all proportion to the value of the land." This cannot be true, since it would require us to believe that the chiefs, who by then were more and more becoming ambitious to take over their clans' land for themselves (and many of whom were engaging in any commercial pursuit they could think of), stood contentedly aside and watched their tacksmen-tenants pocket lots of money which the chiefs/landlords could easily have appropriated for themselves. This is not a likely outcome anyway, but certainly not in the eighteenth century when the chiefs/landlords were devoting themselves whole-heartedly to the gratifying task of getting rich as quickly as possible. No doubt MacCulloch got his "facts" about the tacksmen, whose supposed misbehaviour justified the chiefs in driving them out of the Highlands, from MacLeod of MacLeod, to whom MacCulloch gave a sycophantic dedication – "what chief is there who is so beloved of his clansmen all over the world as you?", and who, said MacCulloch, had interested himself in the book's "making and in its publication". The attention paid by landlords to authors is certainly explicable, since the resulting books, as in this instance, stick closely to the politically correct view of history (see the reference, p. 219 fn, to "Skye, where it is doubtful how far clearances were resorted to", though of course it is in reality not "doubtful" in the slightest).
[276] O.S.A. II 453, Fortingall Perth.
[277] See above, chapter one notes, subsection 62, *Less fine feelings*, note 322.
[278] Adam Smith (Smith 1895, 118), in *The Wealth of Nations*, said that as early as 1776, "the rents of many Highland estates have been tripled and quadrupled"; and that was only the beginning.

42. Small farmers dispossessed
[279] O.S.A. III 25, Petty Inv.
[280] O.S.A. XIII 517, Kiltarlity Inv.
[281] O.S.A. VIII 62 fn, Gigha & Cara Arg.
[282] O.S.A. VII 254, Urray Ross.

[283] O.S.A. II 560, Rosskeen Ross.
[284] O.S.A. XIV 241-2, Kilfinan Arg.
[285] O.S.A. VIII 96-8 fn, Kilmartin Arg.
[286] MacKenzie 1813, 83.
[287] Wordsworth 1894, 141.
[288] Stewart 1822, I 156.
[289] Stewart 1822, I 176.
[290] Lord Teignmouth, *Sketches of the Coasts of Scotland*, Parker, London, 1836, I 44.

43. Designedly inadequate
[291] "Sir John Sinclair . . . reckoned that the typical crofter had to be able to obtain at least 200 days of additional work outside his holding in order to avoid chronic destitution and crofts were in fact reduced in size in order to force the crofter and his family into other employments. The holding itself should only provide partial subsistence and to make ends meet and afford the rental the crofter and his family had to have recourse to supplementary jobs" (Devine 1998, 47-48).
[292] An *Undiscovered Scotland* website said that during the Sutherland clearances an eye-witness saw "250 crofts on fire" in Strath Naver, implying that this happened before 1816. Firstly, the eye-witness, Donald MacLeod, saw this in 1819; secondly, a croft was a piece of land, not a habitation, or anything else which could be burnt; and thirdly, the small tenants being put out were the old joint-farmers, not crofters at all.
[293] M. Campbell, *Argyll, the Enduring Heartland*, Turnstone, London, 1977, 176.
[294] Simpson 1975, 107-8, evictions in Lewis; & 18, 26, 27, 28, 29, crofts & crofting.

44. A patch of ground
[295] Gray 1957 (2), 31.
[296] Somerset Fry 1985, 199.
[297] Lynch 1996, 377.
[298] Way & Squire 1994, 15.
[299] C. V. Wedgwood, *Montrose*, A. Sutton, Stroud, 1995, 140.
[300] Moncreiffe 1967, 27.
[301] Schama 2001, 386.
[302] M. Adam, *Scottish Historical Review*, XVI, 1919, 296.
[303] Compare MacLeod 1910, 135: "The 'upper' and 'lower' classes in the Highlands were not separated from each other by a wide gap."
[304] Trevelyan 1946, 447.

45. Lochiel's tribute
[305] Selkirk 2010, 66.
[306] Adam 1972, I 229.
[307] J. S. Gibson, *The Gentle Lochiel*, NMS, Edinburgh, 1998, gives the figure of 800 (page 38), and the figure of 900 (page 36) as the number of soldiers Lochiel brought to the Jacobite army. In an earlier book (Gibson 1995, 71) he put the number at 700. I have taken 800, as the average of the three figures. 800 was also the figure given in the 1746 memorial about the clans as the number of soldiers which the Cameron clan could muster.
[308] Hopkins 1998, 59.
[309] Or perhaps somewhat more: Gibson 1995, 35.
[310] Smith 1895, 314.
[311] Stewart 1822, I 62-3 fn; & see I 146 – formerly an ox was thirty shillings, & a sheep half-a crown.

46. Violence in Scalpay

[312] Burt 2005, 193.
[313] O.S.A. XVII 384, Killin Perth.
[314] Atholl 1908, I 444.
[315] Richards 1999, 250.
[316] Adam 1972, II 82.
[317] Fraser 1892, I 1105.
[318] O.S.A. VIII 443, Kilmallie Inv.
[319] O.S.A. XIX 22, Halkirk Caith.
[320] Pennant 1998, 366 fn.
[321] O.S.A. VIII 402, Kilmartin Arg.
[322] O.S.A. XX 33, Boleskine Inv.
[323] O.S.A. VI 295, Eddrachillis Suth.
[324] Johnson & Boswell 1930, 96.

47. *Rent-collecting in Kintail*
[325] O.S.A. VI 245-6 fn, Kintail Ross.
[326] O.S.A. VII 129, Glenshiel Ross.

48. *Safely lodged in the bank*
[327] Stewart 1822, II xxxix-xl fn.
[328] Hogg 1981, 86-7.
[329] Stewart 1822, II xxxix.
[330] Thomson 1970, 115.

49. *Rob Roy MacGregor*
[331] *Oxford D.N.B.* Stewart 1822, II xvi, gives another account of the origin of the quarrel.
[332] Stevenson 1954, 58.
[333] Johnson & Boswell 1930, 85, 85-6.

50. *Keppoch and Glengarry*
[334] Larkin 2010, 104-5.
[335] Lang 1898, 96.
[336] Lang 1898, xxxviii.
[337] O.S.A. VI 256, North Knapdale Arg.
[338] O.S.A. X 540 fn, Campbeltown Arg.

51. *Most cordial manner*
[339] Jamieson 2005, xxx-xxxi.
[340] Pennant 1998, 745, appendix XI, by Rev. Donald MacQueen.
[341] Burt 2005, 193.
[342] Johnson & Boswell 1930, 116.
[343] Chauncy H. Townshend (T.H.C.), *Descriptive Tour in Scotland* 1840, 108.
[344] N.S.A. XIII 127, Duthil Moray. (The O.S.A. put Duthil in Inverness-shire.)
[345] Selkirk 2010, 7.

52. *Fostering of the chief's heir*
[346] MacLeod 1910, 114 (1867 ed., 155).
[347] Stewart 1822, I 304 fn.
[348] Stewart 1822, II 48 fn.

[349] Geddes 1955, 140. See Carmichael 1928-71; W. C. MacKenzie, *The Western Isles*, Gardner, Paisley, 1932; and Arthur Geddes: *Songs of Craig and Ben*, volume two, Wm. Maclellan, Glasgow, 1961.

53. Stories of despotism
[350] Collier 1953, 47; O.S.A. XIX 297, Aboyne Aberd.
[351] O.S.A. XIX 292, Rhynie Aberd.
[352] Stewart 1822, II viii.

54. Despotism in a former age
[353] Johnson & Boswell 1930, 40-41; Burt 2005, 193, 200, 260, 262, 263. Collier 1953, 39.

55. Lowland education
[354] Hunter 1999, 176.

56. Clan Ranald
[355] Shaw 1880, 202.
[356] Fulton 1991, 14.
[357] MacDonald 1904, III 159; & see Alice MacDonald, *House of the Isles*, printed privately, Edinburgh, 1925?, 64.

57. MacLeods of Harris
[358] MacLeod 1905, 356-7.

58. MacPhersons and Clan Chattan
[359] Shaw 1880, 527.

59. Stewarts of Appin; Cameron of Lochiel
[360] Stewart 1822, II 368-9 fn.

60. Keppoch, Glengarry, Lewis
[361] Lang 1898, 97.
[362] Lang 1898, 105.

61. Chief and tacksmen
[363] MacKenzie 1908, 405.

62. Tacksmen with charters
[364] D. MacKinnon & A. Morrison, *The MacLeods*, Clan MacLeod Society, Edinburgh, 1968, 10.

63. Other names in the clan
[365] MacLeod 1910, 182 fn.
[366] MacMillan 1971, 51, 105, 157-9, & 163; & see MacDonald 1994, 237, 246-7.
[367] MacLeod 1910, 182 fn.
[368] MacLean 1988, 225.
[369] MacMillan 1971, 146.
[370] MacMillan 1971, 158-9.
[371] MacMillan 1971, 163.
[372] MacMillan 1971, 105.
[373] MacMillan 1971, 51.
[374] Rev. W. Forsyth, *Origin of the Kincardine Camerons*, website lochiel.net/archives.

64. *Newcomers to the clan*
[375] Celtic Monthly, I 89.
[376] Brand Commission, P.P. 1895, XXXVIII 213.
[377] Shaw 1880, 586, 591.
[378] Macaulay 1907, 431.
[379] MacMillan 1971, 95.
[380] Shaw 1880, 551, 551 fn.

65. *Movement within the Highlands*
[381] Shaw 1880, 556 fn.
[382] Shaw 1880, 150 fn.
[383] Adam/Innes 1965, 243.
[384] Adam Gunn & John MacKay, *Sutherland & the Reay Country*, 1893, 43.
[385] MacLean & Carrell 1986, 87.
[386] Johnson & Boswell 1930, 359.

66. *Clan and name*
[387] Stewart 1822, I 25 fn.
[388] *Recollections of Marshal MacDonald*, 1825, chapter one, website electricscotland.com. Neil MacEachan came from Clan Ranald country, he bore a Clan Ranald sept name, his relatives lived in Clan Ranald country, he was Clanranald's children's tutor, and when he went outside the Highlands he was known as MacDonald; yet, astonishingly, Fitzroy MacLean (MacLean 1988, 259) claimed he was "in fact a MacLean"! This can only be put down to clan prejudice.
[389] Blundell 1917, 44.
[390] Blundell 1917, 154.
[391] Smollett 1967, 278.
[392] N.S.A. XIV 287, Kilmuir Inv.
[393] Burt 2005, 199.
[394] N.S.A. XIV 272, Rosskeen Ross.

67. *Identity of name*
[395] Stewart 1822, I 24.
[396] Stewart 1822, II xxix.
[397] Stewart 1822, II xxii.
[398] Stewart 1822, II ii.
[399] Stewart 1822, II xxix & II 278 fn.
[400] Stewart 1822, II 139.
[401] Moncreiffe 1967, 39. Norman MacLeod of MacLeod, 1754-1801, had raised a company of his clansmen to join the second battalion of the 42nd Regiment, and when it was proposed to put the men of this battalion into other regiments, Norman protested because of the unpopularity this would cause him among his "own name and clan". The proposal was dropped.
[402] Burt 2005, 192.
[403] Atholl 1908, 391-3.
[404] Thomson 2010, 62, quoting Cunningham 1787.
[405] Argyll 1887, 250.
[406] Malcolm MacLennan, *Gaelic Dictionary*, Acair, Stornoway, 1979: Nic stands for Nighean Mhic.
[407] O.S.A. V 584, Greenock Renfr.
[408] Robertson 1808, iv-v.

68. *Twelve generations*

[409] Alasdair Alpin MacGregor, quoted in Adam/Innes 1965, 117. MacGregor wrote many books about the Highlands. In the 1950s he was living in north London, where I was able to hear his views on the Highlands and the Highlanders when by chance I had lunch with him at the house of a mutual friend (F. L. Stevens) in Hampstead Garden Suburb.

[410] Blackie 1885, 11.

[411] J. Shaw Grant, *Highland Villages*, Robert Hale, London 1977, 49.

[412] Hugh G. Allison, *Roots of Stone*, Mainstream, Edinburgh, 2004, 151-7.

[413] Burt 2005, 200.

69. *No foundation*

[414] Argyll 1887, 480-1 (MacPherson or Grant).

[415] William MacPherson Grant, landlord, 1781-1846.

[416] If it was essential to be known by the surname of a direct male ancestor, Winston Churchill would have been called Spencer, Arthur Wellesley (the Duke of Wellington) would be known as Colley, Oliver Cromwell – Williams, Gladstone – Gladstanes, Napoleon – Buonaparte, Hitler – Schicklgruber, Stalin – Djugashvili, Lenin – Ulyanov, Trotsky – Bronstein, Bill Clinton – Blythe, Mark Twain – Clemens, Charlotte & Emily Brontë - Brunty or Prunty, Frances Burney – MacBurney, Lewis Carroll – Dodgson, Ivor Novello – Davies, Richard Burton – Jenkins, John Cleese - Cheese, George Orwell – Blair, Donald Bradman – Bradnam, and so on. In fact many famous Hollywood actors and actresses operate under names other than those they were born with; and it is not unknown in well-to-do families for someone to take on a different surname in order to inherit a family position and the property that goes with it, one example being Edward Austen or Knight, Jane Austen's brother. Earlier, in 1770, Lord George Sackville changed his name to Germain to inherit an estate.

[417] Geddes 1955, 132 – in Gaelic, companas, ceartas, saorsa.

CHAPTER FOUR

CHIEFS AND CHARTERS

1. The coming of the charter

So far we have dealt with the realities of society and of political organization in the Highlands – the Highland facts of life. Now we come to some activities of the chiefs, in association with the authorities and the lawyers in Edinburgh, which were in the beginning of purely theoretical interest, and of no practical effect whatever: but which in the end had such cataclysmic consequences that they destroyed the whole of Highland society. These activities were the obtaining of charters to the clan lands by the chiefs. The charters were like a slumbering volcano, which is safely ignored for generations; but which then erupts with great ferocity, wiping out all those in its vicinity.

Cosmo Innes, speaking of the Lowlands as well as the Highlands, described how the process was carried on. At first only narrow strips of the cultivated land were appropriated to the local lord: then, in Scotland generally, "the lawyers lent themselves to appropriate the poor man's grazing ground to the neighbouring baron". Although "the lord had never possessed any of the common, when it came to be divided, the lord got the whole that was allocated to the estate, and the poor cotter none. The poor had no lawyers!"[1]

The Lowland lawyers also considered the Highland area, which of course the Edinburgh kings claimed to rule, and applied to it the theory of "feudal investiture". Crown charters were given to many chiefs, who were said to hold the whole land of the clan in barony, in return for present favours, or past help, or promises of future support for the Lowland king. The strength of the position of the chiefs vis-à-vis the Edinburgh authorities lay in the fact that the latter were always eager to gain the support of the physically tough and mentally agile Highlanders who were produced by the clan system. (This eagerness to enlist the Highlanders is yet further evidence of what kind of people they were: the help of the half-starved, cowering nonentities who – according to the orthodox historians – populated the old Highlands would of course have been of no use to anyone.) The Highlanders could not be indifferent to what was happening in the Lowlands, since the Lowland authorities could – and often did, if they were so minded – cause much trouble in the small clan countries of the Highlands by interference, military or otherwise, in Highland affairs. The Scottish kings knew that the chief's advice on whether to engage in or to ignore a particular Lowland war, or whether to take part in any struggle (on whichever side) as to the succession to the Edinburgh throne, carried weight with his clan, and therefore they often attempted to win the chiefs over by granting them charters which claimed that the land occupied by their clans belonged to them, the chiefs, as their own personal property. The kings were the readier with a gift of this kind since it cost them nothing; to make a present of what belongs to someone else has always been an easy way to show one's generosity. Besides that, in Lowland society private property had triumphed. Increasingly in the Lowlands, every yard, every foot, every inch, of the earth's surface was "owned by" some lucky individual or other: every hump or hillock, every plain or plateau, every rock, rill or ridge, had its exultant individual possessor. Human beings are so vainglorious that each human society commonly regards its own rules as being self-evidently supreme, beyond question, while other countries' rules are manifestly erroneous: and wherever and whenever it can, it tries to force all other societies to adopt its own laws. Thus the Lowland kings regarded the communal ownership of land in the Highlands as being barbaric, immoral, and unnatural. So at every opportunity, they did what they could to introduce and enforce private property in land in the Highlands. And the clan chiefs were the most obvious candidates to be transformed into private landowners, apart from the fact that they could be the most useful to the Lowland authorities. David Stewart recounted how a foster-brother of an earlier Stewart of Garth had been injured by one of the MacIvors who then occupied much of Glen Lyon; the Stewarts gathered to avenge this grievance, defeating and ousting the MacIvors. They then occupied the MacIvors' land, and "law confirmed what the sword had won" – by giving the chief (not, of course, the clan) a charter to the territory.[2]

When it became known that Crown charters were obtainable, more and more it became the fashion among the Highland chiefs to attempt to obtain one. It became possible, and therefore it was often done. In order to acquire a charter, the chiefs were frequently prepared to play the shabbiest games of Edinburgh politics, to use the backstairs way to the king's ear, to intrigue, beguile, double-cross, and deceive. When one chief had obtained a charter to his clan land, the neighbouring chiefs would be stimulated to emulation, and would come to Edinburgh to learn, often all too successfully, how the trick was performed. As Shakespeare put it, "How oft the sight of means to do ill deeds/makes deeds ill done!"[3]

John Mackintosh, in his *History of Civilization in Scotland*, said that Crown charters were being granted as early as the twelfth century: they were a great instrument of injustice, fraud and cruelty: and "the mass of the Celtic people were thrust down by a process of slow robbery".[4]

This process, of course, was not completed in a day. As late as 1597 Parliament summoned the clan chiefs to Edinburgh to produce their titles to "their" lands, but the response was poor, because few chiefs could produce such written charters.[5] Sometimes a claim was made of "sword-right" to the land; in other words, an assertion that the land belongs to those who can defend it with their swords. No chief could have been so swollen-headed as to claim that he alone, one swordsman, could defend land against the hundred, or 200, or 300 swordsmen of another clan; so this claim again shows the clan ownership of the land – the clan then in possession of a district had the right to it because the swords of the clansmen who lived there could hold it against any attackers.

2. Practical effect of the charters

Although the process of the chiefs obtaining fanciful "charters to the clan lands" began very early in Scottish history, the practical effect – to repeat – of these charters in the Highlands was, for centuries, almost nil. A claim written on a piece of paper lying in a wooden chest, and a claim put into effect in the real world, are two very different things. The documents, as they stood, did nothing except inflate the self-importance of the possessors. They were, in many ways, reminiscent of the musical cheques about which Samuel Butler wrote in *Erewhon*; it was the general pretence that they were of great importance, and they were referred to with great solemnity, but everyone realized that for all practical purposes they were merely window-dressing.[6] The rights claimed in the charters represented a threat which, when and if put into effect, would overturn the whole of Gaelic society, and revolutionize the entire Highlands; but, perforce, the threat had to remain latent. It was quite true that, as Cosmo Innes put it, "a large part of the population of the Highlands had no written charters", and it was also quite true, as Innes continued, that Edinburgh lawyers, factors and so on could, if they wished, describe "those immemorial occupants and dwellers on the land as holding at the absolute will of the first chief who was knowing enough to obtain a Crown charter";[7] but who was to put this "absolute will of the chief" into effect? It would have been a brave lawyer, and indeed a brave chief, who would have dared to make his way into the mountains and solemnly inform a whole clan of hefty and heavily-armed Highlanders that they no longer had any rights whatever in their own clan land, because some alien clerks speaking a foreign language in a town in the Lowlands some forty miles beyond the furthest Highland boundary had made some marks in ink on a fragment of sheepskin. Such a manifestation could not have harmed the clansfolk – unless it made them ill from laughing.

When a child makes a particularly empty threat to one of his fellows that he will do so and so, the retort is often "Oh yes? You and whose army?" This kind of retort would have gone to the heart of the situation visualized above. Even when, in the latter half of the eighteenth and in the nineteenth centuries, the chief and his lawyers had the whole vast extraordinary might of the British Army (and Navy) behind them, supported by the tremendous power of the new multiple industries of the Lowlands and England, which had made Great Britain the first world superpower, master of a quarter of the entire globe, and overlord of a quarter of the entire population of the world, even then there were very many cases when the Highlanders forcibly resisted the attempts to evict them (and very occasionally, when the landlord was particularly afraid of public opinion, the resistance was even successful). In earlier centuries, when the Lowlands were simply one negligible part of one small island off the coast of the smallest continent, and when therefore this overwhelming state power was plainly not available, the opposition to any attempts at eviction would not only have been forcible: it would have been effective.

Those experts who guilelessly claim that because a certain man had a charter saying he had title to a certain stretch of the Highlands in 1500, or 1600, or 1700, he was therefore its absolute owner at that date might as well claim that a player at the game of Monopoly really does own Mayfair or Marlborough Street, because he has acquired the piece of cardboard purporting to represent it. The closest parallel to the pre-Culloden charters would perhaps be the decorative certificates now held by optimists round the world – who have paid good money for the privilege – giving them "ownership" of pieces of the moon, or even (as further crafty operators get in on the act) of sites on Mars or Venus. Of course, if the company which is now selling "plots on the moon's surface" (for only £16.75 an acre, plus £3 for your name on the title deed, a very reasonable price) were in future to obtain actual jurisdiction over the moon, whether by force or cunning, and in some extraordinary way humans were in fact able to settle on the moon, then the title deeds which the company is now marketing could come to represent reality.[8] Those trusting souls who have bought them would turn out to have been very astute instead of very naive, and would be able to make a gigantic profit: a process exactly analogous to what happened to the Highland chiefs after 1746.

3. Precepts of sasine

In the eyes of orthodox historians, however, pieces of paper have enormous power. One reviewer of Fraser Darling's book reproved him, even though Darling's opinions were firmly on the side of the landlords, for having conceded that the clan had owned its own land. "It is perpetuating a popular misconception", said the reviewer resolutely, to say that the clan land "belonged to the tribe". The proof that it was a misconception (he continued) lay in the fact that there are in existence at this moment actual documents confuting it: from the end of the fifteenth century "at least, precepts of sasine exist". Sasine is a Scots law term, meaning the act to give possession of feudal property; and a precept of sasine is a document claiming that this has been done. So if a piece of paper says that an individual owned property in the Highlands, then he did own property in the Highlands.

This belief is a great time-saver: there is no need to study the actual history of the Highlands, to find out how close a connection with reality is demonstrated by these scraps of writing. There is more "proof" still, said the reviewer triumphantly: the chiefs "were borrowing money on the security of their estates from early in the seventeenth century".[9] It is quite true that some Lowlanders, born and bred in the Lowlands, and steeped from birth in the Lowland belief that the Highlands were really just as much part of Scotland as Midlothian was (although unfortunately inhabited at the moment by unbridled and lawless barbarians, who viciously ignored what the gentlemen in Edinburgh told them to do), and that the chiefs' fanciful charters were solidly authentic – it is quite true that some people were prepared to lend money to eminent figures such as Highland chiefs, who, of course, were more and more pushing themselves to prominence in the Lowlands, and "from early in the seventeenth century" – and before – even obtaining houses and furnishings in Lowland cities like Edinburgh, where inescapably they and their Lowland property were vulnerable to Lowland debt-collectors and lawyers, who could invoke the valuable legal tool of imprisonment for debt: but the idea that such transactions changed the Highland facts of life is a mere chimera. No doubt if I had sufficient "gift of the gab" to persuade someone that I owned Westminster Abbey, and that he should lend me money on the strength of my claim, the transaction could subsequently be taken by some simple souls (whether or not book-reviewers) to "prove" my claim of ownership – however strong the other evidence was that I did not own Westminster Abbey.

Any Lowland financier lending money to a Highland chief in the seventeenth century was either astute enough to take a lien on the chief's Lowland property, or gullible enough to think that his Highland charter represented reality. Some moneyed men, indeed, seem to be surprisingly naive, now as well as then. The writer of these pages has from time to time received e-mails (as have many others) solemnly promising thousands of pounds in return for helping various alleged foreign ex-dictators and other worthy characters to move their fortunes to England: sometimes the writers request money to be paid over, so that customs officials etc. can be bribed, sometimes the request is simply for the details of one's bank account, so that the cash "can be paid in". The advance money, once dispatched, of course disappears, and the bank account details simply enable money to be taken out of the account, not put into it. I have also several times "won" large sums in foreign lotteries which I had never even heard of: and the letters or e-mails announcing my good fortune merely wanted my bank details to pay in my winnings. While the great majority of such attempts must meet with incredulous smiles (as they do at this address), it is undeniable that numbers of rich men have lost considerable sums of money to these scams. The theory that anyone who possesses large amounts of currency also necessarily possesses large amounts of common sense has, sadly, no factual basis.

Admittedly, one advantage of having little money is that you do not have much to lose; rogues cannot trick you out of what you have not got – he that is down need fear no fall.

4. Virtually absolute control

Many academics in this field, however, seem to regard anything written as necessarily true. Pilate's jesting question, "what is truth?" presents no difficulty to the true believer: the answer is simply, "whatever is written down". Perhaps because they live in a world of books and journals and monographs and articles, where publication is the prerequisite for prominence and promotion, academics often appear to bestow an over-riding importance upon documents. It is all rather reminiscent of Mr Brooke, in George Eliot's *Middlemarch*, who "with an easy smile", was fond of saying, "I have documents at my back", though he never seemed to do anything with them.[10]

We saw earlier the traps which lie ready for observers who place unquestioning faith in documents, as shown in the field of Highland topography – where reports greatly exaggerating the size of Highland parishes have been accepted without further investigation. Some academic writers appear not only to believe that any contemporary document must be true, they seem to credit documents with extraordinary potency. Written words on pieces of paper, for example, are so powerful that they can "give" extensive powers. Professor T. C. Smout wrote: "The Highland chiefs or chieftains of the late middle ages all held land by feudal charters [although of course, some had no charters at all, as we shall shortly see] accepted from the crown or from each other [!] which gave virtually absolute control over their tenants and their territories. In particular it is necessary to stress that there was in the medieval Highlands no known concept of clan lands to which the peasants [sic] had immemorial prescriptive rights of ownership, though such rights were very widely believed in by nineteenth-century crofters, who held them to be of great antiquity, and the existence of such a belief can be traced even in the eighteenth century. But there is no sign of this before 1600."[11] Professor T. M. Devine agreed, using the same definitive phrase to put the matter beyond dispute.

"Highland elites . . . possessed land by crown charters which gave them virtually absolute control over their territories."[12]

The passage from Professor Smout encapsulates many treasured Lowland beliefs. It relies on the deification of the document: the writing made divine. The "feudal charters" said the chiefs had "absolute control"; therefore they had absolute control. The charters seemingly described the clansfolk as "tenants"; therefore they were tenants. There was "no known concept of clan lands", a fact which, interestingly, "it is necessary to stress" because, one supposes, of its impact on modern policies and measures. The Gaelic clansfolk did not set themselves down in collegiate cloisters to write Latin or English charters or other documents describing the Highland polity, therefore it did not exist.[13] The hunting and herding clansfolk were only "peasants", a term carrying a strong implication of impoverished lives, supplied only by the scanty crops of two or three sterile acres (people, in fact, so low down on the social scale that in American English – and increasingly in British English – the word is used as an insult. An online dictionary obligingly provides eleven synonyms of "peasant", all extremely unflattering: boor, bumpkin, hayseed, hick, hired hand, labourer, peon, provincial, rube, rustic, and serf.) The idea that the clans had owned their own land was held (we are assured) pre-eminently by "nineteenth-century crofters", that is a class of people who had designedly been placed in circumstances at best on the margin of destitution, and sometimes sunk in famine, trying to obtain a meagre living on patches of infertile ground which the landlords found it impossible to rent out to anyone else: people, that is to say, of such an inferior social stratum that their beliefs need not long detain the university scholar or any serious writer. Painstaking academic work, apparently, can "trace" a "concept of clan lands" as early as "the eighteenth century", but (the seventeenth century being ignored) there is "no sign" of any such belief before 1600 – no significant archives of documents survive recording the Gaelic view of society (any Gaelic writings, of course, were regularly destroyed by the Lowlanders, to the point where the great literary panjandrum of the eighteenth century was able to announce that "the Erse never was a written language");[14] therefore the Gaelic view of society can be peremptorily dismissed.

However, the whole history of the clans shows what was the real state of affairs. As lawyers say, res ipsa loquitur – the thing speaks for itself. In chapter three, above, we quoted the opinions of a number of observers who, in some cases reluctantly, had to acknowledge the inescapable facts.

5. MacDonalds of Keppoch

There were frequent demonstrations throughout the history of Highland clanship of the purely theoretical nature of the chiefs' supposed right to the clan lands, this "virtually absolute control" which the chiefs were alleged to exercise over their clans' land, as seen from the Lowlands and as written in the charters. Clans, of course, were (as is remarked on below) completely foreign to the Lowland authorities' way of thinking,[15] and therefore were never given a title to land; but (apart from that) there were numbers of Highland clans whose chiefs or chieftains never obtained a charter, yet which kept possession of their clan countries for centuries, until the coming of the landlord revolution. Examples are the MacLarens of Balquhidder in Perthshire, the MacIntyres of Glen Noe in Argyllshire, the MacRaes of Kintail in Ross-shire, and the Gunns of Kildonan in Sutherland.[16] Another case in point is the history of the MacDonald clan of Keppoch, in Inverness-shire, which for centuries lived in Glen Spean and Glen Roy, without the slightest justification from a charter. The firm belief in Edinburgh, however, was that there was a "virtually absolute" proprietor of the Keppoch lands, a genuine charter-holding, rent-collecting, tenancy-granting landlord – the chief of MacIntosh. (The MacIntosh clan had once lived in Badenoch, before moving over to Strath Dearn and Strath Nairn; therefore the MacIntosh chief could claim an ancestral hankering after what was now Keppoch country.) MacIntosh perhaps felt that as he had obtained a charter to some of the land of the MacIntosh clan, which was not his property, there was no reason why he should not obtain charters to other land which was also not his property: and so he had somehow wheedled a charter to much of the Keppoch land as early as 1431. Indeed, in 1467 the MacIntosh chief also managed to wangle also a charter to Glengarry, in this fanciful paper-chase: so, in the trusting view of an orthodox historian, in 1467 MacIntosh was clearly the "virtually absolute" owner of the Glengarry clan land.[17] However, the MacIntosh chief never did (nor ever could) make any move towards transforming this empty claim on Glengarry into anything approaching reality; he appeared to accept that his Glengarry charter was merely fictional. He did his best to take hold of Keppoch clan land, however. Here was a clear-cut confrontation: the charter right to the land (which could be called the Lowland right) lay in the hands of the MacIntosh chief, while the clan right, the right of occupation (which could be called the Highland right), lay with the Keppoch MacDonald clan. The Lowland theory said the land belonged to the chief of MacIntosh: the Highland fact said it belonged to the Keppoch MacDonalds. The wishful thinking of the Lowland lawyers, and successive MacIntosh chiefs, and many modern academics, said one thing; the reality of the Highlands said another. Throughout the clan era, reality won, as it always does. The MacIntosh chiefs kept explaining to everyone who would listen that they had pieces of paper which gave them "virtually absolute control" (to use the trenchant phrase employed by Smout and Devine) of Brae Badenoch; the MacDonalds rejoined that in the real world they had "absolute control" of their own land. Repeatedly successive MacIntosh chiefs told the MacDonalds to leave; repeatedly the MacDonalds rejected all such requests. Repeatedly the MacIntosh chiefs gathered all the forces they could muster, and buttressed by their Lowland scraps of parchment tried to drive the MacDonalds out by armed assault; repeatedly the MacDonalds defeated the invasions. Whether a MacIntosh chief attempted to assert his right with his own clansmen alone, or with the help of his Clan Chattan allies, or with the assistance of Lowland official commissions against the MacDonalds from the Edinburgh authorities, or even when strengthened by southern soldiery, the result was the same. The struggle continued intermittently for over three hundred years after MacIntosh had obtained the charter, and each venture by the MacIntosh chiefs ended in failure. In 1618, for example, after nearly two centuries of striving on the part of the MacIntosh chiefs, Sir Lachlan MacIntosh, 17th of MacIntosh, "invaded Lochaber with a large force", as A. M. Shaw put it, but was unable to lay his hands on Keppoch; and then, as usual, had to withdraw. Soon afterwards he planned an even larger expedition, but various incidents conspired to frustrate his foray.[18]

6. Invasion of Badenoch

Towards the end of the seventeenth century, the charter holder (as Shaw tells us) made yet another determined attempt to possess "his" land. In 1667, Lachlan MacIntosh, 19th of MacIntosh, "went to Lochaber with a large following", and surrounded by the MacIntosh clansmen actually held some "courts", but as soon as he returned to MacIntosh country matters reverted to where they had been before the invasion (just as a European army, invading a neighbouring country, and even announcing that they really owned it if all had their due, would leave affairs unchanged when they went home again). In 1672 Lachlan sued unsuccessfully "for a commission to eject Keppoch and his people from the Brae Lochaber lands"; in 1681 the chief actually "received a commission against the MacDonalds, but this had no satisfactory result"; while at the end of 1682 Lachlan found the young Coll MacDonald of Keppoch (then a student at St Andrews) in Inverness, and arrested him, imprisoning him in the Inverness Tolbooth – whence he was liberated two months later by the Inverness magistrates, since it was not clear what crime he was supposed to have committed.[19] However, in 1688 MacIntosh obtained the express warrant of the Privy Council against the MacDonalds, besides the help of a company of regular soldiers under the command of Captain Kenneth MacKenzie of Suddie. The Privy Council also ordered the "concurrence", or help, of the people of Inverness-shire and neighbouring counties to be given to MacIntosh, but this was of little use, because the Highlanders, living in effect in their own independent countries, paid no attention to any orders coming from Edinburgh – if on any particular occasion they did what the Edinburgh authorities would have wanted them to, it was only because they had decided unilaterally that it was in their own interests to do so. Nevertheless, MacIntosh set out for Badenoch with his own MacIntosh clansmen, plus the other armed men of Clan Chattan (except the MacPhersons), at his back, together with Captain MacKenzie's regular soldiers – 1200 men in all. The Keppoch MacDonalds had a much smaller array – 700 men, and they had only managed that number by enlisting the help of their kinsmen the MacDonalds of Glengarry and of Glen Coe. However, having a clearer insight into the real value of the vaunted charter right than either MacIntosh or many subsequent historians, they drew up to face the invaders along the ridge of Mulroy. What happened then may be learned from the words of Donald MacBane, an enlisted man who fought that day in Suddie's company (and who later wrote his reminiscences after a lifetime of soldiering, latterly in Marlborough's wars):

"The MacDonalds came down the hill upon us, without either shoe, stocking, or bonnet on their head; they gave a shout, and then the fight began on both sides and continued a hot dispute for an hour. Then they broke in upon us with their sword and target and Lochaber axes, which obliged us to give way. Seeing my captain sore wounded, and a great many more with their heads lying cloven on every side, I was sadly affrighted, never having seen the like before. A Highlandman attacked me with sword and targe, and cut my wooden handled bayonet out of the muzzle of my gun: I then clubbed my gun and gave him a stroke with it which made the butt end to fly off. Seeing the Highlandmen to come fast upon me, I took to my heels and ran thirty miles before I looked behind me. Every person I saw or met I took him for my enemy."[20]

MacKenzie of Suddie, the commander of the Lowland detachment, and several MacIntosh chieftains, were killed in the fighting. (Suddie, according to Stuart MacDonald – a Keppoch descendant – attacked one of the MacDonalds with a pike, "upon which the Highlander hurled an empty pistol at the officer with such force it cracked his skull".[21] Was it "an Highland pistol, all of steel"?) MacIntosh himself was taken prisoner, but was shortly rescued by the MacPhersons, who arrived too late to take part in the battle.

7. Fire and sword

The Privy Council, in face of this total defiance by the Keppoch clansmen, did all that lay within its power: it issued letters of intercommuning against them (i.e., decrees forbidding any dealings with those named, on pain of being regarded as accessories to their crimes and misdemeanours), and gave orders for laying waste the land occupied by the MacDonalds with fire and sword. Two hundred Foot Guards, and a troop of dragoons, were sent to the Braes of Lochaber; and the

MacDonalds took refuge among the mountains. Paul Hopkins wrote: "the troops killed some who remained, besides burning houses and corn, until the reports of invasion recalled them."[22] This was the expedition of William of Orange, invading England; the Lowland expedition into Keppoch was equally an invasion, but was not described as one. In fact the soldiers could not be kept in the Highlands indefinitely, in those simpler days before the economic revolution of the eighteenth century, and so they withdrew, after giving the MacDonalds a fearful foretaste of the house-burning improvements that were to come some decades later, when the chiefs really had become landowners. The MacDonalds resumed their land as soon as the soldiers withdrew.

One account says that Keppoch forced MacIntosh, while he held him prisoner, to renounce his right to the lands; but any such renunciation under duress, if made, could not be recognized by Lowland law. The MacDonalds took their revenge for the wasting of their own townships by harrying the lands of the MacIntosh clan (the attacks on the Keppoch MacDonalds, and the attacks on the MacIntoshes, both being the direct result of Lowland interference in Highland affairs). The removal of James VII and II (who also thought he had "virtually absolute control" of the country, but found he was wrong) in 1688, and his replacement by William and Mary and the Bill of Rights, was seen as a "Glorious Revolution": but of course both regimes, whether glorious or inglorious, had exactly the same attitude towards the Highlands – the desire to impose Lowland rule on the Highlanders. In 1690 the new Williamite Scots Parliament passed two Acts saying that the MacDonalds occupied the Keppoch land illegally, and that the legal possessor of them (for the past 259 years!) was the chief of MacIntosh. But again the power to enforce this Lowland law and even to recompense MacIntosh for the harrying of "his" land, the burning of his house, and so on, was wanting.

In 1697 the Lords Commissioners of Justiciary issued warrants for the arrest of Keppoch and 130 of his clansmen: these, too, were unavailing. MacIntosh took his complaint to the highest quarter, to King William III himself, and the king wrote to his Scots Privy Council ordering them to evict the MacDonalds and put MacIntosh in possession of the land to which he had the charter right. In 1698 the Council renewed the commission of fire and sword against Coll MacDonald, chief of Keppoch, and his clan, in the strongest terms; appointed MacIntosh and the Clan Chattan chieftains to execute the commission; outlawed Coll MacDonald and his clan; sent letters of concurrence and intercommuning to the sheriffs of Inverness, Ross, Nairn, Perth, and Aberdeen, ordering all men between sixteen and sixty to help MacIntosh and forbidding them to help MacDonald; and in every way made it clear that under Lowland law Coll MacDonald and the Keppoch clan were nothing more than outlaws and renegades in possession of stolen property.

And what happened after these tremendous fulminations by the highest authorities of the Lowland law? Nothing whatever. There is no record of so much as a finger being lifted against the MacDonalds after all this paper fury. A. M. Shaw, from whose *Historical Memoirs of Mackintosh and Clan Chattan* many of these details are taken, said that perhaps MacIntosh, no longer a young man, realized that if he wished to prosecute his claim to the Keppoch lands he would have to do so, in the last analysis, by means of his own clansmen; and his attempt to do that in 1688 had ended in failure at Mulroy. "A campaign in wild Lochaber against a warlike race of outlaws [sic] fighting for hearth and home was not to be lightly undertaken"; and so the MacDonalds were in the end left in peaceful possession of their own clan land.[23]

Yet, of course, MacIntosh had a "feudal charter", which gave him "virtually absolute control" of the lands occupied by the Keppoch clan in Badenoch. If only an academic historian had been able to visit the Keppoch clansfolk during the three centuries and more after 1431, he could have tried to persuade them that "there was in the medieval Highlands no known concept of clan lands"; though one feels he could hardly have been more successful than the entire might of the Lowland state, which was also (with completely null and void results) trying to impose the same belief.[24]

8. MacIntosh and Gordon

As a refinement of unreality, MacIntosh continued a separate argument with the Duke of Gordon, who had also obtained some writing on a piece of paper which conflicted not only with the facts, but also with the MacIntosh charters, in giving him "virtually absolute control" over much of the Keppoch land. This fantastical disagreement between two men as to which of them owned what part of a district that neither of them owned was settled about the 1720s, when MacIntosh allowed Gordon to be the owner of Glen Spean, and in return Gordon allowed MacIntosh to be the owner of Glen Roy. The MacDonalds continued in occupation, in the full exercise of the rights of ownership, and in blissful indifference to the presumptuous MacIntosh-Gordon negotiations and decisions and arrangements.

David Stewart, as a successful field officer in the nineteenth-century army of Great Britain, and living at a time when the Lowland charters had been forcibly inflicted on the Highlands, and which therefore gave a completely authentic account of landownership as it existed in the early nineteenth century, was wedded to the idea that these charters had always given an accurate picture, even in the days of the clans. "It is one of the most singular circumstances in the history of the Highlands, that a family without an acre of land in property, tenants [sic] only to the Duke of Gordon and the Laird of MacIntosh, could for so many centuries maintain a power which few chiefs or proprietors could equal. Keppoch could command a body of followers from 200 to 400 men, according as exigencies or circumstances might require."[25] We have seen that the chiefs "commanded" their clansfolk only when the latter wished to be commanded (as the events of the attempted enrolment of the clansmen in 1689, 1715, and 1745, clearly demonstrated, apart from all the other evidence). The clan's ability to put a force of this size in the field (the 1746 memorial gave their strength as 300 men) meant that in reality it was the owner of its lands: to describe (in Stewart's words) the Keppoch men as "tenants only to the Duke of Gordon and the Laird of MacIntosh" cannot be accurate. It would be astounding if "tenants" stayed on someone else's property for well over three centuries (from 1431 to the middle of the eighteenth century), throughout which time the "landlords" were moving heaven and earth – including sending in whole armies against them – to get them to leave.

The position of the chiefs of Keppoch, despite their lack of a charter, was exactly the same as that of other clan chiefs who had obtained a charter. Their powers in both cases depended not on scraps of paper, but on the support and approval of their clans.

9. *Camerons and Clan Chattan*

A similar dispute took place between the chief of MacIntosh on the one hand and the Clan Cameron on the other. Angus MacIntosh, 6th chief of MacIntosh, had married the daughter of the last of the old line of Clan Chattan chiefs, and claimed through her some rights to the charters of the ancient Clan Chattan lands of Glen Loy and Locharkaigside. But early in the fourteenth century, Angus and his clansfolk having departed into Strath Nairn and Strath Dearn, the Camerons had occupied these lands, with other territory. Angus's son William renewed his claim to the lands, and obtained a charter to them from the Lord of the Isles in 1337: the charter was confirmed by King David II in 1359.[26] Here again there could be no doubt, throughout well over three centuries, as to who had the charter right to Glen Loy and the lands round Loch Arkaig; nor as to who had the right by the fact of physical occupation.

A long struggle between the Camerons and the MacIntosh clansfolk (who, unhappily, thought themselves bound to support their chief's pretensions against both the Keppoch clan and the Camerons) ensued. The hostilities included the bloody battle of Invernahavon in 1370, when the Camerons totally defeated the Clan Chattan, almost wiping out the Davidsons. The MacPhersons had refused to take part in the battle (they were often only semi-detached members of the Clan Chattan); but seeing the defeat of their fellow clansmen, they came up and in turn defeated the Camerons.[27] It may be that the Clan Battle at Perth in 1396, between two bands of champions, thirty from each of two clans, was in fact between the Camerons and the Clan Chattan over this dispute.[28] But in spite of the long struggle to evict them, the Camerons remained in possession.

The chiefs of MacIntosh did not give up their claim, and they had the full support of Lowland law. In 1616 the Lords of Council and Session ordered the Camerons to remove themselves from Glen Loy and Locharkaigside, and give possession to MacIntosh. In 1622 a commission was issued to the chief of MacIntosh against the Cameron chief. In 1639 MacIntosh again obtained from the Lords of Council and Session a "decreet of removing" against the Camerons.[29] All these came to nothing, since the Lowland claim to rule the Highlands was not matched by the reality on the ground. The Cameron country, though much smaller than the Lowland kingdom, was in effect an independent entity.

In 1661 the Scots Parliament enacted that Cameron of Lochiel should give up the disputed lands to MacIntosh; in 1662 the Privy Council again enacted a decreet of removing against the Camerons; in 1663 a Royal Commission of fire and sword against the Camerons was issued, along with letters of concurrence and intercommuning.[30] The commission had been issued to many of the greatest nobles in the kingdom, and at last it seemed that MacIntosh could scarcely fail in his claim. The author of *Lochiel's Memoirs* said that Lochiel's position seemed hopeless. "One would now think, that when near one-half of the kingdom was armed against a private gentleman and his family, it was scarcely in the power of fortune to save them from utter ruin."[31] But the author was wrong: if it was true that all this power was directed simply against "a private gentleman and his family", the outcome could not have been in doubt. However, this armament was not against a private gentleman – that is, Lochiel: it was against the whole of the Clan Cameron, and in their own Lochaber land (until the landlord revolution after Culloden) the Camerons were in practice irremovable, whatever the Lowland law or Lowland lawyers (or orthodox historians) might say.

10. Settlement at Loch Arkaig

In 1665 there was a further armed confrontation. MacIntosh collected his forces; supported by the MacPhersons as well as the other clans in the Clan Chattan federation, he had 1500 men. He then invaded Lochaber, coming into the vicinity of the assembled Camerons near Loch Arkaig. Lochiel had mustered 1200 men in all, including 300 men from his allies – the MacGregors and the Glen Coe MacDonalds. As they were preparing to engage, a third force arrived – 500 men commanded by John Campbell younger of Glenorchy, who was related to both MacIntosh and Lochiel. (Lochiel was his first cousin, while MacIntosh's grandfather was Campbell's father's cousin: so MacIntosh was his second cousin once removed.)[32] A settlement was suggested to the effect that MacIntosh would sell his charter right over Locharkaigside and Glen Loy to Lochiel, or to whomever Lochiel might nominate, for 72,500 merks, or just over £4000 in English money. MacIntosh was enraged at the scheme, but since the majority of the chieftains who had come with him refused to support him if he rejected the proposal, and since Glenorchy said he would commit his force to support whichever side accepted the settlement, he was compelled to agree. Lochiel, being only the head of the Clan Cameron and not a landowner, was not able to raise this much money, a derisory amount though it was compared with the real value of the lands when owned and rented by a landlord. Instead the Earl of Argyll (the most prominent Campbell chief, who as a Lowland politician could get his hands on a sum of this size) paid the purchase money, and it was arranged that Lochiel should hold the lands in feu, or on permanent lease, from Argyll, at a microscopic "rent" or feu-duty, which bore no relation to the value of the land under a system of landlordism.[33] A century later, however, after Argyll's superiority was bought off, Lochiel's title was held to be as good as complete private ownership.

MacIntosh would never, of course, have consented to surrender his charter right to Locharkaigside and Glen Loy but for the Cameron clansmen who had gathered to support Lochiel. Lochiel's ability to overturn MacIntosh's undoubted charter right to the land, which had existed for no less than three hundred and twenty-eight years, was due entirely to the fact that the land was occupied by the Clan Cameron, who refused to surrender it.

If any of the Cameron clansmen assembled on that day had been told that, as a result of the agreement which had been reached in their presence, Lochiel now had the right to turn the entire Clan Cameron (the very people who had just won Lochiel his parchment title) out of their ancestral land, they would have flatly refused to believe it. Indeed, Lochiel himself would have flatly refused to believe it. Yet that is exactly what was done by this chief's great-great-grandson, who derived his title solely from the 1665 transaction.

Not only the unfortunate MacIntosh, but also the chief of the Clan Ranald, had laid claim to the Camerons' land on the strength of some piece of Edinburgh writing. But this was before the Highland law was overturned by the Lowland: the Camerons occupied the land, and were prepared (and able) to defend it; so they kept it, irrespective of what a charter might claim.

On another occasion, Dr Johnson wrote, MacLean of Coll obtained a charter of some of the Cameron lands, and went with an armed force to take possession of what the king had given him. The Camerons mustered, "and a battle was fought at the head of Loch Ness, near the place where Fort Augustus now stands, in which

Lochiel obtained the victory, and MacLean, with his followers, was defeated and destroyed".[34]

11. Glenorchy and the Sinclairs

These are all examples of a clan successfully defending its own territory against invaders (the invasions caused in each case by Lowland machinations); and it may be thought that where clansfolk were trying to protect their own homeland against aggressors, the knowledge that they were the aggrieved party – or even merely their feeling of having so much to lose – would lend greater strength to their arms. But victory against assailants was not inevitable; even in Western films, the good guys don't always win. What happened when a battle was fought and the invaders triumphed?

Such an event actually occurred in 1678. As usual, the basic disagreement was caused by Lowland interference in Highland affairs, and the dreamily romantic idea that he who held the charter held the land. The sixth Earl of Caithness, chief of the Sinclairs, had fallen into debt in the reign of Charles II, and Sir John Campbell of Glenorchy, known as Iain Glas in the Highlands, the chief of the Breadalbane Campbells (the second most important Campbell formation), positioned himself – as he hoped – to seize the Sinclair lands by buying up most of the earl's debts. (This was the same man who brought about the settlement of the MacIntosh-Cameron dispute near Loch Arkaig.) The Earl of Caithness had to make a conditional grant of the lands covered by his charters to the Glenorchy chief, the grant (if repayment failed) becoming absolute in six years. "Sir John had Crown confirmation of, and sasine [legal validation] on this disposition", said *Burke's Peerage*. In 1673 a charter was granted by the Edinburgh authorities naming Glenorchy as the owner of the lands which belonged (in reality) to the Sinclair clan, or (in the Lowland theory) to the Earl of Caithness. In 1676 the Sinclair Earl of Caithness died, and the king gave Glenorchy "a new charter, including both the lands and the title of Earl of Caithness" (in the words of *Burke*). In 1678 Glenorchy married the last earl's widow. Glenorchy was now in Lowland eyes possessed of every possible legal claim that he could have to the Sinclair lands in Caithness. He had been granted the estate by the former earl, the Crown had given him a new charter of the lands, the Crown had made him the new Earl of Caithness, and he had even succeeded to the previous earl's claims by marrying his widow. Without question, Glenorchy had (in the eyes of the Lowland authorities) "virtually absolute control" of the Sinclair clan lands. There was no possible obstacle to his taking possession – no obstacle, that is, except the Sinclair clansfolk, who were cross-grained enough to decide that their new chief should be the previous earl's cousin and heir-male, George Sinclair of Keiss.

Glenorchy, being a Highlander, knew that Lowland titles were in reality worth nothing at all in the Highlands, so instead of relying on his (in Lowland terms incontrovertible) charter right, he gathered together an army. David Stewart said he collected "1100 Breadalbane men, including the followers of the immediate descendants of his family, [the Campbells of] Glenlyon, Glenfalloch, Lochdochart, Achallader, etc., and those of his neighbour and brother-in-law, the Laird of MacNab".[35] He marched through the Highlands with this force, a journey commemorated in the pipe tune *The Campbells are Coming*. When they reached Caithness, the Sinclair clan rallied to defend its homeland, and in 1680 the two armed forces met in a pitched battle at Altimarlich, near Wick.

12. Fight at Altimarlich

In the clash between the two clans, the Campbells triumphed. Many Sinclairs were killed. The battle was fought on the banks of a stream, the Allt-nam-meirleach, and it was said that there were so many corpses in the water that a man could walk from one bank to the other dry-shod.[36]

If Lowland ideas, and the decrees of the Lowland Government, could have prevailed anywhere in the Gaelic area, it would have been in Caithness. Along much of the southern and eastern border of the Highlands the boundary with the Lowlands was clearly defined by mountain ranges, allowing entrance only through narrow passes and defiles which were easily defensible; but in Caithness, the hills on the western (or inward) boundary of the Sinclair country were not very high, and as the terrain ran eastwards, the hills became still less imposing. At the boundary between the Gaelic and English languages (which was, as we saw earlier, a line drawn from Easter Clyth burn to Thurso) the land on the western, Gaelic, side was hardly higher than that on the eastern, English-language, side. In fact it was sometimes lower. At the northern end of the boundary line the highest "Highland" hill of 437 feet (133 metres) was matched – across the River Thurso – with a "Lowland" hill twenty-five feet higher, measuring 462 feet (141 metres);[37] at the southern end of the boundary the Cnoc an Earranaiche in Sinclair territory, at 693 feet (211 metres), was opposite to the Hill of Yarehouse in the anglophone district, at 696 feet (212 metres), three feet higher.[38] The Sinclair country of western Caithness was, it appeared, highly vulnerable to penetration by Lowland authorities and Lowland values. (So much so, that – as we noticed earlier – Professor Rosalind Mitchison, Seton Gordon, Lord Napier, Dr Ian Grimble, Sir Archibald Geikie, R. C. MacKenzie, and Allan MacColl, all considered that the whole of Caithness was entirely outside the Gaelic area.) Even the characteristic Highland garb, the plaid, had been abandoned; the Sinclairs wore breeches. (When a regiment of fencibles was raised by a Sinclair chieftain in Caithness in 1794, they wore not the filibeg, but what Stewart called "tartan pantaloons".)[39] To the Campbells this seemed no better than Lowland costume, and in the battle, said Stewart, Glenorchy's piper (one Finlay MacIver) made fun of it; he struck up an improvised melody which irresistibly suggested to Highlanders the Gaelic words "bodach na brigan", etc. – "the Lowland churls with the breeches are running away", thus stimulating the Campbells' efforts. "The tune has ever since been called Lord Breadalbane's March to Battle", wrote Stewart.[40]

13. A conquered country

The victorious Campbells of Breadalbane, their morale bolstered by the fact that they considered the Sinclairs – devoid alike of impregnable mountains and of the true Highland dress – to be not much better than Lowlanders, now spread out across the Sinclair clan territory. But in fact the Sinclairs were true Gaels, and Glenorchy had to overcome the problem of governing a Gaelic people within the Highland line who did not intend to be governed, in the days when the Highland clans were *de facto* independent: when, that is to say, there was no threatening state-power of soldiers and police, lawyers and courts, jails and gallows, to enforce obedience to the Lowland rulers. Glenorchy, wrote Stewart, "having gained the victory, quartered his men in the country for three years, levying rents and taxes, as if in a conquered country". According to the ideas of the Edinburgh and London authorities at the time, and according to the conventional historians ever since, Sir John Campbell of Glenorchy had, without a shadow of doubt, "virtually absolute control" of the Sinclair lands in Caithness.

What happened when this fine hypothesis came into collision with the real world? Stewart rounded off the story. "But though the Sinclairs were forced to yield in the first instance, they so harassed the invaders, and showed such hostility and determined resolution to oppose the claims of Glenorchy, that he at last yielded."[41] Glenorchy was compelled by the Sinclairs' resistance to abandon his claims, including the royally awarded title "Earl of Caithness", and in 1681 the king compensated him by making him Earl of Breadalbane. The clan's choice as the new chief, George Sinclair of Keiss, succeeded to the chiefship, and the authorities deferred to the clan's decision by accepting him as the seventh Earl of Caithness, and charter holder of the Sinclair lands. If Glenorchy, with all his plenitude of power and privilege – legal grant by the former owner, marriage with the former owner's widow, Crown grant of the lands, Crown grant of the earldom, braced and buttressed by over a thousand stalwart Campbell and allied clansmen, in all the potency of a sanguinary victory, and in the highly vulnerable Sinclair country – if Glenorchy and all his compelling claims were to be overthrown in these border-land foothills simply because the clansfolk in possession were not in a mood to accept them, then it is surely obvious that the vaunted charter right had no validity in the practical world, and was nothing more than a pious and unenforceable aspiration, exactly like (to repeat the comparison made earlier) the scraps of paper which some gullible modern citizens are convinced entitle them to building sites on the moon.

The Sinclairs, who had thus incontestably demonstrated who really owned the Sinclair clan territory, were subsequently, after the landlord revolution of the mid-eighteenth century, turned out by the charter holders. Proved worthless in 1680, the charters were used only a century later, after the Lowland conquest of the Highlands, to annihilate the Sinclair clan. The Sinclairs had made clear that private property in land had no place in the Highlands by insisting on Sinclair of Keiss as their chief in defiance of the Lowland law; and by a bitter paradox those to whom the charters descended only because the Sinclairs had established that they were meaningless used those same charters not long afterwards to claim untrammelled private ownership of the clan lands, entitling them to dispossess and banish the clansfolk.

14. Lovat and the Frasers

The Camerons were showing that they were the owners of their own clan country in the 1660s, the Sinclairs were showing the same in the 1680s, as were the MacDonalds of Keppoch in the 1680s and 1690s. Even later, the Frasers were demonstrating the same fact.

Hugh Fraser, seventh Lord Lovat, and thirty-second chief of the Frasers, died in 1646. Two of his sons, Simon and Hugh, died before he did; a third son, Thomas Fraser of Beaufort, lived on for another half century. The eldest-born Simon had no children, so the second-born Hugh's son, another Hugh (grandson of the chief who had just died), became eighth Lord Lovat; he also died early, and was succeeded by *his* son, again called Hugh, ninth Lord Lovat, and thirty-fourth chief. In 1685 Hugh, this ninth Lord Lovat, married Lady Amelia Murray, daughter of the first Marquis of Atholl. They had four daughters, of whom the eldest, called Amelia like her mother, was only ten years old when her father Hugh Fraser died (aged thirty) in 1696. The child Amelia was acknowledged to be "heir to the Fraser estates", or rather to the charters which purported to give possession of the lands of the Clan Fraser, according to the marriage settlement; since by that disposition Hugh (the younger Amelia's father) had left all "his" lands to the "heirs of his body" – his own children. If Hugh had no sons, the eldest daughter was to inherit his property, provided she married a Fraser. Six months before his death, however, Hugh had made a will claiming to overturn the marriage settlement and to leave the Fraser charters instead to his great-uncle and heir male, Thomas Fraser of

Beaufort. On the face of it the will must have been invalid, since by it Hugh was attempting to decide what would happen after his death to the land charters – but that question had already been resolved by the marriage settlement. It seems that Hugh was bowing to the decision of the clan: one of the chief's main duties being to lead the clan in any conflict, the Frasers would prefer a man to a ten-year-old girl as chief – as they demonstrated in 1696, when Hugh died. It would be difficult to explain otherwise why a man should try to disinherit his own family in favour of distant relatives, especially since Thomas (then an old man) and his son Simon were, as their actions proved, self-seeking scoundrels.

On her father's death the youthful Amelia succeeded to her father's position and his charters (subject only to her marrying a Fraser in due course), since obviously the marriage settlement had priority over the ninth Lord Lovat's purported will: Hugh could not leave what he had already bestowed – you cannot give away what you have already given away. So Amelia had all the power in the Fraser clan lands that the legal right to the succession could give her, strongly reinforced as that legal right was by the late Lord Lovat's family influence, all backed up by her own close connection through her mother with the powerful Atholl family. If Lowland law, with its private property and landlordism, had prevailed in the Highlands as early as 1696, the succession would have been quite clear: Amelia would have inherited. However, the correspondence among the Lovat and Atholl families shows that the Fraser clansfolk were still able to decide who should be the next chief, and to prove that, without the support of the Fraser clan, the Lovat charters were completely valueless. Soon after Hugh died, his widow wrote to her brother the Earl of Tullibardine, Atholl's eldest son: "Thomas of Beaufort and his son began interfering and conspiring among the Clan Fraser . . . They are more obdurate than ever and delude the people extremely, especially Strath Errick, for there they have positively denied to pay the rent [sic] till they see who has the best right . . ." Already, however, the clan had made its decision that Thomas Fraser was to be its next chief, and had gone beyond merely denying what Lady Lovat called "rent", that is the chief's tribute, to the Lovat family: they had begun to pay it to Thomas Fraser, as the thirty-fifth chief – a development which was naturally warmly welcomed and encouraged by the Beauforts. (Lady Lovat's use of the word "rent" is clearly mistaken, as the facts of the case show: not many landlords would be happy to accept a definition of "rent" as something that the occupiers of land paid when and if they felt like it, and even then only to the person they thought most deserving.)

The Marquis of Atholl, one of the most potent noblemen in the Lowlands, as well as being a clan chief in the Perthshire Highlands, came to the support of his daughter, the dowager Lady Lovat: as soon as his son-in-law Hugh Fraser died, he projected a marriage between his granddaughter, the ten-year-old Lady Lovat, and

Alexander Fraser, the thirteen-year-old son of Lord Saltoun (who was the head of a Fraser family in the Lowlands). This would comply with the clause of the marriage settlement requiring Amelia to marry a Fraser. Faced with this scheme, Thomas and Simon convened a meeting of the clan at Essich, near Inverness, on 22nd September 1696, only a week or two after Hugh's death, and a warning was issued telling Saltoun and his family to keep out of the Fraser clan country.[42]

15. A remarkable career

Saltoun disregarded this advice and entered Fraser territory, accompanied by Lord Mungo Murray, another of Atholl's sons. The Beauforts (Thomas and Simon) and sixty armed men came up with them in Bunchrew Wood and seized both Saltoun and Lord Mungo, together with their attendants. They were all held hostage at Finellan House for six or seven days, according to the *Atholl Chronicles*, "during which time Captain Simon assembled several hundreds of his clan in arms". On the same day that Saltoun and Murray were taken, the Beauforts captured Castle Downie (the residence of the Fraser chief, which was still held by the former Lovat family), made the young Lady Lovat and her mother prisoners, and put a garrison into the castle. Simon Fraser planned to compel the unfortunate child Amelia to marry him, and apparently carried out this atrocious scheme.

The 1891 edition of *Burke's Peerage*, no doubt conscious of the deference due to a peer of the realm, said respectfully that Simon Fraser "had a remarkable career". After the ninth Lord Lovat's death, it continued, Simon "induced his [Lovat's] eldest daughter to elope with him" – a thirty-year-old (Simon) inducing a ten-year-old (Amelia, who was his cousin's granddaughter) to "elope with him": by describing a kidnapping and an apparent rape in these terms *Burke* debased the English language.

Atholl wrote to his son Tullibardine, proposing that an armed expedition be sent to the Fraser country to avenge what he called the "forced marriage" of the child Amelia, and the capture of Lord Mungo (Tullibardine's brother). He suggested that the leader should be one Capoch (a chieftain from the Atholl clan), "and I will join a hundred of the ablest Atholl men with him, for without they be actors in it, I do not see how we can recover the affront that has been done us".[43] Atholl planned to send members of his own clan on the expedition because he realized that the family of his late son-in-law would get no support from the Fraser clansfolk. Murray of Dollery, who was also an Atholl chieftain, wrote to Tullibardine, "it is certain the generality of the country about Inverness favours them [the Beauforts]".[44] Tullibardine also received a letter from another of his brothers, Lord James Murray, about Simon Fraser: "never was creature so befriended as he is in that country, either out of kindness [kinship] to him, or out of hatred to us and the family of Lovat."⁴⁵ The *Atholl Chronicles* gloomily concluded that the Atholl men found it impossible to get at Simon and his father, from the wildness of the country, and from the fact that all the countrymen, or clansfolk, favoured the Beauforts.

16. This unhappy accident

The support of the Frasers meant that Simon was secure while he was in his own clan country, and that the efforts of the Marquis of Atholl – such as his proposed expedition – would fail; but Simon tried to win the approval of the Lowland authorities as well, for without it any journey beyond the Highland line (or even perhaps into some other parts of the Highlands) would be a risky venture. Writing to Colonel Sir John Hill, the governor of Fort William, Simon had the nerve to pretend to apologize for capturing Saltoun, calling the episode "this unhappy accident". Any Highland chief seeking favour in the Lowlands would often claim that he was able to bring the clan's armed men to support the Edinburgh authorities if they were needed: and Simon boldly promised his clansmen's assistance as if there were no chance of their ever rejecting his advice. He wrote that "if I had, or will have, my birthright preserved, I will always furnish 800 men to the King's service", and pointed out (as we saw above) that "the whole name . . . have unanimously joined with me".⁴⁶ (The 1746 memorial estimated the Frasers' armed strength at 900 men, so either Simon was being too modest, or he did not feel sure of carrying the whole clan with him.)

Simon's further attempt to regularize his position according to Lowland ideas by forcibly marrying the child Lady Lovat received a setback when the girl managed to escape Simon's clutches. According to the *Dictionary of National Biography*, "the clansman who had been entrusted with conveying her [to Simon], for whatever reason, failed to complete his commission, and brought her back to her mother". In other words, the clansman – as usual with clansmen – decided to do what he thought was right, whatever the orders of his "superiors" may have been. Simon's overtures to Sir John Hill were deservedly fruitless; and in 1698 both he and his father Thomas were tried (in their absence) for abducting Amelia and for "illegally" accepting her "rents". They were found guilty of high treason, and were sentenced to death, and attainder (the loss of all their civil rights, including, of course, any claim to landownership). The sentence was never carried out. Having failed to appear at his trial, Simon had even less desire to attend his own execution. (Thomas, however, died soon afterwards, in 1699.) This conviction made the position of Amelia on the one hand and the Beauforts on the other even more crystal clear: according to Lowland law, Amelia was the owner of the Lovat estates, and the Beauforts did not own, and now legally could not own, anything. (Curiously enough, Simon was executed forty-nine years later, as punishment for supporting Prince Charles: not many men have been condemned to death twice – with half a century between the two sentences. Simon's career was certainly "remarkable", to borrow the obsequious language of *Burke*).

17. Forcibly possessed himself

However, surrounded and supported by his clan, Simon could thumb his nose at Lowland judgements. He was quite unabashed. Having failed to keep the luckless child Amelia as his prisoner after their "forced marriage", he raped her mother. This was in October 1697. As the *Burke's Peerage* writer (perhaps feeling that a member of the aristocracy could not be accused of raping anybody) delicately put it, "he next forcibly possessed himself of the person of the widow of the ninth lord, and compelled her to marry him".[47] One account said that Simon "went in the dead of night to Castle Downie, where the Dowager Lady Lovat was living", accompanied by "three or four ruffians", and by "Mr Robert Munro, minister of Abertarff". They pushed out Lady Lovat's maids, and Munro began the marriage service, while a bagpiper played to stifle Lady Lovat's cries. Ignoring Lady Lovat's protests, the minister concluded by declaring the happy pair legally married. Two of Simon's thugs "rent off her clothes, cutting her stays with their dirks, and so thrust her into bed". The bagpipes continued "to play to drown the victim's screams".[48] The Rev. Robert Munro was clearly one of those complaisant Highland ministers who felt that the benefits of supporting the local bigwig over-rode the fine-sounding moral principles that they preached to the rank-and-file on Sundays. The clearance era saw many of these fawning ministerial flatterers, and their sycophantic accounts still make excellent documentary evidence, praised as being completely impartial,[49] and quoted extensively by historians to prove that the clearing landlords were blameless. Two other ministers exhibited the same deference towards Simon, according to a letter sent by Atholl to Tullibardine in December. "There is not any wickedness that can be imagined in sorcery and witchcraft that has not been used, and likewise by two base Ministers Mr Hew and Mr James Fraser, who has wrestled the scriptures to make her believe that she ought in conscience yield to that unworthy man."[50]

This "marriage" of Simon and Lady Lovat, however, does not appear to have convinced even the *Peerage* scribe who tells us of it, for when he lists Simon's wives, Amelia's mother does not appear. Nor does Amelia.

Opinion in the clan seems to have become less firm in its support of Simon; the clansman who took the girl Amelia back to her mother may have done so because feeling was turning against Simon. There was fighting in the Fraser clan country.

The *D.N.B.* said of Simon: "For some time he wandered with a band of trusty followers among the wilds of the northern Highlands, eluding every effort to capture him, and occasionally inflicting severe losses on his pursuers . . ." However, he persevered in his manoeuvres outside the clan as well. He took advantage of the enmity between Atholl (the supporter of Simon's rival for the chiefship) and the Earl of Argyll, and got Argyll on his side: and in 1700 Argyll duly obtained a pardon for Simon from King William III, apparently as to the 1698 verdict of high treason. Next Simon went to France, where he visited the court of the exiled James VII and II at St Germain to intrigue against King William; on the same expedition Simon also met that same King William, and played the loyal courtier to such good effect that William gave him a pardon for all offences against the state. However, the Dowager Lady Lovat complained to the high court of judiciary about Simon's outrage against her; he modestly failed to appear, and was outlawed by the court. Again he went to France, and intrigued with the Jacobites: sent by them as their agent to the Highlands, he found the clans reluctant to rise. At this point the Frasers seem to have turned completely against Simon, no doubt as some of his exploits became more generally known: and he returned to France. There, however, the Old Pretender (the son of James VII and II, and of Mary of Modena) seems to have realized what a lying rogue he was, and kept him as a virtual prisoner in France – in varying degrees of incarceration – for the next ten years.[51]

18. Fraser of Fraserdale

The plan to marry Amelia to Lord Saltoun's son failed for some reason (perhaps Saltoun's capture and imprisonment had given him, as a Lowland Fraser, a distaste for all his Highland cousins), and when Amelia was sixteen she married Alexander MacKenzie, nephew of the Earl of Cromartie. No doubt hoping to make himself acceptable to the clan as a chief – for the son-in-law of a chief had on several occasions been chosen as chief himself in Highland history – MacKenzie changed his name to Fraser of Fraserdale. At the same time the Lowland law was satisfied, for Amelia could now claim that she had married a Fraser, in accordance with the terms of her parents' marriage settlement. Opinion in the clan had veered towards the support of Amelia and her husband: their rival Simon had shown himself to be a serial turncoat, as well as a complete reprobate, and in any case he was now detained in France. For a time Amelia and Fraserdale were accepted by the clan as being the rightful inheritors of the position of chief. But then Fraserdale blotted his copybook. In 1706 he got a deed executed allowing the heirs of Amelia and himself "if they should think fit, in place of the surname of Fraser to bear the name of MacKenzie". This revelation that Fraserdale's transformation of himself into a

Fraser was not apparently genuine turned feeling against him and his wife, and as they went down in the scale, so their rival Simon went up. The *D.N.B.* said: "This procedure [the Fraserdales' apparent plan to change themselves back to MacKenzies] deeply offended the clan, and after several meetings of the gentlemen [or the elders of the clan] had been held they in 1713 despatched Major Fraser of Castle Leathers to France to discover the whereabouts of their chief and bring him home." Simon managed to escape from his detention, and accompany the major back to England; in London Simon was arrested for debt, but again he managed to flee, and made his way north to the Fraser country. By now the 1715 rebellion was brewing, and Simon found that Fraserdale had come out in favour of the Old Pretender.

Fraserdale may well have taken this step to regain the favour of the clan, because there was a strong Jacobite feeling among the Frasers; they had supported James VII and II in 1689, and Thomas Fraser, Simon's father, had even tried to take Edinburgh Castle for the same monarch in 1696. Subsequently, of course, the Frasers came out for Prince Charles in 1745. In fact Fraserdale was able to benefit from this Jacobite enthusiasm to the extent of getting some of the Fraser clan to go with him in 1715 to join the Pretender's army at Perth. Immediately Simon Fraser, who had been in close correspondence with the Stuarts, saw what a heaven-sent opportunity he had been given to push his personal ambitions; and forthwith he declared his support for the house of Hanover, confident that the clan (especially after Fraserdale's faux pas of apparently planning to call himself MacKenzie again) would rally to him. He sent an emissary to speak to the Fraser clansmen who had enlisted with the Jacobites in Perth, and again, when faced with the choice between Fraserdale (who was fortified up to his ears with legal rights and official charters), and Simon, whom they now preferred as chief, they plumped for Simon – even though Fraserdale was appealing to their ingrained Jacobite fervour. Those Frasers who had already rallied to the rebels, said Selkirk, marched off in a body to join their preferred chief.[52] The commander of the Jacobite forces, the Earl of Mar, wrote that "Lovat is the life and soul of the [Hanoverian] party here; the whole Country and his name dote on him; all the Frasers have left us since his appearing in the country."

In the fighting the Fraser clan did good service to George I by cutting off the rear of the main body of rebels under Mar. Simon had, as he intended, turned his position as chief of the Clan Fraser to his own advantage. He had proved that the clan now regarded him, not Fraserdale, as its chief; and he had posed as a guardian of law and order and loyal supporter of the Government. As often happened, the manufactured Lowland "right" of alleged private property in the clan land followed the actual Highland position as chief of the clan. The Government granted the infamous Simon a remission of the sentences which had been passed upon him, deprived Fraserdale and his wife of their charters to the Fraser clan land, and presented them to Simon. The result was, in the words of the *Complete Peerage*, that "Lady Lovat and her numerous family lived in great financial distress for many years".[53]

19. Eloquent tongue

No one could deny that Simon had an eloquent tongue and a winning manner. When another Jacobite rebellion was planned, in 1719, Simon wrote to the Jacobite leader Seaforth promising to join him to fight for the Stuart dynasty. Then he went to London to explain how strongly he supported the house of Hanover, and George I agreed to be godfather to his daughter.

More was yet to come. The title of Lord Lovat had descended since the fifteenth century in the Fraser of Lovat family. It went to the nearest heir, and was not restricted to males. By Lowland law, therefore, both land charters and the peerage should have gone to Amelia, and did go to her. She was called Lady Lovat as soon as her father died in 1696, and when she was sixteen in 1702 she obtained – to make the matter absolutely certain – a decree of the Court of Session affirming her right to the title, as Baroness Lovat. But Simon, by the opportune use of his position as chosen head of the Fraser clan, had now obtained the charters to the land; and by a decision of the Court of Session in 1730 the decree of 1702 was rescinded, and Simon became Lord Lovat. This decision appears to be inexplicable by strict reference to Lowland law, for Amelia was alive and had a son, Hugh, to succeed her. (Hugh lived until 1770.) Even if Amelia was to be deprived of the title because Fraserdale had supported the Old Pretender, it seems that there were still heirs nearer to the ninth Lord Lovat than Simon Fraser. (The ninth Lord Lovat, Amelia's father, had three sisters, all married; and Amelia herself had three sisters, two of them married.)[54] The 1730 decision was a remarkable instance of the vigour of the old Highland polity, and its ability, in the hands of such an unscrupulous scoundrel as Simon Fraser, to overcome the apparently all-conquering Lowland law as late as the second quarter of the eighteenth century.

20. Object of her aversion

Simon had married Margaret, the daughter of Ludovic Grant of Grant, and they had four children. (Simon ignored his previous "marriage" to Lady Lovat, and made no attempt to obtain a divorce.) When Margaret died, Simon's eye fell on Primrose Campbell, a girl of twenty-three who was the cousin of the current (second) Duke of Argyll; later, her brother succeeded as fourth duke. Lovat no doubt thought he would benefit from an alliance with the powerful Argyll family, but his overtures to Primrose Campbell were refused with contempt. It is not surprising that she wanted to have nothing to do with Lovat, who was now sixty-six years old (forty-three years older than she was), and had been practised in villainy from his youth. Lovat had had much experience in how to overcome such difficulties. When Primrose was visiting a relative she received a note "from her mother", in which she was asked to come quickly to a certain house in Edinburgh, where, the note said, her mother lay ill. Primrose went, and there found she was trapped. She came face to face, wrote Alexander (Dean of Guild) MacKenzie, with "the special object of her aversion, Lord Lovat, under conditions which impelled her to listen to his vows of endearment". When she refused to submit, Simon told her that the house to which she had been lured was a brothel, and that if she continued to refuse him he would ruin her reputation for ever by disclosing the fact to everyone. Simon imprisoned Primrose in the house for several days, and finally she gave in and agreed to marry him.[55]

It seems somehow fitting that the nefarious Archibald Fraser, the chief who more than any other was responsible for the rape of the Fraser land, should have been born as the result of this misbegotten and ill-fated union. But that story will come later. Lovat treated Primrose very badly, at the same time unmercifully slandering her in all his letters. After a year or two she succeeded in leaving him, and she survived her blackguard of a husband by half a century, living on until 1796.

When the 1745 rebellion broke out, Simon was still playing his double game with his old skill. He was in regular, friendly correspondence with Duncan Forbes of Culloden, the Hanoverian banner-bearer in the Highlands. Then Prince Charles' army won the Battle of Prestonpans. This made Simon think the Jacobites were likely to prevail, so he sent round the croishtarich to rouse the clan (which had always had Jacobite leanings) in the rebel cause. His son, another Simon, commanded the Fraser contingent that went off to join Prince Charles. At the same time Lord Lovat wrote to Forbes that "nothing ever grieved his soul so much" as his son's coming out for Prince Charles. After Culloden, Lovat was captured and charged with treason. In the end, all Lovat's dexterity and double-dealing could not save him. At his trial, said an eye-witness, he "most piously alluded to passages of Scripture"; but he was found guilty, and he was beheaded in April 1747. Before his execution, he asked to be buried at Kirkhill, in Fraser country, near the grave of his elder brother, who died young, and where "some good old Highland woman might sing a coronach [lament] at his funeral"; but permission was refused, and he was buried at the Tower, where he was executed.

It will be seen that Simon Fraser, the tenth Lord Lovat, was one of the most contemptible characters to have appeared even in the ranks of the eighteenth-century Highland chiefs; and it is easy to feel that the Frasers could scarcely have chosen a worse evildoer to lead them. (Even those who are prepared to accept individuals' documentary testimony to their own excellence may feel misgivings over what Simon Fraser had the immense aplomb to write in 1729: "I bless God I never was in my life guilty of a base or villainous action.")[56] However, it must be confessed that even in modern Britain, where everyone receives a dozen years of full-time education gratis, and where millions boast university degrees, more than one deceitful and corrupt individual has been freely chosen by the electors to represent them in the House of Commons. Electoral democracy, whether in the eighteenth-century Highlands or in twenty-first century Britain, does have these drawbacks, and would be rejected as inadequate – were it not that (as has often been said) every other system is much worse.

In the case of the other clans – the Camerons, the Sinclairs, the MacPhersons, and so on – who during the seventeenth century were demonstrating beyond any question that they, not the person who happened to be named in the Edinburgh writing, were the owners of the clan lands, those who were made chiefs by their clansfolk did not themselves begin to act as landlords; at least a generation or two were allowed to pass before the chiefs started to evict those same clansfolk. In the case of the Frasers, however, the transformation from being a chief owning his position (in flat defiance of Edinburgh) entirely to the support of the clan, to being a landlord in full possession of the Lowland private-property right, which enabled the charter holder to begin clearing out his clansfolk, was complete within a single generation. Simon Fraser, the tenth Lord Lovat, performed in his own personal lifetime the revolutionary volte-face from being a hunted outlaw, subject to the severest penalties of the Lowland law, to being the most prized darling of that law – a landlord. Later it will be seen how this seemingly magic metamorphosis did not prevent Simon embarking upon the same courses as other proprietors, who could at least persuade themselves that not only they, but also their forefathers before them, had always been the preferred objects of Edinburgh's favours.[57]

21. MacNeills of Barra

The history of the MacNeills of Barra also shows how little the boasted "charter-right" had to do with the actual ownership and possession of the lands supposedly governed by it.

The island of Barra had been the country of the MacNeills, the clansfolk said, since the eleventh century, when they had first come from Ireland. The MacNeills claimed to be a very ancient clan indeed. Neil MacNeill, first chief of Barra, was also, according to the genealogies, the twenty-first chief of MacNeill. When the MacNeills had possessed Barra for four centuries, King James IV of Scotland, at Stirling in 1495, gave the chief a charter to the island. James IV, then young and ambitious, was planning to make a sally against England on behalf of the pretender to the English throne, Perkin Warbeck, and needed friendly chiefs behind him. This piece of paper did not alter the fact of the matter, which was that the MacNeill clan owned Barra.

In 1587 Queen Elizabeth of England ordered the execution of the former Scottish monarch, Mary Queen of Scots; the MacNeills of Barra used Mary's death as an excuse to seize an English ship. Elizabeth protested to King James VI of Scotland, and James (who wished to maintain friendly relations with the English queen) summoned the then chief, Roderick, to appear before him. Roderick ignored him. Another chief, however, MacKenzie of Kintail, wished to curry favour with James. He realized that to seize a chief surrounded by his clan would be virtually impossible; so he resorted to dishonourable trickery. He visited Barra, and invited Roderick on board for a friendly meal; then he kidnapped him and delivered him to the king. James took no action against the person of Roderick, but he did annul Roderick's charter, and in its place gave the trickster MacKenzie of Kintail a charter to the lands of the MacNeills.

In Lowland theory, and in the eyes of all those many historians who take the will for the deed (or the other kind of deed for the reality), Kintail was now the owner of Barra. The only way he could in practice exercise any power over Barra, however, was by leading his MacKenzies, MacRaes and the rest to conquer it. The Clan Kenneth, again at the instigation of James VI and I, did conquer Lewis (at the other end of the Outer Hebrides) a few years later, aided by divisions and disputes among the Lewis clansfolk; but the MacKenzies did not think fit to make any move against the united MacNeill clan of Barra. Instead, Kintail gave MacNeill of Barra a Lowland title to the island at the cost of sixty merks Scots (or £3 6s 8d – less than £3½ sterling) annual feu duty. This freed the MacNeills from any immediate fear of conflict and bloodshed following King James' manipulation of the charters, and Kintail for his part got a very small annual income, and some prestige, out of the affair. Later Sir James MacDonald, second baronet of Sleat, married the daughter of Sir Roderick MacKenzie, tutor of Kintail (that is, guardian of the young chief, and temporary regent), and received the superiority, and the minute annual feu duty, of Barra as his wife's dowry.

In 1688 James VII and II, afraid that he was going to lose his throne to William of Orange, attempted to ensure the loyalty of Black Ruari MacNeill, then the chief of Barra, by granting him an exclusive charter to the island, ignoring the preceding claims of MacDonald of Sleat. In the subsequent war between James and William, Ruari in gratitude persuaded his clan to support the former; they fought for James at Killiecrankie in 1689. However, William won the war and established himself and his wife, Mary, as joint sovereigns. The rebel chiefs (that is, those who supported the deposed king) were pardoned, though of course the defeated monarch's charters were annulled; so MacNeill of Barra – in the eyes of the Lowland lawyers – now returned to his earlier position, and held the island as "feudal under-tenant" of MacDonald of Sleat. MacNeill of Barra again raised his clan and joined the rebellion of 1715, no doubt hoping that the Old Pretender would emulate his father, and give him a full charter; but the rebellion failed.

Throughout this time, whether there was a charter to Barra, or whether there was no charter to Barra, whether the Lowland lawyers regarded MacNeill as the charter holder, or whether some other chief (MacKenzie or MacDonald) had that honour, it made no difference on the ground. In the world of fact, as opposed to the domain of fictional records written up by the authorities (and thought highly of by Edinburgh lawyers and by orthodox historians), the MacNeill clansfolk possessed the island of Barra. The story is interesting in that it shows how the charters purporting to give the ownership of or the "superiority" over Barra first arose, and how little they had to do with any actual possession (much less with any care or improvement) of the soil.[58]

22. Fate of Clan Gregor

The fate of the MacGregors was dealt with in *Burke's Peerage*. "When territorial possessions were legally secured by written tenures, the clan imprudently continued to trust to the right of the sword, and thus paved the way for the long train of misfortunes which fell upon them. While they pursued their simple and retired mode of life, the great barons in their vicinity used their court influence to obtain charters over the old MacGregor possessions, and followed up the acquisition of such documentary rights by driving out the true proprietors."[59]

The second of these sentences contains such a clear description of the way in which the clearances were carried out, when the clan chiefs "used their court influence to obtain charters" to what was not theirs – the clan lands – and then exploited their "documentary rights by driving out the true proprietors", thus founding the fortunes of many rich Scottish families, that one is surprised to find the passage in that particular publication. It is not, however, accurate in two ways. Firstly it suggests ("the clan imprudently continued to trust to the right of the sword") that some *clans* did legally secure their territorial possessions by written tenures: but this never happened. When the Lowland state triumphed over the Highlands, and Lowland law was imposed over the whole of Scotland, the very idea of a clan was so foreign to the legal system and the way of life which had now come out on top that Scots law refused even to recognize the legal existence of such an institution. The Lord Ordinary (Ardmillan) pronounced in the MacGillivray succession case in 1862 to that effect: "In more recent times clans are indeed mentioned, or recognized as existing, in several Acts of Parliament. But it is thought that they are not mentioned or recognized as institutions or societies having legal status, legal rights, or legal vocation or functions, but rather as associations of a lawless, arbitrary, turbulent, and dangerous character . . . The purposes for which they once existed, as tolerated but not as sanctioned societies, are not now lawful. To all practical purposes they cannot legally act, and they do not legally exist. The law knows them not."[60]

Societies whose existence the Lowland law refused to recognize, regarding them as "lawless, arbitrary, turbulent, and dangerous", could hardly obtain any title to ownership under that law. Clan chiefs secured written tenures, but never clans.

Secondly, the *Peerage* account suggests that it was because "the great barons in the vicinity" obtained charters to the MacGregor land that they then proceeded to attack the MacGregors, but that puts the cart before the horse. What really occurred was that a number of neighbouring chiefs and great men, who all happened to have grudges at the same time against the MacGregors, combined against them – with the support of their clans. The powerful Campbells were the leading spirits, but the Stewarts, Gordons, Grahams, Drummonds, Buchanans, and MacFarlanes joined in. Of these clans and families, the heads of the first five – Argyll, Atholl, Huntly, Montrose, and Perth – had become imbued with Lowland desires for self-aggrandisement, and their greed at the thought of extending the areas over which they ruled in the Highlands had much to do with this combination against the MacGregors. Being well versed in Lowland ways, and wishing to obtain a veneer of legality, they first obtained charters to the MacGregor lands: nor was this difficult, since they had the ear of the king, and the MacGregor clan did not. The Privy Council, it is true, issued letters of fire and sword against the MacGregors, but we have seen that these commissions were worth nothing unless the particular chiefs to whom they were issued had the power to carry them into effect. This band of chiefs and noblemen did have the power, and ultimately the MacGregors were defeated, and their very surname made illegal. But this fate was due not to any failure of the Clan Gregor, or its chief, to obtain written charters; it was the result of their misfortune in incurring the enmity of so many powerful and unscrupulous neighbours at the same time.

23. *To make an ally*

Edinburgh itself appears to have recognized that, unless the Lowland government intended to provoke dissension (a motive touched on below), it was advantageous to grant a charter to whoever was currently chief. R. W. Munro mentioned this penchant of the Edinburgh authorities. "The MacLeans bypassed the nearest heir in the reign of James IV, and so did the Clan Ranald in accepting John of Moidart [Iain Mudartach] as their chief – in both cases sanctioned by charters from the Crown."⁶¹ In the case of the Clan Ranald the grant of a charter to the de facto chief (contradicting the previous charter) occurred more than once within a few years. Iain Mudartach, when he was chosen as chief of the Clan Ranald in defiance of the rules of landlord descent, was able to secure a charter to the Clan Ranald lands. On Mudartach's imprisonment, when Ranald Gallda was able to interpose himself into the position of chief, the charter given to Mudartach was revoked, and a new charter given to Gallda. After Gallda had been overthrown by the clan, and Mudartach re-instated as chief, the latter apparently obtained yet another charter to the land of Clan Ranald.

The aim and object of these dealings was that the charter holder would feel under an obligation to the king who had granted him the charter, and would do his best to bring his clan to the king's help if help were needed. Hence a king feeling insecure might try to insure against trouble by granting charters. We have seen how the Scottish king in 1495, and the British king in 1688, gave MacNeill of Barra a charter to the island, to secure his support in the immediately imminent struggles. Similarly, in 1542 James V, when about to invade England, gave Ewen MacKinnon of MacKinnon a charter to the lands of the MacKinnon clan in Skye and Mull, clearly hoping that the MacKinnon chief would feel grateful.⁶² James V's invasion ended in disaster at Solway Moss; James died three weeks later, so was not able to demand any return for his grant. But his intention was clear – to make an ally in the Highlands, so as to help keep peace in the north while he made war in the south.

The ordinary member of a clan may well have regarded any desire on the part of the chief to secure a charter to the clan land with an amused tolerance. The charter was only an unintelligible scrap of paper – English or Latin, it was all one to the Gaelic clansfolk – and if it pleased the chief, so much the better, for it certainly made no difference to the position of the clanspeople themselves; nor could it, so far as the members of the clan could see, ever make any difference. This attitude it is easy for us – who know what happened later – to characterize as short-sighted; but the Highlanders were by no means the only people (either then or now) to have believed that the general conditions of the society in which they lived would last for ever. Often the Highlanders may have considered the chief's charter as a positive advantage to themselves. For, as we have seen, where a rival chief had been servile or dishonest enough to have got in first with a charter to a particular clan land, before the clan's own chief, long-drawn-out hostilities and much bloodshed quite often followed. The chief's charter may have appeared to the ordinary clansfolk as making peace more likely for themselves and their families.

The three areas of the Highlands which outsiders (for example Richard Franck, in his *Northern Memoirs* of 1658) sometimes referred to as being particularly "lawless" were Balquhidder, Lochaber, and Badenoch.⁶³ It may be significant that in all these areas lived clans whose chiefs either did not obtain charters to the whole of the clan lands until late in the clan period of history, or did not obtain them at all. The MacGregors were a Balquhidder clan; the Camerons lived in Lochaber, the MacPhersons in Badenoch, and the MacDonalds of Keppoch in the Braes of Lochaber – or, as the district was also called, Brae Badenoch. (The Keppoch MacDonald clan was sometimes known as the Clan Ranald of Lochaber.)

24. Clan Donald land

A king who thought he could "manage" the Highlands would grant charters to the chiefs of the clans in possession. Other kings who were less assured, or less confident of the charter holder adhering to his bargain, would adopt a policy of divide and rule: and would grant land charters to chiefs not because their clans occupied the specified territory, but for exactly the opposite reason – because they did not. If a king despaired of influencing the Highlands, the next best thing was to provoke disagreements among the chiefs, and thus (he hoped) keep them too busy quarrelling to interfere in Lowland affairs. Canon R. C. MacLeod, a member of the chiefly family of Dunvegan, discussed the subject in an article in *The Scottish Historical Review*. "As a matter of fact, however, a very large part of the Highlands was *de facto* in the hands of owners [i.e., in his opinion, clan chiefs: though really it was in the hands of the clans] who *de jure* [as of legal right] had no claim whatever. Sometimes the Kings of Scotland created jealousies and strife between the great chiefs by granting the lands [or rather the charter-right to land] of one powerful laird to another, and even making simultaneous grants of the same estates to different people. In 1498 [as part of his struggle against the MacDonald Lordship of the Isles] James IV granted the Bailliary of Trotternish [which was Clan Donald country] to both MacLeod of Dunvegan and MacLeod of the Lewes, leaving them to fight it out between them. In 1542 [that is, as we saw, just before he invaded England] James V granted the estates which had been for centuries the property of the MacDonalds of Sleat to MacLeod of Dunvegan, a grant which was the cause of endless disputes between these powerful clans. The Kings of Scotland were directly responsible for the turbulence and unrest which prevailed in the Highlands at this period."[64]

The unreality of these charter awards can be seen from the would-be dealings on paper with the land of Clan Donald. In 1495, the Crown granted a charter to North Uist, and to Trotternish and Sleat in Skye, all Clan Donald territories, to the chief of Clan Donald; that chief's son, having no immediate family, bequeathed his charters to the chief of Clan Ranald; at the same time, as we saw, the Crown granted Trotternish simultaneously to two rival MacLeod chiefs (Dunvegan and Lewis); in 1542 the Crown granted these Clan Donald lands to MacLeod of

Dunvegan; in 1597 the Crown granted the lands to the chief of Clan Donald; on 11th June 1614 the Crown granted the lands to MacLeod of Dunvegan; and on 21st July 1614 the Crown granted the lands back again to the chief of Clan Donald. The Rev. Dr Archibald MacDonald said: "How little the Crown and its officials thought of the formal and even solemn terms of the title recorded on sheepskin" when these grants were made may be gathered from the three incompatible awards (one in 1597, and two in 1614) effected in less than a score of years.[65] But all this granting and rescinding and inheriting and transferring (which kept numbers of solemn lawyers very busy, not to mention prosperous) was purely fanciful, as far as the facts of the matter were concerned; in the real world the Clan Donald occupied its lands, and kept them. The rank-and-file MacDonalds probably did not normally even know who – from time to time – could boast of holding this illusory Lowland charter to the lands of Clan Donald. The authoritative Clan Donald history pointed out that though for many years a rival chief had a Lowland title to the MacDonald lands, the Clan Donald was not disturbed, "the strong right arm of the clan proving more than a match for the sheepskin right of the charter holder, MacLeod of Dunvegan".[66]

It is surprising that anyone, knowing all these facts, can bring himself or herself to believe in the literal truth of all these conflicting charters.

25. No formal leases

The idea of a written title percolated no further into the clan than the chief's charter. The right of the clansfolk to a share in the clan land was ensured by custom, by tradition, and by their own undoubted ability to defend it, if a foreign clan should attempt to invade (or, for that matter, if a chief of their own clan should get too big for his boots). And although the chief, having obtained his charter, might be more inclined to call the clan's annual tribute to him by the name of "rent", again, since the sum involved remained the same, there was no reason why the clansfolk should be concerned with questions of nomenclature. Everyone knew, as a matter of practical politics, where the chief stood and where the clansfolk stood. As John Stuart Blackie said, referring to the clansman under the clan system: "Although he may pay some acknowledgement in the shape of what we call rent to the head of the clan, it stands more in the place of what we now call taxation for public purposes, than a price paid for temporary occupancy under the modern relation of landlord and tenant. Formal leases there could be none where the right of every member of the clan to have a share in the property of the clan was practically recognized by both parties."[67]

The clan tribute paid to the chief was really (as Blackie said) much nearer to being a tax, paid to keep up the chief's position as head of state of the clan country.

In 1893 Angus Sutherland, a crofters' delegate, told one of the Brand commissioners "there is no Gaelic word for rent": he said "the Norman French word you give has always been used", that is, màl.[68] In Irish mál means a tribute-tax, in Anglo-Saxon it meant tribute, and in Gaelic it is used to mean either tribute or (later) rent. The same word was used to mean first the tribute paid by the clansfolk to a chief during the clan system, and subsequently the rent paid by a tenant to a landlord when that system was overthrown.

Since the surviving history of the Highlands was written largely by Lowlanders or by those who accepted Lowland ideas and standards, the tribute paid to the chief by the clansfolk was usually called "rent" in the history books. No doubt if the history of the Lowlands had been written largely by Highlanders, and therefore reflected Highland ideas and standards, the amounts paid by the possessors of Lowland land to those who had obtained a charter right to it would have been called "tribute". The important thing (in matters either historical or current) is not the name given to a particular payment (or any other transaction), but the reality behind it.

26. "Sales" of land

If these charters had meant what the clan chiefs (and commentators) subsequently claimed that they meant, that the chiefs had from the date of the charter the complete private property right in the clan land, then land in the Highlands would have been bought and sold in the ordinary commercial way just as freely as land in the Lowlands and in England. But, in fact, ordinary commercial sales of land in the Highlands were non-existent. Dr Johnson in 1773 visited MacLeod of Raasay, who had charters to Raasay and also to much land in Portree parish, and wrote, "the estate has not, during four hundred years, gained or lost a single acre".[69] In the 1790s the minister of Kirkmichael (Banffshire) said the Gordon family had been in possession of a charter since the 1480s, and that to the parish's "detached situation", its "natural barriers", and the "coldness of the climate, it has been owing that the possession of the property has undergone so few changes".[70] But when the landlord revolution was complete, transfers of land came to Kirkmichael as to the rest of the Highlands, without the weather getting warmer or the hills disappearing. What had changed was that the charters, once valueless, were now enforced. Sir George Steuart MacKenzie said of Ross-shire in 1813, "until of late, few estates have changed their owners".[71] Simon, Lord Lovat, in a memorial on the Highlanders, wrote in 1724: "Many of their families have continued in the same possessions during many ages, and very little alterations happen in the property of land; there are few purchases, and securities for debts are very uncertain, where power happens to be wanting to support the legal right."[72]

Lovat here means the legal right according to Lowland law; at that date, the power of the clan was still almost always able to support its legal right according to Highland law. The phrase "securities for debts" refers to the mortgaging of land. A Lowland landowner could always raise funds by giving a charge over part of his land to someone who had lent him money, so that the rents would go to the lender in lieu of interest on his loan (or as a combination of interest and part-repayment). But a Highland chief, even though he possessed a charter which alleged that he was the landowner, found any such transaction very difficult, if not impossible. The clan paid its tribute to the chief, as its head of state; and would refuse to pay it to anyone else, even though the chief asked his clansfolk to do so. Hence Lovat wrote that "securities for debts are very uncertain".

Transactions dignified with the name of "sales of land" were not entirely unknown, although, naturally, they were rare. If one only examined the written evidence, and ignored the truth behind it, one would conclude that in 1666, for example, Lachlan MacIntosh of that ilk had sold Glen Loy and Locharkaigside to Archibald, Earl of Argyll – this being the deal that followed in due course the armed confrontation of the MacIntosh and Cameron clans in 1665.[73] But in fact that episode, so far from showing the existence of private property in land in the Highlands, had shown exactly the opposite – that a clan (in this case the Camerons) was perfectly capable of defending its own land against an Edinburgh charter. The Cameron clan owned the Cameron clan land before 1666 and also after 1666. The reality behind the 1666 transaction was that the Clan Cameron kept its land, yet the "sale" document did not even mention the Camerons: another reminder of the difference between the fact and the appearance.

In the same way, Campbell of Calder "purchased" Dunmaglass in 1414; but, unfortunately for Calder, Dunmaglass had long been possessed by the MacGillivray clan, and they continued in possession, notwithstanding Calder's "purchase". The Edinburgh lawyers got round this clear contradiction between their fanciful theory and the undeniable fact of the matter by saying that in such cases the clan had dùchas, or dùthchas, which means both native land and the hereditary right to that land. In 1626, over two centuries later, the then chief of the MacGillivrays agreed to hold Dunmaglass from the Campbells of Calder as a feu for sixteen pounds (Scots) a year, or £1 6s 8d (one and a third pounds) in English money.[74] He no doubt considered that the payment of a few shillings annually was well worth it, to avoid the annoyance of Calder claiming the clan land as his own. At a time when many of the Highland chiefs had already obtained a charter to their clan lands, probably MacGillivray felt that he too would like to have a Lowland title, and that this was the least troublesome way of obtaining it.

Another of the minor clans in the Clan Chattan, the MacBain clan, came out of Lochaber with the MacIntoshes and occupied some land at Kinchyle, near the north-eastern end of Loch Ness, in the first part of the fourteenth century. And there, without a charter, they stayed. A Campbell of Calder (the Campbell chiefs were always great charter-collectors) obtained a charter to Kinchyle at the latest in the seventeenth century, and here again the Lowland law had to recognize the contradiction between the theory and the fact by saying that the MacBains held the land as dùchas. In 1685 the then MacBain chieftain acquired the feu right from Sir Hugh Campbell of Calder,[75] but it is significant that only fifteen years from the end of the seventeenth century a clan was holding its lands within six miles of Inverness without the slightest countenance from a Lowland charter.

27. MacLeods of Raasay and Glenelg

Similar events took place in Raasay. The Raasay MacLeods, a branch of the Torquil MacLeods of Lewis, held their island off Skye for many generations. But the chief of the MacLeans of Dochgarroch, a small clan that had made its way across the Highlands in course of time to occupy a small territory near Inverness, had inherited a piece of paper which claimed to be a "title to Raasay", granted by the Bishops of the Isles. Alexander MacLean, the chief of Dochgarroch in 1630, was served heir (in the appropriate Lowland manner) to his father as the "owner" of the island;[76] and the documentary record of that event would no doubt convince some true believers that Alexander MacLean of Dochgarroch "owned" Raasay in 1630. The contrast between fact and fiction is quite clear: the academic historians say that in the seventeenth century MacLean of Dochgarroch owned Raasay, and reality says that the MacLeod clansfolk then owned Raasay. (The reader can choose which version to believe.) By 1745 MacLeod of Raasay had obtained the charter (which later enabled his successor to begin clearing out the ordinary Raasay MacLeods) – presumably by buying it, or getting hold of it somehow, from a MacLean of Dochgarroch.

Glenelg is another case in point. In 1598 a company of Lowland adventurers obtained from the Edinburgh authorities a fictitious "title" to the lands of Harris, Dunvegan, and Glenelg. These were the lands of the Tormod MacLeods, and the Lowland company were not, of course, able to enforce their written claim, or to disturb in any way the MacLeods who actually lived in, and possessed, those districts.[77] Lovat, the chief of the Frasers, had got hold of a charter to Glenelg years before, in 1532:[78] he, too, could do nothing to unsettle the MacLeods who were in occupation. There followed another of those transactions which a naive observer might take to be "documentary evidence" that private property in land already existed in the Highlands, the "sale of Glenelg" in 1620 by Lovat to MacLeod of

MacLeod for a few thousand Scots merks (apparently both parties ignored the Lowlanders' charter of 1598).[79] But this was a sale, not of Glenelg, but of a charter to Glenelg. No doubt MacLeod was glad to get it so cheaply. For a chief who had not been cunning or unscrupulous enough to get to Edinburgh first and procure a fabricated charter to his clan land probably without payment at all (except a deferential cringe and deceitful commitments), the buying of a charter for a small sum would be an acceptable alternative. The size of the purchase price, a few thousand merks, indicates conclusively that there was no sale of Glenelg as a piece of private property: the only thing that changed hands was the Edinburgh charter, a kind of insurance that another chief would not get a similar fake title to the clan land and cause trouble, such as the Camerons and the Keppoch MacDonalds experienced from MacIntosh, the Lewis MacLeods from MacKenzie of Kintail, and the MacLeans and MacDougalls from the Campbell chiefs. One thousand Scots merks is £55 10s in English currency; even 5000 merks would only amount to £277 10s. Less than two hundred years later, in 1810, when Glenelg really had become a piece of private property, it was sold to a director of the East India Company for £98,500, which was probably at least 400 times as much as the price given in the 1620 document. Making every allowance for inflation, and for the differing circumstances, it is plain enough that what was sold in 1620 was not what was sold in 1810.

28. MacDougalls of Muckairn

Wherever one is able to delve into the true facts behind what the Lowland lawyers described as "sales of land" in the Highlands before 1745, one uncovers still more evidence that private ownership of land had no place in Highland society. According to the charters, Sir John Campbell of Calder, who flourished in the early sixteenth century, obtained possession of Muckairn by "buying" it from the Bishop of the Isles; in fact, he obtained it by leading his clan of Campbells to conquer it from the MacDougalls, who previously possessed it. The story of how some of the MacDougalls and their septs came to be incorporated in the Calder clan is told in a manuscript, "probably a century and a half old", lent by Campbell of Lochnell to the writer of the report on Muckairn in the New Statistical Account, and quoted there at some length.[80] The story illustrates how a mutually exclusive Lowland charter right (the theory) and Highland clan right (the fact) could exist over the same piece of land for several centuries.

Muckairn lay very close to Loch Awe, the centre of the growing power of the Campbells. It included Ben Cruachan, which looked down on the River Awe and, a little further away, on Loch Awe. The Highland right to Muckairn lay with the MacDougalls, in whose country it was; but the Bishops of the Isles had the charter right. A compromise was attempted, but it broke down. "One of these bishops, called Ferquhard, set the same in tack to MacDougall of Lorn [the chief of the MacDougalls], who was at that time very powerful in these countries. MacDougall, for some considerable time, paid his tack duty to the bishops in victuals . . . but MacDougall, either through insolence, or some private discontent, became an undutiful vassal, and an ill payer of his dues, till, in the end, he refused to pay any thing at all." In other words, for a time MacDougall thought it worth while to pay a small annual fee to the bishop who held a Lowland charter to Muckairn, in order to avoid the possibility of trouble: but it was always open to him to refuse to pay, and after a time he did refuse. The bishop, of course, could do nothing at this point, since the MacDougalls occupied the territory in question.

With hindsight, MacDougall might well have been wise to continue his small payments to the bishop, though in the end the Campbells, expanding their territory with the support and encouragement of the Edinburgh authorities, would probably have caused trouble (in an area so close to Loch Awe) whatever MacDougall did.

29. Campbell of Calder

Then Campbell of Calder (or Cawdor) came on the scene. The Campbell clan was powerful enough to conquer Muckairn; and Calder (like most of the Campbell chieftains) was sufficiently astute to see the advantage of first obtaining the Lowland charter right to his intended conquest, in order to lend it a colour of Lowland legality. "At this time Sir John Campbell, Knight of Calder, and second son to the Earl of Argyll, a valiant, witty, and active man, by the instigation and unwearied endeavours and meditation of one Priest MacPhail, his foster father, (a relation at that time among the Highlandmen no less obliging than that of blood,) did obtain from the Bishop of the Isles a right to this barony and regality of Kilmaronag, or country of Muckairn, which the said priest did carefully manage, both in assisting the advance of the money that was given for it to the bishop, and in obtaining the Pope's confirmation to the right, which was done by his legate, Sylvester Darius, the last legate from the Pope in this kingdom. Thus, [Calder] having obtained a legal right, MacDougall, as he [here the manuscript is illegible] the bishop out of it, thought also to do the same to the knight, and by force to retain the possession of the country in his own hand, many of his kindly men [kinsmen] and followers inhabiting the same, and himself very powerful in these bounds. After several civil messages to MacDougall to no purpose, the knight, being clothed with legal right and authority, is necessitated to possess himself by force, and having gathered a considerable party of men, was met, in his entry to the country, by a numerous party under the command of MacDougall's son, and, both parties engaging, MacDougall's son and some of his adherents were slain, and the rest pursued till the night and woods did separate them. There are yet cairns or some heaps of stones remaining, which were made in the places where the dead were found, denominated from the persons killed. Thus the knight got possession. Not long after this, MacDougall, hearing that the knight had sent a few men to take up the rents [sic] in the country, sent a party to surprise them, and cut them off; but they, getting intelligence hereof, were in readiness to receive them, and repelled them with the loss of two of MacDougall's men. A third encounter they had, but without blood; for, the knight on the one side, and MacDougall on the other, both well appointed, and accompanied with their followers, as they were ready to fight, fell on a treaty, and by message betwixt them they were reconciled: MacDougall yielding up and passing from all his pretensions, desiring only as a favour that the knight would be kind to his clansmen and followers dwelling in these lands, which his successors performed to that degree, that, within a short time, they forsook their dependence on MacDougall, and depended absolutely on the Knight of Calder, of whom there are several branches yet remaining in the country, as the MacCalmans, MacNackands, MacAndeoras, and others. Ever since it hath been peaceably possessed by the Knights of Calder as their proper heritage, without any intermission, and governed by their baillies and chamberlains in their absence, who always were cadets of their own family."[81]

The reality of the matter was that Muckairn was too close (as the MacDougalls found to their cost) to the heart of the Campbell country, at a period when the Campbell chiefs were seeking to expand the Campbell clan land. The Campbell principality was augmented to include Ben Cruachan, and indeed the ben was considered so central by the Campbells that "Cruachan" became the Campbells' war cry. As usual after these clan conquests, Calder made no attempt to evict the defeated clansfolk: instead, he treated them so well that they willingly became part of the Calder clan, and took Calder as their chief (or a "cadet" of his family as chieftain). The ordinary people, the possessors of the land, the MacCalmans and the rest, remained in place: only the ruler changed – just as England changed its ruler from time to time. But all this could scarcely have been deduced from the formal written dealings in the charter right.

30. Argyll and the MacLeans

Another Campbell conquest took place nearly two centuries later, an act of aggression accompanied by the Argyll family gaining the official parchment title to the lands of the main section of the MacLean clan, in Mull, Morvern, and elsewhere. The chief of the MacLeans was MacLean of Duart, so Argyll began his campaign by buying up Duart's debts; he then multiplied them by suing Duart in his (Argyll's) own Argyllshire courts, where the chance of Argyll losing an action was non-existent. Finally, in the time of Charles II, he got a judicial decree for debt against Duart. Duart's land charters now belonged to Argyll, so – in Lowland eyes – Argyll was the legal owner of the greater part of the MacLeans' territory. Sir Allan MacLean of Duart died in 1674, leaving his successor, Sir John, still a child; Argyll seized on such a promising opening, and mounted his final legal assault shortly afterwards. Sir Allan's cousin Lachlan MacLean of Brolas acted as tutor, or regent, and rallied the clan. He "did convocate together" (as one account has it) "armed men with swords, hagbuts [muskets], pistolls, dirks, and other weapons invasive, and munitions bellicall [presumably bellicose, or warlike]". When Argyll directed the sheriff-depute of the county to take possession of the MacLeans' land, that official found waiting for him "seven score armed men, armed with fyrelocks, swords, and targets, in a posture ready to fight, with their plaids throwne from them, standing and drawne up hard by the house of Dowart".[82] A few warning shots from within Duart Castle made the sheriff-depute realize that the mere presentation of some writing on a piece of paper was not going to be enough to persuade the MacLeans to give up their homeland, and he withdrew.

Argyll was now furnished with incontrovertible evidence of the MacLeans' "barbarism" and their resistance to the due processes of "law and order". He was thus able to obtain from the Edinburgh authorities an official order – in the form of a commission of fire and sword against the MacLeans – to do what he had been planning to do all along: to descend with his Campbells upon the MacLeans, with legal proof in his hands that the latter were merely felons and outlaws, and then to conquer them, and to incorporate their land in his own principality. The invasion took place in 1679, but despite the fact that the Campbells considerably outnumbered the MacLeans, it failed. The MacLeans were able to obtain help from their allies, the Camerons and the Glengarry MacDonalds, and they succeeded in fighting off Argyll's assault.

So far Argyll had been no more successful than MacIntosh was in similar attempts to take over the territory of the Keppoch MacDonalds or the Camerons. The outlook for the MacLeans was better still when in 1681 Argyll fell out with Charles II, and just managed to escape abroad with his life. His estate was forfeited to the Crown, so the Crown claimed the lands covered by the Duart charters, as part of that sequestrated estate; but it could no more enforce this paper claim than Argyll had been able to do. However, in 1688 Charles' successor James VII and II fled, and the Whigs returned to power, including the then representative of the noble house of Argyll. Naturally, the land charters of Argyll were now restored to him. Since Argyll was against King James, Sir John MacLean of Duart was for him, and he led the MacLeans to fight for James at Killiecrankie; while they were away English warships (now acting for the new king, William III) bombarded Duart

Castle. Even so, they failed in their attempt to conquer the MacLean lands for Argyll. The defeat of the Jacobites in 1689 enabled Argyll to concentrate on his private war against the MacLeans. He gathered a fleet, and invaded Mull with 2500 clansmen: his superiority in numbers (the MacLeans in the prime of their prosperity could only raise 800) enabled him to conquer all the Duart lands in Mull and Morvern, together with Tiree, the two ends of Coll, and some other small islands.[82] From then until 1746, the annus mirabilis of the charter holders, he exercised an uncertain and often challenged control over them. Even after 1746, the MacLeans were often rebellious.

Lowland lawyers, and Highland landlords (and, sometimes, even orthodox historians), subsequently described these events in more simplistic terms: Argyll, as mortgagee of the Duart estate, had foreclosed upon it, and any further strife or conflict in those areas merely resulted from the innate barbarism of the Highlanders. In fact Argyll, by abusing the clan loyalty of his Campbells, was simply attempting to enlarge still further the area of his own princely power in the Highlands.

31. Struggle in Tiree

The relations between Argyll, and the MacLean clansfolk, in the half-century between this successful Campbell invasion and the overthrow of the old order at Culloden, and even later, were those between a conqueror and would-be ruler, on the one hand, and the populace he hopes to subjugate, on the other. It is impossible to say now what would have happened in the end if the Lowland economic and social system had not been imposed on the Highlands. Perhaps Argyll would have abandoned the attempt to enforce his rule, as Campbell of Glenorchy (in Caithness), MacIntosh of that ilk (in Lochaber), and Amelia Fraser and the Atholl family (in the Fraser country), had abandoned their attempts; or perhaps the Argyll Campbells, who had already succeeded in expanding their territories elsewhere, would have been equally victorious here. But Culloden settled the matter; the Lowlanders triumphantly enforced their economic system on the Highlands, and the Argyll family (along with the other chiefs) were able to rewrite the history of the Highlands as if private landownership had been the accepted routine in the mountains throughout recorded history – the Duke of Argyll's account was *Scotland as it was and is*.[83] But the facts are there, for those who wish to find them.

In Tiree (one of the MacLean territories), for example, in Noel Banks' words, "unrest during and after the '15 had caused the Duke of Argyll to plant Tiree with substantial Campbell tacksmen – more to keep the peace than as agricultural innovators". (To "keep the peace" here means "to consolidate the conquest".) The duke sent in Duncan Forbes of Culloden, who recommended higher "rents", paid directly by the small tenants; but, wrote Banks, "the need for quick returns led to bad farming and sandblow, and much rent remained unpaid . . . squatting became widespread" – which seems to indicate that the MacLeans were still able to live where they wanted to live, on their own clan land. In the '45, the Government attempted to raise a militia to oppose the Jacobite rising. The MacLeans of Coll, who (apart from those living in the two ends of the island) still acknowledged Hector MacLean, 13th of Coll, as their chief, contributed sixty volunteers for this Government force, but in Tiree, wrote Banks, "not a man could be found for the militia"; in fact many men from Tiree tried to join Prince Charles, though few succeeded. "Tiresians relieved their frustration by threatening Factor Campbell of Barnacarry 'in such a manner that he had reason to make the best of his way' off the island, which was 'constantly on the flutter'." After the defeat of the rebellion, the Duke of Argyll took his revenge. "Factor Campbell of Barnacarry returned to Tiree in July 1746 with a detachment of militia and orders to burn some houses – odd instructions for a landlord's agent"; in fact, such instructions merely indicate still further that Argyll had not yet established himself as a landlord. A landlord does not destroy his own property.

Even after the old system was given a mortal blow on the field of Culloden in 1746, the new regime was imposed on Tiree (as it was elsewhere in the Highlands) only gradually. After Culloden there was "active obstruction" when an attempt was made to abolish the joint-farms, wrote Banks. In 1771 Argyll's chamberlain (or manager) reported that "the small tenants of Tiry are disaffected to the family. In this disposition it is thought that long leases might render them too much independent . . . and encourage them to that sort of insolence and outrage to which they are naturally prone and much incited by their chieftains of the MacLean gentry."[84] As late as 1803 there was reported to be "growing unrest and opposition". Argyll, in fact, was not able to operate as a landlord for many years after his 1690s conquest, any more than any of the other chiefs were "landlords" – it was the growing power of the Lowland/English state in the Highlands that enabled the charter holders to make this revolutionary transition after (and sometimes a considerable period after) the final defeat of the Jacobites in 1746.

32. Hostility of the MacLeans

The same holds true of the other territories to which Argyll laid violent claim as the charter holder in the 1690s. When the Campbells had apparently seized control of Mull, said David Graham-Campbell, there was a "specially hated factor called Black John Campbell. Unable to collect his dues from a man called Dewar because he was away from home, the factor seized his far more valuable pair of plough horses and dispatched them to the mainland. When Dewar found Black John he chased him till the oppressor stumbled on a tombstone in the burial-ground of Soroba and was forced to plead for his life. He was only spared on paying the value of the horses and promising never to return to the island. He kept the promise in his lifetime"[85] – the significance of the last three words being that he had made such an impression on the islanders that they thought his ghost returned occasionally.

The dogged greed of the noble family of Argyll to extend their Highland principality in the Inner Hebrides led to similar clashes elsewhere. By assiduous and skilful currying of favour with the sovereign power, the Argyll family gained the ascendancy over, for example, Colonsay, where lived the MacPhees. John Mercer, in *Hebridean Islands*, told how they put in deputies to rule the island. "The Campbells [i.e., the Campbell chief] installed a MacNeill family on Colonsay: the islanders' hostility was such that the incomers had to take refuge in the Loch Sgoltaire fortress."[86] Again, when the ninth Earl of Argyll, by capitalizing on his influence at court in the reign of Charles II, was granted the supremacy over the Garvellach Islands (a MacLean territory) in the Firth of Lorn, here too he interposed an agent to represent him – MacLauchlan of Kilbride. Years later, in 1749, MacLauchlan's grandson John MacLauchlan sent a petition to the ninth earl's grandson, who was then the third Duke of Argyll, relating how his grandfather had been assigned the Garvellach Islands on wadset. "Although he met several obstructions yet at length he forcibly obtained possession of these islands which for several [i.e., a number of] years made no return to the family of Argyll." This seems to mean that until MacLauchlan seized them, the earl's annexation had been purely titular, and he had not been able to obtain any income from them. But MacLauchlan's apparently successful seizure was not the end of the matter: the MacLeans counter-attacked, and "most viciously plundered" the incomers. John MacLauchlan continued: "Although the MacLeans did for some time smother their resentment on account of my grandfather's having thus dispossessed them, yet at length a band of them came fully armed under cloud of night and carried off the whole effects and bestial [property and animals] on these islands to the value of 3000 merks [about £166 sterling], and after destroying the houses and byres, stript the possessors of their vivers [eatables] and left their wives and children stript naked and exposed to the inclemency of the weather . . ."[87] The fact that this petition was made as late as 1749 may indicate that this particular episode of MacLean resistance was successful, at least for a time. There were similar events in other MacLean lands which Argyll was attempting to assimilate. "In the earlier part of the century", wrote Gaskell, "the duke's agents had occasionally been abused and even imprisoned in Morvern."[88]

Eric Cregeen, in his *Changing Role of the House of Argyll*, told the story of what had happened in the Garvellach Islands, and continued: "Over the annexed MacLean lands acts of overt hostility such as this, as well as innumerable acts of secret revenge, ranging from cattle-maiming to arson, were going on fifty years after the actual annexation [i.e., till Culloden – till the landlord revolution]. The position of the tacksmen in Morvern became so untenable that it was hopeless to let farms to any but the original occupants. As will become clear, the existence of widespread 'disaffection to the family' within the Estate was a factor of considerable political and also economic importance throughout the eighteenth century"[89] – that is, as late as perhaps five decades or more after Culloden.

33. Fife adventurers, and Kintail

Again, the formal records might be taken to show that MacKenzie of Kintail obtained Lewis in 1611 as a grant from the Crown; in fact, the MacKenzies – who because of Kintail's covetousness were nicknamed "the Campbells of the North" – took Lewis by conquering the MacLeods who lived there, helped by the fact that the MacLeods were much weakened by internal discord (there was disagreement among the clan as to who the next chief should be). There can be no question that a Crown grant of Lewis in 1611 would have been completely null and void without an army of MacKenzie clansmen to enforce it. Only a few years before James VI of Scotland "granted" Lewis to MacKenzie of Kintail, he had generously "granted" it to the "Fife Adventurers", under the Duke of Lennox, the king's cousin. They were (in Arthur Geddes' respectful quote) a " 'capitalist' fishery enterprise",[90] or (as Derek Cooper more candidly described them) "a bunch of hooligans and chancers".[91] An Act of the Lowland Parliament declared that the Gaels of Lewis were "voyd of any knowledge of God or his religioun", sunk in "all kynd of barbaritie and inhumanitie", and called for the "ruiting out the barbarbous inhabitantis", while the Lowland Privy Council declared that no part of the Highlands and Islands should be "disponit in few, tak, or utterways bot to Lowland men" (should not be disposed of in feu, tack, or other ways unless to Lowlanders). James VI, passionately longing to bring civilized behaviour to the Highlands, cordially told Lennox he could employ whatever "slauchter, mutilation, fyre-raising, or utheris inconvenieities" he wanted to exterminate the Lewis people.[92]

These would-be civilizers of Lewis, with their avowed objectives of spreading the sacred knowledge of "God and his religioun" by means of arson, maiming, and murder, or "other inconveniences", hired six hundred mercenaries, and attacked the island. In November 1598 this professional army landed on Lewis, defeated the MacLeods in a pitched battle, and established a camp near Stornoway. To win a battle was not beyond an invading force; but for Lowlanders to establish a rule over people who did not intend to be ruled (whether they were divided over the chiefship or not) was much harder. Food ran short; messengers sent for help were captured; and a further attack by the MacLeods (described naturally by the defeated Lowlanders as "barbarous, bludie, and wiket Hielandmen") drove the Fife Adventurers off the island in 1601. Another attempt to conquer Lewis was made in 1605; it also failed. So did a third attack, in 1609.[93] Lowland commentators, obviously sympathetic to this savage Lowland onslaught, hinted knowingly at cannibalism; according to Tom Steel (presumably unwilling to miss such a damaging insinuation) the would-be settlers were "massacred . . . by the local inhabitants, and some say eaten".[94] The Fife Adventurers perforce abandoned their pretensions; but a further aggression was now planned.

Kenneth MacKenzie of Kintail was high in royal favour at the time. He was created Lord MacKenzie of Kintail in 1609, and as soon as the Fife Adventurers failed in their final attempt to seize Lewis, James VI told Kintail he could have it – if he could take it. (Kintail also paid a small sum to the Fife Adventurers, and took over their claims.) An army of clansmen, drawn from the various sections of the Kintail clan – MacKenzies, MacRaes, MacLennans, and so on – then invaded Lewis. The MacLeods were still at daggers drawn among themselves over the chiefship: and one of the island clans or septs, the Morrisons, gave their support to the invaders, though another, the MacAulays, gave its support to the MacLeod chief. The united invading force triumphed over the divided defenders, and MacKenzie of Kintail, who was already the chief of a large principality on the mainland part of Ross-shire, established himself also (admittedly after a two-year struggle) as the chief of Lewis.[95] When the formal excuse of a "Crown grant" is stripped away, the episode is seen to be in reality a war between two clans, one of which conquered the other. Whether this and similar wars may be put down simply as a defect of the old clan system, that is to say of the clans without the ambitious Edinburgh-haunting chiefs, may be doubted. It seems unlikely that the MacKenzies would have troubled themselves about Lewis (where the MacLeods continued to live after the conquest, albeit with MacKenzie sub-chiefs or tacksmen), had not the chief of the MacKenzies thirsted after personal glory, and had not the Lowland king urged him on by providing him with a pretence of legality to justify the exploit.

34. Kintail and Assynt

Kintail's descendant, the Earl of Seaforth, got hold of Assynt in the second half of the seventeenth century by (in the Lowland lawyers' version of events) some perfectly legal manoeuvres – buying up the debts of the previous "owner", and thus securing "his estate" for less than half its value. In fact, it was a case of a powerful clan attempting to impose its will on a less powerful one, just as much as the seizure of Lewis had been. It was in fact a logical sequel to that episode.

A branch of the MacLeods of Lewis had long been established on the mainland, in Assynt, with their own chief: in the middle of the seventeenth century the chief was Neil MacLeod of Assynt. In 1650 he captured the royalist general, the Marquis of Montrose, and handed him over to the then ruling Edinburgh authorities, by whom he was executed. The Earl of Seaforth, head of the MacKenzies, wanted to extend his principality to include Assynt, and he zealously propagated the story that in some way MacLeod had promised to help Montrose, so that the handing over of Montrose was in fact not an instance of loyal co-operation with the established authorities in apprehending an enemy of law and order, but a betrayal. He may even have originated the charge: "possibly the original accuser of MacLeod", wrote the *D.N.B.* contributor, "was Kenneth MacKenzie, third Earl of Seaforth."[96]

MacLeod was arrested at the Restoration, and was in jail from 1660 to 1666, despite the fact that he had quickly repented of his part in the Montrose affair, and had obtained an indemnity from the future Charles II himself at Breda in 1650. After MacLeod's release Seaforth continued his campaign against him – ignoring the flavour of hypocrisy deriving from the fact that the Seaforth family themselves had fought against the king (and therefore against Montrose) during the civil wars in Scotland. Seaforth was now in the royal favour, while MacLeod was far away in Assynt; so Seaforth on some pretext (presumably connected with the buying up of MacLeod's debts) successfully pursued a Lowland legal process against him. When the MacKenzies, with this legal colour to their actions, sent officials to demand the handing over of Assynt in 1670, the MacLeods forcibly repelled them. This successful defence of their homeland by the Assynt people meant that Seaforth could now depict the MacLeods as Highland savages, and himself as the virtuous champion of civilized law and order.

"For violently opposing a claim of ejectment against him", says the *D.N.B.*, "at the instance of the MacKenzies, a commission of fire and sword was in July 1672 obtained against MacLeod." These letters of fire and sword issued in the Highlands remained dead letters, as we have seen, unless the grantee commanded sufficient force to put them into effect. Seaforth did command sufficient force – in the shape of the MacKenzies, whose loyalty to their chief misguidedly led them to support his vaulting ambition – and the clansmen duly carried out the commission against MacLeod of Assynt. "His territory was ravaged," the *D.N.B.* continued, "and he was brought south a prisoner to Edinburgh", where on 2nd February 1674 "he was tried on four charges: (1) treachery to Montrose, (2) assisting English rebels, (3) exacting arbitrary taxation upon shipping in his creeks, (4) fortifying and garrisoning his house in 1670 against the king" – that is, against the attempted MacKenzie take-over. The charges were so dishonest that even the Lowland court acquitted MacLeod, but Seaforth continued to harass him, and finally in 1690 MacLeod was "deprived of his estates and forced to quit Assynt".[92] He died probably in 1697, leaving no issue. The MacKenzies' superior power had finally overcome the Assynt MacLeods; and John MacKenzie, the younger son of the third Earl of Seaforth, and brother of the fourth earl, set himself up as the new chief of Assynt. As in other clan conquests, the MacKenzies did not disturb the actual occupants of the land, the Assynt MacLeods. In fact the latter appear to have continued to resist John MacKenzie, and after him his son Kenneth. Kenneth MacKenzie seems to have found his position untenable because of this resistance, and in 1736 he withdrew from Assynt, after making two conflicting dispositions of his claims – one to his cousin the fifth Earl of Seaforth, and one to his wife's relative the Earl of Sutherland, who also had his eye on Assynt.[97] Neither claimant was acceptable to the people of Assynt, and so there was no chief at all in Assynt (and certainly no landlord) during some considerable time before Culloden. (The ruin of Calda House, which the MacKenzies of Assynt built for themselves beside Loch Assynt, is still there.) In the end, a district without an "owner" was too much of an affront to the new private-property society imposed on the Highlands after the '45, and the state authorities took it on themselves to sell off what was not theirs to sell: the land of Assynt.[98] It was bought by the Sutherland family, so far as anyone can be said to "buy" something legally from someone who had no right to sell it.

35. MacNeills of North Knapdale

Parallel claims to Highland land – one, the right by charter granted in Edinburgh, and the other, the Gaelic right, which carried the actual land with it until the middle of the eighteenth century: that is to say one fictional, and one factual – can also be seen in North Knapdale. The N.S.A. report quoted a manuscript in the possession of Malcolm of Poltalloch, which gave the history of the MacNeill territory in Knapdale and of a local stronghold, Castle Swen. "In the end of the thirteenth century, Knapdale appears in the possession [sic] of a certain Swenus de Ergadia, known in tradition as Swen Ruadh, or Swen the Red, Thane of Glassary and Knapdale, and from him it is said the castle took its name; and there are strong grounds for thinking that he was ancestor of the MacNeills [apparently a separate clan from the Barra MacNeills]. John his son took an active part with Balliol, and was forfeited by Bruce." (This is a reference to the struggles between Balliol and Bruce for the Edinburgh crown before and after 1300; after Bruce won, he took John's charters off him.) This Lowland version of the ownership of the district was what was affected by Bruce's decision to forfeit John, son of Swen, and the manuscript went on to describe the subsequent dealings with this Lowland right. "Bruce granted Knapdale to John de Menteth, recorder to the Earl de Menteth, from whom it descended to his eldest son, Sir John Menteth, Lord of Arran and Knapdale. Sir John disponed [conveyed] the greater part of South Knapdale to the Earl of Argyll in 1353, and, on his death in 1360, the rest of Knapdale fell to the Crown, by whom it was granted, in 1372, to John Lord of the Isles, and remained in that family until the forfeiture of the last Lord of the Isles in 1476, when it again came to the Crown, and was granted in 1480, with the keeping of Castle Swen, to the Earl of Argyll." (There was no Earl of Argyll in 1353, though there was one in 1480: the 1353 charter presumably referred to the chief of the Campbells, Campbell of Lochow or Lochawe, whose descendant received the earldom in 1457.) While for the better part of two centuries the Lowland lawyers were hard at work recording how this Lowland right was conveyed, and inherited, and transferred, and forfeited, and re-granted, the actual land was still held by the MacNeills. "Although Swenus de Ergadia and his descendants", the manuscript continues, "were deprived of Knapdale, they seem to have retained actual though not feudal [i.e., charter] possession; for, in 1742, we find Hector MacTorquil MacNeill in possession of the greater part of North Knapdale, and heritable keeper of Castle Swen."[99] To assert in the same sentence that the local Highlanders were "deprived" of their land, and also retained possession of it, is to demonstrate the problems caused when a writer attempted to believe what the Lowland charters said.

It seems that Argyll, after his triumph over the MacLeans of Duart, was able to extend his rule over the MacNeills of South Knapdale, in much the same way, from about 1700: though probably with the same uncertain success until after Culloden.

36. MacIntosh and Cluny

Yet another example of the fictitious character of transfers of land as recorded by Lowland lawyers may be taken from Clan Chattan history. According to the legal writing, Lachlan MacIntosh, 20th of MacIntosh, granted certain lands near Loch Laggan to Lachlan MacPherson, 11th of Cluny, in 1726; in return, Cluny acknowledged MacIntosh to be the rightful chief of Clan Chattan.[100] The transfer, though, was nothing more than a matter of Lowland theory: the lands in question had long been occupied by the MacPhersons. It may be surmised that Cluny was pleased to avert the possibility of any future mischance arising out of MacIntosh's possession of the charter right to some MacPherson lands, in return only for the acknowledgement of MacIntosh's chiefship of Clan Chattan – an acknowledgement which Cluny may have been disposed to grant anyway: his mother was a MacIntosh of the chiefly family.

The fact that so often in the Highlands the land was not possessed by the person stated in the punctiliously crafted Lowland documents to be the owner was (as we saw earlier) comfortably explained away by Lowlanders as being the result of the regrettable "lawlessness" of the Highlanders. It is as if a pauper produced a piece of writing alleging that he was the owner of a billionaire's luxury yacht, and accounted for the discrepancy between his theory and the palpable fact by alleging that the billionaire had stolen it from him.

Various hostile encounters in the Highlands – the armed confrontation at Loch Arkaig in 1665, the battles at Altimarlich in 1680 and at Mulroy in 1688, the tumults in the Fraser country in the late 1690s, the struggles when the MacDougalls and MacLeans tried to defend themselves against Argyll, and the Lewis MacLeods' resistance to Seaforth – were all taken as further evidence of how "lawless" these unruly Highlanders were; yet in reality all were the result of Lowland interference, and the attempted imposition of alien and fictitious Lowland charters on the Highlands.

37. Undoubted legal power

Despite all the evidence, some of which is given above, of the true nature of the charters to land which were held by some Highland chiefs and others, many academic historians have been unable to accept that the Highland polity, in this regard as in many others, was fundamentally different from the social structure in the Lowlands and England. A. J. Youngson, Professor of Economic History at and Vice-Chancellor of Edinburgh University, said resolutely that in the days of the clans "the land was the chief's".[101] After the failure of the '45, "the Highland proprietors began to take advantage of the legal power, which they undoubtedly possessed but had never exercised, of doing with their land as they pleased, renting it to whom they pleased, regardless of" the protests of the Highlanders.[102] So the Highland chiefs (according to Professor Youngson), throughout the heyday of the clan system, had "undoubtedly" possessed "the legal power" to turn their clansfolk out of their clan countries, and rent it out to great farmers, and thus make vast fortunes for themselves, just as by similar operations at the same time the Lowland landlords (as the Highland chiefs well knew) were making vast fortunes for themselves – but for some reason they had refrained from doing so; and this despite the fact that many of these chiefs, in the latter days of clanship, often grumbled about how poor they were. When a whole class of men who it is alleged had the power to become abundantly rich did not use that power, without any apparent reason for this self-sacrifice apart from an altruistic desire to see others happy rather than themselves, one may be pardoned for feeling incredulous: especially when that identical class of men, with it is said exactly the same powers, suddenly started to do (after 1746) what all their forebears (and they themselves in their younger days) had philanthropically abstained from doing. (One is tempted to say that some men, though obviously very clever in some ways, in other ways cannot see what is at the end of their noses.)

If the Highland chiefs had in fact owned the land before the '45 rebellion, they would have begun the clearances much earlier. Well before the arrival of Bonnie Prince Charlie, the chiefs were mixing in Lowland society and doing their best to adopt Lowland ways. They preferred English to Gaelic, they preferred Lowland clothes to Highland, and they engaged in assorted commercial transactions, although necessarily in a marginal way, since they were not yet able to overturn the clansfolk's control of their own clan lands. Cameron of Lochiel was selling timber, as well as trying business ventures in America, trading with the West Indies, and speculating in the Edinburgh money market; MacDonald of Glengarry was providing wood, to be made into charcoal for ironworks; Robertson of Struan was also making money from the local forests; Drummond of Perth was engaged in various merchandising projects;[103] Campbell of Knockbuy started cattle-dealing and raising his rents as early as the late 1720s.[104] The Marquis of Atholl took fees from an outsider who was opening coalmines in Glen Lyon forty years before Culloden.[105] Few people would be so gullible as to maintain that the successive Dukes of Argyll, or equally Simon Fraser of Lovat, would have held back from anything which would bring them in more money. Well before Culloden, many chiefs were engaging in whatever activities would make them a profit.

In fact, the ultimate demonstration of the true ownership of the clan lands is the fact that the chiefs did not dare to evict the clansfolk, when evictions of small tenants were commonplace in the Lowlands of Scotland in and after the seventeenth century. The failure of the attempts – mentioned in the next section – made by the Earl of Moray in the 1620s to eject his small tenants (who were MacIntoshes) from the low-lying lands of Petty, in the Highland marches, show – a fortiori – what would have been the results of similar attempts in the Highlands proper. If the powerful Earl of Moray failed in his endeavours to seize the land in this lower border country, then the chiefs in the mountains would have had no chance whatever.

38. Moray and the MacIntoshes

The Clan Chattan had spread beyond the strict Highland area in north-eastern Inverness-shire, and on the coastal plain of Petty parish east of Inverness there were numbers of Gaelic-speaking MacIntoshes who were small tenants on lands to which the Earl of Moray held the charter right. In the Highlands proper this charter right was, as we have seen, completely fictitious; in the lower country, including the seaboard of Petty parish, the charter-holder sometimes tried to make the charter correspond more closely with reality. In 1622 the Earl of Moray took it into his head to act upon this undeniable (in the Lowland view) right of ownership by evicting his MacIntosh tenants, no doubt because in that year Sir Lachlan MacIntosh, 17th of MacIntosh, died, leaving only his nine-year-old son William as the next clan chief. Moray clearly concluded that with a child as chief, the MacIntosh clan would be easier to maltreat. A. M. Shaw wrote: "The district of Petty, which was under the superiority of the Earls of Moray, had been occupied by the MacIntoshes for some four centuries and a half . . . But they [the MacIntoshes] held their lands in Petty only as duchus [or duchàs], and in 1622 Moray – whose family reckoned their hold on the district for the short period of forty years [i.e., the Moray family had only held a Lowland charter to that land for forty years] – took advantage of their want of a written title to call upon the ancient occupiers to remove. We can imagine the surprise and indignation with which the mandate was received by the tenants, but there was no alternative to obedience."[106]

The evicted MacIntoshes removed, however, only as far as the immediately neighbouring Clan Chattan Highlands, and before long 500 clansmen gathered, the lead being taken by Lachlan MacIntosh of Corribrough (an uncle of the Sir Lachlan who had just died) and by one of the more prominent Petty MacIntoshes. They then attacked Moray's stronghold, Castle Stuart, helped themselves to the earl's rents from the lands which had formerly been occupied by the MacIntoshes, and carried off the possessions of the Lowland tenants who had been given the cleared lands, thus striking at the root of the earl's income and his power. "This yeir", wrote Sir Robert Gordon in 1624 of the MacIntoshes, "they goe to ane hous which he (Moray) hath now of late built in Pettie, called Castell Stuart; they dryve away his servants from thence and doe possess themselves of all the Earl of Moray his rents in Pettie. Thus they intend to stand out against him." John Spalding wrote: "They keeped the feilds in their Highland weid [clothing] upon foot with swords, bowes, arrowes, targets, hagbuttis [muskets], pistollis, and other Highland armour; and first began to rob and spoulzie [despoil] the earl's tennents, who laboured their possessions, of their haill [whole] goods, geir, insight plenishing [household furniture], horse, nolt [oxen], sheep, corns, and cattle, and left them nothing that they could gett within boundes . . . yet still keeped themselves from shedeing of innocent blood."[107] This attempt by the MacIntoshes to resist Moray's evictions was smoothly put down by one author merely as a fight between clans: "In 1624 there was another inter-clan conflict when the Clan Chattan, in effect the MacIntoshes, fell out with the Earl of Moray."[108] This is by no means the only time when strife arising directly from a mischief-making Lowland charter right (which in this case rated a forty-year-old charter as more weighty than a possession which had lasted four hundred and fifty years) has been portrayed as if it arose naturally from the clan system, and can thus be dismissed as merely yet "another" example of savage Highland bellicosity.

39. Moray repulsed

The Earl of Moray, as we shall see below, was one of a small group of noblemen who were balanced uneasily between the Lowlands and the Highlands: they had a two-fold existence, being at the same time proprietors in the Lowlands, and clan chiefs in the Highlands. The Earl of Moray was a Lowland landowner in low-lying Petty and elsewhere, but in the Perthshire Highland district of Menteith, which was populated mainly by MacGregors, he was a Highland chief, in the way that will be explained later; so he called in the Menteith clansmen to help him. In Shaw's words, he "raised a force, chiefly MacGregors", from Menteith, "and making Inverness his headquarters sent out parties in search of the disturbers of the peace" (wrote Shaw, though it may be thought that Moray was the chief peace-disturber). But this counter-stroke was in vain: "the only result of this search was the expense which it brought on the earl." A second expedition also failed: so Moray went to London, where the king made him "Lieutenant in the Highlands, to employ the extreme terrors of the law against the offenders". Letters of intercommuning were issued against the MacIntoshes, threatening condign punishment against any who helped or harboured them. Yet the MacIntoshes held out in their mountains, and continued their campaign against Moray for six years longer: and in the end it was Moray who gave in, and restored the Petty MacIntoshes to their holdings.[109]

Moray was unquestionably the landlord of this Petty estate in the 1620s: the MacIntoshes paid him rent, which was quite distinct from the tribute they gave to their chief. Yet, even on these flat coastal lands outside the high ground, Moray could not succeed in evicting his Gaelic small tenants (since they were able to call upon the help of their fellow-clansmen nearby). It is not surprising that even those chiefs who might have aspired to become landowners did not try similar measures against their clansfolk behind their mountain ramparts, by simply exercising this supposed "legal power which they undoubtedly possessed" (in A. J. Youngson's categorical contention). If they had, they would inevitably have failed.

Almost exactly 200 years later, in about 1819, another Earl of Moray issued ejectment orders against his MacIntosh small tenants in Petty; and, in the changed conditions of the nineteenth century, the clansfolk could no longer defend themselves, and were successfully expelled.[110]

Those who believe that the Highland chiefs could perfectly well have legally driven out all their clanspeople, and could legally have sold "their" lands, before the landlord revolution of the mid-eighteenth century, have apparently forgotten the known character and activities of some of those chiefs, as shown well before that revolution. The Earls of Moray, for example, would without doubt have treated the clan lands to which they had the charter right as their own personal possessions well before 1745, if they had thought they could get away with it.

The failure of the chiefs to sell any of the clan lands before 1745 (as opposed to occasionally buying or selling land charters), their failure to clear out the clansfolk and rent out their possessions to sheep farmers, was not due to any aristocratic altruism or to any modest meekness, but to the fact that the clansfolk were still powerful enough to prevent other people taking their land from them, at a time when the British state was not yet quite dominant enough to impose its will by force of arms upon the Highland clan countries. Proudhon did not deliver his dictum that "la propriété c'est le vol" – "property is theft", or "property is robbery"[111] – until 1840; but he might have been thinking of the times a century or so earlier when many of the chiefs brazenly misappropriated the land of their clans after the defeat of the '45. It is one of the ironies of history that Rousseau penned his famous denunciation of private property in 1754, at the very time when the Highland chiefs were converting themselves into landlords, and making the land which had previously been public property belonging to the clan into private property belonging to themselves. "The first man who, having enclosed a piece of ground, bethought himself of saying 'This is mine', and found people simple enough to believe him, was the real founder of civil society. From how many crimes, wars, and murders, from how many horrors and misfortunes might not anyone have saved mankind, by pulling up the stakes, or filling up the ditch, and crying to his fellows: Beware of listening to this impostor, you are undone if you once forget that the fruits of the earth belong to us all, and the earth itself to nobody."[112]

What an extraordinary piece of presumption it is for a puny two-legged mammal, standing on the flimsy crust covering (often inadequately) the ball of fire that we live upon, and making the palpably untenable claim that he "owns" a bit of it, when he and everyone else knows unequivocally that he could not make so much as a cubic inch of earth to save his life. But in our society, presumption is often the principal provenance of prosperity.

40. Heritable jurisdictions

While one is distinguishing between the theoretical and the actual powers of the chiefs, the heritable jurisdictions should be mentioned. To repeat what was said earlier, the chief was not only the leader of the clan in war, but also the judge of disputes in peace. The Scottish lawyers had to face a situation in which the Edinburgh king's judges were not able to travel, and if they did travel by taking an army with them to protect them while they held a court, were not able to enforce any judgements, over the larger part of what was claimed to be the "kingdom of Scotland"; while at the same time, in those same parts of that supposed kingdom, the clansfolk freely submitted their disputes to the chief of their clan, and freely accepted his rulings.

Lawyers like to have matters arranged neatly and tidily, and the Edinburgh lawyers were no exception. They had already imposed the terms and usages of the quite irrelevant and alien feudal system on to the Highland clans – so far as they had the power to do so. In their charters and enactments on Highland matters, the chiefs were alleged to hold their lands feudally of the king, the tacksmen of the chiefs, and so on. Where one chief had obtained a written title to land which was in reality possessed by another clan, and the chief of that other clan, to give himself a locus standi in Lowland law, had agreed to pay a small feu-duty to the first chief, then in the lawyers' charters the first chief was the "tenant-in-chief" of the king and the second chief his "vassal", and so on down the line.

The problem of the independent jurisdictions exercised by the chiefs in their clans was solved in the same way. The position was regularized in the Lowland legal archives by granting to the chiefs the feudal right of "heritable jurisdiction", that is to say, a right to judge disputes, which right can be inherited in the same way as other property. Like the granting of charters of ownership to the chiefs, at the time it made no difference in practical matters. The chief had judged disputes in his clan before the grant, and he judged them after the grant in exactly the same way. All that had happened was that the Lowland lawyers had found a legal pigeonhole into which they could force this particular exercise of chiefly powers in the Highlands.

But the lawyers in Edinburgh were not always able to make their grants of these feudal powers correspond exactly to the facts of Highland life. Sometimes a chief who was in favour at court would obtain a grant of "heritable jurisdiction" over an area larger than that inhabited by his clan; sometimes a chief not in favour would not even obtain such a grant over his own clan. Neither chief, however, had any more, or any less, jurisdiction for that. The Earl of Selkirk observed this discrepancy: "In fact there were some chiefs who nominally held these jurisdictions over very extensive territories, but never could enforce their authority beyond the limits of their own immediate clannish power. On the other hand, the chiefs who had no legal jurisdiction at all, exercised every power of the highest courts of law."[113] The word "legal" here refers, as usual, to Lowland law.

41. With great equity

Adam Smith, in his *Wealth of Nations*, 1776, made the same point: "It is a mistake to imagine that those territorial jurisdictions took their origin from the feudal law ... It is not thirty years ago since Mr Cameron of Lochiel, a gentleman of Lochaber in Scotland, without any legal warrant whatever, not being what was then called a lord of regality, nor even a tenant-in-chief, but a vassal [sic] of the Duke of Argyll, and without being so much as a justice of peace, used, notwithstanding, to exercise the highest criminal jurisdiction over his own people. He is said to have done so with great equity, though without any of the formalities of justice."[114]

Macaulay told a story demonstrating how ineffectual were attempts by Lowland kings to direct the course of jurisdiction in the Highlands, unless they accepted the status quo by "granting" juridical powers to the chiefs, who already had them by the will of their clans. On one occasion James VII of Scotland (and II of England) directed the sheriff of Inverness-shire to hold a court in Lochaber – in Cameron country. Lochiel, wrote Macaulay, naturally objected to this attempt to overturn the established order of things, and "came to the tribunal at the head of 400 armed Camerons. He affected great reverence for the royal commission, but he dropped three or four words which were perfectly understood by the pages and armour-bearers who watched every turn of his eye. 'Is none of my lads so clever as to send this judge packing? I have seen them get up a quarrel when there was less need of one.' In a moment a brawl began in the crowd, none could see how or where." The court broke up in disorder, "and the terrified sheriff was forced to put himself under the protection of the chief, who, with a plausible show of respect and concern, escorted him safe home".[115]

Not only Lochiel, but all the clan chiefs, necessarily exercised their juridical power "with great equity" (in Adam Smith's words); for their powers, in this as in other directions, came from the clan itself, not from Edinburgh, which was in effect powerless in the Highlands (unless it sent in a military expedition). And just as Edinburgh did not give, so Edinburgh could not take away. The so-called abolition of the heritable jurisdictions in 1747, for which the chiefs were bare-faced enough to claim, and receive, monetary compensation, did not put an end to the chiefly powers of judging disputes within the clan: the chiefs' own betrayals of their clans did that. The fanciful nature of the 1747 act is made clear beyond dispute when we recall that the Lowland government had already passed an Act of Parliament in 1608 "abolishing all the heritable jurisdiction of the chiefs of clans" (in Sir Thomas Innes' words);[116] so the Lowland authorities were claiming to abolish, in 1747, what they had already abolished a hundred and forty years before.

In those clans where the chief did not at once begin to rack-rent and to evict his clansfolk after the failure of the '45, his judicial powers continued until he, too, was converted to the new way of thinking. David Stewart said that the people "admitted the arbitration of their chiefs"[117] when the chiefs possessed, according to the Edinburgh law, no more right to judge and pass sentence than anyone else. Dr Johnson, twenty-seven years after Culloden, also mentioned that this right was still "exercised in lower degrees, by some of the proprietors, when legal processes cannot be obtained".[118] The feudal or Lowland paper right had been withdrawn; but the right according to clan law, which had always been the only genuine one, was only destroyed by the actions of the chiefs themselves, as they changed into landlords (following the rules of the new regime).

42. Compulsion to obey

One writer has remarked, surprisingly, that the abolition of the hereditary jurisdictions "made the whole clan bankrupt; for what was the worth of a clansman who was under no compulsion to obey?"[119] To regard the clansfolk as being "compelled to obey" is to misconceive the whole clan system. The clansfolk were not compelled to obey anybody: there was no one to compel them. The whole burden of the complaints which the Lowlanders made continuously about the Highlanders over centuries was that they would obey no one, not their own chiefs, and certainly not the Lowland king, unless – very exceptionally – it suited them to do so. Nothing could make the clan bankrupt, for the clan never had a financial value; although, certainly, it had a great value in the eyes of the clansfolk who composed it. Indeed, the scattering of the clans by their chiefs in the late eighteenth and the nineteenth centuries was due, not to the fact that the clansfolk were no longer under any "compulsion to obey", but to a process exactly the opposite. The clansfolk had never been compelled to obey anybody: now, with the growth of English and Lowland economic and military power, the chiefs were able to claim that the clan land was theirs, and were able to summon up English soldiers to compel the clan members to obey their eviction orders. The clearances were directly due to this introduction into the Highlands of the power to compel obedience. It is curious how an acceptance of the orthodox clichés about Highland history leads some writers into making statements that are exactly and completely the opposite of the truth.

Macaulay referred to the unpopularity of the Campbells among some neighbouring clans. This unpopularity arose from the activities of the principal Campbell chiefs, the Argyll family, who busied themselves in Lowland politics, and who were often used by the Lowland authorities in schemes that aimed – usually only too successfully – to cause dissension among the Highlanders. The resulting dislike of the Campbells meant that since the Argylls often found themselves in opposition to the Stuart kings, many clans fought for those kings; and were therefore regarded as supporters of absolute as against constitutional monarchy. This, as Macaulay observed, was a long way from the truth. "The Gaelic population was far indeed from holding the doctrines of passive obedience and non-resistance. In fact, disobedience and resistance made up the ordinary life of that population."[120]

43. Chiefs of the clan name

The centuries of ceaseless external pressure from the Lowlands and England, and the ceaseless internal development which goes on in all societies, could not but produce some changes in the Highlands. In the early eighteenth century, the clans could be separated into four groups.

The first group was the largest. This contained the clans who followed a chief or chieftains of their own name, and where no other chief at all had any claim, however nebulous, on the clan or the clan land. (Of course, as we saw earlier, and for the reasons then given, every clan had septs or individuals within it who had different – or alternate – surnames from the main clan surname.) The chiefs of these clans had all been astute enough to obtain charters to the lands of their clans. The Edinburgh lawyers – who were trying to impose a uniform feudal system, at least in name, on the Highlands – dealt with these clans by treating the chiefs as the landowners or land-holders, "holding of the Crown". Among these clans, so far as the discoverable evidence shows, were apparently the MacLachlans, Stewarts of Appin, Clan Donald, MacDonalds of Glengarry, MacLeods of Harris, Skye, and Glenelg, MacKinnons in Skye and Mull, MacFarlanes, MacAulays of Garelochside, Colquhouns, MacCallums, Lamonts, Clan Menzies, Stewarts of Grandtully, Farquharsons, Frasers, Grants of Glen Moriston, Chisholms, Munros of Ferindonald, Rosses, Sinclairs, several clans of MacKenzies, and several clans of Campbells. Also in this group were those MacKays who followed Lord Reay, the Robertsons who followed Robertson of Struan, the MacNabs who followed MacNab of that ilk, and the MacDougalls who followed MacDougall of Dunollie.[121] The Clan Ranald, the MacIntoshes, and the Grants of Strath Spey and Glen Urquhart might also be included; their chiefs were said to "hold" most of the clan land "of the Crown", though a minor part was held "of feudal superiors". On the other hand, it could be said that they should be in the second group of clans, as we shall see below.

44. "Feudal superiors"

In the second group were those clans where the chief had not been quick enough to get a charter to the lands of his clan before another chief had obtained a charter to them. Sometimes the chief who had obtained the charter was at the head of a clan which was strong enough to conquer the clan land to which he had obtained a charter; but if one clan was strong enough, and its chief or its members had the inclination, to conquer the land of another clan, it would have done so anyway. (In the same way, if a twenty-first century country is stronger than another country, and wants to conquer it, it will do so whatever the legal niceties.) In these situations the charter was an external irrelevancy (unless it put ideas into the chief's head which were not there already). In other cases, where the charter right was not supported by the superior strength of the claimant's clan, it was, as has been seen, ignored; at the most, the chief of the clan which actually held the land would give the charter owner a few shillings a year feu-duty to end the nuisance of a rival claimant, and to give himself a title to the clan land under Lowland law. For in these cases the chief of the clan actually holding the land appears to have secured a Lowland title to the clan land which was virtually as good as those of his more artful brethren, and enabled him after Culloden to buy off the "superiority" and to begin evicting his clansfolk and bolstering his bank balance with as much Lowland right to do so as they had. To give these transactions the required feudal terminology, the Lowland lawyers called the charter holder the "tenant-in-chief", and said that the chief of the clan which actually occupied the district "held the land of" the charter holder.

These descriptions were purely fictional. Under the feudal system an under-tenant holding of a tenant-in-chief only held the land while he was loyal to the tenant-in-chief, and supported him in any quarrel by bringing the stipulated number of men to serve under his banner. In the Highlands, no clan chief who was a theoretical "under-tenant" ever brought his clan to support the theoretical "tenant-in-chief" on the grounds that he had a feudal duty to do so: if he had tried it, the clan would have refused to follow him. Sometimes the clan of a so-called "under-tenant" did muster and serve alongside the clan of a so-called "tenant-in-chief", but that was because the clan felt, rightly or wrongly, that its own interests were involved. The feudal system never had any existence within the Highland line. David Stewart has already been quoted as saying: "Nothing can be more erroneous than an opinion, often repeated, and therefore sometimes believed, that whatever side the feudal superior took in any great political question or contest, he was invariably followed by his subservient adherents. Many instances to the contrary have been stated [in his *Sketches of the Highlanders*], and I could produce many more, all highly creditable to the spirit of independence which long distinguished the clansmen."[122]

Among the clans in this group were the Camerons: Lochiel paid a small feu-duty in respect of the Cameron country, most of it to the Duke of Argyll (so Adam Smith called him "a vassal of the Duke of Argyll"), part to the Duke of Gordon. Grant of Grant had the charter to most of the lands of the Clan Grant, but the Earl of Moray had obtained the "feudal superiority" over Abernethy, and was paid a small annual sum to keep him happy. The MacIntosh chieftains in Strath Nairn paid feu-duties to the same earl for the same reason. MacIntosh himself paid a feu-duty on a small part of his land to the Duke of Gordon. The chief of Clan Ranald, also, had the charter to most of the Clan Ranald land, but paid a feu-duty for a part of it. MacDonald of Glencoe paid a few shillings a year to Stewart of Appin. MacNeill of Barra "held of" MacDonald of Sleat.[123]

In all these cases the reigning clan chief, such as Lochiel, seem to have had in Lowland eyes the virtual landownership title to his clan land, not the "feudal superior", such as the Duke of Argyll, in Lochiel's case. The rights of these superiors came down to nothing more than the feu-duty, when it was paid – nothing more than a kind of annuity. Even that had the less value for being virtually unsaleable, since there was no guarantee that the clan chief would ever pay, certainly not to a newcomer to the scene. And there was no power, before the changes following Culloden, to make the clan chief pay.

45. Chiefs not of the clan name

In the third group were the clans who followed chiefs not of their own name. This situation could come about in a number of ways. Sometimes one clan would thrive and multiply, while a neighbouring clan would be afflicted by some of the mischances of human existence, and would decrease in numbers. When that happened, the stricken clan would sometimes be absorbed into the prosperous one, and would after a generation or two consider itself part of the larger clan, although still with its own generic name. Sometimes one clan would conquer the country of another, and this again might lead to the absorption of the conquered clan into the conquering one. (In historical times, this happened only when one clan was egged on to commit such aggression by the Lowland authorities.) Sometimes a particular clan would feel from its arrival in a new area that it was too small to stand on its own feet, especially if there was a very powerful neighbouring clan: here again absorption into the larger clan might follow. Sometimes the smaller clan would keep a chieftain of its own name, sometimes it would follow the chief of the larger clan directly. When any of these things occurred, there was no question of the freedom or social status of the individual being threatened. Each Highlander, whatever his surname, would still be a free and equal member of the clan society. It could not be otherwise, for there was no economic or social machinery in the Highlands for slavery, or the subjugation of one person to another. Just as nation-states in the eighteenth or nineteenth centuries sometimes accepted a foreign king, and were loyal to him, so the smaller clan-states in the Highlands would sometimes accept a foreign chief – that is to say, a chief not of the native breed – as their chief executive. (The English themselves invited over a Dutch prince in 1688; when he, and his wife, and his sister-in-law, had all died without heirs, they brought in a German prince as king in 1714, and gave their allegiance to him and his descendants.)

In this group (for example) were the MacRaes, the MacLennans, and the MacLeods of Lewis, who followed Seaforth, chief of the main body of MacKenzies; the MacQuarries, who followed Duart; the MacGillivrays, MacBains and the others who followed MacIntosh; a number of clans other than the Campbells, such as the MacIntyres, MacTavishes, and MacIvers, who followed the Duke of Argyll or the Earl of Breadalbane (though other MacIvers followed Struan Robertson, while some MacTavishes followed Lovat); the MacColls, other MacIntyres, and some of the MacLarens, who followed Stewart of Appin; and the Murrays, Mathesons, Gunns, and Strath Naver MacKays, who followed the Earl of Sutherland.

The conquest or absorption by a large and powerful clan of part of a neighbouring smaller clan gave rise to situations where men of the same clan surname could be members of either of two clans. A MacKay, for example, could be either in the Reay or the Sutherland clan; a Robertson might be in the Atholl clan or might follow Robertson of Struan; a MacNab might follow either Breadalbane or MacNab of MacNab; and a MacDougall might follow either Campbell of Calder or the chief of his own name.

The author of the *History of Scotland in 1750* gives a picture of a small clan in the process of being drawn into a federation with a larger one: "In Lord Sutherland's lands live a small but fierce clan of the name of Gun. They are about 150 in number, they have a chieftain of their own, who lives upon a small Mortgage not above £20 per annum, but his Clan give him a generous assistance to keep up the Grandeur of a Chieftain . . . The Earls of Sutherland tho' Proprietors of every foot of Land the Guns possess [i.e., they have a Lowland charter to it] have been in former times oblig'd to court their Favour and Friendship [when did a landlord have to court the favour and friendship of his tenants?]; but they [the Gunns] have been entirely at the Devotion of the Sutherland Family since the Revolution [of 1688]."[124]

46. Borderers' enmities

In the fourth group were some of the clans who lived in areas in the southern and eastern Highlands, near the Lowland border. The long contention between the Highlanders and the Lowlanders had produced a more warlike type of clan in these border regions – Dr Johnson was told by a Highlander that the most unruly clans were "those that live next the Lowlands"[125] – and thus knew more conflict, leading to more "broken clans" or "broken names" like the MacGregors. Dr Johnson recorded this opinion of the character of the Highlanders near the Lowland boundary as a laughable example of Highland prejudice: but Tobias Smollett, born close to that boundary, had made much the same point only two years earlier. Referring to the islanders of Islay, Jura, Mull, and Iona, he wrote that "in their manners they are less savage and impetuous than their countrymen on the continent"[126] – the continent he had been speaking of was that of Argyllshire (he himself came from Dumbartonshire). Macaulay, it seems, held the same opinion. He remarked: "National enmities have always been fiercest among borderers; and the enmity between the Highland borderer and the Lowland borderer along the whole frontier was the growth of ages, and was kept afresh by constant injuries."[127]

David Stewart concurred. "When dislikes and jealousies subsist between neighbouring countries or districts, the nearer they are, the more bitter their animosities."[128] He explained why the mutual feeling of hostility between the Highlanders and Lowlanders was worst among those living near the dividing line. It happened, he said, "because, in the first place, the [Highland] borderers lived in a state of perpetual contention with their Lowland neighbours, and had thus the worst propensities of their nature called forth and exasperated; and, secondly, because their more powerful neighbours had been, for ages, in the habit of taking deep revenge for petty injuries . . .[129] Not seventy years ago [i.e. about 1750] antipathies of this nature were very prevalent among this now united people of the Lowland and Highland borders of Angus, Perth, and Stirling; nor was there a town in Scotland where prejudices ran stronger against the mountaineers than in Perth." Though the Highlands (and the Highlanders) were only, he said, ten miles distant from Perth, nowhere were the latter more ridiculed for "their real or supposed characteristics of ferocity, ignorance, indolence, and superstition, than by the people of that city, in the daily view of the Grampians, and in constant communication with the inhabitants [of the mountains]".[130]

In fact the distant English, Irish, and Welsh, were sometimes more prepared to adopt Highland habits and Highland manners than the adjacent Lowlanders were. When the Seaforth Highlanders returned under-strength to Scotland in 1798, and the regiment was temporarily filled up with drafts from England and Ireland, a commentator remarked: "One-fourth of the men and officers were English and

Irish, and three-fourths Scotch Highlanders; and, singular as it may seem, the former were as fond of the kilt and pipes as the latter, and many of them entered completely into the spirit of the national feeling."[131] And when the Inverness-shire Fencible Regiment was embodied in 1794, containing some men from the Lowlands, and a few (about forty) from Wales, even at that late date some of the Lowlanders put on Highland dress (wrote Stewart) "with some degree of sulky dislike, while the young men of Wales wore it with great cheerfulness, and seemed to be quite pleased with their own appearance when they put it on". But the men from the Lowlands disliked the plaid. "To the Lowlanders of Aberdeen, as well as Perthshire, it was more objectionable than to either the English or the Irish."[132]

47. "Lowland nobles' clans"

At the same time these border areas of the Highlands were more open to insidious Lowland influences, and were more likely to attract the attention of powerful nobles who lived just outside the Highland line, but were at the head of powerful Lowland family groups or quasi-clans, such as the Drummonds, Grahams, Ogilvies, Gordons, and Murrays. These factors led to the development of what might be called, though it appears on the face of it to be a contradiction in terms, "Lowland nobles' clans". In several districts of the south and east Highlands a number of small or broken clans lived near to each other, or mingled together; sometimes larger clans lived intermixed. In certain areas the Highlanders all accepted one chief, and were loyal to him to the same extent, and with the same limitations, as clans following chiefs of their own name. In the 1740s, it might be said that there were eight chiefs of this kind, four of them earls, and four dukes: the Earls of Perth, Moray, Airlie, and Bute, and the Dukes of Atholl, Montrose, Gordon, and Hamilton. The nobleman-chief, despite his Lowland origin, and despite the fact that he was still a landowner in the Lowlands as well as a chief in the Highlands, often spoke Gaelic to his Highlanders; and always treated them with the same familiarity and the same careful regard to justice and fairness as any "chief of the name". (If he wished to continue as chief, he could do no other.) David Stewart describes how during the civil war of the 1640s, the Marquis of Montrose (one of these noblemen-chiefs) was so unostentatious among his Highland army, "dressed in the common Highland garb" and with only two attendants, that some royalist soldiers newly arrived from Ireland could not believe he was the great Montrose.[133] Yet Montrose was James Graham, in origin a Lowlander.

The nobleman-chief usually had a Lowland charter to the Highland areas over which he exercised his chiefly powers, just as the other clan chiefs often did, but by Highland law and practice the clansfolk over whom he ruled owned the land as the occupiers and defenders of it, in exactly the same way that the other clans owned their land. And up to the middle of the eighteenth century this ownership could not be challenged as a matter of realistic politics, since, despite their Lowland connections, the noblemen-chiefs had just as little power to do anything contrary to the will of their clan-communities as had the other chiefs.

48. Noblemen-chiefs

Among these chiefs of "Lowland noblemen's clans" was the Earl (and, by a Jacobite title, Duke) of Perth, the head of the Drummonds, who was accepted as chief by the Highlanders of Glen Artney and some neighbouring Perthshire glens. The Duke of Atholl, head of the Murrays in the Lowlands, was chief of the Highlanders in Atholl, including the Stewarts of Atholl, most of the Robertsons, some of the Menzies, and some other less numerous clans, for example the Flemings. As Forbes of Culloden wrote, "likewise the Fergussons, Smalls, Spaldings, Rattrays, MacIntoshes in Atholl, and MacLarens in Balquhidder, with other broken names in Atholl, are all followers of the Duke of Atholl".[134] The Duke of Montrose, head of the Grahams, was chief of the clansfolk on both sides of Loch Katrine and Loch Ard. The Earl of Moray, who was himself a Stewart, had a following (as we saw earlier) among MacGregors and others in Balquhidder and Menteith. The Earl of Airlie, head of the Ogilvies, had a Highland following in Glen Isla and Alyth. The Duke of Gordon was chief of the Highlanders in Strath Avon and Glen Livet, in Banffshire, though elsewhere in the Highlands he was – like the Earl of Moray – only a "feudal superior", not a chief. Two other great noblemen, who were in much the same position as Atholl, Montrose, and the rest, were the Earl of Bute, who is particularly mentioned in the 1746 memorial as having a Highland following – obviously in the island of Bute – and the Duke of Hamilton, who had a corresponding position in Arran. All these noblemen, of course, also owned large estates in the Lowlands (or elsewhere in Great Britain).

These chiefships were obtained in various ways. Sometimes a particular group of clansfolk would agree to accept as chief the son-in-law or the grandson of their last chief. The Stewarts of Atholl and their associated clans originally followed Stewart, Earl of Atholl. When the last Earl of Atholl of the Stewart family died without male issue, the title ultimately went (in 1629) to John Murray, his daughter's son, and the Atholl clansfolk accepted Murray (and subsequently his descendants) as their chief.

The "Duke of Perth – is no clan family", as the clan memorial said, and it repeated the phrase in regard to the Duke of Atholl and the Duke of Gordon.[135] But though the families of these Lowland nobles were not themselves clans, the fact that these family-heads had become chiefs in the Highlands led inevitably to the appearance of Drummonds in Glen Artney, Murrays in Atholl, Grahams around Loch Katrine, Ogilvies in Glen Isla, Gordons in Glen Livet, and so on, who were Gaelic-speaking Highlanders indistinguishable from the clansfolk with longer Highland pedigrees.

There is evidence that up to the year 1715 another "nobleman-chief" could have been added to the roster: the Earl of Mar. He was an Erskine, a Lowlander, whose main estate was seemingly at Alloa, in Clackmannanshire. In Braemar, however, he was apparently a clan chief, and it was there that he raised the standard of revolt for the Old Pretender in 1715. The rebellion being defeated, Mar was deprived of his land charters; but subsequently his brother, Lord Grange, and another relative, Erskine of Dun, bought the charters back from the authorities.[136] For some reason, however, the Earl of Mar decided to give up his position as a Highland chief (or did his erstwhile clansfolk refuse to follow him any longer?). The Highland land charters which had been obtained as reflecting this position were sold off, and in the 1790s, the three Highland parishes of Aberdeenshire (Crathie, Glenmuick, and Strathdon) had only one Erskine landlord, Erskine of Achallader.[137] The family of the Earl of Mar had retreated to their Lowland properties.

Sometimes these noblemen-chiefs with a Lowland background assessed the realities of power in the Highlands more accurately than the orthodox "chiefs of the name". In the civil war, the Marquis of Montrose fought for Charles I, and the Marquis of Argyll fought against him, each with an army of Highlanders. David Stewart compared the two: "Montrose, whose numbers were on every occasion very inferior, never lost a battle. Argyll, with Highlanders equally brave, was constantly worsted. Haughty and overbearing, he kept aloof from his people (who honoured him as their chief, but could not love him as a man), and disregarded those courtesies by which a Highlander can be so easily managed. Montrose, on the contrary, knew every soldier in his army, and while he flattered them by his attention to their songs, genealogies, and traditions, and by sharing in all their fatigues and privations, he roused them to exertions almost incredible."[138]

49. Clan communities

In these larger clan communities in the third and fourth groups, although all the clansfolk accepted the same chief, each individual clan in the grouping still regarded itself as a separate entity, with its own traditions and its own burying-place. In Glen Lyon, in the Breadalbane country, there were about twelve surnames (according to Duncan Campbell's *Reminiscences of an Octogenarian Gael*) and each had separate burial plots in the churchyard.[139]

Even in the clans of the first and fourth groups, it was not always the case that the chief had the charter rights to all his clan's land. The Duke of Argyll and the Earl of Breadalbane, for example, were both followed by a number of chieftains, Campbells and others, who had their own charters. There were several Stewart charter holders besides Appin, and several Frasers other than Lovat. Nor could the chief of a clan, even one of these titled chiefs, who played an important part also on the Lowland stage, always be completely certain who would rally to his banner on any given occasion until the test was made. In 1697 the Duke of Atholl summoned his clan to help him in the dispute he had with the Frasers of Beaufort, and he thought it necessary to write to his son telling him (as the *Atholl Chronicles* put it) "how well their neighbours [i.e., the Atholl clan chieftains] had behaved, and that none had refused to come when he sent to them except Ashintully and Shian".[140] Even in what was considered to be a good clan turnout, two chieftains – Spalding of Ashintully, and Menzies of Shian – were absentees. Forbes of Culloden wrote of the Athollmen that the Stewarts of Atholl were "the readiest to turn out on all occasions",[141] thus clearly implying that some of the other groups were sometimes less eager. (At the same time this comment underlined the point that the "turning out" of the clansmen was not a matter of blind obedience, but depended on their own "readiness", i.e. willingness.)

50. Gordon and Argyll

There were a few areas where wrangling over charters, or the ambitions of powerful noblemen, had produced somewhat complicated situations. In the Keppoch country, the Duke of Gordon owned the charter to Glen Spean, and MacIntosh the charter to Glen Roy. After Culloden, and the replacement of the Highland law by Lowland, they were able to take possession of "their" land, and charge the MacDonalds rent for it: and the Keppoch chiefs found themselves without legal standing, since they had omitted to secure their position under Lowland law, relying on the strength of their status in the previous Highland system. North Morar was in the same case. MacDonald of Glengarry had obtained a charter to the land, a charter that remained ineffective during the days of clanship, since the Clan Ranald continued to occupy and to own North Morar. But after 1746 King George's armies gave a practical effect to what had been no more than a theoretical ambition, and the Clan Ranald clansfolk of North Morar found themselves compelled to pay rent to Glengarry.

As we have seen, in the early 1690s the Campbells had established themselves in a dominant position in the Mull and Morvern lands of the MacLeans who followed MacLean of Duart. Perhaps in time these MacLeans would have accepted the conquest, and become as thoroughly integrated with the Campbells as the

MacRaes were with the MacKenzies, or the Gunns with the Sutherland clan. But this had not been accomplished by 1746 – perhaps because of the unpopularity of the Dukes of Argyll in many parts of the Highlands. Whatever the reason, in 1746 many of the MacLeans still regarded Duart as their chief, even though they lived in territory which had been largely seized by the Campbells. Forbes of Culloden wrote that the MacLeans used to have a strength of 800 men; "but now that the Campbells are possessed of their chief's estate, they will hardly make 500, and even many of that number must be brought out of the Duke of Argyll's estate"[142] – i.e., the lands to which Argyll had the charter right, and in which he had as much power as the Campbell clan could give him. The state of affairs in the old MacLean lands gives no support to any theory that the chiefs were really landlords: it was simply the result of a struggle, still not finally resolved, between two rival clans.

The ambition of the Marquises of Huntly (the then marquis became the Duke of Gordon in 1684) brought about a similar situation in parts of Strath Spey, Badenoch, and Lochaber. The dukes owned much land in the Aberdeenshire Lowlands, but they had also established themselves as Highland chiefs in Strath Avon and Glen Livet, in the way that has already been described. They thirsted after further power in the central Highlands, and had when in favour at court obtained various charters giving them ostensible rights of feudal superiority, rights of jurisdiction, and rights of landownership, in various areas. While the clan system was in full flower, these charters had no effect: but as the state power, directed from Edinburgh and London, began to make itself felt in the Highlands, in a very small way after 1689, somewhat more strongly after 1715, and very powerfully in the years after 1746, so were the Dukes of Gordon increasingly able to take steps to enforce their Lowland-given rights. The transformation was far from complete even in 1746, when Forbes of Culloden wrote that the Duke of Gordon had "Highland followings in Strath Avon and Glen Livet, which are about 300 men; his extensive jurisdictions and superiorities in the centre Highlands, viz. Badenoch, Lochaber, and Strath Spey, do not yield him any followers. The tenants on his own property [i.e., where he possesses land charters], as well as those who hold their lands of him in feu, follow their natural-born chief, of whom they are descended, and pay no regard either to the master or superior of their lands. Thus the Camerons follow Lochiel, the MacPhersons follow Cluny, and other chiefs are followed and obeyed in the same manner from respect, family attachment, and consanguinity."[143]

These two last-mentioned areas – western Argyllshire, and the lands in the central Highlands covered by the Gordon charters – were among the very earliest to experience the change of methods of the new era. The Gordons could have laid claim to the unenviable distinction of being perhaps among the very first of the Highland charter-holding families to introduce the new order. In 1887 the eighth

Duke of Argyll, looking back to the beginning of the transformation in the Highlands, wrote that the Dukes of Gordon began what he shamelessly called "the work of reform" in the north;[144] the first complaint of "the rule of factors" came from the Gordon lands in Badenoch as early as 1699 (this being perhaps the first certain piece of evidence that the changes were beginning); the two conflicts in the 1720s mentioned by Burt, involving some MacPhersons near Ruthven and some MacMartin-Camerons near Fort William, were both on lands to which Gordon held the charters;[145] on the former of these two occasions, the Duke of Gordon became the first landlord to call in troops to evict the Highlanders; and in William MacIntosh's book, published in 1729, the Duchess of Gordon the younger is mentioned, along with two other Gordons, as being among the "improvers" in the north.[146]

51. Gordon and the MacPhersons

The clear statement of Forbes of Culloden that the "extensive jurisdictions and superiorities in the centre Highlands" of the Duke of Gordon "do not yield him any followers" appears to be contradicted by A. M. Shaw in his *Mackintosh and Clan Chattan*, at least so far as concerns the MacPhersons. "We have seen", wrote Shaw, speaking of the 1720s, "that the MacPhersons had for some time been following the house of Huntly, and that Huntly – or more properly the first Duke of Gordon – had been using every means to trouble MacIntosh." Shaw gives only three examples of the relations between the Duke of Gordon (and his eldest son, who after the creation of the dukedom bore his father's second title as Marquis of Huntly) and the MacPhersons – only three instances to support his statement that "the MacPhersons had for some time been following the house of Huntly". In 1689, wrote Shaw, quoting the *Memoirs of Lochiel*, "the MacPhersons had been found 'very keen and hearty in their inclinations for the service' of King James, but could not move without an order from their superior the Duke of Gordon".[147] This seems to be an instance, not so much of the MacPhersons obeying Gordon, as of their using his opposition as an excuse for not doing what King James' supporters thought they would do. (The assertion that Highlanders were so deferential that they "could not move without an order" from a "superior" is of course completely at odds with how they really behaved, as many examples given in this work demonstrate.) Shaw's second example occurred at the time of the 1715 Rising. "The MacPhersons formed a separate battalion", he wrote, "under the orders of the Marquis of Huntly, son of their superior lord; but owing to that noble's jealousy and distrust of Mar they had not much opportunity of exhibiting their prowess. At the indecisive battle of Sheriffmuir they were compelled to remain inactive, either in obedience to Huntly's order or by the enemy's strategy."[148] This seems even more clearly a case of the MacPhersons using Huntly's supposed superiority to excuse their own inaction, following on their own apathy. (Highlanders fighting for causes they believed in did not wait for orders to engage.) Shaw's third example of the relations between Gordon and the MacPhersons took place in 1724. "In imitation", wrote Shaw, "of the policy of his great-grandfather the first Marquis, the Duke [of Gordon] had stirred up the chieftain of Clan Mhuirich [MacPherson of Cluny] to assert his independence of MacIntosh, and to claim the headship of Clan Chattan."[149] Yet despite these efforts of the MacPhersons' so-called "superior lord", in 1724 Lachlan MacPherson of Cluny, supported by the MacPherson chieftains, made an agreement with Lachlan MacIntosh of that ilk in which, among other things, Cluny recognized MacIntosh as "the only undoubted Chief of Clan Chattan".[150] Here again, only twenty-two years before Culloden, we have the MacPhersons clearly asserting their independence of Gordon. Shaw, then, must be held to have failed to prove his contention that the MacPhersons regarded Gordon as their chief.

We are left with the statement of Forbes of Culloden, that Gordon had no followers in the central Highlands: and Culloden was a contemporary witness who clearly was closely acquainted with the personalities of the Highlands in 1746. David Stewart, writing in about 1820, drew attention to the large extent of territory to which the Duke of Gordon had secured charters. Stewart continued: "His feudal power [i.e., his power during the clan system] was indeed small in proportion to the number of people and the extent of territory. The patriarchal sway of the chiefs of families, or, as they were called, natural-born chiefs of their own blood, superseded the authority of the feudal lord of whom several chiefs and lairds held their lands. Independently of any vassalage or subjection, these chiefs commanded their own followers [when they were prepared to be commanded], acknowledging no power as superior except that of the Sovereign. But although they did not publicly acknowledge a superior power in the Chief of the Gordons of whom they held, they, on many occasions, allowed him to influence their actions, particularly if his measures did not run counter to their peculiar feelings and political prejudices. Thus, in 1715, a number of the Badenoch and Lochaber Highlanders were ready to follow the Marquis of Huntly in support of the claims of the exiled Royal Family; but, when the father of the present Duke of Gordon attempted to call out his people in arms to support Government, in the year 1745, none of the Highlanders of his estates moved, except to follow their own immediate Chiefs and Lairds, all of whom took the opposite side."[151] In other words, as Jacobites they were prepared come out in rebellion in 1715, but were not prepared to come out against Prince Charles in 1745 – when, indeed, many of them joined the Pretender's army.

It may finally be remarked that if the Duke of Gordon had succeeded ultimately in ingratiating himself sufficiently with the MacPhersons to induce them to accept him as chief, it still would have offered no indication of the existence of Lowland landownership in the Highlands. If that had happened, it would simply have offered a parallel with the conditions which unquestionably obtained around the southern and eastern fringes of the Highlands, where Graham of Montrose, Drummond of Perth, Murray of Atholl, Stewart of Moray, Ogilvy of Airlie, the Earl of Bute, the Duke of Hamilton, and the Duke of Gordon himself, had succeeded in obtaining Highland followings, not as Lowland landlords, but as Highland chiefs.

52. Memorial of 1746

One of the best-known attempts to list the Highland clans as seen through Lowland eyes was made in about 1746: it has already often been referred to. The Jacobite rebellion of 1745, most of the active supporters of which were Highlanders, had made it a matter of urgency to obtain some reliable facts about this strange and foreign race, dwelling in a country which (as we see elsewhere) was almost completely unknown to, and almost completely out of the power of, those who claimed to be ruling over it. So a memorial was drawn up, probably by Duncan Forbes of Culloden, Lord President of the Court of Session.

Whether he wrote the memorial or not, it is a Lowland document, written from the Lowland point of view. The memorial contains all the usual Lowland errors about Highland life; Highland actuality was described in terms of Lowland theory. Particular law systems apply, and can only apply, to particular sets of social and economic circumstances; the Lowland law system had grown up to cover Lowland conditions, so it was not able to make any meaningful statement about the quite different Highland system. It could only use Lowland legal concepts to cover the alien Highland reality. So in the view of the memorial writer each clan land was owned, not by the clan who lived there and clearly possessed it, but by whichever individual happened to have cheated or wheedled or bribed or bought his way into the ownership of a piece of parchment which brazenly claimed that he owned it. The fact was nothing; the document was everything. Thus the Highlands were full of "estates", each with its owner, and the Highlanders were depicted as mere ciphers, turning out fully armed to war simply on the command of their chiefs – beliefs which were as we have seen blatant contradictions of the real situation.

The author considered each clan in turn, giving the clan name, the name of its chief, and the chief's position as it was adjudged to be in the eyes of an Edinburgh lawyer. Sometimes the author gave the area where the clan lived; always he gave a rough estimate of the number of men he thought each clan might be able to put into the field. As we shall see later, for example when we look at the response of each clan in the '45, the numbers who would actually rally to the chief at his call depended entirely on what the clansfolk felt about the merits of the case. However, the potential maximum armed strength of each clan does provide an approximate guide to the total numbers in the clan.

The author also noted a number of border families, and indicated how far nobles like the Duke of Gordon and the Earl of Moray could properly be considered to be part of the Highland picture, or how far their strengths lay only in the Lowlands. The author obviously knew a great deal about the Highlands, as understood in the Lowlands, although he did get some details wrong.

The date of the memorial can be established to within a few months. Two of the men named in the memorial as currently holding the position of chief were Sir Henry Munro of Foulis, and Sir Alexander MacDonald of Sleat. Sir Henry Munro succeeded his father (Sir Robert, who was killed at Falkirk) on 17th January 1746, while Sir Alexander died on 23rd November 1746, when he was succeeded by his son Sir James. If Sir Henry and Sir Alexander are correctly named, therefore, the memorial must have been composed in 1746, after 17th January but before 23rd November. We know now that this was the culminating era in the history of the clans; so the memorial gives us a most interesting picture (albeit seen through Lowland blinkers) of the independent Highland clans just before they were swept out of history.[152]

Some writers now use the term "chief" as meaning the head of a clan, and the term "chieftain" as meaning the head of a sept within the clan. In the 1746 memorial the two terms appear to be used indiscriminately. I have followed the author of the memorial in calling the head of each clan either a chief or a chieftain, though I have modernized the spelling. Where a word or phrase is in quotation marks, it is a direct citation; where there are no such marks, the words convey the meaning in the memorandum.

53. The roster of clans

The clans were listed as follows:-

Campbell; chief, the Duke of Argyll, or "MacAillain Mor". Argyll "can raise above 3000 men; the Earl of Breadalbane, more than 1000; and the Barons of the name of Campbell, Ardkinglass, Auchenbreck, Lochnell, Inneraw, and others, 1000, so that this clan could bring into the field above 5000 men, besides those barons and gentlemen of the name in Dumbarton, Stirling, and Perthshire, and the Laird of Calder in Nairn". They are "the most numerous clan in Scotland".

MacLean; "Sir Hector MacLean of Douart [Duart]" was their chief; "a very potent clan about 200 years ago, and could have raised 800 men; but now that the

Campbells are possessed of their chief's estate, they will hardly make 500, and even many of that number must be brought out of the Duke of Argyll's estate", that is to say, from the lands where the Duke of Argyll had been able to obtain the charter-right, and which were now in contention between the MacLeans and the Campbells.

MacLachlan; chief, "the Laird of MacLachlan"; 300 men.

Stewart of Appin; chieftain, "the Laird of Appin"; 300.

MacDougall (Lorn); chief, "the Laird of MacDougall". "This was a more potent family of old, but is now much diminished by the Campbells; they can still (I believe) bring out 200 men."

MacDonald (Sleat); chieftain, Sir Alexander MacDonald; "in the Isles of Skye and Uist" – or, more accurately, in two districts of Skye, and in North Uist; 700.

MacDonald (Clanranald); chieftain, Captain of Clan Ranald; "in Moidart and Arisaig on the Continent, and in the Isles of Uist, Benbecula, and Rum"; 700. (The author was mistaken; of the four Small Isles, Rum and Muck were MacLean territory: it was Eigg and Canna which were inhabited by the Clan Ranald. Moreover, in the Outer Hebrides only South Uist and Benbecula were Clan Ranald territory – North Uist belonged to Clan Donald – while "on the Continent" the Clan Ranald also lived in Morar, North and South.)

MacDonald (Glengarry); chieftain, "the Laird of Glengarry"; "in Glengarry and Knoydart"; 500.

MacDonald (Keppoch); "Keppoch is their chieftain"; "in Lochaber"; 300.

MacDonald (Glencoe); chieftain, "the Laird of Glencoe"; 150.

Cameron; chief, "the Laird of Lochiel"; "MacMartin of Letterfinlay, and others, branches of the Camerons", acknowledge Lochiel as chief; 800.

MacLeod; "were two distinct and very potent families of old; viz. MacLeod of Lewis, and MacLeod of Harris, but they are both utterly extinct, and their lands possessed by the MacKenzies"; chief, the Laird of MacLeod; "in Glenelg, on the Continent, and in the Isle of Skye"; 700. (Another mistake: the MacKenzies had seized Lewis, but not Harris. Even in Lewis, the MacLeods were far from extinct, but lived under the MacKenzie chief, Seaforth.) The Tormod MacLeod clan were also far from extinct; they lived in Harris, in parts of Skye, and in Glenelg, their chief being MacLeod of Harris or of Dunvegan.)

MacKinnon; chief, "the Laird of MacKinnon"; "in the Isles of Skye and Mull" (that is, in one part of each island); 200.

"I again pass to the south . . . There are several persons of rank, as well as gentlemen, who are chieftains, and who have the command [sic] of many Highlanders in Argyll, Monteith, Dumbarton, Stirling and Perth shires; such as the Duke of Montrose, the Earls of Moray and Bute, also the MacFarlanes, MacNeill of Barra, MacNab of MacNab, Buchanans and Colquhouns of Luss,

CHIEFS AND CHARTERS

MacNaughtons, Lamont of Lamont, etc. They can raise among them 5,400 men. Besides these there are several border families, those of Kilraick [Rose of Kilravock], Brodie of Brodie, Innes of Innes, Irvine of Drum, Lord Forbes, and the Earl of Airlie, all of whom are loyal, except the Ogilvies. Few or none of them have any followers, except Lord Airlie, from his Highland estate." (Monteith, or Menteith, is not a shire, but a district of Perthshire; while MacNeill of Barra is presumably here in error, since the MacNeills lived in the Outer Hebrides – Barra was in Inverness-shire, not in any of the named counties.)

These clans, therefore, must be added to the 1746 list: the clan of the Duke of Montrose; ditto the Earl of Moray; ditto the Earl of Bute; ditto the Earl of Airlie; MacFarlane; MacNab; Buchanan; Colquhoun; MacNaughton; Lamont; and MacNeill of Barra.

Apart from these clans, mentioned briefly by the memorial, there should be added to the roster three more clans: the MacAulays of Garelochside; the Duke of Hamilton's clan, consisting of the Arran Highlanders; and the Forbes clan of Strath Don (as we shall shortly see). Besides that, David Stewart asserted that "there were a number of independent gentlemen, who had many followers, but being what were called broken names, or small tribes, they are omitted in the Lord President's report".[153]

54. Is no clan family

The list resumes:

Duke of Perth; "is no clan family", although the duke is head of the Drummonds "in the Low country. He is brought in here allenarly [solely] on account of his command of about 300 Highlanders in Glenartnie [Glen Artney] and other glens in the county of Perth." (The title "Duke of Perth" was a Jacobite creation only; it is curious that the writer of the memorial – almost certainly a Hanoverian – used that designation.)

Robertson; chief, "the Laird of Strowan [Struan]"; "in Rannoch in the Braes of Atholl in Perthshire"; 200. "There are 500 men more of the Robertsons in Atholl who never follow their chief, being part of the followers of the Duke of Atholl."

Menzies; "Sir Robert Menzies of Weem is the chief"; "in Rannoch, and Appin Dull in Atholl"; 300.

Stewart (Grandtully); chief, Stewart of Grandtully; "in Strath Bran and Strath Tay in Atholl"; 300.

MacGregor; "this name was called down by Act of Parliament. They are now dispersed under the different names of Drummond, Murray, Graham, and Campbell, and live in the counties of Perth, Stirling, Dumbarton etc."; the chief is elective – "he is chosen on the principle of detur digniori" (let it be given to the more worthy); 700.

Duke of Atholl; "the Murrays is no clan family", though the duke is head of the Murrays in the Lowlands; the duke is chief of the Highlanders "in Atholl, Glen Almond, and Balquhidder. The most numerous of these, and the readiest to turn out on all occasions, are the Stewarts of Atholl, in number more than 1000 men, as also 500 Robertsons . . . likewise the Fergussons, Smalls, Spaldings, Rattrays, MacIntoshes in Atholl, and MacLarens in Balquhidder, with other broken names in Atholl"; in all, 3000.

Farquharson; "the only clan family in Aberdeenshire"; chief, "the Laird of Invercauld"; "both in Perthshire and Brae Mar"; "other barons of the name . . . such as Monaltrie, Inverey, Finzean, etc."; 500. (The Forbes clan of Strath Don also lived in Aberdeenshire; if Duncan Forbes was really the author of this memorial, he might have wished to repudiate any idea of Forbes being a clan name, and thus to distance himself and his immediate relatives from any of the Highland clans, who were often suspected as Jacobite and always considered to be "uncivilized". As we saw above, the memorial asserted that Lord Forbes was loyal, and that he was part of a border family, not the head of a clan: but an official report on the Highlanders who rebelled in 1715 included the name "Forbes of Strathdon", 250 strong, on the list just under the Farquharsons.)[154]

Duke of Gordon; "the Gordons is no clan family, although the duke is chief of a very powerful name in the Lowlands"; he has "Highland followings in Strath Avon and Glen Livet"; 300.

Grant; chief, "the Laird of Grant"; "in Strath Spey and Urquhart"; "several barons of his name . . . such as Dalvey, Ballindalloch, Rothiemurchus, Cullen etc."; 700 (in Strath Spey) and 150 (in Urquhart).

MacIntosh; chief, "the Laird of MacIntosh", or "Captain of Clan Chattan"; Strath Nairn; "including the small neighbouring clans of MacGillivray, MacQueen, MacBean, etc."; 800.

MacPherson; chief, "the Laird of Clunie [Cluny]"; Badenoch; 400.

Fraser; chief, "Lord Lovat"; Aird and Strath Errick; there are "a good number of barons of his name in Inverness and Aberdeen shires", said the memorial, despite having stated earlier that the Farquharsons were "the only clan family in Aberdeenshire"; 900.

Grant (Glen Moriston); chieftain, "Grant of Glenmoriston"; frequently the ally of Glengarry; 150.

Chisholm; chief, "Chisholm of Strathglass"; 200.

MacKenzie; chief, "the Earl of Seaforth"; in "Kintail, Lochalsh, Lochbroom, Lochcarron, on the Continent, and in the Isle of Lewis"; 1000. "The Earl of

Cromarty [Cromartie], with the Lairds of Gairloch, Scatwell, Killcowie [Kilcoy?], Redcastle, Comric, etc. etc. can raise among them 1500 men more."

Munro; chief, "Sir Henry Munro of Foulis"; 300.

Ross; chief, "Lord Ross"; 500.

Sutherland; chief, "the Earl of Sutherland"; 2000.

MacKay; chief, "the Lord Reay"; Strathnaver (here with its general meaning of "north Sutherland", rather than that particular strath); 800.

Sinclair; chief, "the Earl of Caithness"; other Sinclair chieftains are "May, Dunbeath, Ulbster, Freswick, etc. etc."; 1000.

55. Britain as a privately-owned estate

When after 1746 those chiefs who had charters to the lands of their clans suddenly found that they now had the right to drive out the clansfolk, and deal with the clan land in whatever way suited them (the chiefs) best, the clansfolk now being entirely powerless, it was such a demolition of everything in Highland history, such an overturning of the entire social system of the Gaels, that it was only slowly, by very gradual steps, that this power began to be used. The clansfolk found it difficult to believe that it could be done; the chiefs found it difficult to believe that they could do it. Some chiefs, particularly those who had grown up before 1746 – or even those born before that fateful date – realizing the basic injustice of the new regime, were hesitant about grasping the fortunes offered them by that regime. One chief is said to have told Adam Smith about his clansfolk: "Their forefathers got or secured my estates by their blood and their lives and I think they have a natural claim to a share of it."[155] The chief's self-interest not surprisingly made him call the clan land "my estates", but he could not close his eyes to the fact that it was the clansfolk who had held and defended their clan country against all assaults, principally those from the Lowlanders, for centuries past, and who were now going to lose it to their own chief.

If some foreign power conquered Great Britain, and decided for its own ends to make Britain a piece of private property belonging to royalty, with the result that the British monarch could now use the country in any way he wanted for his own individual enrichment, the British people would be as astounded as the Highlanders were when an exactly parallel process gave the chiefs that precise power.[156] And if the British sovereign proceeded to give the whole population of Great Britain – English, Welsh, Scots, everybody – notice to remove, so that he could rent Britain out to say German or Japanese businessmen (for them to turn it perhaps into a series of holiday camps – after all, the country has many scenic splendours and historical attractions), no doubt he, commanding sufficient force from his foreign backers, could succeed in his plan. If in consequence the whole

British population had to flee to whatever place overseas might be found to give them asylum, they might have to accept this decree as a matter of practical politics (assuming that the foreign, conquering state was powerful enough to enforce this new dispensation), but it would be a long time before they admitted that the new way of doing things was in any way lawful or justifiable. They would doubtless continue to believe, for many generations, that if rectitude returned, they should be restored to the country of their forefathers. And so it was with the Highlanders.

The amazement of some commentators at the unbelievable turn of events after 1746 was marked, for example, by Professor F. W. Newman (younger brother of Cardinal Newman), who wrote in 1851: "A king of England might as well claim to drive all his subjects into the sea."[157]

CHAPTER FOUR NOTES

1. The coming of the charter
[1] Innes 1872, 155.
[2] Stewart 1822, II xi.
[3] Shakespeare, *King John*, IV, ii 219.
[4] John Mackintosh, *History of Civilization in Scotland*, I 231 fn.
[5] Adam/Innes 1965, 53-4.

2. Practical effect of the charters
[6] Samuel Butler, *Erewhon*, Dent, London, (1872) 1947, 90. Butler's imaginary country had ordinary banks, but also "musical banks", where people had accounts which were pretended to be of great importance, but which in reality were ignored. ("Musical banks" were Butler's sardonic parody on the churches in the England of his time.)
[7] Innes 1872, 155.
[8] Website moonestates; ten acres of the moon for only £94, and cheap at the price. The action of this company in selling off bits of the moon in the twenty-first century is exactly parallel to the action of the clan chiefs during the eighteenth century. The moon company now, and the clan chiefs then, simply announced that they were now the owners of what up to then had not belonged to them; and proceeded to exercise the rights of ownership. Most people in the late eighteenth century accepted the clan chiefs' claim (which now had the Lowland and English state power behind it), and so it became true; whether the same will happen now in the case of the moon company remains to be seen.

3. Precepts of sasine
[9] Richards 1985, 124, quoting a reviewer in *The Times Literary Supplement*.

4. Virtually absolute control
[10] George Eliot, *Middlemarch*, O.U.P., London, (1871-2) 1950, 14.
[11] Smout 1970, 42.
[12] Devine 1998, 6.
[13] The dinosaurs left no written documents, but no one denies their existence; see Geddes 1955, 106.
[14] Johnson 1930, 104.

5. *MacDonalds of Keppoch*
[15] In 1862, in the case of MacGillivray v. Souter (24 Dunlop 772), Lord Ardmillan said that "clans are not corporations which law sustains, nor societies which law recognizes or acknowledges". Sir Thomas Innes (Adam/Innes 1965, 145) quoted this, but was sure it was completely wrong. My own view is that taking into account the Lowlanders' opinions about the Highlanders and about Highland society, this is an accurate statement of the (Lowland) law.
[16] Stewart 1822, II ii.
[17] Shaw 1880, 155.
[18] Shaw 1880, 302.

6. *Invasion of Badenoch*
[19] Shaw 1880, 388-392.
[20] Shaw 1880, 394-98.
[21] MacDonald 1991, 145.

7. *Fire and sword*
[22] Hopkins 1998, 108.
[23] Shaw 1880, 405-10.
[24] Perhaps unhappy at this demonstration that Highland law ruled in the Highlands, Dr I. F. Grant (Grant 1934, 146) said that "by the middle of the seventeenth century" the MacDonalds of Keppoch "had obtained sole and legal possession" – that is, legal possession according to the Lowland documents; but of course this statement is inaccurate – MacDonald of Keppoch never obtained a Lowland charter to Keppoch. When the Keppoch family, before the end of the eighteenth century, became sheep farmers, they had to rent what had been Keppoch land from the charter-holders who had by then been put in possession by the landlord revolution. It is true that very occasionally, even in the days before Culloden, when a Keppoch chief was preoccupied with other matters, he might send a very small sum to MacIntosh to avoid the necessity of defeating an armed invasion. The *Memoirs of Lochiel* (Shaw 1880, 388 fn.) said that MacIntosh "sometimes received such small sums in name of yearly rents as Keppoch was pleased to give", but these sums can scarcely be called rent, as the term is now understood: a more accurate name would be blackmail – a payment made to avoid violent attacks, such as the Keppoch people suffered at Mulroy and afterwards.

It is interesting that Professor George Pryde fell into the same error as Dr I. F. Grant, when he said that the annexed estates after Culloden included the "large domains of Lovat, Lochiel, Cromartie, and Keppoch" (Pryde 1962, 153). Keppoch never had a "domain", in the Lowland meaning of that term.

8. *MacIntosh and Gordon*
[25] Stewart 1822, II 381 fn.

9. *Camerons and Clan Chattan*
[26] Shaw 1880, 349.
[27] Shaw 1880, 85.
[28] Shaw 1880, 98.
[29] Shaw 1880, 349-50.
[30] Shaw 1880, 351, 355, 357.
[31] Shaw 1880, 358.

10. *Settlement at Loch Arkaig*
[32] Shaw 1880, 378 fn.
[33] Shaw 1880, 371-83.
[34] Johnson & Boswell 1930, 121; & see MacKenzie 1906, 73.

11. *Glenorchy and the Sinclairs*
[35] Stewart 1822, II 327 fn.

12. *Fight at Altimarlich*
[36] Way & Squire 1994, 323. Dr Smout mentioned the battle at Altimarlich (Smout 1970, 205), but he did not say that it was the direct result of the Lowland king's charter-granting; and he described it as the "last major pitched battle between clan armies", a comment which surprisingly ignored Mulroy, eight years later.
[37] I have taken Cairnmore Hillock (133 m.) to be at the edge of the Highlands, and the Hill of Olrig (141 m.) to be at the edge of the Caithness Lowlands: Bartholomew's *National Map Series*, sheet sixty.
[38] Ordnance Survey *One-inch Series*, sheet sixteen.
[39] The full name was "Rothesay and Caithness Fencibles", but they were "principally natives of Caithness" (Stewart 1822, II 325). "Rothesay" was added to the name because Bute and Caithness sent an M.P. to Parliament alternately, and because of a desire to please the Prince of Wales (who was known as the Duke of Rothesay when in Scotland).
[40] Stewart 1822, II 327 fn.

13. *A conquered country*
[41] Stewart 1822, II 327 fn.

14. *Lovat and the Frasers*
[42] Atholl 1908, I 389.

15. *A remarkable career*
[43] Burke 1891, article on Lovat.
[44] Atholl 1908, 401.
[45] Atholl 1908, 422.

16. *This unhappy accident*
[46] Atholl 1908, 389.

17. *Forcibly possessed himself*
[47] Burke 1891, article on Lovat.
[48] *Memoir of the Life of Lord Lovat*, said to be by Duncan Forbes, Cooper, London, 1746, 23.
[49] Fry 2005, 171.
[50] Atholl 1908, 419.
[51] *Oxford D.N.B.*, article on Simon Fraser.

18. *Fraser of Fraserdale*
[52] Selkirk 2010, 75; & *Oxford D.N.B.*, article on Simon Fraser.
[53] G. E. Cokayne, *Complete Peerage*, Bell & Sons, London, 1898, article on Lovat.

19. *Eloquent tongue*
[54] Burke 1891, article on Lovat.

20. *Object of her aversion*
[55] MacKenzie 1896, 442-3.
[56] MacKenzie 1896, 365, & Mitchell 1971, II 20.
[57] Website electricscotland.

CHIEFS AND CHARTERS

21. *MacNeills of Barra*
[58] Website electricscotland.

22. *Fate of Clan Gregor*
[59] Burke 1891, article on Sir Malcolm MacGregor.
[60] MacGillivray vs Souter, 24 Dunlop 772; Adam/Innes 1965, 145 (see above, note to subsection 5, *MacDonalds of Keppoch*); quoted MacKenzie 1908, 304.

23. *To make an ally*
[61] Munro 1977, 15.
[62] Bain 1960, 192.
[63] Rixson 2004, 27, quoting Franck 1694.

24. *Clan Donald land*
[64] MacLeod 1905, 357.
[65] A. MacDonald, *Transactions of Gaelic Soc of Inverness*, XXXVIII 358.
[66] MacDonald 1904, 157-8.

25. *No formal leases*
[67] Blackie 1885, 8.
[68] Brand Commission, P.P. 1895, XXXVIII c. 370.

26. *"Sales" of land*
[69] Johnson & Boswell 1930, 53.
[70] O.S.A. XII 426 fn, Kirkmichael Banff.
[71] MacKenzie 1813, 50.
[72] *Edinburgh Magazine*, July 1817, 399.
[73] Shaw 1880, 384.
[74] Shaw 1880, 578.
[75] Shaw 1880, 538.

27. *MacLeods of Raasay and of Glenelg*
[76] Shaw 1880, 583.
[77] Burke 1838, III 478.
[78] Burke 1838, III 78.
[79] Burke 1838, III 101; www.historyofparliamentonline, P. C. Bruce 1748-1820. Sale of Glenelg 1810, Fraser-Mackintosh 1897, 154.

28. *MacDougalls of Muckairn*
[80] N.S.A. VII 513, Ardchattan Arg. If Sylvester Darius was concerned, this must have been about the 1530s. Darius was involved in the negotiations between Henry VIII and the Pope over Henry's desire to depose his first wife Catherine of Aragon, and marry Anne Boleyn.

29. *Campbell of Calder*
[81] N.S.A. VII 513-14, Ardchattan Arg.

30. *Argyll and the MacLeans*
[82] Moncreiffe 1967, 73.

31. *Struggle in Tiree*
[83] Argyll 1887, passim.
[84] Banks 1977, 63, 65.

32. *Hostility of the MacLeans*
[85] Graham Campbell 1978, 127.
[86] Mercer 1974, 93.
[87] Mercer 1974, 94, & Cregeen 1970, 8.
[88] Gaskell 1980, 5.
[89] Cregeen 1970, 8.

33. *Fife adventurers, and Kintail*
[90] Geddes 1955, 109.
[91] D. Cooper, *Road to Mingulay*, Warner, London, 1992, 16.
[92] Murray 1973, 201.
[93] Thompson 1973, 43-4.
[94] Steel 1994, 111. Steel deplored the violence shown by Highlanders, defending themselves against Lowland attacks (there was little "law and order and firm government . . . north of the Highland line", Steel 1994, 40); but he took a more sympathetic view of the violence done *to* the Highlanders. "The Highland clearances, however sad and traumatic, cannot be seen in isolation . . . It was a restless, changing age, and as in all such periods of history sections of society, often inadvertently, get hurt" (Steel 1994, 257). Strange how violence done by "our side" is generally excusable, while violence done by others is condemned.
[95] Thompson 1973, 44.

34. *Kintail and Assynt*
[96] *Oxford D.N.B.*, article on Neil MacLeod of Assynt.
[97] Ross 1998, 271, makes the extraordinary allegation that "MacKenzie of Assynt went bankrupt because of the collapse of the kelp industry". There was not much of a "kelp industry" in 1736, when John MacKenzie gave up the attempt to impose himself as chief upon the MacLeods of Assynt, and abandoned his pretensions. Orthodox commentators go to extraordinary lengths to show the chiefs overcome by undeserved economic disasters and, blamelessly, "going bankrupt" – and also of course, to avoid showing that in the 1730s the ordinary Highlanders still had the power to decide who, if anyone, was going to be chief.
[98] Groome 1892-6, article on Assynt.

35. *MacNeills of North Knapdale*
[99] N.S.A. VI 637, North Knapdale Arg.

36. *MacIntosh and Cluny*
[100] Shaw 1880, 444-5.

37. *Undoubted legal power*
[101] Youngson 1974, 17.
[102] Youngson 1974, 26.
[103] Devine 1998, 26. Devine surprisingly calls Drummond by his Jacobite title, Duke of Perth.
[104] Youngson 1973, 20; Devine 1998, 16.
[105] Atholl 1908, 502.

38. *Moray and the MacIntoshes*

CHIEFS AND CHARTERS

[106] Shaw 1880, 313.
[107] Shaw 1880, 314.
[108] Pine 1972, 99. "The clansmen took advantage of their chief being only a child to ravage the lands of Moray and his vassals." An extraordinary switch of the facts: Moray took advantage of the MacIntosh chief being only a child to evict the MacIntosh clansfolk; this author said it was "the clansmen" who "took advantage" of that fact – taking advantage to suffer evictions, presumably.

39. *Moray repulsed*
[109] Shaw 1880, 316.
[110] Shaw 2880, 316; for the successful clearance, see volume four of this work (1800-40, except Sutherland).
[111] Pierre-Joseph Proudhon, *What is Property*, Cosimo, New York, (1840) 2007, 3.
[112] Jean-Jacques Rousseau, *Discourse on Inequality*, Kessinger, Montana, (1754) 2004, 41.

40. *Heritable jurisdictions*
[113] Selkirk 2010, 77.

41. *With great equity*
[114] Smith 1895, 315.
[115] Macaulay 1907, 427.
[116] Adam/Innes 1965, 55.
[117] Stewart 1822, I 124.
[118] Johnson & Boswell 1930, 85.

42. *Compulsion to obey*
[119] Linklater 1962, xiii.
[120] Macaulay 1907, 424.

43. *Chiefs of the clan name*
[121] Some of the clansfolk with these names followed other chiefs.

44. *"Feudal superiors"*
[122] Stewart 1822, II i fn.
[123] Stewart 1822, II v-ix.

45. *Chiefs not of the clan name*
[124] Lang 1898, 12-13.

46. *Borderers' enmities*
[125] Johnson & Boswell 1930, 31.
[126] Smollett 1967, 295.
[127] Macaulay 1907, 423.
[128] Stewart 1822, II 347.
[129] Stewart 1822, II xxxv.
[130] Stewart 1822, II 347-8.
[131] Stewart 1822, II 138.
[132] Stewart 1822, II 347-8.

47. *"Lowland nobles' clans"*
[133] Stewart 1822, I 40.

48. *Noblemen-chiefs*
[134] Stewart 1822, II viii.
[135] Stewart 1822, II vii-viii.
[136] O.S.A. XIV 351, Crathie Aberd.
[137] O.S.A. XII 215, Glenmuick Aberd.
[138] Stewart 1822, II lii (Roman 52).

49. *Clan communities*
[139] *Reminiscences of an Octogenarian Gael*, Northern Counties, Inverness, 1908, 229.
[140] Atholl 1908, 109.

50. *Gordon and Argyll*
[141] Stewart 1822, II viii.
[142] Stewart 1822, II vi.
[143] Stewart 1822, II viii; also see Stewart 1822, I 23 fn.
[144] Argyll 1887, 374.
[145] Burt 2005, 225.
[146] William MacIntosh, *Ways & Means for inclosing... Scotland*, Freebairn, Edinburgh, 1729.

51. *Gordon and the MacPhersons*
[147] Shaw 1880, 402.
[148] Shaw 1880, 423.
[149] Shaw 1880, 442.
[150] Shaw 1880, 443-5.
[151] Stewart 1822, II 219-20; I 23 fn.

52. *Memorial of 1746*
[152] Stewart 1822, II v-ix.

53. *The roster of clans*
[153] Stewart 1822, I 26.

54. *Is no clan family*
[154] Hunter 2006, 83.

55. *Britain as a privately owned estate*
[155] Dr John Smith, *General View of the Agriculture of Argyllshire*, Mundell, Edinburgh, 1798, 261.
[156] Some say that Britain now is owned by the Queen *in theory*; but many people (from a duke with thousands of acres, to a heavily mortgaged owner of a terraced house) would be greatly annoyed if this alleged theoretical right was followed up by the arrival of a royal notice to quit.
[157] F. W. Newman, *Lectures on Political Economy*, Chapman, London, 1851, 132.

CHAPTER FIVE

THE LIFE OF THE HIGHLANDERS

1. Staff of life

The major food-source of most nineteenth-century Highland small tenants was a croft, an acre or two of poor land (too poor even to graze sheep – otherwise the landlord would have rented it to the sheep farmers); and on those crofts they tried to grow food for their families. Their main produce was potatoes, because potatoes yield more eatables per square foot of ground than any other food crop. It is, therefore, easy (though painfully unhistorical) for writers to assume that they had always lived in the same way.[1] And yet this assumption is often made. That the Highlanders during the centuries before the Battle of Culloden in 1746 were merely "peasants", scraping a precarious living from an unproductive soil just like their nineteenth-century descendants, became an academic cliché; and like other clichés it was regarded as incontrovertible – evidence not being required.[2]

Here we should recall Malcolm Gray's opinions as to the Highland system before the changes began, as set forth in his book about the Highland economy. Orthodox historians, as we saw earlier, thought highly of this work. Professor Smout called Gray's effort "the only scholarly, dispassionate and comprehensive study" of the period.[3] Professor Richards praised it as "the most penetrating contribution" to the transformation of the Highlands, as "an austere and precise analysis", not to mention being "the most rigorous analysis available", which, fortunately, being "dispassionate", held aloof from "overheated prose";[4] and was written "without recourse to sentimentality".[4] Professor Pryde thought it was "an admirable and dispassionate study of a theme that has too often been charged with emotion in the past"[5] – extravagant praise from the three professors perhaps earned by the fact that the book, mystifyingly, hardly mentioned the clearances, despite being called *The Highland Economy, 1750-1850*. How "penetrating" and "comprehensive" was Gray? He remarked on the "sparse resources" of the Highlands, and "the arable soils on which nearly every family has had to depend". In the Highlands, Gray asserted, "the gravest problem, and the greatest hindrance to productive reform, was over-crowding", and the proof Gray offered was that the arable holdings of the joint-farmers "were tiny" – despite the fact that, according to him, "in eighteenth-century Scotland meal was the staff of life". (The phrase "eighteenth-century Scotland" must be intended to include the Highlands; otherwise there would be no point in mentioning it in a book entitled *The Highland Economy*.) In the south and east of the Highlands, Gray asserted, the average amount of land devoted to arable farming by the clansfolk was ten to fifteen acres per "tenant", while in the north and west even less land (he claimed) was used for arable, down to only two or three acres per "tenant". Since in "eighteenth-century Scotland" oatmeal was "the staff of life", arable holdings of this size indicated – said Gray – a "land scarcity" in the Highlands, which "kept great numbers in a bedrock equality at the minimal levels of independent farming".[6] According to Gray, indeed, peasant society and over-population were like Siamese twins, indissolubly linked. He ran the two smoothly together, declaring that the Highlands after Culloden was an area of "a continuing small peasant system, of over-population". This state of affairs was not the result of the clearances, which really had nothing to do with it: "the extent to which sheep farmers took over land previously occupied by the small tenantry is scarcely relevant to the present discussion . . . except perhaps for accentuating the existing dominant characteristic of the small peasant system – crowding on the land".[7] Professor Smout joined in this version of history: even in the new era in the Highlands, he claimed, in those parishes where the potato had not been introduced, "oatmeal was still the staff of life" – thus indicating clearly that it had already been the "staff of life" before the new era arrived.[8] Professor Smout made clear his view of the Highland economy during the days of clanship; in his 1969 Scottish history he called the clansfolk "peasants" fifteen times on four pages.[9]

Dr Jean Dunlop said that in Kintail "there is so much rain that the crops of oats, which once formed the staple diet of the Highlander, often cannot ripen".[10] (One would have thought that most writers would hesitate before maintaining that the "staple diet" of a people was a crop that "often" could not be grown successfully.) Professor Rosalind Mitchison said that "the basic resource of this mounting population remained a thin, poor soil, soured by cold and wet into peat on the hilltops . . ."[11] John Lister deplored the old "Highland way of life. At its best, it was precarious, with tenants [sic] trying to scrape a subsistence living, using primitive instruments, from an ungrateful land. When crops or labour [i.e. employment – as if the old clansfolk had anyone to employ them, or would ever have considered being employees even if employers had been plentiful] failed, starvation was the inevitable outcome."[12] James Scarlett thought that in the old Highlands, "with no welfare state, a bad harvest means steal or starve".[13] According to Tom Steel, "the people of the glens for the most part had scraped little more than a subsistence living, and famine had never been far away", while "autumn gales ruined one harvest in four".[14] Dr Richard Muir said that during the clan system "the monotonous diet of oats and potatoes was unhealthy at even the best of times".[15] John Lister, too, thought that the Highlanders, "by the mid eighteenth century, had in many cases been reduced to a potato diet".[16] (Despite these confident assertions by Muir and Lister, potatoes were in fact only commonly grown and eaten in the Highlands generally from the 1780s, or at the earliest in the 1770s – when the improvements were beginning to hurt, and the varieties of food previously consumed by the Highlanders were therefore becoming no longer available.)

2. "Monocultural famine"

Douglas Hill, to add some variety, thought that only potatoes and the clearances had rescued the Highlanders from their sufferings in the old days: after the changes, "the potato not only held off starvation for much of the population but also prevented debilitating diseases (like scurvy) that had been prevalent on the thin diet of previous times based mainly on oats. In other words, bluntly, the improvements meant that fewer people died."[17] (That word "bluntly" is a clever touch, with its implication that the author is bravely striking out against what everyone else has said, instead of merely repeating the unfortunately incorrect platitudes which are the standard fare – or, if the reader prefers, the "staple diet", not to say the "staff of life" – in books on the Highlands.) Noel Banks, too, claimed paradoxically that it was the spread of the potato after the 1740s that "eliminated monocultural famine"[18] (though, of course, it was in fact the new era that ended the previous multicultural system and introduced monoculture – the exclusive rearing of sheep – over vast areas of the Highlands, and thus brought about that progressive deterioration of the soil, bemoaned even by the landlords, which is always caused by monoculture). Finlay McKichan wrote that the "clansmen . . . lived mainly on oats".[19] John MacLeod said that "porridge of oats and barley, or cakes – bannocks – of these grains: that was the staple fare of the people".[20] Professor George Pryde (as we see elsewhere) said that in the Highlands "the meagre produce of the soil – the oats and bear painfully extracted from the scattered runrig holdings – had to be supplemented from other sources" – the "other sources", before 1746, having sadly been "war and pillage".[21] John Prebble echoed both the word "meagre" and the usual orthodox thesis when he lamented the Highlanders' "meagre patches of soil", thus plainly asserting that the clansfolk depended on the products of arable farming.[22] Dr Ian Donnachie and Dr George Hewitt said that the old Highlanders relied on "subsistence agriculture".[23] Dr Isabel Grant and Hugh Cheape asserted that the clansfolk had to exist by "subsistence farming" in the "sterile overcrowded"[24] Highlands. In 2002 Professor Richards painted the same picture of Highlanders dependent entirely on their crops: their lives were "bounded by the possibility of a lavish harvest or a famine".[25] In the same year Professor Arthur Herman claimed (in what was described as a "fascinating book") that this fictional oatmeal diet obtained both in the pre-clearance and the post-clearance Highlands: in the 1880s, he said, the Highlanders' "diet had changed little from almost two centuries earlier – oatmeal porridge, bread and oatcakes, a little beef and mutton"[26] (thus ignoring the ubiquitous potato in the Highlands after the improvements, as well as the ubiquitous game, flesh and dairy products before them; and if any fact in these centuries is indisputable, it is that the Highlanders' diet in the new era changed enormously). Denis Rixson, though quoting a traveller of 1535 who said the Highlanders knew nothing of bread, immediately denounced as "myths" the reports that the Highlanders lived on animal products: "these myths . . . are, actually, pure hokum. Highlanders ate oats and barley just like everyone else in Scotland – in fact over the centuries they proved strikingly devoted to grain crops."[27] (So when the contemporary evidence and the modern orthodoxy conflict, it is the contemporary evidence which is denounced as "hokum" and thrown out: an interesting glimpse of the process of producing history acceptable to modern tastes.) Other present-day commentators, whether sympathetic or unsympathetic to the Highlanders, can be found showing themselves "strikingly devoted" to the idea that the Highlanders were simply peasants, and not very clever peasants at that, since they spent their entire lives trying to live on what they could grow on a small patch of infertile land, all the while ignoring their own vast flocks and herds, and the prodigious quantities of freely available wild animals, birds and fish all round them (all eminently catchable with the weapons which every Highlander not only possessed, but used frequently and expertly).

3. Explaining the emigrations

This belief, or at least this allegation, that the clansfolk existed only on arable crops – oats, barley, or whatever – is a very useful one, because it provides a plausible reason for the extrusion of the Highlanders, other than the clearances. John Lister, for example, claimed that "poor land resources have resulted in continuing depopulation of the Highlands for many generations . . ."[28] (For how many of these "many generations" could "continuing depopulation" occur, before no one was left? At least Lister is in this particular aspect striking out on his own, since clearly this hypothesis cannot fit in with the standard belief about "stupendous" over-population, after all these "many generations" of "continuing depopulation".) John MacLeod insisted that "initially, the mass emigration of Gaels was voluntary, and to a large degree necessary"; and it can, seemingly, be shown to be necessary, because (he asserted) "the staple food of the Gael had been such grain crops as oats and bere (a primitive form of barley) and these had been highly vulnerable to the vagaries of weather. A cold wet spring, a wild wet summer and autumn led to poor harvest, winter famine, and widespread death."[29]

Donnachie and Hewitt said there had been an "enforced migration", since the Highlanders' "subsistence agriculture" (that is, tilling the fields) could scarcely feed them. (Like Douglas Hill who had "bluntly" been forced to support the improvements, they put this down as if they had nobly fought against such a conclusion as long as they could: "try as we might, it is hard to escape the fact that subsistence agriculture in the Highlands could hardly support its pre-eighteenth century population."[30] If they had tried just a little harder, by consulting the contemporary records – which is surely what historians are supposed to do – they would have found out that since "subsistence agriculture" had never needed to support the Highlanders, it was irrelevant whether it could or could not have done so.) Grant and Cheape said that as the seventeenth and eighteenth century Highlands got "more and more crowded", the "unreliability and harshness of the Highland climate" was "in the days of subsistence farming a serious threat to the people's well-being", to the health "and even to the lives of the weaker members of the community".[31] Tom Steel was adamant: "the soil of Scotland's most beautiful landscape could not provide a living for the mass of folk who wished to live in the glens."[32] Professor Richards asserted that "famine was endemic", because "crops were likely to fail every third year on the average"[33] (an advance on Tom Steel's one ruined harvest every fourth year). Professor Herman, after claiming that the Highlanders' diet "had changed little from almost two centuries" before the 1880s, immediately added: "No wonder emigrants continued to stream out of the country in record numbers."[34] (Though if "the emigrants" were going because of their poor food, why had they not gone two centuries earlier? – when their food, according to this professor, was pretty much the same.)

In summary, this theory holds that the Highlanders depended on their crops, their arable produce; the Highlands was not a good place for arable farming; the crops often failed; therefore the Highlanders frequently went short of food, and finally they had to leave. It all hangs together, but for the fact that the basic premise, that the Highlanders depended wholly or even to a significant extent on their crops, is – to put it "bluntly" – not true. "Try as we might, it is hard to escape the fact" that the "subsistence agriculture" theory is completely spurious (or, in Denis Rixson's trenchant phrase, "pure hokum": unless we should follow even more decorous academic precedents, and borrow Professor Mitchison's measured expression, "clearly rubbish", or Professor Donaldson's still more judicious remark, "utter rubbish").

4. Hunting, shooting, and fishing

These stories of regular famines make unaccountable reading. Let us use the archive of the head in this matter. Let us tackle the question of the Highlanders' food supplies by ignoring entirely what little food the Highlanders obtained from their insignificant arable patches. Let us also ignore for the moment the wild berries, nuts, herbs, shellfish and other naturally occurring foods that the Highlanders regularly collected.[35] Let us ignore, too, what Tobias Smollett called the "great number of sheep, goats, and black cattle"[36] belonging to the Highlanders, along with Chevalier de Johnstone's statement that the mountainous region "abounds with horned cattle",[36] as well as Daniel Defoe's reference to the Highlanders' "large quantities of black cattle",[37] and all the other assertions by contemporaries that the Highlanders had vast herds and flocks. Let us go back to the basic facts set out in the last chapter. We know that the Highlands covered some 16,300 square miles; we know that the Rev. Alexander Webster's population figure for those 16,300 square miles, in the middle of the eighteenth century, was 295,566; we know that therefore, according to Webster, there were at that time only just over eighteen people per square mile, and that each individual human being had over thirty-five acres to roam in, so that a family of six – two parents and four children, a mild allowance – had nearly two hundred and twelve acres in which to disport themselves. (Let us disregard, for the moment, Malcolm Gray's extraordinary assertion that in a country with thirty-five acres *per head* the "gravest problem . . . was overcrowding",[38] Grant and Cheape's reference to the "overcrowded" Highlands,[39] David Ross's assertion that the Highlands before Culloden were "extensively populated",[40] Professor Mitchison's "mounting population",[41] Professor Smout's "numbers vastly above"[42] what the Highland economy could support, John Prebble's "steady and alarming increase"[43] in the numbers, and all the many similar allegations. They will all be dealt with later.) We know, from numerous accounts, that the Highlands, which had so few people that they were described by Jorevin de Rochefort in 1671,[44] and also by Adam Smith in 1759 (nearly a century later, but significantly using the same phrase) as "almost uninhabited";[45] and we also know that they were full of wild animals, birds, and fish: where humans in temperate climes are sparse, wild life flourishes. (Between de Rochefort and Adam Smith, Defoe in the 1720s said – using that same phrase again – that beyond Inverness the country was "almost uninhabited rocks and steeps fill'd with deer innumerable . . . harts and roebucks, with vast overgrown stags and hinds of the red deer kind, and with fallow-deer also".)[46] There was a veritable standing larder of venison, fresh on the hoof; hares and rabbits abounded;[47] the air was full of winged game – moor-birds, water-birds, shore-birds, all good eating; and the rivers and lochs were crowded with succulent salmon and trout, while the Highland shores, the bays, the sea-lochs, and the deeply penetrating salt-water firths teemed with many species of luscious fish. We also know that the Highlanders always went about armed with muskets and pistols (as well as swords and dirks), and were skilled marksmen as well as expert anglers.

THE LIFE OF THE HIGHLANDERS

The question therefore insistently suggests itself to the curious enquirer – why on earth did the Highlanders, if any question of scarcity ever arose, not simply go out and get themselves some food? Surely that would be the obvious answer to any such shortage of provisions. But when that same curious enquirer goes to look at the contemporary accounts of the Highlanders, he finds immediately that that is exactly what they did. Most readers at this point would conclude that the matter is settled – except for some Lowland/English historians, who presumably feel themselves bound by professional solidarity to believe other Lowland/English historians. It does remind one of the dictum ascribed to Sherlock Holmes – "The world is full of obvious things which nobody by any chance ever observes."[48]

It is strange that anyone examining the contemporary accounts about the Highlands in the years before or just after the landlord revolution (as opposed to reading what some modern historians have said about those times) could conclude that the Highlanders' standard of living was governed by the number of arable acres that each family tended. Such a thesis would have a certain plausibility if promulgated about the Highlands during much of the nineteenth century; but it has little to do with the facts of life during the clan system. The writers who strive to make our blood run cold with their tales of the intermittent failure of harvests cannot – presumably – know that before the Lowland conquest which followed Culloden, it would have made very little difference to the Highlanders if the harvests had failed *every* year. (Anyone studying history has to accept the fact that, putting it at its simplest, as the years pass things change: and that what might have been true in 1840 was by no means necessarily true in 1740, 1640, 1540, or 1440.) The Highlanders, who (as we shall shortly see) were generally accepted as being markedly intelligent and ingenious, and who had after all, successive generations of them, lived in their mountains and glens for centuries, knew better than anyone that the greater part of the Highlands is much more suitable for the pursuit of wild life, and after that for pastoral farming, than for agriculture. Not to mention the fact that hunting – and even herding – were, and are, often considered to be both easier and more pleasant than tilling the fields. (Ask anyone who has ever had to hoe a five-acre field of cabbages.)[49] Rich people, who can choose their own lifestyles, often elect to do almost exactly what the Highlanders (before the landlord revolution) did constantly as a matter of course. As Joseph Mitchell said, the old Highlanders spent their time "enjoying the sports of fishing and shooting which are now esteemed the choice recreation of our aristocracy".[50]

5. Nutting, fiddling, dancing

The Highlanders lived in what was first and foremost a hunter-gatherer economy. Before the anglophone conquest which occurred in the middle of the eighteenth century, the most important source of food among the clansfolk was hunting, shooting, and fishing: they shot deer and game birds, and they caught fish in the rivers and lochs. Of course, the Gaels collected the fruits of the wild as well, berries, nuts, herbs and so forth, which is a kind of less strenuous hunting: in Kenmore the kirk-session – in the days of the clans – had recorded its attempts to rebuke the people because they had gone "to the wood a-nutting" on the Sabbath, as well as to "fiddling and dancing" on Sabbath evenings, rather than to church.[51] A visitor to the Highlands in 1746 said that whortleberries, or bilberries, were abundant, and children collected them "in almost every part of these Mountains in prodigious Quantities"; in fact "they chiefly live on the Fruit, when they are gathering them on the Mountains".[52] Burt also mentioned the gathering of bilberries, "much esteemed by the inhabitants, who eat them with their milk", while in the "mountain woods", harder of access, were "nuts, raspberries, and strawberries".[53] We will see later how women and children gathered hazelnuts in Callander parish.[54] The Kirkmichael (Banffshire) report in the Old Statistical Account said, "indigenous shrubs of different kinds grow wild in the hills, that carry fruit, such as wild strawberries, two kinds of black berries, and two of red berries"; children, in particular, picked and ate them. (Nowadays, of course, in rural areas such as where I live, we know better: people get in their cars and drive for miles to a superstore to buy blackberries, passing on the way many brambles heavy with succulent fruit ready for picking, which line the country lanes.) The Kirkmichael report also mentioned the collecting of "cor", which "grows a little below the surface of the ground . . . carrying larger or smaller knobs". (Can this be truffles, which are found – mostly under beech trees, apparently – in the British Isles?) Till "of late", reported the Kirkmichael minister in the early 1790s, before the woods were "better preserved, the inhabitants used in the month of March to extract a liquid from the birch, called fion-na-uisg, a bheatha, which they considered very salubrious and conducive to longevity."[55] Pennant mentioned the same practice. Describing what he saw in Braemar, he said the "large woods of birch" were very useful, the timber for implements of husbandry and roofing, and the bark for tanning; "and a great deal of excellent wine is extracted from the live tree".[56] Numbers of writers, even in supermarketed twenty-first century Britain, have recently drawn our attention to the tasty and nutritious food which still grows wild (and disregarded) in our countryside; and the minister of Kirkmichael (writing in the O.S.A.) felt that the old Highlanders had known even more than his current parishioners. "In ancient times when the wants of the inhabitants were few, gratified from the spontaneous productions of the field, or the beasts of the forest; as they lived almost constantly in the open air . . . they must necessarily acquire a considerable knowledge of plants and herbs, together with their various and specific qualities . . ."[57] Such knowledge must have helped the clansfolk – in such a large, thinly-peopled area – to benefit fully from "the spontaneous productions of the field". Scott, too, talking of the Highlands in *A Legend of Montrose,* referred to "roots and wild-berries, with which the woods at that season [summer] abounded".[58] (Could these "roots" have been cor, or even an early form of potato, or carrot, or radish?) J. L. Buchanan remarked on the food available on Lewis-with-Harris – not only the cuddies, saithe, cod, herring, salmon, and trout, but the lobsters, crabs, scollops, oysters, whelks, periwinkles, cockles, mussels, limpets and so on.[59]

After hunting the wild animals, birds, and fish, and gathering berries, nuts, and so on, the Highlanders' second most important food-source was pasturing domestic animals: they took meat and milk (and milk's derivatives, such as cream, butter, cheese, curds and whey) from their numerous flocks and herds of cattle, sheep, and goats, as well as eggs and flesh from their poultry. The third and much the least important food source was a little arable farming, from which they obtained a small amount of grain – oats, bere or bear, and wheat: the minister of Campbeltown, as we see below, said that formerly these grain foods were cultivated chiefly to give to infants.[60]

6. Private enjoyment

Later, as the nineteenth century wore on, the Highlands were turned increasingly into a mere pleasure ground for the rich, where wealthy sportsmen came to pursue the game. This was only at the right season of the year, of course: King George V is supposed to have said that "no gentleman would go to Scotland in January", thus implicitly rebuking the Highlanders who had no desire to leave their homeland, whatever the season.[61] The appropriation of the game (one of their main sources of food) for the private enjoyment of the leisured class was a grievous blow to the Highlanders. James Shaw Grant said in his book on Lewis and Harris: "When deer stalking became a private pursuit, confined to the wealthy, the life of the ordinary people of the Highlands was gravely diminished. They lost a recurring social and recreational occasion which added excitement to their lives. They also lost an important source of food. Few things have rankled more with islanders than the expropriation of these ancient rights."[62] Incidentally, according to Cosmo Innes, the landlords were here acting illegally. The appropriation of all game rights by the landlords was unjustified even by their Lowland-granted charters, since these only gave rights over game when pursued "lucri causa" (to make money); fishing for recreation should never have been prohibited, said Innes, and "the most innocent and cheapest of sports wrested from the poor".[63] However, even if the ordinary people had been able to afford skilled lawyers to examine the exact meaning of the proprietors' documentation, it is unlikely that the courts, set up and sustained by the landlords' Parliament, would have offered any relief. Financial (and other) considerations ensured that the law, then as now, in effect protected the rich rather than the poor.[63]

But it was not enough that the Highlanders' hunting, shooting, and fishing, occupations which they found health-giving and enjoyable in themselves, and which provided most of their families' food, should have been altogether transferred in the new regime to opulent outsiders; the new orthodoxy was to deny that the Highlanders had ever hunted or shot on the moors and hillsides, or fished the rivers and lochs (at the same time banishing the Highlanders' flocks and herds from the record), and to claim that the clansfolk had no sources of food other than a few arable acres. The landlord revolution in the Highlands could only be justified by claiming that the old Highlanders were all starving anyway, so that driving them out was really doing them a good turn. Perhaps the fact that the Highlanders had happily spent much of their time, in doing freely and skilfully what had now become the exclusive and expensive entertainment of the rich, was difficult to explain away by those who wished to malign the old society: so the satisfying theory arose that they had never done these things.

If we are to base our belief on the evidence, however, there is little room for doubt.

7. Delight and pleasure

The comments quoted above about "subsistence agriculture" were all written in the second half of the twentieth century or later. Earlier writings, when people were talking about contemporary events, give a much different picture. In former days terrain, of course, dictated diet; and Cassius Dio, the Roman historian, writing about the Highlands well before the Scots ever arrived, said there was no tillage there, the people living "by pasturage, the chase, and certain berries".[64] Later comments about the Highlands, by Gaels and others, say much the same. The Gaelic proverb which enshrines the Highlanders' belief as to the people's prerogatives says, "there is a common right to take a deer from the hill, a tree from the wood, and a fish from the river"[65] – sowing a crop, and even pasturing a domestic animal, are not mentioned. The Hebridean maiden, lamenting her faithless lover, says nothing of tillage: "The hunting field/ The greenwood tree/ The trout, the running deer he loves/ Far more than me."[66] In about 1250 Matthew Paris produced a map of Britain, showing that the central and northern Highlands were occupied by a "wild pastoral people", while the land even further to the north-west was marked as "suitable for cattle and herdsmen". (G. W. S. Barrow, giving this information, added that in the thirteenth-century Lowlands "agriculture already predominated", while "herds, flocks, hunting and fishing gave the Highlander his subsistence" – tillage was not mentioned.)[67] An old poem about "Arran of the many stags", said to have been recorded in the thirteenth century, described the island: "Many hinds are on her hills/ Juicy berries are there for food/ Refreshing water in her streams/ Nuts in plenty in the wood."[68] When MacLeod of Dunvegan fell out with his fairy lover in the traditional tale, her revenge was to cause the cows to produce dead calves, not to make the harvest fail.[69]

In 1521 John Major described the Highlanders as mainly a pastoral people (i.e., their livelihood came from flocks and herds).[70] In 1535 a traveller, Peter Swave, reported that the Highlanders "are ignorant of the use of bread"; instead they ate meat.[71] In 1543 John Elder, a Highland priest, said of his fellow Highlanders that "our delight and pleasure is . . . in hunting of red deer, wolves, foxes, and graies [probably grouse], whereof we abound and have great plenty".[72] In 1578 Bishop Leslie remarked that the Highlanders were a pastoral people.[73] In 1582 George Buchanan did mention grain ("they make a kind of bread . . . of oats and barley, the only grain cultivated in these regions") but the main thrust of his comments was clear: "hunting and fishing supply them with food".[74]

In 1618 John Taylor, the Water Poet, described a hunting trip led by the Earl of Mar and others of the nobility in Braemar: no doubt they fed particularly well, but Taylor's account of the "great variety of cheer" will indicate what was available: "venison baked, sodden, roast, and stewed, beef, mutton, goats, kid, hares, fresh salmon, pigeons, hens, capons, chickens, partridge, moorcoots, heathcocks, capercaillies and termigants [ptarmigan]".[75] In 1630, Sir Robert Gordon made the obvious point that Strathnaver (meaning here the north of Sutherland) was better suited for pasture and fishing than for growing corn.[76] In 1655 Seaforth and some Fraser chieftains, "with a hundred pretty fellows more", made a hunting trip through Strath Glass and Glen Farrar, and around Loch Monar: they "got sight of 6 or 700 deere", and ate (according to the Wardlaw manuscript) "beefe, mutton, foule, fishes, fat venison".[77] So much were the Highlanders a hunter-gatherer people that Franck, in 1658, described the Highlands as "destitute of cultivation".[78] In 1671 Jorevin de Rochefort wrote that in the Highlands there were "great gulfs" or inlets of the sea, where there was "fish, in abundance"; further, "there is no want of game in great quantities; but there grows but very little corn".[79] According to Odo Blundell, a report on the Glengarry people in 1677 said, "all their substance consists in flocks which afford them meat and dairy produce for food and wool for clothing".[80] Blundell also described a visit of a Catholic bishop to Arisaig in 1700: "The arable land is stated to be of small extent", though it did give them "a good return, and that with little labour".[81] When the Lowlanders built a fort at Inverlochy in 1691, the food supplies they obtained locally were described (in

Prebble's words) as "butter and cheese, eggs, milk and beef"[82] – the products of a pastoral way of life: nothing from ploughing the soil.

8. No bread

In the 1720s Burt, whose operations were centred on Inverness, always considered to be a Lowland outpost, spoke of oats and of meal; but things were different (he said) in the Highlands. "In a wild part of Argyllshire, there was no bread of any kind till the discovery of some lead mines, which brought strangers among the inhabitants, who before fed upon the milk of their cows, goats, and sheep."[83] In the same decade Daniel Defoe said that the Highlanders "live dispers'd among the hills... Their employment is chiefly hunting, which is, as we may say, for their food", though they did also "breed large quantities of black cattle".[84] He added that "the mountains are . . . full of deer, harts, roe-bucks, etc.", while "the rivers and lakes also in all this country are prodigiously full of salmon".[85] Game birds were abundant, too; so much so, said Defoe, that travellers in the Highlands could live off the countryside – they could "supply themselves by their guns, with very great plenty of wild fowl".[86] (And if strangers journeying through the mountains could live off the game, the inhabitants – knowing the local wild life and the choice spots for hunting – would of course be still more successful.) Many fish, Defoe continued, were off the coast: "as for herrings indeed the quantity was prodigious", and the sea seemed "one third water, and two thirds fish". What the fishermen did "could hardly be called fishing, for they did little more than dip for them into the water and take them up".[87] (J. L. Buchanan, writing of the 1780s, said the same of the east coast of the Long Island, where the "cuddies" were "taken by hundreds, at one dipping of a bag net".)[88] According to Defoe, "however mountainous and wild the country appear'd, the people were extremely well furnish'd with provisions". They had "venison exceeding plentiful, and at all seasons, young or old, which they kill with their guns wherever they find it; for there is no restraint, but 'tis every man's own that can kill it. By which means the Highlanders [to repeat the earlier quotation] not only have all of them fire-arms, but they are all excellent marksmen." They also had "salmon in such plenty as is scarce credible". Some "they eat fresh in the season"; some they cured by drying them in the sun so as to have a supply all the year round. Besides that "they have no want of cows and sheep". Unlike some other commentators, Defoe found "very good bread, as well oat bread as wheat"; but he had just visited "John a Grot's house",[89] so he may have been thinking particularly of the Caithness Lowlands.

THE LIFE OF THE HIGHLANDERS

9. Doe from the glen

During the Jacobite rebellion of 1745-6 MacLean of Duart is supposed to have invited Prince Charles to dinner. A poet later put the invitation in verse, of which this an English translation:

We'll bring down the black steer, we'll bring down the red deer,
The lamb from the corrie and the doe from the glen;
The salt sea we'll harry, and bring to our Charlie
The cream from the bothy and curds from the pen.

In other words, the fruits of hunting, and fishing, and herding. Not a single grain is mentioned.[90]

In 1746 Duncan Forbes said of the Highlands, "no part is in any degree cultivated, except some spots here and there . . . The Grounds that are cultivated yield small quantities of mean Corns, not sufficient to feed the inhabitants, who depend for their nourishment on milk, butter, cheese, etc., the product of their Cattle."[91] As we saw earlier, the author of the 1747 book on the Highlanders referred to "their continual exercise in hunting, fishing, and fowling".[92] (The other book on the Highlanders published in 1747, by James Ray, said about the country between Inverness and Fort William, "hereabouts is plenty of Red Deer, whose flesh eats exceeding well".)[93]

On the other hand, as we shall see later, the author of the *History of Scotland in 1750* referred several times, as he described the Highlands, to corn, and bread, and barley, oats and rye. This seems to show, along with other references quoted here, that some arable farming was carried on; but when the evidence is considered as a whole, it appears that crops formed comparatively a small part of the Highlanders' food-supplies. When Dr John Walker toured the Hebrides in 1764, the changes were beginning, and he found that the landlords' actions were enforcing a greater reliance on tillage – particularly on the increased use of potatoes; but he wrote that the Highlanders were "still in the Pastoral [i.e., animal-herding] Stage of Society".[94] In those islands where the changes were only in their infancy, the Highlanders kept to their original diet. Previously, said Walker, the North Uist people had eaten "Fowl, Fish and Milk, with little or no Bread"; but as the new regime was able to insist that they should devote much effort to collecting kelp, with naturally much less time and space for hunting and herding, so "they consume a much greater Quantity of Grain".[95] In Jura it was still the case that "the People live mostly on Milk, Butter, Cheese, Fish, Mutton, Venison, and use very little vegetable Aliment".[96] As for the people of Rum, "during all the Summer, they live entirely upon animal Food, and yet are healthy and long lived". One old man there had never tasted bread till he was fifty years old, and used to upbraid the younger people "with their Indulgence in the Article of Bread, and judged it unmanly in them to toil like Slaves with their Spades" to produce grain.[97]

In 1768 Archibald Menzies, who was an agent for the Forfeited Estates commissioners, praised the tenants in Knoydart: "they are good managers of cattle . . . It is remarkable the skill they show in choosing their pasturages for the different seasons . . . Every farmer is so far a botanist as to distinguish the particular season each grass is in perfection." In fact, they "are very attentive to the management of their cattle, which is the principal thing worthy of attention here, as their climate and soil are against agriculture".[98]

In 1771 one of Tobias Smollett's characters wrote that "the Highlanders are used to eat much more animal food than falls to the share of their neighbours in the low country – They delight in hunting; have plenty of deer and other game, with a great number of sheep, goats, and black cattle running wild . . . They have plenty of red deer and roebuck, which are fat and delicious at this season of the year [this was in a letter dated 3rd September] – Their sea teems with amazing quantities of the finest fish in the world." Smollett added: "as the soil and climate of the Highlands are but ill-adapted to the cultivation of corn, the people apply themselves chiefly to the breeding and feeding of black cattle, which turn to good account."[99]

In 1776 Adam Smith wrote, "it is not more than a century ago, that in many parts of the Highlands of Scotland, butcher's meat was as cheap or cheaper than even bread made of oatmeal":[100] common items are always lower-priced than rarer ones.

10. Parcel of rogues

Indeed, Highlanders seem to have regarded tilling the land as an occupation fit merely for those lesser breeds who spoke only English. James ("Ossian") MacPherson derided the efforts of the English writer Thomas Gray (who was a very much better poet than he was), and Gray's incomparable *Elegy in a Country Churchyard*: "To write panegyrics upon a parcel of rogues that did nothing but plough the land and saw [sow] corn!"[101] MacPherson clearly agreed with the old man in Rum, that it was unbecoming in a Highlander to cultivate the soil. The writer of the book of *Genesis* seems to have had similar views: "And Abel was a keeper of sheep, but Cain was a tiller of the ground." The Highlanders (who were well acquainted with the Bible) no doubt found it appropriate that the man regarded as the world's first murderer should have spent his time digging and delving, like the Lowlanders – unlike the guiltless Abel, a herdsman such as themselves.[102]

In 1773 Dr Johnson visited Raasay, and said, "the corn of this island is but little . . . The ground of Raasay seems fitter for cattle than for corn, and of black cattle I suppose the number is very great." Of the Highlands as a whole he maintained, "a tract of land so thinly inhabited, must have much wild-fowl . . . The moorgame is everywhere to be had. That the sea abounds with fish, needs not be told, for it supplies a great part of Europe . . . They sell very numerous droves of oxen yearly to England, and therefore cannot be supposed to want beef at home. Sheep and goats are in great numbers, and they have the common domestic fowls." They also had geese "of a middle race, between the wild and domestic kinds", though they fed in the sea and tasted fishy. There were also some products of tillage, for Johnson added, "I did not observe that the common greens were wanting".[103] The year before Johnson's tour Pennant, landing in Canna, said, "Here are plenty of poultry and of eggs".[104] Dr Walker in 1764 said that Islay "abounds in poultry of all kinds, especially in geese".[105] The minister of Kirkmichael (Banffshire) wrote a much longer report than most of his colleagues, taking up some fifty pages with detailed information: and after the usual list of horses, cows, and sheep, he added that the locals had "some poultry and a few geese".[106] Donald MacLeod said that when the Countess of Sutherland was a young girl living in Edinburgh in the 1770s, "the gentlemen of Sutherland" sent down presents of Sutherland produce to her, "such as fowls, venison, butter, cheese, etc.";[107] no grain was mentioned, even though it would no doubt have stood the journey better. Alexander Cunningham wrote in 1787, in his *History of Great Britain*, that the Highlanders "use but little corn, except in the shires of Moray and Ross [two counties which extend into the flat land at the eastern margin of the Highlands]. Their food, for the most part, is milk, cattle, venison, and fish."[108] William Thomson, writing in 1788, said that in the old system "husbandry [arable farming], and even pasturage [herding], were followed no further than necessity required. It is not long since sheep and goats, in the Highlands, were considered as below the care of a man, and reputed the property of the wife, in the same manner as geese, turkeys, and other poultry, are in the Low Countries, and in England." Their poetry, thought Thomson, showed "they were not so much shepherds as hunters".[109] According to the Rev. J. L. Buchanan in 1793, Thomson also said: "And in those times [before the improvements], the Highlanders were better fed and in general, finer men than they are at present. For now the cattle, the salmon, and the very game, are either carried or driven out of the country: nor has the faint dawn of commerce been yet able to supply that abundance which preceded it."[110] Buchanan wrote at the same time that in the Long Island there were no "partridges, black-cocks, nor many of the granavirous [or graminivorous – grain-eating] fowls; a strong proof that grain has not been long sown here, and that the country has not been so thoroughly cultivated, as to entice them to reside in it".[111] Captain Henderson in 1812 said that in Sutherland "every farmer and cottager's wife has a flock of common poultry"; and, where there were ponds, ducks too, "all for family use".[112]

At much the same time Burns' *Highland Widow* lamented not any lost ploughlands but her "score o' kye [cows]", and her "three score o' yowes [ewes]".[113]

11. Trifling provision

Writers at the end of the eighteenth century and in the first part of the nineteenth, at a time when living Highlanders could still remember clearly how they fared in the days before the improvements had been inflicted upon their homeland, gave exactly the same picture. Several of the O.S.A. reports were highly relevant. According to the Rev. John Grant, minister of Kirkmichael (Banffshire), "in ancient times, in the Highlands, a small portion of land was cultivated, in comparison of the present".[114] Dr John Smith, the minister of Campbeltown, wrote: "Even so late as about the middle of the last century [i.e. about 1650], meal, excepting a trifling provision, reserved, perhaps, for an infant, was rarely to be found in any family throughout the greatest part of the year."[115] The Rev. Andrew Gallie, of Kincardine in Ross-shire, said that the Highlanders lived in that area because "pasture for cattle, with fishing and hunting, the favourite employment of the Highlanders, could be had in the greatest variety".[116] Dr Joseph MacIntyre, the Glenorchy incumbent, recorded (though he regretted) the fact that the clansfolk used to spend much of their time in the "favourite chase".[117] The Rev. Alexander Sage, minister of Kildonan, said that in times past the local "sustenance . . . consisted chiefly of fish, fowls, and venison".[118] At the same time Ailean Dall (Blind Allan) MacDougall, the Glengarry bard, lamented that the new regime had left the Gaels "without food, without money, without pasture" – not without fields to till.[119] When at the end of the eighteenth century Adam Ferguson (who had prospered in Lowland society, becoming a philosophy professor at Edinburgh University) wished to belittle Gaelic, despite his Highland name and his Highland birth at Logierait, he sneered that "its greatest elegancies" were "to be learned from herdsmen and deer-stealers" – not plough-boys.[120] The Rev. Donald Sage said that when (about 1800) a joint service, "the Lord's Supper", was held, attended by people from several Sutherland parishes, the minister kept open house; and to feed the crowds who came, the week before "was occupied in receiving presents of mutton, butter, and cheese. On these occasions I have seen the whole range of a large cellar so closely laid with mutton carcasses, that the floor was literally paved with them."[121] In 1805 the Earl of Selkirk observed, "the greatest part of the country was fit only for pasturage, and the small portions of arable land which fell to the share of any family, could occupy but little of their time".[122] Robert Brown, writing in 1806, commented on the easy conditions of the former Highland society, when the old Highlanders could procure "the luxury of flesh meat, and warm clothing . . . by the chase, or for nothing".[123] Benjamin Meredith, sent by the management to report on the Sutherland estate in 1810, criticized those many Sutherlanders whose "chief employment . . . during the whole year" was "angling, or shooting".[124] In her 1811 book on the Highlands Anne Grant of Laggan described the old Highlanders as "hunters, graziers, and warriors"; in fact so much were the Highlanders regarded as hunters and herdsmen, so much was crop-growing disregarded, that when Anne Grant used the phrase "cultivators of the soil", she meant Lowlanders. Grant described the Highlanders as "inured to all the hardships of the chase, their only . . . means of subsistence".[125] In 1814 Sir John Sinclair pointed out that "cattle, and not corn, are the natural produce of these districts".[126] Robert Southey visited Sutherland in 1819, and deplored the policy of putting the people on the shore, requiring them "to become some cultivators, some fishermen [i.e. commercial sea fishermen], occupations to which they have never been accustomed"; he would have been surprised to find historians solemnly declaring that the Highlanders had always been "cultivators" – and, indeed, had never done anything else.[127] David Stewart said (in about 1820) that "in those primitive times [before the improvements], the forests, heaths, and waters, abounding with game and fish, were alike free to all, and contributed greatly to the support of the inhabitants".[128] He also said that the decree banning the Highland garb after the '45 was felt as a heavy blow, since "the dress of the Highlanders was so peculiarly accommodated to the warrior, the hunter, and the shepherd"[129] (a list of occupations almost exactly echoing that of Anne Grant of Laggan a score of years before). Of the Highlanders' arms, Stewart wrote: "Latterly, the bow and arrow seem to have been but rarely used [in battle]. This is the more remarkable, as these weapons are peculiarly adapted to that species of hunting which was their favourite amusement; I allude to the hunting of deer, or what is commonly called *deer-stalking*, where the great art consists in approaching the animal unobserved, and in wounding him without disturbing the herd."[130] So Stewart used the same adjective as the minister of Kincardine and the minister of Glenorchy, when he said that hunting was the Highlanders' "favourite" pastime. In 1824 one of Sir Walter Scott's characters in *Redgauntlet* (a novel about events half a century earlier) gave a graphic description of a speedy action by saying "they didna mak muckle mair ceremony than a Hielandman wi' a roebuck".[131]

The Highland "warrior", mentioned by both David Stewart and Anne Grant, necessarily appeared because of the frequent Lowland incursions into the Highlands, the result of the oppressive Lowland claim to rule over the Highlands.

If you attack people, they do often defend themselves: and you can then deplore their pugnacity.

12. Animal food

W. F. Skene, writing in 1837, said, "the chief occupation of the ancient Highlanders was that of hunting".[132] Several of the reports in the New Statistical Account, which was written between 1833 and 1844, made much the same point. (And in those years many Highlanders, who lived long, could remember well what they had done before the new arrangements had been imposed.) The minister of Mortlach said that in the old days "the peasant [sic] sportsman, and there is no inconsistency, especially in the Highlands, in one's being both, was wont to range over the fields and hills, with his dog and gun, in manly exercise which gave health to his body and vigour to his mind".[133] The Contin N.S.A. report said: "To the pleasures of the sportsman, who ranges unmolested over moors and mountains, the inhabitants of Contin were long accustomed, in common with their Highland neighbours."[134] The minister of Blair Atholl, also writing in the N.S.A., said of the old Highlanders, "their principal aliment was animal food".[135] Fortingall's N.S.A. report said that in the old days the people had gone in the height of summer each year to their shielings in the remoter pastures, "the men employing themselves chiefly in fishing and hunting, the women in spinning and attending to the dairy".[136] The Rev. Hugh MacKenzie, minister of Tongue, giving evidence to the Poor Law commissioners of 1841, described the condition of his parishioners before the clearances: "they used to eat flesh, fish, milk, butter, and curds and cream; no vegetables; and a few spots of oat and bear; they bought very little meal. Potatoes were only introduced when I was a child [he was born in 1771], now it is their general food."[137] The minister of Portree (the Rev. Coll MacDonald) was a sheep farmer himself, and his own extensive ranch could only have been created after the expulsion of the small tenants (who were, he therefore asserted, "rude" and "savage"); as a beneficiary of the clearances he is a particularly hostile witness. In his N.S.A. report, however, he said that though the old Highlanders "lived in a rude, and almost savage state, they seldom suffered under the pressure of famine or destitution. Situate in localities remote from one another, each family had a sufficient extent of land to support a number of sheep and cattle. At the period to which we allude, the parish abounded with game of all sorts. In the rivers and estuaries, there were salmon in abundance; and, being free from the restraints of the present Game Laws, the people may be said to have had a sufficiency of flesh, fish, milk, and venison [almost exactly the same menu as Alexander Cunningham gave]. They cultivated small portions of the best part of the land, which yielded them some meal. It is, therefore, certain, that in old times, the people were more abundantly supplied with the necessaries and comforts of life than they are at present."[138]

In *The Misty Isle of Skye*, even that champion of the Skye landlords, J. A. MacCulloch, said that "there is no doubt that before the Highlands became available to sporting tenants, the peasantry [sic] had more or less free access to the rivers, lochs, and moors, and subsisted largely on the produce found therein".[139] When a Highland bard was encouraging his countrymen to emigrate to North Carolina, in order to escape the landlords who (he said) "prefer gold to a brave man", his exposition of the new world's advantages did not mention crops, only the hunter's quarry. "We shall find game of every kind, the most beautiful game to be seen. We shall get deer, buck and doe, and the right to take as many as we wish. We shall get woodcock and woodhen, teals, duck and wild geese. We shall get salmon . . . and white fish if it pleases us better." Even the Highlanders' secondary food source, herding, was only introduced incidentally: in the promised land "even every herdsman has his horse".[140] Joseph Mitchell, born in 1803, said of the old days in his *Reminiscences*: "There were then no Game Laws, and no objection was taken to a shot at a stag or a moorfowl. The rivers and sea teemed with fish as they do now, and afforded a plentiful supply for food. Hence in general the people lived comfortably and well in their way."[141] Donald MacQueen, a ninety-year-old catechist, told the Napier Commission that he remembered when the people in the MacLeod country had "plenty of food of all sorts – flesh and fish and milk".[142]

It is not surprising that the Conservative M.P. John Buchan, in his *Montrose* (published in 1928), concluded that in the seventeenth century "the Highlander, accustomed to full meals of meat from the chase, was physically far superior to the bannock-fed Lowland peasant or the apprentice from the foul vennels [alleyways] of the little cities".[143]

13. Ten witnesses

It may be thought that ten witnesses, out of all those quoted above, would be enough to make a convincing case that the Highlanders were hunters and herdsmen, not crop-growers: Peter Swave, who said the Highlanders "are ignorant of the use of bread"; Jorevin de Rochfort, who said "there grows but very little corn" in the Highlands; Dr Walker, who said there was "little or no bread" in the old days in North Uist, and in Jura; Alexander Cunningham, who said the Highlanders "use but little corn", except in Moray and Ross; Archibald Menzies, who said the Highlanders' "climate and soil are against agriculture"; Tobias Smollett, who said the Highlands were "ill-adapted to the cultivation of corn"; the Rev. John Grant, who said that formerly "a small portion of land was cultivated, in comparison of the present"; Dr John Smith, who said meal was "rarely to be found in any family" for most of the year; the Rev. Coll MacDonald, who said the clansfolk only "cultivated small portions" of the land; and the Rev. Hugh MacKenzie, who said his parishioners used to eat only "a few spots of oat and bear" – at the same time that they, and many others, described how the Highlanders obtained their food by hunting, shooting, and fishing.

Why, then, do so many historians ignore the avalanche of evidence given above, and allege that the clansfolk ate only (or mainly) oats, or that they had no resource other than a small patch of arable? The suspicion must be that this untenable view has been adopted in order to supply a plausible explanation ("food being scarce") for the dispersal of the Highlanders, other than the clearances. (Coupled, of course, with historians' lemming-like tendency to follow the conjectures of other historians.)[144]

14. Matter of surprise

One account of Highland history, published in 1987, found it hard to understand why the Highlanders largely ignored the offshore fisheries: "it is a matter of surprise that the Highlanders, suffering as they did from frequent food shortages [sic], should have made so little and such inefficient use of the excellent supplies of fish round their shores."[145] The O.S.A. report on Lochgoilhead, written probably in 1791, implied a similar criticism. The local rivers and lochs, said the writer, were full of fish: Lochs Fyne, Long, and Goil "abound in great variety of excellent fish . . . at all seasons of the year", which could be caught "either with hand line, or the long line", but it was only recently that the people "were sensible of the plenty, which Providence has placed within their reach", and had begun to catch them.[146] Dr John Walker, visiting the Hebrides in 1764, made several equivalent comments. Off the coast of Lewis, he said, mackerel arrived about the beginning of August, "and might then be had ofttimes in large quantities, but the inhabitants are at no pains to catch them".[147] As for Benbecula, he continued, "the shores and sounds about the island abound greatly with mullet; there is cod also to be caught upon the east shore, and in the season the bay of Viskarvay [Uskavagh] upon the east coast, is frequently filled with herrings; yet through the year there is not a fish taken and cured by the inhabitants".[148] Mull was the same. "Though the isle of Mull is almost every year visited by the herring shoals, and though there is plenty of cod and ling upon many parts of its coast, there is not a net or long line in all the island"; the people, Walker added, did fish "with the Rod, and in this way, they procure the most part of their subsistence in summer, by catching great plenty and variety of fish from the sea rocks".[149] In Tiree, too, the islanders ignored the plentiful sea-harvest: "every year, the herrings constantly abound in great shoals all about Tiree, from the beginning of October to the end of

December . . . This however they have always neglected, nor ever take any herrings, though during that season they are thrown up in vast quantities upon the shores, by every violent gale of wind." In fact, said Walker, they might take the chance of "enriching themselves", and driving "a very profitable trade".[150] That people should take only the food they wanted, and miss the chance of making money, was not comprehensible in Dr Walker's eyes. The islanders generally, thought Dr Walker, though "by nature the most acute and sagacious", had left "the most fertile lands I ever saw in my life, without cultivation".[151]

In 1695 Martin Martin said there were many herring in North Uist's Loch Maddy; but though "the natives sit angling on the rocks", often catching herring, still they could catch many more in boats – yet in the whole of North Uist there was "not one herring net to be had".[152] Later, the author of the 1750 report on the Highlanders made the same criticism of the people who lived near Loch Broom, who he said often neglected the herrings in the loch.[153] In 1773, Dr Johnson wrote that some of the "many lochs" on Coll had "never yet been stocked" with freshwater fish; this, he thought, proved "the negligence of the Islanders, who might take fish in the inland waters, when they cannot go to sea".[154] In fact it did not show any "negligence" on the part of the Highlanders; it showed a sufficiency of food. People who were always described as quick-witted and ingenious would not have ignored the fish waiting to be caught off their shores (nor would they have failed to stock their lakes with freshwater fish) if there had been any shortage of supplies. People of that kind (or of any kind) do not starve voluntarily. (In fact hungry people will break the most fundamental rules and inhibitions – including, in the final extremity, eating each other – in order to escape starvation.) This is an interesting example of how evidence can be used to point to two differing conclusions, and how easily the wrong conclusion (as can be shown by other data) is seized upon.

In the same way (as is remarked later) the fact that the highly prolific potato, though commonly used in Ireland, and even in England, in the first part of the eighteenth century (and earlier), was only widely grown in the Highlands after the improvements had begun to bite, shows that the Highlanders had no need of it. People who are short of food do not ignore a prolific crop which is easily grown year after year even in poor soil. Again, Captain Henderson, writing about Sutherland before the improvements were really under way, said that there were rabbits in the north of the county, for example at Durness, and also in south Sutherland, for instance at Dornoch, "but they are little attended to".[155] The disregard of easily available food supplies in the old days, and the subsequent widespread recourse to those supplies, shows both that once they were not needed, and that later they were needed. The only "matter of surprise" is that historians cannot work that out for themselves by using the archive of the head, and –

oblivious to all the evidence – prefer instead to reproduce yet again the allegations of the "frequent failed harvests" and the "meagre subsistence agriculture" during the clan system which they have read about in the standard text-books produced by their colleagues.

When David Stewart wished to emphasize the changes brought about by the new system, it is significant that he said: "many cannot now indulge in animal food."[156]

15. Pig-meat

The old Highlanders were very choosy about what they ate. There were plenty of eels in the Highlands (they were food for herons, gulls, otters and so on): the Highlanders refused to eat them. They could easily have reared pigs (which grow fat on scraps which would otherwise be wasted): the Highlanders refused to touch pork, and ham, and bacon. There were seals on the long Highland coastline: except for a few islanders, they were ignored. There are also some references to the Highlanders' refusal to eat pike, or hares. Their aversion to these foods, particularly to pig-meat, is well documented. It was mentioned (for example) by John Toland, Edmund Burt, Dr Johnson, Sir Walter Scott, and James Robertson (in his *General View of Perthshire*, 1799), as well as by several of the *Old Statistical Account* ministers, such as the Kiltearn and the Ardchattan reporters.[157] These observers made it clear that it was the old clansfolk, before they were struck down by the improvements, who could afford to be so fastidious; when the clearances brought in the new regime of prosperity for all, which is celebrated in so many history books, the Highlanders were glad to eat anything they could lay their hands on. Their hostility to pig-meat, which they shared with some other ethnic groups (perhaps because pigs do not seem to object to wallowing in mud, perhaps because they eat almost anything they can find) was now a thing of the past. Whatever had proved repellent about roast ham, or rashers of bacon (to go with the eggs from the ubiquitous poultry) was forgotten; and a leg of pork was now prized as highly within the Highland line as without.

Yet academics tell us that the Highlanders of 1700, turning their noses up at certain kinds of food, were often starving; and it was the Highlanders of 1800, propelled into prosperity by the new order, who found it necessary to tear themselves away from what their fathers had done, and what they had done themselves in earlier years, and to accept that they would have to eat foods which they had always considered to be unfit for human consumption. Writers should ask themselves – does what I've written really add up?

16. Belted plaid

The Highlandman wore a long undershirt, down to his knees, and over that came his main garment, a large piece of woven cloth, a tartan plaid, known as am breacan feilidh (breacan being tartan, and feilidh being blanket or plaid). This belted plaid, said David Stewart, "was a piece of tartan two yards in breadth and four in length, which surrounded the waist in large plaits or folds, adjusted with great nicety, and confined by a belt, buckled tight round the body; while the lower part came down to the knees, the other was drawn up and adjusted to the left shoulder, leaving the right arm uncovered, and at full liberty. In wet weather, the plaid was thrown loose, and covered both shoulders and body; and when the use of both arms was required, it was fastened across the breast by a large silver bodkin, or circular brooch . . ." These fastenings had another function. "In the Highlands, buttons of large size, and of solid silver, were worn, [so] that, in the event of falling in battle, or dying in a strange country, and at a distance from their friends and their home, the value of the buttons might defray the expenses of a decent funeral."[157] A sporran (in Gaelic, sporan means a purse or pouch) hung from the front of the belt. "A large purse of goat's or badger's skin, answering the purpose of a pocket, and ornamented with a silver or brass mouth-piece, and many tassels, hung before . . . The bonnet, which gentlemen generally wore with one or more feathers, completed the national garb. The dress of the common people differed only in the deficiency of finer or brighter colours, and of silver ornaments, being otherwise essentially the same; a tuft of heather, pine, holly or oak, supplying the place of feathers in the bonnet. The garters were broad, and of rich colours, wrought in a small primitive kind of loom, the use of which is now little known, – and formed a close texture, which was not liable to wrinkle, but which kept the pattern in full display. The silver buttons were frequently found among the better and more provident of the lower ranks, – an inheritance often of long descent. The belted plaid, which was generally double, or in two folds, formed, when let down so as to envelop the whole person, a shelter from the storm, and a covering in which the wearer wrapt himself up in full security, when he lay down fearlessly among the heather . . . In storms of snow, frost, or wind, he would dip the plaid in water, and wrapping himself up in it when moistened, lie down on the heath. The plaid thus swelled with moisture was supposed to resist the wind, so that the exhalation from the body during sleep might surround the wearer with an atmosphere of warm vapour. Thus their garb contributed to form their constitutions in early life for the duties of hardy soldiers, while their habits, their mental recollections, and the fearless spirit they nourished, rendered them equally intrepid in the attack, and firm in resisting an enemy."[158] (As a military man, Stewart often saw things from the point of view of his own profession: just as a hatter looks at headgear and a cobbler at shoes.)

To put on full Highland dress was a matter of some moment. First, the Highlandman laid his belt down on the ground, or floor, and his plaid on top of it. Then he had to lie down on the plaid, so that his knees came about half way along one of the longer sides. After that he rucked up the material on either side of him into pleats or folds, and got hold of the two ends of his belt. Part of the material at each side of the plaid was left flat, and these flat ends the Highlander then brought across his front, fastening his belt to hold them in place. Now he could stand up, and the rest of the plaid he arranged across his top half, according to what he planned to do that day, and whether (for example) he was going out into fine weather or foul. All this was a complicated procedure, and there must have been frequent occasions when a Highlander had to rise hastily from his sleep to attend to some emergency, perhaps among his flocks and herds; so at some time the fairly obvious step was taken of separating the lower part of the plaid, which hung below the belt, from the rest of it, thus making it possible to dress much more quickly. This lower part was then called the feilidh-beag, little plaid, or filibeg. The Lowlanders and English called it a kilt.

17. Trews and arisaid

Another form of Highland dress, said Frank Adam, was "the triubhas or trews. These were always made of tartan. They were cut crossways and worn tight to the skin after the style of breeches. They were often elaborately laced down the seam, sometimes finished with gold braid." The trews were worn by chieftains when on horseback, "and by Highlanders when travelling in the Lowlands."[139]

Highland women wore the arisaid, which (said Martin Martin) was "a white plad, having a few small stripes of black, blue, and red. It reached from the neck to the heels, and was tied before on the breast, with a buckle of silver or brass . . . The plad, being pleated all round, was tied with a belt below the breast, the belt was of leather, and several pieces of silver intermixed with the leather like a chain . . . The head-dress was a fine kerchief of linen straight about the head, hanging down the back taperwise."[160] David Stewart said that "young unmarried women never wore any close head dress, but only the hair tied with bandages or some slight ornament".[161]

The widespread acceptance of the idea that each clan had a particular fixed tartan pattern or patterns for its plaids and filibegs seems to have occurred as a result of the preparations for the visit of George IV to Edinburgh in 1822. It is likely, however, that well before that date local weavers might have found it easier to reproduce a pattern they had already used, and that the predominant colours in each district's tartan might be those which were most easily obtainable in the neighbourhood, from the local mosses, lichens, berries, leaves and bark of trees, and plants of every kind, which were utilized, along with soot, for dyeing the wool. Certainly Martin Martin, writing in 1695, thought that particular places in the Highlands were associated with different tartans. "Every Isle differs from each other in their fancy of making Plads as to the stripes in breadth and colours. The humour is as different thro the mainland of the Highlands, in so far that they who have seen these places are able at the first view of a man's Plad, to guess the place of his residence."[162] Since each clan was closely linked with a specific area, it can be seen how a clan might come to be connected with a particular pattern. The modern clan tartans, however, were mostly recorded by the manufacturing firm Wilson Brothers, of Bannockburn near Stirling, after discussions with the notables of the clan concerned, in the second decade of the nineteenth century.

18. Highland dress forbidden

After the suppression of the '45 rebellion, the Lowland/English forces conquered the Highlands, and so, now being able for the first time to impose their own way of life on the mountaineers, began to compel the Highlanders (so far as they could) to accept the values and the practices of the Lowlanders. After Culloden laws were passed forbidding the Highlanders either to wear Highland dress or to carry arms. Those who wore the plaid, or filibeg, or anything else that might be called part of the Highland dress, were to be imprisoned for six months for the first offence, and transported for seven years for the second.[163] In the first flush of the Lowland conquest, however, clansfolk disregarding the ban were treated as outlaws, and the Government soldiers killed them on the spot. As the Duke of Cumberland's armed and uniformed bandits scoured the country thirsting for blood, they were now considered to be justified in slaying any Highlander they found wearing his normal clothes, without having to tax their brains working out which side he had actually supported in the late conflict – and many clansmen, of course, had in point of fact fought for the Government. Some Highlanders had not heard of the new rules, and others had not had the money or the opportunity to obtain completely different outfits of clothing; but these excuses were cut short by executions, and the statute was enforced by slaughter, as the soldiers introduced the Highlanders to the benefits of Lowland civilization.

After a year or two, the order was less strictly imposed. In the sparsely-populated Highlands, a permanent large and expensive army would have been necessary to ensure prolonged obedience to such a finicky decree. It must be remembered, too, that though there had long been a Lowland/English claim to rule over the Highlands, the anglophone conquest only took place in reality after 1746; and the enforcement of a new-fangled alien rule over some 16,000 square miles of mountainous territory was bound to be a lengthy business. Before long, said David

Stewart, "instead of the prohibited tartan kilt, some wore pieces of a blue, green, or red thin cloth, or coarse camblet [a strong waterproof cloth], wrapped round the waist, and hanging down to the knees like the feal-dag", a garment which "was the same as the filibeg, only not plaited". Others were allowed to comply with the new regime by carrying this strange – but now compulsory – Lowland garment, a pair of breeches, "often suspended over their shoulders upon their sticks; others, who were either more wary, or less submissive, sewed up the centre of the kilt, with a few stitches between the thighs, which gave it something of the form of the trowsers worn by Dutch skippers". As early as 1757 there occurred "the trial of a man of the name of MacAlpin, or Drummond MacGregor, from Breadalbane, who was acquitted, on his proving that the kilt had been stitched up the middle".[164] In the face of such ingenuity, the law fell into disuse.

It is true that Smollett, writing of the Highlands in 1771, said the Gaels had been "deprived of their ancient garb, which was both graceful and convenient . . . and compelled to wear breeches"; and that "the majority wear them, not in the proper place, but on poles or long staves over their shoulders". Immediately afterwards, however, he described (in a fictional letter from Argyllshire) the dress of the local chieftain's piper, who wore "the kilt, or ancient Highland dress, with the purse [no doubt sporran], pistol, and durk".[165] Dr Johnson, too, strangely wrote in 1773 that "the law by which the Highlanders have been obliged to change the form of their dress, has, in all the places that we have visited, been universally obeyed"; but then immediately revealed that the people considered that since the law against plaids was made by Lord Hardwicke, it was "in force only for his life", and added that "the filibeg, or lower garment, is still very common, and the bonnet almost universal".[166] (The usual dress of "a Sky-boy" was "a dirty kilt".)[166] Since the filibeg was "very common", and it was believed that the prohibition of the plaid had lapsed, it is clear that the law was in fact being ignored. On the same journey, indeed, Johnson and Boswell met Malcolm MacLeod, "one of the Raasay family"; Malcolm wore brogues, tartan hose leaving his knees bare, "a purple camblet kilt", "a short green cloth coat bound with gold cord", and "a large blue bonnet", altogether "a perfect representation of a Highland gentleman". The travellers also met Allan MacDonald of Kingsburgh, husband of Flora MacDonald. Boswell said he was "completely the figure of a gallant Highlander . . . He had his Tartan plaid thrown about him, a large blue bonnet with a knot of black ribband like a cockade, a brown short coat of a kind of duffil, a Tartan waistcoat with gold buttons and gold button-holes, a bluish philibeg, and Tartan hose."[167] Kingsburgh, and Malcolm MacLeod, and many others, certainly wore Highland dress, despite Johnson's assertion that the law against it was "universally obeyed". William Gilpin, writing about the Highlands in 1776 (only three years after the Johnson-Boswell visit), wrote of "the Highland dress (which, notwithstanding an Act of

Parliament, is still in general use)".[168] When the Highland Society of London organized its first piping competition, held in Falkirk in 1781, one of the rules was that competitors had to wear Highland dress – still technically illegal.[169] In about 1791 the minister of Lochgoilhead said that the people there had in earlier decades ignored the prohibition. Except the fishermen, they "wear the Highland dress, the bonnet, the phillabeg, and tartan hose; even the authority of an Act of Parliament was not sufficient to make them relinquish their ancient garb".[170]

In the same way, any laws against bagpipes became inoperative well before they were officially abandoned – and that not in a surreptitious or intermittent way, either. In 1775 there was a professional bagpipe maker operating in the middle of Edinburgh: he was called Hugh Robertson, and an Edinburgh directory of that year recorded his ongoing business in Castlehill.[171]

19. Necessary to connive

In 1779 some men who had enlisted to serve in the 71st Highland regiment were ordered to join a Lowland regiment instead; being Highlanders, and therefore unused to submission, they naturally resisted (as we saw earlier). In the subsequent trial, it was stated that the accused could not cope with having to don Lowland wear, for they had always worn Highland dress: "though the philebeg [filibeg] was one of the forbidden parts of the dress, yet it was necessary to connive at the use of it, provided only that it was made of a stuff all of one colour and not of tartan, as is well known to all acquainted with the Highlands, particularly with the more mountainous parts of the country."[172] The mutinous men were pardoned, and joined the Black Watch.

Others failed to obey the law even earlier. An official report was made in 1753 about the chieftain MacDonald of Barrisdale,[173] and his sept of the Glengarry MacDonalds. "They [the clansfolk of his sept] have the insolence, ever since the year 1746, to pay their rents [sic] to the attainted Barrisdale who, since that time, absolutely rules them, and ranges up and down that country and the neighbourhood with a band of men dressed, as well as himself, in the Highland habit."[174] This was Archibald MacDonald, 3rd of Barrisdale, one of the Glengarry tacksmen, who before the rebellion had held a wadset of Barrisdale from Glengarry. Barrisdale's property had been forfeited to the Crown, and no doubt it was the rents payable to Archibald under this wadset (which, of course, could no longer legally be made) that were so annoying the writer. Subsequently Barrisdale was jailed in Edinburgh for his part in the '45; then he made his peace with the new regime, and became an officer in the Queen's Highlanders, after which he transformed himself into an improving farmer on several farms in Barrisdale.

However, those who prefer writing to reality, and allow documents to defeat deeds, were convinced that since an Act of Parliament had banned Highland dress, it must have disappeared. Dr Johnson appears to have reasoned in this way, and so did Hugh Trevor-Roper. Notwithstanding the evidence from 1773 that the filibeg was "very common", the evidence from 1776 that the Highland dress was "in general use", and the failed prosecution in 1779 of some who actually wore it because it was "necessary to connive at" the filibeg, Trevor-Roper asserted that "by 1780 the Highland dress seemed extinct, and no rational man would have speculated on its revival";[175] thus burdening the "rational man" with a most irrational disregard of the evidence.

In the matter of the proscription of Highland dress, as in the question (for example) of the "land charters", it is necessary for the "rational man", and the rational woman, to examine all the evidence carefully, and if necessary to distinguish what actually happened from what the documents said ought to have happened.

20. Origin of the filibeg

In 1782 the abortive attempt to make the Highlanders wear Lowland costume was finally abandoned, and the act prohibiting the wearing of Highland dress was (as we shall see later) repealed. The appearance of Gaels flaunting the hated Highland habit, now not even theoretically illegal, which made it obvious that the great post-Culloden offensive against these old enemies had manifestly not succeeded in wiping them out completely, must have annoyed the Lowlanders intensely; and it is interesting that it was only three years later, in 1785, that the *Edinburgh Magazine* published a letter, supposedly written in 1768, asserting the consoling theory that the filibeg had been invented by an Englishman. The writer of the letter was Evan Baillie of Abriachan, who belonged to a Highland landlord family. His father was the landlord Alexander Baillie of Dochfour, and his brother was the landlord William Baillie of Rosehall. Evan Baillie had (one writer said) given "much useful information during 1745-1746"[176] to the Hanoverian authorities. Baillie's previous activities may be significant: certainly the idea that such an integral part of the Highland dress was only an English invention was very useful to the Hanoverian Government, since any story which helped to pour cold water on the idea that the Highlanders had a separate identity would be of great assistance in the Government campaign to destroy that separate identity. This campaign is still being actively pursued: as we saw earlier, Trevor-Roper said not long ago that "the whole concept of a distinctive Highland culture and tradition is a retrospective invention".[177] When one investigates Evan Baillie, odd facts emerge. Baillie was a writer (a Scots solicitor) in Inverness; he was, according to a recent volume, "Lovat's Inverness businessman", i.e. the agent of Simon Fraser, the eleventh Lord Lovat; and Simon's youngest son, Archie, knew him well because "he was often at home with his father", i.e. with Simon.[178] Now it is against all common sense to condemn anyone because of his associates: but Simon Fraser, at a time and in a class where lying was common, was the master-liar of the age. There are many letters of his still extant in which he solemnly wrote down many thousands of words which (as he well knew) were complete fictions. He lied so often and so comprehensively that clearly in his mind the distinction between truth and falsehood had completely disappeared. All one can say is that it would have been little short of miraculous if anyone regularly associating with Lord Lovat had been able to hang on entirely in his own mind to the separation of fact and fiction.

According to Evan Baillie's account, the man chiefly responsible was one Thomas Rawlinson, a Quaker from Lancashire, who was an ironmaster.[179] The smelting of iron required much fuel, which at that time had to be wood, and many of the English and Lowland forests were rapidly being used up. Some ironmasters therefore established works in the Highlands, where timber was still plentiful. This Lancashire ironmaster Rawlinson was said to have set up an iron foundry about 1727 at Invergarry, in the territory of the MacDonalds of Glengarry. Some Highlanders worked for him, and after discovering (so the story goes) how cumbersome the plaid was for people operating an iron foundry, he decided to try for something more convenient: so he got in touch at some time in the late 1720s with the local regimental tailor at Inverness, called Parkinson, and Parkinson obediently invented the kilt. This account must be true, as John Burke shrewdly asserted in his *Traveller's History of Scotland* in 1990, because "the very word [kilt] is not of even remotely Gaelic origin":[180] in fact, he added as a clinching argument, it is Danish. This is as if a Native Australian, coming across London for the first time, had named it, say, "Corriwarra"; and then another Native Australian had brightly maintained that London could not be English, because Corriwarra (or whatever) was "not of even remotely English origin". The English-speaking Burke finds it difficult to accept that these strange eccentric people, the Highlanders, had their own language; and that it was the anglophone outsiders (like himself) who decided to call the filibeg the "kilt".

21. Ancient Highland dress

It is in fact the ill-concealed joy with which this story is regularly regurgitated by English and Lowland authors (and journalists, when they have nothing else to write about) that makes one slightly suspicious as to its authenticity. Trevor-Roper included the allegation that the filibeg only appeared in the 1720s in his *The*

Invention of Scotland (published in 2008 after Trevor-Roper's death, though he was writing it thirty years before; it seems likely that he may have decided to abandon the accusation that others had accepted "fakes", after his own embarrassing acceptance of the fake "Hitler diaries", which he misguidedly certified as genuine). Book-reviewers in England and the Lowlands wrote as if Trevor-Roper had been the first to make the discovery of this tale; and it is strange, but true, that all three of the reviews which I happened to read were at pains to polish the story still more by yet further post-dating the supposed "invention of the kilt" by the English, which according to the Evan Baillie story happened in the 1720s. *The Times* of London approved of Trevor-Roper's "identification of the Highland kilt as the invention of a Quaker ironmaster in Lancashire [!] in the 1780s [!]";[181] *The Guardian*, giving the Manchester viewpoint, said Trevor-Roper had shown that "the modern kilt" was invented "in the early 1800s";[182] while Edinburgh's *Scotland on Sunday*, perhaps the best of all, said the book dealt with "the invention of the kilt in the 19th century",[183] which could of course mean in the 1890s. The nearer to the Highlands, the further from the facts.

The present writer does not know enough of the circumstances to be able to reach a decision on the matter. However, the evolution of the filibeg from the breacan feilidh does seem so obvious a step among such an astute and inventive people as the Highlanders that one would have expected it to occur without extraneous intervention.[184] Secondly, there seem to be references, in accounts of Highland dress well before 1727 (for example those of Sir William Brereton in 1635, and of Thomas Kirk in 1677, as we see elsewhere), and in illustrations and even sculptured figures, which indicate that the filibeg already existed.[185] Thirdly, Tobias Smollett, who was born in March 1721 on the verge of the Highlands, referred (as we saw earlier) to "the kilt, or ancient Highland dress"; if the kilt was only invented in 1727 (or 1728, or 1729) at distant Invergarry (eighty miles away from where Smollett lived), then the new invention could only have reached the edge of the southern Highlands – at the earliest – at some time after that; so Smollett would himself have observed when he was a boy the gradual introduction of this new-fangled garment (which had only been dreamed up a long way away when he was six years old, or seven, or eight). Yet he regarded the kilt as "the ancient Highland dress".[186] Fourthly, a close reading of the contribution said to have been made by the tailor Parkinson might indicate (as David Stewart suggests) that what he furnished was not the idea of a separate filibeg, but (tailor-like) the admitted improvement of making sewn-in pleats, instead of the wearer having painstakingly to fold them himself each time he put on his filibeg: in other words, to convert the piece of cloth which, put on quickly, would only be a feal-dag (or unpleated kilt), so that it became a permanent filibeg (or pleated kilt).

THE LIFE OF THE HIGHLANDERS

David Stewart wrote: "it may, with as much reason, be supposed, that breeches were never worn till the present cut and manner of wearing them came into fashion. As the Highlanders had sufficient ingenuity to think of plaiting [i.e., pleating] the plaid, it is likely that they would be equally ingenious in forming the kilt; and as it is improbable that an active light-footed people would go about on all occasions, whether in the house or in the field, encumbered with twelve yards of plaid, (to say nothing of the expense of such a quantity,) I am less willing to coincide in the modern opinion, founded on such a slight unauthenticated notice, than in the universal belief of the people, that the filibeg has been part of their garb, as far back as tradition reaches."[187] Stewart returned to the subject: "as it is not probable that a people, at so late a period, would assume a garb totally unknown in the world, and in their climate put away the warm breeches, and expose half their body to the blast, there are the better grounds for the undivided opinion of the people themselves, that, as far back as they have any tradition, the truis [trews], breachan-na-feal (the kilted plaid,) and philibeg, have ever been the dress of the Highlanders." Stewart added that his "grandfather always wore tartans; truis, with the plaid thrown across the shoulders on horseback, and the kilt when on foot, and never any other clothes, except when in mourning."[188]

22. From the beginning

A further point might be this. The filibeg was certainly widely worn in the Highlands in the 1730s, or even the late 1720s, which, if it were only invented after 1727, would indicate an enormously quick acceptance of a completely new invention (if it was completely new). But at that time, without the assistance of a countrywide press, radio, and television, the knowledge about and adoption of new inventions was a very slow process. This is exemplified, curiously enough, by what was happening in the iron industry (the very industry alleged to have spawned the filibeg) at that time. The smelting of iron, the extraction of the pure metal from the naturally occurring iron ore, needed much fuel. Britain, of course, had much fuel, in the form of vast deposits of coal. But when iron smelters attempted to use coal in the smelting process, noxious gases from the burning coal got into the iron, and made it too brittle to use. Therefore iron had to be smelted using wood, or rather wood after it had been turned into charcoal, which burned without such harmful fumes. However, the forests of Britain were swiftly diminishing, and it became clear that unless some way of utilizing coal instead of wood was discovered, the smelting of iron in this country would exhaust the forests and come to an end. All the developing industries relying on iron would be greatly disrupted; and if pig iron (smelted iron) had to be imported, the supply would be liable to interruption by enemy blockades whenever war broke out (as it frequently did). The problem was solved soon after 1709 (as we know now) by Abraham Darby at Coalbrookdale, who avoided the noxious fumes by converting coal into coke before using it to smelt iron.[189] But many years later ironmasters were still in ignorance of this, and were going to all the trouble and expense of establishing foundries in the remote Highlands in order to use the local supplies of timber. That was why Rawlinson himself started a works at Invergarry as late as 1727, nearly two decades after Darby had removed any necessity for going to such a distant and inconvenient spot, far away both from the supplies of ore and from the market for the product. It is true that Darby was not eager to let everyone know what he had discovered: but an iron foundry cannot be operated secretly in a garden shed, and if the machinery for the quick dissemination of new information had existed the Darby process would have been general knowledge within weeks (instead of taking several decades). One can only say that if the filibeg was invented after 1727, the news of this completely new garment spread with astonishing speed.

A further observation may be added. When the act against Highland dress was repealed in 1782, a proclamation was made in the Highlands (as we shall see later), telling the Gaels that they could again wear "the Trews, the Little Kilt" and the other items of Highland dress which "came down to the Clans from the beginning of the world to the year 1746".[190] In 1782 (again, we shall see this later) there were many Highlanders who had reached seventy, eighty, and ninety or more years of age. They would all have been able to remember the costume they wore in their younger days, before 1727 (only fifty-five years earlier). If the filibeg had been invented after 1727, they would have been aware, from their personal knowledge, that it had not come down from ancient times; yet no Highlander, until Evan Baillie produced his story, objected to this account, untrue as they must have known it to be. Many of these ageing Highlanders were referred to in the O.S.A. reports. When the Lochgoilhead minister wrote his account in 1791, the people there (as we saw earlier) still wore "the Highland dress, the bonnet, the phillabeg, and tartan hose"; and furthermore there was in the parish (for example) a man of 93, "who not only enjoys health, and the exercise of his mental faculties, but also strength sufficient to dress his little garden and potato ground".[191] This man, still compos mentis, would have been about thirty if the kilt was first invented in the late 1720s; he could only have worn it first when he was almost entering middle age. Neither he, nor any of the other thousands of Highlanders who must have been able to remember the comparatively recent introduction – if such it was – of the filibeg, ever hinted that it was anything other than "the ancient Highland dress".

Rawlinson was so unpopular (as a southern interloper into a clan territory) that according to one account many attempts were made on his life; and if he had any hand in the "invention" of the filibeg, it seems likely that no Highlander would have worn it on that ground alone, whereas the orthodox story is that this new garment spread with astonishing speed. It is curious, too, how a letter supposedly written in 1768 is eagerly taken as proof of what had happened forty years before; whereas when Highlanders offered evidence about what had occurred decades earlier their testimony is looked at askance, on the grounds that it lacks "contemporary validation".

Altogether, the story of "Rawlinson's kilt" is somewhat unconvincing.

23. Begged his bread

Whenever one is considering the history of a people swept aside by the march of history – as the Highlanders, and their society, were swept aside by the anglophone triumph – one finds how often the vanquished people are slandered by their conquerors. Most human beings want to regard themselves favourably; if one person has treated another harshly, he likes to justify himself by embracing the belief that his victim was bad, or stupid, or in some way deserving of rough treatment. Therefore one naturally becomes distrustful of stories that would show defeated people in a bad light. The name of the reputed ancient Gaelic bard, Ossian, occurs in this connection. The present writer is far from having any pretension to speak about poetry, in particular about Gaelic poetry, or about Gaelic legends; but the supposed Ossianic poems had a great influence during the Romantic revival, and were accepted as valid by many prominent literary and artistic figures in Britain and elsewhere, such as Smollett, and Goethe, who presumably could recognize good work when they saw it. The *D.N.B.* spoke of Thomas Gray's "enthusiasm for James MacPherson's Ossianic productions" (although, as we saw, MacPherson was less fervent about Gray). Sheridan (a classic playwright) put Ossian above Homer and Virgil. William Wordsworth celebrated Ossian's supposed grave[192] in Glen Almond – "In this still place, remote from men, Sleeps Ossian, in the Narrow glen", while his sister Dorothy wrote of "the hills of Morvern, so much sung of by Ossian".[193] Coleridge wrote two poems imitating Ossian.[194] Burns more than once referred to Ossian's poems or his poetic methods.[195] The *D.N.B.* mentioned Burns' "enthusiastic reading of the poems of Ossian"; he gave a friend a two-volume edition of the poems of Ossian; and he visited the supposed site of Ossian's grave. Byron quoted Ossian.[196] Schubert set some of the poems to music; a book of Ossian's poems was supposedly Napoleon's favourite reading; we are told that Thomas Jefferson learned Gaelic so as to be able to translate Ossian; and John Wesley thought Ossian was "little inferior to either Homer or Virgil – in some respects superior to them both".[197] Ossian was translated into half-a-dozen European languages; numbers of artists (including

Ingres) painted scenes from Ossian's stories; and Bernadotte, King of Sweden, called his son Oscar after an Ossianic character. Ossian was also accepted by many others who (one would have thought) should know, such as numbers of the Gaelic-speaking Highland ministers who wrote the O.S.A. reports (one of them was Dr John Smith of Campbeltown, who referred his readers to Ossian's poem *Temora*).[198]

There is, however, virtually no evidence that Ossian ever existed. The Highlander who is supposed to have translated his works, James MacPherson, was certainly untrustworthy, as we shall see later; his achievements culminated in buying a Highland estate and evicting the Highlanders. But lack of evidence is not always fatal to reputation. There is no evidence of the existence of Homer – "nothing is definitely known of Homer", as an encyclopaedia puts it; there is even one theory that the author of the "Homeric" poems was a woman, and another conjecture is that the poems had a variety of authors. However, many places would like to postulate such a poet and (relying on the absence of evidence) claim him (her? them?) as a local worthy. "Seven wealthy towns contend for Homer dead, through which the living Homer begged his bread", as that prolific versifier Anon once declaimed. But Homer (if he ever lived) wrote in classical Greek, the basis of the education of upper-class Englishmen for centuries; while Ossian (if he ever lived) wrote in Gaelic, the language of the "mountain savages", who were considered as surplus to requirements at home, and were steadily being driven out of their glens to serve the British Empire as cannon-fodder in the army and navy, as factory drudges in the congested Lowland towns, or as toiling pioneers in imperial outposts. It is clear which of the two poets, although the evidence of their existence is equally deficient in both cases, would be extensively honoured, and which would be condemned as a sham.

James MacPherson was accused of writing himself much or all of the Ossianic canon, but – as an enthusiast for Gaelic literature – he is a standing target now as much as Ossian is. John Burke (the same author who described the filibeg as a kilt, and then perceptively pointed out that the word "kilt" was not Gaelic), after asserting Ossian's poems were "most of them actually contrived by MacPherson himself" while he was living in the Lowlands, also claimed that he – James MacPherson – "could not speak a word of Gaelic". (If Burke thought that MacPherson had made up the "Fragments of [Gaelic] Poetry" he published in 1760, or the further Gaelic poems he collected on two journeys to the Highlands in 1760-1, then MacPherson must have had the unprecedented skill of composing poetry in a language he could not understand; many of us would be glad to be able to compose poetry in a language we do understand.)[199] The idea that MacPherson knew no Gaelic is not true, of course – anyone born in the MacPherson country in 1736 (at Ruthven in Strath Spey), both parents being MacPhersons, could scarcely avoid facility in Gaelic; and he aroused interest when he met Scots literati and "repeated to them Gaelic verses from memory", as the *D.N.B.* put it.

24. Forfeited lands going cheap

It may be worthwhile to look briefly at John Burke's work, because unless rigorous rectifications are made some of his statements will doubtless be trustingly reincarnated in other books, and by such repetition (as one learned historian copies another) become an accepted part of "Highland history", which is fictitious enough as it is. In fact, however dubious one may feel about the alleged clever foreigners who are supposed to have invented the filibeg, one need have no fears that the well of anglophone inventiveness as to Gaelic affairs is running dry.

It is intriguing to note that Burke's volume was published by John Murray, the celebrated firm founded by a Scotsman, originally called John MacMurray (1737-93). John Murray felt unable to publish the present work, but was happy to bring Burke's effort to the attention of the reading public. Many basic orthodox errors are given another outing by Burke – the "overpopulated" Highlands,[200] the "bleak crofts" in which the pre-Culloden clansfolk had to "scrape a bare living", and the description of those clansfolk as "peasant smallholders".[201] (Here one can only repeat in brief firstly that the old Highlands were very sparsely peopled, more than one observer calling them "almost uninhabited", and secondly that the old Highlanders lived in joint-farms; most of their food came from hunting or collecting, much from herding, and a very little from agriculture. Crofts only appeared when the clearances began: they were small barren plots where some of the evicted Highlanders were allowed to live – and attempt to turn valueless ground into rentable land for the benefit of the proprietor – after they were ejected from their farms.) Again, thought Burke, the Gaels were virtually savages, and cowardly at that. There were "all too frequently . . . internecine feuds".[202] The Highlanders, said Burke, fought "with terrifyingly murderous vigour; but acquired a reputation [no evidence was given for this, of course] for quitting the field the moment they realized that the battle was lost and there would be no profitable pickings. Apart from this opportunism and the love of fighting for its own sake, their main characteristic was a passion for quarrelling interminably and bloodily among themselves."[203] To establish these allegations beyond doubt Burke was able to quote the impartial Lowlander John Major, who naturally was able to point out the contrast between these barbarians and the "tolerably civilized life"[204] (in Burke's words) of the Lowlanders like himself.

Sometimes one wonders whether, if authors had to undergo some legal training, they would have a sharper sense of what does, or does not, amount to convincing evidence.

Occasionally, however, Burke comes up with original variations on these themes, or even ventures into newer strains. Some of his flights of fancy may be numbered, as follows.

1. The filibeg could not have been a Highland invention, because the Lowlanders called it a kilt.

2. James MacPherson "could not speak a word of Gaelic" (and therefore was being dishonest when he claimed to understand the Gaelic poetry he purported to translate), although he was able to travel round collecting Gaelic poetry from Gaelic speakers.

3. The Highlanders were simply "intolerable barbarians",[205] continually slaughtering each other. "Blood feuds were the cause of much of the Highland barbarism so deplored by monarchs in Edinburgh; or was it the innate barbarism that provoked the blood feuds?"[206] Again, this "innate barbarism", a mainstay of Lowland propaganda down the centuries, is discussed on other pages.

4. Seaforth and the MacKenzies seized for a time the chiefship of Assynt from the MacLeod clansfolk, merely because they deplored the chief Neil MacLeod's "breach of Highland hospitality" towards Montrose.[207]

5. In the Highlands after 1746, "London speculators made haste to buy up whatever they could – in this case, forfeited lands going cheap".[208] As we shall see, some dozen Highland estates were confiscated, but they were not sold, cheaply or otherwise, to "London speculators" or to anyone else; they were managed by an official commission, and all were returned to the original families thirty-seven years later. (Burke's book was published in 1990. Curiously, a similar assertion had appeared in another work only a year before: *A Companion to Scottish History*, by two academic historians, Dr Ian Donnachie and Dr George Hewitt, and published by Batsford. They wrote – under the heading "Clans" – that after Culloden, "many Jacobite chiefs lost their lands to Government, a transfer that created the Forfeited Estates. Most were sold off, but some restored in 1784."[209] If this was supposed to apply to the Highlands – as the use of the words "chiefs" and "clans" would presumably indicate – it is misleading: no forfeited Highland estates were "sold off" after the '45.)

6. The Speyside parish of Duthil ("derived from the Gaelic Tuathil, north", according to the New Statistical Account of Scotland) was spelled Duthill by Burke, presumably to make it more acceptable to English eyes.[210]

25. Died in the scuffle

Burke also gives a new version of the Selkirk expedition of 1813.

7. "A group from Kildonan founded a settlement on Hudson Bay, but when it proved unworkable" they went to the Red River, where they "started all over

again" at Fort Douglas.[211] In fact they were always en route for Fort Douglas (which had already been established), having been recruited by Selkirk for the single purpose of joining his new project there, and had to winter at Fort Churchill (on Hudson Bay) in 1813-14 only because the incompetent (or malevolent) captain of the emigrant vessel put them ashore too far north to undertake the final journey to the settlement before winter set in. Even the hardiest of Highlanders would hardly have planned to settle so far north that minus thirty degrees Fahrenheit – sixty-two degrees of frost (or minus thirty-five degrees Celsius) – was a normal January temperature.

8. Burke said that Croick church (which was erected in 1827) and the other "Parliamentary churches" were built "in an effort to woo Papist Jacobites finally to Protestantism".[212] Croick was in Kincardine parish, where there were no Catholics in the 1750s, according to Webster, no Catholics in the 1790s, according to the O.S.A., and no Catholics in the 1830s, according to the N.S.A. In all the thirty-three parishes of Ross and Cromarty Webster found only twenty "papists": the population of the entire county was then recorded as 47,656, of whom 47,636 were Protestants.[213] So Croick church had been erected, according to this account, to do what had already been done.

9. "In 1882", Marines arrested some of the Glendale (Skye) crofters, said Burke: "one of these leaders, John MacPherson, died in the scuffle and became known as the Glendale Martyr".[214] The episode on which this yarn is obviously based occurred in 1883, not 1882; the three men who were sentenced to two months in jail were all known as the Glendale Martyrs; the men were not arrested, so there could have been no "scuffle" – MacPherson and the two others went voluntarily to Glasgow and there gave themselves up; and MacPherson was not killed, but lived nearly another forty years, dying in 1922. So it is not necessary to spend time wondering how anyone could die in a "scuffle".

10. "Towards the end of 1887 one landowner decided to turn the whole of his Eishken estate into a deer park, provoking an invasion of crofters who killed several deer before being forced to withdraw by police and marines."[215] Park Forest, raided in 1887, included the land of a number of townships, not only Eishken (there was no "Eishken estate"); it had been turned into a deer forest de facto in 1883, and formally in 1886, not 1887; the landowner was Lady Matheson, so the estate was hers, not "his"; the invasion was mainly of landless cotters, not crofters; they killed at least 100, probably 200, deer – there were 700 raiders, doubtless including some who had not lost the hunting skills of their youth, armed with fifty rifles; and the raiders withdrew of their own accord on the third day of the raid, before the Lowland police or troops could reach them.[216] Apart from these six errors, this thirty-eight-word sentence is accurate.

26. Highland townships

We may now return to what actually happened in the Highlands. The normal unit of Gaelic society was the township, or hamlet. A number (from three or four up to fifteen or more) of families, who were relations or friends, combined and formed themselves into a small co-operative group, and lived in a separate township. Each such group, as Arthur Geddes says in *The Isle of Lewis and Harris*, "formed a team".[217] Their main efforts, as we saw above, went into hunting, and after that into herding. As the landlord revolution increasingly deprived the clansfolk of the first resource, and increasingly restricted the second, more emphasis had to be laid on tilling the land, which previously had been of negligible importance. The men of the township would collaborate in hunting the wild life, so long as that was still possible, and in herding their animals, so long as they had sufficient pasture; and together they would manage their arable holding. As the landlord revolution began to bite, more and more this would have to include a piece of infield, perhaps in the valley bottom by the river flowing through the glen, which would be cropped every year; and a larger piece of outfield, further up the hillside, of which a third or a quarter would be cropped each year in rotation. Sometimes part of the outfield was cropped each year for several years, then another part, and so on. In what seems to be the older method of operation, the produce of the tilled land would be shared among the farmers; in the later mode, each of the partners would have a number of strips of infield, and a number of strips of outfield, on the township farm. These strips would be changed by lot from year to year, so that each member of the team would have his or her share of the better and worse land on the farm. The earlier mode still survived at the beginning of the nineteenth century, according to Selkirk, although the strip system was then more usual. But both where the whole field was still common, and where it had been divided into strips or "rigs", the men still ploughed the land, planted the seed, and gathered in the harvest, together. Where the strips had been introduced, the system was called "runrig" farming – a rig being a strip of land. To prevent misapprehension, however, it should be repeated that in the days of the clans food was obtained by hunting, shooting, and fishing, and after that by herding; tilling a patch of soil, whether jointly or in runrig, was merely a by-occupation, and only became of any importance as the landlord revolution deprived the clansfolk progressively of their usual means of life.

Until the charter holders began to exclude the Highlanders from their pasture lands, in order to let it separately to large commercial farmers, the animals of the farm would roam freely over the clan's moorland and mountains, along with the cattle and sheep from the other farms of the clan. All this was done in co-operation by the clansfolk. The minister of Kilmartin said in the O.S.A. that the work of the joint-farm was "carried on in common among the whole tenants, with their wives and children".[218] Also together the men rowed their boat on the loch or the arm of the sea, netted the fish, and shared the catch.

The women, too, did much as a team. Together they spun the wool from the sheep's back into yarn, and prepared it, and collected the dyes. Each would weave her piece of cloth with brightly coloured threads in complicated chequered patterns known as tartans; then together they would help in fulling, or "waulking", the cloth. As the occasion arose, the women would also help each other in childbirth and child-care.

27. Leisurely work

Many of the necessary tasks were tackled by the members of the whole family, whatever their age, as the Kilmartin minister indicated. In 1803 Dorothy and William Wordsworth stayed on a farm in Glen Gyle, and although it was a sheep farm the Highlanders who ran it (and who denounced the oppression of the landlords in what Dorothy called "Jacobinical" – i.e. violently subversive – terms)[219] had kept many of their ancestral methods. "We amused ourselves", wrote Dorothy, "with watching the Highlanders at work: they went leisurely about everything, and whatever was to be done, all followed, old men, and young, and little children." Thus children learned the ways of adults in the best manner possible, by direct imitation – by doing what the adults did, alongside them; a contrast to modern customs, when children are hived off into separate, and sometimes not very praiseworthy, institutions or communities, where they are told what to do. Nor had these Highlanders learned that in the new era it was necessary for human beings to work until they dropped from exhaustion. The Wordsworth siblings were surprised to hear the Highlanders all "laughing and talking long after we were in bed; indeed I believe they never work till they are tired".[220] No wonder such a society, and such profit-sapping habits, had to be swept away by the powers-that-be: in the new factories, the owners made sure that everyone certainly did work till they were tired, and for that matter well after they were tired – mill-hands had little energy left for "laughing and talking" after fifteen hours or more at the bench or loom.

Each family had the right to graze its animals on the clan land. As the improvements progressed, and the Highlanders' pasture was increasingly confiscated, so the system arose of each small tenant being allowed only so many units or "soums": one soum was a cow and her progeny, or equivalent numbers of other animals. During the days of the clans, however, each family pastured whatever animals it wished. The men tended their stock in common. Sir George Steuart MacKenzie, writing (in 1808) about Wester Ross during the former system, said that "the hills which bounded the glen were generally occupied in common by all the townships on the banks of the river which flowed through the glen".[221] In winter and spring, said the O.S.A. minister of Boleskine, "the whole pasturage" was in common: poind-fold (the place where stray, or unlawfully grazing, animals were placed) "was a thing totally unknown".[222] The Highlanders had great numbers of black cattle, and as the new restrictions were fastened on the Highlands, these became more and more important, because the sale of some animals in the Lowlands each year was of great help in satisfying the landlords' ever increasing demands for rent. But the clansfolk also had many sheep of the old Highland kind, which provided succulent meat for the table and fine wool for spinning and weaving. The Inveravon minister said the small tenants' sheep grazed on "the hills" – "in general in common".[223] These Highland sheep tend to be overlooked in accounts of the old Highland society, because they were used "only" to help feed and clothe the Highlanders. The new flocks of sheep, which appeared after the clearances, were considered of much greater importance, because they provided great rent increases for the landlords. The former township sheep should not be forgotten: Dr Bangor-Jones said, "it appears that sheep equalled cattle numbers, particularly in the more Highland areas",[224] that is, the more mountainous districts. The Highlanders also had flocks of goats, whose milk expanded their owners' diets; some accounts say the goats were as numerous as the sheep.

Each May or June the associated families, working in teams, cut their peats to provide fuel for the ensuing year.

28. Scarcely a murmur or dispute

Incredible though it seems, over a century after the beginning of the Industrial Revolution, and after more than a century of ferocious attacks by the men of the commercial system on the old Highland society, a few of these "sociable hamlets" still survived, with many of their original features, in the British Isles. Alexander Carmichael saw them in operation in North Uist, and wrote an account of them, which was incorporated by W. F. Skene in his *Celtic Scotland*, 1880.

"Towards the end of autumn, when harvest is over, and the fruits of the year have been gathered in, the constable calls a meeting of the tenants of the townland for Nabachd (neighbourliness). They meet, and having decided upon the portion of land to be put under green crop next year, they divide it into shares . . . Thereupon they cast lots, and the share which falls to a tenant he retains for three years . . . Should a man get a bad share he is allowed to choose his share in the next division." The houses of the tenants were usually in a cluster. "They are placed in a suitable part of the townland, and those of the tenants of the runrig system are warm, good, and comfortable. These tenants carry on their farming operations simultaneously, and not without friendly and wholesome rivalry, the enterprise of one stimulating the zeal of another . . . Whatever may be the imperfections, according to modern notions, of this very old semi-family system of runrig husbandry, those tenants who have least departed from it are the most comfortable in North Uist, and, accordingly, in the Outer Hebrides."[225]

Carmichael even found isolated survivals of the system still older than runrig, where the people farmed the land in common without even dividing it into strips. "Occasionally and for limited bits of ground, the people till, sow, and reap in common, and divide the produce into shares, and draw lots . . . The system was not uncommon in the past, though now nearly obsolete."

The habit of sharing without greed or envy was deeply ingrained in the clansfolk – not because they were "better" human beings (morally or racially), but because that is how their system worked. The minister of North Uist described in 1837 how the people of certain small tenant farms went to catch seals on three rock islands off the west coast. "When successful, the division is made according to ancient rule, with scarcely a murmur or dispute."[226]

29. Shielings

The Highlanders' regular annual move to the upland pasture, where they lived in huts known as shielings, was also a joint undertaking. Here again Alexander Carmichael gave a graphic picture:

"Having finished their tillage, the people go early in June to the hill grazing with their flocks. This is a busy day in the townland. The people are up and in commotion like bees about to swarm. The different families bring their herds together and drive them away . . . The men carry burdens of sticks, heather, ropes, spades, and other things needed to repair their summer huts. The women carry bedding, meal, dairy and cooking utensils . . . Barefooted, bareheaded, comely boys and girls, with gaunt sagacious dogs, flit hither and thither, keeping the herds together as best they can, and every now and then having a neck-and-neck race with some perverse animal trying to run away home. There is much noise. Men – several at a time – give directions and scold. Women knit their stockings, sing their songs, talk and walk as free and erect as if there were no burdens on their backs nor on their hearts, nor sin nor sorrow in this world of ours, so far as they are concerned. Above this din rise the voices of the various animals being thus unwillingly driven from their homes . . . All who meet on the way bless the trial, as this removing is called. They wish it good luck and prosperity, and a good flitting day, and having invoked the care of Israel's Shepherd [having asked for divine protection] on man and beast, they pass on.

"When the grazing ground has been reached and the burdens are laid down, the huts are repaired outwardly and inwardly, the fires are rekindled, and food is prepared. The people bring forward their stock, every man's stock separately and, as they are being driven into the enclosure, the constable and another man at either side of the gateway see that only the proper souming [correct number of animals] has been brought to the grazing. This precaution over, the cattle are turned out to graze." This restriction to "the proper souming" occurred of course only after the chiefs had transformed themselves into landlords, with the help of the Lowland/English state power; in the days of the clans, the evidence shows clearly that the grazing was common to all, and each Highlander put as many animals as he pleased out to pasture.

The people, Carmichael continued, then gathered for their "removing feast", a simple meal, each housewife providing a cheese. "The cheese is shared among neighbours and friends, as they wish themselves and cattle luck and prosperity . . . Every head is uncovered, every knee is bowed, as they dedicate themselves and their flocks to the care of Israel's Shepherd . . . As the people sing their declaration, their voices resound from their shielings, here literally in the wilderness, and as the music floats on the air, and echoes among the rocks, hills, and glens, and is wafted over fresh-water lakes and sea lochs, the effect is very striking."[227]

In the Outer Hebrides, the dedication to "Israel's Shepherd" occurred among the Protestants of North Uist, Harris, and Lewis, where lived the Clan Donald, the MacLeods, and MacKenzies; in Catholic Benbecula, South Uist, and Barra, among the Clan Ranald and the MacNeills, the people invoked the Virgin Mary and the saints. Apart from the actual names of the deities, however, nothing differed in these shieling ceremonies.

The minister of Kintail wrote in the O.S.A. that the people followed the flocks to the hill grazings from 1st June to 12th August (commercial grouse-shooting still begins on the latter day, presumably because the Highlanders' herds then left the remoter hills).[228] In Boleskine, the O.S.A. report says that the inhabitants went to the shielings in the summer; also in the summer they got in their peats, and repaired their dwellings. At harvest time they returned from the shielings to get in their crops; then they often went again to the shielings until driven thence by the first snow.[229] The main visit to the shielings seems to have been regarded almost as a ten-and-a-half week summer holiday.

30. Free from care

The writer of the Kilninian report for the N.S.A., dated 1843, was Francis Clark: he was a landlord and an immigrant Lowlander, a man of the new order who himself carried out clearances (T. Devine called his activities "a relentless process of eviction").[230] Yet he was honest enough to write an almost lyrical account of the days when the Highlanders went every year to the shielings. "It would appear that a custom prevailed in this country [Mull], even so recently as forty years ago, of the inhabitants setting off to the hills with their flocks at the beginning of summer, and bivouacking in the vicinity of the best upland pastures, where all the families of the district took up their residence till it became necessary to descend to the low grounds in the month of August, when the hill pasture became bare, and when their crops required attendance. Frequently has the writer of this listened with delight to the tales of pastoral life led by the people on these occasions, – when free from care, they tended their flocks among the pastures of the upland common. The men occasionally visited the low grounds to attend their simple husbandry then in use, or to procure some of the delicious fish which abound along the coast; some engaged in the chase, or followed the game; and richly did they deem themselves rewarded for their toil. When returning to the family circle, the produce of the flocks and dairy was put before them, and the feast enlivened by the pure essence of mountain dew, joined to the heart-stirring strains of the bagpipe. Nor in this pastoral encampment were the women idle; much of their time was occupied in the labours of the dairy, in preparing an abundant stock of butter and cheese for winter. When baughting [ewe-milking][231] time was over, the females used the distaff and spindle, and, congregating on the sunniest bank, enlivened the task of providing the tartan clothing for the family, by the simple yet innocent strains of their mountain songs."[232]

The Rev. Dr James Robertson wrote about this summer safari to the shielings in his 1808 book on Inverness-shire. "This is the season of contentment, of festivity, of health and joy." The women were occupied in spinning, and in making butter and cheese. "The youth are employed in fishing, and wrestling, or other athletic exercises which put their swiftness and courage to the test, as a preparation for the more serious conflicts of a field of battle. When the various labours of the day are closed, the whole hamlet retires to rest . . .on a bed of heath, whose mellifluous fragrance perfumes the whole dwelling."[233]

Arthur Geddes said that the phrase in the well-known song, "the lone shieling of the misty island", gives a false impression. "Traditional Gaelic songs tell rather of shielings grouped within hail, with their sweethearting and good cheer!" In the shielings there was "fellowship and a gaiety".[234] Even in the early twentieth century, a Lewisman remembered "vividly how life in the shieling restored health and colour after the winter".[235] Carmichael wrote: "The people enjoy this life at the hill pasturage, and many of the best lyric songs in their language are in praise of the loved summer shieling."[236] In 1688 an observer said that "the Laird of Cappagh [Keppoch], after sowing time was over, had gone that summer, as was his custom, to make merry with his clans [sic] on the mountains, till the time of harvest should call him home".[237]

The enjoyments of the annual shieling excursion were, of course, swept away by the clearances. The pleasures of the people, put in the balance against the profits of the proprietor, were found to carry no weight whatever.

The Earl of Selkirk, writing in 1805, claimed that sometimes the joint-tenants in former days had unequal shares in the joint-farm.[238] If that ever did happen it was a late, and an unusual, development. Robert Brown, writing in answer to Selkirk, said such an arrangement was extremely rare: on all well-regulated Highland estates (he wrote) small tenants who had farms in common each had an equal share, since it was very prejudicial to have unequal shares.[239] This was confirmed by the N.S.A. report on Kilmory, in Arran, which described the old times: "All the lands were undivided, and unenclosed. Each farm was leased by a number of individuals, sometimes by as many as ten and fifteen, who were jointly and severally liable for the rent [sic]. Each farm was thus a societas arandi [farming fellowship], or township, containing as many families, having each an equal interest in its cultivation, each field being sub-divided into as many stripes, separated by a narrow ridge, called a 'bone', where the stones, weeds, and other rubbish gathered off the land were accumulated. These stripes generally changed possessors every second or third year, according to arrangement of parties."[240]

Selkirk appears to have been mistaken: all the available evidence indicates equal shares among the joint-holders. Arthur Geddes referred to two judicial "rentals" (in fact two lists of the customary tribute, or local taxation) drawn up by the authorities in Lewis in 1718 and 1726, when the Seaforth charters had been confiscated; in them, it can be seen that each occupier was rated at exactly the same figure as his fellows.[241]

31. Little commonwealths

When the chiefs converted themselves into landlords, these comradely co-operative hamlets or townships were called "small-tenant farms".

The minister of Harris, writing in the O.S.A., said that "a small-tenant farm is a little commonwealth of villagers".[242] And so it was. Decisions on the matters that affected the community were taken after full discussion, by a vote. Arthur Geddes described how the constable, who was a kind of township chairman, was chosen by the free vote of the township members. When the chiefs took on the character of the landlords, these self-governing institutions naturally came under heavy attack (any custom savouring of democracy is a danger to private landownership), and the landlords would often force their own nominees into the position of constable. But even in the new dispensation, the people were still able sometimes to retain the right of electing their constable.[243]

This kind of egalitarian commonwealth was still fully operative on the North Uist runrig farms as late as the 1870s. The people, said Carmichael, "obey the decision of the majority". The small tenants had two kinds of meeting to come to decisions on local affairs: one called Nabac [or Nabachd, as Carmichael called it in 1890], and one named Mod or moot. "When required by the proprietor or the people, the constable convenes a meeting of the tenants. If the constable presides, the meeting is Nabac; if the Maor [steward] presides, the council is the more important Mod or moot. Perhaps the people have met to confer about making or repairing a district road, the digging or deepening of a ditch, or trench, the planting or repairing with bent the drifting sandbanks of their machair [sandy soil], or the buying or selling of a bull. The man who presides explains the business, and makes a motion. If the people assent, the matter is decided; if not, discussion ensues. Some of the people speak well. They reason forcibly, illustrate fittingly, and show complete mastery over their native Gaelic, which with them is plastic, copious, and expressive. Everything calculated to mar neighbourliness is discountenanced. Reasoning, they say, shall obtain hearing, and sooner or later victory; but the most contemptible of contemptible things are doggedliness and vulgar abuse [so they would not have enjoyed modern elections] . . . The subject is decided by votes . . . Should the votes be equal, lots are drawn three times – the two times carrying against the one time."[244]

When Carmichael wrote, he was describing only a stray remnant of a system once universal in the Highlands. This centuries-old active democracy, exercised not merely by putting crosses on ballot papers at long intervals (to elect "leaders" who often ignore their public pledges, implementing instead their personal opinions – "I did what *I* thought was right", as one recent prime minister boasted, putting the voters in their place), but as an integral part of people's daily lives, was destroyed by the landlords during the clearances. It possessed such attractions, however, even in retrospect, that its very existence had to be denied by the landlord version of events. This landowners' propaganda unfortunately convinced John Prebble, who described the Gaelic people as "a monoglot minority accustomed to making no decisions for itself".[245] How erroneous this assessment was has already been seen.

32. Mutual help

While the clan or the hamlet had food, no one starved (and as we shall shortly observe, the Highlanders were much more in control of their own food supply than their contemporaries in the Lowlands, or their own descendants in commercial society). There were no separate "social services", because the old and the sick were looked after as part of the normal course of events. The old widow could be sure of her relatives, or her friends, or those of her name, building her a hut and seeing that she had some poultry, and grass for a cow. If a man was sick, the others in the hamlet saw to it that his land was dug over and planted; his wife and children would not go without their share of the harvest.

"In making their own land arrangements for the year, the tenants set apart a piece of ground towards the support of their poor", said Carmichael. He went on: "Not the least pleasing feature in this semi-family system is the assistance rendered by his neighbours to a tenant whose work has fallen behind through accident, sickness, death, or other unavoidable cause. When death occurs in a family, all the other families of the townland cease working till the dead is buried – till earth is placed under earth. Compassion for the poor, consideration towards the distressed, and respect for the dead, are characteristic traits of these people. This is inculcated in their sayings – 'Succour to the poor, aid to the dead [in burying], and sympathy with the distressed, are three things which a wise man never regretted'."[246] Such "respect for the dead" may seem anachronistic now, when it has been replaced by a hearse speeding along the motorway to the nearest crematorium amid complete indifference, but it may be closer to how human beings would like to behave.

Samuel Smiles, the Victorian apostle of thrusting individualism, had not yet become the guiding light, and mutual assistance, rather than *Self-Help*, was the accepted social behaviour within the clan. John Stuart Blackie remarked: "In a commercial age and among a commercial people, accustomed from the daily practice of their business to be governed by habits of acquisition and aggrandisement, in their nature mainly selfish, it is difficult to make people realize the power of essentially unselfish motives which formed the firm cement of the social architecture under an altogether different system. But that these thoroughly unselfish motives were a living reality, and not a mere unfruitful sentiment, has been universally admitted by all who have even superficially looked into the history of the Highlanders."[247]

It is possible, of course, to take a different view of the apparent unselfishness of these motives. For if the clansfolk wished their clan society to prosper and to endure, which they did, and if the best way to promote the well-being of the clan was to act in a fair and helpful way towards the other members of the clan, which it was, then the clansfolk who acted in that way would be, in the last analysis, selfish rather than unselfish. For the prosperity of the township and of the clan meant the prosperity of the individual clan member: and in promoting the prosperity of the clan and the hamlet, the clan members promoted the prosperity of themselves and their families. The behaviour of the clansfolk would, in this view, be rather enlightened self-interest than unselfishness. But whatever reasoning one adopts as to the motives of the clansfolk, the evidence that they did act in this fair and helpful way is, as we shall see, conclusive.

33. Unity of labour

In this society there was no division of labour, apart from the distinction (justified or not) between the tasks usually performed by men, and those normally done by women. A man was a whole man, and a woman a whole woman. A husband and wife did all the things that were necessary to feed, clothe, and house themselves and their children. Instead of an individual spending his whole working life in the terrifying tedium of one single confined action repeated over and over again every day *ad nauseam*, as if the human being were simply a nerveless machine (the aim is "the reduction of the necessity for thought on the part of the worker and the reduction of his movements to a minimum. He does as nearly as possible only one thing with only one movement", as Henry Ford put it with appalling honesty),[248] he turned his hand to all the employments which society had to offer. Adventurous, open-air activities like hunting, shooting and fishing, which are now the distinguishing badge of the wealthy, that is to say of those who can choose their own life-style, were part of his normal round. He caught his family's trout and salmon in the burn, or cod and turbot in the loch; he brought home a rabbit or a blackcock, a capercaillie or a deer, for the cooking pot. He, and she, found pastures suitable for their flocks and herds, and ensured a supply of milk, cheese, and eggs, for the family. In turn the Highlander was hunter and herdsman, fisherman and farmer, builder and carpenter, stonemason and cobbler. As Dr John Walker remarked in 1808, almost everyone in the Highlands executed "most of the mechanic arts that are necessary for his own accommodation".[249]

In this way the Highlanders developed skills of many kinds, and became self-reliant, adroit, resourceful, and adaptable. As David Stewart observed, "the sagacity and facility of accommodation to novel situations that mark the Highland character may be ascribed to the versatility arising from such varied occupations".[250] The Rev. J. L. Buchanan wrote that "the common people are wonderfully ingenious" – each man had many trades: it was "very common" to find the same man a tailor, shoemaker, stocking weaver, cooper, carpenter, sawyer, metalworker, netmaker, boat-builder and boat-mender, and ploughwright.[251] The minister of Applecross said "every man" was "the architect of his own house."[252]

The clan member, wrote J. S. Blackie, "was thus, in the dexterous adaptability to various cases and varying circumstances, a much more complete and accomplished human being, than the thousands and tens of thousands of creatures who under the much-vaunted system of division of labour succeed in multiplying the product, only by dwarfing the producer".253 He might have gone further, and said they succeed in multiplying the product, only by dividing the producer. For the producer was divided: once a whole man, he became only a machine-attendant, almost a machine-component. His change in status was signalized with frightening precision by the name given to him under the new system: once a man, he was now no more than a "hand". He was disconnected, and nothing was left of him but the manipulations of his fingers and thumb.

It may be argued (and repeatedly is) that economic production is carried out more efficiently under the system where each worker does only one repeated task. But efficiency of economic production cannot be taken as the paramount goal of human society: the goal of human society must surely be the happiness of the human beings who compose it. A society where human beings are happy, and economic production is somewhat less efficient, is surely preferable to a society where economic production is extremely efficient, and human beings are unhappy. This was true in earlier centuries, and it must be even more true now, when economic production has grown so overwhelmingly prolific that its very excellence has become over much of the globe the main problem, to the astounding extent that many able-bodied people are given much money on condition that they promise faithfully to produce nothing (for example, landowners who are paid large sums to "set aside" their fields – that is, to leave them useless, and prevent any food being grown there); and when over-production, leading to economic disaster, means that the old story of the sorcerer's apprentice – who by magic turned his broom into a water-carrier, and then could not stop it, despite his desperate attempts to bring it to a halt – is no longer merely a far-fetched fairy-tale, but the very type and essence of many modern industrial states.

34. Unity of class

The Earl of Selkirk wrote that since everyone in the Highlands had some land, the people there were not separated into distinct classes of farmers, labourers and mechanics – by which categories Selkirk appears to mean farm owners, farm workers, and artisans or town workers.254 In other words, the division in society between the people who owned the land on the one hand, and the people who tilled the land on the other, had not yet arisen. In the Lowlands this distinction was already well established: in much the greater part of Lowland society the owner of the land did not work on it, and the worker on the land did not own it. Comparatively recent though this separation was, it seemed to Selkirk that it was part of the natural order of things; and the absence of the distinction in the

Highlands seemed to him a confusion and intermixing of what should be eternally separate. He wrote: "The excessive division of land arising from the feudal manners, has confounded and intermixed the characters of farmer and labourer." This had "diffused the agricultural capital of the country among a great number of hands": the unspoken remedy was clearly to concentrate it in a few.[255] (Lucky those who were in the "few".) Selkirk's remedy, it will be seen, was achieved in the clearances.

In the old Highland society, however, the co-owner of the land and the co-worker on the land were still the same person. The minister of Dornoch complained in the O.S.A. that too many people – in fact, almost all of them – had land. It was very difficult to procure servants, he grumbled, since this system made "almost every man a master".[256] The new system, then rapidly introducing, reversed this sorry state of affairs, and instead made "almost every man" a menial.

35. Standards of living: comparisons

On the question of the standards of living enjoyed by the Highlander under the clan system, accounts differ. One can find descriptions of the Highlanders as being in the direst poverty: and one can find descriptions that say exactly the opposite. Many historians take the former view, among them Professor George Pryde. "For all but a handful, life in the Highlands was harsh, plain and exacting, with no surplus for comforts or niceties, and with a slender margin of safety from famine and want... Society was held together by common beliefs and mutual loyalties, by the bond of fears and sufferings shared by all."[257]

One great fallacy must be avoided here – comparing like with unlike. Many observers appear, subconsciously, to be comparing the standard of living of the Highlander in the days of the clans with the standard of living of the twenty-first century white-collar worker living in the leafy suburbs of a modern conurbation. In fact there were only three basic choices open to the Highlander in the eighteenth century: to stay with his or her clan, on the clan land; to go and live in the Lowlands, in the urban slums; or to depart overseas, to undertake years of backbreaking pioneering work in a new land, where every facility or resource had to be improvised. (Young, fit men had a fourth choice: to enlist in the armed forces under fierce military discipline, and risk death or injury defending and expanding the British Empire.) The eighteenth-century Highland family, put out of their home and farm, did not have the choice of skipping two or three centuries, and going to live in Hampstead or Morningside with a dishwasher and tumble-drier. One must be careful to compare the standard of living of the Highlander, not with any theoretical optimum standard, but with the alternatives that were actually open to him or her.

A similar pitfall ensnared some eighteenth-century travellers. Themselves fine-living gentlemen from the Lowlands or England, they toured the Highlands, saw how the clansfolk lived, and felt sorry for them on finding that they had few of the comforts to which they (the well-to-do tourists) had always been accustomed. If these observers had gone a much shorter journey, to the back streets of their own Lowland or English cities, they would have found much more to excite their pity. But the urban slums of course were not a romantic and unknown land, tempting the wealthy into exotic journeys, to be recorded later in colourful volumes of reminiscence.

J. E. Bowman, a prosperous banker from Cheshire and North Wales, was travelling in the Highlands in 1825, and in Glen Croe he came across a party of workmen who were repairing the road. While the workmen were on a labouring expedition, they lived in "a large and very broad green caravan", in which there were a number of berths for them to sleep in. Bowman stopped to talk, and found that "their sole food was 'porridge', or oatmeal and water, seasoned with a little salt. Upon such simple food do these hardy people labour hard and brave the rigours of a Scotch winter!" Bowman could not resist pointing the moral – perhaps thinking of his own employees. "A powerful lesson to the pampered inhabitants of England, more than one half of whose diseases are the offspring of luxury and indolence."[258]

36. Crowdie for a week

I cannot resist making a personal digression here. I could not help but think, when I read Bowman's castigation of "the pampered inhabitants of England", about my own forebears. Twenty years after Bowman's rebuke, my great-grandmother on my mother's side (whose father, incidentally, carried on *his* father's shoulders, had been at Peterloo) went to work in a Lancashire silk mill at the age of five, while my maternal grandmother began work at eleven in a Manchester cotton mill. It is not easy to think of them as "pampered". Even more relevantly, on my father's side, my grandfather,[259] who was born in 1850 at Alston, in Cumberland, went to work (like his forebears) in the leadmines, beginning at the age of nine: though when he was seventeen, the leadmines were closing down, and he and his brother (he was the second son) and father had to move over to County Durham to work in the coalmines there (and to quarry stone and build a couple of houses in their spare time, so the rest of the family could join them) – and stayed there throughout their working lives. When I was a boy, I was able to talk to him about his early days (he lived to be nearly ninety-five; he had retired at seventy-three, after a working life of sixty-four years). The lead deposits were becoming exhausted around Alston in the 1860s, and the last leadmining job my grandfather had was near Cross Fell, about ten miles away. He and his fellow-workers went there for a week at a time – going early on Monday morning, returning late on Saturday. They slept on bunks in a workmen's hut, and they laboured though the rigours of the Cumbrian climate. They took with them, he said, their bedclothes, and enough "crowdie" to last for a week. Never having heard of it, I asked him what it was: "crowdie", he said, was cold oatmeal porridge, in slabs. ("Crowdie" is defined in Chambers' dictionary as "a mixture of meal and water"; my grandfather's definition was somewhat different.) So forty years after Bowman's praise (in the 1820s) of the hardy Highlanders and his reproaches to the "pampered inhabitants of England", that is to say in the 1860s, my grandfather was working through the week under much the same conditions, sleeping in much the same way, and eating much the same unappetizing food, as the Highland road-repairers. But Cumberland had not known the rallying of the Jacobite clans under Prince Charles, the tartan plaids and the bagpipes, and Sir Walter Scott's romances: so Cumbrian leadminers, unlike Highlanders, would not have been romantic and exotic enough to attract the attention of travellers. Bowman must have passed quite near to the Cumberland leadmines on his way to Scotland, but did not spend any time on them. As a result, he could draw a comparison between the ill-fed Highlanders and the "pampered inhabitants of England" which turns out to have been quite unfounded. Bowman's comments, however, do underline the fact that many travellers were not comparing like with like – they observed the scattered Highland huts, whose denizens were too hospitable to think of concealment, and compared what they saw not with the poor people among the English-speakers, but with themselves and the people they knew – the ones who could reasonably be described, in comparison with the Lowland and English poor, as "pampered".

Returning from this digression, one ought to look at Selkirk. He gave a useful comparison between the Highlands and the rest of the country – and his book was published in 1805, when the chiefs, by steadily raising rents and worsening conditions, had materially lowered the standards of the clansfolk. Selkirk said that small tenants (by which term Selkirk meant the old joint-farmers, as opposed to the newly-created crofters) were still a considerable proportion of the Highland population. The small tenant might have from three to twenty cows, with a proportionate number of young cattle; he also had horses, a few sheep, agricultural implements, and household articles; by selling these he could embark on undertakings beyond the reach of cotters and of peasantry "even in the more improved and the richer parts of the kingdom".[260] There, the labouring poor had to spend their wages as they got them to support their families; but these Highland clansfolk had property. Later Selkirk repeated that from the "peculiar circumstances" of the Highlands, the proportion of the Highlanders whose property was enough to get them to America was greater than in other parts of the kingdom:[261] the small tenants could usually pay their passages to America, in most instances taking some money with them as well.

It appears from this that the ordinary Highlander was better off than the ordinary Lowlander. It also shows who exactly was better off in "the more improved and the richer parts of the kingdom" – not, obviously, the ordinary people. The Lowlands might have been "more improved and richer": but apparently the Lowland people were less improved, and poorer.

37. John Buchan

The author John Buchan (who was a Lowlander, a Conservative M.P, and in 1935-40 the Governor-General of Canada; he was created Lord Tweedsmuir), said in his *Montrose* – as we saw – that the Highlander, with his "full meals of meat from the chase, was physically far superior to the bannock-fed Lowland peasant".[262] Five years later he returned to the subject in another book, when he described the state of the Highlanders generally and in particular the situation of a branch of the MacDonalds, the MacIains of Glen Coe, towards the close of the seventeenth century:

"Their economy was rudimentary but by no means barbarous. They grew their own corn, which sufficed except in a season of dearth. In summer and autumn hunting gave them ample store of game and fish. For the winter cattle were salted down, and salmon kippered. In actual comfort the society of the glen probably far exceeded that of a Lowland parish of the time. There was not the back-breaking monotonous toil on sour, ill-drained land. The chase gave their men healthy exercise. Their food was better, except in the depth of winter – full meals of flesh as contrasted with the Lowland sowens [a dish of oat-husks] and bear-meal bannocks. Their bodies were better nourished and developed . . . The houses were no worse, and fuel was more plentiful. Occupations were more varied, there was more social freedom, and more light and colour in their lives . . . In their own enclave they had a richer and more wholesome civic life. The keynote of such a society was a sense of ancient civilization and a pride of race, in which every member of the clan shared. The long past of Clan Donald was an intimate thing to the humblest, almost like a living memory . . . The life in the glen, too, had its refinements and its hours of merriment. On the summer evenings on the haughs [riverside meadows] there would be tossing the caber, and races among the young men, and fierce games of shinty [a game not unlike hockey]. Up in the shieling huts in the twilight the girls would spin, or dance to the pipes, or listen to old tales and harpers' tunes. In the winter nights, when the birch billets made the peat fires leap, and the doors were shut, there would be snug gatherings; the old men at their tobacco, the wives at the spinning-wheel, and the young folk at their songs and tales."[263]

After the Glen Coe massacre of 1692, the Government forces (wrote Macaulay) drove away "many sheep and goats, nine hundred kine, and two hundred small shaggy ponies of the Highlands" – a large number of animals if the clan "was not supposed to exceed some two hundred souls", as Macaulay related.[264] (However, the 1746 memorial said – fifty years after the massacre – that MacIain of Glencoe could raise 150 men, so probably the clan had well over a thousand members. And no doubt the clansfolk had some of their animals in inaccessible parts whose whereabouts would not be known to the soldiers.)

38. Hugh Miller

Hugh Miller, in his *My Schools and Schoolmasters*, 1850, wrote of the Highlanders' former living standards, which he himself had seen and experienced when staying with his Gaelic relatives, as compared both with the Highlanders' position after the clearances, and also with the Lowlanders' contemporary situation (these too being matters of which he had personal knowledge). Even before the clearances, it should be remembered, the Highlanders were already in a much less comfortable position than during the days of the clans: they had lost their hunting, their shooting, and their inland fishing, their pasture had been restricted, and their rents had been multiplied. But even after these impoverishments, there is no doubt, from Hugh Miller's evidence, where the "dire poverty" lay.

Miller recalled in one passage the events of the year 1823, when he had been working at Flowerdale, in Wester Ross. Earlier than that, in his boyhood (he was born in 1802), he had seen, in the interior of Sutherland, the Highlanders living "in that condition of comparative comfort" which they enjoyed "till the beginning of the present century, and in some localities for ten or twelve years" longer. Then, in Wester Ross in 1823, "I saw them in a condition – the effect mainly of the introduction of the extensive sheep-farm system into the interior of the country – which has since become general over almost the entire Highlands, and of which the result may be seen in the annual famines. The population, formerly spread pretty equally over the country, now exists as a miserable selvage, stretched along its shores, dependent in most cases on precarious fisheries, that prove remunerative for a year or two, and disastrous for mayhap half a dozen; and, able barely to subsist when most successful, a failure of the potato crop, or in the expected return of the herring shoals, at once reduces them to starvation. The grand difference between the circumstances of the people of the Highlands in the better time and the worse may be summed up in the one important vocable –

capital. The Highlander was never wealthy: the inhabitants of a wild, mountainous district, formed of the primary rocks, never are. But he possessed, on the average, his six, or eight, or ten head of cattle, and his small flock of sheep; and when, as sometimes happened in the high-lying districts, the corn crop turned out a failure, the sale of a few cattle or sheep more served to clear scores with the landlord, and enabled him to purchase his winter and spring supply of meal in the Lowlands. He was thus a capitalist, and possessed the capitalist's peculiar advantage of not 'living from hand to mouth', but on an accumulated fund, which always stood between him and absolute want, though not between him and positive hardship, and which enabled him to rest, during a year of scarcity, on his own resources, instead of throwing himself on the charity of his Lowland neighbours. Nay, in what were emphatically termed 'the dear years' of the beginning of the present [nineteenth] and latter half of the past [eighteenth] century, the humble people of the Lowlands, especially our Lowland mechanics and labourers, suffered more than the crofters and small farmers of the Highlands, and this mainly from the circumstance, that as the failure of the crops which induced the scarcity was a corn failure, not a failure of grass and pasture, the humbler Highlanders had sheep and cattle, which continued to supply them with food and raiment; while the humbler Lowlanders, depending on corn almost exclusively, and accustomed to deal with the draper for the articles of clothing, were reduced by the high price of provisions to great straits."[265]

39. Experienced no want

The diet of the Highlands differed from that of the Lowlands and England. In the Highlands, salmon was more common than beef. Edmund Burt told the story of the Highland gentleman and his servant who went to London. The gentleman ordered beef for himself, and salmon for Duncan; and was astounded to find that his beef was eight pence, while the salmon was nearly as many shillings.[266] But the food, though different, was sufficient. "While the clan retained its own lands", wrote Ian Finlay, "there was enough, if not abundance, of the staple things for every man."[267]

Jamieson said that the Highlanders in the old system used to have small wicker barns or storehouses, "in which they kept their whole stock of hams, butter, cheese (for they then had such things), corn, meal, blankets, webs, yarn, wool, etc."[268]

There is in fact a great deal of evidence to show that although in the simple country life to which they were accustomed the wants of the old Highlanders were few, they lived prosperously enough: in fact their standards of living would have been considered opulent by the mass of the common people at that time either in the Lowlands or in England. Times had changed over much of the Highlands when the O.S.A. was written, but the comforts of life in clan society could still be remembered, and with regret, by the older people. A number of ministers, even though they owed their positions, their stipends, their comforts, and their prospects, to the local landlord or landlords, were honest enough to admit these facts when they came to write their statistical accounts in the 1790s. The minister of Kilmallie said that before 1764, when sheep farming was introduced into his parish, the people "lived very comfortably," with "plenty of milk, butter and cheese, and a good deal of oats".[269] The account of Boleskine (even though it was written by a landlord) said that in the old days, "as the inhabitants experienced no want, and generally lived on the produce of their farms, they were hospitable to strangers".[270] At Halkirk, before the changes, the minister said the "rent" was very low, and "other necessaries" were easily got, so that "very little pains" were "necessary to live and keep credit" by a small farm.[271] The minister of Kilmore, Argyll, wrote that when he first came thirty-three years before, the people lived in "tolerable black farmhouses": the rents were then moderate, and "the people lived comfortably in their line, though on simple fare, and in homely clothing".[272] In Otter, which was the northern part of Kilfinan, Argyll, the O.S.A. report said, "most of the inhabitants of the northern division, occupy the same lands upon which their forefathers lived comfortably for many generations before them".[273]

In the extreme north-west, in Sutherland, where the new order was later in establishing itself, the minister of Eddrachillis wrote of matters as they were as late as the 1790s: "Notwithstanding the ruggedness of the ground, and the wild appearance of this country, scarce any place affords a more commodious habitation to poor people, if there are any such in it. For upon a farm of 20s [i.e., rented at twenty shillings – or £1 – annually] and sometimes only of 10s [half of £1] many families want none of the necessaries of life: having bread and potatoes, fish and some flesh, wool and clothing, milk, butter and cheese, all the fruit of their own industry, and the produce of their farms. Their fuel they have also good, and on easy terms, every farm having plenty of peat mosses free to all."[274] There was also very good fishing there; every man was a fisher, and fished for himself; every village (township), almost every house, had a boat. But the improvements had brought worse conditions. In Kirkmichael (Banffshire), "the sheep were more numerous than formerly", but "the smaller tenants are fewer, and live less at their ease". In the old days "the hill pasture was a common, and there were few of any description who did not occasionally feed upon flesh", but now there was no such indulgence, except "at Christmas, or when any little festivals are celebrated".[275]

David Stewart wrote: "The small tenants in the Highlands generally possessed from two to ten or twenty milch [milk] cows with the usual proportion of young cattle, from two to five horses, and from twenty to one or two hundred sheep, the quantity of arable land being sufficient to produce winter provender for the stock, and to supply every necessary for the family. To each of these farms a cottager was usually attached, who also had his share of land, so that every family consumed their own produce, and, except in bad seasons, were independent of all foreign supplies."[276] Stewart said "two to ten or twenty milch cows" (and followers), "two to five horses", and twenty to two hundred sheep; Selkirk said from three to twenty cows, "and always with a proportionate number of young cattle", with "horses, and a few small sheep";[277] Miller said "six, or eight, or ten head of cattle, and his small flock of sheep";[278] the North Uist minister said six cows (or their equivalents), six horses, and perhaps fifteen sheep.[278] The four estimates are not far asunder.

These small Highland sheep were kept not only for their mutton and wool, but also for their milk, and for the cheese, curds, and butter, made from the milk. Milk and dairy products were also obtained from goats, and, naturally enough, from the black Highland cattle. J. Hicks, a regular sporting visitor to the northern Highlands in particular, wrote in 1855: "Milk has never been tasted in perfection by those who have not visited this portion of Britain, where the only fault that can be raised against it is that it is far too rich for a draught [a drink], which is constantly offered to one at any cottage one may enter. It is more than cream, it has the consistency almost of butter."[279]

40. *Ease of subsistence*

Not only could the clansfolk (even after several decades of the landlord revolution had greatly worsened their position) live in modest comfort on the products of the chase and of their herds: they did not (like the Lowland factory workers) have to work all day and every day in order to survive. They had time enough to enjoy themselves, time for their poetry, music, dancing, and sports. Selkirk said that a family's land could occupy but little of their time. On two or three occasions in the year they had to prepare the soil, gather the crop and so on: "but no regular and continued industry was requisite for providing the simple necessaries of life, to which their forefathers had been accustomed, and beyond which their desires did not extend. The periods of labour were short; and they could devote the intermediate time to indolence, or to amusement, unless when they were called upon by the chief to unite for the common defence, or for an attack on some hostile clan."[280] Selkirk no doubt feared his description of the normal life of the clan would make many people feel sympathetic to clanship, rather than antagonistic, so he felt the need to imply that fighting was frequent: as if the Lowlanders never went to war, or suffered hostile English incursions. As we shall often see, when armed conflict did occur in the Highlands, the basic cause was almost always Lowland interference, carefully planned to bring about just that result.

Robert Brown, although he wrote his book solely in order to attack Selkirk's, could find nothing here with which to disagree: indeed, he stressed the same point. In their own country, he said, the Highlanders could support existence with hardly any labour: the true cause of the "indolence" of the Highlanders (which the apostles of the new order had naturally begun to denounce) was "the ease with which a man in these regions can acquire subsistence". But he was writing in 1806, when he was glad to be able to say that the imposition of "adequate rents" was "every day" operating as a corrective of these "indolent" habits. In the areas where the new system was operating, this ease of living was now a thing of the past: "A Highlander cannot now enjoy the luxury of flesh meat, and warm clothing, unless he create, by his industry, something which he can exchange for them at their market price. He is in a very different situation from his ancestors, who could procure these luxuries by the chase, or for nothing."[281]

Long after the changes had begun, there were groups of small tenants who had been comparatively undisturbed, and were still able to live fairly well. Dr Norman MacLeod, writing in 1863 of his personal experience in Morvern before the clearances had reached every corner of it, said that the small tenants there "lived very comfortably. I remember a group of men, tenants in a large glen, which now has not a smoke in it, as the Highlanders say, throughout its length of twenty miles. They had the custom of entertaining in rotation every traveller who cast himself on their hospitality. The host on the occasion was bound to summon his neighbours to the homely feast. It was my good fortune to be a guest when they received the present minister of 'the Parish' while en route to visit some of his flock. We had a most sumptuous feast – oat-cake, crisp and fresh from the fire; cream, rich and thick, and more beautiful than nectar, whatever that may be; blue Highland cheese, finer than Stilton; fat hens, slowly cooked on the fire in a pot of potatoes, without their skins, and with fresh butter – 'stoved hens', as the superb dish was called; and though last, not least, tender kid, roasted as nicely as Charles Lamb's cracklin' pig. All was served up with the utmost propriety, on a table covered with a pure white cloth, and with all the requisites for a comfortable dinner, including the champagne of elastic, buoyant, and exciting mountain air. The manners and conversation of those present would have pleased the best-bred gentleman. Everything was so simple, modest, unassuming, unaffected, yet so frank and cordial. The conversation was such as might have been heard at the table of any intelligent man."[282]

This particular meal was, of course, on a special occasion. These were Highlanders of the old kind, in the days before individualism had completed its conquest of the Highlands; and thus the guests would have their share of the best that was available. Yet even allowing for the demands of hospitality, this description hardly fits into the orthodox picture of "dire poverty".

41. All conveniency

The manuscript dating from about 1700 and quoted in the N.S.A. report on Muckairn, which has been mentioned elsewhere, had also some interesting comments on the standard of life in that district of the Highlands. "This country lieth leaning to the north, whence the soil is not altogether so fertile in grain nor the grass so kindly as the rest of Mid Lorn marching with it, except in some tenements that lie near the shore side; yet it hath such plenty of grain as not only to suffice itself, but also some every year to sell to the neighbouring glens above it. But its chief increase is in cattle, with which it is furnished plentifully of all sorts, cows, horses, sheep, and goats, and hath this singular advantage, that every rown [perhaps a mistranscription for town, or township] or farm a part hath woods, moss [peat] for fuel, grass, corn, and barley land so commodiously mixed, so that every singular tenement hath all conveniency within itself . . . In the lower places of the country, there are few of these moorfowls called red cocks and their hens, but great plenty of blackcocks and heath hens . . . Besides the greater rivers or waters, Nant, Lonan, Luachragan, Lusragan, there are a great many small rivulets or brooks, all replenished with small trouts at all times, and betwixt Michaelmas and Hallowmas [29th September to 1st November] with greater trouts, of the bigness of herring, or rather larger, which come in from the sea to spawn; and on these greater rivers, there come in good store of salmon fish, some of the largest sort, but most of the smaller, which are grilses . . . There is no considerable take of sea fish here, only at the Connel, and the little island near it called Glash Island, there is good store of young seathes [coalfish – a variety of cod], codlings, and other small fish, caught with rods all summer over."[283]

The author of the *History of Scotland in 1750* referred several times to the food-producing capacity of the regions he dealt with. His intense dislike of the Highlanders, particularly those lately in rebellion, is revealed over and over again. If anyone had then had the idea that the Highlanders were becoming too crowded for their food supply, a state of affairs which would furnish an ideal pretext for driving them all away, he would have seized on it with avidity: but he seems to have had no such suspicion. On the contrary (interspersed among the usual malignant Lowland slanders on the Highlanders), he repeatedly talked of the ample food-supplies of the Highlanders. The MacKay country in north Sutherland, he said, "breeds great numbers of all sorts of cattle, produces some corn, and lies very convenient for fishing";[284] in fact he wrote of Sutherland, "this Country produces Corn enough for the Inhabitants and some for the market." The

Munros "have Bread in Plenty and live Comfortably". In the Long Island, there was "great Plenty of Barley Oats and Rye . . . these islands might be improved to bear Double the Quantity of Grain they at present do". There was very rough country (he said) in Knoydart and Arisaig: but even there, there was a "prodigious number of Cattle of all kinds . . . The people even in these Horrid parts of the Highlands might grow Rich if they were under Proper Management. They have also great Plenty of Venison of all Kinds." The country north of Loch Ness was "very fertile"; Aird had "very rich soil and produces great quantities of Corn". Jura, Islay, Kintyre, Glassary, and Cowal were "famous for Corn and Grass". Lorn was "famous for Barley and fine Pasture for Sheep". Morvern was "a good country for Corn and famous for Grass". And when the author mentioned the MacDonalds of Keppoch who joined the rebels in 1745, he called them "300 stout [robust] fellows", a strange description if the Keppoch men were faint from want of food.[285] Yet Andrew Lang (the grandson of the notorious Sutherland factor, Patrick Sellar), who wrote an introduction for the *Highlands of Scotland in 1750* when it was published in 1898, declared that it went to show that "the population far exceeded the means of subsistence".[286] By 1898 orthodox history had long striven to assert that the reason for the Highlanders leaving the Highlands was not the clearances, but over-population. Therefore anything written about the old Highlands must show that there was over-population. Therefore any commentary on the 1750 work had to ignore the evidence it gave as to the Highlanders having plenty of food, and had to allege that it showed "the population far exceeded the means of subsistence". And historians apparently find it so difficult to challenge what everybody accepts, that no one (so far as this writer has discovered) has ventured to point out that Andrew Lang's introduction flatly contradicts what the book actually says. The Emperor's new clothes are still wearing well.

In the same way what the Earl of Selkirk said has clearly been misinterpreted. Selkirk made clear his belief that the Highlands could support the Highlanders, and that problems arose simply because the landlords now wished to keep in the Highlands only those Highlanders necessary for the work on the new big farms.[287] One historian claimed Selkirk thought emigration necessary to avoid "overcrowding and destitution" in the Highlands, thus implying (incorrectly) that Selkirk believed the Highlands could not support their population. We shall also see later the trenchant assertions of Colin MacKenzie, adviser to the Countess of Sutherland, that "the country is far from being overstocked", and that there were "immense spaces of unimproved ground in Sutherland capable of cultivation".[288] Another historian alleged that this meant that Colin MacKenzie "had thought seriously over the years on the problems of Highland over-population".[289] In other words, if the orthodox view now is that the old Highlands were over-populated, then (according to our present experts) that is what leading figures in the Highlands then must have been saying: what they actually said can be ignored.

42. Muckairn, Ardnamurchan, Rannoch

Further indications that there was no land shortage appear continually as one studies Highland history. The Muckairn manuscript related how a branch of the Campbells under Campbell of Calder conquered Muckairn, previously the land of the MacDougalls; but instead of expelling the MacDougalls (especially considering that they had violently resisted the take-over), to make room for supposedly surplus members of the Clan Campbell, they allowed them to stay, and treated them so well that they became part of the larger clan, and accepted Calder as their chief. The same thing happened, for example, at another Campbell conquest, when Ardnamurchan was over-run. Here the hostility between the Campbells and the MacIains, the old possessors of Ardnamurchan, was such that the MacIains were scattered. But the Campbells did not want the now empty lands for themselves, as they would have done had they been suffering from "over-population"; instead, they brought in MacDonalds from Glen Coe, and some Camerons, and a sept of MacKenzies, to occupy the farms.[290]

A similar incident occurred in Rannoch in the fifteenth century, according to the N.S.A. report on Fortingall. There was at that time a clan in Rannoch called the Clann Jain – or Iain – Buidhe (the children of yellow-haired John). "Two pedlars of the Stewarts of Appin went to Perth for goods, and, upon their return home by Rannoch, were robbed or killed by Clann Jain Buidhe. As soon as tidings reached Argyllshire, the Chief of Appin gathered his clan, and marched immediately to Perthshire." Near where the Stewarts rested the first night lived a MacGregor, "one of the MacGregors of Roro Glen Lyon, who, for some fault, was banished that district by the rest of the clan". Stewart, the Appin chief, sent him a message asking for refreshment, and MacGregor made the Appin men the gift of a fat cow; this pleased Stewart so well that he went to see MacGregor, "and proposed that he should accompany him next day, and that, should they be able to extirpate or banish Clann Jain Buidhe from Rannoch, he should have all their lands to himself". So MacGregor went with the Stewarts the following day. The opposing clan were defeated, and then either slain or put to flight. True to his word, Stewart handed over their land to MacGregor.[291] If the Appin Stewarts had indeed been overcrowded, as we are told the Highlanders were, such a generous offer would have been unthinkable. The Stewarts would have wanted the extra land for themselves.

As we shall see later, there was so much pasture in the Highlands that before the middle of the eighteenth century (and even later than that) the drovers taking their herds south to the Lowland markets were not charged for grazing. This is hardly consistent with the view that the Highlands were over-populated.

43. Tillage and potatoes

The Highlanders were, as will be shown in the next chapter, an active and hardy, a resourceful and ingenious people. If the population was "too large for the glens to support", it seems incredible that people of this character should not have taken steps to remedy the position. The solution to a food shortage would have been obvious. For the amount of Highland land that was actually tilled in the middle of the eighteenth century was an insignificantly small proportion of the total land surface. Some of the Highlands, of course, could hardly ever be turned to food production: neither crops nor animals would thrive on the summit of Ben Nevis. But there were vast areas of moor, and bog, and high glen, which could be reclaimed for tillage – or, failing that, for pasture – by the patient hand-labour which the Highlanders were prepared to bestow on the sacred soil of their native land. The proof of this is that towards the end of the eighteenth century, and later, very large areas of this waste land were in fact reclaimed by the Highlanders, working without encouragement and without capital. It was often remarked in the eighteenth and nineteenth centuries that this available land in the Highlands could be regenerated with much less arduous toil than the densely forested wilderness of Canada demanded.

Yet we are asked to believe that with all this reclaimable land on their doorsteps, these active and ingenious clansfolk allowed themselves, and their children, to sink into a starvation diet.

All this evidence shows that the Highlanders under the clan system had sufficient food, whereas food shortages began to be felt when the improvements were progressively denying the clansfolk their immemorial way of living off the proceeds of hunting and herding. There are other indications which point in the same way. Some surprise has been expressed that the potato was not adopted more quickly at an earlier stage in the Highlanders' history. It was known in the Hebrides in the 1680s, according to Martin Martin,[292] and it was grown and eaten by the Irish early in the eighteenth century. But all the evidence indicates that it began to be introduced by the Highlanders generally only in the 1770s, becoming commonly accepted only in the 1780s. One historian wrote that "potatoes were grown in Ireland, and also in England", long before they were taken up in the Highlands, the reason being the Highlanders' "obstinacy", since "Highlanders by temperament and by habit resisted change"[293] – an interesting example of a writer's knowing a fact, but completely failing to realize its significance. The Highlanders, as will be shown at length later, were generally accepted as being sharp-witted and knowledgeable, particularly about their own affairs; and it cannot be doubted that if the Highlanders had been short of food in the days of the clans, then the new near-miraculous crop, which gave much greater supplies of food for the same extent of ground, even poor ground, would have been very quickly embraced. The fact that the Highlanders took a century to take up this new food is yet another piece of evidence showing that they had no need of it in the days of the clans – whereas when the new privations descended on them with the improvements, they did not hesitate to utilize it (even though this sad "obstinacy ... by temperament" of the Highlanders was the same in 1780 and 1800 as it was in 1750).

44. Blackhouses

The mere sight of a Highlander's house, or hut, was enough to send the sophisticated Sassenach traveller into a paroxysm of horror at such a wretched habitation; though they could have found many worse in the poor quarters of the Lowland and English towns, much nearer to where they lived themselves. In reality, the blackhouse had many features which long experience had shown would give protection against the wind and the rain. It was built, said James Shaw Grant in his *Lewis and Harris*, "low and snug, like a sheltering animal. The thatched roof, and even the corners of the stone walls, were rounded, denying a fingerhold to the wind. The black house was streamlined before the word was invented or the concept known." It usually had double walls, the space between being packed with earth. The thatched roof rested on the inner wall, so there was no projection, no eaves, which would allow the wind to get under the roof and lift it off. The rain drained off the thatch into the space between the double walls, "where a blanket of moist earth effectively sealed out the draughts, which otherwise would have blown through the chinks in the drystone walls". Grant said that the thick walls and central fire kept it cosy and snug; it was much harder, he added, to maintain the same warmth in a modern council house.

This method of building, wrote Grant, "provided a broad walk around the house at roof level, facilitating the regular removal and replacing of the fertilising thatch. Steps, after the manner of a stile, were often built into the wall to make the roof walk (or 'tobhta') more accessible. 'In suitable sunny weather', wrote Alexander Carmichael, 'the women of the family take possession of these grassy wall-tops, and sew, spin, or knit, and look about them, while the household dogs sleep beside them in the sun'."[294]

Where the thatch of the roof did overhang the walls, perhaps in times or places where building materials were short (or, in more recent times, were denied to the

Highlanders), it was held down against the wind by putting long ropes across from one side to the other, the ends weighed down with heavy stones.

The crofter's dwelling was called a blackhouse because of the blackening of the rafters by the smoke from the peat fire, which (latterly) had no chimney to let it out. Thomas Garnett claimed in 1811 that the blackhouses he saw were so smoky that it was almost impossible for one not used to them to breathe in them.[295] The modern city dweller, whose air is so heavily tainted with dust, smoke, industrial emissions, and petrol and diesel fumes, may think that mere peat smoke is not so bad as Garnett considered it, especially when the purest of mountain air was available immediately outside the door. Peat, said Grant, "is clean to handle. The smoke is aromatic and inoffensive; indeed, medical men have claimed for it valuable antiseptic properties". The Highlanders claimed that cold and other germs did not easily survive the "peat reek".[296] J. E. Bowman (though he deplored the huts where the Highlanders lived, just as he was honest enough to deplore the huts where the Lowlanders lived) said that "where peat fuel is used", it was "a well ascertained fact, that bugs are never found" – though they re-appeared where fires were made with coal instead of peat.[297]

45. Smoke and filth

There is some evidence that in earlier times, when the Highlanders' food supplies came from hunting and fishing, and from the herds on their wide pastures, more of the smoke was allowed to escape through a hole in the roof; but when they had lost their hunting and fishing rights, and the greater part of their pasture, and therefore most of their farm animals, they were forced to rely mainly on a small patch of arable. Thus the soot-filled thatch which they took off their houses each year (to improve the poor land on to which they had been driven) became so important that the smoke was intentionally kept inside for as long as possible – the more smoke, the more sooty thatch for humus on the land. Grant suggested that "the design of the blackhouse changed: the chimney holes which had previously existed were stopped up to conserve the smoke. The value of soot was rising: not in money terms but as an imperative of existence."[298] In the same way, when the prosperous small farmer had been reduced to living as a penurious crofter, the ordure of his one remaining cow was so important to put heart into the small piece of waste land to which he had been confined, and which had to grow most of his family's food, that even if he had had room to keep it outside (in the same way that his ancestors had, naturally, had to keep all their flocks and herds outside, since there was clearly no room for scores of animals in a Highland hut), the crofter could not have afforded to do it; the ordure, left outside in a rainy climate, would lose much of its goodness, while if kept inside the house, it conserved the fertility so necessary to provide next season's harvest.²⁹⁹ Grant said that "in the old blackhouse, the manure, on which the crops depended, was kept indoors: protected from the leaching rain. Not because people were indifferent to dirt or smells, but because they knew the price of survival."³⁰⁰

The landlords who had deprived the Highlanders of their land, and thus forced them to conserve even the smoke from their fires, and the manure from the few remaining animals, were naturally not at all apologetic. Nor did they have to be: the proprietors and their allies had the education and the leisure (and of course the incentive) to write innumerable documents defending the clearances – which documents are still used as unimpeachable sources by orthodox historians. In fact they seized the chance to castigate the Highlanders for the living conditions that the landlords' clearances had imposed upon the crofters. Sir George MacKenzie of Coul, a clearing landlord, wrote disdainfully in 1808 that "the Highland tenantry are universally ill-accommodated. They live in the midst of smoke and filth; that is their choice."³⁰¹ The landlords first pauperized the Highlanders, and then sneered at them for being paupers. Indeed Coul was here making the unlikely claim that the Highlanders actually preferred being poor. Yet some modern writers, as they dutifully replicate the landlords' propaganda, still cannot understand why Highland landlords came to be unpopular.

46. Lowlanders' habitations

The Highlander who went to work in the Lowlands in the eighteenth or even in the nineteenth century found that the Lowlanders' habitations were very similar to his own. An account of two Lowland villages just south of Perth quotes a description of the local houses there in about 1775. "The cottages were all alike – walls of stone and clay cemented together with chopped straw; roofs thatched with the reeds which grow in great abundance close by at the junction of the Tay and the Earn; the inside divided by box beds into a but and a ben [two rooms], and the hallan, a clay partition at the entrance door to exclude the wind . . . The fireplace was at one end of the cottage, and consisted of some neat stones placed near the wall that the smoke might escape through the lum or hole in the roof . . . In one corner stood a cow . . . in the other sat a hen with a brood of five chickens nestling under her . . ."³⁰² So these cottages had stone and clay walls, thatched roofs, and holes in the roof for the smoke to escape; and they sheltered animals as well as humans, just like the Highland blackhouses had to do after the clearances.

But though the Lowland house or hut was very similar to its counterpart in the Highlands, there was the very great added Lowland disadvantage that in the towns thousands of these huts were crowded together. The absence of modern sanitation was comparatively unimportant in the Highlands, where the huts were isolated or in small groups, and where a small amount of human waste helped the fertility of the soil, and contributed to a rational eco-system: but in the crowded towns, where there was no space to grow anything, and where many thousands of people had to live cheek-by-jowl, the lack of proper mains sewerage meant an extremely unpleasant environment, plus typhus and cholera.

CHAPTER FIVE NOTES

1. *Staff of life*
[1] That the old Highlanders were merely subsistence farmers is a central plank of orthodox theory: "The Highland economy was based largely on subsistence farming", said *The Scotsman* on 8th February 2005. The contemporary evidence shows how far from the truth this is. Professor Williams, in volume eleven of the *Oxford History of England*, i.e. *The Whig Supremacy* 1949, 243, said the Highlanders whom Prince Charles met in 1745-6 were "mostly poor fishermen and crofters [!] on the edge of starvation".
[2] In fact Dr J. Hunter made the position clear when he wrote that "it was only under the impact of capitalism and the associated imposition of a commercialized agricultural structure that a peasantry in the usual sense of the word was created from the lower strata of traditional society" (quoted Richards 1985, 148).
[3] Smout 1970, 541.
[4] Richards 1985, 127, 128, 129, 133, 132.
[5] Pryde 1962, 156 fn.
[6] Gray 1957 (1), 4, 24, 31, 25.
[7] Gray 1957 (2), 32 fn.
[8] Smout 1970, 349. On p. 270 Smout said that when potatoes were introduced to the Highlands, they "tended to displace the older staple" – oatmeal, in his view.
[9] Smout 1970, 347-50.
[10] Jean Dunlop, *Clan MacKenzie*, Johnston & Bacon, (1953) 1987, 11.
[11] Mitchison 1971, 376.
[12] Lister 1978, 19. This author was not the only one to think that since most people in the modern world are employees, working for employers, it must have been the same during the clan system: Janet Glover said that one advantage which the chiefs obtained from the clearances was "the reduction in wage bills" (Glover 1966, 225); in fact, of course, a chief who cleared usually had greater wage bills – now that he had a large income in rent to replace the previous small clan tribute he could afford to set himself up as a country gentleman with a rural mansion, staffed by numerous servants – so he had a bigger wage bill, not a smaller one. This is an extraordinary example of a historian taking a present-day circumstance, and locating it in the past.
[13] Scarlett 1975, 26.
[14] Steel 1994, 243, 60. Steel roundly denounced what he called the bards' "invention" of "often mythical history"; assertions which unavoidably recall the adage about people in glass houses.
[15] Muir 1985, 161.
[16] Lister 1978, 20.

2. *"Monocultural famine"*
[17] Hill 1972, 46.
[18] Banks 1977, 67.
[19] F. McKichan, *The Highland Clearances* (1977), Longman, Harlow, 1987, 7. McKichan cited five "books written after the clearances" (p. 91): the five authors were Prebble, Richards, Gray, Youngson, and Donaldson – a carefully balanced selection, including one writer who attacked the clearances (though in somewhat scattergun fashion), and four times as many writers who defended (or ignored) them.
[20] MacLeod 1997, 102. MacLeod did add (to do him justice) that the Highlanders also had milk, cream, and cheese, and kept poultry; however, he asserted that grain was "the staple fare of the people".
[21] Pryde 1962, 151.

[22] Prebble 1971, 21.
[23] Donnachie & Hewitt 1989, 44.
[24] Grant & Cheape 2000, 153.
[25] Richards 1982, 85. Richards had just quoted Eric Cregeen's remarks on the "exquisite and highly elaborate music and poetry" which were "vigorously alive" among the ordinary people, and since Richards affirmed that the Highlanders were often half-starving, he felt he had to explain these accomplishments away. "Privation may have caused them to sing the better", he said (p. 85), an observation which scarcely indicates a sufficiently serious frame of mind.
[26] Herman 2002, 350. It was *The Times*, 13th February 2006, which described it as a "fascinating book"; there is no fascination in inaccuracy.
[27] Rixson 2004, 18.

3. *Explaining the emigrations*
[28] Lister 1978, 5.
[29] MacLeod 1997, 184.
[30] Donnachie & Hewitt 1989, 43-4.
[31] Grant & Cheape 2000, 164.
[32] Steel 1994, 256.
[33] Richards 2005, 37. Professor Richards reproached Alexander MacKenzie for having said "without the benefit of evidence" (Richards 2005, 24) that the Strath Conon people, before the evictions, were in "comfortable circumstances"; a dozen pages later, in the same book, Richards told us the old Highlanders' "crops were likely to fail every third year on the average", similarly "without the benefit of evidence" – no reference was given. But perhaps this point is hardly worth making. During the clearance era almost every landlord, or member of a landlord's family, or factor, or sheep farmer, or professional working for a landlord, who could find pen and ink, must have made similar allegations about failing harvests in their eagerness to justify the expulsion of the small tenants. Indeed, Patrick Sellar repeatedly said something very much of this kind, and who could doubt Patrick Sellar? Professor Richards' comment appears to be a curious conflation of two desirable thoughts: surely crops were either "likely to fail every third year", or they did "fail every third year on the average"? This kind of comment is particularly useful to those who wish to exonerate the landlords, since it ignores the fact that the old Highlanders lived mostly by hunting, and then by herding; their crops, failing or not, were comparatively insignificant.
[34] Herman 2002, 350. One should add that Michael Fry (Fry 2005, 135) alleged that the "Highland population" suffered a "rapid rise" between 1755 and 1801, from 337,000 to 382,000 (though elsewhere, as we have seen, he gave different figures). "The old social structure could not hold such numbers . . . a breaking point had to come." The figures that Mr Fry gives here, if they were correct, would show that the "old social structure" had to deal with an extra two and three-quarter people in each square mile: or an extra eleven people in every four square miles. No wonder such an enormous increase in the population made the "old social structure" reach "breaking point" (or, presumably, such must be the reaction of the respectful reader who makes the effort to accept what the politically correct commentators assert).

4. *Hunting, shooting, and fishing*
[35] Smollett 1967, 276-7.
[36] MacLean 1988, 226, quoting de Johnstone.
[37] Defoe 1974, 411.
[38] Gray 1957 (1), 24.
[39] Grant & Cheape 2000, 153.
[40] Ross 1998, 210.
[41] Mitchison 1971, 376.

[42] Smout 1970, 349.
[43] Prebble 1971, 70.
[44] Rixson 2004, 21, quoting Jorevin de Rochefort, it seems in 1671 (see J. Hughes, Learning to Smoke, University of Chicago Press 2003, 50).
[45] Richards 1985, 16, quoting Adam Smith.
[46] Defoe 1974, 408.
[47] Colonsay, and Islay, had so many rabbits that in 1764 they were exporting rabbit skins to Glasgow – see Walker 1980, 100 & 125. Hares are mentioned passim, e.g. Burt 2005, 132, "the hares, with which, as I said before, the country [the Highlands] abounds"; & see Burt 205, 66, 75. As for the wild animals, birds, and fish, of the Highlands generally, the reader should look at the 162 Highland parish reports in the O.S.A. and the N.S.A., where he will find regular accounts of the teeming local wild life. At one time I began collating all these reports of the superabundant Highland wild life, but gave up – there was too much material. But they are all there in the O.S.A. and N.S.A. reports on the Highland parishes, for anyone who wishes to consult the contemporary evidence, rather than the standard narrative.
[48] Sir Arthur Conan Doyle, *Sherlock Holmes Complete Novels*, Chancellor, London, (1987) 1988, 225.
[49] This sour remark recalls my own experience working as a farm labourer in 1949. (I can't be sure that the particular field I am thinking of was exactly five acres; but it seemed like it.)
[5] Mitchell, 1971, I 12.

5. *Nutting, fiddling, dancing*
[51] N.S.A. X 486, Kenmore Perth.
[52] Ray 1747, 172.
[53] Burt 2005, 177.
[54] O.S.A. XI 578, Callander Perth.
[55] O.S.A. XII 451-2, Kirkmichael Banff.
[56] Pennant 2000, 84. In *The Times 2*, 21st November 2012, pages 2-3, there was an article claiming that "xylitol, a natural type of sugar alternative that comes from birch trees", had an "almost incredible effect . . . preventing and reversing tooth decay". Are the moderns re-discovering something that the Highlanders knew centuries ago?
[57] O.S.A. XII 453 fn, Kirkmichael Banff.
[58] Scott 1925, 49.
[59] Buchanan 1997, 10.
[60] O.S.A. X 543, Campbeltown Arg.

6. *Private enjoyment*
[61] It may be necessary to remind readers that when the Highlands passed into private ownership, the autumn was pre-eminently the season for the gentry to go shooting and fishing. King George was here presumably talking of wealthy Englishmen (or Lowlanders), who would in those days usually go to Highland moors or deer forests (their own or others') in the autumn, but who would normally return to their English (or Lowland) paternal acres for Christmas and the New Year.
[62] Grant 1987, 139.
[63] Innes 1872, 158. Elsewhere I have quoted Adam Smith (*Wealth of Nations*, Book V, Chapter 1, Part II): "Civil government, so far as it is instituted for the security of property, is in reality instituted for the defence of the rich against the poor, or of those who have some property against those who have none at all."

7. *Delight and pleasure*
[64] Quoted W. Mackay, *Urquhart & Glenmoriston*, Northern Counties, Inverness, 1893, 438.
[65] Grant 1980, 7 fn –
Breac a linne, slat a coille

Is feadh a fireach
Meirle anns nach do ghabh
Gaidheal riamh nàire.

Grant translates this as "a Highlander has a right to take a stag from the hill or a salmon from the pool", and Hunter (Hunter 2000, 218) as "all Highlanders have a right to a deer from the hill, a tree from the wood and a fish from the river". It could also be more literally translated as "a trout from the lake, a stick from the wood, and a deer from the moor, a Gael has the right to take". Generally, the meaning is clear.

[66] Website sundown.pair.com.
[67] Barrow 2003, 336.
[68] Website rampantscotland.com (for one version).
[69] A. Smith, *A Summer in Skye*, Sampson Low, London, (1865) 1912, 370.
[70] Smout 1970, 46, quoting John Major in 1521.
[71] Rixson 2004, 18, quoting Peter Swave in 1835.
[72] Rixson 2004, 315, quoting John Elder in the 1540s; grayhen in Scots dialect is the female black grouse – *Concise Scots Dictionary*, 1991, 245.
[73] Smout 1970, 46, quoting Bishop Leslie in 1578.
[74] Buchanan 1827, I 40.
[75] Seton Gordon 1949, 382, quoting J. Taylor, *The Penniless Pilgrimage*, 1618.
[76] Richards 1973, 222.
[77] Rixson 2004, 229, quoting the Wardlaw Manuscript, 1655.
[78] Rixson 2004, 337, quoting Franck 1694.
[79] Rixson 2004, 21, quoting J. de Rochefort, 1661.
[80] Blundell 1917, 173.
[81] Blundell 1917, 123.
[82] Prebble 1970, 100.

8. *No bread*
[83] Burt 2005, 271.
[84] Defoe 1974, 411.
[85] Defoe 1974, 409.
[86] Defoe 1974, 417.
[87] Buchanan 1997, 10.
[88] Defoe 1974, 418.
[89] Defoe 1974, 414.

9. *Doe from the glen*
[90] Website lyricsmania.com.
[91] Youngson 1973, 23, quoting Duncan Forbes.
[92] Anon. 1747, 20.
[93] Ray 1747, 175.
[94] Walker 1980, 35.
[95] Walker 1980, 65.
[96] Walker 1980, 115.
[97] Walker 1980, 196.
[98] Rixson 2004, 160-1, quoting V. Wills, *Reports on Annexed Estates*, 100.
[99] Smollett 1967, 276-7, 290.
[100] Adam Smith 1895, 118.

10. *Parcel of rogues*

[101] Barrow 2003, 336, quoting J. MacPherson.
[102] *Genesis*, ch. 4 v. 2.
[103] Johnson & Boswell 1930, 55-6, 48-9, 72.
[104] Pennant 1998, 272.
[105] Walker 1980, 100.
[106] O.S.A. XII 434, Kirkmichael Banff.
[107] MacLeod 1892, 181.
[108] Thomson 1788, 215, & Thomson 2010, 62, quoting Cunningham 1787.
[109] Thomson 2010, 64.
[110] Buchanan 1997, 21 (Buchanan's quotation from Thomson actually said "the Highlands were better fed, and, in general, finer men", and I have assumed "Highlands" to be a misprint for "Highlanders").
[111] Buchanan 1997, 9.
[112] Henderson 1812, 110. The remark about ducks appears to refer mainly to the south-east of Sutherland, but the "common poultry" seem to have been present across the county.
[113] Burns 1839, III 176.

11. *Trifling provision*
[114] O.S.A. XII 428, Kirkmichael Banff.
[115] O.S.A. X 543, Campbeltown Arg.
[116] O.S.A. III 505, Kincardine Ross.
[117] O.S.A. III 360, Glenorchy Arg.
[118] O.S.A. III 410, Kildonan Suth.
[119] Prebble 1986, 86, quoting Ailean Dall MacDougall.
[120] James Buchan, *Capital of the Mind*, John Murray, Edinburgh, 2003, 153, quoting A. Ferguson.
[121] Sage 1975, 97.
[122] Selkirk 2010, 6.
[123] Brown 1806, 57.
[124] Adam 1972, I 17, quoting Meredith 1810.
[125] Grant 1811, 27 (quoted in Stewart 1822, I 107).
[126] Youngson 1973, 69, quoting Sir John Sinclair.
[127] R. Southey, *Journal of a Tour in Scotland 1819*, Murray, London, 1929, 137.
[128] Stewart 1822, I 87.
[129] Stewart 1822, I 76.
[130] Stewart 1822, I 70.
[131] Scott, *Redgauntlet*, Collins, London, (1824) n.d., 143 (chapter eleven).

12. *Animal food*
[132] Skene 1837, I 238.
[133] O.S.A. XVII 437, Mortlach Banff.
[134] N.S.A. XIV 240, Contin Ross.
[135] N.S.A. X 569, Blair Atholl Perth.
[136] N.S.A. X 557, Fortingall Perth.
[137] Hunter 2006, 116, quoting Rev. H. MacKenzie.
[138] N.S.A. XIV 225, Portree Inv.
[139] MacCulloch 1905, 221 fn.
[140] Hunter 1999, 224-5.
[141] Mitchell 1971, II 82.
[142] Napier 1884, I 339, qu. 6085, Donald MacLean.
[143] Buchan 1938, 158. Buchan became Conservative M.P. for the Scottish Universities in 1927. On this topic, it is interesting that the widespread idea that starchy foods, such as potatoes and grains, form the

healthiest diet is now being rejected by some experts, who claim that a much better regime is "eggs, red meat, butter, and cheese" (*The Times*, 1st February 2012) – in other words, very much what the old Highlanders ate for centuries. And in the same paper (*Times 2*, page 2) on 16th May 2012, there was an article on a Danish restaurant where only what might be called hunter-herdsman food was supplied – that is, meat, eggs, fish, vegetables, nuts, berries, and native fruit. There is no sugar, alcohol, processed foods, potatoes or grains. The restaurant's slogan is "bread is suicide". I do not know enough to have an opinion as to which view is right.

13. *Ten witnesses*
[144] Dr Johnson has already been quoted to the effect that it is easier to go along with what others have written than to do any original research, Boswell 1928, I 467.

14. *Matter of surprise*
[145] Grant & Cheape 2000, 235.
[146] O.S.A. III 172, Lochgoilhead Arg.
[147] Walker 1980, 45.
[148] Walker 1980, 69.
[149] Walker 1980, 161.
[150] Walker 1980, 188-9.
[151] Walker 1980, 8.
[152] Martin 1703, 55.
[153] Lang 1898, 34.
[154] Johnson & Boswell 1930, 113. Later we shall see that Janet Glover (Glover 1960, 223) knew that potatoes were introduced in the Highlands much later than elsewhere; but was happy to put the delay down to the "fact" that the "Highlanders by temperament and by habit resisted change".
[155] Henderson 1812, 109.
[156] Stewart 1822, II xii fn.

15. *Pig-meat*
[157] O.S.A. I 265, Kiltearn Ross; O.S.A. VI 177, Ardchattan Arg.

16. *Belted plaid*
[158] Stewart 1822, I 78 fn.; Stewart 1822, I 77-9. William Gilpin 1789, II 136-7, said that "the plaid" was "three yards in length and half that measure in breadth", which were rather smaller dimensions than those indicated by Stewart (four yards by two yards).

17. *Trews and arisaid*
[159] Adam/Innes 1965, 357.
[160] Martin 1703, 208-9.
[161] Stewart 1822, I 91.
[162] Martin 1703, 208. The minister of Morvern, N.S.A. VII 176, said "the top of the heather was used for dyeing green; the bark of the alder and root of the bramble and water-lily, for black; crotal, or a spongy substance growing on rocks and trees, for brown, etc."

18. *Highland dress forbidden*
[163] Stewart 1822, I 115-16.
[164] Stewart 1822, I 118-19.
[165] Smollett 1967, 276, 278.
[166] Johnson & Boswell 1930, 45. Hugh Trevor-Roper said: "In the whole of their tour, Johnson recorded, they had never seen the tartan worn." Trevor-Roper, being of the ipse dixit school, accepted

the claim at face value: if Johnson said that (p. 45), if his words were sanctified in an actual document, there was no need to investigate to find out if it was true (this being, of course, a much easier way of writing history). So Trevor-Roper did not point out that Johnson and Boswell had certainly seen "tartan worn" by Allan MacDonald, who was wearing the complete Highland costume when they met him (279); or that Malcolm MacLeod was also wearing tartan when they saw him (264); or that the travellers had found that "the filibeg, or lower garment [which is made of tartan cloth], is still very common, and the bonnet almost universal" (46); or that the "usual" dress of a "Sky-boy" was "a dirty kilt" (305). Trevor-Roper wished to allege that "by 1780 the Highland dress seemed extinct, and no rational man would have speculated on its revival" (Hobsbawm & Ranger 2008, 24), so this evidence that "Highland dress" was regularly worn in 1773 was ignored. Thus is history written.

[167] Johnson & Boswell 1930. Why some of Johnson's words were directly contradicted by other statements he made is hard to explain. Perhaps he wanted to extol the triumphant Lowland/English triumph over the Highlands, and yet felt unable to conceal the things that he had personally seen, despite the fact that some assertions he made plainly belied other comments.

[168] Gilpin 1789, II 136-7.

[169] Grant & Cheape 2000, 207.

[170] O.S.A. III 190, Lochgoilhead Arg.

[171] Grant & Cheape 2000, 255.

19. *Necessary to connive*

[172] Stewart 1822, II 411.

[173] There were several successive MacDonald chieftains of Barrisdale. The first was Archibald, "old Barrisdale", younger brother of Alexander, the chief of Glengarry who fought at Killiecrankie. His son was Coll Ban, 2nd of Barrisdale, "young Barrisdale", a Jacobite who died imprisoned in Edinburgh Castle in 1750. His son Archibald, 3rd of Barrisdale, who was a rebel, and subsequently an army officer and an improver, died in 1787. His son was Coll, 4th of Barrisdale, sheep farmer, who was still active in 1817. His son was Archibald, 5th and last of Barrisdale.

[174] (Hunter 1999, 201.)

[175] Trevor-Roper in Hobsbawm & Ranger 1983, 24.

20. *Origin of the filibeg*

[176] Pine 1972, 60; the authority was J. G. Mackay in *Romantic Story of the Highland Garb*, 1924. p. 207 or 209. According to Pine (p. 61), John MacCullough also claimed, in 1824, that "an Englishman named Rawlinson" invented the filibeg, but MacCullough's "Rawlinson" was a lead miner in Perthshire – not quite the same thing as an Argyllshire ironmaster.

[177] Trevor-Roper in Hobsbawm & Ranger 1983, 15.

[178] Sarah Fraser, *The Last Highlander*, HarperPress, London, 2012, 252, 316-17.

[179] Dunbar 1977, 33. I have not seen much in the way of precise identification of this inventive ironmaster Rawlinson. There was a Thomas Hutton Rawlinson, a Quaker eighteenth-century ironmaster at Cator in Lancashire, who devoted most of his energies to the highly remunerative occupation of slave-trading; but he was born in 1712, so would have been only a teenager when this supposed discovery came about. According to Alistair Moffat, indeed (Moffat 2010, 123), the ironmaster's name was Thomas Rowlandson, and he came from Barrow in Lancashire.

[180] Burke 1990, 204.

21. *Ancient Highland dress*

[181] *The Times*, 27th Jan 2008.

[182] *The Guardian*, 19th April 2008.

[183] *Scotland on Sunday*, 25th May 2008.

[184] It is sometimes hard to deduce a person's opinions from what he has written: for example, Sir Walter Scott. In *A Legend of Montrose*, published in 1819, which is set in the civil wars of the 1640s, one of his characters considered "plaids, and dirks, and kilts" to be representative of the old Highlanders (Scott 1925, 68). Yet, writing in the *Quarterly Review* in 1816, Scott accepted the story of Rawlinson's invention (*Miscellaneous Prose Works*, Baudry, Paris, 1838, *The Culloden Papers*, VII 89-90). Edmund Burt, writing in about 1726, described the "common habit of the ordinary Highlanders", in which the part of the plaid worn below the waist was described as a "short petticoat" (Burt 2005, 232, 234). He added "this dress is called the quelt" (Burt 2005, 232). It is possible that Burt, an outsider, was in fact describing a filibeg. The dates given for Parkinson's alleged contribution differ considerably. Trevor-Roper said that the interloper Rawlinson inaugurated his ironworks at Invergarry in 1727, and wound it up in 1734 (Hobsbawm & Ranger 2008, 21). Evan Baillie said Rawlinson had his brainwave about 1718 (in 1768 he thought it was "about fifty years ago") – that is, some nine years before he started his iron foundry (and therefore the same period of time before he had any interest in Highland dress); Sir John Sinclair said it was about 1770 (writing in 1830, he put the invention "about sixty years ago" – Dunbar 1977, 34), that is to say, some thirty-six years after Rawlinson left the Highlands; and (as we saw) *The Times* said it was in the 1780s, *The Guardian* in the early 1800s, and *The Scotsman* in the 19th century. Burt (Burt 2005, 112) printed a letter supposedly written by one Donald MacPherson, who had emigrated to Maryland; it was written in English, in the dialect of the eastern Highlands. In it Donald asks his father to send "as muckle cloths" as would make a "Quelt". This is defined in John Jamieson's Etymological Dictionary of the Scots Language (Vol. I, Gardener, Paisley, 1879) as "A sort of petticoat worn in the Highlands. V. Kilt". If "quelt" is an early spelling of "kilt", it would mean that the kilt was known in the eastern Highlands, near Inverness, at the same time as it was supposedly being invented many miles away in Glengarry. It is highly unlikely that the knowledge of any new invention would have travelled so many miles across the Highlands so quickly.

[185] Sir William Brereton wrote of a journey to Leith in 1635: "Many Highlanders we observed in this town in their plaids, many without doublets [close-fitting upper garments], and those who have doublets have a kind of loose flap garment hanging loose about their breech [the lower back, or buttocks], their knees bare" (Hume Brown, 142). Thomas Kirk went to Scotland in 1677: "Here we may note the habit of a Highlander: their doublets slashed in the sleeves, and open on the back; their breeches and stockings are either all on a piece, and straight to them [close to the body], plaid colour [this must be trews]; or otherwise a sort of breeches, not unlike a petticoat, that reaches not so low, by far, as their knees, and their stockings are rolled up about the calves of their legs, and tied with a garter, their knee and thigh being naked" (*Tours in Scotland 1677 and 1681*, ed. P. Hume Brown, Douglas, Edinburgh, 1892, 28.) If this garment "not unlike a petticoat" was merely part of the all-enveloping plaid, then Kirk (it will be observed) would not have been able to see that the Highlander's doublet was "open on the back". Both these authors could be taken to be describing the filibeg, or at least the feal-dag (with pleats having to be formed by the wearer each time he put it on).

[186] Smollett 1967, 278.
[187] Stewart 1822, I 118 fn.
[188] Stewart 1822, II xxiv.

22. *From the beginning*
[189] Williams 1949, 110, 109.
[190] Bain 1960, 320.
[191] O.S.A. III 190, 164, Lochgoilhead Arg.

23. *Begged his bread*
[192] Wordsworth, *Glen Almain, or the Narrow Glen*.
[193] Wordsworth 1894, 156, and see 159.
[194] Coleridge "wrote in 1793 two poems in imitation of Ossian", *D.N.B.*, pre-Oxford.

[195] Burns 1839, I 2, 80, 84, & II 14; Burns spoke of e.g. Ossian's *Fingal, Cath-Loda, & Caric-thura*.
[196] Byron 1863, 318, 371, 385.
[197] John Wesley, Journal, 15th May 1784.
[198] Dr. John Smith: O.S.A. X 517 fn, Campbeltown Arg. The Rev. William MacKenzie, minister of Assynt, also referred to *Temora*, O.S.A. XVI 163 fn. A number of other ministers accepted Ossian, e.g. O.S.A. XII 449 fn, Kirkmichael Banff.
[199] Burke 1990, 204.

24. *Forfeited lands going cheap*
[200] Burke 1990, 178.
[201] Ditto, 179.
[202] Ditto, 155.
[203] Ditto, 157.
[204] Ditto, 157.
[205] Ditto, 204.
[206] Ditto, 157.
[207] Ditto, 195.
[208] Ditto, 178.
[209] Donnachie & Hewitt 1989, 43.
[210] N.S.A. XIII 124, Duthil Moray.

25. *Died in the scuffle*
[211] Burke 1990, 183.
[212] Burke 1990, 183.
[213] See Kyd 1952, 62; O.S.A. III 505, & N.S.A. XIV 403, both Kincardine Ross.
[214] Burke 1990, 27. See J. Hunter, *Skye the Island*, Mainstream, Edinburgh, 1986, 128.
[215] Burke 1990, 227. It was hers, not "his": see Walford's *County Families of the U.K.*, 1881, article "Lady Matheson of Achany, Sutherlandshire and of the Lews, Ross-shire".
[216] Hunter 2000, 239.

26. *Highland townships*
[217] Geddes 1955, 7-8, 172.
[218] O.S.A. VIII 97 fn, Kilmartin Arg.

27. *Leisurely work*
[219] Wordsworth 1894, 92.
[220] Wordsworth 1894, 90, 91.
[221] MacKenzie 1810, 134, 148.
[222] O.S.A. XX 25, Boleskine Inv.
[223] N.S.A. XIII 136, Inveravon Banff.
[224] Dr M. Bangor-Jones, *Agricultural History Review*, volume fifty, part 2, 2002, 182.

28. *Scarcely a murmur*
[225] Skene 1890, III 380-1, 393.
[226] N.S.A. XIV 164, North Uist Inv.

29. *Shielings*
[227] Napier 1884, V 469-70, 472, Alexander Carmichael.

[228] O.S.A. VI 251, Kintail Ross. A poem by Duncan Ban showed how Highlanders kept sheep not only for their mutton and wool, but for their milk, and the cheese, curds and whey derived from it: *Gaelic Society of Inverness* XXXVIII 238.
[229] O.S.A. XX 25, Boleskine Inv.

30. *Free from care*
[230] Devine 1998, 60.
[231] Burns wrote in *My Ain Kind Dearie O*, "When o'er the hill the eastern star/ Tells bughtin-time is near, my joe", and the Aldine Edition of Burns defines "bughtin-time" as "the time of collecting the sheep in the pens to be milked". Neither "baughting" (Clark's word) nor "bughtin" (Burns') is in the *Concise Scots Dictionary*, 1991, but it does have "buchting" or "bouchting", which it defines as collecting ewes into a fold to be milked.
[232] N.S.A. VII 346, Kilninian Arg.
[233] Robertson 1808, 198-9.
[234] Geddes 1955, 62-3.
[235] Geddes 1955, 83.
[236] Napier 1884, V 472, Alexander Carmichael.
[237] MacDonald 1994, 143.
[238] Selkirk 2010, 13.
[239] Brown 1806, 107.
[240] N.S.A. V 60, Kilmory Bute.
[241] Geddes 1955, 117.

31. *Little commonwealths*
[242] O.S.A. X 368, Harris Inv.
[243] Geddes 1955, 131, 240.
[244] Napier 1884, V 453, Alexander Carmichael.
[245] Prebble 1971, 22. Prebble's criticism of the Highlanders as a "monoglot minority" is particularly remarkable, since it is often said that the English are perhaps the most pre-eminent of all peoples in their reluctance to learn any language but their own.

32. *Mutual help*
[246] Skene 1890, III 393.
[247] Blackie 1885, 9.

33. *Unity of labour*
[248] Henry Ford, *My Life and Work*, Classic House, New York, (1922) 2009, 61.
[249] Walker 1808, 152.
[250] Stewart 1822, I 206 fn.
[251] Buchanan 1997, 35-6.
[252] O.S.A. III 374, Applecross Ross.
[253] Blackie 1885, 15.

34. *Unity of class*
[254] Selkirk 2010, 12; Selkirk 1806, 41.
[255] Selkirk 2010, 17; Selkirk 1806, 58-9.
[256] O.S.A. VIII 18, Dornoch Suth.

35. *Standards of living: comparisons*
[257] Pryde 1962, 152.

[258] Bowman 1986, 50, 52.

36. *Crowdie for a week*
[259] David Edgar 1850-1945, leadminer 1859-67, coalminer 1867-1923. He told me himself that he began work in the leadmines at the age of nine. Legally, it should have been ten, but the law was often ignored if a boy looked a bit older.
[260] Selkirk 2010, 41.
[261] Selkirk 2010, 17.

37. *John Buchan*
[262] Buchan 1938, 158.
[263] Buchan 2009, 48-50.
[264] Macaulay 1907, 587.

38. *Hugh Miller*
[265] Miller 1854, 301-2.

39. *Experienced no want*
[266] Burt 2005, 68.
[267] Finlay 1976, 24.
[268] Burt 2005, introduction, xxxvi.
[269] O.S.A. VIII 443, Kilmallie Inv.
[270] O.S.A. XX 23, Boleskine Inv.
[271] O.S.A. XIX 22, Halkirk Caith.
[272] O.S.A. XI 136, Kilmore Arg.
[273] O.S.A. XIV 236, Kilfinan Arg.
[274] O.S.A. VI 289, Eddrachillis Suth.
[275] O.S.A. XII 468, Kirkmichael Banff.
[276] Stewart 1822, I 210 fn.
[277] Selkirk 2010, 14.
[278] Miller 1912?, 301; O.S.A. XIII 307-11, North Uist Inv.
[279] J. Hicks, *Wanderings by the Lochs & Streams of the Highlands*, Blackwood, London, 1855, 188.

40. *Ease of subsistence*
[280] Selkirk 2010, 6; Selkirk 1805, 288.
[281] Brown 1806, 57.
[282] MacLeod 1910, 144-5.

41. *All conveniency*
[283] N.S.A. VII 511, Ardchattan & Muckairn Arg.
[284] Lang 1898, 9; Sutherland 15-16, Munros 23, Long Island 44, Knoydart 67-8, north of Loch Ness 113, Aird 115, Jura Islay etc. 134, Lorn 134, Morvern 70.
[285] Lang 1898, 102.
[286] Lang 1898, xi.
[287] Selkirk 2010, e.g. 9, 11, 27; Selkirk 1806, e.g. 28, 37, 93.
[288] Adam 1972, II 70.
[289] Adam 1972, I xxxv.

42. *Muckairn, Ardnamurchan, Rannoch*
[290] N.S.A. VIII 513-14, Ardchattan Arg.

THE LIFE OF THE HIGHLANDERS

[291] N.S.A. X 546-7, Fortingall Perth.

43. *Tillage and potatoes*
[292] Martin 1703, 201.
[293] Glover 1966, 223.

44. *Blackhouses*
[294] Grant 1987, 97-99.
[295] Garnett 1811, I 121.
[296] Grant 1987, 101-2.
[297] Bowman 1986, 61.

45. *Smoke and filth*
[298] Grant 1987, 98.
[299] See chapter one, subsection 17, *Under the same roof*.
[300] Grant 1987, 97.
[301] MacKenzie 1810, 163, 169.

46. *Lowlanders' habitations*
[302] Graham-Campbell 1979, 123, quoting Rev. James Ballingal, *The Rhynd & Elcho*, Douglas, Edinburgh, 1905.

CHAPTER SIX

CHARACTER OF THE HIGHLANDERS

1. A retrospective invention

Some historians take the view that the distinction between Highlanders and Lowlanders in the Scotland of the eighteenth century and earlier has been exaggerated, or even that it did not exist, having been subsequently invented. Hugh Trevor-Roper, elevated to the peerage as Lord Dacre, scouted the whole idea (in words quoted earlier) that there was a separate and different Highland way of life: "the whole concept of a distinctive Highland culture and tradition is a retrospective invention."[1] This may be bound up with Trevor-Roper's attempted defence of the role of the Highland landlords during the Highland clearances: if there was no distinctive Highland way of life, then no one can be blamed for having destroyed it. As we shall see later, Trevor-Roper assured his readers that one aim behind the Sutherland clearances, for example, was "a constructive policy of re-settlement".[2]

However, many travellers in the nineteenth, eighteenth, and earlier, centuries, went to the Highlands and wrote about them precisely because they seemed so different, like the author of the 1818 *Sketch of a Tour in the Highlands*, who thought when he crossed the Highland line (in words quoted above) that he had been transported "as if by magic into some remote foreign region".[3] There are many indications suggesting that there was, before the clearances, "a distinctive Highland culture and tradition", and we shall now examine some of the evidence.

There is no better criterion of a society than the character of the people who live in that society: one assumes that there would be general agreement on that point. A society, for example, which produced people who were honest, just, kind, and happy, would clearly be preferable on almost any score to a society that produced people who were devious, unfair, cruel, and miserable. People suffering from dire poverty and frequent famines, cringing in fear of the will and whim of their masters, could not be expected to develop characteristics of a very praiseworthy kind. An oppressive, harsh, and narrow, society – and that is the authoritative modern view of clan society – would inevitably produce downtrodden, servile, and stunted, people. So what kind of people did the old Highlands produce?

David Stewart thought that "firmness in decision, fertility in resource, ardour in friendship, and a generous enthusiasm, were the natural result" of the Highlanders' form of society and of their geographical location.[4] Some modern authors, on the contrary, take a much gloomier view of the character of the old Highlanders. John Prebble said they were "frequently subservient, scheming or dissimulating".[5] Moreover, they were given to extreme violence. Prebble poured scorn on writers who, he claimed, had failed to recognize this true quality of the Highlanders. In his *Glencoe* Prebble said "David Stewart of Garth . . . and Walter Scott, with their imitators, created a Highlander who was an amalgam of Knight Templar and Paladin".[6] James Scarlett was of the same opinion, saying that in his *Sketches of the Highlanders* Stewart "set out to extol the virtues of the Highlander to the exclusion of any faults".[7] (Strange that no criticism was offered of all those many histories that have presented the clearing Highland landlord as "an amalgam of Knight Templar and Paladin"; and have "set out to extol the virtues" of those same Highland landlords to "the exclusion of any faults".)

2. Fire and sword

This view misrepresents what Stewart wrote, of course. David Stewart, as we see elsewhere, stressed how the Highlander, with an inimical environment, became (like the Lowlander in the same adverse circumstances) all too often merely a coward and a criminal.[8] As for Sir Walter, he did a great deal to reinforce the Lowland-cum-landlord fabrication of the Highlanders as schizophrenic outpatients – unbridled killers and destroyers abroad, and obsequious serfs at home: Genghis Khan and Uriah Heep united in a single persona. In Scott's best-selling poem *The Lady of the Lake* both these mutually exclusive characteristics are crammed together in only six lines of verse. In the poem the "Clan Alpine" gathers:

Till at the rendezvous they stood
By hundreds prompt for blows and blood;
Each trained to arms since life began,
Owning no tie but to his clan,
No oath, but by his chieftain's hand,
No law, but Roderick Dhu's command.[9]

– while the chief's despotic decree to muster the clan was so incontestable that "he who failed to appear, suffered the extremities of fire and sword", as Sir Walter wrote in an excited note to the same poem.[10] (The Rev. James MacKenzie, in his *History of Scotland*, used exactly the same phrases – "He who failed to appear . . . suffered the extremities of fire and sword", though without acknowledging the loan.[11] Perhaps using Walter Scott's words meant that the matter was beyond dispute: or perhaps it was merely an example of the plagiarism which is not unknown in history-writing.)

In that very same note which Scott wrote about "the extremities of fire and sword", he was unlucky enough to give as an example the rapid passage across Breadalbane of the croishtarich in 1745:[12] when, as we know, it was ignored by the Breadalbane clansfolk because they disagreed with their chief. (They had obviously forgotten that any absentees were going to suffer "the extremities of fire and sword"; no doubt that kind of thing easily slips one's mind.) In fact, as we will see in due course, almost every element of Scott's description is incorrect: they were not "prompt for blows and blood", they did not reject every tie but to their clans, they did not regard their chieftain's command as law, and they often "failed to appear", if they thought the quarrel not worth turning out for – and were then reproached for their unreliability and for their disobedience to their masters by the same writers who had already condemned them for their blind obedience to those identical chiefs. Scott himself said (in *A Legend of Montrose*) that the Highlanders could not be "induced to consider themselves as regular soldiers, or to act as such". In the '45, for example (Scott continued), the clansmen could not see how anyone could be penalized "for merely going home when it did not suit him to remain longer with the army" – after a battle they simply went back to the mountains to foster their families and care for their cattle.[13] So Scott simultaneously believed that the clansman always obeyed his chief, and also that he often did not obey his chief. Such are the mental contortions that necessarily follow the attempt to believe the unbelievable fictions invented by those who crafted the politically correct narrative of those years; and which is still accepted and reinforced by orthodox historians.

However, even if Stewart and Scott had created such a plaster saint as John Prebble alleges, the retort frames itself: the Lowland historians, and Prebble, on the contrary, created a Highlander who was a vicious amalgam of murderer, robber, and rapist – and yet who, in some miraculous way, was simultaneously a weak-willed helot who would not say boo to a goose. There cannot be two such opposite characters in one body. The Scottish author Conan Doyle said: "It is a fool's plan to teach a man to be a cur in peace, and think that he will be a lion in war. Fleece them like sheep, and sheep they will remain."[14]

3. War rather than peace

A great deal depends on the sources that a particular writer uses. The sources which Lowland and English writers use when writing the history of the Highlands are (perhaps not surprisingly) overwhelmingly Lowland and English. Even where on the face of it they seem to be of impeccably Highland origin, they are sometimes seen to be suspect on further investigation. "A hundred years ago", wrote Prebble in 1965, "a woodsman of Argyll, John Dewar, spent the last years of his life putting . . . Highland memories to paper"; but, as Prebble also wrote, these memories were "collected . . . for the 8th Duke of Argyll", and were preserved "in the archives of Inveraray Castle".[15] It is not surprising, therefore, that some of Dewar's recollections, as instigated, protected, and no doubt compensated, by the Duke of Argyll, are such as to confirm the duke's highly unfavourable view of the Highland clansfolk. He who recommends and regulates the research is routinely rewarded by its results.

Before the Lowland conquest of the Highlands (and for that matter after it), Lowland propaganda against the Highlanders was unremitting. In the fourteenth century, John of Fordun naturally praised the Lowlanders, such as himself, as being "domesticated and cultured, trustworthy, patient and urbane, decent in their attire, law-abiding and peaceful", not to mention "home-loving, civilized . . . tolerant and polite", while he felt compelled to admit that the Highlanders were "a wild and untamed race, primitive and proud, given to plunder and the easy life".[16] John Major, the most prominent Lowland intellectual of the sixteenth century, made a ferocious onslaught upon the Highlanders, just as the élite of stronger countries have always denounced the weaker neighbours whom they hope to conquer. Major, like other Lowland writers, insisted that there was an entity called "Scotland", whose inhabitants all owed allegiance to the Edinburgh authorities, and that therefore those people living in this "Scotland" who did not obey those authorities were wild and lawless. "One-half of Scotland speaks Irish, and all these as well as the Islanders we reckon to belong to the Wild Scots. In dress, in the manner of their outward life, and in good morals, for example, these come behind the householding Scots [like me]." In fact, thought Major, the Gaelic-speakers were totally despicable. "They live upon others, and follow their own worthless and savage chief in all evil courses sooner than they will pursue an honest industry. They are full of mutual dissensions, and war rather than peace is their normal condition."[17] All clearly impartial conclusions. (Even in the twenty-first century, a commentator writing the usual partisan Lowland-based account of the Highlanders chose to take his title, "Wild Scots", from these comments of the unbiased and objective Major.)[18]

Despite the protestations of Professor Lord Dacre, Sir Robert Rait, Sir Thomas Innes of Learney, and Michael Fry, which we examined earlier, King James VI certainly believed there were two different kinds of people in Scotland – the civilized Lowlanders, and the savage Highlanders. In his *Basilikon Doron*, a thoughtful treatise of government published in 1599, James judiciously divided the Highlanders into two groups: those who were bad enough, in all conscience, and those who were still worse. He wrote: "As for the Highlands, I shortly comprehend them all in two sorts of people: the one, that dwelleth in our mainland that are barbarous, and yet mixed with some show of civility; and the other than dwelleth in the Isles and are all utterly barbarous, without any sort of show of civilities." Concerning the first sort he advised his son to put the laws into execution (an apt word, in connection with James VI's attitude to the Highlanders). "As for the other sort, think no more of them than of wolves or wild beasts, and therefore follow forth the course that I have begun, in planting colonies among them of answerable inlands subjects, that within short time may reform and civilize the best inclined among them, rooting out or transporting the barbarous and stubborn sort, and planting civility in their room."[19] In 1603 this unprejudiced James VI became also James I of England; and in 1616 the Privy Council decided "that the vulgar English tongue be universally planted, and the Irish language, which is one of the chief and principal causes of the continuance of barbarity and incivility among the inhabitants of the Isles and Highlands, may be abolished and removed".[20] In 1695 an Act of Parliament ruled that where a Highland parish had no minister, the stipend should be used to establish schools "for rooting out the Irish language, and other pious uses". Piety could go no further.[21]

Even Highlanders sometimes repeated these calumnies. John MacKay, author of *The Church in the Highlands*, said of the members of the "Highland Host", who were sent to the covenanting south-west of Scotland in 1678, that the king made use of "their propensity for taking what did not belong to them", and called them "professional robbers". It seems that there are people of every nation who are prepared to parrot the opinions of the powerful, even when it means adopting the role of quisling.[22]

4. Murder and pillage

Lowland historians, writing for an English-speaking readership, still follow the enlightened lead of James VI, and routinely accuse the Highlanders of shameless violence and lawlessness. Professor Rosalind Mitchison in 1970 said clan society was "grouped under its chiefs for cattle-raiding and war".[23] In 1982 P. and F. Somerset Fry said that Glasgow University was founded in 1450 "on the edge of the Highlands [in fact about seventeen miles away] . . . and it offered education to people of the clans who might care to learn rather than fight or steal cattle".[24] (Did the university send a mailshot out to the clansfolk offering this prized education? It would presumably have had to be in English, a language unknown in the Highlands. Or did the university recruit Gaelic-speaking professors? – a rare breed in 1450: or now, for that matter. Otherwise, it would be like offering a university education to English people – the tuition being exclusively in Estonian. This information is either too much or too little.) Janet Glover, writing in 1960, said "the chieftains maintained interminable vendettas against each other, in the interests of which they called out their clans for prolonged and bloody wars. Organized cattle-raiding and wife-stealing were accompanied by murder, betrayal and cruelty."[25] Tom Steel, writing in 1984, found himself in close agreement with the 1960 author, even in phraseology: he said "the chiefs frequently called upon their followers to fight vendettas. Often these were prolonged and bloody wars. They were frequently the consequence of the theft of wives or cattle; and murder and pillage were commonplace." Steel went on to allege that "most Highlanders made a living by hunting, stealing and fighting"; a little later in his book he seems to have become worried that the reference to hunting might have been letting the Gaels off too lightly (besides which, in another chapter he had asserted that the old Highlanders "had scraped little more than a subsistence living", which appeared to rule out any hunting), so when he returned to the charge he dropped any reference to hunting – "most Highlanders, however, made a living by raiding and protection rackets", while "clan society was only viable through battle and theft, usually at the expense of Lowland Scotland".[26] These anglophone historians offered interesting résumés of the Highland way of life, obviously written by disinterested observers.

When savagery and barbarity, employed in profuse quantities by the Lowlanders and English, actually did come to the Highlands after Culloden, some orthodox historians suddenly became more lenient in their comments; it turned out that slaughter and plunder, oppression and devastation, are not necessarily to be deplored; and the rape and spoliation of the Highlands by the unified Lowland/English state was treated as a highly meritorious matter of "law and order" (reminiscent of Bernard Levin's heroine, "Laura Norder"). Professor Mitchison said "law and order had come into this area [the Highlands] gradually after the '45".[27] Dr I. F. Grant thought the same: after 1745 in the Highlands, "law and order was a phrase which came to be more clearly understood".[28] Professor Smout thought the changes brought "law and order into the hills", accompanied by a "moral reformation";[29] and Professor Donaldson saw the imposition of the anglophone yoke on the Highlands merely as the "growth of law and order".[30] The military subjugation of a neighbouring country has often been justified in this way by the aggressors' publicity machine. The Nazi propaganda offensive in 1938-9 depicted the consecutive German conquests of Austria, the Sudetenland, Czechoslovakia, and Poland, merely as a question of putting down lawless disturbances and establishing proper Teutonic "law and order". To those who know something of history, contemporary events are frequently reminiscent of past times (often unhappily so); while a knowledge of previous episodes often helps in the understanding of current affairs. Such are some of the many consequences of studying history.

5. Violence and bloody murder

Prebble reinforced Lowland perspectives by asserting that "violence and bloody murder are part of the history of the Gael".[31] Professor Mitchison, too, shook her head sadly over the violence of the old Highlands, remarking of the Lord Lovat beheaded in 1746: "his long life of intrigue and violence is a picture of the excesses which clanship could tolerate."[32] It is of course true that independent states (which the clan countries in essence were until 1746) do fight each other, and that wars, sadly, do consist precisely of "violence and bloody murder" (though the carnage is usually described more delicately by politicians and newsmen, at least the part in it played by one's own side). Later we shall examine the unfortunately plentiful "violence and bloody murder" in the Lowlands, including the episode when the great Lowland hero, Robert the Bruce, solved one thorny problem by murdering a rival for the kingship at a peaceful conference before the high altar of a church. Of course the conflicts are not usually called by such opprobrious names for domestic consumption: normally when a state clashes with another state the battles are described (for the benefit of the home populations) as glorious victories or tragic but explicable defeats, each encounter – whether triumphant or the reverse – being the scene of heart-warming heroism on the part of "our boys".

However, if "violence and bloody murder", and the "excesses which clanship could tolerate", are to be scrutinized, perhaps a wider reference would be helpful. When the larger states of modern Europe collided, the "excesses" of "violence and bloody murder" were on a very much greater scale. The author's father (to add yet another personal note), as a private – a volunteer! – in the Durham Light Infantry, was unfortunate enough to be present at the Battle of the Somme, which began with the Allied offensive on 1st July 1916; on 2nd July he received injuries (a German shell burst above him: it killed his friend, who was standing next to him, and peppered his head and shoulder with shrapnel) from which he suffered – always economically, and often physically – for the rest of his days. However, he knew that he was lucky to be alive. On the first day of the battle some *20,000 men* of the British army were killed (or were sacrificed to "violence and bloody murder", if Prebble's phrase is to be preferred): in the whole battle, lasting from July to November, the British lost 420,000 men, the French 194,000, and the Germans 465,000 – a total of 1,079,000 killed, wounded, missing, and prisoners, in one battle.[33] (In the British and French armies alone, 146,431 were recorded as killed or missing.) Shakespeare's Hamlet stood appalled to contemplate "the imminent death of twenty thousand men" in a war[34] – the whole of the war, on both sides; but on the Somme twenty thousand was the roll of the slain on only one day, in only one of the three armies involved in the conflict. It was a striking example of "the excesses" which modern states "could tolerate", to borrow Professor Mitchison's forcible phrases. Any Highlander during the clan days would not only have refused to believe that such a sanguinary slaughter would in due course come about, but he would not have conceded that it was even remotely within the bounds of possibility. Even to imagine such an event, he would have thought, must be beyond the nightmares of the most diseased mind. And yet it happened. 100,000 men of the British army attacked the enemy on the first day of the carnage on the Somme; before nightfall, 57,000 of them were casualties (dead, injured, missing, or prisoners) – that is, nearly twice as many as the entire fighting strength of every clan in the Highlands in 1745 (which was about 32,000, according to Duncan Forbes' *Memorial*).

Though not often achieving the wholesale massacres of the dreadful bloodbath of 1914-18, wars were regular occurrences within the Lowland-English polity. From 1739 to 1815 Britain was fighting an officially declared war three-fifths of the time, in Europe and elsewhere in the world, plus undeclared but frequent imperial hostilities, during the two-fifths of the time when it was formally "at peace";[35] in the nineteenth century, colonial wars were constant; the first half of the twentieth century saw two monstrously destructive world wars, and the second half saw repeated instances of strife – as have the opening years of the twenty-first century. (And, of course, throughout that time there were not infrequent cases of violent crime in the Lowlands and England, as there are today.) It is curious in view of these facts that Prebble did not confess that "violence and bloody murder are part of the history of the Lowlander and the Englishman"; curious that Mitchison did not deplore "the excesses" of modern society. At least the Highlander had the excuse that nearly all of his battles could be traced to the intentionally mischievous intervention of the Lowland and English authorities. But since the Massacre of Glen Coe can be (however erroneously, as we shall see later) ascribed by Lowland propagandists to the "barbarism" of the old clansfolk, the forty Highlanders who were killed in the onslaught are probably better remembered by most of those whose historical knowledge has been conventionally acquired than the 20,000 British soldiers (five hundred times as many) killed on a single day of the Somme offensive – not to mention the many millions of others who were killed in the battles of the two world wars).

Some writers, then, insist on the supposed delinquent traits of the Highlanders, as we have just seen. In some other sources, however, a different picture emerges. What can the dispassionate enquirer now discover about the characteristics of the Highlanders, and about the society that gave rise to such features? (To enable objective comparisons to be made, conditions and events in the Lowlands during the centuries when the clan system was flourishing in the Highlands – conditions and events which are, for some mystifying reason, usually ignored by writers making the routine denunciations of Highland barbarism – will be discussed later.)

6. Report of the Royal Commission

One trusts that one will not be accused of evading the issue if one tries to discover the character of the Highlanders from all the available evidence, rather than exclusively from often hostile foreign (e.g., Lowland or English) sources. If evidence is to be preferred to prejudice, the testimony is almost embarrassingly rich. A start may be made with the report, issued in 1884, of the Royal Commission on the Highlands and Islands – the Napier Commission. This directly compared the people of the Highlands with those of the Lowlands: and the commission cannot be considered as biased in favour of the ordinary Highlanders, since of its six members no fewer than four belonged to the class of landlords who had destroyed the Highlanders' society (two were the direct descendants of evicting Highland chiefs, and in fact had done some evicting themselves), and the fifth was the lawyer son of a clearing landlord. The secretary appointed to the commission was a member of a landlord family which had cleared the land it owned. (The sixth member of the commission, no doubt chosen to provide balance, was a Tory academic.) A Royal Commission composed entirely of crofters or crofters' sons (and enough of the latter had become eminent in the world to make such a structure quite possible) would have been instantly denounced by most historians as hopelessly warped; it is odd that a commission so strongly weighted towards the opposite end of society should so seldom have been criticized on similar grounds.

Despite its composition, the commission was (as we shall see) simply echoing the evidence from a century, two centuries, and three centuries, earlier, when (having seen and listened to hundreds of humble Highlanders) it felt obliged to say: "In no part of Her Majesty's dominions are there to be found, among the humbler ranks of society, more intelligence, better manners, purer morals, than in the remotest parts of the Highlands and Islands, from the Mull of Kintyre" northwards.[36]

"The stock" of crofters, the report goes on, "is exceptionally valuable. By sound physical constitution, native intelligence, and good moral training, it is particularly fitted to recruit the people of our industrial centres, who without such help from wholesome sources in rural districts would degenerate under the influences of bad lodging, unhealthy occupations, and enervating habits. It cannot be indifferent to the whole nation, constituted as the nation now is, to possess within its borders a people, hardy, skilful, intelligent, and prolific, as an ever-flowing fountain of renovating life."[37]

These words are of extraordinary significance, not only in their portrayal of the Highlanders, but in their depiction of "our industrial centres". For well over a century Highland landlords had been urgently recommending the Highlanders to better themselves by going to the supposedly alluring Lowland towns, and sampling the delights of factory life (and, obediently, orthodox historians still routinely describe the urban Lowlands as being magnetically attractive, manifestly more desirable than the mountains, and shamelessly claim that the Highlanders had bettered themselves by sinking into the crammed hovels of the city slums); and after all that time, and all that advice, and all that opportunity for municipal improvement, the commission could think of no more seductive phrases to describe those very towns than "bad lodging, unhealthy occupations, and enervating habits".

7. Comradeship and independence

The Highlanders helped each other. There are many examples of this, as there are of other facets of Highland character, in the Highland parish reports in the O.S.A. If any were reduced to poverty by accident, disease or calamity, said the Kilmallie minister, "an extraordinary collection" was "made for their relief":[38] and since by the 1790s the clan system had been under heavy attack for half a century, the mutual help of the Highlanders had had all too many occasions to come into play. In South Uist, where there were 2950 Roman Catholics, and only 500 Protestants, the minister said that both groups were "attentive and generous to the poor":[39] and for a Presbyterian minister of that generation to praise the Catholics, there must have been good cause indeed. In Cromdale, when anyone was reduced by accident or illness to poverty a general collection was made; and "the liberality on such occasions far exceeds what might be expected".[40]

The Highlanders did not accept charity easily. Even at the end of the eighteenth century, they were still very much aware of their status as clansfolk, with an equal right to a share in the clan land. But by that time the clearances were reducing many of them to beggary. In Cromdale, where "the union of farms is frequent", and where flocks of sheep "everywhere covered the face of the country", many of the poor were "reduced householders"; and the minister said that they "would starve rather than beg".[41] In Monzievaird, too, some of the small farms had been put together to make large ones: and there too the poor were reluctant to accept charity. "This spirit of independence prevails most among the oldest set of tenantry in the parish; who, having a kind of family character to support, are averse from doing anything that would seem to degrade it."[42]

David Stewart quoted from letters written by two Perthshire Highland ministers. The minister of Moulin (where, according to the O.S.A. report, many small-tenant farms "have been denuded of their inhabitants, and converted into sheep walks and grazings", including one whole glen)[43] wrote: "I have witnessed many singular instances, and have been astonished and gratified, to see how long poor creatures will struggle with their fate before they submit to that painful degradation [of accepting charity]."[44] The Little Dunkeld minister (where the O.S.A. account said "the uniting of farms" had led, for example, to one great farmer displacing eight small-tenant townships, another six, another four, and so on)[45] confirmed that experience: "I must always search for objects of charity in my parish. When questioning individuals on their state, I have seen a blush of shame and confusion spread over their countenances; and while they endeavoured to conceal their wants, and pointed out to me others more needful, I knew that they were in great necessity."[46]

Dr James Robertson, in his report on the *Agriculture of Inverness* in 1808, had naturally (after several decades of clearances) to deal with those who had recently been made poorer, who "from affluence . . . had fallen into want". "The poor in most parts of the Highlands have an honest pride, which disdains to descend in the scale of society; and a laudable shame, which blushes at everything unbecoming a former reputation. Hence, an extreme reluctance to go about begging; insomuch, that persons who, from affluence or even from easy circumstances, have fallen into want, suffer often the most excruciating distress, to the very danger of perishing, rather than assume the garb of mendicants."[47]

Having been members of egalitarian clan societies, where every person had a stake in the land and therefore in the community based upon that land, the Highlanders felt it a hard blow to their pride when they had to accept anything in the nature of public charity. Mutual help, of course, within the circle of the family, or the joint-farm, or the clan, was part of their way of life; and help for those who needed it was always forthcoming. In Dunkeld, "sympathy for the distressed" was "prompt and lively",[48] and in Fortingall "it would be deemed impious to refuse an alms, or a night's quarters, to a poor person".[49] Sixty miles away, the minister of Knockbain said almost exactly the same: "it would be deemed impious to refuse alms, or a night's quarters, to any".[50] The Kirkmichael (Banffshire) minister said, "the indigent and the stranger found them [the Highlanders] always ready to sympathize with their distress".[51] In Avoch, when in 1792 a crew of fishermen drowned at sea leaving seven widows and a good many dependants, a "liberal supply" was obtained for them through collections there and in nearby places, mostly unsolicited.[52]

The poor were cared for by their relations and by their neighbours, said the Jura reporter.[53] Selkirk, coming from the new commercial and hard-headed society, was obviously amazed at these old-fashioned kindly ways, when people did not seize every opportunity to make money out of the needs of others. He wrote perplexedly that the relatives of small tenants would be given crofts of land "from mere charity".[54] The minister of Tongue said in biblical terms that the people of the country made the heart of the widow to rejoice, and granted to the poor his desire;[55] while, more prosaically, Arthur Geddes said that when one was "in distress or sickness", the others supported him.[56] In 1803 Dorothy Wordsworth stayed at a ferryman's house on the shore of Loch Katrine. A "feeble paralytic old woman" was sitting by the fire: she had married an English soldier, but all their children were "dead or in foreign countries". Returning to her native place, all the neighbours looked after her. "Pointing to the ferryman and his wife, she said they were accustomed to give her a day of their labour in digging peats, in common with others, and in that manner she was provided with fuel, and, by like voluntary contributions, with other necessaries."[57]

8. Romantic excess

Selkirk thought that this fulfilment by the Highlanders of precepts which every society preaches but which few (very few) societies practise was taking matters much too far. He said that the Highlanders carried their sentiments of hospitality and generosity to "a romantic excess".[58] Many of the ministers who wrote their reports in the O.S.A. mentioned this Highland trait of charitableness, and some shared Selkirk's opinion. In Harris, the parishioners were hospitable and charitable "even to excess".[59] In Kilfinan, the tenants "liberally supplied" those who begged.[60] In Kildalton, "the natives are very hospitable to strangers; and are often imposed upon by vagrant beggars, who are very capable of working for their own support".[61] The tone here is authentically modern: the words could almost be taken from a speech by a contemporary Chancellor of the Exchequer. And the minister of Strachur says helplessly, "no fine will prevent some people from giving alms to whoever asks it for the love of God".[62] One can only conclude that there were very few misdemeanours (as indeed was the case) in a district where the giving of alms was considered almost in the light of a punishable offence. It is provocative that some ministers (such as the Kildalton incumbent) appeared to be pained by what the New Testament appears to praise.

These ministers could console themselves with the attitude of those other members of their flocks, the chiefs. They needed no fine to discourage them from the excessive giving of alms. Despite, or perhaps one should say because of, the fact that they had pauperized many of their clansfolk by evicting them from their joint-farms on the good land, compensating some of them only with small plots of waste ground, they rejected every proposal that a regular assessment should be made to provide a poor rate, as was done in England. The refusal was on the grounds that they did not wish to destroy the moral fibre of the poor by giving them any money. Instead they graciously contributed, as a gesture of pure generosity, a minute fraction of the profits they made every year from the clan land they had purloined, to the accompaniment of extravagant rhapsodies about their munificence from the local minister. The villainous fourth Duke of Atholl, for example – evictor, clearer, and press-ganger, as we shall see later – had distributed some free food to the poor of Dowally in 1783. Fifteen years later the minister had still not recovered: "Inhabitants of Dowally! Let your grateful language to your Benefactor be that of Elisha to the Shunamite, 'Behold, thou hast been careful for us with all this care, what shall be done for thee?' "[63] (As if anything could have been "done for" the fourth Duke of Atholl to make him wealthier, which he had not already done for himself.) The minister of Little Dunkeld remarked that the heritors there "have very wisely declined burdening their lands with a permanent assessment", but "they make the poor an object of much attention" – mainly, apparently, by magnanimously allowing them "to beg from door to door" in the parish.[64]

Who were "the poor" mentioned in these comments? Many of the quoted remarks were made towards the end of the eighteenth century, or later still, when the new methods introduced by the landlords had indeed produced a new class of poor people, those evicted from their land, or rack-rented out of it. Even during the clan system, there were those who could have been regarded as poor in comparison with the small tenants: perhaps childless old men or women no longer able to work; or older single women, with no close family; those crippled, or otherwise maimed, from birth or by accident; and the simple-minded. (These were, in technical language, "idiots", born with mental deficiencies: "lunatics", those who go mad under the pressure of events, still largely belonged to the post-clan future, as did the society whose events exerted such destructive pressure.)

Of the last two groups, the physically and mentally handicapped, some would stay in or near the place of their birth, and would be regularly supported by their families or by the community, as we have seen; others, of both groups, would prefer a wandering life, and would be given food and lodging at the small-tenant farms they came across on their travels. In return they would dispense the news they had gleaned as they journeyed (news being a valuable commodity in all societies, and these itinerants could supply it at a time when there were few more sophisticated means of spreading it), or they would recite traditional tales and verse, while the eccentricities of the simple-minded would arouse pity or occasionally amusement. Dozens of stories of such people have survived. For example, one individual is said to have displayed his simplicity by always choosing the smaller sum whenever anyone offered to give him either a shilling or a halfpenny; those who asked did not realize that in this way he obtained a steady supply of halfpennies, whereas if he once chose a shilling, the whole subsidy would cease.

9. Rallying the clansmen

The clansfolk were prepared to assist each other with more vigorous means than money if it were necessary. If any enemy was sighted in Kintail (as, for example, when the Edinburgh authorities tried to make the Kintail people pay "rent" after the 1719 rising), a burning barrel was placed on the topmost ridge of Tullochard, the highest mountain in the district: the next morning all the serviceable Kintail clansmen – MacRaes, MacLennans and the rest – would appear armed and ready at Castle Donan to see off the threat.[65]

Each clan had a similar signal when assistance was needed. Often the token was the fiery cross, one end burnt, and the other bloodstained, no doubt symbolizing the dangers to be warded off. In a country "over-populated" and "congested", as the history books monotonously allege the Highlands to have been, news would have spread as quickly as it did in a teeming Lowland town; but since the Highlands were always only sparsely peopled (*pace* the historians), populated only with small groups living far from their nearest neighbours, some other device was necessary. David Stewart wrote that "the nature of the country, over a large extent of which they lived scattered and distant from one another, rendered some signal necessary to give the alarm, and assemble the warriors. The principal signal was the Cross Tarie [croishtarich] or Fiery Cross . . . The cross was sent round the country from hand to hand, each person who bore it running at full speed, shouting as he went along the war-cry of the tribe, and naming the place of rendez-vous [often the war-cry, or slogan, was in fact the place to assemble]. At each hamlet a fresh man took it up, so that an alarm was given, and the people assembled, with a celerity almost incredible."[66]

In modern civilized societies young men are conscripted, and expected to fight against any enemy selected by their government; individuals who would prefer to choose their own adversaries can expect rough treatment. However, in those "barbarous" days in the Highlands, the response to the summons of the fiery cross depended on the opinion of the clansfolk. In 1745, Stewart continued, "by the orders of Lord Breadalbane, it [the croishtarich] was sent round Loch Tay, (a distance of thirty-two miles, in three hours,) to raise his people and prevent their joining the rebels, – but with less effect than in 1715, when it went the same round, and when five hundred men assembled the same evening under the command of the Laird of Glenlyon, acting under the orders of the Earl of Breadalbane, to join the Earl of Mar",[66] who was the Jacobite commander. Since there was a considerable amount of pro-Jacobite feeling in the Breadalbane country around Loch Tay, the croishtarich which was sent round in 1715 to summon help for the rebels was much more effective than the same croishtarich sent on the same circuit in 1745, when the chief (Breadalbane) was asking the clansmen to join the Government forces against the Jacobites. In the Lowlands and England, the common people had to do what their "betters" told them; in the Highlands, the response to a chief's appeal was substantial or not according to the judgement of the clansfolk. Yet many histories tell us that the Highlanders were mere serfs, slavishly obeying the orders of their chiefs (while, we are also told, it was the English-speakers who revelled in their freedom).

The O.S.A. report on Crathie and Braemar, in the Farquharson country, said that everyone capable of bearing arms was expected to keep his weapons, and a bag with an emergency supply of food and new-mended shoes in it, always ready: at the appearance of the croishtarich, the clansman would seize these, and repair to a certain cairn on the north bank of the Dee, called Carn-na-cuimhne.[67] (If, that is, the clansfolk thought the summons justified.) The name of the cairn was the watchword. Even at the end of the eighteenth century, said the report, if there was any fray or squabble at a market or meeting, the slogan (slogan is itself a Gaelic word) "Carn-na-cuimhne!" would rally all the country people round to the help of the person assailed. In the same way, in the Grant country Craig Elachaidh was both the place where the able-bodied men of the clan convened in time of danger, and the clan's rallying cry when trouble threatened. Among other clans, the Clan Donald slogan was Fraoch Eilean; the MacPhersons' Creag an Dhubh; the MacGregors' Ard-choille; the MacFarlanes' Loch Slòigh; the Campbells' Cruachan; and the Buchanans' Clar Innis – all of them prominent geographical features in the countries of those clans.[68]

10. Fair and friendly

While these usages had of necessity grown up to help the Highlanders fend off the strife which as a rule arose from the Lowlanders' deliberate attempts to stir up trouble in the Highlands, the normal state of the clansfolk was much more pacific. In fact, the friendliness of the Highlanders to each other was often remarked on. They lived "in peace and harmony among themselves", and were "very ready to oblige and assist one another" when the need arose,[69] wrote the Buchanan reporter. In Eddrachillis, "the native inhabitants are all connected by blood, and few strangers dwell among them, so that they assist each other, and scarcely any are in want of bread".[70] The minister of the neighbouring parish of Assynt said that the inhabitants had "a regard" for "their departed friends" and relatives, which they showed by "doing all the good possible to the survivors of the departed": so the poor were not "a burden to the parish". They also dealt with the problem of age: "When anyone becomes old and feeble, their nearest relations build a little comfortable house for them, close to their own residence; and even there the distaff and spindle is well managed [i.e., even the aged still spin the wool into yarn]. These old matrons nurse the children of their relations; the songs and airs of Fingal, and ancient heroes, are sung in the Gaelic tongue, to which the little children dance. Old men are prudently engaged in some domestic affair, such as repairing the houses of neighbouring tenants, etc. In short, they share with their relatives all the viands of the family."[71]

A number of accounts say that there were few quarrels or disputes. At Alvie, it was "very uncommon" to have "recourse to the sheriff", and still more to go to the judiciary courts.[72]

One of the keys to the Highland character was the clansfolk's love of their families. The Rev. J. L. Buchanan wrote that an "illegitimate" child "is as much esteemed as the lawfully begotten child".[73] Edmund Burt said the same: "the love of kindred, so honourable to the Highland character, procures for natural [i.e. 'illegitimate'] children in that country a kindness and attention which they do not meet with elsewhere."[74] The Highlanders (unlike their contemporaries in the Lowlands and England, not to mention some people in those places now) were too rational to blame human beings for something that had happened before they were born. A strong feature of the Highland character, and the best proof of true civilization, said Robert Jamieson, was "the kind-hearted, sensible, and considerate good-nature and indulgence which they everywhere manifested towards women and children".[75] Perhaps one indication of this feeling was the fact that in the Highlands a married woman kept her own name, as can be seen in official documents such as emigrant schedules, and even more permanently on Highland gravestones. The account of Kincardine in the O.S.A. said that Highlanders still retained their "sacred regard for the clan and family they are sprung from".[76] According to the minister of Avoch, an immense crowd of both sexes attended at all funerals: "the lamentations of the women, in some cases, on seeing a beloved relative put in to the grave, would almost pierce a heart of stone."[77] In Callander, this great attendance had led to a much greater tragedy: a lake there was called Lochan-nan-corp, the lake of corpses, where a funeral company had "dropped through the ice" and drowned. The "most numerous clan" among the funeral party were the Kessanachs, which "were formerly a considerable people" there; but since the disaster, they had "dwindled very much away".[78]

It appears that much as the Highlander loved his immediate family, he was even more devoted to the larger family, his clan. Alexander Cunningham wrote: "they are more attached by a similarity of manners and dress, and the sameness of name, than by the ties of kindred and nature."[79] The phrase "ties of kindred and nature", used in a society based on the small family of parents and children, seems likely to mean the immediate family; while "sameness of name" indicates the clan.

11. Love of country

Equalling the Highlanders' love of the family and clan was their love of their clan country. Like other peoples who are in the stage of development that the Highland clans had reached, the Highlander regarded the land with a reverence that had almost an element of mysticism in it. The land was the all-provider – there was no other source from which his livelihood could be obtained. The animals he hunted or herded grazed upon it; the fruits he gathered and the crops he harvested grew on it. The fish he caught swam in the waters running over or round it; the birds of the air took their sustenance from it. His clothes came from the back of his grazing animals, coloured with dyes from the earth and its produce. The land was the great mother, which gave birth to all that he lived by: and the Highlander's veneration for his land, the land of his clan, is tinged with a quasi-religious devotion which must be almost incomprehensible to the people of an industrialized society (many of whom move into a different area – or even into a different country – not infrequently, being forced into this restless nomadism by economic pressures).

Many observers commented on this attitude on the part of the Highlanders. Anglophone people then thought otherwise. Burt admitted that the Highland mountains served "for the breeding and feeding of cattle, wild fowls, and other useful animals", but little else could be said for them. The mountains were "monstrous excrescences", of "stupendous bulk, frightful irregularity, and horrid gloom" offering only "horrid prospects", of "a dismal gloomy brown drawing upon a dirty purple, and most of all disagreeable when the heath is in bloom"; these "hideous productions of nature" formed a "disagreeable subject". It was "the deformity of the hills that makes the natives conceive of their naked straths and glens, as of the most beautiful objects in nature".[80] (This was before the cult of the Highlands arose in the nineteenth century, which made admiration of the Highlands fashionable, and Burt clearly thought the Highlanders misguided.) Dr John Walker said, "no people in the world have a stronger attachment to their native spot, which nothing but singular occurrences, or very strong motives, could oblige them to abandon".[81] The O.S.A. has many references to this facet of character: the report on Kirkmichael in Perthshire talked of "the ardour of patriotism, that attachment to his native soil, which glows spontaneously with such warmth in the breast of a Highlander".[82] The minister of Strachur maintained that this attachment was to the Highlander's own clan land alone. If the Highlander had to leave his own native area, the minister said, he did not care how far he went; going to another parish, or to a "district of another clan", was "to him entire banishment"; "he would as soon cross the Atlantic" as "an arm of the sea".[83] It is true that for centuries the clansfolk considered themselves as members of a particular clan, with a rightful home in the country of that clan, rather than merely as Highlanders. A MacDonald was a member of the Clan Donald, and a citizen of the MacDonald country: the Cameron country, for example, was foreign ground to him. Yet when the final agonizing wrench of the clearances came, the Highlander would snatch at any opportunity, and do anything, rather than leave the Highlands altogether. The account of Dores described Fort Augustus as being "in the mouth of the Highlands, where many, who were distressed by the extension of the sheep farms, still continue to reside, from an invincible attachment to their native country, though they have scarce sufficient employment to maintain them".[84] Again, at Urray, in the coastal plain of Easter Ross, the report said a number of people came annually from the west coast (where, as we know, the sheep farms were spreading), instead of crossing the Atlantic, because "they feel themselves within reach of their relations and sepulchres of their fathers".[85] After a prolonged absence, returning to any part of Scotland was enough to kindle this fervour. When the Black Watch returned from overseas in 1775 after an absence of thirty-two years, even though they landed in Galloway, in the Lowlands, many of its soldiers (said Stewart) "leaped on shore with enthusiasm, kissing the earth, and holding it up in handfuls".[86]

12. Forefathers' graves

It was in the Urray reporter's "sepulchres of their fathers" that the two ruling passions of the Highlander's life – his love of his family and clan, and his love of the land – came together. When after the 1745 rebellion the Highlanders were forbidden to have arms, or to wear Highland dress, the authorities produced an oath which any Highlander could be compelled to swear, an oath which must have been devised by someone who had a very deep insight into their character: "I, _____, do swear, and as I shall have to answer to God at the great day of Judgement, I have not, nor shall have, in my possession any gun, sword, pistol or other arm whatever; and never use tartan, plaid, or any part of the Highland garb; and if I do so, may I be cursed in my undertakings, family and property – may I never see my wife and children, father, mother or relations – may I be killed in battle as a coward, and lie without Christian burial in a strange land, far from the graves of my forefathers and kindred; may all this come across me if I break my oath."[87] These were exactly the eventualities which the Highlander would most wish to avoid – and most were those which, by an obnoxious quirk of fate, many a Highlander was forced to undergo as a result of the clearances shortly afterwards – to be cursed in his everyday dealings, never to see many of his near relations again, and to lie in a strange land, far from the graves of his forefathers and kindred: the oath builds up powerfully towards this most awful of destinies.

For it was, to the Highlander, the most appalling fate. Those of his family and kindred, those of his friends, who had died, lay buried in one particular spot of his dear native soil: and that spot became sacred to him. At Weem, the minister said that the people did not necessarily bury in the nearest churchyard, nor in the parish churchyard, "but they always endeavour, at whatever distance, to bury with their ancestors".[88] The parish of Altyre in Moray, at the eastern edge of Gaeldom, had long been incorporated with the parish of Rafford: but Altyre was the burying place of the Cummings of Altyre "time out of mind", and most of the "ancient residenters", said the report, still buried there.[89] The minister of Portree said the people used to bury near an old Catholic chapel in a retired situation; a new cemetery had been marked out at the church of Portree about forty-five years before, but the people had only just begun to bury their dead there.[90] At Dornoch, the churchyard was very unsuitable for burials – it was also a market place, and the county road ran through it. The proprietors and magistrates prohibited burials there from a certain date, and marked out a new cemetery outside the town; but "the prejudices of the people prevailed", and the novel project had to be relinquished.[91] Stewart wrote: "to be consigned to the grave among strangers, without the attendance and sympathy of friends, and at a distance from their family, was considered a heavy calamity."[92] Even the graves of Highlanders not of one's own clan were held sacred. The account of Knockbain, in the Black Isle (not, of course, MacDonald country) tells of a battle there between the MacDonalds and the people of Inverness in the thirteenth or fourteenth century. The place where the battle was fought, Blair-na-coi, was in tillage at the time; but since then, the cairns marking the graves of the dead had been left untouched, even though the neighbouring ground was cultivated.[93]

13. Hospitality

Almost all the parish reports in the O.S.A. that describe the character of the Highlanders mention their remarkable hospitality. For the clansfolk did not confine their kindness to themselves. In the account of Assynt we read that "the poorest stranger, even though unacquainted, finds charity and safe shelter".[94] Pennant, "from experience", speaks of the Highlanders' "disinterested assistance to the distressed traveller, either in directing him on his way or affording their aid in passing the dangerous torrents of the Highlands"; they were "hospitable to the highest degree, and full of generosity". In the Highlands, Pennant said, every house gave a welcome to the traveller.[95] Dr Johnson experienced this hospitality for himself, on his journey in 1773: "Along some miles of the way, in the evening, a gentleman's servant had kept us company on foot with very little notice on our part. He left us near Glenelg, and we thought on him no more till he came to us again, in about two hours, with a present from his master of rum and sugar. The man had mentioned his company, and the gentleman had this attention to two men, whose names perhaps he had not heard, by whom his kindness was not likely to be ever repaid, and who could be recommended to him only by their necessities."[96] Richard J. Sulivan visited the Highlands five years later, and then wrote: "Many Highlanders would be offended at the offer of a reward; accept of their services, appear satisfied, and they are usuriously repaid for everything they can do for you: nay, what is more surprising, this extends itself to many of the lowest servants, one of whom, from Lord Breadalbane, having been pressed to accept of an instance of our thanks for bringing us some fruit, flew out of the house with all the trepidation imaginable, resolutely declining the offer, and seemingly hurt that he should be supposed capable of accepting a pecuniary gratification."[97] In 1803 Dorothy and William Wordsworth, driving their horse and trap towards Ballachulish, came to a bridge that had been damaged by a flood a few days before, and was no longer usable. Several Highlanders came along "by great good luck", unharnessed the horse (which had been made skittish by its trip on a ferry-boat), and dragged the trap through the river. The travellers felt fortunate "in having met with such true good-will and ready kindness in the Highlanders".[98]

According to John Toland, writing in 1709, the Highlanders were "hospitable beyond expression, entertaining all strangers of whatever condition gratis".[99] The O.S.A. report on Gigha and Cara said that the people were "ready by every exertion to relieve the distress of seafaring men".[100] In Kilfinichen, in Mull, there had been two shipwrecks in the previous six years, and the sailors had been treated "with kindness and humanity".[101] As late as 1835, the *Inverness Courier* reported that a Prussian ship had foundered off St Kilda. The crew of eleven got to land, and stayed there as the guests of the inhabitants until they could cross to Skye. When they offered to pay for their fourteen days' stay, the St Kilda people would only accept a few pence from each of them.[102] The account of Glenorchy said that the inhabitants there never refused charity to the needy whether they were newcomers or natives. About twenty years before, a stranger and his family had come to reside there. By an "accident, his house and his all were destroyed by fire. A collection was made for them at the church doors", which came to £21, although none of the landlords "were resident at the time".[103] This was at a period when a whole year's rent for a small tenant would have been from one pound down to only a quarter of that (five shillings).

Alexander Nicolson said that the Skye people were always hospitable. He quoted Lord Mahon, who had visited the island: "Here we seemed suddenly to have become the near relatives, or intimate friends, of every individual we saw; while I almost began to fancy we must have recently succeeded to the whole island, and were come to take possession."[104]

14. He is a stranger

A low country shepherd, in the service of a gentleman near Glen Coe, was drinking whisky at the annual fair at Portnacroish, in Appin, about 1788. At this time the Highland clans were everywhere being turned off their land, and their farms given to graziers, some of them Lowlanders. The Lowland shepherd, having had too much to drink, became abusive, and struck several of a party of Highland shepherds. One of them turned him out of the inn, and the Lowlander again hit him with his staff. The Highlander seized the staff and snapped it in two; but he prevented another man attacking the Lowlander, saying, "He is a stranger, and has none to take his part." One can only contrast this attitude with the current behaviour of some of our modern citizens towards immigrants, even when those immigrants have only taken the worst jobs and the worst accommodation, whereas the Highland improvers, some of whom were Lowlanders, were often taking the land itself, the root and foundation of the old clan society.

The minister of Dunoon wrote in the N.S.A. of an earlier chief of Lamont who went to stay with MacGregor of Glenstrae. Lamont went hunting with some of the MacGregors, including the only child of Glenstrae, a youth of Lamont's age. They sheltered for the night in a cave. "During the night, unhappily, the two had a quarrel, when the young MacGregor fell, mortally wounded, under the sword or the dirk of Lamont." Lamont fled to escape the anger of the MacGregors. Seeing a light, he made for it, "and did not, in his perturbation, perceive till he had entered the house, that it was the house of the father whose only son had fallen, but a few hours before, – the victim of his unhappy anger". But even when Glenstrae found what had happened, the laws of Highland hospitality prevented him harming his guest. Glenstrae protected Lamont from the anger of the MacGregor men when they returned later that night, and before dawn he aroused Lamont, and took him the long journey to Loch Fyne; there he gave him a boat to take him across to Cowal. "Go", he said, "flee for your life – land in your own country, and there we shall pursue you – save yourself if you can." Lamont reached home safely, and thus escaped retribution. The duty of hospitality had over-ridden even the rage of a man bereaved of his only child.[105]

J. Mawman wrote, in his *Excursion to the Highlands of Scotland*, 1805: "We doubted if the traveller could be more safe from harm, even among the simple and innocent Laplanders."[106] Thirty years earlier Dr Johnson remarked: "To enter a habitation without leave seems to be not considered here as rudeness or intrusion. The old laws of hospitality still give this licence to a stranger."[107]

According to the old Highland code, not only had hospitality to be freely offered: it seems it also had to be readily received. John Bristed, in his tour of the Highlands in 1801, stayed with one MacDiarmaid and his wife, who kept an inn at Dunkeld. "The hostess, indeed", Bristed wrote, "abated a little of her regard for me, when she found that I could not be prevailed upon to drink any whisky with her at parting, when she brought out her bottle and dram-glass . . . telling her husband, that he in the hairy cap did not like her, for he would drink no whisky with her."[108]

The Lowlander Bristed was so impressed with the Highlanders he met on his tour that only Biblical language could express his feelings: "When I forget to reverence and to honour the manly and dignified character of the Highlander, *may my tongue cleave unto the roof of my mouth, and may my right hand forget her cunning.*"[109]

15. Highlanders as soldiers

One of the greatest tests of the character of a people comes at times of conflict, when the able-bodied men among them become soldiers. Again in modern times, we have seen the transformation which all too often occurs when an apparently decent citizen is given a gun, a uniform, and an army number, and is sent into a foreign country. This test, however, the Highlander passed with flying colours.

When the Highlanders joined the Young Pretender's army for the march to Derby in 1745, Jamieson wrote that their conduct was "not only orderly and proper, but in innumerable instances, in the highest degree humane and magnanimous".[110] English people, who had billetted on them first the rebels, and then the government forces, sometimes told the Hanoverians, "When the rebels, as they are called, were here, *they* behaved very differently – they behaved like gentlemen – quite like gentlemen – God help them", and one Cheshire widow told a party of Cumberland's officers, "If I am not a Jacobite, it certainly is not your fault - Ye have done all ye could to make me one!"[111] Dr Robert Jackson wrote that "their conduct in the year 1745 proves that they are neither a ferocious nor a cruel people; for no troops probably ever traversed a country which might be esteemed hostile with fewer traces of outrage".[112] David Stewart said that the rebel army "conducted itself throughout with a moderation, forbearance, and humanity, almost unexampled in any civil commotion". Despite the fact that they marched through "fertile and rich districts", and needed food and shelter, yet "private revenge, or unprovoked massacre, wanton depredation, the burning of private houses, or destruction of property, were entirely unknown".[113] The best testimony to this is the gratitude of the people of Derby (for example) themselves. As we shall see later, when Keith's and Campbell's Highlanders were ordered home from the Continent seventeen years later, they marched through Derby on the way back to Scotland; but the local people had not forgotten the exemplary behaviour of the Highlanders fighting for Prince Charles. According to David Stewart they refused to take payment from the soldiers for their quarters, and subscriptions were raised to give gratuities to the men.[114]

Many examples will be given subsequently of the high opinions won by the Highland regiments from friends and foes, in Britain and overseas.

More than one commentator has remarked on the enormous difference between the restrained behaviour of the Highlanders on the march to Derby, and the pandemonium of murder and destruction which was unleashed when the civilized English-speaking soldiers reached the Highlands, following up their war-crimes at Culloden with an orgy of slaughter, looting, rape, and devastation – later described as a "moral reformation".

16. Loyalty

The loyalty and steadfastness of the ordinary Highlanders was remarked on earlier. These qualities were clearly displayed during and after the 1745 rebellion. Those clans who were convinced that the Stuarts were their lawful kings went out to fight for them even though some of their chiefs stayed at home: the clansmen fought, but some chiefs – equally Jacobite in theory – prudently held back until they were sure which way to jump.

When the rebellion had been defeated, Prince Charles was at large in the Highlands for five months, during which time many of the clansfolk became aware of his whereabouts. They all knew of the terrible brutality of the revenge taken by "Butcher" Cumberland and his men on all they thought were rebels; and on the other hand, they knew that the Government had offered £30,000 reward for Prince Charles – a sum which would have been a fantastic fortune to any Highlander, or any Lowlander for that matter (it would equal more than £10,000,000 now). And yet not one of them betrayed him. As Dr Johnson wrote, "Quantum cedat virtutibus aurum" – With virtue weighed, what worthless trash is gold.[115] The ordinary Highlanders often showed their belief in this maxim by acting on it: it was left to the chiefs, during the clearances, to show how much they had risen above such primitive sentiments.

Among those who protected Charles, at enormous risk to themselves, were two MacIains, alias Kennedies. The O.S.A. report of Glenorchy praised the loyalty of one of these lowly Highlanders, even though it was written by the Rev. Dr Joseph MacIntyre, who moved in much higher circles. (His daughter married the brother of the clearing landlord Sir James Colquhoun of Luss). MacIain, MacIntyre wrote, watched over the defeated Prince Charles "with inviolable fidelity for weeks, and even robbed at the risque of his life for his support, at the very time that he and his family were in a state of starvation, and that he knew he could gain £30,000 for betraying his guest. This poor man was afterwards executed at Inverness for stealing a cow. A little before his execution, he took off his bonnet and thanked God that he had never betrayed trust, never injured the poor, and never refused a share of what he had to the stranger and needy."[116] Now, to claim good qualities is not the same thing as proving you have them: although, as we will see during the succeeding volumes, a landlord's testimony to his own merit has frequently been accepted without question by orthodox chroniclers. Yet it must be said that a man going to his immediate death by public strangulation might be thought likely not to waste time on lies; if nothing else, for a man to profess these virtues at such a solemn, culminating moment of his existence does indicate that – at the lowest estimation – they were what he felt his contemporaries in the Highlands would applaud.

MacIain and his fellow Highlanders refused thirty thousand pounds to betray one man; but the chiefs took the thirty pieces of silver offered to them by modern commerce, and betrayed whole clans for it.

At the full tide of the clearances, some of the landlords' propagandists denigrated everything connected with the Highlanders. Dr MacCulloch, in his *Tour in the Highlands*, 1824, even tried to devalue the undoubted records of the Highlanders' loyalty to Prince Charles. "Unless Highlanders themselves", MacCulloch wrote, "had been his bloodhounds, he could scarcely have been discovered in any one of the places where he took refuge. English soldiers might have hunted him in vain till now."[117] As in much else that he wrote, MacCulloch allowed his dislike of the Highlanders to make him ignore the plain facts, and to write what he must have been aware was deceitful. Highlanders were, as MacCulloch well knew, among Prince Charles' "bloodhounds". Many soldiers from the Munro, the MacKay, the Argyll Campbells, and other "Hanoverian" clans, were among those who hunted the Prince. But to talk of "bloodhounds" at all is to miss the point. Many Highlanders – some thousands of them – knew where the Prince was at various times in his wanderings; not one could be induced to inform on him. In South Uist, for example, Prince Charles hid in a cave in the rock face on the north side of Glen Corodale. "Chambers says that about ninety persons knew that the Prince was in Corodale", wrote Alexander Carmichael. "He might safely have said 900, yet no one attempted to betray him."[118]

Thousands of Highlanders could have claimed the enormous reward offered for betraying Prince Charles, but they refused to do so: a circumstance which must be a great embarrassment to some modern historians, who appear to claim that all human actions follow from, and are therefore justified by, the "economic imperative".[119] Money, they seem to say, excuses everything. Perhaps one advantage of studying history is to cheer oneself up by observing that even in the earlier stages of our present society, where gain is the greediest of the gods, the fact remains that some human beings (despite extreme temptation) have chosen higher ideals than mere personal profit. All honour to them!

17. "Pacification" of the Highlands

The deportment of the so-called Highland barbarians in the rebel army of 1745-6 was in marked contrast to the savage behaviour of the Government troops on their "pacifying" and "civilizing" mission. (The brutal military suppression of clanship after the '45 was often called the "pacification" of the Highlands, and still is, by orthodox thinkers: "pacification" was a defensive slogan used almost as often as "law and order". Hitler's savage conquest of neighbouring countries in the 1930s and 1940s was called – by the Nazis – the pacification of Europe, with equal justification.) The Hanoverian army was commanded by the Duke of Cumberland, one of George II's sons, a callous scoundrel – still celebrated in the twenty-first century (with a gate to Hyde Park, a flower, and Highland place-names) – who set the tone of the whole operation. When Duncan Forbes (who during the rebellion had done more than any man to uphold Hanoverian rule) hinted to him that the laws of the country should be observed even by the army, the duke is reported to have replied: "The laws of the country, my Lord! I'll make a brigade give laws, by God!" (Presumably these were the same "laws" which the Highlanders unfortunately lacked, according to Dr Johnson – as we shall see below.) Cumberland described Forbes as "that old woman who spoke to me of humanity". When the Whig anti-Jacobite Provost of Inverness hinted at forbearance, and actually uttered the word "mercy" to General Hawley, Cumberland's alter ego, Hawley had him literally kicked downstairs. A previous Provost of Inverness, equally Whig and anti-Jacobite, who also bravely hinted about compassion, was ordered to "muck out General Hawley's stables". Wounded Highlanders were murdered out of hand, clubbed or shot; in one case they were burnt alive, as the hut in which they had taken refuge was deliberately burnt down.[120] Peter Anderson quoted one account: "Some were handcuffed, especially Major Stewart and Major MacLachlan. Their handcuffs were so tight that their hands swelled, and at last broke the skin, so that the irons could not be seen."[121] Lowlanders were to the fore in this reign of terror, as we saw earlier. Even some Highland chiefs, or members of their families, had adopted the anglophone ethos so whole-heartedly that they are named as having been part of the Hanoverian revenge on the Highland Jacobites – Sir Alexander MacDonald of Sleat, Norman MacLeod of Dunvegan, Ludovick Grant (son of Sir James Grant of Grant), Ludovick Grant younger of Knockando, John Campbell younger of Mamore, and George Munro of Culcairn,[122] were not ashamed to take part in the ferocious repression: their names should be remembered. This epoch was merely a precursor of that time, very soon to come, when virtually all the Highland chiefs embraced the moral standards of the Lowlands so enthusiastically as to filch their clansfolks' property, and transform themselves into landlords.

CHARACTER OF THE HIGHLANDERS

After Culloden the Lowlanders' hatred of the Highlanders was given free rein in a sweeping campaign of spoliation and terror. Some writers appear to blame Cumberland's German parentage for his post-Culloden ferocity (the frequent glib excuse – it was the foreigners' fault!): but nearly all those involved in the thuggery came from the sceptred isle of Britain. The English General "Hangman" Hawley was even more bloodthirsty than Cumberland: in fact Lord Mahon said that on arriving in Edinburgh to take over the command, Cumberland "immediately arrested the course of Hawley's savage executions".[123] (So Hawley may be given what some would have thought an impossible accolade – being more vicious than Cumberland.) When after Culloden Hawley thought he might be moved out of Scotland, he wrote in his disappointment, "There's still so many more houses to burn and I hope still some more to be put to death."[124] A number of Lowlanders were named earlier as being to the fore in this brutal offensive: Major Lockhart of Cholmondley's Regiment, Captain Caroline Scott of Guise's Regiment, Captain Dunlop of Blakeney's Regiment, Captain Ferguson R.N., in command of the *Furnace*, Captain Robert Duff R.N. and Captain John Hay R.N. – along with the Lowland Regiment, the Royal Scots.[125] Lockhart had been taken prisoner at Falkirk by the Jacobites, and was mercifully released on parole:[126] but he now repaid this kindly treatment by showing that Lowland soldiers had sterner views of warfare. (Cumberland had decided that the solemn promises to stay out of the conflict made by those given parole could be ignored.) Lockhart led his men, murdering and ravaging, through the lands of the Grants of Glenmoriston, and the Frasers, and the Chisholms.[127] Captain Scott, said Fitzroy MacLean, "had by his punitive operations in the Western Highlands won a reputation for exceptional brutality".[128] Captain Ferguson R.N., "born in the country of Aberdeen and naturally of a furious savage disposition",[129] landed parties of sailors and marines in the islands and the coastal districts, and led them to many atrocities, so that the British navy can share with the British army whatever credit is due for this campaign. The English Lord George Sackville, son of the Duke of Dorset, tried to equal the Lowlanders. When he was marching with his regiment through MacDonald country, the rear of his column was attacked by raiders, who carried off Lord George's baggage and supplies.[130] (This may have been the work of the faithful Highlanders who were looking after the fugitive Prince Charles: David Stewart said that about this time Charles' helpers "plundered an officer's baggage to supply him with shirts and linen, – a luxury to which he had for some time been a stranger. This robbery made a noise at the time, and was frequently mentioned as an instance of the thievish disposition of the Highlanders.")[131] Sackville retaliated viciously against the nearest Highlanders, ignoring irrelevant questions of guilt or innocence. "For this outrage [said Fitzroy MacLean] his men took their revenge on the next village they came to, first raping the women and then making them watch while their men were bayoneted and shot."[132] The noble Lord George was less brave when he had to face men who could fight back. At Minden thirteen years later the British won a crushing victory against the French, but Lord George cravenly refused to lead the cavalry against the retreating enemy, and was dismissed the service in disgrace.[133] His atrocities against the Highlanders, of course, had not occasioned any repercussions from the authorities; they were quite to the taste of the Lowland and English rulers.

18. Most deplorable way

Another British regiment rampaged through the MacPherson country, destroying any shelter, slaughtering men, raping women, looting and driving off the Highlanders' cattle, horses and sheep, and one of the plunderers wrote that they had done a good job: "for the space of Fifty Miles neither House, Man nor Beast was to be seen."[134] Other soldiers went out every day, terrorizing the country around Fort Augustus. One officer wrote: "the people are deservedly in a most deplorable way, and must perish either by the sword or famine, a just reward for traitors"[135] (a verdict which naturally ignored the fact that as many Highlanders had fought for George II as had fought for Prince Charles). Another officer said, "we hang or shoot everyone that is known to conceal the Pretender, burn their houses and take their cattle, of which we have got 8000 head within these few days past".[135] A third boasted of the plunder of the Highlanders' cows: "we bring them to our camp in great quantities, sometimes about 200 in a drove."[135] The devastation was authorized and duly regulated. James Wolfe, then a brigade-major in the occupying army, wrote to a colleague: "The general bid me tell you that when any seizures were made of cattle or otherwise in this part of the world, the commanding officer and every person concerned have shares in proportion to their pay."[136] The great herds of looted cattle were sold off cheaply to Lowland and English traders, and the money shared out among the robbers. Hugh Miller (born as we saw in 1802) had known in his youth an old man who had been in the Hanoverian army at Fort Augustus, and who became angry at the memory of what he had seen done by his own comrades. "While scores of cottages", wrote Miller, "were flaming in the distance, and blood not infrequently hissing on the embers", the victorious soldiers, and their camp followers, engaged in pony-races. "Gold circulated and liquor flowed in abundance; and in a few weeks there were about twenty thousand head of cattle brought in by marauding parties of the soldiery from the crushed and impoverished Highlanders; and groups of drovers from Yorkshire and the south of Scotland – coarse vulgar men – used to come every day to share in the spoil, by making purchases at greatly less than half-price."[137]

An officer of the invading army wrote: "there were found last week two women and four children dead in the hills who perished through want, their huts being burnt."[138] A minister wondered how he would get his stipend, "as the most of this parish is burnt to ashes and all the cattle belonging to the rebels carried off by His Majesty's forces", so that "there is no such thing as money or a pennyworth to be got in this desolate place".[138]

19. Very wanton excesses

The N.S.A., which appeared in the 1840s, was more forthcoming than the O.S.A., written in the 1790s, about Cumberland's reign of terror. As the atrocities committed by "our" side recede into history, it becomes more forgivable to mention them. Among the N.S.A. references to the events after Culloden, five may be quoted. The Dunkeld report reads: "The Duke of Cumberland, early in 1746, made Dunkeld and Blair in Atholl his advanced posts. These detachments lived on the inhabitants, plundered the houses of the rebels, and committed very wanton excesses."[139] This was despite the fact that the people of Dunkeld had remained loyal to the Government: it was enough that they were considered (with dubious accuracy) to be Highlanders. According to the minister of Kilmallie, "the royal army, after the Prince was finally defeated at Culloden, pitched their camp at Fort Augustus, and sent plundering parties to Lochaber, who drove away all the cattle in the country, burnt the houses, and drove the miserable inhabitants, old and young, without food or clothing, to the hills. They killed several persons in cold blood."[140] In Ardnamurchan, wrote the minister, the various districts of the parish "were laid waste with fire and sword, and subjected to the fullest measure of the vengeance which, although perpetrated by the army of civilized Britain, rivalled the savage cruelty of the most barbarous age".[141] In Morvern, so much timber was burnt when the district was sacked that people alive at the time (according to the parish minister) saw the country "as one red ember".[142] The minister of Croy (in whose parish lay Culloden Moor) wrote: "Early in the morning after the battle, orders were given by the Duke of Cumberland or General Hawley, par ignobile fratrum [a wretched pair of brothers], to inspect the wounded and mangled, in whom there remained any symptoms of life, and collect them into two heaps, and apply a six pounder to each heap: yet, wonderful as it may appear, one MacIver, a private . . . though mutilated in several parts of the body, survived this massacre a dismal memorial of Cumberland's tender mercies. The man died near Beauly, about the year 1796, where many are still living, who may have known him; but to put the bloody deed beyond the shadow of doubt, the writer of this account knew for several years a John Reid, who fought that day in the second battalion of the Royal Scots [in the Government army], and heard from his lips, that he saw the cruel deed, and thanked God that he had nothing to do with the *black wark*."[143] None of the O.S.A. reports on these parishes mentioned these interesting episodes. Veracity can be overdone.

Another illustration of the way that increasing distance from an event allows increasing honesty about it comes in Lord Mahon's *History of England*. The publication of Mahon's seven volumes began in 1836, and they were much more informative than comparable writings issued nearer to 1746. "Quarter was seldom given to the stragglers and fugitives, except to a few considerately reserved for public execution. No care or compassion was shown to their wounded; nay more, on the following day most of these were put to death in cold blood, with a cruelty such as never perhaps before or since has disgraced a British army. Some were dragged from the thickets or cabins where they had sought a refuge, drawn out in line and shot, while others were dispatched by the soldiers with the stocks of their muskets. One farm-building, into which some twenty disabled Highlanders had crawled, was deliberately set on fire the next day, and burnt with them to the ground. The native prisoners were scarcely better treated; and even sufficient water was not vouchsafed to their thirst . . . The rebels' country was laid waste, the houses plundered, the cabins burnt, the cattle driven away. The men had fled to the mountains, but such as could be found were frequently shot; nor was mercy always granted even to their helpless families. In many cases, the women and children, expelled from their homes and seeking shelter in the clefts of the rocks, miserably perished of cold and hunger."[144] Thus were treated the members of a minority people, who had contumaciously, over the centuries, refused to submit to the rule of the English-speaking majority.

The army which had brought civilized man's methods of warfare to the Highlands brought also entertainments appropriate to such a pacifying mission: and there were held "races of naked women on horseback for the amusement of the camp at Fort Augustus".[145]

Four peers were beheaded, numbers of less important rebels were made to rue their inferior social status while they were being were hanged, drawn and quartered, and some hundreds were shipped to the colonies in de facto slavery; apart from all those Highlanders who died from ill-treatment, from the refusal to attend to their wounds, from the disgusting conditions in which they were held, or who – found to be ill or verminous on the ships transporting them to London – were simply thrown overboard (with a stone tied to their legs) and so drowned by honest British tars.[146] One ship, the *Liberty and Property*, took on board 157 prisoners; and landed forty-nine, fewer than a third.[147] ("Oh, *Liberty*", one might say, "what crimes were committed, to thy shame!")

These events are sometimes treated blandly, if treated at all, by modern respectable commentators. Lord George Sackville's 5000-word entry in the *D.N.B.*, written by a Lowlander, found room for a lengthy defence of his behaviour at Minden, but did not mention his atrocities against innocent Highlanders.[148] If the victims had been English, would they have been ignored? The relevant volume (*The Whig Supremacy 1714-1760*) in the *Oxford History of England*, penned by the Edinburgh University professor Basil Williams, did mention Cumberland's "savage repression", though giving few details; however, it cautioned against accepting all the accounts of the savagery – "some are obviously exaggerated". How he knew that some accounts were "obviously exaggerated" Professor Williams chose to conceal in the recesses of his anglophone brain. Perhaps the vicious campaign of the Lowlanders and English was covered by the professor's genial comment: "The suppression of the '45 rebellion and the wise measures of appeasement which ensued completed the good work of the Union for Scotland as well as for England."[149] The Highlanders murdered or raped by Cumberland's men would probably have felt that "wise measures of appeasement" was hardly an adequate description of the British government's savagery.

Those who think that Englishmen or Scots Lowlanders could not be guilty of war crimes, or that British soldiers and sailors would not commit atrocities, should study the Culloden campaign.

20. Stinking Billy

Prince William Augustus, the Duke of Cumberland ("Bloody Butcher Cumberland", or "Stinking Billy", as he was more accurately known to those who suffered from his barbarity), was not even an efficient soldier. He was only twenty-five years old at the Battle of Culloden, and he owed his advancement simply to being a member of the royal Hanoverian family, having shown such promise that he was made a companion knight of the Bath at age four, a duke, marquis, earl, viscount, and baron a year later (no fewer than five grandiose titles at only five years old), and a knight of the Garter at nine. He achieved an income of £6000 a year at age ten, and £12,000 a year at eighteen: clearly a promising lad. He was a major-general at twenty-one, and commander-in-chief of the forces abroad at twenty-five. Having serenely accepted all these rightful rewards of having been born into the ruling family, he successfully avoided one of the few apparent duties of royalty, that is, the obligation to marry and produce legitimate heirs, though he found the time to console himself, says the *D.N.B.*, with "many mistresses". (They found a princess for him, but he greedily demanded so much extra money to carry out this solitary royal duty of marrying her that his father, George II, had to give up the idea.)[150]

He reluctantly refrained from executing prisoners at first, "as they have so many of our prisoners in their hands"; but he wrote affably, "I have encouraged the country people to do it as they may fall in their way".[150] He thought that the Almighty had had a hand either in his appointment or in the battle on Drummossie Moor: "I thank God most heartily that I was an instrument in the affair . . ."[151] He commanded the army in half-a-dozen battles, and lost them all except Culloden. (Perhaps the Almighty withdrew his approval after that one.) If he had a taste for atrocity he may have felt he should seize what turned out to be his only chance of triumphal brutality. The Highlanders assuaged their grief (accurately, as it happened) forecasting his future failures. One wrote:

Though once by a terrible error in strife
He victory gained over us Highlandmen
In devil a battle throughout his whole life
Will Cumberland ever be victor again.

In Lowland Scotland, and England, however, this revolting blackguard was regarded as a hero. The General Assembly of the Church of Scotland, like Cumberland himself, obviously saw the hand of God in the matter, and composed a fawning official address referring to the "public blessings . . . on mankind" vouchsafed by the Hanoverian Royal Family.[152] St Andrews University (the third oldest in the English-speaking world, after Oxford and Cambridge), invited Cumberland to become its Chancellor: another triumph of academic scholarship.[153] The Anglicans agreed with the Presbyterians, and the Archbishop of York rivalled the General Assembly: Cumberland, he thought, had done "singularly great" things for the country, and "his manner of performing them was still more to be admired".[154] The archbishop sadly left it uncertain as to which "manner of performing" he admired most – whether it was robbery or destruction, or perhaps murder or rape, which most took his fancy. Parliament gave Cumberland (and his heirs, not that he had any) a further £25,000 a year on top of his civil list income; a medal was struck and a ballet, *Culloden*, composed in his honour; a gate in Hyde Park (appropriately, the portal nearest to the Tyburn gallows) was christened the Cumberland Gate, to commemorate this vile scoundrel – and it still honours him in the twenty-first century; and *a flower*, the fragrant sweet william – was named after him. (To have, at this day, a flower named after such a villain, could only be equalled by dubbing another flower "sweet adolf".) Handel complimented him with "See the Conquering Hero comes" (performed first at a thanksgiving religious service in St Paul's Cathedral), and dedicated an oratorio, *Judas Maccabeus*, to this war criminal. Fort William and Fort Augustus were both named after him (and both still proudly proclaim his name), as were several places in America (such as the Cumberland Gap); Glasgow University gave him an honorary doctorate; and Sir Joshua Reynolds painted him, sword in hand. He could do no wrong: in Fitzroy MacLean's words, he "gave a ball at Vauxhall in honour of a well-known whore called Peggy Banks, landing there from the Royal Barge amid cheering crowds to the strains of the National Anthem".[155] Altogether, atrocities directed against Highlanders seemed, and still seem, to be much to the anglophone public's taste. The *Dictionary of National Biography* said: "few people were moved to enquire into the slaughter of enemies who were widely regarded as being subhuman." Even in London, however, when someone suggested making Cumberland a freeman of a City company, some daring individual hinted it should be the Butchers.[156]

As long as twenty-three years later, Thomas Pennant was no more critical of this orgy of savagery than to say, "let a veil be flung over a few excesses consequential of a day, productive of so much benefit to the united kingdoms".[157] A veil, of a sort, has been flung over the battle, and the "few excesses" which Pennant was prepared to concede. "For many years thereafter", said Fitzroy MacLean, "Culloden was included in the battle honours of the British regiments engaged."[158] They are not now included: one hopes that it is because the regiments concerned are ashamed of their disgusting reign of terror.

21. A little bloodletting

Cumberland described his campaign against the Highlanders as "a little bloodletting", and went on to express his "fear that this vile spot may still be the ruin of this island and our family".[159] This fear no doubt helps to explain his horrific actions; if the royal family had to return to the modest German principality they had left only thirty-two years before, there would be no more dukedoms at the age of five, no more showers of honours and public acclaim, no more vast incomes at the age of ten, no more religious services giving thanks for criminal atrocities, and probably fewer mistresses. Fear is often a basic cause of inhuman misconduct.

The campaign in the Highlands after Culloden was in fact the conquest of the Highlands by the Lowlanders and English; the transformation of the previous subjective theory (that the Highlands had always been ruled by Edinburgh, or since 1603 by Edinburgh and London) into objective fact. This conquest was clearly defined by Cumberland when he explained why he had marched his army from Inverness through the Great Glen to Fort William; it was, he said, to show "that it is as much in His Majesty's power to march his forces into the country which they have hitherto boasted as inaccessible as into any other part of his dominions".[160] Cumberland told his army that they were there "to crush the insolence of a set of thieves and plunderers who have learned from their fathers to disturb every government they have lived under"[161] – an exact description of the whole of Gaeldom as it was seen from the Lowlands: not the slightest hint that many of the Highlanders had fought for the Hanoverian king – all were "thieves and plunderers", to be crushed.

The merciless campaign of the British armed forces against the Highlanders after Culloden made possible the subsequent merciless campaign by the clearing chiefs against the Highlanders, and the two campaigns were worthy of each other. Cumberland wanted "to transport to the colonies several entire clans, such as the Camerons and most of the MacDonalds and several others".[162] Forbes of Culloden (who by Lowland standards was a moderate) also benignly suggested "that entire clans should be transported to the American colonies".[163] Cumberland was succeeded as commander in Scotland by the Earl of Albemarle, and he, said Devine, "concluded the only way to ensure permanent stability was to devastate whole areas and deport large numbers of their inhabitants".[164] The sentiments of Cumberland, Forbes, and Albemarle could almost have been used as a blueprint by the Highland proprietors in their clearance operations. Professor G. M. Trevelyan ridiculed the idea that the landlords were in any way to blame for driving out the Highlanders, saying that those who criticized the clearances must believe that the chiefs had had "a sudden access of wickedness"; perhaps he thought that a similar argument might be used to exonerate the brutality of the British army and navy in the Highlands after Culloden.

22. Honesty and fidelity

Let us leave the painful topic of the behaviour of the English and Lowland invaders after the defeat of Prince Charles, and return to a less stressful theme, the disposition of the Highlanders. Dr Joseph MacIntyre, minister of Glenorchy, praised his parishioners' character, even when they were impoverished. "The simple promise of the poor to pay, without any other obligation, will, generally, procure from those who know them, the loan of money in their straits, and family necessaries from the shop-keeper."[165] Dr Robert Jackson (who, said David Stewart, had served – though a Lowlander himself – "in many campaigns with Highland regiments", and thus became "intimately acquainted with their character") affirmed that the Highlanders' "character is conspicuous for honesty and fidelity".[166] Stewart wrote: "The integrity and capability of the numerous bands of Highlanders which supplied Edinburgh with *Caddies* is proverbial. These Caddies were, during the last [eighteenth] century, a species of porters and messengers plying in the open street, always ready to execute any commission, and to act as messengers to the most distant corners of the kingdom, and were often employed in business requiring secrecy and dispatch, and frequently had many sums of money entrusted to their care. Instances of a breach of trust were most rare, indeed almost unknown. These men carried to the South the same fidelity and trustworthiness which formed a marked trait in the character of the Highlanders of that period, and formed themselves into a society, with regulations of their own."[167] Smollett, too, noted in 1771 that these Highland caddies were "wonderfully acute, and so noted for fidelity, that there is no instance of [a] cawdy's having betrayed his trust".[168]

One of these caddies was called Ned Burke. Like the others he was a Highlander; he had been born in North Uist. In the '45 he was one of Prince Charles' attendants, and he was with him for more than two months after Culloden, until the prince himself sent him away. Ultimately – after further great sufferings on the run – he returned to his job as caddy in Edinburgh. He was poor all his life, and when he died his epitaph said that he "preferred a good conscience to thirty thousand pounds".[169] There have been less persuasive tributes.

Dr James Anderson wrote in 1785 a report for the Treasury on a tour he had made in the Highlands. He commented: "The natives of the Highlands and Isles are at this present moment as much civilized in their manners, and under as just a subordination to the laws, as any people whatever; so that in no part of the world is property more secure, or lawless violence more rare among the body of the people, than there; insomuch that a single peace-officer, unattended and unarmed, can execute, without difficulty, or danger to himself, any commission that the law may require. A stranger also in those regions may go where he will, in perfect safety; and if he behaves with decent politeness, he will not only not be insulted, but will be kindly entertained wherever he goes, with a cheerful and unaffected hospitality."[170]

23. Property secured and preserved

When shipwrecks occurred (wrote Dr Anderson), not only were the sailors saved wherever possible, and "kindly entertained, but their property is secured and preserved with a degree of care, that reflects the highest honour on the natives". During the American War of Independence (1775-83), a Liverpool ship, damaged at sea, entered Loch Tarbert in Harris. The master had to leave the ship there and seek fresh instructions in Liverpool. The ship remained in Loch Tarbert, guarded by a single sailor, while the master was away for nearly two years, "without sustaining the smallest loss, either by violence or pilfering". In the winter of 1784-5 a foreign crew abandoned their ship near Iona; some Iona men, "seeing the vessel rolling, without being under proper management, put off to the ship, and, finding nobody on board, took possession of her, and carried her into Loch Scridain in Mull. The mariners, seeing their vessel safely moored, went and claimed her, and, without hesitation or dispute, obtained full possession, without any salvage or other charge being made, save a few shillings to the men who brought her in." (Men who saved an abandoned ship were legally entitled to claim high compensation under the law of salvage.) The ship and its cargo were left in the care of a neighbouring farmer for several months, without loss or charge, except a "very trifling consideration" to the farmer. Another vessel, which went ashore on Coll at the same time, was similarly saved, without any return, by the islanders. Also at the same time, two vessels from the Clyde ran aground on Islay; there was an epidemic of sickness among the crew, so the cargoes (including "ten thousand pounds in specie") were heaped on the shore. When the ships were refloated, and the cargoes collected, nothing whatever was missing "save one barrel of tar, which had probably been hove overboard, or lost through carelessness". Even more remarkable was another case. "A vessel from Ireland, laden with linen yarn, was stranded in Islay. The weather happened to become easy, and the cargo was got out; but as it was drenched in salt water, it became necessary to have the whole washed in fresh water. This was done in a river that was near, and the yarn spread about along some extensive fields near the shore. Several hundred persons were employed in this work for several weeks. Yarn is the staple manufacture of the island, so that the temptation for embezzlement was very great, as a discovery in these circumstances would have been extremely difficult. Yet when the whole was collected together, to the utter astonishment of the parties concerned, a very few hanks of the yarn (about five or six to the best of my recollection), value about two or three shillings, were wanting."

The author summed up his feelings. "I gladly record these instances of honesty and friendly care of the unfortunate. How different from what I have been witness to on the coast of England and Ireland!"[171]

Dr John Walker, in his 1764 journey to the Hebrides, said shipwrecks around Coll were not infrequent, but "the unfortunate sufferers are sure of being treated with the greatest honour and humanity by the inhabitants".[172]

24. Civilized the people

Many of the Lowland and English travellers who went to the Highlands in the later part of the eighteenth century "knew" that the mountains were populated exclusively by thieves, rogues, and barbarians – or at least, that they had been so populated up to very recently. Yet as soon as they crossed the Highland line they found that they (and their property) were much more secure, and in much less danger, than they had been in the sophisticated areas down south. They could only conclude that there had been an amazingly rapid reformation in the character of the Highlanders. Dr Anderson, for example, quickly deduced that this almost extravagant honesty of the Highlanders was a modern phenomenon. It had been the suppression of the two rebellions of 1715 and 1745, he wrote, that had led to the introduction of "a system of civil government which has entirely civilized the people". Thus this fantastic transformation in manners (if transformation there had been), from what Anderson called "perpetual wars and lawless disorder" to the most extreme integrity, had been accomplished in little more than thirty years (Dr Anderson's first example of the Highlanders' scrupulous honesty was dated "during the late war", that is between 1775 and 1783).[173]

In fact, as we have seen, there was no wondrous volte-face in behaviour. Anderson's comments were paralleled by the earlier observers, well before the '45 and the '15 rebellions. His story of the ship in Loch Tarbert in particular echoes even in detail an episode recounted by Martin some eighty years earlier, which is mentioned below. And Burt, as we will see later, wrote of the Highlanders' rigorous rectitude well before the '45 rebellion.

James Hogg, on his Highland journey in 1803, was told in the Long Island – no doubt by the landlords and sheep-farmers who gave him hospitality – that "the poorer sort are much addicted to pilfering", and at first he believed it. Yet when he came to Stornoway, despite his Lowland background, he was candid enough to confess that he "saw a striking evidence to the contrary in the inhabitants of this town. During the daytime there were thousands of white fish spread on the shores, drying on the sand. When night came they were gathered and built up in large heaps, and loosely covered with some coarse cloth, and when the sun grew warm next day they were again spread." The safety of the fish, unguarded though they were, made Hogg tell Sir Walter Scott, to whom he was writing: "I'll wager you durst not have exposed your fish in such a manner at Edinburgh, for as fine a place as it is."[174]

Ten years earlier, the minister of Kilfinichen in Mull had referred to a similar incident. In a recent shipwreck, he said, "a quantity of cork" was "scattered over" the beach for more than a mile. Cork was "much wanted" by the people for their nets, but they did not touch the wreckage, although many of them "were too poor to buy" the cork even if they had had the chance.[175]

Despite all this, it remained common knowledge – in the Lowlands – that the Highlanders before the modern "improvements" were all thieves. The Scottish histories of the Lowland Professor Gordon Donaldson, Historiographer Royal in Scotland, were still serenely repeating the calumny near the end of the twentieth century.[176]

Dr Anderson's boast about this extraordinary supposed achievement in the Highlands brought about by the central British administration does make one curious. If the London and Edinburgh authorities were able (as Dr Anderson claimed) to effect this miraculous amelioration of behaviour in the far-off (and almost impenetrable) Highlands in only three decades, why did they refrain from doing the same in the areas much closer at hand (and much easier of access), in the crime-ridden cities of the English-speaking parts of Britain? And where, moreover, they had had a much longer time to operate, but had all too conspicuously failed to work a similar miracle. Commentators using the archive of the head would not have fallen into such an error.

25. Ridiculously small

Those writers of the O.S.A. Highland parish reports who described the Highland character nearly all (there were very few exceptions) said that there had been no serious crime, or no crime at all, in their parishes within living memory, or for many years: the minister of Monzie remarked that there had been no suicide or conviction for crime "these forty years".[177] Jamieson said that the Highlanders often used to leave their houses and barns unprotected for days together, at the peat-cutting or hay seasons, or when they were tending cattle, yet nothing was ever stolen or disturbed.[178] He added that the very lasting impression made by robberies and murders showed how rare they were: the Highlanders, who knew their history, told of these uncommon deeds for centuries; and some Lowland travellers, hearing these stories, went back to Edinburgh with the impression that they were everyday occurrences.

Hugh Miller, born in 1802, made the same point. As we shall see later, he said that when in his youth he stayed with his uncle and aunt in Sutherland, their cottage door had no lock or bar, but opened with a latch, "because at that comparatively recent period the crime of theft was unknown in the district".[179]

The evidence is conclusive. As late as the second half of the nineteenth century, Sheriff Nicolson said that the criminal calendar in Skye was "ridiculously small".[180] David Stewart wrote that among the Highlanders in the old days, theft, as a sneaking and cowardly vice, was altogether unknown: "In the interior of their own society," he said, "all property was safe, without the usual security of bolts, locks, and bars."[181] Edmund Burt had put it almost as strongly a hundred years earlier. "Personal robberies are seldom heard of among them: for my own part, I have several times, with a single servant, passed the mountain way from hence [Inverness] to Edinburgh, with four or five hundred guineas [perhaps £200,000 in C.E. 2000 money] in my portmanteau, without any apprehension of robbers by the way, or danger in my lodgings at night, though in my sleep, any one, with ease, might have thrust a sword, from the outside, through the wall of the hut and my body together." He added ruefully that he wished he could say as much of his "own country, civilized as it is said to be, though one cannot be safe in going from London to Highgate".[182] And one can see that the practice of raising a cairn to commemorate robberies, which was the custom of the Highlanders, would very soon become impossible in modern society. The streets of our great cities, for example, would quickly become impassable.

Dr James Robertson, in his *Survey of the County of Inverness* (1808), made the same point. Speaking of the high moral character of the Highlanders, he said that there is "perhaps less thievery and picking in the Highlands than in any part of the King's dominions ... Single individuals travel unarmed, in all directions, through the Highlands, with thousands of pounds in their pockets, to purchase cattle, without dread or annoyance."[183] In the O.S.A. the Glenelg minister said his people were "strictly honest",[184] while the Lochgoilhead minister said his parishioners had "long been remarkable for their strict honesty"[185] – both ministers thus echoing the Glenorchy minister's testimony which we saw earlier.[186] As early as 1577 Raphael Holinshed similarly praised the Highlanders: "as for their faith and promise, they hold it with great constancie."[187]

A dislike of breaking promises is closely allied to a dislike of telling lies. Alexander MacKay wrote: "Apart from the guilt and horror felt from taking human life, no crime was considered so dreadful by our faithful and honest forefathers in Sutherland as that of perjury (mionnan éithich) [a false oath], and any individual known, or even suspected, to be guilty of such a gross violation of the moral law, was ever after shunned, and held in utter contempt."[188] It was even believed that the soul of any perjurer would continue to haunt its earthly habitation until recompense could be made for the transgression.

William Marshall, who wrote about the *Agriculture of the Central Highlands* in 1794, was no friend to the Gaels, and looked forward to the extinction of Gaelic, which event, he thought, "will be fortunate for the country"; but even he felt compelled to make some dispassionate remarks on the absence of crime. "Murder, cruelty, or even theft, is rarely heard of; nor are riotings, drunkenness, or any kind of debaucheries, at present prevalent among them; comparatively, at least, with other districts of the island."[189] Donald MacLeod said that in Sutherland any "violation of the laws of God and rules of society" was virtually unknown, and "there was no need for fiscal [the local prosecutor], constables, thief-catchers, or policemen to keep us quiet and protect property; till of late years these hateful names were not known in the Gaelic language".[190]

26. No traveller could pass

Dr Johnson noted the safety of the Highland roads, but assumed (like Dr Anderson) that it was a modern phenomenon: no doubt he had been plentifully favoured, by those who were profiting from the new order, with tales about the barbarism of the old clansfolk. He said that "the roads are secure in those places through which, forty years ago, no traveller could pass without a convoy". On another page he put the happy change even later: "Thirty years ago no herd had ever been conducted through the mountains, without paying tribute in the night, to some of the clans; but cattle are now driven, and passengers travel without danger, fear, or molestation."[191] Perhaps Dr Johnson had not had the opportunity of reading Burt, whose letters show that travellers were perfectly safe in the Highlands not thirty, or forty, but fifty years before Dr Johnson's visit. Dr Johnson did, however, take with him on his journey a copy of Martin Martin's *Description of the Western Islands of Scotland*, published in 1703, which demonstrated that the same state of affairs existed even earlier, in the seventeenth century. Martin wrote: "I am not ignorant that foreigners have been tempted, by the sight of so many wild hills, to imagine that the inhabitants, as well as the places of their residence, are equally barbarous, and to this opinion their habit [clothing] has contributed. The like is supposed by many that live in the south of Scotland; but the lion is not so fierce as he is painted, neither are the people so barbarous as people imagine. The inhabitants have humanity, and use strangers hospitably and charitably. I could bring several instances of barbarity and theft by stranger seamen in the Isles, but there is not one instance of any injury offered by the islanders to any seamen or stranger." In fact "there are some pedlars, from the shire of Moray, and other parts, who of late have fixed their residence in the Isle of Skye, and travel [carrying tempting goods to sell] through the remotest isles without any molestation; tho' some of those pedlars speak no Irish". (The fact that Dr Johnson ignored what Martin said in the book he had with him on his expedition perhaps shows that Johnson preferred voicing his own opinions to considering the evidence of others.)

Martin related a case which occurred about 1687 of an English ship which sprang a leak; its skipper, Captain Jackson of Whitehaven, left her fully loaded, with only two men aboard, in a bay in the island of Scalpay, near Harris; twelve months later the captain returned to find the vessel – after a year when it was at the mercy of the Highland barbarians – quite untouched. Another English ship, "the *Dromedary* of London, of 600 tons burthen", was lost off Skye. Captain Lotch and his men, who escaped, were kindly entertained by the chief and clan of MacLeod, and although the cargo which the seamen had rescued included six boxes of gold dust, "there was not the least thing taken from them by the inhabitants".[192]

Even if Dr Johnson had not read Burt, and disbelieved Martin, a moment's consideration would have convinced him that a government which was unable to control the brigands and robbers who operated almost with impunity at the very gates of the English capital (in Johnson's time highwaymen infested Finchley Common, Hampstead Heath, Epping Forest, Blackheath, Shooters Hill, Thornton Heath, Hounslow Heath, and Turnham Green, among other delectable spots all within a mile or two of London) – such an impotent authority could hardly take any credit for the safety of wayfarers in the wildest recesses of the Grampian Mountains, five hundred miles away. In 1774, the year after Dr Johnson's tour, and his praise of the English government for having made the remote Highland "roads . . . secure" for travellers, Edmund Burke, a well-known politician, was robbed by two Finchley highwaymen.[193] Sir Gilbert Elliott, Burke's friend, said he would not "trust my throat on Finchley Common after dark". In 1775, two years after Dr Johnson's astute discovery of the anglophone achievement in ensuring the security of the far-distant Highland trackways, the Norwich coach was held up in Epping Forest, a few miles outside London: three of the band of highwaymen were shot dead by the guard of the coach, before he fell himself to the bullets of the other four.[194] These matters were so commonplace in England that in 1725 one "knight of the road" took another one to court, alleging that he had been cheated out of some of the plunder: this, however, was too much for even the eighteenth-century judicial system. The solicitors involved were heavily fined, and both plaintiff and defendant were hanged a year or two later. [195]

27. The want of law

Dr Johnson was convinced that peoples who have a different law from one's own have no law at all. In James Boswell's *Life of Dr Johnson* he is quoted as agreeing with Lord Lyttelton that the Highlanders had many wants: "but you have not mentioned the greatest of them all, – the want of law." Only a page or two earlier he had felt it necessary to explain away the apparently surprising fact that he was not robbed whenever he ventured out of doors at night into the virtuous thoroughfares of London, the blameless capital city of the fortunately law-abiding English. "He walked the streets at all hours, and said he was never robbed, for the rogues knew he had little money, nor had the appearance of having much." The clear implication of Dr Johnson's words was that if "the rogues" had thought he had any money, he would have been pillaged as soon as he stepped out of his front door. In fact Boswell recorded that on one occasion Johnson was assailed in the public thoroughfare: "he told me himself that one night he was attacked in the street by four men, to whom he would not yield, but kept them all at bay, till the watch came up" and rescued him. Yet Johnson considered that it was the Highlanders who suffered from "the want of law".[196]

Only seven years after Dr Johnson's visit to the Highlands (so recently devoid of "law"), riotous and uncontrollable mobs roamed the praiseworthy streets of London for more than a week, robbing pedestrians, looting and burning down public buildings (including four jails) and a number of private houses. Boswell himself called it "the most horrid series of outrage that ever disgraced a civilized country".[197] If Dr Johnson had found a Highlander in the metropolis at that time he could have lectured him as to the sad "lawlessness" of the clan system against a background of the plunder and destruction wreaked by the Gordon Riots.

Presumably because he was unwilling to give too much credit to the peaceable Highlanders for the undisturbed progress of their tour, Johnson – having honestly confessed that in the Highlands "the night and the day are equally solitary and equally safe" – added his own explanation: "for where there are so few travellers, why should there be robbers."[198] By that criterion, when there were still fewer travellers (in the days of the clans), there should have been still less pillage; yet according to Johnson himself, the Highlands then were infested with bandits. It seems that great luminaries love to settle matters with plausible explanations – even if the plausibility falls apart when scrutinized.[199]

28. Macaulay's History

When Lord Macaulay wrote his *History* in 1848-55 it had become the fashion to regard the Highlands as the most picturesque part of Great Britain, so he felt he had to justify the philistine distaste of the eighteenth-century Sassenachs for the mountains, which Edmund Burt (for example, as we saw) denounced as "monstrous excrescences", revolting in their "frightful irregularity and horrid gloom".[200] Macaulay achieved this by falling back on the Lowlanders' unshakeable belief that all Highlanders were thieves and cut-throats: no one, said Macaulay, could be expected to enjoy the scenery while travelling among the bloodthirsty and rapacious Highlanders during the clan system. "A traveller must be freed from all apprehension of being murdered or starved before he can be charmed by the bold outlines and rich tints of the hills." Aesthetic admiration, he contended, had to wait until the Highlanders were civilized, and the Highlands had become as secure as the capital city, when "there was as little danger of being slain or plundered in the wildest defile of Badenoch or Lochaber as in Cornhill".[201] The necessary implication was that in London all citizens were safe from criminal outrages; otherwise, the satisfying contrast between the behaviour of the barbarian Highlanders and that of the virtuous Londoners would be lost. Unfortunately, only a page or two later Macaulay himself referred to "the pickpockets who infested Drury Lane Theatre", and "the highwaymen who stopped coaches on Blackheath"[202] – Drury Lane being only a mile and a half, and Blackheath only seven miles, from Cornhill – without, it seems, realizing that he had destroyed his own argument. In fact, as we have seen, so far as the ordinary peaceful wayfarer was concerned, Cornhill was a much more dangerous place to be than "the wildest defile of Badenoch", both when Macaulay wrote and for centuries before, and after. It is curious to observe how a belief firmly held by all those whose opinion matters will be unthinkingly set down by an illustrious historian, despite the fact that the same writer makes clear in the same few pages that the belief cannot be correct.

Macaulay was the leading intellectual of his day: essayist, poet, politician, member of the Cabinet, author of a code of law for India, and historian – "like a book in breeches",[203] said Sidney Smith. But he must have felt embarrassed by his own Highland descent, at a time when the perpetual propaganda of the Highland landlords insisted that the Highlanders were all savages, in order to justify their actions in driving many Highlanders out of the Highlands, and even out of Britain. Yet by the time Victoria ascended the throne many people were prepared to accept the old clansfolk as being colourful and romantic, at least so far as their unflinching loyalty to the ill-fated Prince Charles was concerned. Unfortunately Macaulay could not claim any reflected glory from that apparently glamorous episode. (And who would have known his own family history more thoroughly than the renowned historian Lord Macaulay?) When Lord Macaulay's grandfather, the Rev. John MacAulay, minister of South Uist, found out that the prince was in the Outer Hebrides, he immediately sent a warning to *his* father, the Rev. Aulay MacAulay, minister of Harris. The unfeeling and covetous Aulay thereupon got together a band of armed men, and descended on Scalpay near Harris, to try and capture the fugitive (who had taken shelter there), so as to claim the £30,000 reward. But the tacksman of Scalpay, Donald Campbell (even though he himself supported the Hanoverian succession), being a Highlander, refused to give up the man who had trusted in his hospitality, and MacAulay had to retreat, baffled and not a penny richer. "So far as we know", wrote Hugh Douglas, "in spite of the price on his head, this was the only attempt to betray the Prince throughout the Rising and flight"[204] – a notable achievement on the part of the MacAulay family.

Fourteen years later, in 1760, when the Rev. John MacAulay had moved from South Uist to become the incumbent at Lismore and Appin, a petition from the small tenants there accused him of trying to encourage a clearance in Appin, in the hope of getting some of the cleared land for himself.[205] It appears that the members of the MacAulay family, Thomas Babington and the rest of them, knew which side their bread was buttered on.

29. Accumulated filth of years

Macaulay must have felt under great pressure to distance himself from his forebears – perhaps like some modern immigrants, who after they have safely established themselves in Britain demonstrate their respectability by being more opposed to immigration than anyone else. Presumably driven by similar motives,

Macaulay became outspokenly critical of the Highlanders. The unromantic and mercenary attempt by Macaulay's own forebears, alone in the whole Highlands, to sell Prince Charles – for immediate execution – in return for the blood-money, must have given him all the more incentive to adopt the Lowland and English views of the Highlanders. Macaulay, writing for English readers, certainly made it clear that he accepted the growing English belief that they – the English – were now the supreme nation of all time: "The English have become the greatest and most highly civilized people that ever the world saw, [and] have spread their dominion over every quarter of the globe."[206] And again: "The history of England is emphatically the history of progress."[207] (One almost expects him to add, "Can I have my money now?")

Much of what Macaulay said about the Highlands was factual – for example his comments on the independence of the clan countries, on the powerlessness of the Lowland authorities beyond the Highland line, and so forth, possibly because these facets of Highland life were useful to "prove" to his readers that the old clan society was so outlandish that it could not have been allowed to survive. But elsewhere he merely confirmed the official propaganda. He satisfied his readers' prejudices, and supplied some of the purple prose his audience was looking for, by castigating the Highlanders as unclean – they were filthy, he said, and in the Highland huts "every nook would have swarmed with vermin"[208] (not the definite "did swarm", but the conjectural "would have swarmed"); "their clothes were begrimed with the accumulated filth of years". In fact washing clothes in the pure water of the mountain streams or the unpolluted rivers would have been easy enough – much easier of course than trying to do laundry in the foul slums of the great cities, where the (not always uncontaminated) water had to be carried from the nearest pump: other commentators mentioned how clean the Highlanders' clothes were, and how dirty those of the city poor.

Macaulay's strictures may owe something (as remarked above) to his need to distance himself from his Highland ancestors; something to a desire to fortify the satisfying belief that all foreigners (which in an English context included the Gaels) are disgustingly dirty; something to an unconscious comparison of like with unlike – of the English upper class with the rank-and-file clansfolk (certainly, in the houses of the English lower orders when Macaulay wrote, and long afterwards – as I remember from my own childhood – objectionable insects often flocked freely, while travellers in the Highlands noted as a prosaic observable fact that bugs could not survive in the peat-reek of the Highland hut, so that so far from dramatically "swarming in every nook", they were not there at all); and something to a failure to realize that all societies, and all strata within all societies, have their own standards of cleanliness, by which standards they judge themselves and all others. In the very decade when Macaulay was condemning the

Highlanders, it was suggested (at the Oxford college of which I later became a member) that some baths should be installed to allow the undergraduates to clean themselves: the Master thought it was quite unnecessary – "they are only here for eight weeks at a time", he said.[209] And the Master was not talking about the poorer members of the community. Cleanliness is not an absolute, but a convention. While Macaulay ostentatiously held his nose at the thought of the old Highlanders, we hold our noses (perhaps with more justification) at the thought of Macaulay and his fellow citizens.

30. Eighteen times more honest

Clan society was not destroyed in a day; its destruction took many years. The behaviour and the moral code engendered by clan society were even more persistent. (Economic circumstances can change overnight, but patterns of behaviour, although originally emerging from such circumstances, usually take much longer to alter.) Certainly they lasted well into the nineteenth century, if not later still. Thus there is great significance in some figures given by David Stewart, in which he counted up the numbers of convicted criminals in the Highlands from 1747 to 1817.[210] Ninety men and women were in that time executed for such crimes as murder, cattle stealing, theft, and infanticide. Nine of these (ten per cent of the total) were strangers, either soldiers stationed in the Highlands, or others passing through. Of the natives, two were the MacIains who protected Prince Charles at the risk of their lives after Culloden, and were later hanged for stealing a cow. Seventeen of them altogether, including the two MacIains, were executed for cattle stealing between 1747 and 1765 – there were no executions for that crime after 1765. Most of these cattle rustlers had been concerned in the rebellion, for example Donald Cameron, or Donald Ban Leane, who was executed at Kinloch Rannoch in 1752. These men had been unable to return to their homes after Culloden because of the ferocious savagery with which the Duke of Cumberland's army (which, luckily, did not suffer from Dr Johnson's "want of law") treated the Gaels – behaviour which was in marked contrast to the forbearance and humanity of the "barbarous" Highlanders in the Jacobite army. Thus driven from their homes, their crimes of cattle lifting could more justly be put at the door of the new society than the old.[211] The same is true of the supposed crime of another of the ninety, James Stewart of the Glen, who was hanged for the murder of Campbell of Glenure. Glenure was the Government factor on the Appin estates, and was shot dead on the eve of large-scale evictions of Jacobite tenants. Most of those who have studied the "Appin murder" think that James Stewart was not guilty of the killing.

It is true that one Highlander called MacIntosh, an unregenerate villain, formed a gang, and took to highway robbery.[212] His father, said David Stewart, "had usurped possession of an estate to which he had no right", and "lived, after the death of his wife, in a kind of seraglio", shunned by his neighbours. The son was as bad as the father, and his "last exploit" was to try, with his gang, to rob Sir Hector Munro, when the latter was returning to the north in 1770. MacIntosh escaped to America, and joined the rebels there, but three of his gang were "taken and executed at Inverness".[213]

However, it is a striking indication of the general character of the Highlanders that all the serious crime committed among some 389,000 people – David Stewart had to take his figures from the official judicial circuits, so that his figures covered some Highland border districts as well as the strict Gaelic area – over a period of *seventy years* can be analysed almost by individual offences. Many might wish that crime were as infrequent as that in a modern British city of the same population! Stewart himself made the comparison: as against ninety offenders in the whole Highlands in seventy years, "the number of criminals convicted in one year, 1817, at the spring and summer assizes at Lancaster [which would have included the industrial towns of Lancashire], was eighty-six" – very nearly the same number.[214]

Taking all ninety of these criminals in the Highlands, however, including the strangers and the men impelled to rob in order to live after the '45, the proportion works out as one criminal per year for every 302,502 of the population. Stewart also calculated the corresponding figure for all England and Wales, for the seven years up to 1817. There, the proportion worked out as one criminal per year for every 16,903 of the population. That is to say, the people of the Highlands, in 1747-1817, were about eighteen times more honest, or less criminal, than the people of England and Wales were in 1810-17.[215] This extraordinarily low Highland criminal figure can obviously not be attributed to the new order that was being forced upon the Highlands in the second half of the eighteenth century. One supposes that even Dr Johnson would not have had the audacity to credit the English Government with being some eighteen times more successful at fighting misconduct in the far-off and impermeable Highlands than it was on its own doorstep.

31. Racial assumptions

Professor Richards said that "racial assumptions underpinned Stewart's ideology". In the Stewart world-view, said Richards, the Highlanders were a "pure stock", who "could not adapt to the world of industry"; in fact Stewart (he continued) was "prepared to depict the entire problem in terms of Saxonism against the Celts".[216] If this is intended to imply that (in Stewart's opinion) the Highlanders, being a "pure stock", were free from crime and immorality, all such bad behaviour being left to the Saxons, it is not what David Stewart wrote; in fact it shows a remarkable failure to understand Stewart's manifest message. Stewart, rightly, never tried to assert that the lack of crime among the Highlanders was the result of superior racial characteristics, or of "better" genes. Quite the opposite: just as clan society was a milieu which produced people who did not commit crimes, so commercial society was a milieu which acted as a criminal breeding ground, whether the people influenced by it were originally Lowlanders or Highlanders, Saxons or Celts. He repeatedly made clear the non-racial, or even anti-racial, basis of his comments. He pointed out "how rapidly such cruel measures [the clearances] lead to poverty, immorality, and crime".[217] (and the victims of the clearances were the Gaels, not the Saxons – so it was the Gaels who were led into "immorality and crime"). The villages which were set up to house the evicted Highlanders were far from being the abodes of rectitude: in fact they were the "seats of misery and vice".[218] Ireland (and its Celtic population) showed us, said Stewart, "how fertile poverty and misery are in crimes".[219] If the improvements were to continue, "may we not dread lest they realize in the north of Scotland the lawless turbulence of the sister island of Celts".[220] Contemporary towns, then populated by immigrants from all over Scotland (Highlanders and Lowlanders) were, said Stewart, "the resorts of immorality and crime".[221] Again, Stewart asked, "Will the Highlanders, as cottagers, without employment, refrain from immorality and crime? Can we expect from such men the same regularity of conduct as when they were independent, both in mind and in circumstances?"[222] He supplied his own answer: "how idleness and poverty generate vice in populous towns, the records of the criminal courts sufficiently evince. These show, likewise, how numerous the crimes committed by Highlanders, or, at least, persons with Highland names, and of Highland descent, have become in cities."[223] He returned to the subject, pointing out that Highlanders were being driven to places where "poverty, and the too frequent attendants, vice and crime, will lay the foundation for a character which will be the disgrace, as that already obtained has been an honour, to this country".[224]

Clearances, in fact, led directly to crime, even among those Highlanders still in the Highlands. "When the stock graziers got possession of the pasture grounds", one result was law-breaking: "many sheep were stolen at that period."[225] Stewart emphasized the point. "When the engrossing system commenced in the North, and the people [i.e. the Highlanders] were removed from their farms, a spirit of revenge was strongly evinced among those who were permitted to remain in the country. They saw themselves reduced to poverty", and the result was "thefts from the pastures" of the new big farmers. But since these crimes "commenced only when they were reduced to poverty, and [were] instigated by vindictive feelings for the loss of their ancient habitations, may it not be believed that, if these irritating causes had not occurred, neither would the crimes which seem to have resulted from them? And if circumstances confirm the justness of this supposition, may we not ask what degree of responsibility attaches to those whose plans led on to these crimes?"[226]

So Stewart insisted that the Highlanders, so far from being "a pure stock" which could never fall from grace, were being led into crime by the new social system. At the same time the Saxons, though more often found in the towns and cities where the new economic arrangements frequently pushed people into criminality, were – in a different social milieu – as crime-free as the original Highlanders. Though the city of Lancaster, said Stewart, suffered a heavy criminal calendar, "the agricultural parts of the neighbouring county of Westmorland [populated entirely by Saxons] . . . equal any part of the kingdom in morality and exemption from crime."[227]

Stewart could scarcely have made it more obvious that in his opinion it was not race, or genes, but the form of society, that was the determining factor in how people behaved. It is extraordinary how anyone (however academically eminent) reading what Stewart repeatedly wrote, can have failed to see this.

32. How did they survive?

If we take seriously the historical narratives of orthodox writers, the inevitable conclusion is that the Highlanders must surely have died out as a separate race many years ago. If the accepted version of Highland history is true, there could not have been any problem about what to do with the ordinary Highlanders when the small group of charter holders had seized the Highlands as private property, and rented it out to large commercial farmers, and subsequently to hunting, shooting and fishing "sportsmen". As we saw at some length earlier, the "sterile overcrowded" Highlands are depicted as having been hostile to any human survival. The Highlanders (so runs the scholastically correct version of history) were meagre peasants, depending on "subsistence agriculture". They had to live on their crops, though their holdings were "tiny"; adverse weather, inescapable in the Highlands, led to "widespread death"; crops often failed, so that "starvation was the inevitable outcome"; famine was a regular occurrence, and only the arrival of the improvements "meant that fewer people died". If any stray members of the human race had survived such conditions, they must clearly have been wiped out by the perpetual wars and regular massacres that (as we are assured by Professor Donaldson, for example) constituted their social system.[228]

Yet the same writers tell us that despite the Highlanders being doomed to live on sterile soil, suffering frequent famine and unceasing slaughter, the Highlands "became more and more crowded", in the words of Grant and Cheape.[229] That, as we have seen elsewhere, may be an exaggeration; but it is a fact that, after centuries of supposedly continuous starvation and carnage, there were nearly 300,000

Highlanders still in existence at the time of Culloden. Not only that, but as we shall see later they were extremely tough and resilient.

It is worth repeating that a narrative will only carry conviction if it is consistent. Readers who know nothing of the different historical approaches will automatically use the archive of the head; and if some of the facts alleged do not chime smoothly with the rest of the account, incredulity inevitably ensues.

33. Place of refuge

Lowlanders were fond of comparing themselves, whom they naturally described as exquisitely peaceful and impeccably honest, with the bloodthirsty ruffians who lived in the Highlands. John Major, writing in 1521, sadly admitted that the Highlanders hated the Lowlanders, that is to say people like Major himself, the "house-holding Scots, or quiet and civil-living people – that is, all who lead a decent and reasonable life".[230] In *Rob Roy* Sir Walter Scott makes Bailie Nicol Jarvie (the character who repeatedly voices Scott's own beliefs about early eighteenth century Scotland) point the distinction between the two peoples: the Highlands "are, and hae been for this thousand years by-past", the home of "the maist lawless unchristian limmers [scoundrels] that ever disturbed a douce [peaceable], quiet, God-fearing neighbourhood, like this o' ours in the west here [i.e., the Glasgow area, which still does not quite have the reputation of being douce, quiet, and God-fearing]".[231] A recent historian contrasted the wild Highlands with "the doucer, more peaceable central parts of Scotland".[232] Professor Smout affirmed that the conquest of the Highlands after 1746 was best described as "a slow assimilation of the Lowland norms of behaviour, brought about by the increasing strength of the forces of law and order in the hills"; it was the introduction of a "new moral world", a "triumph of order and of Lowland ethics", led by Highland landowners in a "spirit of economic zeal and moral reformation". Professor Smout unblushingly presented the Duke of Argyll, the outstanding gangster chief, the superlative robber baron, whose family fortunes were built by incessant plunder and shameless thievery (backed up by the Lowland authorities) as the champion of this new lawfulness, this "new moral world" and "Lowland ethics".[233]

Yet ironically, the Highlands, so often depicted as the stamping ground of lawlessness, were in fact (in reality, as opposed to the history books) – compared with the Lowlands, and despite the best efforts of appalling brigands like the Dukes of Argyll – the abode of peace and security; while the Lowlands, so far from being "douce, quiet, [and] God-fearing", were during the centuries before Culloden in almost constant violent turmoil. In fact prominent Lowlanders (according to the old manuscript quoted in the Muckairn N.S.A. report) used to take refuge in the Highlands from the lawlessness of the Lowlands. "Of old, because of the frequent incursions of the English into this kingdom [of Scotland], and other commotions, it was usual that men of quality, whose interest lay in the low countries, did purchase some small parcel of lands in the Highlands, into which, in time of these public calamities, they used to withdraw for a while, when they could not, without hazard, reside at home."[234] The reference to "purchasing" does not invalidate what was said earlier on the subject of "sales of land". In such a thinly populated country as the Highlands, enough land for a temporary hide-out would be easy enough to come by, provided it was in no one's occupation at the time; and no doubt if some artful dodger had acquired a charter claiming "ownership" of that area, a small sum of money would have kept him happy. The Highlanders, of course, would no doubt have treated such temporary Lowland refugees with the hospitality they always displayed to strangers.

The N.S.A. report on Inveraray mentioned what seems to have been the same phenomenon. In 1650 (it said) an English service, as well as the Gaelic one, was instituted in the parish church, because at that time "many persons came here from the low country, probably as a place of refuge".[235] And David Stewart, after referring to the grievous state of the Lowlands following the murder of James I in 1437, wrote that the Highlands "may be said to have lived in a state of peace and repose, compared with the distractions and turbulence in the south, whenever the laws and the executive authority were for a time suspended."[236] Eric Linklater remarked that "from the fourteenth to the seventeenth century life was probably safer in the northern Highlands than in the southern Lowlands".[237]

The Lowlands' economic and political system meant that there was a constant jockeying for power and property among the nobility; and just as the Highlanders suffered from their ambitious neighbours in the Lowlands, so the Lowlanders suffered from their ambitious neighbours in England. The result was that during the centuries when the clan system was in full flower throughout the Highlands there were in the contemporary Lowlands repeated outbreaks of civil commotion, complicated and exacerbated by aggressive interventions – political and military – from England. To make this point clear, a short survey will now be made of conditions during the four centuries when the Bruces and the Stewarts were ruling in the "douce, quiet, God-fearing, civil-living" Lowlands (in what A. G. MacDonell called the "civilized counties"), while the clan system held sway in the Highlands. This will enable us to see the "Lowland norms of behaviour", and the "Lowland ethics" at work in their homeland, and it will become clear how justified (or otherwise) is the boast that – in contrast to the Highlands – the Lowlands were "doucer", "more peaceable", and in a state of "moral reformation", exhibiting the "triumph of order".

34. Disorder and misery

Histories of Scotland often say or imply that the thirteenth century was a tranquil time of peace in the Lowlands (and in England), before the outbreak of the troubles following on the uncertainty about the kingly succession which arose in the last decade of that century. J. Glover described it as "a time of hope", and said, "Scotland enjoyed a stability in the thirteenth century which contrasted sharply with what was to happen later on."[238] That was history seen through rose-tinted spectacles. The Scottish King Alexander II (1214-49) took advantage of the armed conflicts in England, at the time of the barons' war against King John, to invade northern England, killing and burning in the normal fashion of civilized armies. Only a little later King John marched with his destructive army of mercenaries – recruited from the most savage cut-throat bands which could be found across civil-living northern Europe – through the north of England, whence came many of the barons who had opposed him. "The chroniclers record terrible ravaging, plundering, and burning during this triumphant march, scenes of atrocity such as events in the reign of Stephen alone in English history afford a parallel",[239] said A. L. Poole in the *Oxford History*. Since that was how King John behaved in his own country, it may be imagined how he operated north of the border, when (said Poole) "for nine days his troops harried the Lowlands of Scotland to punish Alexander II": no doubt the unfortunate Lowlanders welcomed the fact that it was nothing personal. A novel set in those years said that "while John burned Roxburgh – a royal burgh and castle at the junction of the Teviot and the Tweed – the mercenaries pursued the King of Scots to the gates of Edinburgh, and, during their return, deliberately burned Haddington, Dunbar, Berwick, and the fair abbey of Coldingham".[240] The rest of Alexander's reign was occupied with (not very "douce" nor extraordinarily "quiet") rebellions in Galloway and Moray, as well as war with the Norwegians, and an aggressive expedition into Argyll.

So much for the first half of the thirteenth century. More Lowland suffering came in the next reign, said the Rev. James MacKenzie (who painted a strange picture of J. Glover's thirteenth-century Lowland "hope" and "stability"). "During the minority of Alexander III [from 1249] great disorder and misery prevailed. Rival factions made war on each other. Castles and villages were burned. Tillage was interrupted, and famine aggravated the miseries of war. The great object of the contending parties was to have possession of the king . . . To get hold of him they did not hesitate to use violence";[241] one night the young king was seized in his bed at Kinross, and carried by his captors to Stirling before morning. When the king was older, the violence abated for the time; but the deaths of Alexander III in 1286 (his horse fell over a cliff on a dark night), and of his granddaughter the Maid of Norway in 1290 (while sailing back to Scotland), and the resulting claims of no fewer than thirteen nobles to the crown of Scotland, led to more than thirty years of mayhem – the reign of John Balliol, as a humiliated underling to Edward I of England, the heroic defiance of William Wallace, and the long struggle of Robert the Bruce (who became king in 1306 after murdering one of his main rivals, Sir John Comyn, in a church at Dumfries, and then fought against the English, though he had earlier supported the English overlordship). For example, in 1295 the Scots invaded and plundered the English border counties, and the following year Edward I captured Berwick (then a Scottish town) and slaughtered most of the inhabitants. One historian said that "the years 1298 to 1305 were some of the most miserable in Scottish history"[242] – that is, Lowland history: Lowland historians often say "Scotland" when they mean "the Lowlands". In the last few years of the thirteenth century and the first few of the fourteenth there were many pitched battles – Dunbar, Stirling Bridge, Falkirk, Methven, Dalry, Loudon Hill, Bannockburn, and so on; and frequent English incursions, together with at least half a dozen reprisal invasions of the north of England, all of them wreaking death and destruction among the "enemy" populations. This melancholy epoch ended with the death of Edward II of England in 1327, and of Robert I (the Bruce) of Scotland in 1329. The long war, as Hume Brown said, "had certainly done much evil. Thousands of Scotsmen [i.e., Lowlanders] had been slain in the many battles that had been fought; towns and villages and the lands of the nobles and gentry had been burnt and plundered . . . and so at the end of the war Scotland [i.e., the Lowlands] was far poorer than it had been" in Alexander's time.[243]

Next came David II (1329-71), Robert I's son, but things got no better: David was "a very unworthy son of his father, and his reign a very unhappy one for Scotland",[243] (that is, the Lowlands) said Hume Brown. Edward Balliol (son of John) landed with an army, beat King David's forces at Dupplin Moor (1332), where "an English chronicler noted with bloodthirsty glee that the pile of Scottish dead stood more than a spear's length high".[244] Balliol was crowned king, but later was chased back to England. Then he returned, with English support, and beat David's party at Halidon Hill (1333), where "six Scottish earls, seventy barons and nearly 500 knights were killed",[244] not to mention the carnage among the less carefully counted commoners. Balliol and the English King Edward III divided the Lowlands between them; but when England became involved in the long struggle (the Hundred Years' War) against France, in 1339, Balliol was again driven out, and David II was brought back from France, where he had had to flee. In 1346 David's men invaded England, and (said Glover) "carried out horrible acts of cruelty in defenceless villages".[245] The English then won the Battle of Neville's Cross, where they inflicted heavy casualties, and captured King David. He was eleven years a prisoner in the Tower of London, and was only released on the payment of a heavy annual ransom, which was exacted by England every year for the next twenty years, until 1377. Apart from that, there were several rebellions by

Scottish nobles; perhaps a third of the Lowlanders died from the Black Death in 1349-50; and in 1356, when Edward III invaded, the defence was a "scorched earth" policy, while Edward laid waste the Lowlands from the border to Edinburgh and back – the so-called "burnt Candlemas".[246] Not surprisingly, the poet Dunbar said these were "dark and drublie [abusive] days";[247] and one historian described David's reign as "decades of misery for ordinary people".[248]

35. Robert II, Robert III

King David, who was a Bruce, was succeeded by his nephew Robert II (1371-1390), the first of the Stewart dynasty. The usual strife and devastation continued. The English invaded in 1385, and burned Melrose, Edinburgh, Perth, and Dundee – abbeys, homes, workplaces, farms, were all destroyed. Three years later Robert's men invaded England, beat the English at Chevy Chase, and caused much destruction and many deaths. A contemporary could see nothing but chaos. "In those days there was no law in Scotland [i.e., the Lowlands]; but the great man oppressed the poor man and the whole kingdom was one den of thieves. Slaughters, robberies, fire-raisings and other crimes went unpunished, and justice was sent into banishment, beyond the kingdom's bounds."[249] John Buchan wrote that "the Scottish [i.e. Lowland] nobles from the fourteenth to the sixteenth century were probably the most turbulent, rapacious, and ignorant in Europe".[250]

Robert II's son was Robert III (1390-1406). This reign was no better. A Scots invasion of England led to many commoners being slain, and many lords being killed or captured, at Homildon Hill in 1402. One historian wrote: "These were very unruly times for Scotland [i.e., the Lowlands] . . . The descriptions do give a gloomy picture of anarchy and lawlessness, of 'horrible destructions, burnings and slaughters'."[251] The king's own brother, Alexander, Earl of Buchan, seized some of the lands of the Bishop of Moray, and, when the bishop objected, he burned down the episcopal cathedral at Elgin. Robert's son David behaved so badly that in 1401 the king had him arrested and imprisoned in a castle belonging to another of the king's brothers, the Duke of Albany. The next year it was announced that he had died, and the rumour was that he had been starved to death. Robert then sent his only other son, James, aged twelve, by ship to France, probably thinking he might be safer there than at home in the Lowlands when his father should die. He was captured by English pirates, handed over to the English king, and put in the Tower of London (like his great-great-uncle). He did not return to Scotland for eighteen years. Robert was prostrated by the news of his son's capture, and died within days.[252]

36. James I

James I (1406-37), Robert's son, was nominally king at the age of twelve, as soon as his father died in 1406, but as he was imprisoned in England his uncle the Duke of Albany was the real ruler until 1424, when James was finally allowed to return. In the interim, "the land [i.e., the Lowlands] was filled with oppression and violence"; the nobles "held the laws in open contempt. They kept the whole country in confusion with their feuds and revenges, their fierce wars on one another, and their cruel oppressions of the people. Outrage and violence filled the land."[253] An "ancient chronicler" said the kingdom (i.e., the Lowlands) was "little else than a wide den of robbers".[254] One new horror was introduced to the Lowlands in this reign. Different ideas were abroad, and doubt was being cast on some of the doctrines taught by the Catholic Church. An Englishman, James Resby, and later a Bohemian, Paul Crawar, preached these new principles. The result of these attempts at free speech was that Resby was burnt alive at Perth in 1407 ("an ugly omen of much that was to follow"),[255] and Crawar "in 1433 at St Andrews, later the scene of many similar executions".[256] Many were tortured to death in the name of religion in the Lowlands in the following century and a half. Even in the Highlands, Lowland land charters and Lowland honours were causing great trouble. Donald, Lord of the Isles, claimed the earldom of Ross in right of his wife, and led an army across the Highlands to get it; but he was met by the Earl of Mar, and defeated at the Battle of Harlaw in 1411 – "one of the bloodiest battles ever fought on Scottish ground"[257] (no small distinction, as we have seen). King James returned from England to Edinburgh in 1424, and proceeded to execute or imprison a number of nobles whom he suspected of having been insufficiently enthusiastic about his return. He then invaded the Highlands, and asked the Highland clan chiefs to come to a peaceful conference at Inverness; when they arrived he imprisoned them, beheading two and hanging one without the irrelevance of a trial, in a practical demonstration of the historians' "Lowland ethics" and "moral reformation".[258] In 1436 James spent his happy Christmas-tide at the Blackfriars' monastery in Perth. A group of nobles whom he had earlier put in jail (led by his own Stewart relatives) came at night, found him hiding in the privy outlet where he had fled, and murdered him after a fist fight amid the excrement.[259]

James' queen hunted down and arrested all the conspirators. What happened to them was described by Ian Grimble. "The Earl of Atholl, about seventy-five years old and the son of a king, was tortured in public for three days in Edinburgh before he was allowed to die. A diadem of red-hot iron was placed on his head in fulfilment of the prophecy that one day he would wear a crown. But the worst torment was to have his body wrapped in cloth after a day's flogging through the streets, and then to have this covering ripped off the following morning, so that he was partially flayed before the beating began again."[260] Sir Robert Graham was subjected to similar savage tortures, and "before they suffered him to die they disembowelled his son, living, before his eyes",[261] in a further demonstration of the Lowlanders' "decent and reasonable" deportment. It seems to have been James I's queen who insisted on this ferocious revenge.

Similar abominations were enacted in England. Sir John Oldcastle became a Lollard – that is, a Protestant. Persecuted by the Catholic church, Oldcastle led a rebellion. He was executed in 1417. According to several depictions of the execution, he was fastened to a gibbet with a fire underneath him: presumably so as to prolong as much as possible the almost inconceivable torture of being burned alive.[262]

As the large crowd of English spectators enjoyed the spectacle of his protracted dying agonies, some of them no doubt consoled themselves with the patent superiority of English customs to those of the Highland barbarians.

37. James II

James II (1437-60), son of James I, came to the throne aged six, after his father was murdered. As one account says, "his minority years saw much bloodshed as rival factions vied to control Scotland [i.e., the Lowlands] through controlling the young king".[263] One of the squabbling nobles, Lord Crichton, in 1440 invited the Earl of Douglas, a rival for power, to dinner in Edinburgh Castle, then seized him and his brother, along with a third Douglas, and beheaded them all – the "black dinner".[264] Another of the competitors for dominance, the Earl of Crawford, harried the lands of the Bishop of St Andrews (the king's cousin), destroying farms and villages (which suffered for the grievous fault of being owned by the wrong person): the bishop excommunicated him; and when Crawford died in a fracas at Arbroath soon after, it was thought to be by divine intervention.[265]

One commentator wrote about this period: "Through this manner the whole youth of Scotland [i.e. the Lowlands] began to rage in mischief; for as long as there was no man to punish, much herships [armed raids] and slaughter was in the land and boroughs, great cruelty of nobles among themselves, for slaughters, theft, and murder, were their patent; and so continually, day by day, that he was esteemed the greatest man of renown and fame that was the greatest brigand, thief, or murderer ... Traitors became so proud and insolent, that they burned and herried [plundered] the country wherever they came, and spared neither old nor young, bairn nor wife, but cruelly would burn their houses and them together if they made any obstacles. Thus they raged through the country without any respect either to God or man."[266] Another author wrote: "Prodigious disorders sprang up . . . the laws fell into contempt, and robbery and outrage passed unpunished ... The miseries which the country [i.e. the Lowlands] suffered from the feuds of the nobility pass description."[267]

When James II was old enough to take real power, he played the same game. For example, in 1452 he gave a safe-conduct to the new Earl of Douglas to Stirling Castle: after supper he stabbed him to death. The earl's brother got his "revenge" by sacking the town of Stirling (whose inhabitants may have felt that it was hard to blame them). Later, at Arkinholm, James destroyed the power of the Douglas family in a pitched battle: one of the new earl's brothers was killed, another captured and executed.

Like many of the Stewart kings, James II died violently; in 1460 he was besieging the castle of Roxburgh, which was occupied by the English, when a cannon burst and killed him.

38. James III

James III (1460-88) came to the throne when he was eight: he was the son of James II, and the story of his reign is not dissimilar. "The nobles of Scotland [i.e., the Lowlands], no doubt, were for many generations the cause of immense mischiefs – outrage in every form, miseries and wreck of civil war . . ."[268] A group of nobles seized the king in 1466, held him in Edinburgh Castle, and collected honours and lands for themselves. One of them, Thomas Boyd, became Earl of Arran, and married the king's sister; so he was now allied to the king, and helped to exercise the royal power. Acting for the king, he went to Norway to arrange the king's marriage with the Norwegian king's daughter; but when he was away, his enemies seized power, and Boyd's uncle was executed. (Subsequently James took the charter to the island of Arran, and his youthful sister Princess Mary, from Boyd, and gave them both to the aged head of the Hamilton family – so *Hamilton* became the Earl of Arran, and the king's brother-in-law. This interesting episode is dealt with in volume two of this work.) In 1478 James arrested and imprisoned his own teenage brothers Albany and Mar. Mar soon died (rumour said James had killed him); Albany escaped from jail, and returned accompanied by an English army. Marching to attack this army in 1482, James was seized again at the town of Lauder by a group including his own uncle, who objected to James' "low-born" ministers. The group vindicated the "high-born" right to rule by capturing all the king's unaristocratic ministers and favourites and hanging them all "in one dismal row" over Lauder Bridge, and then incarcerating James again in Edinburgh Castle.

James and Albany were reconciled, and James regained his freedom; then the pair fell out again, and the king managed to force Albany to flee. James beat one group of rebels; later another group raised rebellion, and got the king's fifteen-year-old son on their side. James marched against the rebels, but was defeated at

Sauchieburn in 1488; he fled, and hid in a cottage, but (according to most accounts) was discovered there and stabbed to death.[269]

39. James IV

James IV (1488-1513) succeeded his father at the age of fifteen. There were frequent conflicts with England: two sea-battles in the Firth of Forth in 1489, and a plundering invasion of England (on behalf of Perkin Warbeck, the pretended Duke of York) in 1493. There was also strife with other countries. Andrew Barton, a naval commander and privateer or pirate, in 1506 demonstrated contemporary Lowland standards when he sent a present to James IV consisting of three barrels full of salted Dutch seamen's heads.[270] There were more sea-battles with the English from 1511, in one of which Barton was killed: this fight took place when England and "Scotland" (i.e. the Lowlands) were nominally at peace with each other.

The taxes paid by the Lowlanders were often wasted in extravagance. For example, in 1511 James ordered the construction of *The Great Michael*, a monster ship for those days: 240 feet long, carrying 300 sailors, 120 gunners, and 1000 soldiers. The king being short of money, this great craft then had to be sold cheaply to James's ally, France, when she went to war with England. (The French ran it aground.)[271] The French alliance also dictated yet another invasion of England by the Lowland army, which culminated in the disastrous Battle of Flodden Field, 1513, where the king and 10,000 of his soldiers lost their lives. After describing the slaughter at Flodden, J. Glover said that "since 1295, Scotland (i.e. the Lowlands) had known no reasonably long period unbroken by warfare . . . the two countries fought each other unmercifully, and the wars, which afflicted the least prosperous part of England, wrecked the towns, villages, monasteries and farmlands of the districts most vital to Scotland's [i.e., the Lowlands'] well-being. They also killed many of the best leaders and finest young men of a country [i.e., the Lowlands] so limited in population that such personalities were greatly needed and hard to replace."[272]

40. James V

James V (1513-42) was only a year old when he came to the throne on his father's death. The perpetual warfare among members of the nobility to gain power and property continued to be as fierce as ever. "The nobles traversed the country [i.e., the Lowlands] at the head of large bodies of their armed vassals, and carried on their wars against each other with a fury which defied all control."[273] This was exacerbated from about 1525 by growing religious dissension (which may have been genuine in individual cases, though it only became politically significant when it was used as a cover for other aims). There were two Lowland factions, one pro-English, and one pro-French; the second clique was heartened by the appointment of the king's cousin, the Duke of Albany, who had grown up in France, as Regent. The Douglases, who looked to the Earl of Angus as their leader, belonged to the pro-English party, and the Hamiltons, whose head was the Earl of Arran, belonged to the pro-French. The Douglases and the Hamiltons clashed in a bloody battle in the middle of the Lowland capital city, in Edinburgh High Street. The Douglases won, and the combat was remembered as "Cleanse the Causeway". After Albany retired and returned to France, Arran's faction seized control of the young king; but in 1528 the king escaped, and took over the government himself. He subdued various Border lords, and then attacked the Highlands, sailing northwards in yet another unsuccessful attempt to establish Lowland rule over the Highlanders. The ideas of the new religious reformers were banned, and Patrick Hamilton, who preached Luther's doctrines, was burned at the stake – inexpertly: the officials took six hours to incinerate him.[274] Nine more reforming preachers followed him to the stake, some while the king watched them being burnt alive. James seems to have been particularly sadistic, even for a Lowland ruler: he once ordered a thief to be fastened to a stake and consumed by fire. He was hostile to the Douglases, so he had one of them, Lady Glamis, burnt to death on the Castle Hill of Edinburgh on a charge of "witchcraft"; her son was forced to watch. She was described as "young and beautiful",[275] but if she had been old and ugly it would have been just as cruel. The English were equally brutal; while James V was king north of the border, a man who had tried to poison the Bishop of Rochester (and did poison two others) was taken to the favourite execution ground of the English authorities, Smithfield in London, and there boiled to death while the crowds watched the entertainment.[276]

When James V was only a promising youth of eighteen, he ordered every man of Clan Chattan to be slaughtered, and their wives and children to be deported to Shetland and Norway.[277] Since in reality he was only King of the Lowlands, not of the Highlands, this forward-looking scheme, sadly from a Lowland perspective, could not be implemented.

James fell out with Henry VIII of England, and an English army invaded the Lowlands, burning Kelso, Roxburgh and a score of smaller places. The Scottish Catholics financed an army against the English king (since Henry had broken with the Pope); James led it to the border, then stayed behind while it invaded England. The Scottish leaders quarrelled with each other, and they were beaten by a much smaller English army at Solway Moss, 1542; two earls, five barons, and 500 lairds were captured by the English. (Numbers of Scots were drowned, either in the moss – a peat bog – or in the River Esk: commoners, who did not live to fight another day, unlike their betters.) It was a disgraceful defeat, and James never recovered, dying soon afterwards.

41. Mary Queen of Scots

Mary, who reigned from 1542 to 1567, succeeded her father when she was a few days old. Her reign, like those of her predecessors, was a catalogue of disasters and devastation. There were "numberless fierce and bloody skirmishes which took place about Edinburgh at this wretched time"; besides which "there was, of course, a total interruption of justice at this miserable period, and for the most brutal oppression no redress".[278] Henry VIII of England had proposed that his son Edward should be betrothed to the baby Queen Mary; and in two successive years Henry sent armies on murderous expeditions into the Lowlands to support his kindly marriage proposal – the "Rough Wooing". In 1544 Leith and Edinburgh were burnt down, the surrounding country laid waste, and the English, returning home, naturally burnt every village on their route.[279] "Whole districts of the country [i.e. the Lowlands] were reduced to a desert."[280] The invaders reported their successes to the English king, Henry VIII, in a stolidly business-like way. "Towns, towers, steads, parish churches, castle houses, cast down or burnt, 192; Scots slain, 403; prisoners taken, 816; nolts, i.e. horned cattle, taken, 10,386; sheep, 12,498; nags and geldings, 1296; goats, 200; bolls of corn, 850; insight gear (i.e. household furniture) not reckoned." In 1545 the English came again into Berwickshire in harvest time, destroying all the crops and many buildings. "Monasteries and friars' houses, 7 [including the magnificent abbeys of Kelso, Melrose, Dryburgh, and Eccles]; castles, towers, and piles, 16; market towns, 5; villages, 243; milns, 13; hospitals, 3. All these were cast down or burnt."[281]

The violence was now made worse by religious discord. The government of the Lowlands was in the hands of Mary of Guise, James V's French Catholic widow. Protestant preachers were burnt alive: in 1546 George Wishart went to the stake at St Andrews, one interested spectator of this horrifying, lengthy torture, being Cardinal Beaton. Two months later a band of ruffianly noblemen broke into Archbishop Beaton's palace, the Castle of St Andrews, murdered him, and hung his body from the castle walls; and then fortified themselves in the castle against reprisal.[282] A French fleet arrived, stormed the castle, and carried its defenders as captives to France: the nobles were put in prison, the commoners (including John Knox) made into galley slaves.

In 1547 the English invaded again, and beat the defending forces at Pinkie, slaying thousands of men and capturing 1500, and then occupying Lowland strongholds; the Lowland rulers sent the infant Mary to France, where in 1548 she was married to the French Dauphin. Protestantism spread; Catholic friaries were burnt by earnest mobs of religious reformers; and the Protestant Covenant was drawn up in 1557. War broke out between Protestants and Catholics – the French supporting the latter, and the English the former. In 1560 the Protestants won, the French left, and Catholicism in the Lowlands was made illegal. Mary's French husband having died, she returned to Scotland in 1561. A Catholic rebellion under Huntly was quashed in a battle at Corrichie, 1562. In 1565 Mary married her cousin, the Catholic Darnley (both of them were grandchildren of Margaret Tudor, Henry VIII's sister); the Earl of Moray rebelled, but was defeated by Mary. In 1566 Mary's favourite, Riccio, at supper with Mary and her attendants at Holyrood, was stabbed to death in Mary's presence by Mary's husband Darnley and other lords. Soon afterwards Mary's baby James was born. By then she had a new favourite, Bothwell. In 1567, Darnley was ill, and was brought to a house at Kirk o' Field, in Edinburgh; Mary sat with him one evening, but then said she had to leave to go to the wedding of one of her servants. A few hours later, in the middle of the night, the house was blown up (barrels of gunpowder having been secreted in the cellarage); the bodies of Darnley and his page were found in the garden – they were thought to have been strangled. It was widely believed that Bothwell was responsible, perhaps with Mary's connivance. Bothwell proceeded to abduct Mary, and probably raped her; he then divorced his wife, and immediately married Mary, two or three months after Darnley's murder. Another rebellion ensued, and Mary was forced to abdicate in 1567. Mary was imprisoned, but escaped in 1568, and raised an army. This army was beaten at Langside, and Mary fled to England, hoping Elizabeth would help her recover her throne. (Bothwell, once Lord High Admiral of Scotland, went to Orkney and took to piracy; apprehended, he spent the last ten years of his life as a prisoner in Denmark.)

George Thomson lived in the late sixteenth century, and wrote about it: "From that time [1560] the kingdom [i.e. the Lowlands] was so on fire with civil wars, was so polluted with massacre and bloodshed, that nought else seemed to exist but a perpetual shambles."[283]

42. James VI and I

James VI (1567-1625) succeeded to the throne as a baby, when his mother abdicated. But some wished to restore Mary, and soon the Lowlands was the grip of a struggle between those who supported the child James, and those who supported Mary. "The civil war raged with increasing cruelty and ferocity. The whole country [i.e., the Lowlands] was divided into King's men and Queen's men, and Scotchmen [i.e., the Lowlanders] slaughtered each other in the names of the mother and her son. Both parties hanged their prisoners without mercy . . . The bloody strife . . . was carried on by means of numberless skirmishes, surprises, and barbarous ravagings. Some of the atrocities committed were savage beyond description." For example, an adherent of Mary demanded the surrender of Towie Castle, held by the wife of a partisan of James; being refused, he burned it down, when "the unfortunate lady, with her children and whole household, to the number of thirty-seven persons, perished amid the wild, roaring flames."[284]

Mary's half-brother, the Earl of Moray, was regent; but Mary made the Earl of Arran, head of the Hamiltons, her lieutenant in Scotland. In 1570 one of the Hamiltons murdered Moray by shooting him from a window as he rode down a street in Linlithgow. (When the Hamiltons later raided across the Border, the English invaded and destroyed the town and palace of Hamilton.) Darnley's father (and the king's grandfather), the Earl of Lennox, was made regent in Moray's place. Those who still supported Mary controlled Edinburgh and Dumbarton Castles; but in April 1571 the king's party captured the latter, and took Archbishop Hamilton of St Andrews prisoner. A few days later the archbishop was hanged at Stirling, having been denounced as partly responsible for the murders of Darnley and Moray. The king's party besieged Edinburgh Castle (held for the queen by Kirkcaldy and Maitland), but failed to take it. In August 1571 many lords of the king's party had a meeting at Stirling, where the young king was kept; Kirkcaldy led the queen's men on a sortie from Edinburgh Castle to Stirling, and in the small hours took many of them prisoners. The king's men counter-attacked, and freed them all – except the Regent Lennox, who was shot dead.

The next regent was the Earl of Mar, who, while a peaceable man by the Lowland standards of the time, still contributed to the continuous clashes and slaughters between the queen's and the king's parties. Mar besieged Edinburgh, still in Kirkcaldy's hands, but again the siege failed. Different writers have claimed that different periods represented the Lowland nadir: Hume Brown thought it was now. "There was never a sadder time in the whole history of Scotland [i.e., the Lowlands]. There had been civil war in previous reigns, but never had the contending sides been so cruel and merciless. When prisoners were taken, they were at once put to death."[284] In 1572 Mar died because, it was said, "he loved peace and could not have it". He was succeeded by the Earl of Morton. As with the other Lowland lords, his Protestantism was made more sincerely devout by the lands and revenues he took from the old Catholic Church. There was a further siege of Edinburgh Castle, led by Morton, and with the help of English forces sent by Elizabeth to help him, he took it in 1573; Kirkcaldy was hanged, and Maitland died in prison before he could be executed.

There was another Anglo-Lowland border clash in 1575 at Reidswire, where the Scots beat the English. Then Morton was overthrown and accused of complicity in Darnley's murder; and was beheaded by "the Maiden" – a precursor of the guillotine – in 1581. (France is often thought to have invented the mechanical apparatus for efficiently chopping people's heads off, but the Scottish Lowlands made it first. Credit should be given where it is due.) Of James VI's first four regents, three died violently, and the other one died of despair because he failed to end the violence. The king's advisers now were the Earl of Arran and the Earl of Lennox (nephew of the former Earl of Lennox, who had been shot at Stirling ten years before; this earl had been brought up in France). Another group of nobles, led by Gowrie, seized the fifteen-year-old king in the Raid of Ruthven, 1582, and took the reins of power; Lennox was sent back to France (and soon died). But in 1583 King James escaped, and his favourite, Arran, returned to power; and in 1584 Gowrie was executed. Religious contention continued: James wanted bishops, the established Kirk of Scotland did not. But both sides devoutly believed in witchcraft, a satisfying creed for sadists – James wrote a whole book about it – and old women were solemnly found guilty of performing physically impossible acts, and thereafter piously and publicly burned alive. These included the North Berwick "witches", who had "tried to drown" James by "creating storms" in the North Sea when he went to Denmark to bring home his wife (the "witches" having first achieved the difficult feat of sailing across the Firth of Forth in sieves – conclusive evidence for which, convincing in King James' feeble comprehension, having been obtained by torture).[285] The Lowland nobles continued to pursue their private vendettas. In 1592 the Catholic Earl of Huntly and a band of followers came to the house where the Protestant Earl of Moray (son of James' first regent) and his men were staying, set fire to it, and killed Moray as he rushed out. (A famous ballad commemorated the murder: "They hae slain the Earl o' Moray, and laid him on the green".)[286] Bothwell (nephew of the former Bothwell) made several attempts to attack James; he then took refuge with Huntly, so James led an army against Huntly's castle and drove them both abroad. And in 1600 James claimed that the two sons of the Earl of Gowrie (executed in 1584) tried to kill him – "the Gowrie Conspiracy"; James' attendants killed them instead. Who were the aggressors in this affair, and who the victims, remains a mystery – like much of the intrigue behind the non-stop Lowland violence of these centuries.

In 1603 James VI of Scotland became also James I of England, and henceforth the Lowlands were doubly unfortunate; they were dragged perforce into England's wars and civil strife, as well as keeping up their own murderous quarrels.

43. Union of the crowns

There were a couple of plots to kill James I in England, thought to involve some Catholics, so all Catholics were persecuted. The repression led to the 1605 Gunpowder Plot to blow up king and Parliament together; those responsible were discovered, tortured, and executed. More harsh decrees against Catholics followed. Most of the reign was taken up by struggles between king and Parliament as to who should wield the main power in the united kingdom.

On James' death in 1625, his son became Charles I. Unrest and civil strife were continual; Charles' attempt to rule without Parliaments was followed by the Bishops' Wars in 1639, the civil wars of the 1640s, and the turmoil through the interregnum after Charles' execution. The Restoration of 1660 was followed by the murderous struggles in the Lowlands between the Episcopalians and the Presbyterians, the harsh religious laws ordaining how exactly different sects of the same church were to conduct their worship of what they said was the same God, the persecution and violence against the Covenanters (remembered as "the killing time"), the battles at Rullion Green, Drumclog, and Bothwell Brig, the torture and public hanging of many rebels, the transportation of many more to the West Indies (200 of them were drowned in a shipwreck, having been left below decks under fastened hatches), and the open atrocities (one woman was tied to a stake on the shore, so she drowned slowly when the tide came in, while a deaf man was shot dead for failing to answer a question he had not heard being asked). A leader of the Covenanters, a Presbyterian minister called James Sharp, changed sides to support Charles II's (and the Episcopalians') restoration, and was rewarded with the title of Archbishop of St Andrews. The archbishop persecuted his former Covenanting comrades, and in 1679 he was dragged from his coach on the public road between Edinburgh and St. Andrews and murdered, in front of his daughter. (Bishop Paterson, an Episcopal inventor who is believed to have possessed the interesting intellect which devised the torture device called thumb screws, preached at his funeral.) More hangings followed, of those thought responsible. The Scottish Lowland judicial system seems to have been even harsher than its English counterpart; after the Rye House plot of 1678, which aimed to assassinate Charles II, some of the suspects were taken from England to the Lowlands to be tortured, since there were fewer laws there to discourage such wholesome activities. Later still came the upheavals of William III's accession, and the battles necessary to secure his throne. "The half-century from 1695 onwards formed a wretched period in Scottish [i.e. Lowland] history", said J. Glover.[287] The arrival of the Hanoverian monarchs in 1714 was followed by successive Jacobite rebellions in 1715, 1719, and 1745. We have seen the revenge of the anglophone authorities after Culloden. To punish some of those who supported the wrong ruling house, the agonies of slow strangulation were not enough. In James Shaw Grant's words, "many of the prisoners of the '45 were taken down from the gallows while still alive, revived with cold water, and then cut open so that the intestines of the living prisoner could be ripped out and burnt, before the body was hacked in four and exhibited in a public place".[288] This was done by the Lowland authorities at a time when the general Lowland opinion was that the *Highlanders* were savages.

As to the condition of the ordinary Lowlanders, Fletcher of Saltoun (wrote David Stewart) gave "a deplorable view of the state to which thousands of the people were reduced at the end of the seventeenth century. His statement seems to refer only to Fife and the counties southwards and westward [that is, an area much the same as the Lowlands], which at that period did not contain beyond 900,000 inhabitants. Of this population, he states that 200,000 went about in bands of sturdy beggars, or sorners, as they were called, without house or habitation, living on the public by begging, open plunder, and private stealing. This frightful number of beggars and outcasts of society, in so small a population, is almost incredible..."[289]

The basis of the economic system of the Scottish Lowlands (and England) was the private ownership of land, and the basis of the political system was autocratic monarchy. The possession of the land by private owners meant that there was always liable to be strife as each individual proprietor strove to maintain and extend his estates, to defeat others who wished to take his property from him, and to subdue the unpropertied. In the same way monarchical or autocratic rule meant that conflict was always likely, as each monarch strove to maintain and extend his power, to hold off those who wished to take his power from him, and to put down the powerless.

Since the Highlands did not have either of these systems, economic or political, there was naturally less conflict there. However, Lowland historians have always tried to disguise this fact. One murder in the Highlands, though committed as a direct result of Lowland interference which was intended to cause conflict and which succeeded in causing conflict, was put at the forefront of any account of Highland affairs. Hundreds of murders committed at the same time in the Lowlands, though arising directly and inevitably from the very nature of Lowland society, were considered to be much less significant, and are blandly brushed over in the eulogies as to how "douce" and "moral" that society was.

It may be thought unnecessary to recount such well known events in Lowland history, but it is essential to remember that all this was happening in the Lowlands during the very years when Lowland propagandists were bewailing the "lawlessness" of the Highlands, and it shows how hypocritical it was of the Lowlanders to claim that they were bringing "law and order" to the Highlands when they could not even bring them to their own Lowlands. At any rate the reader will now know what the conventional historians mean when they claim that the Lowlanders were establishing their "quiet and civil-living" standards, their "decent and reasonable" models of behaviour (in the Lowlander John Major's words), in the Highlands.

After this depressing but essential excursion, we may resume our survey of the Highlanders in the society before Culloden.

44. Public opinion

Why was there so little crime in the old clan society? It is what one would expect in a society where there was so little insistence on the right of individual exclusive private property: where the land was held in common by the clan, where the farms were tilled in common by a group of joint-farmers, where all the labour necessary for the well-being of society was performed together by groups of neighbours and friends; where one had only to go to visit another to be given the best that was in the house. For in such a society it would be clearly seen that theft, robbery, assault, and so on were not only against the interests of the victim, but against the common interest. In such circumstances a public opinion would arise, and did arise, that was just as effective against crime as the expensive machinery that we maintain in modern societies. In fact much more effective: now, we have many crimes, and in a small minority of cases (apparently only two out of every hundred crimes result in a conviction, not a reassuring proportion), find and punish the criminal[290] – or, from time to time, complacently punish some innocent person in error; then, crime was almost unknown.

The first barrier to criminal activity in such a society was the conscience of the individual, which was not stifled (as it often is in other environments) by the structure of society. Donald MacLeod, who helped Prince Charles during his flight, was later captured and brought before General John Campbell of Mamore (who later became Duke of Argyll), one of those pursuing the prince. The general reminded him that for betraying the prince he could have got "thirty thousand pounds sterling, which would have made you and all your children happy for ever". Donald differed, and made it clear why he differed. "Conscience would have gotten up upon me: that money could not have kept it down." He could not have done it, he said, "though I could have got all England and Scotland for my pains". General Campbell was part of the army which was then murdering and destroying throughout the Highlands; but as a member of a Highland chief's family, he knew the different standards of clan society, and when MacLeod gave his defiant answer, General Campbell replied, in words which did him credit, "I will not say that you are wrong".[291]

Once a pattern of behaviour has been established by the economic and social conditions in any particular society, the behaviour becomes a tradition, which in turn reinforces the pattern. Religious beliefs, too, provide supernatural support for prevailing secular standards. The innkeeper at Blair Atholl, one MacNaughton, said to John Bristed on his Highland tour, "it is a noble and an elevating sensation to be conscious that our blood has run pure and uncontaminated for many generations through the veins of the upright and honourable [i.e., that our ancestors have done no wrong]. It is a great incitement to do well, when we know that the spirits of our fathers are looking upon our actions from their habitations of bliss."292 (These are not expressions one would expect to hear from a modern pub licensee.) But social habits and manners have to be in existence before tradition and religion can come to their aid. Public opinion was the sanction that sustained and vindicated the social code.

45. Banished themselves

The minister of Dull, after giving the usual list of the virtues of the Highlanders – they were sober, regular, industrious, lively, cheerful, hospitable – went on to say that "gross offenders" were "held in great disgrace"; even "a notorious drunkard" was "despised in the highest degree".293 Burt said that a sheep stealer was infamous among the Highlanders.294 And the force of public opinion had its effect. The minister of Lismore and Appin, after saying that no inhabitant had been executed or banished for twenty-five years past (and this was when the purloining of some insignificant article was penalized by death) added significantly that one or two, guilty of irregularities, had banished themselves.295 The minister of Kilmuir, in Skye, told a story which indicates even more clearly the state of affairs. He wrote: "Crimes are rarely committed. About twenty-five years ago, a man was overtaken with a stolen sheep on his shoulder, by two neighbouring tenants. The thief declared to them, that this was his first trespass; and offered a reward, if they would keep it a profound secret. But they declined to accept of the one, or to do the other. The sheep was set at liberty: and the poor wretch hung himself, next morning, to the roof of his own house."296

That was a case where the fear of a hostile public opinion led to an offender punishing himself. Much more often, it seems, and much more satisfactorily, it prevented the offence in the first place. David Stewart, who served at various times in the 42nd, the 77th, the 78th, and the 90th, Highland regiments, said that the Highland soldier had a "sense of duty". Stewart had "generally found, that a threat of informing their parents of misconduct has operated as a sufficient check on young soldiers, who always received the intimation with a sort of horror. They knew that the report would not only grieve their relations, but act as a sentence of banishment against themselves, as they could not return home with a bad or a blemished character. Generals MacKenzie Fraser and MacKenzie of Suddie, who successively commanded the 78th Highlanders, seldom had occasion to resort to any other punishment than threats of this nature, for several years after the embodying of that regiment."297 The soldiers knew that if they tarnished their good name "they would bring shame on their country and kindred", and the result would be "perpetual banishment from a country to which they could not return with a bad character".[298]

46. A grievous punishment

Stewart gave a number of examples of the operation of this Highland public opinion. Nearly 300 men in the 78th (the Ross-shire Highlanders of 1793) came from Lewis. Of this contingent, Stewart wrote: "Several years elapsed before any of these men were charged with a crime deserving severe punishment. In 1799 a man was tried and punished. This so shocked his comrades that he was put out of their society as a degraded man, who brought shame on his kindred. The unfortunate outcast felt his own degradation so much, that he became unhappy and desperate; and Colonel MacKenzie [of Suddie], to save him from destruction, applied and got him sent to England, where his disgrace would be unknown and unnoticed. It happened as Colonel MacKenzie had expected, for he quite recovered his character."[299] (Apparently the colonel shared the opinion of Shakespeare's grave-digger, who asserted that Hamlet "is mad, and sent into England . . . 'Twill not be seen in him there; there the men are as mad as he.")

Another example Stewart gave came from Breadalbane. "Several years ago, two men, one old and the other young, stepped into a small boat to cross Loch Tay. On the middle of the lake they were seen to stand up, as if struggling, and then quickly to sit or fall down, the people from the distance could not distinguish which. When the boat arrived at the shore, the young man was missing. The account which his aged companion gave was, that the youth was in liquor, and wished to quarrel with him, and got up in the boat to strike him, but his foot slipped and he fell overboard. This story was not believed. The man was sent to Perth jail, tried at the ensuing assizes, and acquitted for want of evidence. The impression of his guilt, however, was not to be effaced from the minds of the people. This belief was further confirmed by the character of the man, who was quarrelsome and passionate. On his return to Breadalbane no person would speak to him. He was not upbraided for his supposed guilt, nor was any attempt made to insult or maltreat him; but he found every back turned upon him, and every house he entered instantly emptied of its inhabitants. He withstood this for a short time, when he left the country, and never returned, or was seen afterwards. I was present at this man's trial. His name was Ewen Campbell, or Ewen Laider, or the Strong, from his great strength."[300]

There was also the case of a young woman found dead, murdered, in Strath Bran, in Highland Perthshire. The people of the strath believed she had been killed by her sweetheart. He was tried, but acquitted for want of proof: "He happened to reach home late on a Saturday night, and next morning went to church, and took his seat in one end. In a moment he had it wholly to himself. Every person moved away to a distance, and left the whole range of seats empty. When he came out after service, and stood in the churchyard, all shunned him, and when he walked homewards, those that were in his front hurried on and those behind walked slow, leaving the road to himself. This was too much to bear, and his resolution not holding out so long as the old man's, he disappeared that night, and like him, has never since been heard of."[301]

47. Nobody would speak to me

One of the Highlanders who had known of Prince Charles's movements after the '45, when asked why he had not given the information in return for the £30,000 reward, answered: "Of what use would the money be to me? A gentleman might take it, and go to London or Edinburgh, where he would find plenty of people to eat the dinners and drink the wine which it would purchase; but as for me, if I were such a villain as to commit a crime like this, I need not return to my own country, where nobody would speak to me, but to curse me as I passed along the road."[302]

This system of "punishment by public opinion" is, of course, quite clearly liable to error. It is possible that Ewen Campbell, and the young man from Strath Bran, had not been guilty of the crimes attributed to them. Yet who should know better whether an accused man is likely to have committed a crime imputed to him than those who have known him since he was born? In the close-knit and co-operative society of the clan, the character of each must soon have become known to all. In the English criminal system, which (for good historical reasons) in some ways leans over backwards to be fair to the defence, the past record of an accused is normally not allowed to be brought up unless he brings it up himself, or unless the evidence of the crime under consideration necessarily involves such revelations, or in one or two similar cases. And yet as a matter of hard-headed fact, few people would deny that the previous behaviour of the accused is among the most relevant of facts. If two individuals are both suspected of an instance of burglary, the one who has been a professional burglar for years is more likely to be the culprit than the one who has lived a blameless life. People so often act as they have done before, even in detail, that an experienced policeman can sometimes tell who has committed a particular housebreaking by seeing how it was done. The value of knowing the previous history of an accused person gave rise to one of the most prized institutions of the English legal system. Now a man would be thought unfit for jury service if he had any personal knowledge of the crime or of the accused; but originally the jury was twelve local men who could be supposed to know all about the circumstances of the crime. The qualification of a juryman was not that he knew nothing about the crime, but that he probably knew all about it. And this knowledge of a person's character and past is what a Highlander's fellow-clansfolk would have.

As for the possibility of error, no system yet devised is free from that: least of all our own, under which a number of people have been imprisoned, some for long terms, for crimes they did not commit, and a few, at least, hanged by mistake. The possibility of error works, perhaps just as often, in favour of the accused. Every year men who, it is as certain as it can be, are guilty of the crime with which they are charged, and who are strongly suspected of guilt by the judge, the police, most of the lawyers engaged, and probably the court reporters (all, in other words, who know the men's record), are found not guilty by juries who think they are impeccable citizens and should get the benefit of the doubt. This second kind of error may well be a good thing in the conditions of modern society, but that is not the point: the fact is that there is a very large margin of error in both directions.

If we are to compare the Highland system of ostracism in the conditions of clan society, and the system of imprisonment and (for many years) execution in the commercial society that existed in England, there is no doubt which was the most effective. The only period for which a comparison can be made is the second half of the eighteenth, and the early nineteenth, centuries: before that there are no figures for the Highlands, and after it the clan code of behaviour was no longer fully operative. Stewart's figures, covering this period, show that the Highland system, as was shown earlier, was eighteen times more effective.

48. Lawlessness

Why, then, was there such a widespread belief in the "lawlessness" of the Highlands? The belief was still held by many twentieth-century historians. Trevelyan relished calling the Highlanders "barbarians",[303] and said they were (as we saw earlier) "a population that had always lived for and by war".[304] Eric Linklater said that to the Highlanders "war was a natural exercise".[305] A. G. MacDonell said that after 1746 there was introduced into the Highlands the "new idea . . . that the law is, or ought to be, stronger than the sword", and it was that idea (he declared) which destroyed all the clans – except the Campbells, thought MacDonell: the Duke of Argyll, unleashing his Campbells in aggressions against several neighbouring clans, was not really guilty of violence, because he had got pieces of paper from the Lowland authorities to justify his attacks. But this very profitable new idea was not, said MacDonell sadly, grasped by "the less intelligent and less cultured clans further north".[306]

There were several reasons behind the Lowland accusation of Highland "lawlessness". The first lay in the difference of attitude of the Highlander and the

Lowlander to the territories north of the Tweed. To the Lowlander, Scotland was, or should have been, all one country: to the Highlander, his country was his clan land. And just as the Lowlanders saw nothing wrong in attacking the English from time to time, or in defending themselves against the aggressions of the English, so the clansfolk saw nothing wrong in pursuing any bone of contention they might have with a neighbouring clan, or for that matter with the Lowland state, by force of arms.

It should be remembered that these bones of contention were very largely provided by the astute Lowland authorities, precisely because they would lead to trouble among the clans. Ian Finlay asserted that "tribal feuds continued to be settled by blood down to 1688, when MacDonell of Keppoch revenged himself on the Mackintoshes over a land dispute".[307] Prebble, too, talked of Keppoch's "interminable feud with the MacIntoshes".[308] This conflict was not a "tribal feud"; as we have seen, it came about because the MacIntosh chief was given, by the alien Lowland authorities, an obviously fictional charter over much of the land inhabited by the Keppoch MacDonalds. Spurred on by continuous Edinburgh incitement over 300 years, the MacIntosh chiefs tried repeatedly to conquer the Keppoch country – one result being the Battle of Mulroy. The conflict did not arise from the clan system; it was solely the result of Edinburgh trying – successfully – to cause trouble in the Highlands.

A similar – equally successful – attempt occurred when the Lowland authorities gave the Marquis of Argyll a charter to the lands of the MacLeans, which not surprisingly led to fighting, as the Campbells tried to enforce the charter: this made Thomas Kirk (a Lowlander travelling in 1679) shake his head sadly over the Highlanders' "feuds, some of which are in agitation at this day, viz. Argyll with the MacLeans".[309] In the same way, one author described the unjust execution of James Stewart of the Glen in 1752 for the murder of Colin Campbell of Glenure as a "grim incident in Scottish clan history";[310] in fact it showed, as we have seen, that the Highlands had now been conquered by the English/Lowland state, with the result that the Duke of Argyll was able to hold a kangaroo court to obtain the inevitable conviction of James Stewart; under the clan system such a flagrant injustice would have been impossible. Campbell of Glenure had been actively ejecting Jacobite small tenants on the lands of Cameron of Callart and Cameron of Lochiel, "troops having been called in to collect rents and effect evictions while he factored those forfeited estates", as the *Oxford D.N.B.* put it, and he was about to do the same on the estate of Stewart of Ardshiel. He could be called one of the first "improvers", and he was doing what afterwards became, in the new era, standard practice throughout the Highlands.

It is true that under the old clan system each clan ran the risk that in the event of a quarrel between itself and another clan, it might be attacked and defeated. If a clan was defeated, it might be put to flight and dispersed by the victorious clan, and its land occupied by the victors. There are examples of this happening, although it was rare, and then mainly in the earlier history of the Highlands. More often, a clan that had been defeated by an implacable enemy found its land incorporated in the clan land of the victor: the defeated clansfolk stayed on their land, but under tacksmen or sub-chiefs placed there by the chief of the victorious clan. Usually, neither of these things happened after a clan war; a pitched battle, whichever side won, was considered as settling the matter, at least for the time being, and no land changed hands. The worst that could happen, then, and it happened very seldom over the centuries during which the history of the Highland clans is known, was that the clan could lose its land. When the defeated clan became a kind of sub-clan or sept of the victors, it involved little more than a change in the name of the chief, for as has been said the clansfolk remained free people, with a share in the soil: slavery or subjugation was not possible in the social organization of the Highlands. It is true that the new commercial system ended the possibility of either of these eventualities (the loss of land to a rival clan, or an incorporation in a more powerful clan): but it also produced a state of affairs in which, instead of one clan in a hundred years or so losing its land, that was the fate (in the decades after Culloden) of every clan in the Highlands and Islands, without exception. The greatest evil that could befall a clan was the loss of its lands: and the clans were saved from the remote possibility of this fate – in return for the certainty of it.

49. Wars of Great Britain

It is also true that the deaths and injuries caused by the very occasional clan conflicts were ended; but at the price of many more deaths and injuries caused to the Highlanders through their being involved in the much more frequent and much more destructive wars of Great Britain. Trevelyan says that the people were "effectively disarmed".[311] This, of course, was not so. They were given more modern and more efficient weapons, and sent out to fight the wars of the rulers of Britain – for example, the trade and imperial wars against France, and the war in which the American colonies, previously governed by the British ruling class, successfully replaced that authority by an American ruling class. In the new society the young Highland men fought much more often, and, moreover, for ends which were none of their choosing. As the minister of Campbeltown said, referring to Kintyre: "Yet we are not to suppose that the MacDonalds, or their predecessors, the fierce sovereigns of this country, ever sported wantonly with the lives of their subjects, otherwise than by exposing them to the calamities of war;

and in this respect it is hardly necessary to remark, that the politest people of *our own times* will match them" (original italics).[312]

Reading the history of the Highland regiments, one can scarcely believe that the total casualties of the Highlanders were any the less as a result of the change. The minister of North Knapdale wrote of the old clan wars: "It is remarkable, that no considerable family was ever annihilated by these intestine broils; a proof, that they were not so destructive as, at this distance of time, we are apt to believe."[313]

The Battle of Culloden was remembered by the Highlanders as the worst disaster of the clans, and that, clearly, was nothing to do with warfare among the clans: it was the result of the clansfolk being dragged into the politics of England and the Lowlands. At Culloden Prince Charles's army lost a thousand men killed, among the various clans.[314] In comparison, David Stewart gives the official figures of the officers and men killed outright in action in one regiment alone, the Black Watch; from 1740 to 1815, the officers and men killed were 850. He does not give the total figures of soldiers who died from wounds and disease, but he does say that while in the official lists 280 privates were killed between 1793 and 1815, 1135 more "died by sickness, wounds, and various casualties" – just over four times as many. If the proportion was the same for officers and men in all the wars from 1740 to 1815, it would mean that in that period over 3500 died from wounds and disease. If this supposition is correct, the total number dead in this one regiment from 1740 to 1815 would be something of the order of 4300[315] – four times as many as the death-roll at Culloden.

50. Went to destruction

Dr Johnson confirmed the view that the Black Watch ("the old Highland regiment") and the other Highland corps suffered heavy casualties. He wrote that the Highlanders who went to America to fight in the Seven Years' War (1756-63) "went to destruction. Of the old Highland regiment, consisting of 1200, only seventy-six survived to see their country again."[316] This seems to have been an exaggeration, but there were certainly severe losses. David Stewart said that the Black Watch, the 42nd Regiment, in its American operations from 1758 to 1765, lost 25 officers and 386 men killed, while 55 officers and 526 men were wounded.[317] At Ticonderoga (1758) alone, the regiment lost half its men – eight officers, nine sergeants, and 299 private soldiers were killed attacking the French in an "impenetrable stockade" during a whole summer day, while the British commander Abercromby remained safely at the base.[318] (In the next year Abercromby was promoted to lieutenant-general, and some years later to general. Then and now, standing well with the powers-that-be is more important than mere success at your job.)

During the next war, the War of American Independence, in 1781 the Seaforth Highlanders sailed for India (to attack the French there, who were allies of the Americans – as well as being colonial rivals to Britain): on the voyage, from scurvy and without a shot being fired, Seaforth himself and 230 out of 1110 men died before reaching Madras.[319] It would have been a sanguinary clan fight indeed for the casualties to reach this figure.

What were the chances of survival for the individual recruit? During the French wars from 1793 to 1815, 3563 men (in total) served in the first battalion of the Black Watch – they were either in the regiment in 1793, or joined later. The strength of the regiment in 1815 was 530 (these figures are given by David Stewart). Thus the total decrease in the first battalion during these years was 3033 (3563-530). Of these over half were dead, or missing believed dead. (The others had been discharged through injury, or had left the colours for other reasons.) As we have seen, 280 were killed, 1135 died of sickness and wounds, and 138 were "unaccounted for, having been left sick in an enemy's country, prisoners, etc." – a total of 1553 – just over half of 3033. Similarly, the total number in the first battalion of the 78th Regiment, the Seaforth Highlanders, who belonged to the regiment in 1793 or were recruited between 1793 and 1820, was 4369, of whom 638 still belonged in 1820. The total decrease was therefore 3731 (4369-638). Of these the "killed and dead" (not counting the missing, prisoners, etc.) numbered 2051 – this figure alone being over half the decrease.

After giving these facts about the 78th, Stewart wrote that "similar statements respecting the other Highland regiments would give similar results". More specifically he said that "the service of the 42nd [Black Watch], 79th [Cameron Highlanders], and 92nd [Gordon Highlanders], was very similar, the regiments having been much employed together, and subject to the same casualties" – although, he said, the 92nd "was not employed in the West Indies" (an unhealthy posting) with the other two regiments during the French wars, and therefore had fewer casualties.[320] After the war, however, the 92nd was sent to Jamaica, and Stewart had to add the melancholy information that in four months the regiment lost by disease more than 240 men.[321] If the casualty lists of the 42nd and the 79th are as typical as Stewart says, it seems that a recruit joining a Highland regiment, at least during the French Revolutionary and Napoleonic Wars, stood rather less than a fifty-fifty chance of coming out alive; and even some of the survivors were maimed or crippled. When one recalls that between 1740 and 1815 fifty battalions of infantry were raised mainly from the Highlands (a Highland regiment consisted usually of one, sometimes of two battalions), besides many fencible or militia regiments, it becomes clear that the total casualty list must have been long. Ten battalions served for all or a substantial part of the French wars (an average of seventeen years per battalion, of the twenty years – 1793-1815, less about two years of peace – that those wars lasted): as we have seen, two of those battalions lost altogether some 3500 men killed, or dead, or missing, during that time. The total killed, and dead of disease and wounds, in the fifty battalions embodied during the eighty years after 1740 can scarcely be fewer than 25,000, and may be higher. Alexander Sutherland may not have been exaggerating in a comment he made in 1825. "Few are the Highland families", he wrote, "that have not sons laid in a soldier's grave."[322]

The 1740s did not, as has been commonly supposed, mark a change from war and bloodshed to peace and tranquillity among the Highlanders: the evidence shows that it was exactly the other way round. Jamieson wrote that in the battles of the French wars (1793-1815) alone "there was twice as much Highland blood spilt . . . as was shed by the Highlanders on their own account, in any way whatsoever, during the three centuries that preceded the abolition of the feudal system among them in 1748".[323]

In view of these figures, it is hard to believe that what took place after 1746 is still being described as "the pacification of the Highlands".

However, even if the deaths and injuries among Highland fighting men had ceased altogether, instead of being multiplied, the accompanying destruction of clan society would still have been considered a grievous loss by the Highlanders.

51. Small-scale warfare

The second reason for the belief in the "lawlessness" of the Highlanders was that they and the Lowlanders were not infrequently involved in little local wars against each other. Since the Highland society produced more valorous men, they usually had the better of any fighting; but the hatred on each side, and the moral guilt, were probably fairly equal. As part of this more or less perpetual warfare there was a great deal of what the Lowlanders called thieving, and what the Highlanders considered plundering an enemy. Formal declarations of war were not necessary; in the same way, the Americans and British invaded Iraq in 2003 without declaring war. The Lowland government in Edinburgh had often tried by violent aggression (without declaring war) to extirpate the Highlanders' language and their way of life, and indeed the Highlanders themselves; and had frequently passed Acts of Parliament which openly announced their destructive ambitions. In these circumstances it is not surprising that the Highlanders thought the Lowlanders and their form of society so objectionable and so hostile, and their incursions so destructive, that any raid on them was a justifiable act of war. Drake, and Hawkins, and the other sea rovers whom English children were for long taught to regard as heroes, acted on exactly the same principle: their enemy being not the Lowlands but Spain. (In parallel with events in the petty

CHARACTER OF THE HIGHLANDERS

Highland/Lowland warfare, the Spaniards said the English sailors were barbarous thieves, while the English said they were merely plundering an enemy.) Selkirk, in a passage already quoted, drew the same parallel.[324] The English sailors' passions were inflamed by the savage treatment dealt out by the Spaniards to their captured comrades; in the same way, the Highlanders were enraged by the reprisals – summary executions and worse – taken by the Lowlanders against any clansmen who were caught.

This small-scale warfare between Highlands and Lowlands was certainly stopped in the eighteenth century, along with the infrequent battles between the clans. Clan warriors were thenceforward to be killed, not in Scotland where at least there was a chance of their bones lying in their native glens, but (in much greater numbers) in America, India, Africa, and on the continent of Europe.

The third reason, one presumes, is the great and often riotous resistance put up by the Highlanders when the chiefs, and their Lowland allies, were thrusting them out of their country. (One of the minor mysteries of the clearances is the origin of the oft-repeated tale that there was virtually no opposition on the part of the Highlanders to the men who finally destroyed their society.) This violent resistance of the Highlanders no doubt reinforced the theory of the "lawlessness" of the Highlands.

Even in wars between the clans, a distinction was drawn between taking a man's wealth, and taking his provisions. A Highlander's wealth was in cattle: his sheep were thought of as merely means of subsistence. Thus sheep, even in clan wars, were not considered as proper booty: cattle were. Burt said that the Highlanders thought it less shameful to steal 100 cows than one sheep.[325] The stealing of cows, of course, was something restricted to raids on other clans. It would be just as shameful to steal a cow as a sheep within the clan.

Even outside the clan, during a war against a foreign clan, the Highland expeditionary forces conducted themselves according to strict rules. The minister of Glenorchy said that in times past, the Highlanders would "purloin" from the wealthy, but "avoided the cattle of the poor".[326] Any contemporary European army would have considered such distinctions ridiculous. (Voltaire's *Candide*, published in 1759, did not exaggerate.)

52. Peaceable and polite

Leaving aside the question of the "lawlessness" between the separate states which the clan countries in effect were – a lawlessness which, it is sobering to reflect, has not been conquered in the twenty-first century, despite the enormous advances in our knowledge, our expertise and our power – and returning to the conduct of the Highlander as a citizen of the clan, we find that these "savages", as the Lowlanders called them, were in fact "peaceable and gentle", as they were described in the Duirinish report of the Old Statistical Account.[327] The minister of North Uist called them "obliging and peaceable in their dispositions",[328] and the minister of Comrie said that "like the generality of the common Highlanders, the lower ranks here are modest, peaceable, and very obliging".[329]

They were also consistently polite and courteous. The point was frequently made in the O.S.A. The Kingussie minister said of his parishioners that "like most of the natives of the Highlands, they are brave, hospitable, and polite".[330] The daughter of one of the Sutherland clan tacksmen wrote about society before the clearances (in a passage later quoted more fully in volume three) that "the humble orders of the community had a degree of external polish and manly mildness of deportment in domestic life that few of the present generation have attained to, much as has been said of modern improvements".[331]

Jamieson said that "in 1745 the Scottish Highlanders, of all descriptions, had more of that polish of mind and sentiment, which constitutes real civilization, than in general the inhabitants of any other country we know of . . ."[332] Sir Walter Scott wrote that "there are few nations, by the way, who can boast of so much natural politeness as the Highlanders".[333] Pennant reported that they "are much affected with the civility of strangers, and have in themselves a natural politeness and address which often flows from the meanest when least expected".[334] Sir John Dalrymple gave it as his opinion that "the Highlanders, whom more savage nations call savage, carried in the outward expression of their manners the politeness of courts without their vices, and in their bosoms the high point of honour without its follies".[335] The common Highlanders, he wrote, "were as polite and as guarded in their behaviour as the gentry of other countries."[336] Burt himself, though (as a Lowlander) convinced that the Highlanders were "savage", said "I never had the least reason to complain of the behaviour towards me of any of the ordinary Highlanders, or the Irish [the Highlanders' cousins]; but it wants a great deal [i.e. it is not the case] that I could truly say as much of the Englishmen or Lowland Scots that were employed in the same business".[337]

Dr Johnson stayed with the family of MacLeod of Raasay, and said: "More gentleness of manners, or a more pleasing appearance of domestic society, is not found in the most polished countries."[338] Johnson ascribed the courtesy of the Highlanders to their system of chiefship. "Civility seems part of the national character of the Highlanders. Every chieftain is a monarch, and politeness, the natural product of royal government, is diffused from the laird through the whole clan."[339] One may or may not agree with the royalist Johnson's explanation, but it is significant that he agrees with all the other witnesses as to the character of the Highlanders.

53. Healthy, vigorous, agile

It seems to have been generally accepted that the Highlanders were brave, as well as vigorous and tough: the minister of Kilmonivaig said the Highlanders had much courage, which was "derived from their ancestors".[340] The Kilmuir (Skye) report said they had "signalized themselves, in the last [1775-83], and in the former [1739-48, and 1756-63], wars, by their valour, and their ability in bearing every species of hardship and fatigue".[341] The records of the Highland regiments must lead an observer to the same conclusion. Certainly the clan life of the Highlands produced healthy and active people. In about 1500 a writer described the Lowlanders, and then continued: "A race of men, much the hardiest and rough, inhabits the other northern and mountainous part [of Scotland], and they are called wild."[342] In the sixteenth century Raphael Holinshed wrote that the Highlanders were "hard of constitution and bodie"; "they are kind, bold, nimble, and thereto more skilful in the wars".[343] In 1630 Captain Dymes visited Lewis, and found that the inhabitants had "lustie and able bodyes".[344] In 1688 William Sacheverell was sent to the Highlands, and wrote: "During my stay I generally observed the men to be large-bodied, stout [robust], subtle, active, patient of cold and hunger."[345] John Toland wrote in 1709 that "they are stout and active, dextrous in all their exercises".[346] The Glengarry men who emigrated in 1786 were described as "young, stout, hale and hearty".[347] The O.S.A. ministers agreed. The people were "tall, robust, and well-limbed", according to the Kintail report;[348] they were, wrote the Halkirk minister, "in general very healthy, vigorous, firm, agile, well proportioned";[349] and "of a shapely firm make" wrote the minister of Moulin.[350] The Tiree account said that the islanders were "remarkable for agility", with "not above two or three of either sex corpulent".[351] The Lochgoilhead reporter attributed the people's good health to the fact that they were "not crowded together in towns or villages".[352] So did the minister of Glenisla, who said that his parishioners were "in general very healthy", which he "ascribed to their manner of living. They are not pent up in houses, nor employed in sedentary occupations like many others [Glenisla was on the edge of the Highlands, and its minister would know well how the Lowlanders in adjoining parishes lived], but roam at large in the open air, tending flocks of sheep and cattle."[353] The Lismore and Appin account used the same phrase ("not pent up") to make the same point: "The inhabitants are, on the whole, abundantly healthy, owing, probably, in part to their not living pent up in towns or villages, or being more or less employed in sedentary occupations. They live mostly in houses detached from each other; and are industrious, cheerful, and constantly engaged in active employments in the open air, which greatly tends to the preservation of their health. The constant sea-breezes likewise prove very favourable to their constitutions."[354] Burt thought that "the air of the Highlands is pure, and consequently healthy; insomuch that I have known such cures done by it as might be thought next to miracles – I mean in distempers of the lungs, as coughs, consumptions, etc."[355]

Alexander Carmichael, writing in 1883, recorded the belief of the Long Island crofters that the shielings (when they were still allowed to have them) had been beneficial to their health. They said that "the bracing air of the hills was of benefit to themselves, and that as a consequence complaints common among them now were then unknown. They talk with delight of the benefit they derived in mind, body, and substance, from their life among the hills. I entirely agree with them."[356]

The Highlanders "often work very keenly" for short periods when the season of the year demanded it, in the words of the Lismore account.[357] Not infrequently, whether engaged in their normal peaceful pursuits, or where necessary in martial ones, they performed feats which called for great stamina, such as negotiating flooded rivers or mountain torrents, sailing in storms, crossing mountains in winter, sleeping on the hill in rain or snow, and so on. And here the Highlanders showed that their bravery was not only of the kind that reveals itself in headlong charges upon an enemy: it was also of the enduring kind which will cheerfully outlast difficulty and discomfort. The account of Assynt called the people "patient of hunger, cold, and fatigue", by land or sea, "as emergencies may require";[358] in Kincardine they were "extremely patient under hunger, cold and other distresses";[359] and in Kilmallie "invincible by fatigue, cold, or hunger".[360] The Kilmuir (Skye) report said they were "very economical, industrious, and humane".[361] The Rev. Dr John Smith, in his survey of Argyllshire in 1798, wrote that the natives "are, in general, a sober, active, frugal, and industrious, race of men".[362] Dr James Robertson, in his report on Inverness-shire in 1808, said that the Highlanders "have uniformly proved themselves to be warm in their attachments, true to the cause they espouse, steady in their engagements, patient under many privations, vigorous in their constitution, inured to toil, active in their motions, indefatigable in exertion, and fearless in the hour of danger".[363] Earlier, Dr John Walker had asserted that in Mull were "a people capable of powerful industry",[364] while the Hebrides generally were "inhabited by a sensible, hardy, and laborious race of people".[365]

54. A lion and a lamb

Historians assure us that the Highlanders were feeble creatures who did not know where the next meal was coming from, while giving us to understand, at least by necessary implication, that the Lowlanders, invigorated by their their douce, moral, and lawful lives, were much finer men. Yet these findings are not borne out by the facts. The Duke of Argyll wrote in 1715: "a Lamb is not more afraid of a Lyon, than these Low Country people are of the Highlanders."[366] And

Sir Walter Scott, though as a Lowlander he shared many of the Lowland misconceptions about the Highlanders, was prepared to accept the evidence about the Highlanders' physical excellence. In *A Legend of Montrose* he said that during Montrose's campaigns, once the Highlanders came up to the Lowland ranks, "the Lowlanders were utterly unable to contend at close quarters with their more agile and athletic enemies".[367]

Queen Victoria thought the Highland women were better looking, a belief which may indicate that they were healthier. On her 1844 visit she wrote, "near Dunkeld, and also as you get more into the Highlands, there are prettier faces".[368] This observation could be connected with the facts that the Highlanders usually still had some cattle, so many Highland women would help to look after them; and milkmaids were often thought to be better looking than other girls. Smallpox was common, and it disfigured the faces of sufferers even when they survived; but milkmaids apparently got smallpox much less often than others, because many of them had caught cowpox from their animals, which then acted as a shield against smallpox. (It was the observation of this fact, for example by Edward Jenner, that led to the introduction of vaccination, a mild injection of cowpox which defeated subsequent smallpox infection.)

55. Wonderfully swift of foot

Dr Robertson's assertion that the Highlanders were "active in their motions" was supported by other commentators. Their normal pace was sprightly. In the 1720s Edmund Burt wrote to a friend that the Highlanders believed the Highland dress was the most appropriate to their country, and "that they would not be so free to skip over the rocks and bogs with breeches as they are in the short petticoat" – the normal mountain garb.[369] David Stewart said of the old Highlanders, when summoned to arms as in 1715 and 1745, that "their advance to battle was a kind of trot".[370] Thomas Thornton, touring the Highlands in 1804, spoke of the "lively gait peculiar to a Highlander".[371] Robert Somers visited Glen Tilt in 1847, where, he wrote, "a gamekeeper or a gillie hurried past me occasionally, at the jog-trot peculiar to hill-men".[372]

When necessary, they were more than brisk. Nicolay d'Arfeuille, in 1583, said the Gaels could run fast. "They are very swift of foot, and there is no horse so swift as to outstrip them, as I have seen proved several times both in England and Scotland."[373] Daniel Defoe, in his *Memoirs of a Cavalier*, gave his opinion of the Highlanders in General Leslie's army in 1640. This was, of course, a work of fiction, though it pretended otherwise – but many novelists, e.g. Sir Walter Scott, have often been quoted by historians, as we have seen earlier; so we may follow suit. Defoe wrote: "They were generally tall swinging-looking fellows ... They have large bodies, and prodigious strong, and two qualities above all other nations, viz. hardy to endure fatigue, hunger, cold, and hardships, and wonderfully swift of foot. The latter is such an advantage in the field, that I know none like it, for if they conquer, no enemy can escape them, and if they run, even the horse can hardly overtake them."[374] The same author, speaking of groups of cavalry in the 1640 Scots army, said, "I observed that these parties had always some foot with them, and yet if the horses galloped or pushed on ever so forward, the foot were as forward as they, which was an extraordinary advantage. These were those they call Highlanders; they would run on foot with all their arms and their accoutrements, and keep very good order too, and kept pace with the horses, let them go at what rate they would."[374] The anonymous 1747 author said "the Highlander wears a sort of thin pump or brogue, so light that it does not in the least impede his activity in running"; as a result the Highlanders "are able to advance or retreat with incredible swiftness, so that if they have the better in any engagement it is scarce possible to escape from them, and on the other hand, if they are overpowered they soon recover [get back to] their hills, where it is impossible to reach them".[375]

At Fontenoy in 1745, to reconnoitre the ground before the battle, the Black Watch (said a history of the regiment) was chosen "to accompany a squadron of Austrian Hussars [cavalry], for the Highlanders were perfectly able to keep up with horses for hours on end".[376] The rapid summoning of the armed strength of the clan by means of the croishtarich implied that each successive runner could take the message with some speed to the next township. Stewart, as we saw, said that in 1745 the croishtarich went round Loch Tay, at least thirty-two miles, in three hours. The path which successive messengers would take round Loch Tay is probably further than thirty-two miles; but even accepting that minimum figure, this speed means that the couriers, carrying the fiery cross and their weapons, and periodically shouting the clan slogan, were running each mile across uneven ground in just over five and a half minutes – not counting any delay in finding the next runner at each stage. It can be accepted that this was quick work. Not many modern men would be able to match that pace when suddenly called from their usual avocations.

In the Battle of Falkirk, fought in January 1746, a thousand dragoons (heavily-armed cavalrymen) in the Hanoverian army charged the Highlanders. They were repulsed after a "pell-mell" combat, and forced to retire. "The Highlanders", said an eye-witness, the Chevalier de Johnstone, "did not neglect the advantage they had obtained, but pursued them keenly with their swords, running as fast as their [the dragoons'] horses, and not allowing them a moment's time to recover from their fright."[377] (This recalls the comments about the Highlanders in 1583, in 1640 and in 1745, that they were able to keep up with the horses.) In the Seven Years' War (1756-63) the 87th and 88th Regiments, Keith's and Campbell's Highlanders, served on the Continent, and the *Vienna Gazette* remarked "they run with a surprising degree of swiftness".[378] After facing the Black Watch in the field, during the capture of Guadeloupe in 1759, the French (according to private correspondence, quoted by David Stewart) came to believe that the Highlanders "were so nimble, that, as no man could catch them, so nobody could escape them" (and, furthermore, that "no man had a chance against their broadswords").[379] When in 1773 Dr Johnson and Boswell left Inverness, to ride on horseback to the western sea, Johnson wrote: "We took two Highlanders to run beside us, partly to show us the way, and partly to take back from the sea-side the horses, of which they were the owners. One of them was a man of great liveliness and activity, of whom his companion said, that he would tire any horse in Inverness."[380] Eleven years later another traveller, Faujas de Saint Fond, hired horses in Mull, and with him and his friend went two guides, who "pushed forward with such speed as to outrun our horses, though these went at a good speed". (The guides were "well-made, light, and indefatigable; they made nothing of streams, pools, bogs, or mountains; and I admired their courage, gaiety, and graceful figure".)[381] J. L. Buchanan said of the Outer Hebrideans in 1793, "however astonishing it may appear to strangers, it is a known fact that those nimble fellows can catch the wildest sheep that feeds on the highest hills by swiftness of foot, and that in the night as well as by day"; boys of twelve would run a sheep down, then let it go for the pleasure of catching it again.[382] In 1813, when the men of Kildonan gathered to rebuke some Lowland shepherds for coming to prepare the way for the next round of the Sutherland clearances, two of the sheepmen rode off on horseback at a speed proportionate to their fear; yet the Highlanders, on foot, were apparently not far behind them for some eight miles.[383]

56. Hardy and intrepid

They walked, Burt said, "nimbly and upright", with a "kind of stateliness"[384] (a curious gait for a people who supposedly could at any moment be thrown into fetid dungeons at the slightest whim of their chiefs). We saw earlier that the man who described the Colquhoun clansmen at the time of the '15 spoke of the same quality, calling them "forty or fifty stately fellows".[385] James Wolfe, later the victor of Quebec, was in Scotland during the Jacobite rebellion and afterwards; and though he still regarded the Highlanders as the "enemy" he realized how useful they would be as soldiers, characterizing them as "hardy" and "intrepid".[386] A year or two later the Prime Minister, the elder Pitt, speaking in the Commons, used identical adjectives: the Highlanders, he said, were "a hardy and intrepid race of men".[387] Dr Richard Pococke, writing of his *Tour* in Sutherland and Caithness in 1760, said: "They are mostly well-bodied men, of great activity, and go the

Highland trot with wonderful expedition."[388] Dr Johnson, describing the Highlanders on his visit in 1773, said "they are accustomed to run upon rough ground, and therefore can with great agility skip over the bog, and clamber the mountain".[389] Joseph Mawman wrote in 1805: "All the Highlanders walked with firmness and agility . . . We remarked that, north of Glasgow [the last large Lowland factory-town on the route to the Highlands, some seventeen miles from the Highland border], we had not beheld one individual man, woman, or child, crooked."[390] Burt, writing in Inverness in the 1720s, said much the same: "there are hardly any crooked people (except by accidents)."[391] In *Humphry Clinker* (1771), by Tobias Smollett, who was born on the edge of the Highlands, one of the characters observed of the Highlanders: "They do not walk like the generality of mankind, but trot and bound like deer, as if they moved upon springs. They greatly excel the Lowlanders in all exercises that require agility; they are incredibly abstemious, and patient of hunger and fatigue; so steeled against the weather, that in travelling, even when the ground is covered with snow, they never look for a house, or any other shelter but their plaid, in which they wrap themselves up, and go to sleep under the cope of heaven."[392]

A German observer, seeing the 42nd (Black Watch) and 92nd (Gordon Highlanders) regiments leaving Brussels at dawn on their way to Waterloo, was highly impressed. "They were men!" he said later. "All strong, nimble and free as if they had come straight from the hand of God. They carried their heads so freely and gaily and marched so lightly, swinging along with their bare knees, that you would have thought they had never heard of original sin or the primal curse." Another observer who saw the Highlanders marching out for the battle at four o'clock that momentous midsummer morning, said: "One could not but admire their fine appearance, their firm, collected, steady, military demeanour, with their bagpipes playing before them, and the beams of the rising sun shining upon their glittering arms."[393] All this, despite the fact that they were going into imminent action, well aware that many would (as many did) meet their deaths.

57. Rapidity peculiar to Highlanders

Three decades afterwards, the same physical qualities recommended the Highlanders to Queen Victoria and Prince Albert. When the Queen came into the Farquharson country of Braemar in 1849, the royal carriage had been accompanied by some "Farquharson men", whom she described (unconsciously echoing Burt over a hundred years earlier) as "skipping over stones and rocks with the rapidity and lightness peculiar to Highlanders".[394] This dexterity in movement was one of the traits which the royal couple approved in John Brown, born and brought up on the Deeside hills. Prince Albert, one commentator wrote, "admired the incredible toughness of the man, his fast and untiring walk, the way he forded burns and strode on unheeding of wet clothes".[395] As for Queen Victoria, she observed in her diary how Brown walked "with that vigorous, light, elastic tread which is quite astonishing".[396]

Sir Archibald Geikie travelled regularly in the Highlands from the middle of the nineteenth century onwards, staying with Highland families, and becoming friendly with many Highlanders; and he wrote of one acquaintance that he "had the true 'Highlandman's ling' – the elastic, springy and swift step of the mountaineer, accustomed to traverse shaking bog and rough moor".[397] ("Ling" is a Scots word meaning a forward surge.)

All this talk by contemporaries about the Highlanders being "wonderfully swift of foot", "skipping over rocks and stones", their "surprising degree of swiftness", and how they "bound like deer" (not to mention their sagacity and ingenuity) – did not convince one modern Lowland historian, who instead said, without offering any evidence, that "the Highland people were lethargic in mind and slow in movement".[398] It will be seen, in the face of the orthodox opinions, why it was necessary to quote so many people who knew the old Highlanders.

The Highlanders in General Leslie's army ("tall, swinging-looking fellows" with "large bodies") were not exceptional. Alexander Cunningham's remark about the Highlanders, that "most of them are tall, and produce tall children", has already been quoted.[399] Sir Walter Scott described the 1779 Sutherland Fencibles as a "regiment of Sutherland giants".[400] David Stewart wrote that in about 1808 a detachment of recruits left to join the Ross-shire Highlanders in Bombay: 350 of them were volunteers from "Perthshire, Ross-shire, and other Scotch militia regiments; and of these," he said, "280 were six feet and upwards, with strength of limb and person equal to their height".[401] It is curious that the *Vienna Gazette* in 1762 seemed to say the opposite. According to this journal, the Highlanders then fighting in the Seven Years' War "are of low stature . . . Broglio [presumably the Duc de Broglie, who commanded the French several times against the Highlanders] himself has lately said, that he once wished that he was a man of six feet high, but that now he is reconciled to his size, since he has seen the wonders performed by the little mountaineers."[402] This account was written by someone who thought the Highlanders were heathen savages running wild in the mountains, who had to be caught and instructed in Christianity, so he or she did not appear to be over conversant with the reality. But there are two other relevant comments, which are quoted fully below: the Gordon Fencibles of 1793 were described as "not in general tall", and the Fraser Fencibles, raised the following year, were also portrayed as "not in general large". It does make one wonder if the otherwise widespread opinion that the Highlanders were tall was really a tribute to their free, independent, and upright stance, when compared with the (laboriously earned) bowed backs and the (socially necessary) cringing attitudes of all too many other inhabitants of Great Britain at that time. Scott described Lowland villagers in *Waverley* as "bent as much by toil as years".[403]

The good health of the Highlanders may have owed something to their attitude to contemporary doctors (and, for that matter, lawyers). Alexander Cunningham wrote disapprovingly of them: "the sick among them will neither let blood, nor suffer a physician to be sent for, lest their health should thereby be more impaired than recovered: and lawyers they mortally hate."[404] Since Lowland and English doctors know now, rather belatedly, that the Highlanders were quite right when they believed that to drain out people's blood weakened rather than strengthened them, and since it was lawyers who had expertly drawn up the charters which introduced private property in land, and thus provided the vehicle for depriving the Highlanders of their own Highlands, it may be thought that the clansfolk's opinion of contemporary doctors and lawyers is hardly surprising.

CHARACTER OF THE HIGHLANDERS

CHAPTER SIX NOTES

1. *A retrospective invention*
[1] Trevor-Roper 1983, 15. A. N. Wilson, writing in *The Observer* on 11th July 2010, claimed that Trevor-Roper was "at home . . . with prime ministers and duchesses", and that (perhaps as a result?) he was "a historian who never lost sight of the function of history: to tell the truth". The first of these observations is no doubt true; whether the second is equally valid these pages may help to decide.
[2] H. Trevor-Roper, *Sunday Times*, 26th October 1969.
[3] Larkin 2010, 14.
[4] Stewart 1822, I 7-8.
[5] Prebble 1971, 22.
[6] Prebble 1970, 262 fn.
[7] Scarlett 1975, 74.

2. *Fire and sword*
[8] See below, chapter six, subsection 30, *Eighteen times more honest*.
[9] Scott c. 1890, 132.
[10] Scott c. 1890, 587.
[11] MacKenzie 1911, 640.
[12] Scott c. 1890, 587.
[13] Scott 1925, 169-70. This question is looked into more fully above, in chapter one, *The clearances in history*, subsection 17, *Petty tyrants*, and in chapter three, *Power in the clan*, subsection 26, *In all things subservient*.
[14] A. Conan Doyle, *The White Company*, Murray, London (1891) 1938, 69.

3. *War rather than peace*
[15] Prebble 1970, 39-41.
[16] Iain MacDonald, *Clerics & Clansmen,* Brill, Leiden, 2013, 8, quoting John of Fordun.
[17] Steel 1994, 60, quoting John Major, *Historia Majoris Britanniae*, 1521.
[18] Fry 2005, title-page.
[19] Munro 1977, 36.
[20] Website scottishhistory.com/articles/highlands.
[21] Website scottishhistory.com/articles/highlands.
[22] MacKay 1914, 156.

4. *Murder and pillage*
[23] Mitchison 1971, 375.
[24] Somerset Fry 1985, 106.
[25] Glover 1966, 93.
[26] Steel 1994, 61, 60, 110, 243, 256.
[27] Mitchison 1971, 375.
[28] Grant & Cheape 2000, 234.
[29] Smout 1970, 340, 347.
[30] Donaldson 1993, 166.

5. *Violence and bloody murder*
[31] Prebble 1970, 261.
[32] Mitchison 1971, 379.

[33] A. J. P. Taylor, *English History 1914-1945*, Clarendon Press, Oxford 1965, 61 fn. My father was in the 18th battalion of the Durham Light Infantry, the "Durham Pals", which (according to what my Uncle Anthony told me before he died) had four companies: A, B, C, and D. My father (and my Uncle Anthony) were both in C company. On that fateful day, lst July 1916 (my uncle said), A, B, and D companies were sent "over the top" as part of the great Somme offensive, somewhere near the village of Serre, at the northern end of the onslaught; C company was held in reserve to "consolidate the expected gains" later on. In fact there were no gains: the three companies were largely wiped out. As C company stood on the step that evening ready to "go over the top" on the projected "consolidation", the brigadier came along the trench ordering them to stand down; there was to be no further attack. The brigadier was weeping, so my Uncle Anthony said (not a spectacle a private soldier would soon forget), having just heard what had happened to so many of the men involved in the great assault. Since my father and uncle were in the "reserve" C company, they both survived the carnage of that first day: a matter of pure chance (the odds about anyone in that battalion being in C company, rather than A, B, or D, were three to one against; the odds about any two brothers in that battalion both being in company C were fifteen to one against). The official records appear to state that on 1st July 1916, the 18th Battalion, D.L.I., "lost over half their strength killed or wounded" (and only three-quarters of the battalion's men were actually in the offensive: which must mean that over two-thirds of those who "went over the top" were killed or injured). On one day! All this happened within Prebble's lifetime (he was born in 1915); so it was remarkable that he did not mention it, when he chose to accuse the Gaels of "violence and bloody murder". My father was badly injured the next day, 2nd July; my Uncle Anthony survived the war uninjured. A third brother, my Uncle Jack, actually became a sergeant (so he must at the least have kept his nose clean in all his time at the front), but was gassed, and died many years later from the after effects. When Jack, after years in the trenches, was able to "gan hyem" to the little coalminers' terraced house on the Medomsley hillside outside Consett in County Durham, he was greeted by his mother with the welcoming words "Ah've put your pit clothes oot" (i.e., you can go straight down the mine again). Economic pressure means that members of the lower orders have less time for emotion than their betters.

When my father enlisted in the army he was a probationary minister in the Wesleyan Methodist church (which some years later became and still remains part of the united Methodist Church); after his injuries at the front the church officials (who were afraid he would be a financial liability) skilfully prevented him, by scarcely legal and indeed by illegal means, from ever becoming a full minister. The result was that he did the whole work of a full minister but for only one-fifth of the salary, a pleasant profit for Methodism. This family background was so far useful to the author (let us look on the bright side) that he realized early on the paramount necessity of discriminating between what people say and what they do – a skill absolutely essential for a historian (not to mention people generally). It is essential to listen to people's words: but then you must compare their words with their actions. And indeed you must work out whether people's statements at certain times are compatible with what they say at other times.

[34] Shakespeare, *Hamlet*, IV, iv 60.

[35] In the early 1800s, Sydney Smith declared that since the Treaty of Utrecht, 1713 (which itself had closed the eleven-year "War of the Spanish Succession"), Britain "had been at war thirty-five minutes out of every hour" (Hesketh Pearson, *Smith of Smiths*, Right Book Club, London, 1934, 135).

6. *Report of the Royal Commission*

[36] Napier 1884, V 67, report of the commissioners.

[37] Napier 1884, V 110, ditto.

7. *Comradeship and independence*

[38] O.S.A. VIII 435, Kilmallie Inv.

[39] O.S.A. XIII 298, South Uist Inv.

[40] O.S.A. VIII 256, Cromdale Moray.
[41] O.S.A. VIII 255, 252, 256, Cromdale Moray. So the clansfolk, who had for centuries supposedly suffered under tyrannical rulers, whose slightest whim (historians say) could condemn their clanspeople to foul imprisonment or the hangman's rope, had under the economic disasters of the later eighteenth century suddenly discovered a sturdy independence. Why do not historians ever ask themselves if what they are saying is remotely consistent, or even humanly possible?
[42] O.S.A. VII 575 & 575 fn, Monzievaird Perth.
[43] O.S.A. V 54, Moulin Perth.
[44] Stewart 1822, II xlvii.
[45] O.S.A. VI 368, 364, Little Dunkeld Perth.
[46] Stewart 1822, II xlvii.
[47] Robertson 1808, 92. Wherever did Robertson find these people, descending in the scale "from affluence or even from easy circumstances . . . into want"? Surely orthodox history tells us that the clearances were making everybody better off? P. Gaskell (Gaskell 1980, 1) said under the heading "Morvern in 1800" that the Highlanders were poor then, but staunchly affirmed "they had been poorer before"; in other words, they were better off, in comparison with earlier years. That clearly means that they were ascending in the scale of society. Many modern writers make similar allegations, though contemporary observers often have a different tale.
[48] O.S.A. XX 446, Dunkeld Perth.
[49] O.S.A. II 455, Fortingall Perth.
[50] O.S.A. XII 271, Knockbain Ross.
[51] O.S.A. XII 470, Kirkmichael Banff.
[52] O.S.A. XV 634, Avoch Ross.
[53] O.S.A. XII 331, Jura Arg.
[54] Selkirk 2010, 14.
[55] O.S.A. III 530, Tongue Suth.
[56] Geddes 1955, 124.
[57] Wordsworth 1894, 234-5.

8. *Romantic excess*
[58] Selkirk 2010, 7.
[59] O.S.A. X 387, Harris Inv.
[60] O.S.A. XIV 250, Kilfinan Arg.
[61] O.S.A. XI 294, Kildalton Arg.
[62] O.S.A. IV 571, Strachur & Strathlachlan Arg.
[63] O.S.A. XX 467, Dunkeld Perth.
[64] O.S.A. VI 370, Little Dunkeld Perth.

9. *Rallying the clansmen*
[65] O.S.A. VI 244 & 246 fn, Kintail Ross.
[66] Stewart 1822, II ix.
[67] O.S.A. XIV 352, Crathie Aberd.
[68] Adam/Innes 1965, 545, & Stewart 1822, II x.

10. *Fair and friendly*
[69] O.S.A. IX 23, Buchanan Stir.
[70] O.S.A. VI 302, Eddrachillis Suth.
[71] O.S.A. XVI 203, Assynt Suth.
[72] O.S.A. XIII 378, Alvie Inv.
[73] Buchanan 1997, 47.

74 Burt's *Letters*, 1822 edition, 149 fn.
75 Burt 2005, xxxiii.
76 O.S.A. III 516, Kincardine Ross.
77 O.S.A. XV 636 fn, Avoch Ross.
78 O.S.A. XI 583, Callander Perth.
79 Thomson 2010, 62, quoting Cunningham 1787.

11. *Love of country.*
80 Burt 2005, 156-8, 294-5.
81 Walker 1980, II 399.
82 O.S.A. XV 522, Kirkmichael Perth. The Boleskine reporter was amazed at "the attachment the natives of this country bear to their natale solum [natal soil]", O.S.A. XX 34, Boleskine Inv.
83 O.S.A. IV 577, Strachur & Strathlachlan Arg.
84 O.S.A. III 484, Dores Inv.
85 O.S.A. VII 256, Urray Ross.
86 Stewart 1822, I 364 fn.

12. *Forefathers' graves*
87 Grant & Cheape 2000, 205.
88 O.S.A. XII 137, Weem Perth.
89 O.S.A. XVI 345, Rafford Moray.
90 O.S.A. XVI 145, Portree Inv.
91 O.S.A. VIII 12 fn, Dornoch Suth.
92 Stewart 1822, I 82.
93 O.S.A. XII 273 fn, Knockbain Ross.

13. *Hospitality*
94 O.S.A. XVI 204, Assynt Suth.
95 Pennant 2000, 152.
96 Johnson & Boswell 1930, 43.
97 R. J. Sulivan, *Tour Through Parts of England Scotland & Wales*, Becket, London, 1780, 210.
98 Wordsworth 1894, 164-5.
99 Stewart II 13, quoting Toland 1709.
100 O.S.A. VIII 67, Gigha & Cara Arg.
101 O.S.A. XIV 209, Kilfinichen & Kilvickeon Arg.
102 Inverness Courier, 5th August 1835, Barron 1903-13, volume two, electricscotland website. The total charge was five shillings (sixty pence); since there were eleven rescued seamen, that made five and a half pennies each.
103 O.S.A. VIII 357, Glenorchy & Inishail Arg.
104 Nicolson 1930, 308.

14. *He is a stranger*
105 N.S.A. VII 601, Dunoon Arg.
106 Mawman 1805, 156.
107 Johnson & Boswell 1930, 27.
108 Bristed 1803, II 121.
109 Bristed 1803, II 122. (Bristed borrowed two phrases from Psalm 137, v & vi.)

15. *Highlanders as soldiers*
110 Jamieson, Burt 2005, xxxii.

CHARACTER OF THE HIGHLANDERS

[111] Jamieson, Burt 2005, xxxiii.
[112] Stewart 1822, I 239, quoting Jackson 1804.
[113] Stewart 1822, I 113.
[114] Stewart 1822, II 33.

16. *Loyalty*
[115] Johnson & Boswell 1930, 281.
[116] O.S.A. VIII 359 fn, Glenorchy Arg.
[117] MacCulloch 1824, 456.
[118] Napier 1884, V 461, Alexander Carmichael.
[119] Richards 1982, 14, & passim elsewhere in his work.

17. *"Pacification" of the Highlands*
[120] MacLean 1988, 215, 222, 223, 234, 282-288, 296. Culloden was ungrateful as well as graceless to Duncan Forbes, who had done as much as anyone to keep Cumberland's father on the throne. When someone suggest Forbes's service had not been worth five shillings, Forbes is reported to have said that some thought they were worth three crowns (MacKenzie 1908, 253), three coins which were then of course worth fifteen shillings.
[121] Anderson 1920, chapter six, *Events after the battle*, website queenofscots.co.uk.
[122] Grant & Cheape 2000, 203-4: "Companies under the command of Lord Loudoun, MacDonald of Sleat, and MacLeod of MacLeod" went to Glen Moriston, murdering, destroying and driving off the cattle.
[123] Mahon 1853, III 436.
[124] *Oxford D.N.B.*, article "Henry Hawley".
[125] MacDonald 1994, 177; Gaskell 1980, 3, 4; N.S.A. XIV 452, Croy Inv.
[126] MacLean 1988, 283.
[127] MacLean 1988, 283.
[128] MacLean 1988, 285.
[129] MacLean 1988, 283.
[130] MacLean 1988, 285.
[131] Stewart 1822, I 64 fn.
[132] MacLean 1988, 285.
[133] C. Grant Robertson, *England under the Hanoverians*, Methuen, London (1911) 1934, 151.

18. *Most deplorable way*
[134] MacLean 1988, 283.
[135] MacLean 1988, 284.
[136] John G. Gibson, *Traditional Gaelic Bagpiping*, Birlinn, Edinburgh 2000, 40.
[137] Miller 1854, 135, apparently basing account on Ray 1747, 179.
[138] MacLean 1988, 285.

19. *Very wanton excesses*
[139] N.S.A. X 979, Dunkeld Perth.
[140] N.S.A. XIV 121, Kilmallie Inv.
[141] N.S.A. VII 143, Ardnamurchan Arg.
[142] N.S.A. VII 176, Morvern Arg.
[143] N.S.A. XIV 452, Croy Inv.
[144] Mahon 1853, III 309.
[145] Mahon 1853, III 311.
[146] Forbes 1834, 343.

[147] Forbes 1834, 300.
[148] *Oxford D.N.B.*, article Lord George Sackville.
[149] Williams 1949, 243 fn, & 269.

20. *Stinking Billy*
[150] *Oxford D.N.B.*, article Duke of Cumberland.
[151] MacLean 1988, 282.
[152] MacLean 1988, 223, 287.
[153] MacDonald 1994, 177.
[154] MacLean 1988, 287.
[155] MacLean 1988, 287, 290, & *Oxford D.N.B.*
[156] *Oxford D.N.B.*, article Duke of Cumberland.
[157] Pennant 2000, 103.
[158] MacLean 1988, 215.

21. *A little bloodletting*
[159] MacLean 1988, 223.
[160] *Oxford D.N.B.*, article Duke of Cumberland.
[161] *Oxford D.N.B.*, article Duke of Cumberland.
[162] MacLean 1988, 288.
[163] MacLean 1988, 296.
[164] Devine 1998, 30.

22. *Honesty and fidelity*
[165] O.S.A. VIII 361, Glenorchy Arg.
[166] Stewart 1822, I 239, quoting Jackson 1804.
[167] Stewart 1822, I 200 fn.
[168] Smollett 1967, 263. The name "caddy" now survives only as the title of a golfer's assistant.
[169] Linklater 1976, 126.
[170] Anderson 1785, vi-vii fn.

23. *Property secured and preserved*
[171] Anderson 1785, vi & vi fn.
[172] Walker 1980, 171.

24. *Civilized the people*
[173] Anderson 1785, vi & vi fn.
[174] Hogg 1981, 109.
[175] O.S.A. XIV 209, Kilfinichen & Kilvickeon Arg.
[176] Donaldson 1993, 155, 165, 166.

25. *Ridiculously small*
[177] O.S.A. XV 258, Monzie Perth.
[178] Burt's *Letters*, 1822 edition, xlviii (2005 edition, xxxvi), R. Jamieson.
[179] Miller 1854, 106-7.
[180] Blackie 1885, 18.
[181] Stewart 1822, I 35.
[182] Burt 2005, 254-5.
[183] Robertson 1808, 83.
[184] O.S.A. III 190, Lochgoilhead Arg.

CHARACTER OF THE HIGHLANDERS

[185] O.S.A. XVI 273, Glenelg Inv.
[186] O.S.A. VIII 361, Glenorchy Arg.
[187] Stewart 1822, II xii, & I 61 fn, quoting R. Holinshed.
[188] MacKay 1889, 331.
[189] Marshall 1794, 18, 19.
[190] MacLeod 1892, 123.

26. *No traveller could pass*
[191] Johnson & Boswell 1930, 85 & 40.
[192] Martin 1703, 345-6.
[193] G. O. Trevelyan, *The American Revolution*, Longmans, London, 1905-12, V 246.
[194] Trevelyan 1946, 383. Dickens mentioned this incident in *A Tale of Two Cities*. That was a novel, of course, but those who regularly quote the fiction of (e.g.) Walter Scott should not ignore Dickens' diatribe on the state of England in "the year of our Lord one thousand seven hundred and seventy five". He said: "Daring burglaries by armed men, and highway robberies, took place in the capital itself every night; families were publicly cautioned not to go out of town without removing their furniture to the upholsterers' warehouses for security; the highwayman in the dark was a City tradesman in the light, and, being recognized and challenged by his fellow-tradesman whom he stopped in his character of 'the Captain', gallantly shot him through the head and rode away; the mail was waylaid by seven robbers, and the guard shot three dead, and then got shot dead himself by the other four, 'in consequence of the failure of his ammunition': after which the mail was robbed in peace; that magnificent potentate, the Lord Mayor of London, was made to stand and deliver on Turnham Green, by one highwayman, who despoiled the illustrious creature in sight of all his retinue; prisoners in London's gaols fought battles with their turnkeys, and the majesty of the law fired blunderbusses in among them, loaded with rounds of shot and ball; thieves snipped off diamond crosses from the necks of noble lords at Court drawing rooms; musketeers went into St Giles's, to search for contraband goods, and the mob fired on the musketeers, and the musketeers fired on the mob, and nobody thought any of these occurrences were much out of the common way. In the midst of them, the hangman, ever busy and ever worse than useless, was in constant acquisition; now, stringing up long rows of miscellaneous criminals; now hanging a housebreaker on Saturday who had been taken on Tuesday; now, burning people in the hand at Newgate by the dozen, and now burning pamphlets at the door of Westminster Hall; today, taking the life of an atrocious murderer, and tomorrow of a wretched pilferer who had robbed a farmer's boy of sixpence."

On hanging days, the doomed felons were taken (often splendidly dressed) the three miles from Newgate to Tyburn through a great roistering rabble who had come to enjoy the holiday show for the mob (paradoxically giving welcome opportunities to pickpockets), to applaud or jeer the last speeches of the condemned, and then not infrequently joining in the free fights as the friends of the executed criminal (planning an appreciative funeral) battled with those who tried to grab the body to sell it to the surgery schools for dissection. All in all, a most improving day-long display to demonstrate the majesty of the law.
[195] Everett vs Williams, 9 L. Q. Rev., 197.

27. *The want of law*
[196] Boswell 1928, I 392, I 388, I 517, II 304.
[197] Boswell 1928, II 304. The Gordon Riots began on 2nd June 1780, and "London was not brought back to normal until 12th June" (Watson 1960, 239). Order was only restored when over 200 been killed, over 200 wounded, and twenty hanged. (Some accounts say over 1000 died in the riots.)
[198] Johnson & Boswell 1930, 12.

¹⁹⁹ See *Tristram Shandy*, Penguin, London, (1759-67) 2003, 171, which was published only a year or two before the Highland journey of Johnson and Boswell: "My father, who had an itch in common with all philosophers, of reasoning upon everything which happened, and accounting for it too."

28. *Macaulay's History*
²⁰⁰ Burt 2005, 157-8.
²⁰¹ Macaulay 1907, 421.
²⁰² Macaulay 1907, 423. G. M. Trevelyan approved of his great-uncle Macaulay's sentiments (Trevelyan 1949, 98), about the dangers of a traveller in the Highlands getting his throat cut at the next turn of the track.
²⁰³ S. Smith, *Oxford Dictionary of Quotations*, 505.
²⁰⁴ Douglas 1975, 173; see Buchanan 1997, 28-9.
²⁰⁵ *Journal of the MacColl Society*, at or near volume thirteen, page 15.

29. *Accumulated filth of years*
²⁰⁶ Fenyo, *Contempt, Sympathy, & Romance*, Tuckwell, East Lothian, 2000, 39, quoting Macaulay, *Critical, Historical, & Miscellaneous Essays*.
²⁰⁷ Macaulay, *Historical Essays Contributed to the "Edinburgh Review"*, "*Sir J. Mackintosh's History of the Revolution*", July 1835. A great friend of mine, Eddie Grant, whose own family background included the Baltic states and South America, was working in an office, and became involved in discussions about immigration; and was amused to observe that those who were immigrants themselves were more opposed to it than the natives. ("Pull up the ladder, I'm inboard", as they say in the Navy.) Incidentally, when I have sometimes hinted in discussions that some things done by some English people at some times in the past were not necessarily completely praiseworthy, I have occasionally been told that anyone who would dare to say such things must be of foreign extraction. But since I have been able to give details of eight wholly English great-grandparents, all born, bred, and died in England, I usually found that my opponent was not so English as I was (or sometimes that he was not even able to say who all his great-grandparents were).
²⁰⁸ Macaulay 1907, 422.
²⁰⁹ The Master of University College, Oxford; I think F. C. Plumptre.

30. *Eighteen times more honest*
²¹⁰ Stewart 1822, II xli-xliii.
²¹¹ Stewart 1822, I 43 & I 114.
²¹² Johnson & Boswell 1930, 82.
²¹³ Stewart 1822, I 35 & 35 fn.
²¹⁴ Stewart 1822, I 233.
²¹⁵ To be exact, the Highlanders were 17.89 times more honest than the Lowlanders and the rest of Britain's inhabitants.

31. *Racial assumptions* (see Appendix B)
²¹⁶ Richards 1999, 260.
²¹⁷ Stewart 1822, I 150.
²¹⁸ Stewart 1822, I 159.
²¹⁹ Stewart 1822, I 209.
²²⁰ Stewart 1822, I 213.
²²¹ Stewart 1822, I 233.
²²² Stewart 1822, I 208.
²²³ Stewart 1822, I 232.
²²⁴ Stewart 1822, II 252.

CHARACTER OF THE HIGHLANDERS

[225] Stewart 1822, II xlii fn.
[226] Stewart 1822, I 208-9 fn.
[227] Stewart 1822, I 233.

32. *How did they survive?*
[228] Donaldson 1993, 165. Donaldson believed that the Highlanders were perpetually raiding the Lowlands, obviously entailing casualties (without such raids they would not have had enough food, pp. 155 & 166, so the raids must have been frequent – the human frame does not last long without food); and besides that, the Massacre of Glen Coe was nothing unusual – "more bloody massacres had taken place before in the course of Highland feuding and Glen Coe might have been forgotten like them" (p. 165) but for opponents of William III making a meal of it. (An interesting example of the theory that people often get worked up unnecessarily, and make a fuss about nothing, really.) So what with these perpetual raids on the Lowlands (which must have been every few days at least, since otherwise starvation ensued), and the deaths from the apparently regular massacres in this unfortunate "Highland feuding", there must have been considerable loss of life. See also Trevelyan 1946, 453; Eric Linklater1962, xi; Glover 1966, 93; Steel 1984, 61 (Glover and also Steel, "prolonged & bloody wars"). See also J. Anderson 1785, vii-ix fn, "perpetual wars and lawless disorder".
[229] Grant & Cheape 2000, 164, 153.

33. *Place of refuge*
[230] Rixson 2004, 34.
[231] Scott 1995, 307.
[232] Richards 1982, 42, quoting Annette M. Smith in 1977-8.
[233] Smout 1970, 340, 344, 345, 347. The Duke of Argyll had seized the position as landlord of Tiree by fraudulent illegalities, backed up by force; hypocritically he insisted that the Tiree people should be "peaceable and apply to industry" – the exact opposite of the means he had himself used to seize power in the island (Smout 1970, 344-5). Dr Smout thought Argyll was a supporter of "the new moral world".
[234] N.S.A. VII 512-13, Ardchattan & Muckairn Arg.
[235] N.S.A. VII 20, Inveraray Arg.
[236] Stewart 1822, I 45 fn.
[237] Linklater 1962, xii.

34. *Disorder and misery*
[238] Glover 1966, 68, 70. Hume Brown 1955 (97-8) wrote of "the peaceful days of Alexander III". Perhaps they could be thought so, in comparison with what came afterwards.
[239] A. L. Poole, *From Doomsday Book to Magna Carta*, Clarendon Press, Oxford, (1951) 1958, 480.
[240] J. G. Edgar, *Runnymede & Lincoln Fair*, Everyman, London, (1908) 1923, 118. (No relation, I believe.)
[241] MacKenzie 1911, 92.
[242] Glover 1966, 79.
[243] Hume Brown 1955, 97, 99.
[244] Steel 1994, 53.
[245] Glover 1966, 89.
[246] Hume Brown 1955, 103.
[247] Somerset Fry 1985, 84, quoting William Dunbar.
[248] Glover 1966, 88.

35. *Robert II, Robert III*
[249] Glover 1966, 90, quoting an un-named "contemporary" witness.
[250] Buchan 1938, 56.

[251] Somerset Fry 1985, 91.
[252] Hume Brown 1955, 112-13.

36. *James I*
[253] MacKenzie 1911, 199.
[254] MacKenzie 1906, 70-1.
[255] Glover 1960, 96.
[256] Glover 1960, 101.
[257] Hume Brown 1955, 115.
[258] Hume Brown 1955, 119.
[259] Mitchison 1971, 68.
[260] Grimble 1980, 87.
[261] MacKenzie 1911, 217.
[262] Several early illustrations were made of Oldcastle's execution, e.g. in *Fox's Book of Martyrs*.

37. *James II*
[263] BBC Scotland's History website.
[264] Hume Brown 1955, 131.
[265] Hume Brown 1955, 132.
[266] Stewart 1822, I 45 fn.
[267] MacKenzie 1911, 217, 221.

38. *James III*
[268] MacKenzie 1911, 233.
[269] Somerset Fry 1985, 112. The general course of the reigns of these Lowland kings can be found in many textbooks.

39. *James IV*
[270] MacKenzie 1911, 237. Barton's exploit was celebrated in a ballad – A. L. Lloyd, *Folk Song in England*, Laurence & Wishart, London, 1967, 275.
[271] Mitchison 1971, 83, 85.
[272] Glover 1966, 119.

40. *James V*
[273] MacKenzie 1911, 267.
[274] Glover 1966, 127.
[275] Grimble 1980, 100.
[276] *The Times*, 21st August 2007, *Law* supplement: the execution was in 1531.
[277] Grimble 1980, 100.

41. *Mary Queen of Scots*
[278] MacKenzie 1911, 433, 429.
[279] Hume Brown 1955, 173.
[280] MacKenzie 1911, 294.
[281] Stewart 1822, I 37 fn.
[282] Johnson & Boswell 1930, 6. Dr Johnson said, "he was murdered by the ruffians of the reformation, in the manner of which Knox has given what he himself calls a merry narrative".
[283] George Thomson, *Antiquity of the Christian Religion among the Scots*, 1594, Scottish History Society, XVIV, *Miscellany*, II 131.

CHARACTER OF THE HIGHLANDERS

42. *James VI and I*
[284] MacKenzie 1911, 436; Hume Brown 1955, 204.
[285] *Oxford D.N.B.*, article James VI & I. There are members of the American establishment, it is reported (e.g. in *The Times*, 24th April 2018), who are still convinced that accurate evidence can be obtained by torture, which is therefore justified.
[286] Sylvia Wright, an American author, misheard this ballad as a child, and thought there were two victims, the second being "Lady Mondegreen". She therefore suggested that this kind of verbal misunderstanding should be known as a "mondegreen".

43. *Union of the crowns*
[287] Glover 1966, 200.
[288] Grant 1987, 45-6.
[289] Stewart 1822, I 216.

44. *Public opinion*
[290] A letter in *The Times* on 10th February 2006, from the Chief Executive of the Probation Boards' Association, said that "only some two per cent of all known crime results in a conviction (most of it never reaches a court)".
[291] MacLean 1988, 245.
[292] Bristed 1803, II 231.

45. *Banished themselves*
[293] O.S.A. VI 155, Dull Perth.
[294] Burt 2005, 254.
[295] O.S.A. I 502, Lismore & Appin Arg.
[296] O.S.A. II 555, Kilmuir Inv.
[297] Stewart 1822, I 89.
[298] Stewart 1822, II 180.

46. *A grievous punishment*
[299] Stewart 1822, II 189 fn.
[300] Stewart 1822, II 1 (i.e., Roman 50).
[301] Stewart 1822, II 1 (i.e., Roman 50).

47. *Nobody would speak to me*
[302] Stewart 1822, I 62.

48. *Lawlessness*
[303] G. M. Trevelyan, *England under the Stuarts*, Methuen, London, 1938, 455.
[304] Trevelyan 1946, 453.
[305] Linklater 1962, xi.
[306] MacDonell 1937, 11 & 12.
[307] Finlay 1966, 37.
[308] Prebble 1970, 63.
[309] Rixson 2004, 22, quoting Thomas Kirk.
[310] Peter MacNab, *Mull & Iona: Highways etc.*, Luath, Edinburgh, 2003, 71.

49. *Wars of Great Britain*
[311] Trevelyan 1946, 453.
[312] O.S.A. X 532, Campbeltown Arg.

313 O.S.A. VI 257, North Knapdale Arg.
314 Williams 1949, 243.
315 Stewart 1822, I 588, & II lix.

50. *Went to destruction*
316 Johnson & Boswell 1930, 89.
317 Stewart 1822, II lviii.
318 Williams 1949, 339; & *Oxford D.N.B.*
319 Stewart 1822, II 130.
320 Stewart 1822, II lxxxiii-lxxxv.
321 Stewart 1822, II 238-9.
322 Sutherland 1825, 105.
323 Jamieson 2005, xxxiv.

51. *Small-scale warfare*
324 Selkirk 2010, Appendix A, 76.
325 Burt 2005, 253-4.
326 O.S.A. VIII 359, Glenorchy & Inishail Arg.

52. *Peaceable and polite*
327 O.S.A. IV 136, Duirinish Inv.
328 O.S.A. XIII 323, North Uist Inv.
329 O.S.A. XI 186, Comrie Perth.
330 O.S.A. III 41, Kingussie & Inch Inv.
331 This was written in an 1828 letter by Mrs MacKay Scobie, wife of the sheep farmer of Keoldale: it was printed in an 1829 edition of Rob Donn's poems – *Poetry of Rob Donn*, ed. MacIntosh MacKay, Douglas, Inverness, 1829, lix.
332 Jamieson 2005, xxxi.
333 Scott 1900, 227-8.
334 Pennant 2000, 127.
335 Stewart 1822, I 49, quoting Dalrymple 1771.
336 Stewart 1822, I 98, quoting Dalrymple 1771.
337 Burt 2005, 200.
338 Johnson & Boswell 1930, 53.
339 Johnson & Boswell 1930, 25.

53. *Healthy, vigorous, agile*
340 O.S.A. XVII 545, Kilmonivaig Inv.
341 O.S.A. II 555, Kilmuir Inv.
342 Gilpin 1789, II 139, quoting author c. 1500: "qui sylvestres dicuntur", "who are called wild".
343 Stewart 1822, II xii, quoting R. Holinshed.
344 W. C. MacKenzie, *History of the Outer Hebrides*, Gardner, Paisley, 1903, 591, quoting Captain Dymes 1630.
345 Sacheverell 1859, 98.
346 Stewart 1822, II xiii, quoting Toland 1709.
347 Bumsted 1982, 73.
348 O.S.A. VI 246, Kintail Ross.
349 O.S.A. XIX 12, Halkirk Caith.
350 O.S.A. VI 369 fn, Moulin Perth.
351 O.S.A. X 414, Tiree Arg.

352 O.S.A. III 164, Lochgoilhead Arg.
353 O.S.A. VI 391, Glenisla Angus.
354 O.S.A. I 485, Lismore & Appin Arg.
355 Burt 2005, 268.
356 Napier 1884, V 439, Alexander Carmichael.
357 O.S.A. I 485, Lismore & Appin Arg.
358 O.S.A. XVI 209, Assynt Suth.
359 O.S.A. III 516, Kincardine Ross.
360 O.S.A. VIII 447 fn, Kilmallie Inv.
361 O.S.A. II 555, Kilmuir Inv.
362 Smith 1798, 33.
363 Robertson 1808, iv-v.
364 Walker 1980, 161.
365 Walker 1980, 35.

54. *A lion and a lamb*
366 Ferguson 1994, 67.
367 Scott 1925, 169.
368 Victoria 1868, 47; Duff 1994, 38.

55. *Wonderfully swift of foot*
369 Burt 2005, 234.
370 Stewart 1822, I 71.
371 Youngson 1974, 229, quoting T. Thornton.
372 R. Somers 1847, 19.
373 Rixson 2004, 54, & Skene 1837, I 237 fn, quoting Nicolay d'Arfeuille.
374 Stewart 1822, II xxii, & I 75, quoting Defoe 1720.
375 Anon. 1747, 19.
376 L. Cope Cornford & F. W. Walker, *The Black Watch*, Dent, London, 1915, 20.
377 MacDonald 1994, 60.
378 Stewart 1822, II 31, quoting *Vienna Gazette*.
379 Stewart 1822, I 320 fn.
380 Johnson & Boswell 1930, 25.
381 Rixson 2004, 307, quoting Saint Fond 1907.
382 Buchanan 1997, 43.
383 See volume three, *Sutherland Clearances*, chapter four, *Countess Young & Sellar 1813*.

56. *Hardy and intrepid*
384 Burt 2005, 200.
385 Stewart 1822, I 69 fn.
386 W. T. Waugh, *James Wolfe, Man & Soldier*, Carrier, Montreal, 1928, 101.
387 Stewart 1822, II 18.
388 Kemp/Pococke 1888, 18.
389 Johnson & Boswell 1930, 75.
390 Mawman 1805, 151, 152.
391 Burt 2005, 76.
392 Smollett 1967, 292.
393 Stewart 811, II 238 fn, quoting Near Observer, *Battle of Waterloo*, Booth London 1815, iii.

57. *Rapidity peculiar to Highlanders*

[394] Duff 1994, 68.
[395] Brown seems to have become Albert's favoured servant even before he was Victoria's.
[396] Victoria 1868, 182.
[397] Geikie 1908, 378.
[398] Glover 1966, 222.
[399] Thomson 2010, 63, quoting Cunningham 1787.
[400] Sir Walter Scott, *Journal*, Douglas, Edinburgh, 1890, entry 13th May 1828.
[401] Stewart 1822, II 284 fn.
[402] Stewart 1822, II 31, quoting *Vienna Gazette* 1762.
[403] Scott 1900, 91. Most of the evidence depicts the Highlanders as tall; and one can certainly say that they were taller than their descendants living in the slums and factories of the Lowlands and England. The new urban environment did not produce a tall working class. The combined cities of Manchester and Salford, for example, which have been called "the first industrial society", were said to have supplied in the First World War "the smallest soldiers in the British forces"; 90% of the soldiers in the Bantam Regiments, set up to embody the shortest men, came from Manchester (Robert Roberts, *A Ragged Schooling*, Fontana/Collins, 1976/9, 138 fn).

When the change came in the economic basis of society from hunter-gathering to agriculture (and a similar change was forced through in the Highlands from the mid-eighteenth century) humans suffered. "Farmers were shorter and less healthy than foragers. They had less varied diets and were more susceptible to disease." Things changed as agriculture diversified, but this was what happened at first (*The Times*, 29th June 2017).

[404] Thomson 2010, 62, quoting Cunningham 1787.

CHAPTER SEVEN

CUSTOMS OF THE HIGHLANDERS

1. Harp and violin

In times of social distress and deprivation resulting from the break-up of a once stable and orderly body politic, the most severe forms of religion often find fruitful ground, while at the same time other members of the abused communities find the refuge of oblivion in alcohol. Both of these customary reactions to the collapse of a settled society occurred when the old Highland order was being destroyed during the eighteenth century; indeed, their joint appearance is strong evidence of that destruction. But the subsequent triumph of the most grim and austere type of Presbyterianism, and the over-indulgence in drink which was the other side of the same coin, should not be allowed to obscure our understanding of social conditions in the old clan society.

The qualities of the clansfolk detailed so far – their honesty, fair-dealing, mutual help, gentleness, hospitality, politeness – together with the practical absence of crime, may have suggested an almost puritanical society. But that, whatever happened after the clans were broken up, would be very wide of the mark. The Highlanders knew how to enjoy themselves. The author of *Certayne Matters Concerning Scotland*, 1597, said that "they delight much in music, but chiefly in harps and clairsshoes ['clàrsach' is Gaelic for harp] of their own fashion", while "in place of a drum they use a bagpipe".[1]

While the clàrsach was in favour, a chief would have his own harper as well as his bard. "One of the last of the harpers", said Seton Gordon, "was Murdo MacDonald, harper to MacLean of Coll until 1734. He had received his musical tuition from that famous harper Roderick Morrison, commonly named Ruaraidh Dall, Blind Rory, he who was MacLeod's harper."[2] As time went on the harp was displaced by the trump (an instrument shaped like a lyre, played against the teeth), the bagpipe, and the fiddle. The latter instrument appears to have been ubiquitous. Elizabeth Grant of Rothiemurchus said that at the family's Highland home "Simon Ross the butler . . . played extremely well on the violin",[3] while at Kinrara, nearby, one of the footmen "played the violin remarkably well; and as every tenth Highlander at least plays on the same instrument tolerably",[4] they could always get up a good band for dancing. Anne Grant of Laggan said, "there are, indeed, few houses in the Highlands where there is not a violin".[5] When many people do the same thing, then usually some of them do it very well. Two of the greatest Highland fiddle-players were Iain Ruadh [Ian Roy] Kennedy, from Sleat in Clan Donald country, and Neil Gow, from Atholl.

2. Piping families

In the heyday of clanship the more expert players on the bagpipes achieved wide fame in the Highlands, and often a special status within the clan. Not infrequently the skills were handed on from father to son, and families would produce eminent pipers for several generations, or even several centuries. As the fame of the great pipers spread, others came to them to learn the art, and schools of piping emerged, where the master musicians taught their pupils the ceol beag (little music), ceol meadhonach (middle music), and ceol mor (big music). The ceol beag (also called ceol aotrom, light music) consisted for example of reels and strathspeys; the ceol meadhonach of jigs and airs;[6] while the ceol mor, the big music or piobaireachd (pibroch), could be (said Seton Gordon) "a Salute, a Welcome", a rowing tune, "a Taunt, a March, a Lament".[7] For many years a family of MacArthurs, for example, were noted bagpipers in the Clan Donald; successive members of the family were pipers to the MacDonald chiefs.[8] The MacArthurs lived and conducted their piping college (which some say was older than the MacCrimmons') on the lands of Peingown and Hunglader in Trotternish, Skye; they paid no tribute, since their contribution to the clan was their excellence in piping, not financial support for the clan's chief executive. The MacArthurs and their pupils practised on a hillock at Peingown called Cnoc Phàil. Angus MacArthur piped inspiration to the MacDonalds of Skye at the Battle of Sheriffmuir, in 1715; his successor, Charles MacArthur, was, said Seton Gordon, considered "the most illustrious" of the family.[9] The Clan Donald had official pipers in each of their three home districts – North Uist, Trotternish, and Sleat: at Sleat the MacIntyres were the clan pipers – in 1723 Malcolm MacIntyre represented the family. Sir Alexander MacDonald (the seventh baronet, who died in 1746) once had three master pipers staying with him at Monkstadt: Charles MacArthur, Padraig Og MacCrimmon, and Eain Dall MacKay, the blind piper to MacKenzie of Gairloch.[10] The hereditary pipers to MacDonald of Keppoch were a family called MacGlashan, who had originally been Campbells (as we saw earlier), while another Campbell family were pipers to Campbell of Mochaster.[11] Other famous piping families were the MacGregors of Fortingall; the MacKays of Gairloch; the Rankins of Mull and of Coll,[12] and the MacGillivrays of Barra. Dr Johnson met one of the Rankin pipers when he dined with Coll: "the bagpiper played regularly when dinner was served, whose person and address made a good appearance, and brought no disgrace on the family of Rankin, which has long supplied the Lairds of Coll with hereditary music."[13]

Indeed, Dr Johnson wrote, "I have had my dinner exhilarated by the bagpipe, at Armadale, at Dunvegan, and in Coll".[14]

Several surnames occur more than once in lists of the great piping families. "The best known pipers in Mull", according to David Graham-Campbell, "were the Rankins, hereditary pipers to Duart."[15] (According to Dr Johnson, the Rankins had a "college of pipers" in Mull, "which expired about sixteen years ago" – i.e. about 1757.)[16] They may have been the same as, or at least related to, the Rankins of Coll (at their closest, Coll and Mull are only seven miles apart). On Ulva, Graham-Campbell continued, lived a "family of MacArthurs, who maintained a college of piping though several generations". W. H. Murray wrote that there was also a MacArthur piping school at Proaig, in Islay.[17] The Ulva family, at least, was related to the Trotternish MacArthurs. The Reay country produced two famous piping families: the MacKays who were pipers to MacLeod of Raasay, as well as the MacKays who were pipers to MacKenzie of Gairloch. John MacKay, one of the eighteenth-century MacKay pipers of Raasay, had a repertoire of some 250 pibrochs.[18] The MacIntyres of Rannoch were notable pipers, and MacIntyres were pipers to the chief of Menzies,[19] to MacDonald of Clanranald,[20] and to MacDonald of Kinlochmoidart,[21] as well as to the chief of Clan Donald in Sleat.

3. MacCrimmons in Skye

One of the most notable of all the piping families, the MacCrimmons, pipers of the Clan Leod, lived in Duirinish.[22] The MacCrimmons appeared in Skye in the sixteenth century. Some say that the first of the family came from Harris; some say he came from Ireland; others again maintain (more dramatically) that he was an Italian Protestant musician fleeing from the Inquisition in Cremona (later the home of great violin makers such as the Stradivari, Amati, and Guarneri families). According to this version, MacCrimmon really signified "son of Cremona", and his provenance helped to explain his profession. The MacCrimmons (wherever they came from) appear to have lived and taught their pupils for over two centuries on the shore of Loch Dunvegan, first at Galtrigill, then at Boreraig, paying no material tribute to the chiefs. One of their students was the first MacArthur piper of Ulva. From 1540 the MacCrimmons were hereditary pipers to MacLeod at Dunvegan, and one account is that no fewer than ten generations filled that office. Three of the sixteenth-century MacCrimmons were said to be Finlay, Iain Odhar (odhar is dun or sallow), and Pàdraig Donn (donn meaning brown-haired). After them came Donald Mor (he lived from about 1570 to 1640, and he developed the form of theme and variations now known as piobaireachd); his son Patrick Mor (1595-1670); his son Patrick Og (1645-1730), who moved the MacCrimmon school to Boreraig; his son Malcolm, 1690-1769 (another son,

Donald Ban, was killed in the '45); and Malcolm's sons Iain Dubh (1730-1822) and Donald Ruadh (1740-1825). If these dates are accurate, they would appear to indicate that the MacCrimmons were hale and hearty and long-lived, having children well into middle age. The approximate ages of these five generations were: Donald Mor 70, Patrick Mor 75, Patrick Og 85, Malcolm 79, Iain Dubh 92, Donald Ruadh 85.

According to the Rev. Donald MacQueen, minister of Kilmuir in Skye, at least two of the prominent piping families were still occupying lands in Skye as late as 1774, in return, not for money, but for their services as pipers: "the MacKarters and MacKrumens, the pipers of the family of MacDonald and MacLeod, who still preserve their appointments." Kilmuir, of course, was part of the Clan Donald country, so MacQueen may be supposed to have local knowledge.[23] Indeed, according to J. L. Buchanan the MacCrimmons were still officiating as pipers to MacLeod in 1793.[24]

4. MacKays, MacGregors, MacIntyres, MacDougalls

The MacKays of Gairloch were another great piping family, and they also had a piping school. The first of the line, Ruairidh Dall (Blind Rory) MacKay, was born in Sutherland in 1592, and when he was only seventeen became piper to MacKenzie of Gairloch. His son Eain, born in 1656, as a child also became blind; known as Eain Dall, he was a pupil of Patrick Og MacCrimmon, and achieved fame as a piper and as a poet. Hearing that his old master had died, he wrote *Lament for Padraig Og MacCrimmon*, described by Seton Gordon as "one of the greatest pibroch compositions in existence";[25] the report turned out to be false, so Patrick Og himself was able to hear it. When Ruairidh Dall MacKay died in 1689, aged not far short of a hundred, Eain succeeded him as Gairloch's piper. Eain's son Angus followed him in that post in 1754 (Eain having died at the age of ninety-eight). Angus' son, John Roy, born 1753, also became piper to Gairloch.

One "family of distinguished pipers" named MacGregor, said Seton Gordon, lived in Glen Lyon. They were known as Clann an Sgeulaiche, the Race of the Story-teller, and they were "not only pipers, but fiddlers and bards". Some MacGregors were pipers to Campbell of Glenlyon, and others to MacGregor of MacGregor. The latter piping family lived at Druimcharaidh or Drumcharry, and the tradition was that they sent their best pupil each year for finishing to the MacCrimmons at Boreraig. "In 1706, Patrick MacGregor was piper to the Duke of Atholl." Another MacGregor, Alpin, played to Rob Roy as he lay dying at Balquhidder in 1734. A third MacGregor, Iain, was Prince Charles's piper, and was wounded at Culloden. MacGregors were often among prize-winners in the early piping competitions. The first competition of which records remain was at Falkirk

Tryst in 1781, when Patrick MacGregor won the first prize, and John MacGregor the third.[26]

The family of MacIntyres who were pipers to the chief of Menzies began with Donald Mor, who was said to have studied with MacCrimmon on Skye about 1650; after him came his son Iain, who wrote many tunes, including *My King has Landed at Moidart*; and Iain's son Donald Ban.

The hereditary pipers to MacDougall of Dunollie were also called MacDougall, said Seton Gordon. "By virtue of their office" they occupied land rent-free at Moleigh, while "their school of piping was held in Tigh nam Piobairean, House of the Pipers, near Dunach which is situated a little to the south of Oban". They included Alasdair Mor, 1635-1709; his son Ronald Ban; and his son Ronald Mor.[27]

The pipe music was originally recorded, as Seton Gordon explained, by "canntaireachd – a specialized type of singing by which these ancient tunes were memorized before the use of modern staff notation";[28] there were three different systems, used by three piping families, the MacCrimmons, the MacArthurs, and the Campbells. The Campbell pipers had begun to write down their pibroch notation by 1816.

5. Music and dance

David Stewart said that the Highlanders were "enthusiastically fond of music and dancing, and eagerly availed themselves of every opportunity of indulging this propensity. Possessing naturally a good ear for music, they displayed great agility in dancing." They appreciated the solemn airs, or laments "for their deceased friends . . . while their sprightly reels and strathspeys were calculated to excite the most exhilarating gaiety". In fact, "at harvest-home, halloween, christenings, and every holiday, the people assembled in the evenings to dance. At all weddings, pipes and fiddles were indispensable." Throughout the day when a wedding was taking place, to repeat an earlier reference, "the fiddlers and pipers were in constant employment. The fiddlers played to the dancers in the house, and the pipers to those in the field."[29]

A lullaby to Donald Gorm MacDonald of Sleat (who died in 1617), probably composed by his foster-mother in the mid-sixteenth century, said that wherever "you came to rest . . . there will be there, as is customary, music and storytelling/ Pipe and harp, merriment and dancing . . ."[30] The temporary absence of an instrument was no obstacle; then the Highlanders danced to port-a-beul, which means mouth music, sung by a bystander or one of the performers.[31] A traveller through Glen Dochart in 1784 passed "numerous herds of cattle and sheep, while the young shepherds and shepherdesses who tend them make the air resound with their songs, and animate the delightful scene with their dances".[32]

In the O.S.A. the minister of Monzie wrote: "They meet together at times, and make merry. Their chief amusement at public meetings is dancing; and, upon these occasions, there is a pleasing cheerfulness and innocence among them."[33] In Tiree, the people "frequently entertain themselves by composing and singing songs, by repeating Fingalian and other tales, by dancing assemblies at different farms by turns", in which they are "remarkably neat".[34] The minister of Kincardine said that in the old society "the tale, the song, and the dance" gilded "the horrors of the winter night".[35] The Kilchoman reporter observed: "The dance and the song, with shinty and putting the stone, are their chief amusements. Numbers of them play well on the violin and the bagpipe. They have a natural ease and gracefulness of motion in the dance, which is peculiar to themselves."[36] The minister of Strachur said that the old Highlanders "were passionately fond of music and poetry. The song and the dance soon made them forget their toils."[37] The report on Kirkmichael, Banffshire, said that in the days of the clans the Highlanders "passed the vacant hour in social enjoyment, in song and festivity, and in listening to the tale of other years".[38] Dr Johnson, on his visit to Raasay, said that in the evening "the musician was called, and the whole company was invited to dance, nor did ever fairies trip with greater alacrity".[39] If it is objected that the guests at Raasay were exclusively gentry, it should be noted that the O.S.A. reports quoted above were obviously speaking of the ordinary Highlanders; and the same is true of a visitor to Arran a decade earlier. Charles Hutcheson, who visited the island in 1783, said that his landlord's servants, after a hard day's labour digging peats, spent the evening dancing in a barn to a fiddle; the landlord declared that "they usually had a dance after their work was over".[40] Sir John Stoddart, touring the Highlands in 1799-1800, said of the Highlanders that despite the "general gravity of their behaviour", dancing was "the favourite amusement of the North", and the dancers showed "a Life and Spirit that few but the native Highlanders could attain". When the piper, or the fiddler, strikes up, their "exertions are continued for several hours . . . Perhaps the same causes, which produced in the Highlanders their fondness for the song and the tale, also cherished their partiality for the dance."[41]

6. Vigour and agility

The shinty matches were followed by an evening dance, according to an eye-witness of these amusements in Durness, who was quoted by Alexander MacKay: this "was continued for several hours to the music of the violin, or the pipes, with much grace, vigour, and agility, reels and strathspeys being the favourite dances, varied in form and steps to the cadence of the tune".[42]

A few of the accounts gave the numbers in the parish by their occupations: Knockbain had one fiddler and four pipers,[43] Killean three fiddlers and two pipers,[44] Gigha one fiddler and two pipers.[45] These would no doubt be the full-time musicians; as we saw, in Kilchoman "numbers" played well "on the violin and bagpipe"; Elizabeth Grant (to repeat) said that one in ten Highlanders could play the violin; and Anne Grant said there were few Highland houses without a violin. The minister of Avoch described local weddings. The hosts provided bread, ale and whisky, and the relatives and neighbours convened in great numbers. "A fiddler or two", and "perhaps a boy to scrape on an old violoncello", were engaged. A barn was "allotted for the dancing", and "the house for drinking". The company "made merry for two or three days" until Saturday night. On the Sunday, "after returning from church", the married couple gave a "dinner or entertainment" to their "friends on both sides".[46]

In 1793 the Rev. J. L. Buchanan said the Outer Hebrideans "have a fine vein for poetry and music, both vocal and instrumental", and "had the language been so generally understood, the Gaelic music would have been introduced, with admiration and delight, on every stage on which taste and elegance prevailed... In their agility in the dance, they stand almost unrivalled by any people." They met regularly to dance, showing "amazing alertness and spirit . . . The violin is used more regularly on these occasions than the small pipes. This last, with the great pipe, is mostly used in the field, at weddings, funerals, and other public meetings."[47]

An old soldier of the 42nd, retired to his native glen, recalled the old days before the lairds brought in the new society; he said, "we had then no complaints of lord or lairds . . . and were all merry and happy, and had plenty of piping, and dancing, and fiddling, at all the weddings".[48] Peggy MacCormack, remembering her childhood in South Uist before the clearances, said: "How we enjoyed ourselves in those faraway days – the old as much as the young. I often saw three and sometimes four generations dancing together on the green grass in the golden summer sunset. Men and women of fourscore or more – for they lived long in those days – dancing with boys and girls of five on the green grass."[49] But all that (she said) was before "the clearances came upon us", and the "sorrows, hardships, oppressions we came through".

7. Clearly rubbish

Professor Rosalind Mitchison quoted Peggy MacCormack's comments in order to condemn them: she said briskly that they were "clearly rubbish, and it is the prime duty of the historian to label rubbish as such when he [or she, doubtless] meets it".[50] It is interesting to observe that even those historians who regard documents as almost unchallengeable, no doubt because they usually emerge from the richer circles in society, and therefore support the views of those richer circles, are prompt to reject documents which do not support their views: despite having treated documents as almost incontrovertible sources, it turns out – when they come across a document which defies their views – that documents are very controvertible indeed, and can be rejected out of hand if they do not support the orthodox account. It will be seen that there is a great deal of evidence about the Highlanders' disposition to dance, so that can scarcely be denied, even by a conventional historian. If Mitchison thought that "boys and girls of five" would not dance, she cannot have recalled the O.S.A. report of the minister of Assynt, who described (as we saw above) how the old matrons sang Gaelic songs, "to which the little children dance", or Sir John Stoddart's reference to "young boys" dancing "the hornpipe and the reel".[51] If on the other hand she was taking exception to the references about the number of old people there were, and their vigour, there is much evidence on that topic also, and later in this work the reader will find a passage on that very subject when the state of the Highlands in the late eighteenth century is considered. Some of these ageing yet still active Highlanders may be referred to more briefly here. There was the man who *joined* the army at 62; the man who fought in the ranks at Quebec, aged 70[52] (following the example of that earlier Highlander who wielded his broadsword in the battle at Auldearn, when he was over 70);[53] the man who emigrated to Glasgow at 80; the man aged about 80 with many children and descendants, who (said his minister) was still "able to add to their number by his own personal exertions", and another Highlander who was indeed having children when well over 80; the precentor (psalm-leader in the kirk) of 81; the woman of 91 who walked home overnight more than twenty miles through the snow (for fear of dying among the foreigners in the Lowlands); the clockmaker of 92 who "can travel many miles in a day" pursuing his calling; the man of 93 who "comes to church the coldest day in winter"; the 97-year-old who walked twenty-six miles *in one day*; the man who headed a shinty team at 100, and then carried the colours in the victory procession (and died at 115); the gravedigger of 101; and (perhaps most relevant of all) the Tiree man who had – said his O.S.A. minister – just died at 106, and who had supported himself (and his wife) by herding till he was 99, and whose "liveliness appeared to the last, not only by walking *but dancing*" [my italics].[54] Some people exaggerate their ages: but these Highlanders lived in a society where many people could (as Stewart phrased it) "give a connected, and minutely accurate detail of the history, genealogy, feuds, and battles of all the tribes and families in every district, or glen, for many miles round, and for a period of several hundred years".[55] It would have been hard to overstate one's age in the eighteenth century Highlands, when the Gaels' familiarity with their own history was supported by systematic parish registers. It was indeed a Highlander who first coined the word "statistics".[56]

However, to search for, assemble, and evaluate evidence on this theme is perhaps (from some points of view) supererogatory. There are not a few writers whose work shows that they see their "prime duty" as defending the landlords: the landlords' clearances can only be excused if the clan society they swept away is depicted as barren, unhappy, and famine-stricken; so that is what it must have been. To discover and consider the data as to the real nature of that society, and as to the character of the people who lived in it, is merely to introduce irrelevancies. If any indication emerges that would tend to disprove the orthodox version of history, one could try to counteract it by rational methods, such as collecting and discussing the available evidence; but dismissing what one does not agree with as "clearly rubbish" does save time.

One cannot be blamed for one's family connections, but it is possible (to put it no more strongly) that one's views are coloured by what one's friends and relatives think. Professor Mitchison's sister-in-law came from the family of Martin of Husabost, an earlier member of which – Dr Martin of Husabost – was not only a clearing landlord himself, but acted as spokesman for other clearing landlords. It was Dr Martin who, for example, told the Napier Commission that "I would give £500 today if all the crofters on my place went away . . . I would not give the sum I mentioned for a partial emigration."[57] It is tempting to wonder if Professor Mitchison would have been quite so brusque with her "clearly rubbish" denunciation of Peggy MacCormack's memories (and presumably her equally abrupt rejection of all the many other testimonies pointing in the same direction) if she had been equally closely related to a crofting family.

8. Sweet airs

We may now return to the facts of the matter, as shown by the evidence. Along with dancing and poetry, song was an integral part of the Highlanders' lives. Burt said that when the women worked together at the harvest, they kept time by "several barbarous [they were not civilized, you see] tones of the voice, or by a piper";[58] they did the same when they were fulling, or scouring, the newly woven plaiding; and so did the men, when they were, for example, launching a large boat. Apparently (despite Burt) it was melodious: Dr John Walker, touring the Hebrides in 1764, heard women singing in Lewis, and said it "gave me more pleasure, if it be safe to own such an impolite notion, than any concert I was ever at".[59] In 1769 Thomas Pennant found that "vocal music was much in vogue among" the Highlanders.[60] Three years later, Pennant saw corn being ground by the quern (a little hand-mill) in the Small Isles, and declared "the island lasses are as merry at their work . . . as those of Greece were in the days of Aristophanes". Then in Skye he saw a dozen women "waulking" the cloth, "singing at the same time, as at the quern", and "as they grow very earnest in their labours, the fury of the song rises", till it is almost demonic. "They sing in the same manner when they are cutting down the corn, when thirty or forty join in chorus, keeping time to the sound of a bagpipe."[61] Buchanan mentioned the "waulking" songs: "one of them sings the stanza, while all the rest unite in the chorus, which they repeat twice or thrice after each stanza. The sweet melody of their music seldom fails to attract a number of hearers, who join in the song."[62] Highland milkmaids, according to Carmichael, sang lullabies to please their cows. The animals "become so accustomed to these milking lilts that they will not give their milk without them; nor, occasionally, without their own favourite airs".[63] Thomas Wilkinson passed a Highland woman, reaping alone while she sang a Gaelic song, and said it was "the sweetest human voice I ever heard". The Glenorchy minister warned in the O.S.A. that if Highland women took tobacco or snuff they would lose "their powers of song and sweet cadence".[64]

In 1773 Dr Johnson and Boswell were rowed across from Skye to Raasay, with Malcolm MacLeod and the Rev. Donald MacQueen. MacLeod (wrote Boswell) sang a Gaelic song: "the boatmen and Mr MacQueen chorused, and all went well." As they approached the shore, Boswell added, "the singing of our rowers was succeeded by that of reapers . . . while they worked with a bounding activity".[65] Dr Johnson watched Highlanders harvesting, and said "the strokes of the sickle were timed by the modulation of the harvest song, in which all their voices were united. They accompany in the Highlands every action, which can be done in equal time, with an appropriated strain, which has, they say, not much meaning; but its effects are regularity and cheerfulness." At Raasay House, wrote Dr Johnson, "the ladies sung Erse songs, to which I listened as an English audience to an Italian opera, delighted with the sound of words which I did not understand".[66] Another more prosaic view of Gaelic song came from the English servant who went with a MacLeod to Skye in the 1780s: "All kinds of labour is accompanied by singing. If it is reaping the women sing; if it is rowing in a boat the men sing. I think if they were in the deepest distress they would all join in a chorus."[67] This sturdy Englishman, coming from a society where "time is money", and where the working day – for the lower class, that is, of course – lasted from early morning till late at night, was scandalized by the Gaels' love of literature and romance: "They also spend much of their time in telling idle stories, and singing doggerel rhymes and nonsense." (Even Professor Mitchison could not have put it more forthrightly.)

William Thomson remarked in 1788 on the Highlanders' "passionate love and genius for music, as well as the kindred strains of moving, though simple, poetry".

Like Dr Johnson thirteen years earlier, he told how the Highlanders had special songs and music "not only on occasions of merriment and diversion, but also during almost every kind of work which employs more than one person, such as milking cows, watching the folds, fulling of cloth, grinding of grain with the quern or hand-mill, haymaking, and reaping of corn . . . In travelling through the Highlands, in the season of autumn, the sounds of little bands of music on every side, joined to a most romantic scenery, has a very pleasing effect on the mind of a stranger."[68] The O.S.A. report on Callander said that in the Trossachs, "every grove is vocal, by the melodious harmony of birds, or by the sweet airs of women and children, gathering filberts [hazelnuts], in their season".[69] James Hogg and two companions, travelling through "the braes of Ardnamurchan" in June 1803, were "rivetted to a certain spot a good while, listening to the most mellifluous music, which came floating on the breeze from a neighbouring wood, sometimes in a cadence so soft and low as scarcely to be heard, and at other times in full concert, so loud that all the hills rang again. This proceeded from a great number of people, of both sexes, who were cutting and peeling wood at that place; and being assembled at their breakfast, had joined in singing a Gaelic song, in the chorus of which they all joined . . . the effect was excellent."[70] (A comment reminiscent of Carmichael's description of the "striking effect" of the shieling hymn, as "the music floats on the air, and echoes among the rocks, hills, and glens".)[71]

9. A voice so thrilling

Hogg and his friends, a little later on the 1803 expedition, were rowed over Loch Nan Uamh in a small boat, the "rough sea" washing over it; "the man at the rudder however always bid us fear nothing, and, to encourage us, sung several Erse songs".[72]

Three months later in that same year Dorothy and William Wordsworth were rowed across Loch Lomond by a youth "fresh from the Isle of Skye": "he could not speak a word of English, and sang a plaintive Gaelic air in a low tone while he plied his oar."[73] William wrote an oft-quoted poem about a "solitary Highland lass, reaping and singing by herself":

No nightingale did ever chaunt
More welcome notes to weary bands
Of travellers in some shady haunt,
Among Arabian sands;
A voice so thrilling ne'er was heard
In spring-time from the cuckoo-bird,

Breaking the silence of the seas
Among the farthest Hebrides.

Will no one tell me what she sings?
Perhaps the plaintive numbers flow
For old, unhappy, far-off things,
And battles long ago.

The next four lines may be still more significant:

Or is it some more humble lay,
Familiar matter of today?
Some natural sorrow, loss, or pain,
That has been, and may be again!

As Wordsworth speculated, it might have been that the reaper was singing about what was happening to the Highlanders then and there: and the topic that would be most likely to produce "plaintive numbers" was the current activity of the landlords. But whatever the words were about, the singer's melody stayed in the poet's mind. "The music in my heart I bore, long after it was heard no more."[74]

Byron wrote, in his *Hours of Idleness*, in 1808: "I breasted the billows of Dee's rushing tide,/ And heard at a distance the Highlander's song."[75] In 1825 the two English travellers Bowman and Dovason, with other tourists, went (partly sailing, partly being rowed) from Oban to Fort William in an open wherry: the two rowers "occasionally sung in Gaelic very sweetly, in parts", while the passengers "amused ourselves for a while listening to the harsh guttural Gaelic of the boatmen and to their songs . . . in such wild cadence as the breeze, makes through December's leafless trees".[76] Seventeen years later Queen Victoria did not find Gaelic so harsh. She recorded in her diary how she was rowed sixteen miles up Loch Tay by a crew of Highlanders: "the boatmen sang two Gaelic songs, very wild and singular; the language so guttural and yet so soft."[77]

10. Rustic strains

The N.S.A. report on Kilmuir in Skye also remarked on the people singing when about their daily tasks. The women, co-operatively fulling the cloth, would sing an "òran-lùaidh", a waulking song. "The work goes on so regularly, and the various voices are blended together in such complete unison and harmony, that a stranger would be highly delighted with the scene. In the same manner also, the natives sing when rowing a boat, or in harvest, while reaping their fields. It is rather surprising how nature inspires them with such skill in the modulation of their rustic strains, that their music often appears as if composed by connoisseurs in the science. They observe sharps and flats with much precision, and also not infrequently change their tunes from major to minor keys, and vice versa."[78] By the middle part of the nineteenth century, under the impact of the improvements, these skills were naturally becoming rarer. A tourist who journeyed through the Highlands (mainly south of the Great Glen) in 1818 was happy to relate that this unthrifty resort to melody was dying out as the old communal joint-farms were broken up: he thought that the Highlanders' practice of singing at their work "seems almost incompatible with laborious exertion".[79] It is true that travellers in the Lowland towns did not find it necessary to reproach the people there for singing at their labour: the toil demanded of workers in the new dispensation left them no energy for such wasteful customs. In fact in many of the new industrial mills and mines the continuous frenzied noise of the machines was unavoidably so great that the workers found it difficult even to speak to each other, never mind to join in song (they had to develop a form of lip-reading to communicate at all); but the long hours, and heavy labour, would have made melody highly unlikely, even if the machines had been mute. The 1818 tourist was quite right: the "laborious exertion" of the Industrial Revolution was in fact "incompatible" with singing. Alexander Carmichael said of the Highlanders in 1883: "If they sing less now, their silence is due to repression from without."[80] (And, as with singing, so with dance: Stoddart said that "the recent changes in the Highland modes of living have operated much to the restraint of this amusement".)[80]

The observations on the harmonization of Gaelic song, implicit in many of these reports (and others), and explicit in the comments of 1793 ("sweet cadence", that is the chords closing a musical phrase or melody), of 1825 (when the Gaels sang "very sweetly, in parts") and 1840 (when the minister spoke of the Gaels' "harmony") did not deceive the Lowland historian T. Steel. He asserted that "Gaelic song harmony was also an invention, first performed in 1875 by the Glasgow St Columba church choir". The "also" is explained by the fact that Steel had just revealed his discovery that there was no MacCrimmon school of piping in Skye; the claim that there was ever such a school was, he affirmed, "probably a hoax".[81] As is remarked elsewhere in this work, if you are accused of destroying something valuable, it is a tempting defence to claim that it never existed.

Professor Mitchison's denunciation of Peggy MacCormack's recollections, and her caustic complaint that Peggy's memories were "clearly rubbish", was only one example of the industrious endeavours of Lowland historians as they worked to re-fashion the Highland facts to fit their Lowland feelings; and to adjust the performances of the past to correspond with the prejudices of the present.

11. Sports and games

The clan system gave the Highlanders the leisure time, and the fitness and health, to engage frequently in physical contests and similar recreations. This circumstance does not chime well with the standard picture of puny Highlanders, enfeebled by constant famines, but it is difficult to ignore the evidence (though many writers do their best). As early as 1543 John Elder, a Highland priest, wrote to Henry VIII of England (the spelling in this section has been modernized): "our delight and pleasure is . . . in running, leaping, swimming, shooting, and throwing of darts."[82] An observer in 1574 spoke of the young men of the Fraser clan: "at intervals they used swimming, arching [presumably archery], football, throwing of the barr [the caber?], fencing, dancing, wrestling and such manly, sprightly exercises and recreations, very fit for polishing and refining youth."[83] In 1655 the Wardlaw Manuscript described how one hunting party camped on the banks of the River Farrar for four days: "what is it that could cheer and recreate men's spirits but was gone about, jumping, arching, shooting, throwing the barr, the stone, and all manner of manly exercise imaginable."[84] When two companies of soldiers from Argyll's regiment were billeted on Glen Coe in 1692, they were there for thirteen days before they did their best to carry out their Lowland orders to murder their hosts. In the mornings the MacDonalds went about their normal business while the soldiers drilled, but in the afternoons the soldiers and the clansfolk ran races, or wrestled, or competed against each other at archery or at shinty.[85] In 1774 the minister of Kilmuir, Skye, said that the old Highlanders were "all bred to the use of arms, to hunting, to the exertion of their strength in several amusements, games, and feats of activity".[86]

In the 1790s the O.S.A. minister of Moulin said that forty or fifty years before – that is, before clan society began to be broken up – "gymnastic exercises" were "the chief pastime of the Highlanders". "At every fair or meeting" there was "racing, wrestling, putting the stone, etc." "On holidays all the males" of the district, young and old, played football or, more often, shinty.[87] By the time the N.S.A. was written, the improvements were in full swing, and the Highland sports and games were therefore often mere matters of memory. What is regarded as normal and familiar, like breathing, is sometimes unrecorded by contemporary observers; but what was once routine and therefore unremarkable becomes noteworthy when it has just disappeared, or is disappearing. Perhaps for this reason, or because the N.S.A. reports were more extensive than those in the O.S.A., more of the later accounts carried references to these past enjoyments. The Kilmuir Easter account of the people mentioned "those popular amusements which formerly engrossed much of their time";[88] Dull, "the once popular games";[89] Kilbride, the "ancient games and amusements of the Highlander";[90] Kilmory, "many of the games . . . peculiar to the Highlands";[91] Inverness, "games of football, shinty, throwing the stone, hammer, and bowls";[92] Duirinish, "shinty playing, or throwing the putting-stone";[93] Lochs, "jumping, putting the stone, the shinty or club" (from this, "club" seems to be a similar game to shinty, or an alternative name for it);[94] and Uig, "public games or amusements".[95] The reports, however, mostly said that all these things had vanished, or nearly so. The minister of Dingwall said "the taste for amusements would seem to be declining here; even the Christmas and New Year shinty matches, in which but recently, both old and young used to indulge with eager interest, are now abandoned".[96] The Clyne report summed it up: it remarked on the "popular games and amusements" of the Highlanders, but mourned that "the few remnants of the merry olden times are fast passing from among them".[96] However, all these remarks (and others elsewhere) make it clear what the Highlanders had done in the flourishing days of clanship.

12. Amusing themselves

These "games and amusements" of the Highlanders, often ignored by well-behaved commentators, were pervasive enough to be the frequent bane of sabbatarians. The result is that more evidence has survived of the athletic pleasures of the old Highlanders – at least when they were enjoying themselves at the weekend. A number of the ministers who wrote the N.S.A. reports had examined their parish records dating from the years before 1745, and they revealed, with appropriate expressions of evangelical horror, the enjoyments which the people had got up to in those heathen times. The parish of Croy, according to its minister, was then rife "with every species of abomination": and first in the "black catalogue" was "drying and grinding corn and killing salmon [i.e., going fishing] on the Sabbath".[97] The schoolmaster of Monzie wrote that a hundred and fifty years before (i.e., in about 1690) "the parishioners were in the practice of assembling upon the Green of Monzie on the Sabbath mornings to play at football".[98] The first Presbyterian minister of Moy was settled about 1727: the first time he went to preach, "he found a great multitude of people putting the stone, and amusing themselves otherwise about the church".[99] (The new dispensation was soon to demonstrate that "amusing themselves" was not a seemly occupation for the lower orders.) A new minister arriving in Rosskeen in 1717, said the N.S.A. report, had a nasty shock when he discovered that "it was the practice for the people to meet at Ardross, in the heights of the parish, on Sunday, to play at shinty".[100] The minister of Kenmore, as we saw earlier, wrote that the records of the kirk-session referred to attempts in times past to "reprimand the people, because they had gone on the Sabbath to the wood a-nutting, rather than to church", not to mention having "devoted the evening of that hallowed day to the unsabbatical pastime of fiddling and dancing".[101] In Lismore, the minister said that his predecessor had been able to abolish the practice of publishing marriage banns on a Sunday only twenty or thirty years before,[102] while the minister of Edinkillie took such a stern view of the Sabbath that he seemed to regard even Sunday funerals as an illicit form of light relief, and had very nearly stamped them out.[103] The Rev. Donald Sage, too, in his memoirs, spoke of a minister who was transferred to Nigg in 1729, only to find that Sunday was "the day of all others on which the parishioners assembled to exercise themselves in athletic games"[104] – and naturally tried his best to abolish such pagan pursuits. Coincidentally, Nigg was also mentioned by Hugh Miller in his memoirs; he confirmed that the games "were usually played on the Sabbath".[105] Donald Sage's grandfather, Aeneas Sage, was minister of Lochcarron from 1726: when he arrived there "the people assembled every Lord's day in a plat of ground about twenty yards from the church door for the practice of athletic games", while "the Highlanders observed" the Christmas holidays "by assembling to play at club and shinty".[106] So much did the Highlanders use Sundays to enjoy themselves in their energetic games and amusements that one writer said sourly, "Sabbath never got aboon [above] the Pass of Killiecrankie":[107] at least the grim Lowland Sabbath never seems to have made that journey – until, that is, the improvements destroyed the old society and its pleasures. And the Lowland Sabbath was grim. Burt said that a minister in the Moray Lowlands, "between Spey and Findhorn, made some fishermen do penance for Sabbath-breaking" when they had put to sea on a Sunday to try to rescue a vessel in distress in a storm.[108] Obviously attempts to save people from drowning would have annoyed the Almighty.

John Murdoch was brought up (from 1827, when he was nine) in Islay, where the clearances came later than in many other places. When he was a youth (that is, in the 1830s), he wrote, "as elsewhere, stone throwing, shinty playing, leaping and running were leading pastimes". They had regular games of shinty at Traigh an Luig. He wrote this in 1889, when of course all had changed. "Traigh an Luig is silent under the feet of cattle. And the small farms from which the keen shinty players of those days came are consolidated into the large farms."[109]

13. Work and play

John Murdoch wrote about the township of Kilchiaran in Islay, before it was cleared, and his account revealed how these pastimes grew naturally out of the lives of the Highlanders. When Murdoch was a boy in the 1820s, of course, the Highlanders of Islay, though they still had their small-tenant farms, were already in many ways much worse off than in the days of the clans. The small tribute which they had paid before Culloden to the chief, as a species of tax paid by the members of a community to its government, had now become the much greater rent, forcibly exacted from all the small farmers for the benefit of those who had now seized ownership of the land. In addition, the Highlanders' main food supply had been confiscated – game, animals, birds, and fish. In the case of Islay, for example, Murdoch said that its owner, Walter Frederick Campbell (with whose son Murdoch was friendly), had some good qualities. "To the folly of shooting and game preservation, however, he was devoted to an excessive degree. He carried this craze so far that there was no offence so great, in his eyes, as to meddle with game and salmon."[110] And, of course, "game and salmon" had once provided a large part of the Highlanders' food supplies – not to mention their acquisition having contributed to the people's healthy enjoyment.

However, the Islay clansfolk still adhered as far as possible to the customs of the clan days. After seed-time came peat-cutting for the next year's fuel, wrote Murdoch. "All the able-bodied men in the community, and others from neighbouring hamlets, came with their implements to the scene of operations – the principal battalion of them, in all probability, headed by a piper. The work was regarded as a pleasant contribution of good neighbourhood and a day's amusement. Nor, in the midst of this co-operation, was the spirit of competition wanting. There was a happy union of what are now, in improved society, regarded as incompatible principles. While this light-hearted body worked as one for the party whose turf was being cut, there was ample scope for competition among the members as to who should do most and best. At a word, too, the scene of labour was turned into that of sport and the instruments of industry were thrown aside in order that the best leaper, the best runner, the best thrower of the stone might be made manifest on the spot – while work and sport were duly relieved by sallies of wit and staves of song both old and new. The turf cut, home they hied to the house for which they had thus provided a year's fuel, to be entertained at supper and to conclude the day's 'foregathering' with a dance, the neighbouring damsels being duly invited to participate in the same." This was in Islay, described in 1859; thirty years later, at the other end of the Highlands, Alexander MacKay published his account of Sutherland's peat-cutting, which was remarkably similar. "Then it was seen how neighbours helped neighbours . . . how cheerfulness and goodwill lighten labour, and how co-operation makes short work of it, – the fuel for a whole township cut and spread to dry, in less than a fortnight; and we who have taken a part in this work, though 'tis 'sixty years since', still love to recall the joyous time." MacKay remembered "the over-flowing mirth and jollity of the workers . . . the superabundance of food for the occasion, with an occasional glass of aqua vitae, during the long day of vigorous toil, that closed with a reel or two on the green to the music" of the bagpipe. In fact " 'Latha buain na moine' ('the peat-cutting day') was not only a day of hard work, it was a festive occasion."

"In this way", said Murdoch, "the fuel of the little community was, in one, two or three weeks, all cut" – and it is clear from Murdoch's account that money never came into it.[111] (Such a flagrant phrase as the one I have just suggested – "money never came into it" – would have struck horror into the hearts of the new men: and, possibly, still does.) Clearly the improvers had to destroy a society which operated on such lines, in defiance of what we are now told is deep-rooted, immutable, "human nature". This kind of co-operative effort was work as surely everyone would prefer it – "a day's amusement . . . mirth and jollity . . . a festive occasion": the long labours in the grim factories of the congested mill-towns were never recalled in such terms.

It is strange that the music, the dances, the songs, the sports and the games, of the Highlanders, though they were so often recorded and described in genuine undeniable documents, are so little acknowledged by orthodox historians. They would, of course, scarcely fit in with the conventional picture of the famine-wracked Highlander, weakening and dying every time the weather was somewhat adverse (as we saw above, a cold spring or summer was supposed to lead inexorably to "widespread death"). There have been many accounts in the newspapers in the last few decades of the conditions in areas, whether in Asia or Africa, which really have been stricken with famine; they have not often included descriptions of the local people's vigorous physical sports and amusements, and their extensive musicianship.

14. Gaelic culture

Since the Highlanders were not proletarians, that is people who have to devote most of their energies to unremitting wage-work for employers in order to exist, they were naturally able to spend more time on the pleasures of life. One result was that they were skilful in their use of language, and the more proficient people are in speech, the nearer it approaches to poetry. Poetry, in fact, is only a more dexterous, a more telling, or a more beautiful, form of language – ideally combining two or all of those traits. In clan society, therefore, "cultural activities" were not pursued only by a few. The culture of the Highlanders was something that grew naturally out of their everyday life and normal pursuits, and it was shared by all. The minister of Callander described the old Highlanders as "wrapped in their plaids all day long . . . on the brow of a hill, attending their cattle, and composing sonnets".[112] Toland wrote that the Highlanders had "a strong inclination to poetry and music",[113] and William Thomson said the Highlanders were "fond of poetry and music".[114] Martin agreed: "Several of both sexes have a quick vein of poesy; and in their language (which is very emphatic) they compose rhymes and verse, both of which powerfully affect the fancy, and, in my judgement, (which is not singular in this matter,) with as great force as that of any ancient or modern poet I ever yet read. They have generally very retentive memories", and "are able to form a Satyr or Panegyrick ex tempore" (a critical verse, or a eulogy, impromptu). [115] The Tongue N.S.A. report spoke of the "poetic talent and sprightly wit" once possessed by the clansfolk.[116] Sometimes there would be living in a chieftain's family a clàrsach-ùrlair, an old woman whose task was simply to tell the traditional stories.

Stewart said, "the recitation of their traditional poetry was a favourite pastime with the Highlanders when collecting round their evening fire. The person who could rehearse the best poem or song, and the longest and most entertaining tale, whether stranger, or friend, was the most acceptable guest. When a stranger appeared, the first question, after the usual introductory compliments, was 'Bheil dad agud air na Fian?' ('Can you speak of the days of Fingal?') If the answer was in the affirmative, the whole hamlet was convened, and midnight was usually the hour of separation."[117] Stewart added: "When a boy I took great pleasure in hearing these recitations, and now reflect, with much surprise, on the ease and rapidity with which a person could continue them for hours, without hesitation and without stopping, except to give the argument or prelude to a new chapter or subject."[118] Duncan Ban MacIntyre, the bard of Glen Orchy, was (said Stewart) outstanding. "His memory was most tenacious; and the poems, songs, and tales, of which he retained a perfect remembrance to the last, would fill a volume."[119] MacIntyre himself, though, said that there were many in his early days who knew much more than he did. Again, when a researcher came to Stewart's house to collect some "remains of Gaelic poetry . . . a young woman in the immediate neighbourhood was sent for, from whose recitations he wrote down upwards of 3000 lines; and, had she been desired, she could have given him as many more".[120]

One would be surprised now by a twenty-first century young person who could recite from memory as much as thirty lines of poetry – or even three.

15. Ancient poems and tales

In the early years of the Black Watch, said Stewart, "when the ancient habits of the people remained unchanged, the soldiers retained much of these habits in their camps and quarters. They had their bards for reciting ancient poems and tales, and composing laments, elegies, and panegyrics on departed friends". Another long-serving Black Watch officer said that when the regiment was first formed, "there were many poets and bards among the soldiers. Their original compositions were generally in praise of their officers and comrades who had fallen in battle, or who had performed some gallant achievement, but they had great stores of ancient poetry. Their love songs were beautiful; and their laments for the fallen brave, and recollections of absent friends and their distant glens and rocks, have often filled my eyes with tears. There were four sergeants of the names of MacKinnon, MacLean, MacGregor, and MacDonald, who had a peculiar talent for these repetitions and songs."[121] Duties permitting, several of the officers, said Stewart, "indulged their taste for poetry and music. Major Reid was one of the most accomplished flute-players of the age." The major was the last of the Atholl family of the Robertsons of Strath Loch or Straloch; they were known in the Highlands as the Barons Rua, or Roy (i.e., Red), and they took the patronymic "Reid" as their more particular surname in the second half of the eighteenth century. When Major Reid was a young lieutenant in the loyalist Loudoun's Highlanders during the '45, a detachment under his command captured some silver intended for Prince Charles, which a French ship had put ashore at Tongue. Reid composed many pieces of music, including "The Garb of Old Gaul", which became the regimental march of the Black Watch. He died in 1806, a general in the army. He married an heiress and left one daughter, who had no family; after she died, General Reid's money, £52,000, went to the "college of Edinburgh, where he was educated", to establish a Professorship of Music, in return for having a concert once a year at which a piece written by Reid was to be included.[122]

Selkirk remarked that the Highlanders were "of acute feelings, habituated to sentiments of a romantic and poetical cast":[123] and Sir John Stoddart, at the beginning of the nineteenth century, mentioned the "singular attachment to poetry, which, until the changes of modern manners, even the poorest of the Highlanders possessed".[124] Jamieson said of the old breed of Highlanders, "history, poetry, and music, were the favourite recreations of their leisure, among the lowest vulgar". He told how Ewen MacLauchlan (a Gaelic scholar) had translated the first four books of Homer into Gaelic, and had read them to groups of "the very lowest class", mechanics and shepherds, near Fort William, who could not read. "They listened to him with such enthusiasm as showed that the beauties of the composition had their full effect, and made such remarks as would have put to shame the comments of better instructed critics."[125]

One wonders if the reading of Homer at that time to groups of "the very lowest class" of Lowlanders or Englishmen would have had such pleasing effects.

16. Copious and expressive

As a result of their knowledge of their own literature, songs and folklore, and of their own practice in composing songs and poetry, the Highlanders had a high regard for their language, and a great skill in using it. The O.S.A. minister of Tiree said that Gaelic had "this great advantage, that the lowest peasant easily comprehends the highest style".[126] In fact the language, like the society that produced it, knew little of class-distinctions (whether the minister realized the full import of what he was saying or not). The minister of Kilmallie observed that "the illiterate Highlander who knows only Gaelic speaks it more fluently, elegantly, and purely than the scholar".[127] The Greenock report said of the Gaelic language, which could be heard everywhere in the town at that time: "Of this, their native tongue, which is said to be copious and highly expressive, the Highlanders are amazingly fond. They seem to be all orators."[128] Carmichael, as we saw earlier, chose similar words when he said the Highlanders' Gaelic is "plastic, copious, and expressive".[129]

It is not surprising that the Highlanders could be eloquent, for the Highlanders, being masters of their lands and of their lives, were naturally also masters of their language. They would achieve and practise self-expression as they discussed the communal work of the township with their neighbours, and as they debated the future plans of the farm or the district at the Nabachd or Mod meetings called by the constable. They also spoke for themselves before the chief if there was a disagreement between members of a clan. Toland wrote: "They have no lawyers or attorneys. The men and women plead their own causes, and every decision is made by the proprietor [or, more accurately, chief], who is perpetual president in their courts: or by his bailiff as his substitute."[130] The minister of North Uist said that although they were of peaceable disposition, "if any difference or quarrels subsist among them, they plead their own cause before the baron-bailie, who is the only magistrate in the parish, with surprising eloquence and address; and rest quite satisfied with his decisions, without ever appealing to any higher tribunal".[131] James MacDonald, writing of the Hebrides in 1811, mentioned the same courts. "The powers displayed by the natives in their pleadings at the baron-bailie courts, are truly astonishing. The eloquence exhibited there ... is unequalled in the British Empire; excepting perhaps in a few corners of Ireland" (where lived, of course, the Highlanders' cousins). The islanders, MacDonald continued, frequently gave vent to "political speculations, some of which would astonish a man not accustomed to the amazing powers of the common Hebridean in conversation, interlarded with reflections upon the character and conduct of their superiors, and upon the hardships of their own condition". One Hebridean "poor tenant", when faced with a rental agreement containing forty-seven mandatory clauses, was articulately scornful. "The commandments of our Great Master are only ten in number, and a reward is offered if we keep them; but those of our insular tyrant here ... are forty-seven, many of which are inconsistent with each other, and impossible to be observed; and all the reward we can expect, is to live slaves, and to die beggars."[132]

17. Powerful and pathetic eloquence

Stewart said that the Highlanders used their language well. They were accustomed (as we saw earlier) to recount the history and genealogy of all the neighbouring families, "for many miles around, and for a period of several hundred years", referring to "every remarkable stone, cairn, tree, or stream within the district", and this with "a powerful and pathetic eloquence", which enlivened and preserved the narrative. "By this manner of passing their leisure time", they acquired "a fluency of nervous, elegant, and grammatical expression", and "their conversations were carried on with a degree of ease, vivacity, and freedom from restraint, not usually to be met with in the lower orders of society [a phrase which, of course, had in the Highlands nothing like its Lowland connotations]. The Gaelic language is singularly adapted to this colloquial ease, frankness, and courtesy . . ." A Highlander "was accustomed, without showing the least bashful timidity, to argue and pass his joke (for which the language is also well adapted) with the greatest freedom, naming the person whom he addressed by his most familiar appellation. Feeling thus unembarrassed before his superior, he never lost the air of conscious independence and confidence in himself."[133]

These eloquent Highlanders, with their command of language, were naturally of a different stamp from the landless farmworkers and factory drudges outside the mountains, who in their working lives, at any rate, would find little scope for any more skill in expression than the single phrase, "Yes, sir".

To the Highlanders of the late eighteenth century, English was the language of the soldiers who had savaged the Highlands and their people after Culloden with murder, destruction, and plunder, and the language of the people some of whom (then as now) exercised their talents in excusing these atrocities. It was also, increasingly, as we will see later, the chosen language of the chiefs and landlords who were completing the work of "Butcher" Cumberland by remorselessly demolishing the old Gaelic society. It was also the language of people who had difficulty turning their thoughts into poetry. It seemed a poor rival to their own language, and Dr Johnson's achievement in producing his *Dictionary* of the Sassenachs' speech was therefore not particularly inspiring. Moray MacLaren wrote that an old Highlander, observing the excitement caused by the arrival of Dr Johnson in 1773, asked "Co an duine mor tha sud?" ("Who is that great man?") The reply was "Sin am fear a rinn a' Bheurla" ("That is the man who made the English language"). The old man was not impressed, and replied dismissively: "Bha beagan aige ri dheanamh!" ("Well, he hadn't much to do!")[134]

18. Inoffensive language

The Highlanders' oratory was not of the kind that can only impress by descending into profanity. One of the old Highlanders would have been astonished if he could have suddenly been made fluent in English, and then been thrust into the crowded city streets of modern Britain, to hear people whose mastery of their native language is so feeble, and whose vocabulary so meagre, that their speech has to be padded out with the same few swearwords, used indiscriminately as nouns and verbs, adjectives and adverbs, pronouns and interjections. Dr Johnson was talking of the lack of seditious opinions among the Highlanders, but also it seems of the tone of their language, when he said of them: "Their conversation is decent and inoffensive ... I never heard a health offered by a Highlander that might not have circulated with propriety within the precincts of the king's palace."[135] Alexander Carmichael, who preserved for posterity large amounts of the Highlanders' oral literature, testified to the Napier Commission that the Highlanders' many songs were decorous as well as delightful, and that in all the many rhymes and legends he had written down he had never come across, "either in this or among the people, an unbecoming word or an impure story".[136] One traveller, in a boat sailing along the rocky coast of Coll, said the boatmen were uneasy, not knowing those waters: they "began to talk loud in Gaelic, and damn in English, for there is no such oath in the Gaelic language".[137]

This was even observable in the all-male society of the barracks. David Stewart said of the first Highland regiment, the Black Watch, that their common conversation was "so correct and so free from all indecency, that I do not recollect an instance of a man making use of improper language, without being reproved by his companions, and taxed with bringing disgrace upon himself and the corps".[138] One can imagine the uproar that would follow if a soldier objected to the use of "improper language" in a modern Scots or English barrack-room.

The Highlanders' skill in language meant that when the clearances came, they often expressed their sorrow and their anger in poetry, which is a vivid and persuasive form of language more likely to be memorable, and therefore with more chance of surviving, than a prose account of the same events. But there are few circumstances that cannot be turned to good account by an adroit spin-doctor. Just as the greater leisure enjoyed by the Highlanders in their society, compared with the Lowlanders in their society, was turned into a reproach ("they are lazy and indolent, and need to be forced into wage-labour"), so the Highlanders' verse, which bore witness to the sufferings brought about by the clearances in a form which demonstrated the superior linguistic abilities conferred by clan society, was itself converted into a condemnation – "those attacking the clearances are merely romantic and sentimental (they even write poetry!) as opposed to the hard-headed business-like commentators who support them".

Such unfounded criticisms, of course, are still the staple of the orthodox histories of the Highlands.[139]

19. Education valued

In such a society, education would be held in great esteem, and was. It was not uncommon for several poor families to club together to get some lad who could read and write to come and teach their children, at each cottage in turn.[140] In Strachur the inhabitants of two or more farms would join and employ a young man to teach their children: they gave him "board and lodging alternately" at their homes, together with wages.[141] There are a number of similar references, for example in the Lismore[142] and the Kilfinichen accounts.[143] Two young men were employed in this way by the Strath Glass tenants (Kiltarlity),[144] and six in Fortingall.[145] There were schools of the same kind, but only in the winter, at Glenmuick[146] and at Lochgoilhead.[147]

To repeat a point made earlier, about fiddle-players, when many people follow the same pursuit, some usually achieve excellence in it. Among the Highland poets whose mastery was acknowledged by their fellows a few may be mentioned here.[148] Mary MacLeod, or Mairi Nighean Alasdair Ruaidh (c.1615-c.1707), was one of the MacLeod of Harris clan. Ian Lom, or John MacDonald, of the Keppoch clan, was a descendant of Ian Aluinn, the chief deposed in 1497. Born about 1620, he lived to be nearly a hundred, and wrote many Jacobite songs. Niall MacMhuirich (or MacVurich), c.1637-1726, was one of a family who successively provided bards to Clanranald. Roderick Morrison (c.1656-1714), known as An Clàrsair Dall, the blind harper, was one of the Morrisons of Lewis; part of his life he spent at Dunvegan, part in touring the houses of Highland gentry. William, Alexander, and John MacKenzie, three brothers who lived in Lochcarron, flourished in the 1720s. The famous Alasdair Mac Mhaighstir Alasdair, or Alexander MacDonald[149] (c.1695-c.1770), was best known for his sea poem *Clanranald's Galley*. Iain Ruadh Stiùbhard (John Roy – the Red – Stewart), 1700-52, came from Strathspey, fought for Prince Charles, was for long a hunted fugitive, and then escaped to France; David Stewart said "he composed with equal facility in English, Latin, and Gaelic".[150] Rob Donn MacAoidh (Robert Donn – brown-haired – MacKay), 1714-78, was born in Durness, and was known as the bard of the Reay country. Donnchadh Bàn Mac-an-t-Saoir (Duncan Ban – the fair – MacIntyre), 1724 to 1812 (or 1816), was the bard of Glen Orchy; though he could not speak English, nor write in either English or Gaelic, he could repeat, it was said, all his own poetry, about 7000 verses.[151] Iain MacCurchi, or John MacRae, of Kintail, flourished in the 1760s and 1770s, and died in America (regretting he had ever left the Highlands).[152] Iain MacCodrum, or John

MacDonald, of North Uist, 1693-1779, was appointed bard to Sir James MacDonald of Sleat in 1763 – the last such officer-holder. Allan MacDougall, c.1750-1829, was born in Glen Coe; he was a tailor, and after being blinded in an accident became a strolling poet and fiddler: he was known as the Blind Bard of Glengarry. William Ross, a noted poet, bard, and fiddler, was born in Broadford, Skye, in 1762; his mother came from Gairloch, and was the daughter of the famous blind piper of Gairloch, An Piobhaire Dall. James Shaw of Ardchattan, "Lochnell's bard", died about 1823. Uilleam MacDhun-léibhe (William Livingstone), 1808-70, was known as the Islay Bard. Iain Mac a'Ghobhainn (John Smith), 1848-81, the Earshader Bard, from Uig, Lewis, wrote for example about landlordism.[153]

Another poet, Charles MacKay, 1814-89, who wrote in English ("Old Tubal Cain was a man of might, in the days when Earth was young"), was the grandson of Captain Hugh MacKay of Strath Naver. (Charles' daughter, Mary MacKay, became a best-selling author under the name Marie Corelli.)

20. Intelligent and ingenious

After the new society had overthrown the clan system, the Lowlanders took pleasure in looking down on the defeated Gaels, and calling them "dreamy, improvident Highlanders" (who were, at the same time, savage and uncontrollable). The historians were either Lowlanders, or came from that small band of Highlanders who had gained from the new society; so these are the views that became accepted. But, as a matter of fact, although the Highlander was a countryman, living in nothing larger than a hamlet, no one has ever given the lie more directly to the cherished belief of some city-dwellers that everyone living outside a town is a clown (the very word means a rustic) and a "country bumpkin".[154] The Highlander's sharpness of mind arose from the society in which he lived. At Crathie the people were "intelligent, humane, obliging, and much given to hospitality";[155] at Killin, they were "lively and intelligent, without being turbulent".[156] The minister of Kilchoman said the people there were "subtle and ingenious";[157] in Tiree, they were "subtle, not easily deceived"; they were also "mannerly, lively, and ingenious".[158] The account of North Uist described the people as "sagacious and acute, in discovering their own interest".[159] The minister of North Knapdale said that Highlanders were "naturally of quick and clear understanding, with lively passions".[160] The Duirinish minister wrote that "the common people of Skye are blessed with excellent parts; a liberal share of strong natural sense, and great acuteness of understanding".[161] The Kirkmichael reporter said of the old Highlanders, "address and stratagem marked their enterprises".[162] Obviously comparing his Highlanders with the Lowlanders, the minister of Portree said that "the common people are naturally endowed with a strength of mind and a sprightliness of disposition that greatly distinguish them from others of the same rank and condition";[163] an opinion reinforced by the minister of Daviot, who said that the people are "remarkable for that acuteness of judgement which has been peculiarly attributed to Highlanders".[164] The Kilmuir (Skye) minister asserted that "the people of this country, and indeed of all the Western Highlands, have signalized themselves, in the last, and in the former wars, by their valour, and their ability in bearing every species of hardship and fatigue. They are possessed of vivacity and penetration in a high degree."[165] The Rev. J. L. Buchanan said that the western Hebrideans in general were of "strong parts, quick and penetrating in their apprehensions"; and, again, they were "an acute, shrewd, and penetrating people: they have, particularly, a quick discrimination of character".[166] Toland said the Highlanders were "remarkably sagacious",[167] while the Rev. Dr Norman MacLeod wrote that "the real Highland peasantry are, I hesitate not to affirm, by far the most intelligent in the world".[168] The Tongue N.S.A. report (to repeat) spoke of the "poetic talent and sprightly wit for which their ancestors, in common with most Highlanders, were distinguished".[169] Dr Jackson, writing in 1804, said "the Highlanders, formed with sound minds, and susceptible of good impressions, discover more natural sagacity than any other class of people in the kingdom, perhaps than any other people in Europe".[170] Sir John Sinclair called the Highlanders "sagacious and hospitable".[171]

John Buchan compared "the Highlander" with the peasants and townsmen in the Lowlands. "He was swift where they were slow, cunning where they were simple, adroit where they were blundering, daring when they were supine."[172] Bishop Nicolson, in 1700, praised the Highlanders. "By nature they are of very lively spirits and they are wonderfully successful when they have a little education. Even the common people seem to be far more open and confiding than those of the Lowlands."[173] Dr John Walker, on his 1764 journey to the Hebrides, said Lewis girls were being taught to spin flax fibres to make linen, at a school set up by the Commissioners of Forfeited Estates: the Lowland mistress at the school said her pupils were "extremely quick and docile, and is certain, that such girls in the low country could not make equal proficiency under a person who was ignorant of their language".[174] Walker (to repeat) thought that the Hebrideans were "a people by nature the most acute and sagacious"; they were "an acute and sensible people, extremely desirous of instruction, and capable of great attainments, both in knowledge and industry". In fact he essayed a topographical interpretation: "the mind of man is to be observed more and more perfect as one moves northwards", thus ascribing to geography a contrast which reasoned thought would suggest to have been the outcome of differing forms of society.[175] (In Walker's view, presumably the North Pole would be the place to look for new Shakespeares or Einsteins.)

As opposed to all this testimony, given by people who themselves knew the Highlanders, there was the carefully considered verdict of Janet Glover who claimed, as we saw above, that the Highlanders were "lethargic in mind".[176]

21. Of quick parts

Nor did the Highlanders have intellects merely inward-turning. They were "of quick parts", as well as "inquisitive and fond of information" (Kincardine),[177] and "full of curiosity" (North Uist).[178] The minister of Portree said they were inquisitive and fond of news: their "questions and shrewd remarks" were often surprising.[179] William Marshall, writing in 1794, said the Highlanders were "inquisitive to gain information; cautious to retain it; and artful and active in applying it to advantage."[180] Dr James Robertson remarked of the Highlanders in 1808 that "the desire of being well informed gives them an inquisitive turn, which is often censured by strangers";[181] in the low country, he said, people were often ill informed, whereas in the Highlands one could obtain detailed information. Many stories were told to show how sharp and quick-witted the Highlanders were. David Stewart remarked on a Highland lad who, together with a Lowland farmer, was crossing a stream in a glen. The lad had reached the far side, while the farmer paused on the stepping stones in the middle of the stream, trying to account for a sudden noise he had heard. The Highlander realized that a waterspout must have fallen further up the glen, and that the noise was caused by a fast-approaching torrent of water. Afraid that the Lowlander might be struck immobile by panic if he revealed this fact, the Highlander shouted instead, "Help, help, or I am a dead man", and fell to the ground. Hardly had the farmer sprung to his side when the torrent rushed down with a force that would have swept away anyone in its path. Thus the Highlander's presence of mind had saved his companion.[182]

Equal perspicacity was shown by Allan MacPherson, a soldier in the 77th, Montgomerie's Highlanders, in the Seven Years' War in America. He and others were taken prisoner in an ambush by the native American Indians. Their captors decided to kill them, slowly, one by one, and MacPherson had to watch several of his comrades being tortured to death. When it was his turn, he told his executioners that if they spared him a few minutes he would tell them of a marvellous potion, which, when applied to the skin, would render it impervious to "the strongest blow of a sword, or tomahawk". They took him into the woods, where he picked plants at random, then boiled them, and rubbed his neck with their juice. He laid his head on a log of wood, and said if the strongest man there would strike him with a tomahawk, it "could not make the smallest impression". This was done, and, of course, his head flew off. The Amerindians realized that MacPherson had tricked them, and had succeeded in escaping the torture that they were preparing for him: David Stewart said "they were so pleased with his ingenuity, that they refrained from inflicting further cruelties on the remaining prisoners".[183]

22. Enterprise and initiative

Earlier in this work it was shown how the Highlanders co-operated in their daily lives, and also in time of war. But it would be wrong to deduce from this that the Highlander could not act on his own. The ability to combine with others for a common end, and the ability to show individual enterprise and initiative, were merely two aspects of a single entity, the resourceful and proficient character of the clansfolk. In 1777 in America, the Black Watch was at Pisquatua, in New Jersey, when the Americans attacked the British forward posts. One Sergeant MacGregor was badly wounded, and fell unconscious, being left behind while the Americans advanced. Then the Black Watch counter-attacked, and drove the Americans back. As the Americans were retreating, one of them saw the insensible body of MacGregor, who had on a new jacket with silver lace, silver shoe buckles, and a watch. Not having time to detach all these valuables, he hoisted the unconscious MacGregor on to his back, to bear him off as a prize. MacGregor, however, came to, and realized what was happening; then (said David Stewart), despite the fact of his injuries, he "drew his dirk, and, grasping him [his captor] by the throat, swore that he would run him through the breast, if he did not turn back and carry him to the camp". The American, perforce, agreed. On the way they met Lord Cornwallis, the British commander, who thanked the American for helping the wounded Highlander; the rebel, however, said honestly what had happened, and Cornwallis "gave him liberty to go whithersoever he chose".[184] Again, later that year, when the army was in Philadelphia, parties were sent out foraging. "In an excursion through the woods, a Highland soldier came unexpectedly in sight of an American, while their pieces [single-shot guns] happened to be unloaded. Each flew behind a tree to cover himself while loading." Neither wished to show himself; but the Highlander put his bonnet on the end of his bayonet, and cautiously pushed it out from behind his tree: the American put his single shot through the middle of it. The Highlander immediately went forward and made the now weaponless American his prisoner.[185]

Thirty years before, after the defeat of the Jacobite rebellion, a corporal and eight soldiers of the occupying army were in the autumn of 1746 marching northwards through Perthshire, bound for Inverness. After passing Tummel Bridge they "halted on the roadside", wrote Stewart, "and placed their arms against a large stone some yards behind them". Robert Ban Robertson, a local Jacobite who had fought at Falkirk and Culloden, saw them there. As a defeated rebel, many of whose erstwhile comrades were being killed on sight by the Government forces, Robertson might have been expected to refrain modestly from any flamboyance. Not a bit of it. "None of his neighbours were at home to assist him, but he sallied out by himself, armed with his gun, pistols, and broadsword; and, proceeding with great caution, got close to the party undiscovered, when he made a sudden spring, and placed himself between the soldiers and their guns." Covering them with his gun, he demanded their immediate surrender, "or he would call his party, who were in the wood behind, and would kill them all". The soldiers were "so alarmed and taken by surprise" that they let Robert Ban carry off their arms, which he claimed he was going to hand over to his companions in the wood. Then he returned, and escorted them all to Tummel Bridge inn: leaving them there, he went back to the wood, collected the soldiers' weapons, and made off. When they discovered that their adversary had been only a single Highlander, the soldiers gave pursuit; but Rob Ban was nowhere to be found.[186]

If clan society was merely a cloak for tyranny, it must have been the first tyranny ever to produce common citizens with this much presence of mind.

23. Pride and independence

But tyrannies do not produce men who are proud, jealous of their honour, and independent to a fault. The Highlanders were all these. Selkirk, who was writing in 1805, said: "Pride, which formerly pervaded even the lowest classes, has always been a prominent feature of their national character."[187] The Highlanders were "of a spirit somewhat independent" (Kirkmichael Perthshire),[188] "impatient of restraint" (Kilmallie),[189] and had "a sense of honour and shame, in a high degree for their station" (Daviot and Dunlichity).[190] They were "regardless of toil and danger" to earn "honour" (North Knapdale).[191] The minister of Campbeltown had a tale of a MacDonald, who was in Ireland, dining with the Lord Lieutenant. He sat at the foot of the table, near the door. The Lord Lieutenant asked him to come to the head of the table. When the message had been translated for MacDonald, who had no English, he replied, "Tell the carl [churl], that wherever MacDonald sits, that is the head of the table".[192] Defoe (in his so-called *Memoirs of a Cavalier*) said that Leslie's Highlanders in 1640 "scorn to be commanded but by one of their own clan or family. They are all gentlemen, and proud enough to be kings."[193] Dr John Walker, in Skye during the 1760s, had found there a "warlike, faithful and high-spirited people".[194] Not only were all the men gentlemen; all the women were ladies. Dr Johnson was much taken with at least one of the latter, who was the daughter of his host in Glen Moriston. "Her conversation, like her appearance, was gentle and pleasing. We knew that the girls of the Highlands are all gentlewomen, and treated her with great respect, which she received as customary and due, and was neither elated by it, nor confused, but repaid my civilities without embarrassment . . . I presented her with a book, which I happened to have about me, and should not be pleased to think that she forgets me."[195]

This pride was not confined to the well-to-do. Buchanan, on his travels in the 1780s, saw that even when the Highlanders had been reduced to poverty, the poorest still addressed each other as "bheanuasle" and "duinuasle", lady and gentleman.[196] To anyone from England, where pride was something which could be afforded only by the rich, this trait was laughable. Daniel Defoe, writing in 1706 from Edinburgh to Harley, a government minister, said of the Highlanders: "They are formidable fellows and I only wish Her Majesty had 25,000 of them in Spain [this was during the War of the Spanish Succession], as a nation equally proud and barbarous like themselves. They are all gentlemen, will take affront from no man, and insolent to the last degree. But certainly the absurdity is ridiculous to see a man in his mountain habit, armed with a broadsword, target, pistol, at his girdle a dagger, and staff, walking down the High Street as upright and haughty as if he was a lord, and withal driving a cow!"[197] A little cringing from men who were only herding cows would have been more to the sophisticated taste of the civilized Defoe. On the other hand, as Sir Walter Scott wrote in *Rob Roy*, "it must be granted that the air of punctilious deference and rigid etiquette which would seem ridiculous in an ordinary peasant has, like the salute of a corps-de-garde, a propriety when tendered by a Highlander completely armed".[198] (Despite his acceptance of the conventional phraseology, Scott was here revealing that the Highlander was neither "ordinary" nor a "peasant".)

24. Erect martial air

David Stewart contrasted the present and the former appearance of the Highlanders. "The clumsy, vulgar, ill-made clothes, now so much worn by the young men of the Highlands, give them a clownish appearance, altogether different from, and forming a marked contrast to the light airy garb, gay with many colours, and the erect martial air and elastic step of the former race of Highlanders."[199]

John MacNaughton, from Glen Lyon, described as a servant of James Menzies of Culdares (or, at least, such was the Lowland portrayal of an attendant of a chief), was executed during the '45 rebellion (as will be seen later) rather than betray his trust and inform on his chieftain.[200] MacNaughton's brother, so David Stewart wrote, lived for many years on the estate of Garth, dying in 1790. "He always went about armed, at least so far armed, that when debarred wearing a sword or dirk, he slung a large knife in his belt. He was one of the last I recollect of the ancient race, and gave a very favourable impression of their general manner and appearance.

He was a smith by trade, and although of the lowest order of the people, he walked about with an air and manner that might have become a field-marshal. He spoke with great force and fluency of language, and, although most respectful to those to whom he thought respect was due, he had an appearance of independence and ease, that strangers, ignorant of the language and character of the people, might have supposed to proceed from impudence."[201] (And Defoe, as we saw, made this very mistake, describing the Highlanders as "insolent to the last degree".) MacNaughton belonged, said Stewart in 1822, to a previous generation, and an observer "will not now see any of those martial patriarchal figures, with an erect independent air, at the same time with an ease of manners, and fluency of language and expression, rarely to be found among any peasantry [sic]".[202]

Dr Robert Jackson wrote that "the character of ardour belongs to the Highlander; he acts from an internal sentiment, and possesses a pride of honour, which does not permit him to retire from danger with a confession of inferiority . . . when an enemy is before the Highlander, the authority of the officer may be said to cease." The Highlander "still sustains the approaching point of a naked weapon with a steadier eye than any other man in Europe. Some nations turn with fear from the countenance of an enraged enemy: the Highlander rushes towards it with ardour; and if he can grasp his foe, as man with man, his courage is secure."[203]

25. Self-respect

The minister of Callander, who lived on the edge of the Highlands and therefore had many opportunities to compare his parishioners with the nearby Lowlanders, said that the Callander people had not the "sullenness of those" in the open country further south and east (that is, in the Lowlands).[204] The Lowlanders' sullenness was their substitute for self-respect: the Highlanders did not need it.

Any blows or corporal punishments were considered degrading by the Highlanders, although they were common currency in the "civilized" areas outside the mountains, and therefore in the British army. David Stewart found this feeling an impediment to recruiting. The Highlanders, he wrote, regarded corporal punishment with more "horror and shame than death itself. When a Highlander is brought to the halberts [i.e., is flogged, the standard and frequent British army punishment] he considers himself as having lost caste. He becomes, in his own estimation, a disgraced man, and is no longer fit for the society of his friends. To them, therefore, or to his native countrymen, he can never return."[205] The mutinies in both the Breadalbane Fencibles and the Grant Fencibles in 1795 – and a mutineer, it must be remembered, then risked and often received the penalty of death – were caused (as we shall see later) by some of the soldiers being confined and threatened with corporal punishment.[206]

The Black Watch regiment fought with such gallantry at Fontenoy in 1745 that the commander-in-chief, the Duke of Cumberland, told the Highland soldiers he would grant any favour they chose to ask. The Highlanders asked for a pardon for one of their number who had been tricked into allowing a prisoner to escape, and was therefore going to be flogged; the pardon (as we shall see later) was immediately granted.[207]

It is a measure of the change which came over the Highlands that when the Gaelic society was finally crushed by the Lowlanders, the Highlanders had to learn to submit even to this disgrace. The Rev. J. L. Buchanan, in his book on the western Hebrides in the 1780s, said that "formerly, a Highlander would have drawn his dirk against even a laird, if he had subjected him to the indignity of a blow"; but when he wrote a tacksman "may strike" a servant, or even a sub-tenant, "with perfect impunity".[208] Though the Hebrideans (to repeat) "still address one another by the title of gentleman or lady (duinuasle and bheanuasle)", that is merely "part of their former state and dignity . . . part of their former importance".[208]

Even when a Highlander was miles away from his clan land and the support of his fellows, and was subject to the savage discipline of the British armed forces, an officer of a Highland regiment who ordered an unjust punishment was treading on extremely dangerous ground. The death of Colonel Cameron of Fassfern at Quatre Bras, and the services rendered to him by his foster-brother, Ewen MacMillan, were mentioned earlier. The evidence is that the Fassfern chieftains (as we shall see in a later volume) were foremost among the Cameron gentry to carry out evictions and raise rents; and it seems that Colonel Cameron had given further offence. According to Somerled MacMillan, the local tradition in Lochaber is that Colonel Cameron was shot "by one of his own men who had been flogged earlier for some petty offence". When Cameron was hit, he said to Ewen MacMillan, "I'm afraid it wasn't the enemy who fired that shot"; MacMillan replied, "No, and he wasn't your friend either". This occurred during an assault on a strong French position. After Cameron's death, the Highlanders (as could have been expected) completed the job in hand, and drove the French out. The general opinion among the Highland soldiers was clearly that Colonel Cameron had deserved what he got: they must all have been aware of the "improvements" on Fassfern's estate, as well as the harsh punishment inflicted. The man who killed him had been seen to have one particular button missing from his coat; so all the other soldiers tore the same button off their coats as well, thus rendering identification of the culprit impossible.[209]

The Highlanders were sensitive of slights on their honour in other ways. George II had never seen a Highland soldier, so in 1743 two privates of the Black Watch "performed the broadsword exercise, and that of the Lochaber axe", before the king. "Each got a gratuity of one guinea, which they gave to the porter at the palace gates as they passed out", said the account in the *Westminster Journal*.[210] The Black Watch soldiers thought that to accept a tip, even from the king, was not consonant with the dignity of a Highlander.

There was a similar case in 1815. After the defeat of Napoleon, the Tsar of Russia reviewed Wellington's army in Paris. He asked for six Highlanders to be brought for closer inspection; and said, "No wonder Wellington won victories with such soldiers". He told his aide-de-camp to give each man a gold coin; each Highlander respectfully declined the gift. The Tsar said, "Ces braves Ecossais, quell gentilhommes!" – "These gallant Scotsmen, what gentlemen!"[211]

This pride and independence of the Highlanders sprang from their position in Highland society, as free and equal members of the clan. It could never have arisen if the clansfolk had been "subordinate" to their chief, merely "peasants" dependent on his whim. In the Highlands there was no division into well-born and ill-born, no such thing as "good breeding" or the lack of it, for it was the unquestioned belief of the Highlanders that in each clan all the clansfolk were related to each other and to the chief. Sir John Dalrymple, in his *Memoirs of Great Britain*, said that the meanest of the clan, believing himself to be as well-born as the head of it, revered his chieftain and respected himself.[212]

Self-respect is not a trait that flourishes under tyranny.

26. *"Habituated to domination"*

When the society which produced these Highlanders – resourceful, independent, and proud to a fault – had been destroyed, and when many of the erstwhile clansfolk had been driven to the factory towns or to the colonies, leaving only a poverty-stricken remnant under enormous pressure to accept the obsequious role of a grovelling rural proletariat, then Lowland historians were free to complete the character assassination of the Highlanders. Professor Dr Gordon Donaldson, for example, ignored the evidence in a quite imperious way, and insisted that the Highlanders were spineless creatures unable to act without someone telling them what to do. Emigration, he wrote, was "usually a movement under leadership, as one would expect of people accustomed to clan life". Of one particular emigration, in 1817, during which a minister, the Rev. Norman MacLeod, became prominent, he wrote: "one can only conclude that the Highlanders were so habituated to leadership and domination that they meekly acquiesced in Norman's tyranny."[213] (What actually happened will be shown later.) Of the land agitation of the 1880s, Donaldson claimed that "the Highlanders themselves did not throw up a leader, and were probably not capable of doing so, for they had always depended on leadership of chief, tacksman, priest or minister".[214] In fact any "lack of leaders" is easily explained: self-governing, self-respecting, and capable people like the Highlanders did not need leaders, and were accustomed to act on their own initiative. John Stewart, one of the Black Watch soldiers who had been brought to London in 1743 by successive deceits, and who therefore set off to walk back to the Highlands, said when interrogated: "I had no leader or commander; we had not one man over the rest."[215] This was a succinct and accurate statement of the Highland attitude towards leaders: leaders, after all, can only appear when people submit themselves to leadership. Donaldson himself, as the Historiographer Royal for Scotland, could be described as the leader of the academic historians of his era: or perhaps one should adopt Donaldson's language, and say that the Lowland chroniclers of the late twentieth century "were so habituated to leadership and domination that they meekly acquiesced in" Donaldson's "tyranny".

When these were the allegations of the pre-eminent Lowland historian, it will be seen how important it is to establish the facts of the Highlanders' very different character. While no writer would venture to deny that (for example) the Highlanders swept away the Hanoverian army at the Battle of Killiecrankie, as will be shown below, the Lowland historians take as much credit away from the Highland clansmen as they can by insisting that it was only done under the leadership of James Graham, "Bonnie Dundee"; and that though he was killed in the battle, it must have been only when the victory was already won. That, therefore, is the unvarying account given of the triumph. In fact, James VII and II wrote to Stewart of Ballechin, who (as we saw earlier) was chosen by the Athollmen to be their general, congratulating him on the Highland success, and commiserating with him on the loss of Dundee "at your entrance into action".[216] It appears from this letter that the Highlanders were as usual not depending on anyone's leadership. Even if Dundee had survived to the end of the battle, it has to be agreed that while generals can decide tactics, they cannot fight a battle themselves; and the repeated success of the Highlanders in the military field can only be explained by the attitudes and attributes which grew naturally out of the old clan society. The Highlanders were so little reliant on leadership, that (to repeat Dr Jackson's words) "when an enemy is before the Highlander, the authority of the officer may be said to cease". Of how many among the European soldiers of those days could that have been said? Indeed, of how many present-day soldiers anywhere in the world could it be said?

27. Highland soldiers

If the Highland chiefs and chieftains had really been tyrants in the Highlands, where their power lay solely in the goodwill of the clansfolk, how much more tyrannical they must have been as officers of Highland regiments, when the clansmen were under full military discipline, and had been marched down into the Lowlands or even overseas, far from the support of their friends and neighbours. In fact, however, the chiefs and chieftains, and their sons and brothers, who made up the complement of officers in a Highland regiment, had to be just as careful about their behaviour towards the clansmen as they were in the Highlands. The minister of Abernethy noted that "a man that is harsh and austere, and fond of severity and punishment, is not fit to command a Highland corps": in the Highland regiments, he continued, the Highland soldiers' officers "speak to them in a discreet friendly manner, and encourage them by a little familiarity".[217]

David Stewart said that the Highland soldier must be given "kind treatment". "A Highland regiment, to be orderly and well disciplined, ought to be commanded by men who are capable of appreciating their character, directing their passions and prejudices, and acquiring their entire confidence and affection. The officer to whom the command of the Highlanders is entrusted must endeavour to acquire their confidence and good opinion. With this view he must watch over the propriety of his own conduct. He must observe the strictest justice and fidelity in his promises to his men, conciliate them by an attention to their dispositions and prejudices, and, at the same time, by preserving a firm and steady authority, without which, he will not be respected."

So independent were the Highlanders, Stewart continued, that "in some instances, when the misconduct of officers, particularly in the field, was not publicly censured, the soldiers who served under them made regular representations that they could not and would not remain longer under their command, and that, if they were not relieved from the disgrace of being so commanded, they would lay their complaints before the highest authority".[218] A "modern major-general" or any other officer would be astounded to find such an attitude among the lower ranks today – Privates Tommy Atkins, Jack Smith and Bert Robinson deciding who was going to command them.

The "firm and steady authority" mentioned by Stewart had to be exercised fairly and justly, and it had to be seen that it was exercised fairly and justly. If promises were made they had to be kept, or trouble would follow. The first of the Highland regiments, the Black Watch, was formed in 1740, and it was understood that they were to be employed only in their own country. But in 1743 it was decided to send them to Flanders. Instead of the authorities informing the soldiers of this change of plan, which perhaps they were reluctant to do through a fear that these supposed subservient helots would simply refuse to obey orders, they were told that they were to be reviewed in Edinburgh by the king; in Edinburgh they were told that the review was to take place at Berwick, on the Scots border; in Berwick they were told that it was going to be in London. When they arrived in London, the king had already left for Hanover. Being greatly discontented over this repeated deception, about a hundred of them set out to return to the Highlands, but were surrounded by a large military force in Northamptonshire, and three of them were tried and executed.[219] (None of those who had been telling repeated lies were even reprimanded, of course.)

The authorities did not take the lesson from this episode that Highland soldiers, who were in their own eyes all gentlemen, had to be treated fairly and openly. In 1778 the Seaforth Highlanders were quartered at Leith (the port of Edinburgh) prior to embarkation; but promises made to them had not been kept, and their pay was in arrears. So the regiment marched up to Arthur's Seat above Edinburgh, with pipes playing and their own temporary colours flying, and took possession of it. These MacKenzies and MacRaes were popular with the people of Edinburgh, though popularity was an accolade rarely bestowed by civilians on eighteenth-century soldiers; and they were kept supplied with provisions and ammunition. The Earl of Seaforth himself had to settle their just grievances; and then they marched down from Arthur's Seat again and embarked for the Channel Islands, without any charge being laid against any of them.[220] In the following year, 1779, much the same thing happened. The 76th Regiment, MacDonald's Highlanders, were quartered at Burntisland, on the Firth of Forth, where they were going to embark. But (as with the Seaforths) their pay was in arrears, and other promises made had not been kept: so the regiment marched away in an orderly body, and camped on a hill above the town, sending down parties regularly for provisions, all of which were paid for. (The locals were astounded: non-Highland soldiers, even when under full military discipline, were seldom so punctilious in their commercial transactions.) When the matter was investigated, the complaints were found to be completely justified: Lord Macdonald himself made up the pay that was due; and no charge was made against the mutineers.[221]

28. Free pardon

In that same year of 1779, when two strong detachments of Highlanders who had been recruited specifically for two Highland regiments reached Leith, they were told (as was remarked above) that they had to join Lowland regiments. Lowland or English soldiers at that time could have been ordered about in this high-handed fashion without repercussion – which, of course, is why the authorities thought they could do the same with Highlanders. But the Highland recruits refused to accept this blatant disregard of the terms on which they had volunteered: so soldiers were sent to take them prisoners to Edinburgh Castle. Such an enterprise was easier to envisage than to execute, and in the melee that ensued, an officer and nine men were killed, and thirty-one wounded. Finally the Highlanders were overpowered, and three of them court-martialled, and sentenced to be shot. They were, however, given a free pardon; the authorities had to abandon their attempt to bully the Highlanders; and the detachments joined their Highland regiments.[222]

At the end of the War of American Independence in 1783, the Atholl Highlanders were marched to Portsmouth to be sent to the East Indies, although their engagements had been for the duration of the war only. The Duke of Atholl, it was believed, had sold the regiment to the East India Company. At Portsmouth the men of Atholl mutinied, and took over their barracks. They spurned their colonel (and chief), the Duke of Atholl, when he came down in person, and defied the Government. In the end the authorities gave way, and the regiment was returned to Scotland, where it was disbanded: no one was charged or punished.[223]

At the same time and place the Government was also attempting to send the Aberdeenshire Highlanders abroad, in breach of the terms on which the men had enlisted. They also refused to go, and again the Government had to give way, and disband the regiment without any punishment being attempted.[224]

Similar mutinies occurred on other occasions when the Government attempted to treat the Highlanders who had been produced by clan society in the same oppressive way as they treated the men produced by the new commercial and industrial society: for example, the mutinies of the Breadalbane Fencibles and the Grant regiment in 1795, and that of the Canadian Fencibles in 1804.[225]

Two Highland regiments raised in 1759 were the 87th, Keith's Highlanders, and the 88th, Campbell's Highlanders. They were reduced at Linlithgow in 1763, at the end of the war. Stewart described what happened on that occasion. The Highland soldier, he wrote, was "attached to officers who merited respect. But then, in order to ensure this respect, strict justice must have been done him, great regard must have been had to his feelings, and, in all his pecuniary transactions with his officers, he must have observed in them the most perfect accuracy. Let these pre-requisites exist, and a Highlander will abandon his post and his life together. In the hurry of the campaign, new clothing had not been served out to the soldiers [in Keith's and Campbell's regiments] for the year 1763, and when they were disbanded, it was thought they had no occasion for military uniforms. The soldiers thought otherwise, and said that they were fully entitled to pay, clothing, and all that had been promised, and due to them. The thing was at first resisted, but the men persevering, it was at length acquiesced in, and an allowance in money given in lieu of the clothing. In this resistance to authority, for the support of what they considered their rights, some indications of violence, very opposite to their previous exemplary conduct, were manifested."[226]

Later in his book, Stewart wrote again: "I have seen Highland soldiers spring forward to cover their officers from the shot of the enemy; I have seen them endeavouring to restrain their officers, and to keep them back, and under cover, while they fully exposed themselves, in the expectation of diverting the attention of the enemy from their commanders; and I have seen the same soldiers disputing a penny in their accounts with the same officers, and this, perhaps, only a few days after this voluntary hazard of their lives to shelter them."[227]

If these men were really down-trodden serfs at home, it must be the only occasion on record when the dreaded severities of drumhead discipline and the horrifying harshness of military punishment have made men not less, but more, independent-spirited. After reading about what the Highlanders actually did, the reader must decide for himself whether to accept the facts or the orthodox theory.

29. Religious tolerance

Independence was not bigotry. The Highlanders' religious beliefs were uncomplicated and inoffensive. Carmichael said that they "had special prayers and hymns for every occasion"; in fact the prayers were almost poetry, being put into rhyme and rhythm to make them easier to memorize. "There was a special prayer on going to sea, a special prayer on going to the shieling, a special prayer for resting the fire at night, for kindling it in the morning, for lying down at night, for rising up in the morning, for taking food, for going in search of sheep, cattle, and of horses, for setting out to travel, and for other occasions."[228] (Such simple repetitions, of course, would also help to reinforce social bonding.) But the kindly conditions of clanship afforded no scope for the growth of intolerance. Dalrymple wrote, "the Highlands of Scotland is the only country of Europe that has never been distracted by religious controversy, or suffered from religious persecution".[229] The English Catholic historian Odo Blundell referred to "those principles of toleration which distinguished many districts of the Highlands long before they were known elsewhere in Britain".[230] David Stewart said that in the Highlands "there was no religious or political persecution".[231]

The minister of Urray (a Presbyterian of course), writing in the 1790s, said that an Episcopal minister served three local churches belonging to that communion. Urray's Episcopalian Highlanders were far from narrow-minded: when their minister was absent "his ordinary hearers attend the parish church as punctually as the other parishioners".[232] In Mortlach, most belonged to the established church, except for a minority of thirty or forty Roman Catholics; but "any ill-will or violence of temper, arising from a difference in religious sentiment, is rare".[233] The Daviot minister thought that "in no country are different religious persuasions attended with more mutual forebearance and charity than in this".[234] An observer at the turn of the century said that "the religion of a Highlander is peaceable and unobtrusive. He never arms himself with quotations from Scripture to carry on offensive operations. There is no inducement for him to strut about in the garb of piety, in order to attract respect, as his own conduct insures it ... Protestants and Papists, so often pronounced to be eternally inimical, live here in charity and brotherhood." Fort William, he continued, had chapels for the Presbyterians, Episcopalians, and Roman Catholics. On Sunday morning the Highlanders could be seen in the streets, conversing amiably, until they separated, each to his own church; afterwards, "they meet again as cordially as they parted. The advocate for intolerance will say, such a people must either be lukewarm and indifferent, or the thing is impossible. Not at all. They are truly earnest in their devotion. I visited a family, where the master of the house and his sons are Roman Catholics, the wife and daughter Episcopalians, and the tutor a Presbyterian. What a mixture! And does it not lead to confusion and wrangling? By no means; quite the contrary. It is a daily lesson of goodwill and kind-hearted forbearance, and everyone in the house is benefited by it."[235]

In 1772 Pennant wrote about the Small Isles, in particular about Canna. "The [Protestant] minister and the Popish priest reside in Eigg; but, by reason of the turbulent seas that divide these isles, are very seldom able to attend their flocks. I admire the moderation of their congregations, who attend the preaching of either indifferently as they happen to arrive."[236] (Some of the remarks in Pennant's book, the ones which can by careful selective quotation be made to discredit the old system, are recited in hundreds of histories; his testimony to the extraordinary tolerance of the Highlanders – which could only arise out of a basically fair and open-minded society – is hardly mentioned at all. Curious.) This moderation was the more remarkable when compared with the attitudes in the "civilized" Lowlands and England. Seven years after Pennant praised the magnanimity of the Canna Highlanders, who were prepared to listen to either Protestant or Catholic cleric as the weather allowed them access, there were savage anti-Catholic riots in the Lowlands (in Edinburgh, in Glasgow and even in smaller towns), and a year later still came the Gordon Riots in London, when enthusiastic, progressive theologians in a "No Popery" mob damaged or destroyed several Catholic churches and chapels and attacked numbers of "Papists" and their houses.[237] The minister of Morvern said in 1843 that there were a few Episcopalians in the parish who were occasionally visited by an Episcopalian clergyman from Fort William: but otherwise "with enlightened liberality, they join in the ordinances as dispensed in the parish church".[238] Sir Archibald Geikie, in his *Reminiscences*, was probably referring to the 1850s when he remembered the three men of the cloth on Eigg – Catholic, Established Church, and Free Church. "The three clergymen, Protestant and Roman Catholic, when I first visited the island, were excellent friends, and used to have pleasant evenings together over their toddy and talk." Geikie found the same in his journeys through the west of the Highlands: "there has always appeared to me to be in the West Highlands far less of the antagonism which in

Ireland separates Catholics and Protestants. They live together as good neighbours, and, unless you actually make enquiry, you cannot easily discriminate between them."[239]

The Rev. James MacGrigor was the Catholic priest in Barra, said Alexander Carmichael; the Presbyterian minister of the parish was the Rev. Roderick MacLean. "He and Mr MacGrigor were warm friends." MacGrigor made a lot of improvements to his croft, so naturally the factor planned to evict him (an improved croft fetched higher rent); but fortunately his friend the minister used his influence with the "absent proprietor", and MacGrigor was reprieved.[240]

The Highlanders were too contented under the clan system to provide likely converts for fanatics of any kind (intolerance is usually a reaction to misery), and these unbigoted attitudes, like other commendable traits, survived many years after the clan system was under attack.

30. Catholic clans

Many writers have said that all, or most of, the Highlanders were Catholic: others have strongly implied it. As long ago as 1911, the Rev. James MacKenzie, speaking of the reign of William III, said that "the clans, when they had any religion at all [the true flavour of Lowland scholasticism comes through here], were mostly Popish".[241] In 1969 James MacMillan asserted that "the Highlander was an unregenerate Papist", and that "the Highlands . . . were Catholic",[242] and a review in *The Times* in 1996 declared that the clearances could be seen as an assault by the "Protestant Scots-speaking Lowlanders" on their "Catholic Gaelic-speaking neighbours".[243] Ten years later the same newspaper said of Gaelic: "as 'the Catholic tongue', it was suppressed for decades."[244] A. G. MacDonell said the Reformation had divided the Highland clans "into two separate factions, the Protestant and the Catholic", as if they were of much the same size: an impression strengthened by his references to "the Catholic clans of the North and West", and to "the Catholicism of the seaboard clans or of the islands of the Hebrides" (including, presumably, the rigidly Protestant Lewis, Skye, North Uist and so on).[245] MacDonell also described Prince Charles' army as "Catholic soldiers"; in fact both religions were represented among the rebels.[246] Sir Thomas Innes of Learney alleged that "the clans, for the most part, were Episcopalians or Catholics".[247] Janet Glover remarked that in 1700 "loyalty to the Roman church . . . was assured in the Highlands".[248] Ian Finlay claimed that in the early seventeenth century "the inhabitants of the Black Isle were Protestant, when all their Highland neighbours were Catholic".[249] L. G. Pine said that as a result of religion "the rift between Highland and Lowland inhabitants became more pronounced", since "many of the clans, especially in the Isles, adhered to Catholicism, while the rest of

Scotland devoted itself to Protestantism".[250] Peter and Fiona Somerset Fry explained the savagery of the post-Culloden onslaught on the Highlanders by this supposed religious difference: "the devastation of the Highlands was ... applauded by many Lowland and Presbyterian Scots who hated Highlanders more for their stubborn adherence to the Roman Catholic faith than their loyalty to the Stewarts."[251] John Burke affirmed that "during the century after Culloden more than forty 'Parliamentary churches' were built throughout the Highlands to designs by Thomas Telford, in an effort to woo Papist Jacobites finally to Protestantism".[252] Professors Donnachie and Hewitt said there were "divided loyalties among the clans – many had remained Catholic", while "the Jacobite clans, notably the MacGregors, MacDonalds, MacPhersons, Stewarts and Robertsons, continued to support the Catholic cause after the Hanoverian succession".[253] David Ross thought that "most central and western clans remained Catholic".[254] Arthur Herman, an American professor of history, writing in 2002, said that while in 1700 the Lowlanders had embraced Presbyterianism, "the clansmen in the north tended to remain loyal to the Catholic faith or followed their chieftains into the Episcopalian Church".[255] Jeff Fallow declared that the Highlanders' "religion at that time [was] mainly Catholic or Episcopalian".[256] Tom Steel said "James VI and his successors continued to see it as a mission to civilize the Highlander and stamp out his general intransigence and Papist ways".[257] Even Hugh Miller, writing in 1854, said that "the Stuarts, exiled for their adherence to Popery, continued to found almost their sole hopes of restoration on the swords of their co-religionists the Highlanders".[258] A website, in 2006, claimed that "Catholicism was the predominant religion" in the Highlands and Islands.[259]

As we have seen before, and shall see again, many historians place more reliance on other historians than on the facts of history. When we look at these repeated statements that the Highlanders, or most of them, were Catholic, all of which assertions defied the clear reality, it becomes more understandable how other fictions about the Highlands – the tyrannical clan-rulers, the chiefs who were already landlords decades and centuries before that concept had any place in the Highlands, the "crofting" clansfolk, and all the other assertions that not only did not happen but could not have happened in clan society as it existed before the eighteenth century – can have lasted so long when the facts were palpably otherwise.

The reality must be revealed. It is not true to say that the Highlands were Catholic, nor that they were "mostly Catholic", nor "mostly Catholic and Episcopalian". (The MacGregors, MacPhersons, Stewarts, and Robertsons, named in one text, along with many of the MacDonalds, who were also mentioned, were Protestant.) In 1750, there were certainly a few Highlanders who were Catholic – for that matter, there were still a few Lowlanders, and a few English people, who were Catholic: but the Highland Catholics were a very small proportion of the whole. In 1691 the Master of Stair wrote that "the MacDonalds" were "the only popish clan in the kingdom", which (he thought) justified the attempted extirpation of the Glen Coe people:[260] but he was erring on the other side of the balance. There were a few Roman Catholic clans. They included the MacNeills of Barra, the Grants of Glenmoriston (though not the members of the main Grant clan), the Chisholms, and the clansfolk acknowledging the Duke of Gordon in the Banffshire Highlands. The MacDonalds of Clan Ranald, of Glengarry, of Keppoch, and of Glencoe,[261] were also Catholic, although their kinsmen and comrades the MacDonalds of Clan Donald had adopted the reformed religion. The Farquharsons, too, were members of the older church, although their close allies in the Clan Chattan (MacIntoshes, MacPhersons, Davidsons, and so on) were Protestant. Besides these, the Camerons[262] and the MacRaes were Catholics for some time after the Revolution of 1688. The great majority of the Highlanders, however, were Protestant.

31. A small minority

The Roman Catholic Highlanders, in 1750 and for years before that, were in a small minority. When Dr Webster took his census (1743-55), he asked each parish minister for the total number living in his parish, and also how many Protestants and Catholics were included in that number. According to the figures returned to him, in only sixty-one of the 162 Highland parishes were there any Catholics *at all*: the greater part of the Highlands was solidly Protestant. Of the sixty-one parishes which were not wholly Protestant, thirty-six numbered their Catholic populations in single figures – between one and eight. (So in 137 Highland parishes, out of 162, there were either no Catholics whatever, or fewer than nine.) In only twenty-five parishes (fifteen per cent of the total) were Catholics present in double figures – Dores had twelve, Callander thirteen, and so on. In only seventeen parishes (out of 162, or just over ten per cent) were there as many as seventy Catholics. These parishes were Ardnamurchan, South Uist, and Small Isles, which included areas where the Clan Ranald lived; Kilmonivaig, Glenelg, Boleskine, and Laggan, in some parts of which the Keppoch and Glengarry MacDonalds were found; Barra, the home of the MacNeills; Inveravon, Kirkmichael (Banffshire), and Mortlach, which contained members of the Duke of Gordon's clan; Crathie, Glenmuick, and Strathdon, where lived the Farquharsons; Kilmorack and Kiltarlity, which included parts of the Chisholm clan country; and the parish of Urquhart and Glenmoriston, which contained the country of the Grants of Glenmoriston.

In only three Highland parishes were most of the inhabitants Catholics – Barra, South Uist, and Small Isles. 159 out of the 162 Highland parishes had a majority of

Protestants – virtually all of them (as the later, O.S.A., reports showed) Presbyterians. At the middle point of the eighteenth century, in less than a tenth of the Highland parishes – fifteen, out of 162 – were there as many as 100 Catholics. In other words, in over ninety per cent of the Highland parishes there were fewer than 100 Catholics. Indeed, in 101 Highland parishes (which covered probably two-thirds of the Highlands) there was not a single Catholic. So in more than three-fifths (62.3%) of the Highland parishes there were no Catholics whatever.

To sum up, of the 162 Highland parishes, only 61 had *any* Catholics; only 25 had ten or more; only 17 had seventy or more; only 15 had 100 or more; and only three had a majority of Catholics.[263]

A. G. MacDonell's reference to "the Catholic clans of the North and West" was particularly misleading, since the further north one went, the fewer Catholics there were. In the whole of Ross-shire only twenty Catholics appeared in the Webster returns, despite the claim mentioned above that the (Ross-shire) neighbours of the Black Isle's Protestants were "all . . . Catholic". One writer, listing the areas where there were "Catholic populations", which were "almost intuitively Jacobite", included Morvern;[264] but according to Webster, Morvern had a mere six Catholics to savour their intuitive Jacobitism, as opposed to 1217 Protestants (two hundred times as many). In Sutherland, and in the Gaelic part of Caithness, there were no Catholics whatever. Catholicism, that is to say, was particularly rare north of the Beauly River and Glenelg Bay, and completely unknown north of the Dornoch Firth and Loch Kirkaig. As for the Black Isle's defiant Protestantism, "when all their Highland neighbours were Catholic", the fact is that none of their neighbours – MacKenzies, Munros, Frasers – were Catholic. Throughout the whole of the Highlands, those Highlanders who adhered to the old church in 1750 were a minute proportion of the total number. In the 162 parishes there were 295,566 people; the Catholics among them numbered 12,831, and the Protestants 282,735. In other words, 4.34% of the Highlanders were Catholics, while 95.66% were Protestants.[265] Of every 10,000 Highlanders, 9566 were Protestant.

It is true that the Webster figures were all supplied by Presbyterian ministers, and perhaps some might suspect them of trying to minimize the number of local Catholics. However, a papal delegate (one William Leslie) estimated in 1678 that there were some 12,000 Highland Catholics: that judgement was considerably earlier than the Webster calculation of 12,831, but was very close to it numerically.[266] Another Catholic estimate, in 1764, only a year or two after Webster's work, was that the Highland Catholics numbered 13,166.[267] This again is very close to the Webster return.

These figures scarcely support the assertion that "the Highlands were Catholic", or that "the Highlander was a Papist", unregenerate or otherwise. However, no doubt it is more exciting to think that the Highlanders still wallowed in the old-fashioned religion associated with the authoritarian states of the European continent, and it fits well with Lowland allegations that the clan chiefs were similarly authoritarian. This linkage was trumpeted by the writer of an article that appeared in the *Gentleman's Magazine* in 1739. He declared that in the Highlands "most of the inhabitants ... are subject to the Will and Command of their Popish disaffected Chieftains, who have always opposed ... the English Tongue"; "they are brought up in Principles of Tyranny and Arbitrary Government", and "depend upon foreign Papists as their main support".[268]

If a historian has convinced himself, by reading other historians, that "most" of the Highlanders were Catholic, and that their chiefs were all "popish" petty tyrants, there is perhaps a temptation to avoid descending to actual facts or authentic numbers, and thus to steer clear of any arduous arithmetic.

32. As if they had been Christians

Returning to the unassailable facts of history, it is clear that the great majority of the Highlanders (95 or 96 out of every 100) had accepted the changes in the predominant religion from Catholicism to Protestantism, and from Episcopalianism to Presbyterianism, changes which echoed what had happened in many other parts of northern Europe, with a forbearance which showed their lack of concern with the minutiae of religious dogma. The minister of Petty wrote in the N.S.A.: "The changes of the national forms of religion seem to have extended to the North Highlands, with comparatively little excitement in the public mind, and without having led to much personal or domestic suffering. Hence we have no places rendered interesting by a martyr's grave."[269] (How fortunate are those places which similarly fall short of "interesting"!) The same thing happened in the South Highlands. John MacVicar, for example, a suitably named sixteenth-century clergyman at Inveraray, ministered alike to Catholics and Protestants: he had a font with two stoups, one containing plain water to baptize Protestants, and one containing holy water to baptize Catholics.[270] One report from the Outer Hebrides, where the people of South Uist and Barra were ostensibly Catholic, said (in Paul Hopkins' words) that "the people generally were neither Protestant nor Catholic, although more inclined to Catholicism".[271] Similar moderation was shown by the Highlanders at the next shift in the religious rotation, when the presbyter ousted the prelate.

While the supposed Highland "barbarians" composed their differences thus amicably, the same distinctions in the urbane and enlightened Lowlands, among the "douce" and "quiet" Lowlanders (as Scott called the Lowlanders, including himself), led to persecution, armed conflict, and the deliberate incineration of live human beings who had a marginally different interpretation of identical sacred writings. Inside the Highland line, forebearance and magnanimity ruled; outside the Highland line, a religion claiming to be based on merciful love and kindness turned out to produce excruciating hatred and venom. Anyone in the Lowlands suspected of rejecting the idea of a deity altogether was of course beyond the pale: in 1697 a twenty-year-old Edinburgh student called Thomas Aikenhead was convicted – on the evidence of a single witness – of uttering atheistical opinions, and was punished for such foolish independent thoughts (not even actions) by being hanged on a gallows specially erected on the road between Edinburgh and Leith.[272] In the same year, a few months later, seven men and women at Paisley were first hanged "for a few minutes", then cut down and burned alive, because the sagacious Lowland authorities had found them guilty of defying true religion by performing physically impossible deeds of "witchcraft": the full story of that and similar events will come later. Thus was Lowland civilization vindicated.[273] The English were not behindhand in such virtuous work. In 1717 a "witch", Mary Hicks, found guilty by the feeble-minded local justices, was hanged at Huntingdon; alongside her, simultaneously suffocating on the gallows, was her nine-year-old daughter Elizabeth – who had been able to raise destructive rainstorms at will. Watching the executions was Edward, Mary's husband and Elizabeth's father, who had informed on both of them.

The Highlanders' religion was less bloodthirsty. Their observances often surprised outsiders. When Prince Charles' army reached Derby during the '45, a gentleman there told a friend of his astonishment "to see these savages [sic], from the officer to the commonest man, at their several meals, first stand up and pull off their bonnets, and then lift up their eyes in a most solemn and devout manner, and mutter something in their own gibberish, by way, I suppose, of saying grace, as if [sic] they had been so many Christians".[274]

33. *Serious and religious deportment*

It is true that where the existing Episcopalian clergyman was personally popular, his parishioners refused to allow him to be replaced by a Presbyterian, as in the case already mentioned of Mr Lindsay of Glenorchy; similar events occurred, as we saw earlier, in Lochcarron, Gairloch, Petty, Rosskeen, Sleat, Snizort, Muthill, and scores of other Highland parishes. But this was personal or political preference, not doctrinal dogmatism: the Highlanders accepted the official religion with a simple piety and devotion which included a readiness to make a round journey of up to twenty-five miles, summer and winter, to attend the Sunday services, but which did not extend to the fervour of the fanatic. David Stewart said the Highlanders had "a strong sentiment of piety"; in the parish where he grew up, "the people travelled six, seven, and twelve miles to church, and returned the same evening every Sunday in summer, and frequently in winter" – and it was the same "in all extensive parishes".275 Dorothy Wordsworth, visiting the Highlands in 1803, asked her Gaelic hosts at Inversnaid on Loch Lomond where the church was: "they replied, 'Not very far"; and when we asked how far, they said, 'Perhaps about four or five miles'." Dorothy Wordsworth added, clearly referring to the Highlands, "in the lonely parts of Scotland they make little of a journey of nine or ten miles to a preaching".276 Odo Blundell even said that Catholics who lived at the western end of Glen Quoich walked thirty miles to attend mass at Fort Augustus, "starting at four o'clock in the morning".277

William Gilpin wrote of his Highland tour in 1776: "Throughout the whole country we found not only a pleasing simplicity, and civility of manners, but a serious, and religious deportment among the common people, which can hardly be conceived by those, who are acquainted with the prophaneness and profligacy of the lower ranks near the capital [Edinburgh, of course, in the Lowlands]. A small Erse bible is the Highlander's usual companion; and it is common to see him reading it, as he tends his cattle, or rests upon the road. We had frequently this pleasing sight. It is common also, when you enter his little cottage, to see the mother spinning, or knitting, and the children standing round either reading in the bible, or repeating their catechism."278

34. No scoffing or insult

The artless approach of the Highlanders to religious observance, together with their own older superstitious beliefs, prompted Alexander Cunningham to write of them: "Their religion is taken partly from the Druids, partly from Papists, and partly from Protestants."279 This obliging laxity on the finer points of theology was made a matter of reproach in some areas as late as the N.S.A. reports. The minister of Morvern said in 1843: "In former times, religious knowledge was, in a great measure, communicated orally, and, not withstanding the exertions of the established clergy and other authorized instructors, it is not surprising that opinions handed down from father to son, among a people 'reformed', it may be said, more by influence than by argument, should be tinged by many errors."280 Like Cunningham, the Kilfinichen reporter (writing in 1842) suspected ancient priesthoods. "A dash of superstition is mixed up with their feelings, and may be traced to some opinions handed down by their ancestors, perhaps from the time of the Druids."281

Stewart affirmed that "the Highlanders, though Presbyterians, did not, in former times, rigidly adhere to the tenets of that church", while, on the other hand, "they were strangers to the very existence of the sects that have branched off from the national church".282 But when, after Culloden, sectaries made their appearance in the Highlands, the Gaels showed their lack of bigotry by giving them a quiet and attentive hearing – conduct which formed a strong contrast to that of the Lowlanders, who thought they displayed their piety by shouting down anyone who differed somewhat from them in matters of canonical interpretation. Thomas Wilkinson, a Lakeland Quaker to whom (or rather to whose shovel) William Wordsworth wrote one of his quaintest poems ("Spade! with which Wilkinson hath tilled his lands . . ."), left his digging and accompanied another Quaker, John Pemberton, on an evangelizing tour through Scotland in 1787.[283] In the Lowlands they met with many difficulties. Of various Lowland meetings, Wilkinson wrote: "Without doors there was much rioting and rudeness . . . The conduct of some was truly painful . . . The people seemed rude, undisciplined . . . The people were at one time so unsettled, that when John Pemberton rose to deliver what came before him, he was obliged to sit down again." At Kilmaurs, in Lowland Ayrshire, "we experienced the rudest conduct I ever beheld on such an occasion; not only many within were unsettled and acted in an unbecoming manner, but a mob collected without, shouting, and giving other proofs of indecorous behaviour. On going to the door at different times to endeavour to still them, and at last taking my stand on the stairs, I was frequently hit by the dirt that was thrown at me." Very different was their experience in the Highlands. The only time they encountered incivility was when a drunk appeared at a meeting at Tarbert, on Loch Lomond; and he quietened down when Wilkinson sat beside him. At Campbeltown, "no scoffing or insult was offered us, nor was anything of a light behaviour observable". At Bunawe, "a considerable number assembled, and behaved with remarkable solidity, without any appearance of lightness or of whispering". This was particularly noteworthy in view of the unusual observances of a Quaker meeting: "We have sometimes seen conduct of a very different kind, even among the well-disposed: it is often no easy matter to make strangers feel the propriety of waiting in silence before the Lord." When the travellers re-entered the Lowlands, and held a meeting at Forres, "it was apparent we had left the Highlands from the want of solidity among the people".[284]

Thomas Wilkinson, wiping the mud from his clothes, can have had no doubt as to where the true barbarians were, or where the true gentility lay.

35. Highland characteristics

In the last few pages we have been surveying some indications of the kind of people produced by clan society. After Culloden the axe was laid to the root of that society, the clan ownership of the land, so the society produced by that economic and social foundation also changed, and with it in due course the behaviour of the Highlanders. However, a society so long and so firmly established, and so ensconced in the hearts of the people, did not transform itself overnight. It took years before even the most covetous charter holders could fully appreciate that their puny pieces of parchment penmanship now had all the irresistible force of the law, which (if the charter holders should request it) would be put into effect, with whatever violence and bloodshed were required, by the authorities in Edinburgh and London: it was many decades before the clansfolk themselves could be persuaded that the whole infrastructure of their lives, a stable system which had endured for centuries, and which if their preferences were to be considered would have endured for ever, was now to be destroyed. For decades the clansfolk continued to live as they had always done, with the same principles and the same patterns of behaviour. As a result they continued to display the same characteristics during the rest of the eighteenth century, and for that matter into the early part of the nineteenth; so the remarks made by David Stewart, writing about 1820, on the soldiers in the eighteenth-century Highland regiments (as well as what he had to say about their predecessors), may fairly be taken to throw a light on the manners and conduct of the Highlanders during the clan system. The quotations given in the next pages are from Stewart's *Sketches of the Highlanders*, except where otherwise ascribed.

It may be thought it has already been demonstrated conclusively what kind of people the old Highlanders were. It should be remembered, however, that by the 1840s many of the Highland small tenants had been reduced to starvation and pauperism, confined to scanty crofts on the worst land, often kept alive only by charity, and told that the Highlands were quite unable to feed them (even though, in the great farms immediately next to them, on the wide lands that used to be theirs, vast amounts of food were being produced and shipped off to supply – for cash down – many thousands in the massive towns now mushrooming in the Lowlands and England). Lady MacAskill, commenting on one of the feeding stations set up after the 1846 potato blight, said: "At the appointed time and place, the poor creatures troop down in hundreds, wretched and thin, starved and wan. Some have clothing, some almost none, and some are a mass of rags . . . they wept aloud as they told of their miseries."[285] To explain away this dreadful state of affairs, and to exculpate the proprietors from any responsibility for it, many writers joined in a sustained onslaught on the Highlanders, their morals, their behaviour, and their character. (It is always more profitable to put down what will please the predominant people; the poor offer no affluence to their allies.) A central argument in the defence of the landlords' new regime was that these unhappy starvelings were typical, that the Highlanders had always been like that – feeble, demoralized, and useless to themselves or to anyone else. It is necessary, therefore, that the facts of the matter should be shown beyond dispute: it is an essential service to historical actuality – to the truth – to make it clear what an appalling catastrophe had overcome the Highland population, and how much these famished paupers differed from their forefathers, only a generation or two before – people strong and well built, active and quick-witted, and (when provoked) such potent fighters that few could withstand them. Much evidence has been given; much more is available.

The irrefutable records of the Highland regiments are an embarrassment to those who claim that the entire Highland population lived perpetually on the edge of famine, at the same time cowering before their chiefs: such men could never have developed the mental and physical qualities that are essential in the make-up of a good soldier. In fact the Highlanders made superlative soldiers. The reasons are simple. The Highlanders came from a society in which there was virtually no "upper class", as the term is now understood, and where therefore they were not condemned to constant arduous toil to make up the landlord's rent, nor had they to scurry round day after day, knuckling their foreheads at the beck and call of an employer: so they had been able to develop a self-confident and independent character, taking decisions for themselves. They came from a population scattered thinly over great stretches of ground; therefore they had learned to be self-reliant. (The constant cries of "congestion" and "over-population", as we see elsewhere, are based not on the indisputable facts but on the defensive propaganda of the proprietors.) They habitually ranged the moors and mountains while hunting, shooting, fishing, herding, and foraging the fruits of nature; therefore they were healthy, active, far-sighted, and resourceful. Their normal daily lives involved co-operating with their fellows in the pursuit of game, and in their joint-farm operations; therefore they were used to combining with each other to effect a common purpose. These characteristics could not fail, when the test came, to make them excellent soldiers.

36. Gratitude, kindness, friendship

David Stewart was brought up among Gaelic-speaking clansfolk, and it is significant that his general opinion of the human race was favourable: "gratitude, kindness, and friendship, are natural to man", he thought.[286] And it is surely true that the adjectives "kind", "humane", "special", and even "generous", are based on the idea that people are benevolent towards others who are related to them, or indeed towards humanity generally. On the other hand, a cynic might say that there have been many places, many times, many environments, during the last three hundred years, in which an observer would have struggled to reach such an encouraging estimate of the human race.

General Sir John Moore was killed at Corunna in 1809, and buried there "at dead of night" – "not a drum was heard, not a funeral note".[287] Moore had given his general opinion of the Highlanders to David Stewart in 1805, it seems at Hythe, Kent, where the two officers had been stationed together in that year: Moore as the brigadier-general, Stewart as a major in the 78th Ross-shire Highlanders. Moore thought (said Stewart) that "under an officer who understands and values their character" the Highlanders made indomitable soldiers. "Under such an officer, they will conquer or die on the spot, while their action, their hardihood, and abstinence, enable them to bear up against a severity of fatigue under which larger, and apparently stronger, men would sink. But it is the principles of integrity and moral correctness that I admire most in Highland soldiers, and this was the trait that first caught my attention. It is this that makes them trustworthy, and makes their courage sure, and not that kind of flash in the pan, which would scale a bastion today, and tomorrow be alarmed at the fire of a picquet."[288] When Sir John had been fighting the Irish rebels in 1798, his forces had included the Dumbarton Fencible Regiment (Dumbartonshire was a border county, covering both Highland and Lowland areas). Stewart wrote that "by the recommendation of General Moore, a detachment of the regiment was ordered as a guard to 400 rebel prisoners sent to Prussia, with directions that 'the detachment should consist entirely of Highlanders, as the service required confidential, trustworthy men'."[289]

Talking to a French general after the end of the Napoleonic wars, Stewart found he had much the same sentiments. The Highlanders, said the general, "are brave soldiers. If they had good officers, I should not like to meet them unless I was well supported."[290] And at the attack on Toulouse in 1814, another French officer saw the 42nd (the Black Watch) and 79th (the Camerons) Highland regiments advancing in their customary dress, and exclaimed "Mon Dieu! How firm these sans culottes are!" (The "sans culottes" of the French Revolution wore full-length trousers instead of knee-breeches, or culottes; the Frenchman used the term for the kilted Highlanders.) The main task of soldiers, unhappily, is to kill the soldiers on the other side; these encomiums on the Highland soldiery are repeated to show their excellent qualities, albeit they were put to such grim uses.[291]

The clan system (said Stewart) "generated and cherished a spirit of independence and self-respect"; the Highlanders "were taught to believe themselves descended of persons distinguished for bravery and virtue from a remote antiquity. Hence the desire of preserving the honour of a respected ancestry stimulated them to daring actions in the field, as the dread of becoming a reproach to their memory deterred from the commission of crime in the common intercourse of life."[292] Dr Jackson wrote: "The Highlander was thus brave as a soldier, decorous and correct in his moral conduct. His exterior aspect might be rugged, but the soul was lofty and enthusiastic; capable at once of receiving and retaining honourable impressions."[293]

37. The Civil Wars

Much of the evidence about the Highlanders' qualities can most conveniently be dealt with chronologically. The same traits of character were displayed and recorded for the better part of two centuries, both while the clan system was in full flower, and then for some time when it was under sustained (but sternly resisted, and therefore only very gradually effective) onslaught from the chiefs.

In 1645 the Marquis of Montrose, fighting for King Charles, commanded a force of 750: some were Highlanders (mostly Athollmen), and the others were their fellow-Gaels from Ireland. He took them from Dunkeld to Dundee (twenty-four miles as the crow flies, and of course further on the ground), and attacked and captured the city; but immediately he heard that a Parliamentary force, more than five times as strong, was almost upon him. So in one continuing operation he led his men back safely to the Highlands by an enormous detour (via Glen Esk), occasionally halting and fighting off his pursuers. In the first twenty-four hours after leaving their Dunkeld base, the soldiers had marched over fifty miles, besides capturing an enemy town: and they still had many more miles to go before reaching safety. (The "wretched and thin, starved and wan" Highlanders of a later era, in 1846, could scarcely have shown such endurance.) Dr Wishart praised "the hardiness of the soldiers in encountering all extremities with patience"; for some ninety miles "they had been often in fight, always upon their march, without either meat [food] or sleep, or intermission, or the least refreshment".[294]

During repeated campaigns in 1644 and 1645, Montrose and the army that he had raised among the Highlanders underwent "exertions almost incredible. So extraordinary were the marches which he [Montrose] performed, that, on many occasions, the appearance of his army was the first notice the enemy had of his approach; and of his retreats, the first intelligence was, that he was beyond their reach." Before the Battle of Inverlochy in 1645, Montrose and his Highland troops "marched thirty miles by an unfrequented route, across the mountains of Lochaber, during a heavy fall of snow, and came at night in front of the enemy, when they believed him in another part of the country". They then "lay upon their arms the whole night" (that is, with their weapons at the ready), cold and wet as they were. When the armies clashed in the morning, the opposing forces had time to fire their muskets only once; then "Montrose's men fell in upon them furiously sword in hand, with a great shout, and advanced with such impetuosity, that they routed the whole army", which was twice as large as their own, "and put them to flight, and pursued them for about nine miles, making dreadful slaughter all the way". Montrose's force lost four killed; the enemy lost 1500. David Stewart added: "Similar to this were six successive battles fought by Montrose, the loss on his side being equally small, and that on the side of the Covenanters proportionately great."[295]

So formidable were the Highlanders that not infrequently their antagonists (after testing their mettle) refused to meet them again. In the 1650s, during the Commonwealth, the victorious Parliamentary army established a fort at Inverlochy in Lochaber with the intention of intimidating the Camerons, and their chief Lochiel. However, after several brushes with the Camerons, it was the garrison who were intimidated, and in the end a report of Lochiel "or his men being in the neighbourhood prevented all egress from the fort", and the Lochaber Highlanders were left undisturbed.[296]

38. Stuart versus Hanover

One of the Hanoverians at the Battle of Killiecrankie, 1689, said that at "the sun's going down . . . the Highlanders advanced on us like madmen".[297] One excuse advanced for the defeat of the Government forces was that the soldiers wasted time fixing bayonets in their muskets after firing a volley. But against such opponents excuses were needless. The author of Lord Dundee's *Memoirs* said: "Then the Highlanders fired, threw down their fusils [guns], rushed in with sword, target, and pistol, upon the enemy, who did not maintain their ground two minutes after the Highlanders were amongst them; and, I dare be bold to say, there were scarce ever such strokes given in Europe, as were given that day by the Highlanders. Many of General MacKay's officers and soldiers were cut down through the skull and neck to the very breast; others had skulls cut off above their ears, like night-caps; some soldiers had both their bodies and cross-belts cut through at one blow; pikes and small swords were cut like willows; and whoever doubts of this, may consult the witness of the tragedy."[298] Another account said that Brigadier-General Balfour, one of the Government commanders, refused quarter, and paid the price: he "spurned mercy with insults and was cleft from collar bone to thigh".[299] (This reminds one of the Blair Atholl minister, who wrote in the O.S.A. that "it is confidently asserted" that two Athollmen, one Robertson and one Stewart, a few years before "cut, each of them, a deer in two, by a single stroke of their broadswords".)[300]

The men who dealt these gigantic blows at Killiecrankie, such as had been "scarce ever . . . given in Europe", were, we know, because our historians regularly tell us, only the emaciated survivors of regular famines; one can only conclude that if the Highlanders had been able to get themselves a few square meals before the battle they would have been awesome warriors indeed.

Sir John Dalrymple said of the Highlanders at this era (1681-92): "To make an opening in regular troops, and to conquer, they reckoned the same thing, because, in close engagements, and in broken ranks, no regular troops would withstand them."[301]

Every contemporary description of the Highlanders that we have appears to say what fine physical specimens they were. At the beginning of the eighteenth century, the Duke of Atholl was said to be "able to raise 6000 of the best men in the kingdom, well armed, and ready to sacrifice their all for the king's service".[302] William Thomson said that the Highlanders had "ever been foremost in the field" of "martial ardour".[303]

In September 1745 the Highland rebels took Fort George, near Inverness. "This was one of the many instances of the terror which the Highlanders, at that period, inspired. When they appeared before the fort, and were preparing to assault it sword in hand, the [Lowland] soldiers could not be kept to their guns, and the commander was obliged to surrender the garrison."[304] Perhaps the Lowlanders' commanders should have told them that the Highlanders, enfeebled (as we are now told) by constant hunger, would clearly hardly be able to lift their weapons; so it is strange that they did not take such an obvious step.

In the same rebellion, Lord Loudoun, with the royal army, marched from Inverness to attack Moy Hall, having been informed that Prince Charles was there. The wife of MacIntosh of MacIntosh was in charge of the hall, though with only two hundred clansmen. However, she marched out with her little force, and put small parties well apart across the line of advance. In this she was aided, said the N.S.A., by a local clansman, Donald Fraser Smith. "When Lord Loudoun came within hearing, a command was passed from man to man, in a loud voice, along a distance of half a mile: the MacIntoshes, MacGillivrays, and MacBeans, to form instantly on the centre, – the MacDonalds on the right, – the Frasers on the left", and so on. That so few Highlanders, facing a whole army, were able calmly to carry out such a manoeuvre shows their firmness, their courage, and their confidence in themselves and their comrades. Loudoun, believing that the clans whose names he heard were then facing him in strength, immediately retreated to Inverness, and then to Sutherland. "Such was the terror inspired by the Highlanders of that day, even in military men of much experience like Lord Loudoun."[305]

39. Fidelity and valour

The bravery of the Highlanders was legendary, and from the 1730s onwards it was turned to advantage by the rulers of Britain: William Pitt the elder boasted that he had recruited the Highland soldiers whose gallantry was profusely displayed in every part of the globe. In a Commons speech in 1766 he said: "I sought for merit wherever it could be found; it is my boast that I was the first minister who looked for it and found it in the mountains of the north. I called it forth, and drew into your service a hardy and intrepid race of men, men who . . . had gone nigh to have overturned the State in the war before the last [in 1745-6].

These men in the last war [1756-1763] were brought to combat on your side; they served with fidelity, as they fought with valour, and conquered for you in every quarter of the world."[306] The original Highland regiment, for example, the Black Watch, fought (and with very few exceptions was victorious) in Flanders, France, and Germany, in Spain and Portugal, in America, Canada, and the West Indies, in Africa, and around the Mediterranean. Even when the army of which they were part was defeated, the performance of the Highlanders could not be faulted – as, for example, at Fontenoy, at Ticonderoga, and at New Orleans, as will be seen below.

The Highlanders who enlisted to fight in the British army were very particular in their enthusiasms, and displayed the independence which was the manifest result of the clan system. They would join the Highland regiments, but refused to join other formations. They would sign up under officers they liked, whether their own chiefs and chieftains or others, but not under those they did not approve of, whatever the inducements. "It is well known that the bounty-money had no influence in the Highlands, when men were raised for the 42nd and other Highland corps" in the Seven Years' War (1756-63) and the American War (1775-83). "In 1776, upwards of 800 men were recruited for the 42nd [Black Watch] in a few weeks, on a bounty of one guinea, while officers who offered ten and twelve guineas for recruits, which they were raising for their commissions, could not get a man till the national corps were completed." Highlanders would even enrol for service abroad under officers they esteemed, for less money than they could have got for service in this country. "Numbers of young Highlanders enlisted for foreign service (and this sometimes in bands together,) on receiving less than one-half the bounty money given at the same time by officers for their commissions in the regular and fencible regiments for home-service, as likewise by others for militia substitutes." When David Stewart was recruiting for the 78th, which was then in the East Indies, and the men knew they would probably be "embarking for that country in a few months; yet they engaged with me, and other officers, for ten guineas, when they could have got twenty guineas as militia substitutes", whose service was limited to this country.[307]

It seems that the Highlanders had not heard of the "economic imperative", the inexorable desire for more money which historians now tell us governs, and therefore excuses, all human actions – particularly, it appears, it regulated the conduct of the Highland landlords. Perhaps it is only the upper class that is ruled by it?[308]

40. Battle of Fontenoy

In 1743 the *Westminster Journal* said that the soldiers of the Black Watch were "certainly the finest regiment in the service [i.e., the entire British army], being tall, well-made men, and very stout [well-built]".[309] Numbers of the Black Watch soldiers, stationed in Ireland a year or two later, defended Methodist preachers against the attacks made on them by raging mobs of civilized city-dwellers in Limerick and Cork, and John Wesley called them "men fit to appear before princes".[310]

At the Battle of Fontenoy in 1745 the Black Watch encountered an enemy for the first time: the regiment won much praise. When they cleared the French outposts before the battle, "the Highlanders were taken great notice of for their spirited conduct". The main conflict opened by an attack on a redoubt held by the enemy, when a force including "the Highlanders with sword, pistol, and dirk, forced them out".[311] The colonel of the regiment at that time was the chief of the Clan Munro. Dr Doddridge wrote, "the gallantry of Sir Robert Munro and his regiment was the theme of admiration through all Britain". The Highlanders, however, very sensibly could not see that there was anything laudable in standing in rows to be shot at, whatever other British soldiers were ordered to do, and Munro therefore obtained leave to fight "according to the usage of his countrymen". So when the French were firing a volley, the Highlanders clapped to the ground. "On receiving the French fire, and instantly after its discharge, they sprang up, and coming close to the enemy, poured in their shot upon them to the certain destruction of multitudes, and drove them precipitately through their own lines; then retreating drew up again, and attacked them a second time after the same manner."[312] A French account said of one of these impetuous charges at Fontenoy that "the Highland furies rushed in upon us with more violence than ever did a sea driven by a tempest".[313] One Highlander "with his broad sword killed nine men, and making a stroke at the tenth, had his arm shot off".[314] Later on in the battle, said one who participated in it, "a brigade of Dutch were ordered to attack a rising ground, on which were posted the troops called the King of France's own Guards. The Highlanders were to support them. The Dutch conducted their march and their attack with great deliberation, halting, and firing, and halting, every twenty paces. The Highlanders, losing all patience with this kind of fighting, which gave the enemy such time and opportunity to fire at their leisure, dashed forward, passed the Dutch, and the first ranks giving their firelocks to the rear rank, they drew their swords, and soon drove the French from their ground." By these tactics the Highlanders not only triumphed in this sector, but suffered fewer losses; about twelve were killed or wounded, while the Dutch lost five times as many.[315]

41. "All or nothing"

However, some of the soldiers among the allies at Fontenoy came from other places and other environments; consequently they were not quite so spirited as the Highlanders, and in the end the allied army was defeated. Many writers have accused the Highlanders of being able to do no more than mount a wild charge; and if the charge failed (they allege) the Highlanders were completely at a loss. A. G. MacDonell (despite his Highland surname) spoke for the Lowland multitude when he wrote, "once the failure had set in, the Highlander would do no more. He was not a defensive soldier. He had not the qualities of the Saxon who fought at Hastings, or the ring of Lowlanders who surrounded the king at Flodden. He had no idea of fighting a rearguard action in the style of Marshal Ney. With the Gael it was all or nothing. There must be either a smashing victory or else a smashing defeat."[316] This is, simply, inaccurate (or, in the stronger language of a history professor, "clearly rubbish"); and there is so much evidence available that such egregious error is inexcusable. MacDonell alleges that the Highlanders (while – he asserted – being quick to boast about their performance in some battles) "were careful to ignore their ancestors' conspicuous absence from",[317] for example, the Battle of Pinkie, in 1547; the fact is that not only were the Highlanders there ("on the right wing the Earl of Argyll with four thousand West Highlanders, and on the left the Islesmen, with MacLeod, MacGregor, and other chieftains", wrote P. F. Tytler),[318] but in the battle they showed exactly those qualities which MacDonell insisted they had not got. Jean de Beaugué's account of Pinkie said, "the Highlanders, who show their courage on all occasions, gave proof of their conduct at this time, for they kept together in one body, and made a very handsome and orderly retreat".[319] In 1645, too, Montrose's Highlanders, withdrawing successfully in one continuous retreat from Dundee to Atholl, and continually fighting off the pursuing enemy, gave the lie to MacDonell's facile sneers.[320] When Prince Charles was comprehensively defeated at the Battle of Culloden in 1746, a London newspaper said: "as to the Highlanders, most of them retreated in such order as to prevent them suffering much in the pursuit."[321] (Many of those who were injured and unable to escape were then casually murdered by the victorious English and Lowlanders, who were presumably demonstrating that, in MacDonell's imposing words, the law was now stronger than the sword.)[322] The Highlanders showed the same tough defensive ability at Falkirk in 1746, when General Hawley sent in a cavalry charge against the Jacobite Highland army. An eye-witness said: "The resistance of the Highlanders was so incredibly obstinate that the English, after having been for some time engaged pell-mell with them in their ranks, were at length repulsed and forced to retire."[323]

The Highlanders displayed the same qualities at Fontenoy. When the order came to draw back, wrote the Black Watch Captain John Munro, "we were ordered to cover the retreat of the army [Saxons, Lowlanders in their rings, and all], as the only regiment that could be kept to their duty". Fortunately the 19th Regiment had the good sense to take pattern from the Black Watch, and in the event the two regiments, the 42nd and the 19th, covered the withdrawal, "the two battalions fronting and forcing back the enemy at every hundred paces" as the official despatches said afterwards.[324] An enemy account called this "a soldier-like retreat".[325] This duty was carried out in such masterly fashion that afterwards Lord Crawford, the commander of the two battalions, in the words of his biographer "pulled off his hat, and returning them thanks, said, they had acquired as much honour in covering so great a retreat, as if they had gained the battle".[326] The commander-in-chief was equally pleased with the Highlanders' staunch defensive achievement, and told them (as we saw above) "he would be happy to grant the men any favour which they chose to ask". Instead of the Highlanders' minds running on money, or drink, "the men assured him that no favour he could bestow would gratify them so much, as a pardon for one of their comrades, a soldier of the regiment, who had been tried by court-martial for allowing a prisoner to escape, and was under sentence of a heavy corporal punishment, which, if inflicted, would bring disgrace on them all, and on their families and country. This favour, of course, was instantly granted."[327]

The cool tenacity of the Highlanders in the withdrawal after Fontenoy (and in many earlier battles) was repeated, for example – as will be shown later – in the retreat after Ticonderoga, and again under the walls of New Orleans. But when a writer (like MacDonell) has an exciting theory to propound, and a theory, moreover, which insults nobody but Highlanders, who needs to worry about facts?

42. Highly disciplined

The onset of the Highlanders was not the wild, undisciplined charge that has sometimes been conjured up by anglophone observers. It is true that G. N. Clark, the Regius Professor of Modern History in the University of Cambridge, kept up the good work of his predecessor G. M. Trevelyan by declaring, in his *Oxford History of England* volume, *The Later Stuarts*, that "the highlanders [as opposed to the not usually lower-cased lowlanders or english, presumably] had dash without discipline or staying power".[328]

Dr Stuart MacDonald gave a different view, describing the "Highland *battle drill* of bringing the charge to the *shock* and the *press*". Many Lowland and English writers, he agreed, preferred a more romantic mythology. "Loving the dramatic, some authors depict Highland battles as frantic braeside rushes of bellowing barbarians swishing axe and claymore, Homeric chiefs and their cadets to the fore, each hero dashing to be first upon the foe. Had this grotesque travesty been enacted, the leading heroes would have been shot down by their followers as all the muskets and pistols were discharged in the customary close-range volley. The truth is very different. The Highland battle charge of the seventeenth and eighteenth centuries was a highly disciplined movement, keeping the leading battle line as straight as possible, as the clans advanced at a steady jog. Only the last few yards were covered at a sprint, after one great single volley. Then the charge 'came to the shock', a shock which *pressed* the enemy tight, an ideal position for the use of dirk, targe and broadsword. Killiecrankie provided the perfect example of the tactic. Dundee, and Montrose before him, were the only two generals fully to appreciate the superiority of the *moving* disciplined Highlanders over the static regulars of their day."[329]

The Black Watch, wrote Stewart, "having sustained so moderate a loss in the battle [of Fontenoy], and having still nearly nine hundred men fit for service, was soon called out again". The enemy made a show of being about to attack Halle, and the Highlanders were sent (with some Dutch cavalry and grenadiers) to its support; but when the allied force arrived, the enemy retreated without a fight. The allies then returned to their original quarters, and "in the last day's march of thirty-eight miles, in a deep sandy road, it was observed, that the Dutch grenadiers and cavalry were overpowered with the heat and fatigue, but that not one man of the Highlanders was left behind".[330]

In 1747 part of the Black Watch was ordered to join an army being sent to Flanders. The *Caledonian Mercury* said that "when it was notified to the men that a part of them was to join the army [in Flanders], all claimed the preference to be permitted to embark, and it was necessary to draw lots, as none would remain behind".[331] The expedition was intended to relieve the town of Hulst, then besieged by the French. Unfortunately Hulst had surrendered to the enemy before these reinforcements could arrive, and so the allied troops had to re-embark. A large French force came up during this operation, and (said the *Hague Gazette*) "attacked 300 of the Highland regiment, who were the last to embark". Again the Highlanders did what MacDonell claimed they could never do, and brought off a successful rearguard action. "They behaved with so much bravery, that they beat off three or four times their number, killing many, and making some prisoners, with only the loss of four or five of their own number."[332]

The valour that the Black Watch had displayed at Fontenoy led the authorities to ask John Campbell, Earl of Loudoun, to raise another Highland regiment. In 1747 Loudoun's Highlanders went to Flanders, where they formed part of the garrison of Bergen-op-zoom when it was besieged by Count Lowendahl. In July it was reported that "the Highlanders, who were posted in Fort Rouro, which covers the lines of Bergen-op-zoom, made a sally sword in hand, in which they were so successful as to destroy the enemy's grand battery, and to kill so many of their men, that Count Lowendahl beat a parley, in order to bury the dead".[333] In the end the besiegers took the town, despite the resistance of the Scotch brigade. "Lieutenants Francis and Allan MacLean of the brigade were taken prisoners, and carried before General Lowendahl, who thus addressed them; 'Gentlemen, consider yourselves on parole. If all had conducted themselves as you and your brave corps have done, I should not now be master of Bergen-op-zoom'."[334]

43. A respect and regard

The kind of men the Highlanders were can be seen by the accounts of what the civilians of various countries thought of them. In those days there were fewer barracks, so regiments were often quartered in the houses of the local population, both in the British Isles and abroad. Civilians thus soon got to know how soldiers behaved. The arrival of soldiers in any locality was usually considered as a ruinous calamity by those who had to endure their churlish and often brutal conduct; yet – in marked contrast – the Highlanders were always popular.

When the Black Watch was in Flanders in 1743, Dr Doddridge wrote, it "was judged the most trustworthy guard of property, insomuch that the people in Flanders chose to have them always for their protection. Seldom were any of them drunk, and they as rarely swore. And the Elector Palatine wrote to his envoy in London, desiring him to thank the King of Great Britain for the excellent behaviour of the regiment while it was in his territories in 1743 and 1744; 'and for whose sake', he adds, 'I will always pay a respect and regard to a Scotchman in future'." In fact people where the Highlanders were stationed on the Continent (in 1743-4) often wanted "to have a Highland soldier quartered in each of their houses, 'as these men were not only quiet, kind, and domestic, but served as a protection against the rudeness of others'."[335] While in the field their actions gained high praise, "in quarters, their conduct was exemplary, and procured them the esteem and respect of those among whom they were stationed".[336] After the peace of 1748, the regiment was sent to Ireland. In that country there was frequent hostility between the local people and the soldiers stationed there; but though the Highlanders "were stationed in small detachments, and associated much with the people, the happiest cordiality subsisted between them".[337]

In 1755 a general war was again looming, and to enrol more men the Black Watch sent recruiting parties to the Highlands under the command of the chief of MacIntosh, who was a captain in the regiment. His mission was very successful, and he "quickly collected 500 men, the number he was desired to recruit: of these he enlisted 87 men in one forenoon. One morning, as he was sitting at breakfast in Inverness, 38 young men of the name of MacPherson, from Badenoch, appeared in front of the window, with an offer of their service to MacIntosh, their own immediate chief, the Laird of Cluny, being then in exile, in consequence of his attainder after the Rebellion."[338] Their "own immediate chief" not being available, the MacPhersons were prepared to serve under MacIntosh, who was the chief of the whole Clan Chattan.

In 1756 the Black Watch was sent to America. Its commander, Lieutenant-Colonel Campbell, later the Duke of Argyll, was promoted to lead another regiment. The Highlanders, naturally, had strong opinions as to who would be a suitable colonel of the regiment: they wanted Major Grant to succeed Campbell, and since often promotion in the army went by purchase, the men "came forward with a sum of money, subscribed among themselves, to purchase the lieutenant-colonelcy for Major Grant; but the promotion going in the regiment without purchase, the money was not required". So Major Grant became the colonel, as the Highlanders wished, without any payment being necessary.[339]

Highlanders had a strong desire to preserve every aspect of their own society, including its habitual dress. The 78th regiment, Fraser's Highlanders, was enrolled in 1757, and went to America. "When the regiment landed in North America it was proposed to change the uniform, as the Highland garb was said to be unfit for the severe winters, and the hot summers of that country. The officers and soldiers vehemently protested against any change, and Colonel Fraser explained to the Commander-in-Chief the strong attachment which the men cherished to their national dress, and the consequences that might be expected to follow, if they were deprived of it. This representation was successful." Fraser's Highlanders were six years in North America, and a soldier in the regiment said that "in the coldest winters our men were more healthy than those regiments who wore breeches and warm clothing".[340]

44. Attack on Ticonderoga

The Highlanders were never prepared to remain in the reserve, or to accept a merely supportive role, while the main effort was being made by other regiments (despite Professor Dr Donaldson's bizarre allegation that the Highlanders "had always depended on leadership"). In 1758, for example, a British army of 15,000 men – including the 42nd Regiment – was ordered to attack an extremely strong French defensive post at Ticonderoga, on Lake Champlain in what is now New York State. The post was defended by a virtually impervious breastwork, nine or ten feet (about three metres) high, the top lined with cannon and heavily armed defenders. The garrison had blocked the approaches by felling great oak trees, to the distance of a cannon shot from the actual fort.

The Black Watch was ordered to stay in the reserve, but remaining in safety while others shouldered the burden of fighting was not to the taste of these soldiers (cowering serfs though they all were, we are now told, at home in the Highlands). Few regiments, then or now, would object to the good fortune of avoiding all casualties: but these were different men. "The Highlanders, impatient at being left in the rear, could not be restrained, and rushing forward from the reserve, were soon in the front, endeavouring to cut their way through the trees with their broadswords." The Highlanders indeed – though the leadership, on which (said Donaldson) they had "always depended", had ordered them to remain in the rear – led the assault. Heavy fire from the fort killed many of them. At length the surviving Highlanders got through to the main fortification. But there was no way to mount the defences, owing to a failure of foresight not unusual among the officers who constituted the "leadership", many of whom owed their exalted rank solely to their parentage or their wealth. "No ladders had been provided for scaling the breastwork. The soldiers were obliged to climb up on each other's shoulders." The few who got through the defensive barrage to reach the top of the breastworks (including John Campbell, one of the two Highlanders who had been presented to George II in 1743) were instantly slain by the defenders. After four hours' onslaught, so many of the attacking force had been lost that the assault was abandoned. The Highlanders, however, "were so obstinate, that it was not till after the third order from the General that the commanding officer, Colonel Grant, was able to prevail upon them to retreat, leaving on the field more than one-half of the men, and two-thirds of the officers, either killed or desperately wounded".[341] Altogether 314 members of the regiment were killed, and 333 wounded. The Black Watch, said Stewart, "was first in the attack, and last in the retreat – which, after all, was made deliberately, and in good order".[342]

An English officer in the battle wrote: "With a mixture of esteem, grief, and envy, I consider the great loss and immortal glory acquired by the Scots Highlanders in the late bloody affair. Impatient for orders, they rushed forward to the intrenchments, which many of them actually mounted. They appeared like lions, breaking from their chains. Their intrepidity was rather animated than damped by seeing their comrades fall on every side." One of the Highlanders' officers, Lieutenant William Grant, wrote: "I have seen men behave with courage and resolution before now, but so much determined bravery can be hardly equalled in any part of the history of ancient Rome. Even those that were mortally wounded cried aloud to their companions, not to mind or lose a thought upon them, but to follow their officers, and to mind the honour of their country. Nay their ardour was such, that it was difficult to bring them off. They paid dearly for their intrepidity. The remains of the regiment had the honour to cover the retreat of the army, and brought off the wounded as we did at Fontenoy."[343]

David Stewart chronicled the bravery of the Highlanders at Ticonderoga, which was carried to the point of refusing orders to retreat, and then said sardonically that the new society in the Highlands was beginning to change matters: the Highlanders were still brave, but perhaps their "officers now may entertain less dread that their men will disobey orders, and persevere in a disastrous and hopeless conflict".[344]

45. West Indies and North America

In the fighting which led to the capture of Guadeloupe from the French in 1759, the 800 men of the Black Watch were so active in "their attacks and annoyance of the outposts of the enemy", constantly harassing the defenders from several different directions, that the French came to believe that there were several thousands of them.[345]

After the taking of Guadeloupe, the Black Watch was sent to North America, where in 1759 it fought under General Wolfe at the capture of Quebec. One account of the battle said that when the attack on the enemy's centre was made, "the Highlanders taking to their broadswords, fell in among them with irresistible impetuosity, and drove them back with great slaughter".[346]

A general officer said after the victory, "the Highlanders seem particularly calculated for this country and species of warfare, requiring great personal exertion. Their patience, sober habits, and hardihood, – their bravery, their agility, and their dress, contribute to adapt them to this climate, and render them formidable to the enemy."[347] In the same year it was decided to mount an expedition against the French West Indian islands, and "General Instructions, dated Whitehall, 1759" suggested that the Highland battalions then in North America were especially suited for the arduous duty envisaged, "as their sobriety and abstemious habits, great activity, and capability of bearing the vicissitudes of heat and cold, rendered them well qualified for that climate, and for a broken and difficult country".[348]

Accordingly three Highland battalions, both battalions of the Black Watch together with the single battalion of Montgomerie's 77th Regiment, were in a force sent to the French island of Martinique in 1762. A dominating height over the capital, St. Pierre, had to be taken, and the attack was described by the *Westminster Journal*. "The Highlanders, drawing their swords, rushed forward like furies"; they were supported by a party of grenadiers and others, and "the hills were mounted and the batteries seized, and numbers of the enemy, unable to escape from the rapidity of the attack, were taken".[349]

46. Seven Years' War

In 1759, during the Seven Years' War, Major Keith was given command of three newly raised companies of Highlanders, each having 105 men. This small force went to Germany as soon as it was formed, and three days after they reached the camp of the allied army under Prince Ferdinand, before there had been time for any serious military training, they joined in the attack on the village of Eyback. Supported by a detachment of German hussars, they routed the enemy, and took many prisoners, "together with two hundred horses and all their baggage. The Highlanders distinguished themselves greatly by their intrepidity, which was the more remarkable, as they were no other than raw recruits just arrived from their own country, and altogether unacquainted with regular discipline."[350]

Prince Ferdinand, naturally impressed, asked for more of these Highlanders, so Major Keith's force was expanded to 800 men, and a second regiment of equal size was also raised, under John Campbell of Dunoon. They came from many parts of the Highlands, including the shires of Argyll, Perth, Inverness, Ross and Sutherland. Sent to Germany in 1760, Keith's and Campbell's Highlanders were in the force which defeated the enemy near Warburg in July: Prince Ferdinand said the Highlanders "did wonders". Six days later the two Highland regiments were in the attack on Zeirenberg; the fortress was captured, the Highlanders leading the assault sword in hand, and one account said "the brigade formed of grenadiers and Highlanders distinguished themselves remarkably upon this occasion".[351]

In October at Campvere the allies were unsuccessful, but it was not the fault of the Highlanders. "They were in the first column of attack, were the last to retreat, and kept their ground in the face of every disadvantage, even after the troops on their right and left had retired." In fact the Highlanders refused to withdraw until they received a direct command from the commander-in-chief, whose message said that to persist in maintaining their position "would be a useless waste of human life".[352] (The same rejection of orders to retreat had happened at Ticonderoga, and was to happen at New Orleans.) The two Highland regiments gained their revenge by their victory at Fellinghausen in 1761, when the commander-in-chief gave "his entire approbation of their conduct on the 15th and 16th of July. The soldier-like perseverance of the Highland regiments in resisting and repulsing the repeated attacks *of the chosen troops of France*, has deservedly gained them the highest honour . . . The intrepidity of the little band of Highlanders merits the greatest praise" (original emphasis). Just before the battle a detachment of the enemy made an unexpected raid, and captured a British general; so Major Archibald Campbell (brother of Achallader) took a small band of Highlanders, and making "a spirited dash . . . dispersed five times his own number", and rescued the general.[353] Major Campbell was killed shortly afterwards at Fellinghausen. Another victory followed in June 1762 at

Graibenstein, where the enemy lost over 4000 men, compared with 700 of the allied army. "Our troops behaved with a bravery not to be paralleled, especially our grenadiers and Highlanders."[354] In the three campaigns, of 1760, 1761, and 1762, in which Keith's and Campbell's Highlanders engaged, they were "uniformly victorious", except at Campvere, though faced with the best troops of France.[355]

47. Humanity and generosity

The Highlanders were pugnacious in battle, but mild and placid out of it. Following the battle at Fellinghausen, where the achievements of Keith's and Campbell's Highlanders won them such praise, they immediately afterwards showed their moderation. Colonel Beckwith, commanding the brigade, said: "The humanity and generosity with which the soldiers treated the great flock of prisoners they took, does them as much honour as their subduing the enemy."

When Keith's and Campbell's Highlanders were in Germany in 1761-2, the *Vienna Gazette* remarked on "the goodness of their dispositions in every thing, for the boors [i.e., the local people] were much better treated by those savages [sic] than by the polished French and English". The *Gazette* added that the "French held them at first in great contempt, but they have met with them so often of late, and seen them in the front of so many battles, that they firmly believe that there are twelve battalions of them in the army instead of two".[356] (Exactly the same thing had happened at Guadeloupe in 1759, where as we saw the excellent soldier-like behaviour of the Black Watch multiplied their numbers in the enemy's estimation.) After the Seven Years' War had ended, in 1763, Keith's and Campbell's Highlanders marched back to Scotland to be disbanded, and their welcome was as warm in Britain as it had been on the Continent. "Though hospitably received in all the towns through which they passed, their reception at Derby was the most remarkable. No payment was taken from them for quarters, and subscriptions were raised to give gratuities to the men." It was only seventeen years since Prince Charles' rebel army of Highlanders had occupied the town: "and the people remembered with gratitude, that the rebels had conducted themselves with unexampled regularity in Derby, and had respected the property and persons of the inhabitants. Nor was it forgotten, though they were in open insurrection, and in situations where the greatest turbulence and licentiousness were to be expected, that nothing of the kind had occurred, and that no ill usage or insult had been offered by those men." These Highland rebels had probably behaved better to the townsfolk than did the soldiers who were supposed to be defending them, and their humane conduct was still remembered.[357]

CUSTOMS OF THE HIGHLANDERS

48. India, America, Ireland, Scotland

The colonial conflicts necessary to preserve and extend the British Empire overseas continued even when the regularly declared and conducted European wars had come to an end. The Seven Years' War ended at the Peace of Paris in 1763, but in India and America hostilities continued. At Buxar in India, in 1764 (a year after "the end of the war"), a British army commanded by Major Hector Munro, which included the 89th Regiment, the Gordon Highlanders, defeated an Indian force five times larger, killing 6000 of the enemy.[358]

In the same year an expedition, which contained the Black Watch, was sent from Fort Pitt (now Pittsburgh) to subdue the Amerindians: "the troops traversed many hundred miles, cutting their way through thick forests, and frequently attacked by, and attacking, skirmishing parties of the Indians", who at length sued for peace. Having set out in July 1764, the detachment returned in January 1765, after the hard winter had set in. "Although forced to march through woods of immense extent, where the snow had attained a depth unknown in Europe, it is a remarkable fact, that in these six months, [in] three of which they were exposed to extreme heat, and [in] two to an equal excess of cold, with very little shelter from either extreme, and frequently disturbed by an active, though not a formidable, enemy, the Highlanders did not leave a man behind from fatigue or exhaustion."[359]

In 1767 the 42nd returned across the Atlantic, to Ireland. When it left America, the *Virginia Gazette* (30th July 1767) said that it had been "distinguished for having undergone most amazing fatigues, made long and frequent marches through inhospitable country, bearing excessive heat and severe cold with alacrity and cheerfulness, frequently encamping in deep snow . . . continually exposed in camp and on their marches to the alarms of a savage enemy, who, in all their attempts, were forced to fly." The article continued: "they have our thanks for that decorum in behaviour which they maintained during their stay in this city, giving an example that the most amiable behaviour in civil life is in no way inconsistent with the character of the good soldier; and for their loyalty, fidelity, and orderly behaviour, they have every wish of the people for health, honour, and a pleasant voyage."[360]

When the regiment arrived in Ireland, many requests "were made by towns and districts to get them stationed among them", rather than other British regiments from the supposedly civilized parts of Great Britain, whose conduct was not so exemplary: the Irish had not forgotten the Highlanders' good behaviour when they were stationed there a dozen years before – or the less praiseworthy conduct of the men from the new industrial towns.[361]

The clansmen were prepared to enlist in the Highland regiments, but not to serve with the Sassenachs. Stewart said, "the recruiting parties of other regiments, in order to allure the Highland youth, frequently assumed the dress of the old Highland regiment [the 42nd], for which they affected to be recruiting". In 1774, for example, a recruiting party from the (Staffordshire) 38th regiment went to the Highlands, the officer and his men all in Highland dress, and they allowed it to be understood that they were recruiting for the Black Watch: "although the 38th was inserted in the attestations [recruiting documents], no explanation was made to the recruits, who, ignorant of the English language, considered that their engagement was to serve in the regiment of their own country, and not among men whose language they did not understand, and whose dress they so much disliked." At that time the 38th was stationed in Cork, and the 42nd in Dublin. When en route for Cork the recruits reached Dublin, and saw the Black Watch, which they thought they were joining, they refused to go any further, unabashed at having to challenge the might of the British military establishment. Several of the men were placed under arrest, but when an inquiry was made and the facts came out, "they were all discharged, when they immediately re-enlisted in the 42nd regiment".[362]

The Black Watch was billeted in Glasgow in 1776,[363] along with the newly raised regiment of Fraser's Highlanders (this time numbered the 71st – the previous Fraser's Highlanders, the 78th, having been disbanded in 1763). "The respectable part of the inhabitants were much struck with the regular conduct of these men, so different from what they had perhaps been led to expect." One account expressed surprise at "the cordial habits these strangers were in with the people, although so many of them spoke no English; and more especially their attachment and respect to their officers, and the kindness and familiarity with which the officers talked to their men".[364]

49. 1775-83 War: the Black Watch

When the American War of Independence broke out, three battalions of Highlanders from these two regiments (one from the 42nd, and two from the 71st) were sent out to defend the Empire. The provisions on the transatlantic voyage were chiefly salt-meat and weevily biscuits, and not a few of the Lowland and English soldiers transported across the North Atlantic fell sick or died. But the Highlanders had stronger constitutions. "In the year 1776 the three battalions of the 42nd and of Fraser's Highlanders embarked 3248 soldiers: after a stormy passage of more than three months, none died: they had only a few sick, and these not dangerously." In contrast, three years later a draft of 150 city dwellers from the streets of London and Dublin were sent out as army recruits, and of them sixty per cent were casualties – ten per cent were dead, and another fifty per cent were ill: "15 died in the passage, and 75 were sent to the hospital from the transports as soon as they disembarked." At the same time many Highlanders were being driven from the Highlands, often to end up in great cities which had much in common with London and Dublin, in order (we are told) to save them from their supposedly unwholesome lives in the glens.[365]

One company of the 42nd, aboard the *Oxford* transport, was taken prisoner when the ship was captured by an American privateer, which put a crew aboard to sail the vessel to a port held by the colonists. The Highlanders, however, overpowered their guards, and took control of their ship. They then sailed to Jamestown, which was (they believed) held by the British. When they arrived they found it was in fact in the hands of the rebels, and again they were taken prisoner. Every effort was made to get them to desert and join the Americans. "When it was found that the offers of military promotion were rejected, they were told that they would have grants of fertile land, to settle in freedom and happiness, and that they would all be lairds themselves, and have no rents to pay." Even these promises, particularly tempting to Highlanders after the recent events in their homeland, were turned down, and finally these incorruptible men had to be sent in small parties to the back settlements. They were exchanged in 1778, and rejoined their regiment.[366]

At Ticonderoga the Black Watch had refused to accept a position in the reserve; a similar refusal to accept a subsidiary role occurred in 1776. The British attacked an American stronghold near New York. On the east of the fort, there was a cliff nearly vertical, with a small creek at the bottom of it; the Black Watch was ordered to make a feint there, while the main assault went ahead on the other more approachable sides of the fort. But when the Highlanders landed, the enemy above (in Stewart's words) "opened a smart fire, which could not be returned, owing to the perpendicular height of the enemy's position". Highlanders could not be expected to come under fire, and make no response: so the Black Watch ignored their orders to make only a pretended foray, and instead climbed the precipice by grasping "the brushwood and shrubs growing out of the crevices of the rocks". Their commander, Major Murray, was so corpulent that he was being left behind by the Highlanders, who as usual had not waited for their "leaders"; but when he called for help the men came down again and got him up between them. At the top they immediately charged forward, taking 200 of the enemy prisoner, and then met their fellow attackers coming from the opposite side. Most of the 3000 defenders were captured. The hill was so steep that one of the Highlanders climbing it was injured by a ball which entered at the back of his neck, and lodged in his lower back; while a piper, who struck up a martial air as soon as he reached the top, was shot and killed by the defenders, and his body fell from rock to rock till it reach the bottom of the cliff.[367]

The Black Watch as a whole fought in America for five years, from 1776 to 1781. (The treaty was signed only in 1783, but there was little in the way of hostilities on the American continent after Cornwallis's surrender at Yorktown in 1781.) During the fighting the rebels tried to win over the British soldiers: "from the promises and allurements which the Americans held out, there were, of course, many inducements to desertion. Desertions from other corps were, indeed, very frequent; but in this regiment it was otherwise; not a man deserted."[368] Subsequently some men were brought into the 42nd from the 26th (non-Highland) regiment, and several of these deserted to the enemy; but these were not the original Black Watch Highlanders.[369]

50. Fraser's Highlanders

In 1775 the 71st Regiment, Fraser's Highlanders, was raised (as we saw above): 2,340 Highlanders were embodied in two battalions. 120 Camerons came up to join the regiment, to get their chief a commission. Lochiel was, however, detained in London, being ill; so the Camerons loudly expressed their reluctance to remain in the regiment. Fortunately a friend and near relation of the chief, Cameron of Fassfern, deputized for him, so the Camerons agreed to go ahead with him as their captain. The Highlanders saw the Highland regiments merely as an extension of the clan rally of former times, when the fit men joined together to defend their clan country; and therefore the clan chief (or a similar respected individual, in whom they could have confidence) was the person they looked to as their natural captain and commander.[370]

More Highlanders appeared in Glasgow than could be taken into the new regiment; so they had to be left behind when the 71st marched to Greenock, to be embarked for the American war. Some of those who had been refused admission to the regiment left Glasgow that night, and secretly joined their friends at Greenock; they then embarked on the troop ship under cover of darkness, and were not discovered till at sea, when it was too late to return them. As Stewart said, "officers who have been in the habit of embarking with troops, on a distant and dangerous service, have perhaps observed individuals who appeared as if they would not have been displeased to remain at home". The Highlanders were from a different background.[371]

Fraser's Highlanders were sent, virtually without training, to fight in the American War of Independence. As soon as they landed they were thrown into battle; and, wrote David Stewart, "on no future occasion, even after the experience of six campaigns, did they display more spirit or soldier-like conduct". They were constantly on campaign. "Little attempt was made to give them the polish of parade discipline till the third year of the war. Field discipline, and forcing their enemy to fly wherever they met him, (except on two occasions, when the fault lay not with them,) they understood perfectly." Finally they were given parade ground training, and Dr Jackson (in his survey of European armies) wrote: "Their conduct was good after they were drilled. It was equally good, perhaps more animated and heroic, before they received this military polish." Stewart said that this demonstrated "how little preparation is necessary for the execution of every military duty, when men possess the proper elements of the soldier".[372] It was the same with Keith's and Campbell's Highlanders – they were sent to the Continent in 1759-60, and thrown into the war before any training could be given. "Could an hypothesis be grounded on a few facts," Stewart wrote, "Fraser's Highlanders would prove, that men without discipline, depending entirely on their native spirit and energy, are capable of performing, in the most perfect manner, every duty of a soldier. Few British regiments ever went into immediate service with less discipline than this regiment, except Keith's and Campbell's Highlanders in Germany."[373]

A Lowland officer could win the same standing in a Highland regiment as a native Gael, provided he could obtain the approval of the Highlanders. Some of the Highlanders in Fraser's regiment came under the command of Sir James Baird. He was from Midlothian, but Stewart said he was very popular with Highlanders – he was "frank and familiar", and "sung their warlike songs". He was very successful in action with the regiment, for "he indulged the propensity of the Highlanders to close upon the enemy".[374] Similarly Colonel Adams, who as a young officer joined the Ross-shire Highlanders. "Though not a Celtic Highlander of Scotland, he was a Celt of Wales; and had he been from the Highlands of Ross, he could not have been more acceptable to the soldiers", since he "so fully appreciated the peculiar traits of their dispositions", and "entered readily into their feelings and peculiarities".[374]

A transport which was taking a detachment of the 71st across the Atlantic sailed into Boston Harbour not knowing it was already held by the rebels. Three rebel ships attacked them, and the 71st men held off the enemy until their ammunition gave out, and their ship was grounded: they then had to surrender (like the Black Watch company which sailed into Jamestown in the same operation). Later they were exchanged with American prisoners, and in 1779 they were part of the British force marching from South Carolina to Georgia. The Americans pushed 2000 men forward: sixty Highlanders under Captain Campbell, son of Glendaruel, were sent to reconnoitre; and when they came across the 2000 Americans, promptly attacked. "This being their first appearance before an enemy, they had not yet learned to retreat, nor had they forgotten what had been always inculcated in their native country, that to retreat was disgraceful."[375] All the officers & N.C.O.s were killed or injured, but when Captain Campbell ordered his men to get back to the main body; they refused. Fortunately "the enemy, either struck with this unexpected check from so significant a force, or waiting till the main body came up, ceased firing"; and seven Highlanders, the only ones still on their feet, retired carrying their wounded officers.

Fraser's Highlanders, like other Highland regiments, rapidly established a fearsome reputation. At the Battle of Guildford, Virginia, in 1781, the struggle was hotly contested, "till towards the end of the action, when a rapid movement of Fraser's Highlanders brought the regiment so conspicuously in view of the enemy, and (as appears by the American General's dispatches) made such an impression, as to induce them to retreat with great precipitation, and never afterwards to attempt a rally. This impression on the nerves of the enemy must have been occasioned by their previous rencontres with the 71st Regiment, as they did not wait an actual attack."[376]

51. Surrender at Yorktown

The 71st Regiment was in the British army which Cornwallis surrendered at Yorktown in 1781. In a hostile country, hemmed in on land by the French and American troops, and blockaded at sea by the French fleet, Cornwallis could see no way out. "And thus ended the military service of this army, which had marched and countermarched nearly two thousand miles in less than twelve months, during which they had no regular supply of provisions, or of necessaries, – had forded many large and rapid rivers, some of them in face of an enemy, – had fought numerous skirmishes and two pitched battles, and in every skirmish and every battle, one affair only excepted, had been victorious."[377] On one occasion, for example, an attack was made on an American post on the South Carolina side of the Savannah River. General Prevost was to make a frontal attack. "The two battalions of the 71st were directed to take a circuit of several miles, with a view of coming on the enemy's rear, while the General advanced on their front. They entered a woody swamp at eleven o'clock at night, and, guided by a party of Creek Indians, penetrated through, the water reaching to their shoulders in the deeper and softer parts of the swamps. In this condition, with their ammunition destroyed, they emerged from the woods at eight o'clock in the morning, less than half a mile in rear of the enemy's position . . ." Unfortunately General Prevost had not yet made his move, but the Highlanders, who had spent the whole night wading through a swamp, which had ruined their ammunition, did not let that affect them: "the Highlanders instantly rushed forward, and drove the enemy from their position at the first charge, and this with such expedition that they suffered no loss."[378]

However, the population of the thirteen colonies were so hostile that the final result was inevitable. "On all occasions where Lord Cornwallis met [the American] General Green, the former gained the day, but afterwards retired and left the country open, surrendering the advantages usually resulting from a victory to the enemy he had beaten."[379]

When the 71st, Fraser's Highlanders, were captured by the Americans like the rest of the army, they held firm to their allegiance. "When [they were] prisoners, and solicited by the Americans to join their standard and settle among them, not one individual violated the oath he had taken, or forgot his fidelity or allegiance; a virtue not generally observed on that occasion, for many soldiers of other corps joined the Americans, and sometimes, indeed, entered their service in a body."[380]

52. MacDonald's Highlanders

The 76th Regiment, MacDonald's Highlanders, was raised in 1778. In 1779 it was ordered to the relief of Jersey in the Channel Islands, which had been attacked by the French. A new commander of the regiment, John Sinclair Lord Berriedale, heir to the earldom of Caithness, "gave orders that the men were not to take their broadswords on shore, nor the officers to land in the Highland dress"; the officers were told of this, but the men were only to hear of it just before disembarkation. During the overnight voyage towards Jersey, the men did not sleep, but prepared for the landing, being particularly careful to sharpen their broadswords. "Next morning", said Stewart, "some of the officers appeared in the Highland dress, and all the men with their broadswords. When they were informed of the orders, they said that it might be so, but they hoped that, God willing, they would be allowed to fight with the arms, and die in the dress, of their country and of their forefathers." In other words, the orders were ignored.[381] Fortunately for Lord Berriedale, the French had already been repulsed; no landing was necessary; and the ship, and the regiment, returned across the Channel. Since this was the regiment which had, earlier that year, left its quarters and occupied a hill above Burntisland, and stayed there till their arrears of pay and bounty money had been handed over, Berriedale was lucky not to have had it demonstrated even more patently that the MacDonalds did not intend to be deprived of their Highland dress and weapons, and did not propose to obey orders which they considered foolish. And these were the men who, according to Professor Donaldson, could do nothing without "leadership".

Sent to America, MacDonald's Highlanders saw no action until 1781, when they joined the army under Lord Cornwallis, in Virginia. There they were attacked by a force of Americans, who "exhibited more than usual bravery and skill", under the Marquis de Lafayette. "A Highland soldier rushed forward and placed himself in front of his officer, Lieutenant Simon MacDonald of Morar." The soldier, who was a MacEachan, said, "when I engaged to be a soldier, I promised to be faithful to the King and to you. The French are coming, and while I stand here neither bullet nor bayonet shall touch you except through my body." Then "Lord Cornwallis, coming up in rear of the regiment, gave the word to charge, which was immediately repeated by the Highlanders, who rushed forward with their usual impetuosity, and decided the matter in an instant".[382]

53. Canada and India

In 1775 two battalions were raised from the Highlanders who had emigrated to Canada, and to the American colonies further south; they composed the Royal Highland Emigrant Regiment, and served throughout the war of 1775-83. The first battalion, under Colonel Allan MacLean (the same man praised as a lieutenant for his behaviour at the siege of Bergen-op-zoom), took part in the successful defence of Quebec against a siege laid by the Americans under General Arnold, and thereafter was "principally employed in small, but harassing enterprises", involving long marches through the trackless Canadian woods. "With every opportunity, and much temptation to desert, in consequence of offers of land, and other incitements held out by the Americans, it is but justice to the memory of these brave and loyal men to state, on the most unquestionable authority, that not one native Highlander deserted." The second battalion was commanded by Major Small, from Strath Ardle in Atholl; five companies served in Nova Scotia, and five in Lord Cornwallis's army. "There was not an instance of desertion in this battalion."[383]

A second battalion of the 42nd was raised in 1780, and later became a separate regiment, the 73rd. These soldiers were in a small British and Indian army which, in 1782 during the war against Hyder Ali, was attacked by a force under the French General Lally nine times as numerous. The British-Indian army was victorious, largely because of repeated bayonet charges by the Highlanders. General Orders, the official record, said that the British-led troops "had nothing to depend on but their native valour, their discipline, and the conduct of the officers. These were nobly exerted, and the event has been answerable. The intrepidity with which Major Campbell and the Highlanders repeatedly charged the enemy was most honourable to their character."[384]

Another instance of the Highlanders turning a planned minor role into a major one took place during the war in India against Tipu Sahib, 1790-2. Seaforth's Highlanders (the 78th Regiment until 1786, and thereafter the 72nd) were in the British army that came up against the strong point of Ootradroog, garrisoned by the enemy. A small party of the 72nd, under Captain John MacInnes, was ordered out to reconnoitre; but the Highlanders, "observing a favourable opportunity, turned this duty into an assault, scaled the walls, and carried the place without loss". Shortage of numbers, and lack of orders, never deterred Highlanders.[385]

54. French Revolutionary War

In 1793 the Black Watch were quartered for some months in Hull. The Highlanders behaved as well as ever, and became popular with the townsfolk; the people of Hull, in fact, "were so well satisfied with their conduct, that, after they embarked for Flanders, the town of Hull sent each man a present of a pair of shoes, a flannel shirt, and worsted socks".[386]

An incident in Flanders in 1793 suggests that, as in one or two earlier instances, enemy forces were sometimes understandably reluctant to face a Highland regiment. The French, with a much greater force than the defendants could muster, were vigorously besieging Nieuport. The Black Watch was sent to relieve the town. "On the appearance of this reinforcement, the enemy seemed to have lost all hopes of success. After keeping up a brisk fire of shot and shells during the whole night, they were seen at daybreak, moving off with great expedition, leaving several pieces of cannon, mortars, and ammunition." Dawn would have been when the enemy first saw clearly that they would now have to face a Highland regiment.[387]

The members of the Gordon Fencible Regiment, 1793, were described as "all of them men of good character, and though not in general tall, yet stout and well made".[388] Much the same was said of the Fraser Fencibles, of whom "300 bore the name of Fraser", and who were raised in 1794. "An able and intelligent officer, who knew them well", commented: "The men were not in general large, but active, well made, and remarkable for steady marching, never leaving any stragglers, even on the quickest and longest marches."[389]

The 78th Regiment, the Ross-shire Highlanders, was embodied in 1793. Twenty-seven years later David Stewart wrote of this regiment: "there has not been one desertion among the men enlisted in the Highlands."[390] In the old, more democratic, days of the clans, as we saw, men had joined a clan array when they felt like it, and had gone home when they felt like it: now, joining a Highland regiment was a much more formal affair, which included swearing an oath to stay with the colours until the regiment was disbanded. After making such a solemn promise, the Highlanders naturally almost never deserted.

The 98th Regiment, or Argyllshire Highlanders, raised in 1794, served in South Africa and in the Peninsula. One soldier of this regiment did desert. He went to America, and settled there; but he could not escape his feeling of remorse for having gone back on his word. "Several years after his desertion, a letter was received from him, with a sum of money for the purpose of procuring one or two men to supply his place in the regiment, as the only recompense he could make for 'breaking his oath to his God, and his allegiance to his King, which preyed on his conscience in such a manner, that he had no rest night nor day'."[391]

In the English and Lowland regiments of the time (and well after that time), there was usually an unbridgeable gulf between the officers and the men; they came from diametrically opposed sections of society. The Highland regiments were different, having come from a different milieu. In the 78th, Ross-shire Highlanders, raised as we saw in 1793, during the war years up to 1815 twenty-three of the rank-and-file were promoted to the rank of officer.[392]

55. Healthy Highlanders

Again, the Black Watch (in which "300 were young men recently recruited") served in Flanders for ten months in 1794-5. This was the ill-fated campaign in which the commander-in-chief, the Duke of York (who was in that post because he possessed the incontestable qualification of being the king's son), helped the Austrians to lose the battle of Turcoing, during which, wrote Steven Watson, "two-thirds of the allied force stood, or counter-marched purposelessly, while the rest of their comrades were being annihilated". As the popular song had it, "he marched them up to the top of the hill, and he marched them down again".[393] This sarcastic comment on the duke's achievements with his "ten thousand men" ignored the reality that there were few hills in Flanders; in fact the flat, marshy land across which the allied armies retreated perhaps contributed to the widespread sickness among the British troops – nor was there any efficient army medical service to restore them to health. Stewart deplored "the state of the hospitals, of which it was observed that whoever entered them never came out till carried to the grave".[394] In this expedition "some of the newly-raised [English and Lowland] regiments had lost more than 300 men by disease, and many who, left behind from exhaustion, fell into the hands of the enemy". As usual the men of the 42nd had better constitutions: the "acknowledged hardihood and capability of the Highlanders" meant that their "deaths in battle and by sickness had been only twenty-five, – a small number, considering the length of the service, the fatigue they underwent, and the severity of the weather to which they had been exposed".[395]

In the winter of 1795-6 many soldiers were sent to the West Indies. Five companies of the Black Watch had a rough crossing, but "none died, and only four men, with trifling complaints, were left on board when the troops were disembarking at St Lucia in April". A number of non-Highland regiments sent across almost at the same time "were not so fortunate in point of health, although they had a good passage and favourable weather. Several officers, and a great number of men, died; and when they reached Barbadoes, the sick were so numerous as to fill the hospitals."[396]

Subsequently the Black Watch was sent to Martinique, and then, in 1797, back to England. "The regiment embarked free of sickness, and landing at Portsmouth on the 30th July, in equally good health, marched to Hillsea Barracks. A body of 500 men landing from the West Indies, and marching, without leaving a man behind, was no common spectacle." Indeed, since the report on the arrival of the troops made no mention of invalids, "directions were given to correct the mistake of omitting the number of sick arrived from the West Indies". In Sherlockian terms, the supposed "curious incident" of the number of sick in the Highland regiment was that there were none.[397]

56. Highlanders in Ireland

It is hard enough for a soldier to be brave when he is part of a victorious, advancing army. An even sterner test of his mettle comes when an army is forced to retreat. The Highlanders passed this test with flying colours, as we saw for example when considering Pinkie, Fontenoy and Ticonderoga. Another instance occurred at Castlebar during the Irish rebellion of 1798. French troops landed, and were opposed by an army composed largely of local militia; the French put them to flight. One Highland regiment, the Fraser Fencibles, was in the defending force; they could not reverse the defeat, but, as could have been expected, they were "the last to retreat". When all seemed lost, one "Highland Fraser sentinel . . . refused to quit his post". He stood his ground. "He loaded and fired five times successively, and killed a Frenchman at every shot; but, before he could charge [his gun] a sixth time, they rushed on him." Stewart added: "If all the soldiers at Castlebar had behaved with equal firmness, the French invasion would have ended on that day."[398]

The Fraser Fencibles were in Ireland from 1795 till 1802. An observer said of them, "the general character of the corps was excellent: they had a high degree of the *esprit de corps*; were obedient, active, and trusty; gaining the entire confidence of the generals commanding, by whom they were always stationed in the most disturbed districts, previous [to] and during the Rebellion. Many attempts were made to corrupt them, but in vain: no man proved unfaithful."[399]

The Highland regiments did good service in Ireland by their upright and pacific behaviour: "it was fully acknowledged, that tranquillity and obedience to the laws prevailed in many disturbed districts, immediately after the Sutherland, Caithness [Stewart called the Caithness men 'a regiment of Fencible Highlanders', so they must have come from Highland Caithness rather than the Lowland part], and other Fencible corps came upon the station. The spirit of revenge and of fierce animosity to the Government was softened by the mild and conciliatory conduct of these men." Not all the British troops in that unhappy country were so successful. "When troops are stationed in an enemy's country, or are ordered to keep down internal insurrection, the influence which their conduct exerts on those whom they are to control is, in general, conspicuous. If troops are insolent, oppressive, or cruel, the hatred and opposition of those who were inimical before are increased and confirmed; and [the occupying forces] may become what an eminent commander said of a part of the troops in Ireland, at that period, 'more dangerous to their friends than to their enemies'." The British Government, however, made good use of the very different demeanour of the Highlanders, who, "in a very considerable degree, contributed to the restoration of the peace and order which ensued".[400]

The fencible and regular Highland regiments were equally successful. The 92nd, Gordon Highlanders, were in Ireland in 1798-9, where they "secured the esteem of the commanders whom they obeyed, and of the people whom they were unhappily sent to coerce . . . In an address to the Marquis of Huntly [who had raised the regiment], by the magistrates and inhabitants, on leaving one of the stations in Ireland, it was said that 'peace and order were established, rapine had disappeared, confidence in the Government was restored, and the happiest cordiality subsisted, since his regiment came among them'."[401]

57. Maida and Merexem

The second battalion of the 78th Regiment, the Ross-shire Highlanders, which was raised in 1804, took part two years later in the Battle of Maida, in the south of Italy; the battle was the first British victory achieved on the Continent during the war, which had (apart from a brief period of peace, 1802-3) lasted since 1793. The victory was so decisive that the enemy lost 1300 killed, and 1100 wounded, while the British loss was forty killed, and 260 wounded. During the fighting the Highlanders, of whom "nearly 600 were under age", presumably under twenty-one, showed "perfect self-possession and coolness".[402]

The French having conquered Portugal in 1807, Goa (Portugal's colony in India) was occupied by the British, to support the Portuguese Prince Regent, who had fled to the other Portuguese colony of Brazil. The first battalion of the 78th, Ross-shire Highlanders, was part of this occupying army in Goa from 1807 to 1811. The Highlanders got on as well with the locals as they always did: David Stewart mentioned "the harmony which so frequently subsisted between Highland corps and the inhabitants of the countries where they have been stationed". In this case, when the Highlanders left Goa the Portuguese Viceroy took the opportunity "to express his sentiments of praise and admiration of the regular, orderly, and honourable conduct of his Britannic Majesty's 78th Highland Regiment"; he eulogized their "exemplary discipline", and said he would never forget "the inviolable harmony and friendship which has always subsisted" between the Goa people "and all classes of this honourable corps".[403] The second battalion of this regiment, the 78th, was in Flanders in 1814-15, and behaved equally well: "the men conducted themselves so as to secure the esteem of the people of Flanders." They were described as "kind as well as brave" – "Enfants de la famille" – "Lions in the field, and lambs in the house". The Mayor of Brussels said they "called forth the attachment and esteem of all", and the inhabitants requested him "to endeavour to detain the 78th (2nd Battalion Ross-shire) Regiment of Scotchmen in town, and to prevent their being replaced by other troops".[404] Thackeray (dealing in *Vanity Fair* with the Waterloo campaign) mentioned how "Donald, the Highlander, billeted in the Flemish farm-house, rocked the baby's cradle, while Jean and Jeanette were out getting in the hay"; this reference was based on reality.[405]

For comparison, one may recall that the contemporary commercial European civilizations had produced armies that were, in the famous phrase, "the sweepings of the jails of Europe". The Duke of Wellington said the British army was "composed of the scum of the earth – the mere scum of the earth, fellows who have enlisted for drink – that is the plain fact". He is also reported to have said, on seeing a draft of troops sent to him in Spain in 1809: "I don't know what effect these men will have upon the enemy, but, by God, they terrify me."[406] It can hardly be contested that the Highlanders had been produced by a different society from these men, and arguably by a preferable one.

The original men of the second battalion of the 78th Regiment, Ross-shire Highlanders, which was raised in 1804 and fought at Maida and in Egypt, were sent in two batches to join the first battalion in India, and a further 400 "healthy country lads" were recruited; most were very young, only forty-three of them being more than twenty-two years old. The newly-embodied battalion went to Holland, where in January 1814 they were part of a force under General Graham which attacked the village of Merexem. The general chose these very young Highlanders, who had never faced an enemy before, to head the attack on an enemy 3000 strong, in a powerful position approachable only by a causeway, and supported by artillery. "The Highlanders leading", the British "advanced in column, both flanks of which were exposed to the fire of the enemy, who occupied the houses to the right and left of the entrance into the village. If the advance, in such circumstances, had been slow or hesitating, the loss must have been considerable"; but (said the general's report afterwards) "an immediate charge with the bayonet by the 78th, ordered by Lieutenant-Colonel Lindsay, decided the contest ... The discipline and intrepidity of the Highland battalion, which had the good fortune to lead the attack on the village, reflect equal credit on the officers and the men." The Highlanders lost eleven killed, and twenty-eight wounded, while the enemy suffered 1100 casualties.[407]

58. Waterloo campaign

A. G. MacDonell wrote, "the Highlander's traditional method of warfare was to attack at a great pace in mass. The clan was a corporate body and it attacked as a corporate body, shoulder to shoulder. Everything was staked on one throw. As I have already said, defensive fighting and rearguard action were outside the Highlander's technical and mental equipment. He had to win or lose quickly."[408] Enough evidence has already been given to show that this was completely inaccurate: Highlanders were versatile and self-reliant, and were eminently able to demonstrate a redoubtable individualism; in fact the Highlanders repeatedly showed more individual initiative than the Lowlanders. (Many Lowland historians have echoed the canard that the Highlanders' only tactic was one mass charge, and to be able to work out whether this allegation was in fact true – despite the clear evidence – was no doubt outside MacDonell's "technical and mental equipment".) The fearless conduct of the Black Watch at the Battle of Quatre Bras showed again the Highlanders' self-reliance. At this engagement in 1815, two days before Waterloo, there were so many of the enemy, coming apparently from every direction, that each regiment had to fight for itself. A body of cavalry, thought (from their uniforms) to be from Wellington's Prussian or Belgian allies, were allowed to approach the British unmolested; then they suddenly revealed themselves to be the French enemy, and launched an immediate attack on the Black Watch at close quarters. The Highlanders had no time to get into the proper defensive formation, so each soldier fought his own battle as an individual. "They stood back to back, every man fighting on his ground till he fell, or forced his enemy to retreat." The French had never seen such a display in quarter of a century of continuous warfare, and their officers called out, "Why don't you surrender? Down with your arms, you see you are beaten."[409] But the Highlanders stood unyielding, not realizing that such independent combat was "outside" their "technical and mental equipment", and in the end it was the enemy who had to retire: it was the enemy who had to "see that they were beaten".

The 92nd, Gordon Highlanders, were actively involved against the enemy in various parts of the Continent and the Near East from 1799 onwards, culminating in the Peninsular campaign, Quatre Bras, and Waterloo. They were never defeated: "on twenty-six occasions, in which they met the enemy, (several of these, to be sure, were very trifling affairs, while others were very desperate,) from 1799 to 1815, the latter invariably gave way before them."[410]

At Quatre Bras on 16th June 1815 the 92nd was deployed along the Namur road. In front of it a detachment of Brunswick hussars was repulsed by the French cavalry, which "forced them to retire hotly pursued, in the direction of the Gordon Highlanders, who were concealed by the ditch along which they had been drawn up. Coolly waiting till the enemy came within reach, they opened a well directed and most destructive fire." The enemy fled, having suffered heavy losses, "as might be expected from repeated volleys of musquetry, aimed with the correctness of such experienced soldiers, as were those of the 92nd Regiment".[411] The British forces maintained their positions throughout the day in face of repeated French attacks, but the Gordon Highlanders lost many men.

The Prussians, on Wellington's left, were beaten by Napoleon at Ligny, while Wellington (in a separate battle, seven miles away) repulsed Ney at Quatre Bras. The defeated Prussians then had to retire northwards to Wavre, so Wellington had to retire in parallel with his allies during the next day. He then took up his position at Waterloo, where on 18th June the decisive battle was fought. At one point during that battle, "the enemy advanced in a solid column of 3000 infantry of the guard, with drums beating". The two British regiments opposed to this advance suffered many casualties. In this crisis, General Pack "ordered up the Gordon Highlanders, calling out, 'Ninety-second, now is your time – charge.' The order was repeated by Major MacDonald, and answered by a shout. The regiment, then reduced to less than 250 men by their losses at Quatre Bras, instantly formed, and rushed to the front, against a column equal in length to their whole line, which was only two men in depth, while the column was ten or twelve. The enemy stood, as if in suspense, till the Highlanders approached, when, panic-struck, they wheeled to the rear, and fled in the utmost confusion." When Napoleon saw that "the small body of Highlanders forced one of his chosen columns to fly in terror and confusion, the feelings of a gallant soldier overcame his disappointment; he openly declared his admiration of 'les braves Ecossais'." A troop of cavalry – the Scots Greys – then came through the Highland ranks to take up the chase; there was a mutual shout of "Scotland for ever!"; and some of the Gordons caught hold of the riders' stirrup leathers and raced forward with them. Most of the men in the French column were killed or taken prisoner. Not surprisingly, Napoleon said: "Qu'ils sont terribles ces chevaux gris!"[412]

Three Highland regiments fought in the final defeat of Napoleon at Waterloo: the 42nd (the Black Watch), the 79th (the Cameron Highlanders), and the 92nd (the Gordon Highlanders). The Duke of Wellington, reporting on the operations at Quatre Bras and Waterloo, complimented five regiments by name, and only five: the 28th, 42nd, 79th, 92nd, and a Hanoverian battalion. Three of the five formations so distinguished were the three Highland regiments – the total Highland force at the battle.[413]

59. Not fit to associate

The Black Watch needed few courts-martial, and for long periods there was no case of corporal punishment. Where, exceptionally, a man's conduct brought him to the halberds (that is, he was flogged), he was no longer considered fit to associate with the soldiers of the Black Watch: "and, in several instances, the privates of a company have, from their pay, subscribed to procure the discharge of an obnoxious individual."[414] In the five years of campaigning during the American War of Independence, only one man was punished. He had asked leave of absence, saying he had important business to attend to; but permission was refused, because a general order had forbidden it. However, the man went away, attended to his business, and then returned to the regiment. For disobeying orders, he was flogged. In fact he endured two punishments: the other soldiers of the Black Watch considered he had brought dishonour to the whole regiment, and refused even to eat with him.[415]

So far were the Highlanders from accepting any autocratic or domineering behaviour from their chiefs or chieftains in civil life, that they would not accept such behaviour even when they were in the army, under the control of officers who had, theoretically and practically, almost unlimited power over them. This was the reason for the repeated mutinies in Highland regiments, despite the fierce punishments that could follow the slightest demur in obeying orders. A contretemps of this kind was, fortunately, avoided in the Sutherland Fencible Regiment of 1793. A non-commissioned officer of the Black Watch, who had been a sergeant-major in that regiment for over twenty years, had (said Stewart) conducted himself well, "though occasionally rather too imperious in his manner towards the soldiers". This tendency was kept under control by the Black Watch officers; but when the same man was given a commission, and appointed adjutant in the Sutherland Fencibles, "his natural disposition broke forth, and although he perfectly knew the character and dispositions of the men, and that no severity was necessary, he irritated the soldiers by his harsh language and manners, to a degree that their spirit would not brook; and had not Colonels Wemyss and Stuart interfered, the consequences might have been that of which there were too many instances in Highland regiments, all originating in the same cause". There were some "men put into confinement on the occasion", but when the commanding officers (who understood the Highlanders) "checked the proceedings of the Adjutant . . . this threatening storm instantly subsided".[416]

60. Highland Host

Even where the Highlanders were engaged on an operation that had the sole purpose of intimidating a civilian population, they showed remarkable restraint. In 1678 a body from both sides of the Highland line, some Highland mercenaries and some Lowland militia, was brought in to intervene in the continuing lawlessness and strife in the Lowlands: a force was sent into south-west Scotland, in order (as was remarked at the time) to "eat up" the Lowland Covenanters, who were virtually in rebellion against the Crown. This body consisted of five or six thousand Highlanders, and three thousand Lowlanders, and was called "the Highland Host", not the Highland/Lowland Host; they were ordered to live on the country, and punish the populace by commandeering their food and houses without compensation, at the same time crushing any opposition. They were given carte blanche by the Privy Council, whose instructions to the occupying force said specifically "we hereby indemnify them" against any retaliation (by civil suit or criminal prosecution) "for anything they shall do in our service by killing, wounding, apprehending or imprisoning such as shall make opposition to our authority". The Lowland authorities could scarcely have used more direct terms to encourage violence, including specifically homicide, against the Lowland population: they were clearly hoping to capitalize on the centuries-long hatred between Highlander and Lowlander. Not surprisingly, many were hurt in this month-long punitive raid, but even a hostile commentator admitted, "yet I hear not of any having been killed".[417] One Lowland observer, though he was clearly convinced the Highlanders were all desperate robbers, honestly said, "Never did 6000 thieving ruffians with uncouth weapons make so harmless a march in a civilized country".[418] In fact the only death reported was that of a Glenorchy Highlander, who was killed by a Lowland mob in Stirlingshire as the clansmen returned to the mountains.[419] No contemporary European army, ordered into a district for the specific purpose of terrorizing and chastising the civilian population, would have been so restrained.

Not infrequently in those times Lowland soldiers were sent on expeditions against the Highlanders, as a punishment for the perceived misbehaviour of the latter, for example in not paying "rent" to some shady operator who had somehow acquired a piece of paper claiming he "owned" a certain area; but while the "Highland host" regularly figures in history books to show the barbarity of the Highlanders, these much more common, and much more savage, incidents featuring aggressive Lowlanders are seldom mentioned. Can it be that the Lowland authorship of such books is the explanation?

61. Bards and pipers

Those Highlanders who entered the king's service carried their culture with them, as we saw above. In the early years their bards related their ancient sagas, and also composed new "laments, elegies, and panegyrics on departed friends".[420] But Stewart, writing his book in 1822, had also to record how things had altered of late. "The recent statistical changes in the Highlands have set to flight poetry, chivalry, and all remembrance of warlike achievements." Highland soldiers in modern times, wrote Stewart, talked of excise officers, smugglers, speculators, "the pretended inspirations of the gospel", distraining for rent, and "the harshness of landlords" – such were the subjects (he added sardonically) which "modern civilizations and improvements have provided for the present generation of Highland soldiers, to educate them and to imbue them with the military spirit".[421] The result was that "the voice of the bard has long been silent, and poetry, tradition, and song, are vanishing away".[422]

The bagpipes for many years had been a favourite instrument of the Highlanders, and the pipes were important to the Highlanders when they had enlisted. The 73rd, MacLeod's Highlanders, fought under General Coote against Hyder Ali at Porto Novo in 1781; it "led all the attacks to the full approbation of General Coote, whose notice was particularly attracted by one of the pipers, who always blew up his most warlike sounds whenever the fire became hotter than ordinary". After the battle Coote presented a pair of silver pipes to the regiment, "with an inscription in testimony of the General's esteem for their conduct and character".[423]

At the sanguinary Battle of Assaye against the Mahratta confederates in September 1803, the musicians (the fife and drum men) were ordered to help carry the wounded to the surgeons in the rear, and the piper of the 78th Ross-shire Highlanders believed himself to be included in the order. After the victory, his comrades reproached him: the piper, they said, should always be in the fiercest part of the fight. But only two months later, the regiment (under Colonel Adams) was in action again against the same enemy. There, the piper "had an opportunity of playing off this stigma, for, in the advance at Argaum, he played up with such animation, and influenced the men to such a degree, that they could hardly be restrained from rushing on to the charge too soon, and breaking the line. Colonel Adams was, indeed, obliged to silence the musician, who now, in some measure, regained his lost fame."[424]

62. Trustworthy

In the society of the Highlanders, a man's word really was his bond. The men of the 42nd, said Stewart, often left sums of money in his hands until they should need it: "I was never asked for a receipt for money so lodged; and when I offered an acknowledgement, it was declined."[425] In this the Highland soldiers were simply acting by the standards of the clan society that produced them. Stewart told how a gentleman of his own surname "had agreed to lend a considerable sum of money to a neighbour". The money was already on the table, when the neighbour offered a receipt. At that the lender took up his money, saying that "a man who could not trust his own word, without a bond, should not be trusted by him, and would have none of his money"; he then pocketed his purse and went home.[426]

In 1795 one of the Breadalbane Fencibles, who had been tricked into letting a prisoner escape, was put in the guardhouse and threatened with corporal punishment. Many of his comrades came and released him, knowing that he had not deserved such degradation. When the authorities decided that some penalties must be exacted, several men offered themselves for trial, taking on themselves the consequences of the actions of the others. Four of them were sentenced to be shot. One of these, John MacMartin, told the officer commanding the guard taking them to Edinburgh for execution that he had some business in Glasgow which he must finish before he died; he declared that after he had gone to Glasgow, he would rejoin the party at Edinburgh. The officer, Captain Colin Campbell of Glenfalloch, being a Highlander himself, knew he could rely on MacMartin's word, and accordingly let him slip away. Two days later the prisoners and the guard had reached Edinburgh, where the prisoners had to be handed over at the castle to be executed; but MacMartin had not re-appeared. In fact he had left Glasgow before daylight to return to his fate. "He took a long circuit to avoid being seen, apprehended as a deserter, and sent back to Glasgow, as probably his account of his officer's indulgence would not have been credited. In consequence of this caution, and the lengthened march through woods and over hills by an unfrequented route, there was no appearance of him at the hour appointed." Glenfalloch went as slowly as he could, but finally he had to march up to the castle: "as he was delivering over the prisoners, but before any report was given in, MacMartin, the absent soldier, rushed in among his fellow prisoners, all pale with anxiety and fatigue, and breathless with apprehension of the consequences in which his delay might have involved his benefactor." The four men, MacMartin and the three others, were taken with their coffins to Musselburgh Sands to be executed by firing squad, but at the last moment three of them, including MacMartin, received a commutation of their sentence. In the event MacMartin and the others were given the 500 lashes that were seen in Lowland eyes as a merciful softening of the sentence, and then had suffer the further punishment of joining a colonial regiment in unhealthy forts in Upper Canada.[427]

In 1803 an Army of Reserve Act was passed, under which more young men were conscripted into the army by ballot; they were to serve only in the United

Kingdom, and were formed into second battalions of the existing regular regiments. David Stewart was in charge of mustering the Highlanders recruited in this way into the second battalion of the 42nd. Many wished to go home to settle their affairs, and applied to Stewart for the necessary permission. Not one Highlander abused this confidence. "The numbers who obtained leave of absence amounted to 235, yet every man returned at his appointed time, except when detained by boisterous weather at ferries, or by other unavoidable causes, which were certified by some neighbouring gentleman."[428]

63. Prudent and sober

In the early years of the Black Watch, each mess was in charge of an N.C.O. or an old soldier, and these small communal bodies were so arranged that "the men were in friendship or intimacy with each other, or belonged to the same glen or district, or were connected by some similar tie. By these means, every barrack-room was like a family establishment. After the weekly allowances for breakfast, dinner, and small necessaries had been provided, the surplus pay was deposited in a stock-purse [a common money-bag], each member of the mess drawing for it in his turn [as required for joint expenditures]. The stock thus acquired was soon found worth preserving, and instead of hoarding, they lent it out to the inhabitants, who seemed greatly surprised at seeing a soldier save money." The accounts were made up every three months. "At every settlement of accounts they enjoyed themselves very heartily, but with a strict observance of propriety and good humour; and as the members of each mess considered themselves in a manner answerable for one another's conduct, they animadverted on any impropriety with such severity, as to render the interference of farther authority unnecessary."[429]

The Argyll, or Western, Fencible Regiment, raised in 1778, also exhibited a "trait of character not uncommon among their countrymen, namely, so much economy in the expenditure of their daily pay of sixpence as to be able to remit considerable sums of money to their relations, and, when disembodied at Glasgow in 1783, to possess so much money, that, if the whole had been reckoned in one sum, it would have appeared very remarkable, considering the moderate means from which it had been saved".[430] Much the same could be said about other Highland regiments, particularly (as we shall see later) about the 93rd, Sutherland Highlanders.

It was a hard drinking age. Wellington, as we saw, thought his men had merely "enlisted for drink", and when he was a young colonel he saw other officers "fling aside" newly arrived despatches, until they should have finished their wine.[431] In the British army generally, drunkenness was endemic and was punished with floggings. General Sir Robert Wilson (1777-1849) wrote about the Flanders campaign of 1793-4, in which he had served as a young ensign. "The halberds were regularly erected along the lines every morning; and the shrieks of the sufferers made a pandemonium, from which the foreigner fled with terror at the severity of our military code. Drunkenness was the vice of officers and men, but the men paid the penalty; and the officers who sat in judgement in the morning were too often scarcely sober from the past night's debauch."[432] As for the duration of the flogging, George III is supposed to have been of the lenient opinion that no more than 1000 lashes should be administered at any one time. One is glad to record this evidence of a more compassionate feeling.[433]

The Highland regiments were different. In such an inebriated milieu, the Highland soldiers stood out as beacons of abstinence. The evidence showed "that, without an exception, their original habits were so temperate, and free from any tendency to excess in the use of liquor, or otherwise, as to attract general observation; that this sobriety withstood many years of example and temptation; that many corps, whose career of service was short, never changed to the last; and that others preserved the same line of conduct till the introduction of men of different characters, the force of example, and the influence of climate, caused a relaxation."[434] We have just seen that the army headquarters in 1759 commended the four Highland battalions then in North America for their "sobriety and abstemious habits". During the service of the Black Watch in America, the soldiers received their regular allowance of spirits twice a week, as the officers did, since they could be trusted not to consume it all immediately; the other regiments got theirs each day, with an officer on duty to check its proper use.[435] And when the 78th Regiment, the Ross-shire Highlanders, was sent to India in 1797, "the temperate habits of the soldiers" attracted much attention. "Their sobriety was such, that it was necessary to restrict them from selling or giving away the usual allowance of liquor to other soldiers."[436] It is ironical that these men came from a society now regularly portrayed – by anglophone commentators – as being addicted to whisky.[437] In the face of so much facile fiction, one feels regretful to have to refer to the facts.

64. Propaganda offensive

Since the Highlanders spoke a strange language, dressed in an odd manner, and lived in a weird way with peculiar principles, it was easy for anglophone observers to make accusations against them. The landlords made full use of these helpful features, when in course of the campaign to clear the Highlanders out of the Highlands it became necessary to mount a propaganda offensive to blacken their characters: the worse the Highlanders could be painted, the less blame would attach to any drive to break up their society, and expel them from their native haunts. It is a sad commentary on the human race that if there is dirty work to be done, there is usually no shortage of people who are prepared to do it. (No tyrant has ever had to give up his sadistic plans because he could not find enough torturers and executioners.) There were writers who in order to curry favour with the Highland landlords were prepared to ignore the reality, and to write what was plainly untrue in order to vilify the Highlanders. One described them as "deficient in intelligence" as well as "slow, heavy-footed, and inert in their movements".[438] One modern historian has chosen (as we saw) to ignore all the evidence, some of which is given above, in order to repeat this calumny, and boldly asserted that "the Highland people were lethargic in mind and slow in movement".[439] Other writers of the time chose to attack supposed religious deficiencies. David Stewart wrote in 1820: "In the reports of some religious societies recently published, the Highlanders are stated to have been guilty of 'the basest vices', – as 'Christians only by name' – as 'Savage Heathens', etc., etc. Many of them 'know not the name of Jesus'."[440]

This last falsehood may have owed much to the needs of getting contributions to the religious societies which sent emissaries into the Highlands. Stewart reported that a gentleman who was interested in such societies, when reproached for such gross duplicity about the Highlanders' religious shortcomings, defended the allegations on the grounds that "a strong case was necessary to make people advance money".[441] And it is clear that religious zealots would get more financial support by painting the Highlanders as heathens: the moral question of veracity was not, apparently, an issue with these doctrinal devotees.

So far did these propagandists leave reality behind them that some even claimed that Highlanders never joined the army. Sir George MacKenzie of Coul was a clearer himself, and wrote much in defence of the clearances generally. He was, however, painfully aware of the strength of the argument against the clearances, that the Highland landlords, for their own personal gain, were driving out many men who were unequalled recruits for the armed forces; and that without their efforts the landlord class in Britain as a whole might have suffered heavy losses. So he attacked the argument head on. "The Highlanders are trumpeted forth as our only resource for soldiers, whilst it is notorious that the inhabitants have a strong aversion to a military life."[442] Dr MacCulloch, another defender of the landlords, clearly wished to decry the efforts of the Highlanders, and to assert that the lower class produced by the new commercial society could defend the country just as well; so he claimed "it may truly be said, that the population of 60,000 Highland insulars . . . was defended, during the late war, by the artisans and manufacturers of England and the low country".[443] These allegations can easily be shown to be wildly untrue, in view of the fifty fighting Highland battalions raised between 1740 and 1815, plus many fencible and militia regiments, but they make clear how important – from the point of view of historical accuracy – was David Stewart's work in recording the military prowess of the Highlanders. They also show, incidentally, how easy it is for prominent writers to continue asserting what can readily be proved to be completely inaccurate, such as the claim that the clan chiefs "owned" their clans' land, that they behaved like brutal dictators, and so forth.

65. Indolent clansfolk

Although all these good qualities of the old Highlanders seem to be incontrovertible, nevertheless they were often accused of having three bad qualities. The first was indolence. The minister of Mortlach in Banffshire, a parish near the Highland-Lowland border, wrote in the O.S.A. (as we shall see later) that among his parishioners, it was the people of Glen Rinnes who most retained the manners of the Highlanders, "as appears from their dress, their vivacity, their social and merry meetings, their warm attachments, their keen resentments, their activity on occasions, and indolence on the whole, their intelligence, and their love of their country".[444]

As we saw earlier, it is undeniable that the Highlanders in the clan system did not have to work anything like so hard as the Lowlanders, or as their own descendants in commercial society. Three observations may be referred to for a second time. "Very little pains" were necessary to "live and keep credit" by a small farm (said the Halkirk O.S.A. minister);[445] "the periods of labour were short: and they could devote the intermediate time to indolence, or to amusement" (wrote Selkirk);[446] and a remarkable feature of the old Highland life was "the ease with which a man in these regions can acquire subsistence" (according to Robert Brown).[447] The Highlanders in the days of the clans lived in a hunter-gatherer economy – a lifestyle which demands many fewer hours of labour a day than more modern arrangements. One observer said, "no society has more leisure time than the hunter-gatherers. On average they spend two hours a day gathering, preparing and cooking food. The rest of the time they sleep a lot, play a lot, make love, and tell stories."[448] The English servant who visited Skye in 1782 (where he grumbled that the people "spend much of their time in telling idle stories, and singing doggerel rhymes and nonsense")[449] was obviously talking about the same kind of society.

The landlords saw that to claim that the Highlanders' way of life was an easy one would be taken by many ordinary folk to be an argument in favour of the old society, rather than an argument against it. And denunciation of the Highlanders for having an easy life was not going to elicit much satisfaction among the operatives of the Glasgow factories, working through every daylight hour and beyond; to hear that the Highlanders had a lot of leisure time could only lead to further discontent with their own laborious lives. The story therefore had to be adjusted. All propagandists have to suit their tidings to their audience. Christian missionaries who told the Inuit of the frozen north in Canada that those not "saved" will burn forever in the fiery furnace of hell were disappointed to find that this information was welcome to many of them. Dwellers in the Arctic were attracted rather than repelled by the idea of perpetual warmth; so in order to become persuasive, the details were adjusted, and hell was portrayed as a place of eternal ice and snow. The message was modified to meet the market. In the same way, when the correct "spin" was applied, the compliment that the Highlanders had an easy life was turned into the accusation that the Highlanders were indolent, and should (in the "national interest") be made to work harder. Some of the O.S.A. ministers supported the indictment. The minister of Farr thought the people were "rather indolent";[450] his fellow of Glenmuick said that his parishioners, "being accustomed from their infancy to a pastoral life, they contract a habit of indolence";[451] and the incumbent of Lochgoilhead, while saying that "the people of this parish have long been remarkable for their strict honesty, the regularity of their manners, their humanity, and their courtesy to strangers", thought that "the cottagers are rather indolent".[452] Historians still make the same point. Professor Richards drew attention to the rank-and-file Highlanders' unfortunate "propensity to inaction and voluntary unemployment".[453] (The professor omitted to deplore the same propensities among people with large amounts of money, who live on the labour of others: perhaps that criticism will come in his next book.) Certainly the men who were revolutionizing Highland society after Culloden were not prepared to allow this leisurely life to continue, since it was unthinkable that the people of Scotland, Highlanders as well as Lowlanders, should evade their obvious duty to spend practically all their waking hours labouring in the new regime, and thus enriching those people who now owned the land and everything else worth owning – whether their toil was in the kelping and fishing of the Highlands, or in the mills and mines of the Lowlands.

The question of "indolence" is bound up with the question of the so-called "over-population" of the Highlands (since, it was alleged, there were more people there than were needed to do the work available), and it will be considered again later, in conjunction with that topic. For the present it should be remembered that the accusation was merely a way in which the landlords (followed by many modern commentators) tried to obscure one of the advantages of clan – as against Lowland – society, and instead to depict it as a drawback of that society.

66. Resentful

The second accusation made against the clansfolk was that they were resentful, and quick to take offence. Many writers refer to this alleged trait in their character – Defoe, for example, in his *Memoirs of a Cavalier*: "The meanest fellow among them is as tenacious of his honour as the best nobleman in the country, and they will fight and cut one another's throats for every trifling affront."[454] Toland said the Highlanders were "choleric" (though, he added, apparently contradicting himself, they were "easily appeased").[455] Smollett said "the Lowlanders are generally cool and circumspect, the Highlanders fiery and ferocious".[456]

Despite this widespread belief, there seems to be much evidence pointing in the opposite direction. The aftermath of the Massacre of Glen Coe is one example. No single episode in the history of the Highlands had ever outraged at one and the same time more tenets of the Highland code of behaviour, or outraged them more blatantly. The soldiers from Argyll's regiment, and their captain Campbell of Glenlyon, sent by the Lowland authorities to lodge in Glen Coe, had been received in peace and friendship by the MacIains. They had thus, with the MacIains, entered into one of the most sacrosanct relationships of any human society: that of host and guest.[457] They were well entertained, each hut taking in two or three soldiers and giving them Highland hospitality for thirteen days. Friendship was shown on both sides: the soldiers and the clansfolk enjoyed races and sports in the afternoons, while Glenlyon and the others played cards with their hosts in the evenings. Glenlyon was actually related by marriage to MacIain, so that family ties, as well as the obligations of guests, were involved. But even though Glenlyon was in the position of guest, and friend, and even relative, he carried out his Lowland orders. At a given signal, in the darkness and intense cold of a February morning at five o'clock, the soldiers turned on their hosts and slew them. The lieutenant of the company, in Macaulay's words, "had knocked at the door of the old Chief and had asked for admission in friendly language. The door was opened. MacIain, while putting on his clothes and calling to his servants to bring some refreshments for his visitors, was shot through the head. Two of his attendants were slain with him. His wife was already up and dressed in such finery as the princesses of the rude Highland glens were accustomed to wear. The assassins pulled off her clothes and trinkets. The rings were not easily taken from her fingers; but a soldier tore them away with his teeth. She died on the following day."[458]

In the very act of hospitality – the door opened to a visitor coming in friendly guise, and refreshments being brought – MacIain was murdered. If the Highlanders had been prone to take deliberate revenge, in cold blood, no act could have called more loudly for retribution. And yet, though Robert Campbell of Glenlyon lived only a few years after the massacre, his son John Campbell of Glenlyon survived many decades in the midst of the friends and relations of the

MacIains of Glen Coe. This, too, in the first half of the eighteenth century, when the so-called "law and order" of the Lowlands had still not been fastened onto the Highlands. It was not for want of the power to do so that no revenge was taken on the Glenlyon family.

The chief author of the massacre was the Master of Stair, a Lowland politician. In 1745 the Jacobite Highland army was encamped near the house of the Earl of Stair, the politician's son. The earl himself was a Hanoverian field-marshal, which was another factor to call forth a Highland "revenge", if such a thing existed. Prince Charles, in order to forestall any move against Stair's house by the Glen Coe men (who were part of his army), sent a guard to protect it. Immediately the MacIains decided to return home, so indignant were they at being thought capable of revenge, and of such an unworthy act as visiting the sins of a father on his child. It would have been perilous in the extreme to separate from the army in the midst of hostile country, but they were only with great difficulty prevailed on to remain.[459] Indeed, the Glen Coe detachment insisted on guarding the house themselves, to prove that they were free from any "vileinye of hate".[460] Again, one can only contrast this behaviour with that of the soldiers of modern armies, who have frequently well-nigh wrecked any houses they happened to be billeted in or near, out of sheer light-heartedness, and without any thought even of hostility, much less any desire for revenge. But they came from a different society.

67. Superior to the meanness of retaliation

The brutalities of the repression, the massacres, and the rapine, inflicted on the Highlands after Culloden by Cumberland and his men must also have called for "revenge", if the Highlanders had been at all vindictive. But in the years following the official campaign of atrocity against the Highlanders which followed the Jacobite defeat, a number of English and Lowland travellers made their way unarmed over the wildest passes of the Highlands, far from the outposts of any soldiers or civil authorities: a single stab with a dirk would have given the quickest of revenges, and quite without risk to the man responsible. Yet none of these travellers was ever touched: on the contrary, as they subsequently testified, they were given assistance and hospitality much beyond anything they could have expected. Pennant, after remarking on this help and friendship, wrote: "Through my whole tour I never met with a single instance of national reflection [i.e., reproach]; their forbearance proves them to be superior to the meanness of retaliation."[461]

Why, then, was it said that the Highlanders were revengeful, and quick to take offence? One can only suppose that travellers coming from England or the Lowlands, where the respect paid to an individual was normally in direct proportion to the amount of wealth he possessed, might have carried over these attitudes into a country where the standards were different. Any ordinary member of a clan, coming down perhaps to sell a stirk in the Lowlands, who was addressed by one of the local worthies in the same way the latter would have addressed one of the lowest class in the Lowlands, would no doubt have taken offence very quickly indeed. The Highlander who so amused Defoe by walking dignified and upright even though he was only driving a cow would certainly, if he had seen Defoe laughing at him, have felt the slight to his honour as quickly as an English gentleman under ridicule.

Consider, too, what Defoe said in his *Memoirs of a Cavalier* – that the Highlander would fight for "every trifling affront": he jeered that the Highland soldiers looked, "when drawn out, like a regiment of Merry Andrews [clowns], ready for Bartholomew fair", in their strange Highland garb.[462] One wonders if Defoe had ever given one of the Highlanders the benefit of his opinion. If he had, he might even have had a personal encounter to support his view that the Highlanders took offence for what he considered to be a "trifling affront".

This belief that the Highlanders were irascible would be reinforced by their behaviour during the attacks made on the clan system by the chiefs. The people were "keenly alive to" any "injustice" or "oppression", said the Mortlach account,[463] while the Kirkmichael minister wrote that the old Highlanders "resented injuries with vehemence and passion".[464] Perhaps the Highlanders must be regarded in the same light as the animal in the French zoo, on whose cage was a warning notice: "Cet animal est très méchant; quand on l'attaque, il se défend". (This animal is very dangerous: when he is attacked, he defends himself.)

Nevertheless, the unanimous report of the Highlanders as being so proud and independent and jealous of their honour is surely very significant. For serfs groaning under a tyranny cannot afford the luxury of taking quick offence, whether it is justified or not.

68. Superstitious

The third bad quality which the Highlanders were said to possess was superstition. It is true that they were superstitious: that is, they held beliefs which had no rational foundation. Many of them accepted the reality of spirits, fairies, the evil eye, second sight, ancestral giants, and contemporary little beings of various kinds. They thought the ghosts of their fathers still hovered round, to make sure that they adhered to the old clan qualities of comradeship, bravery, honesty, hospitality and so on. The existence of these superstitions cannot cause much surprise. The Highlanders lived in small groups in a very thinly populated and untamed landscape, showing few indications of human occupancy. A

Highlander would often find himself alone, perhaps while hunting or herding, in an uninhabited stretch of country, where no man had left his mark; or making his way deep in a gloomy forest; or it might be at night, amid towering mountains, crashing waterfalls, and tearing winds; or encompassed by one of the wild Highland storms, when the lightning flashes across the heavens, the thunder rocks the crags, and the rain whips the ground. Dorothy and William Wordsworth were walking in 1803 near the shore of Loch Lomond, towards Tarbet, and saw a little boy on the hill, "wrapped up in a grey plaid", seemingly calling home the cattle. "His appearance was in the highest degree moving to the imagination: mists were on the hillsides, darkness shutting in upon the huge avenue of mountains, torrents roaring, no house in sight to which the child might belong; his dress, cry, and appearance all different from anything we had been accustomed to."[465] It need not generate great astonishment that the Highlanders were disposed by the sensational natural phenomena around them to give credence to the tales of the supernatural that were part of the clan tradition. Furthermore, the Highlanders actually believed in a future life; not, as many do in our society, as a mere acquiescence in a form of words, but as a firm reality, just beyond the grave. Taking leave of aged friends, Highlanders would sometimes solemnly send messages to their dead relatives, and an old person would gravely accept the office, adding only that the message would be delivered "if it is permitted".[466]

At two particular times in the year the Highlanders thought they were in especially close touch with the "unseen world" of spectres and phantoms. On 1st May the lighter and warmer six months of the year were greeted by the ceremonies of Bealltainn, or Beltane. The O.S.A. report on Callander, written about 1791, described the ceremony at that time (probably less complicated than it had been earlier). All the boys in a township would meet on the moor round a fire. They would eat a custard of eggs and milk; then divide an oatmeal cake into portions, one for each participant, and blacken one piece. Whoever drew that piece was "sacrificed" to Baal, to bring good luck to the community for the next year. The "sacrifice" was leaping three times through the flames.[467] A counterbalancing festival was held on Samhuinn, or the eve of 1st November, the beginning of the darker and colder half of the year. Again fires were made, and various ceremonies performed – the participants hoping to ward off the hobgoblins and other phantoms of the night which were then all about.

The Highlanders were not alone in these half-yearly celebrations, of course. May Day ceremonies were well known throughout the British Isles, and beyond them; while All Souls (or All Saints, or All Hallows) Day, and the night before, or Hallowe'en, was in many places (and apparently, is now) thought to be a time when unfriendly or mischievous spirits were particularly active, and had unusual influence.

CUSTOMS OF THE HIGHLANDERS

69. Fear of a ghost

If one could bring oneself to believe that some superstitions are more acceptable than other superstitions, one might feel that the Highlanders' beliefs were perhaps less harmful than some which have been known. David Stewart wrote that the Highlanders' creed "taught men to believe, that a dishonourable act attached disgrace to a whole kindred and district, and that murder, treachery, oppression, and all kinds of wickedness, would not only be punished in the person of the transgressor himself, but would descend to future generations. When the Highlander imagined that he saw the ghost of his father frowning upon him from the skirts of the passing clouds, or that he heard his voice in the howlings of the midnight tempest, or when he found his imagination awed by the recital of fairytales, of ghosts, and visions of the second sight, the heart of the wicked was subdued; and when he believed that his misdeeds would be visited on his succeeding generations, who would also be rewarded and prosper in consequence of his good actions, he would either be powerfully restrained or encouraged." Stewart maintained "that the fear of a ghost is as honourable and legitimate a check as the fear of the gallows, and the thoughts of bringing dishonour on a man's country, name and kindred, fully as respectable as the fear of Bridewell, Botany Bay, or of the Constable's whip".[468] Certainly these doctrines seem less opprobrious than some schemes of faith-based belief now widely advocated, which sometimes appear to have as a principal aim the infliction of injury or death on the adherents of competing systems.

The matter may be put in perspective if one recalls that in the Lowlands, and England, at that time, people believed so firmly in witchcraft that they burned many old women alive for being "in league with the devil" – a devil so powerless that he could not rescue his supposed allies from one of the most painful forms of death which even civilized man has yet devised. In the present twenty-first century, in our prosaic modern society, where man's knowledge of the universe has developed to the point at which he has begun to send travellers (and to dispatch machines) to other bodies in the solar system, there are many widely held beliefs about the number thirteen, spilling salt, touching wood, walking under ladders, passing on a staircase, and many other daily objects and events; the newspapers, radio, television, and the internet devote much time and space to astrology and fortune-telling; creeds based on Tarot cards, palmistry, crystal-gazing, numerology, furniture re-arranging, flying saucers and exotic visitants from far-distant worlds fascinate whole populations; and many millions devote large parts of their lives to activities which are based on a belief in the supernatural. In fact we are told that a large number of the citizens of the United

States of America, the most industrially and materially advanced country in the world, are convinced that they have been abducted by aliens, and carried off into space ships (though, fortunately, later restored to their friends and families). The replacement of clanship by commercial society meant as a rule only the acceptance of a new set of superstitions, not necessarily more salubrious, to replace the old.

Although some writers draw a picture of the old Highlands in which second sight, forecasting the future, and similar irrational phenomena, bulk largely, it is unfortunately the fact that there is probably more material based on unreason in one day's editions of our modern mass-circulation newspapers than there was in the life of a Highlander over decades.

70. Happiness

Finally, there seems to be no doubt that in the old clan society the Highlanders were generally contented. Even in the 1790s, amid all the complaints of high rents and the changes for the worse which had occurred in the previous half century, those Highlanders who were still allowed to occupy the land in their native glen or island were, under all the new oppressions, happy, whether they were small tenants or sub-tenants under a tacksman. They were "cheerful and humorous" (Tiree),[469] and seemed "to enjoy life" (Loth).[470] The Mortlach report thought the locals were "disposed to cheerfulness and contentment".[471] Before the new dispensation, when the annual tribute had been low and the chief affable, this trait was even more marked. The minister of Strachur said: "The Highlanders of old did not live either in plenty or in elegance, yet they were happy. They piqued themselves on the capacity of enduring hunger and fatigue."[472] He added (as we saw earlier) that they "were passionately fond of music and poetry. The song and the dance soon made them forget their toils." William Sacheverell, writing about the people he saw during a visit to the Highlands in 1688, concurred in this opinion. "There appeared in all their actions a certain generous air of freedom and contempt of those trifles, luxury and ambition, which we so servilely creep after. They bound their appetites by their necessities, and their happiness consists, not in having much, but in coveting little."[473]

The minister of North Knapdale, writing of the old clan days, (and since he called them the "barbarous ages" it seems he was not prejudiced in their favour), said that philosophers often ignored "the happiness and independence which in some degree is peculiar to this state. Of old, the chieftain was not so much considered the master as the father of his numerous clan. Every individual of these followers loved him with a degree of enthusiasm, which made them cheerfully undergo any fatigue or danger. Upon the other hand, it was his interest, it was his pride, and his chief glory, to requite such animated friendship to the utmost of his power."[474]

Toland, writing well before the changes, at the beginning of the eighteenth century, called the Highlanders (to give his comment more fully) "choleric, but easily appeased, sociable, good natured, ever cheerful".[475] Their preference for their own way of life was so strong that to one observer it seemed to have a flavour of religious belief. "They account it", wrote Alexander Cunningham, "among the most scandalous crimes . . . to alter their dress and way of living: for they think that in dress and ancient customs, there is something sacred."[476] Dr Johnson, writing about his 1773 visit to the Highlands, described "whole neighbourhoods" emigrating, and taking with them their language, their opinions, their popular songs, and their "hereditary merriment".[477] David Stewart said, "a more happy and contented race never existed".[478] Even when the improvements had begun over much of the Highlands, there was enough of the old society left in the more remote parts of Gaeldom for this happiness to have survived. Later in the century Peggy MacCormack of Lochboisdale in South Uist reminisced about her early life. Old and young were fond of dancing, she said. "Those were the happy days and the happy nights, and there was neither sin nor sorrow in the world for us. The thought of those young days makes my old heart both glad and sad even at this distance of time."[479] (As we saw, Peggy's memories did not fit the orthodox version of history, so Professor Rosalind Mitchison crisply denounced them as "rubbish". She was not the only Lowland historian who has expedited the arrival at a desired conclusion by taking such a vigorous short cut.) But the eighth Duke of Argyll himself, that implacable enemy of the clan society, could not deny that the clansfolk were happy. He confessed it as grudgingly as he could by calling their happiness "a mindless contentment with a very low diet",[480] thus implying two things – that the clansfolk had somehow a poorer mental life than their descendants in the nineteenth-century factory towns, and that they had a worse diet than the latter – neither of which was true: but he did make the admission.

The happiness of the old Highlanders was their own verdict on the society in which they lived. They were a pastoral people, and one commentator said that they used their Gaelic word for pasture (one of the basic features of their lives) to convey also the meaning of peace, tranquillity, and happiness. As Alexander Cunningham put it, "They take most pleasure in that course of life which was followed by their ancestors".[481]

CHAPTER SEVEN NOTES

1. *Harp and violin*
[1] Stewart 1822, II xxi, quoting Monniepennie 1597.
[2] Seton Gordon 1951, 13-14.
[3] E. Grant, *Memoirs of a Highland Lady*, Canongate, Edinburgh, 1992, 311.
[4] E. Grant, ditto, 46.
[5] Grant 1811, 202.

2. *Piping families*
[6] Cooper 1970, 19.
[7] Seton Gordon 1951, 14.
[8] N.S.A. XIV 285, Kilmuir Inv.
[9] Seton Gordon 1963, 75.
[10] Seton Gordon 1963, 76.
[11] Adam/Innes 1965, 423.
[12] Adam/Innes 1965, 423.
[13] Johnson & Boswell 1930, 116.
[14] Johnson & Boswell 1930, 93.
[15] Graham-Campbell 1978, 115.
[16] Johnson & Boswell 1930, 93.
[17] Murray 1969, 235.
[18] Cooper 1970, 20.
[19] Adam/Innes 1965, 423.
[20] Grimble 1973, 166.
[21] Seton Gordon 1963, 83; see J. G. Gibson, *Old & New World Highland Bagpiping*, Birlinn, Edinburgh, 2005, 167.

3. *MacCrimmons in Skye*
[22] *Oxford D.N.B.*, article on the MacCrimmons.
[23] Pennant 1998, 755, appendix XI, by the Rev. Donald MacQueen.
[24] Buchanan 1997, 35.

4. *MacKays, MacIntyres, MacDougalls*
[25] Seton Gordon 1963, 85-6.
[26] Seton Gordon 1963, 81-2.
[27] Seton Gordon 1963, 84. He wrote: "The MacDougalls were originally hereditary pipers to the MacDougall chiefs . . . By virtue of their office they held a croft [sic] rent-free at Moleigh, and at Kilbride in the same district they had their college of piping. This school of piping was held in Tigh nam Piobairean, House of the Pipers, near Dunach which is situated a little to the south of Oban."
[28] Seton Gordon 1963, 112, & see 76.

5. *Music and dance*
[29] Stewart 1822, I 84 & 84 fn; Stewart 1822, II xxv.
[30] Grant & Cheape 2000, 136.
[31] Grant & Cheape 2000, 255-6.
[32] Rixson 2004, 341, quoting Saint Fond 1907.

[33] O.S.A. XV 258, Monzie Perth.
[34] O.S.A. X 414, Tiree Arg.
[35] O.S.A. III 516, Kincardine Ross.
[36] O.S.A. XI 285, Kilchoman Arg.
[37] O.S.A. IV 576, Strachur & Strathlachlan Arg.
[38] O.S.A. XII 469, 470, Kirkmichael Banff.
[39] Johnson & Boswell 1930, 52.
[40] *Scottish Historical Review*, XVI, 1919, 108, quoting C. Hutcheson, *Journal to Arran in 1783*.
[41] Stoddart 1801, II 132-4.

6. *Vigour and agility*
[42] MacKay 1889, 342.
[43] O.S.A. XII 265, Knockbain Ross.
[44] O.S.A. XIX 629, Killean & Kilchenzie Arg.
[45] O.S.A. VIII 63, Gigha & Cara Arg.
[46] O.S.A. XV 636 fn, Avoch Ross.
[47] Buchanan 1997, 34-5.
[48] Stewart 1822, I 499 fn.
[49] Carmichael 1928-71, III 328-9.

7. *Clearly rubbish*
[50] Hunter 2000, 15, quoting R. Mitchison's words in a 1981 article in *Scottish Economic and Social History*. Professor Mitchison taught history at Edinburgh University, and was described by the *Daily Telegraph* (24th September 2002) as "the twentieth century's foremost exponent of the social history of Scotland".
[51] O.S.A. XVI 203, Assynt Suth; Stoddart 1801, 133.
[52] Stewart 1822, I 333 fn.
[53] Stewart 1822, II liii.
[54] O.S.A. X 404, Tiree Arg. See volume two of this work.
[55] Stewart 1822, I 96.
[56] O.S.A. XX xiii, foreword by Sir John Sinclair.
[57] Napier 1884, I 435, qu. 7579, Dr Martin of Husabost.

8. *Sweet airs*
[58] Burt 2005, 213.
[59] Walker 1980, 8.
[60] Pennant 2000, 129.
[61] Pennant 1998, 279, 284-5.
[62] Buchanan 1997, 36.
[63] Napier 1884, V 478, Alexander Carmichael; www.kirkbymalham.info.
[64] O.S.A. VIII 340, Glenorchy & Inishail Arg.
[65] Johnson & Boswell 1930, 265-6.
[66] Johnson & Boswell 1930, 56, 53.
[67] Barron 1903-13, III 390.
[68] Thomson 2010, 65.
[69] O.S.A. XI 578, Callander Perth.
[70] Hogg 1981, 141, 142.
[71] Napier 1884, V 472, Alexander Carmichael.

9. A voice so thrilling

[72] Hogg 1981, 142.
[73] Wordsworth 1894, 83.
[74] Wordsworth 1894, 237-8.
[75] Byron 1863, 392.
[76] Bowman 1986, 127.
[77] Victoria 1994, 30.

10. *Rustic strains*
[78] N.S.A. XIV 286, Kilmuir Inv.
[79] Larkin 1819, 93.
[80] Napier 1884, V 460, Alexander Carmichael; Stoddart 1801, 133.
[81] Steel 1984, 298, 297. T. Steel's rigorous rectification of Highland history seems to come from the orthodox horse's mouth: in the "Acknowledgements" at the front of his book (p. 9) Steel thanked his father, the "editor of *Scotland's Magazine*", and also the editors of *The Scotsman* and the *Glasgow Herald*, for their help.

11. *Sports and games*
[82] Rixson 2004, 315, quoting John Elder.
[83] Grant & Cheape 2000, 255.
[84] Rixson 2004, 229, quoting the Wardlaw Manuscript 1655.
[85] Linklater 1982, 111.
[86] Pennant 1998, 751, appendix XI, by Rev. Donald MacQueen.
[87] N.S.A. X 72, Moulin Perth.
[88] N.S.A. XIV 307, Kilmuir Easter, Ross.
[89] N.S.A. X 770, Dull Perth.
[90] N.S.A. V 27, Kilbride Bute.
[91] N.S.A. V 58, Kilmory Bute.
[92] N.S.A. XIV 18, Inverness Inv.
[93] N.S.A. XIV 360, Duirinish Inv.
[94] N.S.A. XIV 165, Lochs Ross.
[95] N.S.A. XIV 154, Uig Ross.
[96] N.S.A. XIV 223, Dingwall Ross; N.S.A. XV 156, Clyne Suth.

12. *Amusing themselves*
[97] N.S.A. XIV 451, Croy Inv.
[98] N.S.A. X 268, Monzie Perth.
[99] N.S.A. XIV 104, Moy Inv.
[100] N.S.A. XIV 272 fn, Rosskeen Ross.
[101] N.S.A. X 486, Kenmore Perth.
[102] N.S.A. VII 143, Lismore Arg.
[103] N.S.A. XIII 188, Edinkillie Moray.
[104] Sage 1975, 9.
[105] Miller 1854, 39.
[106] Sage 1975, 12.
[107] Miller 1854, 373.
[108] Burt 2005, 100.
[109] Murdoch 1986, 51, 52.

13. *Work and play*
[110] Murdoch 1986, 80.

[111] Murdoch 1986, 111; MacKay 1889, 296-7.

14. *Gaelic culture*
[112] O.S.A. XI 620, Callander Perth.
[113] Stewart 1822, II xiii, quoting Toland.
[114] Thomson 2010, 64.
[115] Martin 1703, 13-14, 200.
[116] N.S.A. XV 178, Tongue Suth.
[117] Stewart 1822, I 95.
[118] Stewart 1822, I 95 fn.
[119] Stewart 1822, I 95 fn.
[120] Stewart 1822, I 95 fn.

15. Ancient poems and tales
[121] Stewart 1822, I 361 fn.
[122] Stewart 1822, I 98 fn & I 360 fn.
[123] Selkirk 2010, 21.
[124] Stoddart 1801, II 297.
[125] Jamieson 2005, xxviii & xxxi fn.

16. *Copious and expressive*
[126] O.S.A. X 416 fn, Tiree Arg.
[127] O.S.A. VIII 430, Kilmallie Inv.
[128] O.S.A. V 584, Greenock Renfr.
[129] Skene 1890, III 391.
[130] Stewart 1822, II xiii, quoting Toland.
[131] O.S.A. XIII 323, North Uist Inv.
[132] MacDonald 1811, 129.

17. *Powerful eloquence*
[133] Stewart 1822, I 96-8.
[134] Moray McLaren, *The Highland Jaunt*, Jarrolds, London, 1954, 80; for another narrative of the incident, see *Highlands and Highlanders*, Highlands Committee, Empire Exhibition, Glasgow, 1938, 84.

18. *Inoffensive language*
[135] Johnson & Boswell 1930, 96.
[136] Napier 1884, V 481, Alexander Carmichael.
[137] Rixson 2004, 299, quoting Mrs Murray, *Beauties of Scotland*.
[138] Stewart 1822, II 250.
[139] The records left by the clan poets of the clearances are often ignored. Professor Richards goes near to saying they do not exist: "the poor, the powerless and the illiterate leave very little residue of their lives among which a historian may seek material for their reconstruction" – quoted in Hunter 2000, 16. (None so blind as he who will not see.) Professor Smout brushes off this evidence: "the Gaelic poets vented their feelings in a froth of impotent abuse" (Smout 1970, 357). Professor Bumsted (Bumsted 1982, xiv) warned that the bards, who expressed the "Highlanders' sentiments", unfortunately tended to "hyperbole and exaggeration", and therefore "must be treated with some caution"; though sadly he gave no examples, nor was able to indicate why he knew their productions were hyperbolic or exaggerated.

19. *Education valued*

140 Numbers of schools had been established in the Highlands by the Church of Scotland and by the Scottish Society for the Promotion of Christian Knowledge; in their early days these schools were considered to be part of the struggle against Roman Catholicism and also against the use of Gaelic. But the sparse Highland population (so far from being "congested", as modern commentators copy each other in asserting) was spread so thinly that many townships could not expect to be within reach of a school.

141 O.S.A. IV 569, Strachur Arg.
142 O.S.A. I 493, Lismore Arg.
143 O.S.A. XIV 208 fn, Kilfinichen & Kilvickeon Arg.
144 O.S.A. XIII 521 fn, Kiltarlity Inv.
145 O.S.A. II 456, Fortingall Perth.
146 O.S.A. XII 227, Glenmuick Aberd.
147 O.S.A. III 188, Lochgoilhead Arg.
148 See Thomson 1983 for details of these poets. The new regime was inimical to poetry, certainly to poetry expressing the views of the ordinary Highlanders; and in the end the invaluable manuscripts of the MacMhuirich bards were cut up for tailors' patterns.
149 Thomson 1983, 184.
150 Stewart 1822, II xxxii fn.
151 The dates of Duncan Ban – the Fair – are given as 1724-1812 in Thomson 1983, 159, and as 1723?-1812 by the *Oxford D.N.B*. But Stewart (Stewart 1822, I 95) said he "died in 1816, in his 93rd year", which of course would mean that he was born either in 1723 or in 1724. This seems to confirm that Stewart actually did write 1816 for Duncan Ban's death – that it was not a misprint.
152 O.S.A. VI 254, Kintail Ross. MacCurchi emigrated to America, probably in 1782.
153 Mac a'Ghobhainn means literally the son of the blacksmith or metal-worker; and "Smith" is the English for metal-worker.

20. *Intelligent and ingenious*

154 Some city-dwellers believed that everyone living outside a town was a fool: and that it was the city, where the rulers where normally to be found, and where the acceptable language was fashioned which held all the people who knew how to behave properly. Hence many terms of approval in English (and doubtless other languages) mean simply of the town or city (urbane, civil, civilized, polite, cosmopolitan, polished). Besides that, courteous and courtesy go back originally to "court", an open space surrounded by houses, and therefore mainly found in a town. In contrast lots of demeaning terms mean of the country, e.g. clown, boor, villain, rustic, churl, yokel, clod-hopper, country bumpkin, coward (cow-herd), pagan (which originally meant simply a rustic). Boor, villain, and churl, were all farmers in the old manorial system – bordar, villein, ceorl. Silly at one time meant country-dweller, and therefore came to signify foolish. In modern American usage (as we saw earlier), peasant is an insult. The townsman or city-dweller obviously shaped the language which we all now use. In *The Comedy of Errors*, Shakespeare twice used "peasant" to mean "servant" (II, i 81, & V, i 231).

155 O.S.A. XIV 346, Crathie & Braemar Aberd.
156 O.S.A. XVI 384, Killin Perth.
157 O.S.A. XI 285, Kilchoman Arg.
158 O.S.A. X 414, Tiree Arg.
159 O.S.A. XIII 323, North Uist Inv.
160 O.S.A. VI 264, North Knapdale Arg.
161 O.S.A. IV 136, Duirinish Inv.
162 O.S.A. XII 469, Kirkmichael Banff.
163 O.S.A. XVI 160, Portree Inv.
164 O.S.A. XIV 77, Daviot & Dunlichity Inv.
165 O.S.A. II 555, Kilmuir Inv.

[166] Buchanan 1997, 34 & 107.
[167] Stewart 1822, II xiii, quoting Toland.
[168] MacLeod 1910, 102.
[169] N.S.A. XV 178, Tongue Suth.
[170] Stewart 1822, I 239, quoting Jackson 1804.
[171] Sinclair 1795, 110.
[172] Buchan 1938, 158.
[173] Blundell 1909, 122, quoting Bishop Nicolson.
[174] Walker 1980, 47.
[175] Walker 1980, 8, 9.
[176] Glover 1966, 222.

21. *Of quick parts*
[177] O.S.A. III 516, Kincardine Ross.
[178] O.S.A. XIII 323, North Uist Inv.
[179] O.S.A. XVI 160, Portree Inv.
[180] Marshall 1794, 18.
[181] Robertson 1808, v.
[182] Burt's *Letters*, 1818 or 1822 edition. Stewart 1822, I 44 fn, said the story was "in Mr Jamieson's Fenner, London, 1818, or the even later 1822 edition".
[183] Stewart 1822, II 16-17 fn.

22. *Enterprise and initiative*
[184] Stewart 1822, I 381-2 fn.
[185] Stewart 1822, I 386 fn.
[186] Stewart 1822, I 38-9 fn.

23. *Pride and independence*
[187] Selkirk 2010, 49.
[188] O.S.A. XV 520, Kirkmichael Perth.
[189] O.S.A. VIII 447 fn, Kilmallie Inv.
[190] O.S.A. XIV 77, Daviot & Dunlichity Inv.
[191] O.S.A. VI 246, North Knapdale Arg.
[192] O.S.A. X 533, Campbeltown Arg.
[193] Stewart 1822, II xxii, quoting Defoe 1720.
[194] Walker 1980, 203.
[195] Johnson & Boswell 1930, 32.
[196] Buchanan 1997, 43.
[197] G. H. Healey, *Letters of Daniel Defoe*, O.U.P., London, 1955, 146-7.
[198] Scott 1995, 448.

24. *Erect martial air*
[199] Stewart 1822, I 182 fn. Elsewhere Stewart, like Defoe more than a century earlier, hit upon the Spanish hidalgos when seeking a comparison. The effect of the ancestral garb on the Highlanders, he wrote, "even of the present day, is curious. However clownish a young man appears in his pantaloons, walking with a heavy awkward gait, and downcast look, if he dresses in the kilt and bonnet on a Sunday, he assumes a kind of new character, holds his head erect, throws his shoulders back, and walks with a strut and a mien than might become a Castilian or a knight of old Spain".
[200] Stewart 1822, I 53-4.
[201] Stewart 1822, I 53-4 fn.

[202] Stewart 1822, I 132 fn. "Peasantry" was of course a mistaken term to describe the Highlanders of the old society; but in the 1820s it was the usual term to describe the general run of people in a rural society, which perhaps explains why Stewart used it, inaccurate though it was.
[203] Stewart 1822, I 237-8, quoting Jackson 1804.

25. *Self-respect*
[204] O.S.A. XI 619, Callander Perth.
[205] Stewart 1822, II 173, & see I 292.
[206] Stewart 1822, II 413 & 416.
[207] Stewart 1822, I 275 fn.
[208] Buchanan 1997, 21, 43, 70.
[209] MacMillan 1971, 140.
[210] Stewart 1822, I 250 fn, quoting *Westminster Journal*.
[211] MacKay 1889, 175.
[212] Stewart 1822, I 48-9, quoting Dalrymple 1771.

26. *"Habituated to domination"*
[213] Donaldson 1966, 68.
[214] Donaldson 1993, 171. Donaldson's metaphor, about people "throwing up" a leader, with its suggestion of nausea, is not inappropriate when one considers where many leaders have led.
[215] Stewart 1822, I 260.
[216] Stewart 1822, I 67 fn.

27. *Highland soldiers*
[217] O.S.A. XIII 144, Abernethy & Kincardine Inv.
[218] Stewart 1822, I 236-7, & I 237 fn.
[219] Stewart 1822, I 261.
[220] Stewart 1822, II 409.
[221] Stewart 1822, II 404-5.

28. *Free pardon*
[222] Stewart 1822, II 41-12.
[223] Stewart 1822, II 406, & Prebble 1977, 211 et seq.
[224] Stewart 1822, II 140.
[225] Stewart 1822, II 413, 415, 416.
[226] Stewart 1822, II 34-5.
[227] Stewart 1822, II xiv-xv.

29. *Religious tolerance*
[228] Napier 1884, V 460, Alexander Carmichael.
[229] Stewart 1822, I 101, paraphrasing Dalrymple 1771.
[230] Blundell 1909, 207.
[231] Stewart 1822, I 101, quoting Dalrymple 1771.
[232] O.S.A. VII 253, Urray Ross.
[233] O.S.A. XVII 428, Mortlach Banff.
[234] O.S.A. XIV 73, Daviot Inv.
[235] Stewart 1822, I 103-4, quoting an un-named writer.
[236] Pennant 1998, 274.
[237] Watson 1960, 237-9. I was fortunate enough to have tutorials with Steven Watson at Oxford; this was before he went on to his twenty-year tenure as Principal of St Andrews University in Scotland. I

learned much from him – that goes without saying; but when he retained an essay, to mark it, it was sometimes not promptly returned. I enquired once about an essay of mine. He indicated a column of paper, some feet high, in the corner of his room, inclining dangerously like the leaning tower of Pisa, and said it was there somewhere. Perhaps he was already writing his magnum opus.

[238] N.S.A. VII 191, Morvern Arg.
[239] Geikie 1908, 45 & 46.
[240] Napier 1884, V 462-3, Alexander Carmichael.

30. *Catholic clans*
[241] MacKenzie 1911, 650.
[242] McMillan 1969 187, 183.
[243] Richards 1999, 368, quoting *The Times*, 1996.
[244] *The Times*, 3rd February 2006, 28.
[245] MacDonell 1937, 13, 30.
[246] MacDonell 1937, 172. MacDonell described Prince Charles' army in 1745 as "half-savage, Gaelic-speaking, Catholic soldiers"; three adjectives, all of which were wrong in different ways.
[247] Adam/Innes 1965, 55; the date indicated was "after 1603", but no evidence was given to support the statement, or to explain why (in that case) there was such an enormous conversion by 1750. Another commentator referred to a "sectarian divide of catholic highlander and protestant lowlander".
[248] Glover 1966, 193.
[249] Finlay 1966, 30.
[250] Pine 1972, 14.
[251] Somerset Fry 1985, 197.
[252] Burke 1990, 183.
[253] Donnachie & Hewitt 1989, 42.
[254] Ross 1998, 182.
[255] Herman 2002, 94.
[256] Fallow 1999, 74.
[257] Steel 1994, 110.
[258] Miller 1854, 373.
[259] Website www.litencyc.com.
[260] Prebble 1970, 153. "The MacDonalds will fall into this net. That's the only popish clan in the kingdom . . ." Stair was probably referring only to the Glen Coe clan, but it is possible he meant all the MacDonalds. (In either case he was in error, of course.)
[261] There is some uncertainty about the MacDonalds of Glen Coe. See MacDonald 1994, 155; Blundell 1909, 207; Lang 1898, xxxi (who said they were Episcopalians); & Ferguson 1994, 22 (who said they were probably Episcopalians).
[262] Blundell 1909, 207: "the Camerons having been Catholics for several generations after the Reformation."

31. *A small minority*
[263] Kyd 1952, passim.
[264] Devine 1998, 24. A hundred years after Webster, the minister of Morvern gave his own religious census: "Number of families connected with the Established Church, 370; of Roman Catholic families, 8; of professed Episcopalian families, 2" – N.S.A. VII 191. Perhaps one should add here that this whole section is not concerned with what religion the Highlanders should have had, or to boost one belief over another; it is merely concerned with reality, the actual state of the religious beliefs held by those people at that time.
[265] Kyd 1952, passim.
[266] Blundell 1909, 17.

[267] Lynch 1996, 367.
[268] Devine 1998, 29, quoting *Gentleman's Magazine*, 1739.

32. As if they had been Christians
[269] N.S.A. XIV 406, Petty Inv.
[270] N.S.A. VII 19, Inveraray Arg.
[271] Hopkins 1998, 25.
[272] *Oxford D.N.B.*, article on Aikenhead.
[273] N.S.A. VII 243, Paisley Renfr, & N.S.A. VII 507-8, Erskine Renfr.
[274] Stewart 1822, I 251 fn, & II 34.

33. Serious and religious deportment
[275] Stewart 1822, I 134 & 135 fn.
[276] Wordsworth 1894, 110-11.
[277] Blundell 1917, 189.
[278] Gilpin 1799, 214.

34. No scoffing or insult
[279] Thomson 2010, 63, quoting Cunningham 1787.
[280] N.S.A. VII 192, Morvern Arg.
[281] N.S.A. VII 307, Kilfinichen & Kilvickeon Arg.
[282] Stewart 1822, I 135.
[283] *Poetical Works of William Wordsworth*, Warne, London, ?1878, 277. Wordsworth referred in that poem to "the labouring many and the resting few"; and Wilkinson would have seen in the Highlands a striking example of that sociological phenomenon, in the new class-divided system imposed upon the Highlands after Culloden.
[284] Wilkinson, *Last Journey of John Pemberton*, Parke, Philadelphia, 1811, 66, 64, 10, 33, 17, 36, 49.

35. Highland characteristics
[285] Devine 2004, 253, quoting Lady MacAskill, *12 Days in Skye*, London, 1852, 16.

36. Gratitude, kindness, friendship
[286] Stewart 1822, I 218.
[287] Charles Wolfe, *Burial of Sir John Moore*, Palgrave, *Golden Treasury*, O.U.P., London, 1919, 216.
[288] Stewart 1822, I 525-6 fn.
[289] Stewart 1822, II 332.
[290] Stewart 1822, I 580 fn.
[291] Stewart 1822, I 579.
[292] Stewart 1822, II 24.
[293] Stewart 1822, II 24-5, quoting Jackson 1804.

37. The Civil Wars
[294] Stewart 1822, I 41-2.
[295] Stewart 1822, II liii.
[296] Stewart 1822, II 360.

38. Stuart versus Hanover
[297] Stewart 1822, I 66.
[298] Stewart 1822, I 66 fn, quoting *Memoirs of Lord Dundee*.
[299] Graham-Campbell 1979, 61.

[300] O.S.A. II 479, Blair Atholl Perth.
[301] Stewart 1822, I 72, quoting Dalrymple 1771.
[302] Stewart 1822, I 70.
[303] Thomson 2010, 36.
[304] Stewart 1822, I 588-9 fn.
[305] Stewart 1822, I 111 fn; see also N.S.A. XIV 98 fn, Moy Inv.

39. *Fidelity and valour*
[306] Stewart 1822, II 18.
[307] Stewart 1822, I 186 fn; & see also I 366, I 500 fn, II 445 & II 501.
[308] Richards 1982, 14, & passim in his work, e.g. Richards 1999, 28, 375, 376, 377, 378, 383.

40. *Battle of Fontenoy*
[309] Stewart 1822, I 250, quoting *Caledonian Mercury*.
[310] John Wesley, *Journal*, 5th June 1750.
[311] Stewart 1822, I 262.
[312] Stewart 1822, I 272.
[313] Stewart 1822, I 273.
[314] Stewart 1822, I 274.
[315] Stewart 1822, I 358.

41. *"All or nothing"*
[316] MacDonell 1937, 19.
[317] MacDonell 1937, 18, & 11.
[318] Tytler 1874, 134.
[319] Stewart 1822, II xxi; & Skene 1837, I 238, both quoting Beaugué 1707.
[320] Stewart 1822, I 41-2.
[321] P. Anderson 1920, quoting *National Journal*, London, 7th June 1746; see website queenofscots.co.uk.
[322] *National Journal*, London, 7th June 1746.
[323] MacDonald 1994, 60, quoting de Johnstone 1820.
[324] Stewart 1822, I 270.
[325] Stewart 1822, I 273, quoting a Paris account days later.
[326] Stewart 1822, I 274, quoting Rolt's *Life of the Earl of Crawford*.
[327] Stewart 1822, I 275 fn.

42. *Highly disciplined*
[328] G. N. Clark, *Later Stuarts*, Clarendon Press, Oxford, 1947, 266.
[329] MacDonald 1994, 163.
[330] Stewart 1822, I 278-9.
[331] Stewart 1822, I 286 fn.
[332] Stewart 1822, I 288.
[333] Stewart 1822, II 9.
[334] Stewart 1822, II 11.

43. *A respect and regard*
[335] Stewart 1822, I 262-3, quoting Dr Doddridge, *Life of Colonel Gardiner*, London, 1749.
[336] Stewart 1822, I 290.
[337] Stewart 1822, I 291-2.
[338] Stewart 1822, I 406 fn.

[339] Stewart 1822, I 295 fn.
[340] Stewart 1822, II 22-3.

44. *Attack on Ticonderoga*
[341] Stewart 1822, I 301-2.
[342] Stewart 1822, I 305.
[343] Stewart 1822, I 306-7.
[344] Stewart 1822, I 305.

45. *West Indies and North America*
[345] Stewart 1822, I 320 fn.
[346] Stewart 1822, I 330.
[347] Stewart 1822, I 333.
[348] Stewart 1822, I 340.
[349] Stewart 1822, I 343.

46. *Seven Years' War*
[350] Stewart 1822, II 25.
[351] Stewart 1822, II 27.
[352] Stewart 1822, II 28.
[353] Stewart 1822, II 29.
[354] Stewart 1822, II 30.
[355] Stewart 1822, II 33.

47. *Humanity and generosity*
[356] Stewart 1822, II 29, 31.
[357] Stewart 1822, II 33-4.

48. *India, America, Ireland, Scotland*
[358] Stewart 1822, II 38.
[359] Stewart 1822, I 355.
[360] Stewart 1822, I 357.
[361] Stewart 1822, I 292.
[362] Stewart 1822, I 363.
[363] The Black Watch was reviewed in April 1776, & was found to be "complete and unexceptionable". "Of the soldiers 931 were Highlanders, 74 Lowland Scotch, 5 English (in the band), 1 Welsh, and 2 Irish" (Stewart 1822, I 367 fn); that is 931 Highlanders, and 82 others, a total of 1013. Stewart 1822, I 508 fn, gives more figures. "In 1776 the number embarked for America was 1160 men, all of whom, except 54 Lowlanders, and 2 Englishmen in the band, were Highlanders. In all former periods the proportions were similar . . . At the commencement of the war in 1793 the strength of the regiment was low. The proportions were 480 Highlanders, 152 Lowland Scotch, 4 Irish, and 3 English [a total of 639]. At the present period there embarked from Gibraltar, in 1808, 383 Highlanders, 231 Lowlanders, 7 English, and 5 Irish", a total of 626.
[364] Stewart 1822, II 47.

49. *1775-83 War: the Black Watch*
[365] Stewart 1822, I 391 & 391 fn.
[366] Stewart 1822, I 368 fn.
[367] Stewart 1822, I 376, & 376-7 fn.
[368] Stewart 1822, I 393-4.

[369] Stewart 1822, I 397.

50. *Fraser's Highlanders*
[370] Stewart 1822, II 47-8.
[371] Stewart 1822, II 47.
[372] Stewart 1822, II 50-1.
[373] Stewart 1822, II 49.
[374] Stewart 1822, II 53 fn; Stewart, II 181.
[375] Stewart 1822, I 59.
[376] Stewart 1822, II 50 fn.

51. *Surrender at Yorktown*
[377] Stewart 1822, II 79.
[378] Stewart 1822, II 57.
[379] Stewart 1822, II 79.
[380] Stewart 1822, II 79-80.

52. *MacDonald's Highlanders*
[381] Stewart 1822, II 117-18.
[382] Stewart 1822, II 120, & 120 fn.

53. *Canada and India*
[383] Stewart 1822, II 140-43.
[384] Stewart 1822, II 150-1.
[385] Stewart 1822, II 136.

54. *French Revolutionary War*
[386] Stewart 1822, I 407.
[387] Stewart 1822, I 408.
[388] Stewart 1822, II 324.
[389] Stewart 1822, II 352.
[390] Stewart 1822, II 189.
[391] Stewart 1822, II 218 fn.
[392] Stewart 1822, II 206.

55. *Healthy Highlanders*
[393] Watson 1960, 368-9. The nursery rhyme was much older than the Battle of Turcoing, but it was regarded as so apposite that it was appropriated by the duke's critics.
[394] Stewart 1822, I 413 fn.
[395] Stewart 1822, I 414-15.
[396] Stewart 1822, I 423-4.
[397] Stewart 1822, I 441 & 441 fn, & II 209.

56. *Highlanders in Ireland*
[398] Stewart 1822, II 353.
[399] Stewart 1822, II 352.
[400] Stewart 1822, II 401.
[401] Stewart 1822, II 224.

57. *Maida and Merexem*

[402] Stewart 1822, II 264 & 267.
[403] Stewart 1822, II 199-200.
[404] Stewart 1822, II 288, 289 fn.
[405] Thackeray, *Vanity Fair*, O.U.P., London, 336.
[406] Wellington, *Oxford Dictionary of Quotations*, 564.
[407] Stewart 1822, II 286-7.

58. *Waterloo campaign*
[408] MacDonell 1937, 72.
[409] Stewart 1822, I 585-6, & 585-6 fn.
[410] Stewart 1822, II 224-5.
[411] Stewart 1822, II 231.
[412] Stewart 1822, II 235 – literally, "how terrible they are, these grey horses!"
[413] Stewart 1822, I 587.

59. *Not fit to associate*
[414] Stewart 1822, I 292.
[415] Stewart 1822, I 394.
[416] Stewart 1822, II 322-3 fn.

60. *Highland Host*
[417] MacKay 1914, 156; Stewart 1822, II xxxix.
[418] Grant & Cheape 2000, 165.
[419] Hopkins 1998, 63.

61. *Bards and pipers*
[420] Stewart 1822, I 304.
[421] Stewart 1822, I 303 fn.
[422] Stewart 1822, I 121.
[423] Stewart 1822, II 92 fn.
[424] Stewart 1822, II 198 fn.

62. *Trustworthy*
[425] Stewart 1822, I 363-4.
[426] Stewart 1822, II xxviii.
[427] Stewart 1822, II 414-15.
[428] Stewart 1822, I 501.

63. *Prudent and sober*
[429] Stewart 1822, I 365.
[430] Stewart 1822, II 305, 251, & 307.
[431] Elizabeth Longford, *Wellington The Years of the Sword*, World Books, (1969) 1971, 43.
[432] General Sir Robert Wilson, *Life*, John Murray, London, 1862, 98. Wilson was a young officer in Flanders at the time. Earlier in the same book, at page 75, he had written about "courts-martial adjudging men to be punished for an offence of which the members had often been guilty at the same time, and from which they had frequently not recovered when passing sentence".
[433] George III. In a Parliamentary debate in 1812, Sir Francis Burdett tried to get the House of Commons to abolish flogging; but various generals, along with Lord Palmerston, and William Wilberforce, all spoke up in favour of it, and Burdett's attempt was defeated by 79 votes to 6. The Duke

of Wellington was another supporter, and it was only abolished (and even then, not in military prisons) in 1881.
[434] Stewart 1822, II 335.
[435] Stewart 1822, I 393.
[436] Stewart 1822, II 188-9 fn.
[437] See the judicious and restrained contribution of Auberon Waugh, *Daily Telegraph* 3rd February 1996, quoted by Rob Gibson, *Highland Clearances Trail*, Luath, Edinburgh, 2006, 25.

64. *Propaganda offensive*
[438] Stewart 1822, II 441.
[439] Glover 1966, 222.
[440] Stewart 1822, II 442.
[441] Stewart 1822, II 450 fn.
[442] MacKenzie 1810, 298.
[443] Stewart 1822, II 428 fn, quoting MacCulloch, presumably in MacCulloch's book *Description of the Western Islands of Scotland*, Constable, Edinburgh, 1819.

65. *Indolent clansfolk*
[444] O.S.A. XVII 427, Mortlach Banff.
[445] O.S.A. XIX 29, Halkirk Caith.
[446] Selkirk 2010, 6.
[447] Brown 1806, 57.
[448] Dr Dylan Evans, *The Times 2*, 8th June 2006. Another observer confirmed this: The San (Bushmen) peoples, hunter-gatherers living in Namibia, hunted and foraged for only fifteen hours a week (or two and a half hours a day in a six-day week.) In the new industrial society, factories often operated fifteen hours a day. (James Suzman, *Affluence Without Abundance*, Bloomsbury, London 2017.)
[449] Barron 1903-13, III, see 386-94.
[450] O.S.A. III 543, Farr Suth.
[451] O.S.A. XII 216, Glenmuick etc. Aberd.
[452] O.S.A. III 183, Lochgoilhead Arg.
[453] Richards 1985, 108.

66. *Resentful*
[454] Stewart 1822, II xxii, quoting Defoe 1720.
[455] Stewart 1822, II xiii, quoting Toland.
[456] Smollett 1967, 297.
[457] In 1940, at the time of Dunkirk, my family was living in South Yorkshire, in Mexborough; there was no immediate barrack accommodation for many of the soldiers taken off the Dunkirk beaches, and my parents volunteered (like many other residents) to take in some of them – three in our case. Naturally they were given the best in the house, and they and their families became our friends. (When they left, each of them gave me his knapsack, brought home from Dunkirk. I wish I had kept them!) If they had, early one morning, tried to murder us, our feelings would have been the same as those of the clansfolk of Glen Coe. The relationship between host and guest is almost sacred.
[458] Macaulay 1907, 586.
[459] Stewart 1822, I 102-3 fn; Burt 2005, xxxvi fn.
[460] Buchan 2009, 86.

67. *Superior to the meanness*
[461] Pennant 2000, 127.
[462] Stewart 1822, II xxii, quoting Defoe 1720.

[463] O.S.A. XVII 413 et seq, Mortlach Banff.
[464] O.S.A. XII 469, Kirkmichael Banff.

68. *Superstitious*
[465] Wordsworth 1894, 116.
[466] Stewart 1822, I 84.
[467] O.S.A. XI 620-1, Callander Perth.

69. *Fear of a ghost*
[468] Stewart 1822, I 135-6 fn.

70. *Happiness*
[469] O.S.A. X 414, Tiree Arg.
[470] O.S.A. VI 317 fn, Loth Suth.
[471] O.S.A. XVII 429, Mortlach Banff.
[472] O.S.A. IV 576, Strachur Arg.
[473] Sacheverell 1859, 98-9.
[474] O.S.A. VI 256, North Knapdale Arg.
[475] Stewart 1822, II xiii, quoting Toland.
[476] Thomson 2010, 64, quoting Cunningham 1787.
[477] Johnson & Boswell 1930, 87.
[478] Richards 2005, 35, quoting Stewart 1822.
[479] Carmichael 1928-71, III 328-9.
[480] Argyll 1887, 435.
[481] Thomson 2010, 62, quoting Cunningham 1787.

BIBLIOGRAPHY

Anon., Remarks on the People of Scotland, particularly the Highlanders, n. p., Edinburgh, 1747.

Anon., A Candid Enquiry into the Migrations, Tait, Glasgow, 1771.

Adam, Frank, & Innes of Learney, Thomas, Clans Septs & Regiments of the Scottish Highlands, Johnston & Bacon, Edinburgh, (1908) 1965.

Adam, R. J., Sutherland Estate Management 1802-16, two volumes, Scottish History Society, Edinburgh, 1972.

Anderson, Dr James, Present State of the Hebrides & Western Coasts of Scotland, Robinson, London, 1785.

Anderson, Peter, Culloden Moor & the Story of the Battle, MacKay, Stirling, (1867) 1920.

Argyll, 8th Duke of, Scotland as it was and is, Douglas, Edinburgh, 1887.

Atholl, 7th Duke of, editor, Atholl Chronicles, printed privately, Edinburgh, 1908.

Atkinson, Tom, The Empty Lands, Luath, Barr Ayrshire, (1986) 1987; and The Northern Highlands, Luath, Edinburgh, (1986) 1999 (much of these two books is identical).

Bain, Robert, Clans and Tartans of Scotland, Collins, London, (1938) 1960.

Banks, Noel, Six Inner Hebrides, David & Charles, Newton Abbott, 1977.

Barnes, Major R. M. & Allen, C. K., Uniforms & History of the Scottish Regiments, Seeley, London, 1956.

Barron, James, Northern Highlands in the 19th century, Carruthers, Inverness, volumes one to thirteen, 1903-13.

Barrow, G. W. S., Kingdom of the Scots, University Press, Edinburgh, (1773) 2003.

Beaugué, Jean de, History of the Scotch Campaigns of 1548 & 1549, n. p., Edinburgh, 1707.

Bingham, Caroline, Beyond the Highland Line, Constable, London, 1991.

Blackie, John Stuart, The Scottish Highlanders and the Land Laws, Chapman & Hall, London, 1885.

Blundell, Odo, The Catholic Highlands of Scotland, Central Highlands, Sands, Edinburgh, volume one, 1909.

Blundell, Odo, The Catholic Highlands, Western Highlands & Islands, Sands, Edinburgh, volume two, 1917.

Boswell, James, Life of Samuel Johnson, Dent, London, (1791) 1928.

Boswell, James, Tour to the Hebrides, see Johnson, Samuel.

Bowman, John Eddowes, Highlands & Islands, a 19th century tour, Sutton, Gloucester, 1986.

Brander, Michael, The Making of the Highlands, Book Club Associates, London, 1980.

Bristed, John, Pedestrian Tour through Part of the Highlands of Scotland in 1801, two volumes, James Wallis, London, 1803.

Brown, P. Hume, editor, Early Travellers in Scotland, Douglas, Edinburgh, 1891.

Brown, P. Hume, Short History of Scotland, Oliver & Boyd, Edinburgh, (1908) 1955.

Brown, Robert, Strictures on the Earl of Selkirk's Observations, Abernethy, Edinburgh, 1806.

Buchan, John, Lord Tweedsmuir, Montrose, Hodder & Stoughton, London, (1928) 1938.

Buchan, John, Lord Tweedsmuir, Massacre of Glen Coe, LangSyne, Midlothian, (1933) 2009.

Buchanan, John Lanne, Travels in the Western Hebrides, 1782 to 1790, MacLean, Skye, (1793) 1997.

Bumsted, J. M., The People's Clearance, the University Presses of Edinburgh and Manitoba, 1982.

Burke, Sir Bernard, Peerage & Baronetage, Harrison, London, 1891.

Burke, John, History of the Landed Gentry, Colburn, London, 1838.

Burke, John, A Traveller's History of Scotland, John Murray, London, 1990.

Burns, Robert, Poetical Works, Bell & Daldy, London, 1839.

Burt, Edmund, Letters from the North of Scotland, Birlinn, Edinburgh, (1754) 2005; introduction R. Jamieson; preface/introduction, Charles W. J. Withers.

Byron, George Gordon, Lord, Poetical Works of Lord Byron, Nimmo, Edinburgh, 1863.
Cameron, John, J. P., The Clan Cameron, D. MacLeod, Kirkintilloch, 1894.
Campbell, Dr. John Lorne, Canna, Canongate, Edinburgh, (1984) 1994.
Campbell, Patrick, Travels in North America, Greenwood Press, New York, (1793) 1968.
Campbell, Professor R. H., Scotland since 1707, Blackwell, Oxford, (1965) 1985.
Carmichael, Alexander, Carmina Gadelica, Oliver & Boyd, Edinburgh, (1900-41) 1928-71.
Carr, E. H., What is History? G. M. Trevelyan lectures, Cambridge, 1961.
Chambers, Robert, Picture of Scotland, Tait, Edinburgh, (1827) 1828.
Chambers, Robert, History of the Rebellion in 1745-6, Chambers, London, (1827) 1869.
Chambers, Robert, see Bishop Robert Forbes.
Clapperton, Chalmers M., editor, Scotland A New Study, David & Charles, Newton Abbott, 1983.
Collier, Adam, The Crofting Problem, University Press, Cambridge, 1953.
Cooper, Derek, Skye, Routledge, London, 1970.
Cregeen, Eric R., ed., Argyll Estate Instructions, Scottish History Society, Edinburgh, 1964.
Cregeen, Eric R., Changing Role of the House of Argyll, see Mitchison, Rosalind, 1970.
Cregeen, Eric R., Highlands since 1745, in David Daiches, editor, New Companion to Scottish Culture, Polygon, Edinburgh, (1981) 1993.
Cunningham, Alexander, History of Great Britain, Strachan, London, 1787.
Daiches, David, see Cregeen, Eric R.
Darling, F. Fraser, West Highland Survey, O.U.P., London, 1955.
Dalrymple, Sir John, Memoirs of Great Britain, Strachan & Cadell, London, 1771.
Davidson, Basil, see Strand, Paul.
Day, J. P., Public Administration in the Highlands & Islands of Scotland, University Press, London, 1918.
Defoe, Daniel, Memoirs of a Cavalier, Bell, London, 1720.
Defoe, Daniel, Tour through the Whole Island of Great Britain, Dent, London, (1724-7) 1974.
Devine, T. M., Great Highland Famine, John Donald, Edinburgh, (1980) 2004.
Devine, T. M., Clanship to Crofters' War, University Press, Manchester, (1994) 1998.
Donaldson, Gordon, The Scots Overseas, Robert Hale, London, 1966.
Donaldson, Gordon, The Shaping of a Nation, David & Charles, Newton Abbott, (1974) 1993.
Donaldson, Mary, Wanderings in the Western Highlands & Islands, Gardner, Paisley, 1920.
Donnachie, Ian & Hewitt, George, A Companion to Scottish History, Batsford, London, 1989.
Douglas, Hugh, Charles Edward Stuart, Robert Hale, London, 1975.
Doyle, Sir Arthur Conan, Sherlock Holmes Short Stories, Chancellor, London, (1891-1927) 1986.
Duff, David, see Victoria, Queen.
Dunbar, J. Telfer, Highland Costume, Blackwood, Edinburgh, 1977.
Dundee, Earl of, 1965 Memo re Highland Development Bill, printed as Appendix in Moncreiffe 1967.
Dunlop, Dr Jean, The Clan MacKenzie, Johnston & Bacon, Stirling, (1953), 1987.
Dunlop, Dr Jean, The Clan Gordon, Johnston & Bacon, Stirling, 1955.
Dunlop, Dr Jean, The Clan Mackintosh, Johnston & Bacon, Edinburgh, 1960.
Elton, Sir Geoffrey R., The Practice of History, Collins Fontana, London, 1967.
Evans, Sir Richard J., In Defence of History, Granta Books, London, 1997; 2nd edition, 2001.
Fallow, Jeff, Scotland for Beginners, Writers and Readers Ltd, London, 1999.
Ferguson, Dr William, Scotland 1689 to the Present, Mercat Press, Edinburgh, (1968) 1994.
Finlay, Campbell K., We Go To The Western Isles, Harrap, London, 1959.
Finlay, Ian, The Highlands, Batsford, London, (1963) 1966.
Finlay, Ian, The Central Highlands, Batsford, London, 1976.
Fisher, Andrew, A Traveller's History of Scotland, Cassell, London, (1990) 2002.
Forbes, David, The Sutherland Clearances: 1806-20, Craigie College of Education, Ayr, 1976.
Forbes, Bishop Robert, Jacobite Memoirs, ed. Robert Chambers, Chambers, Edinburgh, 1834.

BIBLIOGRAPHY

Franck, Richard, Northern Memoirs written in 1658, Mortlock, London, 1694.
Fraser of Reelig, C. I., The Clan Cameron, Johnston & Bacon, Stirling, (1953) 1987.
Fraser of Reelig, C. I., The Clan Munro, Johnston & Bacon, Stirling, 1954.
Fraser-Mackintosh, Charles, Antiquarian Notes, n. p., Inverness, 1865.
Fraser-Mackintosh, Charles, Antiquarian Notes, Mackenzie, Inverness, 1897.
Fry, Michael, Scottish Empire, Tuckwell, East Lothian, & Birlinn, Edinburgh, 2001.
Fry, Michael, Wild Scots, John Murray, London, 2005 (1).
Fry, Michael, Scottish Review of Books, I, issue 2, 2005 (2).
Fulton, Alexander, Scotland and her Tartans, Hodder & Stoughton, London, 1991.
Gardiner, Juliet, & Wenborn, Neil, History Today Companion to British History, Collins & Brown, London, 1995.
Garnett, Thomas, Tour of the Highlands, J. Stockdale, London, (1800) 1811.
Gaskell, Philip, Morvern Transformed, University Press, Cambridge, (1968) 1980.
Geddes, Arthur, The Isle of Lewis and Harris, University Press, Edinburgh, 1955.
Geikie, Sir Archibald, Scottish Reminiscences, Maclehose, Glasgow, 1908.
Gibson, John Sibbald, Lochiel of the '45, University Press, Edinburgh, (1994) 1995.
Gibson, Rob, Highland Clearances Trail, Luath, Edinburgh, 2006. An earlier (much shorter) edition was "printed by Phil Greene", Glasgow, 1985.
Gilpin, William, Picturesque Scenery in 1776, Blamire, London, volume one (1789) 1792, volume two 1789.
Gittings, Bruce, Gazetteer for Scotland, (based on Groome, Gazetteer 1882-5) 2002-13.
Glover, Janet R., The Story of Scotland, Faber & Faber, London, (1960) 1966.
Goodall, George, ed., Philips' Modern School Atlas, George Philip & Son, London, 1952.
Gordon, John, editor, The New Statistical Account of Scotland, n. p., n. l., 1845.
Gordon, Seton, Central Highlands, Macmillan, London, 1949.
Gordon, Seton, Highlands of Scotland, Robert Hale, London, 1951.
Gordon, Seton, Highland Days, Cassell, London, 1963.
Graham-Campbell, David, Portrait of Argyll & the Southern Hebrides, Robert Hale, London, 1978.
Graham-Campbell, David, Portrait of Perth, Angus and Fife, Robert Hale, London, 1979.
Grant, Anne, of Laggan, Letters from the Mountains, Longmans, London, (1806) two volumes, 1845.
Grant, Anne, of Laggan, Essays on the Superstitions of the Highlanders, Longmans, London, 1811.
Grant, Dr Isobel F., Economic History of Scotland, Longmans, London, 1934.
Grant, Dr Isobel F., The Clan MacLeod, Johnson & Bacon, Stirling, 1953.
Grant, Dr Isobel F., The Clan Grant, Johnston & Bacon, Stirling, (1955) 1984.
Grant, Dr Isobel F., Highland Folk Ways, Routledge & Kegan Paul, London, (1961) 1980.
Grant, Dr Isobel F., & Cheape, H., Periods in Highland History, Shepheard-Walwyn, London, (1987) 2000.
Grant, James Shaw, Discovering Lewis & Harris, John Donald, Edinburgh, 1987.
Gray, Malcolm, The Highland Economy 1750-1850, Oliver & Boyd, Edinburgh, 1957 (1).
Gray, Malcolm, Consolidation of the Crofting System, Agricultural History Review, V part 1, 1957 (2).
Green, John R., A Short History of the English People, Dent, London, (1874) 1945, 673-4.
Grimble, Dr Ian, Trial of Patrick Sellar, Routledge, London, 1962.
Grimble, Dr Ian, Scottish Clans & Tartans, Hamlyn, London, 1973.
Grimble, Dr Ian, Clans & Chiefs, Blond & Briggs, London, 1980.
Groome, Francis H., Gazetteer of Scotland, (1882-5) 1892-6.
Halliday, James, Scotland, A Concise History, Gordon Wright, Edinburgh, (1990) 1996.
Hamilton, Professor Henry, Industrial Revolution in Scotland, Frank Cass, London, 1966.
Haswell-Smith, H., Scottish Islands, Canongate, Edinburgh, 1996.
Henderson, Captain John, General View of the Agriculture of Sutherland, Board of Agriculture, London, 1812.

Herman, Professor Arthur, The Scottish Enlightenment, Fourth Estate, London, 2002.
Hill, Douglas, The Scots to Canada, Gentry Books, London, 1972.
Hogg, James, Highland Tours, Byways, Hawick, 1981.
Hopkins, Paul, Glencoe & the End of the Highland War, John Donald, Edinburgh, 1998.
Houston, R. A., & Knox, W. W. J., New Penguin History of Scotland, Penguin, London, 2001.
Hunter, Dr James, The Making of the Crofting Community, John Donald, Edinburgh, (1976) 2000.
Hunter, Dr James, Last of the Free, Mainstream, Edinburgh, 1999.
Hunter, Dr James, essay in Land & Legacy, NMS Enterprises, Edinburgh, 2006.
Innes, Cosmo, Scotch Legal Antiquities, Edmondson & Douglas, Edinburgh, 1872.
Jackson, Dr Robert, Systematic View of the Formation, Discipline, and Economy of Armies, John Stockdale, London, 1804.
Jamieson, R., introduction to Burt, Edmund, Letters from the North of Scotland, Birlinn, (1754) 2005.
Johnson, Dr Samuel, Journey to the Western Isles, & Boswell, James, A Tour to the Hebrides, editor R. W. Chapman, O.U.P., London, (1775, 1785) 1930.
Johnstone, Chevalier James de, Memoirs of the Rebellion in 1745-6, Longmans, London, 1820.
Kemp, Daniel W., editor, Tour of Dr Pococke in 1760, Sutherland Association, Edinburgh, 1888.
Keay, John & Julia, Collins Encyclopaedia of Scotland, HarperCollins, London, 1994.
Kyd, James G., Scottish Population Statistics, Constable, Edinburgh, 1952.
Lang, Andrew, editor, The Highlands of Scotland in 1750, Blackwood, Edinburgh, 1898.
Larkin, (P?), Sketch of a Tour in the Highlands 1818, Baldwin Cradock & Joy, London, 1819; reprinted General Books, Memphis, 2010.
Lenman, Bruce, Jacobite Clans of the Great Glen, Scottish Cultural Press, Aberdeen, (1984) 1995.
Linklater, Eric, introduction to Grimble, Trial of Patrick Sellar, Routledge, London, 1962.
Linklater, Eric, The Prince in the Heather, Panther, St Albans, 1976.
Linklater, Magnus, Massacre: The Story of Glen Coe, Collins, London, 1982.
Lister, John A., The Scottish Highlands, Bartholomew, Edinburgh, 1978.
Lynch, Michael, Scotland, A New History, Century, London, (1991) 1996.
Lynch, Michael, editor, Oxford Companion to Scottish History, O.U.P., Oxford, 2001.
Macaulay, Thomas Babington, Lord, The History of England, Routledge, London, (1848-55) 1907.
MacCulloch, J. A., The Misty Isle of Skye, Eneas MacKay, Stirling, (1905) 1948.
MacDonald, Rev. Angus (minister of Killearnan) & Rev. Archibald MacDonald (minister of Kiltarlity), The Clan Donald, Northern Counties Publishing Company, Inverness, 1904.
MacDonald, Donald J., of Castleton, Clan Donald, Macdonald publishers, Loanhead, 1978.
MacDonald, Iain S., Glencoe and Beyond, John Donald, Edinburgh, 2005.
MacDonald, James, General View of the Agriculture of the Hebrides, Board of Agriculture, London, 1811.
MacDonald, Stuart, Back to Lochaber, Pentland, Edinburgh, 1994.
MacDonell, A. G., My Scotland, Funk & Wagnalls, New York, 1937.
MacKay, Alexander, Sketches of Sutherland Characters, Gemmell, Edinburgh, 1889.
MacKay, John, The Church in the Highlands, Hodder & Stoughton, London, 1914.
MacKay, Robert, History of the House and Clan of MacKay, n. p., Edinburgh, 1929.
McKay, Margaret M., see Walker, John.
MacKenzie, Agnes Mure, Scotland in Modern Times 1720-1939, Chambers, Edinburgh, 1941.
MacKenzie, Alexander, History of the Highland Clearances, Melven Press, Perth, (1883) 1986.
MacKenzie, Alexander, History of the Frasers of Lovat, MacKenzie, Inverness, 1896.
MacKenzie, Sir George Steuart, General View of the Agriculture of Ross-shire, Phillips, London, 1810, Board of Agriculture, London, 1813.
MacKenzie, Rev. James, History of Scotland, Nelson, London, 1911.
MacKenzie, R. F., A Search for Scotland, Collins, London, 1989.
MacKenzie, W. C., Short History of the Scottish Highlands, Gardner, Paisley, (1906) 1908.

BIBLIOGRAPHY

MacKenzie, W. C., The Highlands and Isles of Scotland, Moray, Edinburgh, (1937) 1949.
MacKinnon, C. R., of Dunakin, The Clan MacKinnon, printed Culross, Coupar Angus, 1958.
MacKinnon, C. R., of Dunakin, The Highlands in History, Collins, London, 1961.
MacLaren, Moray see MacNie.
MacLean, Fitzroy, Bonnie Prince Charlie, Guild Publishing, London, (1988) 1988.
MacLean, Fitzroy, Highlanders, Adelphi, London, c. 1995.
MacLean, Dr John P., A History of the Clan MacLean, Robert Clarke, Cincinnati, 1889.
MacLean, Malcolm & Carrell, Christopher, As an Fhearann, Mainstream, Edinburgh, 1986.
MacLeod, Donald, Gloomy Memories in the Highlands, Sinclair, Glasgow, etc., (1841) 1892.
MacLeod, John, Highlanders, Hodder & Stoughton, London, (1996) 1997.
MacLeod, Rev. Dr Norman, Reminiscences of a Highland Parish, Partridge, London, (1867) 1910.
MacLeod, R. C., Dunvegan Charter Chest, in Scottish Historical Review, II 1905, 356.
McMillan, James, Anatomy of Scotland, Leslie Frewin, London, 1969.
MacMillan, Somerled, Bygone Lochaber, printed privately, 1971.
MacNicol, Rev. Donald, Remarks on Dr Johnson's Journey, Cadell, London, 1779.
MacNeill, Sir John, Report to Board of Supervision (Poor Law), P.P. 1851, XXVI.
MacNie, Donald Lamond, editor, The New Shell Guide to Scotland, Book Club Associates, London, 1977; Historical Introduction by Moray McLaren.
Magnusson, Magnus, Story of a Nation, HarperCollins, London, 2000.
Mahon, Lord, 5th Earl of Stanhope; History of England 1713-83, seven volumes, Murray, London, 1853.
Marshall, William, General View of the Agriculture of the Central Highlands of Scotland, Board of Agriculture, London, 1794.
Martin, Martin, A Description of the Western Isles of Scotland c. 1695, n. p., London?, 1703.
Mathieson, Robert, The Survival of the Unfittest, John Donald, Edinburgh, 2000.
Mawman, Joseph, An Excursion to the Highlands of Scotland, J. Mawman, London, 1805.
Meek, Donald E., Tuath is Tighearna, Scottish Academic Press, Edinburgh, 1995.
Miller, Hugh, My Schools & Schoolmasters, Collins, London (1854), 1912?.
Mitchell, Joseph, Reminiscences of my life in the Highlands, 1884, two volumes, David & Charles Reprints, Newton Abbot, 1971.
Mitchison, Rosalind, Agricultural Sir John, Bles, London, 1962.
Mitchison, Rosalind, & Phillipson, N. T., Scotland in the Age of Improvement, University Press, Edinburgh, 1970. This consisted of ten essays, including Mitchison, Rosalind, The Government & the Highlands 1707-45, & Cregeen, Eric, The Changing Role of the House of Argyll in the Scottish Highlands.
Mitchison, Rosalind, History of Scotland, Methuen, London, (1970) 1971.
Mitchison, Rosalind, Scotland from 1830, (in Alistair MacLean Introduces Scotland), Deutsch, London, 1972.
Mitchison, Rosalind, Scotland 1750-1850, in Cambridge Social History, editor F. M. L. Thompson, (1990) 1993.
Moffat, Alistair, The Highland Clans, Thames & Hudson, London, 2010.
Moncreiffe, Sir Iain, The Robertsons, Johnston & Bacon, Stirling, 1954.
Moncreiffe, Sir Iain, The Highland Clans, Barrie & Rockliff, London, 1967.
Monniepennie, John, Certain Matters Concerning Scotland, Robert Waldegrave, Edinburgh, 1597.
Muir, R., & Philip, G., editors, Philips' New School Atlas of Universal History, Philip, London, 1946.
Muir, Dr Richard, Lost Villages of Britain, Book Club Associates, London, 1985.
Munro, R. W., Highland Clans and Tartans, Octopus, London, 1977.
Murdoch, John, For the People's Cause, editor James Hunter, H.M.S.O., Edinburgh, 1986.
Murray, W. H., The Hebrides, Heinemann, London, (1966) 1969.
Murray, W. H., Companion Guide to the West Highlands of Scotland, Collins, London, 1968.

Murray, W. H., The Islands of Western Scotland, Eyre Methuen, London, 1973.
Newte, Thomas, see Thomson, William.
Nicolson, Alexander, History of Skye, MacLaren, Glasgow, 1930.
Omand, Donald, The Caithness Book, Highland Printers, Inverness, (1972) 1973.
Omand, Donald, The New Caithness Book, North of Scotland Newspapers, Wick, 1989.
Paterson, David, The Highlands, Alan Sutton, Stroud, 1993.
Pennant, Thomas, Tour in Scotland 1769, Birlinn, Edinburgh, (1771) 2000.
Pennant, Thomas, Tour in Scotland & Voyage to the Hebrides 1772, Birlinn, Edinburgh, (1774-6) 1998.
Phillipson, N. T., see Mitchison, Rosalind.
Pine, L. G., The Highland Clans, David & Charles, Newton Abbot, 1972.
Pococke, Tour in 1760, see Kemp.
Pryde, Dr George S., Scotland from 1603 to the Present Day, Nelson, London, 1962.
Prebble, John, Glencoe, Penguin, London, (1966) 1970.
Prebble, John, The Highland Clearances, Book Club Associates, London, (1963) 1971.
Prebble, John, The Lion in the North, Book Club Associates, London, (1971) 1973.
Prebble, John, Mutiny, Penguin, London, (1975) 1977.
Prebble, John, John Prebble's Scotland, Penguin, London, (1984) 1986.
Pryde, George S., Scotland from 1603, Nelson, London, 1962.
Ray, James, A Journey through part of England & Scotland in 1746, Osborne, London, 1747.
Richards, Eric, The Leviathan of Wealth, Routledge & Kegan Paul, London, 1973.
Richards, Eric, Problems on the Cromartie Estate 1851-3, Scottish Historical Review, volume fifty-two, 1973.
Richards, Eric, A History of the Highland Clearances, volume one, Croom Helm, London, 1982.
Richards, Eric, A History of the Highland Clearances, volume two, Croom Helm, London, 1985.
Richards, Eric, Patrick Sellar & the Highland Clearances, Polygon, Edinburgh, 1999.
Richards, Eric, The Highland Clearances, Birlinn, Edinburgh, (2002) 2005.
Richards, Eric, Debating the Highland Clearances, University Press, Edinburgh, 2007.
Rixson, Denis, Arisaig and Morar, Birlinn, Edinburgh, (2002) 2011.
Rixson, Denis, Hebridean Traveller, Birlinn, Edinburgh, 2004.
Robertson, Dr James, General View of the Agriculture of the County of Inverness, Board of Agriculture, London, 1808.
Ross, David, Scotland, The History of a Nation, Lomond Books, n. l., 1998.
Sacheverell, William, An Account of the Isle of Man, Manx Society, Douglas Isle of Man, (1702) 1859.
Sage, Rev. Donald, Memorabilia Domestica, Albyn Press, Edinburgh, (1889, Rae, Wick) 1975.
Saint Fond, Faujas de, Journey through Scotland to the Hebrides, Hopkins, Glasgow, 1907.
Scarlett, James D., Scotland's Clans and Tartans, Lutterworth, Guildford, 1975.
Schama, Simon, History of Britain 1603-1776, BBC, London, 2001.
Scobie, Captain I. H. M., An Old Highland Fencible Corps, Blackwood, Edinburgh & London, 1914.
Scott, Sir Walter, Scott's Poetical Works, Yardley & Hanscomb, London, c. 1890.
Scott, Sir Walter, Waverley, Boots, Nottingham, (1814) probably 1900.
Scott, Sir Walter, A Legend of Montrose, Nelson Classics, London, (1819) 1925.
Scott, Sir Walter, Rob Roy, Penguin, London, (1817) 1995.
Selkirk, Earl of, Observations on the Highlands of Scotland, Longman, London, & Constable, Edinburgh, (1805), 1806; General Books, Memphis, (1805) 2010.
Shairp, John Campbell, notes to Dorothy Wordsworth's Tour in Scotland 1803, see below.
Shaw, Alexander M., Mackintosh & the Clan Chattan, printed for the author, London, 1880.
Sillar, Frederick C., & Meyler, Ruth M., Skye, David & Charles, Newton Abbott, 1973.
Simpson, W. Douglas, Skye and the Outer Hebrides, Robert Hale, London, (1967) 1975.
Sinclair, Sir John, General View of the Agriculture of the Northern Counties, Board of Agriculture, London, 1795.

BIBLIOGRAPHY

Sinclair, Sir John, editor, The Statistical Account of Scotland, Creech, Edinburgh, 1791-9.
Skene, W. F., Highlanders of Scotland, John Murray, London, 1837.
Skene, W. F., Celtic Scotland, David Douglas, Edinburgh, (1886) 1890.
Smith, Adam, The Wealth of Nations, Routledge, London, (1776) 1895.
Smith, John, General View of the Agriculture of the County of Argyll, n. p., Edinburgh, 1798.
Smollett, Tobias, Humphry Clinker, Penguin, London, (1771) 1967.
Smout, T. C., A History of the Scottish People 1560-1830, Collins, London, (1969) 1970.
Smout, T. C., A Century of the Scottish People 1830-1950, Fontana, London, (1986) 1997.
Somerset Fry, P. & F., History of Scotland, Ark, London, (1982) 1985.
Stanhope, 5th Earl of, see Mahon, Lord.
Steel, Thomas, Scotland's Story, HarperCollins, London, (1984) 1994.
Stevenson, Robert Louis, Kidnapped, Hamlyn Press, London, (1886) 1954.
Stewart, David, Sketches of the Character, Manners, & the Present State of the Highlanders of Scotland, with details of the Military Service of the Highland Regiments, Archibald Constable, Edinburgh; Longman, Hurst, Rees, Orme, & Browne; & Hurst, Robinson & Co., London, 1822, volumes one & two. The publication date is usually given as 1822. My copy has that date, but is clearly marked "Second Edition". It begins with the "Preface to the First Edition", which is dated 24th April 1821, so perhaps the first edition was in 1821. This is followed by the "Preface to the Second Edition", which is dated 25th June 1822. A third edition came out in 1825.
Stoddart, Sir John, Remarks on Local Scenery & Manners in Scotland in 1799, Miller, London, 1801.
Strand, Paul, & Davidson, Basil, Tir A'Mhurain, Aperture, New York (1962) 2002.
Strang, Tom, Northern Highlands, Scottish Mountaineering Club, Edinburgh, 1975.
Sutherland, Alexander, A Summer Ramble in the North Highlands, n. p., Edinburgh, 1825.
Swire, Otta F., Skye, The Island and Its Legends, Blackie, London, (1952) 1961.
Thompson, Francis M. L., Cambridge Social History 1750-1950, University Press, Cambridge, (1990) 1993.
Thompson, Francis G., Lewis and Harris, David & Charles, Newton Abbot (1968) 1973.
Thompson, Francis G., The Highlands & Islands, Robert Hale, London, 1974.
Thomson, D. S., editor, Companion to Gaelic Scotland, Blackwell, Oxford, 1983.
Thomson, George Malcolm, A Kind of Justice, Hutchinson, London, 1970.
Thomson, William, A Tour in England & Scotland in 1785, General Books, Memphis, (1788) 2010; first published by G. G. J. & J. Robinson, London, 1788, as by "Thomas Newte".
Toland, John, Critical History of the Celtic Religion, Banton Press, Largs, (1726) 1990.
Trevelyan, George Macaulay, English Social History, Longmans, London, (1942) 1946.
Trevelyan, George Macaulay, An Autobiography & Other Essays, Longmans, London, 1949.
Trevor-Roper, Hugh, Lord Dacre, Highland Tradition of Scotland, in E. Hobsbawm & T. Ranger, The Invention of Tradition, University Press, Cambridge (1983) 2008.
Tytler, Patrick Fraser, Memorable Wars of Scotland, Nimmo, Edinburgh, 1874.
Victoria, Queen, Leaves from the Journal, Smith Elder, London, 1868.
Victoria, Queen, Highland Journals, editor David Duff, Lomond Books, London, (1980) 1994.
Walker, John, Economical History of the Hebrides & Highlands of Scotland, University Press, Edinburgh, 1808.
Walker, John, Report on the Hebrides 1764 & 1771, editor M. M. McKay, John Donald, Edinburgh, 1980.
Watson, J. Steven, The Reign of George III, Clarendon Press, Oxford, 1960 (Oxford History of England, volume twelve).
Way, G., & Squire, R., Scottish Clan and Family Encyclopaedia, HarperCollins, Glasgow, 1994.
Wilkinson, Clennel, Bonnie Prince Charlie, Harrap, London, (1932) 1936.
Williams, Basil, The Whig Supremacy 1714-1760, Clarendon Press, Oxford, (1939) 1949 (Oxford History of England, volume eleven).

Withers, Charles W. J., Urban Highlanders, Tuckwell, East Lothian, 1998.
Withers, Charles W. J., see Burt, Letters.
Wordsworth, Dorothy, Tour in Scotland, Douglas, Edinburgh, 1894.
Youngson, A. J., After the Forty-five, University Press, Edinburgh, 1973.
Youngson, A. J., Beyond the Highland Line, Collins, London, 1974.

Bartholomew *Gazetteer of Great Britain*, 1977.
Macmillan *World Almanac*, 1994.
Nelson's *World Gazetteer*, T. Nelson, London (1932) 1941.
Reader's Digest *World Atlas*, 1965.
Celtic Magazine, editor Alexander MacKenzie, Inverness, 1875-88.
Concise Scots Dictionary, University Press, Aberdeen, (1985) 1991.
Dictionary of National Biography, editor L. Goldman, O.U.P., London, 2005-8.
Edinburgh Magazine, Blackwood, Edinburgh, 1817 etc.
Gazetteer for Scotland, 2002-13, www.scottish-places.info/parishes.
Napier Commission Report, Parliamentary Papers, Session 1884, volumes thirty-two to thirty-six
Transactions of the Gaelic Society of Inverness, volume thirty-eight, 1937-41.
Old Statistical Account of Scotland, Editor Sir John Sinclair, Wm. Creech, Edinburgh 1791-9.
New Statistical Account of Scotland, Editor John Gordon, n.p, n.l, 1845.

n. p. = no publisher given.
n. l. = no location given for publisher.
n. d. = no date given.

APPENDIX A

Professor Lynch (Lynch 1996, 367) gave these figures for the Highland population: 1755, 115,000: 1831, 201,000. That would mean an increase between those two dates of 74.8% – interestingly, this is almost exactly double the real value of the increase, which was 37.3%. None of the figures offered by writers I have seen for the Highland population had the effect of lessening the rate of increase of that population; all of them had the effect of augmenting it. Now why should that be?

Here are some statements made by historians about the supposed "great increase" in the Highland population after 1755. The increases claimed are all much higher than they were in reality. Other statements by historians are also inaccurate, but not quite so much above the facts. I have never come across any commentator who gave figures which showed a smaller increase than actually occurred: all the figures I have seen show a bigger increase than what really happened. Perhaps some academics will claim that the only figures as to the numbers in the Highlands which are easily obtainable refer to whole counties, and no fewer than ten counties covered both Highland and Lowland areas: which means that a lot of hard work is necessary to work out which parishes were in the Highlands, and which in the Lowlands, so that accurate figures can be obtained as to the Highland population in various years. But (as I said earlier) if observers are not prepared to undergo the necessary toil in order to obtain reliable results, perhaps the writing of history books is not the most suitable career for them.

(The figures given below for the real increase in population were maximum figures; in reality – as I have explained earlier – they were probably less than that.)

R. Mitchison 1993, 180: 1755, 115,000 & 1831, 201,000 – a 74.8% increase: really it was 37.3%.

M. Lynch 1991, 367: 1755, 115,000 & 1801, 154,000 – a 33.9% increase; really 12.1%.

M. Lynch ditto: 1755, 115,000 & 1831, 201,000 – 74.8% increase; really 37.3%.

I. Moncreiffe 1967, 35: 1755, 216,952 & 1801, 255,993 – 18.0% increase; really 12.1%.

I. Moncreiffe ditto: 1801, 255,993 & 1851, 334,475 – 30.7% increase; really 21.1%.

I. Moncreiffe ditto: 1755, 216,952 & 1851, 334,475 – 54.2% increase; really 35.7%.

(A small subsidiary point is that the 1851 population of Sir Iain's chosen "Highlands" area appears to be 333,007 – the total of the official figures given for the 1851 populations of Argyllshire, Inverness-shire, Ross & Cromarty, Sutherland, and Caithness, the five counties selected by Sir Iain to represent "the Highlands"). Sir Iain gave a figure a thousand and a half more than that; relatively, it's a very

small error, but I am still hoping to see an error, large or small, which had the effect of minimizing the Highland population increase, instead of exaggerating it.)
Adam/Innes 1965, 77: 1747, 230,000 & 1795, 325,000 – 41.3% increase; really 10.1%.
Adam/Innes ditto: 1795, 325,000 & 1821, 447,000 – 37.5% increase; really 18.7%.
Adam/Innes ditto: 1747, 230,000 & 1821, 447,000 – 94.3% increase; really 30.6%.
I. F. Grant 1961, 53: 1755, 257,153 & 1811, 362,000 – 40.8% increase; really 17.5%.
I. F. Grant ditto: 1755 257,153 & 1841, 396,000 – 54.0% increase; really 37.3%.
J. Lister 1978, 19: 1750 255,000 & 1850, 396,000 – 55.3% increase; really 35.7%.
M. Fry 2005 (2): 1755, c. 250,000 & 1841, "near" 400,000 – "near" 60% increase; really 37.33%.
J. Halliday 1996, 115: 1755 to 1830, Highland population rose "about 50%"; really 37.29%.
C. W. J. Withers 1998, 26: 1755 194,707 & 1801, 233,384 – 19.9% increase; really 12.1%.
Adam Collier 1953, 48: 1755-1801, H. pop. increased 48%; in fact 12.07%.

Then there are the writers who claim that the Highland population "doubled" (Mitchison 1971, 376 & 378), or "perhaps" doubled (Cregeen 1970, 13 & 22), or "almost" doubled (Finlay 1966, 38), when in fact the very highest increase in the Highland population that could be asserted (and this figure is probably too high, as we have seen) is 37.3% – just over one-third. Even further from the facts were the writers alleging a "population explosion", e.g. the Earl of Dundee and Sir Iain Moncreiffe (see Moncreiffe 1967, 35 & 251).

APPENDIX B

Edmund Burt (sometimes called Edward Burt) makes a curious study. He was in the Highlands representing the British authorities in connection with the estates forfeited after the 1715 rebellion. His account of the Highlanders and their "barbarous customs", as he called them (p. 300) – and indeed, of the Scots Lowlanders and their customs (e.g. on p. 118) – reminds one strongly of accounts written by local British officials in the days of imperial triumph, describing for the delectation of the master race the brown or black subject peoples, inhabitants of conquered provinces of that far-flung realm. An Inverness magistrate indeed said that Burt was part of the "haughty, keen, and insupportable government of these military and stranger judges set over us" (*Oxford D.N.B.*). According to Burt's account, the local inhabitants were all dirty, of course, and disgusting in their filth. (The same criticisms could have been made of the English lower classes at that time, in the days before hot water on tap and sufficient cheap soap in the shops, not to mention the washing machines of later days, but that was ignored.) The Highlanders, as Burt saw it, were all credulous fools, accepting nonsensical superstitions such as second sight and witchcraft (Burt's demolition of these unpersuasive beliefs on pp. 245 & 274, though completely reasonable, again ignored the fact that educated English people were strong upholders of the reality of witchcraft – e.g. John Wesley half a century after Burt wrote: and one wonders what Burt would have said if he had known that three centuries later, in civilized Great Britain, respectable newspapers would regularly print supposed forecasts of future events, based on the alleged position of the stars in the sky at the moment the enquirer was born). The Gaels took easily to crime, wrote Burt, if they thought they could get away with it, but as soon as they were met by solid British defiance, they turned out to be cringing cowards (e.g., the story of the Highlander who threatened to rob the British officer, till the latter took out his pistol, whereat the Highlander "fell on his knees, and squalled out" that he was only joking, p. 256). Indeed, Burt claimed to have known "several instances of common Highlanders, who finding themselves likely to be worsted, having crouched and howled like a beaten spaniel" (p. 256). The local improvers, accepting and upholding anglophone standards of behaviour, were also victorious against stupendous odds when assailed by the deceitful Gaels (see the story – p. 225 – of the armed MacPhersons, "five or six of them, young fellows, the sons of gentlemen", who entered the hut of Gordon of Glenbucket and "in fawning words, told him they were sorry any dispute had happened", and then treacherously attacked him – but Glenbucket, despite being covered with "a multitude of wounds", simply seized his sword and "drove all the assassins before him"; perhaps there could be a film version starring the latest Hollywood actor to play James Bond.) Their local culture could be disregarded; Burt, who seemingly had some French (pp. 197, 277) and Latin (pp. 297, 305), still after years in the Highlands had no Gaelic (p. 284), despite the drawbacks of having to deal everyday with people, and frequently having to depend in difficult country upon guides, of whose language he was ignorant. But Gaelic hardly deserved much notice, being merely "a corruption of the Irish tongue" (p. 182 – Burt perhaps unaware of the fact that all languages are merely "corruptions" of earlier languages; in one view, English is merely a "corruption" of the German tongue). As with all officials of an imperial occupying power, Burt was able to derive some harmless amusement from the foolish attempts of the subject people to speak the ruling power's language (pp. 112, 254).

In some things, Burt was clearly wrong. He said: "They have no diversions to amuse them" (p. 207). This was well wide of the mark, as the vast body of evidence as to the Highlanders' song, dance, fiddle-playing, bagpiping, poetry, story-telling, games and athletic competition shows. He joined in the allegations of the "slavish attachment" (p. 28) of the Highlanders to their chiefs (which have furbished forth a hundred history books): this belief is also mistaken, as we have shown elsewhere. Curiously, Burt himself made the point that when an assertion is "repugnant to reason", then it is impossible to accept it, whatever "the number and reputed probity of the witnesses to the truth of" the assertion may be (pp. 148-9). He said "the Highlanders, for the most part, are cruel" (pp. 226 & 130); this goes against much evidence. During and following the '45, only a year or two after Burt wrote, the contrast between the restrained behaviour of the Highlanders, and the headlong brutality of the Lowlanders and the English, was clearly demonstrated. Again, Burt said the Highlanders "had ever a dread of the cavalry" (p. 250); we have already seen how baseless this idea was. Burt said the people were "often boasting of the great hospitality of the Highlanders to strangers", and said he had found the opposite (p. 240); but again, there is so much evidence to the contrary that Burt cannot be believed. (Burt himself described how wanderers in the mountains were automatically given food and a night's lodging wherever they arrived, p. 259.) Burt also had the ludicrous idea (p. 251) that the croishtarich was accompanied by "directions in writing, to signify the place of rendezvous", surprisingly over-estimating the literacy of contemporary Highlanders.

One last point. The editor of Burt's *Letters* tells us that Burt's writings only described what Burt himself had been involved in: "*he* has seen these things. This is not a tale relayed either from the words of others, or from hearsay, or distilled from earlier accounts without corroboration" (p. viii). Burt says much the same himself (ipse dixit, p. 5). But in fact much of what Burt says is, and can only be, what other people have told him. Very few of us have much to say based solely on our own experience. All we can do is to examine carefully what others have said, and then make a rational decision as to its truth. In fact much of Burt's account (as

APPENDIX B

the text makes clear) is, and has to be, hearsay: he is telling his correspondent what other people have told him. There are numerous instances where Burt himself explained that this had happened. Here are some of them, followed by the page-number. "I have been told by several" (13); "I am told by the people of the town" (18); "I was told by an English lady" (30); "I have been credibly informed" (32); "I have several times been told" (55); "some words I have heard over a bottle" (78); "I have heard it from several in Edinburgh" (87); "and I have been told" (97); "in his turn, he told me" (110); "I have been told by several people of this town" (112); "and by the way, I have been often told" (119); "I am told there was formerly" (128); "she told me it was" (133); "an old officer in the army, who thereupon told me" (135); "I have been credibly assured" (197); "I very well remember he then told me" (200); "an English lady [. . .] told me lately" (212); "I have, indeed, heard of one [hut]" (240); "we stopped; and there he described to me" (250); "he further told me" (250); "yet I have been certainly informed" (251); "this I have often heard" (251); "if I am mistaken in that part of my account [. . .] which is beyond my own knowledge [. . .] you may lay the blame on those gentlemen who gave me the information" (254); "he told me, a long while ago" (256); "I have heard great complaint of this custom" (259); "I have heard of several other examples of the same kind" (260); "I have heard several of them ['Highland gentlemen'] vaunt" (260); "I . . . have been often told" (261); "I have heard say of him, by a very credible person" (261); "what was told me by a near relation of a certain attainted lord" (262); "I remember to have heard, a good while ago" (262); "he was telling me his father's estate was much embarrassed" (265); "I have been assured" (271); "a gentleman of my acquaintance told me that" (272); "it is often said, that some of the lairds of those [western] islands" (272); "they tell you that some of the lairds in the islands of Shetland . . . they give you an instance" (273).

However, as with other witnesses, Burt's words, after strict scrutiny by the archive of the head, are certainly worth consideration. The dimensions he gave of the Highlands were surprisingly close to the truth (in an age when such accuracy was rare).

A postscript: most of what Burt writes gives one the vivid impression that he is having to rough it in primitive conditions, without any civilized appurtenances, among the ignorant natives. However, he was able to write some 120,000 words in his lengthy letters to his friend in London, and it is difficult to write even a short letter without some basic requirements. Certainly it would be difficult to write so many words without a table and a chair, or at least a place to sit and a place to support the paper, not to mention pen and ink, all of it in a place reasonably well defended from the weather (the cold, or the heat, or the rain) and other impediments.

INDEX

A Legend of Montrose, 162, 247, 259, 416, 480, 487, 562, 697
Aberdeen, 36, 39, 42, 116, 136, 141, 142, 155, 168, 170, 194, 200, 243, 319, 336, 388, 399, 510, 695, 699
Aberdeen University, 142
Aberdeenshire, xi, xii, 128, 168, 169, 170, 175, 180, 182, 287, 304, 307, 390, 392, 399, 618
Aberfoyle, 148, 156, 173, 181
Aberlour, 176, 182, 204
Abernethy & Kincardine, xii, 181, 683
Aboyne, 225, 287, 314, 323
Achany, 481
Acton, Lord, 16
Adam/Innes, Frank, 33, 128, 132, 135, 136, 138, 146, 205, 218, 313, 314, 317, 318, 324, 325, 401, 402, 404, 406, 431, 478, 570, 677, 684, 701
Africa, 22, 26, 58, 159, 195, 558, 599, 635, 654
Agincourt, 126
Agriculture of the Central Highlands, 522, 696
Aikenhead, Thomas, 626
Aird, 169, 309, 399, 466, 483
Albany, Duke of, 536, 537, 541
Albemarle, Earl of, 517
Albert, Prince, 565
Alexander II, 534
Alexander III, 534, 576
Alloa, 390
Alness, 181, 202, 239
Alston, 457
Altyre, 503
Alvie, 181, 500, 570
Alyth, 173, 181, 203, 389
America, 121, 148, 164, 195, 208, 266, 268, 270, 319, 376, 459, 515, 529, 555, 558, 575, 605, 608, 609, 635, 641, 643, 646, 649, 652, 654, 666, 675, 681, 687, 693
American War of Independence, 518, 647, 649, 661
Amulree, 167
Anderson, Dr James, 191, 518
Anderson, Peter, 509
Andorra, 68
Anglians, 158

Angus MacLeod Archive, 219
Annals of Agriculture, 137
Anne, Queen, 238, 268, 273, 275, 277, 280
Apocrypha, 12
Appin, xii, 105, 149, 181, 197, 204, 224, 252, 253, 279, 295, 296, 306, 323, 383, 385, 386, 391, 397, 398, 467, 505, 526, 528, 549, 560, 578, 580
Appin Dull, 398
Applecross, 181, 454, 482
Arbroath, 538
Archbishop of York, 515
Ardchattan & Muckairn, xii, 181, 483, 576
Ardclach, 176, 182
Ardersier, 177, 181, 202
Ardgour, 105, 148, 202, 223, 304, 309
Ardkinglass, 197, 223, 396
Ardmeanach, 177, 178
Ardmore, 166, 167, 168, 172
Ardnamurchan, 59, 78, 130, 137, 166, 181, 197, 202, 223, 274, 302, 467, 483, 512, 572, 592, 623
Argyll, Duke of, 97, 98, 143, 187, 217, 236, 237, 238, 239, 245, 256, 263, 309, 351, 367, 368, 369, 381, 385, 386, 391, 392, 393, 396, 397, 488, 532, 548, 552, 553, 561, 576, 641, 676
Argyll, Earl of, 97, 98, 143, 187, 217, 236, 237, 238, 239, 245, 256, 263, 309, 351, 367, 368, 369, 381, 385, 386, 391, 392, 393, 396, 397, 488, 532, 548, 552, 553, 561, 576, 641, 676
Argyllshire, xi, xii, 35, 39, 77, 87, 97, 127, 130, 148, 157, 158, 168, 170, 171, 180, 181, 200, 202, 225, 236, 245, 304, 306, 333, 366, 387, 392, 407, 419, 433, 467, 479, 561, 654, 700
Argyllshire Highlanders, 654
Arisaig, 197, 202, 397, 418, 466, 697
Armadale, 129, 155, 235, 584
Armenians, 25
Arnold, General, 653
Arran, 5, 96, 120, 155, 167, 168, 171, 181, 374, 389, 398, 418, 451, 539, 541, 544, 545, 587, 678
Arran, Earl of, 539, 541, 544, 545
Arrochar, 167, 168, 172, 181
Arthur's Seat, 617
Assynt, 21, 37, 64, 181, 304, 371, 372, 373, 405, 443, 481, 499, 503, 561, 570, 571, 580, 589,

INDEX

678
Athelstan, King,   161
Athenaeum, The,   215
Atholl,   106, 130, 149, 156, 170, 181, 197, 235, 243, 244, 245, 264, 265, 275, 288, 306, 307, 319, 322, 324, 344, 345, 346, 347, 348, 349, 356, 367, 376, 386, 388, 389, 390, 391, 395, 398, 399, 403, 405, 407, 425, 477, 497, 512, 537, 548, 583, 585, 601, 618, 633, 634, 637, 653, 686, 692
Atholl Chronicles,   346, 347, 391, 692
Atholl, Duke of,   106, 244, 245, 288, 389, 391, 398, 399, 497, 585, 618, 634
Atholl, Earl of,   389, 537
Atholl, Marquis of,   243, 275, 344, 345, 347, 376
Atkinson, Tom,   100, 220
Auchtergaven,   174, 175, 203
Austria-Hungary,   126
Avoch,   177, 181, 203, 239, 495, 500, 570, 571, 588, 678
Aztec Empire,   26
Badenoch,   229, 264, 294, 304, 333, 334, 335, 337, 357, 358, 392, 393, 394, 399, 402, 525, 640
Baillie of Dochfour, Alexander,   435
Baillie of Rosehall, William,   435
Bain, Robert,   220
Baird, Sir James,   650
Bakewell, Thomas, 91
Balfour, General,   633
Ballater,   166, 175
Ballingal, Rev. James,   484
Balliol, Edward,   535
Balliol, John,   114, 116, 535
Balloch,   166, 236
Balmaha,   156, 166
Balquhidder,   149, 168, 181, 295, 333, 357, 358, 389, 399, 585
Banff, xi, 36, 117, 167, 168, 170, 176, 200, 203, 404, 475, 477, 481, 483, 570, 678, 681, 683, 690, 691
Banffshire,   xi, 128, 170, 176, 180, 182, 287, 304, 360, 389, 415, 422, 423, 462, 495, 587, 623, 668
Bangladesh, 26
Bangor-Jones, Dr M.,   481
Banks, Basil,   24
Banks, Joy,   24
Banks, Noel, 367, 410

Barra,   101, 104, 107, 108, 130, 147, 166, 181, 224, 234, 353, 354, 355, 357, 373, 385, 397, 398, 404, 449, 583, 621, 623, 625
Barron, James,   129
Barrow, G. W. S.,   417
Barton, Andrew,   540
Barvas,   181, 305
Basilikon Doron,   488
Battle drill, Highland,   638
Bawden, Liz-Anne,   24
Beaton, Cardinal,   542
Beauly,   177, 512, 624
Beauly Firth,   177
Beauly River,   624
Beauties of Scotland,   680
Belgium,   36, 126
Ben Cruachan,   363, 365
Ben Lomond,   148, 167
Ben Nevis,   164, 468
Benbecula,   130, 309, 397, 427, 449
Bendochy,   174
Berries, wild,   413
Berwick,   53, 59, 115, 117, 155, 161, 200, 534, 535, 545, 616
Berwick-on-Tweed,   53, 155
Berwickshire,   542
Bible, the,   3, 21, 237, 273, 293, 421
Birmingham,   23, 163, 312
Birnam Hill,   156, 173
Black Isle,   31, 169, 177, 178, 269, 304, 503, 621, 624
Black Watch,   161, 180, 319, 434, 502, 555, 556, 563, 564, 565, 580, 600, 601, 604, 609, 613, 614, 615, 616, 631, 635, 636, 637, 638, 639, 640, 641, 642, 643, 645, 646, 647, 648, 649, 650, 654, 655, 656, 659, 660, 661, 665, 666, 687
Black, Conrad,   62
Blackheath,   523, 525
Blair Atholl,   106, 130, 149, 181, 425, 477, 548, 633, 686
Blairgowrie,   31, 166, 167, 174, 203
Blakeney's Regiment,   510
Blucher,   126
Blundell, Odo,   134, 418, 619, 627, 692
Boleskine & Abertarff,   xii, 181
Book of Grant,   282

Book of MacKay, 218, 313
Bookseller, The   3
Boreraig,   584, 585
Boston,   186, 650
Boswell, James,   42, 155, 241, 524
Botfield, Beriah,   91
Bower,   179
Bowman, J. E.,   260, 457, 470
Boyd, Thomas, Earl of Arran,   539
Boyles,   301
Bracadale,   181
Braemar,   xii, 133, 175, 182, 203, 254, 390, 415, 418, 499, 565, 681
Braes of Balquhidder,   168
Brahan Castle,   236
Brazil,   657
Breadalbane,   72, 80, 87, 170, 197, 223, 244, 245, 257, 270, 306, 341, 342, 343, 386, 390, 391, 396, 433, 487, 498, 504, 550, 612, 618, 664
Breadalbane Fencibles,   612, 618, 664
Breadalbane, Earl of,   79, 244, 245, 343, 386, 391, 396, 498
Brereton, Sir William,   437, 480
Bridge of Bruar,   265
British Empire,   28, 51, 59, 208, 441, 456, 602, 646
British Museum,   2
Britons,   3, 157, 158, 250
Broadford,   606
Brodie of Brodie,   398
Brora,   31, 86, 161
Brown, John,   565
Brown, Robert,   424, 451, 464, 668
Bruce, Robert,   114, 116
Brussels,   565, 658
Buchan,   35, 157, 426, 459, 477, 483, 536, 576, 607, 682, 690, 692
Buchan, James,   477
Buchanan, John, Lord Tweedsmuir,   41, 45, 62, 66, 131, 134, 135, 148, 167, 173, 181, 223, 398, 416, 418, 419, 422, 426, 454, 459, 475, 476, 477, 482, 483, 499, 500, 536, 564, 570, 575, 580, 585, 588, 591, 607, 611, 613, 677, 678, 682, 683, 692
Buchanan, Daisy,   45
Buchanan, George,   62, 134, 418
Buchanan, Rev. J. L.,   66, 422, 454, 500, 588, 607, 613

Buchanans, the,   499
Budge, Robert,   180
Buidhe,   297, 467
Bunawe,   628
Bunchrew Wood,   346
Burial of Sir John Moore,   685
Burke, Edmund,   524
Burke, John,   121, 436, 441, 442, 622
Burke, Ned,   302, 518
Burke's Peerage,   220, 341, 346, 348, 355
Burkes,   301
Burleigh, Michael,   17
Burns, Archibald,   82
Burntisland, 617, 652
Burt, Edmund,   62, 157, 163, 166, 171, 189, 190, 212, 429, 461, 480, 500, 521, 525, 562, 702
Burton, John Hill,   167
Bute,   xi, 33, 35, 167, 168, 171, 181, 215, 288, 388, 389, 395, 397, 398, 403, 482, 679
Bute, Earl of,   389, 395, 398
Bute, Marquess of,   215
Buteshire,   xi, xii, 128, 168, 169, 171, 180, 181, 200
Butter of Pitlochry, 149, 150
Caddies,   517
Caird, J. B.,   219, 313
Cairnmore Hillock,   403
Caithness,   10, xi, 22, 31, 36, 37, 96, 113, 124, 128, 142, 143, 159, 161, 162, 166, 167, 168, 169, 170, 178, 179, 180, 182, 200, 203, 204, 218, 304, 341, 342, 343, 367, 400, 403, 419, 564, 624, 652, 656, 697, 700
Caithness Lowlands,   403, 419
Calda House,   373
Calder,   197, 223, 294, 361, 362, 363, 364, 365, 386, 396, 404, 467
Caledonian Canal,   105
Caledonian Mercury,   639, 686
Caledonians,   158, 191, 221, 313
Callander,   43, 78, 106, 137, 148, 149, 166, 167, 173, 174, 181, 240, 260, 316, 415, 475, 500, 571, 592, 599, 612, 623, 673, 678, 680, 683, 691
Cally, bridge of,   159, 160
Cambridge University,   9, 113, 124, 231
Cambuskenneth,   117
Cameron,   x, 21, 81, 105, 142, 149, 164, 165, 225, 230, 246, 261, 262, 274, 279, 285, 295,

INDEX

296, 302, 303, 305, 306, 319, 321, 323, 338, 339, 340, 341, 361, 376, 381, 385, 397, 502, 528, 553, 556, 613, 649, 660, 693, 694
Cameron Highlanders, the,   660
Cameron of Callart,   553
Cameron of Fassfern, Colonel,   285, 613, 649
Cameron of Lochiel,   x, 81, 105, 246, 274, 279, 295, 296, 323, 339, 376, 381, 553
Cameron, Donald (Donald Ban Leanne),   149, 225, 528
Cameron, Dougal Roy,   261, 262, 319
Campbell family,   583
Campbell of Asknish,   306
Campbell of Barnacarry,   368
Campbell of Calder,   294, 361, 362, 363, 364, 386, 404, 467
Campbell of Dunoon, John,   200, 257, 318, 339, 341, 343, 363, 364, 368, 509, 548, 639, 642, 644, 670, 697
Campbell of Glendaruel,   105, 149
Campbell of Glenfalloch, Colin,   213, 252, 261, 275, 279, 553, 664
Campbell of Glenlyon,   80, 585, 670
Campbell of Glenlyon, John,   200, 257, 318, 339, 341, 343, 363, 364, 368, 509, 548, 639, 642, 644, 670, 697
Campbell of Glenlyon, Robert,   80, 670
Campbell of Glenorchy, John,   341, 343
Campbell of Glenure,   213, 252, 253, 259, 261, 279, 528, 553
Campbell of Glenure, Colin,   213, 252, 261, 279, 553
Campbell of Lochnell,   x, 363
Campbell of Mamore, General John,   548
Campbell of Mochaster,   583
Campbell of Otter,   295
Campbell of Stonefield,   307
Campbell of Strachur,   105, 149, 150, 306
Campbell younger of Mamore, John,   509
Campbell, Black John,   368
Campbell, Colin,   213, 252, 261, 275, 279, 553, 664
Campbell, Colonel,   641
Campbell, Donald,   221, 313, 526
Campbell, Dougal,   236, 306
Campbell, Dr J. L.,   211
Campbell, Duncan,   390
Campbell, Ewen,   550, 551
Campbell, General,   156, 548
Campbell, John,   200, 257, 318, 339, 341, 343, 363, 364, 368, 509, 548, 639, 642, 644, 670, 697
Campbell, Lieutenant Patrick,   164
Campbell, Marion,   76
Campbell, Primrose,   351, 352
Campbell, Professor R. H.,   31, 84, 119
Campbell, Sheriff J. MacMaster,   218
Campbell, Walter Frederick,   598
Campbells are Coming, The   342
Campbell's Highlanders,   266, 506, 563, 618, 644, 645, 650
Campbeltown,   97, 181, 192, 207, 282, 322, 416, 423, 441, 475, 477, 481, 554, 578, 610, 628, 682
Campsie Fells,   167
Canada,   120, 224, 302, 459, 468, 635, 653, 664, 669, 688, 695
Canisbay,   179
Canna,   xi, 67, 148, 197, 211, 312, 397, 422, 620, 693
Cape Wrath,   155, 163, 166
Capital of the Mind,   477
Caputh,   203
Cardiff docks,   215
Cardross,   167, 172, 202, 227
Carlisle,   116
Carmichael, Alexander,   135, 447, 448, 469, 481, 482, 508, 561, 572, 580, 594, 604, 621, 678, 679, 680, 683, 684
Carroll, Lewis,   30, 110, 127, 141, 231, 325
Cassius Dio,   417
Castillon,   184
Castle Downie,   346, 348
Castle Stuart,   377
Castle Swen,   373, 374
Catholic church,   538
Catholics,   61, 123, 249, 444, 494, 541, 543, 545, 619, 620, 621, 623, 624, 625, 627, 684
Cawdor,   176, 182, 203, 364
Celtic Scotland,   447, 697
Celts,   159, 161, 529, 530
Central,   96, 142, 157, 214, 522, 692, 693, 694, 696
Certayne Matters Concerning Scotland, 582
Chamberlain, Joseph,   216, 312

Chambers, Robert, 693
Changing Role of the House of Argyll, 370, 693, 696
Channel Islands, 212, 617, 652
Charles I, 390, 546
Charles II, 258, 297, 341, 366, 369, 372, 546
Charles, Prince, 47, 51, 68, 81, 187, 189, 193, 230, 241, 242, 243, 244, 248, 249, 250, 252, 259, 274, 302, 348, 350, 352, 368, 394, 420, 458, 473, 506, 507, 508, 510, 511, 517, 518, 526, 527, 528, 548, 551, 555, 585, 601, 605, 621, 626, 634, 637, 645, 671, 684
Chatham, Lord, 228
Cheape, Hugh, 410
China, 50, 267
Chisholm clan, 302, 623
Chisholm of Strathglass, 399
Chisholm, Donald, 302
Chisholms, the, 302, 303, 510, 623
Church in the Highlands, The 237, 489, 695
Church of Scotland, 172, 515, 681
Clackmannanshire, 390
Clan Andrish, 303
Clan Cameron, 246, 274, 296, 338, 339, 340, 361, 693, 694
Clan Chattan, 104, 197, 246, 294, 295, 303, 304, 323, 334, 335, 336, 337, 338, 339, 362, 374, 376, 377, 393, 394, 399, 402, 541, 623, 641, 697
Clan Chattan chief of, 295, 303, 374
Clan Donald, 119, 120, 135, 218, 226, 233, 235, 276, 292, 358, 359, 383, 397, 404, 449, 459, 499, 501, 583, 584, 585, 623, 695
Clan Fraser, 344, 345, 350
Clan Gordon, 693
Clan Grant, 225, 243, 244, 385, 694
Clan Gunn, 223
Clan MacKenzie, 102, 473, 693
Clan MacKinnon, 696
Clan MacLean, 148, 218, 317, 696
Clan MacLeod, 146, 147, 323, 694
Clan MacPherson, 294
Clan Menzies, 383
Clan Ranald, xi, 67, 119, 134, 135, 207, 291, 292, 303, 306, 323, 324, 340, 356, 357, 358, 383, 385, 391, 397, 449, 623
Clan Ranald, chief of, 292, 358, 385
Clan Revan, 303
Clann an Sgeulaiche, 585
Clanranald's Galley, 605
Clanship to Crofters' War, 170, 693
Clark, Francis, 449
Clio, 25
Clunie, 173, 174, 181, 203, 204, 399
Cluny MacPherson, 224
Clyde, 117, 162, 166, 167, 168, 169, 171, 172, 519
Clyne, 113, 181, 596, 679
Coalbrookdale, 439
Colbost, 226
Coll, xii, 65, 97, 105, 108, 130, 148, 157, 181, 202, 204, 223, 283, 297, 305, 306, 334, 336, 340, 367, 368, 425, 427, 428, 479, 519, 582, 583, 584, 604
Collier, Adam, 33, 96, 287, 290, 701
Collins, Wilkie, 129
Colonsay, xii, 105, 108, 130, 167, 181, 202, 215, 369, 475
Colquhoun of Luss, 105, 147, 224, 255, 507
Columbia University, 139
Commons, House of, 123, 353, 689
Companion to Gaelic Scotland, 168, 179, 201, 202, 698
Companion to Scottish History, 34, 112, 128, 152, 443, 693, 695
Complete Peerage, 351, 403
Comrie, 106, 149, 173, 181, 559, 579
Comyn, John, 115, 116, 535
Congestion, 43, 47, 131
Contin, 130, 181, 425, 477
Coote, General, 663
Cork, 520, 636, 647
Cornhill, 525
Cornwall, 163, 194
Cornwallis, Lord, 609, 649, 651, 652, 653
Corunna, 630
Council, Privy, 211, 239, 246, 247, 334, 335, 336, 339, 356, 370, 489, 662
County Durham, 15, 457, 569
Covenanters, 172, 546, 632, 662
Cowal, 97, 167, 171, 202, 304, 466, 505
Craig, David, 145
Craigellachie, 166, 175, 176
Craigie Barns, 156, 173

INDEX

Craignish, 97, 181
Crathie & Braemar, xii, 182, 203, 681
Crawar, Paul, 537
Crawford, Earl of, 538, 686
Creative Scotland, 141
Creek Indians, 651
Cregeen, Eric, 70, 370, 474, 696
Creich, 181
Cremona, 584
Crichton, Lord, 538
Crieff, 31, 156, 166, 167, 174, 203, 204
Crimean War, 141, 216, 251
Crofters, x, 21, 55, 94, 133, 145, 170, 693
Crofters' War, x, 94, 170, 693
Croick, 444
Cromar, 130, 175, 202
Cromartie, Earl of, 100, 145, 349
Cromarty, xi, 31, 35, 39, 127, 130, 157, 167, 168, 169, 170, 177, 181, 202, 204, 269, 313, 400, 444, 700
Cromarty Firth, 169, 177
Cromdale, 176, 182, 202, 203, 494, 570
Cross Fell, 458
Crown charters, 326, 327
Croy & Dalcross, xii, 181
Culgower, 122
Culloden, 2, 10, 27, 43, 50, 51, 52, 53, 56, 59, 62, 63, 68, 74, 76, 78, 82, 88, 89, 121, 139, 187, 188, 192, 193, 195, 206, 212, 214, 218, 220, 224, 234, 240, 241, 242, 246, 252, 253, 256, 259, 261, 268, 272, 277, 278, 279, 281, 282, 286, 295, 297, 300, 302, 318, 329, 339, 352, 367, 368, 370, 373, 374, 376, 382, 384, 385, 389, 391, 392, 393, 394, 395, 402, 408, 409, 413, 414, 432, 435, 442, 443, 480, 490, 507, 510, 512, 514, 515, 516, 517, 518, 528, 532, 546, 547, 554, 555, 572, 585, 597, 603, 609, 622, 627, 628, 637, 669, 671, 685, 692
Culloden Moor, 188, 212, 512, 692
Cumberland, 51, 68, 158, 161, 187, 188, 206, 241, 432, 457, 458, 506, 507, 509, 510, 512, 514, 515, 516, 517, 528, 572, 573, 603, 613, 671
Cumberland Gap, 515
Cumberland Gate, 515
Cumberland, Butcher, 514
Cumberland, Duke of, 206, 432, 509, 512, 514, 528, 573, 613

Cumming, Laura, 16
Cumming, Peter, 129
Cunningham, Alexander, 247, 252, 307, 422, 425, 426, 500, 566, 567, 627, 676
Cupertino, Joseph of, 13
Dacre, Lord, 16, 485, 488, 698
Daily Telegraph, 62, 678, 690
Dallas, 176
Dalrymple, Sir John, 257, 559, 614, 633
Darby, Abraham, 439
Darling, Dr Fraser, 218
Dartmoor, 3
Davidson, Basil, 34, 129
Daviot & Dunlichity, xii, 181, 681, 682
Day, J. P., 145
Dean of Guild, 1, 352
Deeside, 565
Defoe, Daniel, 23, 172, 255, 256, 263, 307, 318, 413, 419, 562, 611, 682
Derby, 189, 248, 250, 252, 266, 506, 507, 626, 645
Derbyshire, 164
Description of the Western Islands of Scotland, 523, 690
Description of the Western Isles of Scotland, 134, 696
Deutscher, Isaac, 23
Devine, Professor T. M., 39, 170, 193, 221, 331
Dewar, John, 488
Dickens, Charles, 20, 22, 25, 126, 141
Dingwall, 181, 596, 679
Discourse on Inequality, 406
Dochgarroch, 304, 362
Donald, Lord of the Isles, 537
Donaldson, Professor Gordon, 2, 9, 95, 520, 614
Donnachie, Dr Ian, 410, 443
Dores, 181, 502, 571, 623
Dornoch, 169, 181, 304, 428, 456, 482, 503, 571, 624
Dornoch Firth, 169, 624
Dorset, Duke of, 510
Douglas, Earl of, 538, 539
Douglas, Hugh, 249, 526
Doune, 167, 174, 260
Doune pistol-smiths, 260
Doutelle, 248
Doyle, Conan, 21, 475, 487, 568

Drainage Act,   71
Druids,   627
Drumcharry,   585
Drumfin,   283
Drummond of Perth,   149, 376, 395
Drummond-Moray of Abercairney,   149
Drummonds, the,   388, 389, 398
Drumochter Pass,   169
Drury Lane Theatre,   525
Drymen,   41, 131, 148, 171, 173, 181
Duart Castle,   366
Dublin,   206, 647, 648
Duirinish,   102, 108, 147, 181, 226, 559, 579, 584, 596, 606, 679, 681
Duke of Gordon's clan,   623
Dull,   181, 398, 549, 578, 595, 679
Dumbarton,   xi, 36, 59, 166, 167, 168, 169, 172, 280, 396, 397, 398, 544, 631
Dumbarton Castle,   172
Dumbartonshire,   xi, 128, 157, 161, 168, 169, 171, 172, 180, 181, 182, 387, 631
Dumfries,   165, 200, 535
Dunach,   586, 677
Dunbar,   188, 479, 480, 534, 535, 536, 576, 693
Dunbar, the poet,   536
Dunbar, William,   188, 576
Duncanson, Major,   80
Dundee,   21, 42, 45, 117, 127, 131, 136, 142, 146, 160, 200, 221, 243, 255, 313, 536, 615, 632, 633, 637, 639, 685, 693, 701
Dundee, Earl of,   45, 136, 142, 221, 701
Dundee, Lord,   243, 633, 685
Dundee's Memoirs,   633
Dunkeld,   xii, 77, 137, 156, 159, 160, 161, 166, 167, 168, 173, 181, 182, 199, 203, 495, 497, 505, 512, 562, 570, 572, 632
Dunkeld & Dowally,   xii, 181
Dunkeld, parish of,   173
Dunlop, Captain,   188, 510
Dunlop, Dr Jean,   409
Dunmaglass,   361
Dunnet,   163, 179
Dunoon & Kilmun,   xii, 181
Duntreath,   280
Duntulm,   235
Dunvegan,   224, 229, 244, 260, 319, 358, 359, 362, 397, 418, 509, 584, 605, 696

Dunvegan Castle,   244, 260, 319
Durham,   15, 161, 457, 491, 569
Durham Light Infantry,   491, 569
Durness,   36, 100, 129, 181, 304, 428, 587, 605
Duthil & Rothiemurchus,   xii, 181
Dymes, Captain,   560, 579
Earth Changes (website),   138
East Anglia,   35, 151
East India Company,   363, 618
East Ruston,   138
Easter Clyth,   159, 166, 180, 342
Easter Moy,   303
Easter Rising,   26
Easter Ross,   178, 502
Edderton,   181
Eddrachillis,   36, 68, 100, 129, 181, 275, 300, 322, 462, 483, 499, 570
Edgar, David,   24, 483
Edinburgh,   4, 27, 28, 31, 32, 38, 40, 42, 49, 50, 51, 57, 58, 91, 92, 95, 128, 129, 134, 135, 139, 141, 152, 155, 162, 185, 186, 191, 193, 194, 195, 196, 203, 204, 207, 215, 219, 236, 237, 239, 240, 242, 245, 246, 250, 254, 255, 256, 260, 278, 280, 282, 289, 291, 292, 299, 313, 316, 317, 318, 319, 321, 323, 325, 326, 327, 328, 330, 333, 334, 335, 340, 341, 343, 347, 350, 352, 353, 355, 356, 361, 362, 363, 364, 366, 371, 372, 373, 375, 376, 380, 381, 382, 383, 392, 395, 404, 407, 422, 423, 431, 434, 435, 437, 443, 477, 479, 480, 481, 484, 488, 498, 510, 514, 516, 517, 518, 520, 521, 534, 536, 537, 538, 539, 541, 542, 543, 544, 546, 551, 553, 557, 572, 575, 578, 581, 601, 611, 616, 617, 620, 626, 627, 629, 664, 677, 678, 690, 692, 693, 694, 695, 696, 697, 698, 699, 704
Edinburgh Castle,   282, 350, 479, 538, 539, 544, 617
Edinburgh Magazine,   207, 318, 404, 435, 699
Edinburgh University,   31, 40, 375, 423, 514, 678
Edinkillie,   176, 182, 203, 204, 597, 679
Edward I,   114, 116, 535
Eigg,   xi, 67, 197, 397, 620
Eishken,   444
Elder, John,   418, 476, 595, 679
Elector Palatine,   640
Elegy in a Country Churchyard,   421

INDEX

Elgin, 36, 92, 115, 167, 168, 240, 315, 536
Eliot, George, 138, 331, 401
Elizabeth, Queen, 354
England, 13, 26, 27, 29, 30, 35, 50, 51, 58, 59, 72, 79, 83, 85, 90, 92, 110, 114, 115, 118, 126, 132, 143, 155, 158, 161, 162, 163, 164, 165, 176, 184, 186, 187, 194, 195, 199, 205, 208, 211, 213, 214, 217, 227, 237, 243, 265, 267, 277, 279, 280, 284, 286, 288, 292, 293, 300, 303, 329, 330, 336, 350, 354, 357, 358, 360, 365, 375, 381, 383, 387, 401, 422, 428, 437, 457, 458, 461, 468, 473, 489, 492, 496, 498, 500, 513, 514, 515, 519, 524, 527, 529, 533, 534, 535, 536, 537, 538, 540, 541, 542, 543, 545, 546, 547, 548, 550, 552, 555, 562, 571, 572, 574, 575, 577, 578, 581, 595, 611, 620, 629, 638, 656, 667, 671, 674, 695, 696, 697, 698
English language, 49, 92, 175, 180, 346, 603, 647
English, the, 11, 27, 28, 31, 49, 50, 52, 53, 57, 79, 82, 83, 92, 93, 115, 123, 129, 132, 156, 157, 159, 160, 161, 162, 164, 172, 176, 178, 180, 184, 185, 187, 188, 190, 194, 195, 196, 204, 208, 210, 220, 243, 254, 267, 279, 289, 346, 354, 388, 421, 436, 437, 458, 482, 499, 513, 515, 517, 521, 523, 524, 527, 529, 533, 535, 536, 539, 540, 541, 542, 543, 544, 551, 553, 558, 591, 603, 625, 637, 647, 655, 681, 694, 702, 703
Episcopalianism, 625
Episcopalians, 239, 546, 620, 621, 684
Erewhon, 126, 328, 401
Erskine of Achallader, 390
Erskine of Dun, 390
Esdras, 12
Essich, 346
Ettlinger, Brian, 312
Ettrick Shepherd, 156
European Union, 68
Evans, Bergen, 12, 22
Evans, Eric, 91, 140
Excursion to the Highlands of Scotland, 505, 696
Eyre-Todd, George, 80, 137
Falkirk Tryst, 585
Fallow, Jeff, 34, 622, 693
Farquharson of Invercauld, 105, 148, 224
Farr, 38, 130, 141, 181, 669, 690
Fearn, 181, 277
Ferguson, Adam, 423

Ferguson, Dr William, 193
Fergussons, the, 389, 399
Fettercairn, 167
Fife Adventurers, 370, 371
Finchley Common, 523, 524
Findhorn, 167, 597
Finellan House, 346
Fingal, 481, 500, 600
Finlay, Ian, 71, 77, 168, 260, 461, 553, 621
Firth of Forth, 540, 545, 617
Firth of Lorn, 369
Flanders, 14, 616, 635, 639, 640, 654, 655, 658, 665, 689
Fletcher of Saltoun, 547
Flowerdale, 460
Fochabers, 167
Fodderty, 78, 137, 181
Forbes of Culloden, Duncan, 256, 352, 368, 395
Forbes, David, 37
Forbes, Lord, 398, 399
Ford, Henry, 454, 482
Forres, 167, 169, 628
Forss Water, 204
Fort Augustus, 164, 340, 502, 511, 512, 513, 515, 627
Fort Churchill, 444
Fort Douglas, 444
Fort Rouro, 639
Fort William, 137, 164, 165, 307, 347, 393, 420, 515, 516, 593, 601, 620
Forth, 117, 152, 162, 176, 540, 545, 617
Fortingall, 38, 66, 129, 130, 135, 165, 181, 201, 254, 258, 274, 319, 320, 425, 467, 477, 484, 495, 570, 583, 605, 681
Fowlis Wester, 77, 137, 173, 181, 202, 204
France, 13, 14, 28, 67, 115, 116, 138, 163, 184, 189, 194, 195, 205, 211, 230, 263, 278, 293, 305, 306, 349, 350, 535, 536, 540, 541, 542, 544, 545, 554, 605, 635, 636, 644, 645
Franck, Richard, 357
Frank, 33, 141, 218, 431, 692, 694
Fraser of Lovat, 98, 223, 286, 351, 376
Fraser Professor of Scottish History, 38, 95
Fraser, Alexander, 346
Fraser, Amelia, 367
Fraser, Sarah, 479

Fraser, Sir William, 38, 91, 95, 119, 282
Fraser, William Sutherland, 145
Fraser's Highlanders, 266, 286, 641, 647, 649, 650, 651, 652, 688
Frasers, the, 142, 307, 344, 345, 346, 348, 350, 351, 352, 367, 375, 566, 595, 654, 656
Frederick Duke of Brunswick, 13
Fry, Michael, 9, 33, 64, 71, 94, 95, 99, 108, 113, 122, 133, 142, 185, 318, 474, 488
Fuller, Thomas, 19, 23
Fulton, Alexander, 44, 45
Furnace, 510
Gaelic language, 88, 92, 174, 204, 211, 522, 602, 603, 604
Gaels, 28, 44, 52, 64, 67, 83, 111, 128, 138, 157, 158, 159, 163, 186, 187, 189, 204, 205, 211, 217, 277, 301, 343, 370, 400, 411, 415, 417, 423, 433, 435, 439, 442, 490, 522, 527, 528, 530, 562, 569, 589, 591, 594, 606, 628, 632, 702
Gairloch, 38, 100, 108, 129, 130, 145, 181, 223, 239, 314, 400, 583, 584, 585, 606, 626
Galbraith Dr J. J., 219
Gallie, Rev. Andrew, 423
Galloway, 59, 116, 171, 502, 534
Galtrigill, 584
Garb of Old Gaul, The 601
Gare Loch, 172, 173
Garnett, Thomas, 260, 470
Garvellach Islands, 369, 370
Gazetteer for Scotland, 38, 39, 40, 41, 130, 694, 699
Geddes, Arthur, 286, 323, 370, 445, 450, 451, 496
Geikie Dr, 169
Geikie, Sir Archibald, 165, 178, 342, 566, 620
Geisslerin, Catharina, 13
General Assembly, 236, 515
General View of the Agriculture of Sutherland, 124, 694
Geneva Convention, 26
Gentleman's Magazine, 625, 685
George I, 12, 237, 238, 240, 350, 351
George II, 51, 240, 244, 509, 511, 514, 613, 642
George, Arthur, 24
Georgia, 650
Germans, 126, 159, 491

Germany, 25, 46, 67, 126, 196, 205, 207, 208, 254, 266, 635, 644, 645, 650
Ghosh, Peter, 17
Gibson, R., 21
Gigha & Cara, xii, 130, 181, 320, 571, 678
Gillanders, Farquhar, 220
Gilpin, William, 257, 258, 433, 478, 627
Glamis, Lady, 541
Glasgow, 21, 25, 42, 92, 119, 129, 134, 139, 141, 147, 148, 155, 167, 186, 194, 205, 230, 312, 319, 323, 444, 475, 489, 515, 532, 555, 589, 594, 620, 647, 649, 664, 665, 668, 679, 680, 692, 694, 696, 697, 698
Glasgow Herald, 679
Glasgow University, 489, 515
Glassary, xi, 97, 181, 301, 373, 466
Glen Almond, 156, 174, 399, 440
Glen Artney, 149, 169, 389, 390, 398
Glen Cannich, 302, 303
Glen Clova, 175
Glen Coe, x, 79, 80, 81, 82, 137, 197, 221, 292, 335, 339, 459, 460, 467, 492, 505, 576, 595, 606, 623, 670, 671, 684, 690, 692, 695
Glen Croe, 457
Glen Dochart, 586
Glen Esk, 175, 203, 632
Glen Fernat, 199
Glen Finnan, x, 249
Glen Gyle, 168, 446
Glen Isla, x, 166, 175, 389, 390
Glen Kingie, x
Glen Livet, 389, 390, 392, 399
Glen Lochy, 156
Glen Lyon, 156, 327, 376, 390, 467, 585, 611
Glen Moriston, 98, 242, 302, 316, 383, 399, 572, 610
Glen Ogle, 156
Glen Orchy, 260, 600, 605
Glen Pean, 305
Glen Prosen, 175
Glen Quoich, 627
Glen Rinnes, 668
Glen Roy, 82, 197, 333, 337, 391
Glen Shee, 174, 304
Glen Spean, 197, 333, 337, 391
Glen Tilt, 304, 562
Glendale Martyrs, 444

INDEX

Glendaruel, 105, 149, 304, 650
Glenelg, x, 130, 181, 362, 363, 383, 397, 404, 503, 522, 574, 623, 624
Glenelg Bay, 624
Glengarry, x, 135, 189, 193, 197, 223, 225, 231, 244, 252, 281, 282, 296, 297, 300, 303, 322, 323, 333, 335, 366, 376, 383, 391, 397, 399, 418, 423, 434, 436, 479, 480, 560, 606, 623
Glenmoriston, xii, 98, 163, 181, 197, 223, 302, 399, 475, 510, 623
Glenmuick Tullich & Glengairn, xii, 182
Glenorchy & Inishail, xii, 181, 571, 579, 678
Glentrool, 116
Gloomy Memories, 86, 696
Glover, J., 231, 534, 540, 546
Glover, Janet, 63, 131, 192, 237, 248, 473, 478, 489, 608, 621
Goa, 657, 658
Godalming, 11
Goethe, 440
Golspie, 181, 288
Gorbachov, 26
Gordon Fencible Regiment, 654
Gordon Highlanders, x, 285, 556, 565, 646, 657, 659, 660
Gordon Riots, 525, 574, 620
Gordon, Duke of, 104, 170, 246, 282, 337, 338, 385, 389, 391, 392, 393, 394, 395, 396, 399, 623
Gordon, Seton, 36, 80, 99, 129, 137, 144, 178, 203, 222, 224, 314, 318, 342, 476, 582, 583, 585, 586, 677
Gordon, Sir Robert, 377, 418
Gordons, the, 104, 107, 288, 394, 399, 660
Gower, Earl, 90
Gower, Lord Ronald Sutherland, 127
Gowrie Conspiracy, 545
Gowrie, Earl of, 545
Graham-Campbell, David, 368, 584
Graham, General, 658
Graham, James, Bonnie Dundee, 388, 615
Graham, Sir Robert, 538
Grahams, the, 389
Grampians, 156, 168, 267, 387
Grange, Lord, 390
Grant Fencibles, 612
Grant of Ballindalloch, 150
Grant of Glenmoriston, 98, 223, 302, 399

Grant of Grant, Ludovic, 351
Grant of Grant, Sir James, 509
Grant of Knoc-ceanach, 261, 262
Grant of Rothiemurchus, 98, 144, 582
Grant, Anne, 189, 190, 424, 582, 588
Grant, Edmund, 24
Grant, James Shaw, 219, 309, 416, 469, 546
Grant, John, 302, 423, 426
Grant, Ludovick, 509
Grant, Major, 641
Gray, Malcolm, 69, 76, 134, 221, 272, 408, 413
Gray, Thomas, 421, 440
Great Britain, 27, 51, 59, 68, 72, 74, 83, 85, 89, 146, 158, 163, 165, 179, 186, 187, 194, 199, 200, 208, 215, 263, 265, 277, 279, 329, 337, 389, 400, 422, 525, 554, 567, 578, 614, 640, 646, 693, 699, 702
Great Glen, 97, 516, 594, 695
Great Highland Famine, 170, 201, 693
Great Sheep Tenement, 124
Greenock, 308, 324, 602, 649, 680
Greshornish, 103
Gretna, 92
Groome's Gazetteer, 169, 200
Gruids, 100, 145
Guadeloupe, 564, 643, 645
Guardian, The 23, 437, 479, 480
Guisachan, 67
Guise's Regiment, 510
Gunn, Mrs M., 218
Gurkhas, 116, 196
Guy's Hospital, 12
Haddington, 534
Hague Gazette, 639
Haig, Earl, 22
Halkirk, 62, 134, 179, 182, 204, 275, 322, 462, 483, 560, 579, 668, 690
Halle, 639
Halliday, James, 34, 47, 230
Hamilton, Duke of, 389, 395, 398
Hamilton, Patrick, 541
Hamilton, Professor Henry, 96
Hamiltons, the, 541, 544
Hamlet, 14, 491, 550, 569
Handel, 515
Hanover, 216, 350, 351, 616, 633, 685
Hanoverians, 51, 187, 244, 245, 250, 262,

506, 572, 633
Hardcastle, Edgar (Hardie), 24
Harding D. W., 151
Harley, 611
Harlosh, 303
Harper, Dr Marjory, 142
Harris, 39, 40, 112, 130, 181, 219, 227, 260, 293, 300, 303, 304, 323, 362, 383, 397, 416, 445, 449, 451, 469, 482, 496, 518, 523, 526, 570, 584, 605, 694, 698
Hawley, General, 250, 509, 512, 637
Hebridean Islands, 369
Hebrides, 5, 10, 39, 62, 66, 77, 96, 97, 107, 120, 130, 143, 146, 155, 157, 164, 167, 169, 197, 211, 241, 271, 301, 354, 369, 397, 398, 420, 427, 448, 449, 468, 519, 526, 561, 579, 590, 593, 602, 607, 613, 621, 625, 692, 694, 695, 696, 697, 698
Helensburgh, 166, 170, 172
Helmsdale, 168
Henry VIII, King, 404, 541, 542, 543, 595
Heritable jurisdictions, 379, 406
Herman, Professor Arthur, 410
Heron, Robert, 175
Hewitt, Dr George, 410, 443
Hicks, J., 463, 483
Highgate, 521
Highland Clearances 1840-1900, x
Highland Host, the, 662
Highland Jaunt, The 680
Highland line, 31, 53, 156, 157, 163, 165, 166, 167, 169, 170, 171, 172, 173, 174, 175, 176, 177, 180, 184, 186, 189, 192, 196, 199, 201, 276, 278, 288, 295, 343, 347, 384, 388, 405, 429, 485, 519, 527, 626, 662
Hill of Olrig, 403
Hill of Yarehouse, 342
Hill, Colonel Sir John, 347
Hill, Douglas, 70, 98, 120, 410, 412
Hillman, Ellis, 24
Historians in Trouble, 113, 152
Historical Memoirs of Mackintosh and Clan Chattan, 294, 337
Historiographer Royal, 2, 4, 19, 21, 40, 95, 132, 185, 205, 520, 615
History of Britain, 139, 697
History of Civilization in Scotland, 327, 401

History of England, 126, 227, 473, 513, 514, 638, 695, 696, 698
History of England 1377-1485, 126
History of Moray, 235
History of Scotland in 1750, 252, 282, 297, 386, 420, 465
History of Skye, 235, 696
History of the Clan MacLean, 218, 696
History of the Rebellion of 1715, 255
Hobbs Jay, 24
Hogg, James, 156, 159, 225, 278, 520, 592
Hogmanay, 189, 206
Holborn Head, 155, 166
Holland, 23, 99, 188, 658
Holland, Sir Richard, 188
Holland, T., 23
Holmes, Sherlock, 3, 414, 475, 693
Holy Roman Empire, 227
Homer, 440, 441, 601
Hopkins, Paul, 192, 274, 336, 625
Hours of Idleness, 593
House of Commons, 123, 353, 689
Howard John (midwife), 12
Hudson Bay, 443, 444
Hull, 654
Hulst, 639
Hume Brown, 63, 131, 134, 199, 206, 318, 480, 535, 544, 576, 577, 578
Hume Brown, P., 63, 131, 480
Humphry Clinker, 160, 265, 565, 698
Humpty-Dumpty, 94
Hunglader, 583
Hunt, Lynn, 17
Huntly, Marquis of, 393, 394, 657
Hutcheson, Charles, 587
Hyder Ali, 653, 663
Hythe, 631
I.R.A., 26
Iain Lom, 296
Inch Ewan, 159, 173
Independent, The, 23, 146
India, 26, 82, 146, 267, 363, 526, 556, 558, 618, 646, 653, 657, 658, 666, 687, 688
Indian Mutiny, 26, 129, 251
Industrial Revolution, 29, 74, 194, 195, 208, 267, 447, 594, 694
Ingres, 441

INDEX

Innes Munro of Poyntzfield, 100, 145
Innes of Innes, 398
Innes of Learney, Sir Thomas, 33, 70, 77, 185, 381, 402, 488, 621
Innes, Cosmo, 695
Institute of Historical Research, 18
Invention of Scotland, The 436
Inver, 130, 160, 167, 202, 695
Inveraray, 167, 181, 227, 488, 533, 576, 625, 685
Inveravon, 176, 182, 203, 447, 481, 623
Inverchaolain, 181
Invercoe, 80
Invergarry, 436, 437, 439, 480
Inverlochy, 418, 632, 633
Inverness, 1, xi, xii, 21, 32, 35, 39, 85, 104, 106, 127, 129, 130, 147, 149, 150, 167, 168, 170, 171, 177, 178, 180, 181, 202, 208, 225, 239, 264, 288, 312, 313, 322, 333, 334, 336, 346, 362, 376, 378, 381, 388, 398, 399, 404, 407, 413, 419, 420, 435, 436, 450, 475, 480, 482, 495, 503, 504, 507, 509, 516, 521, 522, 529, 537, 561, 564, 565, 571, 579, 595, 609, 634, 640, 644, 679, 692, 694, 695, 697, 699, 700, 702
Inverness Courier, 504, 571
Inverness-shire, xi, xii, 32, 35, 39, 106, 127, 130, 147, 150, 168, 177, 178, 180, 181, 202, 208, 225, 239, 264, 288, 322, 333, 334, 376, 381, 388, 398, 450, 561, 700
Inverness-shire Fencible Regiment, 388
Iona, 211, 254, 291, 387, 518, 578
Ionian Islands, 113
Ireland, 25, 26, 50, 126, 155, 157, 163, 184, 186, 200, 205, 301, 309, 353, 387, 388, 428, 468, 519, 530, 584, 602, 610, 621, 632, 636, 640, 646, 656, 657, 687, 688
Irish, the, 25
Irvine of Drum, 398
Islay, 39, 97, 130, 165, 167, 197, 202, 205, 235, 256, 260, 282, 304, 305, 387, 422, 466, 475, 483, 519, 584, 597, 598, 606
Isle of Lewis, 100, 399, 445, 694
Isle of Lewis and Harris, 445, 694
Isle of Sanda, 155
Isle of Wight, 165
Israel, 448, 449
Jackson, Captain, 523
Jackson, Dr Robert, 506, 517, 607, 612, 615, 631, 650
Jacobites, 51, 187, 244, 250, 265, 277, 303, 349, 350, 352, 367, 368, 394, 444, 498, 509, 510, 622
Jamaica, 104, 556
James I, 192, 489, 533, 537, 538, 545, 577
James II, 538, 539, 577
James III, 51, 539, 577
James IV, 192, 353, 356, 358, 540, 577
James V, 292, 357, 358, 540, 541, 542, 577
James VI, 176, 207, 298, 354, 370, 371, 488, 489, 543, 545, 578, 622
James VI & I, 578
James VII and II, 236, 238, 246, 303, 336, 349, 350, 354, 366, 615
Jamestown, 648, 650
Jamieson, Robert, 500
Japan, 208
Jarvie, Bailie Nicol, 210, 532
Jarvie, Grant, 220
Jefferson, Thomas, 440
Jenkins, Keith, 17
Jenner, Edward, 562
Jersey, 609, 652
Jewish schools, 25
Jews, 46, 84, 207, 208
John Balliol, 114, 116, 535
John Murray, 304, 305, 389, 442, 477, 689, 692, 694, 697
John of Fordun, 488, 568
Johnson & Boswell 1930, 126, 134, 199, 203, 207, 314, 316, 318, 320, 322, 323, 324, 402, 404, 406, 477, 478, 479, 571, 572, 574, 575, 577, 579, 580, 677, 678, 680, 682, 691
Johnson, Dr, 5, 20, 24, 28, 110, 126, 139, 155, 158, 177, 189, 190, 193, 230, 233, 241, 257, 263, 271, 272, 276, 281, 283, 289, 305, 340, 360, 382, 387, 422, 428, 429, 433, 435, 478, 503, 505, 507, 509, 522, 523, 524, 525, 528, 529, 555, 559, 564, 565, 577, 583, 584, 587, 591, 592, 603, 604, 610, 676, 696
Johnstone, Chevalier de, 158, 199, 413, 563
Joseph Andrews, 132
Journal of Scottish Historical Studies, 141
Journal to Arran in 1783, 678
Judas Maccabeus, 515
Jupiter, 14
Jura, 5, xii, 96, 120, 130, 167, 181, 197, 202, 387,

716

420, 426, 466, 483, 495, 570
Keith, Major, 644
Keith's and Campbell's Highlanders, 266, 506, 563, 618, 644, 645, 650
Kelso, 541, 542
Kenmore, 181, 415, 475, 596, 679
Kent, Pen, 24
Kenya, 26
Kerr, Andrew, 138
Kessanachs, the, 500
Kidnapped, 252, 281, 698
Kilarrow & Kilmeny, xii, 181
Kilbrandon & Kilchattan, xii, 181
Kilbride, xii, 181, 369, 595, 677, 679
Kilcalmonell & Kilberry, xii, 181
Kilchiaran, 597
Kilchoman, 78, 97, 137, 181, 202, 587, 588, 606, 678, 681
Kilchrenan & Dalavich, xii, 181
Kilcreggan, 169
Kildalton, 97, 181, 202, 496, 570
Kildonan, 86, 87, 127, 169, 181, 216, 333, 423, 443, 477, 564
Kilfinan, 97, 181, 269, 321, 462, 483, 496, 570
Kilfinichen & Kilvickeon, xii, 181, 571, 573, 681, 685
Kilgour, Jack, 140
Killean & Kilchenzie, xii, 181, 678
Killearnan, 78, 137, 181, 695
Killiecrankie, attdle of, 156, 159, 255, 354, 366, 479, 597, 615, 633, 639
Killiecrankie, Battle of, 615, 633
Killin, 106, 122, 149, 168, 182, 258, 275, 292, 319, 322, 606, 681
Kilmadock, 174, 203
Kilmallie, 37, 38, 40, 129, 130, 181, 202, 261, 262, 274, 275, 319, 322, 462, 483, 494, 512, 561, 569, 572, 580, 602, 610, 680, 682
Kilmartin, 181, 269, 275, 321, 322, 445, 446, 481
Kilmaurs, 628
Kilmichael, xii, 181
Kilmodan, 97, 181, 202
Kilmonivaig, 38, 129, 181, 560, 579, 623
Kilmorack, 38, 130, 181, 239, 623
Kilmore & Kilbride, xii, 181
Kilmuir, xi, xii, 103, 181, 239, 260, 283, 306, 324, 549, 560, 561, 578, 579, 580, 585, 593, 595, 607, 677, 679, 681
Kilmuir Easter, 181, 595, 679
Kilninian & Kilmore, xii, 181
Kilninver & Kilmelfort, xii, 181
Kilpatrick Hills, 167
Kiltarlity, 181, 269, 320, 605, 623, 681, 695
Kiltearn, 181, 226, 240, 314, 316, 429, 478
Kincardine, xii, 167, 174, 181, 203, 204, 302, 323, 423, 424, 444, 477, 481, 500, 561, 571, 580, 587, 608, 678, 682, 683
Kincardineshire, 169, 170
Kinchyle, 362
King John, 401, 534
King's House, 81
Kingarth, 181
Kingussie & Inch, xii, 181, 579
Kinloch Rannoch, 528
Kinrara, 582
Kinross, 200, 534
Kintail, 101, 102, 159, 181, 199, 224, 225, 259, 277, 278, 279, 302, 319, 322, 333, 354, 363, 370, 371, 399, 405, 409, 449, 482, 498, 560, 570, 579, 605, 681
Kintyre, 58, 155, 166, 167, 168, 171, 197, 282, 466, 493, 554
Kirk, Thomas, 318, 437, 480, 553, 578
Kirkcaldy, 544
Kirkhill, 181, 226, 314, 352
Kirkmichael, xi, 159, 176, 181, 182, 203, 360, 404, 415, 422, 423, 462, 475, 477, 481, 483, 495, 501, 570, 571, 587, 606, 610, 623, 672, 678, 681, 682, 691
Kirkwall, 162, 194
Knapdale, 97, 133, 167, 181, 282, 322, 373, 374, 405, 555, 579, 606, 610, 675, 681, 682, 691
Knockando, 176, 182, 203, 509
Knox, John, 101, 146, 293, 542
Knoydart, 197, 397, 421, 466, 483
Kray twins, 281
Kurds, 25
Kyles Paible, village of, 309
Kylesku, 37
Lachlan MacIntosh of Corribrough, 377
Lachlan MacPherson of Cluny, 394
Lady of the Lake, 162, 486
Lafayette, Marquis de, 652
Laggan, 130, 181, 189, 190, 225, 234, 314,

717

INDEX

315, 374, 424, 582, 623, 694
Lairg, 127, 181, 239, 274
Lairg sheep farm, 274
Lake Champlain, 641
Lakeland, 628
Lally, General, 653
Lament for Padraig Og MacCrimmon, 585
Lamont of Lamont, 398
Lanark, 116, 200
Lang, Andrew, 230, 237, 244, 282, 466
Later Stuarts, The 638
Latheron, 159, 179, 180, 182, 199, 204
Lauder, 539
Lauder Bridge, 539
Lawlessness, 552, 578
Lawrence, Pieter, 24
Legend of Montrose, 162, 247, 259, 416, 480, 487, 562, 697
Leith, 141, 180, 480, 542, 617, 626
Lenman, Professor Bruce, 10
Lennox, Earl of, 544, 545
Leny, 156
Leslie, Bishop, 418, 476
Leslie, General, 562, 566
Leslie, William, 624
Lewis, Isle of, 30, 39, 59, 65, 100, 101, 102, 107, 108, 110, 127, 130, 141, 145, 219, 227, 231, 271, 272, 296, 298, 300, 305, 307, 308, 321, 323, 325, 354, 358, 362, 363, 370, 371, 372, 375, 386, 397, 399, 416, 427, 445, 449, 451, 469, 550, 560, 590, 605, 606, 607, 621, 694, 698
Lewis and Harris, 416, 445, 469, 694, 698
Lewis Carroll, 30, 110, 127, 141, 231, 325
Liberty and Property, 513
Liechtenstein, 68
Life of Dr Johnson, 524
Limerick, 636
Ling, 566
Linklater, Eric, 189, 191, 219, 264, 533, 552
Linklater, Magnus, 9, 10, 21, 95
Linlithgow, 544, 618
Lismore & Appin, xii, 181, 578, 580
Lister, John, 33, 76, 85, 409, 411
Little Dunkeld, 173, 182, 495, 497, 570
Livingstone, David, 308
Livingstone, Sir Thomas, 80

Livingstone, William, 606
Loch Ard, 389
Loch Arkaig, xi, 262, 303, 338, 339, 341, 375, 402
Loch Awe, 363, 364
Loch Broom, 225, 428
Loch Crinan, 167
Loch Duich, 101
Loch Eil, x
Loch Finlaggan, 235
Loch Fyne, 167, 169, 304, 505
Loch Gilpin, 167
Loch Katrine, 168, 389, 390, 496
Loch Kirkaig, 624
Loch Lomond, 28, 156, 160, 166, 167, 168, 169, 172, 173, 592, 627, 628, 673
Loch Long, 168, 172
Loch Maddy, 428
Loch Nell, x
Loch Ness, 169, 340, 362, 466, 483
Loch Rannoch, x
Loch Scridain, 518
Loch Tarbert, 518, 520
Loch Tay, xi, 236, 498, 550, 563, 593
Loch, James, 63, 122, 124, 185, 205, 215, 275, 312
Lochaber, 135, 234, 253, 254, 255, 258, 261, 262, 274, 297, 301, 302, 303, 304, 305, 334, 335, 337, 339, 357, 358, 362, 367, 381, 392, 394, 397, 512, 525, 613, 632, 633, 695, 696
Lochalsh, 106, 150, 181, 399
Lochan-nan-corp, 500
Locharkaigside, xi, 261, 303, 338, 339, 340, 361
Lochbroom, 38, 130, 181, 399
Lochcarron, 181, 238, 316, 399, 597, 605, 626
Lochgilphead, 167
Lochgoilhead & Kilmorich, xii, 181
Lochiel, Cameron of, x, 81, 105, 246, 274, 279, 295, 296, 323, 339, 376, 381, 553
Lochiel's Memoirs, 339
Lochnell, x, 197, 223, 363, 396, 606
Lochs, 181, 427, 483, 596, 679
Lochtayside, xi
Lockhart, Major, 188, 206, 510
Loftus, Captain, 188
Logie Easter, 181
Logie Wester, xi, 78, 137, 181
Logierait, 182, 235, 423

718

Lom, Ian,   605
London,   2, 4, 12, 21, 22, 23, 24, 51, 57, 60, 110, 113, 115, 116, 121, 126, 127, 129, 131, 132, 136, 137, 140, 141, 146, 160, 163, 164, 184, 194, 195, 200, 201, 205, 206, 207, 208, 224, 227, 236, 237, 242, 245, 280, 281, 289, 291, 312, 313, 315, 317, 318, 319, 321, 325, 343, 350, 351, 378, 392, 401, 403, 405, 407, 434, 436, 437, 443, 461, 475, 476, 477, 479, 483, 513, 516, 520, 521, 523, 524, 525, 535, 536, 541, 551, 568, 569, 571, 572, 574, 575, 576, 577, 578, 580, 615, 616, 620, 629, 637, 640, 647, 648, 649, 680, 682, 685, 686, 689, 690, 692, 693, 694, 695, 696, 697, 698, 699, 704
London School of Economics,   110
Long Island,   135, 419, 422, 466, 483, 520, 561
Lord Breadalbane's March to Battle,   343
Lord of the Isles,   292, 338, 374, 537
Lord Reay, Eric,   99
Lords Reay, MacKay chiefs,   99
Lorn,   364, 369, 397, 465, 466, 483
Lotch, Captain,   523
Loth,   87, 181, 675, 691
Loudoun, Lord,   250, 572, 634
Loudoun's Highlanders,   601, 639
Lowlanders the,   23, 27, 28, 42, 50, 51, 52, 53, 56, 58, 59, 61, 83, 84, 85, 89, 92, 93, 118, 123, 124, 138, 158, 159, 161, 162, 172, 178, 185, 186, 187, 188, 189, 190, 191, 193, 194, 195, 196, 204, 205, 210, 219, 236, 248, 250, 253, 254, 264, 267, 271, 272, 288, 289, 330, 332, 343, 360, 363, 367, 370, 371, 375, 382, 387, 388, 400, 402, 418, 421, 424, 431, 432, 435, 442, 443, 460, 461, 463, 470, 471, 475, 484, 485, 488, 490, 499, 505, 509, 510, 514, 516, 525, 530, 532, 533, 534, 535, 536, 538, 540, 543, 547, 553, 557, 558, 560, 561, 562, 565, 575, 601, 604, 606, 612, 613, 621, 622, 625, 628, 634, 637, 638, 659, 662, 668, 669, 670, 687, 702, 703
Lowlands the,   27, 29, 30, 31, 36, 49, 50, 51, 57, 58, 59, 61, 72, 75, 83, 84, 85, 89, 92, 118, 155, 156, 157, 158, 160, 161, 162, 163, 164, 168, 169, 170, 171, 172, 173, 174, 176, 178, 179, 182, 183, 184, 187, 188, 189, 190, 191, 192, 194, 195, 196, 199, 200, 202, 206, 207, 210, 213, 217, 227, 236, 237, 238, 246, 261, 267, 268, 272, 277, 280, 286, 288, 291, 292, 294, 297, 301, 303, 306, 308, 326, 327, 328, 329, 330, 333, 342, 345, 346, 347, 360, 375, 376, 378, 383, 387, 388, 389, 392, 396, 399, 403, 417, 419, 431, 437, 441, 447, 452, 455, 456, 457, 459, 461, 471, 491, 492, 493, 494, 498, 500, 502, 509, 517, 520, 532, 533, 534, 535, 536, 537, 538, 539, 540, 541, 542, 543, 544, 545, 546, 547, 555, 557, 558, 576, 581, 589, 597, 607, 612, 616, 620, 625, 626, 627, 628, 629, 662, 669, 671, 672, 674, 700
Luss,   78, 105, 137, 147, 148, 160, 172, 181, 202, 224, 255, 397, 507
Lynch, Professor Michael, 32
MacAlister of Glenbarr,   147
MacAlister of Torrisdale,   103
MacAndeoras,   365
MacArthur piping school,   584
MacArthur, Charles,   583
Macaulay, Lord,   227, 314, 525, 526
MacAulay, Rev. Aulay,   526
MacAulay, Rev. John,   526
MacAulays,   227, 371, 383, 398
MacAulays of Garelochside,   383, 398
MacBane, Donald,   335
MacCalmans,   365
MacColl, Hugh,   222
MacCormack, Peggy,   588, 590, 594, 676
MacCrimmon, Padraig Og,   583, 585
Macdonald Lord, Clan Donald chief,   102, 103, 112, 119, 120, 297, 617
MacDonald of Achtriochtan,   81
MacDonald of Barrisdale,   282, 300, 434
MacDonald of Clanranald,   106, 112, 120, 152, 223, 584
MacDonald of Glengarry, John,   244
MacDonald of Keppoch,   121, 234, 334, 402, 583
MacDonald of Kingsburgh, Allan,   433
MacDonald of Moidart,   303
MacDonald of Scottas,   300
MacDonald of Sleat,   118, 119, 225, 297, 354, 355, 385, 396, 509, 572, 586, 606
MacDonald of Sleat, Donald Gorm,   586
MacDonald of Sleat, Sir James,   606
MacDonald, Alexander,   119, 216, 297, 316, 396, 397, 509, 583
MacDonald, Dr D. F.,   66, 135

INDEX

MacDonald, Flora, 241, 433
Macdonald, Iain S., 137
MacDonald, James, 77, 119, 354, 602, 606
MacDonald, John, 81, 118, 119, 216, 244, 316, 605
MacDonald, Marshal, 306, 324
MacDonald, Murdo, 582
MacDonald, Rev. Angus, 218
MacDonald, Rev. Coll, 425, 427
MacDonald, Simon of Morar, 653
MacDonald, Stuart, 82, 188, 335, 638
MacDonald's Highlanders, 81, 617, 652, 688
MacDonalds of Islay, 305
MacDonalds of Keppoch, 135, 203, 253, 255, 296, 332, 344, 358, 402, 404, 466
MacDonell of Keppoch, 553
MacDonell, A. G., 91, 196, 219, 245, 533, 552, 621, 624, 637, 659
MacDougall of Dunollie, 383, 586
MacDougall of MacDougall, 223
MacEachan, 260, 306, 319, 324, 653
MacEachan, Neil, 306, 324
MacFarlanes, the, 224, 304, 356, 383, 397, 499
MacFriar, Donald, 241
MacGregor of Glenstrae, 505
MacGregor, Alastair Alpin, 308, 325
MacGregor, Drummond, 433
MacGregor, John, 586
MacGregor, Patrick, 585, 586
MacGregor, Rob Roy, 279, 322
MacGregor, Sergeant, 609
MacGregor, Sir Malcolm, 404
MacGregors of Roro, 467
MacGrigor, Rev. James, 621
MacIains of Ardnamurchan, 302
MacInnes, John, 230, 653
MacIntosh chiefs, 104, 333, 334, 553
MacIntosh of MacIntosh, 634
MacIntosh, John, 82
Macintyre, Ben, 126
MacIntyre, Dr Joseph, 423, 507, 517
MacIntyre, Duncan Ban, 51, 187, 206, 259, 319, 600
MacIntyres of Glen Noe, 333
MacIver, Evander, 96, 141
MacIver, Finlay, 343
MacKays, The 585

MacKay pipers, 584
MacKay, Alexander, 62, 522, 587, 598
MacKay, Angus, piper, 218, 313
MacKay, Captain Hugh, 606
MacKay, Charles, 606
MacKay, Eain Dall, 583
MacKay, Elizabeth, 216
MacKay, General, 633
MacKay, John, 237, 239, 324, 489, 584
MacKay, Robert, 37
MacKay, Ruairidh Dall, 585
MacKay, William, Lewis factor, 101, 146
MacKellar, Mary, 303
MacKenzie of Coul, Sir George, 471, 667
MacKenzie of Cromartie, 100
MacKenzie of Fairburn, 132
MacKenzie of Gairloch, 100, 145, 314, 583, 584, 585
MacKenzie of Kintail, 224, 354, 363, 370, 371
MacKenzie of Redcastle, 223
MacKenzie of Scatwell, 223
MacKenzie of Seaforth, 102, 108, 277
MacKenzie of Strathgarve, x
MacKenzie of Suddie, 334, 335, 549
MacKenzie, Agnes Mure, 233, 315
MacKenzie, Alexander, 1, 21, 87, 223, 349, 474, 699
MacKenzie, Colin, 64, 466
MacKenzie, John, 102, 241, 373, 405, 605
MacKenzie, R. C., 178, 342
MacKenzie, Rev. Hugh, 425, 427
MacKenzie, Rev. James, 162, 486, 534, 621
MacKenzie, Sir George Steuart, 215, 269, 360, 446
MacKenzie, W. C., 145, 298, 323, 579
MacKenzie, William, 122, 481
MacKenzies, The 100, 101, 373
MacKinnon of MacKinnon, 357
MacKinnon, Peter, 66, 135
MacKinnon, Rev. Donald, 66, 103, 135
MacLachlan, John, 189, 206, 246
MacLachlan, Major, 509
MacLaren, Duncan, 218, 313
MacLaren, Moray, 603
MacLatchie, Gilbert (Gilmac), 24
MacLauchlan of Kilbride, 369
MacLauchlan, Ewen, 601

MacLean Donald, younger of Coll, 283, 477
MacLean of Ardgour, 105, 148
MacLean of Coll, 105, 108, 148, 223, 283, 305, 340, 582
MacLean of Dochgarroch, 362
MacLean of Drimnin, 246
MacLean, Allan, 366, 640, 653
MacLean, John, 216, 366
MacLean, Malcolm, 220
MacLean, Rev. Roderick, 621
MacLean, Sorley, ix, 94, 144, 149, 216, 312
MacLeans, the 304, 356, 366, 368
MacLeod of Assynt, Neil, 372, 405
MacLeod of Harris, 112, 397, 605
MacLeod of Lewis, 397
MacLeod of Raasay, 105, 360, 362, 559, 584
MacLeod, Angus, 219
MacLeod, Canon R. C., 293, 358
MacLeod, Donald, 85, 91, 300, 321, 422, 522, 548
MacLeod, Dr Norman, 285, 301, 464, 607
MacLeod, Iain, 219
MacLeod, John, 21, 34, 84, 146, 168, 178, 239, 260, 300, 310, 410, 411
MacLeod, Malcolm, 241, 300, 433, 479, 591
MacLeod, Mary, 605
MacLeod, Rev. Norman, 162, 167, 614
MacLeod's Highlanders, 663
MacLeods of Harris, 293, 300, 323, 383
MacLeods of Raasay, 108, 362, 404
MacLeods of Suardal, the, 260
MacMartin of Letterfinlay, 397
MacMartin-Camerons, the, 393
MacMartin, John, 664
MacMillan, Ewen, 285, 613
MacMillan, James, 621
MacMillan, Somerled, 301, 302, 613
MacNab of MacNab, 386, 397
MacNackands, 365
MacNaughton, John, 611
MacNeill, Captain, 278
MacNeill, Sir John, 170, 215
MacNeills of Barra, 353, 354, 404, 623
MacNicol, Rev. Donald, 233
MacPhail, Priest, 364
MacPhee, Ewen, 230
MacPhees, the, 369
MacPherson of Cluny, 224, 394

MacPherson, Donald, 480
MacPherson, James, 440, 441, 443
MacPherson, John, 444
MacPhersons, the, 224, 228, 230, 264, 265, 294, 295, 323, 335, 338, 339, 353, 358, 374, 392, 393, 394, 395, 407, 441, 499, 622, 623, 641, 702
MacQueen, Donald, 239, 283, 322, 426, 585, 591, 677, 679
MacQueen, Rev. Donald, 283, 322, 585, 591, 677, 679
MacRae, Christopher, 307
MacRaes of Kintail, 277, 279, 333
MacRory family, the, 260
MacTavish, Rev. John, 220, 313
MacVicar, John, 625
Magnusson, Magnus, 91
Mahon, Lord, 504, 510, 513
Maid of Norway, 534
Maitland, 544
Major, John, 133, 418, 442, 476, 488, 532, 547, 568
Malawi, 67
Malcolm of Poltalloch, 105, 108, 148, 373
Mallory, George, 19
Mamore, 165, 509, 548
Manchester, 13, 437, 457, 581, 693
Manitoba, 143, 302, 692
Manning, Cardinal, 7
Mar, Earl of, 133, 263, 350, 390, 418, 498, 537, 544
Marshall, William, 214, 522, 608
Martin of Husabost, 590, 678
Martin, Dr Nicol, 135
Martin, Martin, 255, 257, 428, 431, 432, 468, 523
Martinique, 643, 656
Marx Brothers, 64
Mary of Guise, 542
Mary of Modena, 349
Mary Queen of Scots, 354, 542, 577
Mary, Princess, 539
Maryland, 480
Master of Stair, 79, 623, 671
Matheson, Lady, 145, 444, 481
Matheson, Sir James, 100, 101, 112, 271
Mathieson, Robert, 34, 83, 218
Mau Mau, 26, 126
Mawman, Joseph, 505, 565, 696
Maxwell, Robert, 21

INDEX

Melrose, 536, 542
Melvich, 169, 178
Memoir of the Life of Lord Lovat, 403
Memoirs of a Cavalier, 307, 562, 610, 670, 672, 693
Memoirs of Great Britain, 614, 693
Memoirs of Lochiel, 393
Memorial of 1746, 395, 407
Menteith, 148, 156, 171, 173, 182, 307, 378, 389, 398
Menzies of Culdares, James, 240, 611
Menzies of Shian, 391
Menzies, Archibald, 421, 426
Mercer, John, 369
Meredith, Benjamin, 424
Methven, 174, 535
Mexico, 67
Mikes, George, 132
Miller, Hugh, 64, 91, 218, 263, 313, 460, 483, 511, 521, 597, 622, 696
Milton of Tullich, 166
Misty Isle of Skye, The 426, 695
Mitchell, Donald, 176
Mitchell, Joseph, 63, 106, 414, 426
Mitchison, Professor Rosalind, 10, 32, 178, 342, 409, 489, 588, 676,696
Moidart, xi, 197, 202, 248, 292, 303, 356, 397, 586
Moleigh, 586, 677
Monaco, 68
Moncreiffe of Moncreiffe, Sir Iain, 10, 221
Moneydie, 174
Montgomerie's Highlanders, 608
Montrose, Marquis of, 105, 148, 150, 157, 162, 209, 247, 248, 254, 259, 272, 279, 280, 313, 321, 356, 372, 388, 389, 390, 395, 397, 398, 416, 426, 443, 459, 480, 487, 562, 632, 637, 639, 692, 697
Monzie, 156, 173, 182, 521, 573, 587, 596, 678, 679
Monzievaird & Strowan, xii, 182
Moonstone, The 129
Moore, General Sir John, 630
Moore, Patrick, 14
Morar, xi, 197, 391, 397, 653, 697
Moray, xi, 31, 104, 105, 129, 147, 149, 161, 167, 168, 169, 170, 176, 177, 200, 202, 203, 235, 287, 315, 322, 376, 377, 378, 379, 385, 388, 389, 395, 396, 397, 398, 405, 406, 422, 426, 481, 503, 523, 534, 536, 543, 544, 545, 570, 571, 597, 603, 679, 680, 695, 696
Moray Firth, 177
Moray, Earl of, 104, 147, 376, 377, 378, 385, 389, 396, 398, 543, 544, 545
Morayshire, xi, 128, 161, 170, 176, 180, 182
Morer, Thomas, 188
Morrison, John, 260
Morrison, Roderick, 582, 605
Morrisons, 260, 371, 605
Mortlach, 176, 182, 203, 204, 425, 477, 619, 623, 668, 672, 675, 683, 690, 691
Morton, Earl of, 544
Morvern, 69, 181, 188, 215, 260, 274, 304, 365, 367, 369, 370, 391, 440, 464, 466, 478, 483, 512, 570, 572, 620, 624, 627, 684, 685, 694
Moulin, 79, 137, 182, 199, 494, 560, 570, 579, 595, 679
Moy & Dalarossie, xii, 181
Moy Hall, 634
Mr Dick, 25
Muck, 67, 397
Muckairn, xii, 97, 181, 202, 363, 364, 365, 404, 465, 467, 483, 532, 576
Muir, Dr Richard, 409
Mull, 59, 67, 77, 130, 155, 166, 168, 208, 304, 305, 318, 357, 365, 367, 368, 383, 387, 391, 397, 427, 450, 493, 504, 518, 520, 561, 564, 578, 583, 584
Mull of Galloway, 59
Mull of Kintyre, 155, 166, 168, 493
Munro of Culcairn, 244, 262, 509
Munro of Culcairn, George, 262, 509
Munro of Foulis, Sir Henry, 396, 400
Munro of Poyntzfield, 100, 145
Munro younger of Foulis, John, 226, 637
Munro, R. W., 356
Munro, Rev. Robert, 348
Munro, Sir Hector, 529
Munro, Sir Robert, 636
Munros, the 465
Munslow, Professor, 17, 18
Murdoch, John, 174, 176, 218, 260, 597
Murray of Dollery, 346
Murray, Lady Amelia, 344

Murray, Lord George,   245, 252, 264, 265
Murray, Lord Mungo,   346
Murray, Sarah,   81, 137
Murrays, the,   386, 388, 389, 390, 399
Muslim schools,   25
Muthill,   106, 149, 173, 182, 240, 316, 626
My King has Landed at Moidart,   586
Nabachd,   447, 452, 602
Nairn,   xi, 28, 36, 104, 164, 165, 166, 167, 168, 170, 176, 177, 200, 203, 204, 333, 336, 338, 385, 396, 399
Nairnshire,   xi, 128, 168, 176, 180, 182
Napier Commission,   x, 63, 66, 93, 101, 103, 135, 145, 161, 203, 219, 220, 226, 426, 493, 590, 604, 699
Napier, Lord,   150, 178, 342
Napoleon,   306, 325, 440, 614, 660
National Journal,   686
Nazis,   46, 207, 208, 509
Nennius,   21
Nepal,   116, 196
Netherlands, the,   36, 99, 113
New Brunswick,   46
New Jersey,   609
Newby, Andrew,   70, 136
Newman, Cardinal,   401
Ney, Marshal,   637
Nicholson, Bishop,   255, 257, 318
Nicolson, Alexander,   235, 504
Nicolson, Bishop,   134, 607, 682
Nieuport,   654
Nigg,   181, 597
Night at the Opera,   64
No clearances,   104, 147
Normans,   157, 158, 160
Norsemen,   157, 158
North Atlantic Drift,   163
North Carolina,   426
North Esk,   156, 166
North Knapdale,   97, 133, 181, 282, 322, 373, 374, 405, 555, 579, 606, 610, 675, 681, 682, 691
North Morar,   391
North Uist,   64, 66, 119, 120, 134, 135, 153, 181, 196, 216, 257, 260, 302, 358, 397, 420, 426, 428, 447, 448, 449, 452, 463, 481, 483, 518, 559, 579, 583, 602, 606, 608, 621, 680, 681, 682
Northamptonshire,   617

Northern Ireland,   25, 155
Northern Memoirs,   357, 693
Northumberland,   161
Northumbrians,   158
Norway,   534, 539, 541
Norwich Mercury,   13
Nova Scotia,   46, 653
Oban,   586, 593, 677
Observer, The,   22, 134, 207, 568
Ogilvies, the,   388, 389, 390, 398
Old Pretender,   349, 350, 351, 355, 390
Oldcastle, Sir John,   538
Olrig,   179, 403
Oman, Sir Charles,   126
Omand, Donald,   179, 218
Ootradroog,   653
Orkney,   128, 155, 162, 168, 169, 170, 309, 543
Orwell, George,   25, 93, 126, 140, 325
Ossian,   421, 440, 441, 480, 481
Otter,   295, 462
Oxford Dictionary of National Biography,   22, 100, 138, 199, 206, 225, 322, 403, 405, 553, 572, 573, 578, 579, 677, 681, 685, 702
Oxford Dictionary of Quotations,   575, 689
Oxford History of England,   473, 514, 638, 698
Oxford University,   110
Pack, General,   660
Paisley,   42, 323, 480, 579, 626, 685, 693, 695
Pakistan,   26
Paris, Matthew,   417
Park Forest,   444
Parker, Stan,   24
Paterson, Bishop,   546
Peingown,   583
Pemberton, John,   628, 685
Penguin,   23, 92, 126, 129, 131, 140, 201, 205, 207, 575, 695, 697, 698
Pennant,   175, 203, 204, 213, 214, 226, 266, 275, 312, 314, 322, 415, 422, 475, 477, 503, 516, 559, 571, 573, 579, 590, 620, 671, 677, 678, 679, 683, 690, 697
Pennant, Thomas,   175, 204, 266, 516, 590
Pentland Firth,   59, 179
Perth,   xi, 21, 36, 42, 106, 129, 135, 137, 149, 160, 162, 168, 170, 174, 199, 200, 201, 202, 203, 206, 316, 319, 320, 322, 336, 339, 350,

INDEX

356, 376, 387, 388, 389, 395, 397, 398, 405, 467, 471, 475, 477, 484, 536, 537, 550, 570, 571, 572, 573, 578, 579, 644, 678, 679, 680, 681, 682, 683, 686, 691, 694, 695
Perth, Earl of, 149
Perthshire, xi, xii, 31, 66, 106, 128, 142, 149, 150, 156, 157, 158, 159, 162, 168, 169, 170, 171, 173, 174, 175, 180, 181, 186, 197, 200, 203, 240, 244, 245, 285, 288, 302, 307, 333, 345, 378, 388, 389, 396, 398, 399, 429, 467, 479, 494, 501, 550, 566, 609, 610
Peter, John, 63, 134, 144
Peterloo, 457
Pharos, 36, 129
Philadelphia, 135, 186, 609, 685
Picts, 189
Pine, L. G., 697
Piping families, 583, 677
Pisquatua, 609
Pitt, William the elder, 634
Pittsburgh, 646
Pius IX, Pope, 7
Pluto, 14
Pococke, Dr Richard, 179, 564
Poetry, 312, 441, 579, 599
Poland, 13, 50, 207, 208, 490
Poole, A. L., 534, 576
Pope the, 7, 116, 196, 224, 364, 404, 541
Porson, Richard, 82, 138
Port of Menteith, 148, 171, 173, 182
Portnacroish, 505
Portree, 181, 360, 425, 477, 503, 571, 606, 608, 681, 682
Portsmouth, 618, 656
Portugal, 14, 635, 657
Portuguese, 16, 657
Potatoes, 425
Prebble, John, 3, 19, 33, 34, 84, 87, 97, 99, 410, 413, 452, 486, 487, 697
Presbyterianism, 238, 239, 240, 582, 622, 625
Presbyterians, 236, 515, 546, 620, 624, 627
Prevost, General, 651
Prince Charles, 47, 51, 68, 81, 187, 189, 193, 230, 241, 242, 243, 244, 248, 249, 250, 252, 259, 274, 302, 348, 350, 352, 368, 394, 420, 458, 473, 506, 507, 508, 510, 511, 517, 518, 526, 527, 528, 548, 551, 555, 585, 601, 605,

621, 626, 634, 637, 645, 671, 684
Princeton University, 16
Privy Council, 211, 239, 246, 247, 334, 335, 336, 339, 356, 370, 489, 662
Proaig, 584
Protestant Covenant, 543
Protestants, 25, 61, 123, 444, 449, 494, 543, 620, 621, 623, 624, 625, 627
Proudhon, Pierre-Joseph, 406
Prussia, 631
Public opinion, 548, 549, 578
Purkiss, Diane, 17
Quarterly Review, 91, 480
Quebec, 564, 589, 643, 653
Queen Victoria, 286, 562, 565, 566, 593
Raasay, 105, 108, 241, 300, 360, 362, 404, 422, 433, 559, 584, 587, 591
Raasay House, 591
Rafford, 503, 571
Raid of Ruthven, 545
Rainy, George, 105
Rait, Professor Sir Robert, 185
Ramsay of Ochtertyre, 263
Ranald Gallda, 292, 357
Rannoch, x, 104, 157, 274, 398, 467, 483, 528, 584
Rannoch Moor, 274
Rattrays, the, 389, 399
Rawlinson, Thomas, 436
Rawlinson, Thomas Hutton, 479
Ray, James, 420
Reader's Digest Atlas, 130
Reading Room, 2
Reay, 21, 36, 37, 38, 73, 98, 99, 100, 113, 120, 129, 136, 144, 168, 169, 178, 179, 182, 197, 204, 218, 224, 324, 383, 386, 400, 584, 605
Reay country, 99, 100, 129, 144, 584, 605
Reay, Lord, 36, 73, 98, 99, 100, 113, 120, 129, 136, 144, 218, 383, 400
Red River, 443
Redgauntlet, 205, 424, 477
Regius Professor, 9, 15, 124, 231, 638
Reid, John, 512
Reid, Major, 601
Reminiscences of an Octogenarian Gael, 390, 407
Renfrewshire, xi, 171

724

Resby, James, 537
Rhu, 172, 173, 181, 204
Rhynie, 287, 323
Richard III, 231, 289
Richards, Professor Eric, 8, 170, 193
River Bran, 173
River Dee, 175
River Farrar, 595
River Leven, 167
River Nairn, 176
River Tay, 173
River Thurso, 342
Rixson, Denis, 77, 411, 412, 697
Road Through the Isles, 139
Road to Mingulay, 405
Rob Roy, 210, 279, 280, 322, 532, 585, 611, 697
Robert Bruce, 114, 116
Robert II, 536, 576
Robert III, 536, 576
Robertson, Dr James, 450, 495, 522, 561, 608
Robertson, Robert Ban, 609
Rochester, Bishop of, 541
Rogart, 181, 239
Roman Catholicism, 681
Roman Catholics, 123, 494, 619, 620
Roots of Stone, 309, 325
Rose of Kilravock, 398
Rosemarkie, 177, 181
Rosneath, 169, 172, 173, 202, 204
Ross & Cromarty, 130, 202, 313, 700
Ross of Easter Fearn, 277
Ross-shire, xi, xii, 39, 130, 157, 177, 178, 180, 181, 203, 239, 261, 288, 302, 304, 307, 333, 360, 371, 423, 481, 550, 566, 624, 631, 650, 654, 655, 657, 658, 663, 666, 695
Ross-shire Highlanders, 307, 550, 566, 631, 650, 654, 655, 657, 658, 663, 666
Ross, David, 88, 413, 622, 697
Ross, Donald Roy, 263
Ross, Lord, 400
Ross, Major, 307
Ross, Simon, 582
Ross, William, 606
Rosskeen, 181, 238, 269, 306, 316, 321, 324, 596, 626, 679
Rothesay, 181, 403
Rothesay and Caithness Fencibles, 403
Rothesay, Duke of, 403
Rough Wooing, 542
Rousseau, Jean-Jacques, 406
Rowling, J. K., 20
Rowse, A. L., 15, 22
Roxburgh, 115, 200, 534, 539, 541
Royal Highland Emigrant Regiment, 653
Rum, 5, 67, 96, 97, 105, 120, 121, 143, 148, 149, 397, 420, 421
Rushdie, Salman, 23
Russia, 13, 26, 50, 208, 614
Ruthven, 393, 441, 545
Sacheverell, William, 318, 560, 675
Sackville, Lord George, 188, 325, 510, 513, 573
Saddell & Skipness, xii, 181
Sage, Aeneas, 597
Sage, Rev. Donald, 423, 597
Saint Fond, Faujas de, 564
Saltoun, Lord, 346, 349
Samhuinn, 673
San Marino, 68
Savannah River, 651
Saxons, 52, 159, 161, 162, 185, 189, 529, 530, 531, 638
Scalpay, 275, 276, 277, 320, 321, 523, 526
Scarlett, James, 409, 486
Schama, Professor Simon, 88, 139, 272
Scone, 115, 116
Scotland in Modern Times, 141, 233, 695
Scotland on Sunday, 142, 437, 479
Scotland's Magazine, 679
Scots, 22, 34, 37, 67, 83, 84, 91, 92, 115, 116, 129, 157, 160, 161, 163, 186, 188, 189, 190, 192, 195, 196, 199, 206, 208, 221, 236, 237, 264, 279, 281, 290, 307, 313, 330, 336, 339, 354, 355, 361, 363, 400, 417, 435, 442, 476, 480, 482, 488, 510, 512, 514, 532, 534, 535, 536, 541, 542, 544, 559, 563, 566, 577, 604, 616, 621, 622, 642, 660, 692, 693, 694, 695, 699, 702
Scots merks, 363
Scotsman, The, 80, 95, 128, 131, 137, 138, 139, 141, 142, 143, 153, 473, 480, 679
Scott Fitzgerald, 131
Scott, Alastair, 220
Scott, Captain Caroline, 188, 510
Scott, Sir Walter, 36, 37, 129, 139, 156, 158, 162,

INDEX

189, 199, 228, 247, 255, 257, 314, 424, 429, 458, 480, 520, 532, 559, 562, 566, 581, 611
Scottish Arts Council,   10, 22, 95, 141
Scottish Chamber of Agriculture,   127
Scottish Historical Review,   127, 141, 273, 321, 358, 678, 696, 697
Scottish Poor Law,   183
Scottish Population History,   131
Seaforth Highlanders, the,   146, 387, 556, 617
Seaforth, Earl of, chief of clan MacKenzie,   224, 226, 236, 286, 371, 372, 373, 399, 617
Seaforth's Highlanders,   653
Seathwaite,   164
Selkirk, Earl of,   192, 214, 226, 284, 380, 423, 451, 455, 466, 692
Sellar, Patrick,   78, 122, 150, 230, 275, 466, 474, 694, 695, 697
Selwyn, Lionel,   24
Serbia,   126
Seton Gordon,   36, 80, 99, 129, 137, 144, 178, 203, 222, 224, 314, 318, 342, 476, 582, 583, 585, 586, 677
Seven Years' War,   555, 563, 566, 608, 635, 644, 645, 646, 687
Shaftesbury, Earl of,   124
Shairp, John Campbell,   200
Sharman, Mike,   24
Sharp, James, Archbishop of St Andrews,   546
Shaw of Tordarroch, C. J.,   141, 147
Shaw, Bernard,   143
Shaw, James,   219, 309, 416, 469, 546, 606, 694
Shaw, Rev. Lachlan,   235
Sheffield,   23
Sheriffmuir, battle of,   263, 393
Shetland,   128, 155, 162, 163, 168, 169, 170, 541, 704
Short History of the Scottish Highlands and Islands,   298
Sibbald, Sir Robert,   179
Sinclair of Keiss, George,   341, 343
Sinclair of Ulbster,   22, 105
Sinclair, Hon. R. M.,   142, 149
Sinclair, John, Lord Berriedale,   652
Sinclair, Sir John,   22, 37, 42, 105, 108, 269, 321, 424, 477, 480, 607, 678, 699

Sismondi, Simone de,   91
Skeabost,   103
Skene, W. F.,   697
Sketch of a Tour in the Highlands 1818,   695
Sketches of the Highlanders,   384, 486, 629
Skye,   65, 67, 68, 97, 102, 103, 107, 108, 130, 131, 145, 147, 155, 164, 192, 196, 220, 226, 230, 235, 239, 241, 260, 271, 272, 276, 283, 300, 303, 313, 320, 357, 358, 362, 383, 397, 426, 444, 476, 481, 504, 521, 523, 549, 560, 561, 583, 584, 585, 586, 591, 592, 593, 594, 595, 606, 607, 610, 621, 668, 677, 685, 692, 693, 695, 696, 697, 698
Sleat,   118, 119, 135, 181, 223, 225, 239, 297, 354, 355, 358, 385, 396, 397, 509, 572, 583, 584, 586, 606, 626
Small Isles,   67, 130, 181, 397, 590, 620, 623
Small, Major,   653
Smiles, Samuel,   453
Smith, Adam,   48, 55, 132, 133, 274, 320, 381, 385, 400, 413, 421, 475, 476
Smith, Donald Fraser,   634
Smith, Dr John,   77, 192, 407, 423, 426, 441, 561
Smith, John,   77, 192, 407, 423, 426, 441, 481, 561, 606
Smith, Sidney,   526
Smith, William,   260
Smollett, Tobias,   160, 161, 189, 190, 236, 387, 413, 421, 426, 437, 565
Smout, Professor,   33, 40, 44, 69, 70, 96, 98, 120, 121, 143, 144, 148, 169, 178, 192, 332, 408, 409, 413, 490, 532, 680
Snizort,   181, 239, 626
Society for the Promotion of Christian Knowledge,   164, 681
Solway Firth,   53
Somers, Robert,   562
Song to the Breeches,   132
Soroba,   369
South Africa,   26, 654
South Carolina,   650, 651
South Esk,   175, 203
South Knapdale,   97, 181, 374
South Uist,   xi, 79, 108, 119, 137, 152, 181, 197, 227, 287, 303, 306, 397, 449, 494, 508, 526, 569, 588, 623, 625, 676

South Wales, 15
Southend, 181
Southey, Robert, 424
Spain, 26, 138, 258, 263, 557, 611, 635, 658, 682
Spalding of Ashintully, 391
Spalding, John, 254, 377
St Andrews University, 40, 515, 683
St Andrews, Bishop of, 116, 538
St Kilda, 126, 166, 168, 504
St Paul, 267, 320, 515
St. Andrews, 546
Stair, Master of, 79, 623, 671
Stalin, Joseph, 94
Statutes of Iona, The, 254, 291
Steel, Tom, 69, 167, 192, 237, 248, 371, 409, 412, 490, 622
Stenscholl, 226
Sterne, Laurence, 165
Stevens F. L. (Len.), 325
Stevens, Sheila, 24
Stevenson, Robert Louis, 129
Stewart of Achnacone, 149
Stewart of Ardshiel, 252, 279, 553
Stewart of Ballechin, 243, 615
Stewart of Grandtully, 398
Stewart of Strathgarry, 149
Stewart, John, 615
Stewarts of Appin, 197, 224, 295, 296, 306, 323, 383, 467
Stirling, 31, 36, 129, 167, 248, 280, 353, 387, 396, 397, 398, 432, 534, 535, 539, 544, 545, 692, 693, 694, 695, 696
Stirling Castle, 539
Stirling University, 31
Stirlingshire, xi, 128, 170, 171, 173, 180, 181, 662
Stoddart, Sir John, 587, 589, 601
Stone of Destiny, 115
Stone, Lawrence, 15
Stonehaven, 169, 170
Stornoway, 21, 181, 324, 370, 520
Strachey, Lytton, 7
Strachur, xii, 105, 149, 150, 181, 185, 197, 202, 205, 223, 306, 496, 501, 570, 571, 587, 605, 675, 678, 681, 691
Strachur & Strathlachlan, xii, 181, 570, 571, 678

Stralachlan, xii
Straloch, 199, 601
Strand, Paul, 693, 698
Strath, 8, x, xi, 64, 65, 66, 98, 104, 132, 134, 152, 167, 169, 173, 174, 178, 181, 224, 304, 307, 314, 321, 333, 338, 345, 383, 385, 386, 389, 392, 398, 399, 418, 441, 474, 550, 551, 601, 605, 606, 653
Strath Allan, 167
Strath Ardle, 174, 304, 653
Strath Avon, 389, 392, 399
Strath Bran, 173, 174, 398, 550, 551
Strath Carnach, xi
Strath Carron, xi
Strath Dearn, 333, 338
Strath Errick, x, 345, 399
Strath Farrar, 98
Strath Garve, x
Strath Glass, 418, 605
Strath Nairn, 104, 333, 338, 385, 399
Strath Naver, 8, x, 64, 152, 321, 386, 606
Strath Peffer, x
Strath Spey, 383, 392, 399, 441
Strath Tay, 398
Strathaird, 103
Strathcarnach, xi
Strathcarron, xi
Strathclyde, 157
Strathdon, 175, 176, 182, 203, 390, 399, 623
Strathglass, x, 302, 399
Strathlachlan, xii, 181, 185, 202, 224, 570, 571, 678
Strathmore, 169
Strathnaver, x, 400, 418
Strathpeffer, x
Strathspey, Lord, 144, 225
Stuart kings, 51, 383
Suddie, xi, xii, 181, 334, 335, 549, 550
Sulivan, Richard J., 504
Sunday Times, The, 21, 208
Surrey, 11
Survey of the County of Inverness, 522
Sutherland, 4, 8, 9, x, xi, 21, 24, 35, 36, 37, 39, 62, 63, 64, 65, 69, 72, 75, 84, 86, 87, 90, 91, 94, 96, 98, 99, 100, 104, 106, 107, 113, 119, 120, 122, 124, 125, 127, 128, 129, 130, 138, 141, 144, 145, 149, 150, 151, 152, 153, 157, 161, 167,

INDEX

168, 169, 170, 177, 178, 179, 180, 181, 182, 193, 197, 199, 200, 202, 203, 207, 215, 216, 218, 225, 239, 244, 274, 275, 288, 304, 307, 312, 321, 324, 333, 360, 373, 386, 392, 400, 406, 418, 422, 423, 424, 428, 460, 462, 465, 466, 477, 483, 485, 521, 522, 557, 559, 564, 566, 579, 580, 585, 598, 624, 634, 644, 656, 661, 665, 692, 693, 694, 695, 698, 700
Sutherland Clearances, 4, ix, 37, 580, 693
Sutherland Fencible Regiment, 307, 661
Sutherland, Alexander, 91, 157, 161, 216, 557
Sutherland, Captain Sackville, 307
Sutherland, Duke of, 72, 90, 91, 98, 106, 113, 120, 127, 150
Sutherland, Earl of, 90, 99, 244, 373, 386, 400
Sutherland, Josie, 24
Swire, Otta, 192
Swiss Guard, 116
Switzerland, 36, 116
Tacitus, 143
Tacksmen, 299, 323
Tain, 181
Talisker, 300
Tarbat, 181, 223
Tarbert, 518, 520, 628
Tarbet, 160, 167, 168, 673
Tartan History website, 139
Taylor, A. J. P., 15, 18, 207, 569
Taylor, John, 318, 418
Taylor, Richard, 24
Tayside, 157
Teignmouth, Lord, 270, 321
Telford, Thomas, 622
Temora, 441, 481
Thompson, Francis, 119, 136
Thomson, George, 543, 577
Thomson, William, 81, 158, 191, 258, 422, 591, 599, 634
Thornton, Thomas, 562
Thurso, 22, 142, 149, 162, 166, 169, 179, 180, 182, 204, 342
Tibet, 25, 50
Tigh nam Piobairean, 586, 677
Times, The, 22, 23, 95, 113, 126, 139, 141, 150, 151, 152, 153, 401, 437, 474, 475, 478, 479, 480, 577, 578, 581, 621, 684, 690
Timothy, 267, 320
Tindley, Dr Anne Marie, 119
Tiree, xii, 65, 97, 130, 157, 181, 202, 204, 216, 217, 367, 368, 405, 427, 560, 576, 579, 587, 589, 601, 606, 675, 678, 680, 681, 691
Tiree & Coll, xii, 181
Tobermory, 283
Toland, John, 134, 429, 504, 560, 571, 579, 599, 602, 607, 670, 676, 680, 682, 690, 691, 698
Tongue, 36, 100, 129, 181, 425, 495, 570, 600, 601, 607, 625, 680, 682
Tormod MacLeods, 293, 362
Torosay, 78, 97, 137, 181
Torquil MacLeods of Lewis, 298, 362
Toulouse, 631
Tower of London, 60, 116, 535, 536
Towie Castle, 544
Trabb's boy, 94
Traigh an Luig, 597
Transactions of the Gaelic Society of Inverness, 699
Traveller's History of Scotland, 436, 692, 693
Tristram Shandy, 126, 165, 201, 575
Trotternish, 226, 358, 583, 584
Trumpan, 303
Tsar of Russia, 614
Tummel Bridge, 609, 610
Turcoing, battle of, 655
Tytler, Patrick Fraser, 698
Uig, 181, 596, 606, 679
Uist, xi, 64, 66, 79, 101, 107, 108, 119, 120, 134, 135, 137, 152, 153, 181, 196, 197, 216, 227, 257, 260, 287, 302, 303, 306, 309, 358, 397, 420, 426, 428, 447, 448, 449, 452, 463, 481, 483, 494, 508, 518, 526, 559, 569, 579, 583, 588, 602, 606, 608, 621, 623, 625, 676, 680, 681, 682
Uists, 118, 119, 120, 130, 152, 153
Ulva, 309, 584
United States of America, 208, 674
University College, Oxford, 575
Urquhart, xi, xii, 78, 98, 137, 169, 181, 202, 244, 383, 399, 475, 623
Urquhart & Glenmoriston, xii, 181, 475
Urquhart Castle, 169
Urray, 181, 269, 320, 502, 571, 619, 683
Vanity Fair, 658, 689

Venice, Doge of, 116, 196
Vienna Gazette, 564, 566, 580, 581, 645
Virginia, 646, 651, 652
Virginia Gazette, 646
Voltaire, 55, 558
Wade, General, 159, 224, 256, 257
Wainwright, A., 80, 137
Wales, 15, 114, 388, 403, 457, 529, 571, 650
Walker, Dr John, 204, 420, 427, 454, 501, 519, 561, 590, 607, 610
Wallace, Sir William, 50
War of American Independence, 81, 556, 618
War of the Spanish Succession, 569, 611
Warbeck, Perkin, 354, 540
Ward, Stephen, 6
Wardlaw Manuscript, 258, 319, 476, 595, 679
Watson, Steven, 655, 683
Watten, 179, 180, 182, 204
Waugh, Auberon, 62, 690
Waverley, 255, 257, 259, 567, 697
Wedgwood, C. V., 272, 321
Weem, 182, 398, 503, 571
Weir, Tom, 220, 313
Wellington, Duke of, 325, 658, 660, 689
Welsh, the, 12, 186, 190, 298
Wenborn, N., 46
Wesley, John, 440, 481, 636, 686, 702
West Highland Free Press, 147
West Highland Survey, 127, 136, 218, 693
West Indies, 376, 546, 556, 635, 643, 655, 656, 687
Wester Ross, 1, 100, 101, 137, 225, 446, 460
Western Front, 13
Western Highlands, 220, 272, 313, 510, 607, 692, 693
Western Isles, 120, 134, 136, 303, 323, 693, 695, 696
Westminster Abbey, 115, 330
Westminster Journal, 614, 636, 643, 683
What is Property, 406
White Queen, 30
Wick, 159, 179, 194, 342, 697
Wiener, John, 113
Wigtownshire, 116, 163
Wild Scots, 488, 694
Wilde, Oscar, 127, 140
Wilkinson, Thomas, 591, 628
William III, 79, 238, 336, 349, 366, 546, 576, 621
William of Orange, 303, 336, 354
Wilson Brothers, 432
Wishart, George, 542
Wolfe, General, 643
Wolfe, James, 511, 564, 580
Wordsworth, Dorothy, 81, 160, 172, 270, 496, 627, 697
Wordsworth, William, 440, 446, 504, 592, 628, 673, 685
Wotton, Lord Henry, 30
York, Duke of, 540, 655
Yorkshire, 162, 511, 690
Yorkshiremen, 116
Young Pretender, 506
Young, Arthur, 137
Young, William, 86, 106, 150
Youngson, Professor A. J., 70
Zambia, 67, 694

www.ingramcontent.com/pod-product-compliance
Lightning Source LLC
Chambersburg PA
CBHW071723080526
44588CB00013B/1876